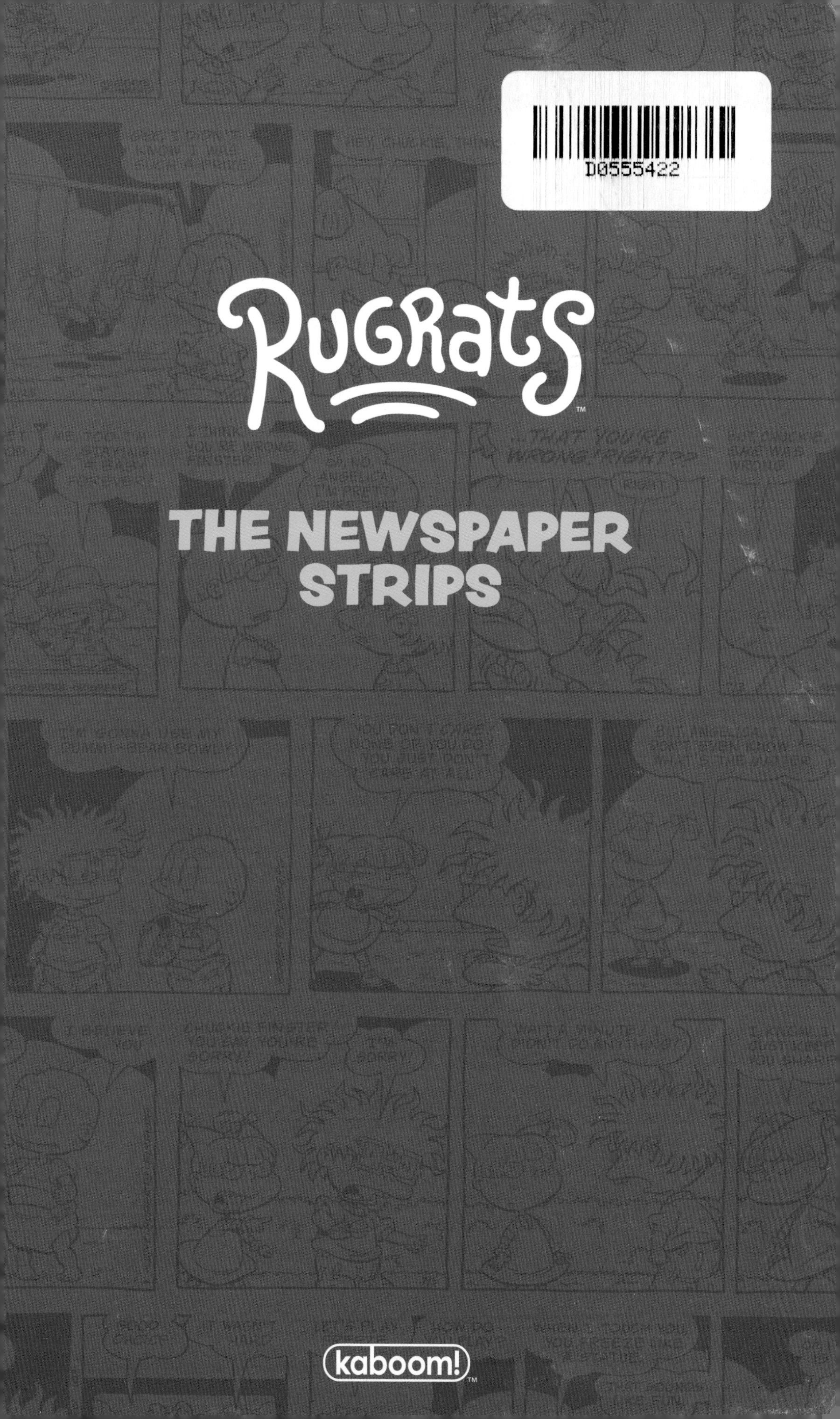

Rugrats™

THE NEWSPAPER STRIPS

kaboom!™

COLLECTION DESIGNERS
Jillian Crab + Chelsea Roberts

COLLECTION EDITOR
Matthew Levine

Ross Richie CEO & Founder
Joy Huffman CFO
Matt Gagnon Editor-In-Chief
Filip Sablik President, Publishing & Marketing
Stephen Christy President, Development
Lance Kreiter Vice President, Licensing & Merchandising
Arune Singh Vice President, Marketing
Bryce Carlson Vice President, Editorial & Creative Strategy
Scott Newman Manager, Production Design
Kate Henning Manager, Operations
Spencer Simpson Manager, Sales
Elyse Strandberg Manager, Finance
Sierra Hahn Executive Editor
Jeanine Schaefer Executive Editor
Dafna Pleban Senior Editor
Shannon Watters Senior Editor
Eric Harburn Senior Editor
Chris Rosa Editor
Matthew Levine Editor
Sophie Philips-Roberts Associate Editor
Amanda LaFranco Associate Editor
Gavin Gronenthal Assistant Editor

Michael Moccio Assistant Editor
Gwen Waller Assistant Editor
Allyson Gronowitz Assistant Editor
Jillian Crab Design Coordinator
Michelle Ankley Design Coordinator
Kara Leopard Production Designer
Marie Krupina Production Designer
Grace Park Production Designer
Chelsea Roberts Production Design Assistant
Samantha Knapp Production Design Assistant
Paola Capalla Senior Accountant
José Meza Live Events Lead
Stephanie Hocutt Digital Marketing Lead
Esther Kim Marketing Coordinator
Cat O'Grady Digital Marketing Coordinator
Amanda Lawson Marketing Assistant
Holly Aitchison Digital Sales Coordinator
Morgan Perry Retail Sales Coordinator
Megan Christopher Operations Coordinator
Rodrigo Hernandez Mailroom Assistant
Zipporah Smith Operations Assistant
Breanna Sarpy Executive Assistant

kaboom! nickelodeon

RUGRATS: THE NEWSPAPER STRIPS, December 2019. Published by KaBOOM!, a division of
Boom Entertainment, Inc., 5670 Wilshire Boulevard, Suite 400, Los Angeles, CA 90036-5679. ©
2019 Viacom International Inc. All Rights Reserved. Nickelodeon, Rugrats and all related titles,
logos, and characters are trademarks of Viacom International Inc. Created by Klasky Csupo and
Germain. KaBOOM!™ and the KaBOOM! logo are trademarks of Boom Entertainment, Inc.,
registered in various countries and categories. All characters, events, and institutions depicted
herein are fictional. Any similarity between any of the names, characters, persons, events, and/
or institutions in this publication to actual names, characters, and persons, whether living or
dead, events, and/or institutions is unintended and purely coincidental. KaBOOM! does not
read or accept unsolicited submissions of ideas, stories, or artwork.

BOOM! Studios, 5670 Wilshire Boulevard, Suite 400, Los Angeles, CA 90036-5679. Printed in
China. First Printing.

ISBN: 978-1-68415-461-6, eISBN: 978-1-64144-578-8

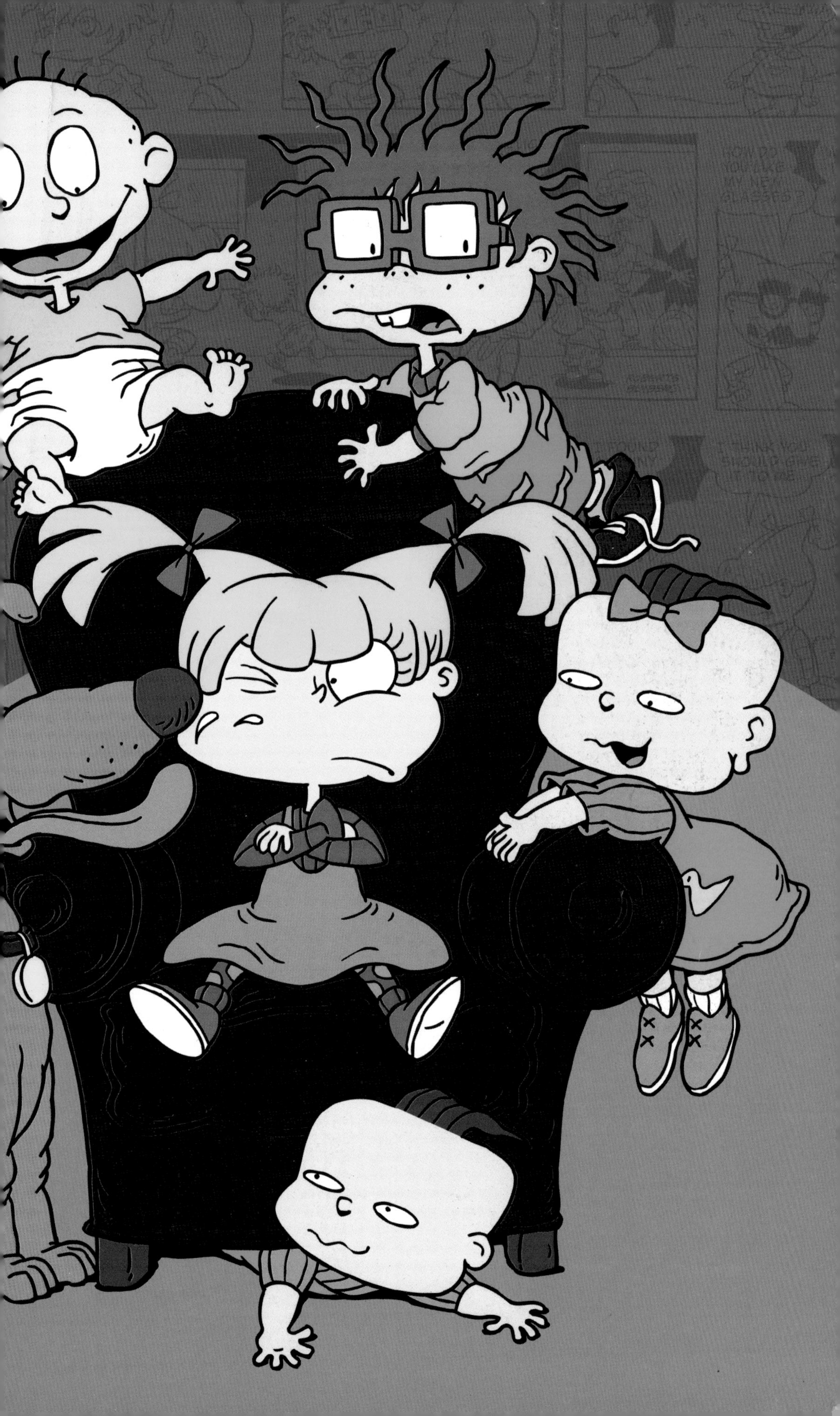
HOW DO YOU LIKE MY NEW GLASSES?
I THINK YOU SHOULD GIVE IT TO ME

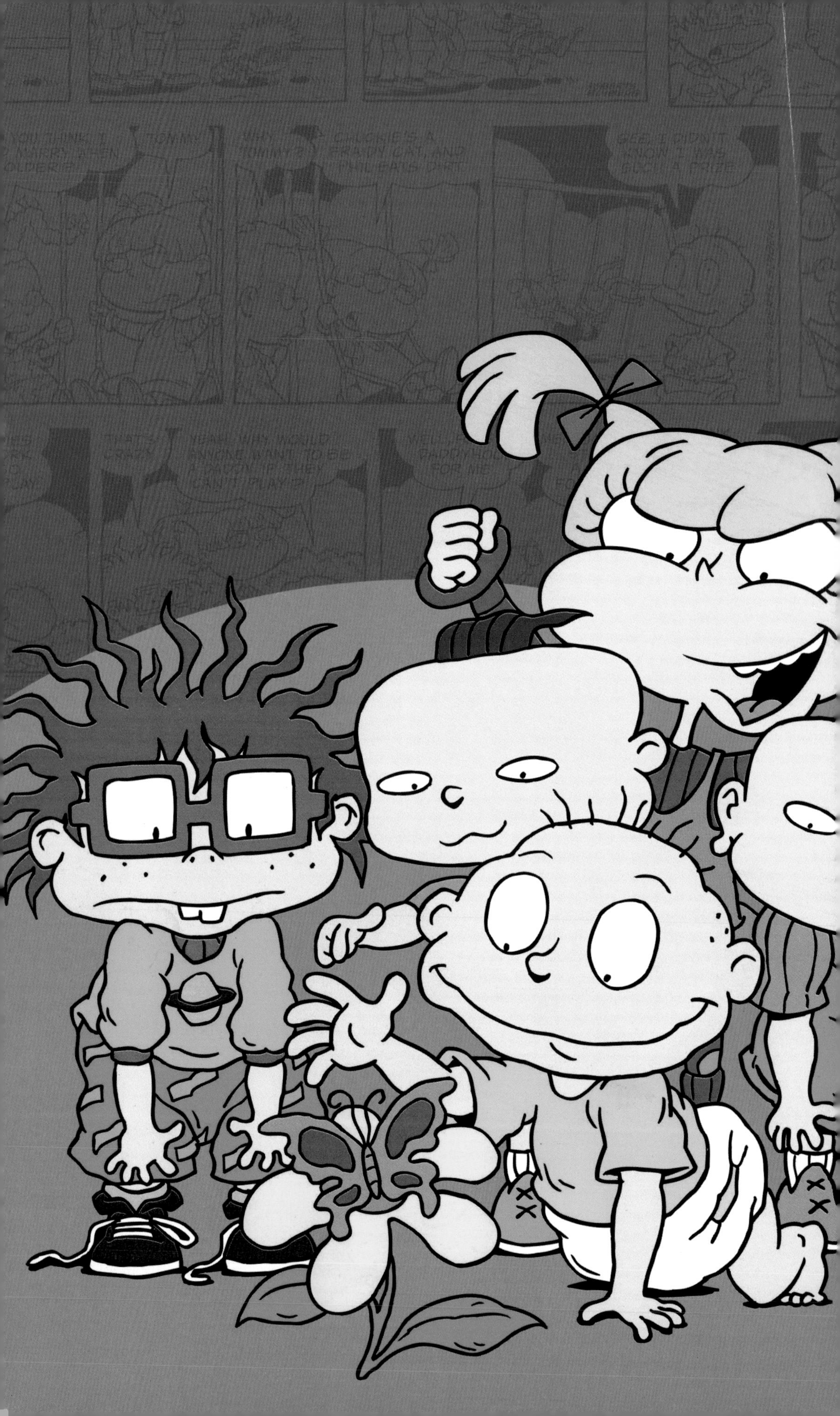

RUGRATS™

THE NEWSPAPER STRIPS

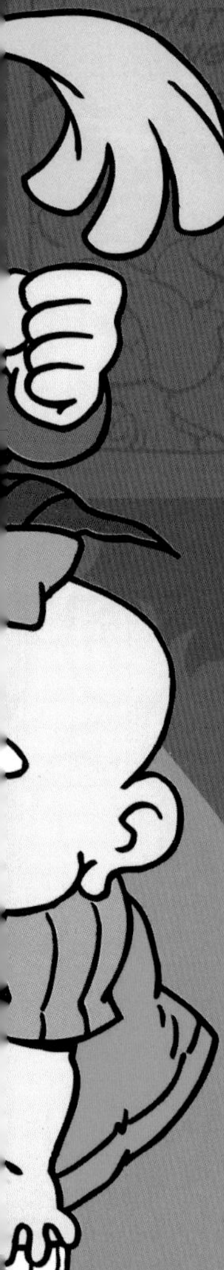

WRITERS

Scott Gray + Gordon Kent + Lee Nordling
Chuck Kim + Scott Roberts + J. Torres
Mark Bilgrey + John Zakour + Rob Moran

ARTISTS

Steve Crespo + Will Blyberg + Gary Fields
Kyle Baker + Rodrigues + Tim Harkins
Vince Giarrano + Scott Roberts

SPECIAL THANKS TO

Joan Hilty + Linda Lee
James Salerno + Alexandra Maurer
THE WONDERFUL TEAM AT Nickelodeon
AND Creators Syndicate.

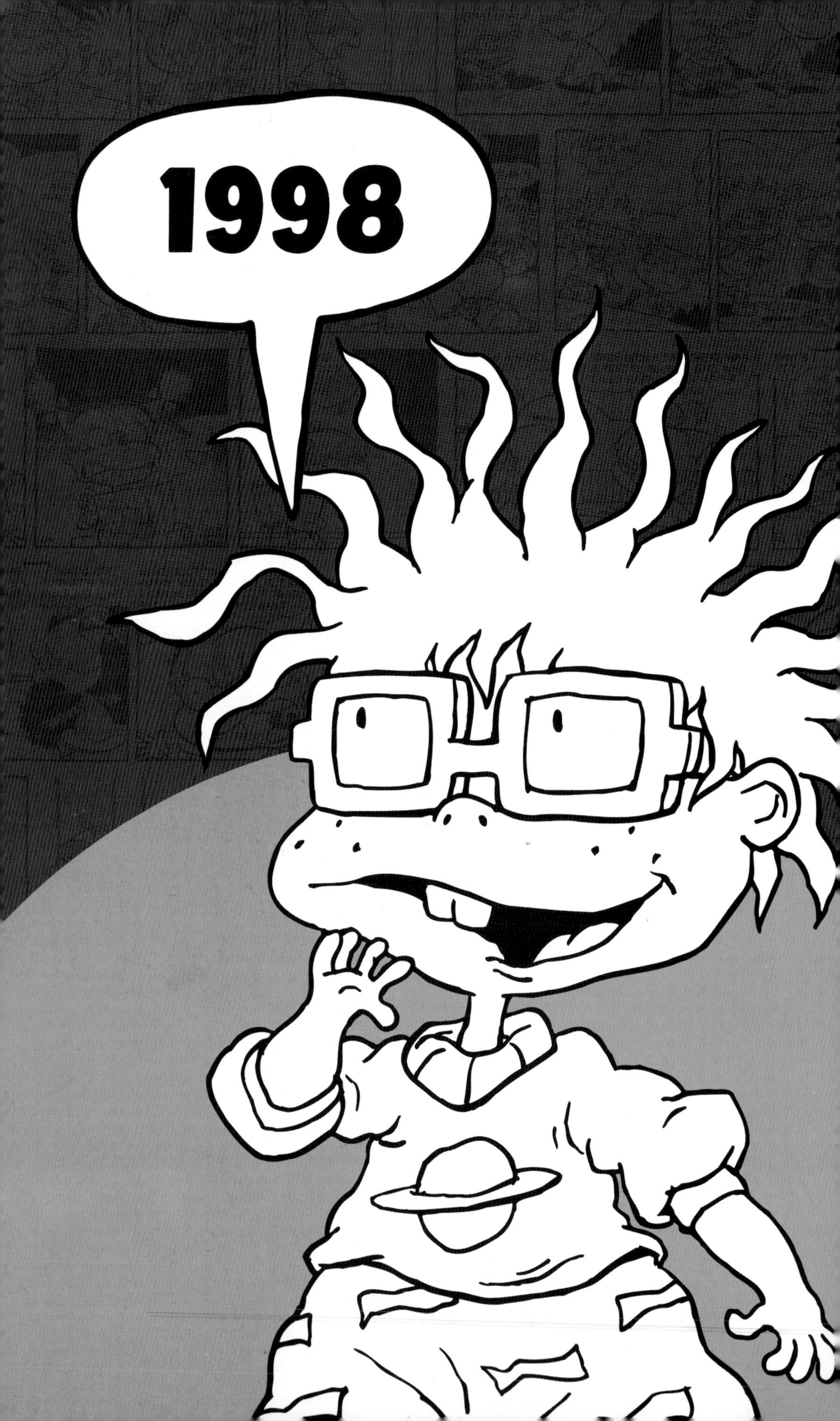
1998

Panel 1: TOMMY'S GOT YOUR EYES, DEED. / HE HAS YOUR NOSE.

Panel 2: HE HAS MY DAD'S EARS, THOUGH. / AND HIS HAIR, TOO.

Panel 3: BOY, ALL MY PARTS BELONG TO OTHER PEOPLES!

Panel 4: I WONDER WHEN THEY'RE GONNA WANT 'EM BACK!...

LOOK, STU, TOMMY ATE ALL HIS BEET GHOULASH, AND HE DIDN'T EVEN MAKE A MESS!

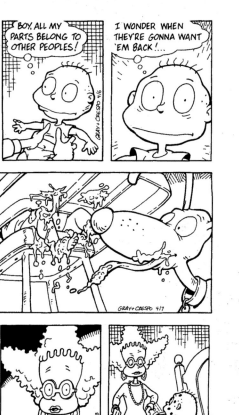

GRAY + CRESPO 4/7

HAVE YOU SEEN MY RED PEN? / NO, HONEY.

GRAY + CRESPO 4/6

AND TOMMY PICKLES IS IN THE LEAD!

UH OH, LOOKS LIKE PICKLES IS SLOWING DOWN!

4/4 GRAY + CRESPO

NOW IT LOOKS LIKE PICKLES HAS PULLED OVER BECAUSE HIS CAR... ...NEEDS TO EAT?!

RELAX, IT'S JUST A PHASE.

GRAY + CRESPO

TOMMY, NOOO!!

THIS PLANET MOBILE SHOULD HELP YOU SLEEP.

HOW AM I S'POSED TO SLEEP WHEN I GOTS ALL THIS NEAT STUFF TO LOOK AT?

GRAY + CRESPO 4/11

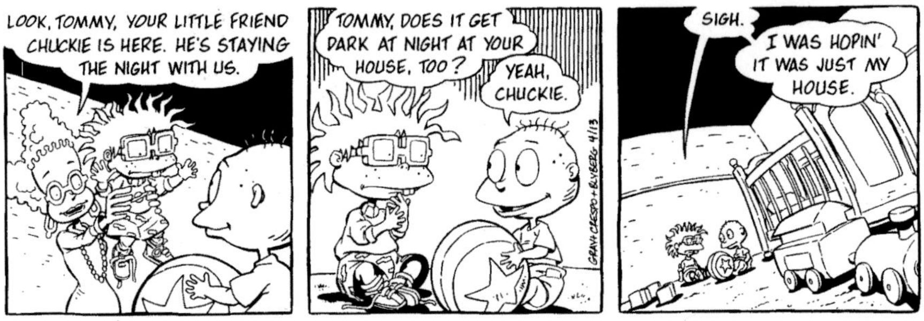
LOOK, TOMMY, YOUR LITTLE FRIEND CHUCKIE IS HERE. HE'S STAYING THE NIGHT WITH US.
TOMMY, DOES IT GET DARK AT NIGHT AT YOUR HOUSE, TOO?
YEAH, CHUCKIE.
GRAY+CRESPO+BLYBERG 4/13
SIGH.
I WAS HOPIN' IT WAS JUST MY HOUSE.

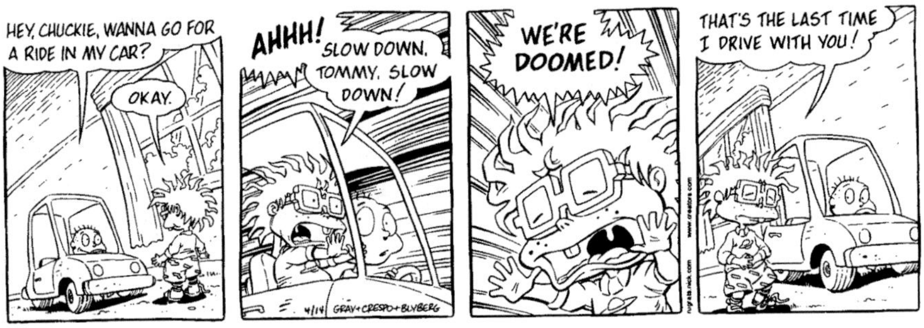
HEY, CHUCKIE, WANNA GO FOR A RIDE IN MY CAR?
OKAY.
AHHH!
SLOW DOWN, TOMMY, SLOW DOWN!
4/14 GRAY+CRESPO+BLYBERG
WE'RE DOOMED!
THAT'S THE LAST TIME I DRIVE WITH YOU!

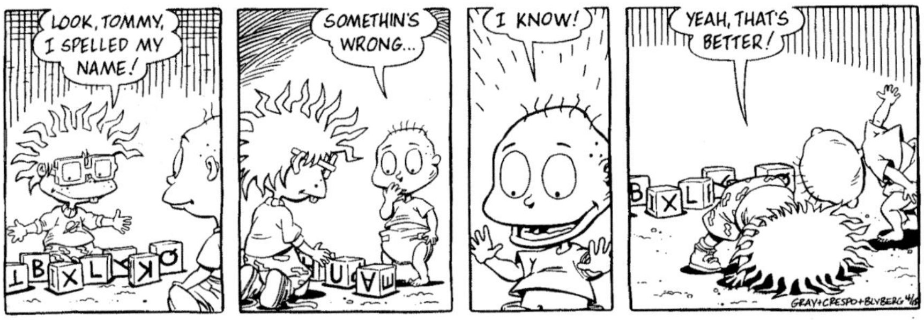
LOOK, TOMMY, I SPELLED MY NAME!
SOMETHIN'S WRONG...
I KNOW!
YEAH, THAT'S BETTER!
GRAY+CRESPO+BLYBERG 4/15

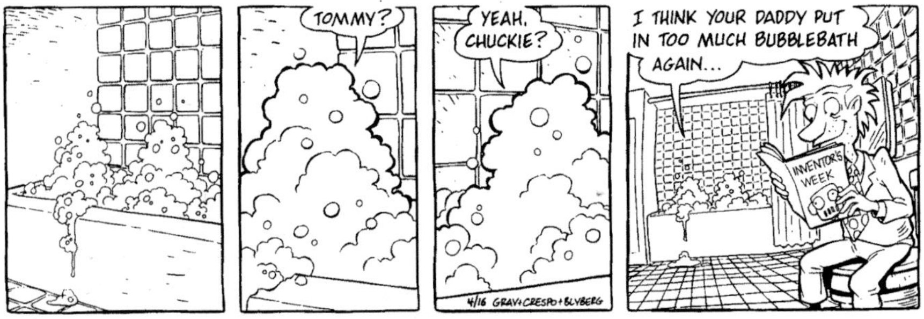
TOMMY?
YEAH, CHUCKIE?
4/16 GRAY+CRESPO+BLYBERG
I THINK YOUR DADDY PUT IN TOO MUCH BUBBLEBATH AGAIN...
INVENTOR'S WEEK

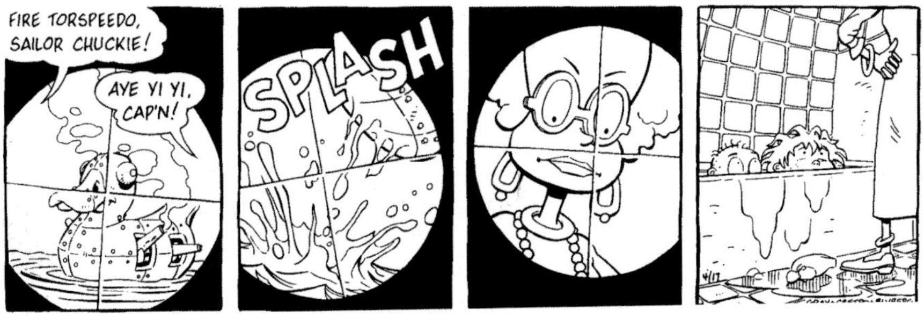
FIRE TORSPEEDO, SAILOR CHUCKIE!
AYE YI YI, CAP'N!
SPLASH
4/17

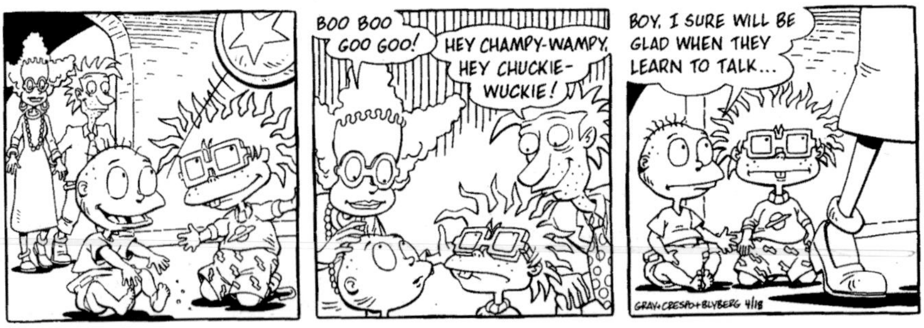
BOO BOO GOO GOO!
HEY CHAMPY-WAMPY, HEY CHUCKIE-WUCKIE!
BOY, I SURE WILL BE GLAD WHEN THEY LEARN TO TALK...
GRAY+CRESPO+BLYBERG 4/18

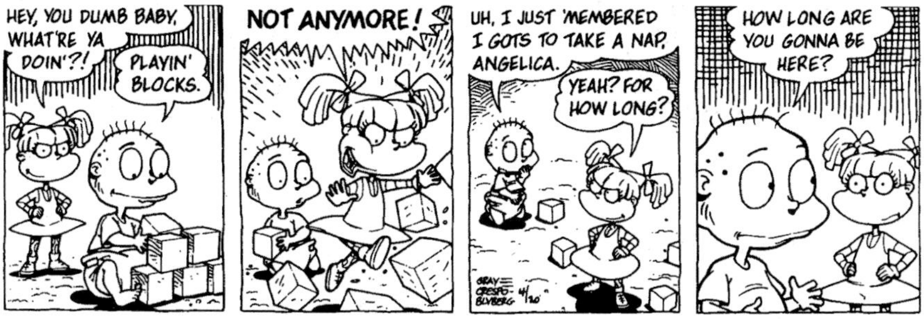
HEY, YOU DUMB BABY, WHAT'RE YA DOIN'?!
PLAYIN' BLOCKS.
NOT ANYMORE!
UH, I JUST 'MEMBERED I GOTS TO TAKE A NAP, ANGELICA.
YEAH? FOR HOW LONG?
GRAY CRESPO BLYBERG 4/20
HOW LONG ARE YOU GONNA BE HERE?

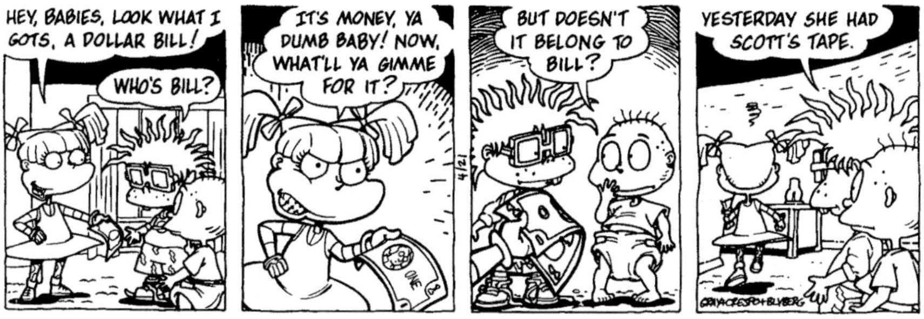
HEY, BABIES, LOOK WHAT I GOTS, A DOLLAR BILL!
WHO'S BILL?
IT'S MONEY, YA DUMB BABY! NOW, WHAT'LL YA GIMME FOR IT?
ONE
4/21
BUT DOESN'T IT BELONG TO BILL?
YESTERDAY SHE HAD SCOTT'S TAPE.
GRAY CRESPO BLYBERG

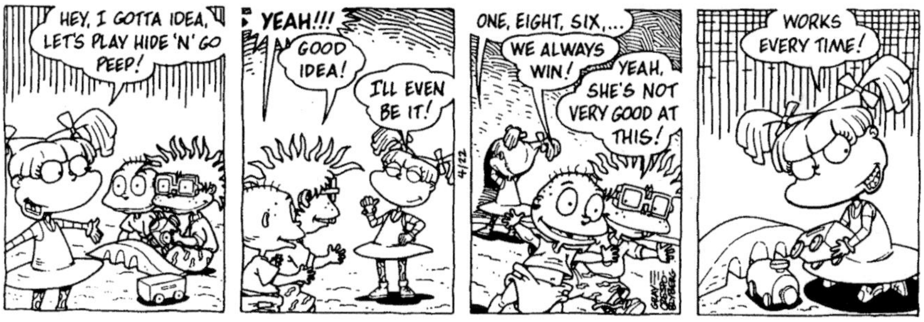
HEY, I GOTTA IDEA, LET'S PLAY HIDE 'N' GO PEEP!
YEAH!!!
GOOD IDEA!
I'LL EVEN BE IT!
4/22
ONE, EIGHT, SIX,...
WE ALWAYS WIN!
YEAH, SHE'S NOT VERY GOOD AT THIS!
GRAY CRESPO BLYBERG
WORKS EVERY TIME!

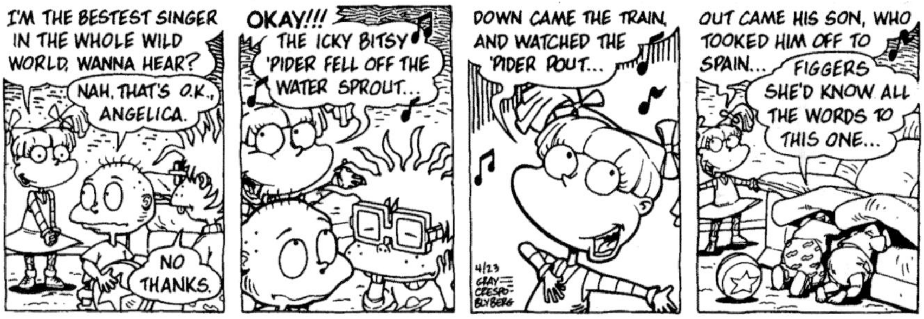
I'M THE BESTEST SINGER IN THE WHOLE WILD WORLD, WANNA HEAR?
NAH, THAT'S O.K., ANGELICA.
NO THANKS.
OKAY!!!
THE ICKY BITSY 'PIDER FELL OFF THE WATER SPROUT...
DOWN CAME THE TRAIN, AND WATCHED THE 'PIDER POUT...
4/23 GRAY CRESPO BLYBERG
OUT CAME HIS SON, WHO TOOKED HIM OFF TO SPAIN...
FIGGERS SHE'D KNOW ALL THE WORDS TO THIS ONE...

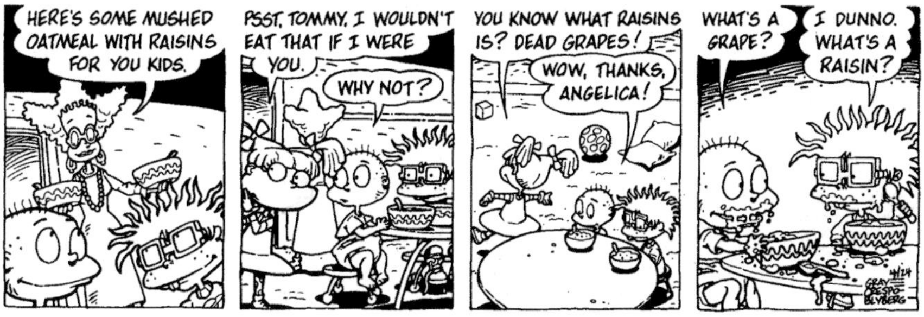
HERE'S SOME MUSHED OATMEAL WITH RAISINS FOR YOU KIDS.
PSST, TOMMY, I WOULDN'T EAT THAT IF I WERE YOU.
WHY NOT?
YOU KNOW WHAT RAISINS IS? DEAD GRAPES!
WOW, THANKS, ANGELICA!
WHAT'S A GRAPE?
I DUNNO. WHAT'S A RAISIN?
4/24 GRAY CRESPO BLYBERG

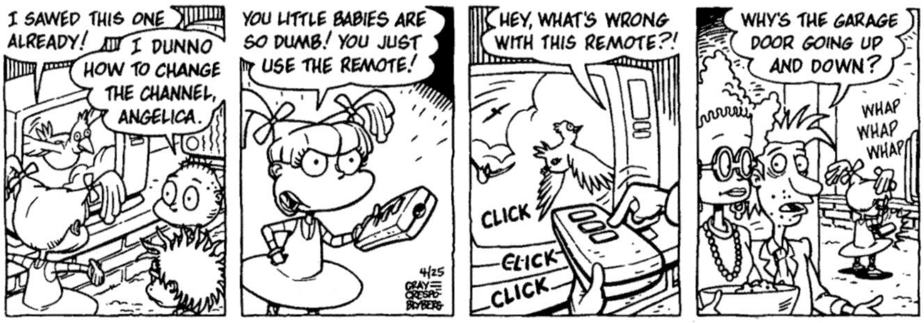
I SAWED THIS ONE ALREADY!
I DUNNO HOW TO CHANGE THE CHANNEL, ANGELICA.
YOU LITTLE BABIES ARE SO DUMB! YOU JUST USE THE REMOTE!
4/25 GRAY CRESPO BLYBERG
HEY, WHAT'S WRONG WITH THIS REMOTE?!
CLICK
CLICK
CLICK
WHY'S THE GARAGE DOOR GOING UP AND DOWN?
WHAP WHAP WHAP

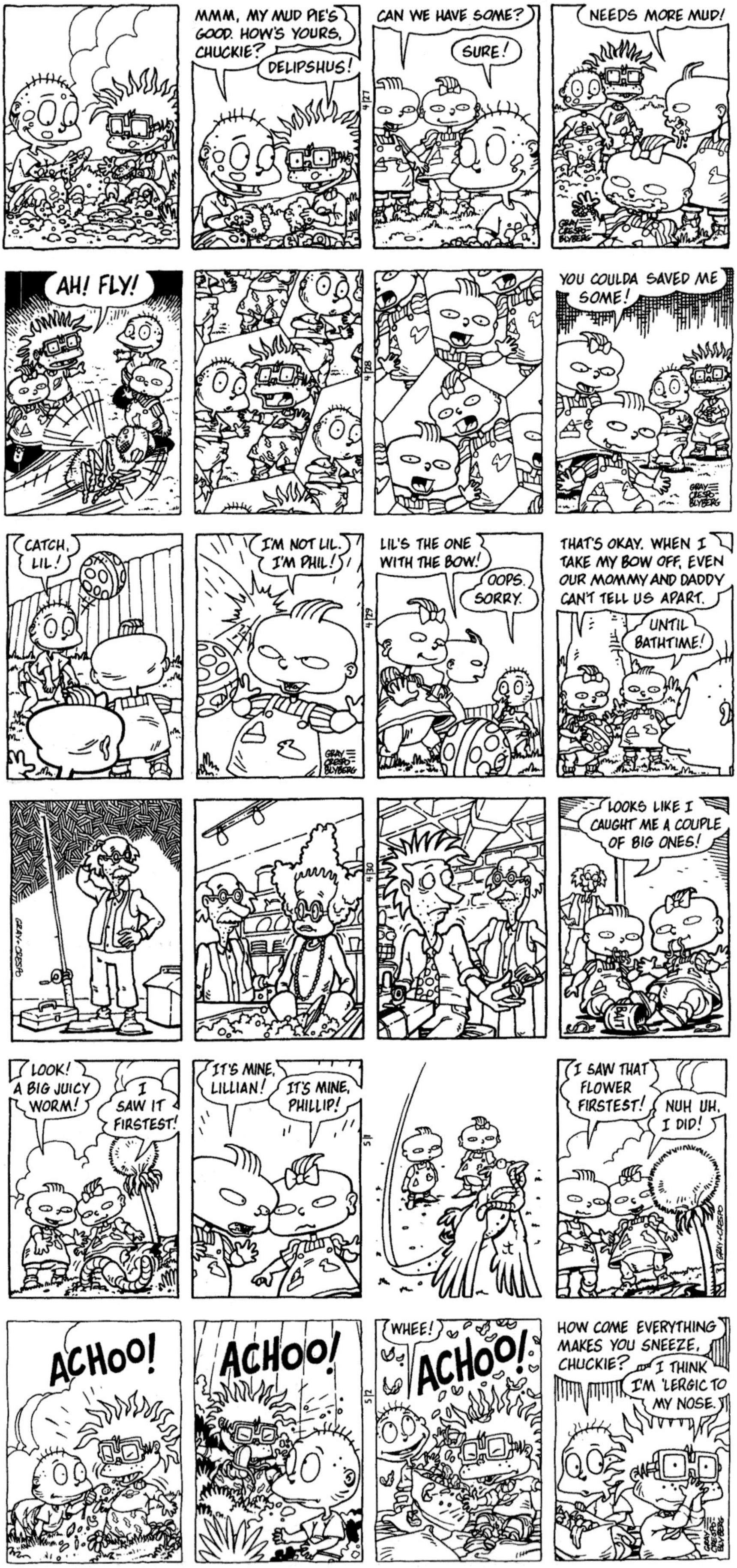
MMM, MY MUD PIE'S GOOD. HOW'S YOURS, CHUCKIE?
DELIPSHUS!
CAN WE HAVE SOME?
SURE!
NEEDS MORE MUD!
AH! FLY!
YOU COULDA SAVED ME SOME!
CATCH, LIL!
I'M NOT LIL. I'M PHIL!
LIL'S THE ONE WITH THE BOW!
OOPS. SORRY.
THAT'S OKAY. WHEN I TAKE MY BOW OFF, EVEN OUR MOMMY AND DADDY CAN'T TELL US APART.
UNTIL BATHTIME!
LOOKS LIKE I CAUGHT ME A COUPLE OF BIG ONES!
BAIT
LOOK! A BIG JUICY WORM!
I SAW IT FIRSTEST!
IT'S MINE, LILLIAN!
IT'S MINE, PHILLIP!
I SAW THAT FLOWER FIRSTEST!
NUH UH, I DID!
ACHOO!
ACHOO!
WHEE!
ACHOO!
HOW COME EVERYTHING MAKES YOU SNEEZE, CHUCKIE?
I THINK I'M 'LERGIC TO MY NOSE.

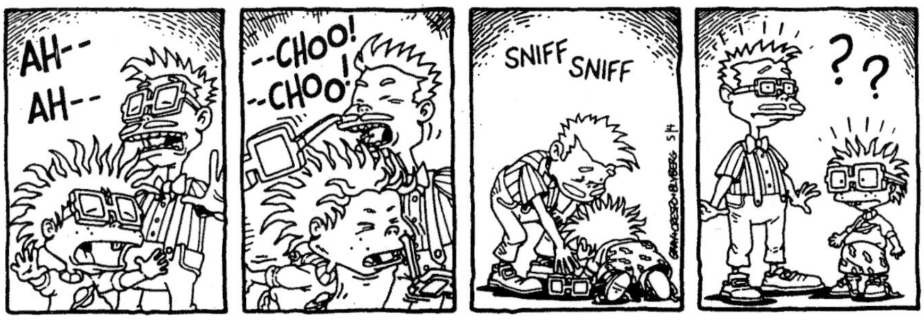
AH--
AH--
--CHOO!
--CHOO!
SNIFF SNIFF
??

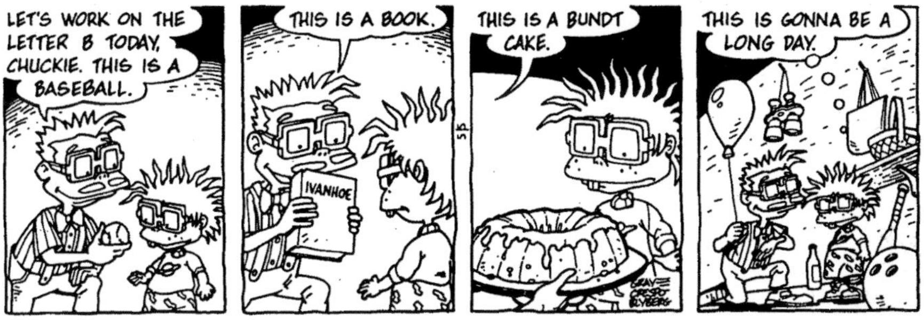
LET'S WORK ON THE LETTER B TODAY, CHUCKIE. THIS IS A BASEBALL.
THIS IS A BOOK.
IVANHOE
THIS IS A BUNDT CAKE.
THIS IS GONNA BE A LONG DAY.

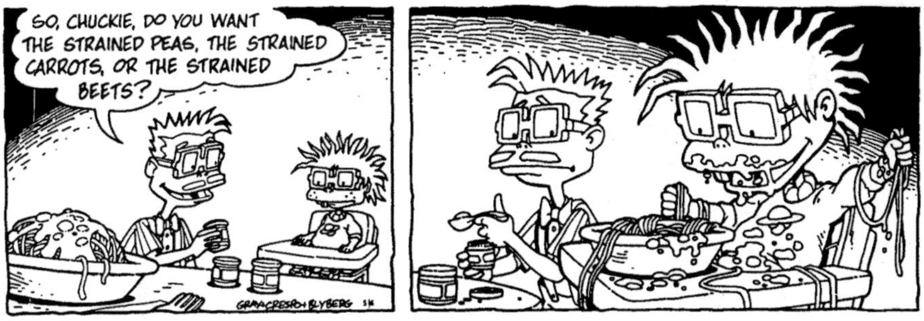
SO, CHUCKIE, DO YOU WANT THE STRAINED PEAS, THE STRAINED CARROTS, OR THE STRAINED BEETS?

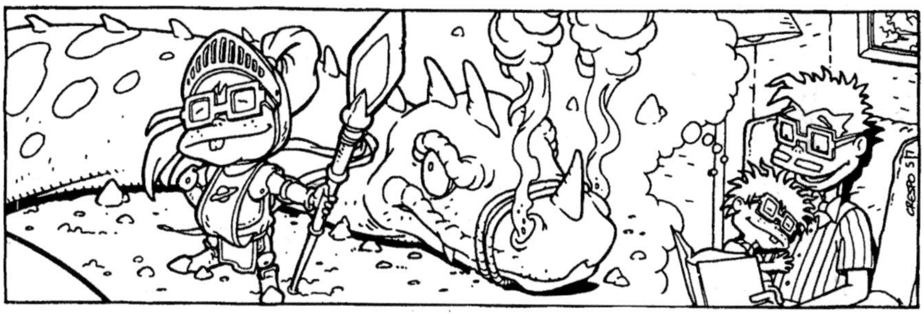

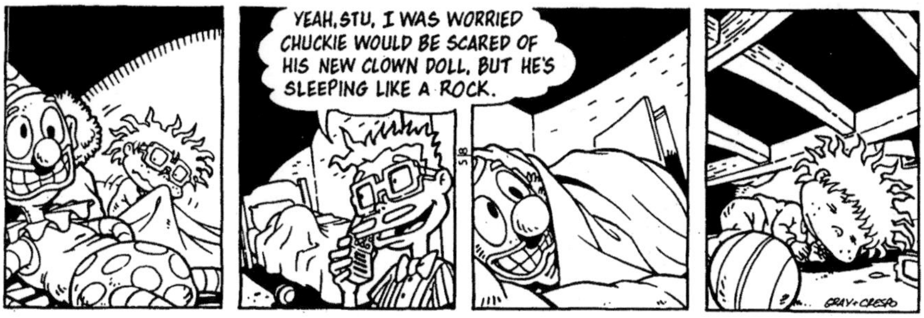
YEAH, STU, I WAS WORRIED CHUCKIE WOULD BE SCARED OF HIS NEW CLOWN DOLL, BUT HE'S SLEEPING LIKE A ROCK.
GRAY+CRESPO

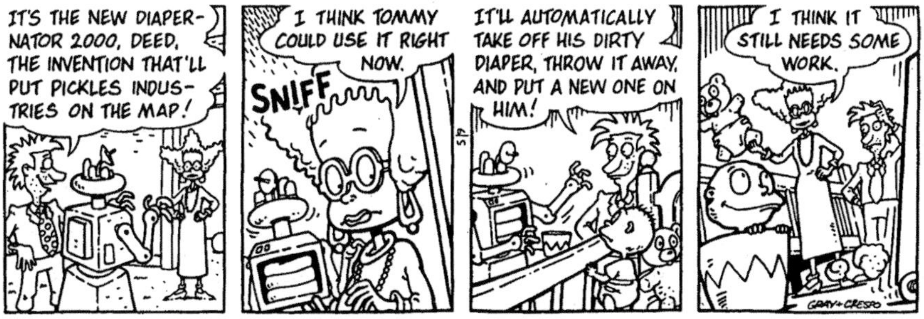
IT'S THE NEW DIAPER-NATOR 2000, DEED, THE INVENTION THAT'LL PUT PICKLES INDUS-TRIES ON THE MAP!
I THINK TOMMY COULD USE IT RIGHT NOW.
SNIFF
IT'LL AUTOMATICALLY TAKE OFF HIS DIRTY DIAPER, THROW IT AWAY, AND PUT A NEW ONE ON HIM!
I THINK IT STILL NEEDS SOME WORK.
GRAY+CRESPO

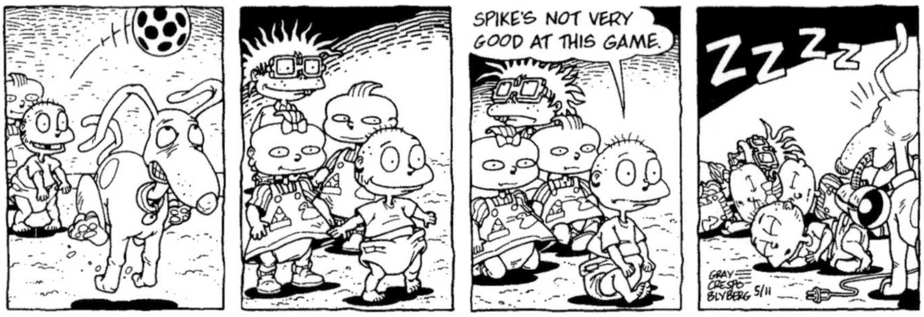
SPIKE'S NOT VERY GOOD AT THIS GAME.
Z Z Z z
GRAY CRESPO BLYBERG 5/11

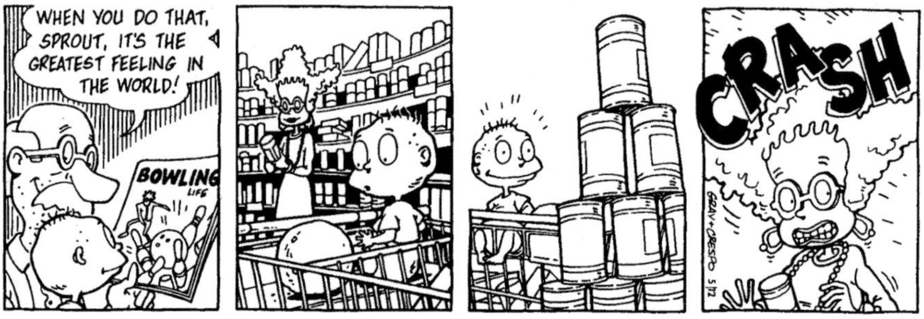
WHEN YOU DO THAT, SPROUT, IT'S THE GREATEST FEELING IN THE WORLD!
BOWLING LIFE
CRASH
GRAY+CRESPO 5/12

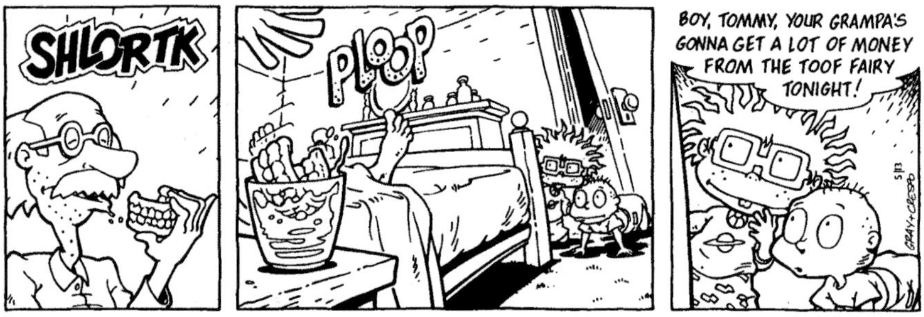
SHLORTK
PLOOP
BOY, TOMMY, YOUR GRAMPA'S GONNA GET A LOT OF MONEY FROM THE TOOF FAIRY TONIGHT!
5/13 GRAY+CRESPO

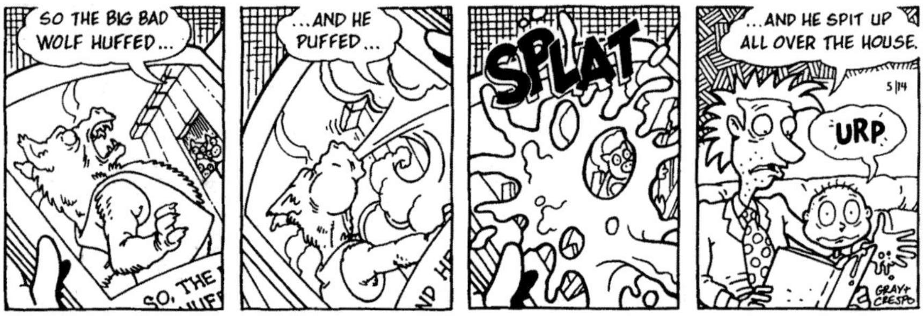
SO THE BIG BAD WOLF HUFFED...
...AND HE PUFFED...
SPLAT
...AND HE SPIT UP ALL OVER THE HOUSE.
5/14
URP
GRAY+CRESPO

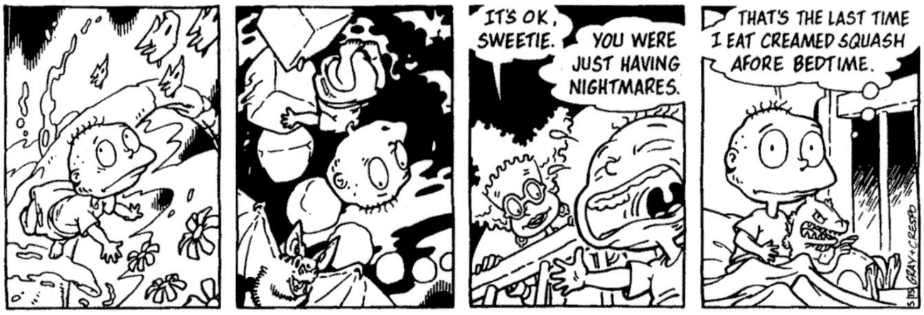
IT'S OK, SWEETIE.
YOU WERE JUST HAVING NIGHTMARES.
THAT'S THE LAST TIME I EAT CREAMED SQUASH AFORE BEDTIME.
5/15 GRAY+CRESPO

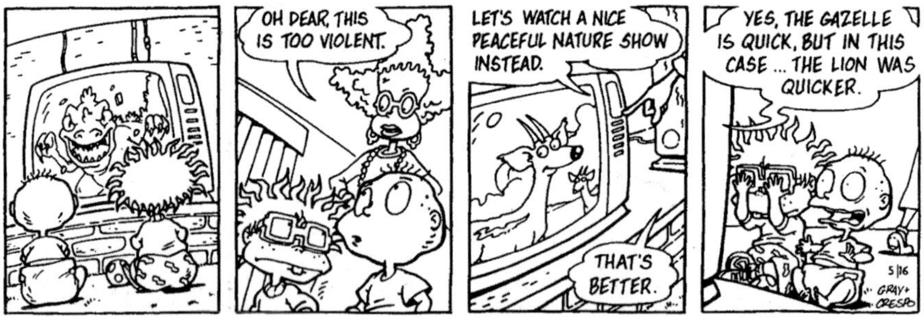
OH DEAR, THIS IS TOO VIOLENT.
LET'S WATCH A NICE PEACEFUL NATURE SHOW INSTEAD.
THAT'S BETTER.
YES, THE GAZELLE IS QUICK, BUT IN THIS CASE ... THE LION WAS QUICKER.
5/16 GRAY+CRESPO

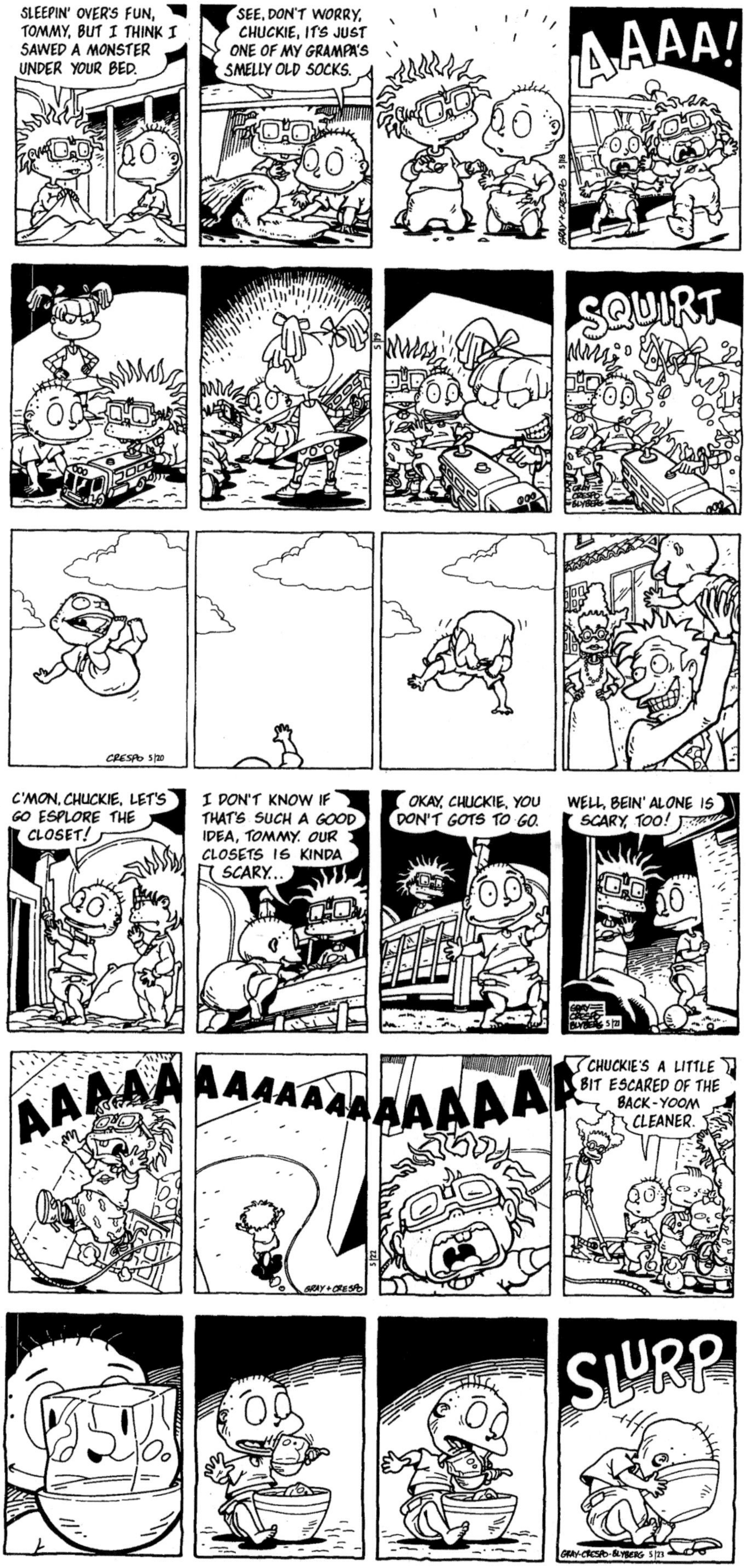
SLEEPIN' OVER'S FUN, TOMMY, BUT I THINK I SAWED A MONSTER UNDER YOUR BED.
SEE, DON'T WORRY, CHUCKIE, IT'S JUST ONE OF MY GRAMPA'S SMELLY OLD SOCKS.
GRAY + CRESPO 5/18
AAAA!
SQUIRT
GRAY CRESPO BLYBERG
CRESPO 5/20
C'MON, CHUCKIE, LET'S GO ESPLORE THE CLOSET!
I DON'T KNOW IF THAT'S SUCH A GOOD IDEA, TOMMY. OUR CLOSETS IS KINDA SCARY...
OKAY, CHUCKIE, YOU DON'T GOTS TO GO.
WELL, BEIN' ALONE IS SCARY, TOO!
GRAY CRESPO BLYBERG 5/21
AAAAAAAAAAAAAAAAA
GRAY + CRESPO 5/22
CHUCKIE'S A LITTLE BIT ESCARED OF THE BACK-YOOM CLEANER.
SLURP
GRAY-CRESPO-BLYBERG 5/23

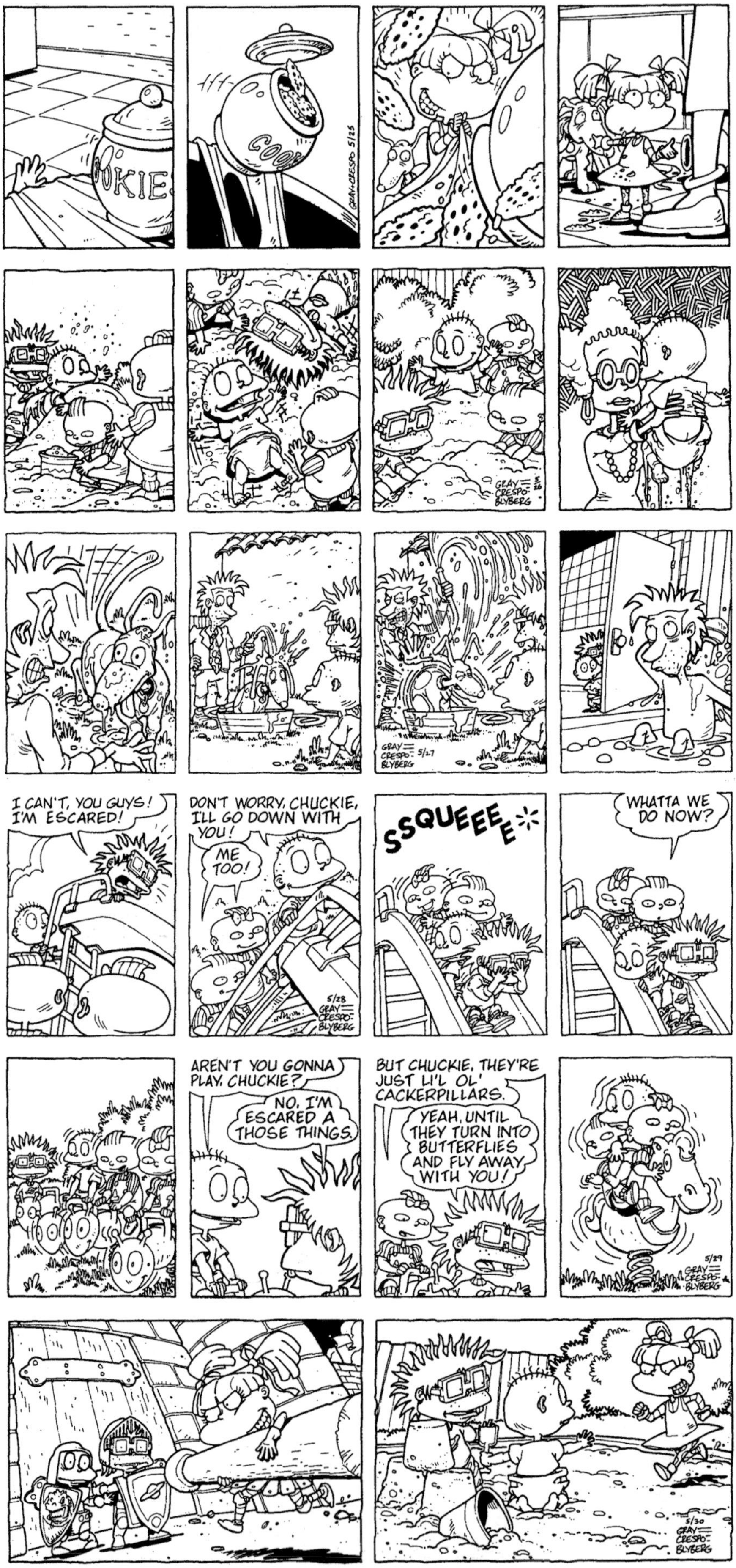
I CAN'T, YOU GUYS! I'M ESCARED!
DON'T WORRY, CHUCKIE, I'LL GO DOWN WITH YOU!
ME TOO!
SSQUEEEEE
WHATTA WE DO NOW?
AREN'T YOU GONNA PLAY, CHUCKIE?
NO. I'M ESCARED A THOSE THINGS.
BUT CHUCKIE, THEY'RE JUST LI'L OL' CACKERPILLARS.
YEAH, UNTIL THEY TURN INTO BUTTERFLIES AND FLY AWAY WITH YOU!

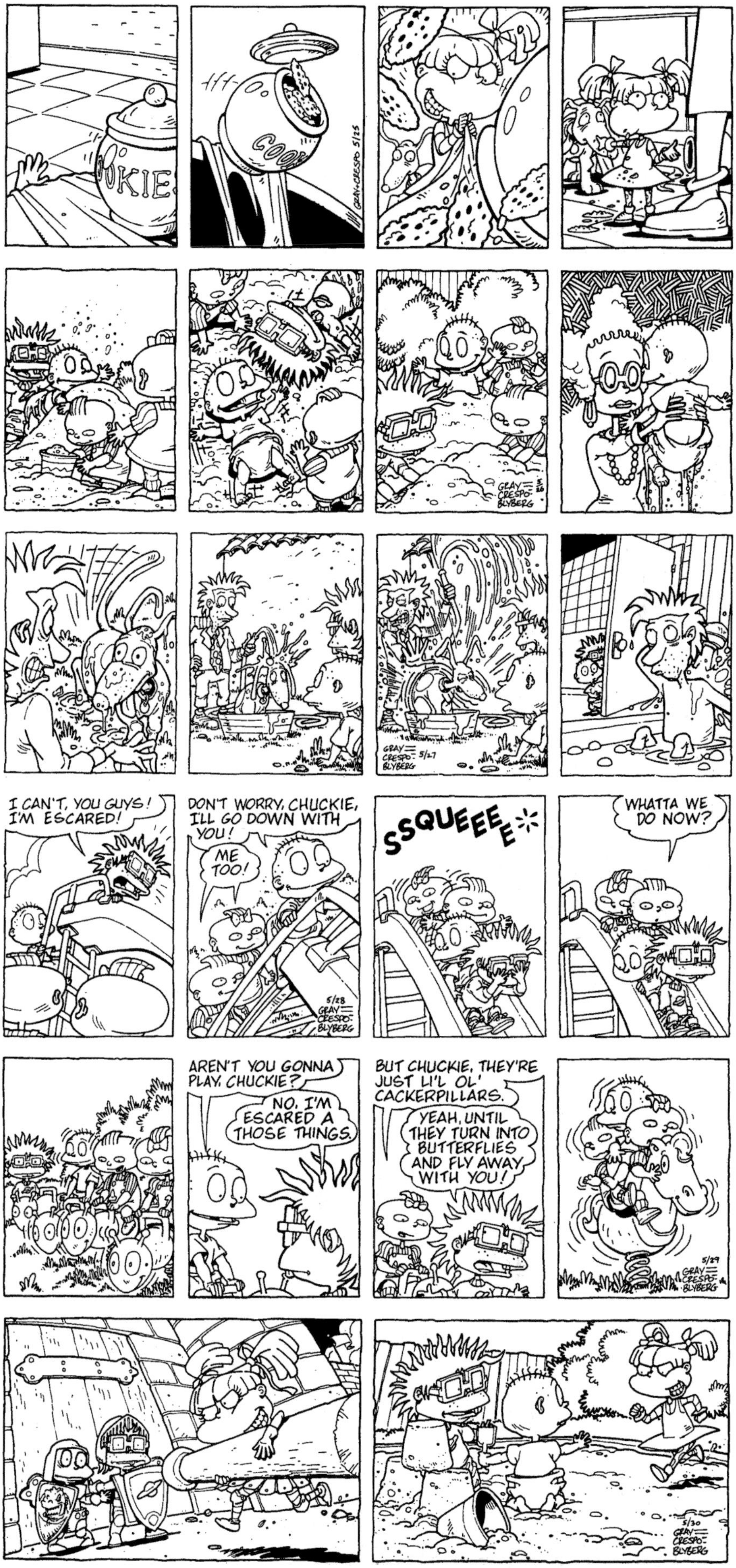
GRAY-CRESPO 5/25
GRAY-CRESPO-BLYBERG 5/26
GRAY-CRESPO-BLYBERG 5/27
I CAN'T, YOU GUYS! I'M ESCARED!
DON'T WORRY, CHUCKIE, I'LL GO DOWN WITH YOU!
ME TOO!
5/28 GRAY-CRESPO-BLYBERG
SSQUEEEEE
WHATTA WE DO NOW?
AREN'T YOU GONNA PLAY, CHUCKIE?
NO, I'M ESCARED A THOSE THINGS.
BUT CHUCKIE, THEY'RE JUST LI'L OL' CACKERPILLARS.
YEAH, UNTIL THEY TURN INTO BUTTERFLIES AND FLY AWAY WITH YOU!
5/29 GRAY-CRESPO-BLYBERG
5/30 GRAY-CRESPO-BLYBERG

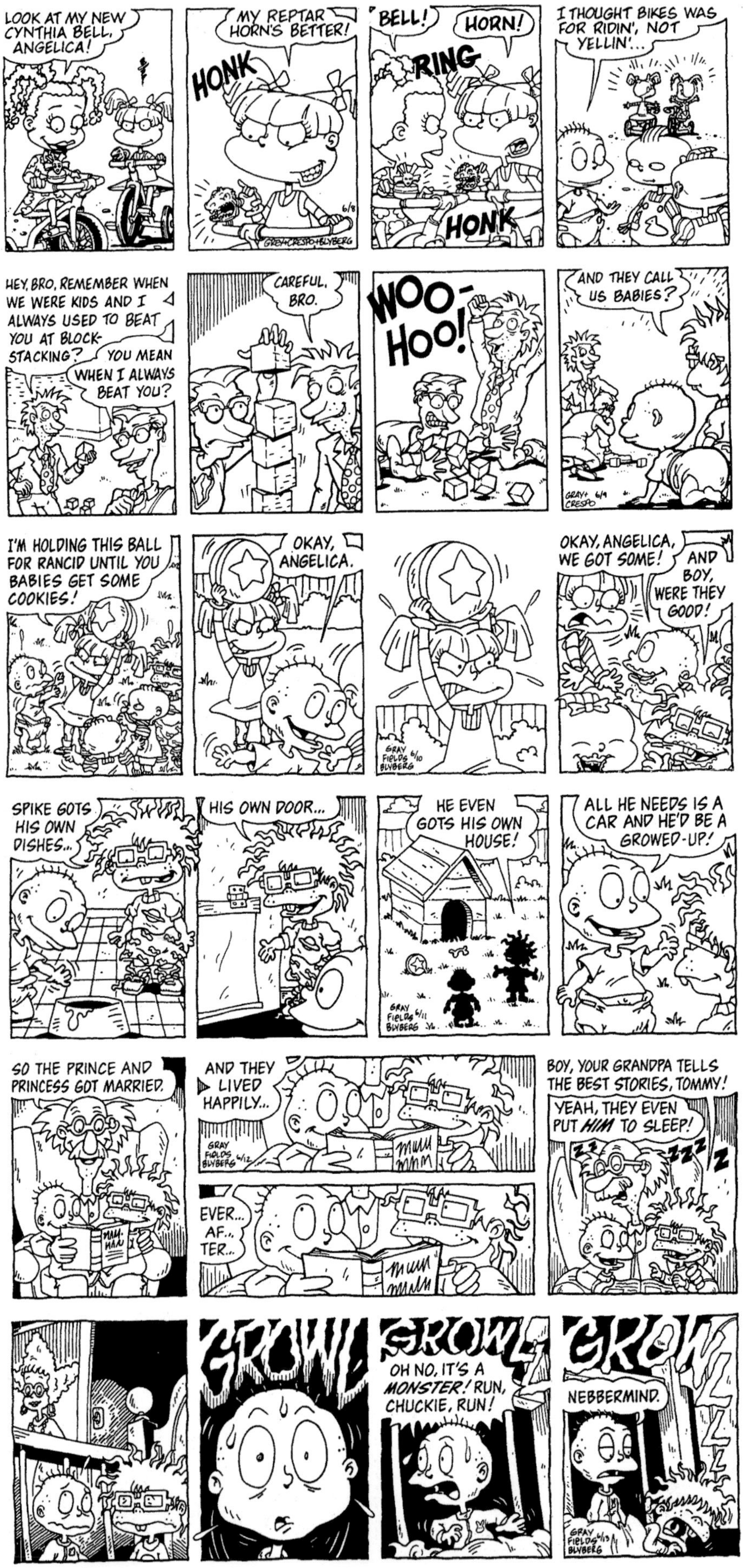
LOOK AT MY NEW CYNTHIA BELL, ANGELICA!
MY REPTAR HORN'S BETTER!
HONK
BELL!
HORN!
RING
HONK
I THOUGHT BIKES WAS FOR RIDIN', NOT YELLIN'...
HEY, BRO, REMEMBER WHEN WE WERE KIDS AND I ALWAYS USED TO BEAT YOU AT BLOCK-STACKING?
YOU MEAN WHEN I ALWAYS BEAT YOU?
CAREFUL, BRO.
WOO-HOO!
AND THEY CALL US BABIES?
I'M HOLDING THIS BALL FOR RANCID UNTIL YOU BABIES GET SOME COOKIES!
OKAY, ANGELICA.
OKAY, ANGELICA, WE GOT SOME!
AND BOY, WERE THEY GOOD!
SPIKE GOTS HIS OWN DISHES...
HIS OWN DOOR...
HE EVEN GOTS HIS OWN HOUSE!
ALL HE NEEDS IS A CAR AND HE'D BE A GROWED-UP!
SO THE PRINCE AND PRINCESS GOT MARRIED.
AND THEY LIVED HAPPILY...
EVER... AF... TER...
BOY, YOUR GRANDPA TELLS THE BEST STORIES, TOMMY!
YEAH, THEY EVEN PUT HIM TO SLEEP!
GROWL
GROWL
OH NO, IT'S A MONSTER! RUN, CHUCKIE, RUN!
GROWL
NEBBERMIND.

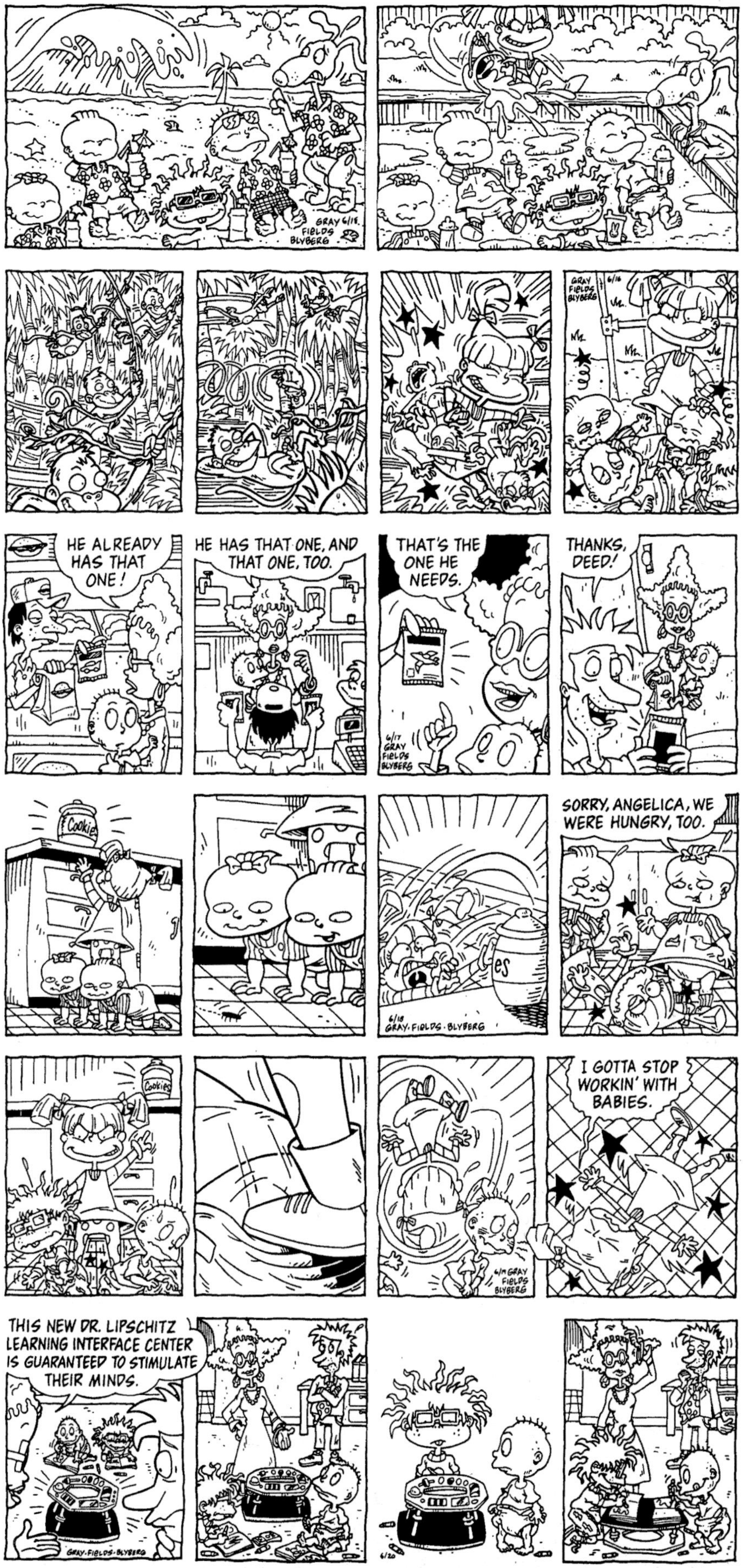
GRAY 6/15
FIELDS
BLYBERG
GRAY
FIELDS
BLYBERG
6/16
HE ALREADY HAS THAT ONE!
HE HAS THAT ONE, AND THAT ONE, TOO.
THAT'S THE ONE HE NEEDS.
6/17
GRAY
FIELDS
BLYBERG
THANKS, DEED!
Cookies
6/18
GRAY · FIELDS · BLYBERG
SORRY, ANGELICA, WE WERE HUNGRY, TOO.
Cookies
6/19 GRAY
FIELDS
BLYBERG
I GOTTA STOP WORKIN' WITH BABIES.
THIS NEW DR. LIPSCHITZ LEARNING INTERFACE CENTER IS GUARANTEED TO STIMULATE THEIR MINDS.
GRAY · FIELDS · BLYBERG
6/20

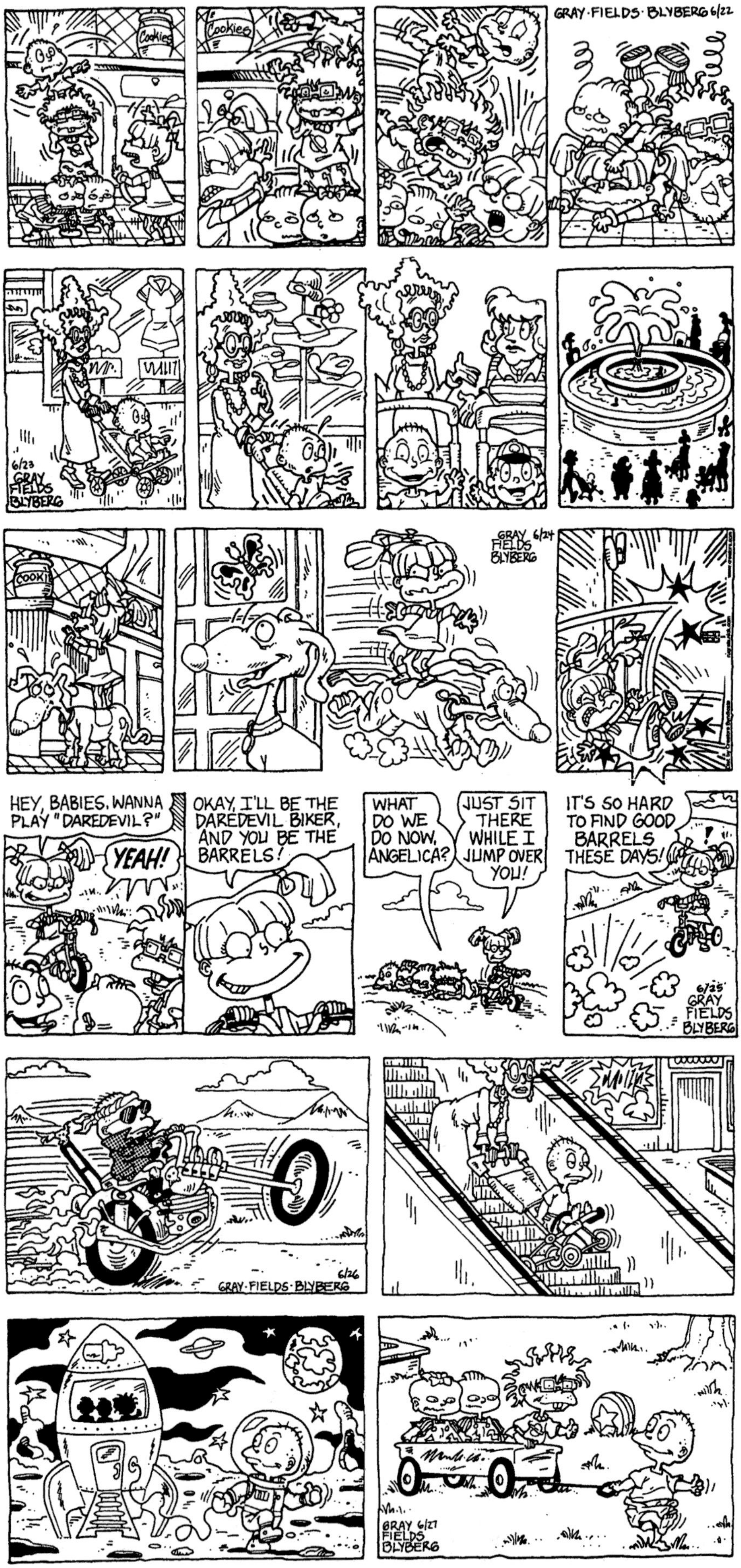
Cookies
Cookies
GRAY·FIELDS·BLYBERG 6/22
6/23 GRAY FIELDS BLYBERG
GRAY 6/24 FIELDS BLYBERG
HEY, BABIES. WANNA PLAY "DAREDEVIL?"
YEAH!
OKAY, I'LL BE THE DAREDEVIL BIKER, AND YOU BE THE BARRELS!
WHAT DO WE DO NOW, ANGELICA?
JUST SIT THERE WHILE I JUMP OVER YOU!
IT'S SO HARD TO FIND GOOD BARRELS THESE DAYS!
!
6/25 GRAY FIELDS BLYBERG
6/26 GRAY·FIELDS·BLYBERG
GRAY 6/27 FIELDS BLYBERG

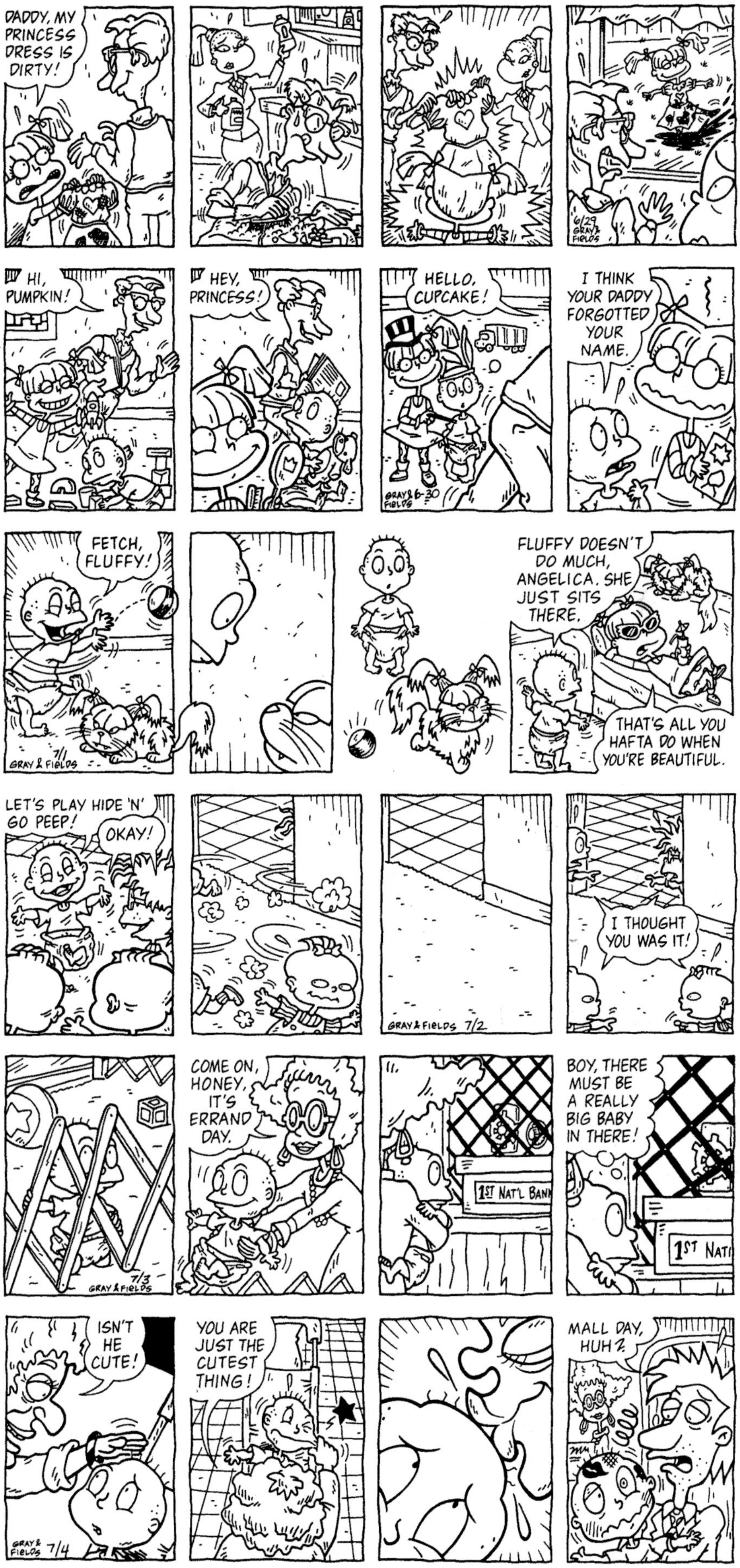
DADDY, MY PRINCESS DRESS IS DIRTY!
6/29 GRAY & FIELDS
HI, PUMPKIN!
HEY, PRINCESS!
HELLO, CUPCAKE!
GRAY & FIELDS 6-30
I THINK YOUR DADDY FORGOTTED YOUR NAME.
FETCH, FLUFFY!
7/1 GRAY & FIELDS
FLUFFY DOESN'T DO MUCH, ANGELICA. SHE JUST SITS THERE.
THAT'S ALL YOU HAFTA DO WHEN YOU'RE BEAUTIFUL.
LET'S PLAY HIDE 'N' GO PEEP!
OKAY!
GRAY & FIELDS 7/2
I THOUGHT YOU WAS IT!
7/3 GRAY & FIELDS
COME ON, HONEY, IT'S ERRAND DAY.
1ST NAT'L BANK
BOY, THERE MUST BE A REALLY BIG BABY IN THERE!
1ST NAT
ISN'T HE CUTE!
GRAY & FIELDS 7/4
YOU ARE JUST THE CUTEST THING!
MALL DAY, HUH?

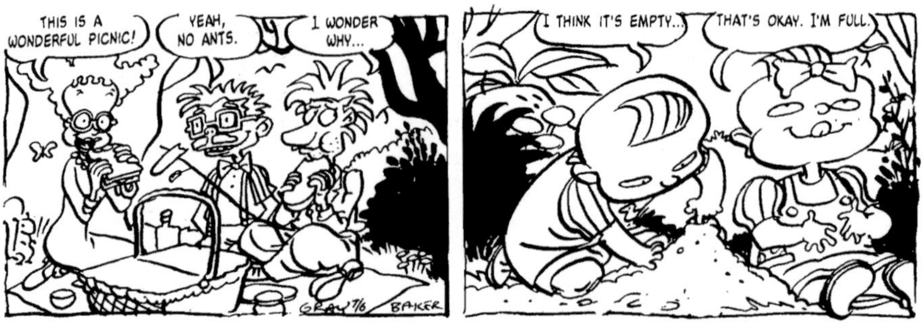
THIS IS A WONDERFUL PICNIC!
YEAH, NO ANTS.
I WONDER WHY...
GRAY 7/6 BAKER
I THINK IT'S EMPTY...
THAT'S OKAY. I'M FULL.

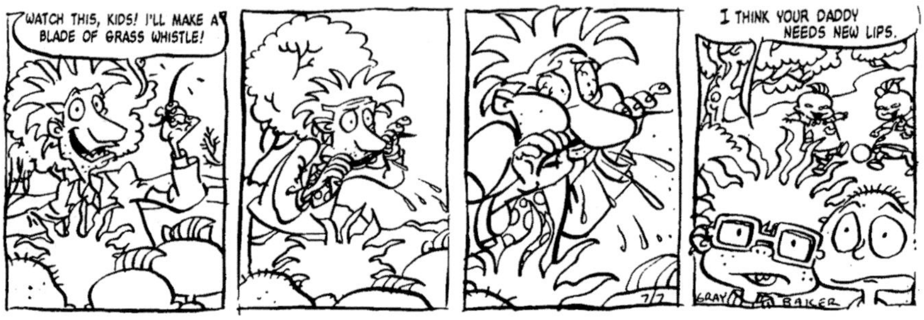
WATCH THIS, KIDS! I'LL MAKE A BLADE OF GRASS WHISTLE!
7/7
I THINK YOUR DADDY NEEDS NEW LIPS.
GRAY BAKER

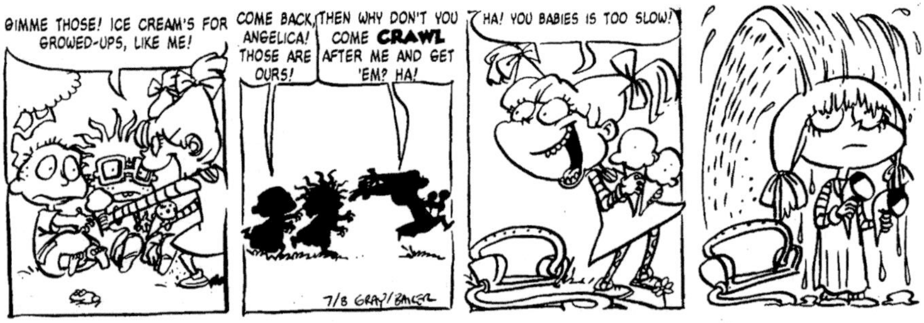
GIMME THOSE! ICE CREAM'S FOR GROWED-UPS, LIKE ME!
COME BACK, ANGELICA! THOSE ARE OURS!
THEN WHY DON'T YOU COME CRAWL AFTER ME AND GET 'EM? HA!
7/8 GRAY/BAKER
HA! YOU BABIES IS TOO SLOW!

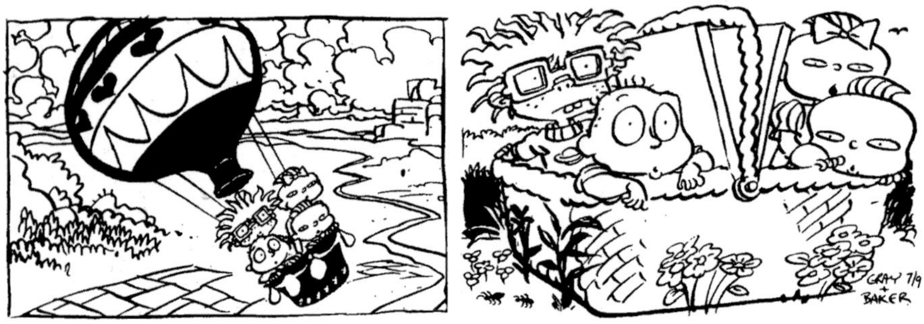
GRAY 7/9 + BAKER

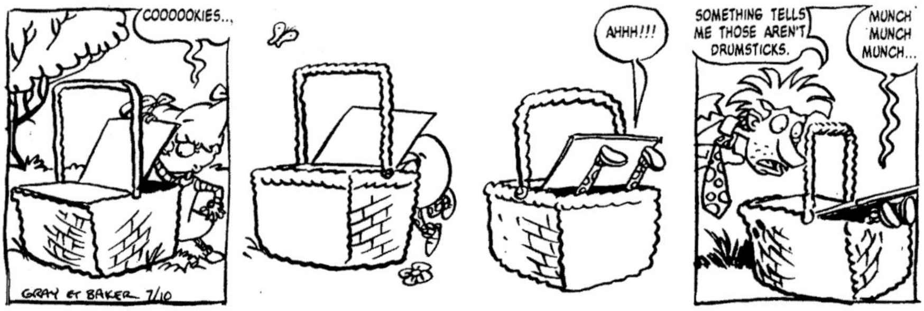
COOOOOKIES...
GRAY ET BAKER 7/10
AHHH!!!
SOMETHING TELLS ME THOSE AREN'T DRUMSTICKS.
MUNCH MUNCH MUNCH...

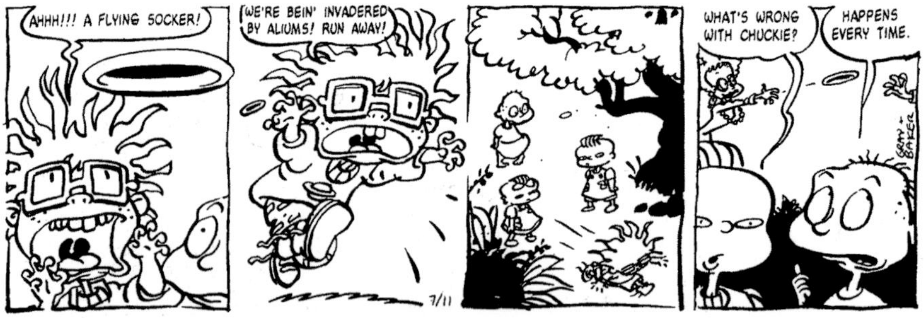
AHHH!!! A FLYING SOCKER!
WE'RE BEIN' INVADERED BY ALIUMS! RUN AWAY!
7/11
WHAT'S WRONG WITH CHUCKIE?
HAPPENS EVERY TIME.
GRAY + BAKER

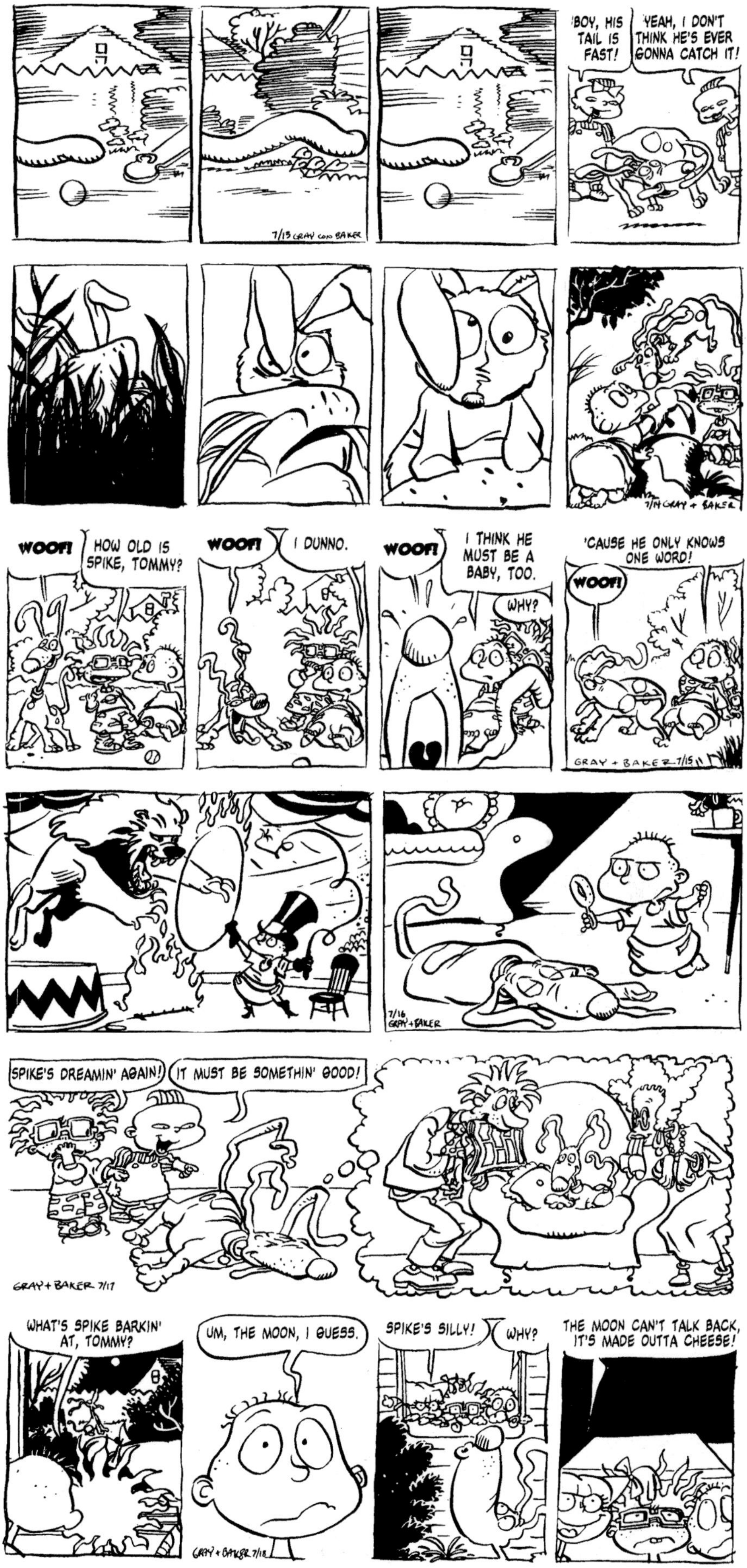
BOY, HIS TAIL IS FAST!
YEAH, I DON'T THINK HE'S EVER GONNA CATCH IT!
7/13 GRAY con BAKER
7/14 GRAY + BAKER
WOOF!
HOW OLD IS SPIKE, TOMMY?
WOOF!
I DUNNO.
WOOF!
I THINK HE MUST BE A BABY, TOO.
WHY?
'CAUSE HE ONLY KNOWS ONE WORD!
WOOF!
GRAY + BAKER 7/15
7/16 GRAY + BAKER
SPIKE'S DREAMIN' AGAIN!
IT MUST BE SOMETHIN' GOOD!
GRAY + BAKER 7/17
WHAT'S SPIKE BARKIN' AT, TOMMY?
UM, THE MOON, I GUESS.
SPIKE'S SILLY!
WHY?
THE MOON CAN'T TALK BACK, IT'S MADE OUTTA CHEESE!
GRAY + BAKER 7/18

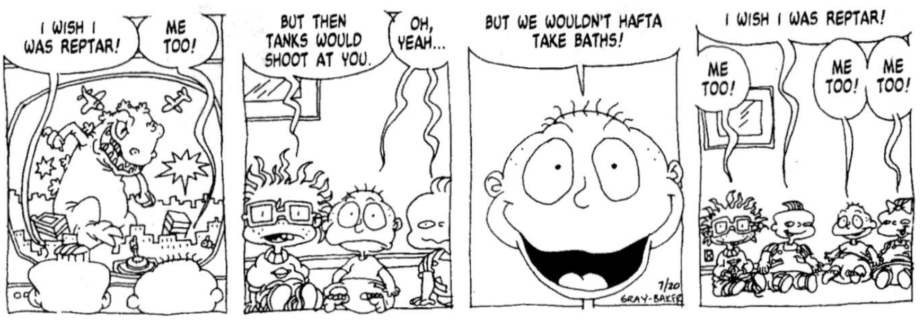
I WISH I WAS REPTAR!
ME TOO!
BUT THEN TANKS WOULD SHOOT AT YOU.
OH, YEAH...
BUT WE WOULDN'T HAFTA TAKE BATHS!
7/20 GRAY-BAKER
I WISH I WAS REPTAR!
ME TOO!
ME TOO!
ME TOO!

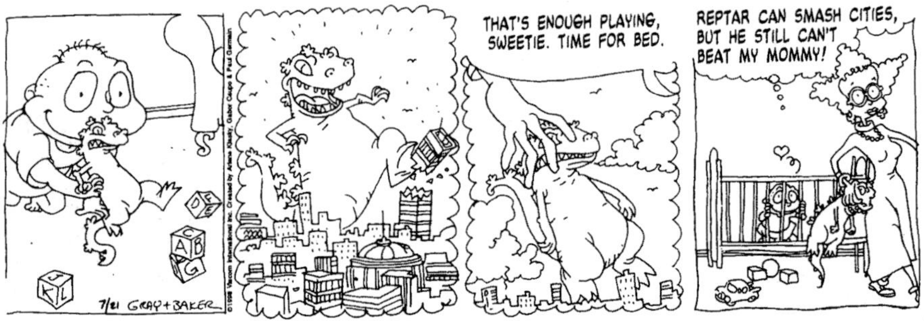
7/21 GRAY+BAKER
THAT'S ENOUGH PLAYING, SWEETIE. TIME FOR BED.
REPTAR CAN SMASH CITIES, BUT HE STILL CAN'T BEAT MY MOMMY!

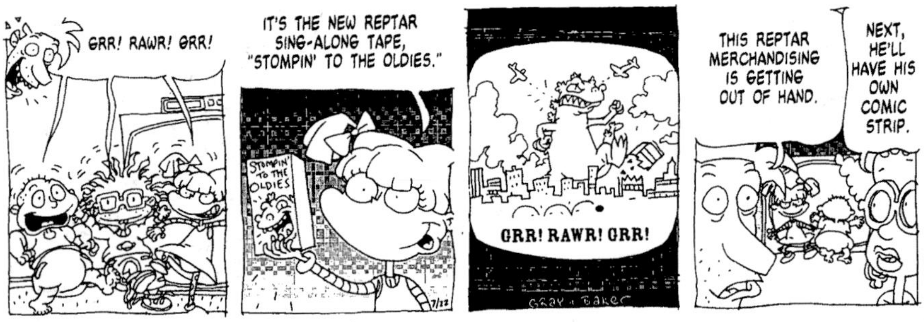
GRR! RAWR! GRR!
IT'S THE NEW REPTAR SING-ALONG TAPE, "STOMPIN' TO THE OLDIES."
STOMPIN' TO THE OLDIES
7/22
GRR! RAWR! GRR!
GRAY + BAKER
THIS REPTAR MERCHANDISING IS GETTING OUT OF HAND.
NEXT, HE'LL HAVE HIS OWN COMIC STRIP.

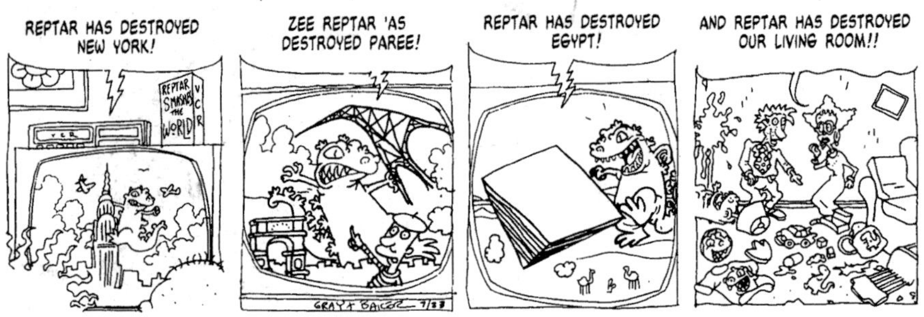
REPTAR HAS DESTROYED NEW YORK!
REPTAR SMASHES THE WORLD
ZEE REPTAR 'AS DESTROYED PAREE!
GRAY + BAKER 7/23
REPTAR HAS DESTROYED EGYPT!
AND REPTAR HAS DESTROYED OUR LIVING ROOM!!

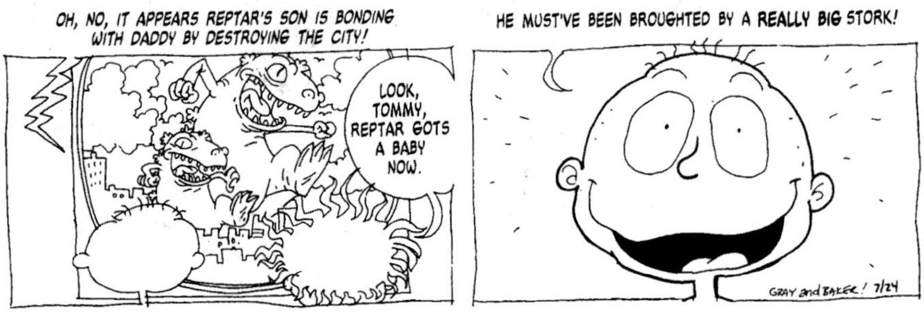
OH, NO, IT APPEARS REPTAR'S SON IS BONDING WITH DADDY BY DESTROYING THE CITY!
LOOK, TOMMY, REPTAR GOTS A BABY NOW.
HE MUST'VE BEEN BROUGHTED BY A REALLY BIG STORK!
GRAY and BAKER! 7/24

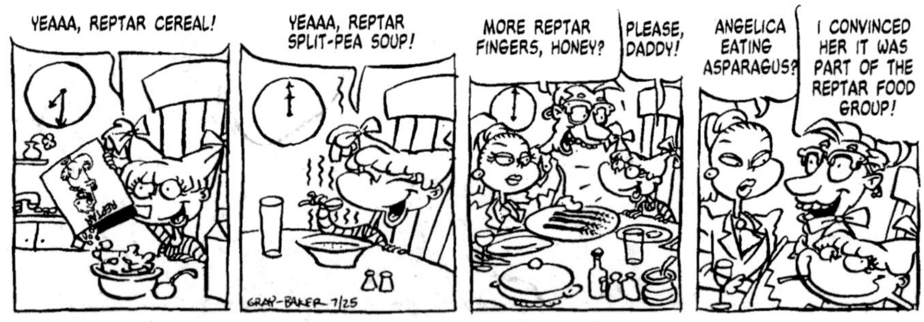
YEAAA, REPTAR CEREAL!
YEAAA, REPTAR SPLIT-PEA SOUP!
GRAY-BAKER 7/25
MORE REPTAR FINGERS, HONEY?
PLEASE, DADDY!
ANGELICA EATING ASPARAGUS?
I CONVINCED HER IT WAS PART OF THE REPTAR FOOD GROUP!

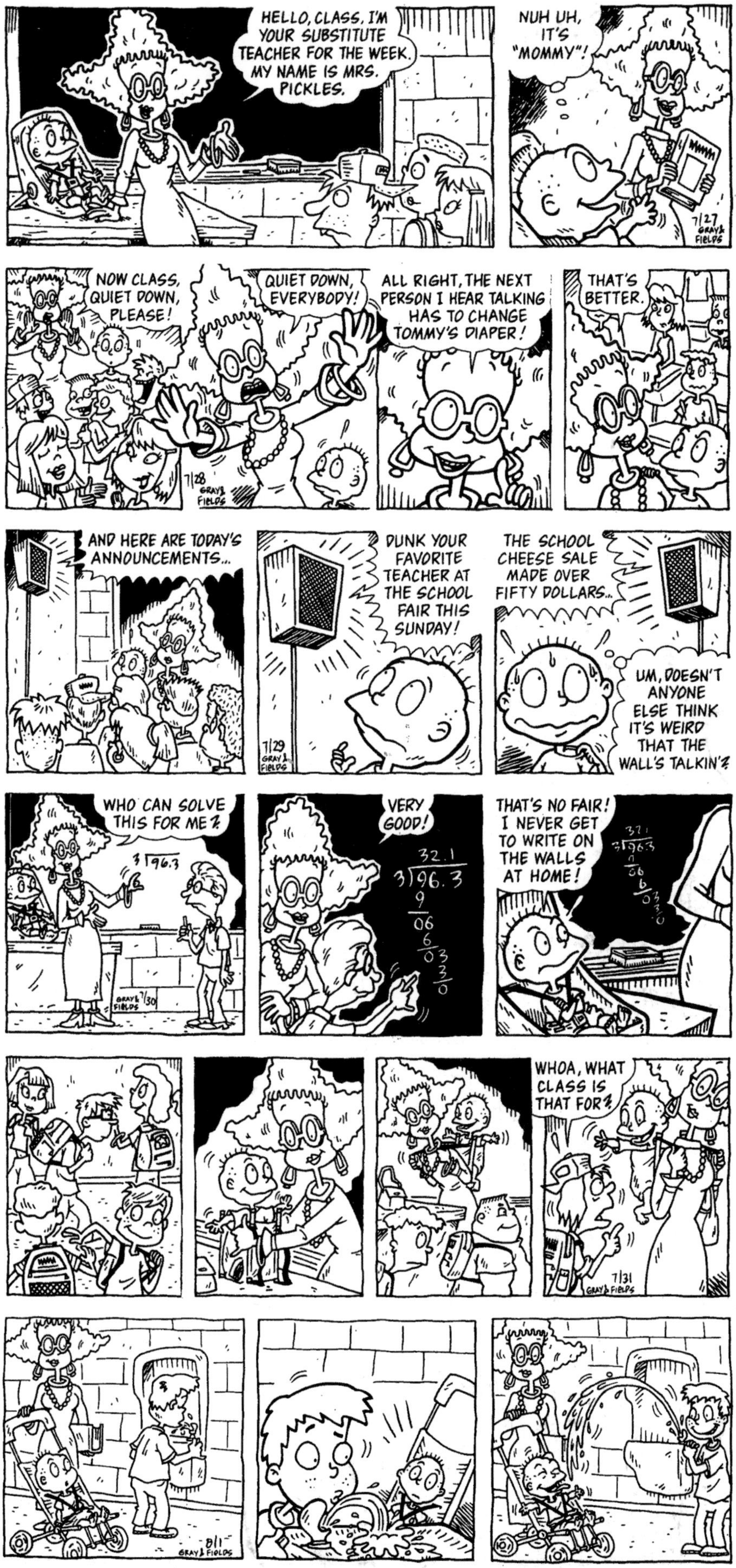
HELLO, CLASS. I'M YOUR SUBSTITUTE TEACHER FOR THE WEEK. MY NAME IS MRS. PICKLES.
NUH UH, IT'S "MOMMY"!
7/27 GRAY & FIELDS
NOW CLASS, QUIET DOWN, PLEASE!
7/28 GRAY & FIELDS
QUIET DOWN, EVERYBODY!
ALL RIGHT, THE NEXT PERSON I HEAR TALKING HAS TO CHANGE TOMMY'S DIAPER!
THAT'S BETTER.
AND HERE ARE TODAY'S ANNOUNCEMENTS...
DUNK YOUR FAVORITE TEACHER AT THE SCHOOL FAIR THIS SUNDAY!
7/29 GRAY & FIELDS
THE SCHOOL CHEESE SALE MADE OVER FIFTY DOLLARS...
UM, DOESN'T ANYONE ELSE THINK IT'S WEIRD THAT THE WALL'S TALKIN'?
WHO CAN SOLVE THIS FOR ME?
GRAY & FIELDS 7/30
VERY GOOD!
THAT'S NO FAIR! I NEVER GET TO WRITE ON THE WALLS AT HOME!
WHOA, WHAT CLASS IS THAT FOR?
7/31 GRAY & FIELDS
8/1 GRAY & FIELDS

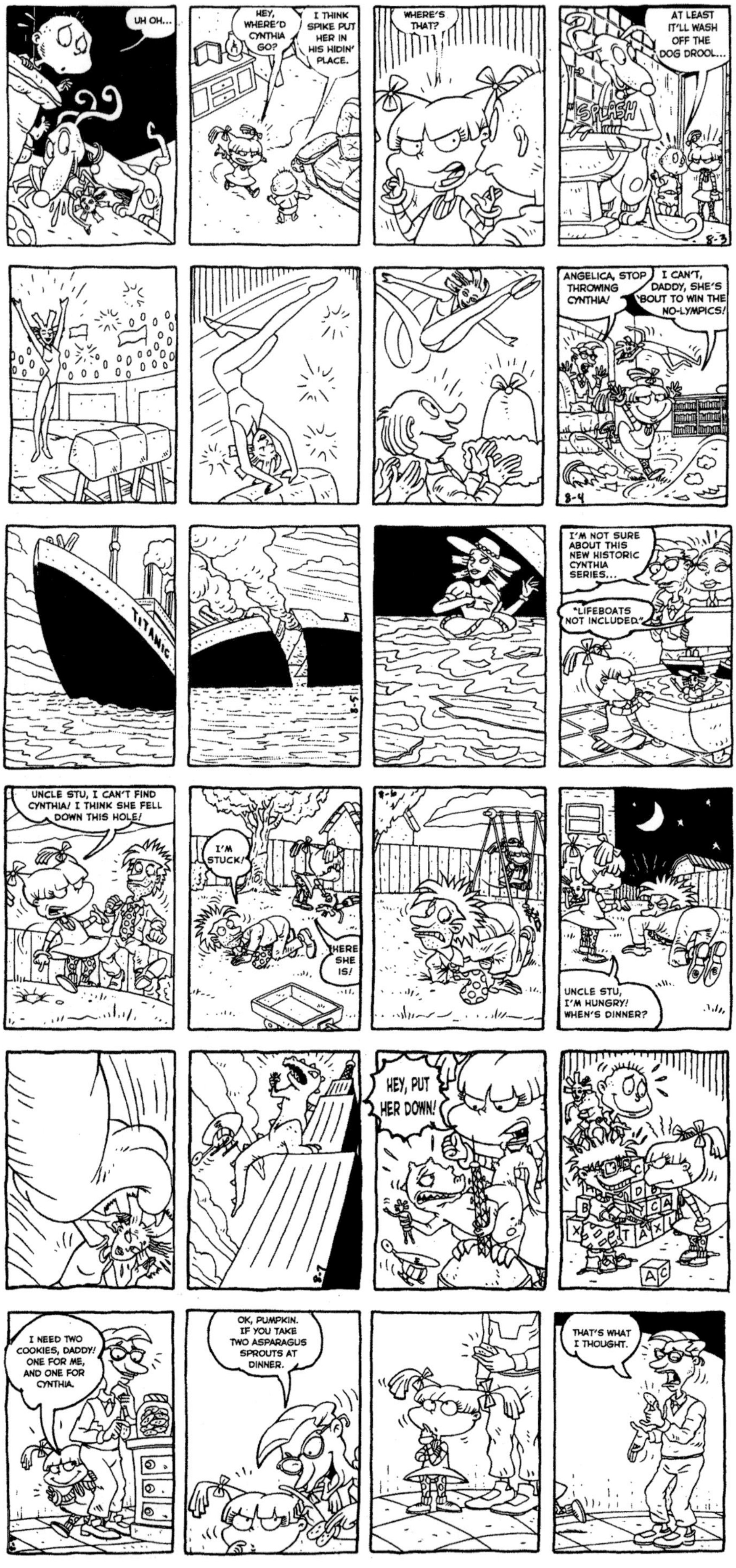
UH OH...
HEY, WHERE'D CYNTHIA GO?
I THINK SPIKE PUT HER IN HIS HIDIN' PLACE.
WHERE'S THAT?
AT LEAST IT'LL WASH OFF THE DOG DROOL...
SPLASH
8-3
ANGELICA, STOP THROWING CYNTHIA!
I CAN'T, DADDY, SHE'S 'BOUT TO WIN THE NO-LYMPICS!
8-4
TITANIC
I'M NOT SURE ABOUT THIS NEW HISTORIC CYNTHIA SERIES...
"LIFEBOATS NOT INCLUDED."
UNCLE STU, I CAN'T FIND CYNTHIA! I THINK SHE FELL DOWN THIS HOLE!
I'M STUCK!
HERE SHE IS!
8-6
UNCLE STU, I'M HUNGRY! WHEN'S DINNER?
8-7
HEY, PUT HER DOWN!
I NEED TWO COOKIES, DADDY! ONE FOR ME, AND ONE FOR CYNTHIA.
OK, PUMPKIN. IF YOU TAKE TWO ASPARAGUS SPROUTS AT DINNER.
THAT'S WHAT I THOUGHT.

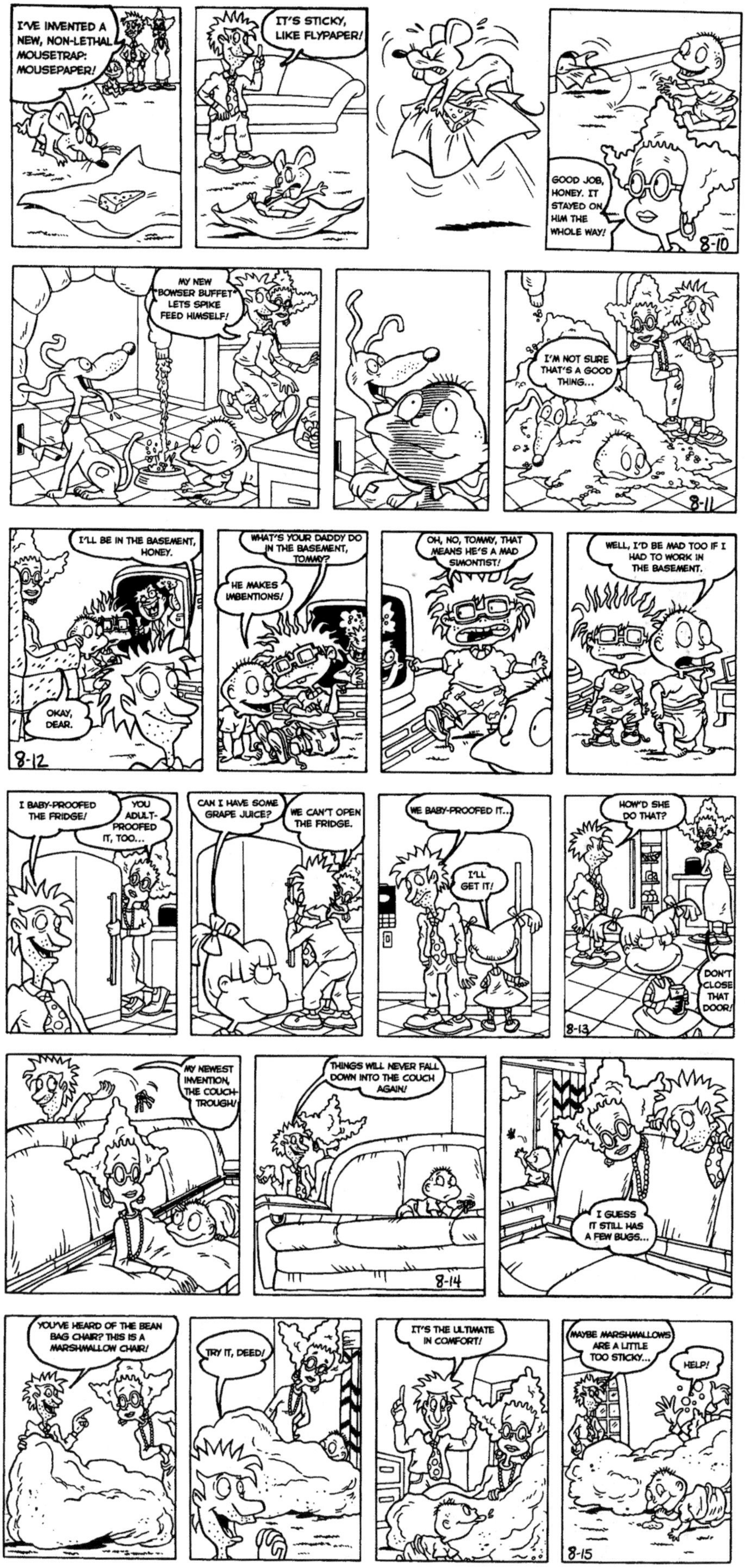
I'VE INVENTED A NEW, NON-LETHAL MOUSETRAP: MOUSEPAPER!
IT'S STICKY, LIKE FLYPAPER!
GOOD JOB, HONEY. IT STAYED ON HIM THE WHOLE WAY!
8-10
MY NEW "BOWSER BUFFET" LETS SPIKE FEED HIMSELF!
I'M NOT SURE THAT'S A GOOD THING...
8-11
I'LL BE IN THE BASEMENT, HONEY.
OKAY, DEAR.
8-12
WHAT'S YOUR DADDY DO IN THE BASEMENT, TOMMY?
HE MAKES IMBENTIONS!
OH, NO, TOMMY, THAT MEANS HE'S A MAD SIMONTIST!
WELL, I'D BE MAD TOO IF I HAD TO WORK IN THE BASEMENT.
I BABY-PROOFED THE FRIDGE!
YOU ADULT-PROOFED IT, TOO...
CAN I HAVE SOME GRAPE JUICE?
WE CAN'T OPEN THE FRIDGE.
WE BABY-PROOFED IT...
I'LL GET IT!
HOW'D SHE DO THAT?
DON'T CLOSE THAT DOOR!
8-13
MY NEWEST INVENTION, THE COUCH-TROUGH!
THINGS WILL NEVER FALL DOWN INTO THE COUCH AGAIN!
8-14
I GUESS IT STILL HAS A FEW BUGS...
YOU'VE HEARD OF THE BEAN BAG CHAIR? THIS IS A MARSHMALLOW CHAIR!
TRY IT, DEED!
IT'S THE ULTIMATE IN COMFORT!
MAYBE MARSHMALLOWS ARE A LITTLE TOO STICKY...
HELP!
8-15

1998

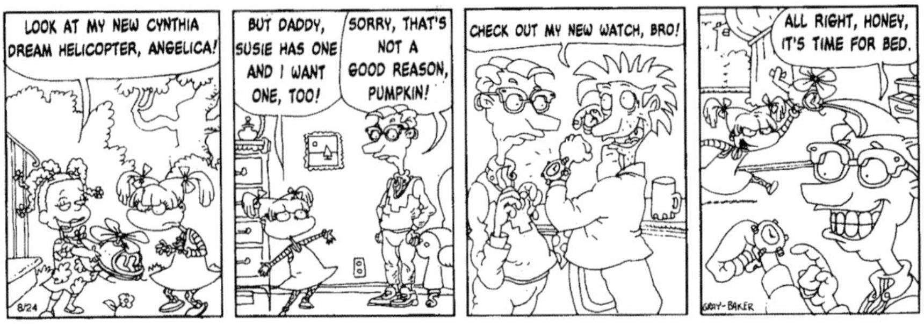
LOOK AT MY NEW CYNTHIA DREAM HELICOPTER, ANGELICA!
BUT DADDY, SUSIE HAS ONE AND I WANT ONE, TOO!
SORRY, THAT'S NOT A GOOD REASON, PUMPKIN!
CHECK OUT MY NEW WATCH, BRO!
ALL RIGHT, HONEY, IT'S TIME FOR BED.
8/24
GRAY-BAKER

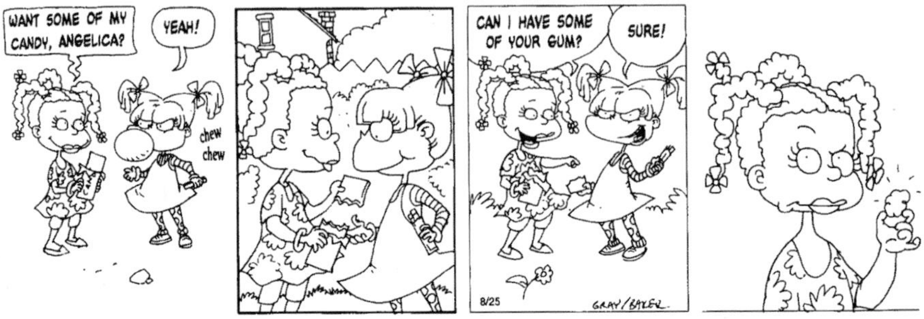
WANT SOME OF MY CANDY, ANGELICA?
YEAH!
chew chew
CAN I HAVE SOME OF YOUR GUM?
SURE!
8/25
GRAY/BAKER

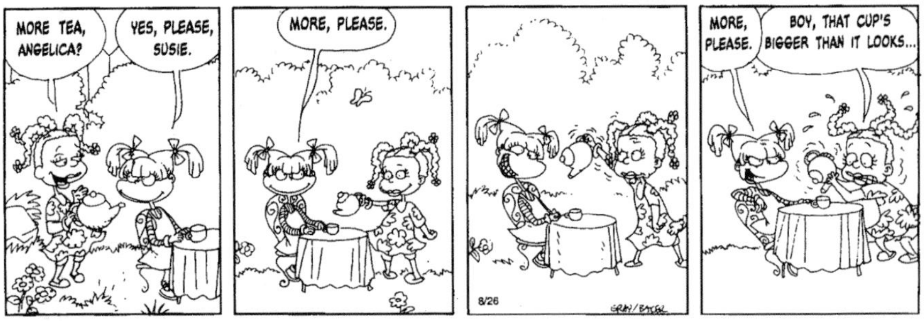
MORE TEA, ANGELICA?
YES, PLEASE, SUSIE.
MORE, PLEASE.
MORE, PLEASE.
BOY, THAT CUP'S BIGGER THAN IT LOOKS...
8/26
GRAY/BAKER

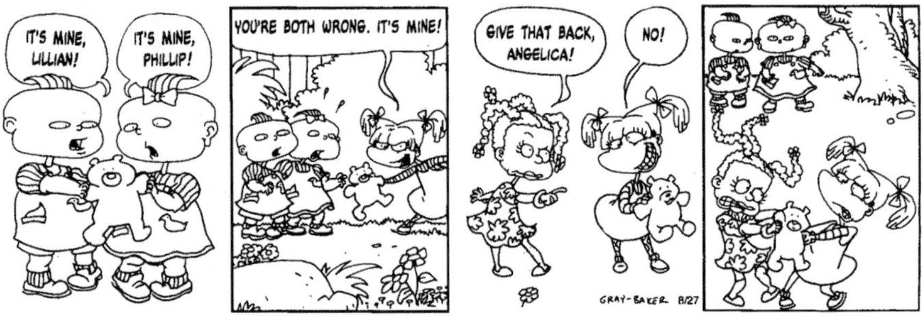
IT'S MINE, LILLIAN!
IT'S MINE, PHILLIP!
YOU'RE BOTH WRONG. IT'S MINE!
GIVE THAT BACK, ANGELICA!
NO!
GRAY-BAKER 8/27

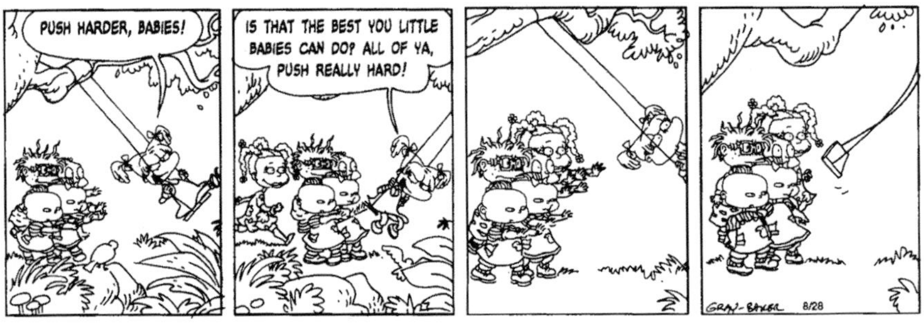
PUSH HARDER, BABIES!
IS THAT THE BEST YOU LITTLE BABIES CAN DO? ALL OF YA, PUSH REALLY HARD!
GRAY-BAKER 8/28

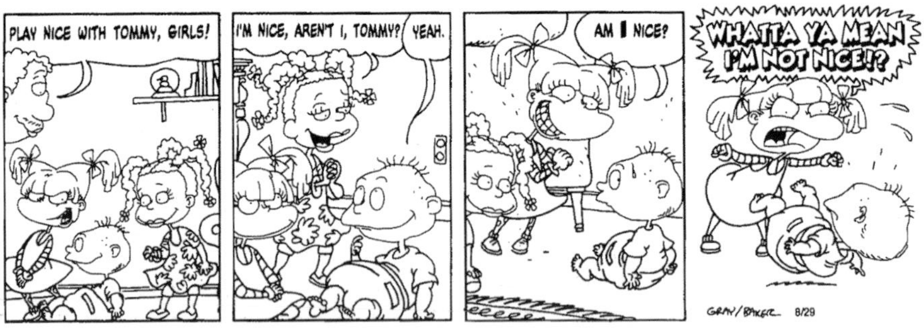
PLAY NICE WITH TOMMY, GIRLS!
I'M NICE, AREN'T I, TOMMY?
YEAH.
AM I NICE?
WHATTA YA MEAN I'M NOT NICE!?
GRAY/BAKER 8/29

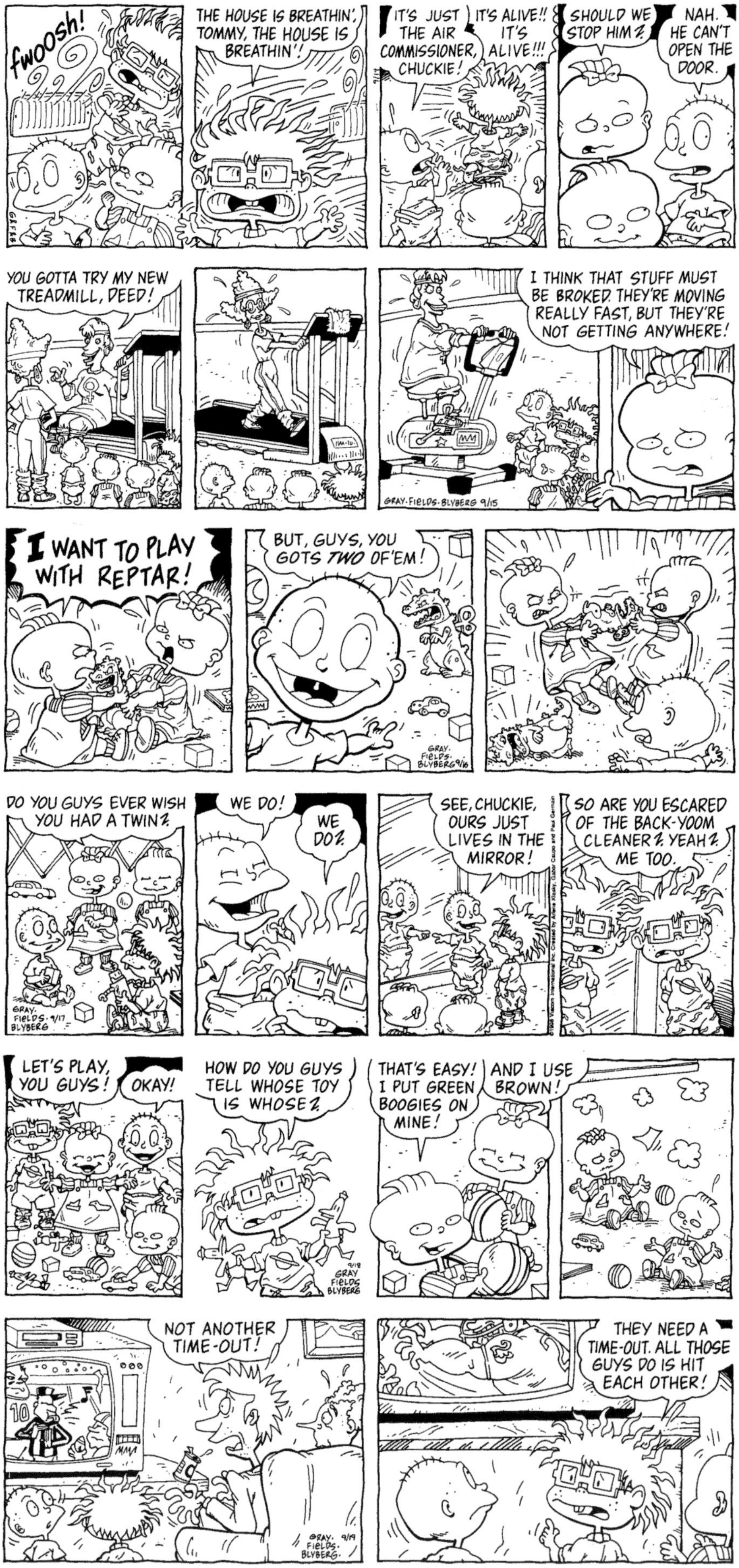
fwoosh!
THE HOUSE IS BREATHIN', TOMMY, THE HOUSE IS BREATHIN'!
IT'S JUST THE AIR COMMISSIONER, CHUCKIE!
IT'S ALIVE!! IT'S ALIVE!!!
SHOULD WE STOP HIM?
NAH. HE CAN'T OPEN THE DOOR.
YOU GOTTA TRY MY NEW TREADMILL, DEED!
I THINK THAT STUFF MUST BE BROKED. THEY'RE MOVING REALLY FAST, BUT THEY'RE NOT GETTING ANYWHERE!
GRAY·FIELDS·BLYBERG 9/15
I WANT TO PLAY WITH REPTAR!
BUT, GUYS, YOU GOTS TWO OF'EM!
GRAY. FIELDS. BLYBERG 9/16
DO YOU GUYS EVER WISH YOU HAD A TWIN?
GRAY. FIELDS. 9/17 BLYBERG
WE DO!
WE DO?
SEE, CHUCKIE, OURS JUST LIVES IN THE MIRROR!
SO ARE YOU ESCARED OF THE BACK-YOOM CLEANER? YEAH? ME TOO.
LET'S PLAY, YOU GUYS!
OKAY!
HOW DO YOU GUYS TELL WHOSE TOY IS WHOSE?
9/18 GRAY FIELDS BLYBERG
THAT'S EASY! I PUT GREEN BOOGIES ON MINE!
AND I USE BROWN!
NOT ANOTHER TIME-OUT!
GRAY. 9/19 FIELDS. BLYBERG.
THEY NEED A TIME-OUT. ALL THOSE GUYS DO IS HIT EACH OTHER!

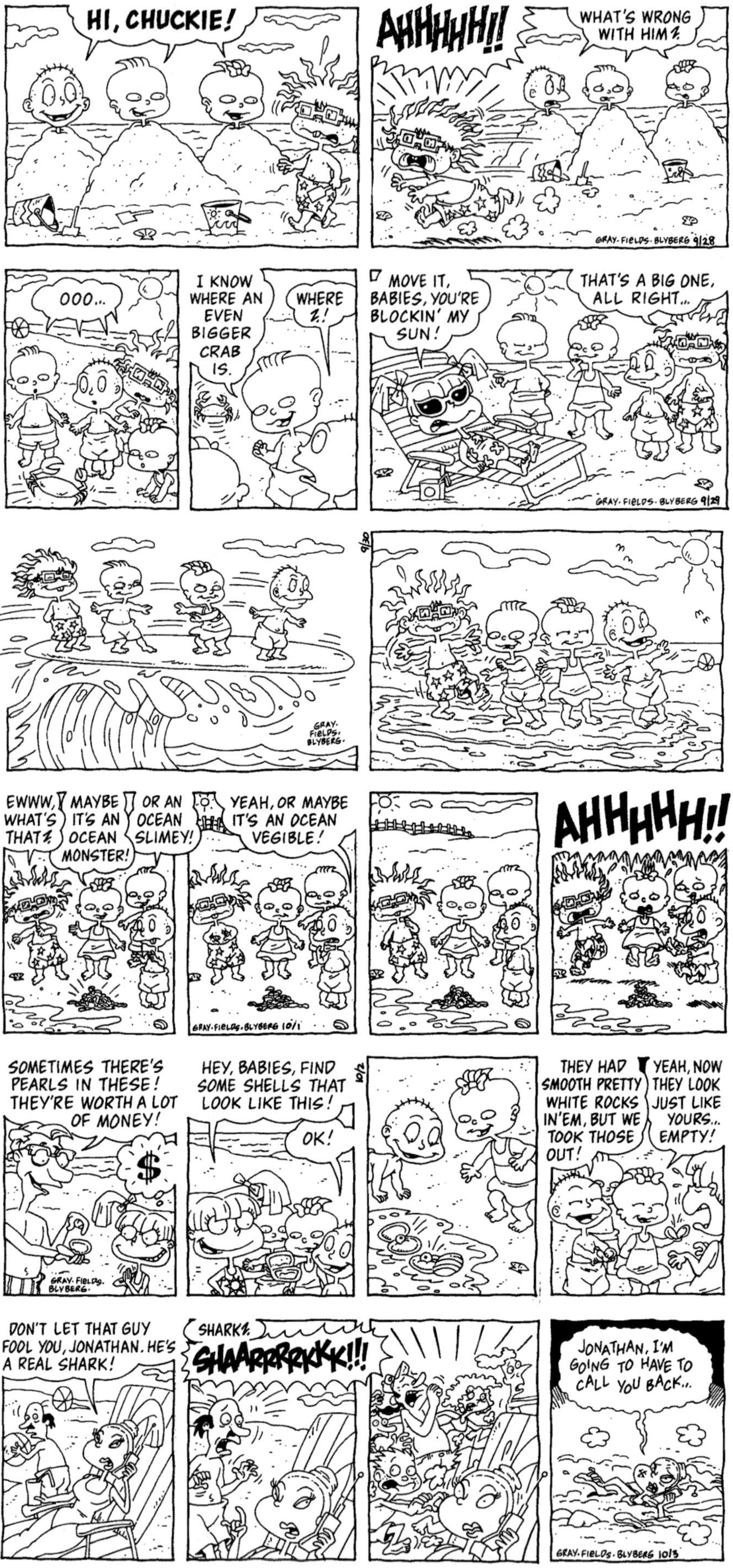
HI, CHUCKIE!
AHHHHH!!
WHAT'S WRONG WITH HIM?
GRAY·FIELDS·BLYBERG 9/28
OOO...
I KNOW WHERE AN EVEN BIGGER CRAB IS.
WHERE?!
MOVE IT, BABIES, YOU'RE BLOCKIN' MY SUN!
THAT'S A BIG ONE, ALL RIGHT...
GRAY·FIELDS·BLYBERG 9/29
9/30
GRAY·FIELDS·BLYBERG·
EWWW, WHAT'S THAT?
MAYBE IT'S AN OCEAN MONSTER!
OR AN OCEAN SLIMEY!
YEAH, OR MAYBE IT'S AN OCEAN VEGIBLE!
AHHHHH!!
GRAY·FIELDS·BLYBERG 10/1
SOMETIMES THERE'S PEARLS IN THESE! THEY'RE WORTH A LOT OF MONEY!
$
GRAY·FIELDS·BLYBERG·
HEY, BABIES, FIND SOME SHELLS THAT LOOK LIKE THIS!
OK!
10/2
THEY HAD SMOOTH PRETTY WHITE ROCKS IN'EM, BUT WE TOOK THOSE OUT!
YEAH, NOW THEY LOOK JUST LIKE YOURS... EMPTY!
DON'T LET THAT GUY FOOL YOU, JONATHAN. HE'S A REAL SHARK!
SHARK?!
SHAARRRRKKK!!!
JONATHAN, I'M GOING TO HAVE TO CALL YOU BACK...
GRAY·FIELDS·BLYBERG 10/3

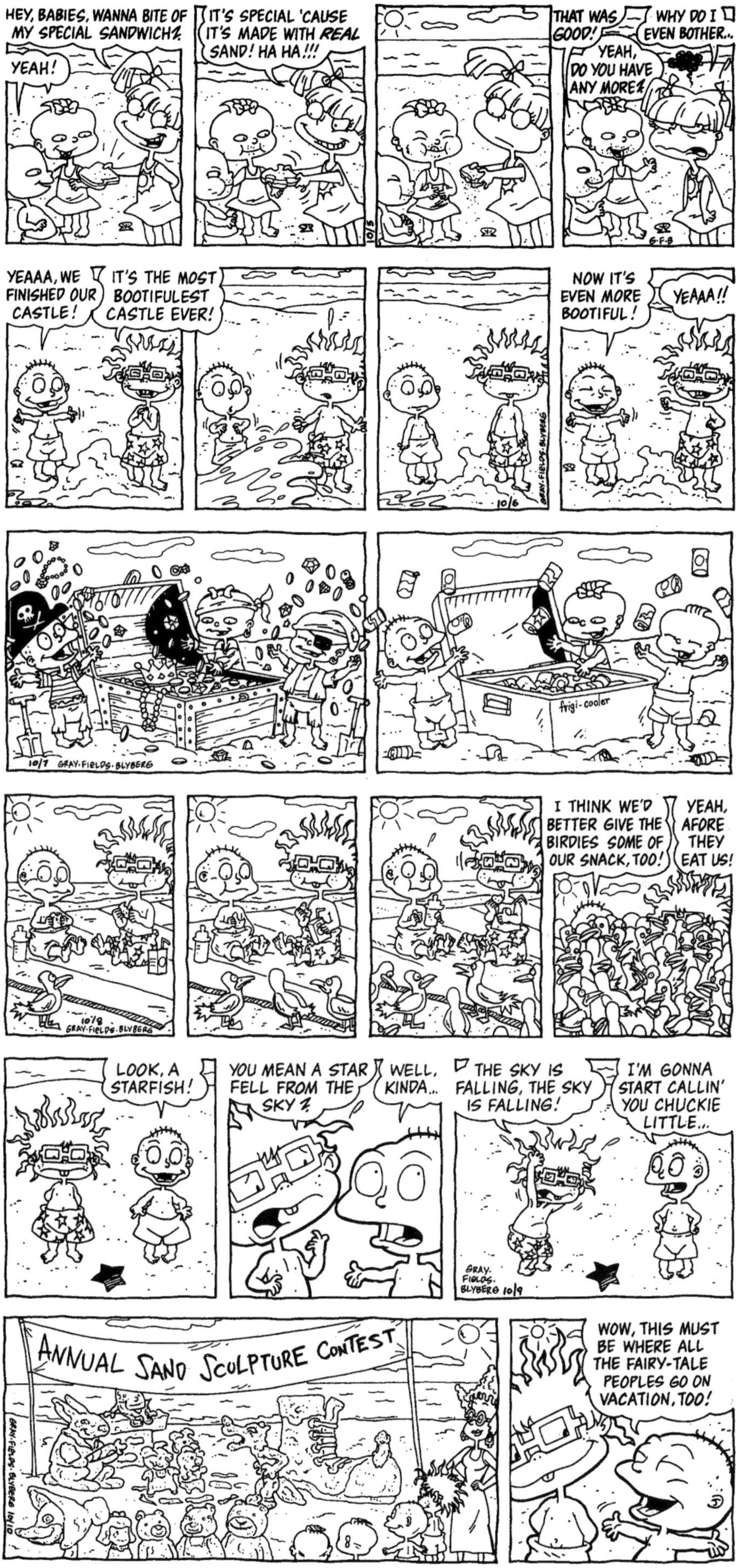
HEY, BABIES, WANNA BITE OF MY SPECIAL SANDWICH?
YEAH!
IT'S SPECIAL 'CAUSE IT'S MADE WITH REAL SAND! HA HA!!!
10/5
THAT WAS GOOD!
WHY DO I EVEN BOTHER...
YEAH, DO YOU HAVE ANY MORE?
YEAAA, WE FINISHED OUR CASTLE!
IT'S THE MOST BOOTIFULEST CASTLE EVER!
10/6
NOW IT'S EVEN MORE BOOTIFUL!
YEAAA!!
frigi-cooler
10/7 GRAY·FIELDS·BLYBERG
10/8 GRAY·FIELDS·BLYBERG
I THINK WE'D BETTER GIVE THE BIRDIES SOME OF OUR SNACK, TOO!
YEAH, AFORE THEY EAT US!
LOOK, A STARFISH!
YOU MEAN A STAR FELL FROM THE SKY?
WELL, KINDA...
THE SKY IS FALLING, THE SKY IS FALLING!
I'M GONNA START CALLIN' YOU CHUCKIE LITTLE...
GRAY. FIELDS. BLYBERG 10/9
ANNUAL SAND SCULPTURE CONTEST
GRAY·FIELDS·BLYBERG 10/10
WOW, THIS MUST BE WHERE ALL THE FAIRY-TALE PEOPLES GO ON VACATION, TOO!

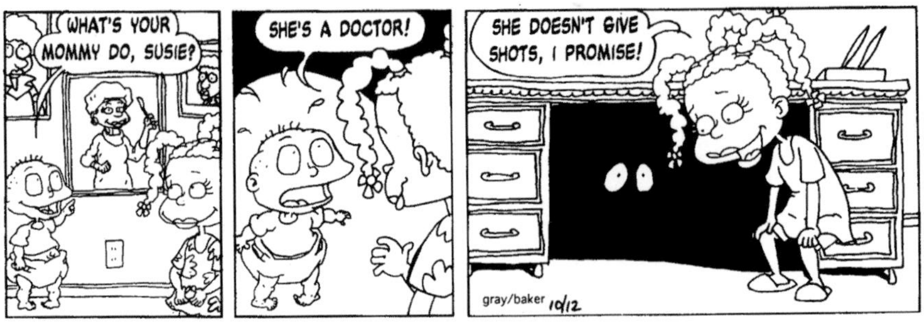
WHAT'S YOUR MOMMY DO, SUSIE?
SHE'S A DOCTOR!
SHE DOESN'T GIVE SHOTS, I PROMISE!
gray/baker 10/12

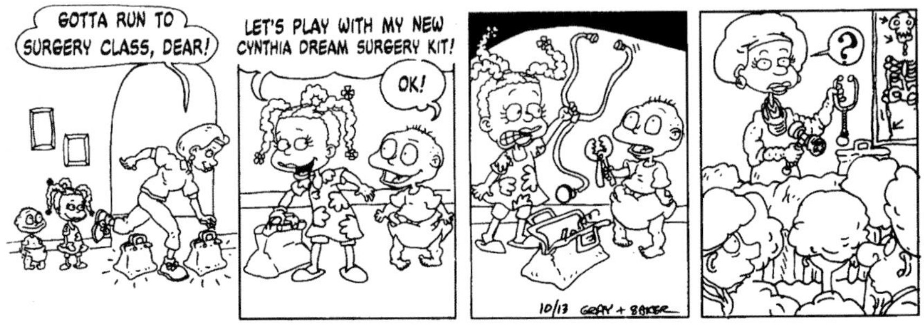
GOTTA RUN TO SURGERY CLASS, DEAR!
LET'S PLAY WITH MY NEW CYNTHIA DREAM SURGERY KIT!
OK!
10/13 GRAY + BAKER
?

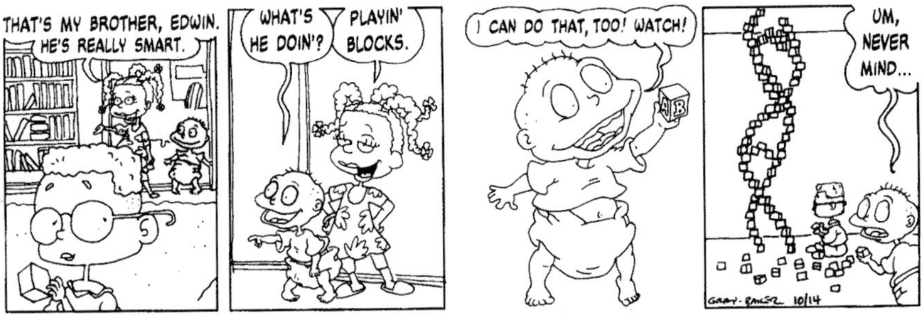
THAT'S MY BROTHER, EDWIN. HE'S REALLY SMART.
WHAT'S HE DOIN'?
PLAYIN' BLOCKS.
I CAN DO THAT, TOO! WATCH!
UM, NEVER MIND...
GRAY-BAKER 10/14

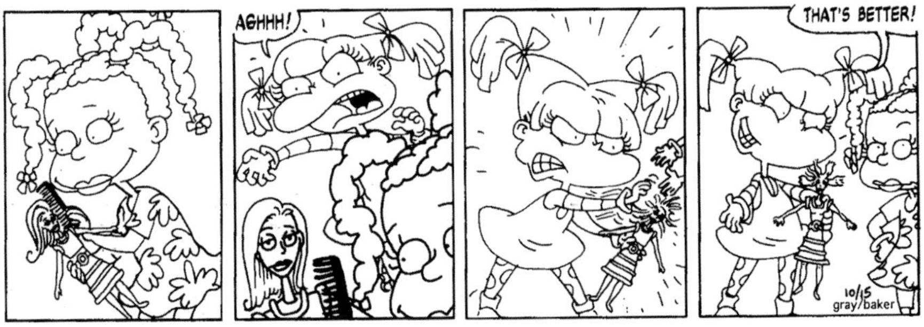
AGHHH!
THAT'S BETTER!
10/15 gray/baker

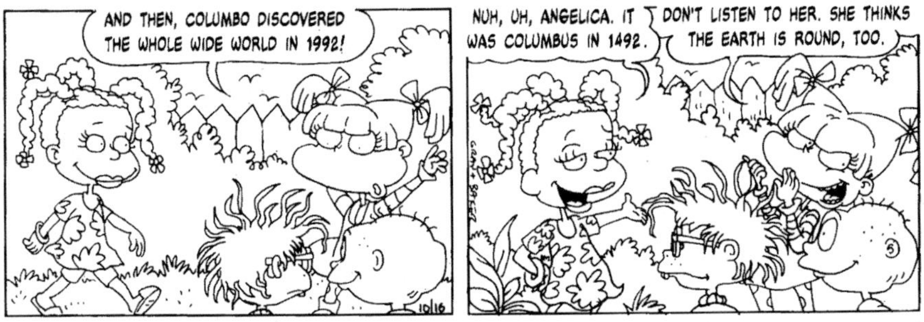
AND THEN, COLUMBO DISCOVERED THE WHOLE WIDE WORLD IN 1992!
10/16
NUH, UH, ANGELICA. IT WAS COLUMBUS IN 1492.
DON'T LISTEN TO HER. SHE THINKS THE EARTH IS ROUND, TOO.

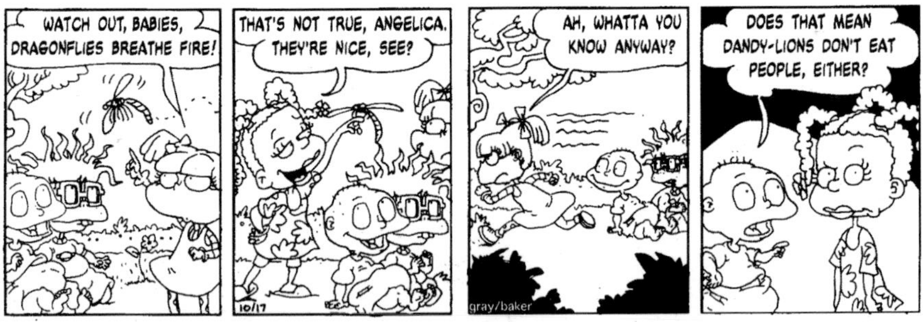
WATCH OUT, BABIES, DRAGONFLIES BREATHE FIRE!
THAT'S NOT TRUE, ANGELICA. THEY'RE NICE, SEE?
10/17
AH, WHATTA YOU KNOW ANYWAY?
gray/baker
DOES THAT MEAN DANDY-LIONS DON'T EAT PEOPLE, EITHER?

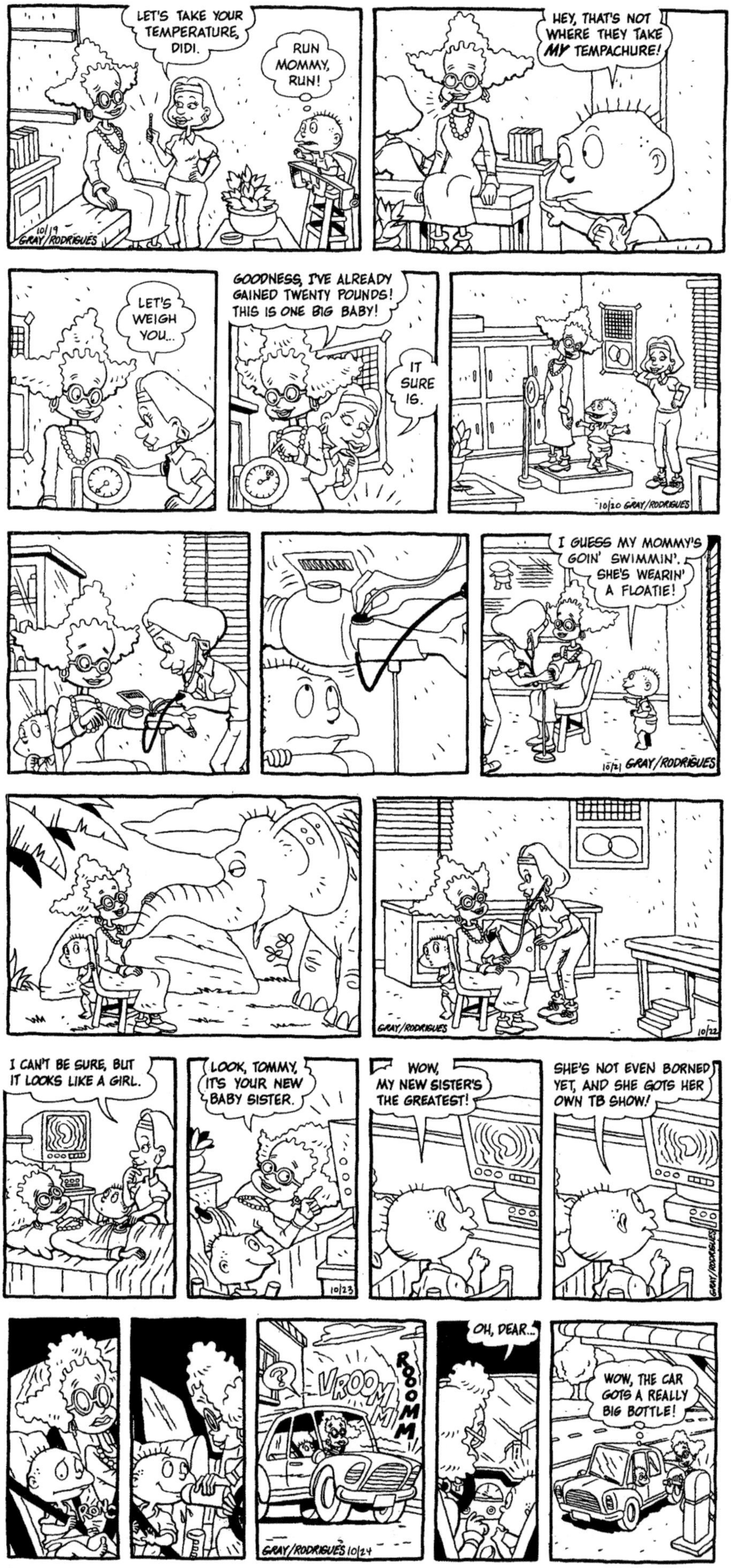
LET'S TAKE YOUR TEMPERATURE, DIDI.
RUN MOMMY, RUN!
10/19 GRAY/RODRIGUES
HEY, THAT'S NOT WHERE THEY TAKE MY TEMPACHURE!
LET'S WEIGH YOU...
GOODNESS, I'VE ALREADY GAINED TWENTY POUNDS! THIS IS ONE BIG BABY!
IT SURE IS.
10/20 GRAY/RODRIGUES
I GUESS MY MOMMY'S GOIN' SWIMMIN'. SHE'S WEARIN' A FLOATIE!
10/21 GRAY/RODRIGUES
GRAY/RODRIGUES
10/22
I CAN'T BE SURE, BUT IT LOOKS LIKE A GIRL.
LOOK, TOMMY, IT'S YOUR NEW BABY SISTER.
10/23
WOW, MY NEW SISTER'S THE GREATEST!
SHE'S NOT EVEN BORNED YET, AND SHE GOTS HER OWN TB SHOW!
GRAY/RODRIGUES
?
VROOM
ROOOMM
GRAY/RODRIGUES 10/24
OH, DEAR...
WOW, THE CAR GOTS A REALLY BIG BOTTLE!

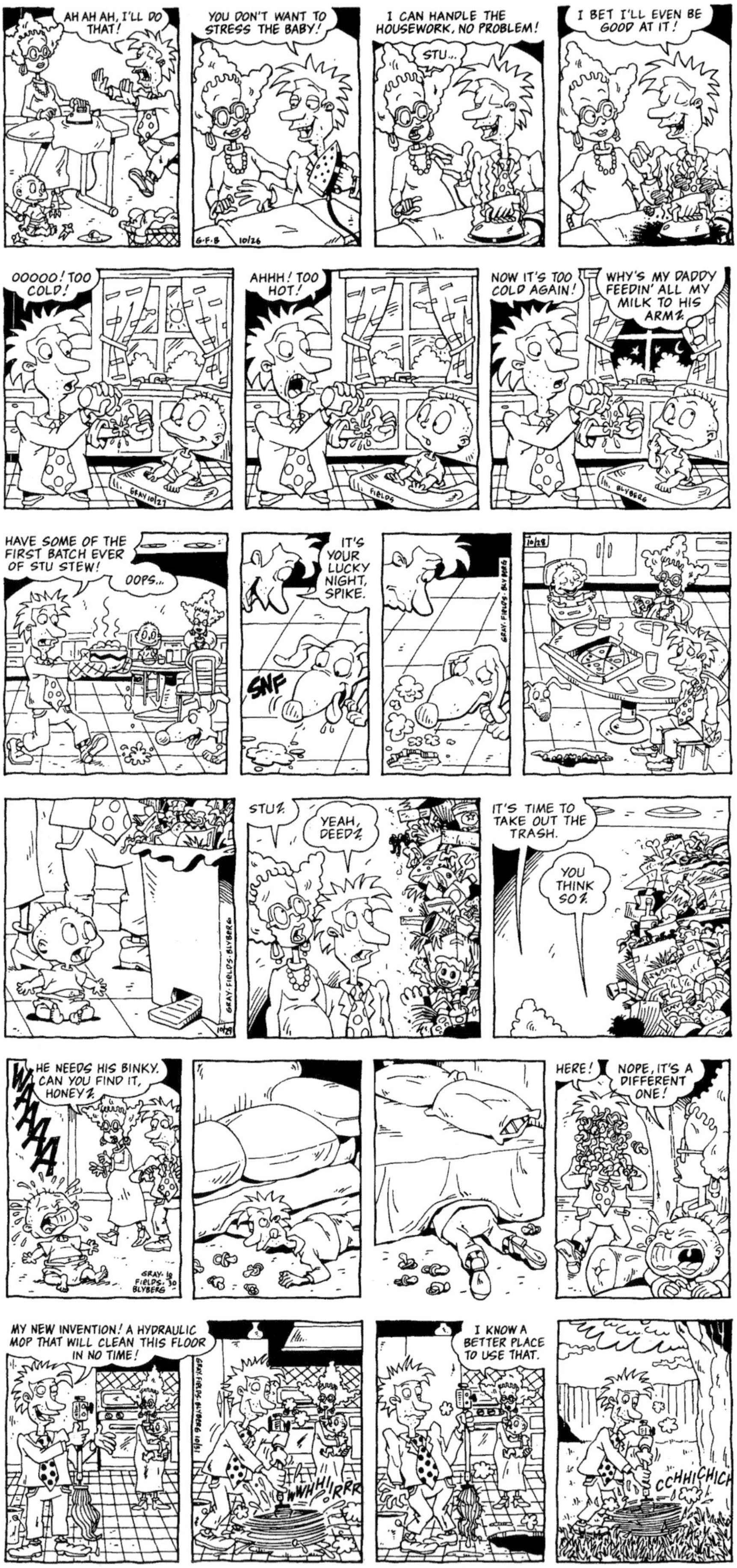
AH AH AH, I'LL DO THAT!
YOU DON'T WANT TO STRESS THE BABY!
G.F.B 10/26
I CAN HANDLE THE HOUSEWORK, NO PROBLEM!
STU...
I BET I'LL EVEN BE GOOD AT IT!
OOOOO! TOO COLD!
GRAY 10/27
AHHH! TOO HOT!
FIELDS
NOW IT'S TOO COLD AGAIN!
WHY'S MY DADDY FEEDIN' ALL MY MILK TO HIS ARM?
BLYBERG
HAVE SOME OF THE FIRST BATCH EVER OF STU STEW!
OOPS...
IT'S YOUR LUCKY NIGHT, SPIKE.
SNF
GRAY·FIELDS·BLYBERG
10/28
GRAY·FIELDS·BLYBERG
10/29
STU?
YEAH, DEED?
IT'S TIME TO TAKE OUT THE TRASH.
YOU THINK SO?
HE NEEDS HIS BINKY. CAN YOU FIND IT, HONEY?
WAAAAA
GRAY·10 FIELDS·30 BLYBERG
HERE!
NOPE, IT'S A DIFFERENT ONE!
MY NEW INVENTION! A HYDRAULIC MOP THAT WILL CLEAN THIS FLOOR IN NO TIME!
GRAY·FIELDS·BLYBERG 10/31
WHHHIRRR
I KNOW A BETTER PLACE TO USE THAT.
CCHHICHICH

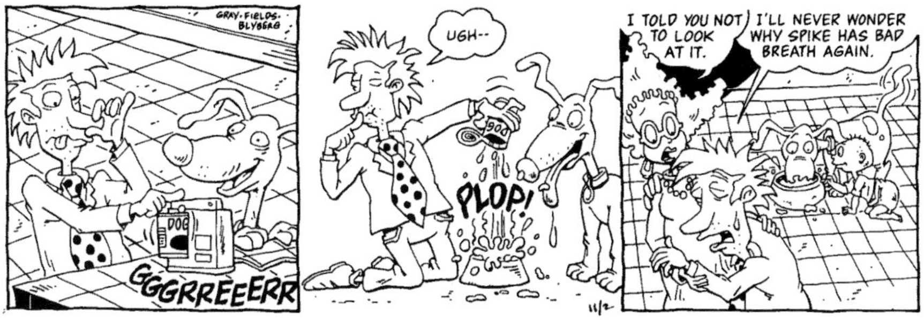
GRAY·FIELDS·BLYBERG
GGGRREEERR
UGH--
PLOP!
I TOLD YOU NOT TO LOOK AT IT.
I'LL NEVER WONDER WHY SPIKE HAS BAD BREATH AGAIN.

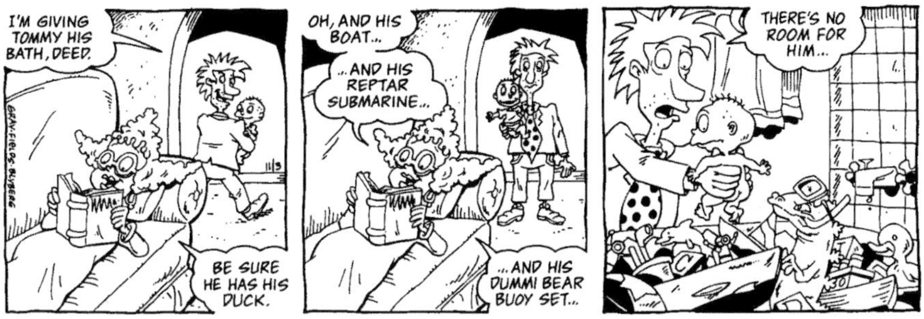
I'M GIVING TOMMY HIS BATH, DEED.
BE SURE HE HAS HIS DUCK.
OH, AND HIS BOAT...
...AND HIS REPTAR SUBMARINE...
...AND HIS DUMMI BEAR BUOY SET...
THERE'S NO ROOM FOR HIM...

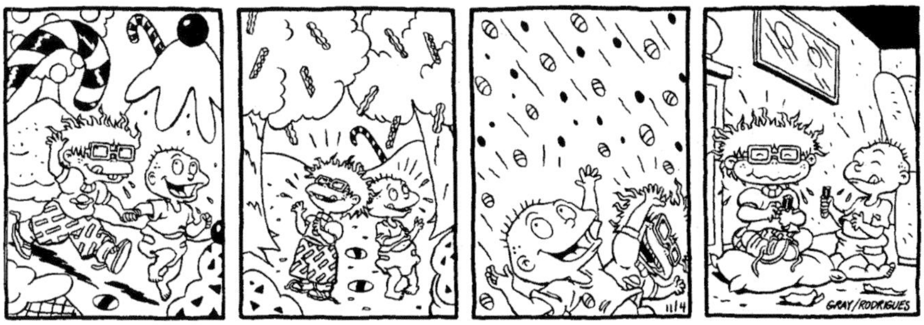
GRAY/RODRIGUES

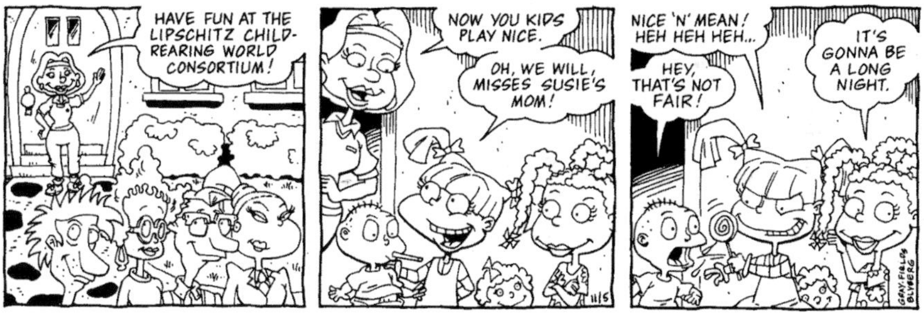
HAVE FUN AT THE LIPSCHITZ CHILD-REARING WORLD CONSORTIUM!
NOW YOU KIDS PLAY NICE.
OH, WE WILL, MISSES SUSIE'S MOM!
NICE 'N' MEAN! HEH HEH HEH...
HEY, THAT'S NOT FAIR!
IT'S GONNA BE A LONG NIGHT.

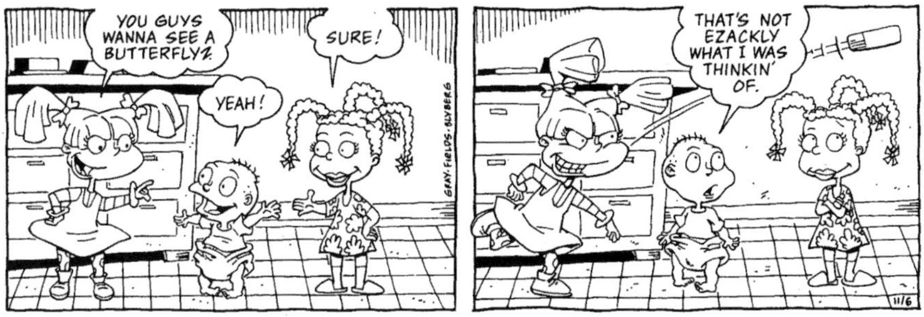
YOU GUYS WANNA SEE A BUTTERFLY?
YEAH!
SURE!
THAT'S NOT EZACKLY WHAT I WAS THINKIN' OF.

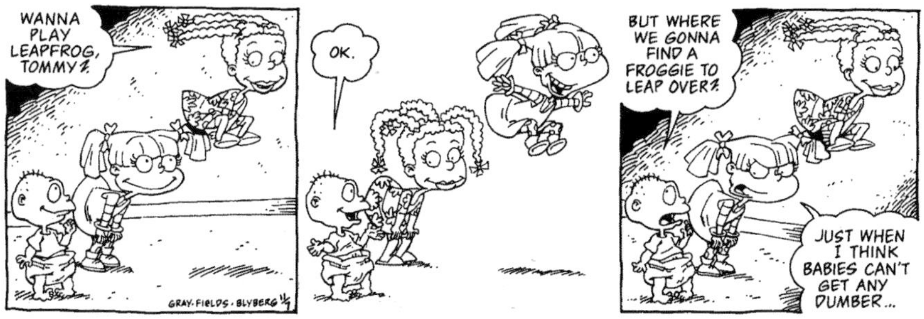
WANNA PLAY LEAPFROG, TOMMY?
OK.
BUT WHERE WE GONNA FIND A FROGGIE TO LEAP OVER?
JUST WHEN I THINK BABIES CAN'T GET ANY DUMBER...
GRAY·FIELDS·BLYBERG

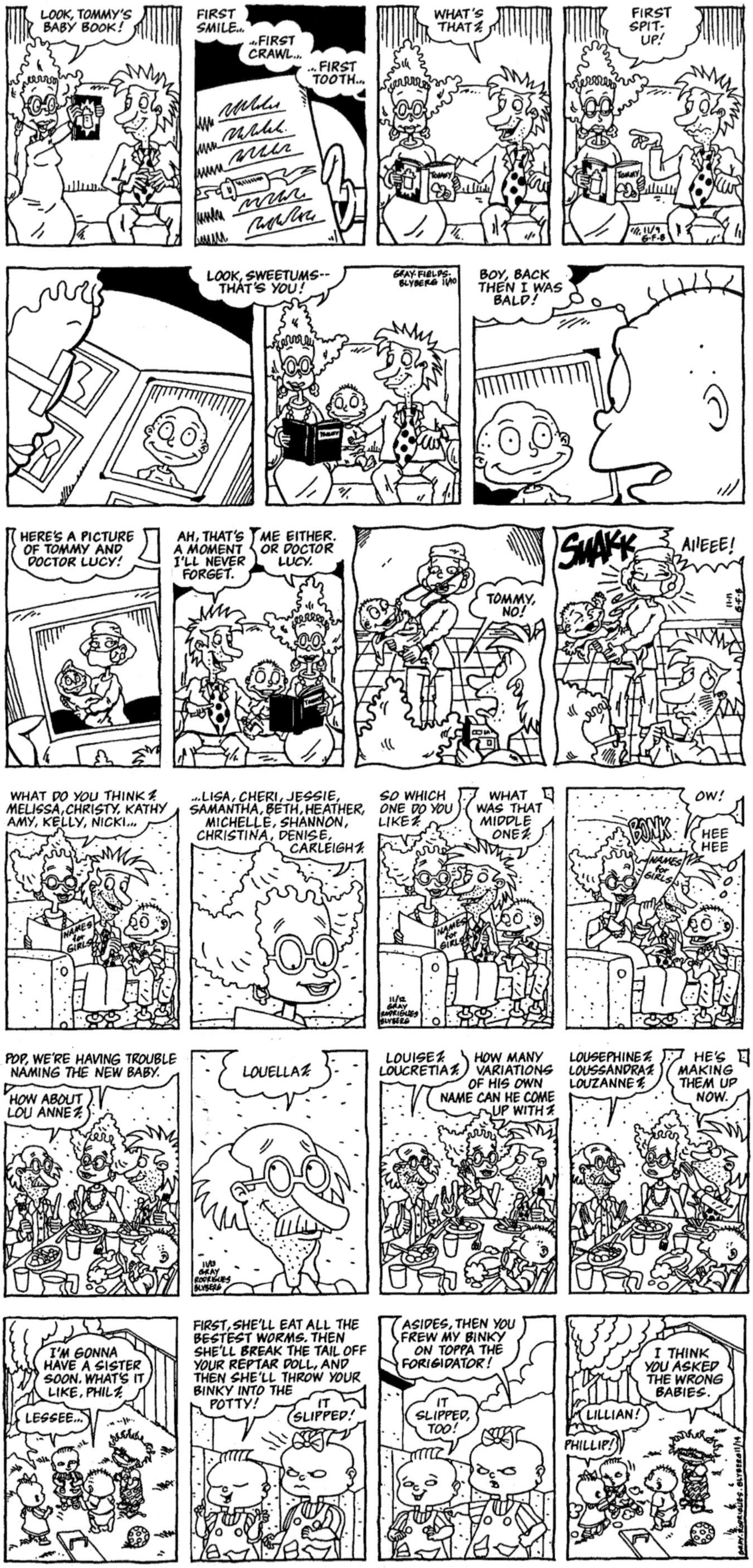
LOOK, TOMMY'S BABY BOOK!
FIRST SMILE...
...FIRST CRAWL...
...FIRST TOOTH...
WHAT'S THAT?
FIRST SPIT-UP!
LOOK, SWEETUMS-- THAT'S YOU!
BOY, BACK THEN I WAS BALD!
HERE'S A PICTURE OF TOMMY AND DOCTOR LUCY!
AH, THAT'S A MOMENT I'LL NEVER FORGET.
ME EITHER. OR DOCTOR LUCY.
TOMMY, NO!
SMAKK
AIIEEE!
WHAT DO YOU THINK? MELISSA, CHRISTY, KATHY AMY, KELLY, NICKI...
...LISA, CHERI, JESSIE, SAMANTHA, BETH, HEATHER, MICHELLE, SHANNON, CHRISTINA, DENISE, CARLEIGH?
SO WHICH ONE DO YOU LIKE?
WHAT WAS THAT MIDDLE ONE?
BONK
OW!
HEE HEE
NAMES for GIRLS
POP, WE'RE HAVING TROUBLE NAMING THE NEW BABY.
HOW ABOUT LOU ANNE?
LOUELLA?
LOUISE? LOUCRETIA?
HOW MANY VARIATIONS OF HIS OWN NAME CAN HE COME UP WITH?
LOUSEPHINE? LOUSSANDRA? LOUZANNE?
HE'S MAKING THEM UP NOW.
I'M GONNA HAVE A SISTER SOON. WHAT'S IT LIKE, PHIL?
LESSEE...
FIRST, SHE'LL EAT ALL THE BESTEST WORMS. THEN SHE'LL BREAK THE TAIL OFF YOUR REPTAR DOLL, AND THEN SHE'LL THROW YOUR BINKY INTO THE POTTY!
IT SLIPPED!
ASIDES, THEN YOU FREW MY BINKY ON TOPPA THE FORIGIDATOR!
IT SLIPPED, TOO!
I THINK YOU ASKED THE WRONG BABIES.
LILLIAN!
PHILLIP!

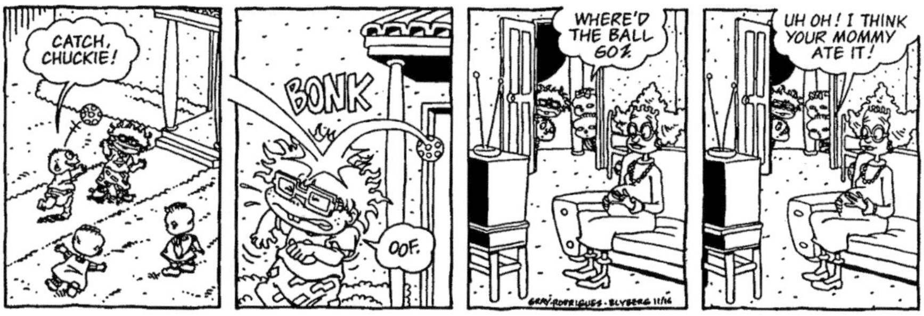
CATCH, CHUCKIE!
BONK
OOF.
WHERE'D THE BALL GO?
UH OH! I THINK YOUR MOMMY ATE IT!
GRAY·RODRIGUES·BLYBERG 11/16

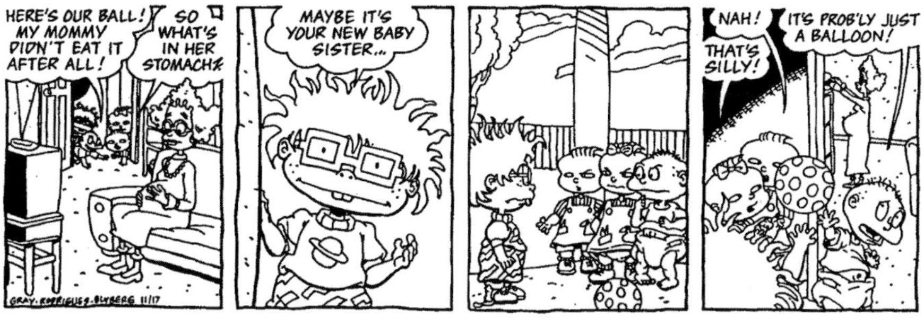
HERE'S OUR BALL! MY MOMMY DIDN'T EAT IT AFTER ALL!
SO WHAT'S IN HER STOMACH?
GRAY·RODRIGUES·BLYBERG 11/17
MAYBE IT'S YOUR NEW BABY SISTER...
NAH!
THAT'S SILLY!
IT'S PROB'LY JUST A BALLOON!

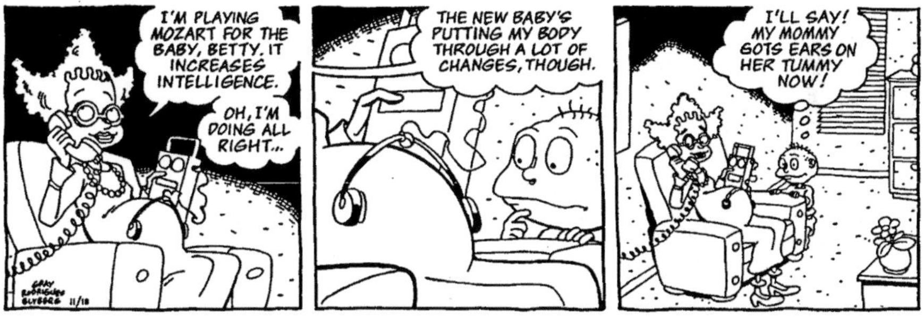
I'M PLAYING MOZART FOR THE BABY, BETTY. IT INCREASES INTELLIGENCE.
OH, I'M DOING ALL RIGHT...
GRAY RODRIGUES BLYBERG 11/18
THE NEW BABY'S PUTTING MY BODY THROUGH A LOT OF CHANGES, THOUGH.
I'LL SAY! MY MOMMY GOTS EARS ON HER TUMMY NOW!

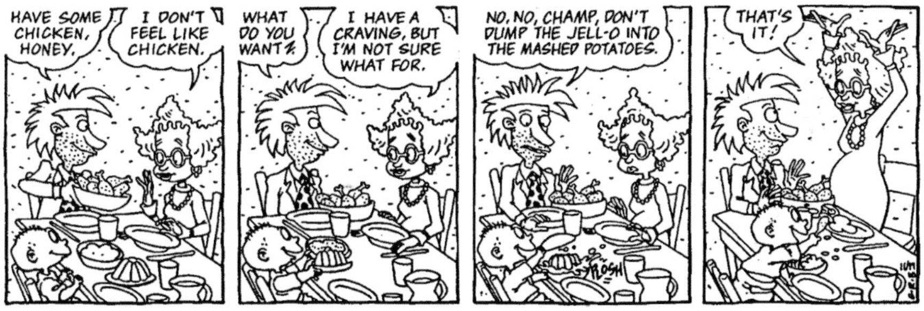
HAVE SOME CHICKEN, HONEY.
I DON'T FEEL LIKE CHICKEN.
WHAT DO YOU WANT?
I HAVE A CRAVING, BUT I'M NOT SURE WHAT FOR.
NO, NO, CHAMP, DON'T DUMP THE JELL-O INTO THE MASHED POTATOES.
SPLOSH
THAT'S IT!

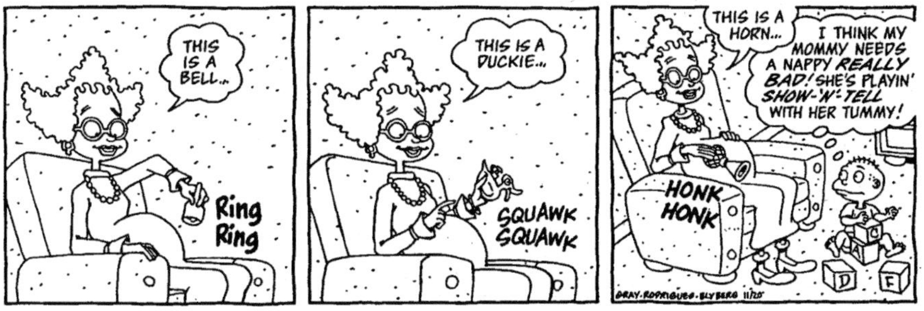
THIS IS A BELL...
Ring Ring
THIS IS A DUCKIE...
SQUAWK SQUAWK
THIS IS A HORN...
I THINK MY MOMMY NEEDS A NAPPY REALLY BAD! SHE'S PLAYIN' SHOW-'N'-TELL WITH HER TUMMY!
HONK HONK
GRAY·RODRIGUES·BLYBERG 11/25

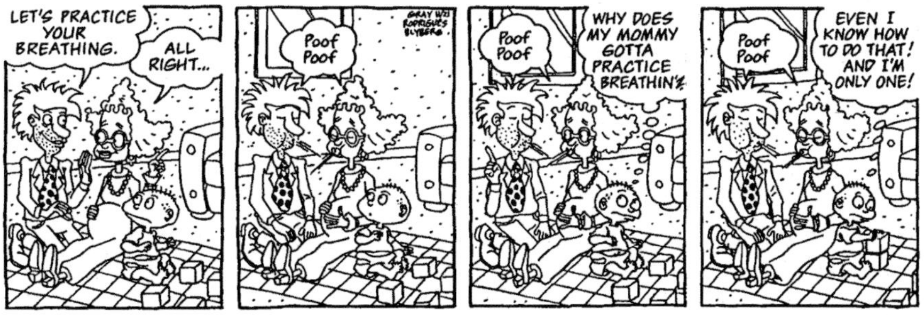
LET'S PRACTICE YOUR BREATHING.
ALL RIGHT...
Poof Poof
Poof Poof
WHY DOES MY MOMMY GOTTA PRACTICE BREATHIN'?
Poof Poof
EVEN I KNOW HOW TO DO THAT! AND I'M ONLY ONE!

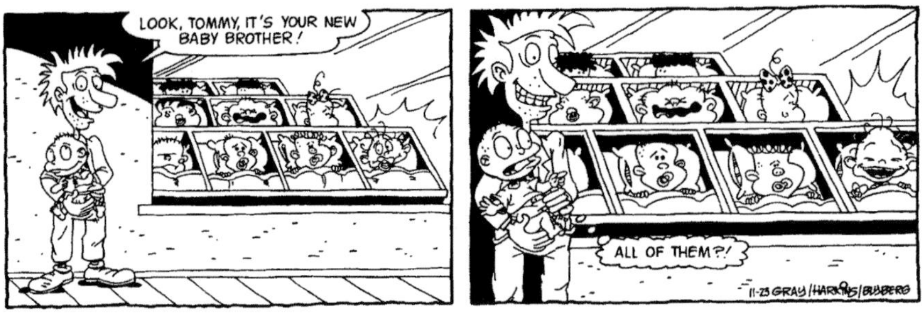
LOOK, TOMMY, IT'S YOUR NEW BABY BROTHER!
ALL OF THEM?!

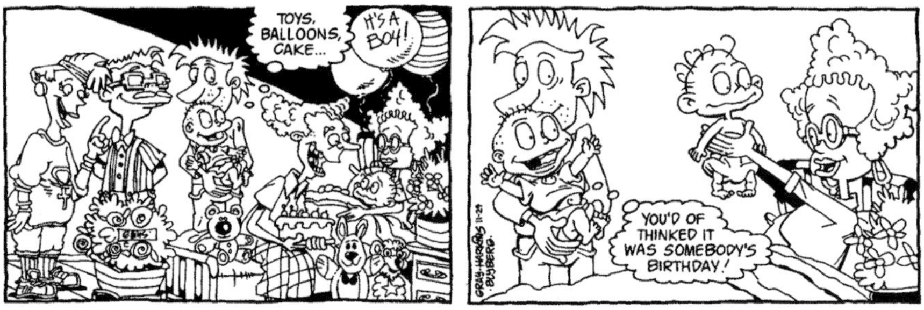
TOYS, BALLOONS, CAKE...
IT'S A BOY!
YOU'D OF THINKED IT WAS SOMEBODY'S BIRTHDAY!

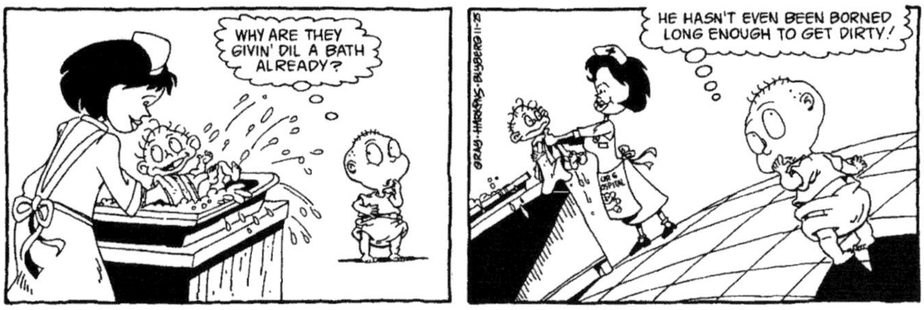
WHY ARE THEY GIVIN' DIL A BATH ALREADY?
HE HASN'T EVEN BEEN BORNED LONG ENOUGH TO GET DIRTY!

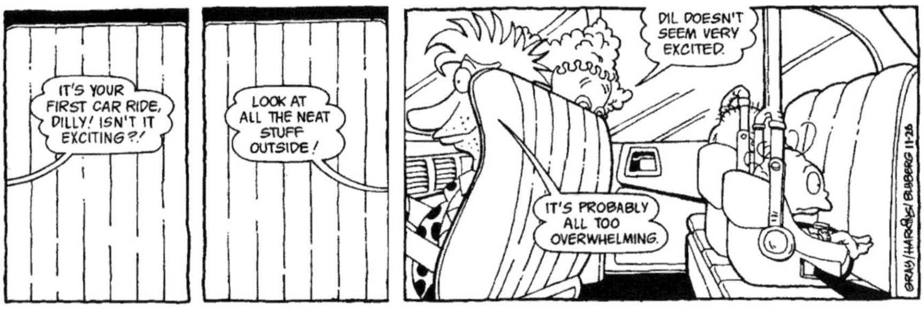
IT'S YOUR FIRST CAR RIDE, DILLY! ISN'T IT EXCITING?!
LOOK AT ALL THE NEAT STUFF OUTSIDE!
DIL DOESN'T SEEM VERY EXCITED.
IT'S PROBABLY ALL TOO OVERWHELMING.

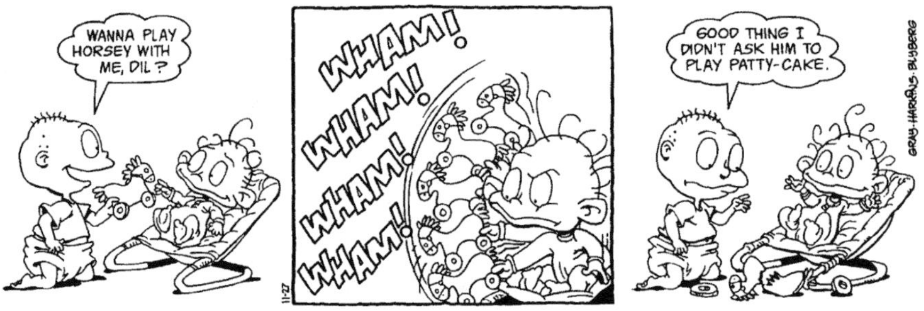
WANNA PLAY HORSEY WITH ME, DIL?
WHAM! WHAM! WHAM! WHAM!
GOOD THING I DIDN'T ASK HIM TO PLAY PATTY-CAKE.

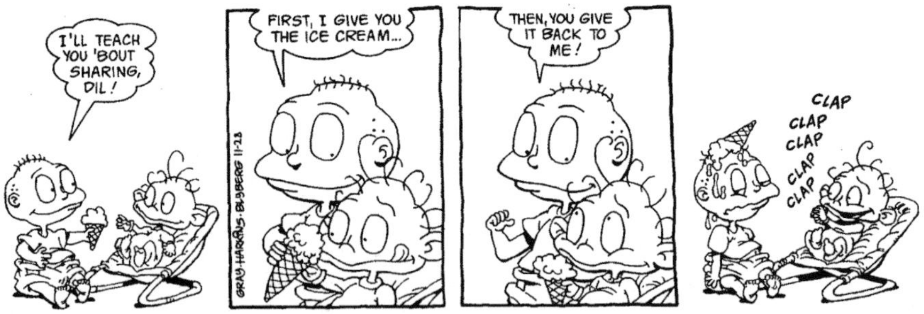
I'LL TEACH YOU 'BOUT SHARING, DIL!
FIRST, I GIVE YOU THE ICE CREAM...
THEN, YOU GIVE IT BACK TO ME!
CLAP CLAP CLAP CLAP CLAP

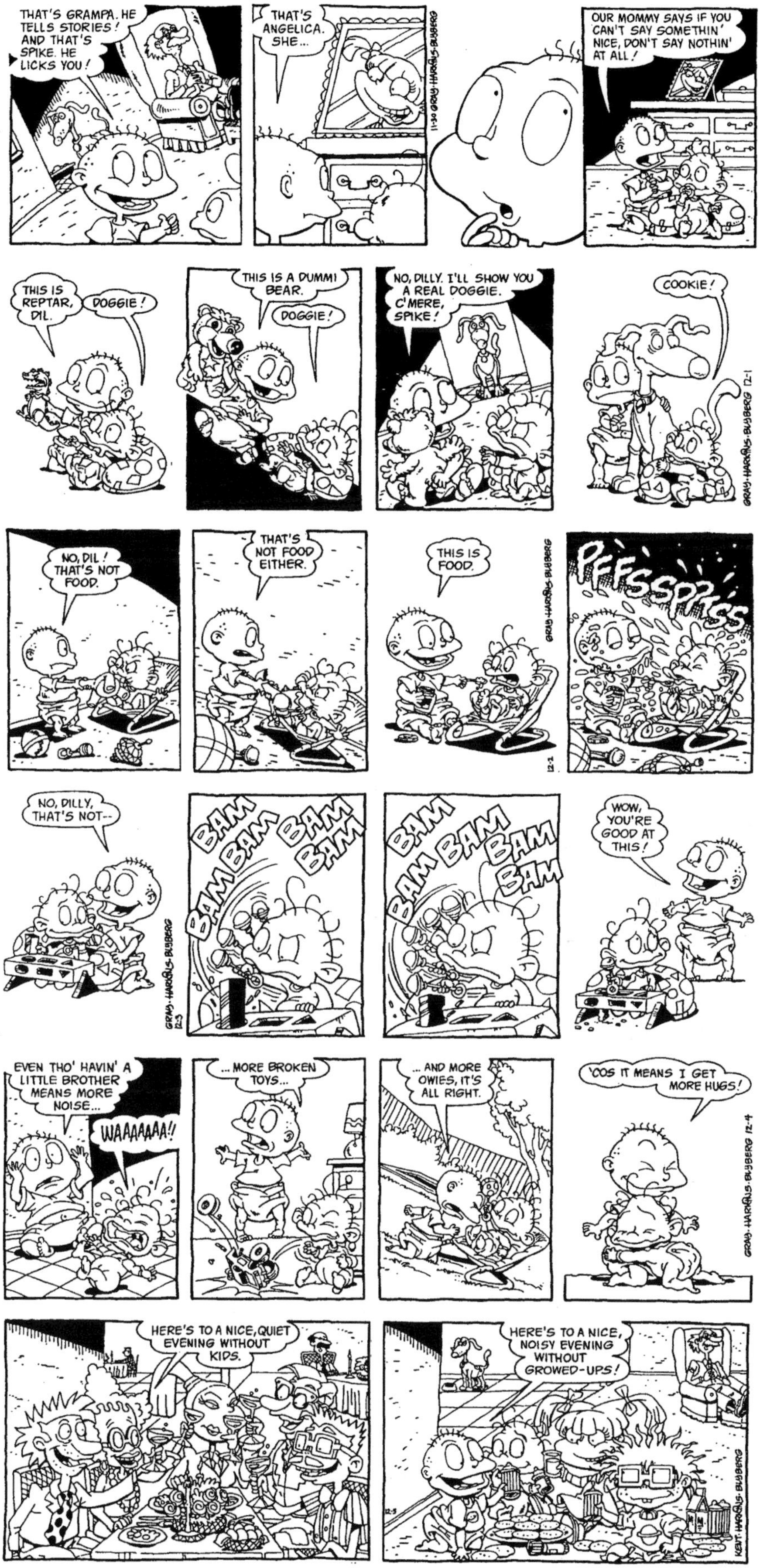
THAT'S GRAMPA. HE TELLS STORIES! AND THAT'S SPIKE. HE LICKS YOU!
THAT'S ANGELICA. SHE...
OUR MOMMY SAYS IF YOU CAN'T SAY SOMETHIN' NICE, DON'T SAY NOTHIN' AT ALL!
THIS IS REPTAR, DIL.
DOGGIE!
THIS IS A DUMMI BEAR.
DOGGIE!
NO, DILLY. I'LL SHOW YOU A REAL DOGGIE. C'MERE, SPIKE!
COOKIE!
NO, DIL! THAT'S NOT FOOD.
THAT'S NOT FOOD EITHER.
THIS IS FOOD.
PFFSSPPSS
NO, DILLY, THAT'S NOT--
BAM BAM BAM BAM
BAM BAM BAM BAM BAM
WOW, YOU'RE GOOD AT THIS!
EVEN THO' HAVIN' A LITTLE BROTHER MEANS MORE NOISE...
WAAAAAAA!!
... MORE BROKEN TOYS...
... AND MORE OWIES, IT'S ALL RIGHT.
'COS IT MEANS I GET MORE HUGS!
HERE'S TO A NICE, QUIET EVENING WITHOUT KIDS.
HERE'S TO A NICE, NOISY EVENING WITHOUT GROWED-UPS!

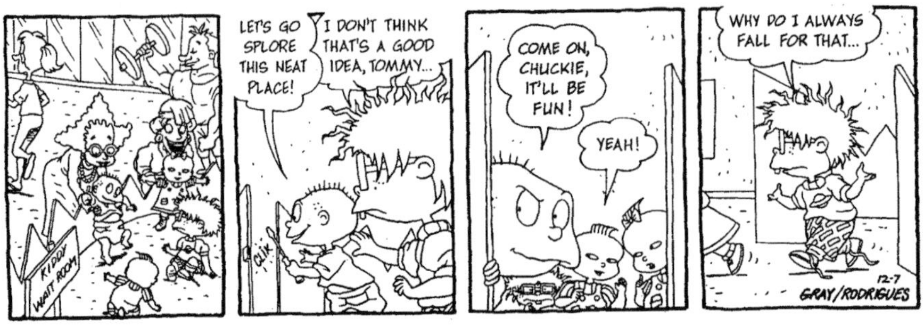
KIDDY WAIT ROOM
LET'S GO SPLORE THIS NEAT PLACE!
I DON'T THINK THAT'S A GOOD IDEA, TOMMY...
CLIK
COME ON, CHUCKIE, IT'LL BE FUN!
YEAH!
WHY DO I ALWAYS FALL FOR THAT...
12-7
GRAY/RODRIGUES

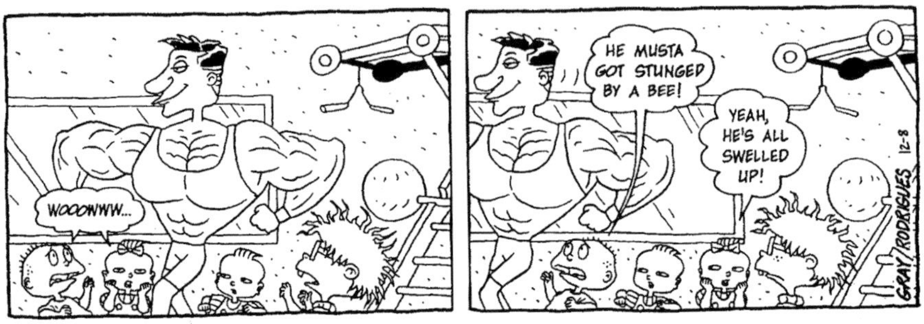
WOOOWWW...
HE MUSTA GOT STUNGED BY A BEE!
YEAH, HE'S ALL SWELLED UP!
12-8
GRAY/RODRIGUES

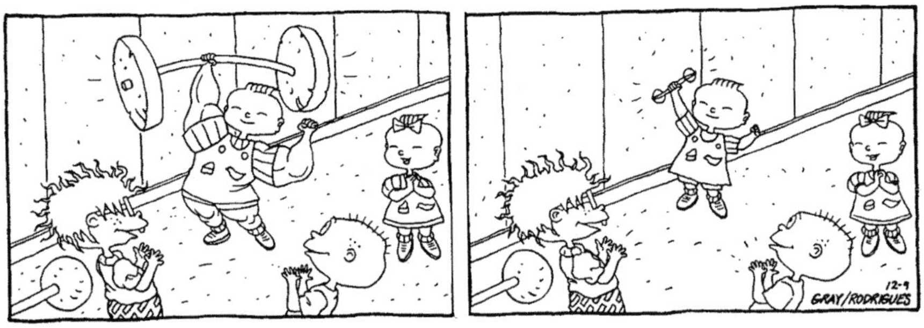
12-9
GRAY/RODRIGUES

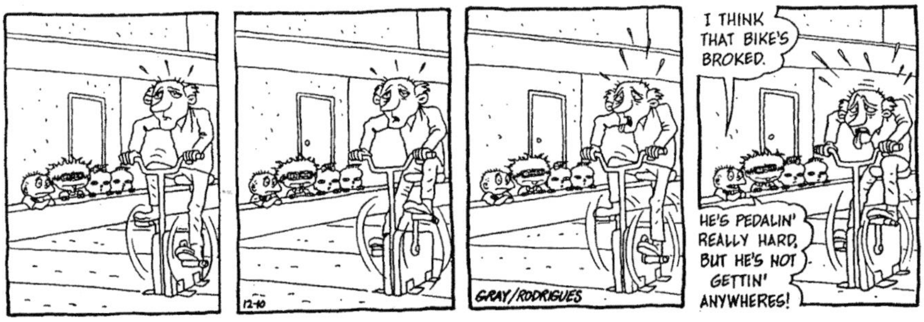
12-10
GRAY/RODRIGUES
I THINK THAT BIKE'S BROKED.
HE'S PEDALIN' REALLY HARD, BUT HE'S NOT GETTIN' ANYWHERES!

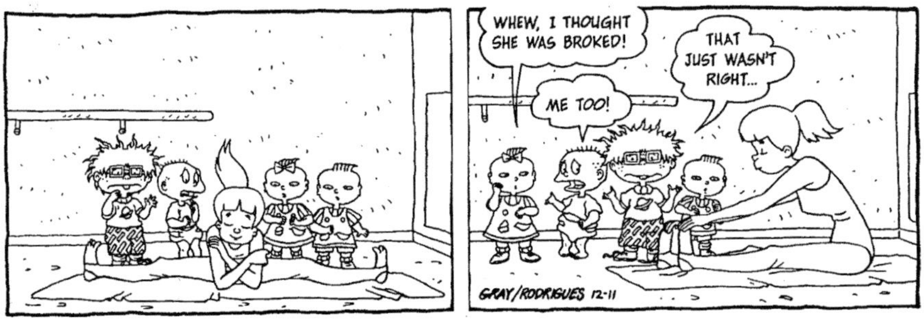
WHEW, I THOUGHT SHE WAS BROKED!
ME TOO!
THAT JUST WASN'T RIGHT...
GRAY/RODRIGUES 12-11

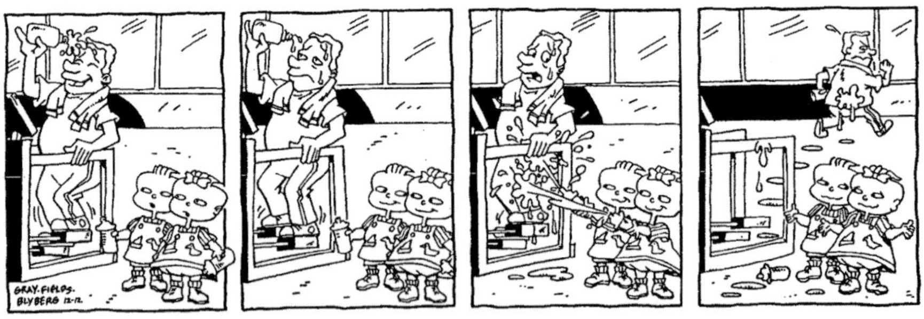
GRAY·FIELDS· BLYBERG 12-12

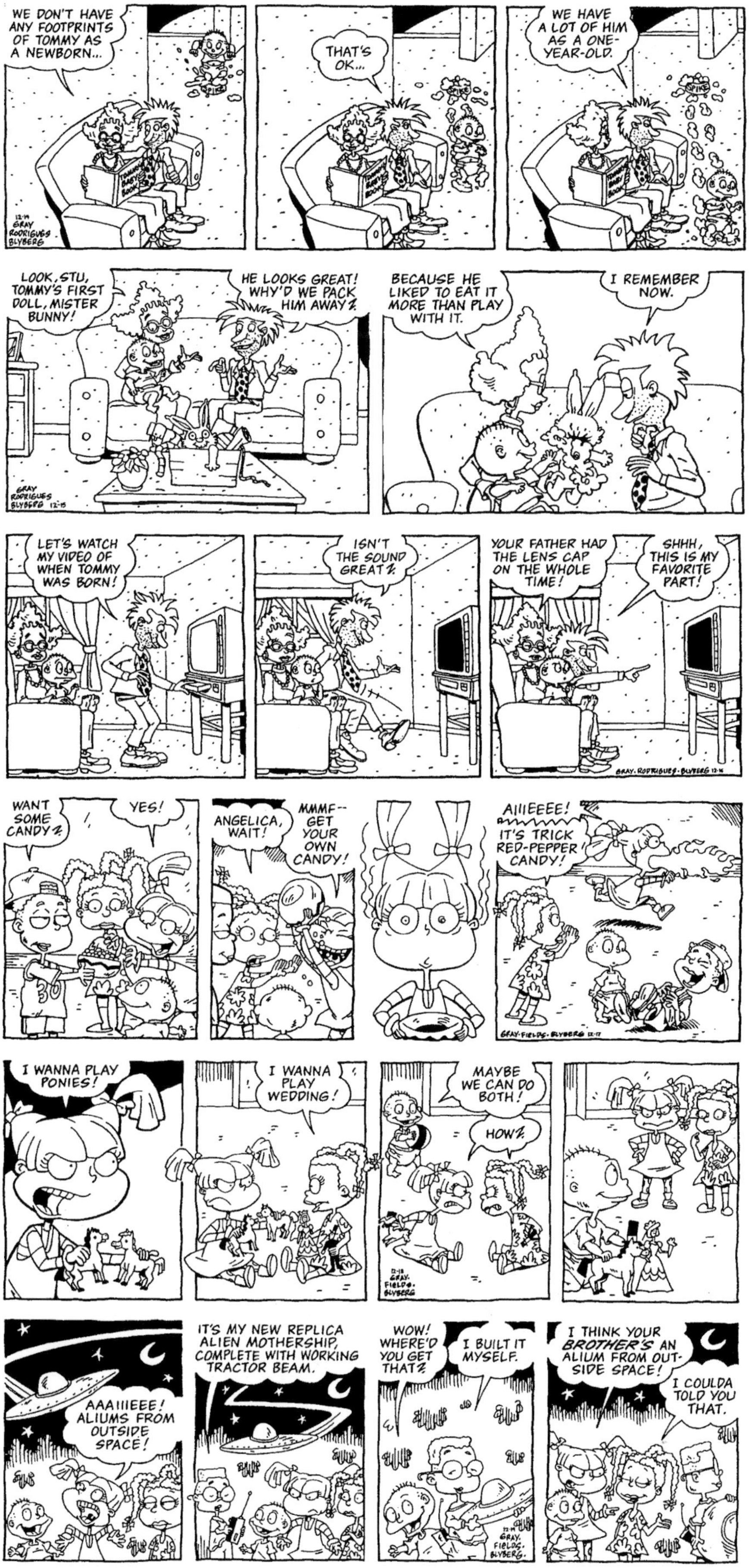
WE DON'T HAVE ANY FOOTPRINTS OF TOMMY AS A NEWBORN...
SPIKE
THAT'S OK...
WE HAVE A LOT OF HIM AS A ONE-YEAR-OLD.
LOOK, STU, TOMMY'S FIRST DOLL, MISTER BUNNY!
HE LOOKS GREAT! WHY'D WE PACK HIM AWAY?
BECAUSE HE LIKED TO EAT IT MORE THAN PLAY WITH IT.
I REMEMBER NOW.
LET'S WATCH MY VIDEO OF WHEN TOMMY WAS BORN!
ISN'T THE SOUND GREAT?
YOUR FATHER HAD THE LENS CAP ON THE WHOLE TIME!
SHHH, THIS IS MY FAVORITE PART!
WANT SOME CANDY?
YES!
ANGELICA, WAIT!
MMMF-- GET YOUR OWN CANDY!
AIIIEEEE!
IT'S TRICK RED-PEPPER CANDY!
I WANNA PLAY PONIES!
I WANNA PLAY WEDDING!
MAYBE WE CAN DO BOTH!
HOW?
AAAIIIEEE! ALIUMS FROM OUTSIDE SPACE!
IT'S MY NEW REPLICA ALIEN MOTHERSHIP, COMPLETE WITH WORKING TRACTOR BEAM.
WOW! WHERE'D YOU GET THAT?
I BUILT IT MYSELF.
I THINK YOUR *BROTHER'S* AN ALIUM FROM OUTSIDE SPACE!
I COULDA TOLD YOU THAT.

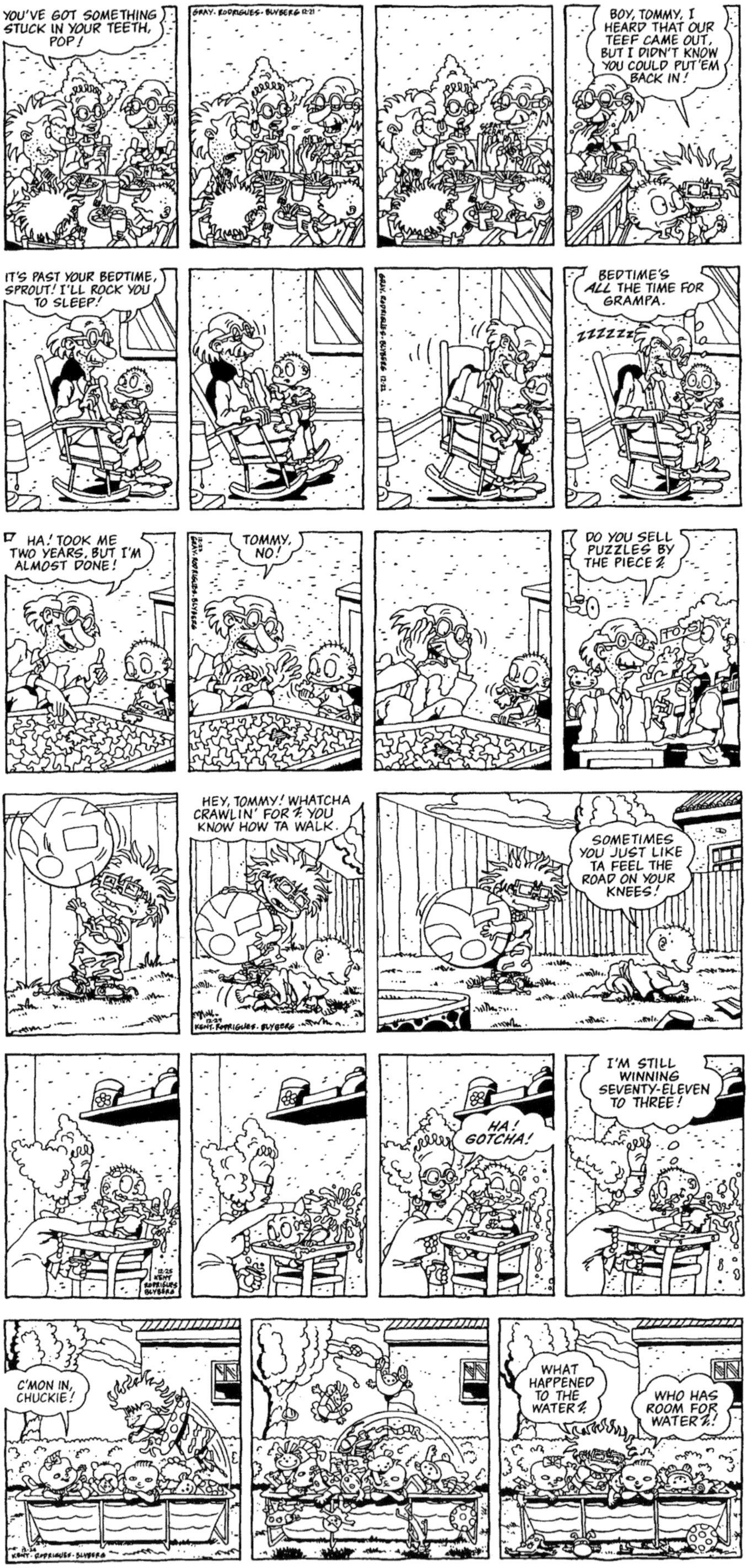
YOU'VE GOT SOMETHING STUCK IN YOUR TEETH, POP!
BOY, TOMMY, I HEARD THAT OUR TEEF CAME OUT, BUT I DIDN'T KNOW YOU COULD PUT 'EM BACK IN!
IT'S PAST YOUR BEDTIME, SPROUT! I'LL ROCK YOU TO SLEEP!
BEDTIME'S ALL THE TIME FOR GRAMPA.
ZZZZZZ
HA! TOOK ME TWO YEARS, BUT I'M ALMOST DONE!
TOMMY, NO!
DO YOU SELL PUZZLES BY THE PIECE?
TOYS
HEY, TOMMY! WHATCHA CRAWLIN' FOR? YOU KNOW HOW TA WALK.
SOMETIMES YOU JUST LIKE TA FEEL THE ROAD ON YOUR KNEES!
HA! GOTCHA!
I'M STILL WINNING SEVENTY-ELEVEN TO THREE!
C'MON IN, CHUCKIE!
WHAT HAPPENED TO THE WATER?
WHO HAS ROOM FOR WATER?!

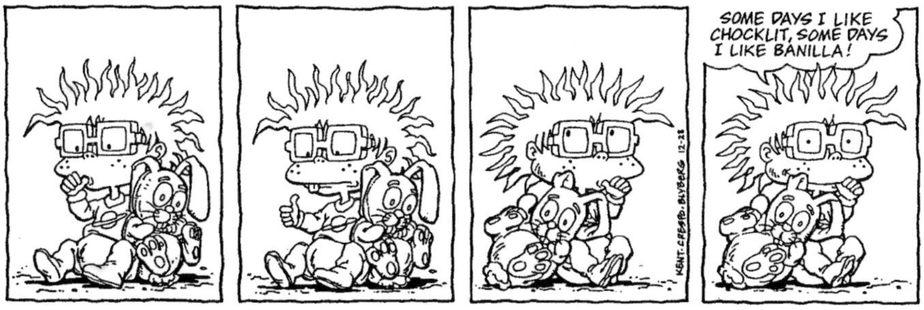
SOME DAYS I LIKE CHOCKLIT, SOME DAYS I LIKE BANILLA!
KENT·CRESPO·BLYBERG 12-28

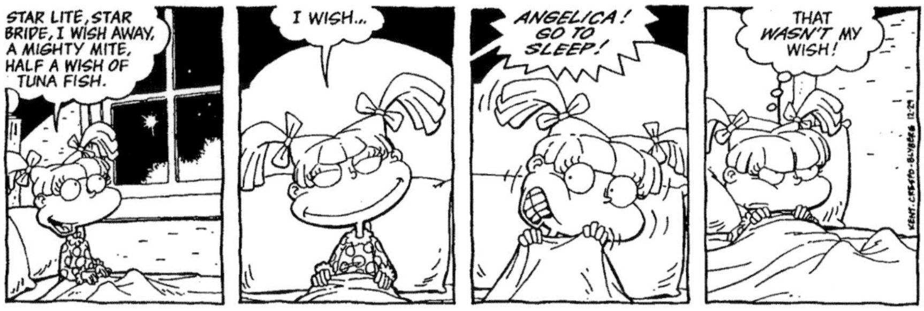
STAR LITE, STAR BRIDE, I WISH AWAY, A MIGHTY MITE, HALF A WISH OF TUNA FISH.
I WISH...
ANGELICA! GO TO SLEEP!
THAT WASN'T MY WISH!
KENT·CRESPO·BLYBERG 12-29

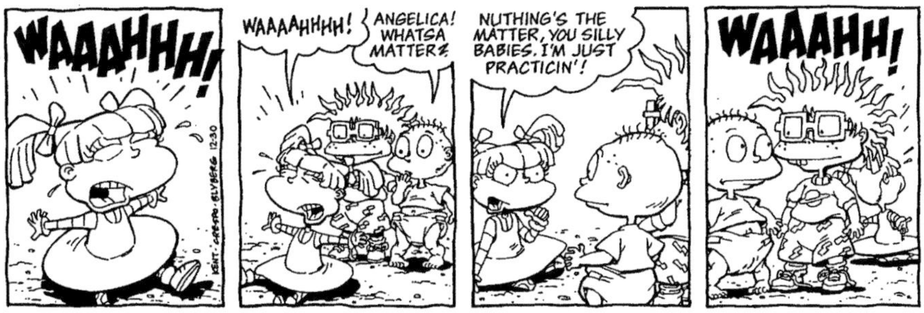
WAAAHHHH!
KENT·CRESPO·BLYBERG 12-30
WAAAAHHHH!
ANGELICA! WHATSA MATTER?
NUTHING'S THE MATTER, YOU SILLY BABIES. I'M JUST PRACTICIN'!
WAAAHH!

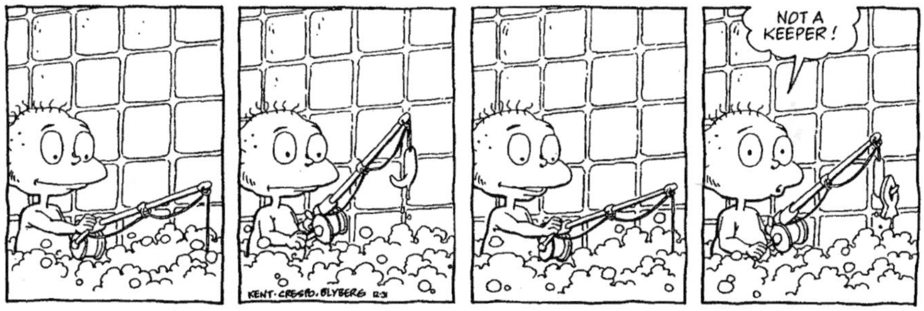
KENT·CRESPO·BLYBERG 12-31
NOT A KEEPER!

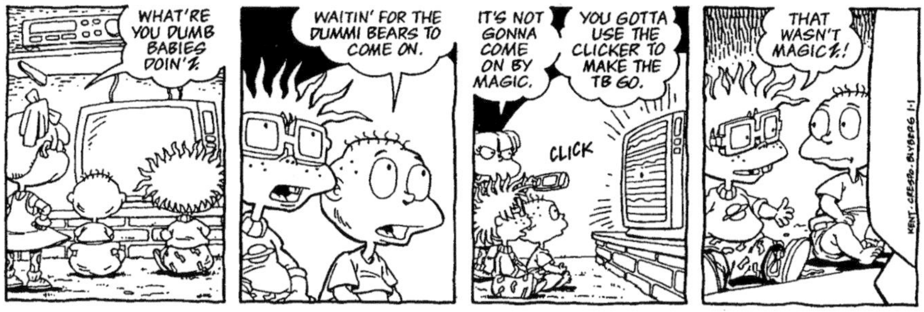
WHAT'RE YOU DUMB BABIES DOIN'?
WAITIN' FOR THE DUMMI BEARS TO COME ON.
IT'S NOT GONNA COME ON BY MAGIC.
YOU GOTTA USE THE CLICKER TO MAKE THE TB GO.
CLICK
THAT WASN'T MAGIC?!
KENT·CRESPO·BLYBERG 1-1

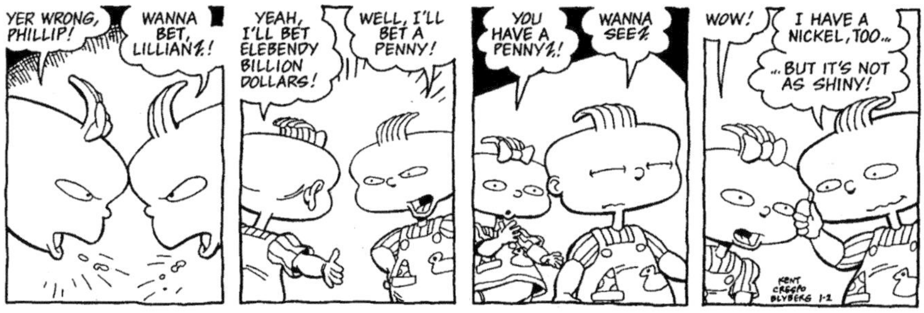
YER WRONG, PHILLIP!
WANNA BET, LILLIAN?!
YEAH, I'LL BET ELEBENDY BILLION DOLLARS!
WELL, I'LL BET A PENNY!
YOU HAVE A PENNY?!
WANNA SEE?
WOW!
I HAVE A NICKEL, TOO...
...BUT IT'S NOT AS SHINY!
KENT CRESPO BLYBERG 1-2

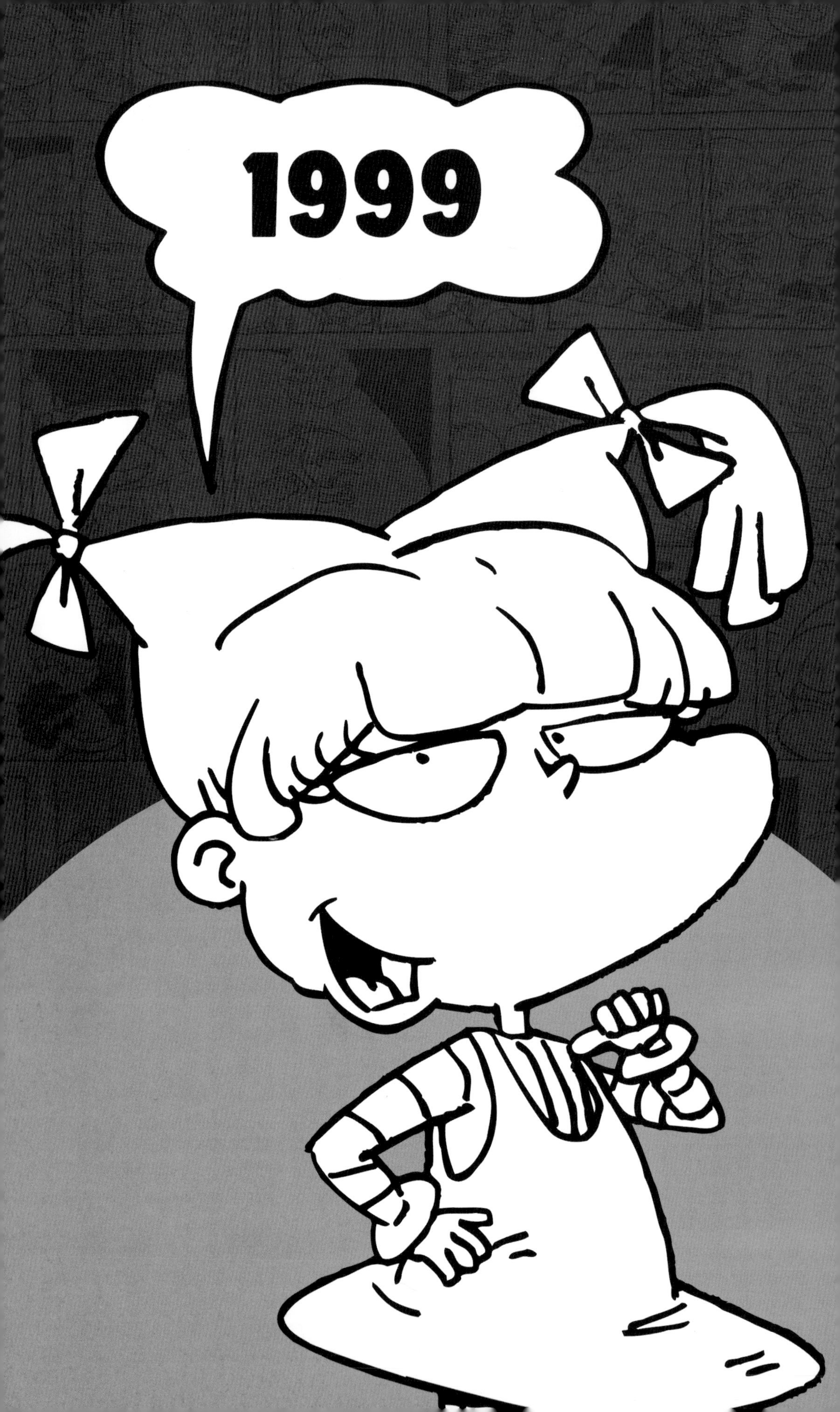
1999

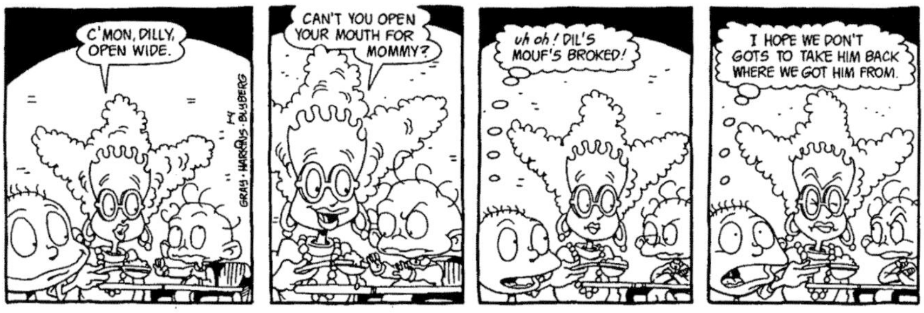
C'MON, DILLY, OPEN WIDE.
1-4
GRAY·HARKINS·BLYBERG
CAN'T YOU OPEN YOUR MOUTH FOR MOMMY?
uh oh! DIL'S MOUF'S BROKED!
I HOPE WE DON'T GOTS TO TAKE HIM BACK WHERE WE GOT HIM FROM.

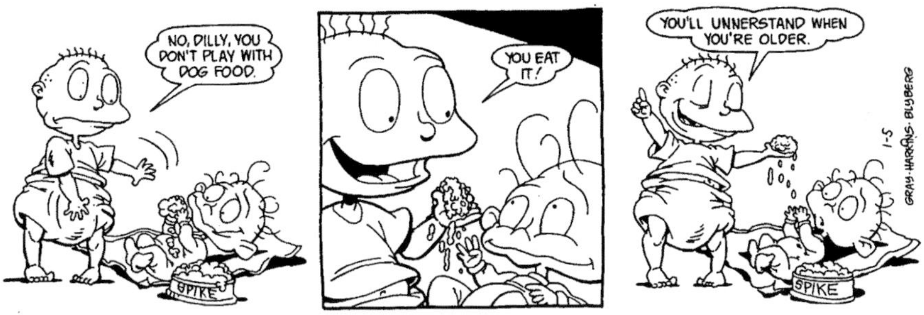
NO, DILLY, YOU DON'T PLAY WITH DOG FOOD.
SPIKE
YOU EAT IT!
YOU'LL UNNERSTAND WHEN YOU'RE OLDER.
1-5
GRAY·HARKINS·BLYBERG
SPIKE

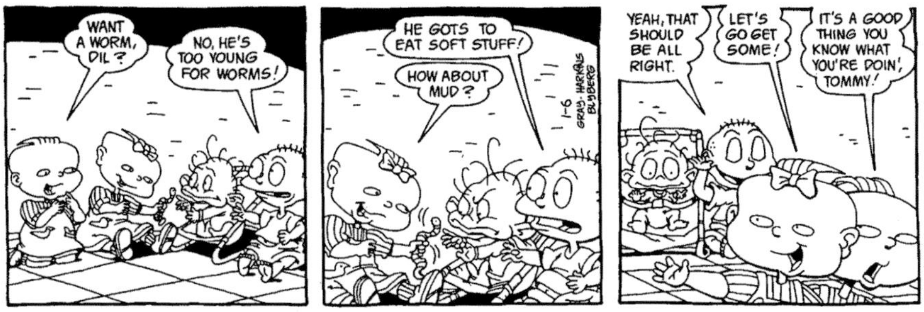
WANT A WORM, DIL?
NO, HE'S TOO YOUNG FOR WORMS!
HE GOTS TO EAT SOFT STUFF!
HOW ABOUT MUD?
1-6
GRAY·HARKINS·BLYBERG
YEAH, THAT SHOULD BE ALL RIGHT.
LET'S GO GET SOME!
IT'S A GOOD THING YOU KNOW WHAT YOU'RE DOIN', TOMMY!

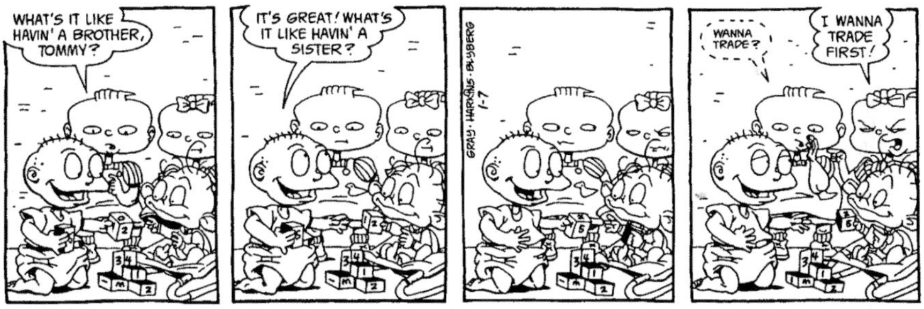
WHAT'S IT LIKE HAVIN' A BROTHER, TOMMY?
IT'S GREAT! WHAT'S IT LIKE HAVIN' A SISTER?
GRAY·HARKINS·BLYBERG
1-7
WANNA TRADE?
I WANNA TRADE FIRST!

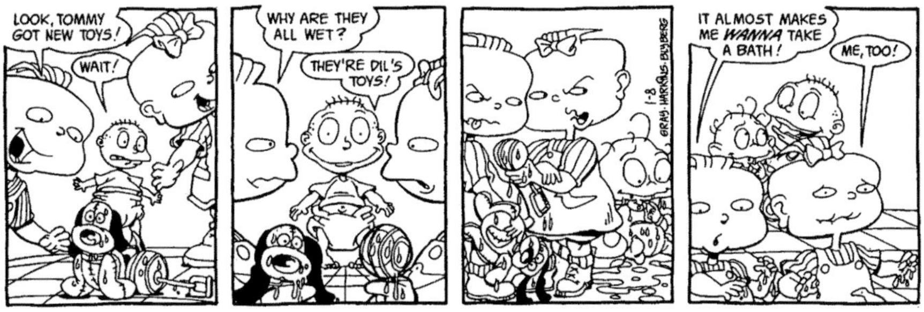
LOOK, TOMMY GOT NEW TOYS!
WAIT!
WHY ARE THEY ALL WET?
THEY'RE DIL'S TOYS!
1-8
GRAY·HARKINS·BLYBERG
IT ALMOST MAKES ME WANNA TAKE A BATH!
ME, TOO!

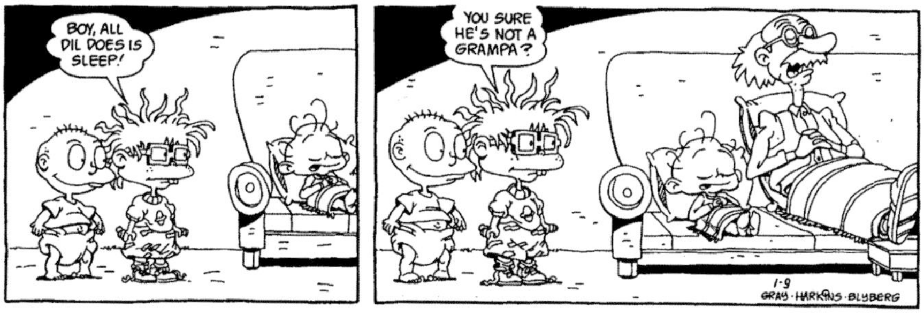
BOY, ALL DIL DOES IS SLEEP!
YOU SURE HE'S NOT A GRAMPA?
1-9
GRAY·HARKINS·BLYBERG

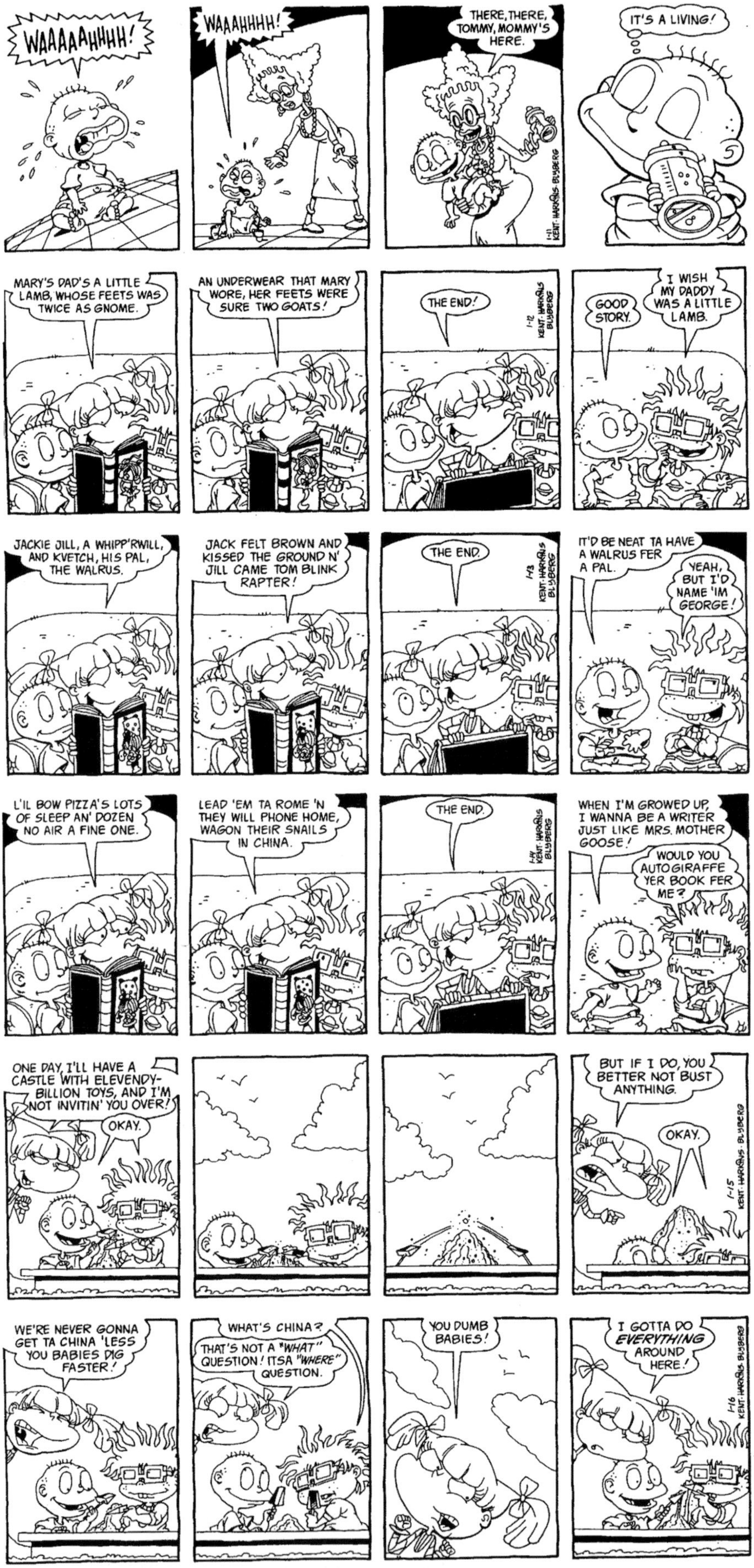
WAAAAAHHHH!
WAAAHHHH!
THERE, THERE, TOMMY, MOMMY'S HERE.
IT'S A LIVING!
MARY'S DAD'S A LITTLE LAMB, WHOSE FEETS WAS TWICE AS GNOME.
AN UNDERWEAR THAT MARY WORE, HER FEETS WERE SURE TWO GOATS!
THE END!
GOOD STORY.
I WISH MY DADDY WAS A LITTLE LAMB.
JACKIE JILL, A WHIPP'RWILL, AND KVETCH, HIS PAL, THE WALRUS.
JACK FELT BROWN AND KISSED THE GROUND N' JILL CAME TOM BLINK RAPTER!
THE END.
IT'D BE NEAT TA HAVE A WALRUS FER A PAL.
YEAH, BUT I'D NAME 'IM GEORGE!
L'IL BOW PIZZA'S LOTS OF SLEEP AN' DOZEN NO AIR A FINE ONE.
LEAD 'EM TA ROME 'N THEY WILL PHONE HOME, WAGON THEIR SNAILS IN CHINA.
THE END.
WHEN I'M GROWED UP, I WANNA BE A WRITER JUST LIKE MRS. MOTHER GOOSE!
WOULD YOU AUTOGIRAFFE YER BOOK FER ME?
ONE DAY, I'LL HAVE A CASTLE WITH ELEVENDY-BILLION TOYS, AND I'M NOT INVITIN' YOU OVER!
OKAY.
BUT IF I DO, YOU BETTER NOT BUST ANYTHING.
OKAY.
WE'RE NEVER GONNA GET TA CHINA 'LESS YOU BABIES DIG FASTER!
WHAT'S CHINA?
THAT'S NOT A "WHAT" QUESTION! ITSA "WHERE" QUESTION.
YOU DUMB BABIES!
I GOTTA DO EVERYTHING AROUND HERE!

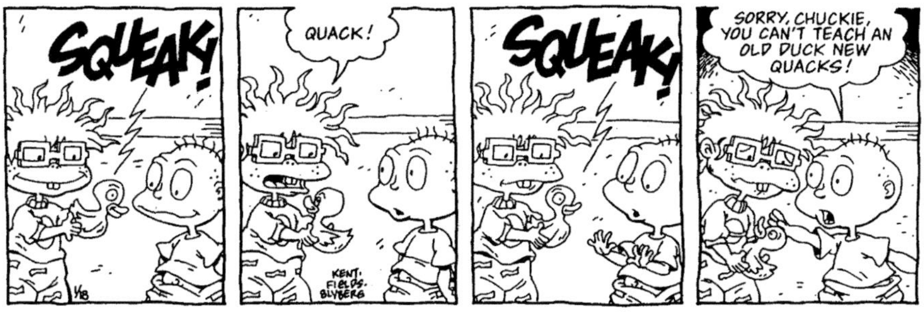
SQUEAK!
1/18
QUACK!
KENT·FIELDS·BLYBERG
SQUEAK!
SORRY, CHUCKIE, YOU CAN'T TEACH AN OLD DUCK NEW QUACKS!

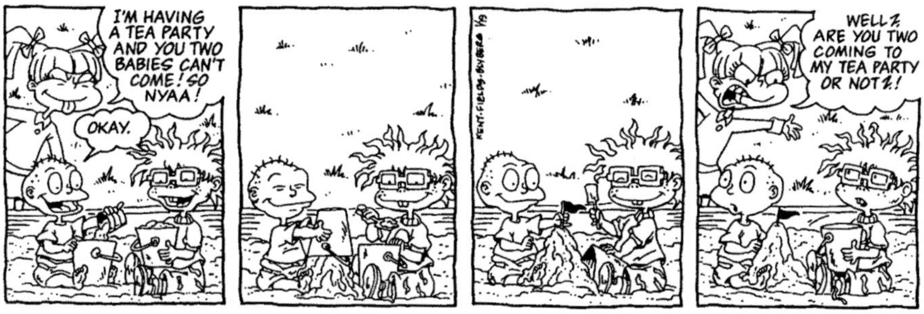
I'M HAVING A TEA PARTY AND YOU TWO BABIES CAN'T COME! SO NYAA!
OKAY.
KENT·FIELDS·BLYBERG 1/19
WELL? ARE YOU TWO COMING TO MY TEA PARTY OR NOT?!

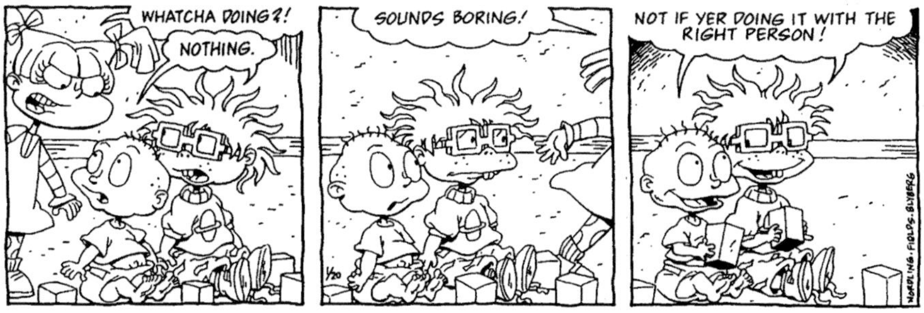
WHATCHA DOING?!
NOTHING.
SOUNDS BORING!
1/20
NOT IF YER DOING IT WITH THE RIGHT PERSON!
NORDLING·FIELDS·BLYBERG

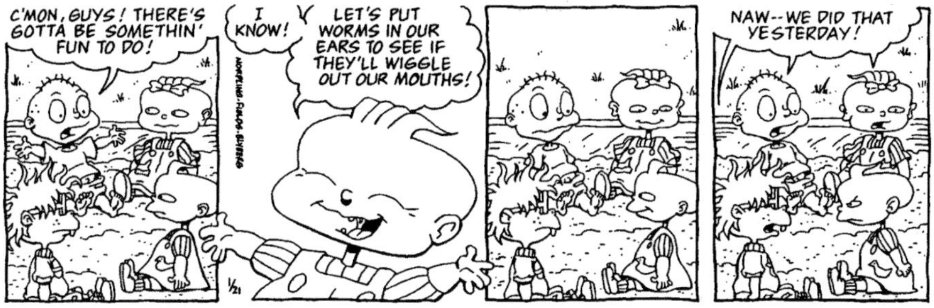
C'MON, GUYS! THERE'S GOTTA BE SOMETHIN' FUN TO DO!
NORDLING·FIELDS·BLYBERG
I KNOW!
LET'S PUT WORMS IN OUR EARS TO SEE IF THEY'LL WIGGLE OUT OUR MOUTHS!
1/21
NAW--WE DID THAT YESTERDAY!

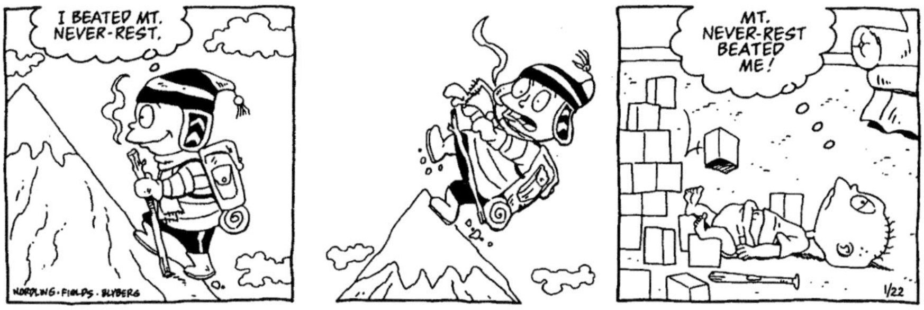
I BEATED MT. NEVER-REST.
NORDLING·FIELDS·BLYBERG
MT. NEVER-REST BEATED ME!
1/22

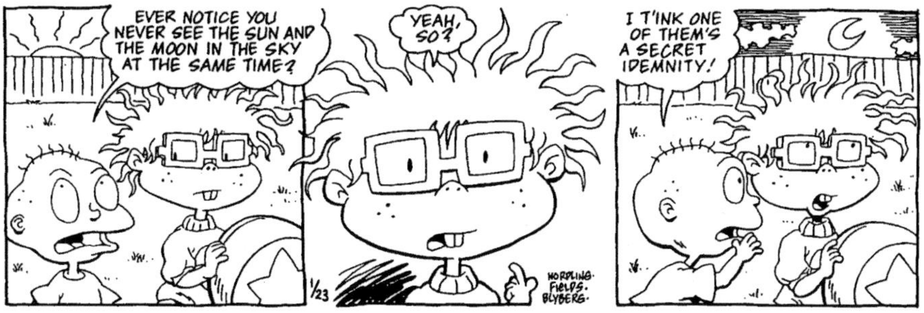
EVER NOTICE YOU NEVER SEE THE SUN AND THE MOON IN THE SKY AT THE SAME TIME?
YEAH, SO?
1/23
NORDLING·FIELDS·BLYBERG
I T'INK ONE OF THEM'S A SECRET IDEMNITY!

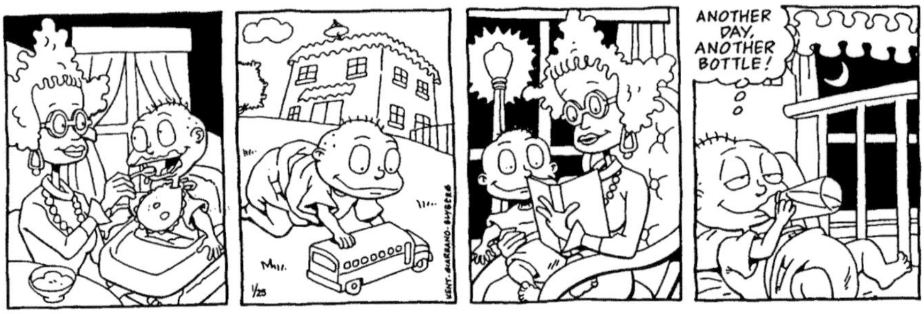
ANOTHER DAY, ANOTHER BOTTLE!
1/25
KENT·GIARRANO·BLYBERG

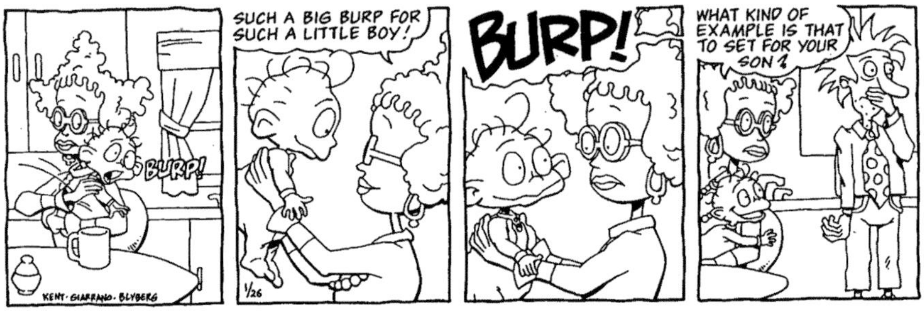
BURP!
KENT·GIARRANO·BLYBERG
SUCH A BIG BURP FOR SUCH A LITTLE BOY!
1/26
BURP!
WHAT KIND OF EXAMPLE IS THAT TO SET FOR YOUR SON?

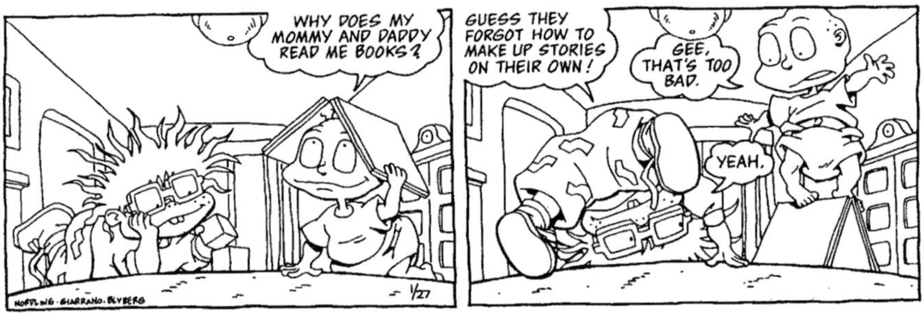
WHY DOES MY MOMMY AND DADDY READ ME BOOKS?
NORDLING·GIARRANO·BLYBERG
1/27
GUESS THEY FORGOT HOW TO MAKE UP STORIES ON THEIR OWN!
GEE, THAT'S TOO BAD.
YEAH.

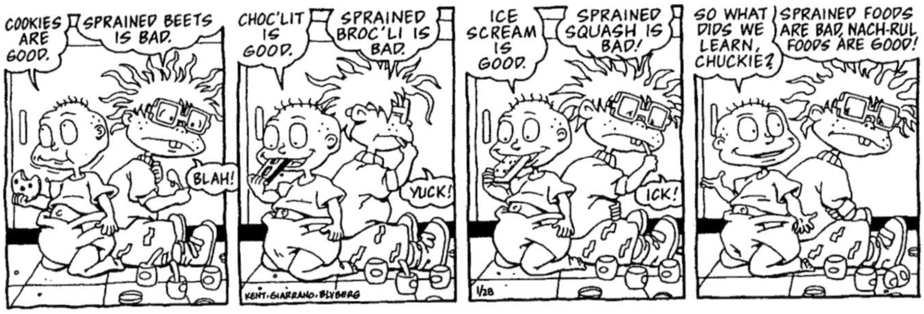
COOKIES ARE GOOD.
SPRAINED BEETS IS BAD.
BLAH!
CHOC'LIT IS GOOD.
SPRAINED BROC'LI IS BAD.
YUCK!
KENT·GIARRANO·BLYBERG
ICE SCREAM IS GOOD.
SPRAINED SQUASH IS BAD!
ICK!
1/28
SO WHAT DIDS WE LEARN, CHUCKIE?
SPRAINED FOODS ARE BAD, NACH-RUL FOODS ARE GOOD!

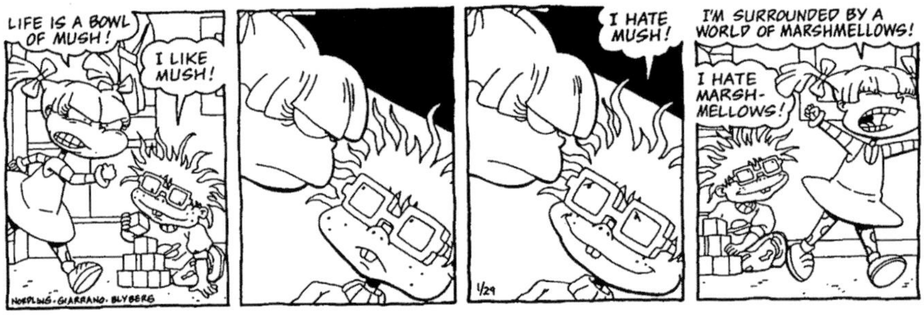
LIFE IS A BOWL OF MUSH!
I LIKE MUSH!
NORDLING·GIARRANO·BLYBERG
I HATE MUSH!
1/29
I'M SURROUNDED BY A WORLD OF MARSHMELLOWS!
I HATE MARSH-MELLOWS!

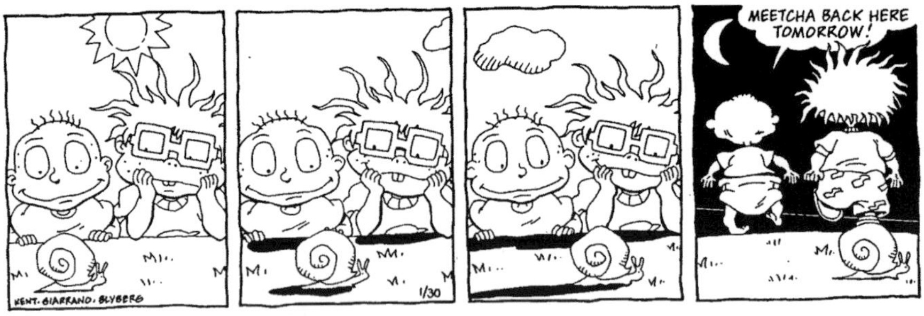
KENT·GIARRANO·BLYBERG
1/30
MEETCHA BACK HERE TOMORROW!

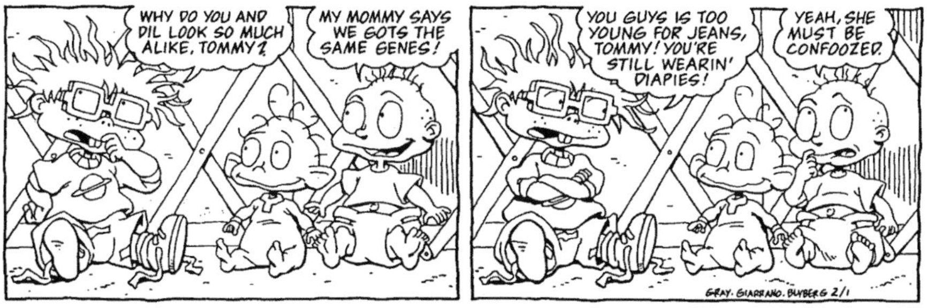
WHY DO YOU AND DIL LOOK SO MUCH ALIKE, TOMMY?
MY MOMMY SAYS WE GOTS THE SAME GENES!
YOU GUYS IS TOO YOUNG FOR JEANS, TOMMY! YOU'RE STILL WEARIN' DIAPIES!
YEAH, SHE MUST BE CONFOOZED.
GRAY·GIARRANO·BLYBERG 2/1

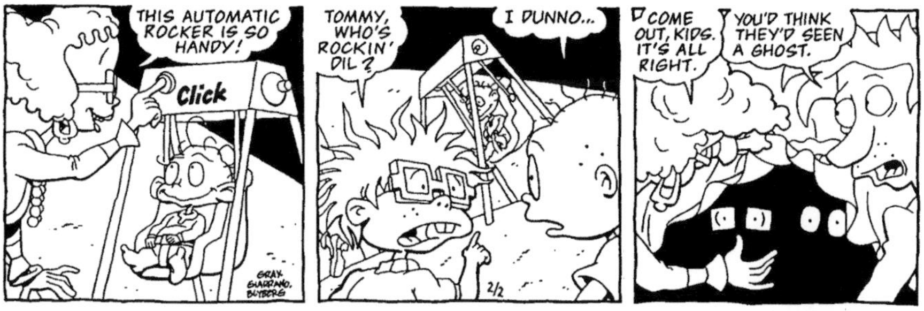
THIS AUTOMATIC ROCKER IS SO HANDY!
Click
GRAY· GIARRANO· BLYBERG
TOMMY, WHO'S ROCKIN' DIL?
I DUNNO...
2/2
COME OUT, KIDS. IT'S ALL RIGHT.
YOU'D THINK THEY'D SEEN A GHOST.

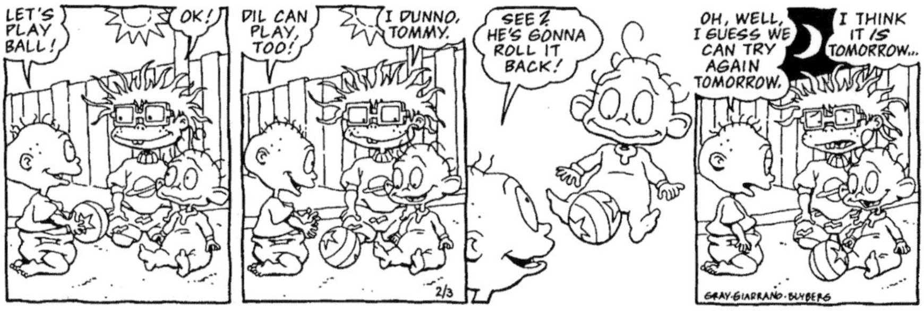
LET'S PLAY BALL!
OK!
DIL CAN PLAY, TOO!
I DUNNO, TOMMY.
SEE? HE'S GONNA ROLL IT BACK!
2/3
OH, WELL, I GUESS WE CAN TRY AGAIN TOMORROW.
I THINK IT *IS* TOMORROW...
GRAY·GIARRANO·BLYBERG

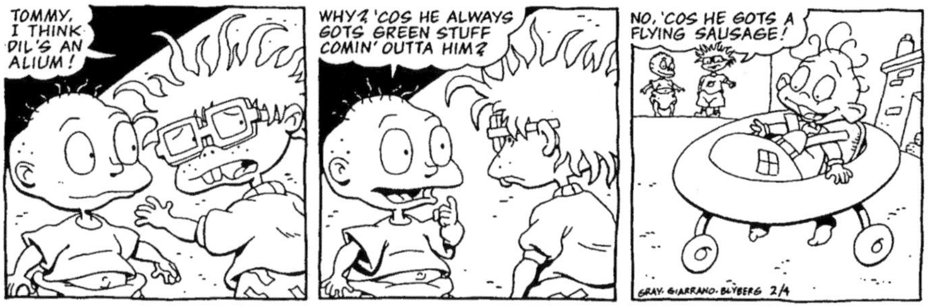
TOMMY, I THINK DIL'S AN ALIUM!
WHY? 'COS HE ALWAYS GOTS GREEN STUFF COMIN' OUTTA HIM?
NO, 'COS HE GOTS A FLYING SAUSAGE!
GRAY·GIARRANO·BLYBERG 2/4

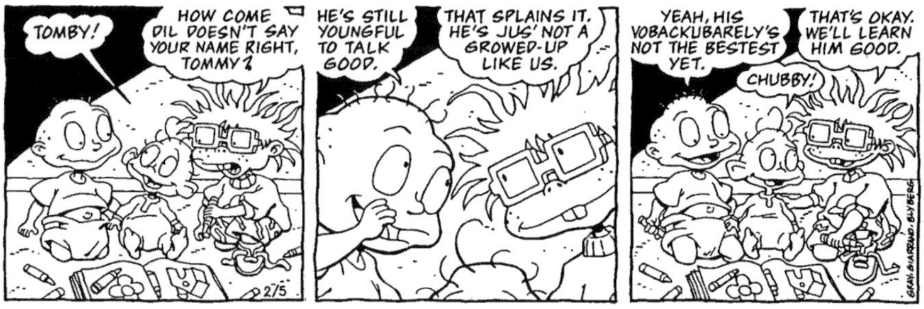
TOMBY!
HOW COME DIL DOESN'T SAY YOUR NAME RIGHT, TOMMY?
2/5
HE'S STILL YOUNGFUL TO TALK GOOD.
THAT SPLAINS IT. HE'S JUS' NOT A GROWED-UP LIKE US.
YEAH, HIS VOBACKUBARELY'S NOT THE BESTEST YET.
THAT'S OKAY. WE'LL LEARN HIM GOOD.
CHUBBY!
GRAY·GIARRANO·BLYBERG

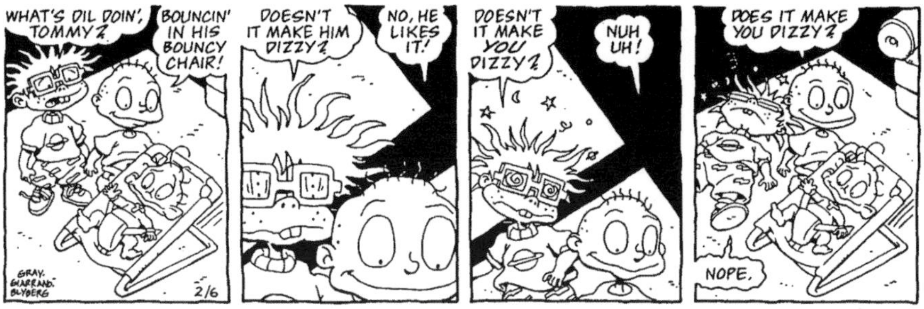
WHAT'S DIL DOIN', TOMMY?
BOUNCIN' IN HIS BOUNCY CHAIR!
GRAY· GIARRANO· BLYBERG
2/6
DOESN'T IT MAKE HIM DIZZY?
NO, HE LIKES IT!
DOESN'T IT MAKE *YOU* DIZZY?
NUH UH!
DOES IT MAKE YOU DIZZY?
NOPE.

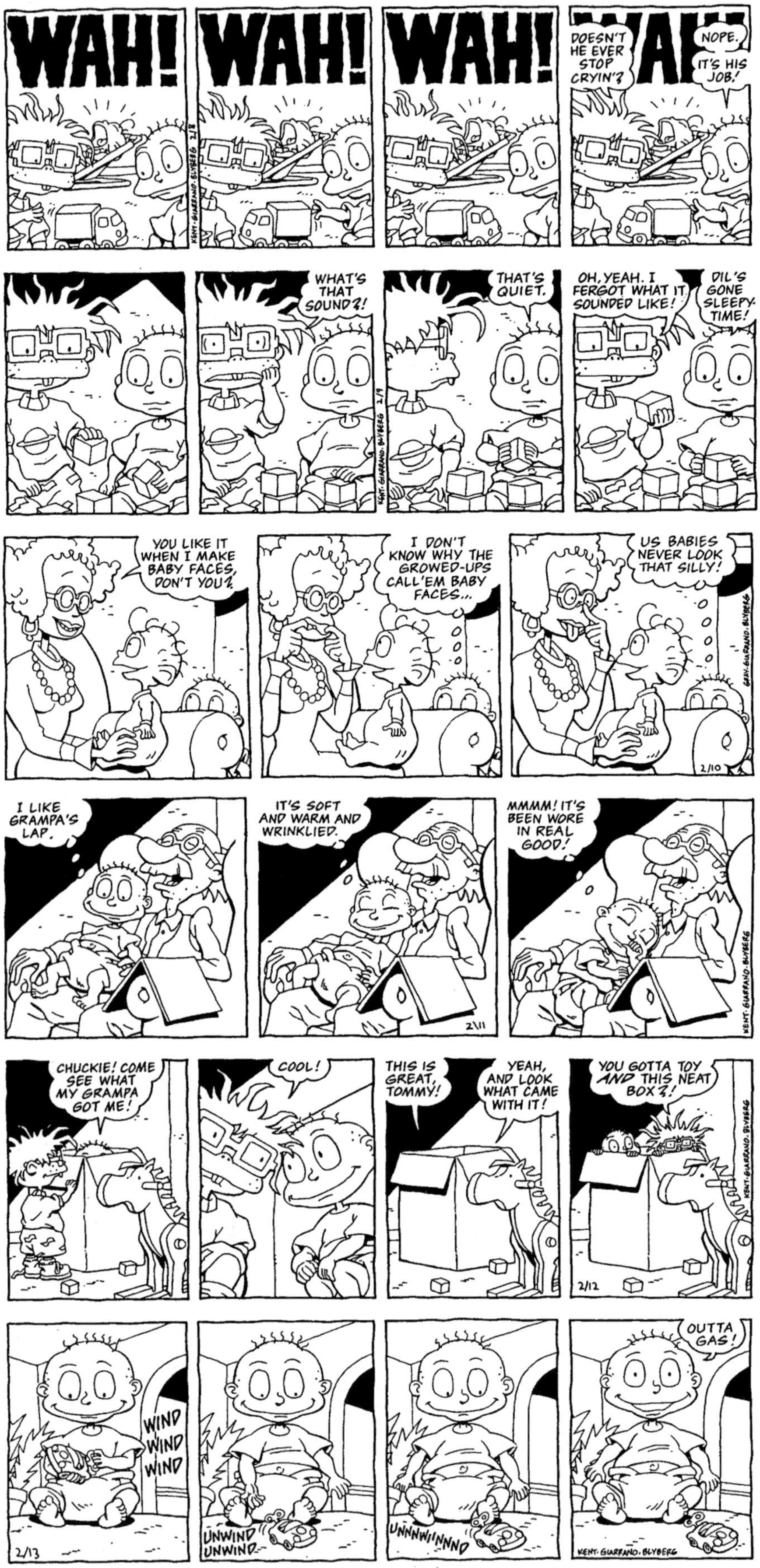

WAH!
KENT·GIARRANO·BLYBERG 2/8
WAH!
WAH!
DOESN'T HE EVER STOP CRYIN'?
NOPE.
IT'S HIS JOB!
WHAT'S THAT SOUND?!
KENT·GIARRANO·BLYBERG 2/9
THAT'S QUIET.
OH, YEAH. I FERGOT WHAT IT SOUNDED LIKE!
DIL'S GONE SLEEPY-TIME!
YOU LIKE IT WHEN I MAKE BABY FACES, DON'T YOU?
I DON'T KNOW WHY THE GROWED-UPS CALL'EM BABY FACES...
US BABIES NEVER LOOK THAT SILLY!
2/10
I LIKE GRAMPA'S LAP.
IT'S SOFT AND WARM AND WRINKLIED.
2/11
MMMM! IT'S BEEN WORE IN REAL GOOD!
KENT·GIARRANO·BLYBERG
CHUCKIE! COME SEE WHAT MY GRAMPA GOT ME!
COOL!
THIS IS GREAT, TOMMY!
YEAH, AND LOOK WHAT CAME WITH IT!
YOU GOTTA TOY AND THIS NEAT BOX?!
KENT·GIARRANO·BLYBERG
2/12
WIND WIND WIND
2/13
UNWIND UNWIND
UNNNWINNNNND
OUTTA GAS!
KENT·GIARRANO·BLYBERG

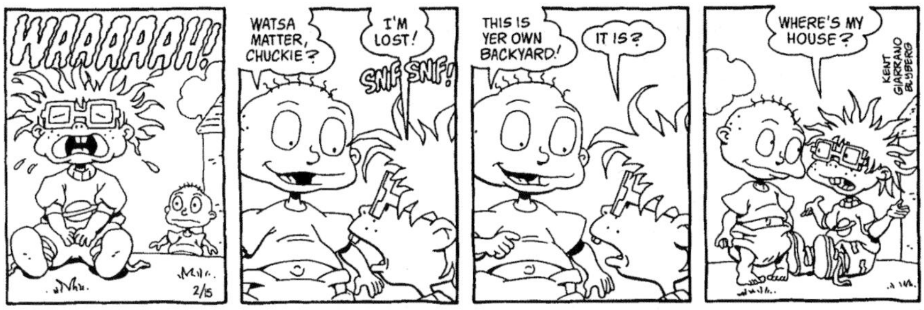
WAAAAAH!
2/15
WATSA MATTER, CHUCKIE?
I'M LOST!
SNIF SNIF!
THIS IS YER OWN BACKYARD!
IT IS?
WHERE'S MY HOUSE?
KENT GIARRANO BLYBERG

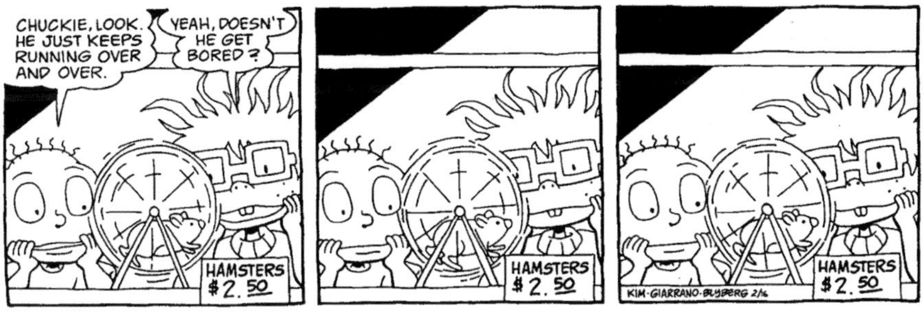
CHUCKIE, LOOK. HE JUST KEEPS RUNNING OVER AND OVER.
YEAH, DOESN'T HE GET BORED?
HAMSTERS $2.50
HAMSTERS $2.50
KIM·GIARRANO·BLYBERG 2/16
HAMSTERS $2.50

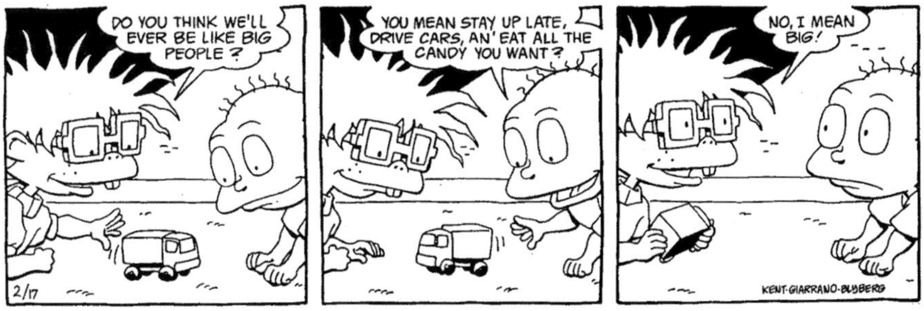
DO YOU THINK WE'LL EVER BE LIKE BIG PEOPLE?
2/17
YOU MEAN STAY UP LATE, DRIVE CARS, AN' EAT ALL THE CANDY YOU WANT?
NO, I MEAN BIG!
KENT·GIARRANO·BLYBERG

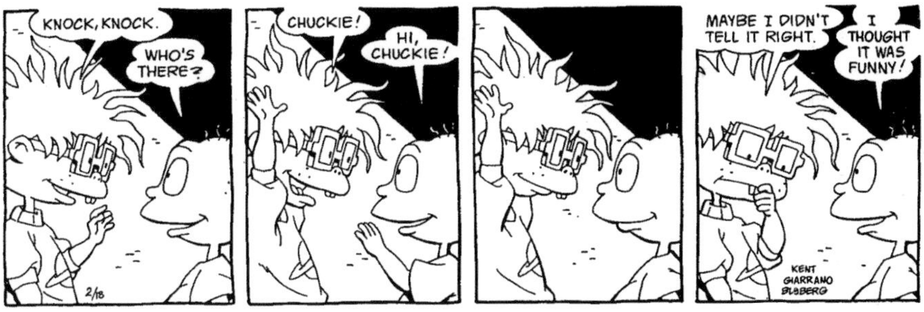
KNOCK, KNOCK.
WHO'S THERE?
2/18
CHUCKIE!
HI, CHUCKIE!
MAYBE I DIDN'T TELL IT RIGHT.
I THOUGHT IT WAS FUNNY!
KENT GIARRANO BLYBERG

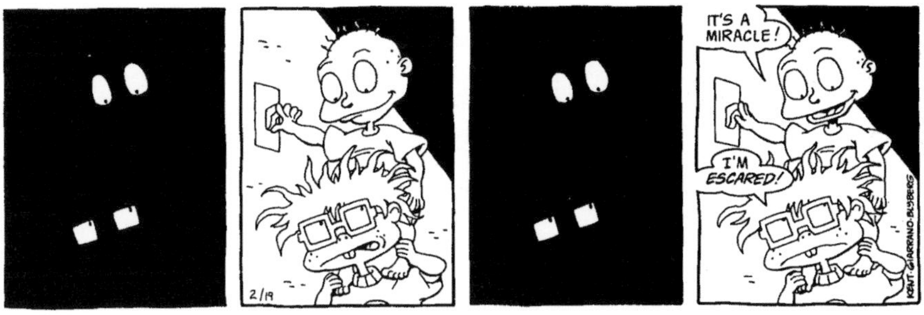
2/19
IT'S A MIRACLE!
I'M ESCARED!
KENT·GIARRANO·BLYBERG

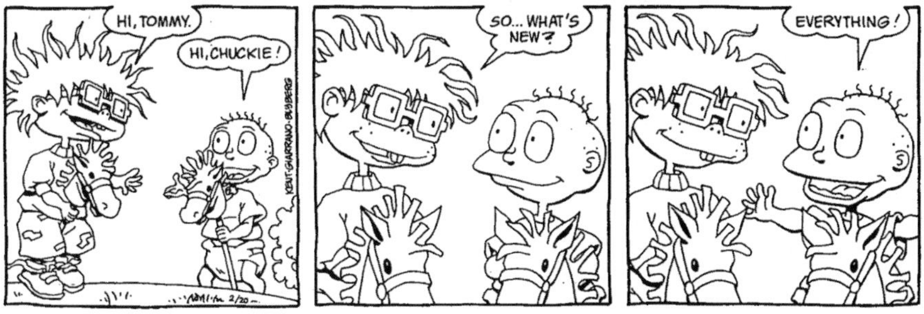
HI, TOMMY.
HI, CHUCKIE!
KENT·GIARRANO·BLYBERG
2/20
SO... WHAT'S NEW?
EVERYTHING!

1999

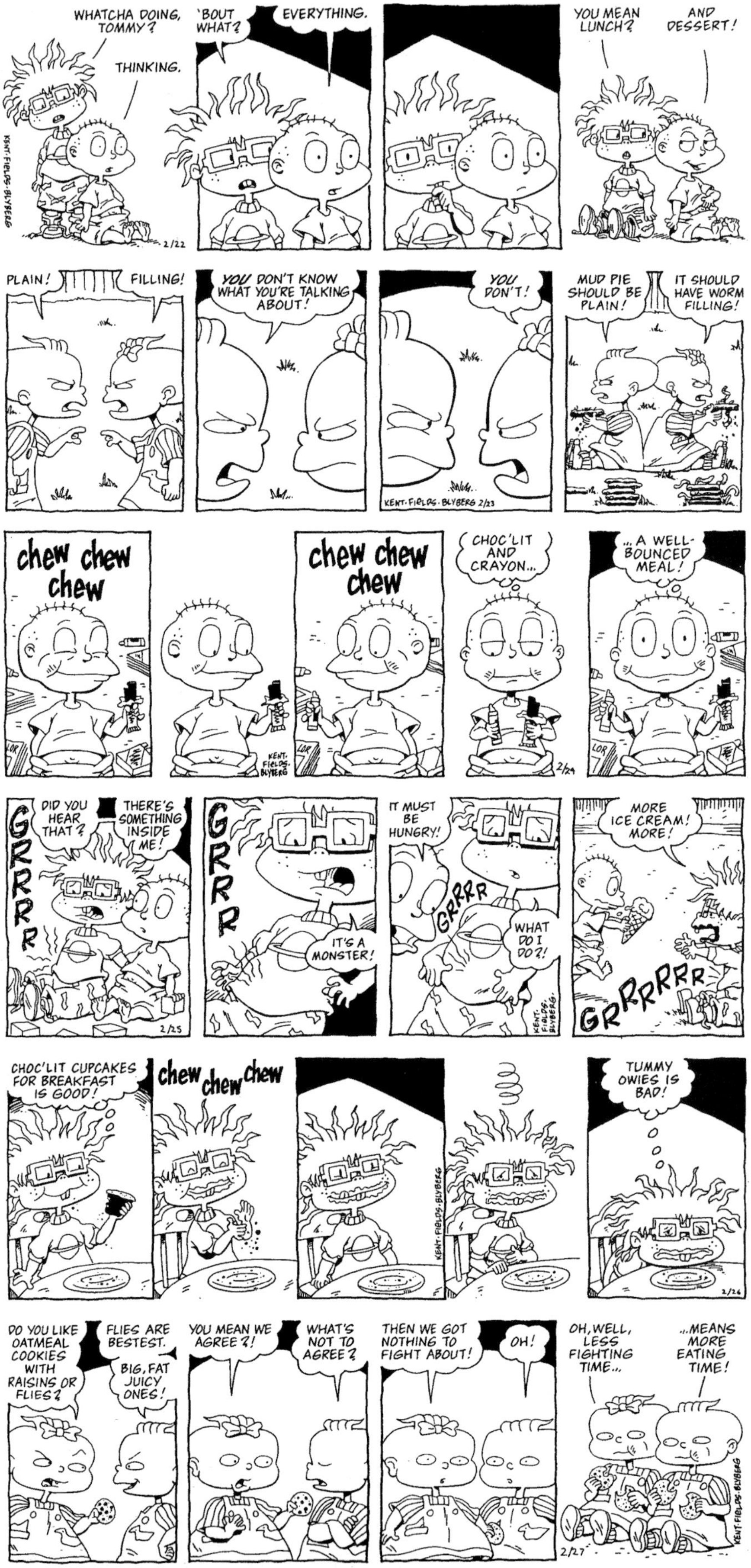

WHATCHA DOING, TOMMY?
THINKING.
KENT·FIELDS·BLYBERG
2/22
'BOUT WHAT?
EVERYTHING.
YOU MEAN LUNCH?
AND DESSERT!
PLAIN!
FILLING!
YOU DON'T KNOW WHAT YOU'RE TALKING ABOUT!
YOU DON'T!
KENT·FIELDS·BLYBERG 2/23
MUD PIE SHOULD BE PLAIN!
IT SHOULD HAVE WORM FILLING!
chew chew chew
KENT·FIELDS·BLYBERG
chew chew chew
CHOC'LIT AND CRAYON...
2/24
... A WELL-BOUNCED MEAL!
GRRRRR
DID YOU HEAR THAT?
THERE'S SOMETHING INSIDE ME!
2/25
GRRR
IT'S A MONSTER!
IT MUST BE HUNGRY!
GRRRR
WHAT DO I DO?!
KENT·FIELDS·BLYBERG
MORE ICE CREAM! MORE!
GRRRRRRR
CHOC'LIT CUPCAKES FOR BREAKFAST IS GOOD!
chew chew chew
KENT·FIELDS·BLYBERG
TUMMY OWIES IS BAD!
2/26
DO YOU LIKE OATMEAL COOKIES WITH RAISINS OR FLIES?
FLIES ARE BESTEST.
BIG, FAT JUICY ONES!
YOU MEAN WE AGREE?!
WHAT'S NOT TO AGREE?
THEN WE GOT NOTHING TO FIGHT ABOUT!
OH!
OH, WELL, LESS FIGHTING TIME...
...MEANS MORE EATING TIME!
KENT·FIELDS·BLYBERG
2/27

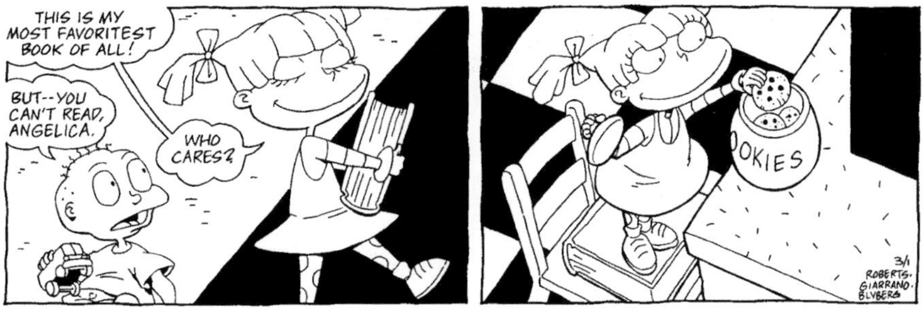
THIS IS MY MOST FAVORITEST BOOK OF ALL!
BUT--YOU CAN'T READ, ANGELICA.
WHO CARES?
OOKIES
3/1
ROBERTS·GIARRANO·BLYBERG

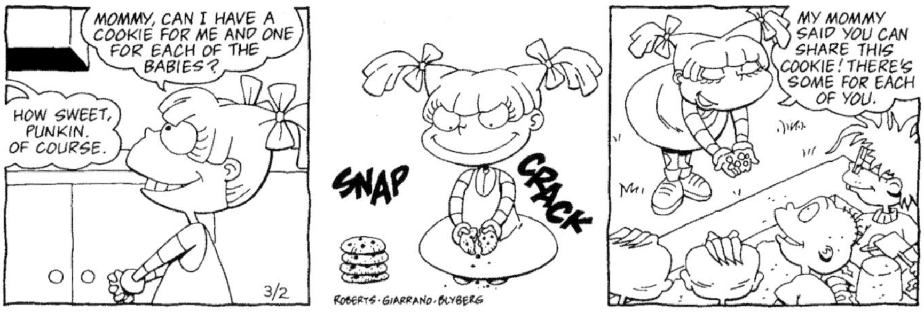
MOMMY, CAN I HAVE A COOKIE FOR ME AND ONE FOR EACH OF THE BABIES?
HOW SWEET, PUNKIN. OF COURSE.
3/2
SNAP
CRACK
ROBERTS·GIARRANO·BLYBERG
MY MOMMY SAID YOU CAN SHARE THIS COOKIE! THERE'S SOME FOR EACH OF YOU.

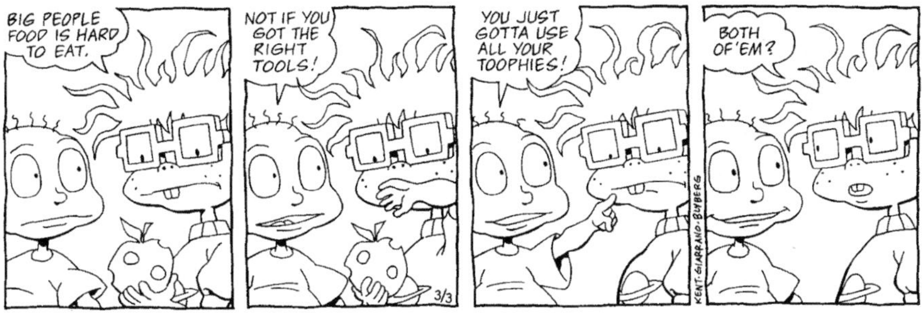
BIG PEOPLE FOOD IS HARD TO EAT.
NOT IF YOU GOT THE RIGHT TOOLS!
3/3
YOU JUST GOTTA USE ALL YOUR TOOPHIES!
KENT·GIARRANO·BLYBERG
BOTH OF 'EM?

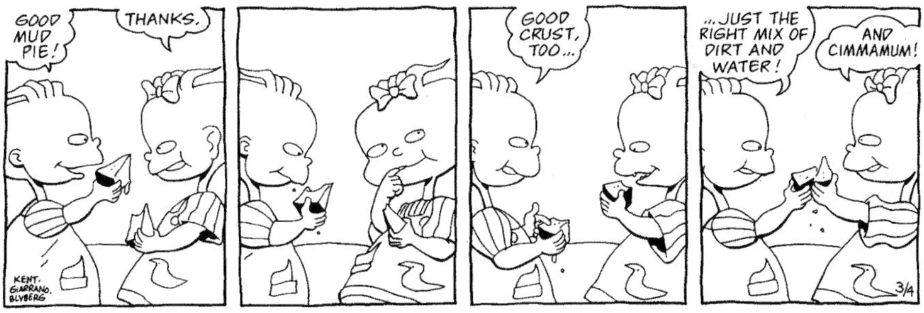
GOOD MUD PIE!
THANKS.
KENT·GIARRANO·BLYBERG
GOOD CRUST, TOO...
...JUST THE RIGHT MIX OF DIRT AND WATER!
AND CIMMAMUM!
3/4

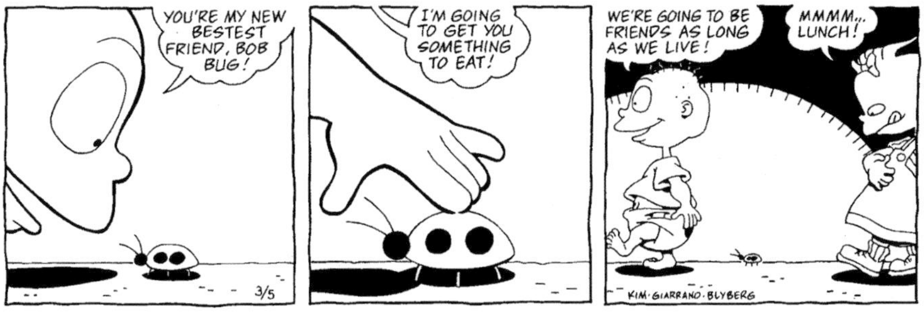
YOU'RE MY NEW BESTEST FRIEND, BOB BUG!
3/5
I'M GOING TO GET YOU SOMETHING TO EAT!
WE'RE GOING TO BE FRIENDS AS LONG AS WE LIVE!
MMMM... LUNCH!
KIM·GIARRANO·BLYBERG

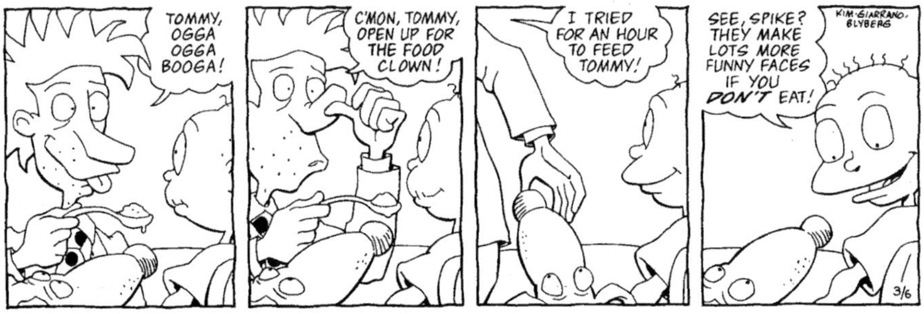
TOMMY, OGGA OGGA BOOGA!
C'MON, TOMMY, OPEN UP FOR THE FOOD CLOWN!
I TRIED FOR AN HOUR TO FEED TOMMY!
SEE, SPIKE? THEY MAKE LOTS MORE FUNNY FACES IF YOU DON'T EAT!
KIM·GIARRANO·BLYBERG
3/6

1999

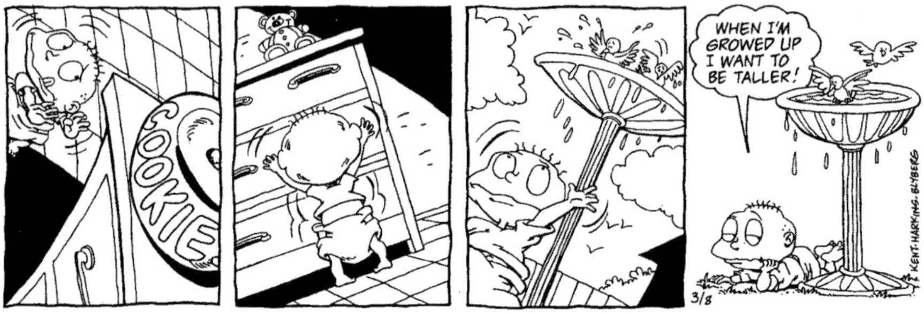
COOKIE
WHEN I'M GROWED UP I WANT TO BE TALLER!
KENT·HARKINS·BLYBERG
3/8

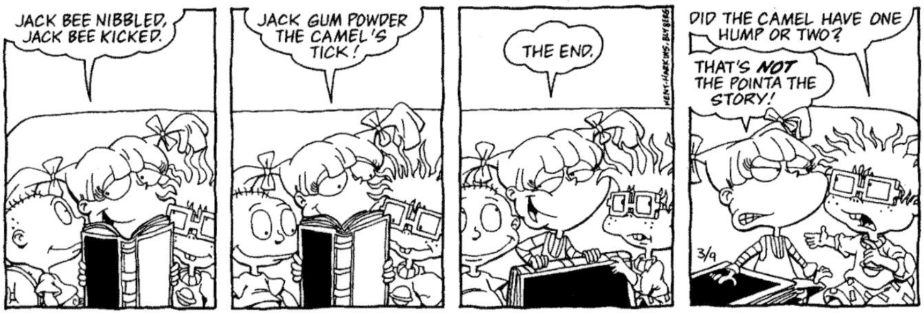
JACK BEE NIBBLED, JACK BEE KICKED.
JACK GUM POWDER THE CAMEL'S TICK!
THE END.
KENT·HARKINS·BLYBERG
DID THE CAMEL HAVE ONE HUMP OR TWO?
THAT'S **NOT** THE POINTA THE STORY!
3/9

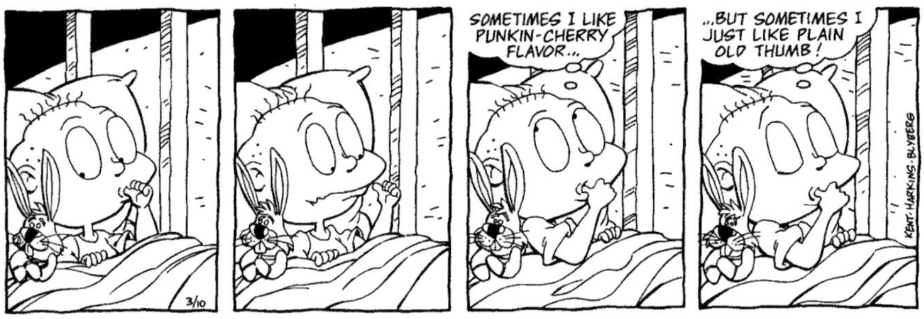
3/10
SOMETIMES I LIKE PUNKIN-CHERRY FLAVOR...
...BUT SOMETIMES I JUST LIKE PLAIN OLD THUMB!
KENT·HARKINS·BLYBERG

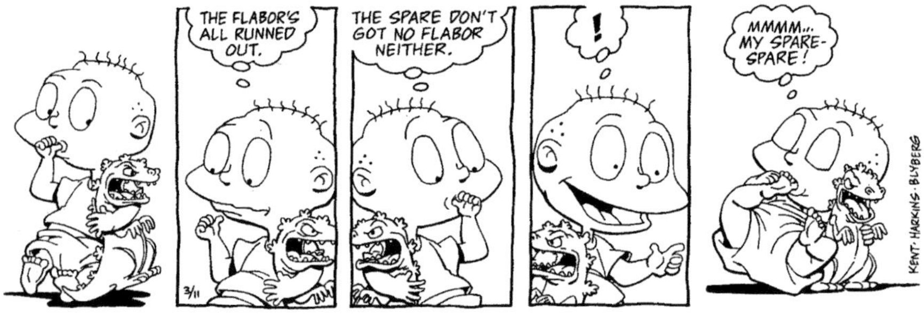
THE FLABOR'S ALL RUNNED OUT.
3/11
THE SPARE DON'T GOT NO FLABOR NEITHER.
!
MMMM... MY SPARE-SPARE!
KENT·HARKINS·BLYBERG

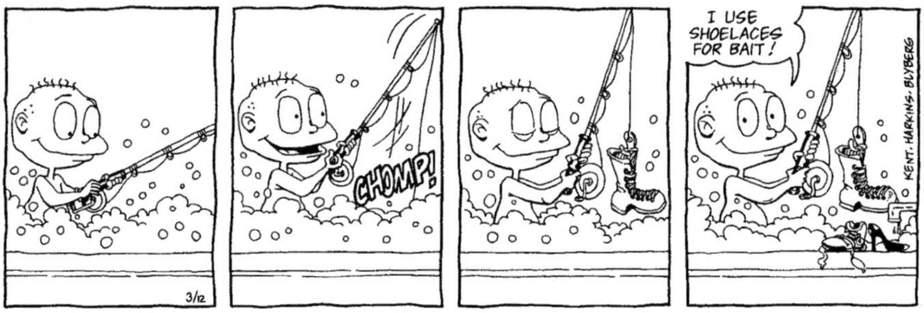
3/12
CHOMP!
I USE SHOELACES FOR BAIT!
KENT·HARKINS·BLYBERG

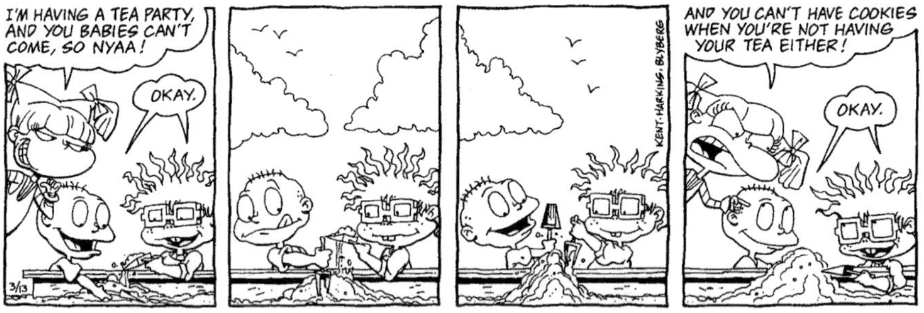
I'M HAVING A TEA PARTY, AND YOU BABIES CAN'T COME, SO NYAA!
OKAY.
3/13
KENT·HARKINS·BLYBERG
AND YOU CAN'T HAVE COOKIES WHEN YOU'RE NOT HAVING YOUR TEA EITHER!
OKAY.

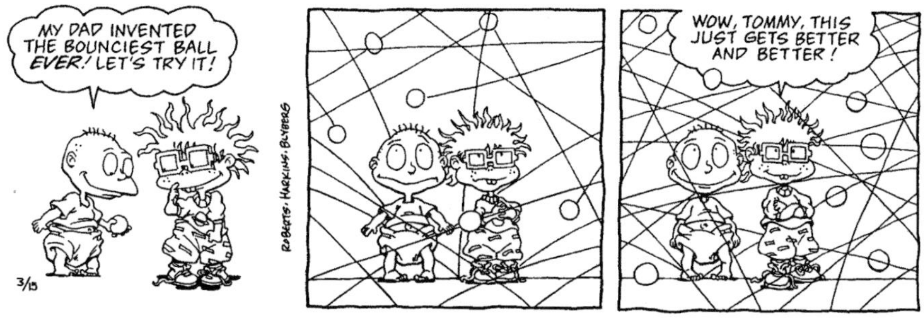
MY DAD INVENTED THE BOUNCIEST BALL *EVER!* LET'S TRY IT!
ROBERTS·HARKINS·BLYBERG
3/15
WOW, TOMMY, THIS JUST GETS BETTER AND BETTER!

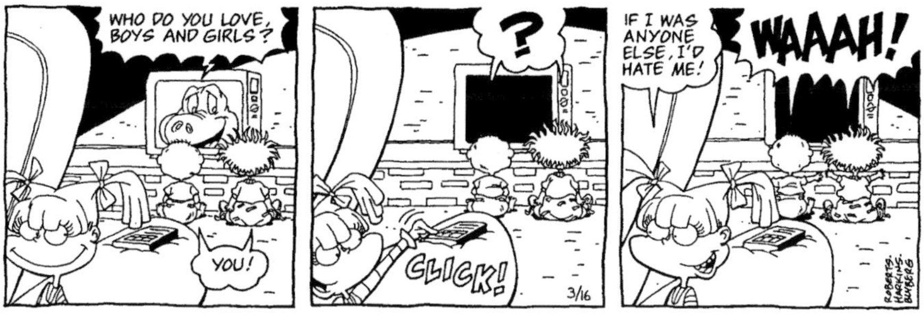
WHO DO YOU LOVE, BOYS AND GIRLS?
YOU!
?
CLICK!
3/16
IF I WAS ANYONE ELSE, I'D HATE ME!
WAAAH!
ROBERTS·HARKINS·BLYBERG

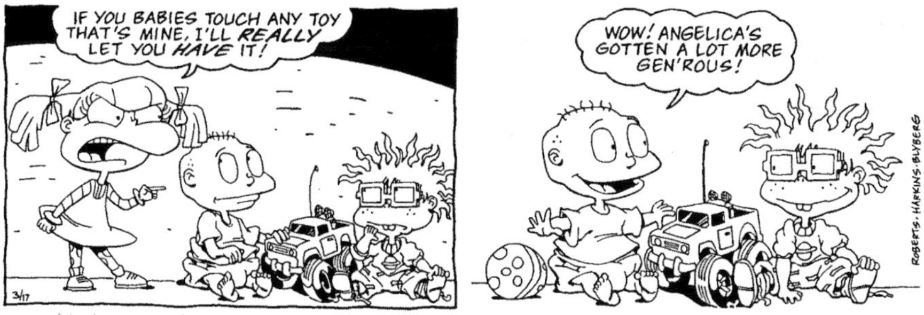
IF YOU BABIES TOUCH ANY TOY THAT'S MINE, I'LL *REALLY* LET YOU *HAVE* IT!
3/17
WOW! ANGELICA'S GOTTEN A LOT MORE GEN'ROUS!
ROBERTS·HARKINS·BLYBERG

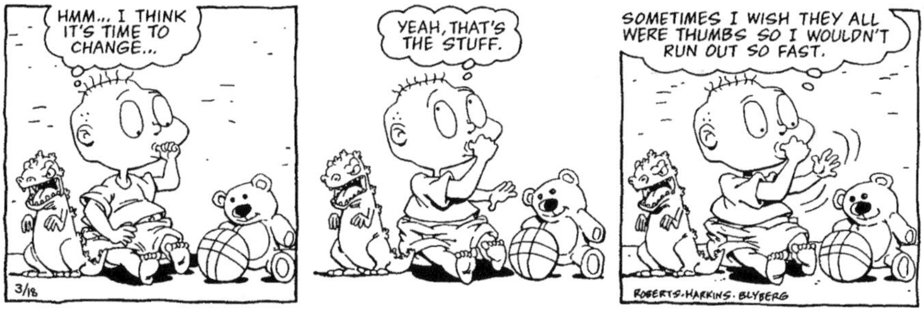
HMM... I THINK IT'S TIME TO CHANGE...
3/18
YEAH, THAT'S THE STUFF.
SOMETIMES I WISH THEY ALL WERE THUMBS SO I WOULDN'T RUN OUT SO FAST.
ROBERTS·HARKINS·BLYBERG

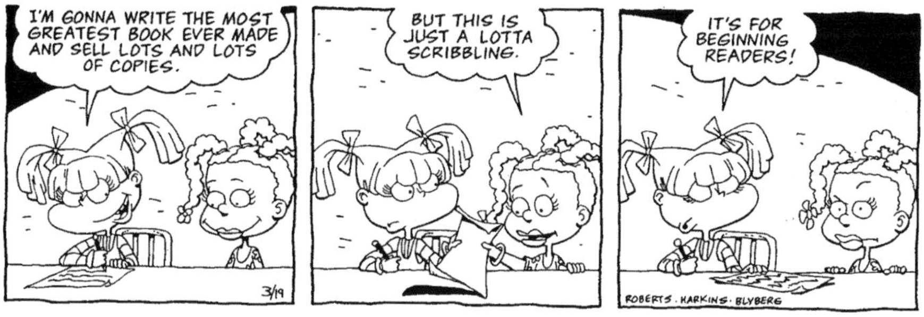
I'M GONNA WRITE THE MOST GREATEST BOOK EVER MADE AND SELL LOTS AND LOTS OF COPIES.
3/19
BUT THIS IS JUST A LOTTA SCRIBBLING.
IT'S FOR BEGINNING READERS!
ROBERTS·HARKINS·BLYBERG

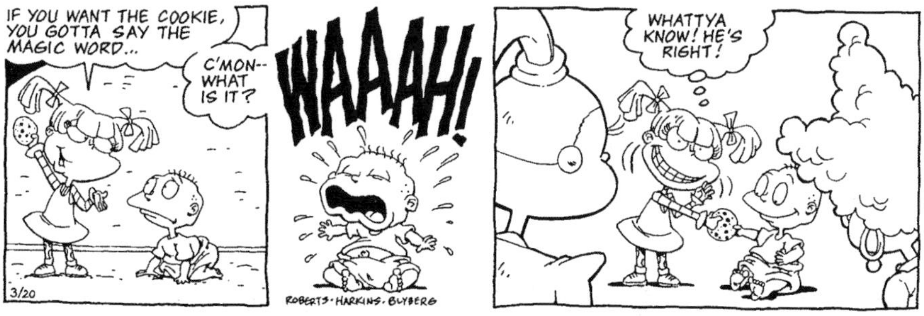
IF YOU WANT THE COOKIE, YOU GOTTA SAY THE MAGIC WORD...
C'MON-- WHAT IS IT?
3/20
WAAAH!
ROBERTS·HARKINS·BLYBERG
WHATTYA KNOW! HE'S RIGHT!

1999

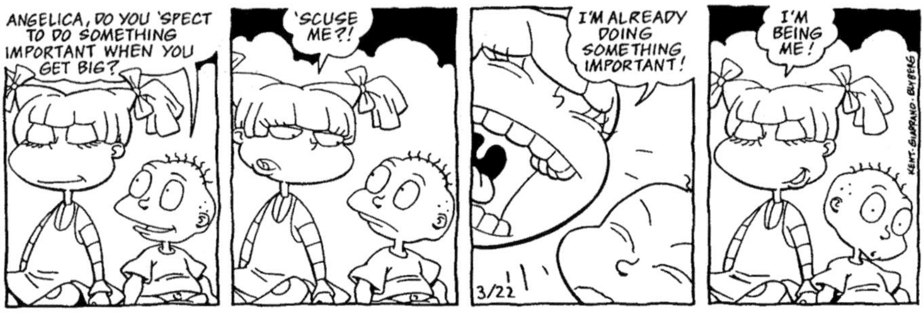
ANGELICA, DO YOU 'SPECT TO DO SOMETHING IMPORTANT WHEN YOU GET BIG?
'SCUSE ME?!
I'M ALREADY DOING SOMETHING IMPORTANT!
3/22
I'M BEING ME!
KENT·GIARRANO·BLYBERG

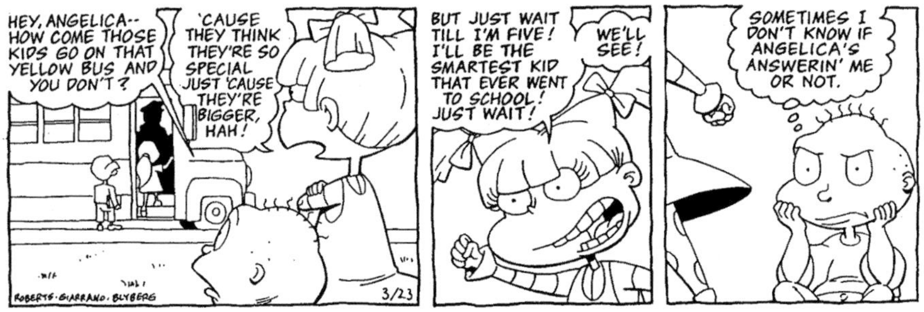
HEY, ANGELICA-- HOW COME THOSE KIDS GO ON THAT YELLOW BUS AND YOU DON'T?
'CAUSE THEY THINK THEY'RE SO SPECIAL JUST 'CAUSE THEY'RE BIGGER, HAH!
ROBERTS·GIARRANO·BLYBERG
3/23
BUT JUST WAIT TILL I'M FIVE! I'LL BE THE SMARTEST KID THAT EVER WENT TO SCHOOL! JUST WAIT!
WE'LL SEE!
SOMETIMES I DON'T KNOW IF ANGELICA'S ANSWERIN' ME OR NOT.

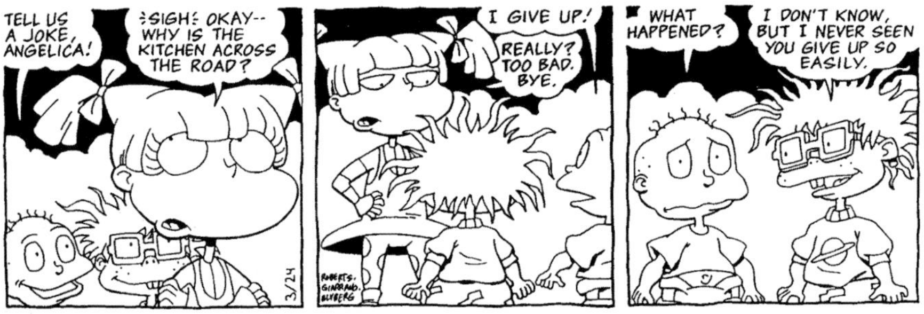
TELL US A JOKE, ANGELICA!
-SIGH- OKAY-- WHY IS THE KITCHEN ACROSS THE ROAD?
3/24
I GIVE UP!
REALLY? TOO BAD. BYE.
ROBERTS·GIARRANO·BLYBERG
WHAT HAPPENED?
I DON'T KNOW, BUT I NEVER SEEN YOU GIVE UP SO EASILY.

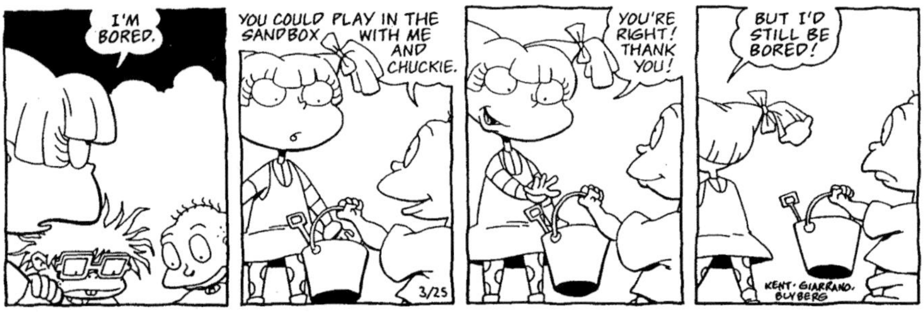
I'M BORED.
YOU COULD PLAY IN THE SANDBOX WITH ME AND CHUCKIE.
3/25
YOU'RE RIGHT! THANK YOU!
BUT I'D STILL BE BORED!
KENT·GIARRANO·BLYBERG

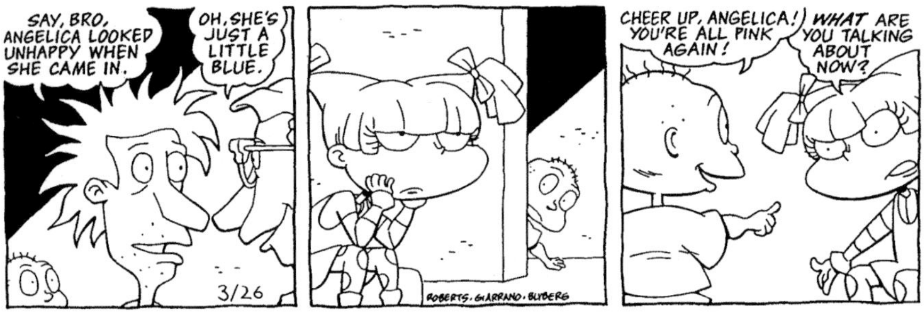
SAY, BRO, ANGELICA LOOKED UNHAPPY WHEN SHE CAME IN.
OH, SHE'S JUST A LITTLE BLUE.
3/26
ROBERTS·GIARRANO·BLYBERG
CHEER UP, ANGELICA! YOU'RE ALL PINK AGAIN!
WHAT ARE YOU TALKING ABOUT NOW?

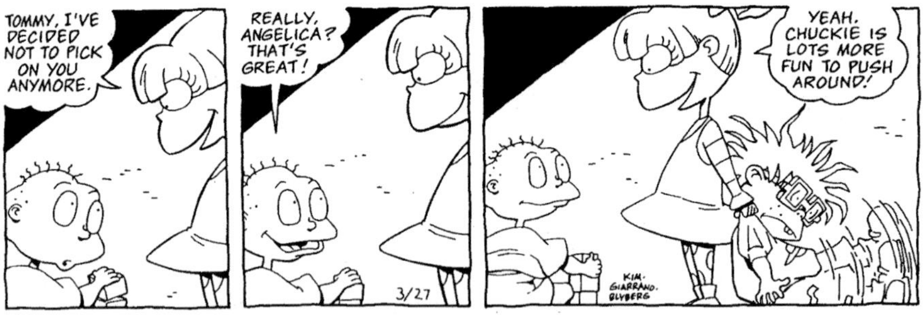
TOMMY, I'VE DECIDED NOT TO PICK ON YOU ANYMORE.
REALLY, ANGELICA? THAT'S GREAT!
3/27
YEAH. CHUCKIE IS LOTS MORE FUN TO PUSH AROUND!
KIM·GIARRANO·BLYBERG

1999

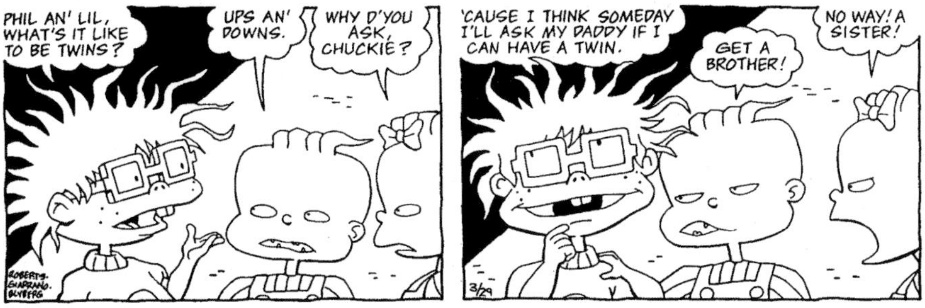

PHIL AN' LIL, WHAT'S IT LIKE TO BE TWINS?
UPS AN' DOWNS.
WHY D'YOU ASK, CHUCKIE?
ROBERTS. GIARRANO. BLYBERG
'CAUSE I THINK SOMEDAY I'LL ASK MY DADDY IF I CAN HAVE A TWIN.
GET A BROTHER!
NO WAY! A SISTER!
3/29

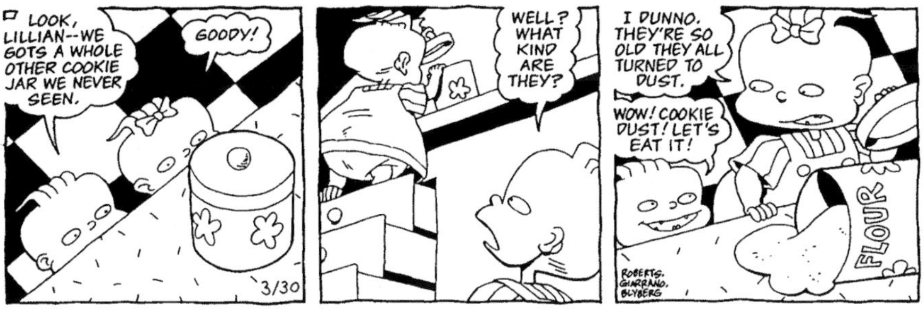

LOOK, LILLIAN--WE GOTS A WHOLE OTHER COOKIE JAR WE NEVER SEEN.
GOODY!
3/30
WELL? WHAT KIND ARE THEY?
I DUNNO. THEY'RE SO OLD THEY ALL TURNED TO DUST.
WOW! COOKIE DUST! LET'S EAT IT!
FLOUR
ROBERTS. GIARRANO. BLYBERG

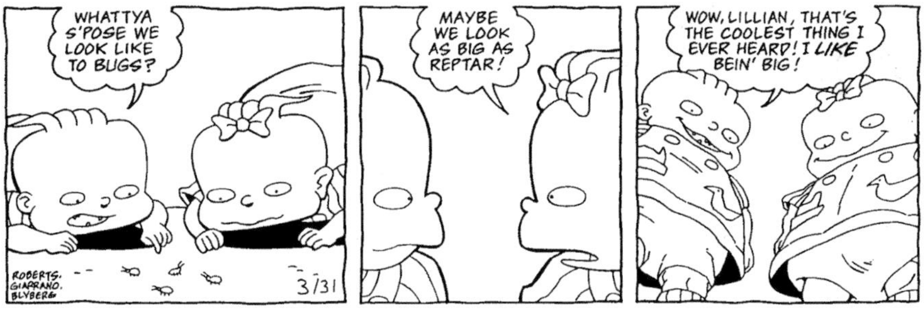

WHATTYA S'POSE WE LOOK LIKE TO BUGS?
ROBERTS. GIARRANO. BLYBERG
3/31
MAYBE WE LOOK AS BIG AS REPTAR!
WOW, LILLIAN, THAT'S THE COOLEST THING I EVER HEARD! I *LIKE* BEIN' BIG!

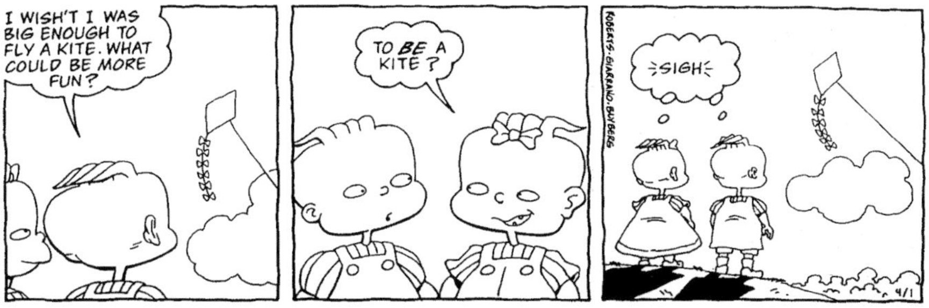

I WISH'T I WAS BIG ENOUGH TO FLY A KITE. WHAT COULD BE MORE FUN?
TO *BE* A KITE?
ROBERTS. GIARRANO. BLYBERG
SIGH
4/1

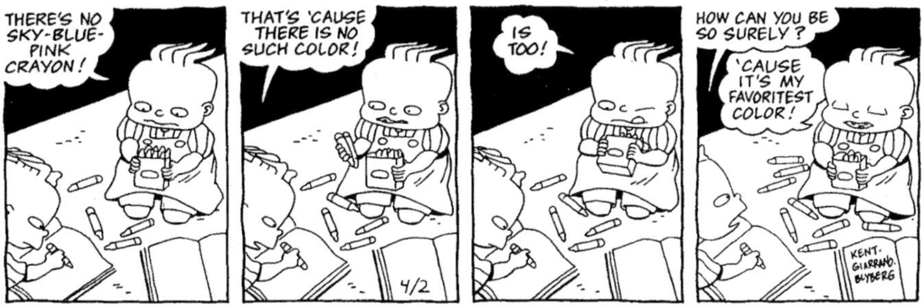

THERE'S NO SKY-BLUE-PINK CRAYON!
THAT'S 'CAUSE THERE IS NO SUCH COLOR!
4/2
IS TOO!
HOW CAN YOU BE SO SURELY?
'CAUSE IT'S MY FAVORITEST COLOR!
KENT. GIARRANO. BLYBERG

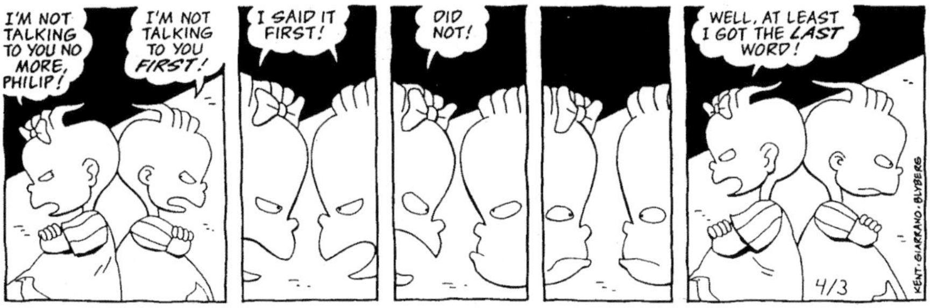

I'M NOT TALKING TO YOU NO MORE, PHILIP!
I'M NOT TALKING TO YOU *FIRST*!
I SAID IT FIRST!
DID NOT!
WELL, AT LEAST I GOT THE *LAST* WORD!
4/3
KENT. GIARRANO. BLYBERG

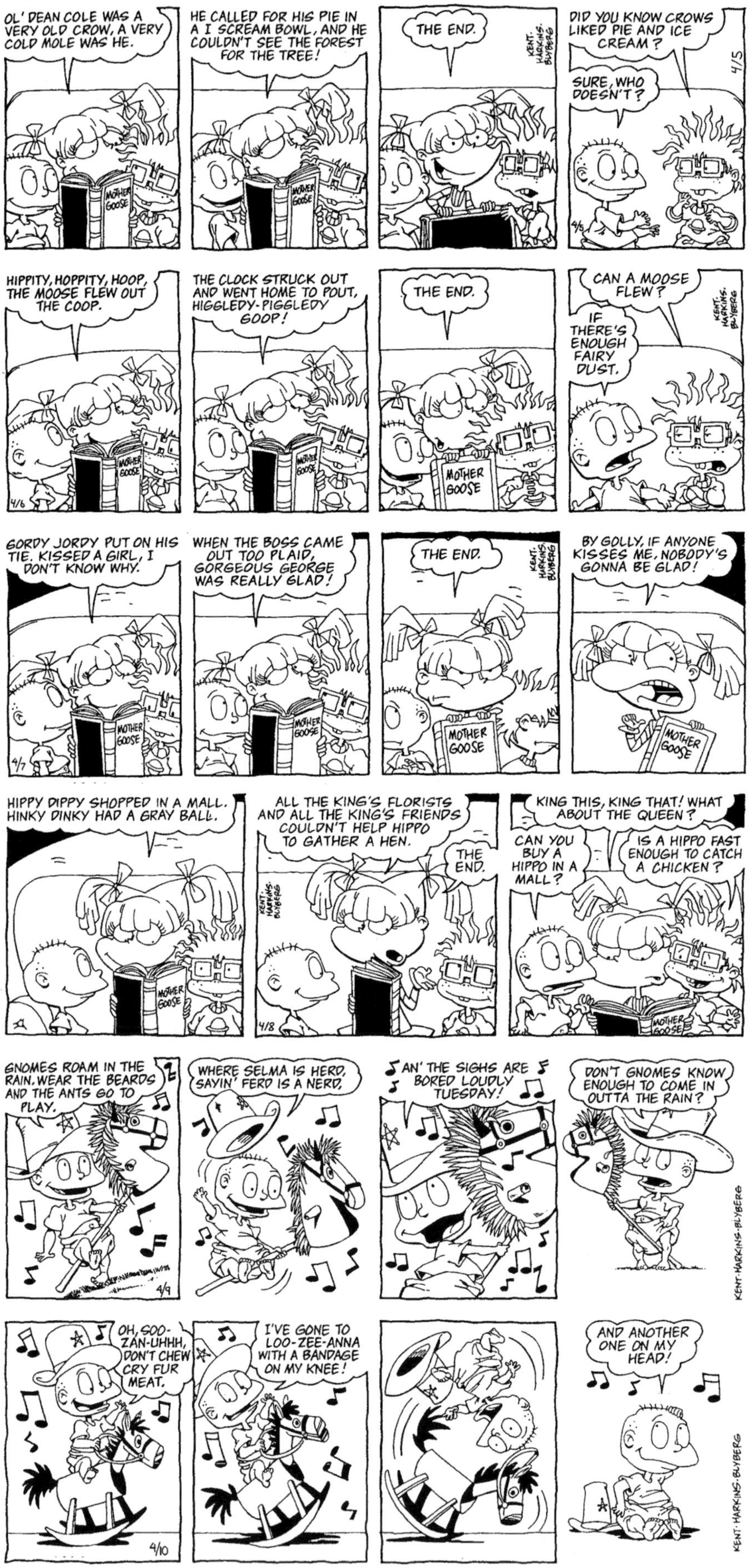

OL' DEAN COLE WAS A VERY OLD CROW, A VERY COLD MOLE WAS HE.
HE CALLED FOR HIS PIE IN A I SCREAM BOWL, AND HE COULDN'T SEE THE FOREST FOR THE TREE!
MOTHER GOOSE
THE END.
KENT. HARKINS. BLYBERG
DID YOU KNOW CROWS LIKED PIE AND ICE CREAM?
SURE, WHO DOESN'T?
4/5
HIPPITY, HOPPITY, HOOP, THE MOOSE FLEW OUT THE COOP.
THE CLOCK STRUCK OUT AND WENT HOME TO POUT, HIGGLEDY-PIGGLEDY GOOP!
THE END.
CAN A MOOSE FLEW?
IF THERE'S ENOUGH FAIRY DUST.
4/6
GORDY JORDY PUT ON HIS TIE. KISSED A GIRL, I DON'T KNOW WHY.
WHEN THE BOSS CAME OUT TOO PLAID, GORGEOUS GEORGE WAS REALLY GLAD!
THE END.
BY GOLLY, IF ANYONE KISSES ME, NOBODY'S GONNA BE GLAD!
4/7
HIPPY DIPPY SHOPPED IN A MALL. HINKY DINKY HAD A GRAY BALL.
ALL THE KING'S FLORISTS AND ALL THE KING'S FRIENDS COULDN'T HELP HIPPO TO GATHER A HEN.
THE END.
KING THIS, KING THAT! WHAT ABOUT THE QUEEN?
CAN YOU BUY A HIPPO IN A MALL?
IS A HIPPO FAST ENOUGH TO CATCH A CHICKEN?
4/8
GNOMES ROAM IN THE RAIN. WEAR THE BEARDS AND THE ANTS GO TO PLAY.
WHERE SELMA IS HERD, SAYIN' FERD IS A NERD,
AN' THE SIGHS ARE BORED LOUDLY TUESDAY!
DON'T GNOMES KNOW ENOUGH TO COME IN OUTTA THE RAIN?
4/9
KENT·HARKINS·BLYBERG
OH, SOO-ZAN-UHHH, DON'T CHEW CRY FUR MEAT.
I'VE GONE TO LOO-ZEE-ANNA WITH A BANDAGE ON MY KNEE!
AND ANOTHER ONE ON MY HEAD!
4/10
KENT·HARKINS·BLYBERG

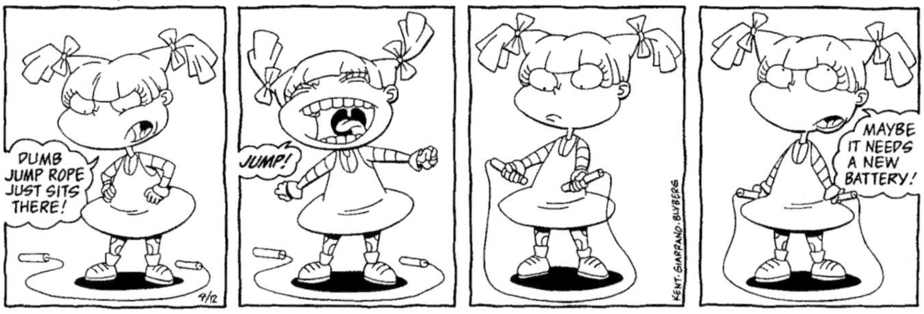
DUMB JUMP ROPE JUST SITS THERE!
4/12
JUMP!
KENT·GIARRANO·BLYBERG
MAYBE IT NEEDS A NEW BATTERY!

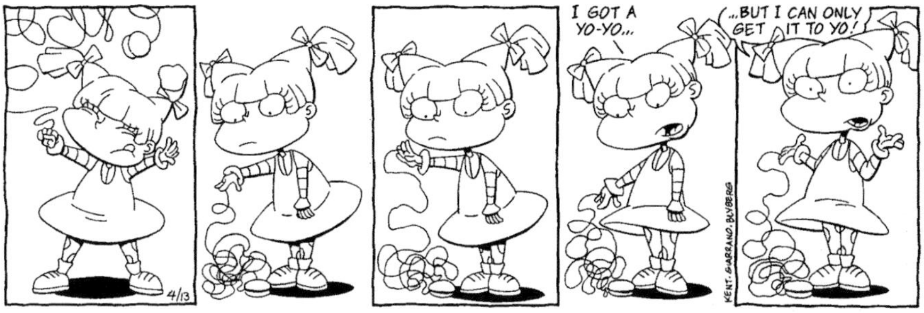
4/13
I GOT A YO-YO...
KENT·GIARRANO·BLYBERG
...BUT I CAN ONLY GET IT TO YO!

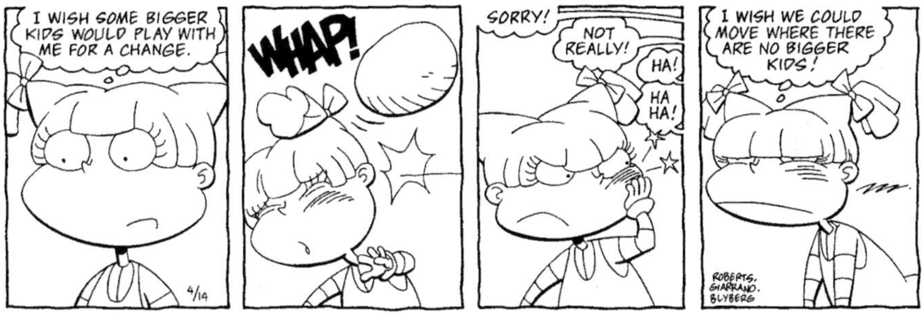
I WISH SOME BIGGER KIDS WOULD PLAY WITH ME FOR A CHANGE.
4/14
WHAP!
SORRY!
NOT REALLY!
HA!
HA HA!
I WISH WE COULD MOVE WHERE THERE ARE NO BIGGER KIDS!
ROBERTS·GIARRANO·BLYBERG

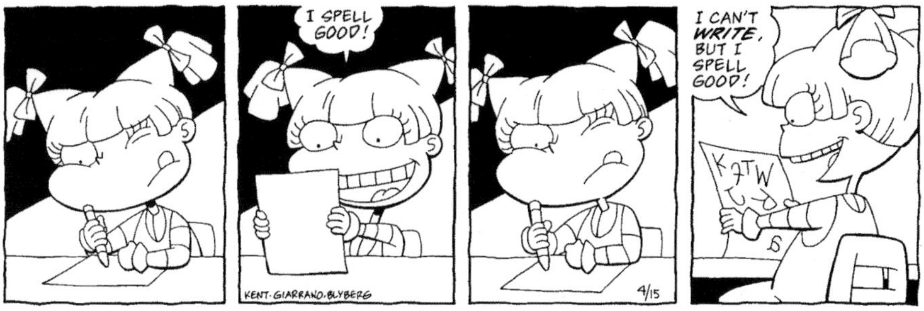
I SPELL GOOD!
KENT·GIARRANO·BLYBERG
4/15
I CAN'T WRITE, BUT I SPELL GOOD!

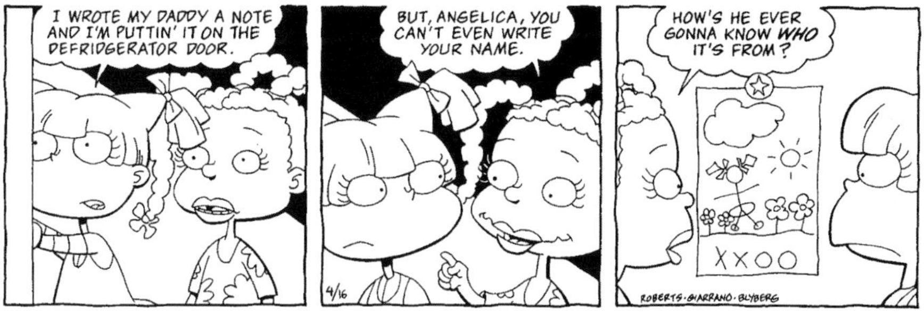
I WROTE MY DADDY A NOTE AND I'M PUTTIN' IT ON THE DEFRIDGERATOR DOOR.
BUT, ANGELICA, YOU CAN'T EVEN WRITE YOUR NAME.
4/16
HOW'S HE EVER GONNA KNOW WHO IT'S FROM?
XXOO
ROBERTS·GIARRANO·BLYBERG

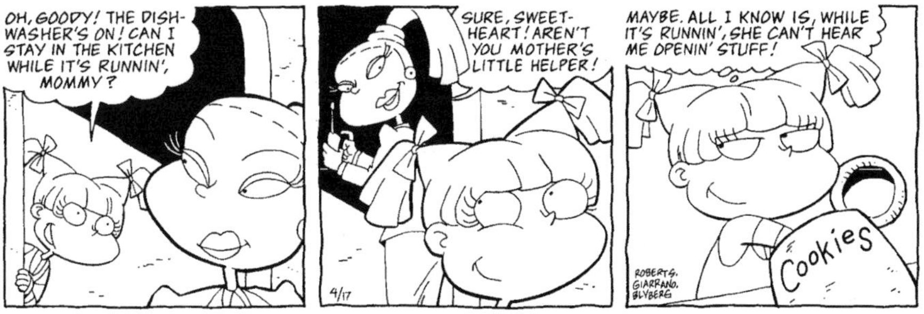
OH, GOODY! THE DISH-WASHER'S ON! CAN I STAY IN THE KITCHEN WHILE IT'S RUNNIN', MOMMY?
SURE, SWEET-HEART! AREN'T YOU MOTHER'S LITTLE HELPER!
4/17
MAYBE. ALL I KNOW IS, WHILE IT'S RUNNIN', SHE CAN'T HEAR ME OPENIN' STUFF!
ROBERTS·GIARRANO·BLYBERG
Cookies

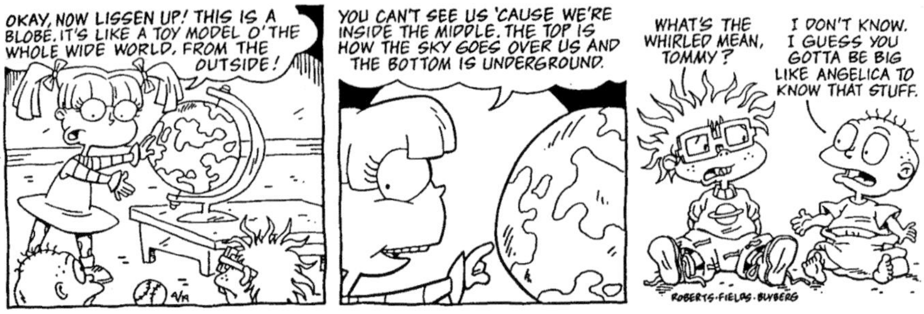
OKAY, NOW LISSEN UP! THIS IS A BLOBE. IT'S LIKE A TOY MODEL O' THE WHOLE WIDE WORLD, FROM THE OUTSIDE!
4/19
YOU CAN'T SEE US 'CAUSE WE'RE INSIDE THE MIDDLE. THE TOP IS HOW THE SKY GOES OVER US AND THE BOTTOM IS UNDERGROUND.
WHAT'S THE WHIRLED MEAN, TOMMY?
I DON'T KNOW. I GUESS YOU GOTTA BE BIG LIKE ANGELICA TO KNOW THAT STUFF.
ROBERTS·FIELDS·BLYBERG

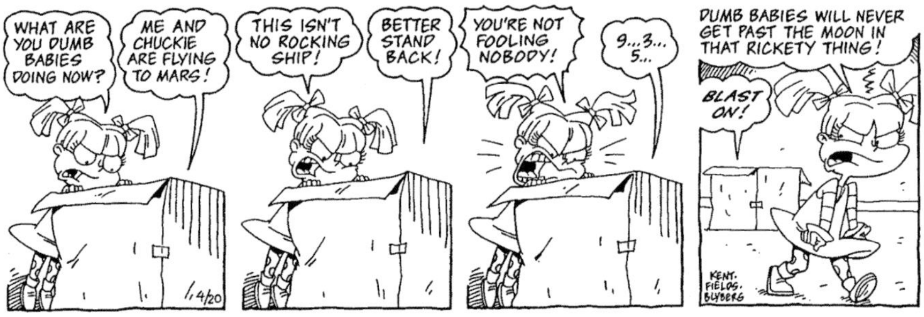
WHAT ARE YOU DUMB BABIES DOING NOW?
ME AND CHUCKIE ARE FLYING TO MARS!
4/20
THIS ISN'T NO ROCKING SHIP!
BETTER STAND BACK!
YOU'RE NOT FOOLING NOBODY!
9...3... 5...
DUMB BABIES WILL NEVER GET PAST THE MOON IN THAT RICKETY THING!
BLAST ON!
KENT. FIELDS. BLYBERG

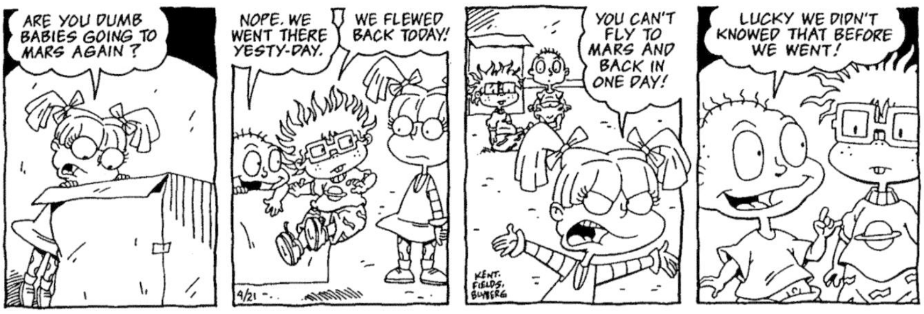
ARE YOU DUMB BABIES GOING TO MARS AGAIN?
NOPE. WE WENT THERE YESTY-DAY.
WE FLEWED BACK TODAY!
4/21
YOU CAN'T FLY TO MARS AND BACK IN ONE DAY!
KENT. FIELDS. BLYBERG
LUCKY WE DIDN'T KNOWED THAT BEFORE WE WENT!

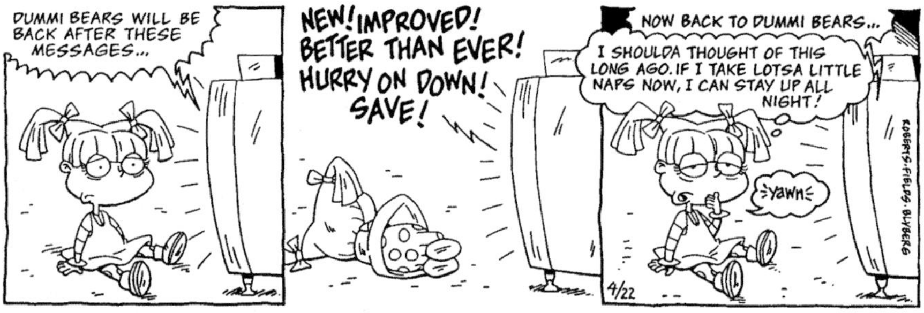
DUMMI BEARS WILL BE BACK AFTER THESE MESSAGES...
NEW! IMPROVED! BETTER THAN EVER! HURRY ON DOWN! SAVE!
NOW BACK TO DUMMI BEARS...
I SHOULDA THOUGHT OF THIS LONG AGO. IF I TAKE LOTSA LITTLE NAPS NOW, I CAN STAY UP ALL NIGHT!
YAWN
4/22
ROBERTS·FIELDS·BLYBERG

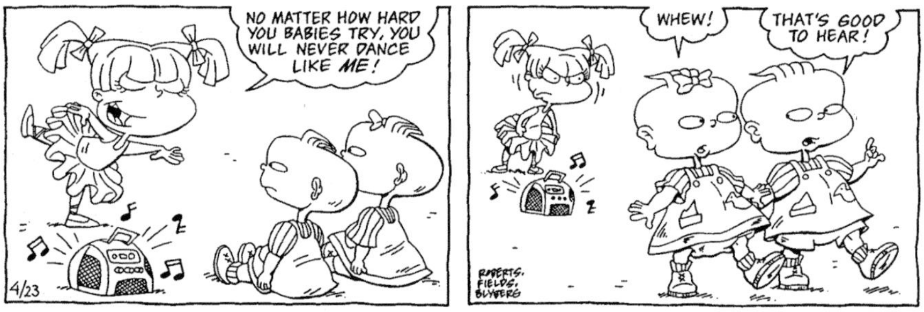
NO MATTER HOW HARD YOU BABIES TRY, YOU WILL NEVER DANCE LIKE ME!
4/23
WHEW!
THAT'S GOOD TO HEAR!
ROBERTS. FIELDS. BLYBERG

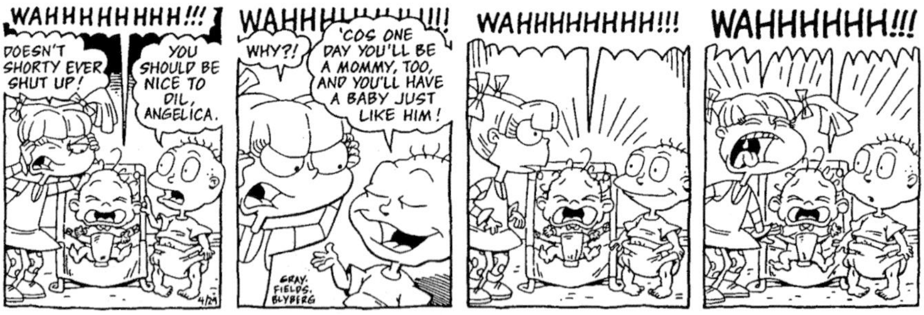
WAHHHHHHHH!!!
DOESN'T SHORTY EVER SHUT UP!
YOU SHOULD BE NICE TO DIL, ANGELICA.
4/24
WHY?!
'COS ONE DAY YOU'LL BE A MOMMY, TOO, AND YOU'LL HAVE A BABY JUST LIKE HIM!
GRAY. FIELDS. BLYBERG
WAHHHHHHHH!!!
WAHHHHHH!!!

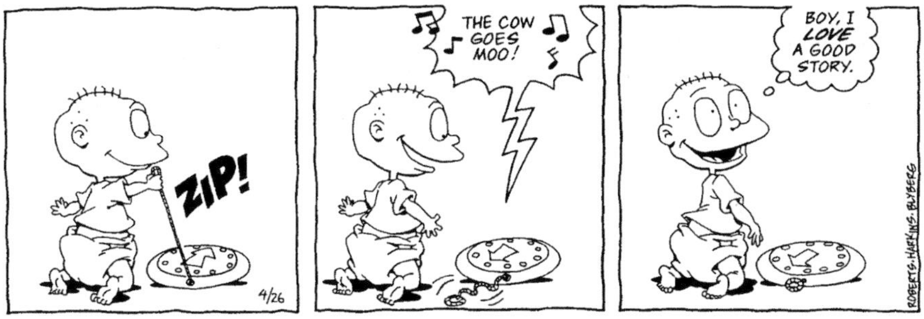
ZIP!
4/26
THE COW GOES MOO!
BOY, I LOVE A GOOD STORY.
ROBERTS·HARKINS·BLYBERG

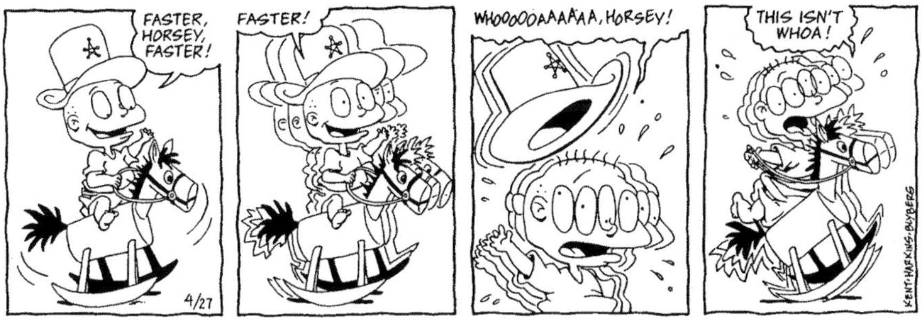
FASTER, HORSEY, FASTER!
4/27
FASTER!
WHOOOOOAAAAA, HORSEY!
THIS ISN'T WHOA!
KENT·HARKINS·BLYBERG

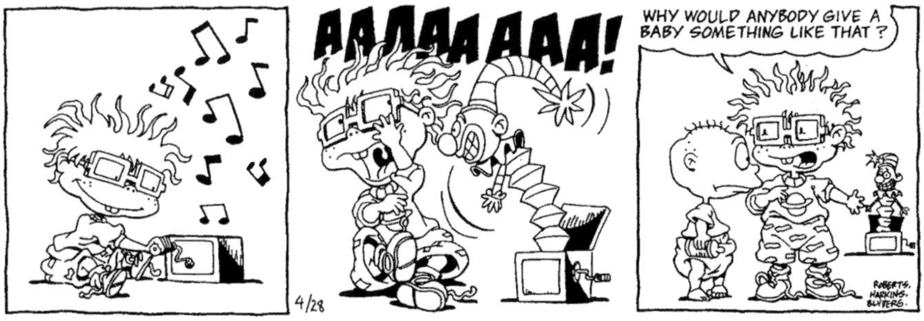
AAAAAAAA!
4/28
WHY WOULD ANYBODY GIVE A BABY SOMETHING LIKE THAT?
ROBERTS. HARKINS. BLYBERG.

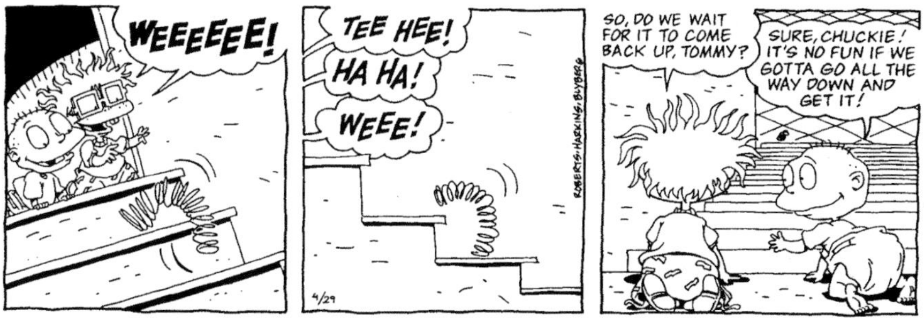
WEEEEEE!
TEE HEE!
HA HA!
WEEE!
4/29
ROBERTS·HARKINS·BLYBERG
SO, DO WE WAIT FOR IT TO COME BACK UP, TOMMY?
SURE, CHUCKIE! IT'S NO FUN IF WE GOTTA GO ALL THE WAY DOWN AND GET IT!

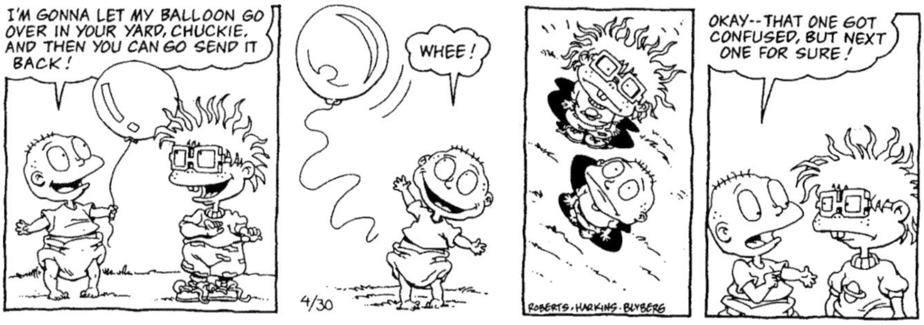
I'M GONNA LET MY BALLOON GO OVER IN YOUR YARD, CHUCKIE, AND THEN YOU CAN GO SEND IT BACK!
WHEE!
4/30
ROBERTS·HARKINS·BLYBERG
OKAY--THAT ONE GOT CONFUSED, BUT NEXT ONE FOR SURE!

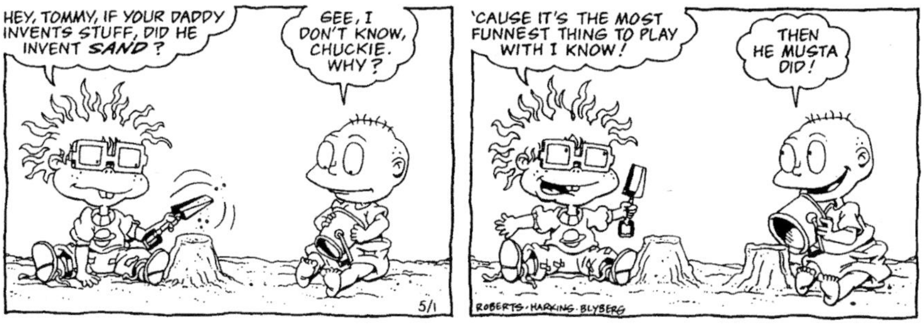
HEY, TOMMY, IF YOUR DADDY INVENTS STUFF, DID HE INVENT SAND?
GEE, I DON'T KNOW, CHUCKIE. WHY?
5/1
'CAUSE IT'S THE MOST FUNNEST THING TO PLAY WITH I KNOW!
THEN HE MUSTA DID!
ROBERTS·HARKINS·BLYBERG

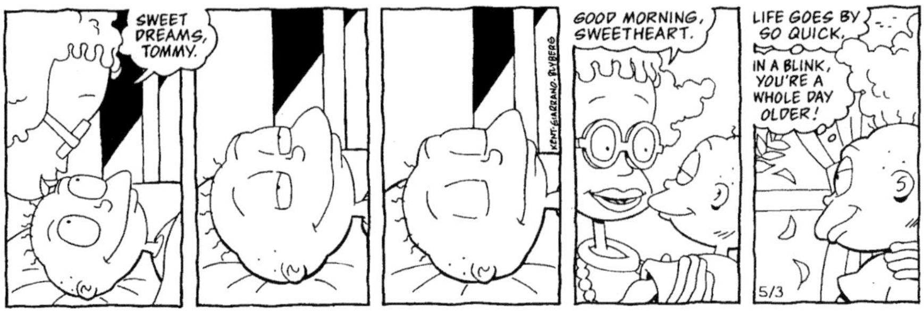
SWEET DREAMS, TOMMY.
KENT·GIARRANO·BLYBERG
GOOD MORNING, SWEETHEART.
LIFE GOES BY SO QUICK.
IN A BLINK, YOU'RE A WHOLE DAY OLDER!
5/3

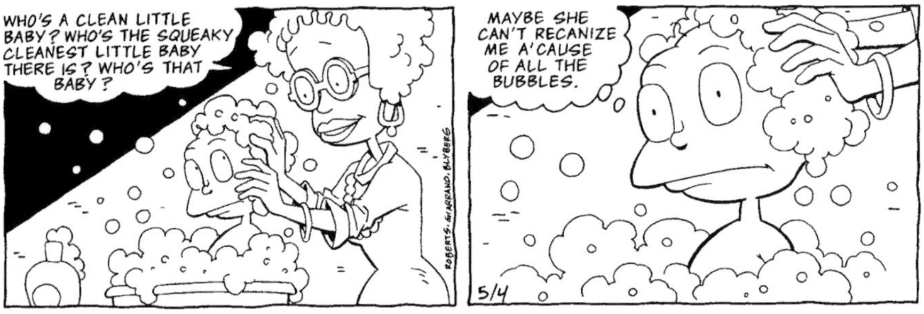
WHO'S A CLEAN LITTLE BABY? WHO'S THE SQUEAKY CLEANEST LITTLE BABY THERE IS? WHO'S THAT BABY?
ROBERTS·GIARRANO·BLYBERG
MAYBE SHE CAN'T RECANIZE ME A'CAUSE OF ALL THE BUBBLES.
5/4

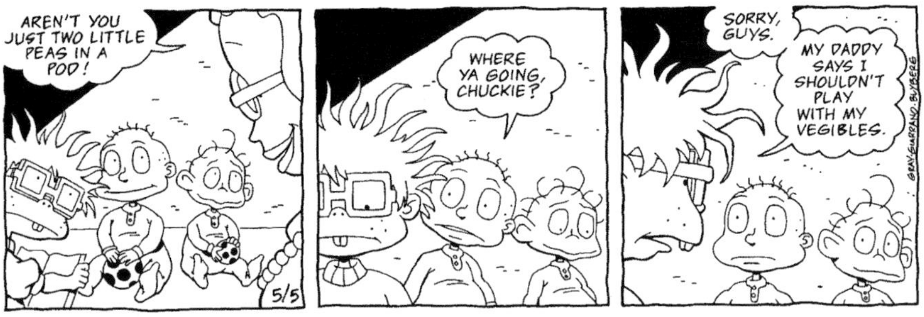
AREN'T YOU JUST TWO LITTLE PEAS IN A POD!
5/5
WHERE YA GOING, CHUCKIE?
SORRY, GUYS.
MY DADDY SAYS I SHOULDN'T PLAY WITH MY VEGIBLES.
GRAY·GIARRANO·BLYBERG

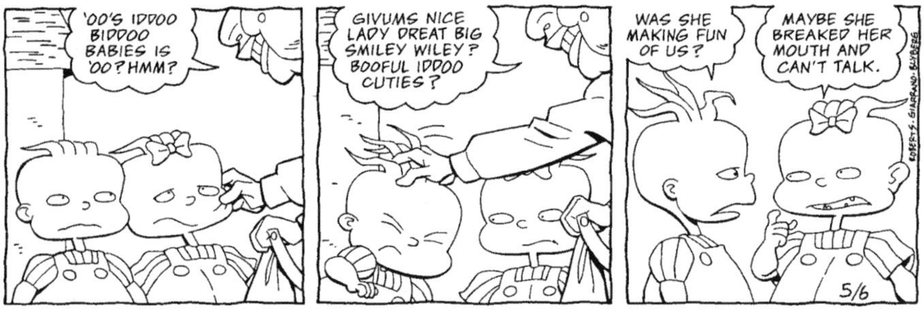
'OO'S IDDOO BIDDOO BABIES IS 'OO? HMM?
GIVUMS NICE LADY DREAT BIG SMILEY WILEY? BOOFUL IDDOO CUTIES?
WAS SHE MAKING FUN OF US?
MAYBE SHE BREAKED HER MOUTH AND CAN'T TALK.
ROBERTS·GIARRANO·BLYBERG
5/6

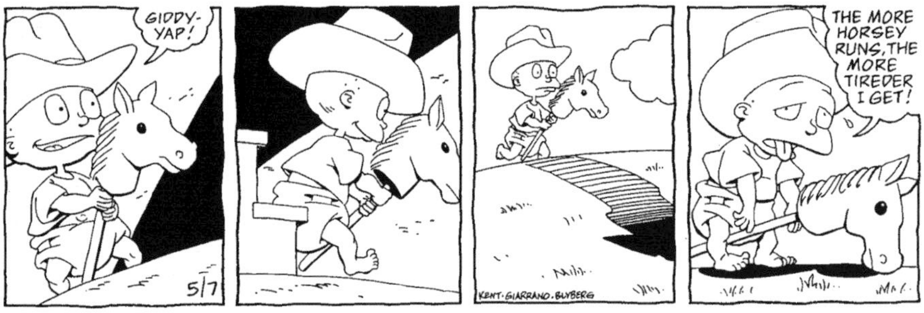
GIDDY-YAP!
5/7
KENT·GIARRANO·BLYBERG
THE MORE HORSEY RUNS, THE MORE TIREDER I GET!

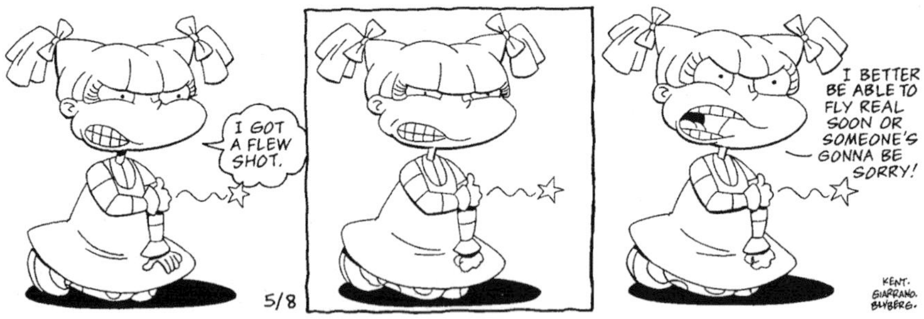
I GOT A FLEW SHOT.
5/8
I BETTER BE ABLE TO FLY REAL SOON OR SOMEONE'S GONNA BE SORRY!
KENT· GIARRANO· BLYBERG·

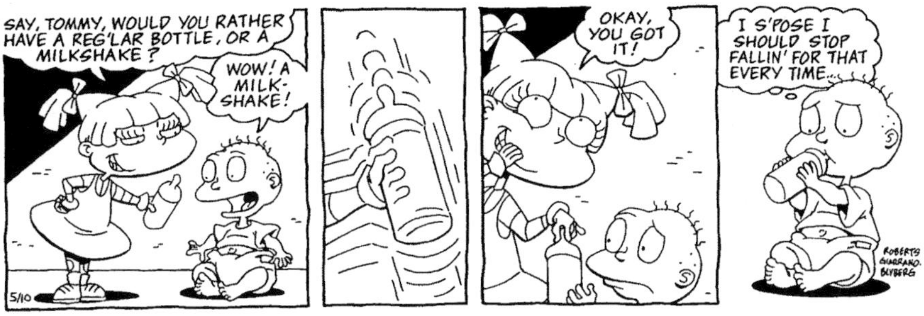
5/10
SAY, TOMMY, WOULD YOU RATHER HAVE A REG'LAR BOTTLE, OR A MILKSHAKE?
WOW! A MILK-SHAKE!
OKAY, YOU GOT IT!
I S'POSE I SHOULD STOP FALLIN' FOR THAT EVERY TIME...
ROBERTS GIARRANO BLYBERG

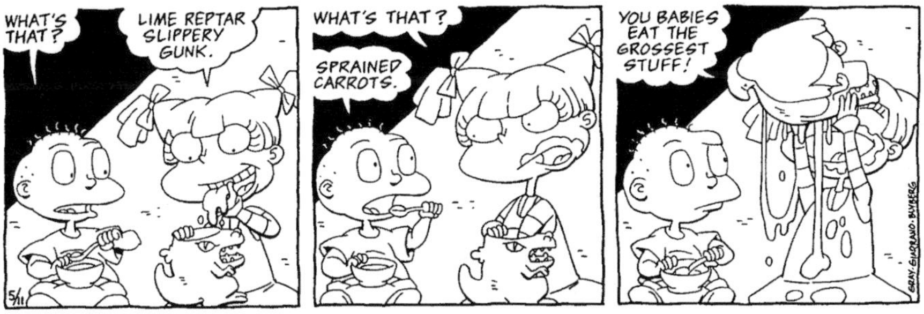
5/11
WHAT'S THAT?
LIME REPTAR SLIPPERY GUNK.
WHAT'S THAT?
SPRAINED CARROTS.
YOU BABIES EAT THE GROSSEST STUFF!
GRAY·GIARRANO·BLYBERG

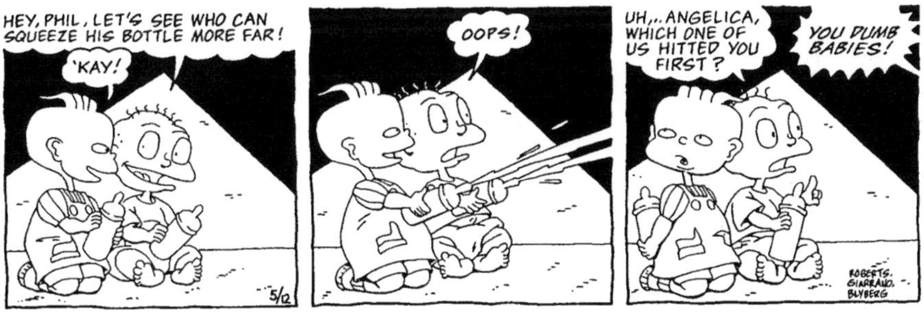
HEY, PHIL, LET'S SEE WHO CAN SQUEEZE HIS BOTTLE MORE FAR!
'KAY!
5/12
OOPS!
UH,.. ANGELICA, WHICH ONE OF US HITTED YOU FIRST?
YOU DUMB BABIES!
ROBERTS GIARRANO BLYBERG

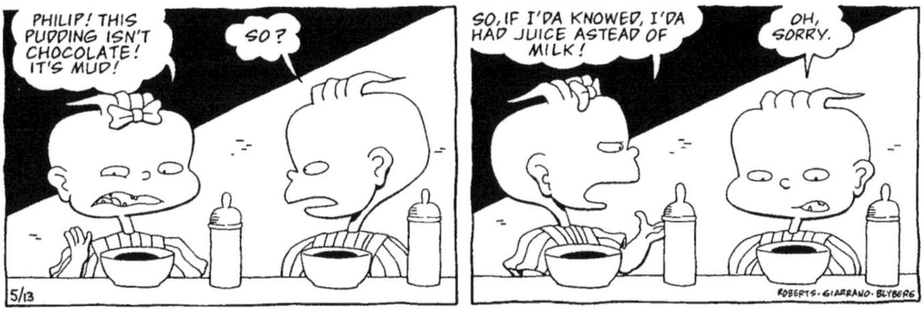
PHILIP! THIS PUDDING ISN'T CHOCOLATE! IT'S MUD!
SO?
5/13
SO, IF I'DA KNOWED, I'DA HAD JUICE ASTEAD OF MILK!
OH, SORRY.
ROBERTS·GIARRANO·BLYBERG

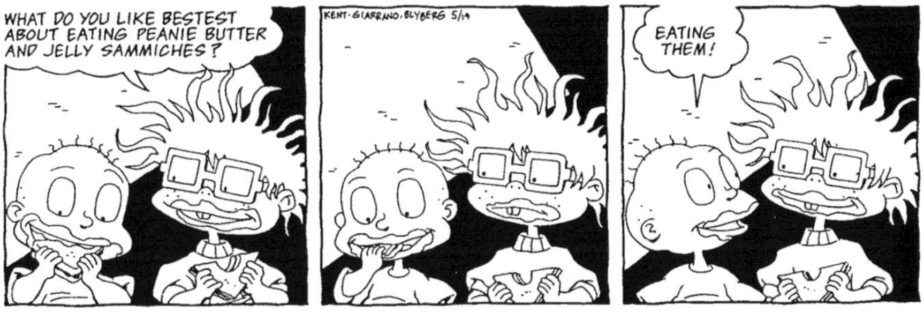
WHAT DO YOU LIKE BESTEST ABOUT EATING PEANIE BUTTER AND JELLY SAMMICHES?
KENT·GIARRANO·BLYBERG 5/14
EATING THEM!

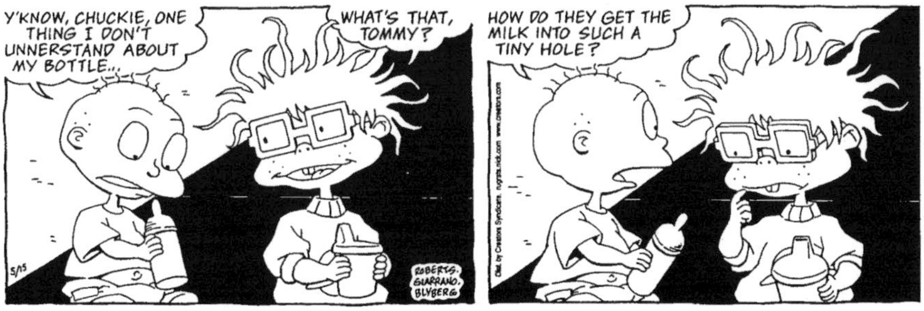
Y'KNOW, CHUCKIE, ONE THING I DON'T UNNERSTAND ABOUT MY BOTTLE...
WHAT'S THAT, TOMMY?
5/15
ROBERTS GIARRANO BLYBERG
HOW DO THEY GET THE MILK INTO SUCH A TINY HOLE?

1999

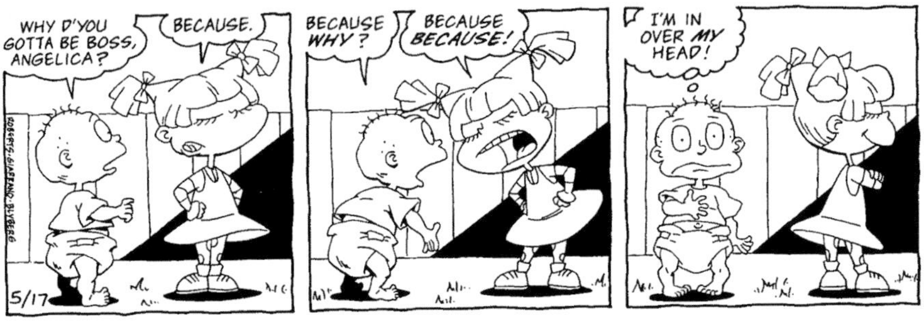

WHY D'YOU GOTTA BE BOSS, ANGELICA?
BECAUSE.
BECAUSE WHY?
BECAUSE BECAUSE!
I'M IN OVER MY HEAD!
5/17

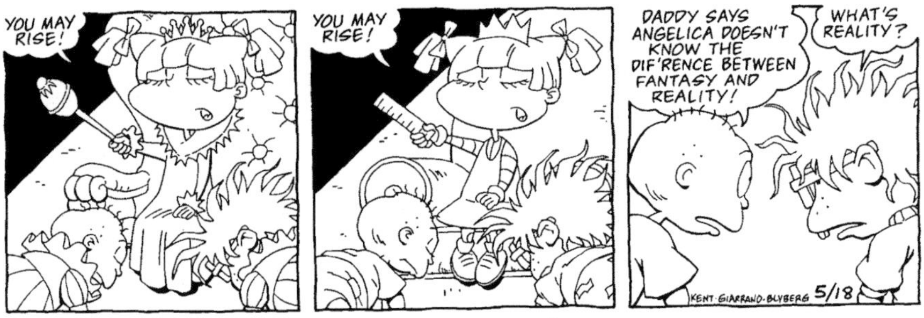

YOU MAY RISE!
YOU MAY RISE!
DADDY SAYS ANGELICA DOESN'T KNOW THE DIF'RENCE BETWEEN FANTASY AND REALITY!
WHAT'S REALITY?
KENT·GIARRANO·BLYBERG 5/18

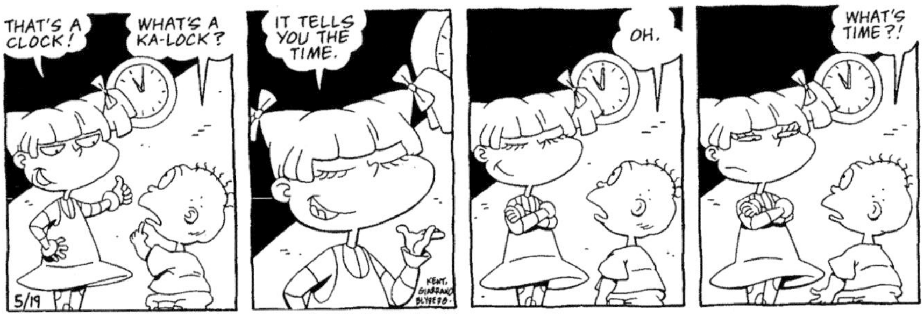

THAT'S A CLOCK!
WHAT'S A KA-LOCK?
IT TELLS YOU THE TIME.
OH.
WHAT'S TIME?!
5/19

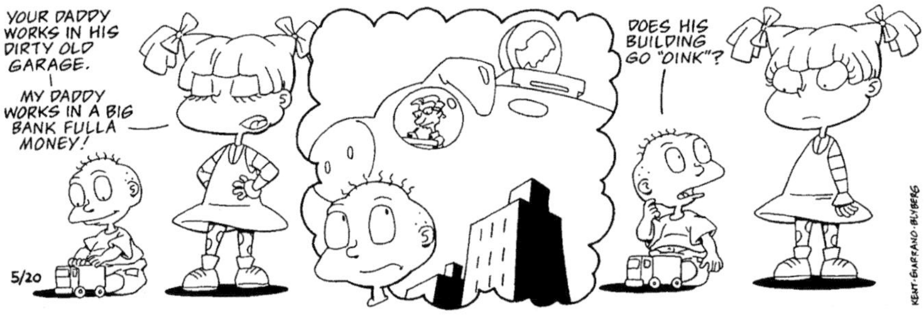

YOUR DADDY WORKS IN HIS DIRTY OLD GARAGE.
MY DADDY WORKS IN A BIG BANK FULLA MONEY!
DOES HIS BUILDING GO "OINK"?
5/20
KENT·GIARRANO·BLYBERG

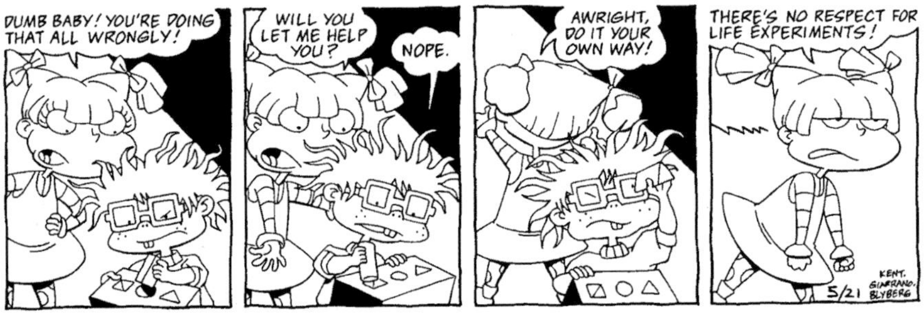

DUMB BABY! YOU'RE DOING THAT ALL WRONGLY!
WILL YOU LET ME HELP YOU?
NOPE.
AWRIGHT, DO IT YOUR OWN WAY!
THERE'S NO RESPECT FOR LIFE EXPERIMENTS!
5/21

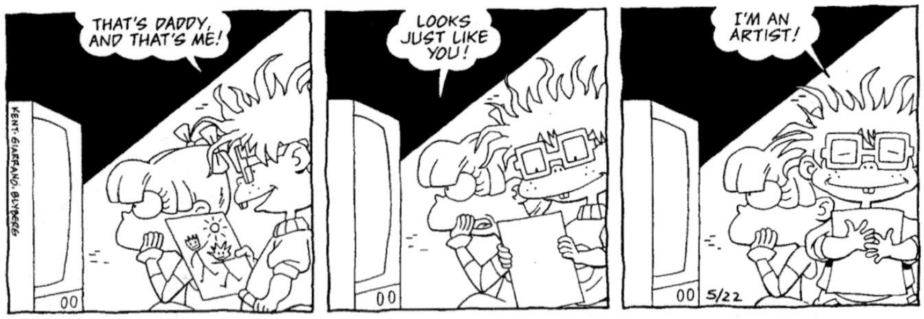

THAT'S DADDY, AND THAT'S ME!
LOOKS JUST LIKE YOU!
I'M AN ARTIST!
5/22

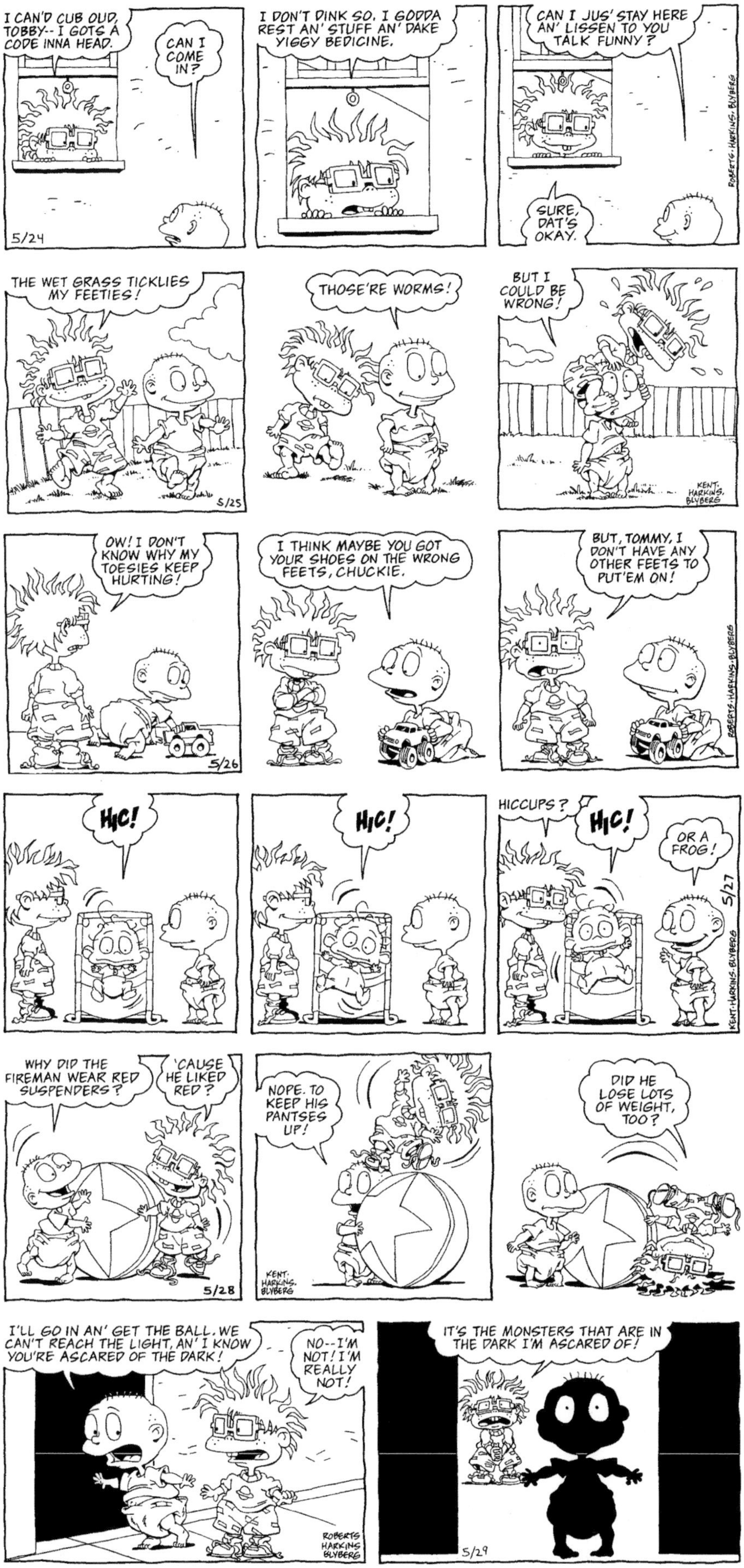
I CAN'D CUB OUD, TOBBY-- I GOTS A CODE INNA HEAD.
CAN I COME IN?
5/24
I DON'T DINK SO. I GODDA REST AN' STUFF AN' DAKE YIGGY BEDICINE.
CAN I JUS' STAY HERE AN' LISSEN TO YOU TALK FUNNY?
SURE, DAT'S OKAY.
ROBERTS·HARKINS·BLYBERG
THE WET GRASS TICKLIES MY FEETIES!
5/25
THOSE'RE WORMS!
BUT I COULD BE WRONG!
KENT·HARKINS·BLYBERG
OW! I DON'T KNOW WHY MY TOESIES KEEP HURTING!
5/26
I THINK MAYBE YOU GOT YOUR SHOES ON THE WRONG FEETS, CHUCKIE.
BUT, TOMMY, I DON'T HAVE ANY OTHER FEETS TO PUT'EM ON!
ROBERTS·HARKINS·BLYBERG
HIC!
HIC!
HICCUPS?
HIC!
OR A FROG!
5/27
KENT·HARKINS·BLYBERG
WHY DID THE FIREMAN WEAR RED SUSPENDERS?
'CAUSE HE LIKED RED?
5/28
NOPE. TO KEEP HIS PANTSES UP!
KENT·HARKINS·BLYBERG
DID HE LOSE LOTS OF WEIGHT, TOO?
I'LL GO IN AN' GET THE BALL. WE CAN'T REACH THE LIGHT, AN' I KNOW YOU'RE ASCARED OF THE DARK!
NO--I'M NOT! I'M REALLY NOT!
ROBERTS HARKINS BLYBERG
IT'S THE MONSTERS THAT ARE IN THE DARK I'M ASCARED OF!
5/29

1999

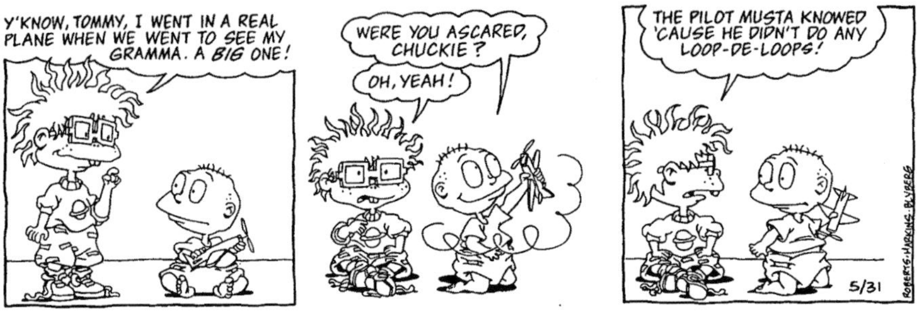
Y'KNOW, TOMMY, I WENT IN A REAL PLANE WHEN WE WENT TO SEE MY GRAMMA. A *BIG* ONE!
WERE YOU ASCARED, CHUCKIE?
OH, YEAH!
THE PILOT MUSTA KNOWED 'CAUSE HE DIDN'T DO ANY LOOP-DE-LOOPS!
5/31
ROBERTS·HARKINS·BLYBERG

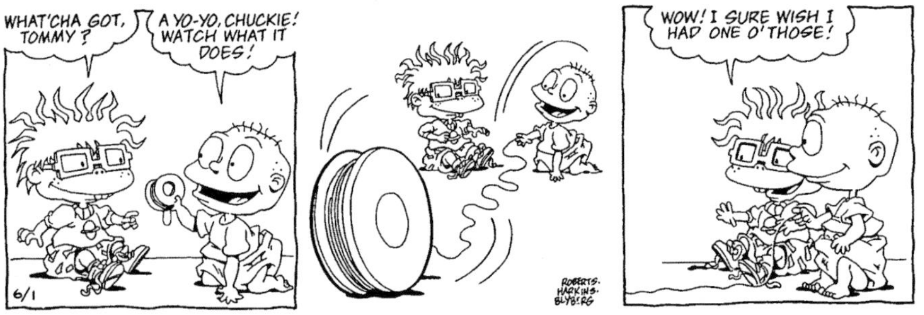
WHAT'CHA GOT, TOMMY?
A YO-YO, CHUCKIE! WATCH WHAT IT DOES!
6/1
ROBERTS·HARKINS·BLYBERG
WOW! I SURE WISH I HAD ONE O'THOSE!

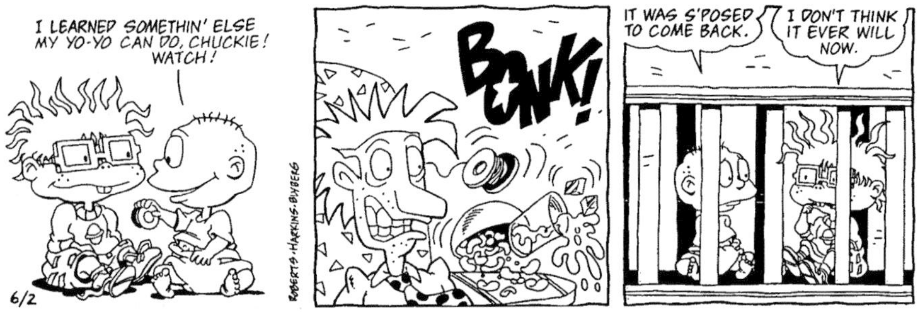
I LEARNED SOMETHIN' ELSE MY YO-YO CAN DO, CHUCKIE! WATCH!
6/2
ROBERTS·HARKINS·BLYBERG
BONK!
IT WAS S'POSED TO COME BACK.
I DON'T THINK IT EVER WILL NOW.

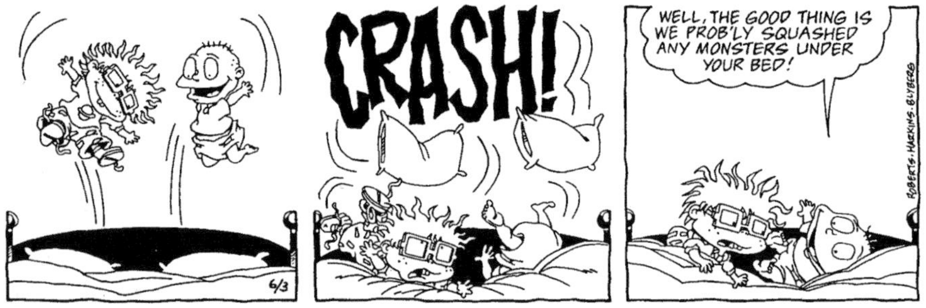
6/3
CRASH!
WELL, THE GOOD THING IS WE PROB'LY SQUASHED ANY MONSTERS UNDER YOUR BED!
ROBERTS·HARKINS·BLYBERG

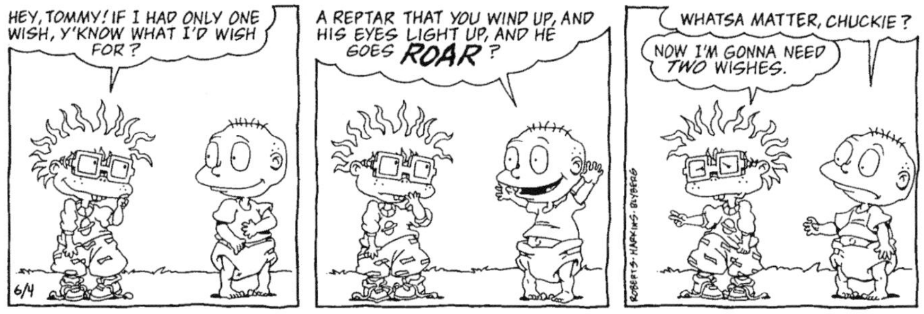
HEY, TOMMY! IF I HAD ONLY ONE WISH, Y'KNOW WHAT I'D WISH FOR?
6/4
A REPTAR THAT YOU WIND UP, AND HIS EYES LIGHT UP, AND HE GOES *ROAR*?
ROBERTS·HARKINS·BLYBERG
WHATSA MATTER, CHUCKIE?
NOW I'M GONNA NEED *TWO* WISHES.

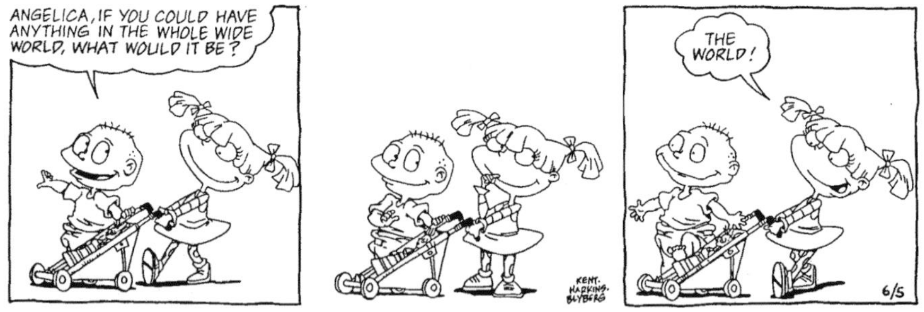
ANGELICA, IF YOU COULD HAVE ANYTHING IN THE WHOLE WIDE WORLD, WHAT WOULD IT BE?
KENT·HARKINS·BLYBERG
THE WORLD!
6/5

1999

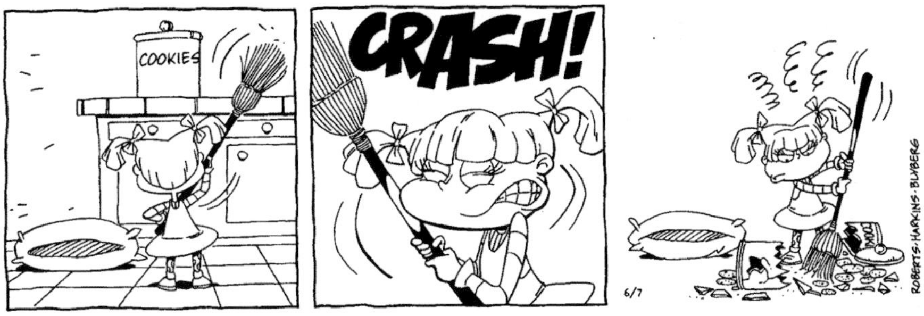
COOKIES
CRASH!
6/7
ROBERTS·HARKINS·BLYBERG

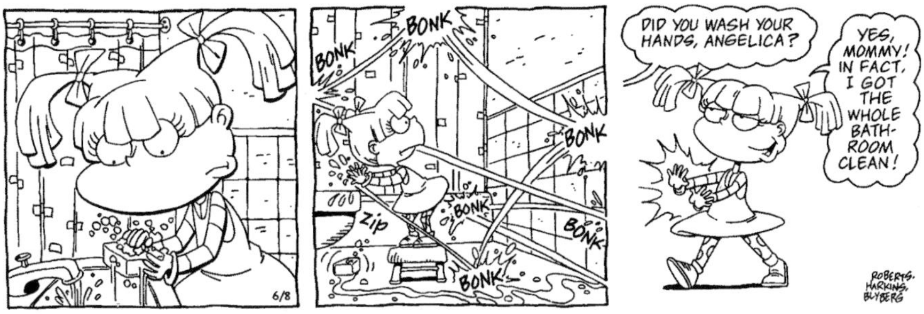
6/8
BONK
BONK
BONK
ZIP
BONK
BONK
BONK
DID YOU WASH YOUR HANDS, ANGELICA?
YES, MOMMY! IN FACT, I GOT THE WHOLE BATH-ROOM CLEAN!
ROBERTS·HARKINS·BLYBERG

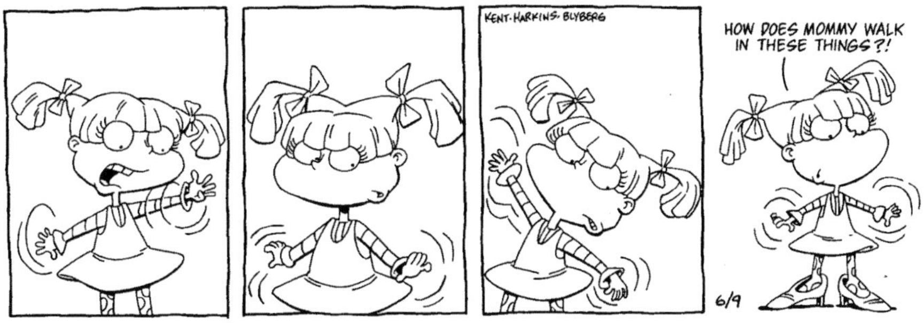
KENT·HARKINS·BLYBERG
HOW DOES MOMMY WALK IN THESE THINGS?!
6/9

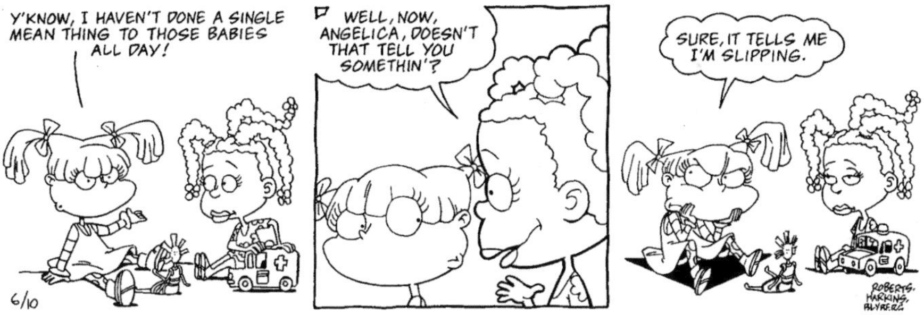
Y'KNOW, I HAVEN'T DONE A SINGLE MEAN THING TO THOSE BABIES ALL DAY!
6/10
WELL, NOW, ANGELICA, DOESN'T THAT TELL YOU SOMETHIN'?
SURE, IT TELLS ME I'M SLIPPING.
ROBERTS·HARKINS·BLYBERG

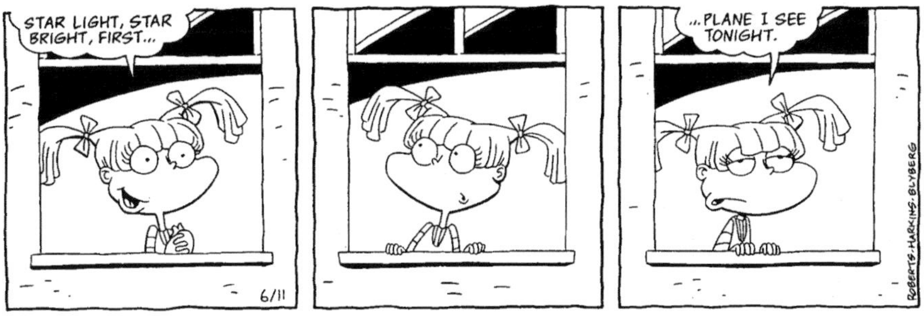
STAR LIGHT, STAR BRIGHT, FIRST...
6/11
...PLANE I SEE TONIGHT.
ROBERTS·HARKINS·BLYBERG

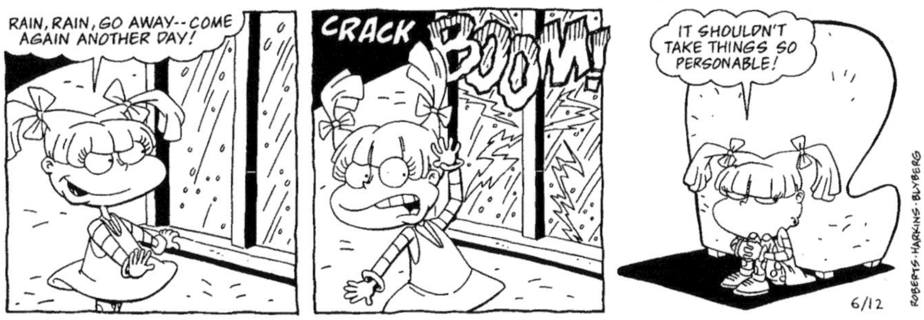
RAIN, RAIN, GO AWAY--COME AGAIN ANOTHER DAY!
CRACK
BOOM!
IT SHOULDN'T TAKE THINGS SO PERSONABLE!
6/12
ROBERTS·HARKINS·BLYBERG

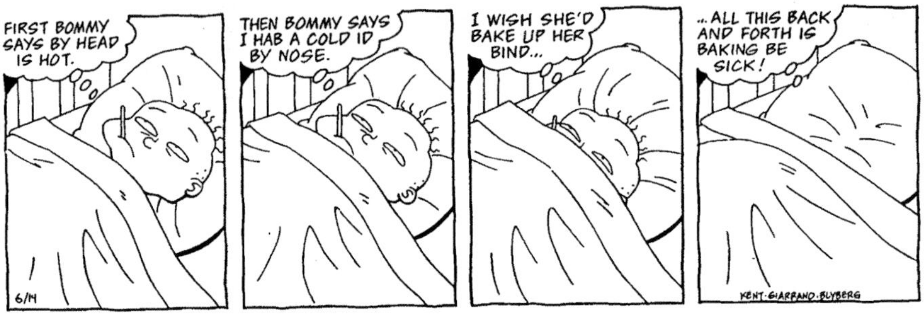
FIRST BOMMY SAYS BY HEAD IS HOT.
THEN BOMMY SAYS I HAB A COLD ID BY NOSE.
I WISH SHE'D BAKE UP HER BIND...
...ALL THIS BACK AND FORTH IS BAKING BE SICK!
6/14
KENT·GIARRANO·BLYBERG

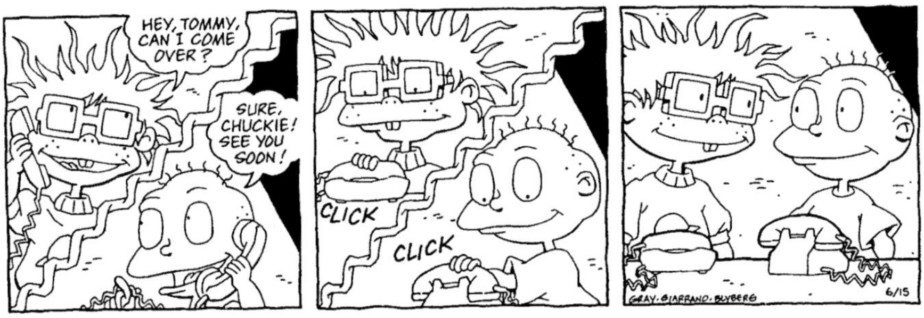
HEY, TOMMY, CAN I COME OVER?
SURE, CHUCKIE! SEE YOU SOON!
CLICK
CLICK
GRAY·GIARRANO·BLYBERG
6/15

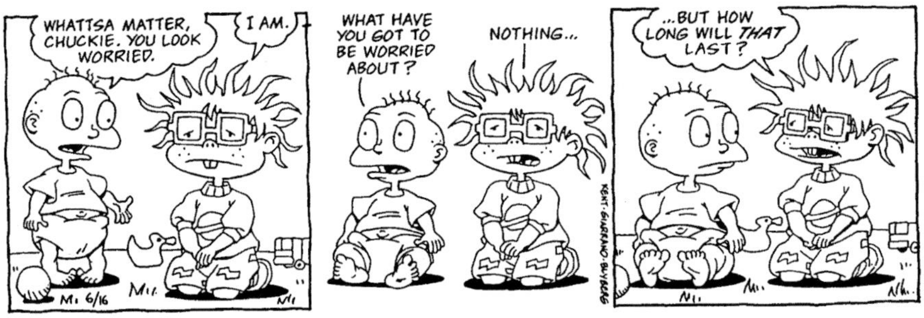
WHATTSA MATTER, CHUCKIE. YOU LOOK WORRIED.
I AM.
6/16
WHAT HAVE YOU GOT TO BE WORRIED ABOUT?
NOTHING...
KENT·GIARRANO·BLYBERG
...BUT HOW LONG WILL THAT LAST?

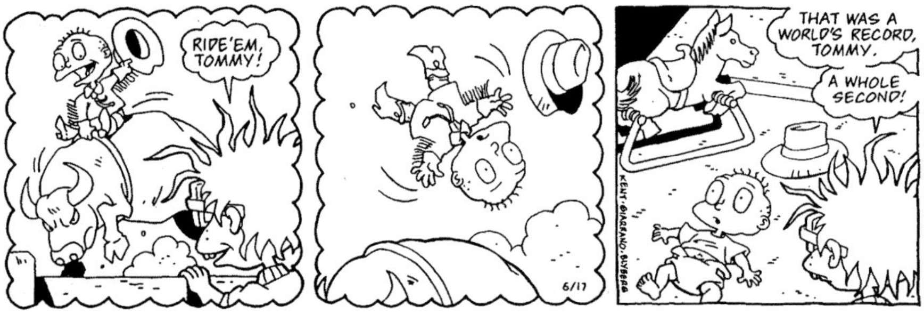
RIDE 'EM, TOMMY!
6/17
THAT WAS A WORLD'S RECORD, TOMMY.
A WHOLE SECOND!
KENT·GIARRANO·BLYBERG

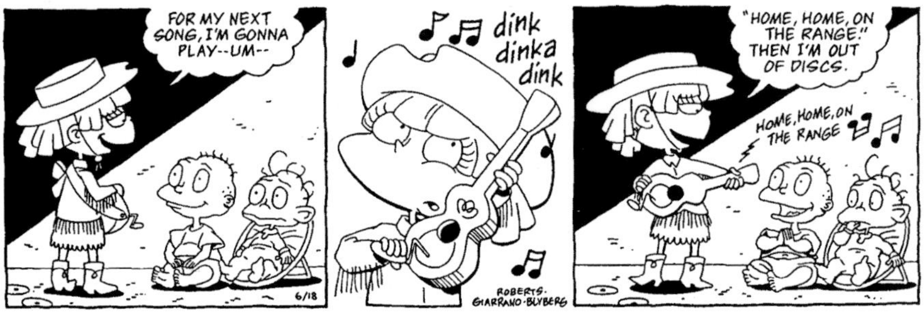
FOR MY NEXT SONG, I'M GONNA PLAY--UM--
6/18
dink dinka dink
ROBERTS·GIARRANO·BLYBERG
"HOME, HOME, ON THE RANGE." THEN I'M OUT OF DISCS.
HOME, HOME, ON THE RANGE

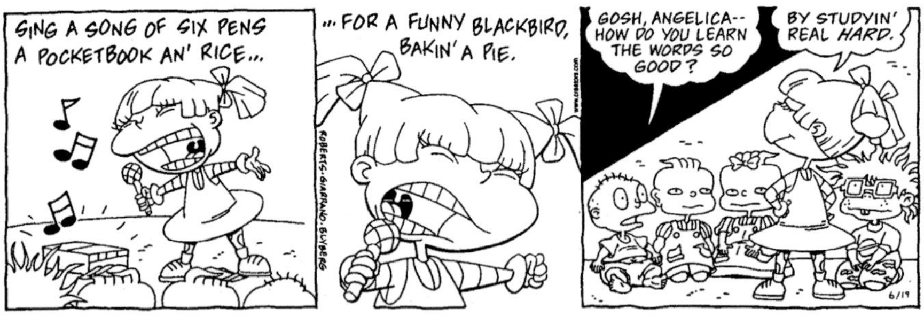
SING A SONG OF SIX PENS A POCKETBOOK AN' RICE...
...FOR A FUNNY BLACKBIRD, BAKIN' A PIE.
ROBERTS·GIARRANO·BLYBERG
GOSH, ANGELICA-- HOW DO YOU LEARN THE WORDS SO GOOD?
BY STUDYIN' REAL HARD.
6/19

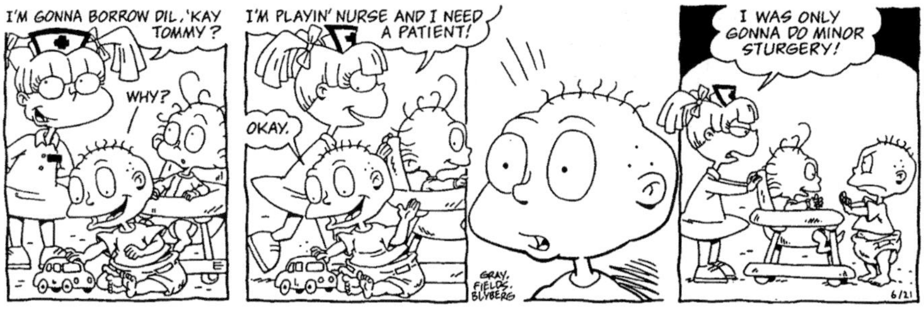
I'M GONNA BORROW DIL, 'KAY TOMMY?
WHY?
I'M PLAYIN' NURSE AND I NEED A PATIENT!
OKAY.
GRAY. FIELDS. BLYBERG
I WAS ONLY GONNA DO MINOR STURGERY!
6/21

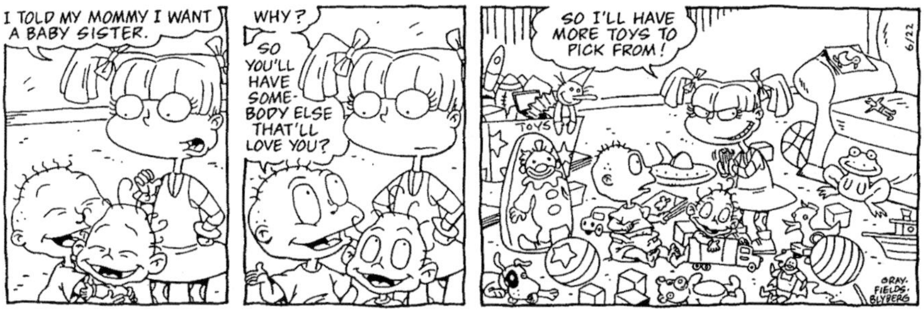
I TOLD MY MOMMY I WANT A BABY SISTER.
WHY?
SO YOU'LL HAVE SOMEBODY ELSE THAT'LL LOVE YOU?
SO I'LL HAVE MORE TOYS TO PICK FROM!
TOYS
6/22
GRAY. FIELDS. BLYBERG

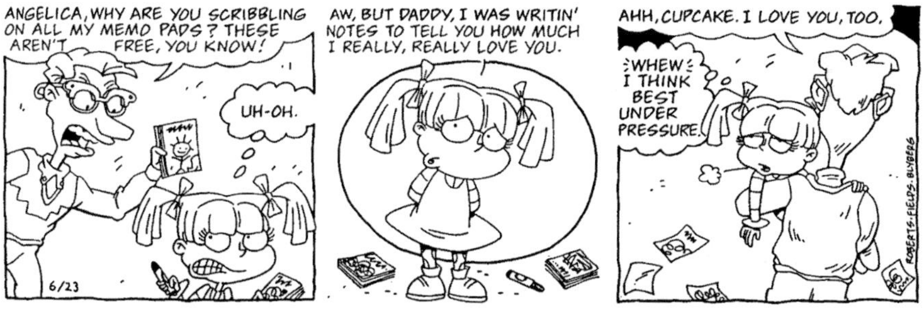
ANGELICA, WHY ARE YOU SCRIBBLING ON ALL MY MEMO PADS? THESE AREN'T FREE, YOU KNOW!
UH-OH.
6/23
AW, BUT DADDY, I WAS WRITIN' NOTES TO TELL YOU HOW MUCH I REALLY, REALLY LOVE YOU.
AHH, CUPCAKE. I LOVE YOU, TOO.
WHEW I THINK BEST UNDER PRESSURE.
ROBERTS·FIELDS·BLYBERG

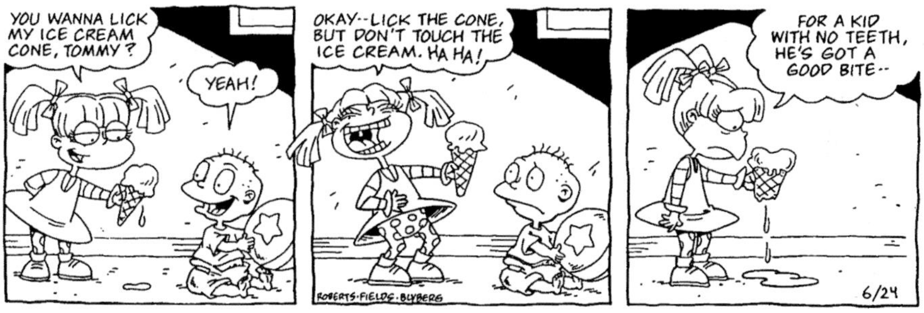
YOU WANNA LICK MY ICE CREAM CONE, TOMMY?
YEAH!
OKAY--LICK THE CONE, BUT DON'T TOUCH THE ICE CREAM. HA HA!
ROBERTS·FIELDS·BLYBERG
FOR A KID WITH NO TEETH, HE'S GOT A GOOD BITE--
6/24

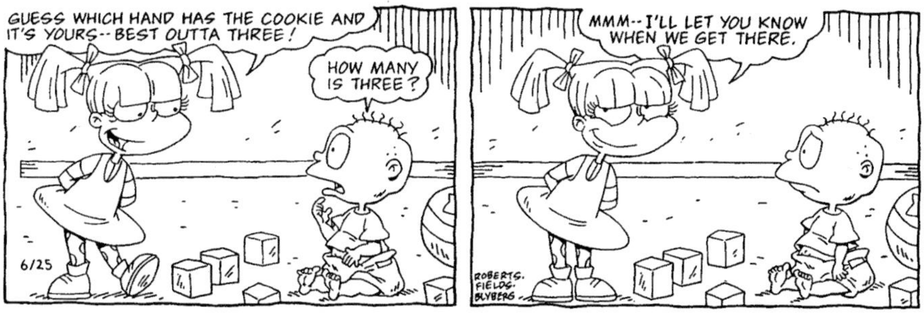
GUESS WHICH HAND HAS THE COOKIE AND IT'S YOURS--BEST OUTTA THREE!
HOW MANY IS THREE?
6/25
MMM--I'LL LET YOU KNOW WHEN WE GET THERE.
ROBERTS. FIELDS. BLYBERG

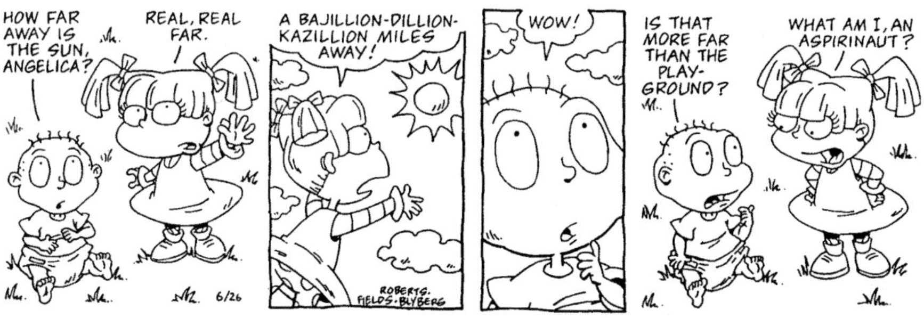
HOW FAR AWAY IS THE SUN, ANGELICA?
REAL, REAL FAR.
6/26
A BAJILLION-DILLION-KAZILLION MILES AWAY!
ROBERTS. FIELDS·BLYBERG
WOW!
IS THAT MORE FAR THAN THE PLAYGROUND?
WHAT AM I, AN ASPIRINAUT?

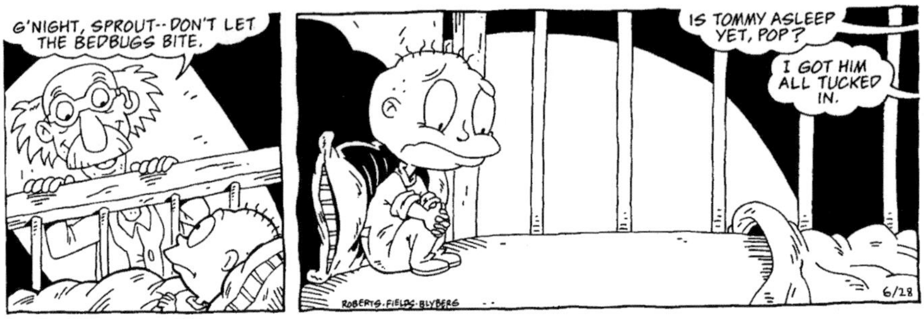
G'NIGHT, SPROUT-- DON'T LET THE BEDBUGS BITE.
IS TOMMY ASLEEP YET, POP?
I GOT HIM ALL TUCKED IN.
ROBERTS·FIELDS·BLYBERG
6/28

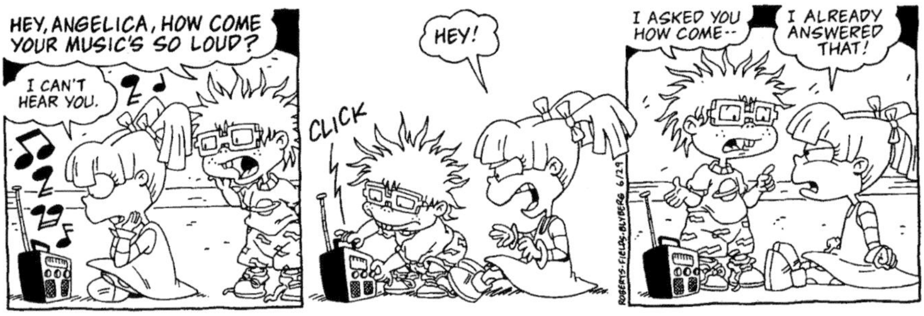
HEY, ANGELICA, HOW COME YOUR MUSIC'S SO LOUD?
I CAN'T HEAR YOU.
CLICK
HEY!
ROBERTS·FIELDS·BLYBERG 6/29
I ASKED YOU HOW COME--
I ALREADY ANSWERED THAT!

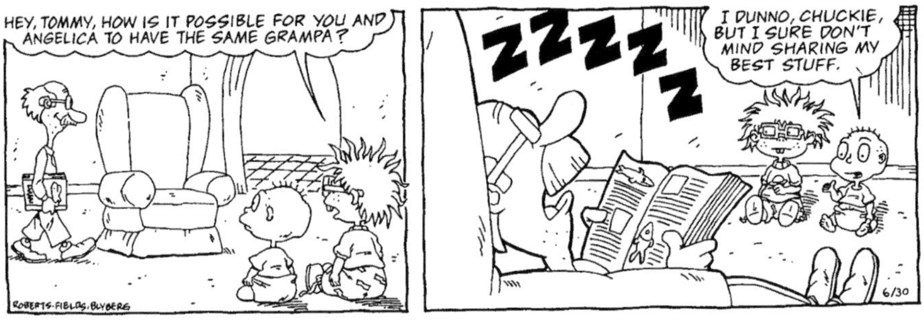
HEY, TOMMY, HOW IS IT POSSIBLE FOR YOU AND ANGELICA TO HAVE THE SAME GRAMPA?
ROBERTS·FIELDS·BLYBERG
ZZZZZ
I DUNNO, CHUCKIE, BUT I SURE DON'T MIND SHARING MY BEST STUFF.
6/30

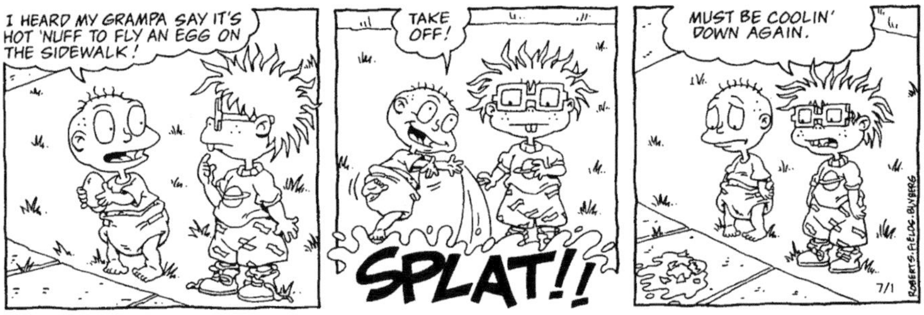
I HEARD MY GRAMPA SAY IT'S HOT 'NUFF TO FLY AN EGG ON THE SIDEWALK!
TAKE OFF!
SPLAT!!
MUST BE COOLIN' DOWN AGAIN.
7/1
ROBERTS·FIELDS·BLYBERG

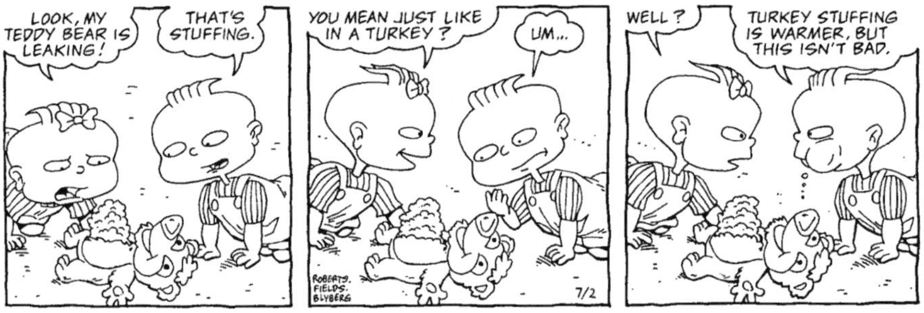
LOOK, MY TEDDY BEAR IS LEAKING!
THAT'S STUFFING.
YOU MEAN JUST LIKE IN A TURKEY?
UM...
ROBERTS· FIELDS· BLYBERG
7/2
WELL?
TURKEY STUFFING IS WARMER, BUT THIS ISN'T BAD.

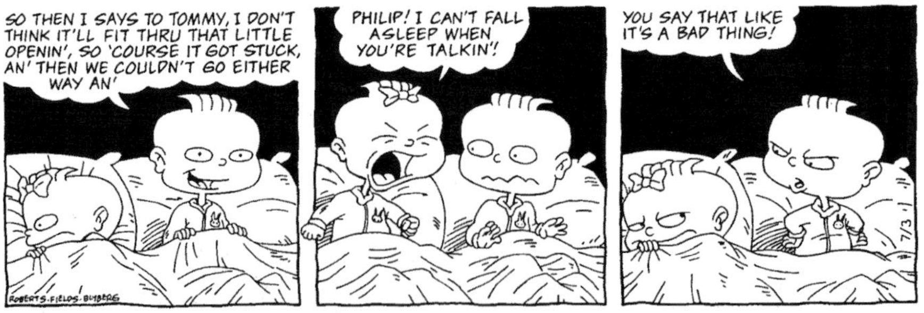
SO THEN I SAYS TO TOMMY, I DON'T THINK IT'LL FIT THRU THAT LITTLE OPENIN', SO 'COURSE IT GOT STUCK, AN' THEN WE COULDN'T GO EITHER WAY AN'
ROBERTS·FIELDS·BLYBERG
PHILIP! I CAN'T FALL ASLEEP WHEN YOU'RE TALKIN'!
YOU SAY THAT LIKE IT'S A BAD THING!
7/3

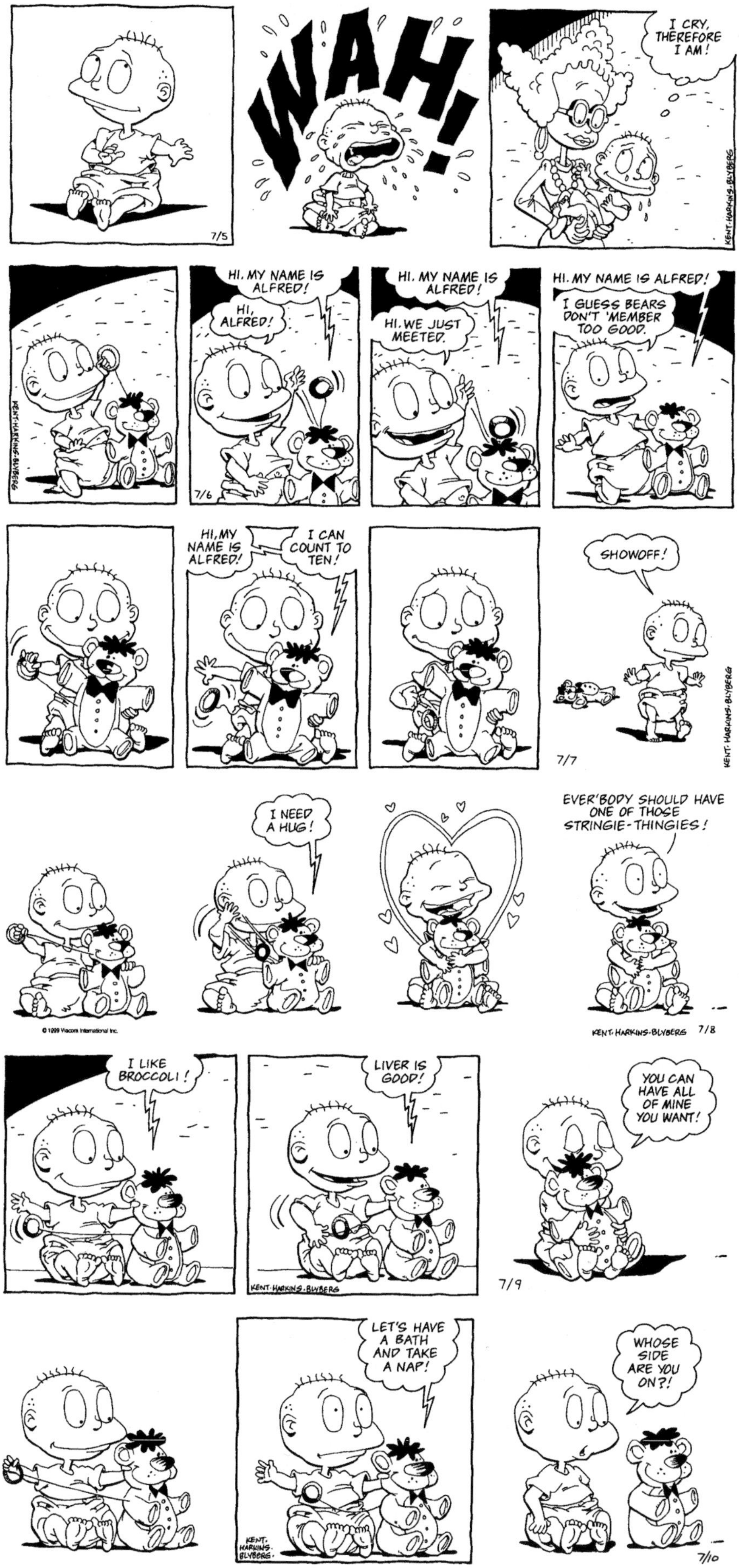
7/5
WAH!
I CRY, THEREFORE I AM!
KENT·HARKINS·BLYBERG
KENT·HARKINS·BLYBERG
7/6
HI. MY NAME IS ALFRED!
HI, ALFRED!
HI. MY NAME IS ALFRED!
HI. WE JUST MEETED.
HI. MY NAME IS ALFRED!
I GUESS BEARS DON'T 'MEMBER TOO GOOD.
HI, MY NAME IS ALFRED!
I CAN COUNT TO TEN!
SHOWOFF!
7/7
KENT·HARKINS·BLYBERG
I NEED A HUG!
EVER'BODY SHOULD HAVE ONE OF THOSE STRINGIE-THINGIES!
© 1999 Viacom International Inc.
KENT·HARKINS·BLYBERG 7/8
I LIKE BROCCOLI!
LIVER IS GOOD!
KENT·HARKINS·BLYBERG
YOU CAN HAVE ALL OF MINE YOU WANT!
7/9
LET'S HAVE A BATH AND TAKE A NAP!
KENT·HARKINS·BLYBERG
WHOSE SIDE ARE YOU ON?!
7/10

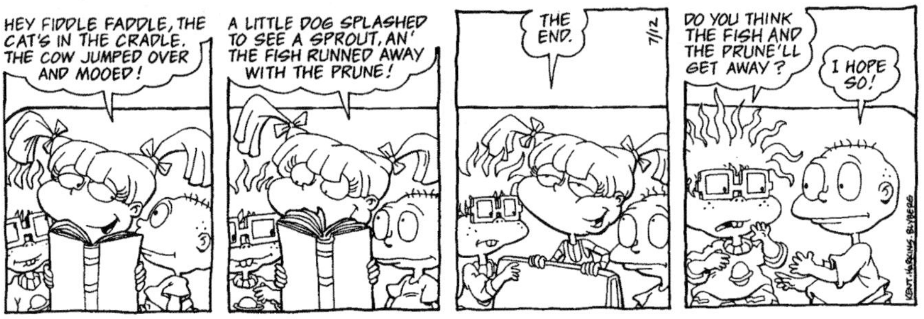
HEY FIDDLE FADDLE, THE CAT'S IN THE CRADLE. THE COW JUMPED OVER AND MOOED!
A LITTLE DOG SPLASHED TO SEE A SPROUT, AN' THE FISH RUNNED AWAY WITH THE PRUNE!
THE END.
7/12
DO YOU THINK THE FISH AND THE PRUNE'LL GET AWAY?
I HOPE SO!
KENT-HARKINS-BLYBERG

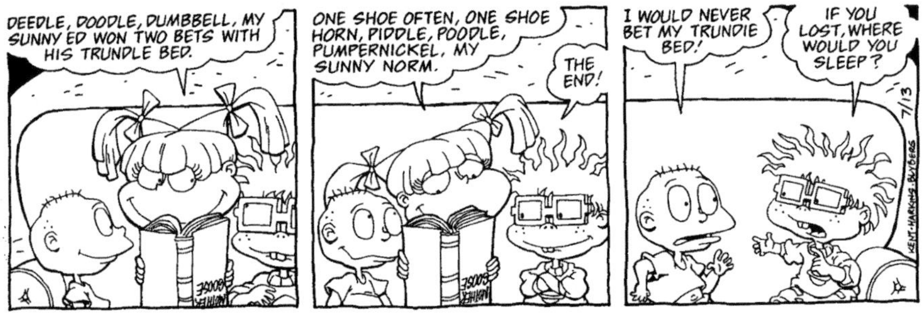
DEEDLE, DOODLE, DUMBBELL, MY SUNNY ED WON TWO BETS WITH HIS TRUNDLE BED.
ONE SHOE OFTEN, ONE SHOE HORN, PIDDLE, POODLE, PUMPERNICKEL, MY SUNNY NORM.
THE END!
I WOULD NEVER BET MY TRUNDIE BED!
IF YOU LOST, WHERE WOULD YOU SLEEP?
7/13
KENT-HARKINS-BLYBERG

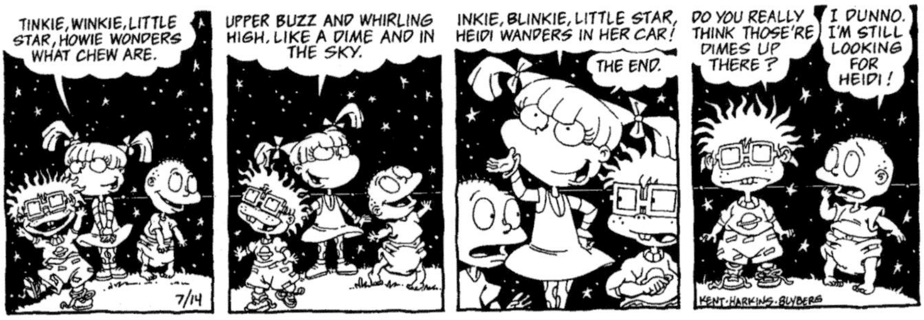
TINKIE, WINKIE, LITTLE STAR, HOWIE WONDERS WHAT CHEW ARE.
7/14
UPPER BUZZ AND WHIRLING HIGH, LIKE A DIME AND IN THE SKY.
INKIE, BLINKIE, LITTLE STAR, HEIDI WANDERS IN HER CAR!
THE END.
DO YOU REALLY THINK THOSE'RE DIMES UP THERE?
I DUNNO. I'M STILL LOOKING FOR HEIDI!
KENT-HARKINS-BLYBERG

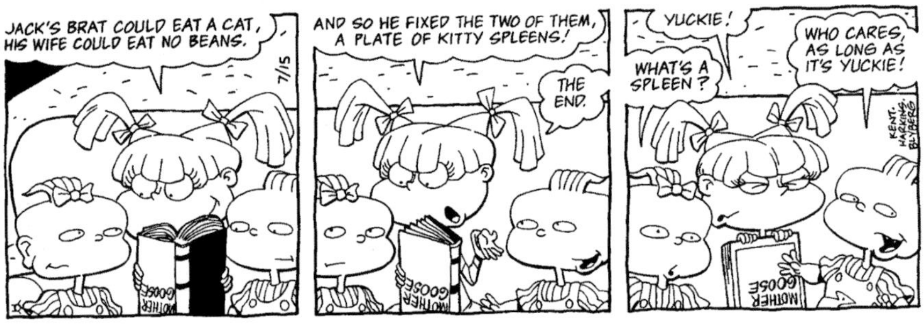
JACK'S BRAT COULD EAT A CAT, HIS WIFE COULD EAT NO BEANS.
7/15
AND SO HE FIXED THE TWO OF THEM, A PLATE OF KITTY SPLEENS!
THE END.
YUCKIE!
WHAT'S A SPLEEN?
WHO CARES, AS LONG AS IT'S YUCKIE!
KENT-HARKINS-BLYBERG

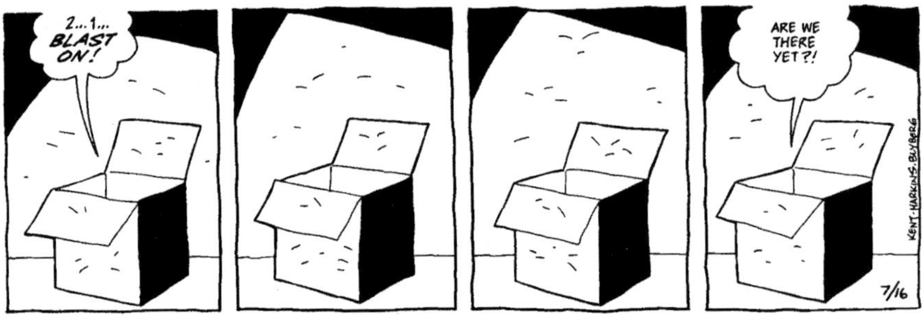
2...1... BLAST ON!
ARE WE THERE YET?!
KENT-HARKINS-BLYBERG
7/16

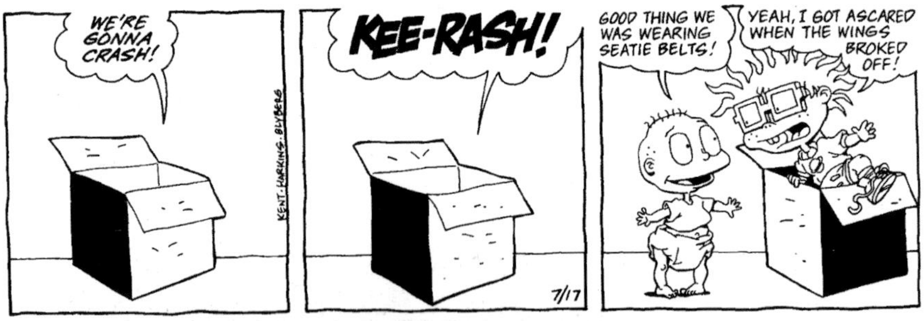
WE'RE GONNA CRASH!
KENT-HARKINS-BLYBERG
KEE-RASH!
7/17
GOOD THING WE WAS WEARING SEATIE BELTS!
YEAH, I GOT ASCARED WHEN THE WINGS BROKED OFF!

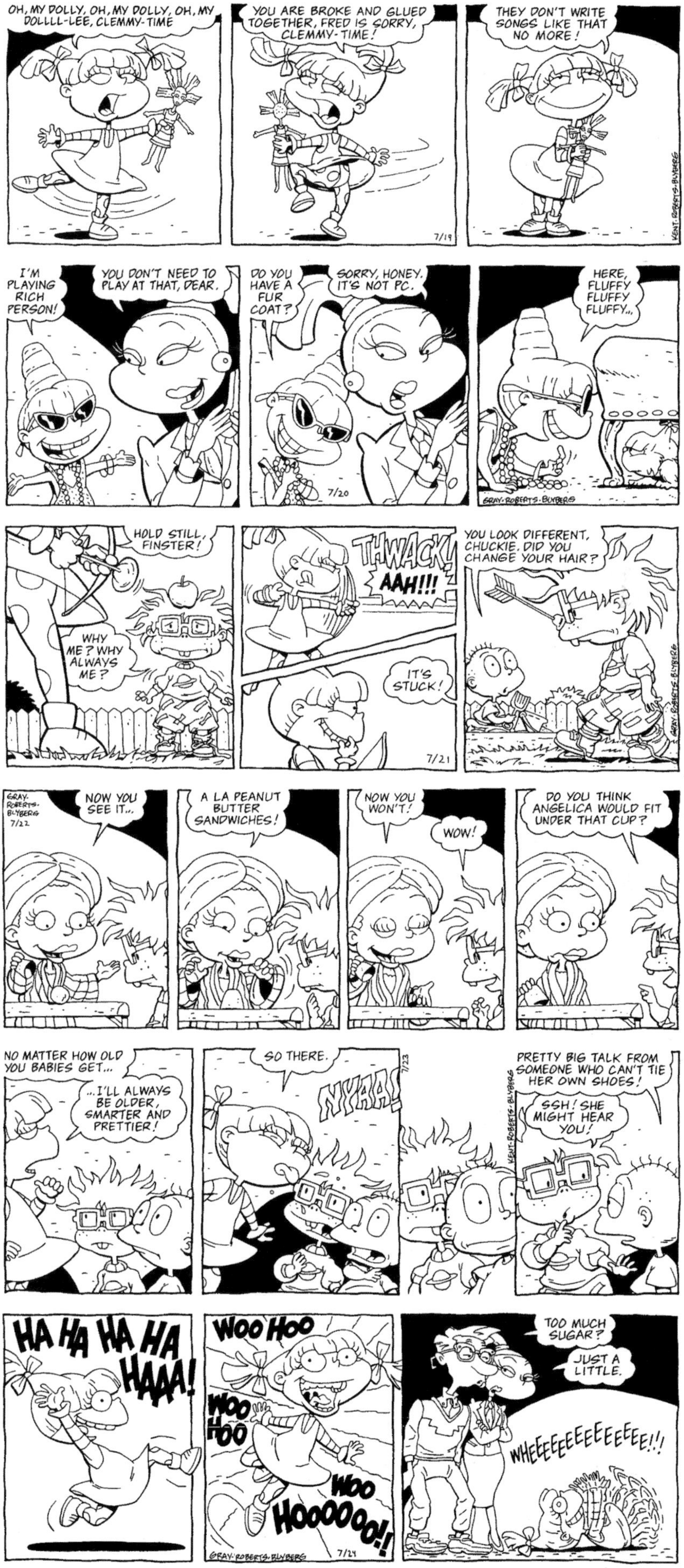

OH, MY DOLLY, OH, MY DOLLY, OH, MY DOLLLL-LEE, CLEMMY-TIME
YOU ARE BROKE AND GLUED TOGETHER, FRED IS SORRY, CLEMMY-TIME!
7/19
THEY DON'T WRITE SONGS LIKE THAT NO MORE!
KENT·ROBERTS·BLYBERG
I'M PLAYING RICH PERSON!
YOU DON'T NEED TO PLAY AT THAT, DEAR.
DO YOU HAVE A FUR COAT?
SORRY, HONEY. IT'S NOT PC.
7/20
HERE, FLUFFY FLUFFY FLUFFY...
GRAY·ROBERTS·BLYBERG
HOLD STILL, FINSTER!
WHY ME? WHY ALWAYS ME?
THWACK!
AAH!!!
IT'S STUCK!
7/21
YOU LOOK DIFFERENT, CHUCKIE. DID YOU CHANGE YOUR HAIR?
GRAY·ROBERTS·BLYBERG
GRAY·ROBERTS·BLYBERG 7/22
NOW YOU SEE IT...
A LA PEANUT BUTTER SANDWICHES!
NOW YOU WON'T!
WOW!
DO YOU THINK ANGELICA WOULD FIT UNDER THAT CUP?
NO MATTER HOW OLD YOU BABIES GET...
...I'LL ALWAYS BE OLDER, SMARTER AND PRETTIER!
SO THERE.
NYAA!
7/23
KENT·ROBERTS·BLYBERG
PRETTY BIG TALK FROM SOMEONE WHO CAN'T TIE HER OWN SHOES!
SSH! SHE MIGHT HEAR YOU!
HA HA HA HA HAAA!
WOO HOO
WOO HOO
WOO HOOOOOO!!
GRAY·ROBERTS·BLYBERG
7/24
TOO MUCH SUGAR?
JUST A LITTLE.
WHEEEEEEEEEEEEE!!!

1999

1999

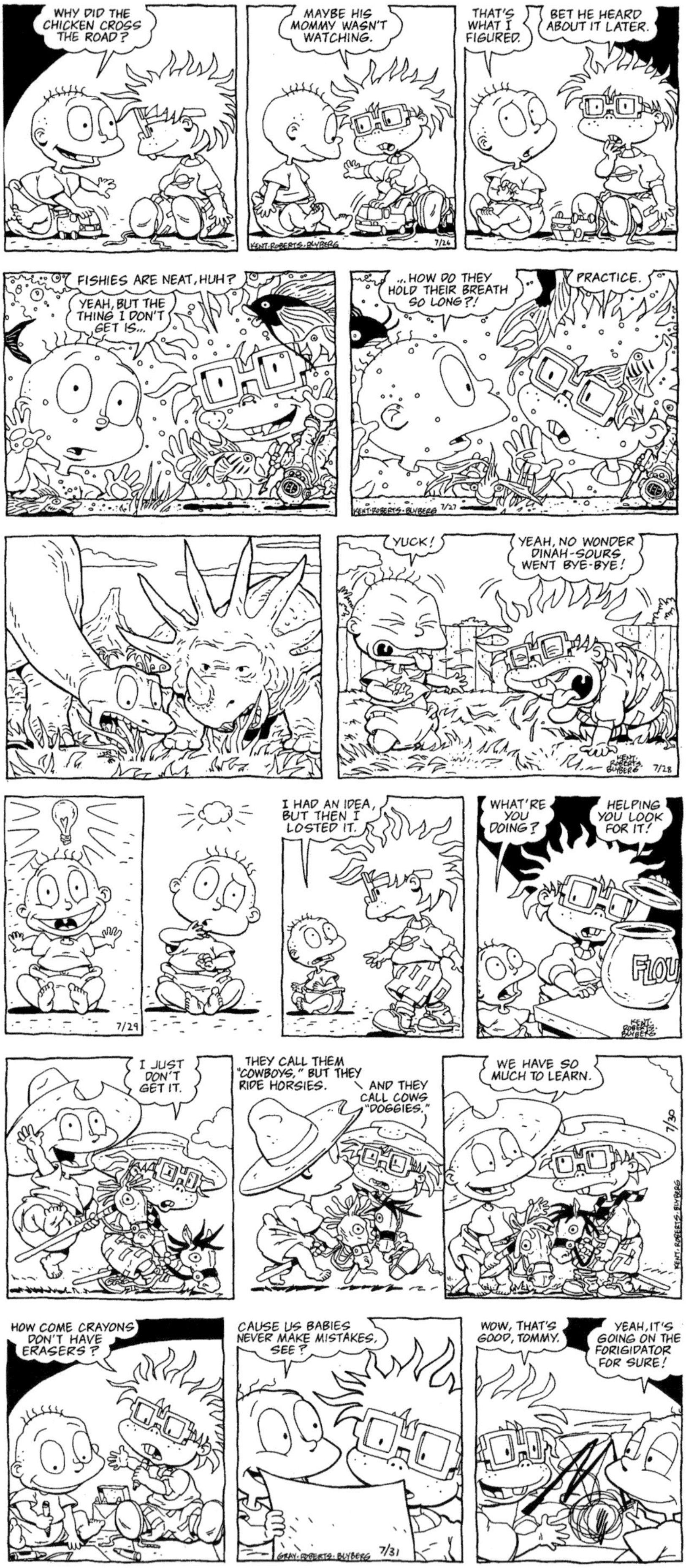
WHY DID THE CHICKEN CROSS THE ROAD?
MAYBE HIS MOMMY WASN'T WATCHING.
THAT'S WHAT I FIGURED.
BET HE HEARD ABOUT IT LATER.
FISHIES ARE NEAT, HUH?
YEAH, BUT THE THING I DON'T GET IS...
...HOW DO THEY HOLD THEIR BREATH SO LONG?!
PRACTICE.
YUCK!
YEAH, NO WONDER DINAH-SOURS WENT BYE-BYE!
I HAD AN IDEA, BUT THEN I LOSTED IT.
WHAT'RE YOU DOING?
HELPING YOU LOOK FOR IT!
FLOU
I JUST DON'T GET IT.
THEY CALL THEM "COWBOYS," BUT THEY RIDE HORSIES.
AND THEY CALL COWS "DOGGIES."
WE HAVE SO MUCH TO LEARN.
HOW COME CRAYONS DON'T HAVE ERASERS?
CAUSE US BABIES NEVER MAKE MISTAKES, SEE?
WOW, THAT'S GOOD, TOMMY.
YEAH, IT'S GOING ON THE FORIGIDATOR FOR SURE!

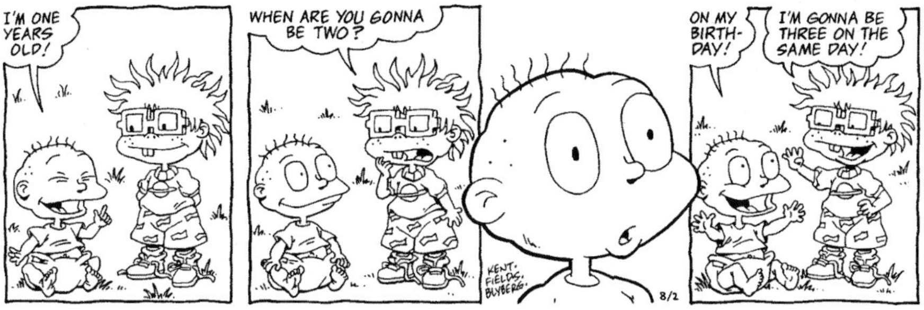
I'M ONE YEARS OLD!
WHEN ARE YOU GONNA BE TWO?
KENT. FIELDS. BLYBERG.
8/2
ON MY BIRTH-DAY!
I'M GONNA BE THREE ON THE SAME DAY!

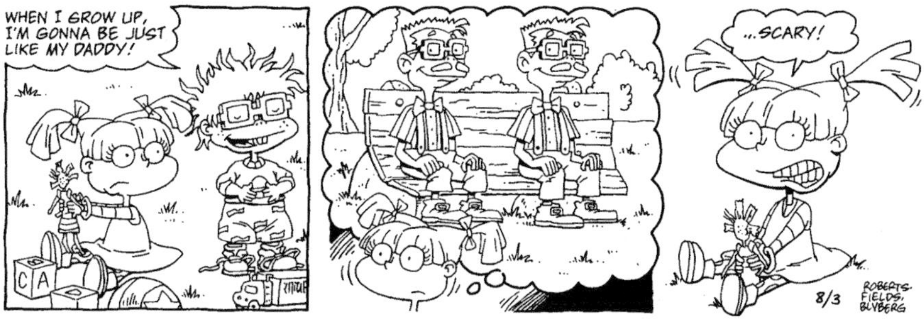
WHEN I GROW UP, I'M GONNA BE JUST LIKE MY DADDY!
..SCARY!
8/3
ROBERTS. FIELDS. BLYBERG

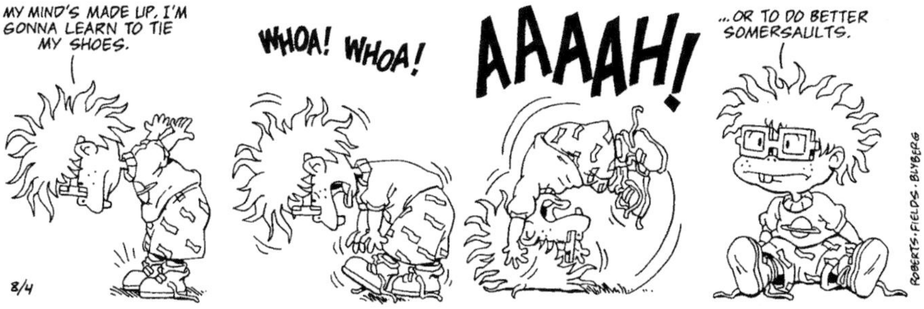
MY MIND'S MADE UP. I'M GONNA LEARN TO TIE MY SHOES.
8/4
WHOA! WHOA!
AAAAH!
...OR TO DO BETTER SOMERSAULTS.
ROBERTS·FIELDS·BLYBERG

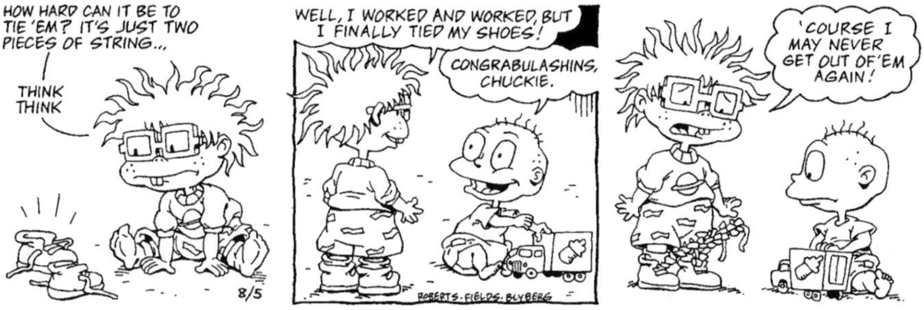
HOW HARD CAN IT BE TO TIE 'EM? IT'S JUST TWO PIECES OF STRING...
THINK THINK
8/5
WELL, I WORKED AND WORKED, BUT I FINALLY TIED MY SHOES!
CONGRABULASHINS, CHUCKIE.
ROBERTS·FIELDS·BLYBERG
'COURSE I MAY NEVER GET OUT OF 'EM AGAIN!

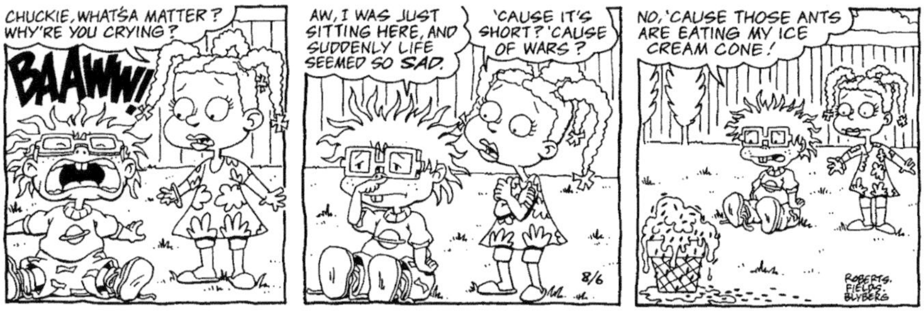
BAAWW!
CHUCKIE, WHAT'SA MATTER? WHY'RE YOU CRYING?
AW, I WAS JUST SITTING HERE, AND SUDDENLY LIFE SEEMED SO SAD.
'CAUSE IT'S SHORT? 'CAUSE OF WARS?
8/6
NO, 'CAUSE THOSE ANTS ARE EATING MY ICE CREAM CONE!
ROBERTS. FIELDS. BLYBERG

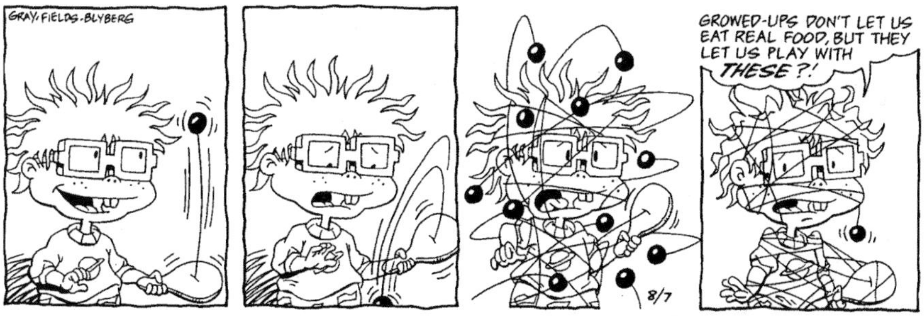
GRAY·FIELDS·BLYBERG
8/7
GROWED-UPS DON'T LET US EAT REAL FOOD, BUT THEY LET US PLAY WITH THESE?!

1999

1999

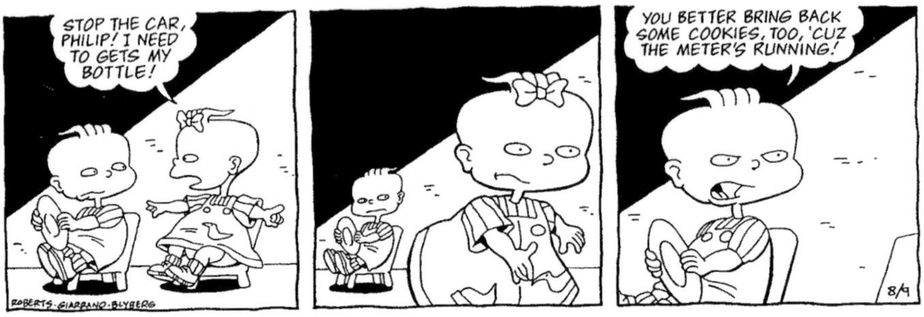
STOP THE CAR, PHILIP! I NEED TO GETS MY BOTTLE!
YOU BETTER BRING BACK SOME COOKIES, TOO, 'CUZ THE METER'S RUNNING!
ROBERTS·GIARRANO·BLYBERG
8/9

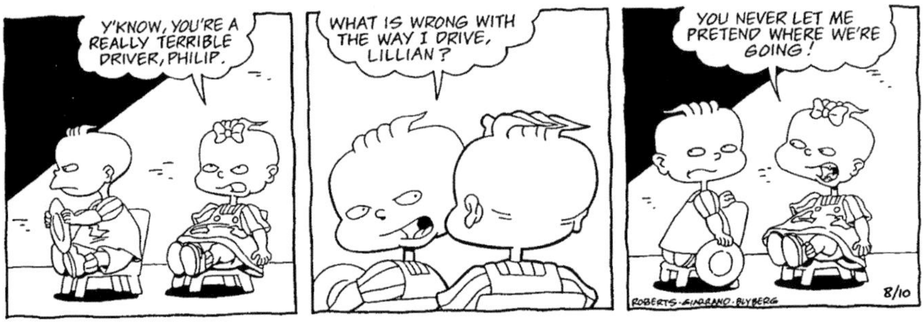
Y'KNOW, YOU'RE A REALLY TERRIBLE DRIVER, PHILIP.
WHAT IS WRONG WITH THE WAY I DRIVE, LILLIAN?
YOU NEVER LET ME PRETEND WHERE WE'RE GOING!
ROBERTS·GIARRANO·BLYBERG
8/10

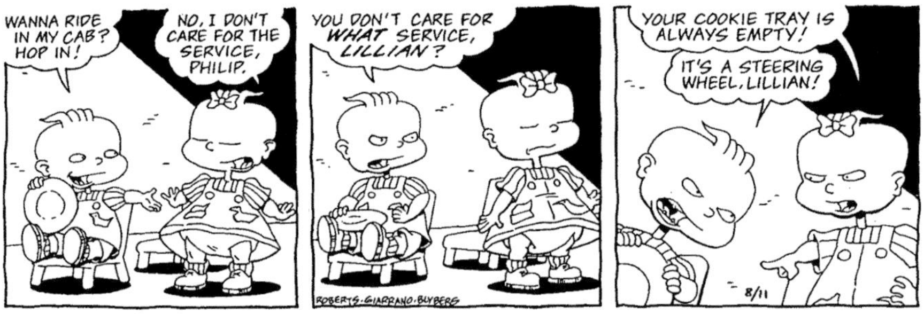
WANNA RIDE IN MY CAB? HOP IN!
NO, I DON'T CARE FOR THE SERVICE, PHILIP.
YOU DON'T CARE FOR WHAT SERVICE, LILLIAN?
YOUR COOKIE TRAY IS ALWAYS EMPTY!
IT'S A STEERING WHEEL, LILLIAN!
ROBERTS·GIARRANO·BLYBERG
8/11

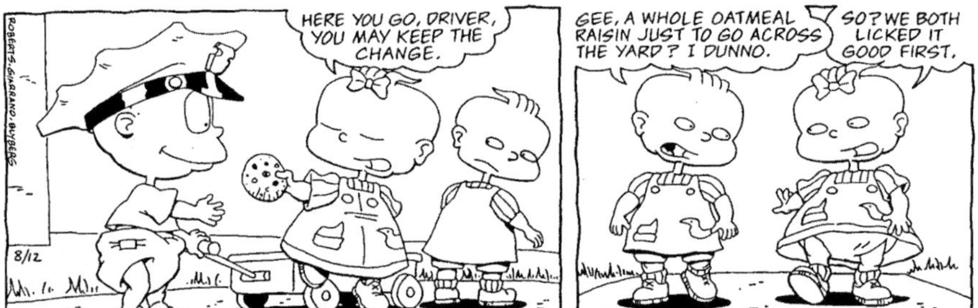
ROBERTS·GIARRANO·BLYBERG
HERE YOU GO, DRIVER, YOU MAY KEEP THE CHANGE.
8/12
GEE, A WHOLE OATMEAL RAISIN JUST TO GO ACROSS THE YARD? I DUNNO.
SO? WE BOTH LICKED IT GOOD FIRST.

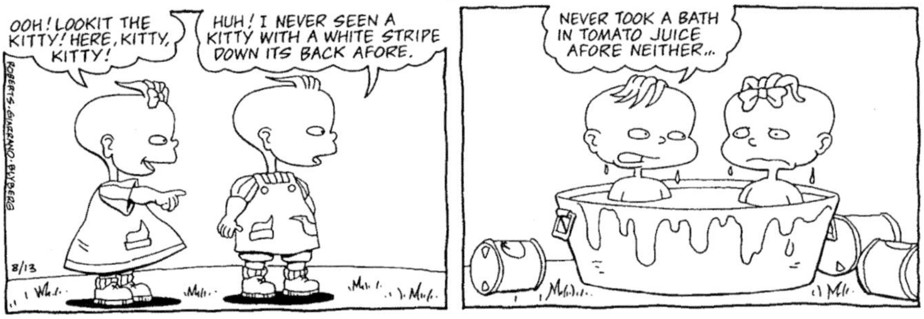
ROBERTS·GIARRANO·BLYBERG
OOH! LOOKIT THE KITTY! HERE, KITTY, KITTY!
HUH! I NEVER SEEN A KITTY WITH A WHITE STRIPE DOWN ITS BACK AFORE.
8/13
NEVER TOOK A BATH IN TOMATO JUICE AFORE NEITHER...

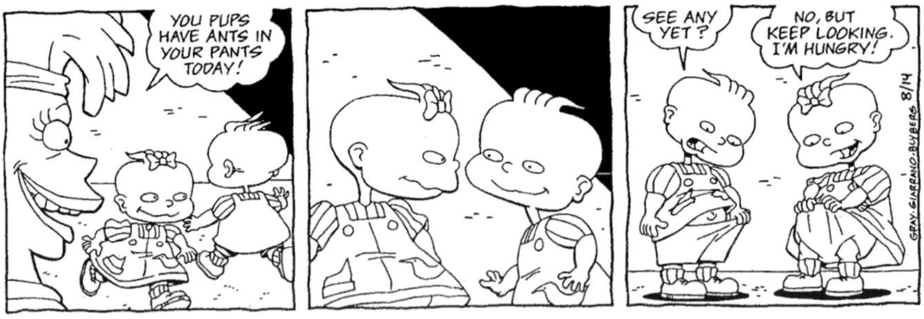
YOU PUPS HAVE ANTS IN YOUR PANTS TODAY!
SEE ANY YET?
NO, BUT KEEP LOOKING. I'M HUNGRY!
8/14
GRAY·GIARRANO·BLYBERG

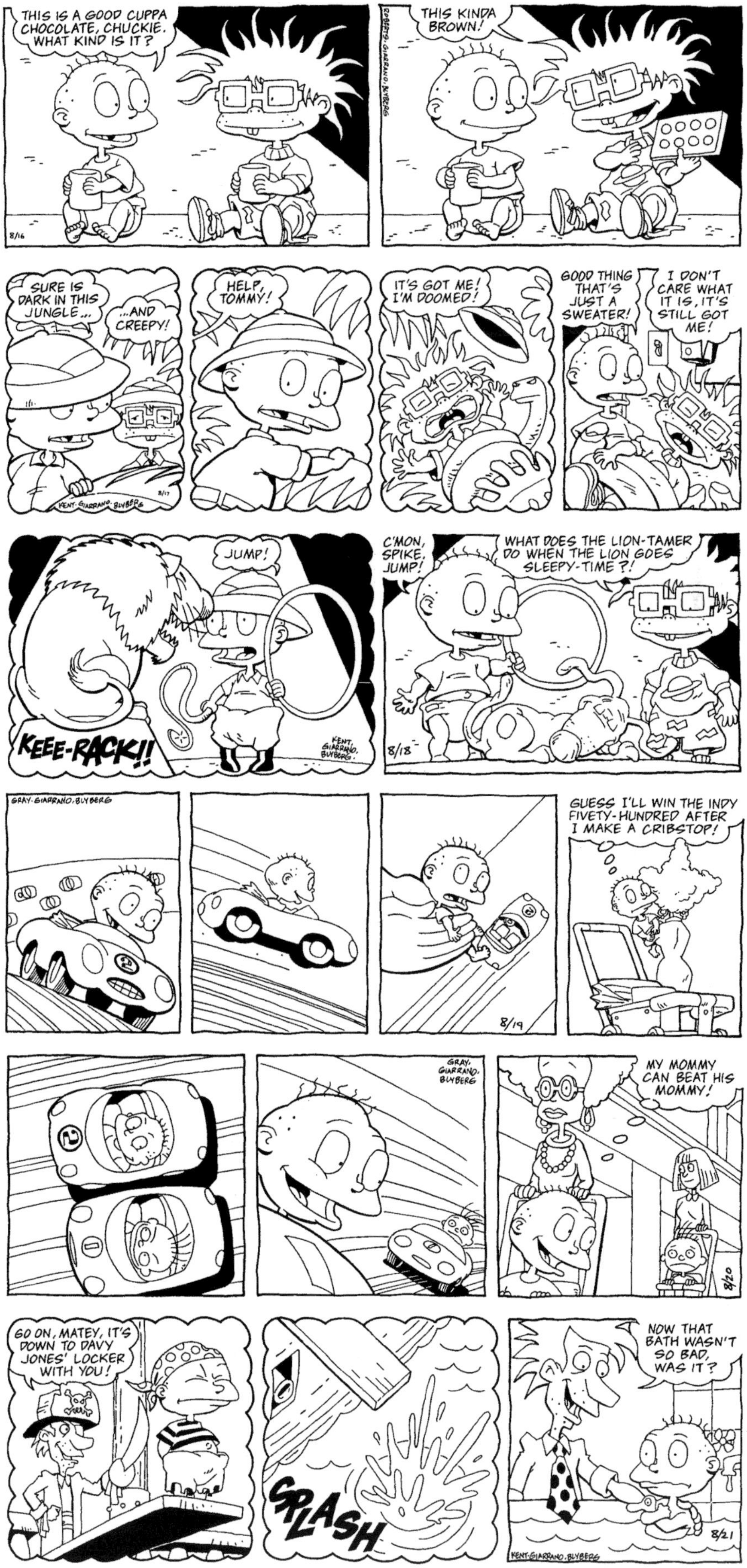
THIS IS A GOOD CUPPA CHOCOLATE, CHUCKIE. WHAT KIND IS IT?
THIS KINDA BROWN!
ROBERTS·GIARRANO·BLYBERG
SURE IS DARK IN THIS JUNGLE...
...AND CREEPY!
KENT·GIARRANO·BLYBERG
HELP, TOMMY!
IT'S GOT ME! I'M DOOMED!
GOOD THING THAT'S JUST A SWEATER!
I DON'T CARE WHAT IT IS, IT'S STILL GOT ME!
JUMP!
KEEE-RACK!!
KENT·GIARRANO·BLYBERG
C'MON, SPIKE. JUMP!
WHAT DOES THE LION-TAMER DO WHEN THE LION GOES SLEEPY-TIME?!
GRAY·GIARRANO·BLYBERG
GUESS I'LL WIN THE INDY FIVETY-HUNDRED AFTER I MAKE A CRIBSTOP!
GRAY·GIARRANO·BLYBERG
MY MOMMY CAN BEAT HIS MOMMY!
GO ON, MATEY, IT'S DOWN TO DAVY JONES' LOCKER WITH YOU!
SPLASH
NOW THAT BATH WASN'T SO BAD, WAS IT?
KENT·GIARRANO·BLYBERG

1999

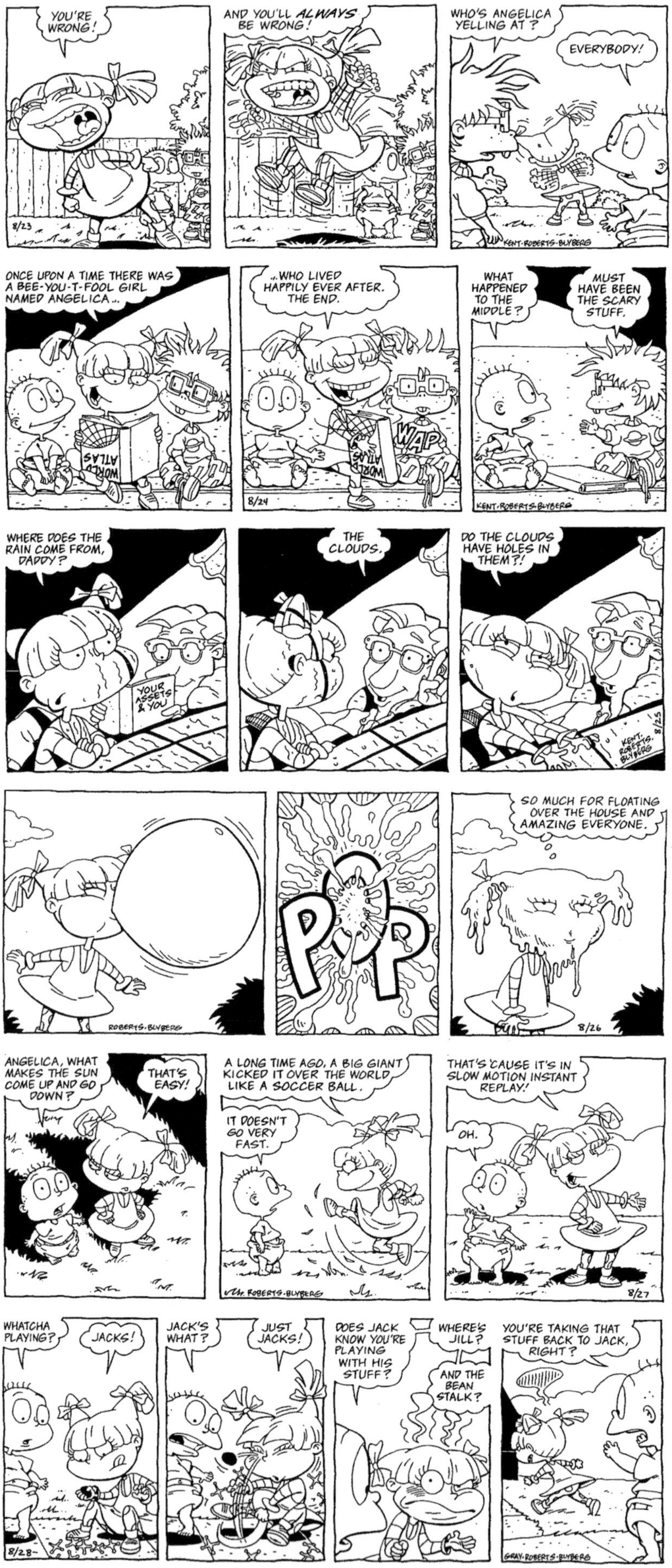
YOU'RE WRONG!
AND YOU'LL ALWAYS BE WRONG!
8/23
WHO'S ANGELICA YELLING AT?
EVERYBODY!
KENT·ROBERTS·BLYBERG
ONCE UPON A TIME THERE WAS A BEE-YOU-T-FOOL GIRL NAMED ANGELICA...
WORLD ATLAS
...WHO LIVED HAPPILY EVER AFTER. THE END.
WAP
8/24
WHAT HAPPENED TO THE MIDDLE?
MUST HAVE BEEN THE SCARY STUFF.
KENT·ROBERTS·BLYBERG
WHERE DOES THE RAIN COME FROM, DADDY?
YOUR ASSETS & YOU
THE CLOUDS.
DO THE CLOUDS HAVE HOLES IN THEM?!
KENT. ROBERTS. BLYBERG 8/25
ROBERTS·BLYBERG
POP
SO MUCH FOR FLOATING OVER THE HOUSE AND AMAZING EVERYONE.
8/26
ANGELICA, WHAT MAKES THE SUN COME UP AND GO DOWN?
THAT'S EASY!
A LONG TIME AGO, A BIG GIANT KICKED IT OVER THE WORLD LIKE A SOCCER BALL.
IT DOESN'T GO VERY FAST.
ROBERTS·BLYBERG
THAT'S 'CAUSE IT'S IN SLOW MOTION INSTANT REPLAY!
OH.
8/27
WHATCHA PLAYING?
JACKS!
8/28
JACK'S WHAT?
JUST JACKS!
DOES JACK KNOW YOU'RE PLAYING WITH HIS STUFF?
WHERE'S JILL?
AND THE BEAN STALK?
YOU'RE TAKING THAT STUFF BACK TO JACK, RIGHT?
GRAY·ROBERTS·BLYBERG

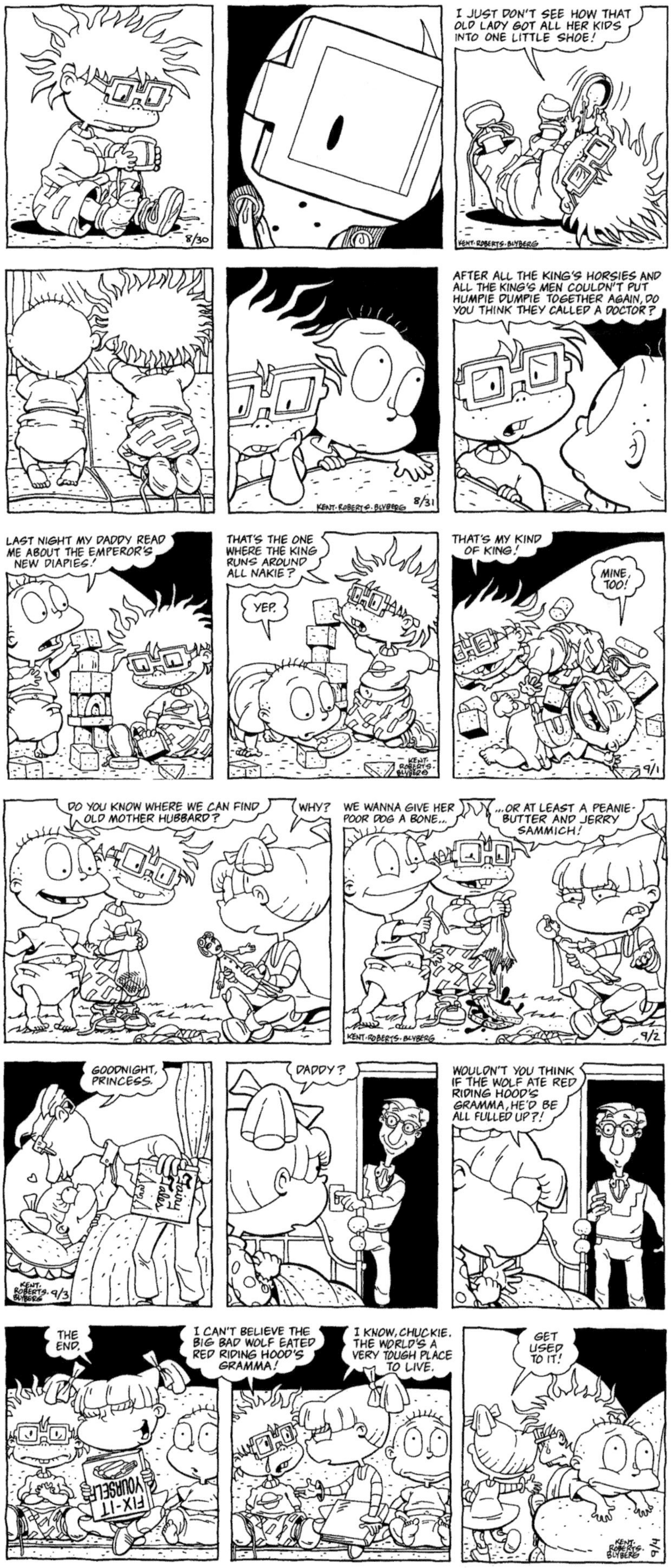
8/30
I JUST DON'T SEE HOW THAT OLD LADY GOT ALL HER KIDS INTO ONE LITTLE SHOE!
KENT·ROBERTS·BLYBERG
8/31
KENT·ROBERTS·BLYBERG
AFTER ALL THE KING'S HORSIES AND ALL THE KING'S MEN COULDN'T PUT HUMPIE DUMPIE TOGETHER AGAIN, DO YOU THINK THEY CALLED A DOCTOR?
LAST NIGHT MY DADDY READ ME ABOUT THE EMPEROR'S NEW DIAPIES!
THAT'S THE ONE WHERE THE KING RUNS AROUND ALL NAKIE?
YEP.
KENT·ROBERTS·BLYBERG
THAT'S MY KIND OF KING!
MINE, TOO!
9/1
DO YOU KNOW WHERE WE CAN FIND OLD MOTHER HUBBARD?
WHY?
WE WANNA GIVE HER POOR DOG A BONE...
...OR AT LEAST A PEANIE-BUTTER AND JERRY SAMMICH!
KENT·ROBERTS·BLYBERG
9/2
GOODNIGHT, PRINCESS.
Fairy Tales
KENT·ROBERTS·BLYBERG 9/3
DADDY?
WOULDN'T YOU THINK IF THE WOLF ATE RED RIDING HOOD'S GRAMMA, HE'D BE ALL FULLED UP?!
THE END.
FIX-IT YOURSELF
I CAN'T BELIEVE THE BIG BAD WOLF EATED RED RIDING HOOD'S GRAMMA!
I KNOW, CHUCKIE. THE WORLD'S A VERY TOUGH PLACE TO LIVE.
GET USED TO IT!
KENT·ROBERTS·BLYBERG 9/4

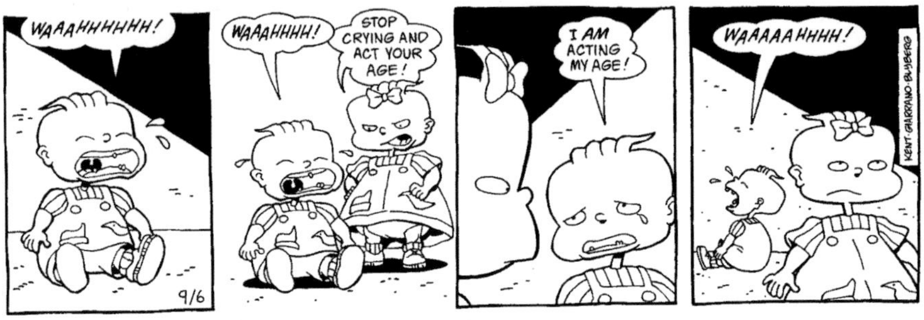
WAAAHHHHHHH!
9/6
WAAAHHHHH!
STOP CRYING AND ACT YOUR AGE!
I AM ACTING MY AGE!
WAAAAAHHHH!
KENT·GIARRANO·BLYBERG

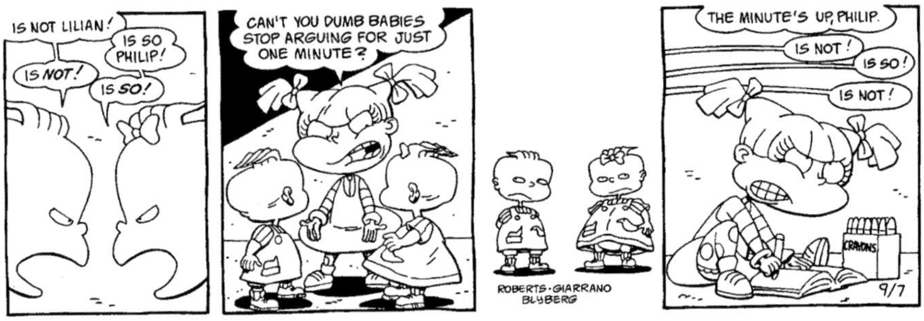
IS NOT LILIAN!
IS SO PHILIP!
IS NOT!
IS SO!
CAN'T YOU DUMB BABIES STOP ARGUING FOR JUST ONE MINUTE?
ROBERTS·GIARRANO BLYBERG
THE MINUTE'S UP, PHILIP.
IS NOT!
IS SO!
IS NOT!
CRAYONS
9/7

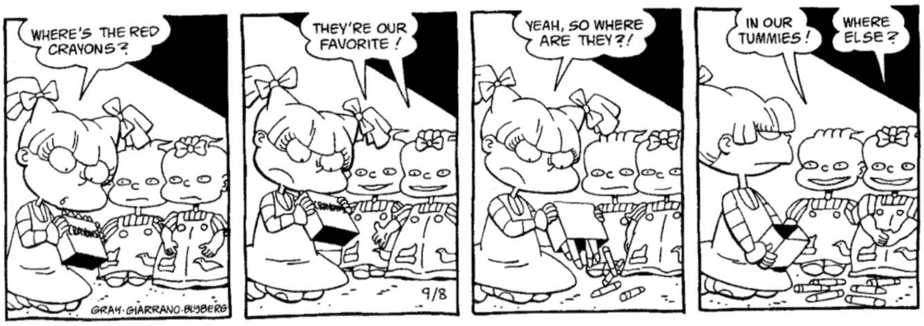
WHERE'S THE RED CRAYONS?
CRAYONS
GRAY·GIARRANO·BLYBERG
THEY'RE OUR FAVORITE!
9/8
YEAH, SO WHERE ARE THEY?!
IN OUR TUMMIES!
WHERE ELSE?

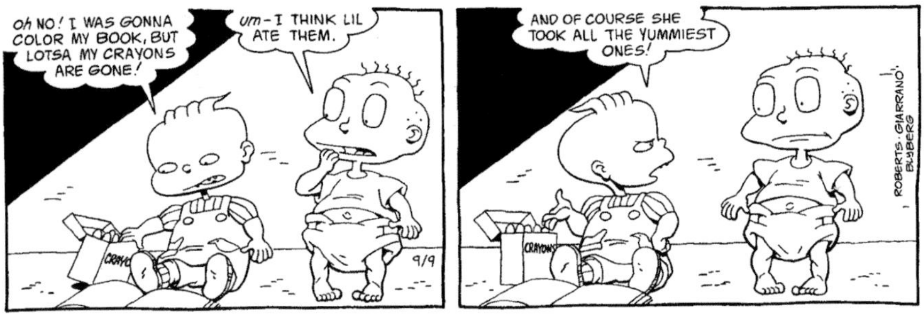
Oh NO! I WAS GONNA COLOR MY BOOK, BUT LOTSA MY CRAYONS ARE GONE!
Um- I THINK LIL ATE THEM.
9/9
AND OF COURSE SHE TOOK ALL THE YUMMIEST ONES!
CRAYONS
ROBERTS·GIARRANO·BLYBERG

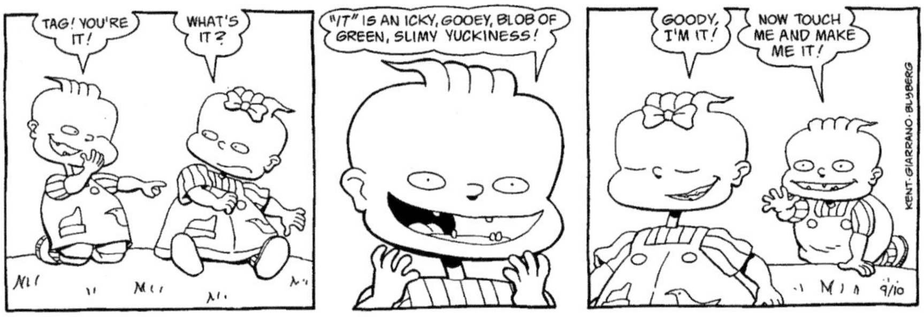
TAG! YOU'RE IT!
WHAT'S IT?
"IT" IS AN ICKY, GOOEY, BLOB OF GREEN, SLIMY YUCKINESS!
GOODY, I'M IT!
NOW TOUCH ME AND MAKE ME IT!
KENT·GIARRANO·BLYBERG
9/10

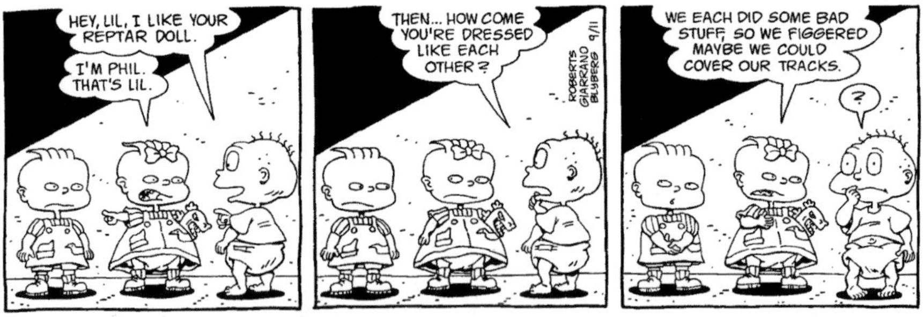
HEY, LIL, I LIKE YOUR REPTAR DOLL.
I'M PHIL. THAT'S LIL.
THEN... HOW COME YOU'RE DRESSED LIKE EACH OTHER?
ROBERTS GIARRANO BLYBERG 9/11
WE EACH DID SOME BAD STUFF, SO WE FIGGERED MAYBE WE COULD COVER OUR TRACKS.
?

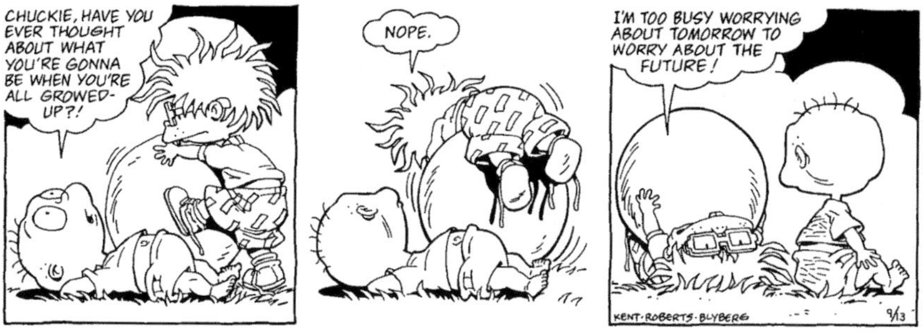
CHUCKIE, HAVE YOU EVER THOUGHT ABOUT WHAT YOU'RE GONNA BE WHEN YOU'RE ALL GROWED-UP?!
NOPE.
I'M TOO BUSY WORRYING ABOUT TOMORROW TO WORRY ABOUT THE FUTURE!
KENT·ROBERTS·BLYBERG
9/13

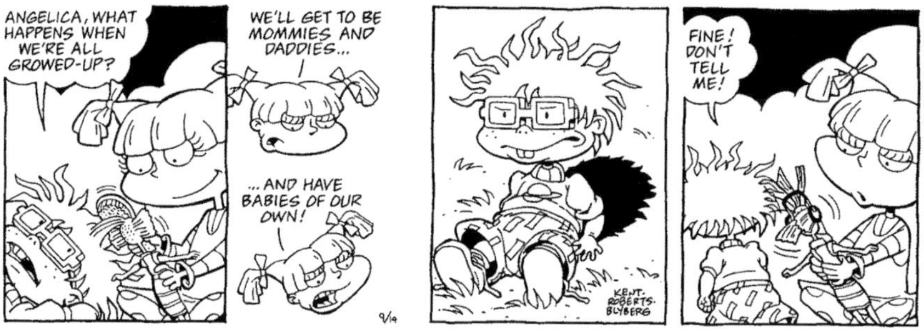
ANGELICA, WHAT HAPPENS WHEN WE'RE ALL GROWED-UP?
WE'LL GET TO BE MOMMIES AND DADDIES...
...AND HAVE BABIES OF OUR OWN!
9/14
KENT·ROBERTS·BLYBERG
FINE! DON'T TELL ME!

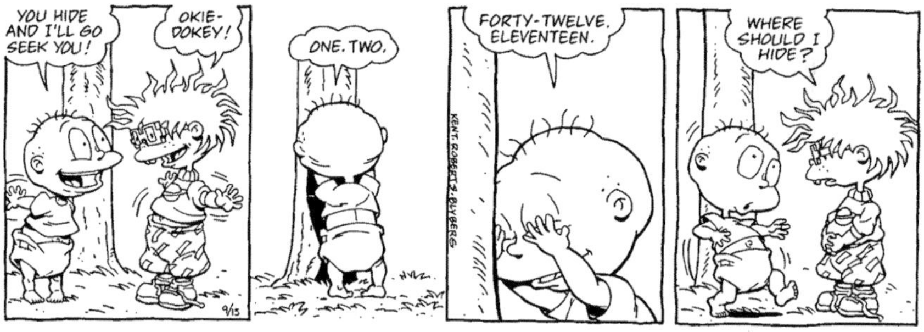
YOU HIDE AND I'LL GO SEEK YOU!
OKIE-DOKEY!
9/15
ONE. TWO.
KENT·ROBERTS·BLYBERG
FORTY-TWELVE. ELEVENTEEN.
WHERE SHOULD I HIDE?

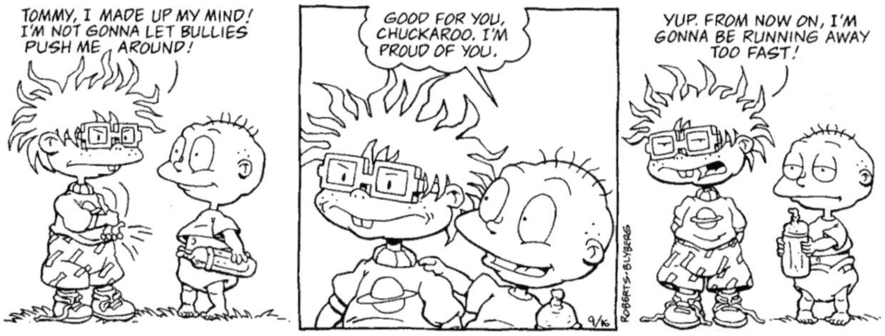
TOMMY, I MADE UP MY MIND! I'M NOT GONNA LET BULLIES PUSH ME AROUND!
GOOD FOR YOU, CHUCKAROO. I'M PROUD OF YOU.
9/16
ROBERTS·BLYBERG
YUP. FROM NOW ON, I'M GONNA BE RUNNING AWAY TOO FAST!

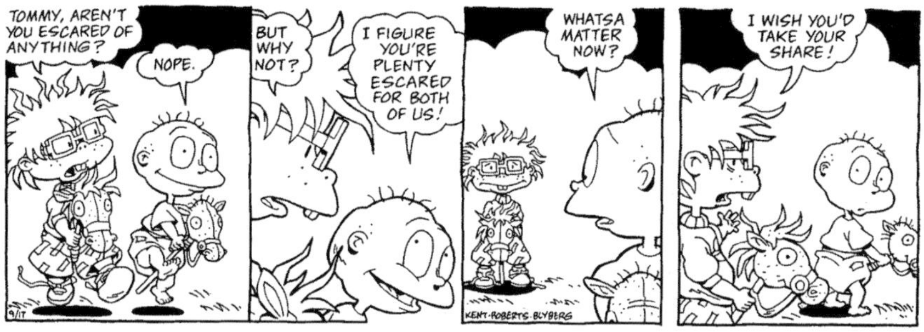
TOMMY, AREN'T YOU ESCARED OF ANYTHING?
NOPE.
9/17
BUT WHY NOT?
I FIGURE YOU'RE PLENTY ESCARED FOR BOTH OF US!
WHATSA MATTER NOW?
KENT·ROBERTS·BLYBERG
I WISH YOU'D TAKE YOUR SHARE!

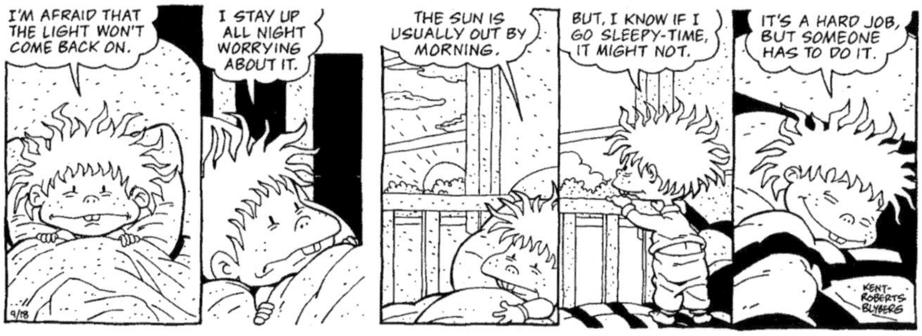
I'M AFRAID THAT THE LIGHT WON'T COME BACK ON.
9/18
I STAY UP ALL NIGHT WORRYING ABOUT IT.
THE SUN IS USUALLY OUT BY MORNING.
BUT, I KNOW IF I GO SLEEPY-TIME, IT MIGHT NOT.
IT'S A HARD JOB, BUT SOMEONE HAS TO DO IT.
KENT·ROBERTS·BLYBERG

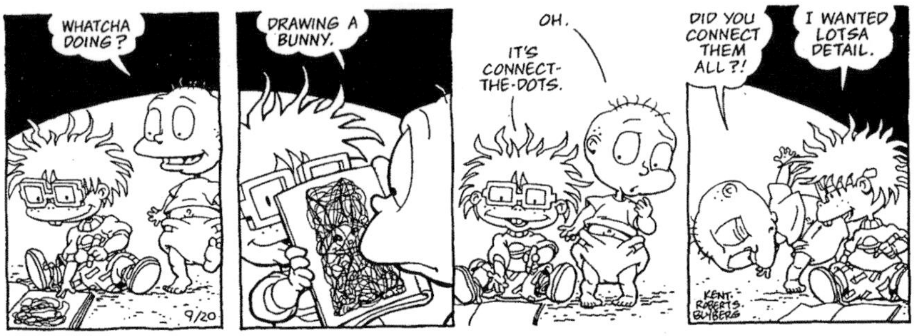
WHATCHA DOING?
DRAWING A BUNNY.
IT'S CONNECT-THE-DOTS.
OH.
DID YOU CONNECT THEM ALL?!
I WANTED LOTSA DETAIL.
9/20
KENT·ROBERTS·BLYBERG

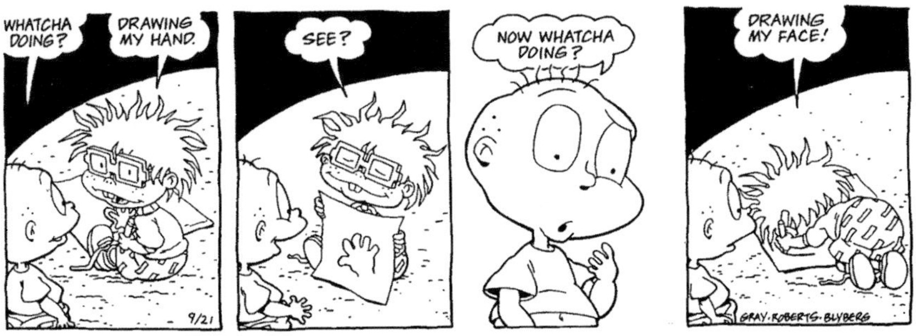
WHATCHA DOING?
DRAWING MY HAND.
SEE?
NOW WHATCHA DOING?
DRAWING MY FACE!
9/21
GRAY·ROBERTS·BLYBERG

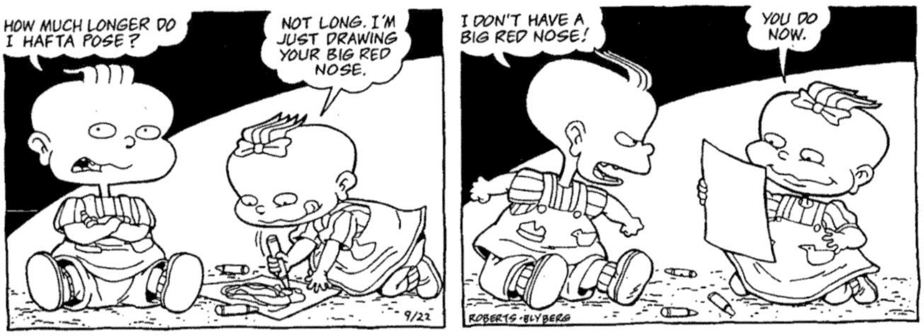
HOW MUCH LONGER DO I HAFTA POSE?
NOT LONG. I'M JUST DRAWING YOUR BIG RED NOSE.
I DON'T HAVE A BIG RED NOSE!
YOU DO NOW.
9/22
ROBERTS·BLYBERG

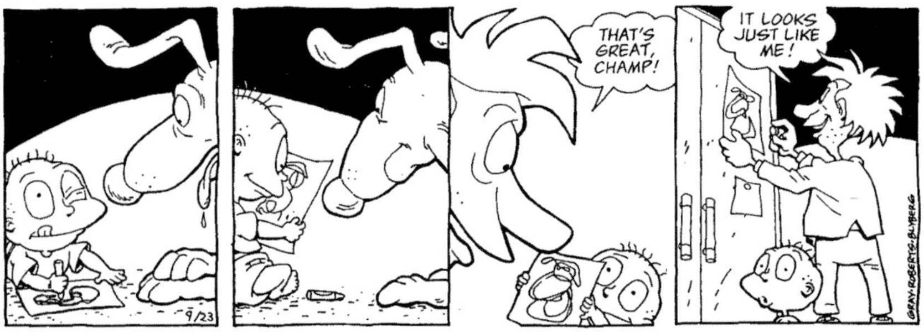
9/23
THAT'S GREAT, CHAMP!
IT LOOKS JUST LIKE ME!
GRAY·ROBERTS·BLYBERG

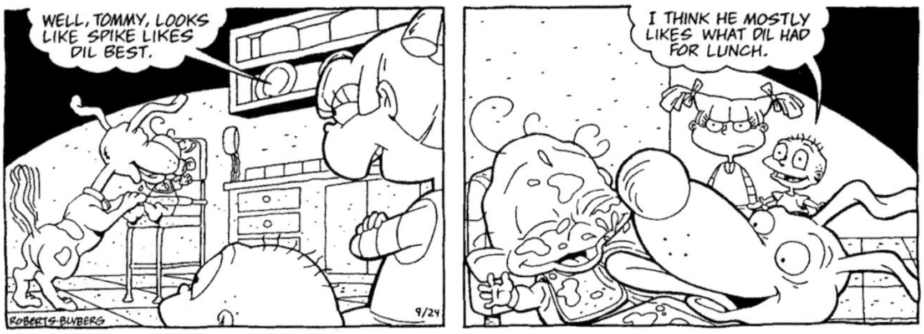
WELL, TOMMY, LOOKS LIKE SPIKE LIKES DIL BEST.
I THINK HE MOSTLY LIKES WHAT DIL HAD FOR LUNCH.
ROBERTS·BLYBERG
9/24

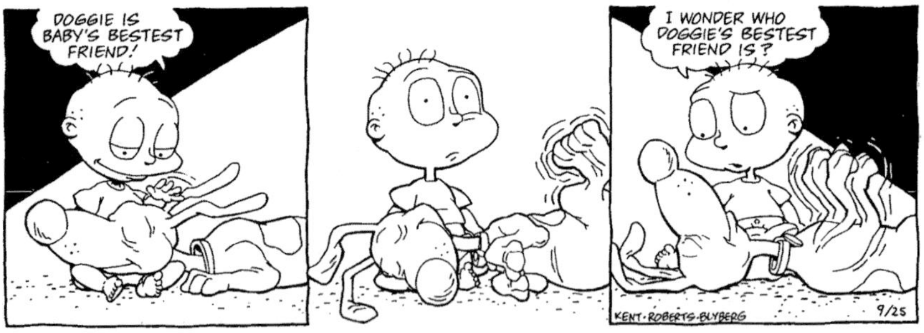
DOGGIE IS BABY'S BESTEST FRIEND!
I WONDER WHO DOGGIE'S BESTEST FRIEND IS?
KENT·ROBERTS·BLYBERG
9/25

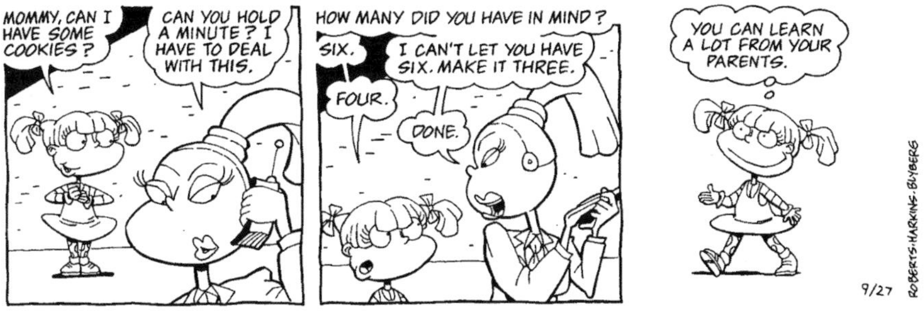
MOMMY, CAN I HAVE SOME COOKIES?
CAN YOU HOLD A MINUTE? I HAVE TO DEAL WITH THIS.
HOW MANY DID YOU HAVE IN MIND?
SIX.
I CAN'T LET YOU HAVE SIX. MAKE IT THREE.
FOUR.
DONE.
YOU CAN LEARN A LOT FROM YOUR PARENTS.
9/27
ROBERTS·HARKINS·BLYBERG

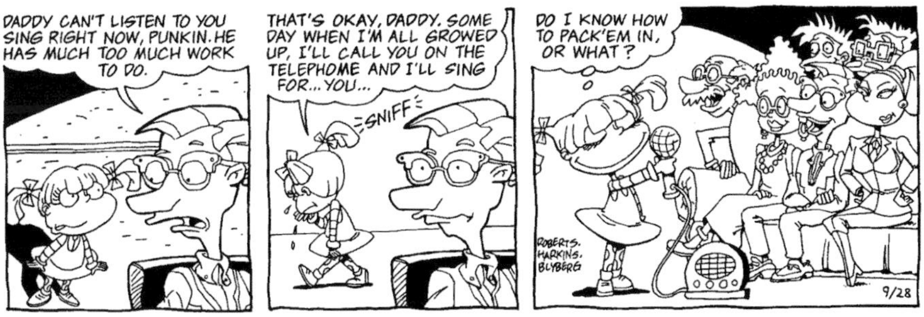
DADDY CAN'T LISTEN TO YOU SING RIGHT NOW, PUNKIN. HE HAS MUCH TOO MUCH WORK TO DO.
THAT'S OKAY, DADDY. SOME DAY WHEN I'M ALL GROWED UP, I'LL CALL YOU ON THE TELEPHOME AND I'LL SING FOR... YOU...
SNIFF
DO I KNOW HOW TO PACK'EM IN, OR WHAT?
ROBERTS· HARKINS· BLYBERG
9/28

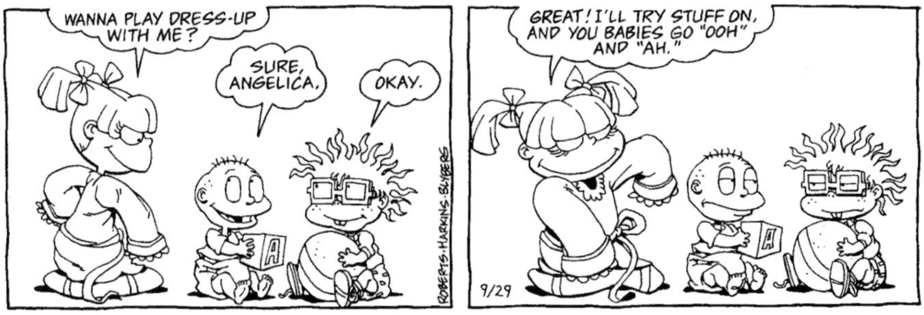
WANNA PLAY DRESS-UP WITH ME?
SURE, ANGELICA.
OKAY.
ROBERTS·HARKINS·BLYBERG
GREAT! I'LL TRY STUFF ON, AND YOU BABIES GO "OOH" AND "AH."
9/29

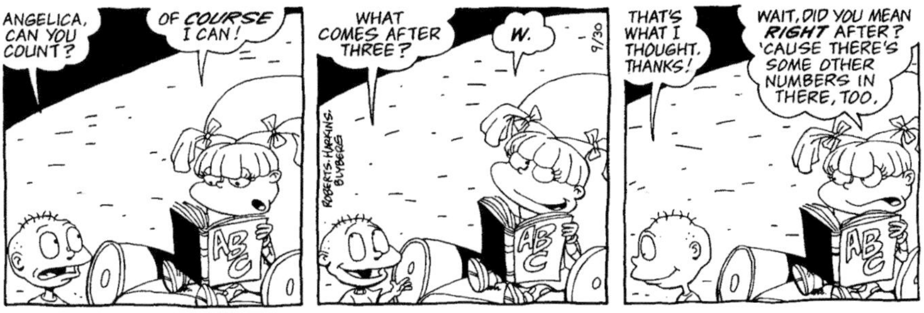
ANGELICA, CAN YOU COUNT?
OF COURSE I CAN!
WHAT COMES AFTER THREE?
W.
9/30
ROBERTS·HARKINS· BLYBERG
THAT'S WHAT I THOUGHT. THANKS!
WAIT, DID YOU MEAN RIGHT AFTER? 'CAUSE THERE'S SOME OTHER NUMBERS IN THERE, TOO.

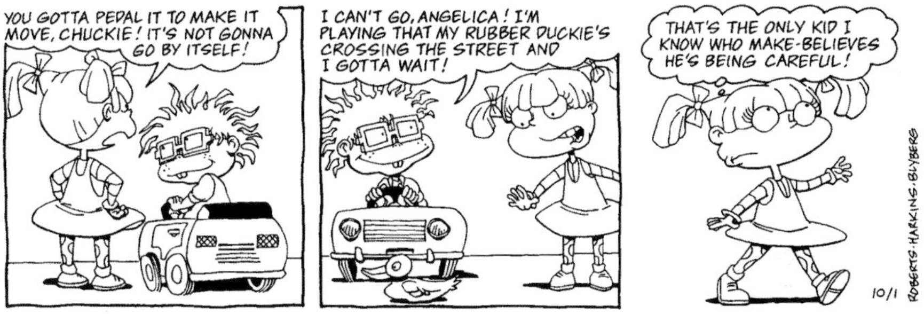
YOU GOTTA PEDAL IT TO MAKE IT MOVE, CHUCKIE! IT'S NOT GONNA GO BY ITSELF!
I CAN'T GO, ANGELICA! I'M PLAYING THAT MY RUBBER DUCKIE'S CROSSING THE STREET AND I GOTTA WAIT!
THAT'S THE ONLY KID I KNOW WHO MAKE-BELIEVES HE'S BEING CAREFUL!
10/1
ROBERTS·HARKINS·BLYBERG

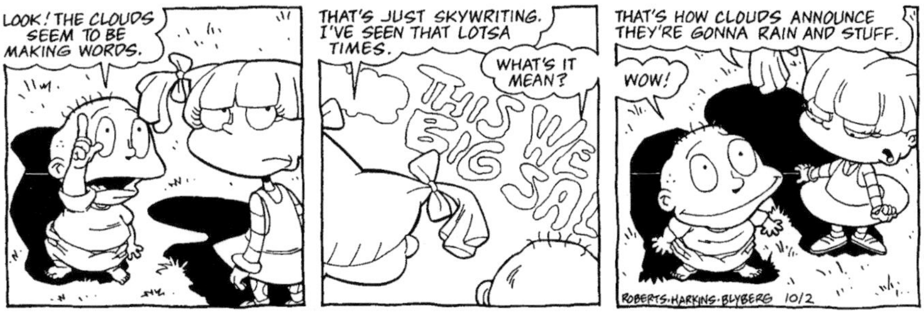
LOOK! THE CLOUDS SEEM TO BE MAKING WORDS.
THAT'S JUST SKYWRITING. I'VE SEEN THAT LOTSA TIMES.
WHAT'S IT MEAN?
THAT'S HOW CLOUDS ANNOUNCE THEY'RE GONNA RAIN AND STUFF.
WOW!
ROBERTS·HARKINS·BLYBERG 10/2

1999

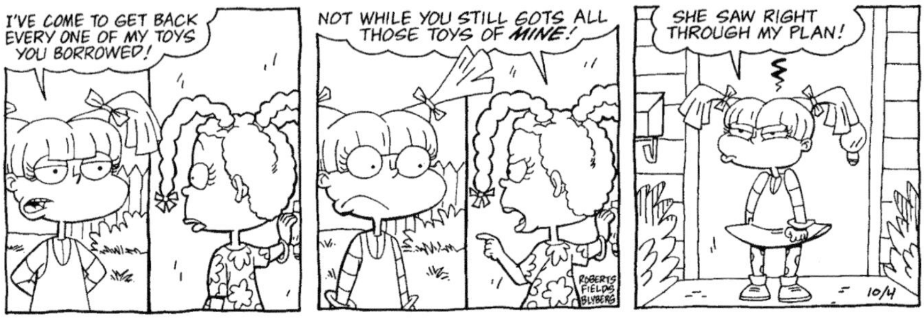
I'VE COME TO GET BACK EVERY ONE OF MY TOYS YOU BORROWED!
NOT WHILE YOU STILL GOTS ALL THOSE TOYS OF MINE!
SHE SAW RIGHT THROUGH MY PLAN!

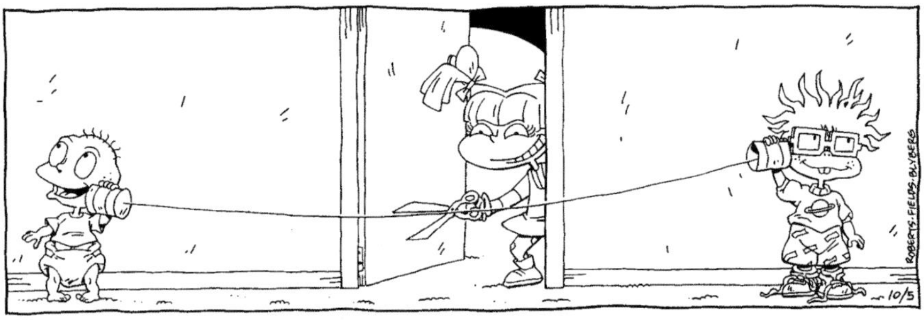

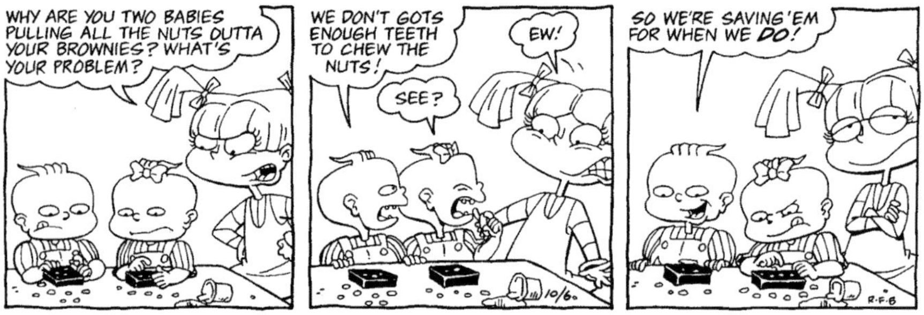
WHY ARE YOU TWO BABIES PULLING ALL THE NUTS OUTTA YOUR BROWNIES? WHAT'S YOUR PROBLEM?
WE DON'T GOTS ENOUGH TEETH TO CHEW THE NUTS!
SEE?
EW!
SO WE'RE SAVING 'EM FOR WHEN WE DO!

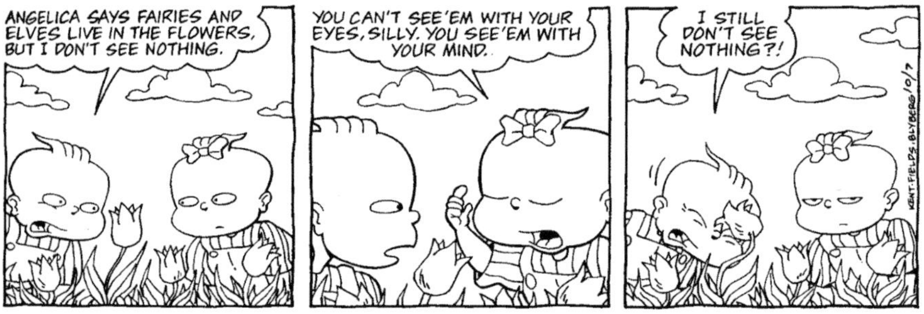
ANGELICA SAYS FAIRIES AND ELVES LIVE IN THE FLOWERS, BUT I DON'T SEE NOTHING.
YOU CAN'T SEE 'EM WITH YOUR EYES, SILLY. YOU SEE 'EM WITH YOUR MIND.
I STILL DON'T SEE NOTHING?!

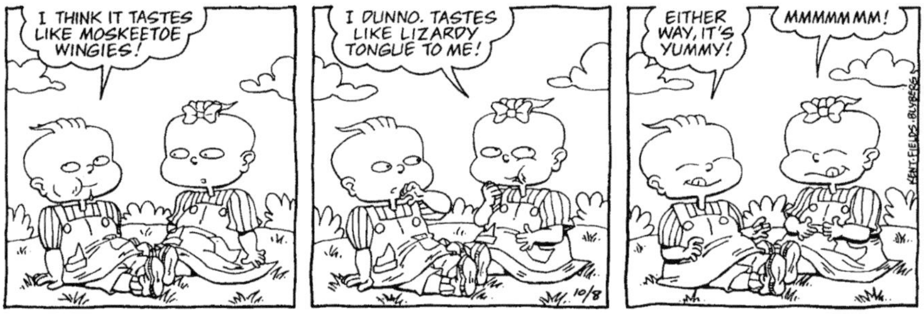
I THINK IT TASTES LIKE MOSKEETOE WINGIES!
I DUNNO. TASTES LIKE LIZARDY TONGUE TO ME!
EITHER WAY, IT'S YUMMY!
MMMMMMM!

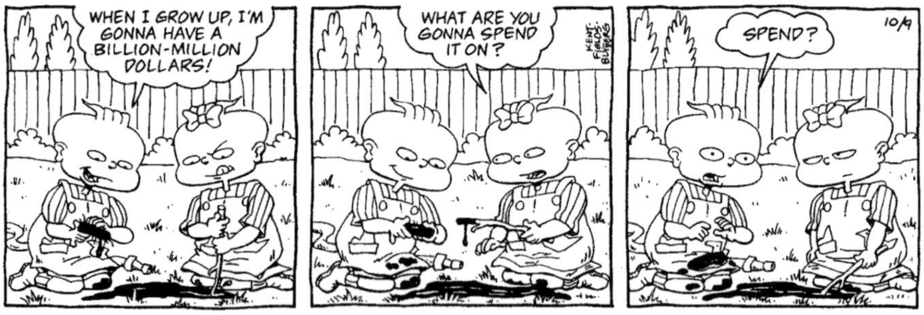
WHEN I GROW UP, I'M GONNA HAVE A BILLION-MILLION DOLLARS!
WHAT ARE YOU GONNA SPEND IT ON?
SPEND?

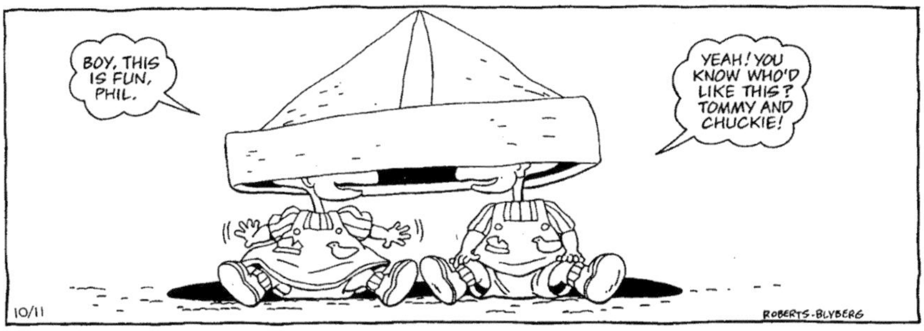
BOY, THIS IS FUN, PHIL.
YEAH! YOU KNOW WHO'D LIKE THIS? TOMMY AND CHUCKIE!
10/11
ROBERTS-BLYBERG

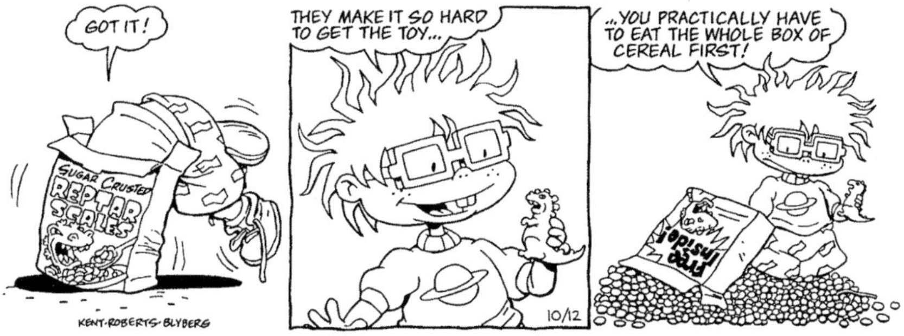
GOT IT!
SUGAR CRUSTED REPTAR SCALES
KENT-ROBERTS-BLYBERG
THEY MAKE IT SO HARD TO GET THE TOY...
10/12
...YOU PRACTICALLY HAVE TO EAT THE WHOLE BOX OF CEREAL FIRST!
Free Inside!

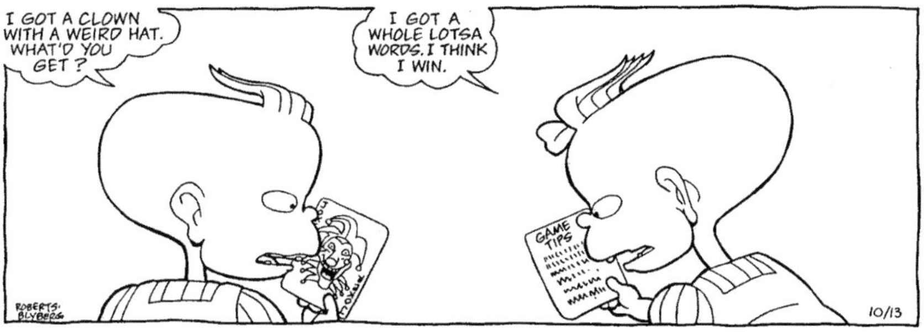
I GOT A CLOWN WITH A WEIRD HAT. WHAT'D YOU GET?
I GOT A WHOLE LOTSA WORDS. I THINK I WIN.
GAME TIPS
ROBERTS-BLYBERG
10/13

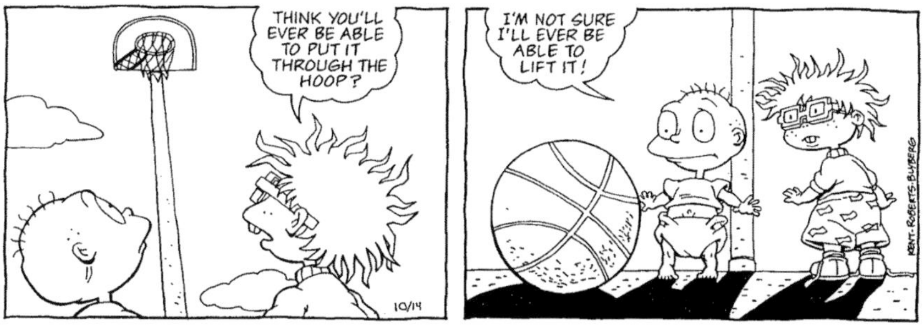
THINK YOU'LL EVER BE ABLE TO PUT IT THROUGH THE HOOP?
10/14
I'M NOT SURE I'LL EVER BE ABLE TO LIFT IT!
KENT-ROBERTS-BLYBERG

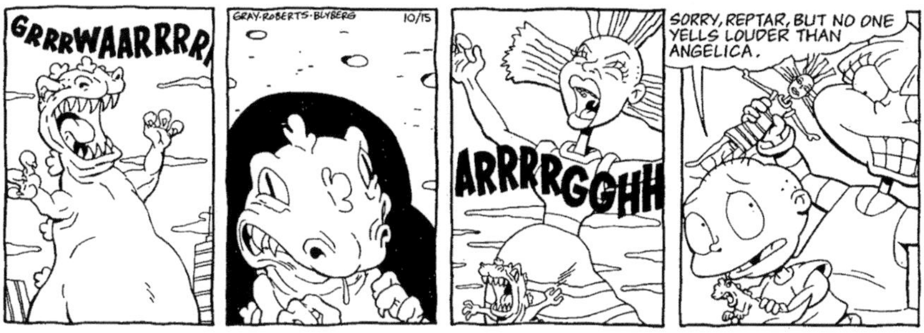
GRRRWAARRRR
GRAY-ROBERTS-BLYBERG
10/15
ARRRRGGHH
SORRY, REPTAR, BUT NO ONE YELLS LOUDER THAN ANGELICA.

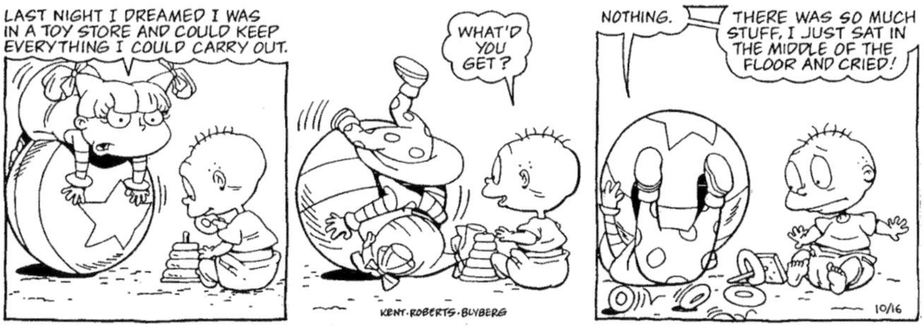
LAST NIGHT I DREAMED I WAS IN A TOY STORE AND COULD KEEP EVERYTHING I COULD CARRY OUT.
WHAT'D YOU GET?
KENT-ROBERTS-BLYBERG
NOTHING.
THERE WAS SO MUCH STUFF, I JUST SAT IN THE MIDDLE OF THE FLOOR AND CRIED!
10/16

1999

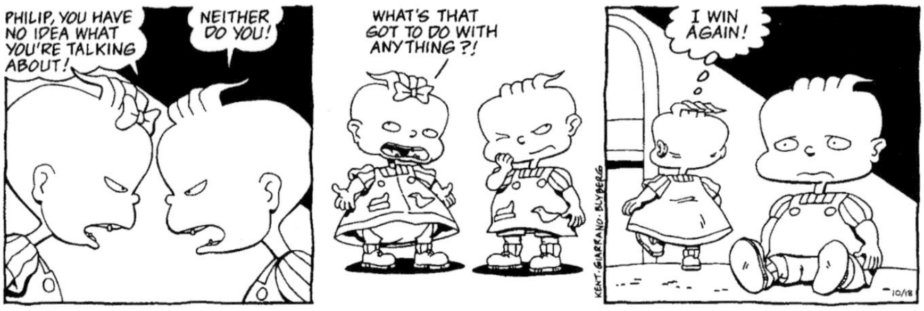
PHILIP, YOU HAVE NO IDEA WHAT YOU'RE TALKING ABOUT!
NEITHER DO YOU!
WHAT'S THAT GOT TO DO WITH ANYTHING?!
I WIN AGAIN!
KENT·GIARRANO·BLYBERG
10/18

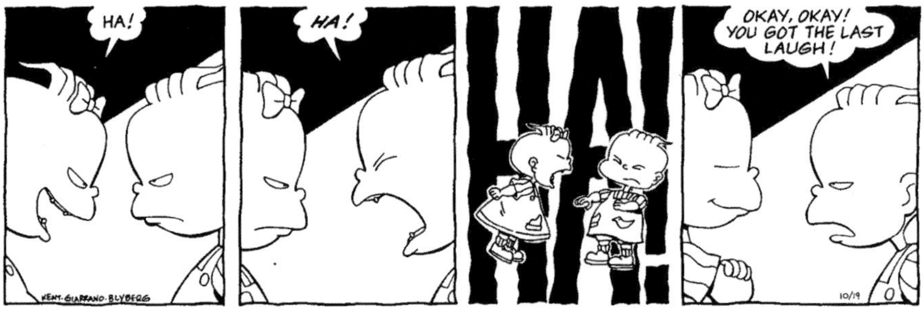
HA!
HA!
HA!
OKAY, OKAY! YOU GOT THE LAST LAUGH!
KENT·GIARRANO·BLYBERG
10/19

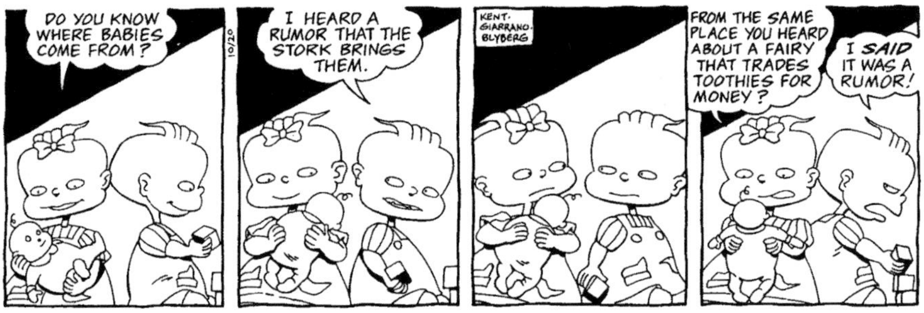
DO YOU KNOW WHERE BABIES COME FROM?
10/20
I HEARD A RUMOR THAT THE STORK BRINGS THEM.
KENT·GIARRANO·BLYBERG
FROM THE SAME PLACE YOU HEARD ABOUT A FAIRY THAT TRADES TOOTHIES FOR MONEY?
I SAID IT WAS A RUMOR!

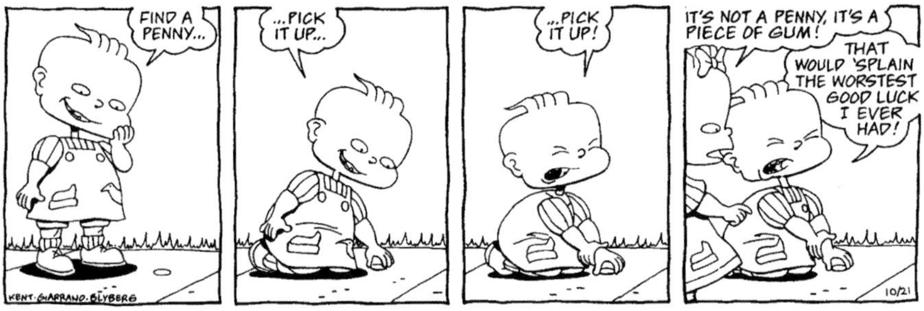
FIND A PENNY...
KENT·GIARRANO·BLYBERG
...PICK IT UP...
...PICK IT UP!
IT'S NOT A PENNY, IT'S A PIECE OF GUM!
THAT WOULD 'SPLAIN THE WORSTEST GOOD LUCK I EVER HAD!
10/21

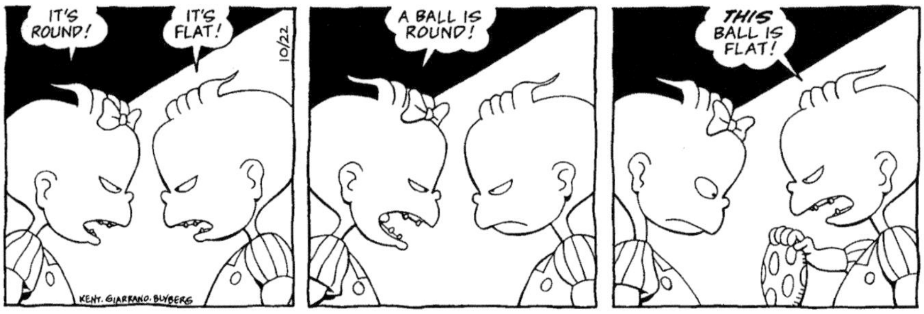
IT'S ROUND!
IT'S FLAT!
10/22
KENT·GIARRANO·BLYBERG
A BALL IS ROUND!
THIS BALL IS FLAT!

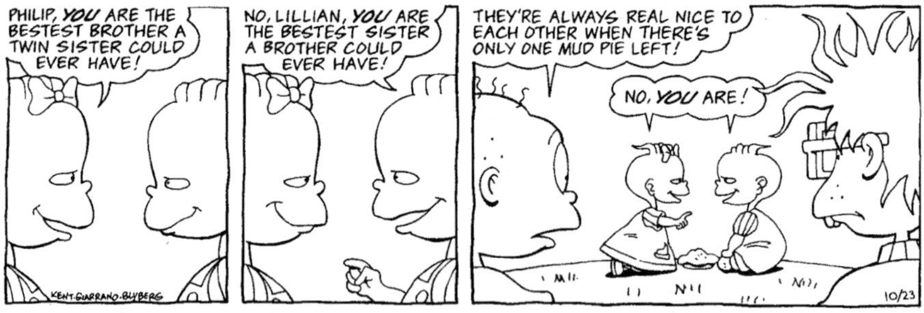
PHILIP, YOU ARE THE BESTEST BROTHER A TWIN SISTER COULD EVER HAVE!
KENT·GIARRANO·BLYBERG
NO, LILLIAN, YOU ARE THE BESTEST SISTER A BROTHER COULD EVER HAVE!
THEY'RE ALWAYS REAL NICE TO EACH OTHER WHEN THERE'S ONLY ONE MUD PIE LEFT!
NO, YOU ARE!
10/23

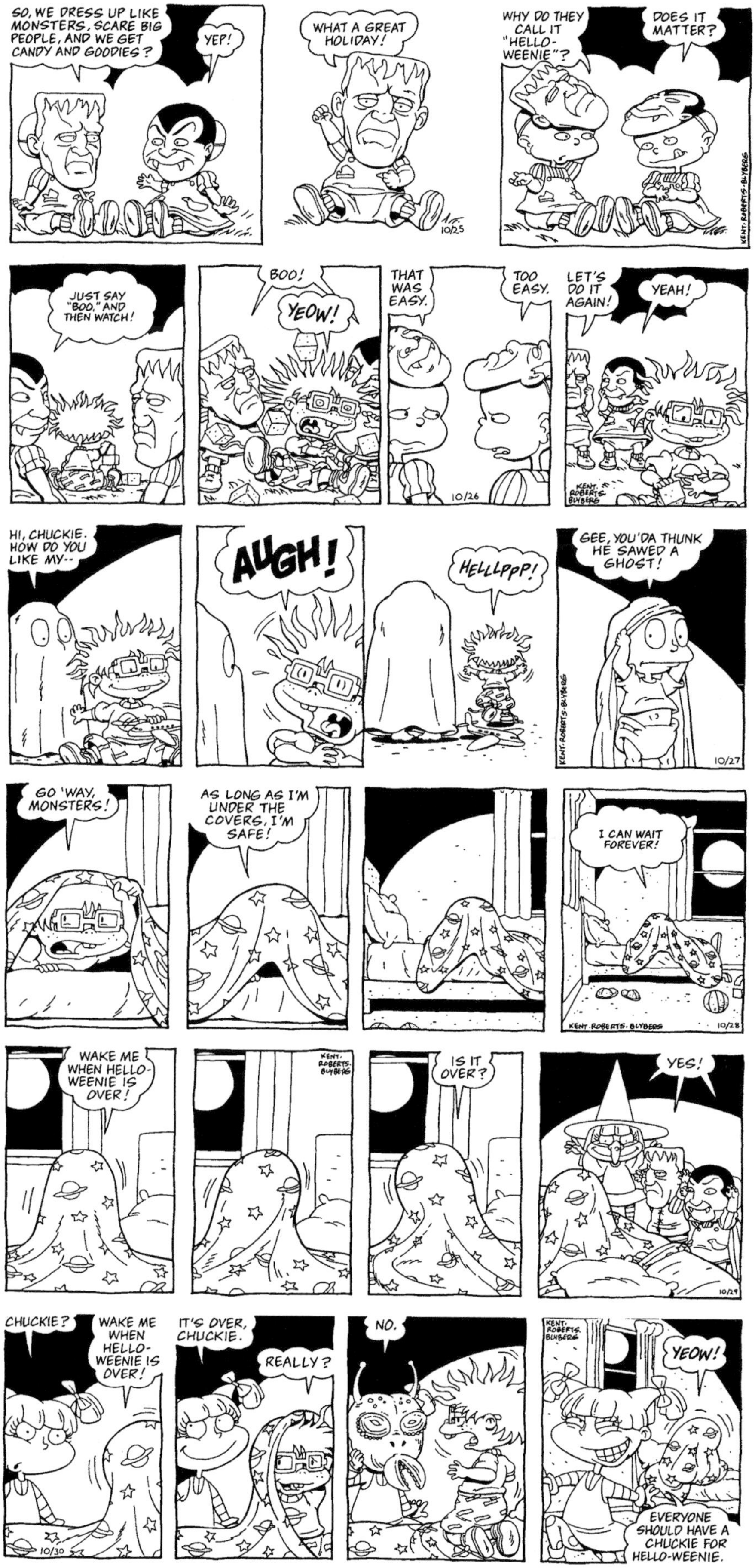
SO, WE DRESS UP LIKE MONSTERS, SCARE BIG PEOPLE, AND WE GET CANDY AND GOODIES?
YEP!
WHAT A GREAT HOLIDAY!
10/25
WHY DO THEY CALL IT "HELLO-WEENIE"?
DOES IT MATTER?
KENT·ROBERTS·BLYBERG
JUST SAY "BOO," AND THEN WATCH!
BOO!
YEOW!
THAT WAS EASY.
TOO EASY.
10/26
LET'S DO IT AGAIN!
YEAH!
KENT·ROBERTS·BLYBERG
HI, CHUCKIE. HOW DO YOU LIKE MY--
AUGH!
HELLLPPP!
KENT·ROBERTS·BLYBERG
GEE, YOU'DA THUNK HE SAWED A GHOST!
10/27
GO 'WAY, MONSTERS!
AS LONG AS I'M UNDER THE COVERS, I'M SAFE!
I CAN WAIT FOREVER!
KENT·ROBERTS·BLYBERG
10/28
WAKE ME WHEN HELLO-WEENIE IS OVER!
KENT·ROBERTS·BLYBERG
IS IT OVER?
YES!
10/29
CHUCKIE?
WAKE ME WHEN HELLO-WEENIE IS OVER!
10/30
IT'S OVER, CHUCKIE.
REALLY?
NO.
KENT·ROBERTS·BLYBERG
YEOW!
EVERYONE SHOULD HAVE A CHUCKIE FOR HELLO-WEENIE.

1999

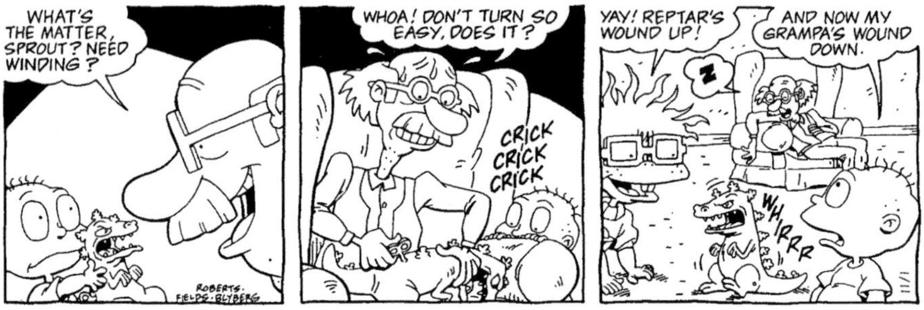
WHAT'S THE MATTER, SPROUT? NEED WINDING?
ROBERTS. FIELDS.BLYBERG
WHOA! DON'T TURN SO EASY, DOES IT?
CRICK CRICK CRICK
YAY! REPTAR'S WOUND UP!
AND NOW MY GRAMPA'S WOUND DOWN.
Z
WHIRRR

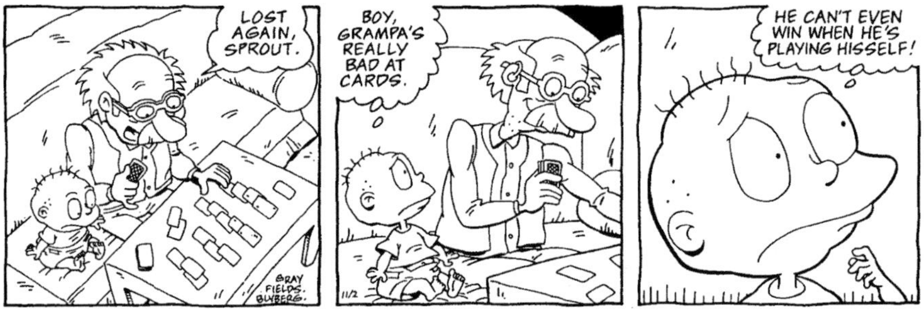
LOST AGAIN, SPROUT.
GRAY FIELDS. BLYBERG.
BOY, GRAMPA'S REALLY BAD AT CARDS.
11/2
HE CAN'T EVEN WIN WHEN HE'S PLAYING HISSELF!

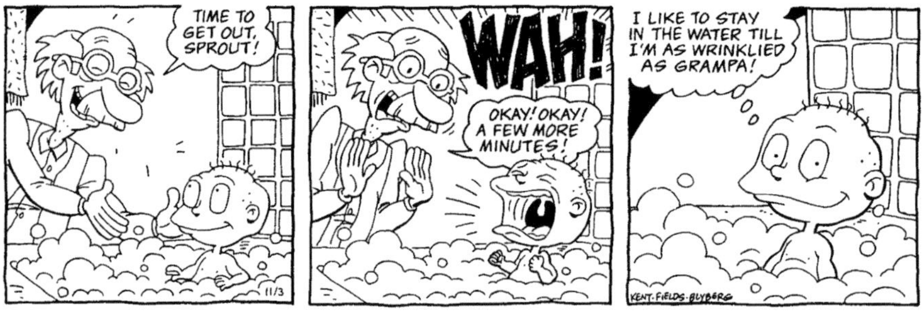
TIME TO GET OUT, SPROUT!
11/3
WAH!
OKAY! OKAY! A FEW MORE MINUTES!
I LIKE TO STAY IN THE WATER TILL I'M AS WRINKLIED AS GRAMPA!
KENT.FIELDS.BLYBERG

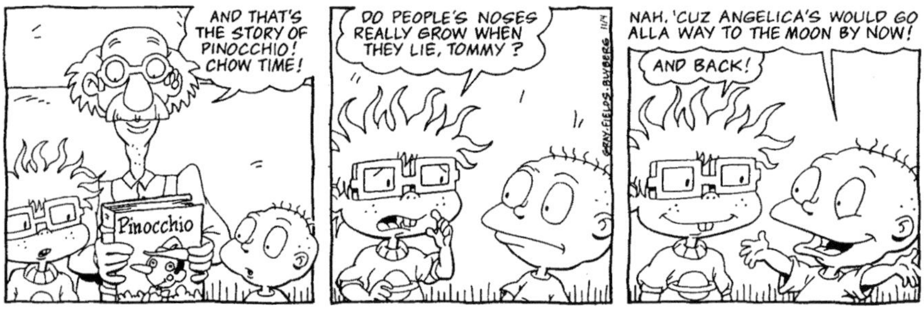
AND THAT'S THE STORY OF PINOCCHIO! CHOW TIME!
Pinocchio
DO PEOPLE'S NOSES REALLY GROW WHEN THEY LIE, TOMMY?
GRAY.FIELDS.BLYBERG 11/4
NAH. 'CUZ ANGELICA'S WOULD GO ALLA WAY TO THE MOON BY NOW!
AND BACK!

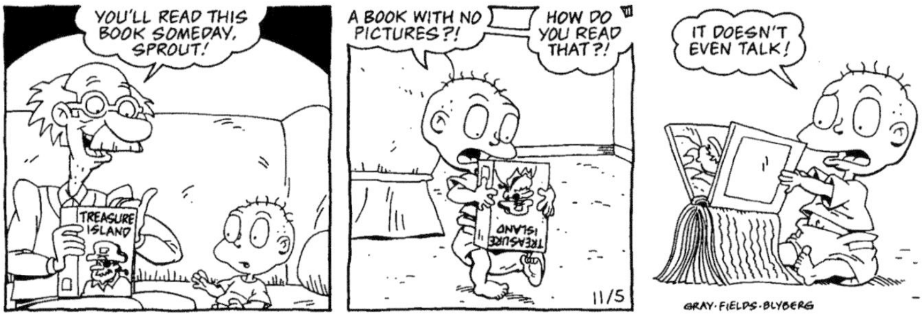
YOU'LL READ THIS BOOK SOMEDAY, SPROUT!
TREASURE ISLAND
A BOOK WITH NO PICTURES?!
HOW DO YOU READ THAT?!
11/5
IT DOESN'T EVEN TALK!
GRAY.FIELDS.BLYBERG

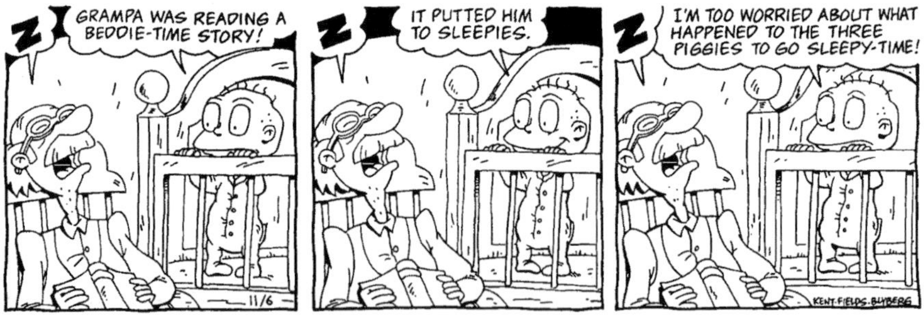
Z
GRAMPA WAS READING A BEDDIE-TIME STORY!
11/6
Z
IT PUTTED HIM TO SLEEPIES.
Z
I'M TOO WORRIED ABOUT WHAT HAPPENED TO THE THREE PIGGIES TO GO SLEEPY-TIME!
KENT.FIELDS.BLYBERG

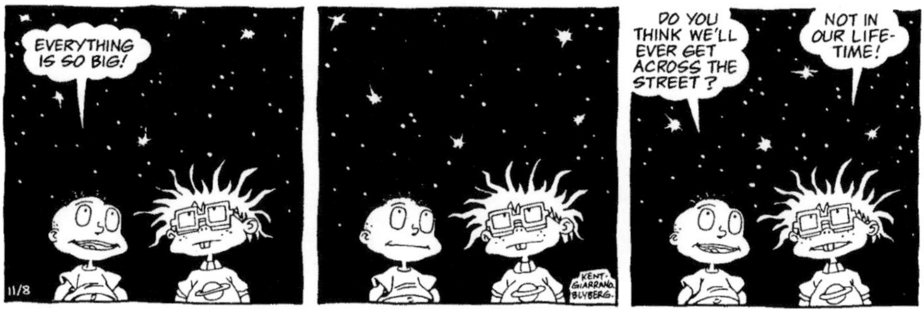
EVERYTHING IS SO BIG!
11/8
KENT. GIARRANO. BLYBERG.
DO YOU THINK WE'LL EVER GET ACROSS THE STREET?
NOT IN OUR LIFE-TIME!

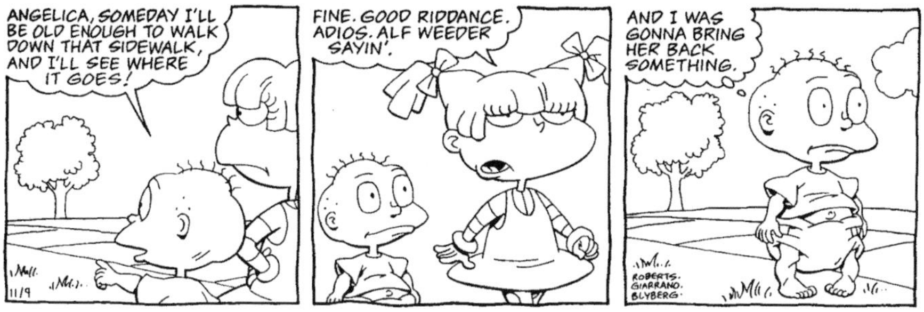
ANGELICA, SOMEDAY I'LL BE OLD ENOUGH TO WALK DOWN THAT SIDEWALK, AND I'LL SEE WHERE IT GOES!
11/9
FINE. GOOD RIDDANCE. ADIOS. ALF WEEDER SAYIN'.
AND I WAS GONNA BRING HER BACK SOMETHING.
ROBERTS. GIARRANO. BLYBERG.

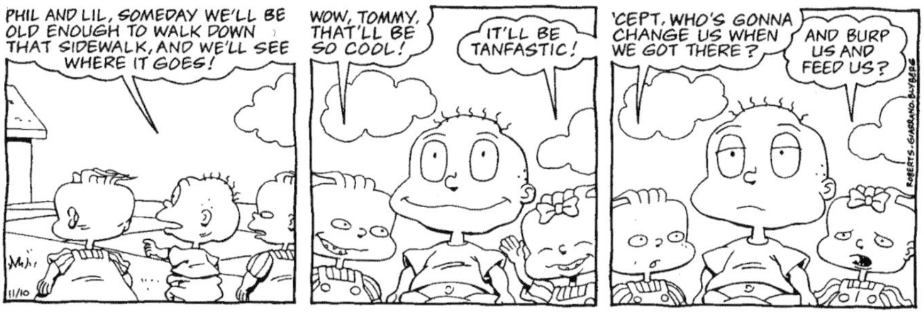
PHIL AND LIL, SOMEDAY WE'LL BE OLD ENOUGH TO WALK DOWN THAT SIDEWALK, AND WE'LL SEE WHERE IT GOES!
11/10
WOW, TOMMY. THAT'LL BE SO COOL!
IT'LL BE TANFASTIC!
'CEPT, WHO'S GONNA CHANGE US WHEN WE GOT THERE?
AND BURP US AND FEED US?
ROBERTS. GIARRANO. BLYBERG

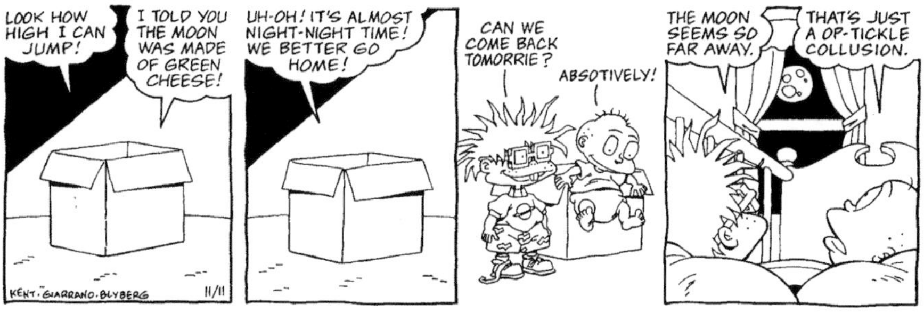
LOOK HOW HIGH I CAN JUMP!
I TOLD YOU THE MOON WAS MADE OF GREEN CHEESE!
KENT. GIARRANO. BLYBERG
11/11
UH-OH! IT'S ALMOST NIGHT-NIGHT TIME! WE BETTER GO HOME!
CAN WE COME BACK TOMORRIE?
ABSOTIVELY!
THE MOON SEEMS SO FAR AWAY.
THAT'S JUST A OP-TICKLE COLLUSION.

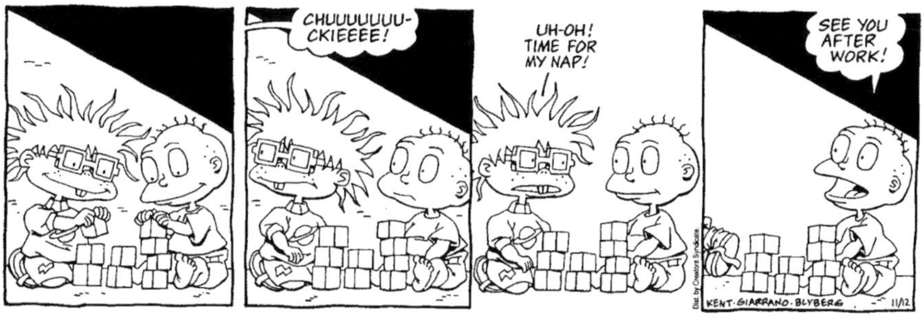
CHUUUUUUU-CKIEEEE!
UH-OH! TIME FOR MY NAP!
SEE YOU AFTER WORK!
Dist. by Creators Syndicate
KENT. GIARRANO. BLYBERG
11/12

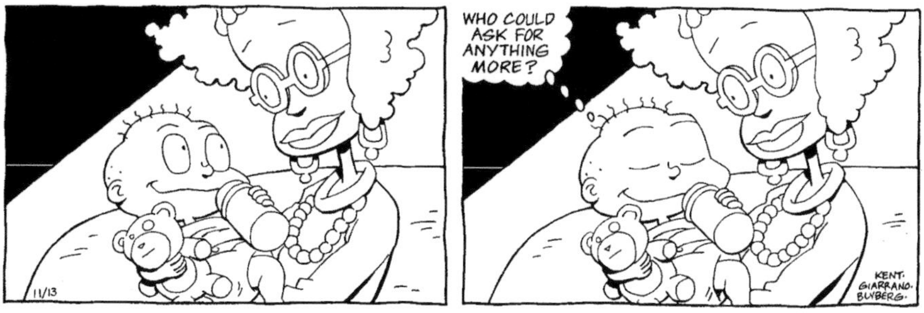
11/13
WHO COULD ASK FOR ANYTHING MORE?
KENT. GIARRANO. BLYBERG.

1999

1999

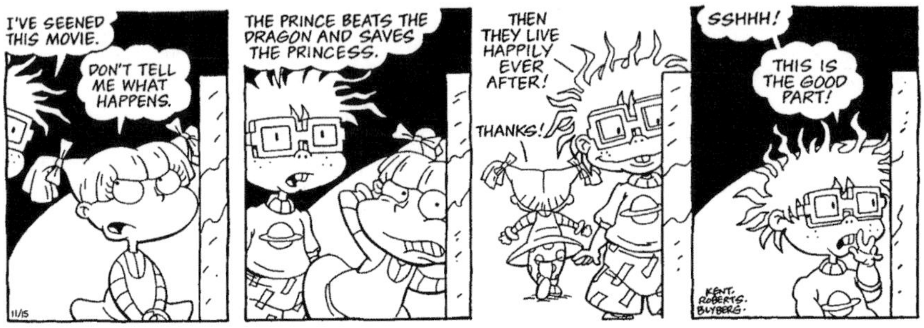
I'VE SEENED THIS MOVIE.
DON'T TELL ME WHAT HAPPENS.
THE PRINCE BEATS THE DRAGON AND SAVES THE PRINCESS.
THEN THEY LIVE HAPPILY EVER AFTER!
THANKS!
SSHHH!
THIS IS THE GOOD PART!
KENT. ROBERTS. BLYBERG.
11/15

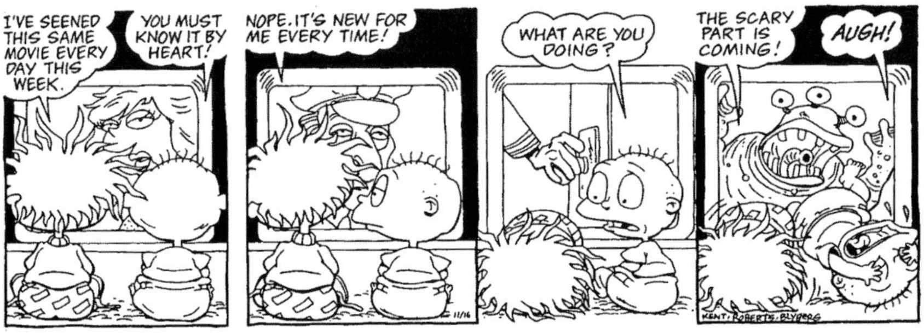
I'VE SEENED THIS SAME MOVIE EVERY DAY THIS WEEK.
YOU MUST KNOW IT BY HEART!
NOPE. IT'S NEW FOR ME EVERY TIME!
WHAT ARE YOU DOING?
THE SCARY PART IS COMING!
AUGH!
11/16
KENT. ROBERTS. BLYBERG

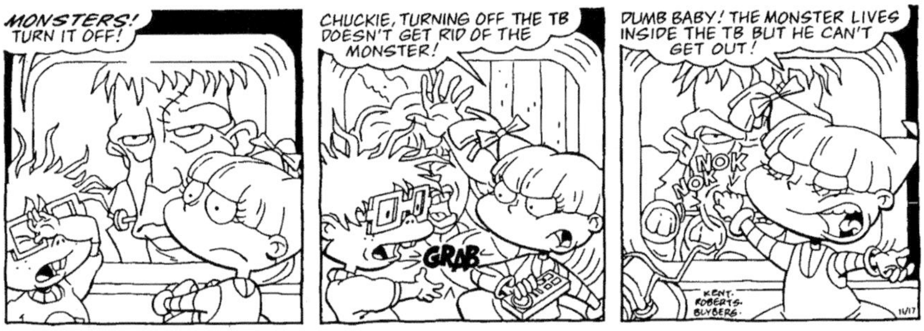
MONSTERS! TURN IT OFF!
CHUCKIE, TURNING OFF THE TB DOESN'T GET RID OF THE MONSTER!
GRAB
DUMB BABY! THE MONSTER LIVES INSIDE THE TB BUT HE CAN'T GET OUT!
NOK NOK
KENT. ROBERTS. BLYBERG.
11/17

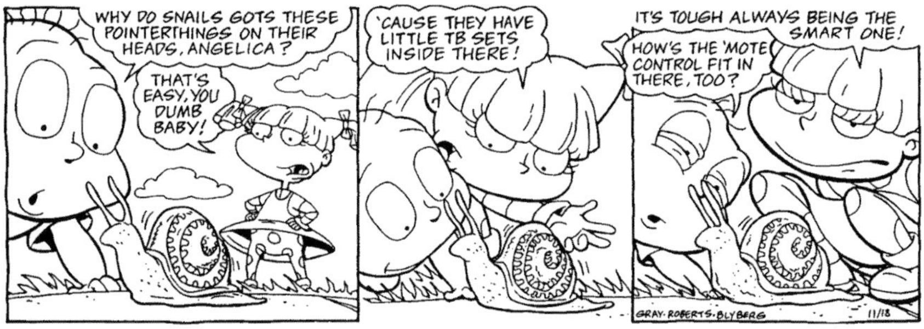
WHY DO SNAILS GOTS THESE POINTERTHINGS ON THEIR HEADS, ANGELICA?
THAT'S EASY, YOU DUMB BABY!
'CAUSE THEY HAVE LITTLE TB SETS INSIDE THERE!
HOW'S THE 'MOTE CONTROL FIT IN THERE, TOO?
IT'S TOUGH ALWAYS BEING THE SMART ONE!
GRAY. ROBERTS. BLYBERG
11/18

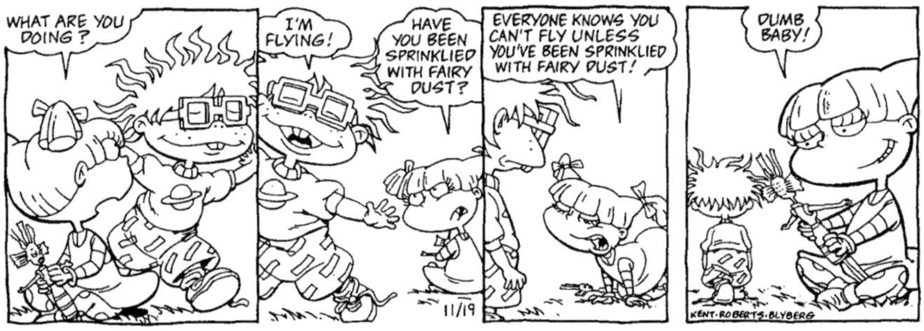
WHAT ARE YOU DOING?
I'M FLYING!
HAVE YOU BEEN SPRINKLIED WITH FAIRY DUST?
EVERYONE KNOWS YOU CAN'T FLY UNLESS YOU'VE BEEN SPRINKLIED WITH FAIRY DUST!
DUMB BABY!
11/19
KENT. ROBERTS. BLYBERG

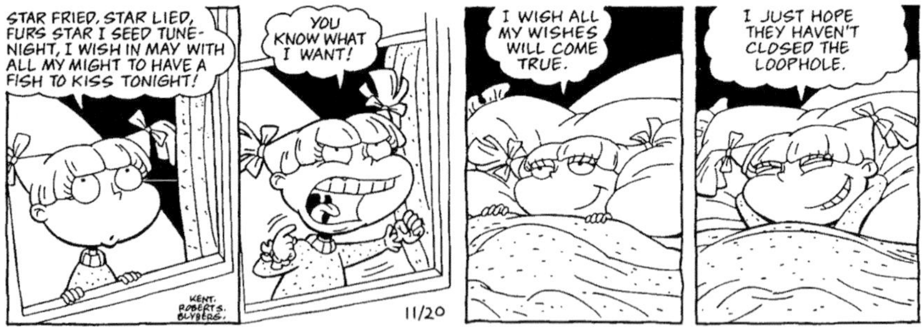
STAR FRIED, STAR LIED, FURS STAR I SEED TUNE-NIGHT, I WISH IN MAY WITH ALL MY MIGHT TO HAVE A FISH TO KISS TONIGHT!
YOU KNOW WHAT I WANT!
I WISH ALL MY WISHES WILL COME TRUE.
I JUST HOPE THEY HAVEN'T CLOSED THE LOOPHOLE.
KENT. ROBERTS. BLYBERG.
11/20

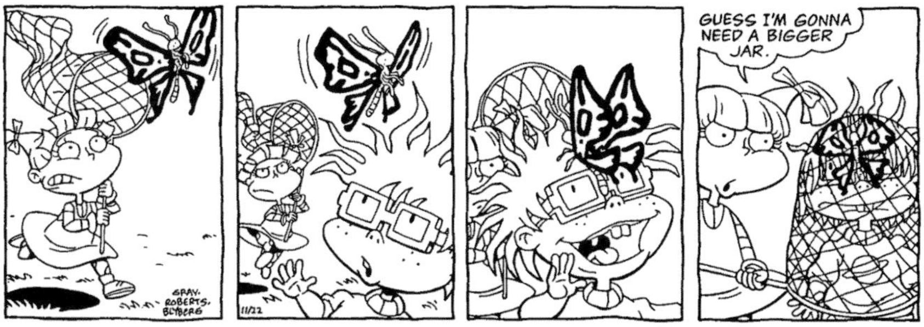
GRAY. ROBERTS. BLYBERG
11/22
GUESS I'M GONNA NEED A BIGGER JAR.

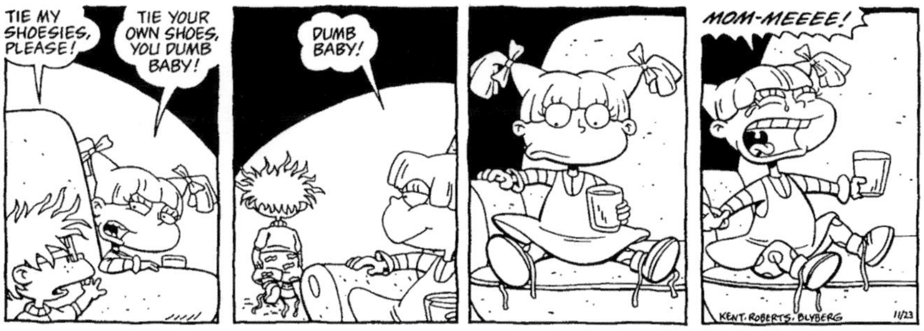
TIE MY SHOESIES, PLEASE!
TIE YOUR OWN SHOES, YOU DUMB BABY!
DUMB BABY!
MOM-MEEEE!
KENT. ROBERTS. BLYBERG
11/23

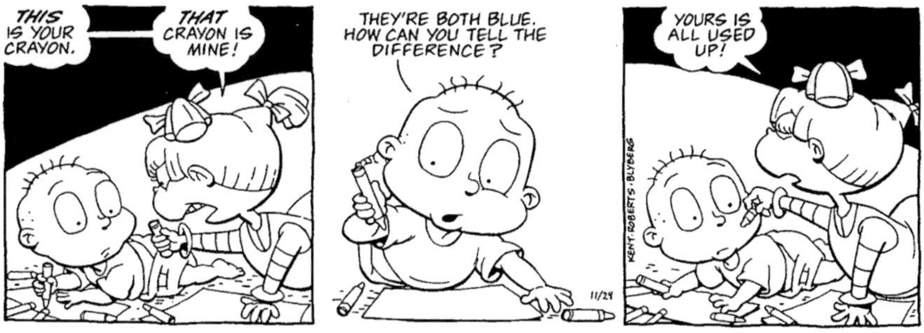
THIS IS YOUR CRAYON.
THAT CRAYON IS MINE!
THEY'RE BOTH BLUE. HOW CAN YOU TELL THE DIFFERENCE?
11/24
KENT. ROBERTS. BLYBERG
YOURS IS ALL USED UP!

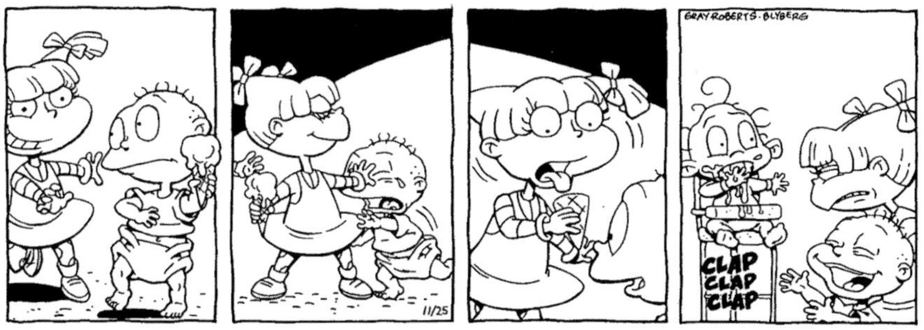
11/25
GRAY. ROBERTS. BLYBERG
CLAP
CLAP
CLAP

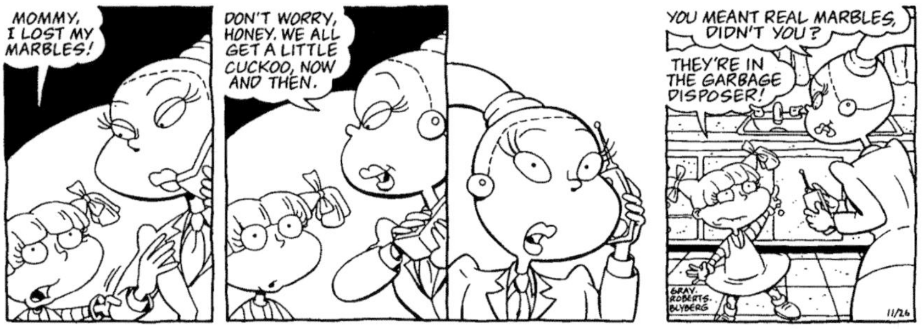
MOMMY, I LOST MY MARBLES!
DON'T WORRY, HONEY. WE ALL GET A LITTLE CUCKOO, NOW AND THEN.
YOU MEANT REAL MARBLES, DIDN'T YOU?
THEY'RE IN THE GARBAGE DISPOSER!
GRAY. ROBERTS. BLYBERG
11/26

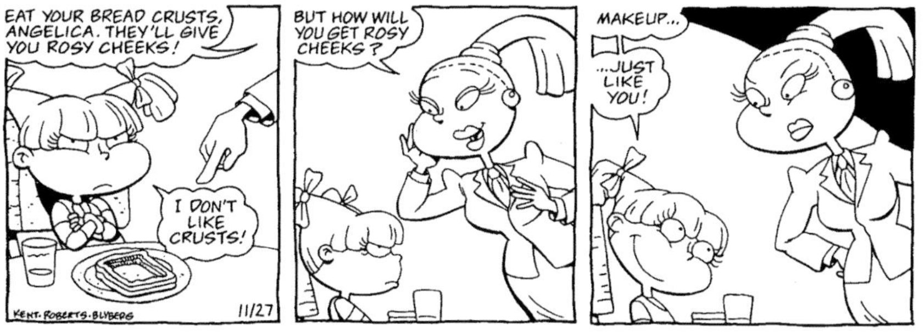
EAT YOUR BREAD CRUSTS, ANGELICA. THEY'LL GIVE YOU ROSY CHEEKS!
I DON'T LIKE CRUSTS!
KENT. ROBERTS. BLYBERG
11/27
BUT HOW WILL YOU GET ROSY CHEEKS?
MAKEUP...
...JUST LIKE YOU!

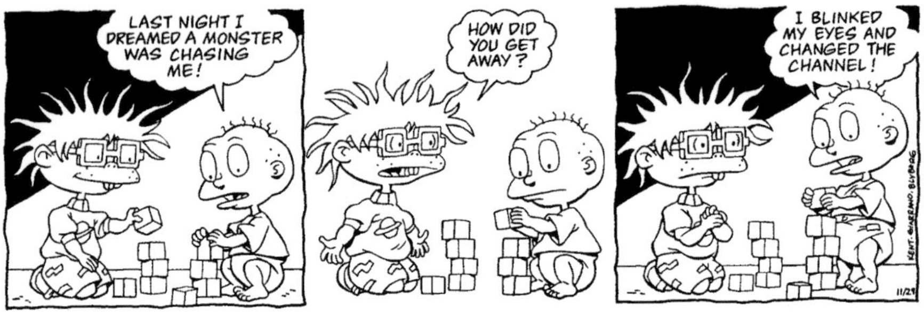
LAST NIGHT I DREAMED A MONSTER WAS CHASING ME!
HOW DID YOU GET AWAY?
I BLINKED MY EYES AND CHANGED THE CHANNEL!
11/29

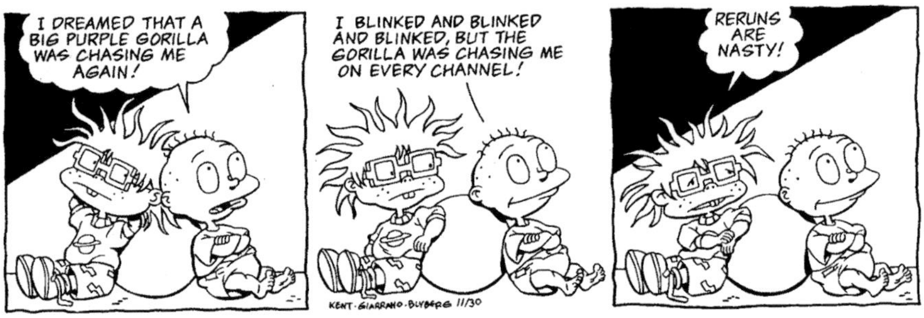
I DREAMED THAT A BIG PURPLE GORILLA WAS CHASING ME AGAIN!
I BLINKED AND BLINKED AND BLINKED, BUT THE GORILLA WAS CHASING ME ON EVERY CHANNEL!
KENT·GIARRANO·BLYBERG 11/30
RERUNS ARE NASTY!

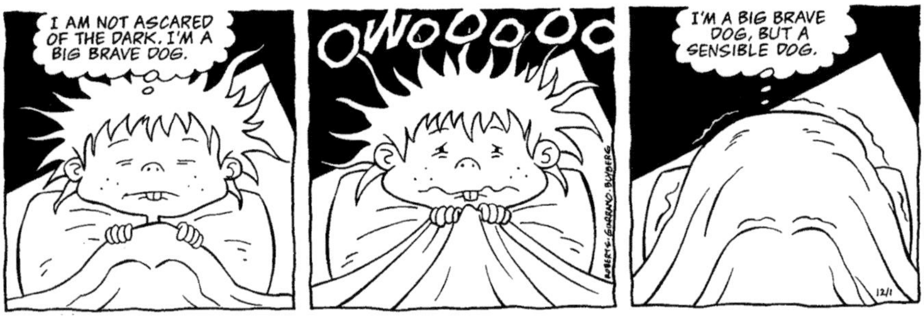
I AM NOT ASCARED OF THE DARK. I'M A BIG BRAVE DOG.
OWOOOOO
I'M A BIG BRAVE DOG, BUT A SENSIBLE DOG.
12/1

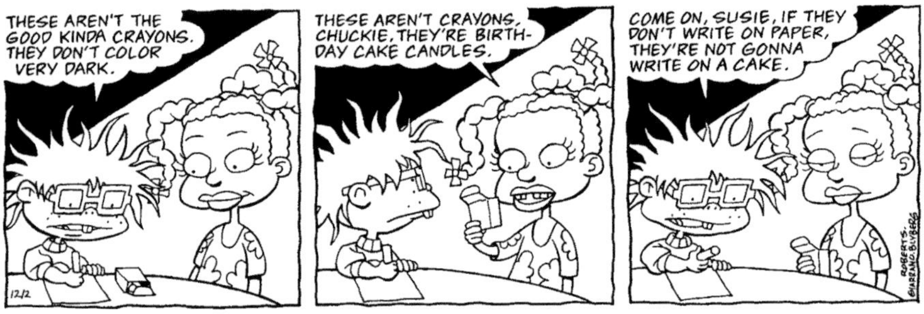
THESE AREN'T THE GOOD KINDA CRAYONS. THEY DON'T COLOR VERY DARK.
12/2
THESE AREN'T CRAYONS, CHUCKIE. THEY'RE BIRTHDAY CAKE CANDLES.
COME ON, SUSIE, IF THEY DON'T WRITE ON PAPER, THEY'RE NOT GONNA WRITE ON A CAKE.

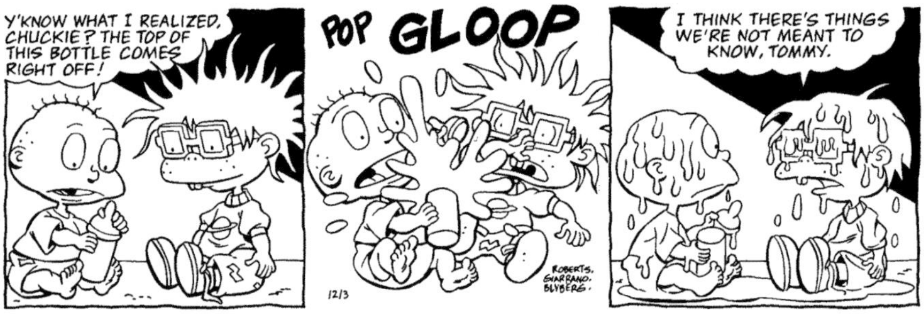
Y'KNOW WHAT I REALIZED, CHUCKIE? THE TOP OF THIS BOTTLE COMES RIGHT OFF!
POP GLOOP
12/3
ROBERTS. GIARRANO. BLYBERG.
I THINK THERE'S THINGS WE'RE NOT MEANT TO KNOW, TOMMY.

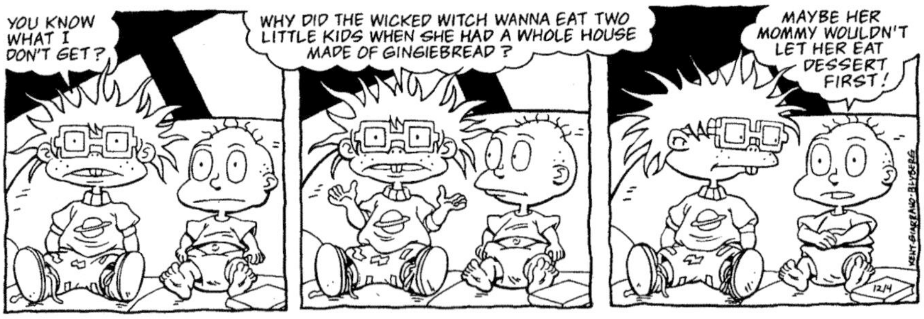
YOU KNOW WHAT I DON'T GET?
WHY DID THE WICKED WITCH WANNA EAT TWO LITTLE KIDS WHEN SHE HAD A WHOLE HOUSE MADE OF GINGIEBREAD?
MAYBE HER MOMMY WOULDN'T LET HER EAT DESSERT FIRST!
12/4

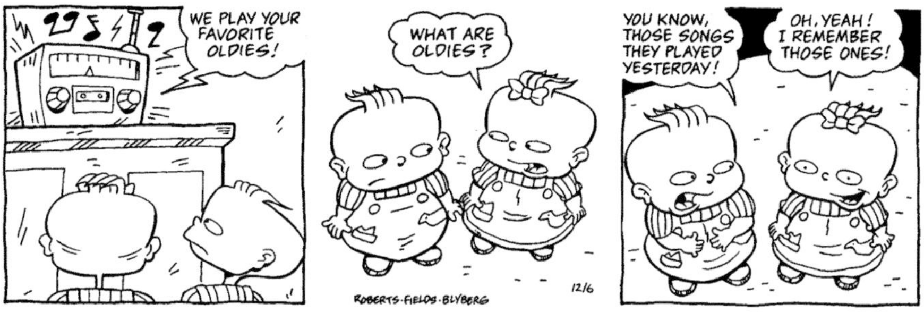
WE PLAY YOUR FAVORITE OLDIES!
WHAT ARE OLDIES?
YOU KNOW, THOSE SONGS THEY PLAYED YESTERDAY!
OH, YEAH! I REMEMBER THOSE ONES!
ROBERTS·FIELDS·BLYBERG
12/6

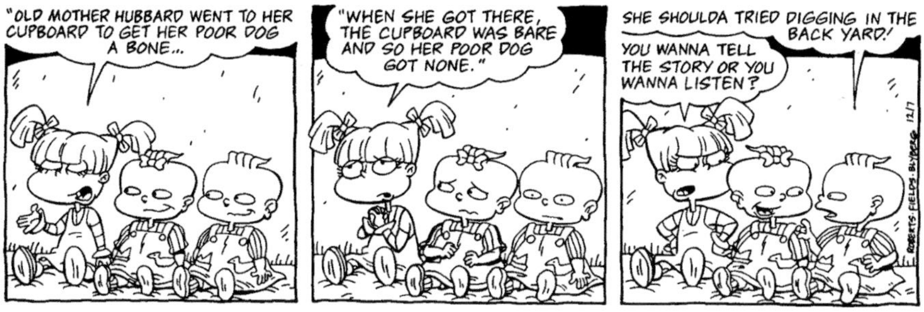
"OLD MOTHER HUBBARD WENT TO HER CUPBOARD TO GET HER POOR DOG A BONE...
"WHEN SHE GOT THERE, THE CUPBOARD WAS BARE AND SO HER POOR DOG GOT NONE."
SHE SHOULDA TRIED DIGGING IN THE BACK YARD!
YOU WANNA TELL THE STORY OR YOU WANNA LISTEN?
ROBERTS·FIELDS·BLYBERG
12/7

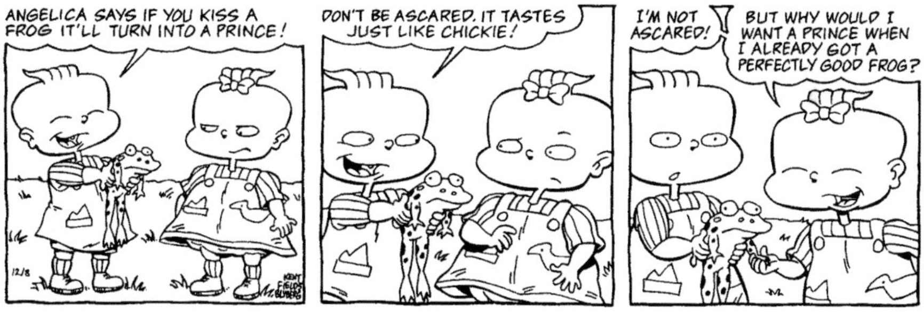
ANGELICA SAYS IF YOU KISS A FROG IT'LL TURN INTO A PRINCE!
12/8
DON'T BE ASCARED. IT TASTES JUST LIKE CHICKIE!
I'M NOT ASCARED!
BUT WHY WOULD I WANT A PRINCE WHEN I ALREADY GOT A PERFECTLY GOOD FROG?

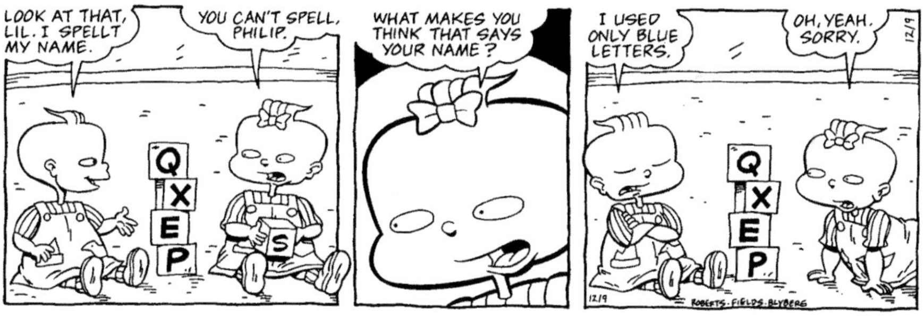
LOOK AT THAT, LIL. I SPELLT MY NAME.
YOU CAN'T SPELL, PHILIP.
Q
X
E
P
S
WHAT MAKES YOU THINK THAT SAYS YOUR NAME?
I USED ONLY BLUE LETTERS.
OH, YEAH. SORRY.
12/9
ROBERTS·FIELDS·BLYBERG

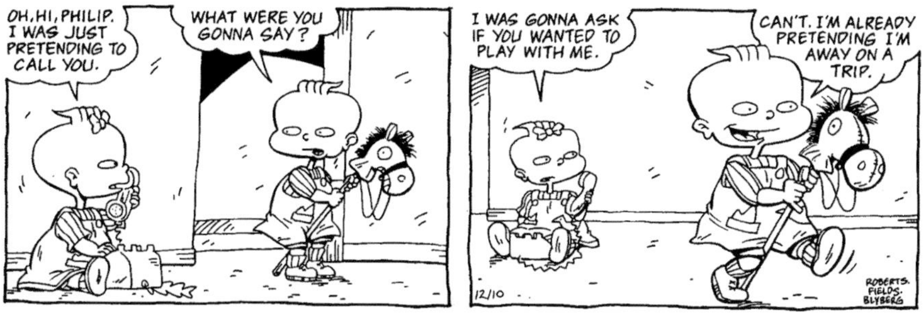
OH, HI, PHILIP. I WAS JUST PRETENDING TO CALL YOU.
WHAT WERE YOU GONNA SAY?
I WAS GONNA ASK IF YOU WANTED TO PLAY WITH ME.
CAN'T. I'M ALREADY PRETENDING I'M AWAY ON A TRIP.
12/10
ROBERTS·FIELDS·BLYBERG

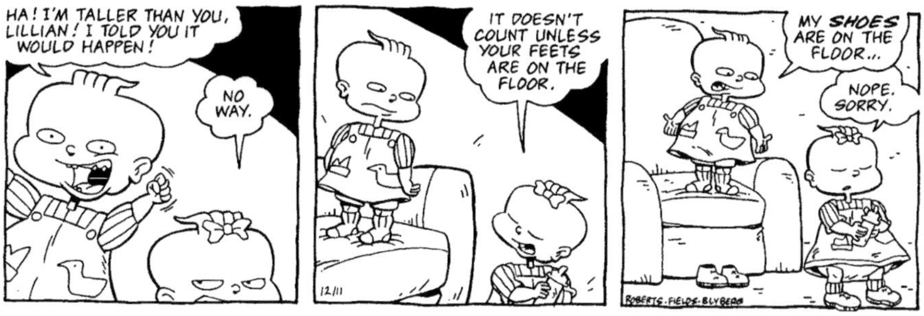
HA! I'M TALLER THAN YOU, LILLIAN! I TOLD YOU IT WOULD HAPPEN!
NO WAY.
IT DOESN'T COUNT UNLESS YOUR FEETS ARE ON THE FLOOR.
12/11
MY SHOES ARE ON THE FLOOR...
NOPE. SORRY.
ROBERTS·FIELDS·BLYBERG

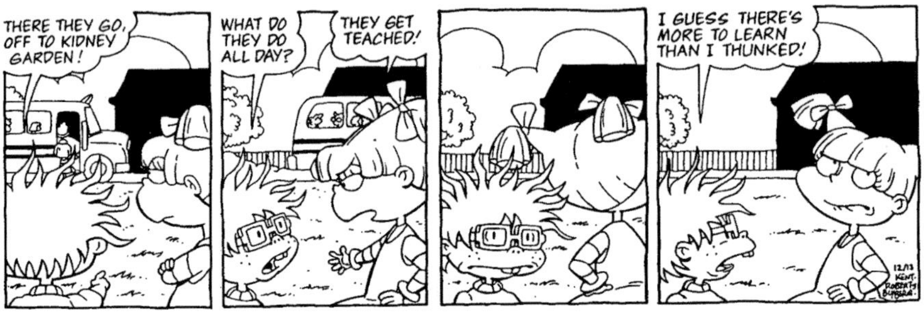
THERE THEY GO, OFF TO KIDNEY GARDEN!
WHAT DO THEY DO ALL DAY?
THEY GET TEACHED!
I GUESS THERE'S MORE TO LEARN THAN I THUNKED!
12/13

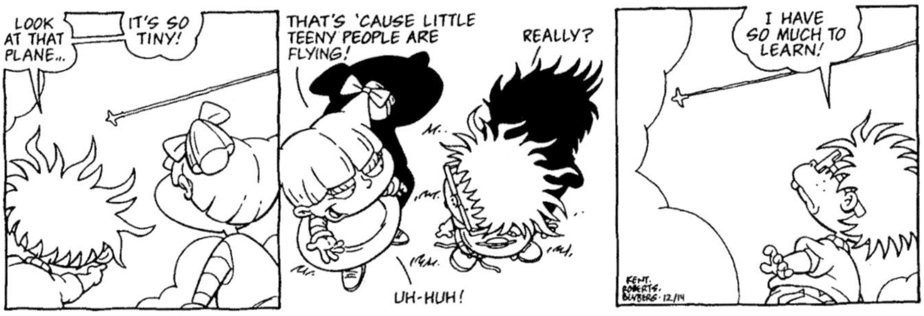
LOOK AT THAT PLANE...
IT'S SO TINY!
THAT'S 'CAUSE LITTLE TEENY PEOPLE ARE FLYING!
REALLY?
UH-HUH!
I HAVE SO MUCH TO LEARN!
KENT. ROBERTS. BLYBERG. 12/14

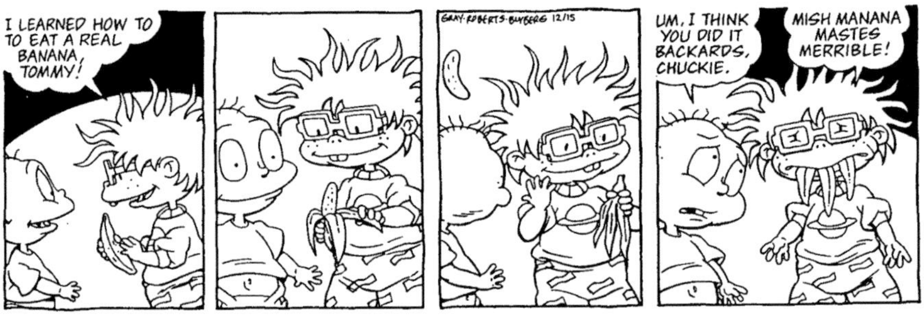
I LEARNED HOW TO TO EAT A REAL BANANA, TOMMY!
GRAY·ROBERTS·BLYBERG 12/15
UM, I THINK YOU DID IT BACKARDS, CHUCKIE.
MISH MANANA MASTES MERRIBLE!

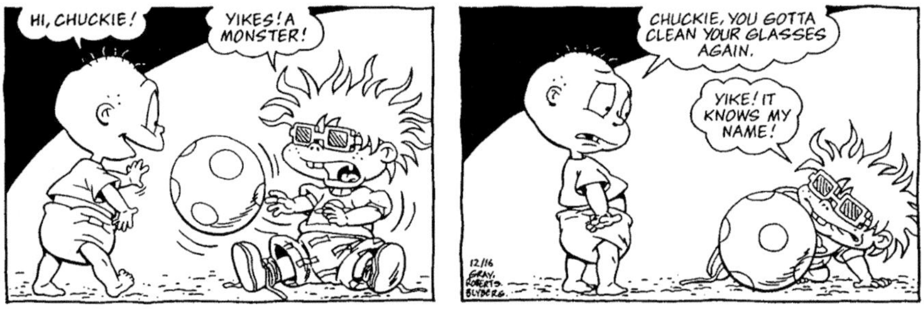
HI, CHUCKIE!
YIKES! A MONSTER!
CHUCKIE, YOU GOTTA CLEAN YOUR GLASSES AGAIN.
YIKE! IT KNOWS MY NAME!
12/16 GRAY. ROBERTS. BLYBERG.

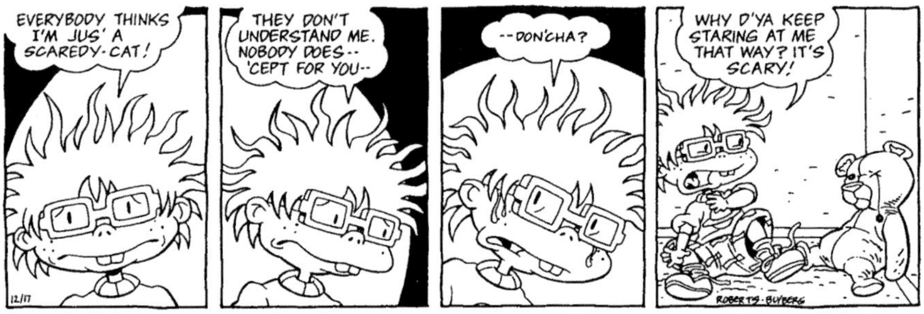
EVERYBODY THINKS I'M JUS' A SCAREDY-CAT!
THEY DON'T UNDERSTAND ME. NOBODY DOES-- 'CEPT FOR YOU--
--DON'CHA?
WHY D'YA KEEP STARING AT ME THAT WAY? IT'S SCARY!
12/17
ROBERTS·BLYBERG

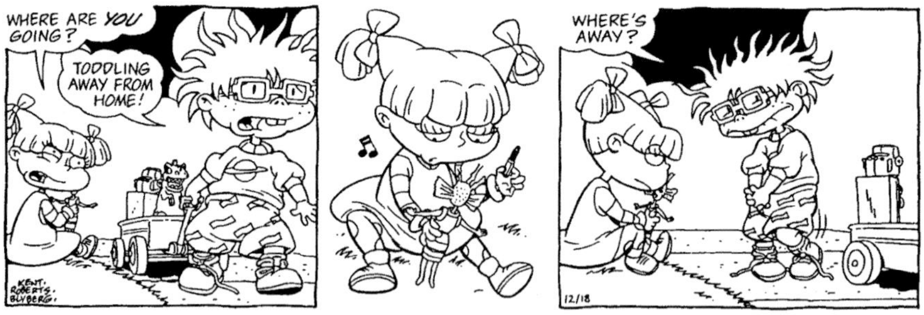
WHERE ARE YOU GOING?
TODDLING AWAY FROM HOME!
WHERE'S AWAY?
KENT. ROBERTS. BLYBERG.
12/18

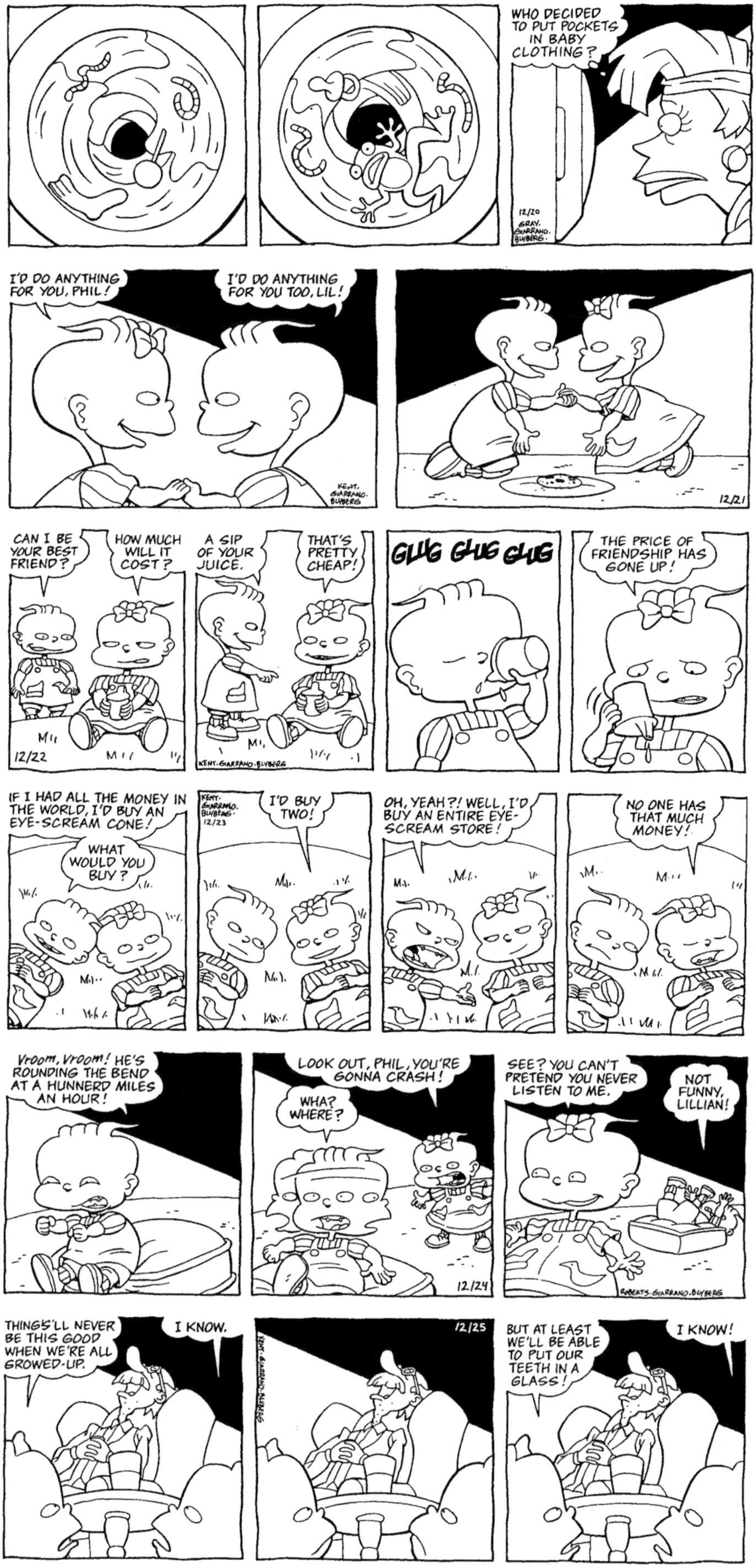
WHO DECIDED TO PUT POCKETS IN BABY CLOTHING?
12/20 GRAY. GIARRANO. BLYBERG.
I'D DO ANYTHING FOR YOU, PHIL!
I'D DO ANYTHING FOR YOU TOO, LIL!
KENT. GIARRANO. BLYBERG
12/21
CAN I BE YOUR BEST FRIEND?
HOW MUCH WILL IT COST?
12/22
A SIP OF YOUR JUICE.
THAT'S PRETTY CHEAP!
KENT. GIARRANO. BLYBERG
GLUG GLUG GLUG
THE PRICE OF FRIENDSHIP HAS GONE UP!
IF I HAD ALL THE MONEY IN THE WORLD, I'D BUY AN EYE-SCREAM CONE!
WHAT WOULD YOU BUY?
KENT. GIARRANO. BLYBERG. 12/23
I'D BUY TWO!
OH, YEAH?! WELL, I'D BUY AN ENTIRE EYE-SCREAM STORE!
NO ONE HAS THAT MUCH MONEY!
Vroom, Vroom! HE'S ROUNDING THE BEND AT A HUNNERD MILES AN HOUR!
LOOK OUT, PHIL, YOU'RE GONNA CRASH!
WHA? WHERE?
12/24
SEE? YOU CAN'T PRETEND YOU NEVER LISTEN TO ME.
NOT FUNNY, LILLIAN!
ROBERTS. GIARRANO. BLYBERG
THING'S'LL NEVER BE THIS GOOD WHEN WE'RE ALL GROWED-UP.
I KNOW.
KENT. GIARRANO. BLYBERG
12/25
BUT AT LEAST WE'LL BE ABLE TO PUT OUR TEETH IN A GLASS!
I KNOW!

1999

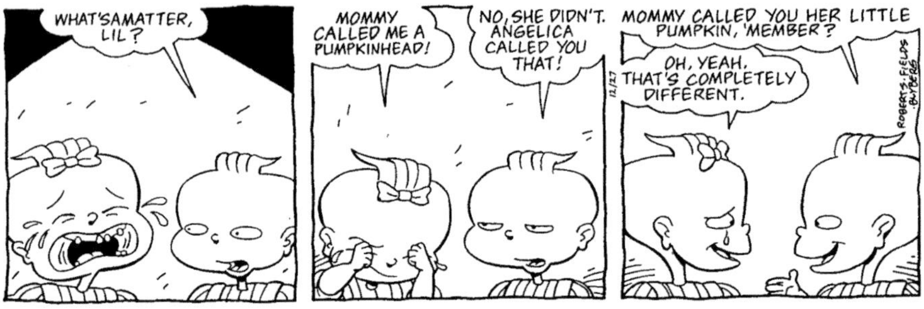
WHAT'SAMATTER, LIL?
MOMMY CALLED ME A PUMPKINHEAD!
NO, SHE DIDN'T. ANGELICA CALLED YOU THAT!
MOMMY CALLED YOU HER LITTLE PUMPKIN, 'MEMBER?
OH, YEAH. THAT'S COMPLETELY DIFFERENT.
12/27
ROBERTS·FIELDS ·BLYBERG

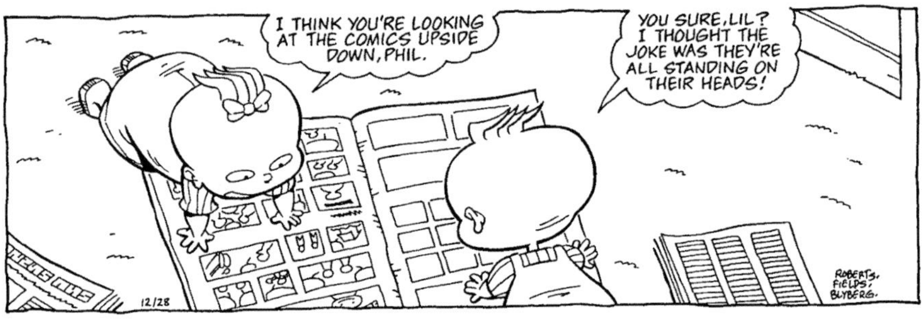
I THINK YOU'RE LOOKING AT THE COMICS UPSIDE DOWN, PHIL.
YOU SURE, LIL? I THOUGHT THE JOKE WAS THEY'RE ALL STANDING ON THEIR HEADS!
12/28
ROBERTS, FIELDS, BLYBERG.

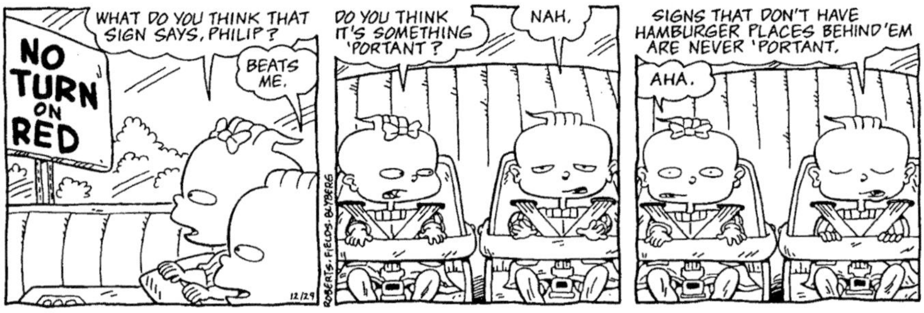
NO TURN ON RED
WHAT DO YOU THINK THAT SIGN SAYS, PHILIP?
BEATS ME.
DO YOU THINK IT'S SOMETHING 'PORTANT?
NAH.
SIGNS THAT DON'T HAVE HAMBURGER PLACES BEHIND'EM ARE NEVER 'PORTANT.
AHA.
12/29
ROBERTS·FIELDS·BLYBERG

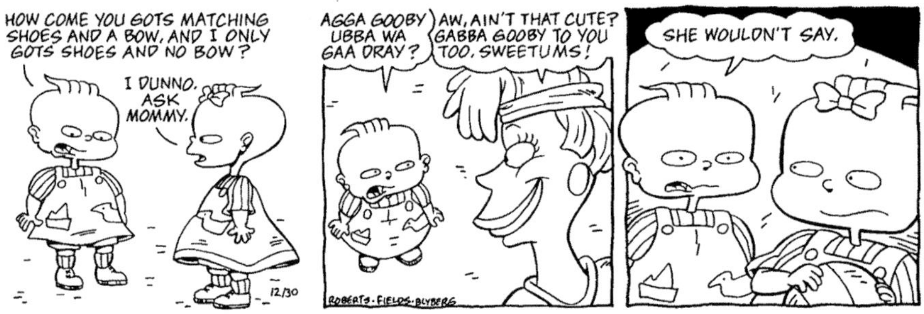
HOW COME YOU GOTS MATCHING SHOES AND A BOW, AND I ONLY GOTS SHOES AND NO BOW?
I DUNNO. ASK MOMMY.
AGGA GOOBY UBBA WA GAA DRAY?
AW, AIN'T THAT CUTE? GABBA GOOBY TO YOU TOO, SWEETUMS!
SHE WOULDN'T SAY.
12/30
ROBERTS·FIELDS·BLYBERG

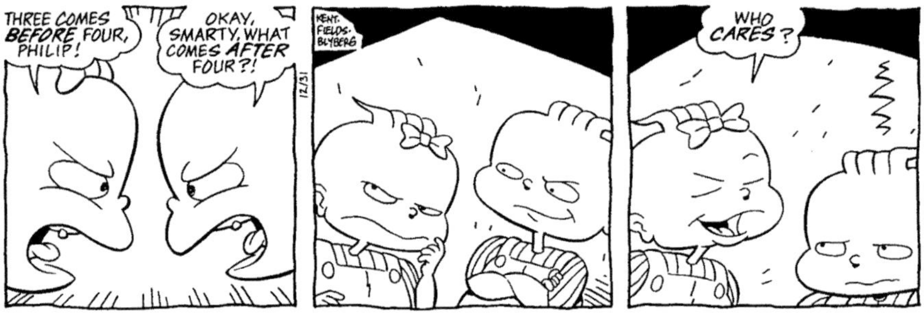
THREE COMES *BEFORE* FOUR, PHILIP!
OKAY, SMARTY, WHAT COMES *AFTER* FOUR?!
KENT· FIELDS· BLYBERG
12/31
WHO *CARES*?

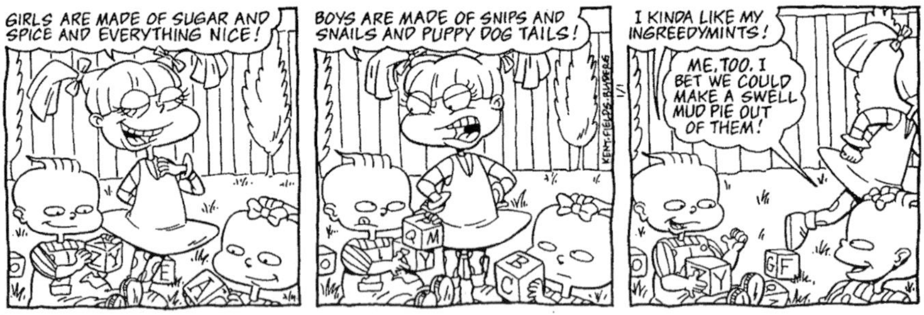
GIRLS ARE MADE OF SUGAR AND SPICE AND EVERYTHING NICE!
BOYS ARE MADE OF SNIPS AND SNAILS AND PUPPY DOG TAILS!
KENT·FIELDS·BLYBERG
1/1
I KINDA LIKE MY INGREEDYMINTS!
ME, TOO. I BET WE COULD MAKE A SWELL MUD PIE OUT OF THEM!

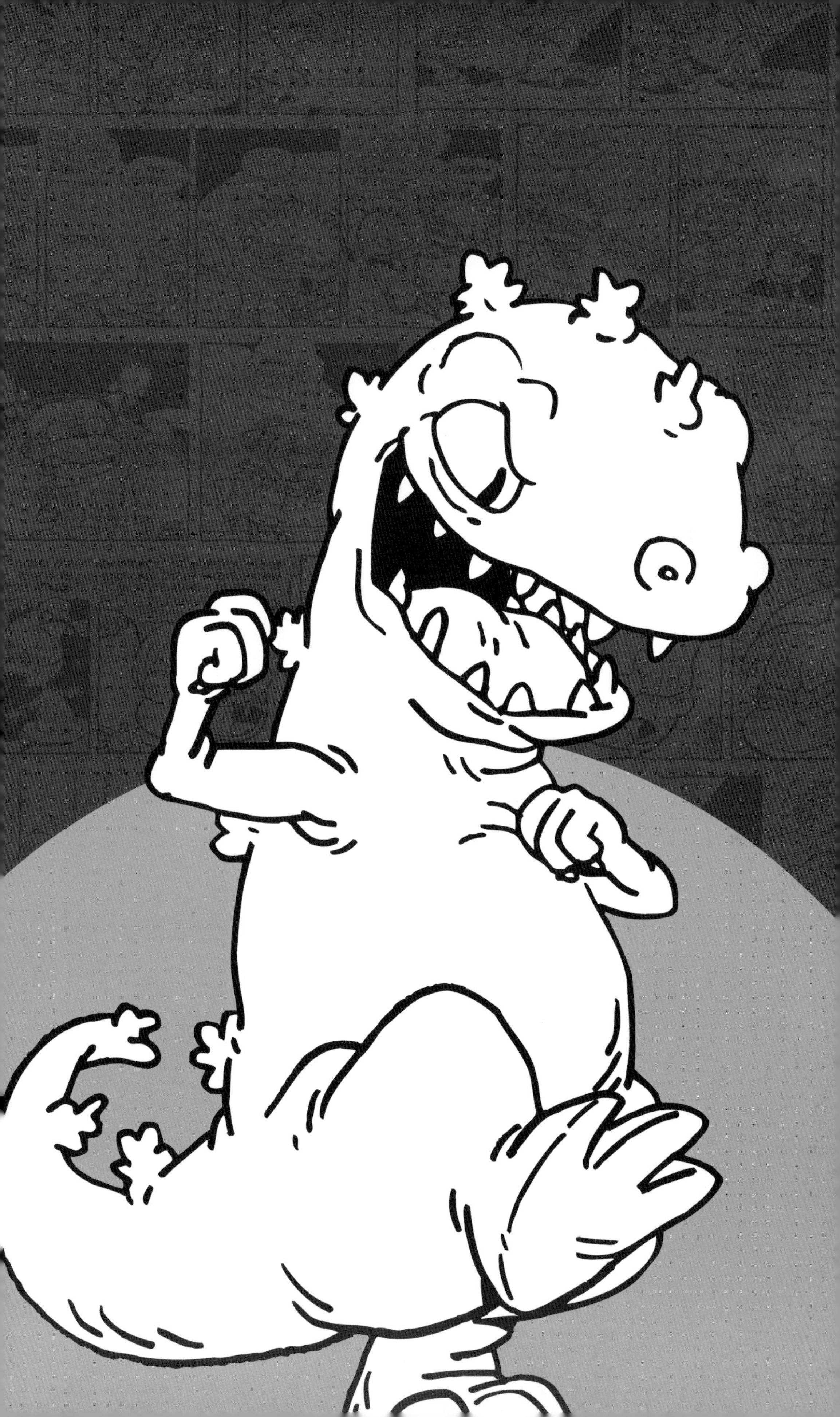

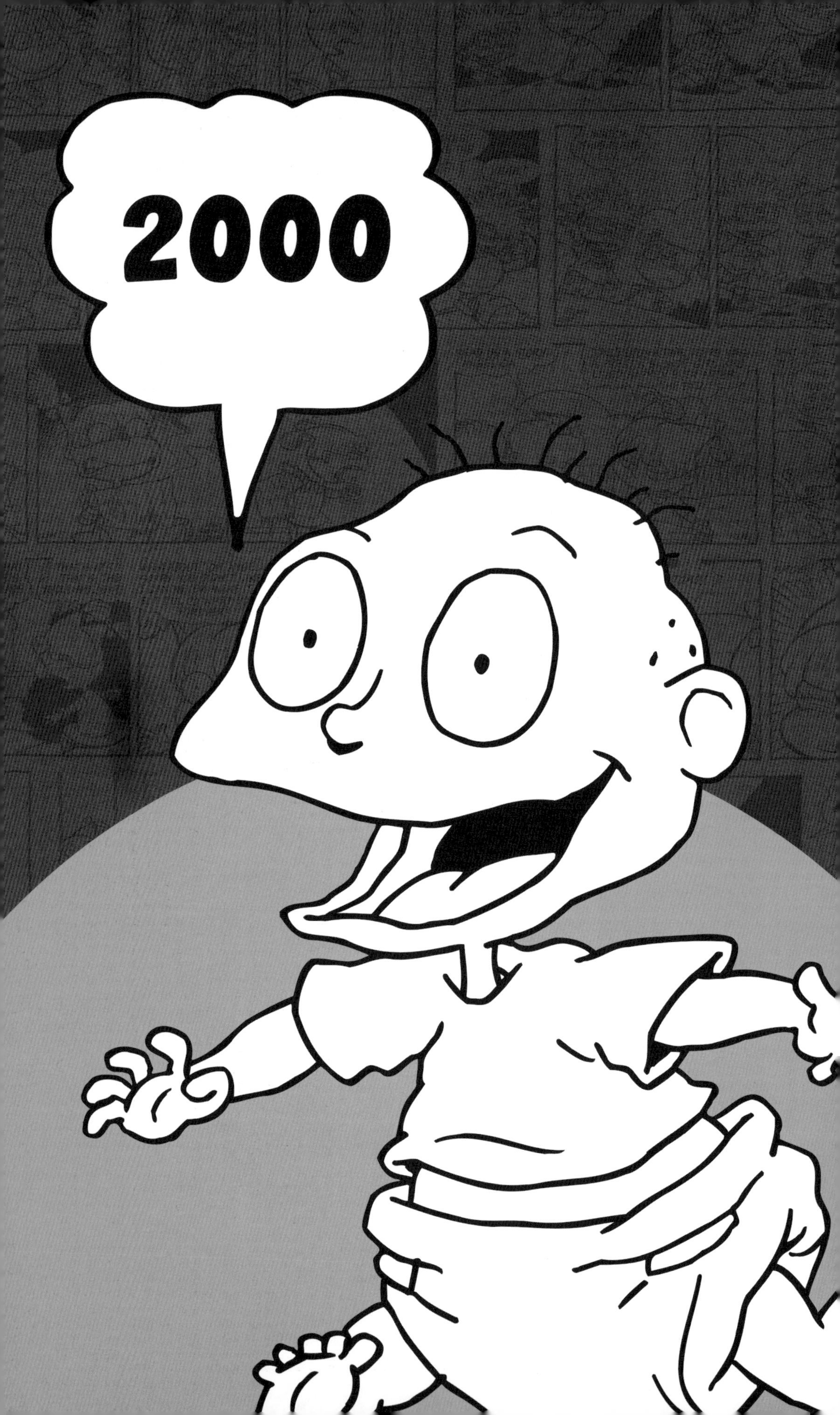
2000

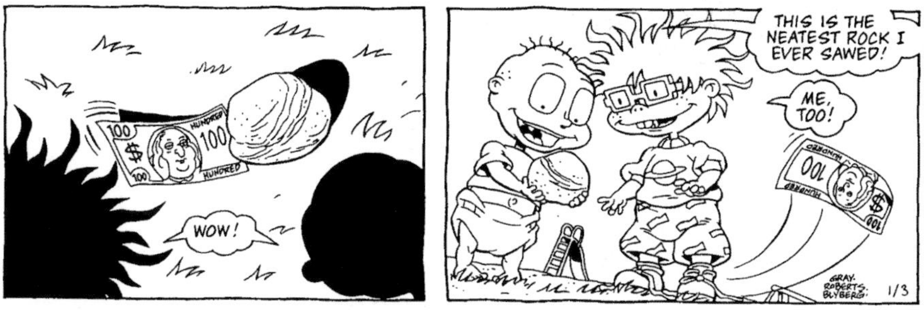
100 $ 100 HUNDRED 100 HUNDRED
WOW!
THIS IS THE NEATEST ROCK I EVER SAWED!
ME, TOO!
GRAY· ROBERTS· BLYBERG·
1/3

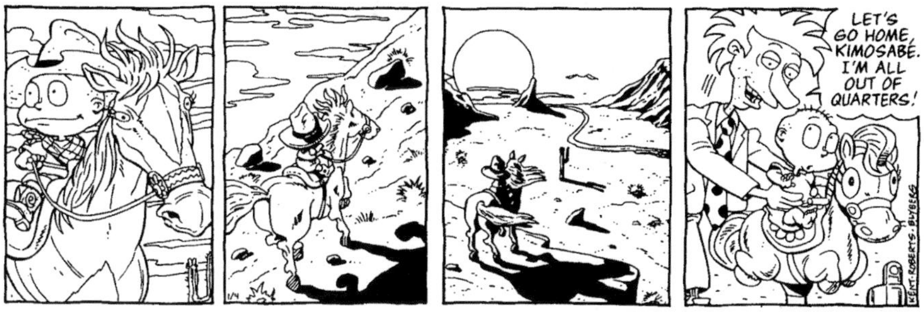
1/4
LET'S GO HOME, KIMOSABÉ. I'M ALL OUT OF QUARTERS!
KENT·ROBERTS·BLYBERG

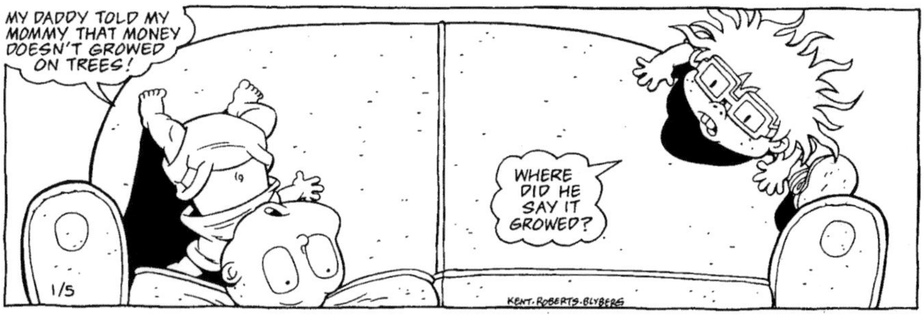
MY DADDY TOLD MY MOMMY THAT MONEY DOESN'T GROWED ON TREES!
WHERE DID HE SAY IT GROWED?
1/5
KENT·ROBERTS·BLYBERG

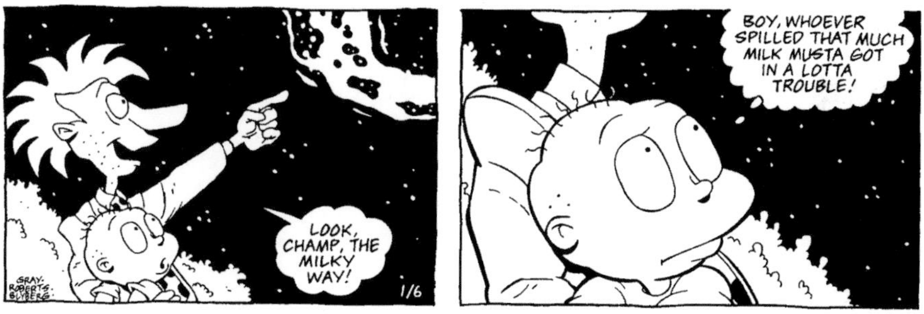
LOOK, CHAMP, THE MILKY WAY!
GRAY· ROBERTS· BLYBERG·
1/6
BOY, WHOEVER SPILLED THAT MUCH MILK MUSTA GOT IN A LOTTA TROUBLE!

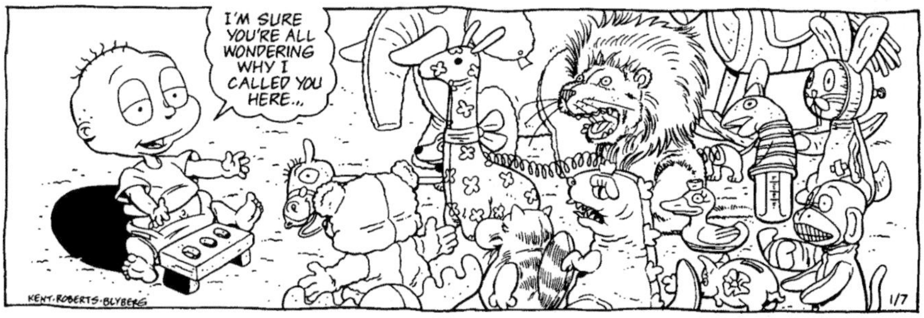
I'M SURE YOU'RE ALL WONDERING WHY I CALLED YOU HERE...
KENT·ROBERTS·BLYBERG
1/7

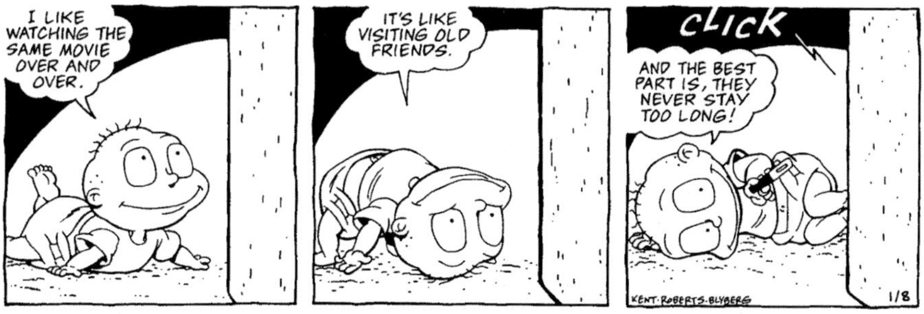
I LIKE WATCHING THE SAME MOVIE OVER AND OVER.
IT'S LIKE VISITING OLD FRIENDS.
CLICK
AND THE BEST PART IS, THEY NEVER STAY TOO LONG!
KENT·ROBERTS·BLYBERG
1/8

2000

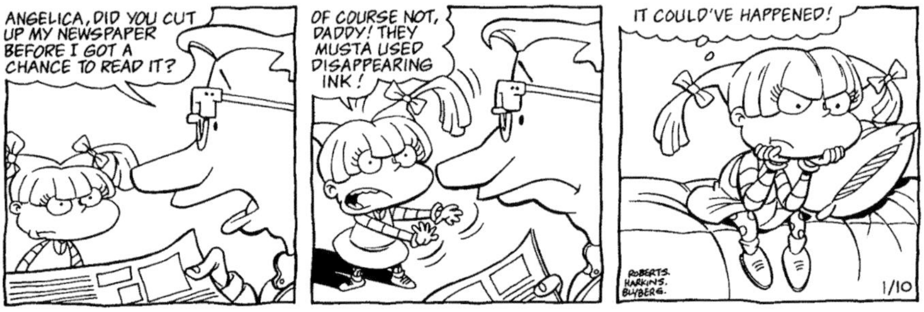
ANGELICA, DID YOU CUT UP MY NEWSPAPER BEFORE I GOT A CHANCE TO READ IT?
OF COURSE NOT, DADDY! THEY MUSTA USED DISAPPEARING INK!
IT COULD'VE HAPPENED!
ROBERTS. HARKINS. BLYBERG.
1/10

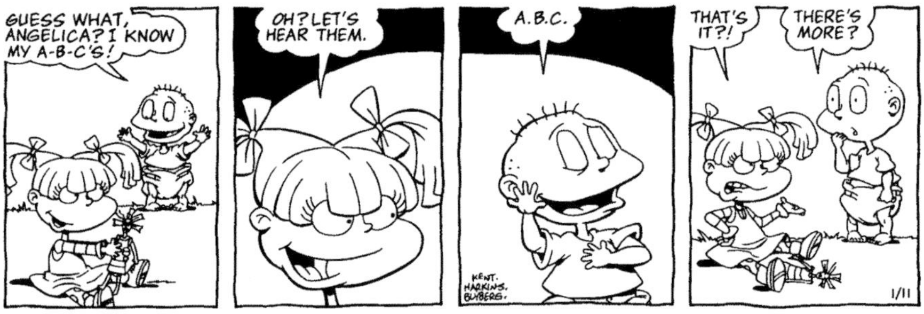
GUESS WHAT, ANGELICA? I KNOW MY A-B-C'S!
OH? LET'S HEAR THEM.
A. B. C.
KENT. HARKINS. BLYBERG.
THAT'S IT?!
THERE'S MORE?
1/11

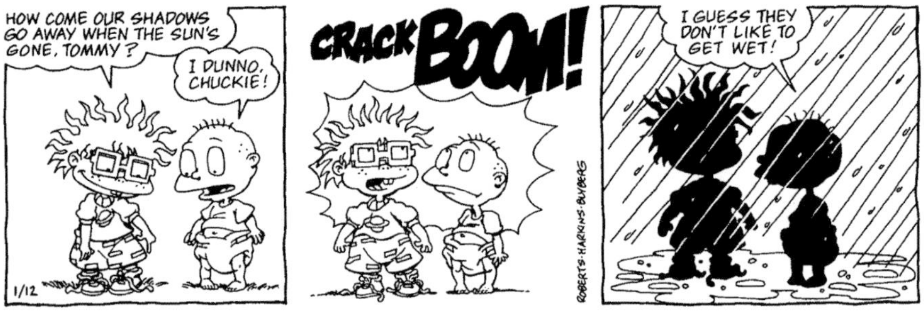
HOW COME OUR SHADOWS GO AWAY WHEN THE SUN'S GONE, TOMMY?
I DUNNO, CHUCKIE!
1/12
CRACK BOOM!
ROBERTS · HARKINS · BLYBERG
I GUESS THEY DON'T LIKE TO GET WET!

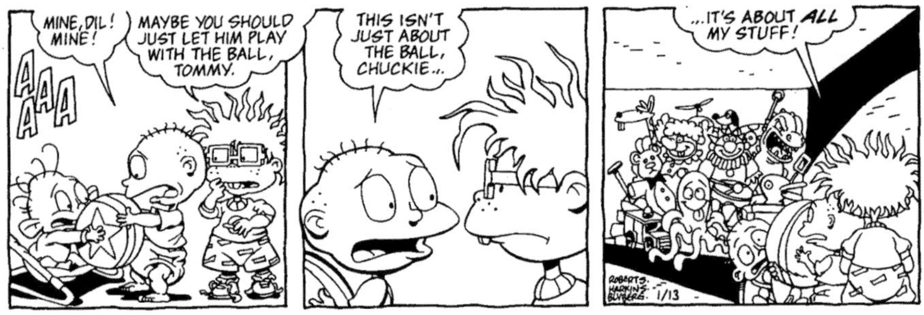
MINE, DIL! MINE!
AAAA
MAYBE YOU SHOULD JUST LET HIM PLAY WITH THE BALL, TOMMY.
THIS ISN'T JUST ABOUT THE BALL, CHUCKIE...
...IT'S ABOUT ALL MY STUFF!
ROBERTS. HARKINS. BLYBERG. 1/13

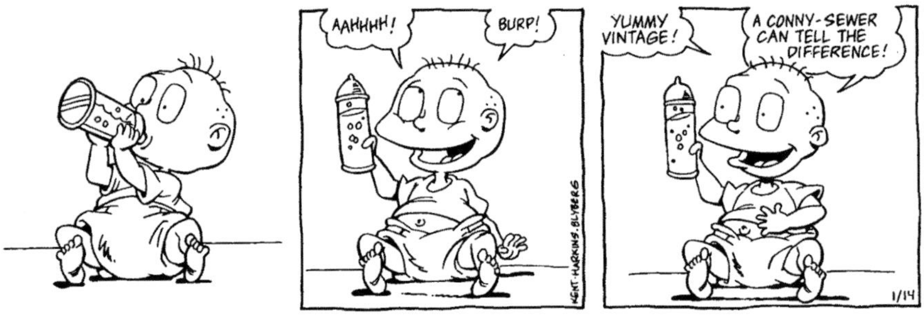
AAHHHH!
BURP!
KENT · HARKINS · BLYBERG
YUMMY VINTAGE!
A CONNY-SEWER CAN TELL THE DIFFERENCE!
1/14

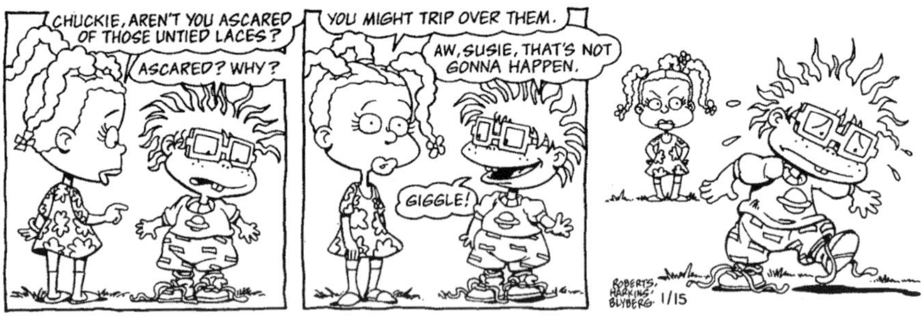
CHUCKIE, AREN'T YOU ASCARED OF THOSE UNTIED LACES?
ASCARED? WHY?
YOU MIGHT TRIP OVER THEM.
AW, SUSIE, THAT'S NOT GONNA HAPPEN.
GIGGLE!
ROBERTS. HARKINS. BLYBERG. 1/15

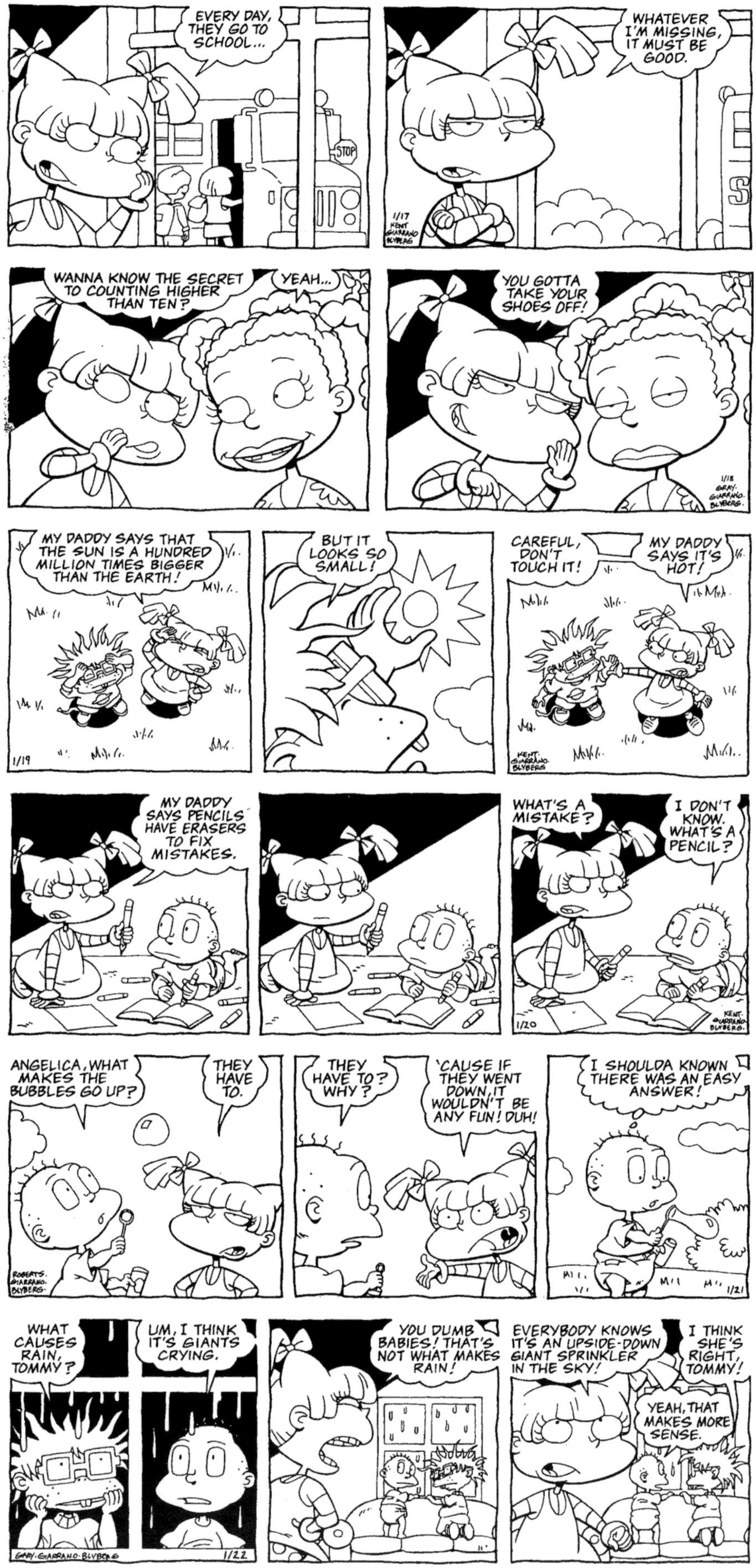

EVERY DAY, THEY GO TO SCHOOL...
STOP
WHATEVER I'M MISSING, IT MUST BE GOOD.
WANNA KNOW THE SECRET TO COUNTING HIGHER THAN TEN?
YEAH...
YOU GOTTA TAKE YOUR SHOES OFF!
MY DADDY SAYS THAT THE SUN IS A HUNDRED MILLION TIMES BIGGER THAN THE EARTH!
BUT IT LOOKS SO SMALL!
CAREFUL, DON'T TOUCH IT!
MY DADDY SAYS IT'S HOT!
MY DADDY SAYS PENCILS HAVE ERASERS TO FIX MISTAKES.
WHAT'S A MISTAKE?
I DON'T KNOW. WHAT'S A PENCIL?
ANGELICA, WHAT MAKES THE BUBBLES GO UP?
THEY HAVE TO.
THEY HAVE TO? WHY?
'CAUSE IF THEY WENT DOWN, IT WOULDN'T BE ANY FUN! DUH!
I SHOULDA KNOWN THERE WAS AN EASY ANSWER!
WHAT CAUSES RAIN, TOMMY?
UM, I THINK IT'S GIANTS CRYING.
YOU DUMB BABIES! THAT'S NOT WHAT MAKES RAIN!
EVERYBODY KNOWS IT'S AN UPSIDE-DOWN GIANT SPRINKLER IN THE SKY!
I THINK SHE'S RIGHT, TOMMY!
YEAH, THAT MAKES MORE SENSE.

2000

2000

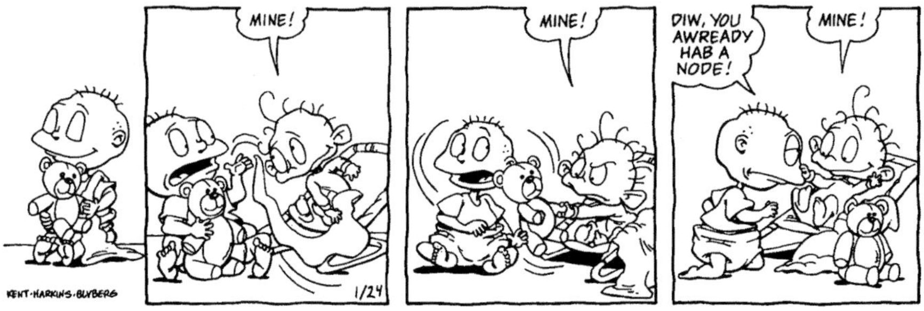
KENT·HARKINS·BLYBERG
MINE!
1/24
MINE!
DIW, YOU AWREADY HAB A NODE!
MINE!

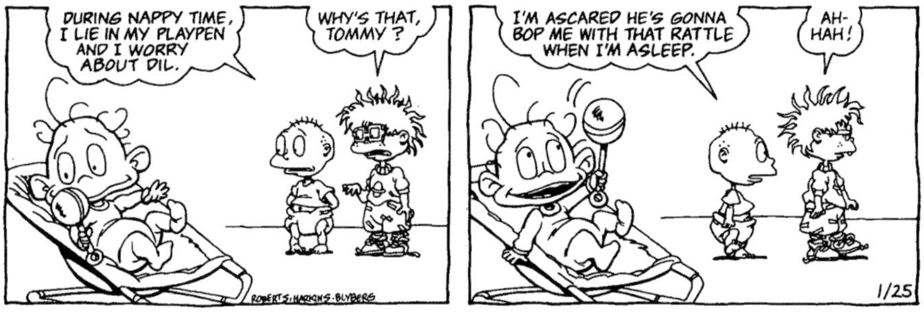
DURING NAPPY TIME, I LIE IN MY PLAYPEN AND I WORRY ABOUT DIL.
WHY'S THAT, TOMMY?
ROBERTS·HARKINS·BLYBERG
I'M ASCARED HE'S GONNA BOP ME WITH THAT RATTLE WHEN I'M ASLEEP.
AH-HAH!
1/25

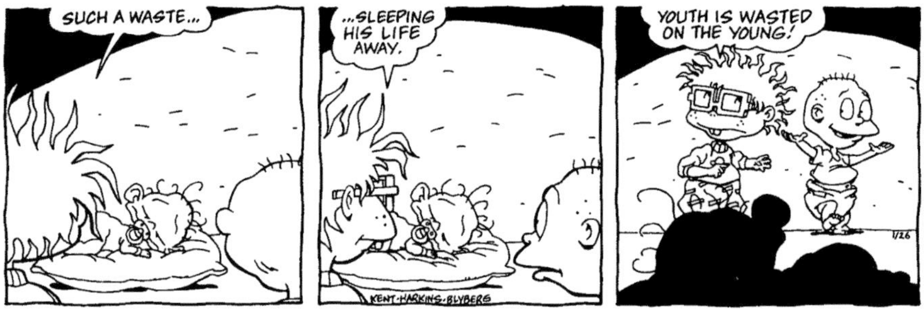
SUCH A WASTE...
...SLEEPING HIS LIFE AWAY.
KENT·HARKINS·BLYBERG
YOUTH IS WASTED ON THE YOUNG!
1/26

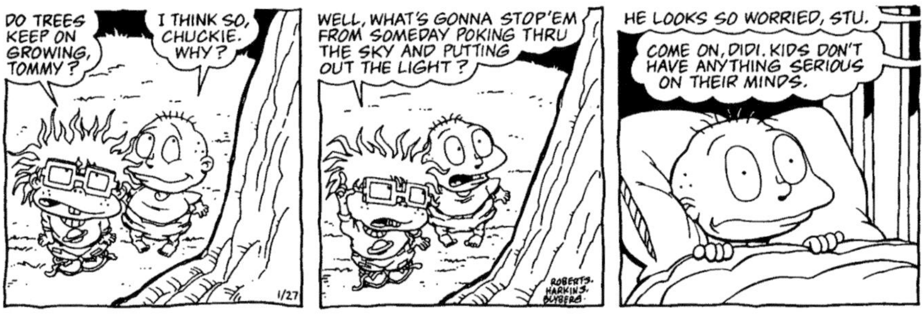
DO TREES KEEP ON GROWING, TOMMY?
I THINK SO, CHUCKIE. WHY?
1/27
WELL, WHAT'S GONNA STOP'EM FROM SOMEDAY POKING THRU THE SKY AND PUTTING OUT THE LIGHT?
ROBERTS·HARKINS·BLYBERG
HE LOOKS SO WORRIED, STU.
COME ON, DIDI. KIDS DON'T HAVE ANYTHING SERIOUS ON THEIR MINDS.

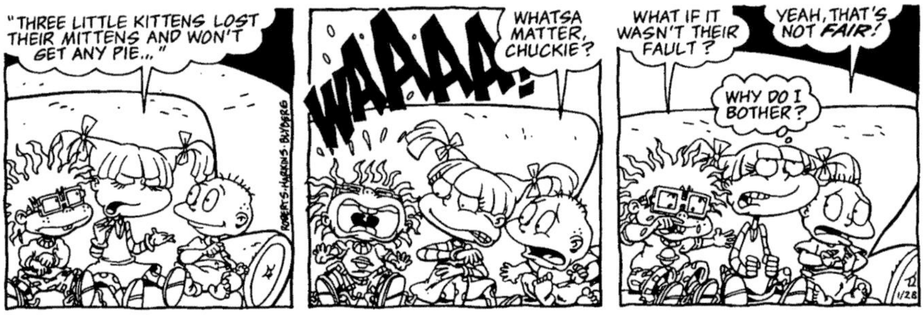
"THREE LITTLE KITTENS LOST THEIR MITTENS AND WON'T GET ANY PIE..."
ROBERTS·HARKINS·BLYBERG
WAAAA!
WHATSA MATTER, CHUCKIE?
WHAT IF IT WASN'T THEIR FAULT?
YEAH, THAT'S NOT FAIR!
WHY DO I BOTHER?
1/28

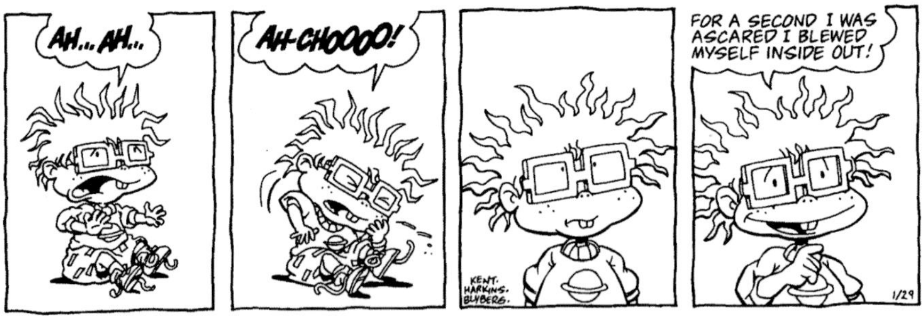
AH... AH...
AH-CHOOOO!
KENT·HARKINS·BLYBERG
FOR A SECOND I WAS ASCARED I BLEWED MYSELF INSIDE OUT!
1/29

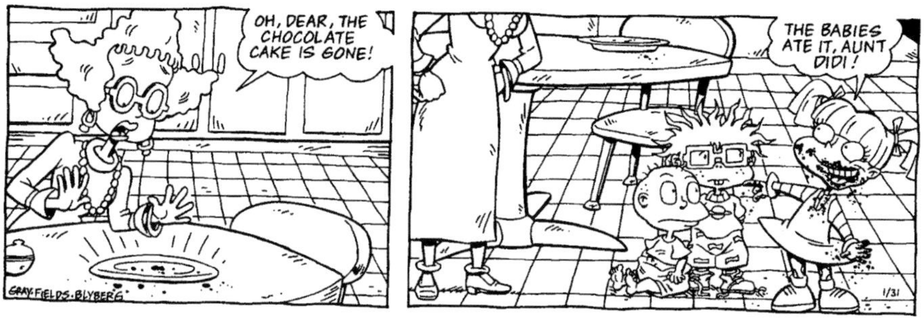
OH, DEAR, THE CHOCOLATE CAKE IS GONE!
THE BABIES ATE IT, AUNT DIDI!
GRAY·FIELDS·BLYBERG
1/31

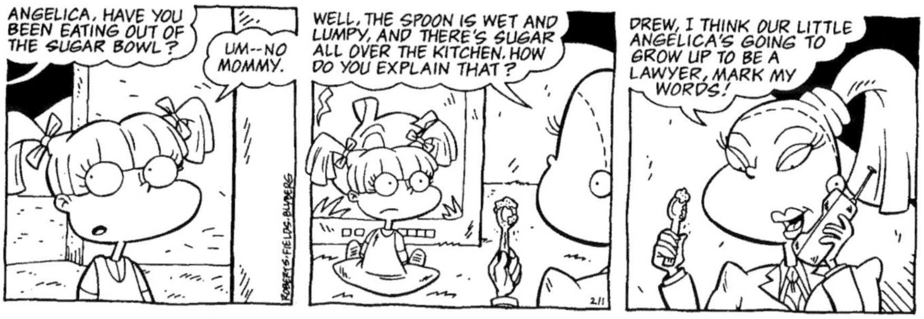
ANGELICA, HAVE YOU BEEN EATING OUT OF THE SUGAR BOWL?
UM--NO MOMMY.
WELL, THE SPOON IS WET AND LUMPY, AND THERE'S SUGAR ALL OVER THE KITCHEN. HOW DO YOU EXPLAIN THAT?
DREW, I THINK OUR LITTLE ANGELICA'S GOING TO GROW UP TO BE A LAWYER, MARK MY WORDS!
ROBERTS·FIELDS·BLYBERG
2/1

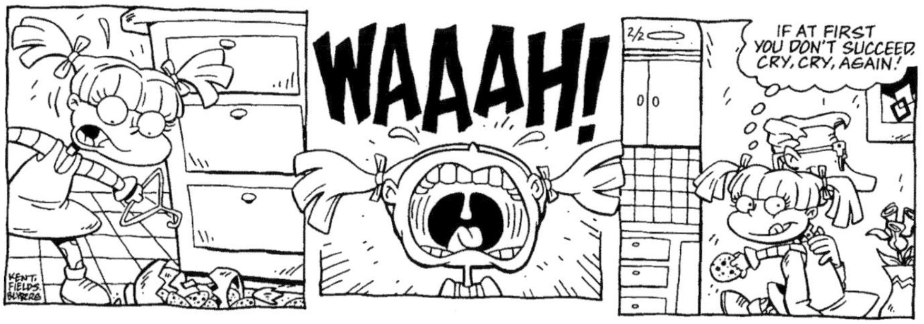
KENT·FIELDS·BLYBERG
WAAAH!
2/2
IF AT FIRST YOU DON'T SUCCEED, CRY, CRY, AGAIN!

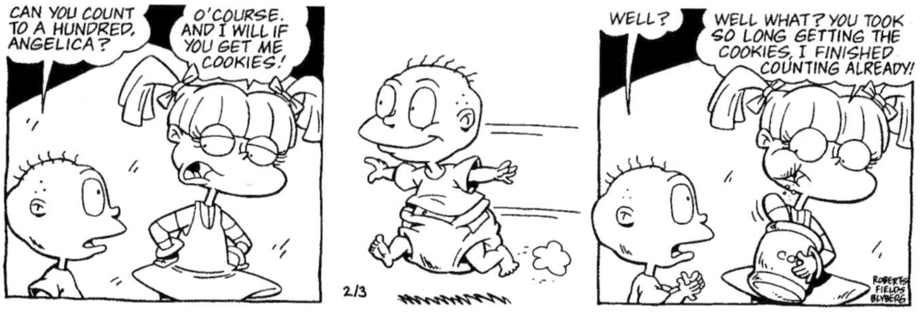
CAN YOU COUNT TO A HUNDRED, ANGELICA?
O'COURSE. AND I WILL IF YOU GET ME COOKIES!
2/3
WELL?
WELL WHAT? YOU TOOK SO LONG GETTING THE COOKIES, I FINISHED COUNTING ALREADY!
ROBERTS·FIELDS·BLYBERG

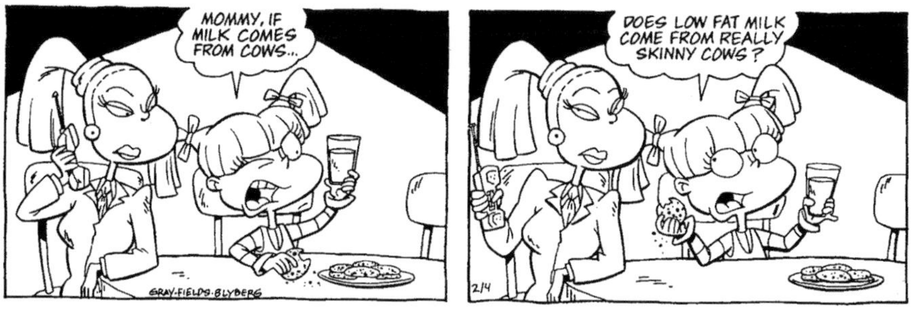
MOMMY, IF MILK COMES FROM COWS...
GRAY·FIELDS·BLYBERG
DOES LOW FAT MILK COME FROM REALLY SKINNY COWS?
2/4

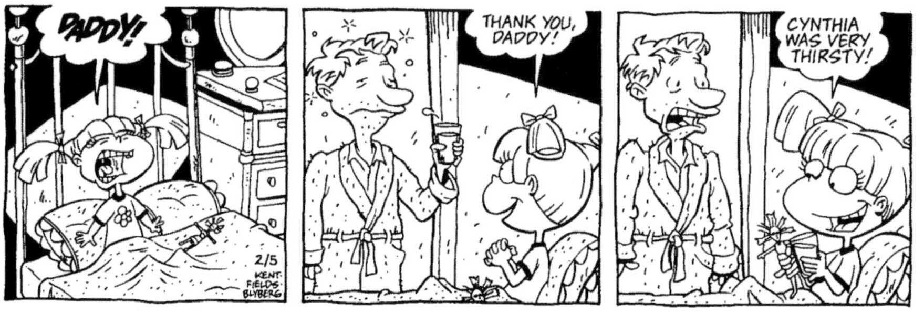
DADDY!
2/5
KENT·FIELDS·BLYBERG
THANK YOU, DADDY!
CYNTHIA WAS VERY THIRSTY!

2000

2000

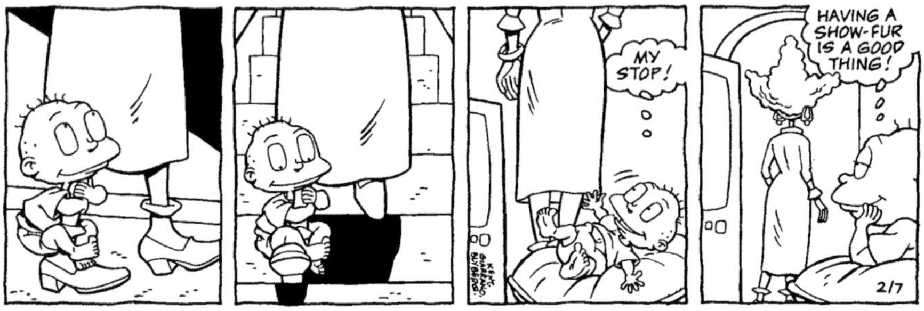
MY STOP!
HAVING A SHOW-FUR IS A GOOD THING!
2/7

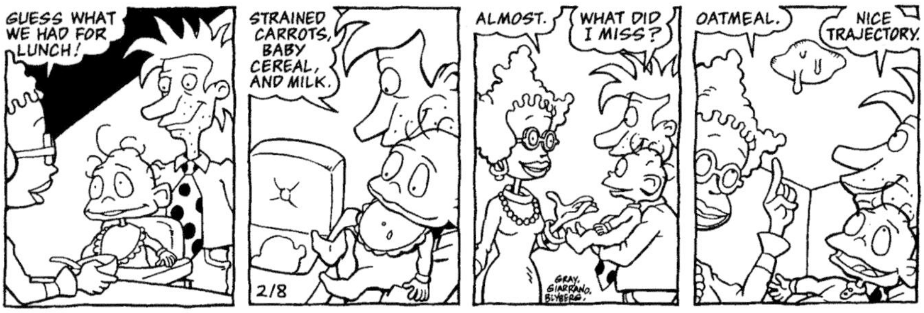
GUESS WHAT WE HAD FOR LUNCH!
STRAINED CARROTS, BABY CEREAL, AND MILK.
2/8
ALMOST.
WHAT DID I MISS?
GRAY. GIARRANO. BLYBERG.
OATMEAL.
NICE TRAJECTORY.

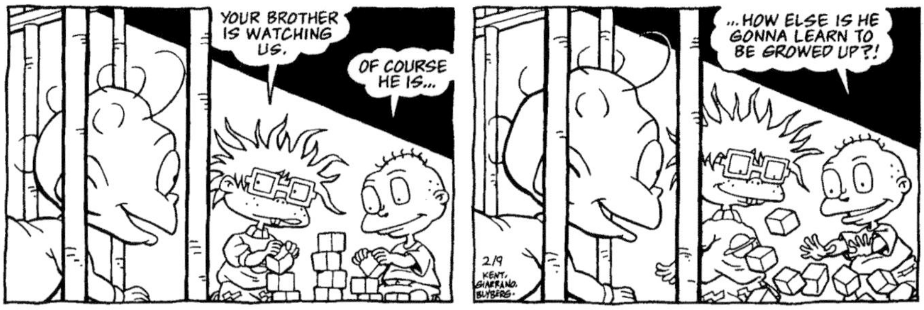
YOUR BROTHER IS WATCHING US.
OF COURSE HE IS...
2/9
KENT. GIARRANO. BLYBERG.
...HOW ELSE IS HE GONNA LEARN TO BE GROWED UP?!

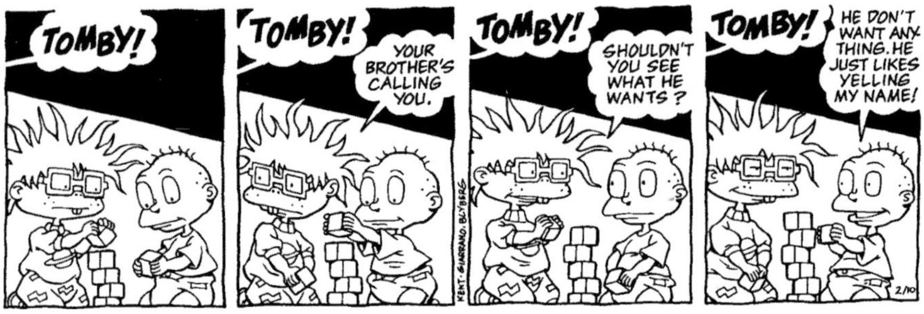
TOMBY!
TOMBY!
YOUR BROTHER'S CALLING YOU.
KENT·GIARRANO·BLYBERG
TOMBY!
SHOULDN'T YOU SEE WHAT HE WANTS?
TOMBY!
HE DON'T WANT ANY THING. HE JUST LIKES YELLING MY NAME!
2/10

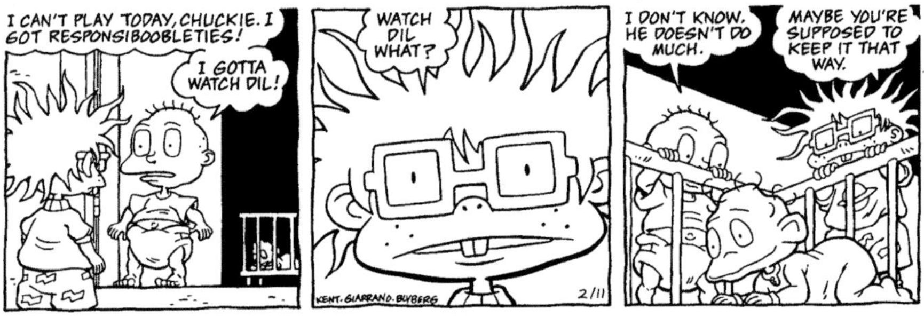
I CAN'T PLAY TODAY, CHUCKIE. I GOT RESPONSIBOOBLETIES!
I GOTTA WATCH DIL!
WATCH DIL WHAT?
KENT·GIARRANO·BLYBERG
2/11
I DON'T KNOW. HE DOESN'T DO MUCH.
MAYBE YOU'RE SUPPOSED TO KEEP IT THAT WAY.

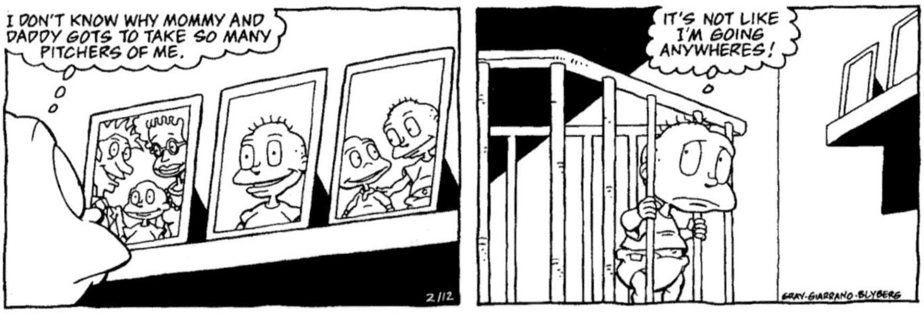
I DON'T KNOW WHY MOMMY AND DADDY GOTS TO TAKE SO MANY PITCHERS OF ME.
2/12
IT'S NOT LIKE I'M GOING ANYWHERES!
GRAY·GIARRANO·BLYBERG

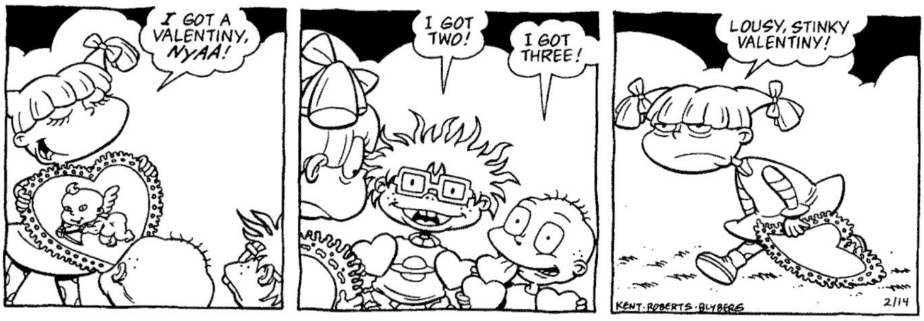
I GOT A VALENTINY, *NYAA!*
I GOT TWO!
I GOT THREE!
LOUSY, STINKY VALENTINY!
KENT·ROBERTS·BLYBERG
2/14

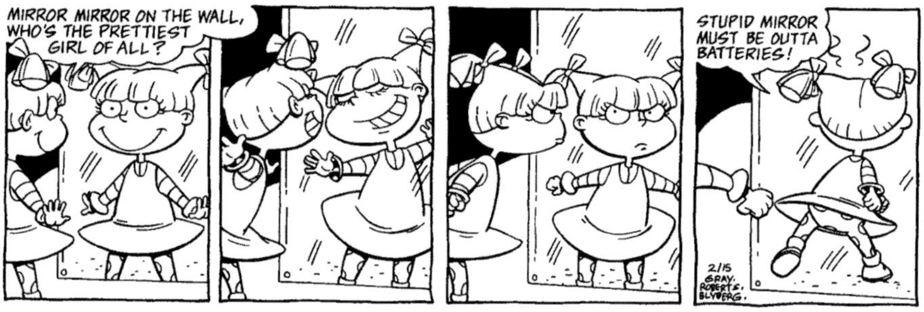
MIRROR MIRROR ON THE WALL, WHO'S THE PRETTIEST GIRL OF ALL?
STUPID MIRROR MUST BE OUTTA BATTERIES!
2/15
GRAY. ROBERTS. BLYBERG.

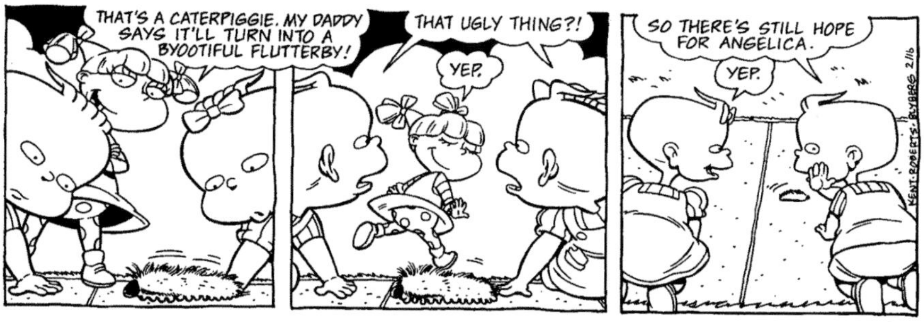
THAT'S A CATERPIGGIE. MY DADDY SAYS IT'LL TURN INTO A BYOOTIFUL FLUTTERBY!
THAT UGLY THING?!
YEP.
SO THERE'S STILL HOPE FOR ANGELICA.
YEP.
KENT·ROBERTS·BLYBERG 2/16

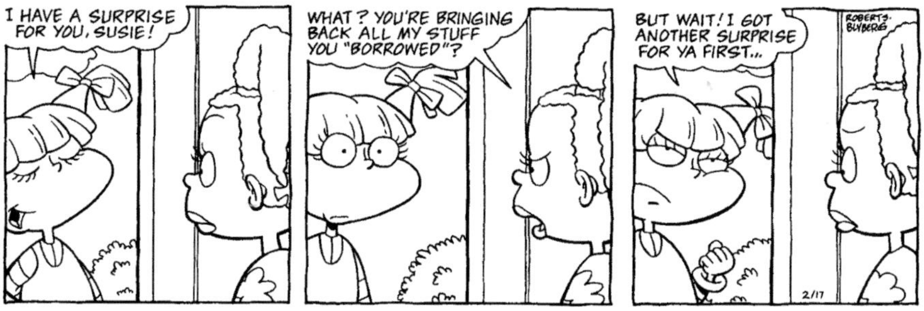
I HAVE A SURPRISE FOR YOU, SUSIE!
WHAT? YOU'RE BRINGING BACK ALL MY STUFF YOU "BORROWED"?
BUT WAIT! I GOT ANOTHER SURPRISE FOR YA FIRST...
ROBERTS. BLYBERG.
2/17

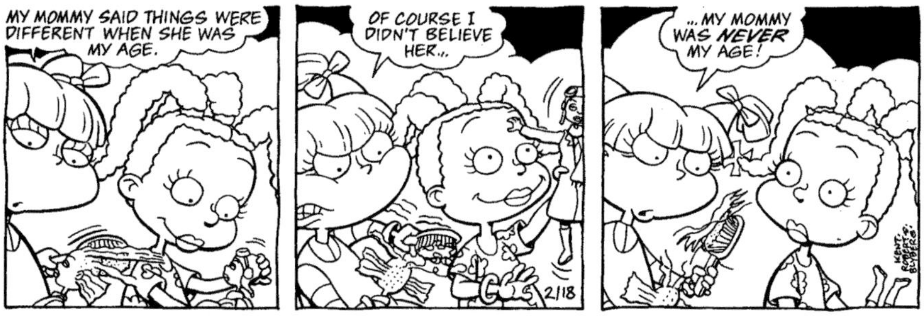
MY MOMMY SAID THINGS WERE DIFFERENT WHEN SHE WAS MY AGE.
OF COURSE I DIDN'T BELIEVE HER...
...MY MOMMY WAS ***NEVER*** MY AGE!
2/18
KENT. ROBERTS. BLYBERG.

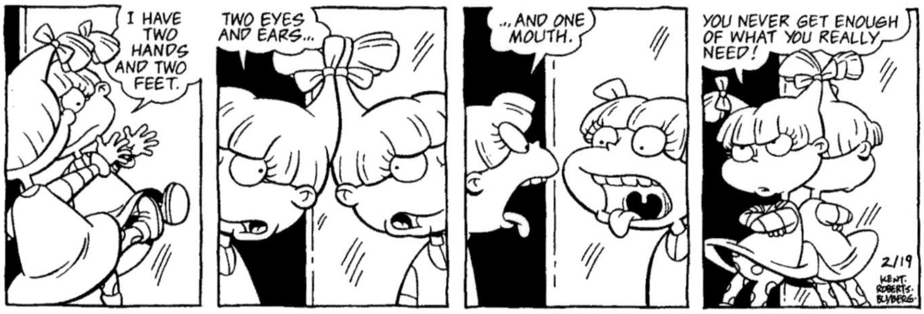
I HAVE TWO HANDS AND TWO FEET.
TWO EYES AND EARS...
...AND ONE MOUTH.
YOU NEVER GET ENOUGH OF WHAT YOU REALLY NEED!
2/19
KENT. ROBERTS. BLYBERG.

2000

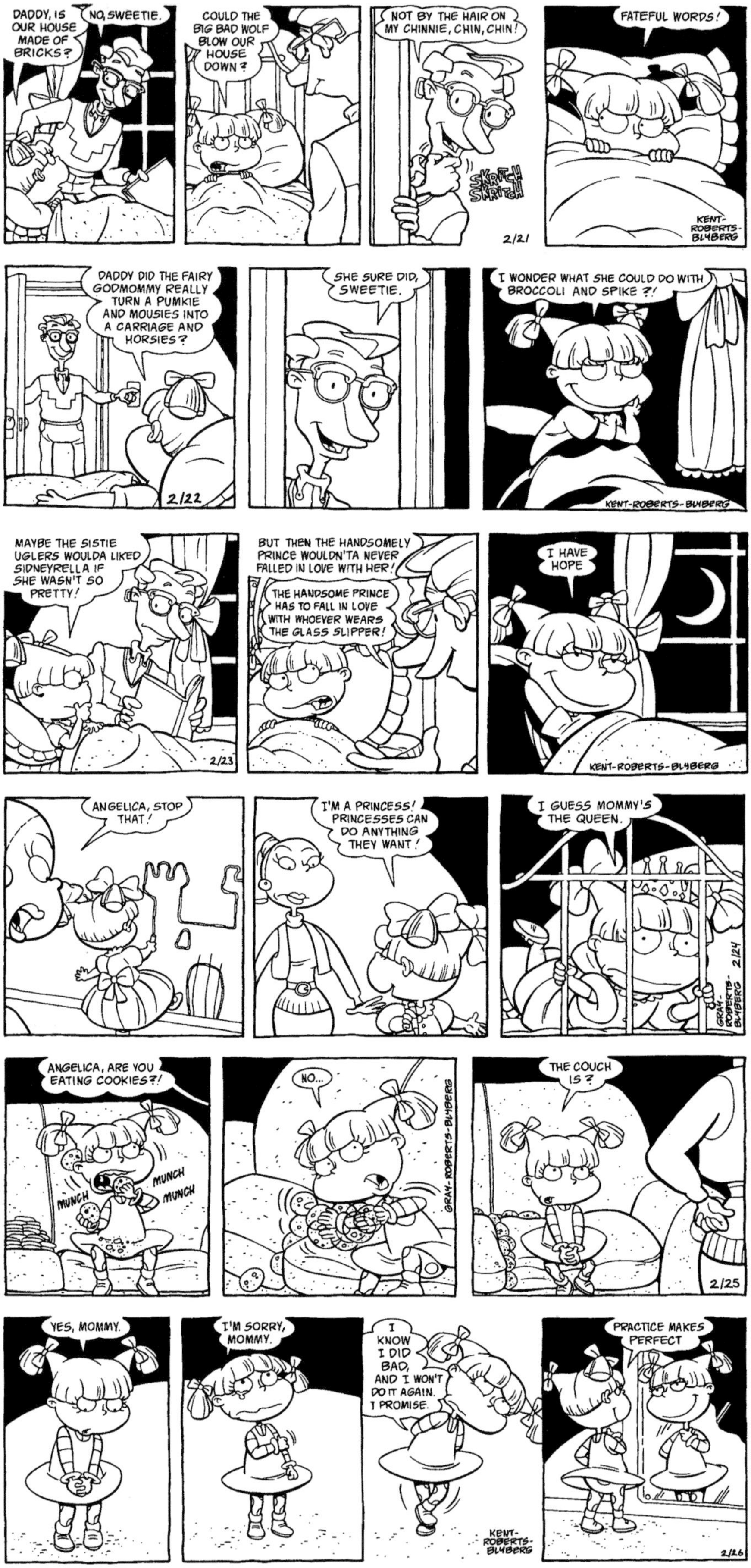
DADDY, IS OUR HOUSE MADE OF BRICKS?
NO, SWEETIE.
COULD THE BIG BAD WOLF BLOW OUR HOUSE DOWN?
NOT BY THE HAIR ON MY CHINNIE, CHIN, CHIN!
SKRITCH SKRITCH
2/21
FATEFUL WORDS!
KENT-ROBERTS-BLYBERG
DADDY DID THE FAIRY GODMOMMY REALLY TURN A PUMKIE AND MOUSIES INTO A CARRIAGE AND HORSIES?
2/22
SHE SURE DID, SWEETIE.
I WONDER WHAT SHE COULD DO WITH BROCCOLI AND SPIKE?!
KENT-ROBERTS-BLYBERG
MAYBE THE SISTIE UGLERS WOULDA LIKED SIDNEYRELLA IF SHE WASN'T SO PRETTY!
2/23
BUT THEN THE HANDSOMELY PRINCE WOULDN'TA NEVER FALLED IN LOVE WITH HER!
THE HANDSOME PRINCE HAS TO FALL IN LOVE WITH WHOEVER WEARS THE GLASS SLIPPER!
I HAVE HOPE
KENT-ROBERTS-BLYBERG
ANGELICA, STOP THAT!
I'M A PRINCESS! PRINCESSES CAN DO ANYTHING THEY WANT!
I GUESS MOMMY'S THE QUEEN.
2/24
GRAY-ROBERTS-BLYBERG
ANGELICA, ARE YOU EATING COOKIES?!
MUNCH MUNCH MUNCH
NO...
GRAY-ROBERTS-BLYBERG
THE COUCH IS?
2/25
YES, MOMMY.
I'M SORRY, MOMMY.
I KNOW I DID BAD, AND I WON'T DO IT AGAIN. I PROMISE.
KENT-ROBERTS-BLYBERG
PRACTICE MAKES PERFECT
2/26

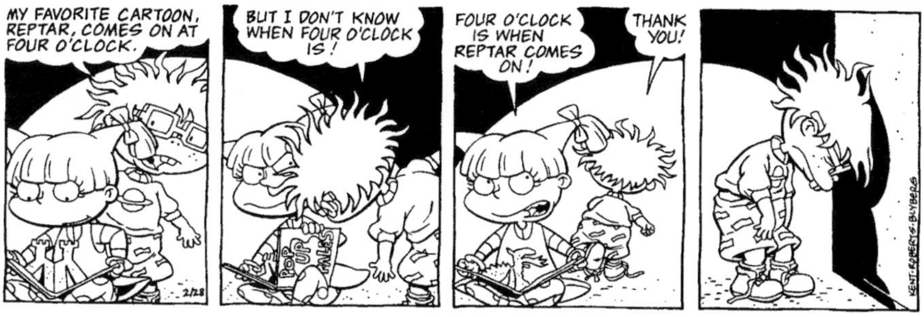
MY FAVORITE CARTOON, REPTAR, COMES ON AT FOUR O'CLOCK.
BUT I DON'T KNOW WHEN FOUR O'CLOCK IS!
FOUR O'CLOCK IS WHEN REPTAR COMES ON!
THANK YOU!
2/28
KENT·ROBERTS·BLYBERG

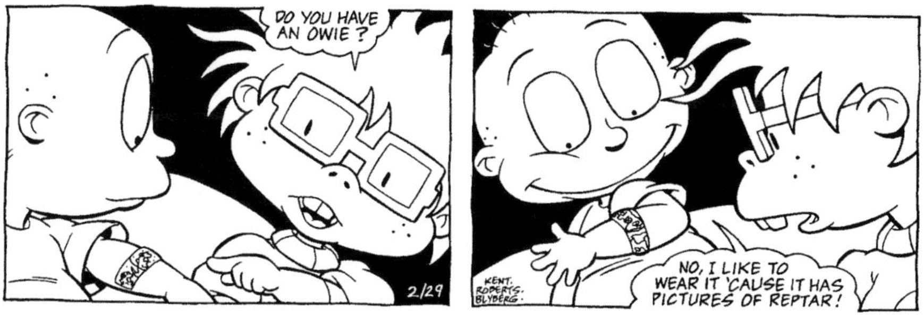
DO YOU HAVE AN OWIE?
2/29
KENT· ROBERTS· BLYBERG·
NO, I LIKE TO WEAR IT 'CAUSE IT HAS PICTURES OF REPTAR!

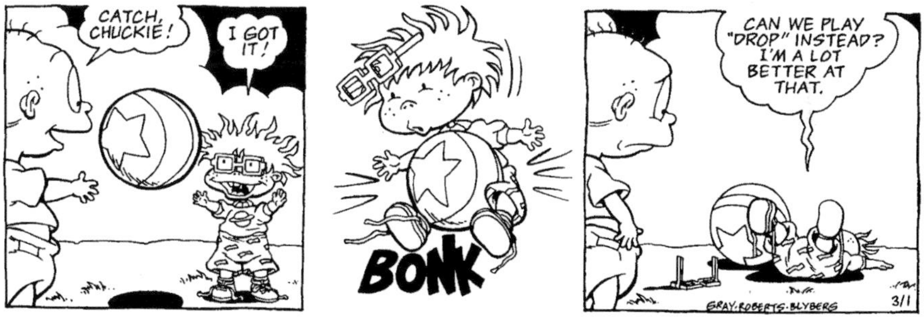
CATCH, CHUCKIE!
I GOT IT!
BONK
CAN WE PLAY "DROP" INSTEAD? I'M A LOT BETTER AT THAT.
GRAY·ROBERTS·BLYBERG
3/1

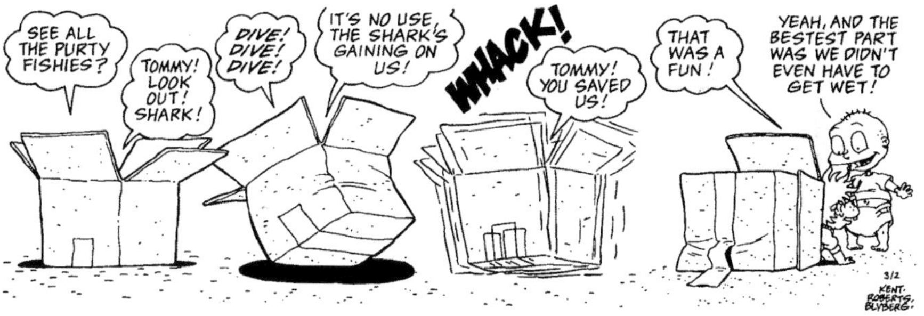
SEE ALL THE PURTY FISHIES?
TOMMY! LOOK OUT! SHARK!
DIVE! DIVE! DIVE!
IT'S NO USE, THE SHARK'S GAINING ON US!
WHACK!
TOMMY! YOU SAVED US!
THAT WAS A FUN!
YEAH, AND THE BESTEST PART WAS WE DIDN'T EVEN HAVE TO GET WET!
3/2
KENT· ROBERTS· BLYBERG·

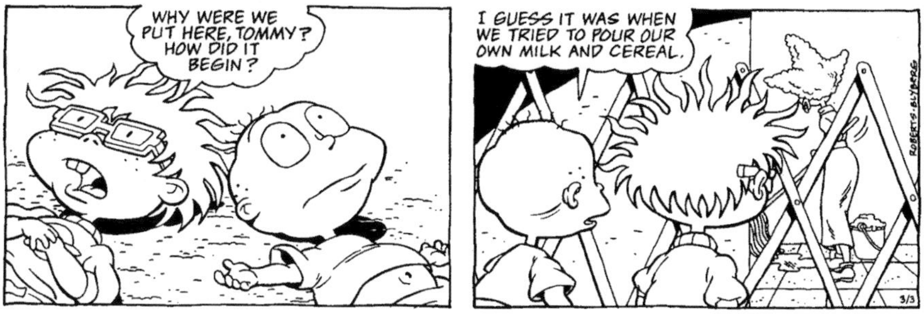
WHY WERE WE PUT HERE, TOMMY? HOW DID IT BEGIN?
I GUESS IT WAS WHEN WE TRIED TO POUR OUR OWN MILK AND CEREAL.
ROBERTS·BLYBERG
3/3

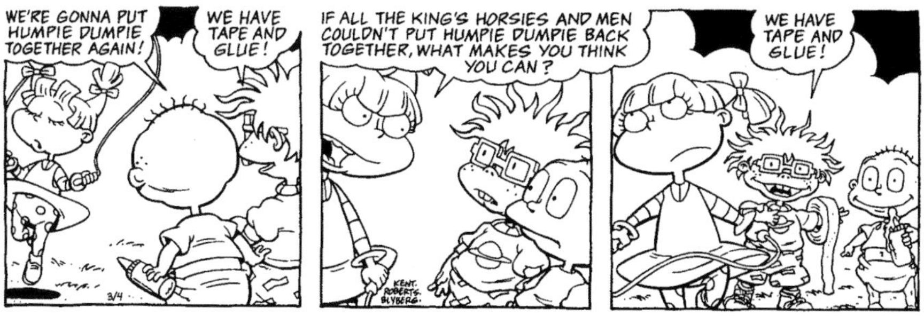
WE'RE GONNA PUT HUMPIE DUMPIE TOGETHER AGAIN!
WE HAVE TAPE AND GLUE!
3/4
IF ALL THE KING'S HORSIES AND MEN COULDN'T PUT HUMPIE DUMPIE BACK TOGETHER, WHAT MAKES YOU THINK YOU CAN?
KENT· ROBERTS· BLYBERG·
WE HAVE TAPE AND GLUE!

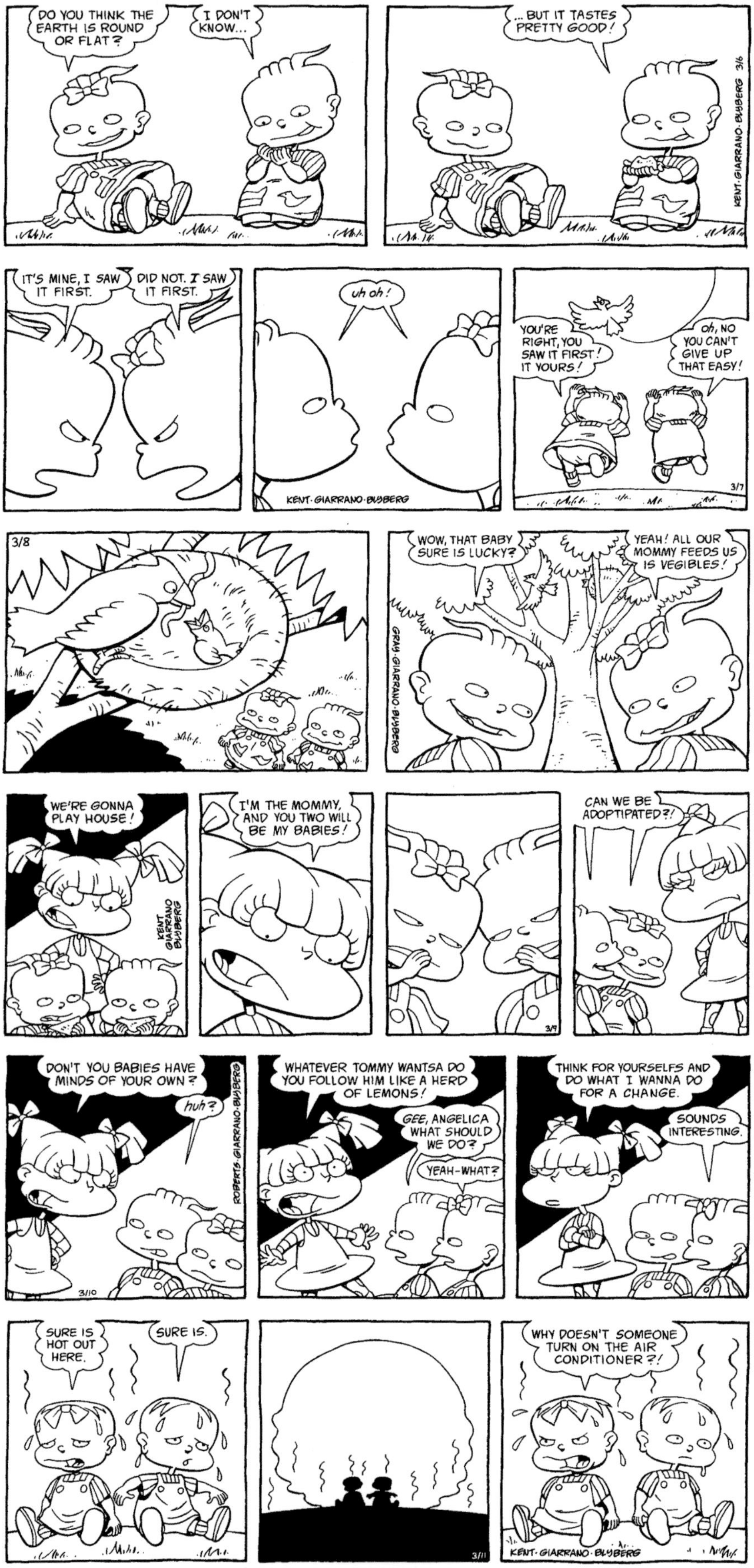
DO YOU THINK THE EARTH IS ROUND OR FLAT?
I DON'T KNOW...
... BUT IT TASTES PRETTY GOOD!
KENT·GIARRANO·BLYBERG 3/6
IT'S MINE, I SAW IT FIRST.
DID NOT. I SAW IT FIRST.
uh oh!
KENT·GIARRANO·BLYBERG
YOU'RE RIGHT, YOU SAW IT FIRST! IT YOURS!
oh, NO YOU CAN'T GIVE UP THAT EASY!
3/7
3/8
WOW, THAT BABY SURE IS LUCKY?
YEAH! ALL OUR MOMMY FEEDS US IS VEGIBLES!
GRAY·GIARRANO·BLYBERG
WE'RE GONNA PLAY HOUSE!
KENT GIARRANO BLYBERG
I'M THE MOMMY, AND YOU TWO WILL BE MY BABIES!
3/9
CAN WE BE ADOPTIPATED?!
DON'T YOU BABIES HAVE MINDS OF YOUR OWN?
huh?
ROBERTS·GIARRANO·BLYBERG
3/10
WHATEVER TOMMY WANTSA DO YOU FOLLOW HIM LIKE A HERD OF LEMONS!
GEE, ANGELICA WHAT SHOULD WE DO?
YEAH-WHAT?
THINK FOR YOURSELFS AND DO WHAT I WANNA DO FOR A CHANGE.
SOUNDS INTERESTING.
SURE IS HOT OUT HERE.
SURE IS.
3/11
WHY DOESN'T SOMEONE TURN ON THE AIR CONDITIONER?!
KENT·GIARRANO·BLYBERG

2000

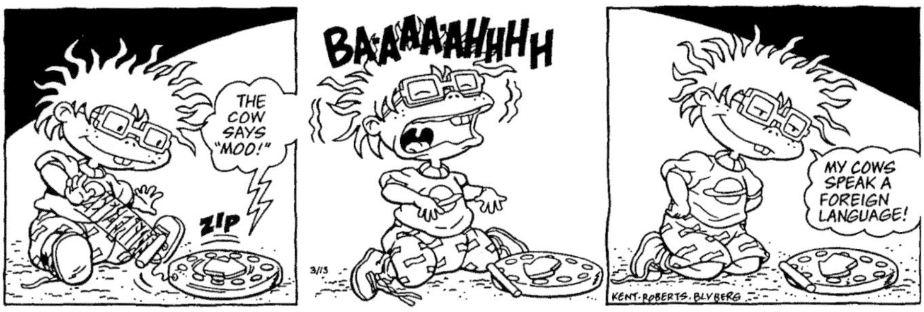
THE COW SAYS "MOO!"
ZIP
BAAAAAHHHH
3/13
MY COWS SPEAK A FOREIGN LANGUAGE!
KENT·ROBERTS·BLYBERG

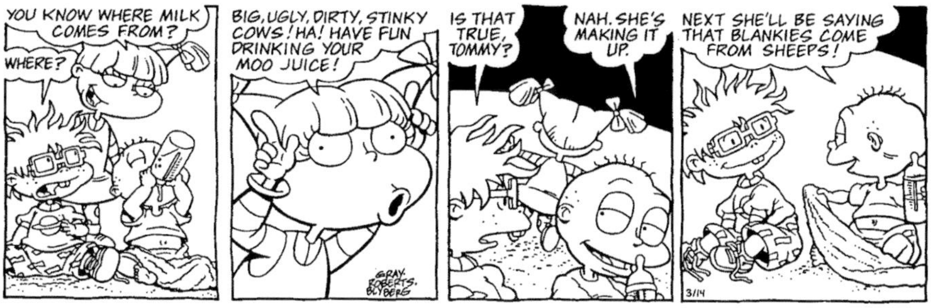
YOU KNOW WHERE MILK COMES FROM?
WHERE?
BIG, UGLY, DIRTY, STINKY COWS! HA! HAVE FUN DRINKING YOUR MOO JUICE!
GRAY·ROBERTS·BLYBERG
IS THAT TRUE, TOMMY?
NAH. SHE'S MAKING IT UP.
NEXT SHE'LL BE SAYING THAT BLANKIES COME FROM SHEEPS!
3/14

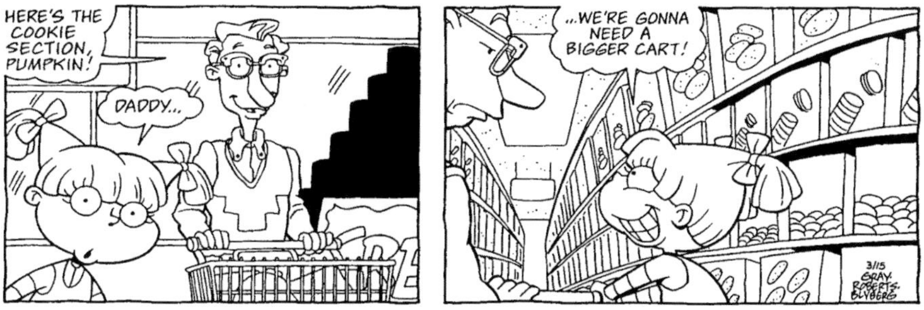
HERE'S THE COOKIE SECTION, PUMPKIN!
DADDY...
...WE'RE GONNA NEED A BIGGER CART!
3/15
GRAY·ROBERTS·BLYBERG

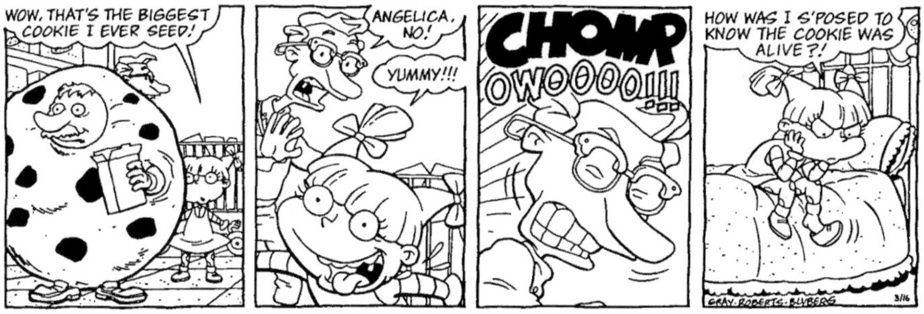
WOW, THAT'S THE BIGGEST COOKIE I EVER SEED!
ANGELICA, NO!
YUMMY!!!
CHOMP
OWOOOO!!!
HOW WAS I S'POSED TO KNOW THE COOKIE WAS ALIVE?!
GRAY·ROBERTS·BLYBERG
3/16

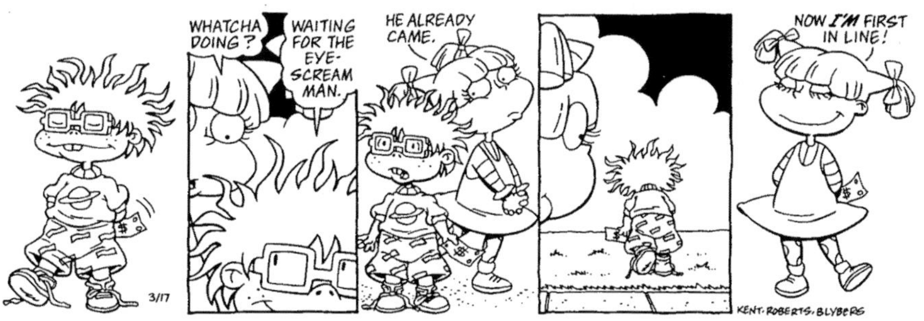
3/17
WHATCHA DOING?
WAITING FOR THE EYE-SCREAM MAN.
HE ALREADY CAME.
NOW I'M FIRST IN LINE!
KENT·ROBERTS·BLYBERG

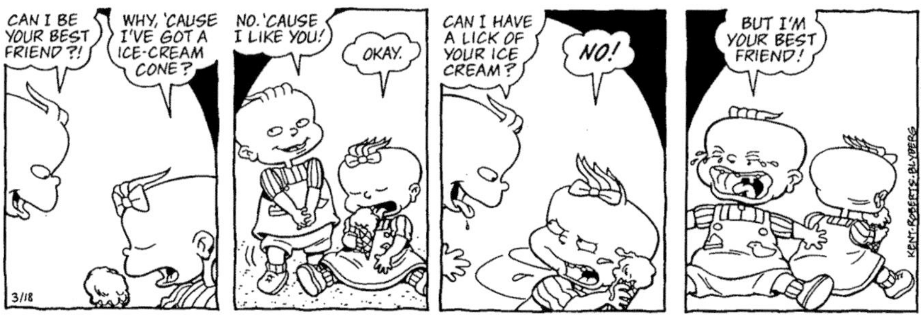
CAN I BE YOUR BEST FRIEND?!
WHY, 'CAUSE I'VE GOT A ICE-CREAM CONE?
3/18
NO. 'CAUSE I LIKE YOU!
OKAY.
CAN I HAVE A LICK OF YOUR ICE CREAM?
NO!
BUT I'M YOUR BEST FRIEND!
KENT·ROBERTS·BLYBERG

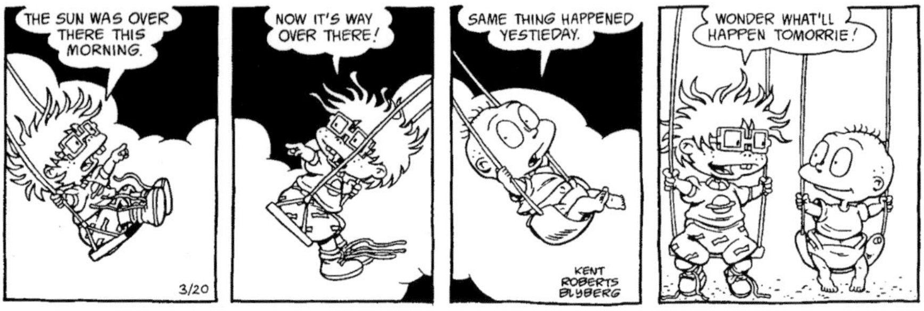
THE SUN WAS OVER THERE THIS MORNING.
NOW IT'S WAY OVER THERE!
SAME THING HAPPENED YESTIEDAY.
KENT ROBERTS BLYBERG
WONDER WHAT'LL HAPPEN TOMORRIE!
3/20

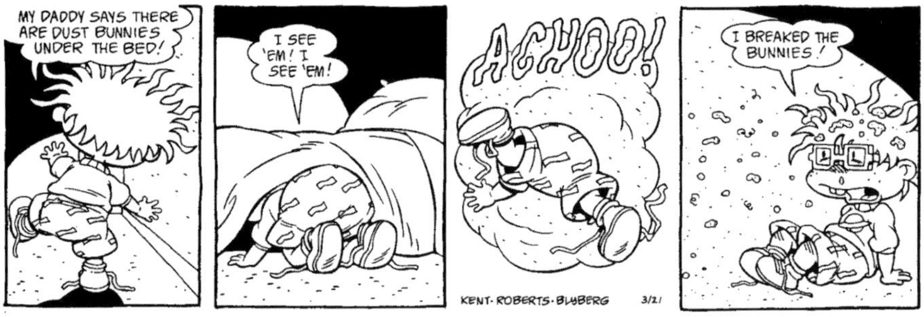
MY DADDY SAYS THERE ARE DUST BUNNIES UNDER THE BED!
I SEE 'EM! I SEE 'EM!
ACHOO!
KENT·ROBERTS·BLYBERG 3/21
I BREAKED THE BUNNIES!

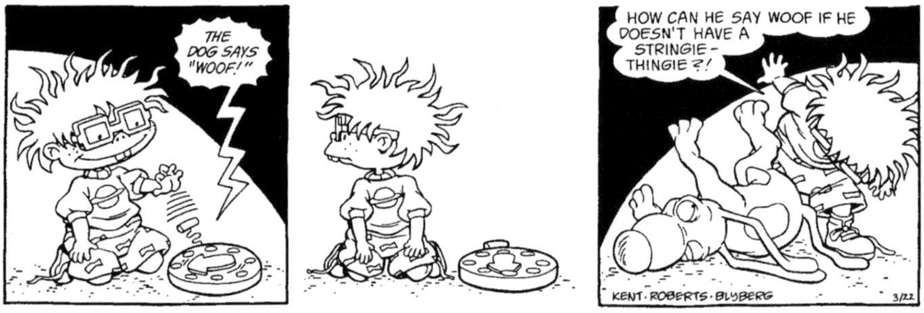
THE DOG SAYS "WOOF!"
HOW CAN HE SAY WOOF IF HE DOESN'T HAVE A STRINGIE-THINGIE?!
KENT·ROBERTS·BLYBERG 3/22

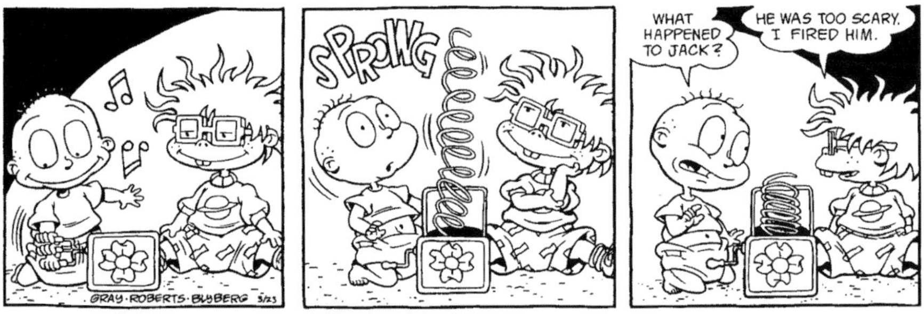
GRAY·ROBERTS·BLYBERG 3/23
SPROING
WHAT HAPPENED TO JACK?
HE WAS TOO SCARY. I FIRED HIM.

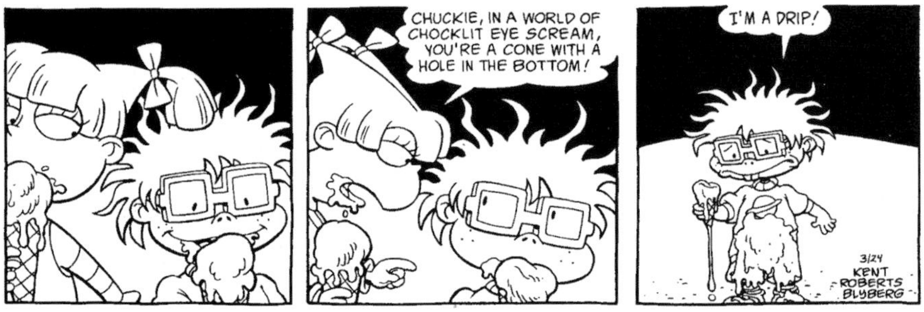
CHUCKIE, IN A WORLD OF CHOCKLIT EYE SCREAM, YOU'RE A CONE WITH A HOLE IN THE BOTTOM!
I'M A DRIP!
3/24 KENT ROBERTS BLYBERG

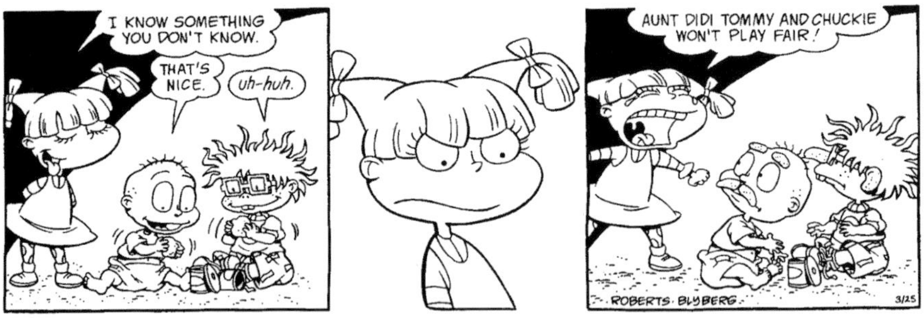
I KNOW SOMETHING YOU DON'T KNOW.
THAT'S NICE.
uh-huh.
AUNT DIDI TOMMY AND CHUCKIE WON'T PLAY FAIR!
ROBERTS·BLYBERG 3/25

2000

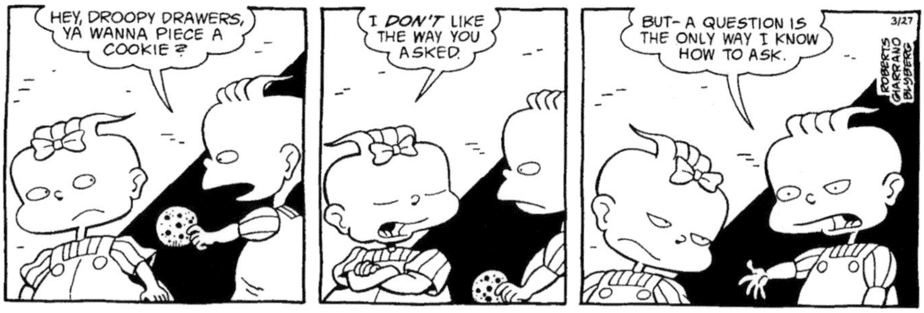
HEY, DROOPY DRAWERS, YA WANNA PIECE A COOKIE?
I DON'T LIKE THE WAY YOU ASKED.
BUT- A QUESTION IS THE ONLY WAY I KNOW HOW TO ASK.
3/27
ROBERTS GIARRANO BLYBERG

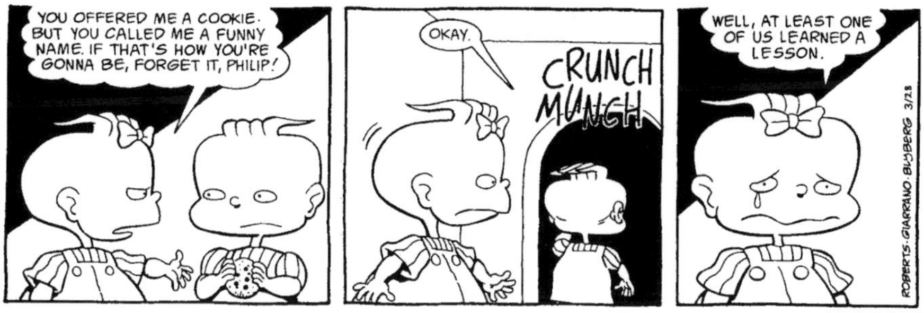
YOU OFFERED ME A COOKIE. BUT YOU CALLED ME A FUNNY NAME. IF THAT'S HOW YOU'RE GONNA BE, FORGET IT, PHILIP!
OKAY.
CRUNCH MUNCH
WELL, AT LEAST ONE OF US LEARNED A LESSON.
ROBERTS·GIARRANO·BLYBERG 3/28

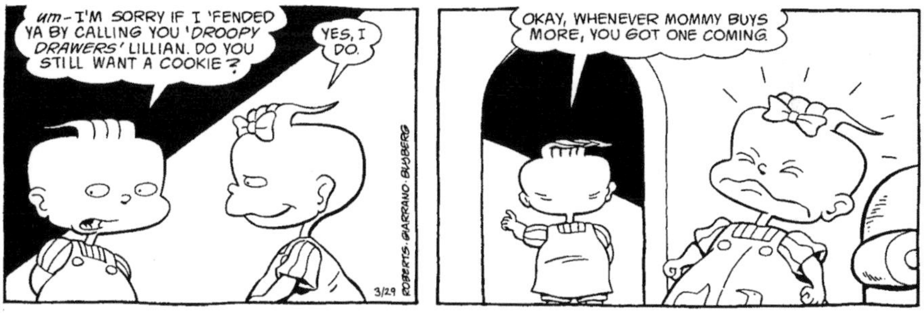
um- I'M SORRY IF I 'FENDED YA BY CALLING YOU 'DROOPY DRAWERS' LILLIAN. DO YOU STILL WANT A COOKIE?
YES, I DO.
ROBERTS·GIARRANO·BLYBERG
3/29
OKAY, WHENEVER MOMMY BUYS MORE, YOU GOT ONE COMING.

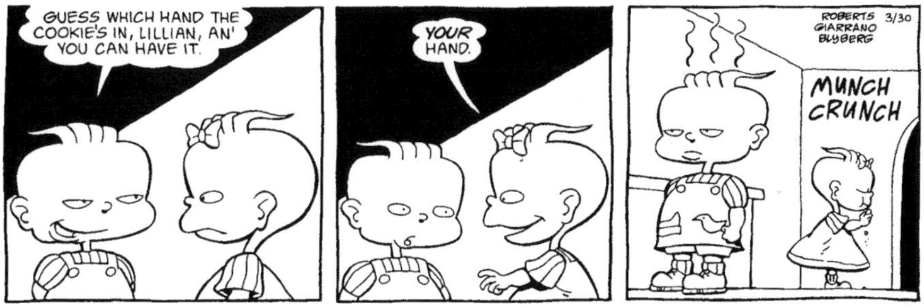
GUESS WHICH HAND THE COOKIE'S IN, LILLIAN, AN' YOU CAN HAVE IT.
YOUR HAND.
ROBERTS GIARRANO BLYBERG 3/30
MUNCH CRUNCH

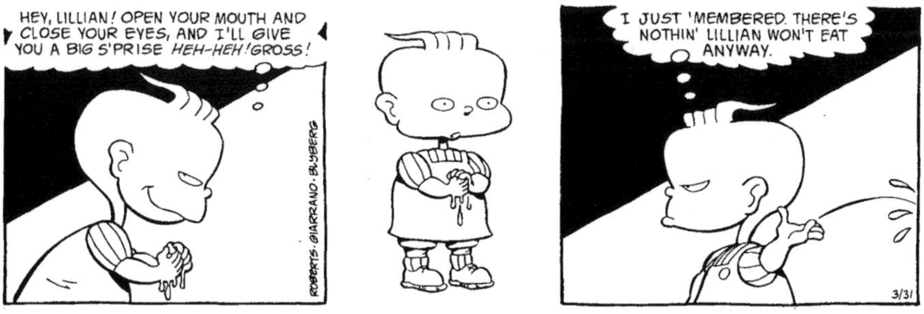
HEY, LILLIAN! OPEN YOUR MOUTH AND CLOSE YOUR EYES, AND I'LL GIVE YOU A BIG S'PRISE HEH-HEH! GROSS!
ROBERTS·GIARRANO·BLYBERG
I JUST 'MEMBERED. THERE'S NOTHIN' LILLIAN WON'T EAT ANYWAY.
3/31

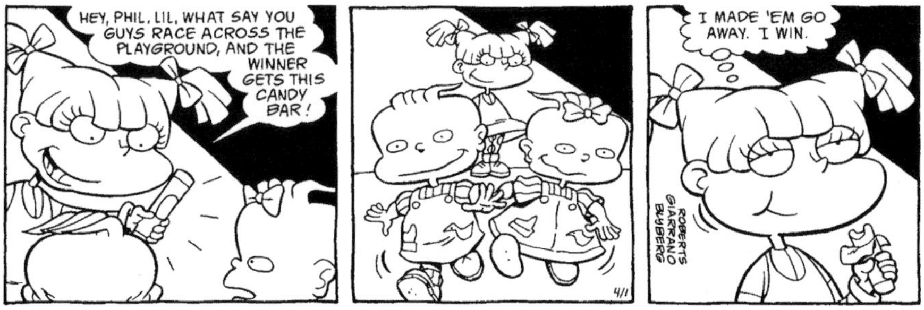
HEY, PHIL, LIL, WHAT SAY YOU GUYS RACE ACROSS THE PLAYGROUND, AND THE WINNER GETS THIS CANDY BAR!
4/1
ROBERTS GIARRANO BLYBERG
I MADE 'EM GO AWAY. I WIN.

2000

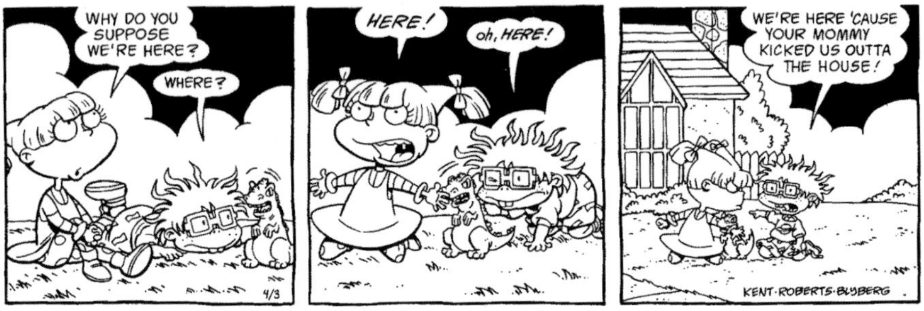
WHY DO YOU SUPPOSE WE'RE HERE?
WHERE?
HERE!
oh, HERE!
WE'RE HERE 'CAUSE YOUR MOMMY KICKED US OUTTA THE HOUSE!
4/3
KENT·ROBERTS·BLYBERG

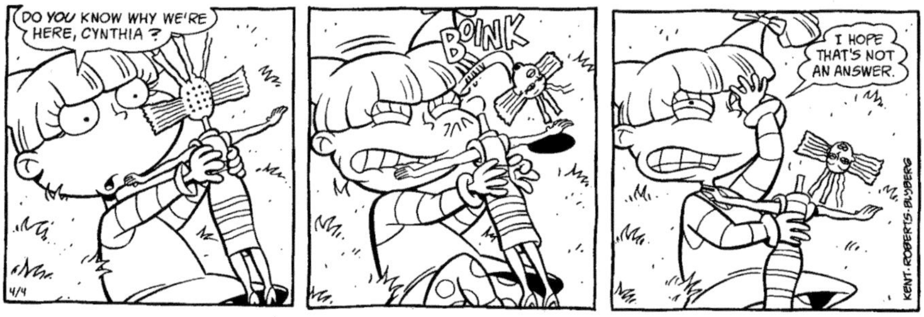
DO YOU KNOW WHY WE'RE HERE, CYNTHIA?
4/4
BOINK
I HOPE THAT'S NOT AN ANSWER.
KENT·ROBERTS·BLYBERG

2000

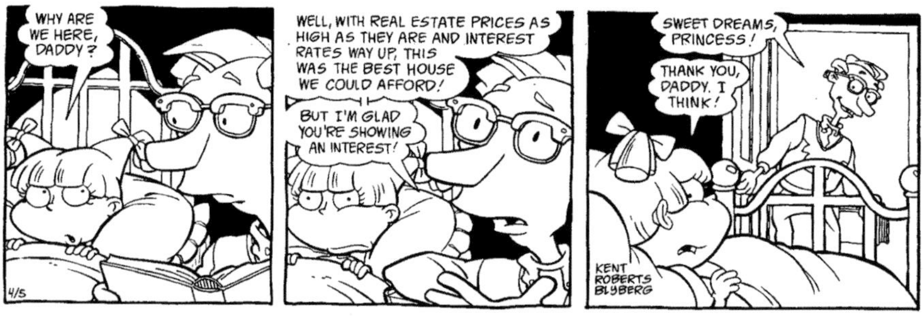
WHY ARE WE HERE, DADDY?
4/5
WELL, WITH REAL ESTATE PRICES AS HIGH AS THEY ARE AND INTEREST RATES WAY UP, THIS WAS THE BEST HOUSE WE COULD AFFORD!
BUT I'M GLAD YOU'RE SHOWING AN INTEREST!
SWEET DREAMS, PRINCESS!
THANK YOU, DADDY. I THINK!
KENT ROBERTS BLYBERG

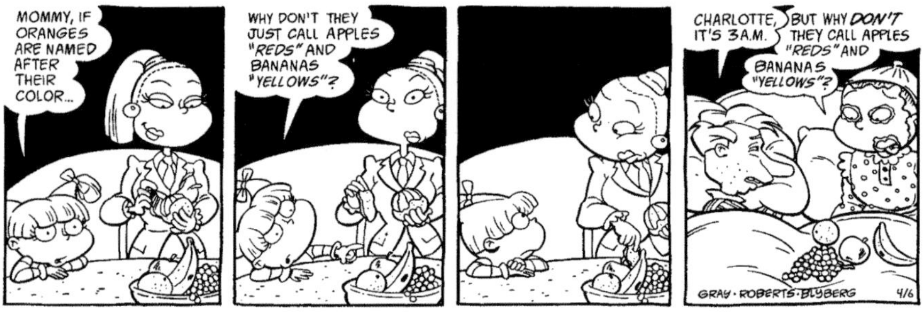
MOMMY, IF ORANGES ARE NAMED AFTER THEIR COLOR...
WHY DON'T THEY JUST CALL APPLES "REDS" AND BANANAS "YELLOWS"?
CHARLOTTE, IT'S 3 A.M.
BUT WHY DON'T THEY CALL APPLES "REDS" AND BANANAS "YELLOWS"?
GRAY·ROBERTS·BLYBERG
4/6

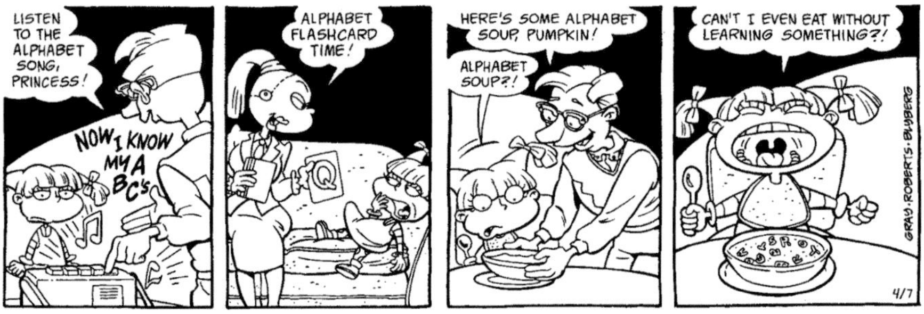
LISTEN TO THE ALPHABET SONG, PRINCESS!
NOW I KNOW MY A B C's
ALPHABET FLASHCARD TIME!
Q
HERE'S SOME ALPHABET SOUP, PUMPKIN!
ALPHABET SOUP?!
CAN'T I EVEN EAT WITHOUT LEARNING SOMETHING?!
GRAY·ROBERTS·BLYBERG
4/7

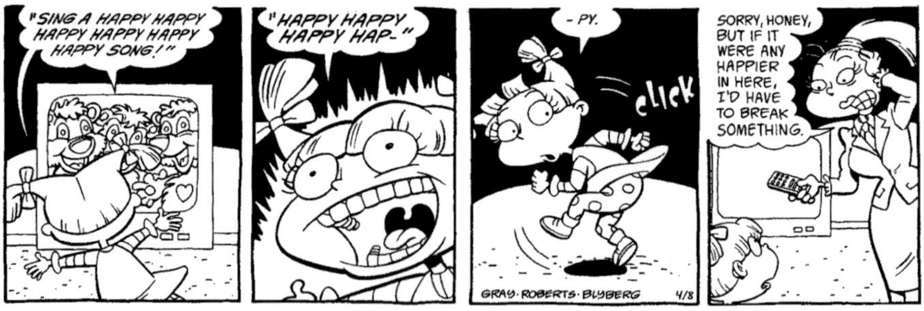
"SING A HAPPY HAPPY HAPPY HAPPY HAPPY HAPPY SONG!"
"HAPPY HAPPY HAPPY HAP-"
-PY.
CLICK
SORRY, HONEY, BUT IF IT WERE ANY HAPPIER IN HERE, I'D HAVE TO BREAK SOMETHING.
GRAY·ROBERTS·BLYBERG
4/8

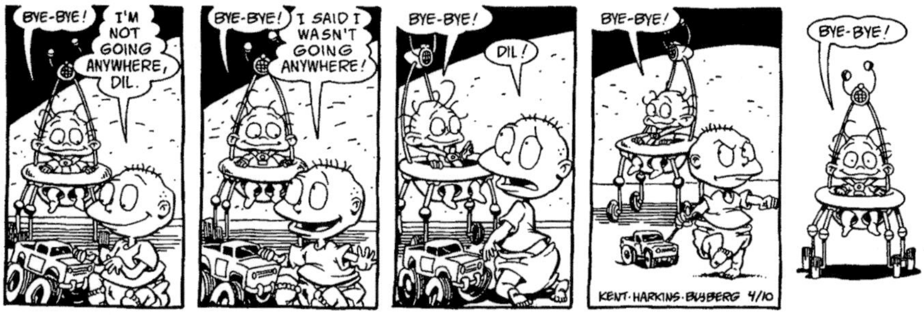
BYE-BYE!
I'M NOT GOING ANYWHERE, DIL.
BYE-BYE!
I SAID I WASN'T GOING ANYWHERE!
BYE-BYE!
DIL!
BYE-BYE!
KENT·HARKINS·BLYBERG 4/10
BYE-BYE!

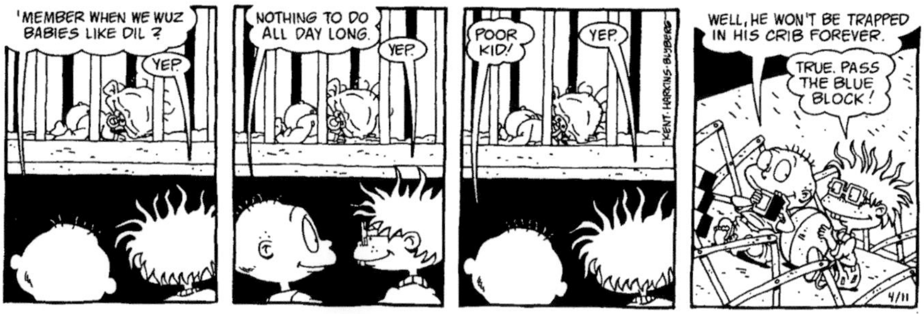
'MEMBER WHEN WE WUZ BABIES LIKE DIL?
YEP.
NOTHING TO DO ALL DAY LONG.
YEP.
POOR KID!
YEP.
KENT·HARKINS·BLYBERG
WELL, HE WON'T BE TRAPPED IN HIS CRIB FOREVER.
TRUE. PASS THE BLUE BLOCK!
4/11

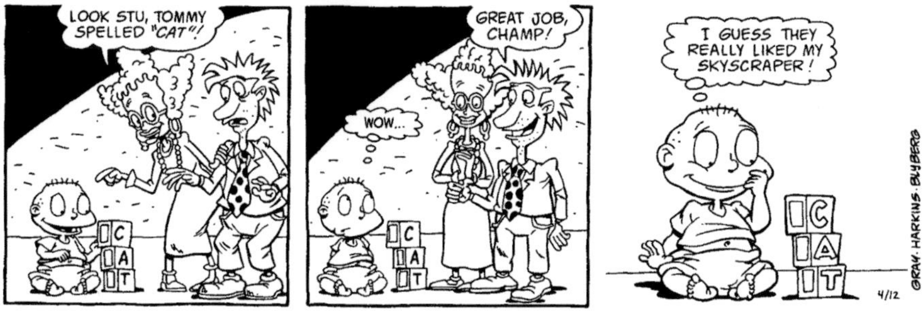
LOOK STU, TOMMY SPELLED "CAT"!
GREAT JOB, CHAMP!
WOW...
I GUESS THEY REALLY LIKED MY SKYSCRAPER!
GRAY·HARKINS·BLYBERG
4/12

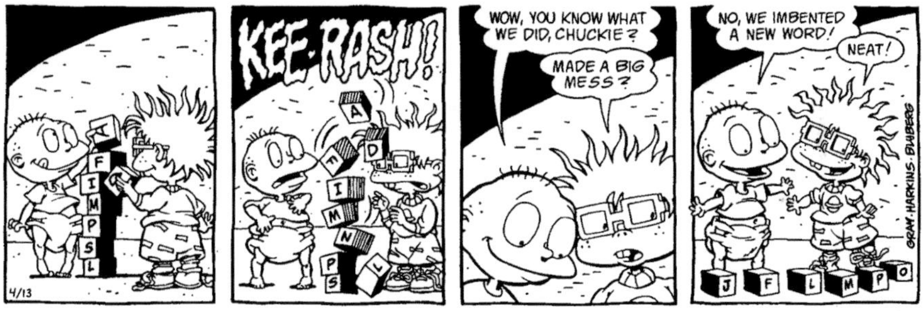
4/13
KEE-RASH!
WOW, YOU KNOW WHAT WE DID, CHUCKIE?
MADE A BIG MESS?
NO, WE IMBENTED A NEW WORD!
NEAT!
GRAY·HARKINS·BLYBERG

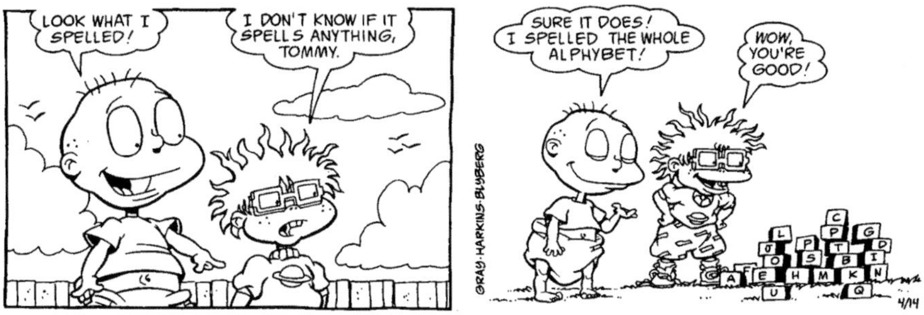
LOOK WHAT I SPELLED!
I DON'T KNOW IF IT SPELLS ANYTHING, TOMMY.
GRAY·HARKINS·BLYBERG
SURE IT DOES! I SPELLED THE WHOLE ALPHYBET!
WOW, YOU'RE GOOD!
4/14

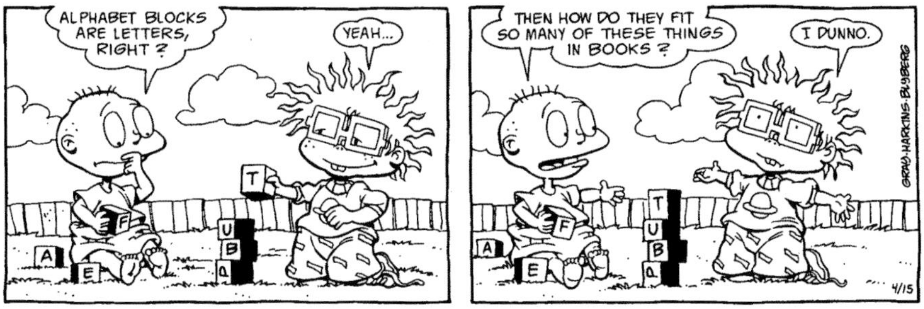
ALPHABET BLOCKS ARE LETTERS, RIGHT?
YEAH...
THEN HOW DO THEY FIT SO MANY OF THESE THINGS IN BOOKS?
I DUNNO.
GRAY·HARKINS·BLYBERG
4/15

2000

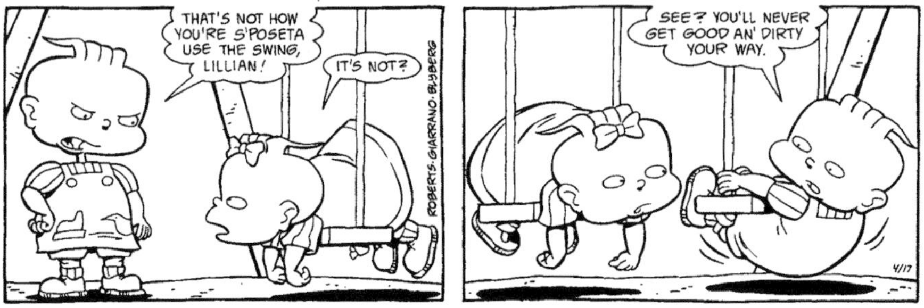
THAT'S NOT HOW YOU'RE S'POSETA USE THE SWING, LILLIAN!
IT'S NOT?
ROBERTS·GIARRANO·BLYBERG
SEE? YOU'LL NEVER GET GOOD AN' DIRTY YOUR WAY.
4/17

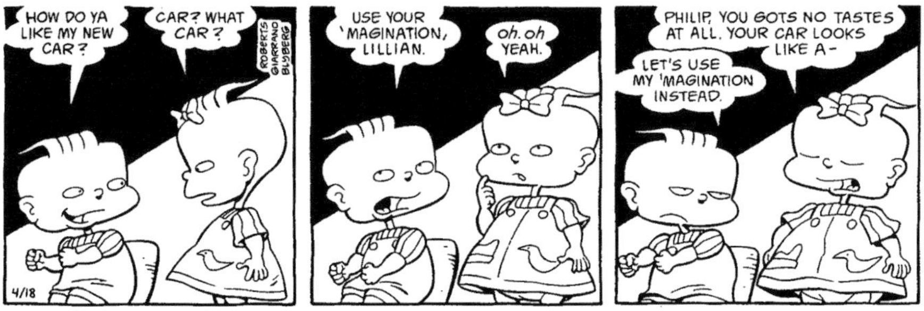
HOW DO YA LIKE MY NEW CAR?
CAR? WHAT CAR?
ROBERTS GIARRANO BLYBERG
4/18
USE YOUR 'MAGINATION, LILLIAN.
oh. oh YEAH.
PHILIP, YOU GOTS NO TASTES AT ALL. YOUR CAR LOOKS LIKE A-
LET'S USE MY 'MAGINATION INSTEAD.

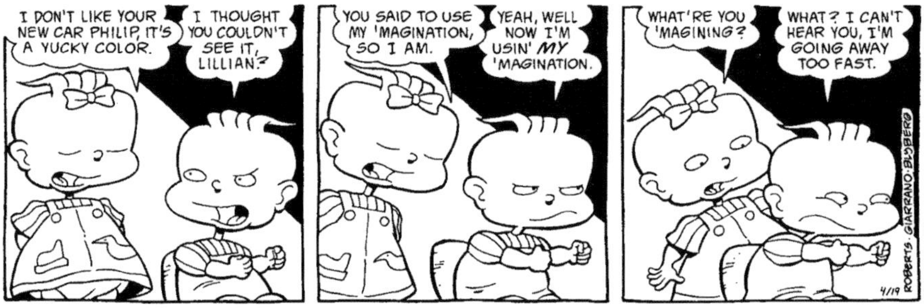
I DON'T LIKE YOUR NEW CAR PHILIP, IT'S A YUCKY COLOR.
I THOUGHT YOU COULDN'T SEE IT, LILLIAN?
YOU SAID TO USE MY 'MAGINATION, SO I AM.
YEAH, WELL NOW I'M USIN' MY 'MAGINATION.
WHAT'RE YOU 'MAGINING?
WHAT? I CAN'T HEAR YOU, I'M GOING AWAY TOO FAST.
ROBERTS·GIARRANO·BLYBERG
4/19

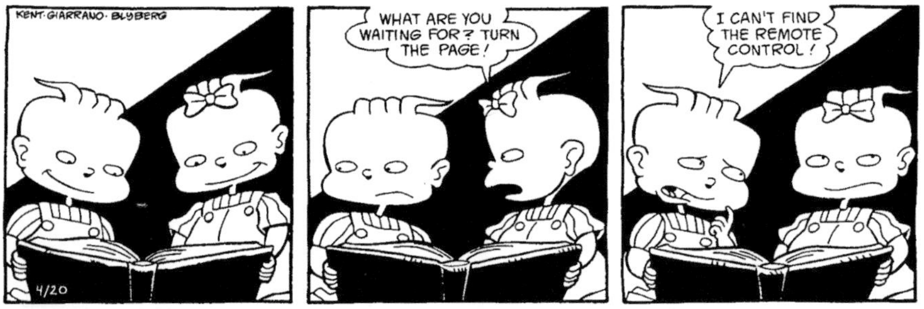
KENT·GIARRANO·BLYBERG
4/20
WHAT ARE YOU WAITING FOR? TURN THE PAGE!
I CAN'T FIND THE REMOTE CONTROL!

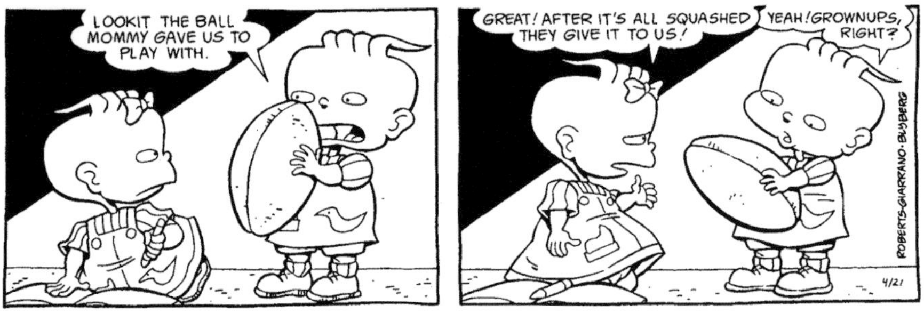
LOOKIT THE BALL MOMMY GAVE US TO PLAY WITH.
GREAT! AFTER IT'S ALL SQUASHED THEY GIVE IT TO US!
YEAH! GROWNUPS, RIGHT?
ROBERTS·GIARRANO·BLYBERG
4/21

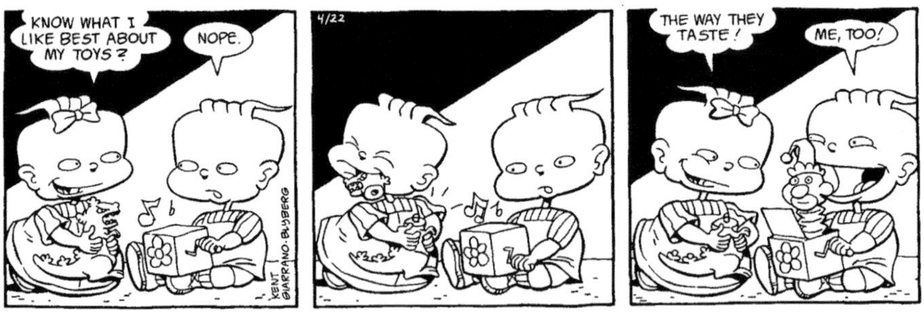
KNOW WHAT I LIKE BEST ABOUT MY TOYS?
NOPE.
KENT·GIARRANO·BLYBERG
4/22
THE WAY THEY TASTE!
ME, TOO!

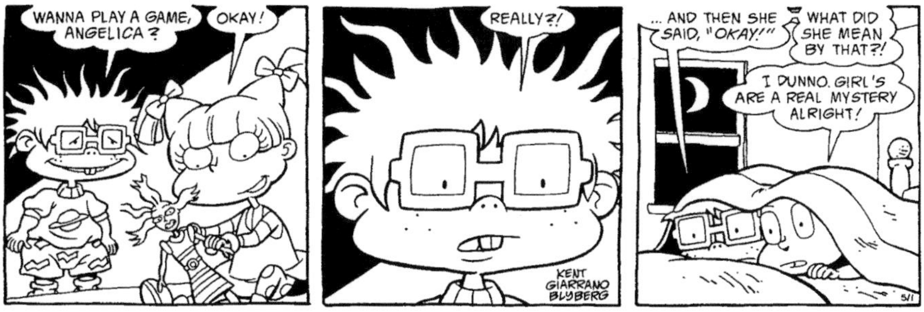
WANNA PLAY A GAME, ANGELICA?
OKAY!
REALLY?!
KENT GIARRANO BLYBERG
... AND THEN SHE SAID, "OKAY!"
WHAT DID SHE MEAN BY THAT?!
I DUNNO. GIRL'S ARE A REAL MYSTERY ALRIGHT!
5/1

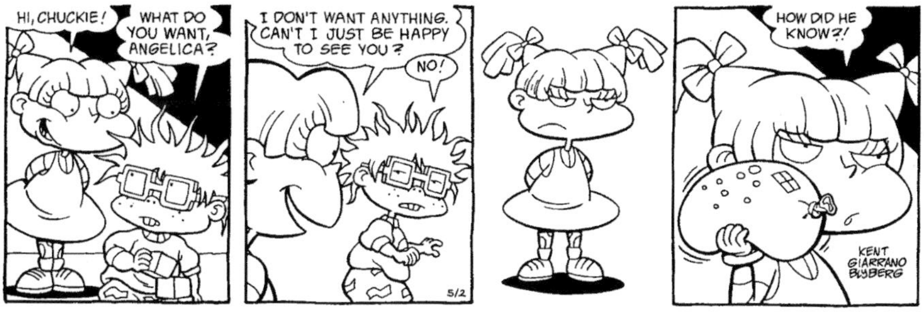
HI, CHUCKIE!
WHAT DO YOU WANT, ANGELICA?
I DON'T WANT ANYTHING. CAN'T I JUST BE HAPPY TO SEE YOU?
NO!
5/2
HOW DID HE KNOW?!
KENT GIARRANO BLYBERG

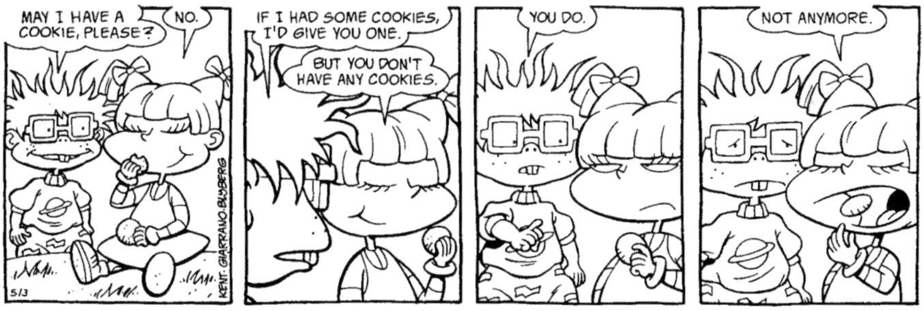
MAY I HAVE A COOKIE, PLEASE?
NO.
KENT·GIARRANO·BLYBERG
5/3
IF I HAD SOME COOKIES, I'D GIVE YOU ONE.
BUT YOU DON'T HAVE ANY COOKIES.
YOU DO.
NOT ANYMORE.

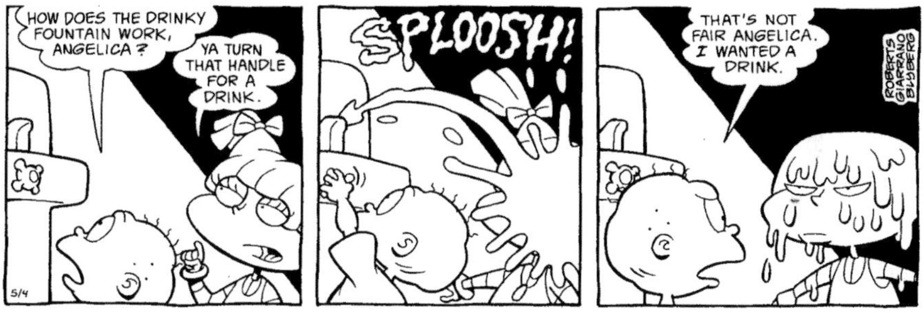
HOW DOES THE DRINKY FOUNTAIN WORK, ANGELICA?
YA TURN THAT HANDLE FOR A DRINK.
5/4
SPLOOSH!
THAT'S NOT FAIR ANGELICA. I WANTED A DRINK.
ROBERTS GIARRANO BLYBERG

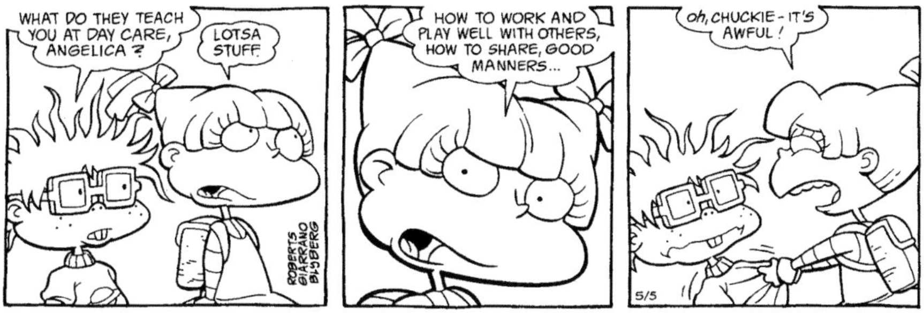
WHAT DO THEY TEACH YOU AT DAY CARE, ANGELICA?
LOTSA STUFF.
ROBERTS GIARRANO BLYBERG
HOW TO WORK AND PLAY WELL WITH OTHERS, HOW TO SHARE, GOOD MANNERS...
oh, CHUCKIE - IT'S AWFUL!
5/5

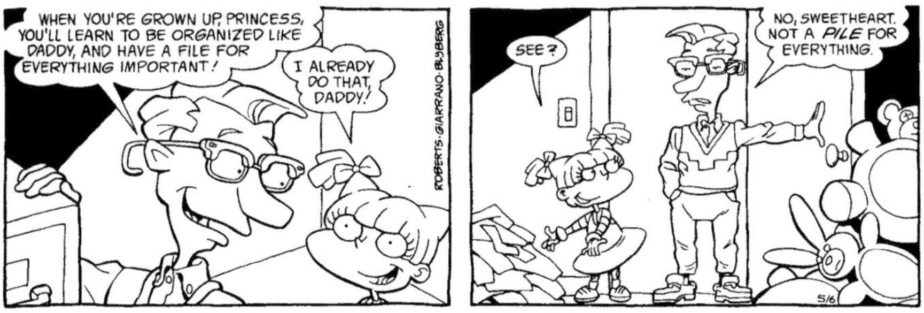
WHEN YOU'RE GROWN UP, PRINCESS, YOU'LL LEARN TO BE ORGANIZED LIKE DADDY, AND HAVE A FILE FOR EVERYTHING IMPORTANT!
I ALREADY DO THAT, DADDY!
ROBERTS·GIARRANO·BLYBERG
SEE?
NO, SWEETHEART. NOT A PILE FOR EVERYTHING.
5/6

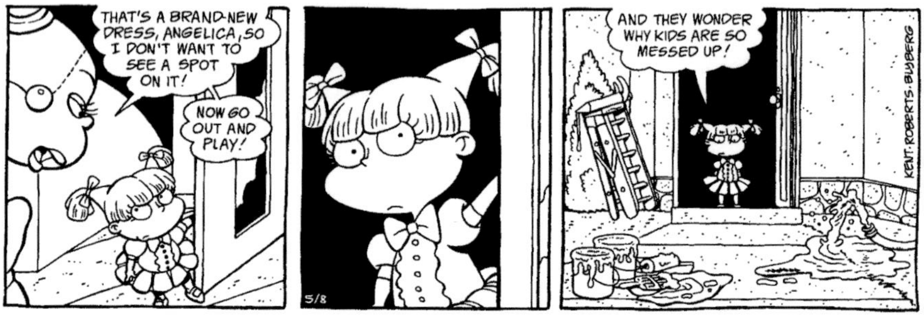
THAT'S A BRAND-NEW DRESS, ANGELICA, SO I DON'T WANT TO SEE A SPOT ON IT!
NOW GO OUT AND PLAY!
5/8
AND THEY WONDER WHY KIDS ARE SO MESSED UP!
KENT·ROBERTS·BLYBERG

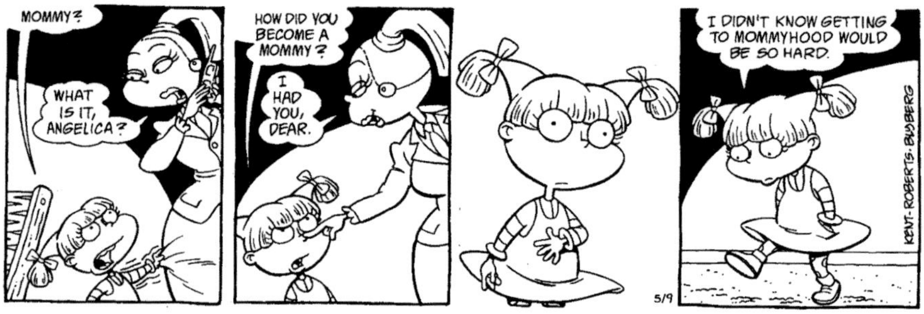
MOMMY?
WHAT IS IT, ANGELICA?
HOW DID YOU BECOME A MOMMY?
I HAD YOU, DEAR.
5/9
I DIDN'T KNOW GETTING TO MOMMYHOOD WOULD BE SO HARD.
KENT·ROBERTS·BLYBERG

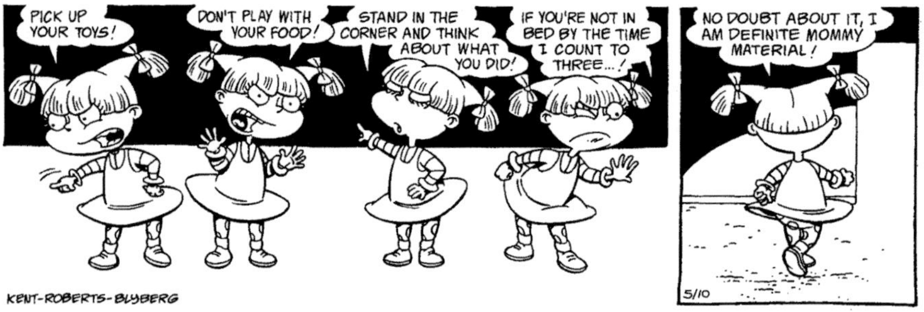
PICK UP YOUR TOYS!
DON'T PLAY WITH YOUR FOOD!
STAND IN THE CORNER AND THINK ABOUT WHAT YOU DID!
IF YOU'RE NOT IN BED BY THE TIME I COUNT TO THREE...!
NO DOUBT ABOUT IT, I AM DEFINITE MOMMY MATERIAL!
KENT-ROBERTS-BLYBERG
5/10

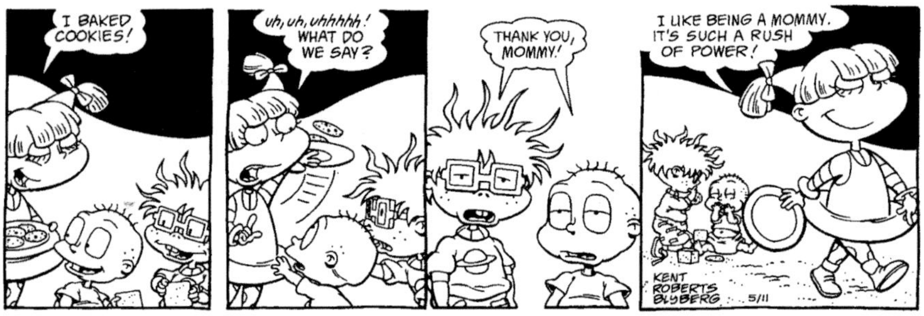
I BAKED COOKIES!
uh, uh, uhhhhh! WHAT DO WE SAY?
THANK YOU, MOMMY!
I LIKE BEING A MOMMY. IT'S SUCH A RUSH OF POWER!
KENT ROBERTS BLYBERG
5/11

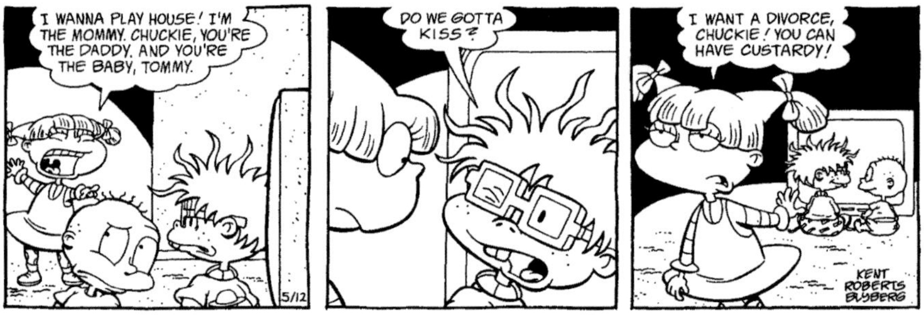
I WANNA PLAY HOUSE! I'M THE MOMMY. CHUCKIE, YOU'RE THE DADDY. AND YOU'RE THE BABY, TOMMY.
5/12
DO WE GOTTA KISS?
I WANT A DIVORCE, CHUCKIE! YOU CAN HAVE CUSTARDY!
KENT ROBERTS BLYBERG

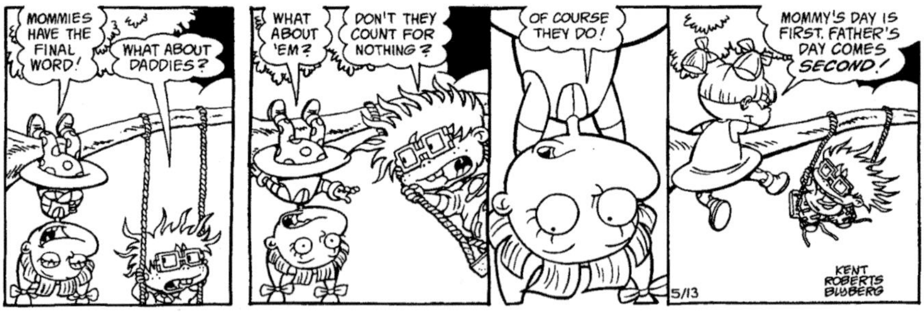
MOMMIES HAVE THE FINAL WORD!
WHAT ABOUT DADDIES?
WHAT ABOUT 'EM?
DON'T THEY COUNT FOR NOTHING?
OF COURSE THEY DO!
5/13
MOMMY'S DAY IS FIRST. FATHER'S DAY COMES SECOND!
KENT ROBERTS BLYBERG

2000

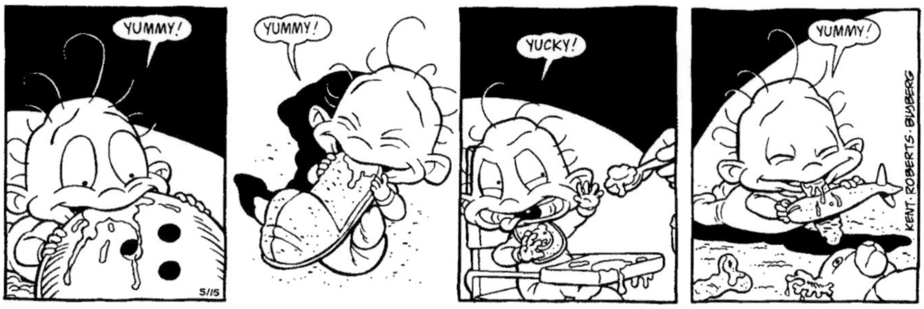
YUMMY!
5/15
YUMMY!
YUCKY!
YUMMY!
KENT·ROBERTS·BLYBERG

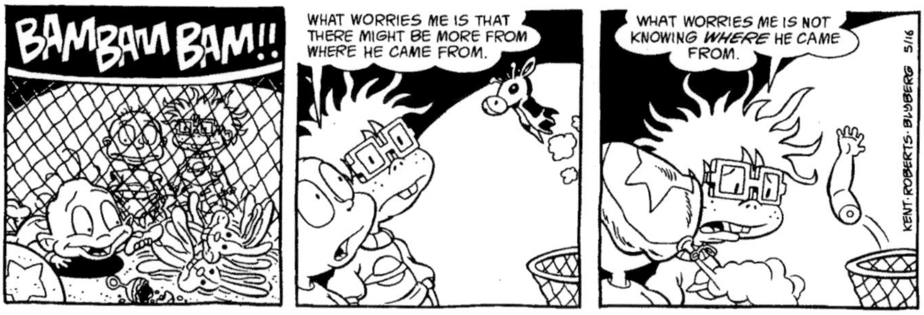
BAM BAM BAM!!
WHAT WORRIES ME IS THAT THERE MIGHT BE MORE FROM WHERE HE CAME FROM.
WHAT WORRIES ME IS NOT KNOWING *WHERE* HE CAME FROM.
5/16
KENT·ROBERTS·BLYBERG

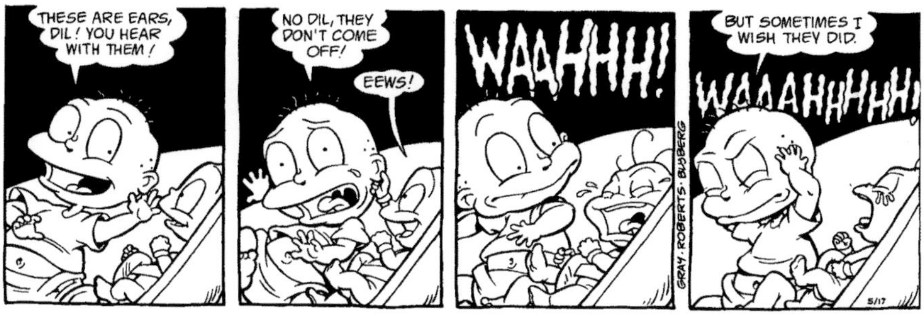
THESE ARE EARS, DIL! YOU HEAR WITH THEM!
NO DIL, THEY DON'T COME OFF!
EEWS!
WAAHHH!
GRAY·ROBERTS·BLYBERG
BUT SOMETIMES I WISH THEY DID.
WAAAHHHHH!
5/17

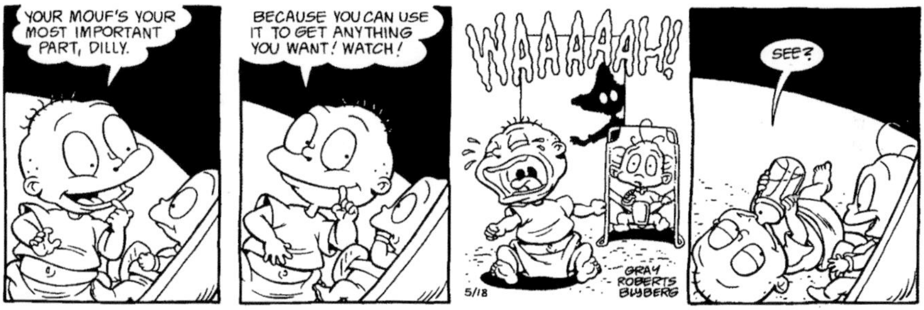
YOUR MOUF'S YOUR MOST IMPORTANT PART, DILLY.
BECAUSE YOU CAN USE IT TO GET ANYTHING YOU WANT! WATCH!
WAAAAAH!
5/18
GRAY ROBERTS BLYBERG
SEE?

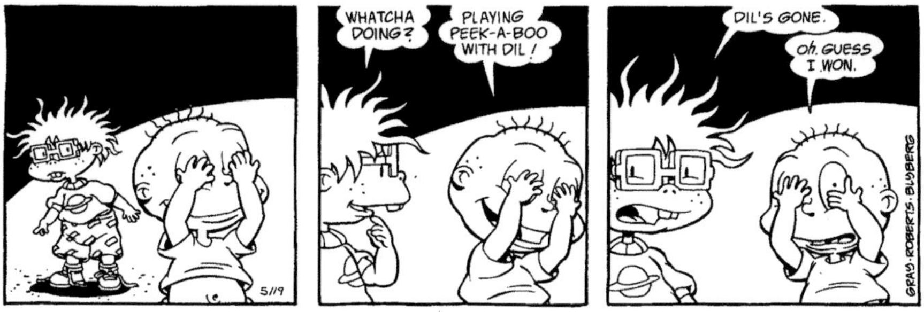
5/19
WHATCHA DOING?
PLAYING PEEK-A-BOO WITH DIL!
DIL'S GONE.
Oh, GUESS I WON.
GRAY·ROBERTS·BLYBERG

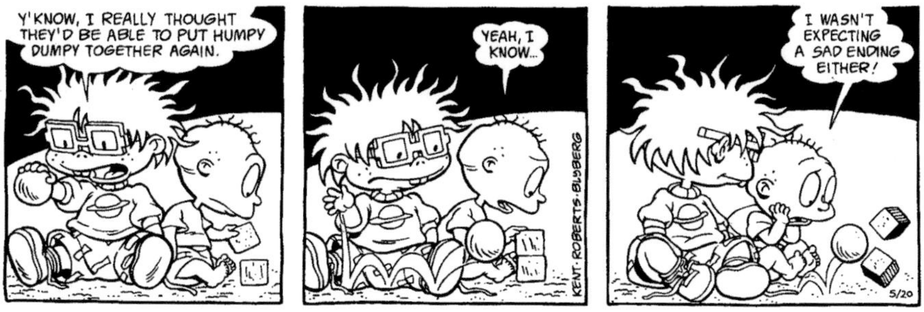
Y'KNOW, I REALLY THOUGHT THEY'D BE ABLE TO PUT HUMPY DUMPY TOGETHER AGAIN.
YEAH, I KNOW...
KENT·ROBERTS·BLYBERG
I WASN'T EXPECTING A SAD ENDING EITHER!
5/20

2000

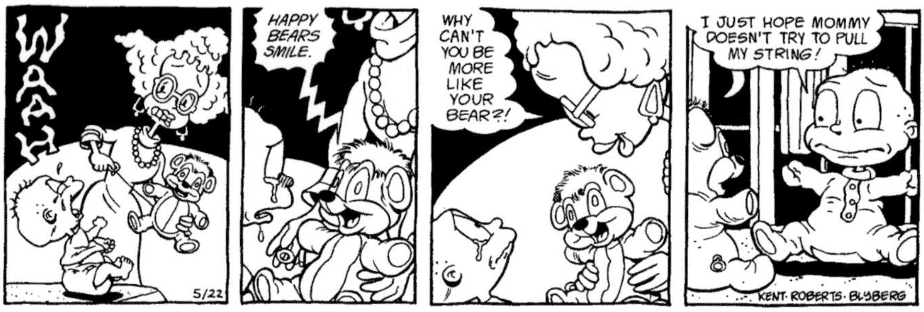
WAAH
5/22
HAPPY BEARS SMILE.
WHY CAN'T YOU BE MORE LIKE YOUR BEAR?!
I JUST HOPE MOMMY DOESN'T TRY TO PULL MY STRING!
KENT·ROBERTS·BLYBERG

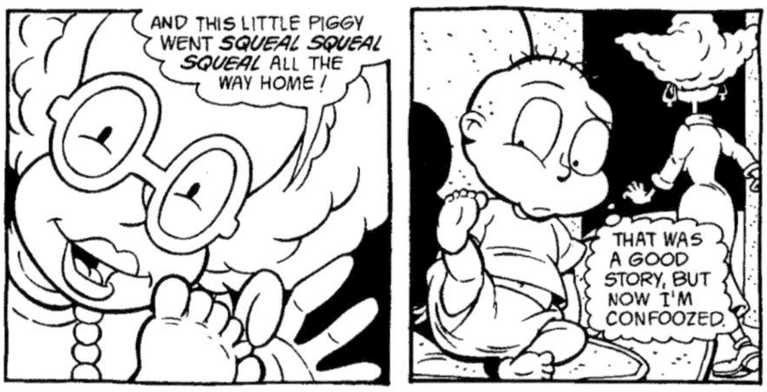
AND THIS LITTLE PIGGY WENT SQUEAL SQUEAL SQUEAL ALL THE WAY HOME!
THAT WAS A GOOD STORY, BUT NOW I'M CONFOOZED.
GRAY·ROBERTS·BLYBERG
DO PIGGIES LIVE ON FARMS, OR ON MY FEETS?
5/23

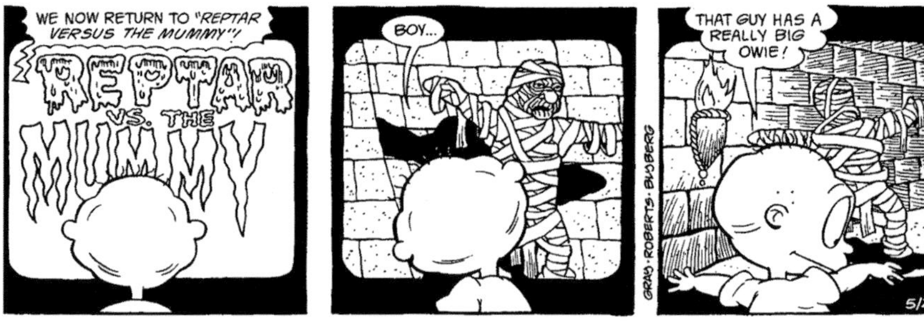
WE NOW RETURN TO "REPTAR VERSUS THE MUMMY"!
REPTAR VS. THE MUMMY
BOY...
GRAY·ROBERTS·BLYBERG
THAT GUY HAS A REALLY BIG OWIE!
5/24

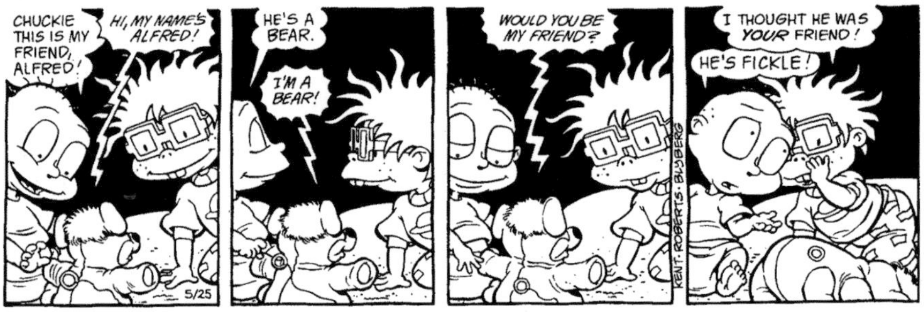
CHUCKIE THIS IS MY FRIEND, ALFRED!
HI, MY NAME'S ALFRED!
5/25
HE'S A BEAR.
I'M A BEAR!
WOULD YOU BE MY FRIEND?
KENT·ROBERTS·BLYBERG
I THOUGHT HE WAS YOUR FRIEND!
HE'S FICKLE!

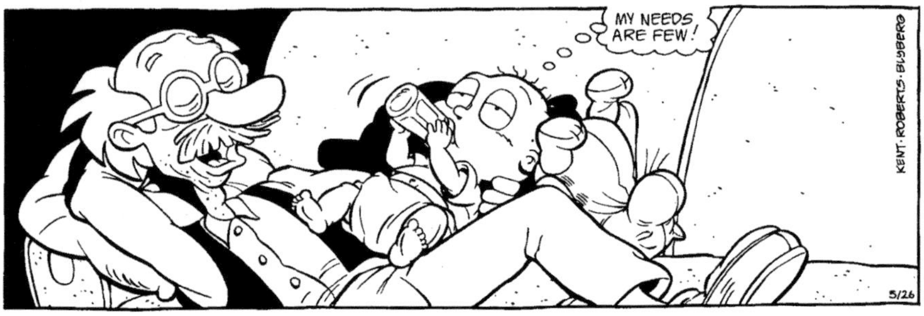
MY NEEDS ARE FEW!
KENT·ROBERTS·BLYBERG
5/26

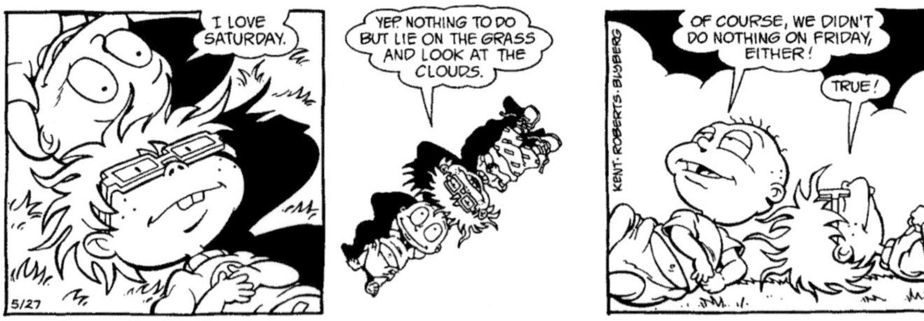
I LOVE SATURDAY.
5/27
YEP NOTHING TO DO BUT LIE ON THE GRASS AND LOOK AT THE CLOUDS.
KENT·ROBERTS·BLYBERG
OF COURSE, WE DIDN'T DO NOTHING ON FRIDAY, EITHER!
TRUE!

2000

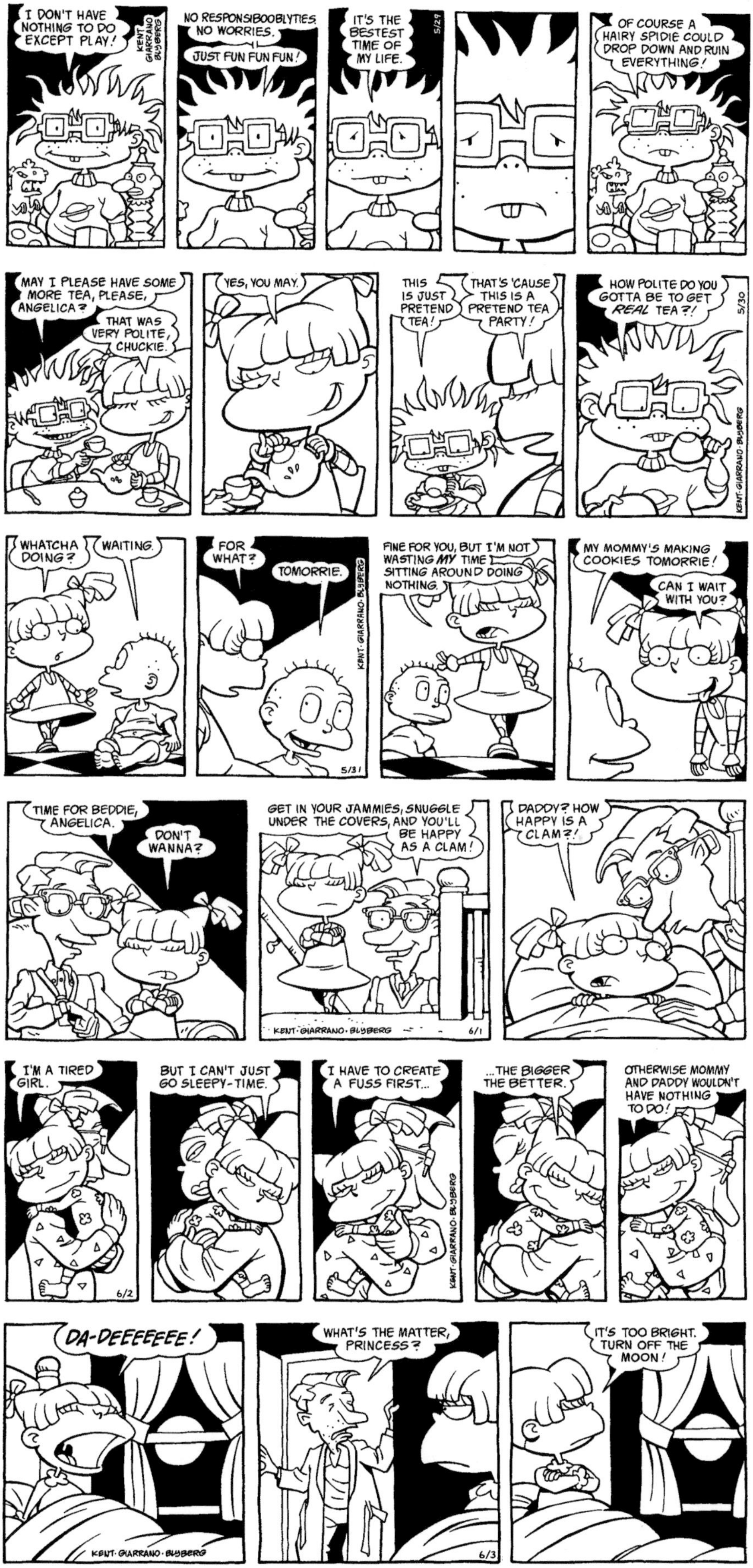
I DON'T HAVE NOTHING TO DO EXCEPT PLAY!
KENT GIARRANO BLYBERG
NO RESPONSIBOOBLYTIES. NO WORRIES.
JUST FUN FUN FUN!
IT'S THE BESTEST TIME OF MY LIFE.
5/29
OF COURSE A HAIRY SPIDIE COULD DROP DOWN AND RUIN EVERYTHING!
MAY I PLEASE HAVE SOME MORE TEA, PLEASE, ANGELICA?
THAT WAS VERY POLITE, CHUCKIE.
YES, YOU MAY.
THIS IS JUST PRETEND TEA!
THAT'S 'CAUSE THIS IS A PRETEND TEA PARTY!
HOW POLITE DO YOU GOTTA BE TO GET REAL TEA?!
5/30
KENT·GIARRANO·BLYBERG
WHATCHA DOING?
WAITING.
FOR WHAT?
TOMORRIE.
KENT·GIARRANO·BLYBERG
5/31
FINE FOR YOU, BUT I'M NOT WASTING MY TIME SITTING AROUND DOING NOTHING.
MY MOMMY'S MAKING COOKIES TOMORRIE!
CAN I WAIT WITH YOU?
TIME FOR BEDDIE, ANGELICA.
DON'T WANNA?
GET IN YOUR JAMMIES, SNUGGLE UNDER THE COVERS, AND YOU'LL BE HAPPY AS A CLAM!
KENT·GIARRANO·BLYBERG
6/1
DADDY? HOW HAPPY IS A CLAM?!
I'M A TIRED GIRL.
6/2
BUT I CAN'T JUST GO SLEEPY-TIME.
I HAVE TO CREATE A FUSS FIRST...
KENT·GIARRANO·BLYBERG
...THE BIGGER THE BETTER.
OTHERWISE MOMMY AND DADDY WOULDN'T HAVE NOTHING TO DO!
DA-DEEEEEEE!
KENT·GIARRANO·BLYBERG
WHAT'S THE MATTER, PRINCESS?
6/3
IT'S TOO BRIGHT. TURN OFF THE MOON!

2000

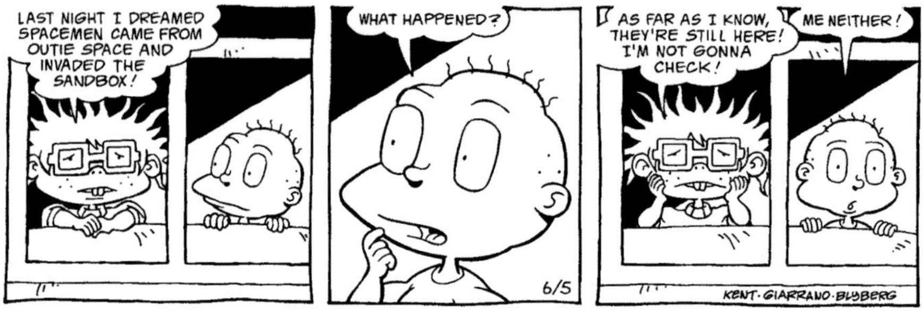
LAST NIGHT I DREAMED SPACEMEN CAME FROM OUTIE SPACE AND INVADED THE SANDBOX!
WHAT HAPPENED?
AS FAR AS I KNOW, THEY'RE STILL HERE! I'M NOT GONNA CHECK!
ME NEITHER!
6/5
KENT·GIARRANO·BLYBERG

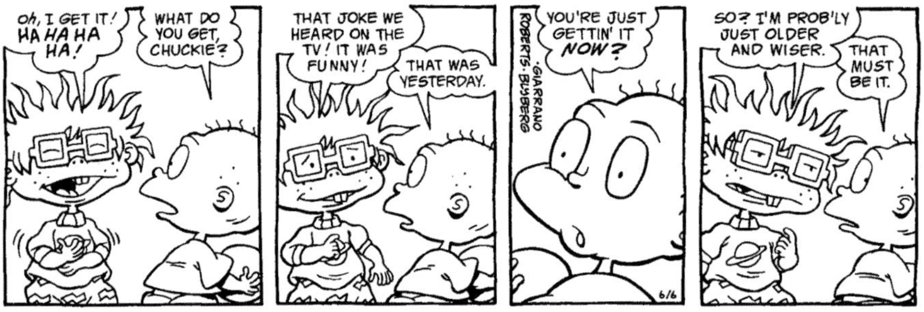
OH, I GET IT! HA HA HA HA!
WHAT DO YOU GET, CHUCKIE?
THAT JOKE WE HEARD ON THE TV! IT WAS FUNNY!
THAT WAS YESTERDAY.
ROBERTS·GIARRANO·BLYBERG
YOU'RE JUST GETTIN' IT NOW?
6/6
SO? I'M PROB'LY JUST OLDER AND WISER.
THAT MUST BE IT.

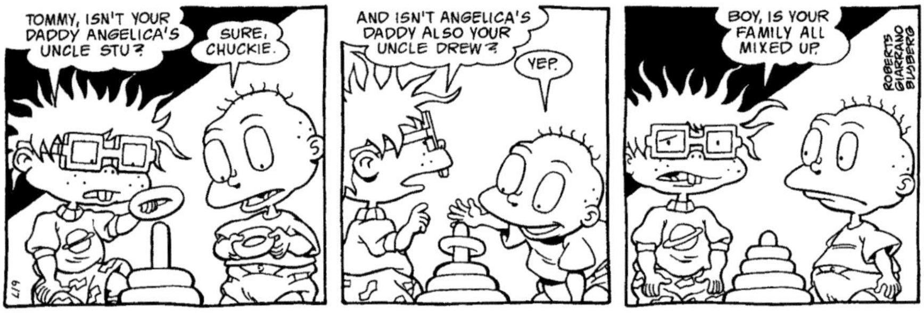
TOMMY, ISN'T YOUR DADDY ANGELICA'S UNCLE STU?
SURE, CHUCKIE.
6/7
AND ISN'T ANGELICA'S DADDY ALSO YOUR UNCLE DREW?
YEP.
BOY, IS YOUR FAMILY ALL MIXED UP.
ROBERTS GIARRANO BLYBERG

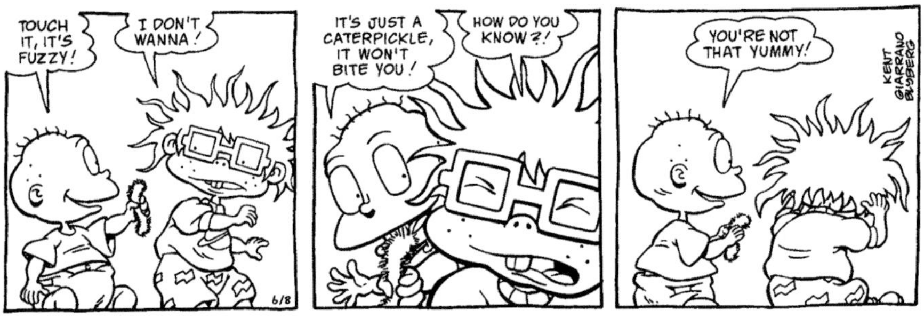
TOUCH IT, IT'S FUZZY!
I DON'T WANNA!
6/8
IT'S JUST A CATERPICKLE, IT WON'T BITE YOU!
HOW DO YOU KNOW?!
YOU'RE NOT THAT YUMMY!
KENT GIARRANO BLYBERG

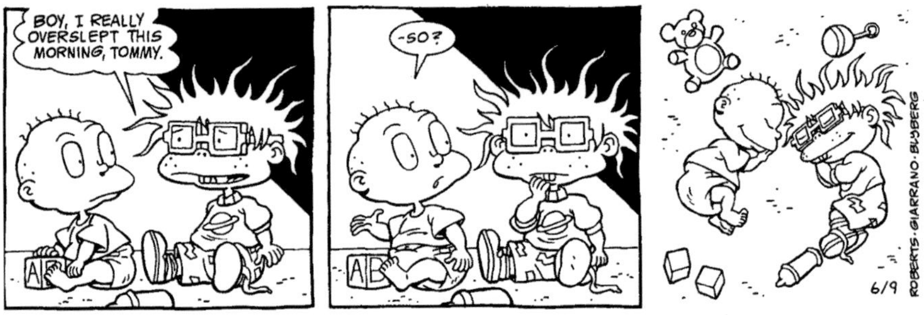
BOY, I REALLY OVERSLEPT THIS MORNING, TOMMY.
-SO?
ROBERTS·GIARRANO·BLYBERG
6/9

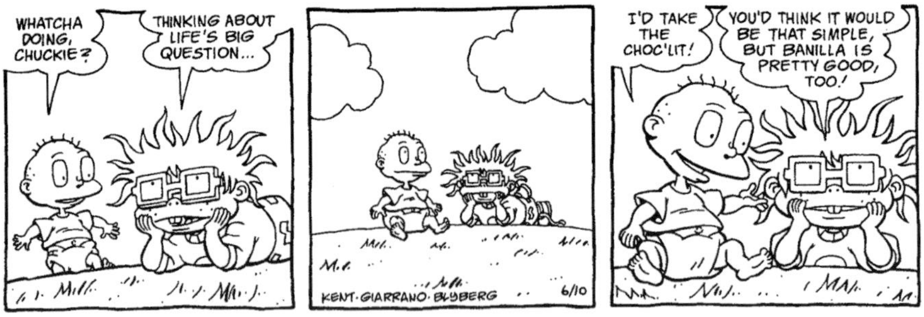
WHATCHA DOING, CHUCKIE?
THINKING ABOUT LIFE'S BIG QUESTION...
KENT·GIARRANO·BLYBERG
6/10
I'D TAKE THE CHOC'LIT!
YOU'D THINK IT WOULD BE THAT SIMPLE, BUT BANILLA IS PRETTY GOOD, TOO!

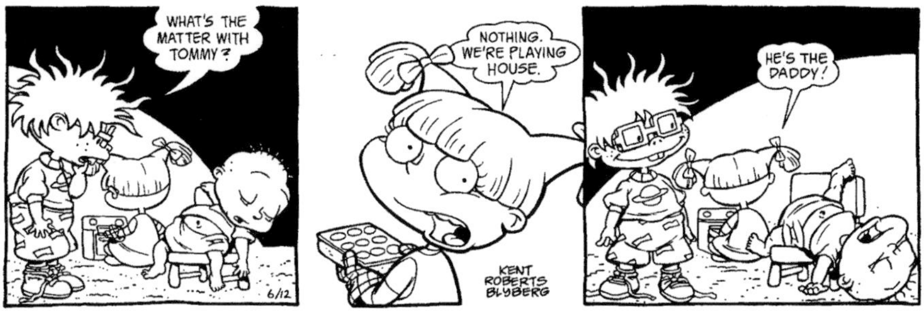
WHAT'S THE MATTER WITH TOMMY?
NOTHING. WE'RE PLAYING HOUSE.
HE'S THE DADDY!
6/12
KENT ROBERTS BLYBERG

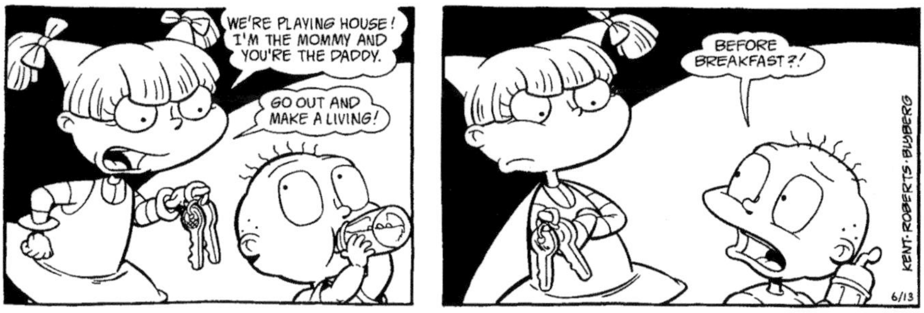
WE'RE PLAYING HOUSE! I'M THE MOMMY AND YOU'RE THE DADDY.
GO OUT AND MAKE A LIVING!
BEFORE BREAKFAST?!
KENT·ROBERTS·BLYBERG
6/13

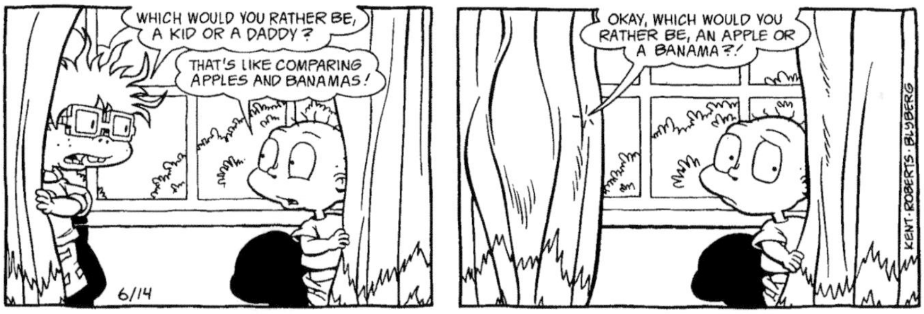
WHICH WOULD YOU RATHER BE, A KID OR A DADDY?
THAT'S LIKE COMPARING APPLES AND BANAMAS!
6/14
OKAY, WHICH WOULD YOU RATHER BE, AN APPLE OR A BANAMA?!
KENT·ROBERTS·BLYBERG

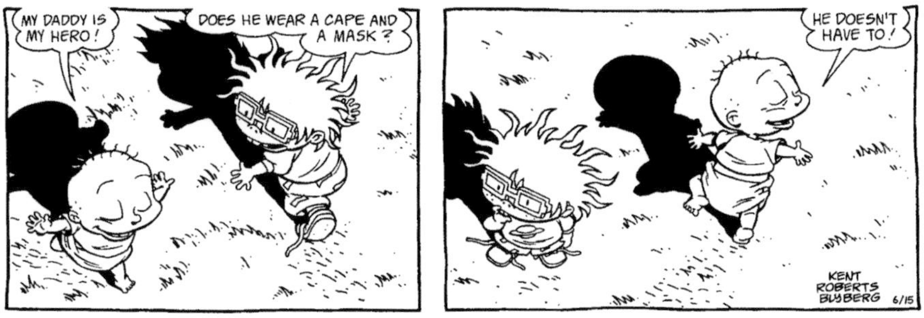
MY DADDY IS MY HERO!
DOES HE WEAR A CAPE AND A MASK?
HE DOESN'T HAVE TO!
KENT ROBERTS BLYBERG 6/15

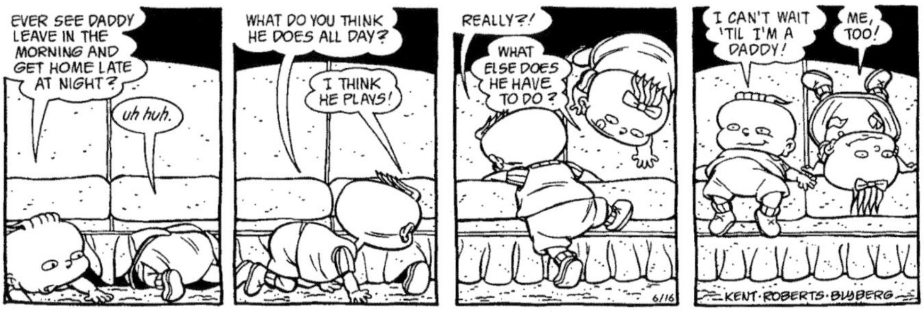
EVER SEE DADDY LEAVE IN THE MORNING AND GET HOME LATE AT NIGHT?
uh huh.
WHAT DO YOU THINK HE DOES ALL DAY?
I THINK HE PLAYS!
REALLY?!
WHAT ELSE DOES HE HAVE TO DO?
6/16
I CAN'T WAIT 'TIL I'M A DADDY!
ME, TOO!
KENT·ROBERTS·BLYBERG

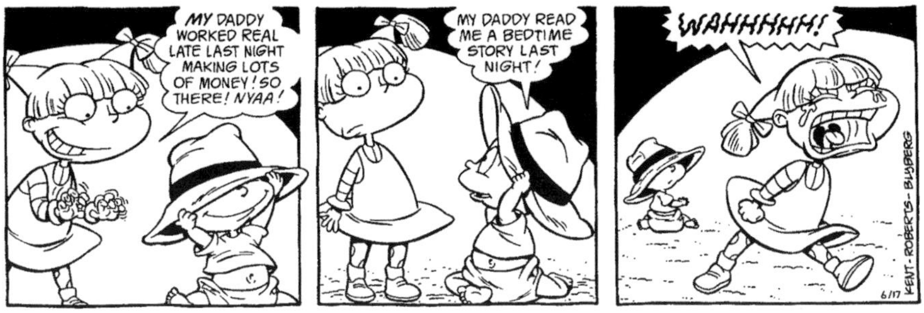
MY DADDY WORKED REAL LATE LAST NIGHT MAKING LOTS OF MONEY! SO THERE! NYAA!
MY DADDY READ ME A BEDTIME STORY LAST NIGHT!
WAHHHHH!
KENT·ROBERTS·BLYBERG
6/17

2000

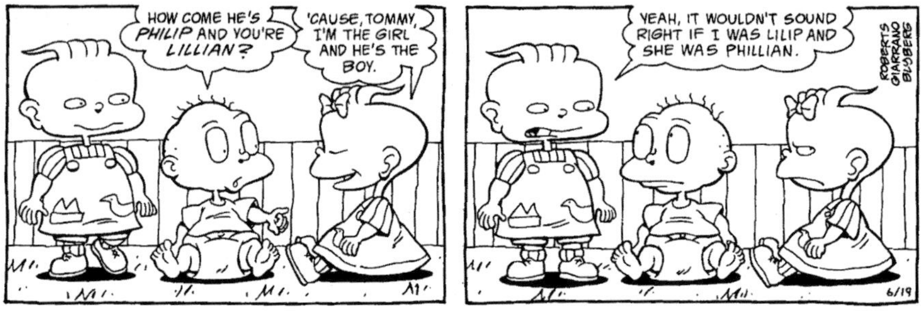
HOW COME HE'S PHILIP AND YOU'RE LILLIAN?
'CAUSE, TOMMY, I'M THE GIRL AND HE'S THE BOY.
YEAH, IT WOULDN'T SOUND RIGHT IF I WAS LILIP AND SHE WAS PHILLIAN.
ROBERTS GIARRANO BLYBERG
6/19

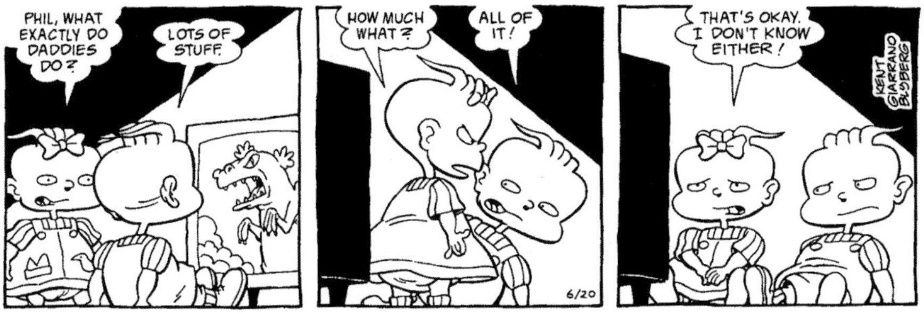
PHIL, WHAT EXACTLY DO DADDIES DO?
LOTS OF STUFF.
HOW MUCH WHAT?
ALL OF IT!
6/20
THAT'S OKAY. I DON'T KNOW EITHER!
KENT GIARRANO BLYBERG

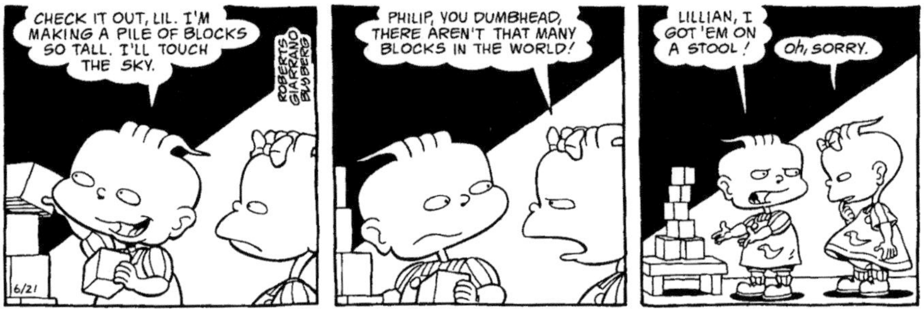
CHECK IT OUT, LIL. I'M MAKING A PILE OF BLOCKS SO TALL, I'LL TOUCH THE SKY.
ROBERTS GIARRANO BLYBERG
6/21
PHILIP, YOU DUMBHEAD, THERE AREN'T THAT MANY BLOCKS IN THE WORLD!
LILLIAN, I GOT 'EM ON A STOOL!
oh, SORRY.

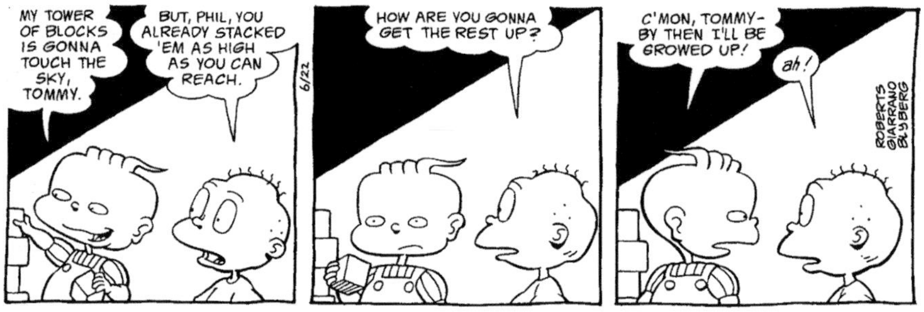
MY TOWER OF BLOCKS IS GONNA TOUCH THE SKY, TOMMY.
BUT, PHIL, YOU ALREADY STACKED 'EM AS HIGH AS YOU CAN REACH.
6/22
HOW ARE YOU GONNA GET THE REST UP?
C'MON, TOMMY- BY THEN I'LL BE GROWED UP!
ah!
ROBERTS GIARRANO BLYBERG

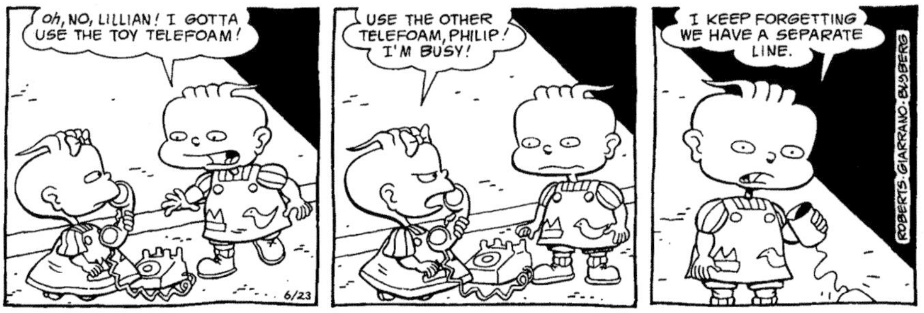
oh, NO, LILLIAN! I GOTTA USE THE TOY TELEFOAM!
6/23
USE THE OTHER TELEFOAM, PHILIP! I'M BUSY!
I KEEP FORGETTING WE HAVE A SEPARATE LINE.
ROBERTS·GIARRANO·BLYBERG

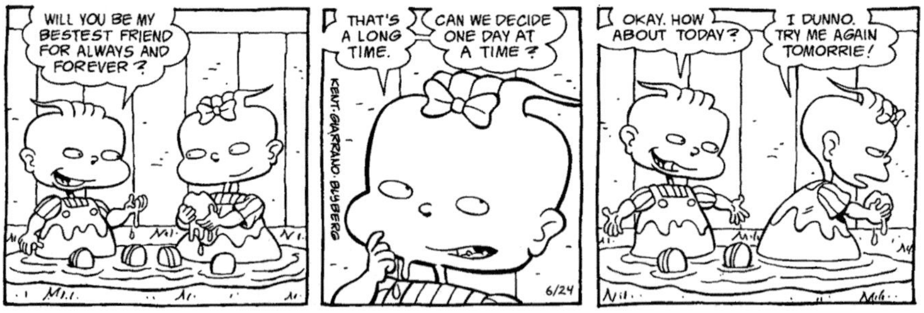
WILL YOU BE MY BESTEST FRIEND FOR ALWAYS AND FOREVER?
THAT'S A LONG TIME.
CAN WE DECIDE ONE DAY AT A TIME?
KENT·GIARRANO·BLYBERG
6/24
OKAY. HOW ABOUT TODAY?
I DUNNO. TRY ME AGAIN TOMORRIE!

2000

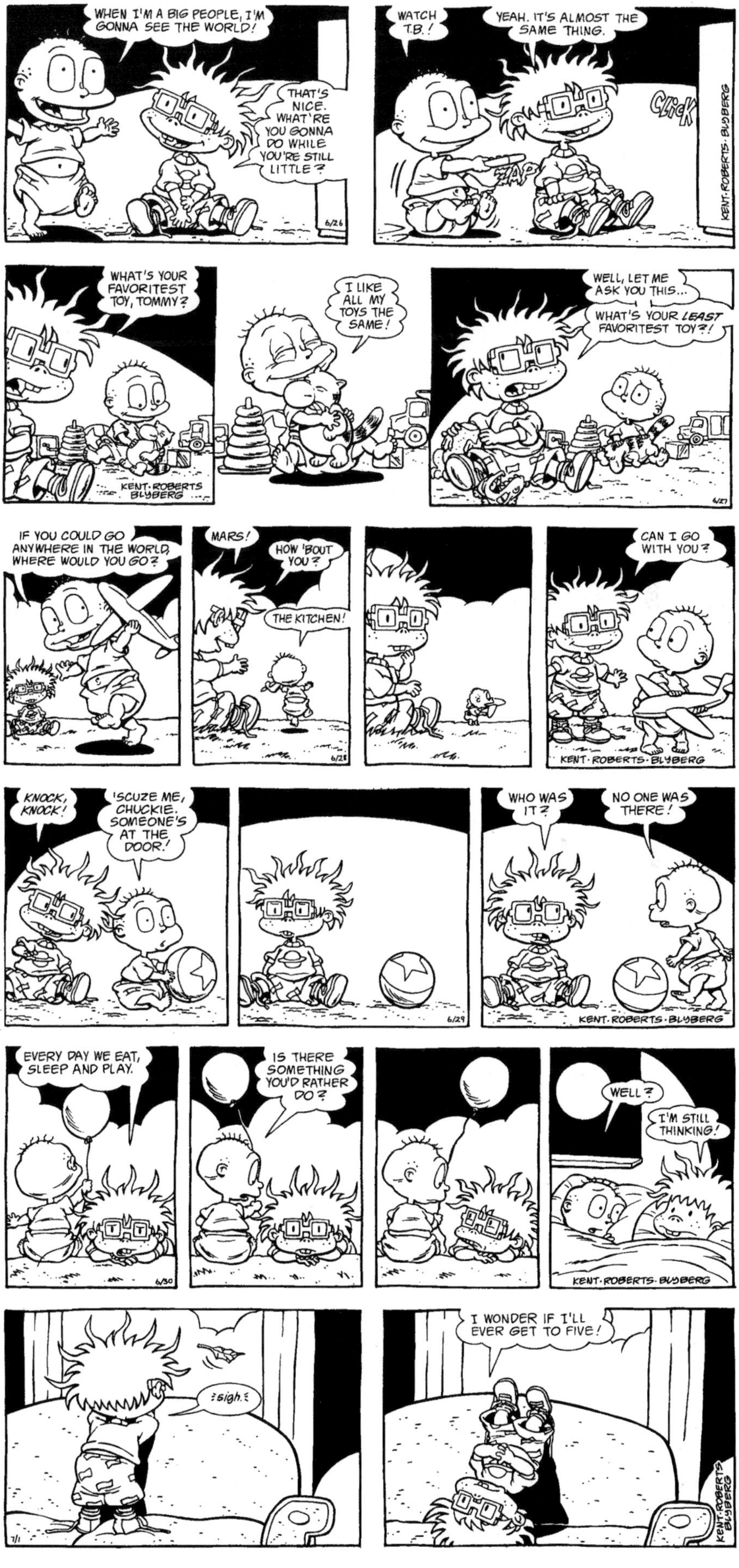
WHEN I'M A BIG PEOPLE, I'M GONNA SEE THE WORLD!
THAT'S NICE. WHAT'RE YOU GONNA DO WHILE YOU'RE STILL LITTLE?
6/26
WATCH T.B.!
YEAH. IT'S ALMOST THE SAME THING.
CLICK
ZAP
KENT·ROBERTS·BLYBERG
WHAT'S YOUR FAVORITEST TOY, TOMMY?
KENT·ROBERTS BLYBERG
I LIKE ALL MY TOYS THE SAME!
WELL, LET ME ASK YOU THIS...
WHAT'S YOUR LEAST FAVORITEST TOY?!
6/27
IF YOU COULD GO ANYWHERE IN THE WORLD, WHERE WOULD YOU GO?
MARS!
HOW 'BOUT YOU?
THE KITCHEN!
6/28
CAN I GO WITH YOU?
KENT·ROBERTS·BLYBERG
KNOCK, KNOCK!
'SCUZE ME, CHUCKIE. SOMEONE'S AT THE DOOR!
6/29
WHO WAS IT?
NO ONE WAS THERE!
KENT·ROBERTS·BLYBERG
EVERY DAY WE EAT, SLEEP AND PLAY.
6/30
IS THERE SOMETHING YOU'D RATHER DO?
WELL?
I'M STILL THINKING!
KENT·ROBERTS·BLYBERG
sigh.
7/1
I WONDER IF I'LL EVER GET TO FIVE!
KENT·ROBERTS BLYBERG

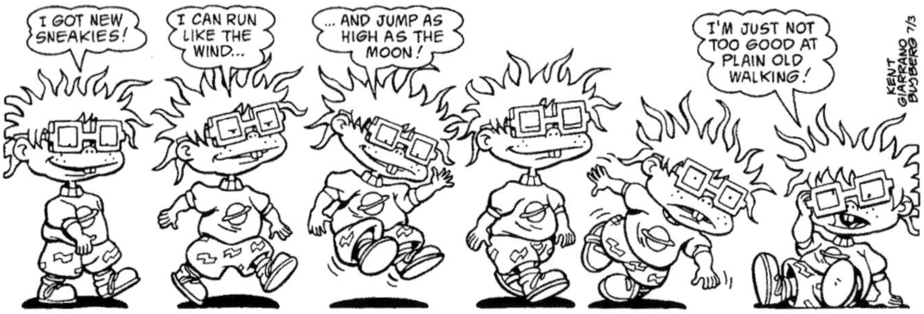
I GOT NEW SNEAKIES!
I CAN RUN LIKE THE WIND...
... AND JUMP AS HIGH AS THE MOON!
I'M JUST NOT TOO GOOD AT PLAIN OLD WALKING!
KENT GIARRANO BLYBERG 7/3

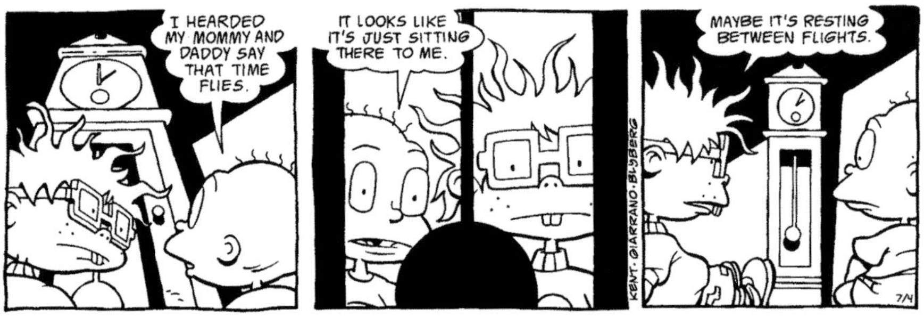
I HEARDED MY MOMMY AND DADDY SAY THAT TIME FLIES.
IT LOOKS LIKE IT'S JUST SITTING THERE TO ME.
KENT · GIARRANO · BLYBERG
MAYBE IT'S RESTING BETWEEN FLIGHTS.
7/4

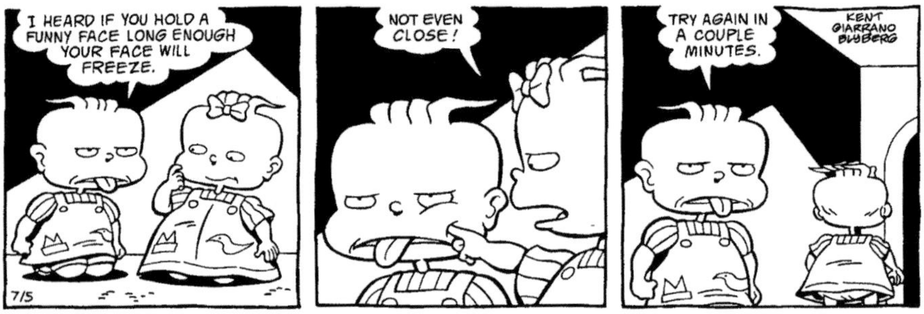
I HEARD IF YOU HOLD A FUNNY FACE LONG ENOUGH YOUR FACE WILL FREEZE.
7/5
NOT EVEN CLOSE!
TRY AGAIN IN A COUPLE MINUTES.
KENT GIARRANO BLYBERG

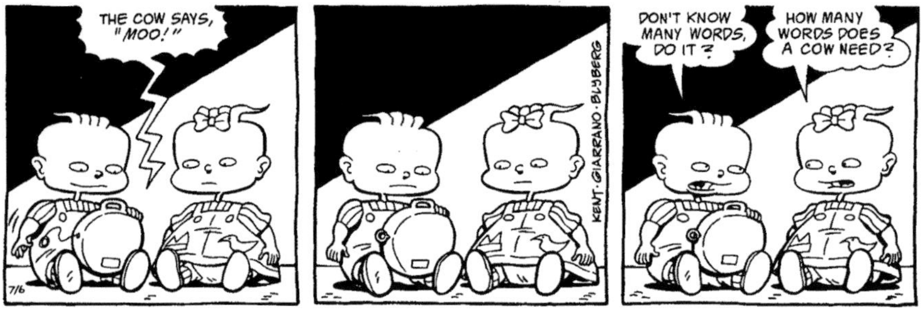
THE COW SAYS, "MOO!"
7/6
KENT · GIARRANO · BLYBERG
DON'T KNOW MANY WORDS, DO IT?
HOW MANY WORDS DOES A COW NEED?

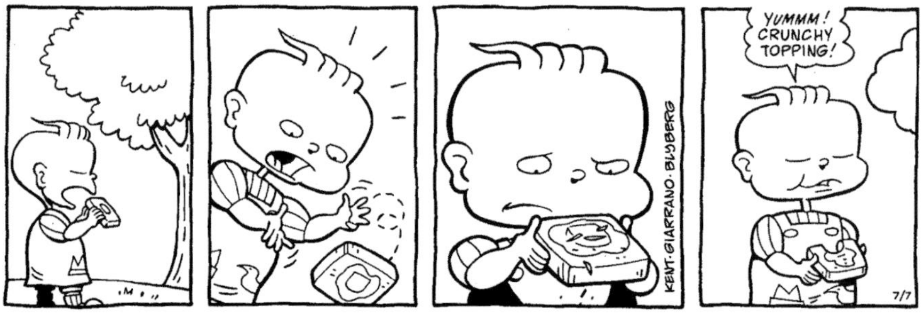
KENT · GIARRANO · BLYBERG
YUMMM! CRUNCHY TOPPING!
7/7

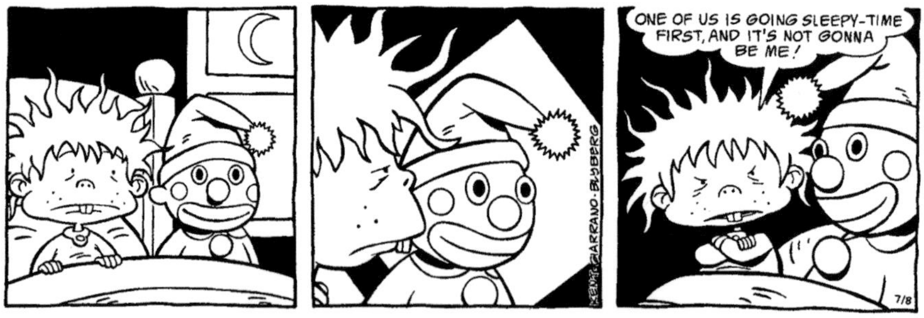
KENT · GIARRANO · BLYBERG
ONE OF US IS GOING SLEEPY-TIME FIRST, AND IT'S NOT GONNA BE ME!
7/8

2000

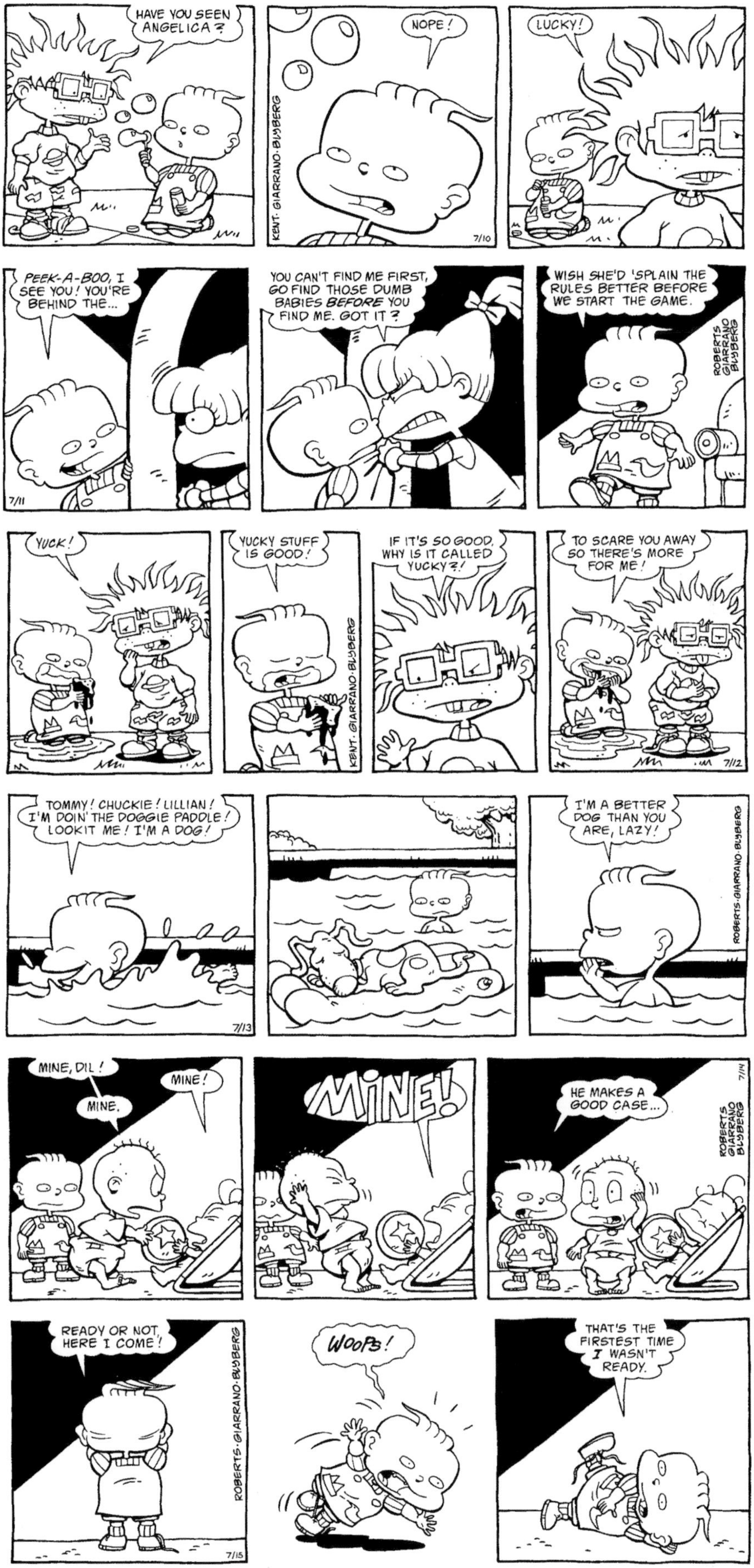

HAVE YOU SEEN ANGELICA?
NOPE!
KENT. GIARRANO. BLYSBERG
7/10
LUCKY!
PEEK-A-BOO, I SEE YOU! YOU'RE BEHIND THE...
7/11
YOU CAN'T FIND ME FIRST, GO FIND THOSE DUMB BABIES *BEFORE* YOU FIND ME. GOT IT?
WISH SHE'D 'SPLAIN THE RULES BETTER BEFORE WE START THE GAME.
ROBERTS GIARRANO BLYSBERG
YUCK!
YUCKY STUFF IS GOOD!
KENT. GIARRANO. BLYSBERG
IF IT'S SO GOOD, WHY IS IT CALLED YUCKY?!
TO SCARE YOU AWAY SO THERE'S MORE FOR ME!
7/12
TOMMY! CHUCKIE! LILLIAN! I'M DOIN' THE DOGGIE PADDLE! LOOKIT ME! I'M A DOG!
7/13
I'M A BETTER DOG THAN YOU ARE, LAZY!
ROBERTS. GIARRANO. BLYSBERG
MINE, DIL!
MINE.
MINE!
MINE!
HE MAKES A GOOD CASE...
7/14
ROBERTS GIARRANO BLYSBERG
READY OR NOT, HERE I COME!
ROBERTS. GIARRANO. BLYSBERG
7/15
WOOPS!
THAT'S THE FIRSTEST TIME *I* WASN'T READY.

2000

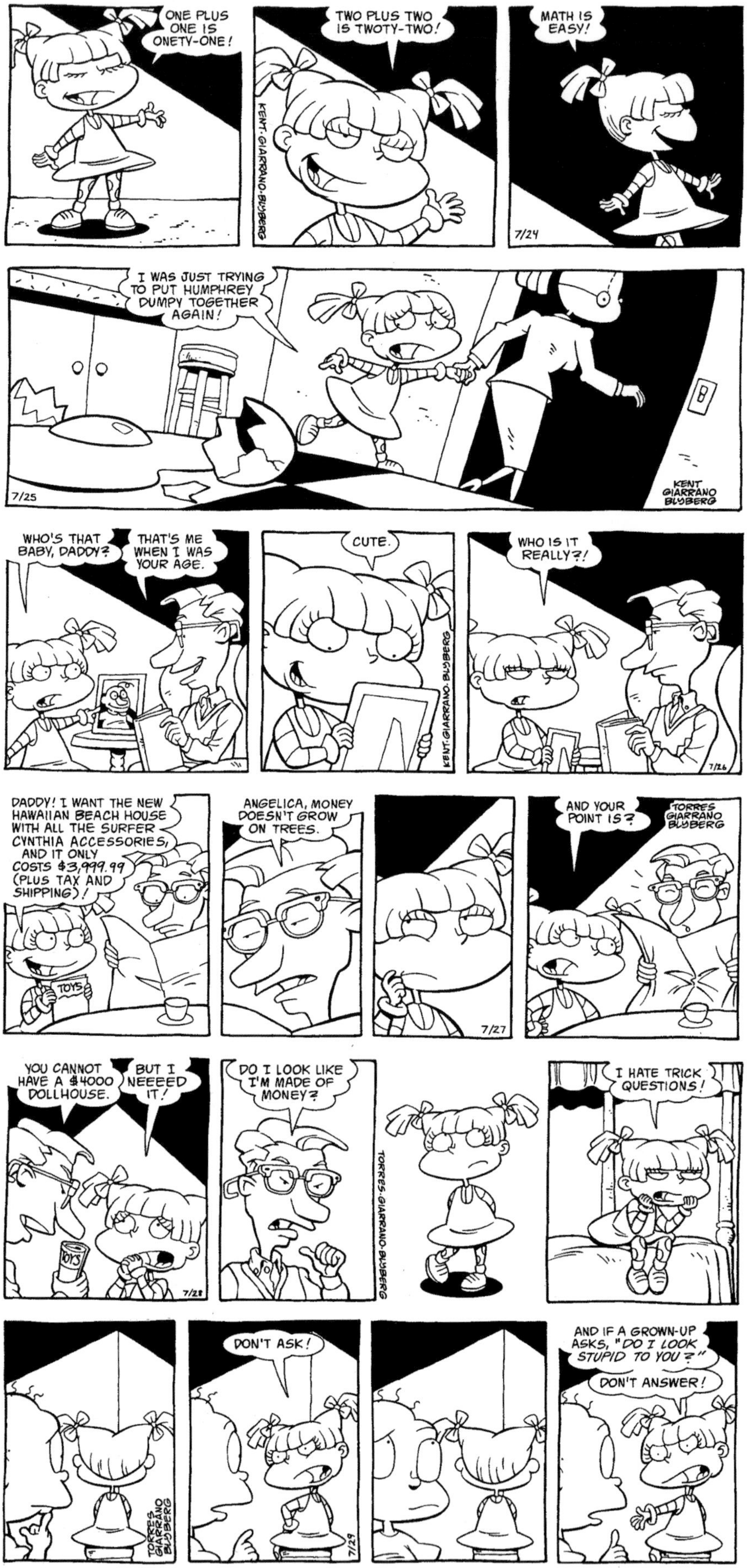
ONE PLUS ONE IS ONETY-ONE!
TWO PLUS TWO IS TWOTY-TWO!
KENT·GIARRANO·BLYBERG
MATH IS EASY!
7/24
I WAS JUST TRYING TO PUT HUMPHREY DUMPY TOGETHER AGAIN!
7/25
KENT GIARRANO BLYBERG
WHO'S THAT BABY, DADDY?
THAT'S ME WHEN I WAS YOUR AGE.
CUTE.
KENT·GIARRANO·BLYBERG
WHO IS IT REALLY?!
7/26
DADDY! I WANT THE NEW HAWAIIAN BEACH HOUSE WITH ALL THE SURFER CYNTHIA ACCESSORIES, AND IT ONLY COSTS $3,999.99 (PLUS TAX AND SHIPPING)!
TOYS
ANGELICA, MONEY DOESN'T GROW ON TREES.
7/27
AND YOUR POINT IS?
TORRES GIARRANO BLYBERG
YOU CANNOT HAVE A $4000 DOLLHOUSE.
BUT I NEEEED IT!
TOYS
7/28
DO I LOOK LIKE I'M MADE OF MONEY?
TORRES·GIARRANO·BLYBERG
I HATE TRICK QUESTIONS!
TORRES GIARRANO BLYBERG
DON'T ASK!
7/29
AND IF A GROWN-UP ASKS, "DO I LOOK STUPID TO YOU?"
DON'T ANSWER!

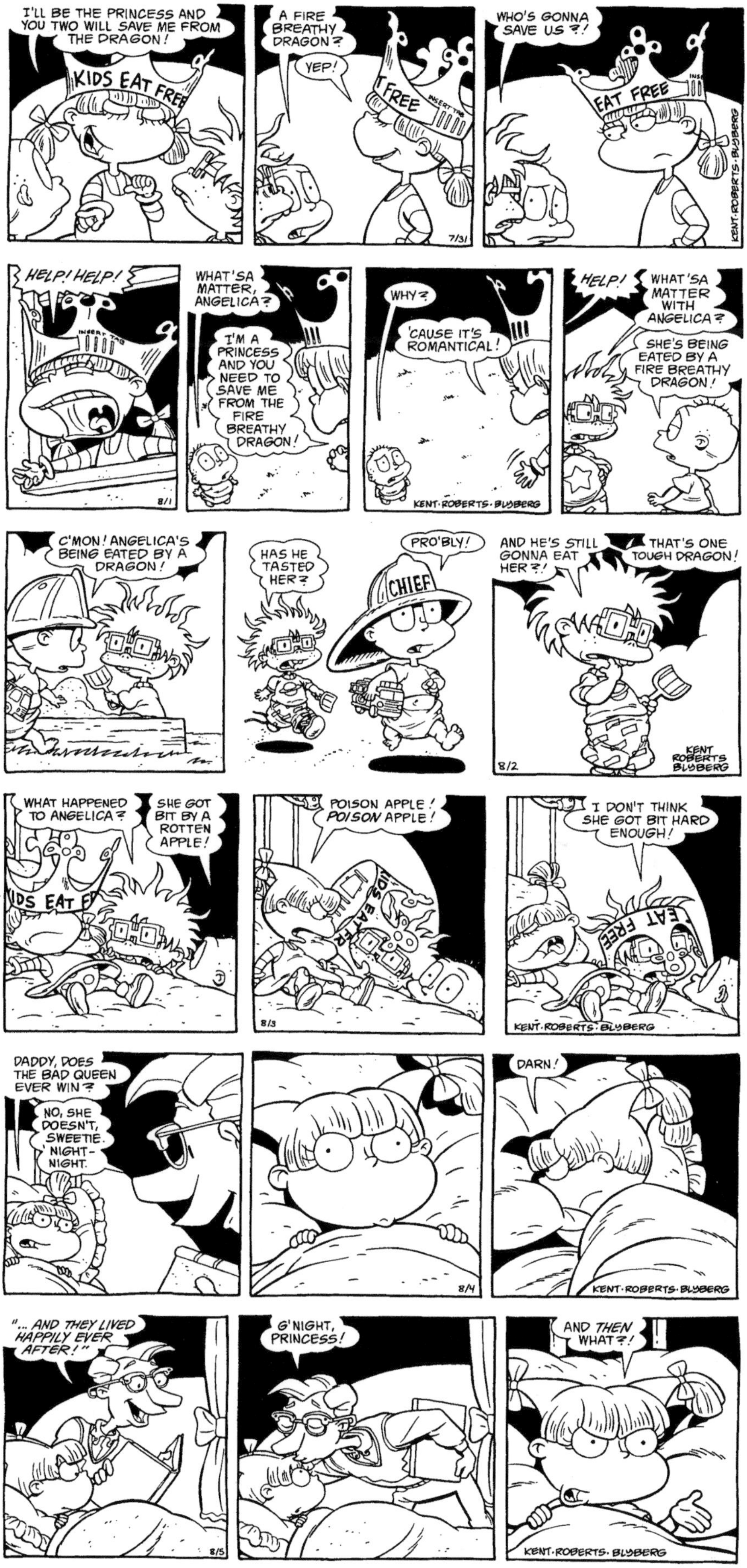
I'LL BE THE PRINCESS AND YOU TWO WILL SAVE ME FROM THE DRAGON!
KIDS EAT FREE
A FIRE BREATHY DRAGON?
YEP!
7/31
WHO'S GONNA SAVE US?!
EAT FREE
KENT·ROBERTS·BLYBERG
HELP! HELP!
WHAT'SA MATTER, ANGELICA?
I'M A PRINCESS AND YOU NEED TO SAVE ME FROM THE FIRE BREATHY DRAGON!
WHY?
'CAUSE IT'S ROMANTICAL!
HELP!
WHAT'SA MATTER WITH ANGELICA?
SHE'S BEING EATED BY A FIRE BREATHY DRAGON!
8/1
KENT·ROBERTS·BLYBERG
C'MON! ANGELICA'S BEING EATED BY A DRAGON!
HAS HE TASTED HER?
PRO'BLY!
CHIEF
AND HE'S STILL GONNA EAT HER?!
THAT'S ONE TOUGH DRAGON!
8/2
KENT ROBERTS BLYBERG
WHAT HAPPENED TO ANGELICA?
SHE GOT BIT BY A ROTTEN APPLE!
KIDS EAT F
POISON APPLE! POISON APPLE!
8/3
I DON'T THINK SHE GOT BIT HARD ENOUGH!
EAT FREE
KENT·ROBERTS·BLYBERG
DADDY, DOES THE BAD QUEEN EVER WIN?
NO, SHE DOESN'T, SWEETIE. NIGHT-NIGHT.
8/4
DARN!
KENT·ROBERTS·BLYBERG
"... AND THEY LIVED HAPPILY EVER AFTER!"
G'NIGHT, PRINCESS!
8/5
AND THEN WHAT?!
KENT·ROBERTS·BLYBERG

2000

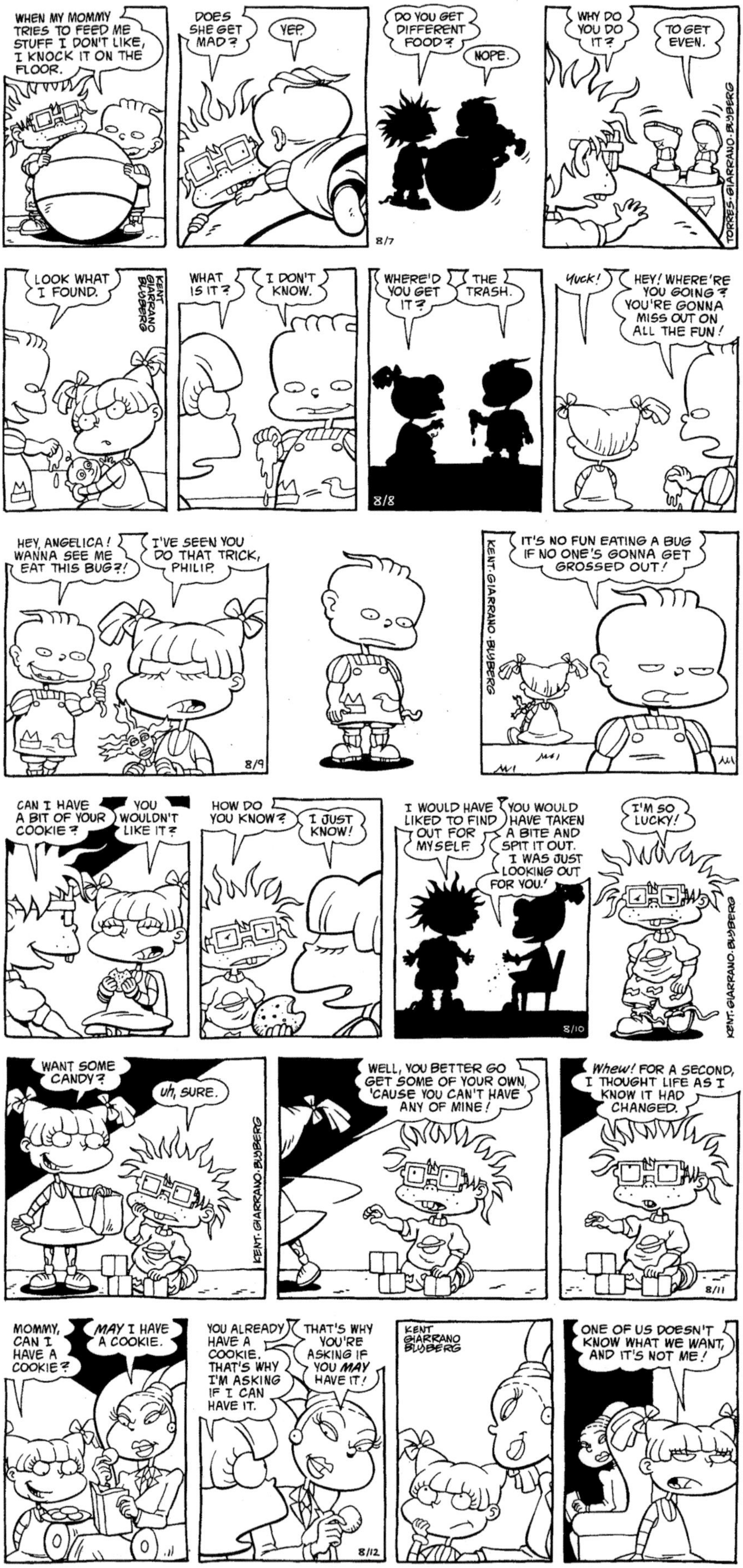
WHEN MY MOMMY TRIES TO FEED ME STUFF I DON'T LIKE, I KNOCK IT ON THE FLOOR.
DOES SHE GET MAD?
YEP.
DO YOU GET DIFFERENT FOOD?
NOPE.
8/7
WHY DO YOU DO IT?
TO GET EVEN.
TORRES·GIARRANO·BLYBERG
LOOK WHAT I FOUND.
KENT GIARRANO BLYBERG
WHAT IS IT?
I DON'T KNOW.
WHERE'D YOU GET IT?
THE TRASH.
8/8
Yuck!
HEY! WHERE'RE YOU GOING? YOU'RE GONNA MISS OUT ON ALL THE FUN!
HEY, ANGELICA! WANNA SEE ME EAT THIS BUG?!
I'VE SEEN YOU DO THAT TRICK, PHILIP.
8/9
KENT·GIARRANO·BLYBERG
IT'S NO FUN EATING A BUG IF NO ONE'S GONNA GET GROSSED OUT!
CAN I HAVE A BIT OF YOUR COOKIE?
YOU WOULDN'T LIKE IT?
HOW DO YOU KNOW?
I JUST KNOW!
I WOULD HAVE LIKED TO FIND OUT FOR MYSELF.
YOU WOULD HAVE TAKEN A BITE AND SPIT IT OUT. I WAS JUST LOOKING OUT FOR YOU!
8/10
I'M SO LUCKY!
KENT·GIARRANO·BLYBERG
WANT SOME CANDY?
uh, SURE.
KENT·GIARRANO·BLYBERG
WELL, YOU BETTER GO GET SOME OF YOUR OWN, 'CAUSE YOU CAN'T HAVE ANY OF MINE!
Whew! FOR A SECOND, I THOUGHT LIFE AS I KNOW IT HAD CHANGED.
8/11
MOMMY, CAN I HAVE A COOKIE?
MAY I HAVE A COOKIE.
YOU ALREADY HAVE A COOKIE. THAT'S WHY I'M ASKING IF I CAN HAVE IT.
THAT'S WHY YOU'RE ASKING IF YOU MAY HAVE IT!
8/12
KENT GIARRANO BLYBERG
ONE OF US DOESN'T KNOW WHAT WE WANT, AND IT'S NOT ME!

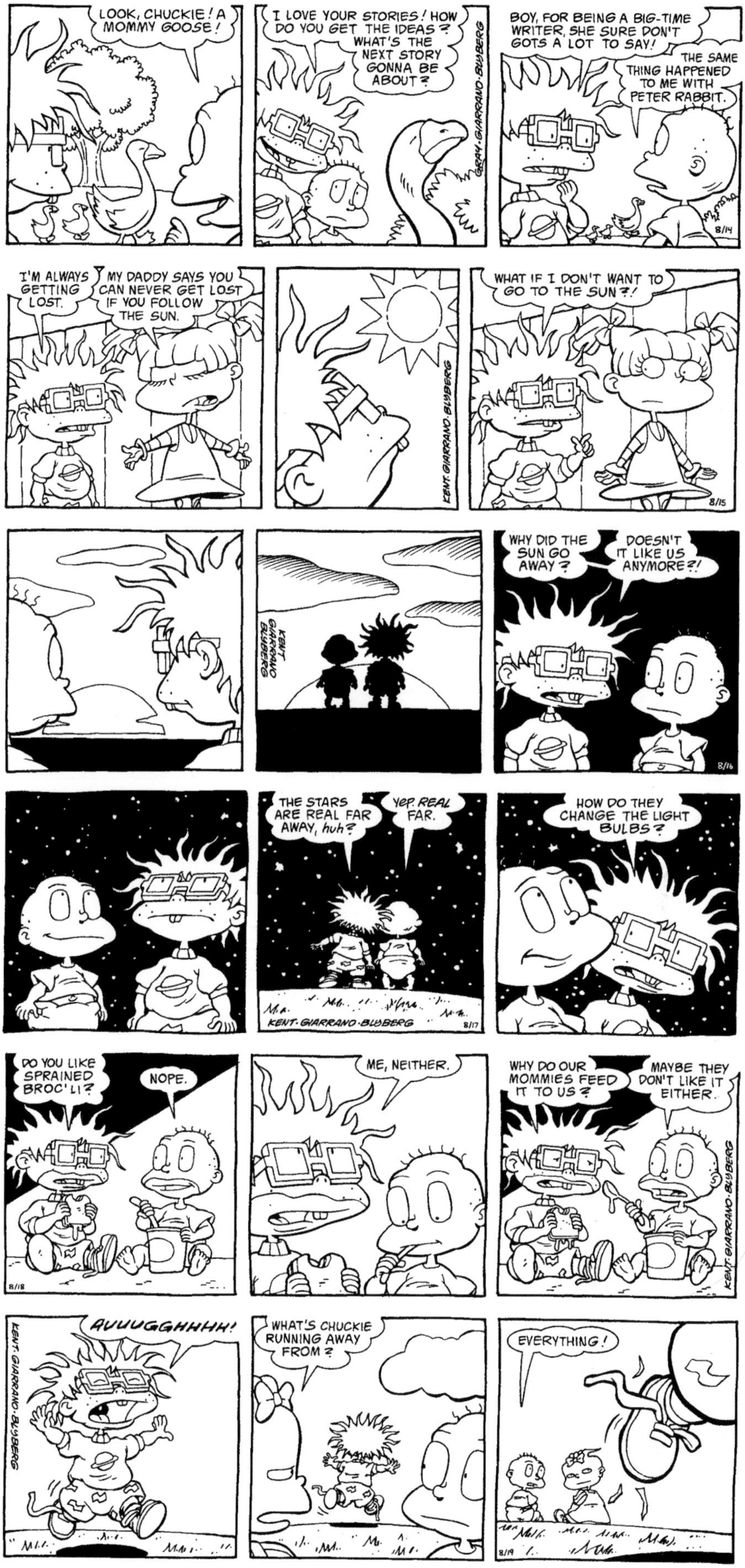
LOOK, CHUCKIE! A MOMMY GOOSE!
I LOVE YOUR STORIES! HOW DO YOU GET THE IDEAS? WHAT'S THE NEXT STORY GONNA BE ABOUT?
GRAY·GIARRANO·BLYBERG
BOY, FOR BEING A BIG-TIME WRITER, SHE SURE DON'T GOTS A LOT TO SAY!
THE SAME THING HAPPENED TO ME WITH PETER RABBIT.
8/14
I'M ALWAYS GETTING LOST.
MY DADDY SAYS YOU CAN NEVER GET LOST IF YOU FOLLOW THE SUN.
KENT·GIARRANO·BLYBERG
WHAT IF I DON'T WANT TO GO TO THE SUN?!
8/15
KENT GIARRANO BLYBERG
WHY DID THE SUN GO AWAY?
DOESN'T IT LIKE US ANYMORE?!
8/16
THE STARS ARE REAL FAR AWAY, huh?
Yep. REAL FAR.
KENT·GIARRANO·BLYBERG
8/17
HOW DO THEY CHANGE THE LIGHT BULBS?
DO YOU LIKE SPRAINED BROC'LI?
NOPE.
8/18
ME, NEITHER.
WHY DO OUR MOMMIES FEED IT TO US?
MAYBE THEY DON'T LIKE IT EITHER.
KENT·GIARRANO·BLYBERG
KENT·GIARRANO·BLYBERG
AUUUGGHHHH!
WHAT'S CHUCKIE RUNNING AWAY FROM?
EVERYTHING!
8/19

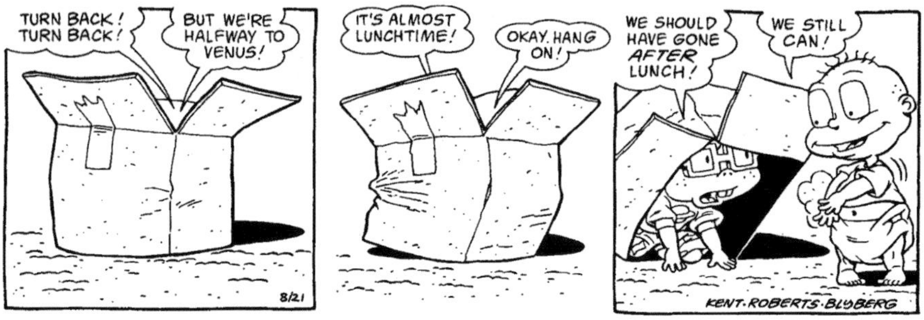
TURN BACK! TURN BACK!
BUT WE'RE HALFWAY TO VENUS!
8/21
IT'S ALMOST LUNCHTIME!
OKAY. HANG ON!
WE SHOULD HAVE GONE AFTER LUNCH!
WE STILL CAN!
KENT·ROBERTS·BLYBERG

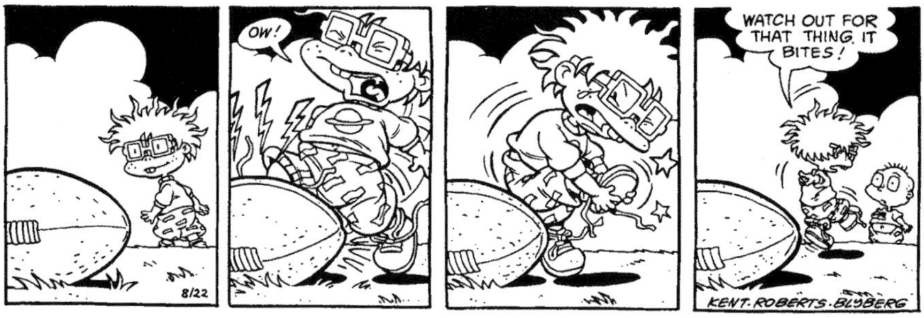
8/22
OW!
WATCH OUT FOR THAT THING. IT BITES!
KENT·ROBERTS·BLYBERG

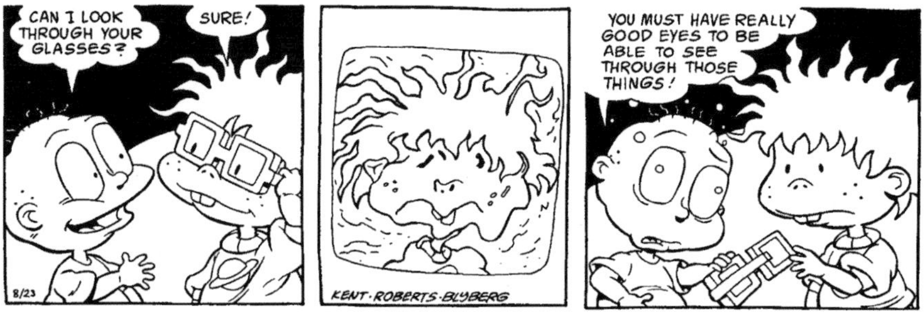
CAN I LOOK THROUGH YOUR GLASSES?
SURE!
8/23
KENT·ROBERTS·BLYBERG
YOU MUST HAVE REALLY GOOD EYES TO BE ABLE TO SEE THROUGH THOSE THINGS!

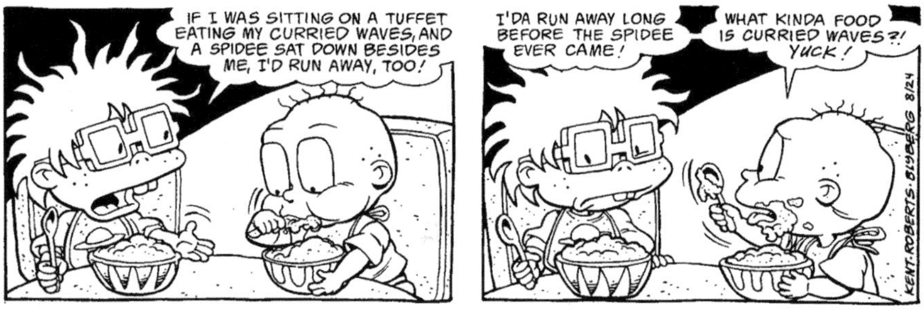
IF I WAS SITTING ON A TUFFET EATING MY CURRIED WAVES, AND A SPIDEE SAT DOWN BESIDES ME, I'D RUN AWAY, TOO!
I'DA RUN AWAY LONG BEFORE THE SPIDEE EVER CAME!
WHAT KINDA FOOD IS CURRIED WAVES?! YUCK!
KENT·ROBERTS·BLYBERG 8/24

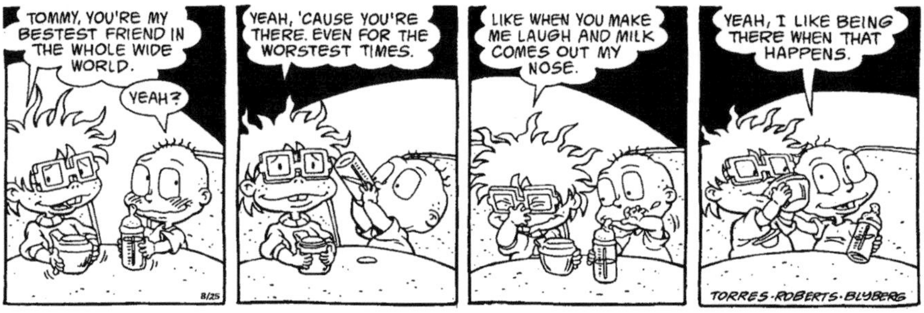
TOMMY, YOU'RE MY BESTEST FRIEND IN THE WHOLE WIDE WORLD.
YEAH?
8/25
YEAH, 'CAUSE YOU'RE THERE. EVEN FOR THE WORSTEST TIMES.
LIKE WHEN YOU MAKE ME LAUGH AND MILK COMES OUT MY NOSE.
YEAH, I LIKE BEING THERE WHEN THAT HAPPENS.
TORRES·ROBERTS·BLYBERG

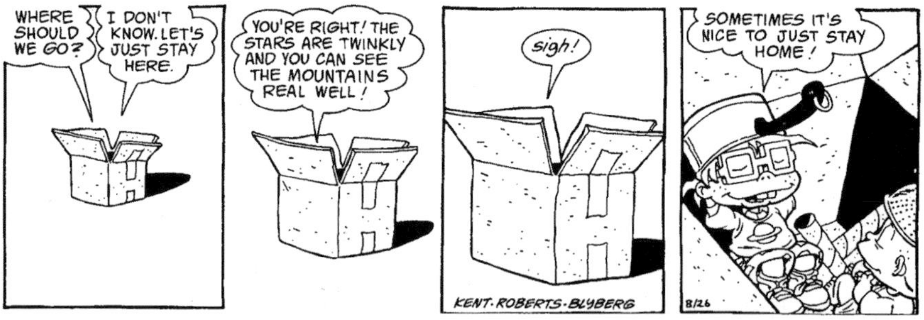
WHERE SHOULD WE GO?
I DON'T KNOW. LET'S JUST STAY HERE.
YOU'RE RIGHT! THE STARS ARE TWINKLY AND YOU CAN SEE THE MOUNTAINS REAL WELL!
sigh!
KENT·ROBERTS·BLYBERG
SOMETIMES IT'S NICE TO JUST STAY HOME!
8/26

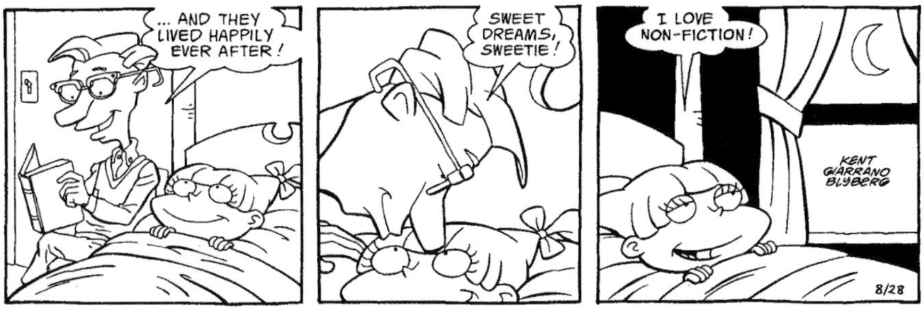
... AND THEY LIVED HAPPILY EVER AFTER!
SWEET DREAMS, SWEETIE!
I LOVE NON-FICTION!
KENT GIARRANO BLYBERG
8/28

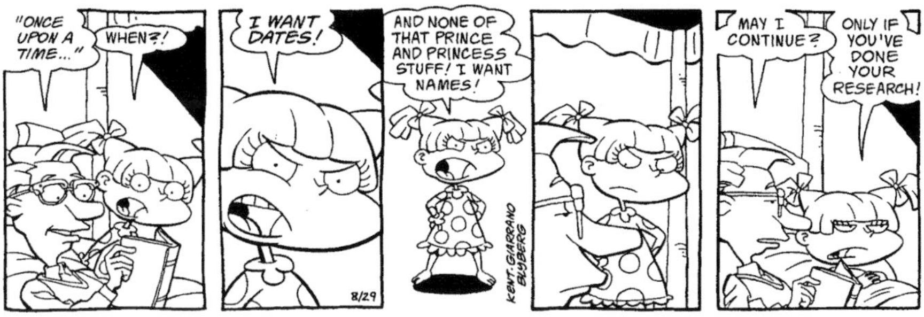
"ONCE UPON A TIME..."
WHEN?!
I WANT DATES!
AND NONE OF THAT PRINCE AND PRINCESS STUFF! I WANT NAMES!
KENT·GIARRANO BLYBERG
8/29
MAY I CONTINUE?
ONLY IF YOU'VE DONE YOUR RESEARCH!

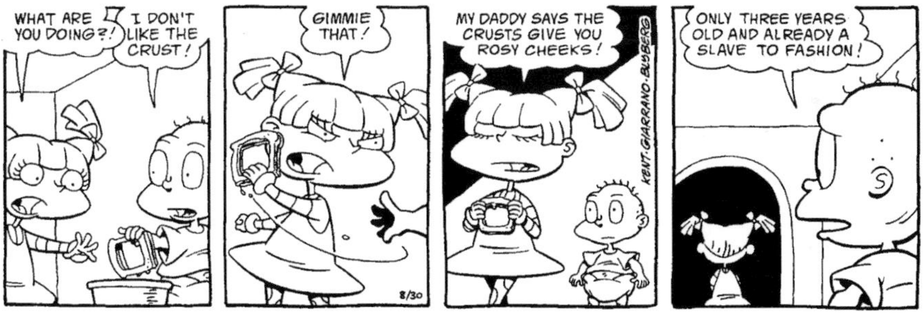
WHAT ARE YOU DOING?!
I DON'T LIKE THE CRUST!
GIMMIE THAT!
8/30
MY DADDY SAYS THE CRUSTS GIVE YOU ROSY CHEEKS!
KENT·GIARRANO·BLYBERG
ONLY THREE YEARS OLD AND ALREADY A SLAVE TO FASHION!

2000

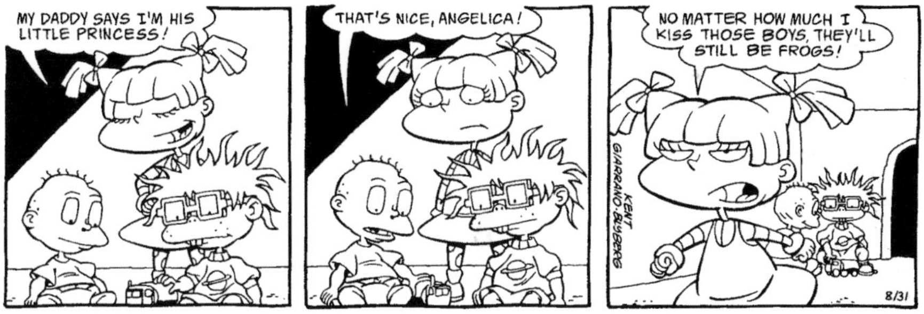
MY DADDY SAYS I'M HIS LITTLE PRINCESS!
THAT'S NICE, ANGELICA!
NO MATTER HOW MUCH I KISS THOSE BOYS, THEY'LL STILL BE FROGS!
KENT GIARRANO·BLYBERG
8/31

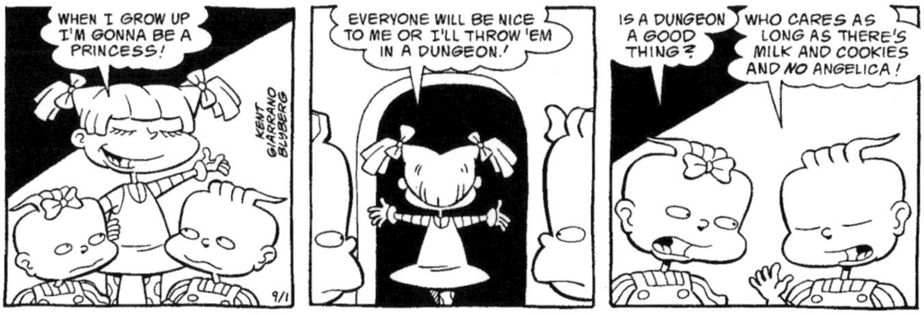
WHEN I GROW UP I'M GONNA BE A PRINCESS!
KENT GIARRANO BLYBERG
9/1
EVERYONE WILL BE NICE TO ME OR I'LL THROW 'EM IN A DUNGEON!
IS A DUNGEON A GOOD THING?
WHO CARES AS LONG AS THERE'S MILK AND COOKIES AND NO ANGELICA!

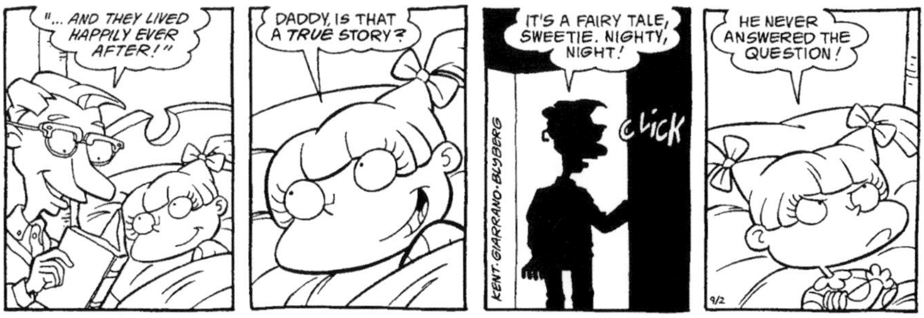
"... AND THEY LIVED HAPPILY EVER AFTER!"
DADDY, IS THAT A TRUE STORY?
IT'S A FAIRY TALE, SWEETIE. NIGHTY, NIGHT!
CLICK
KENT·GIARRANO·BLYBERG
HE NEVER ANSWERED THE QUESTION!
9/2

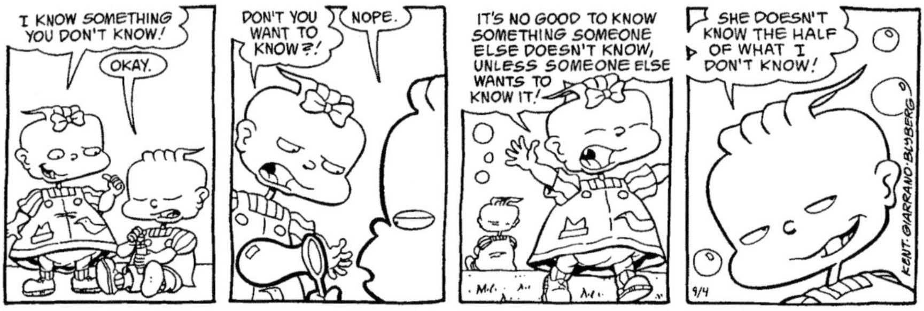
I KNOW SOMETHING YOU DON'T KNOW!
OKAY.
DON'T YOU WANT TO KNOW?!
NOPE.
IT'S NO GOOD TO KNOW SOMETHING SOMEONE ELSE DOESN'T KNOW, UNLESS SOMEONE ELSE WANTS TO KNOW IT!
SHE DOESN'T KNOW THE HALF OF WHAT I DON'T KNOW!
9/4
KENT·GIARRANO·BLYBERG

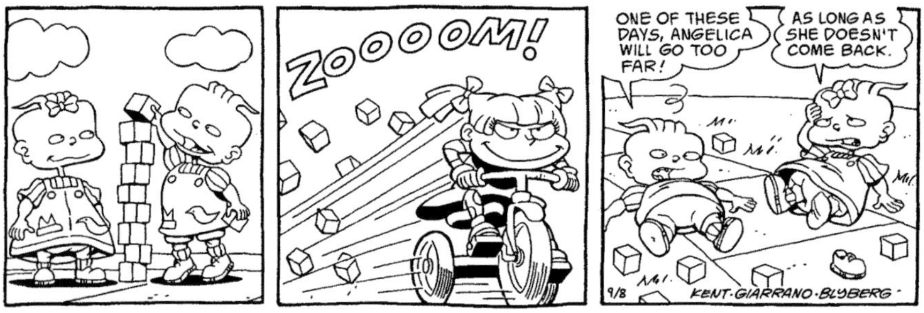
ZOOOOOM!
ONE OF THESE DAYS, ANGELICA WILL GO TOO FAR!
AS LONG AS SHE DOESN'T COME BACK.
9/8
KENT·GIARRANO·BLYBERG

2000

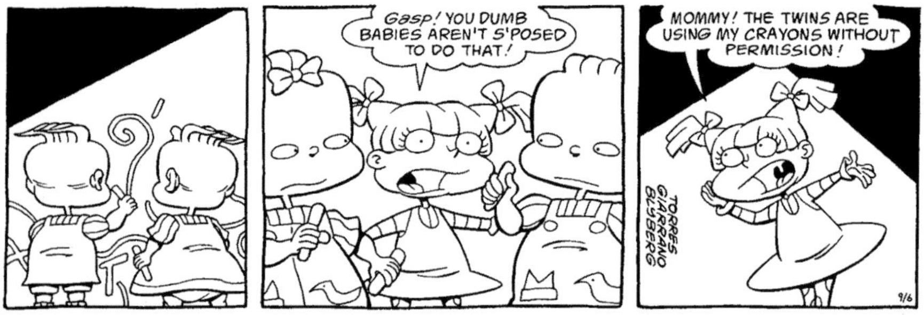
Gasp! YOU DUMB BABIES AREN'T S'POSED TO DO THAT!
MOMMY! THE TWINS ARE USING MY CRAYONS WITHOUT PERMISSION!
TORRES GIARRANO BLYBERG
9/6

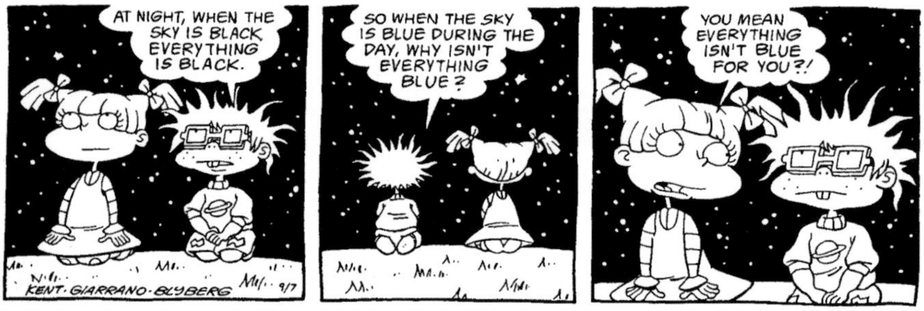
AT NIGHT, WHEN THE SKY IS BLACK EVERYTHING IS BLACK.
KENT·GIARRANO·BLYBERG
9/7
SO WHEN THE SKY IS BLUE DURING THE DAY, WHY ISN'T EVERYTHING BLUE?
YOU MEAN EVERYTHING ISN'T BLUE FOR YOU?!

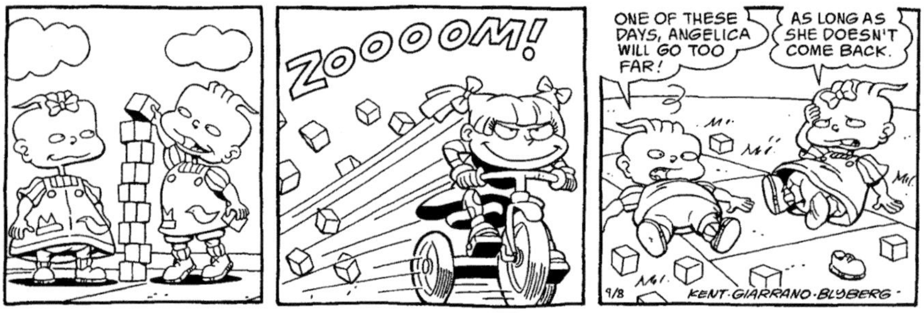
ZOOOOOM!
ONE OF THESE DAYS, ANGELICA WILL GO TOO FAR!
AS LONG AS SHE DOESN'T COME BACK.
9/8
KENT·GIARRANO·BLYBERG

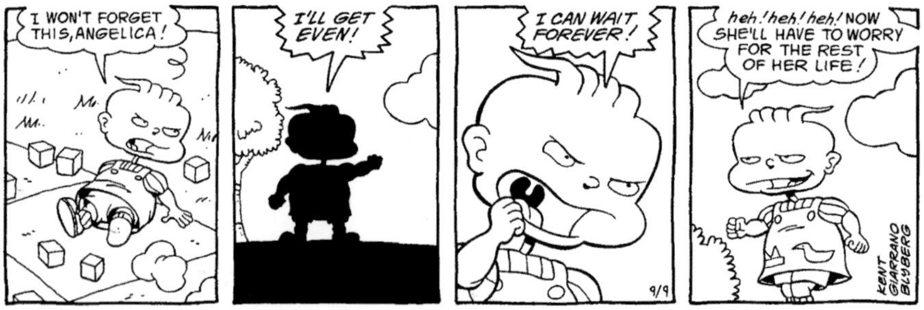
I WON'T FORGET THIS, ANGELICA!
I'LL GET EVEN!
I CAN WAIT FOREVER!
9/9
heh! heh! heh! NOW SHE'LL HAVE TO WORRY FOR THE REST OF HER LIFE!
KENT GIARRANO BLYBERG

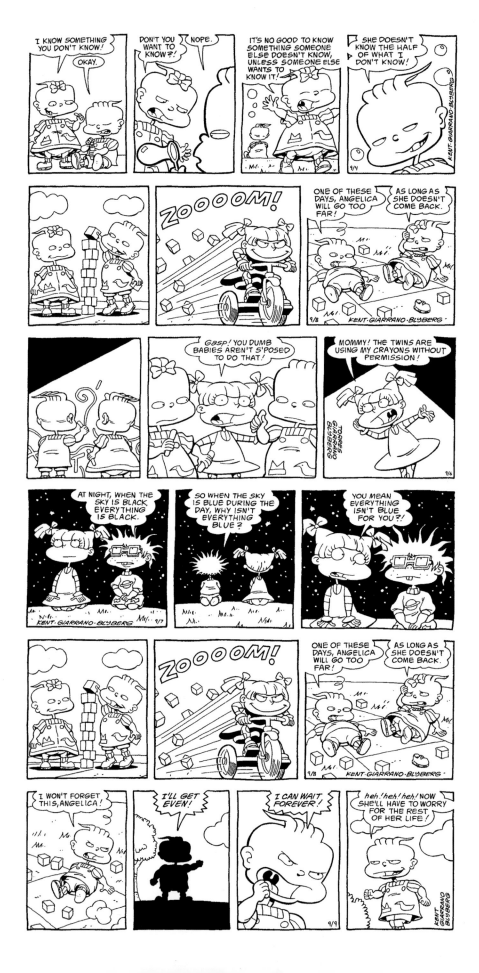

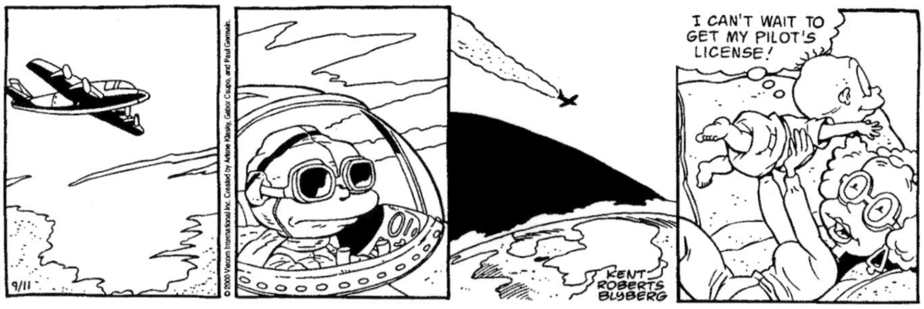
9/11
© 2000 Viacom International Inc. Created by Arlene Klasky, Gabor Csupo, and Paul Germain.
KENT ROBERTS BLYBERG
I CAN'T WAIT TO GET MY PILOT'S LICENSE!

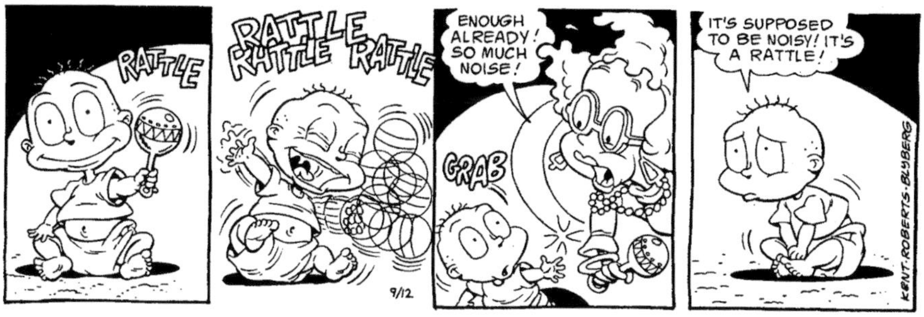
RATTLE
RATTLE RATTLE RATTLE
9/12
ENOUGH ALREADY! SO MUCH NOISE!
GRAB
IT'S SUPPOSED TO BE NOISY! IT'S A RATTLE!
KENT·ROBERTS·BLYBERG

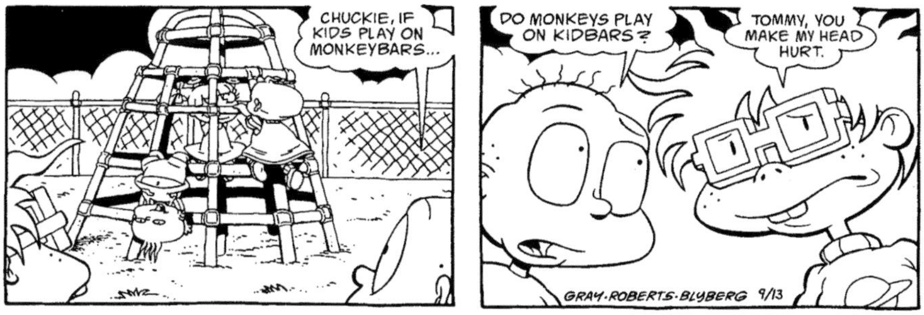
CHUCKIE, IF KIDS PLAY ON MONKEYBARS...
DO MONKEYS PLAY ON KIDBARS?
TOMMY, YOU MAKE MY HEAD HURT.
GRAY·ROBERTS·BLYBERG 9/13

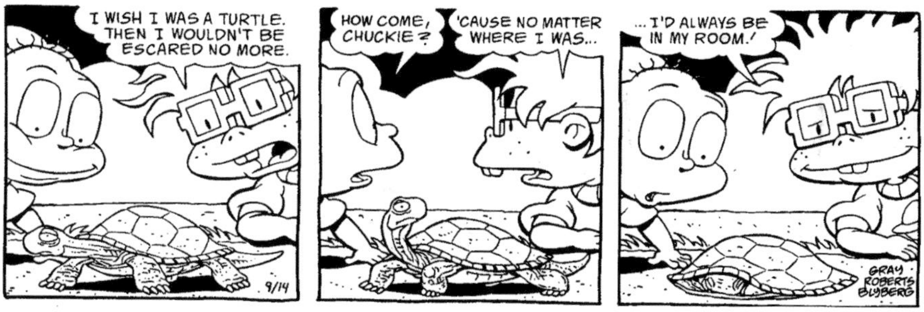
I WISH I WAS A TURTLE. THEN I WOULDN'T BE ESCARED NO MORE.
9/14
HOW COME, CHUCKIE?
'CAUSE NO MATTER WHERE I WAS...
...I'D ALWAYS BE IN MY ROOM!
GRAY ROBERTS BLYBERG

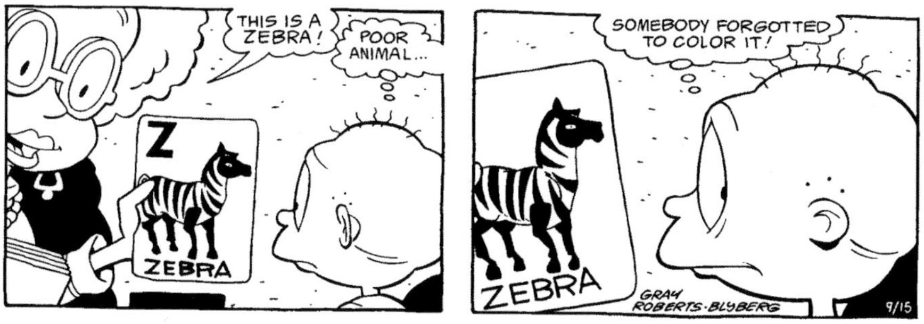
THIS IS A ZEBRA!
POOR ANIMAL...
Z
ZEBRA
SOMEBODY FORGOTTED TO COLOR IT!
ZEBRA
GRAY ROBERTS·BLYBERG
9/15

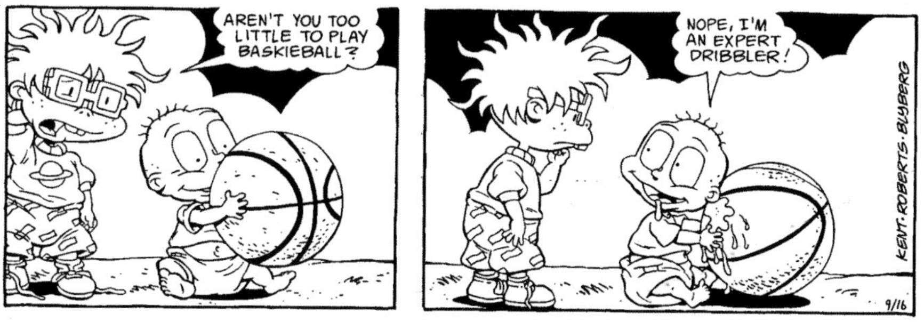
AREN'T YOU TOO LITTLE TO PLAY BASKIEBALL?
NOPE, I'M AN EXPERT DRIBBLER!
KENT·ROBERTS·BLYBERG
9/16

2000

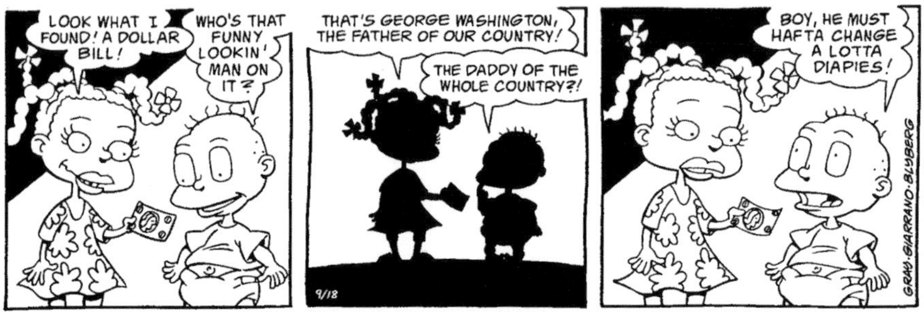
LOOK WHAT I FOUND! A DOLLAR BILL!
WHO'S THAT FUNNY LOOKIN' MAN ON IT?
THAT'S GEORGE WASHINGTON, THE FATHER OF OUR COUNTRY!
THE DADDY OF THE WHOLE COUNTRY?!
9/18
BOY, HE MUST HAFTA CHANGE A LOTTA DIAPIES!
GRAY·GIARRANO·BLYBERG

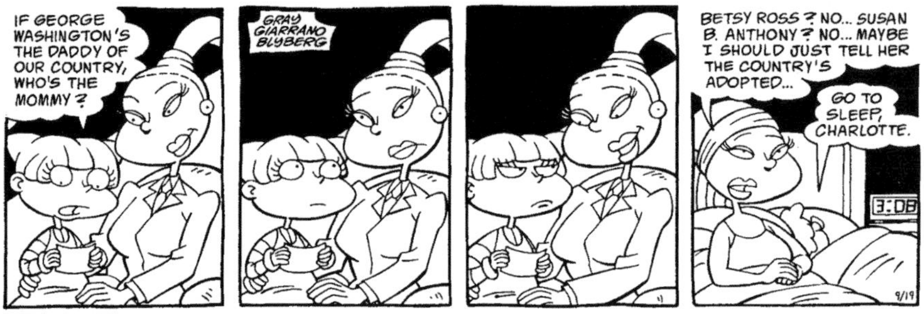
IF GEORGE WASHINGTON'S THE DADDY OF OUR COUNTRY, WHO'S THE MOMMY?
GRAY GIARRANO BLYBERG
BETSY ROSS? NO... SUSAN B. ANTHONY? NO... MAYBE I SHOULD JUST TELL HER THE COUNTRY'S ADOPTED...
GO TO SLEEP, CHARLOTTE.
3:08
9/19

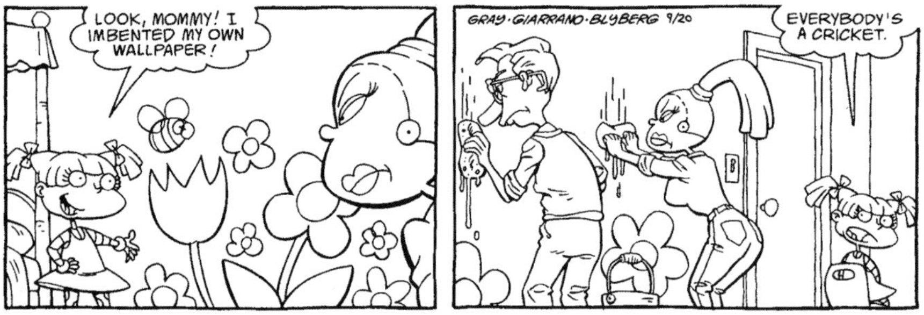
LOOK, MOMMY! I IMBENTED MY OWN WALLPAPER!
GRAY·GIARRANO·BLYBERG 9/20
EVERYBODY'S A CRICKET.

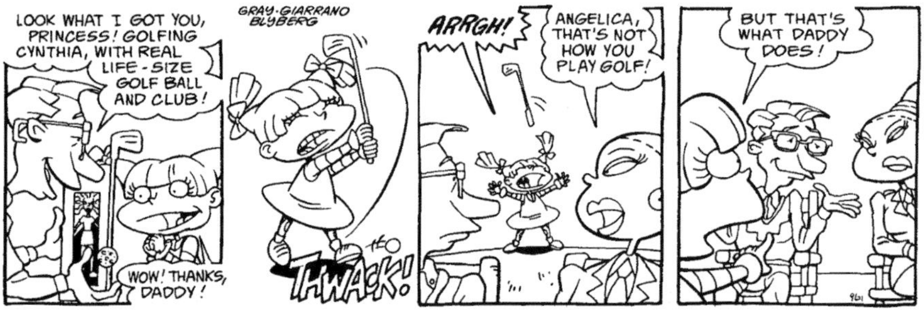
LOOK WHAT I GOT YOU, PRINCESS! GOLFING CYNTHIA, WITH REAL LIFE-SIZE GOLF BALL AND CLUB!
WOW! THANKS, DADDY!
GRAY·GIARRANO BLYBERG
THWACK!
ARRGH!
ANGELICA, THAT'S NOT HOW YOU PLAY GOLF!
BUT THAT'S WHAT DADDY DOES!
9/21

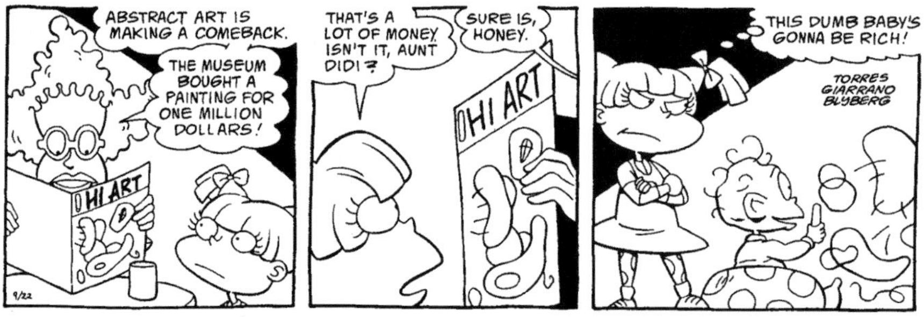
ABSTRACT ART IS MAKING A COMEBACK.
THE MUSEUM BOUGHT A PAINTING FOR ONE MILLION DOLLARS!
HI ART
9/22
THAT'S A LOT OF MONEY, ISN'T IT, AUNT DIDI?
SURE IS, HONEY.
HI ART
THIS DUMB BABY'S GONNA BE RICH!
TORRES GIARRANO BLYBERG

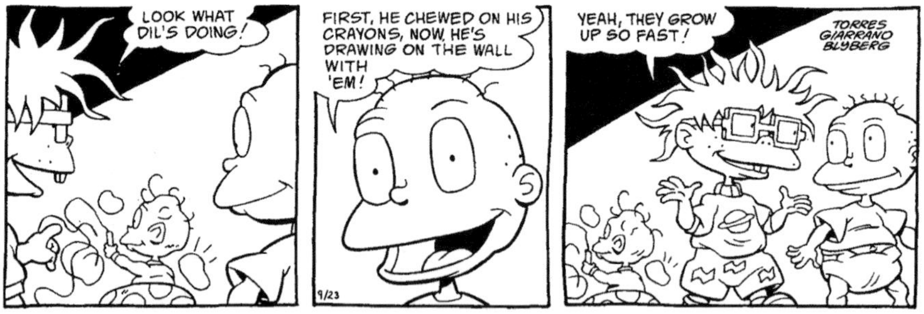
LOOK WHAT DIL'S DOING!
FIRST, HE CHEWED ON HIS CRAYONS, NOW HE'S DRAWING ON THE WALL WITH 'EM!
9/23
YEAH, THEY GROW UP SO FAST!
TORRES GIARRANO BLYBERG

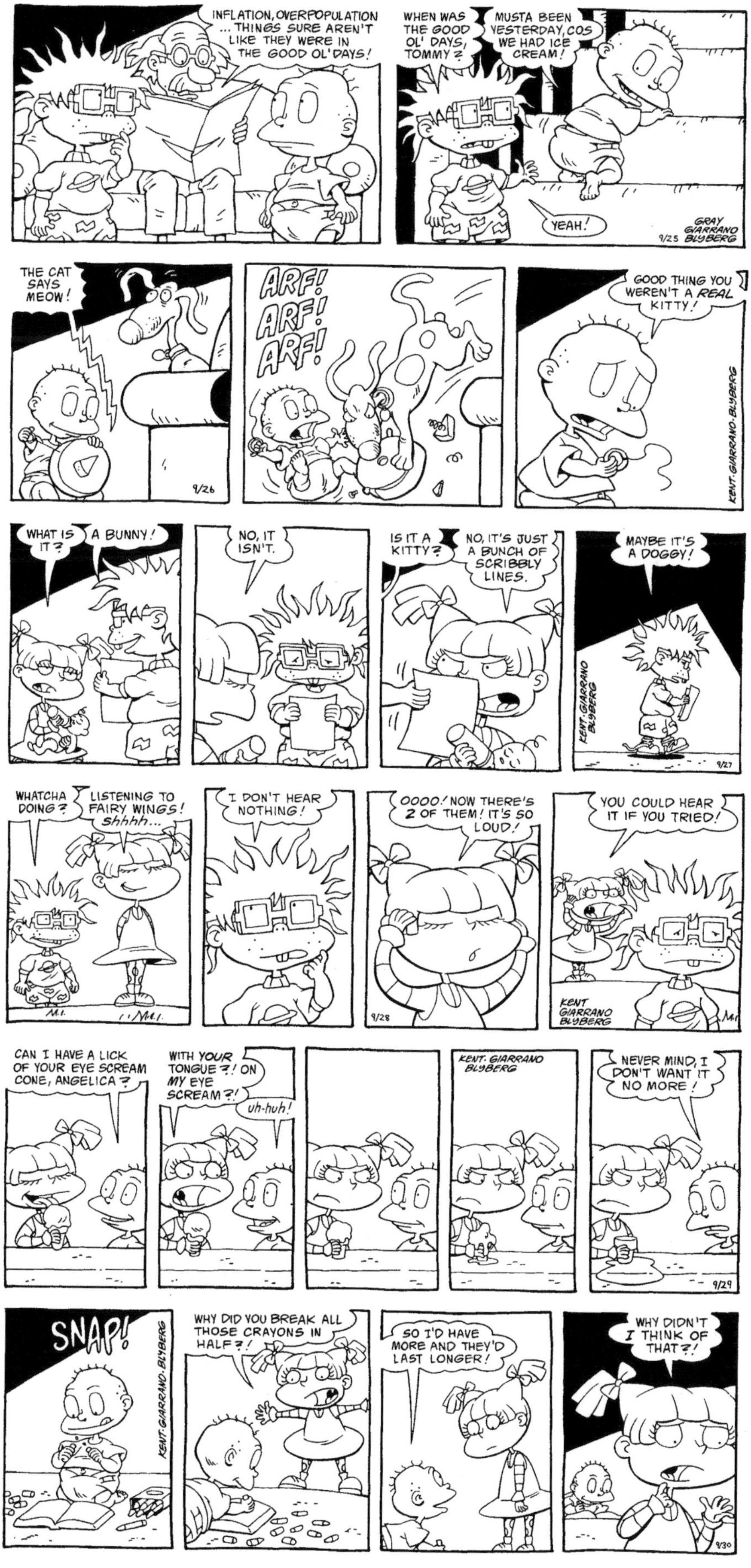
INFLATION, OVERPOPULATION ... THINGS SURE AREN'T LIKE THEY WERE IN THE GOOD OL' DAYS!
WHEN WAS THE GOOD OL' DAYS, TOMMY?
MUSTA BEEN YESTERDAY, COS WE HAD ICE CREAM!
YEAH!
GRAY GIARRANO BLYBERG
9/25
THE CAT SAYS MEOW!
9/26
ARF! ARF! ARF!
GOOD THING YOU WEREN'T A REAL KITTY!
KENT·GIARRANO·BLYBERG
WHAT IS IT?
A BUNNY!
NO, IT ISN'T.
IS IT A KITTY?
NO, IT'S JUST A BUNCH OF SCRIBBLY LINES.
MAYBE IT'S A DOGGY!
KENT·GIARRANO BLYBERG
9/27
WHATCHA DOING?
LISTENING TO FAIRY WINGS! shhhh...
I DON'T HEAR NOTHING!
9/28
OOOO! NOW THERE'S 2 OF THEM! IT'S SO LOUD!
YOU COULD HEAR IT IF YOU TRIED!
KENT GIARRANO BLYBERG
CAN I HAVE A LICK OF YOUR EYE SCREAM CONE, ANGELICA?
WITH YOUR TONGUE?! ON MY EYE SCREAM?!
uh-huh!
KENT·GIARRANO BLYBERG
NEVER MIND, I DON'T WANT IT NO MORE!
9/29
SNAP!
KENT·GIARRANO·BLYBERG
WHY DID YOU BREAK ALL THOSE CRAYONS IN HALF?!
SO I'D HAVE MORE AND THEY'D LAST LONGER!
WHY DIDN'T I THINK OF THAT?!
9/30

2000

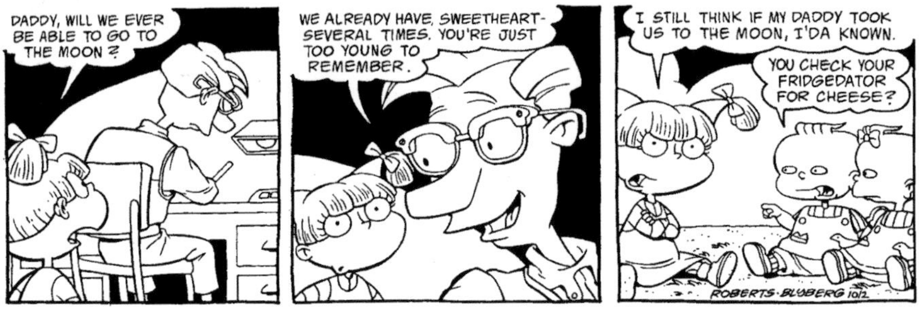
DADDY, WILL WE EVER BE ABLE TO GO TO THE MOON?
WE ALREADY HAVE, SWEETHEART- SEVERAL TIMES. YOU'RE JUST TOO YOUNG TO REMEMBER.
I STILL THINK IF MY DADDY TOOK US TO THE MOON, I'DA KNOWN.
YOU CHECK YOUR FRIDGEDATOR FOR CHEESE?
ROBERTS·BLYBERG 10/2

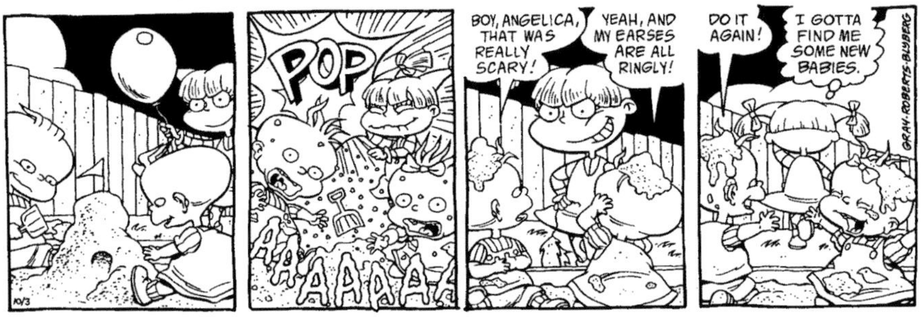
10/3
POP
AAAAAA
BOY, ANGELICA, THAT WAS REALLY SCARY!
YEAH, AND MY EARSES ARE ALL RINGLY!
DO IT AGAIN!
I GOTTA FIND ME SOME NEW BABIES.
GRAY·ROBERTS·BLYBERG

2000

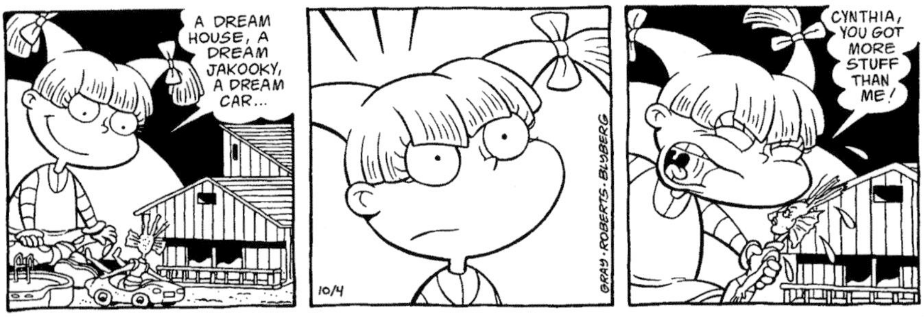
A DREAM HOUSE, A DREAM JAKOOKY, A DREAM CAR...
10/4
GRAY·ROBERTS·BLYBERG
CYNTHIA, YOU GOT MORE STUFF THAN ME!

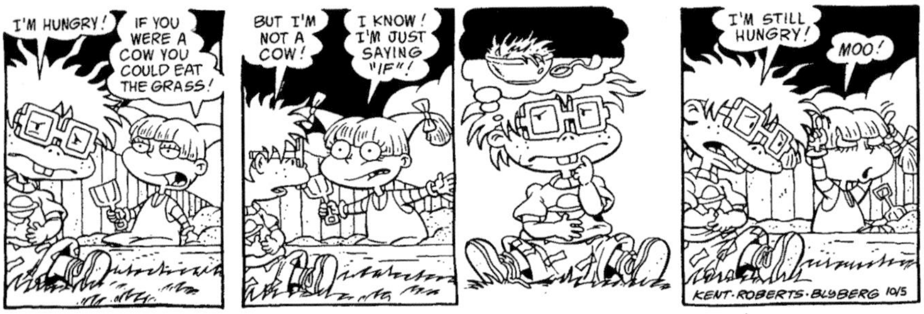
I'M HUNGRY!
IF YOU WERE A COW YOU COULD EAT THE GRASS!
BUT I'M NOT A COW!
I KNOW! I'M JUST SAYING "IF"!
I'M STILL HUNGRY!
MOO!
KENT·ROBERTS·BLYBERG 10/5

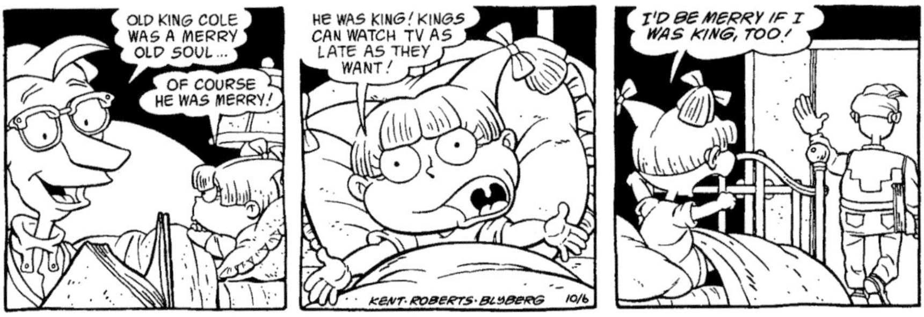
OLD KING COLE WAS A MERRY OLD SOUL...
OF COURSE HE WAS MERRY!
HE WAS KING! KINGS CAN WATCH TV AS LATE AS THEY WANT!
KENT·ROBERTS·BLYBERG 10/6
I'D BE MERRY IF I WAS KING, TOO!

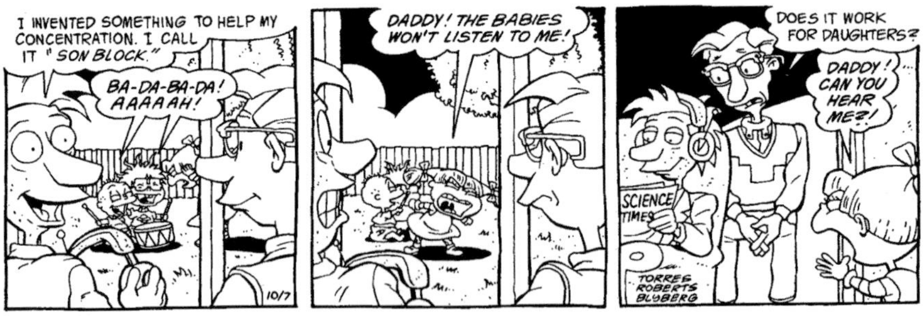
I INVENTED SOMETHING TO HELP MY CONCENTRATION. I CALL IT "SON BLOCK."
BA-DA-BA-DA! AAAAAH!
DADDY! THE BABIES WON'T LISTEN TO ME!
10/7
DOES IT WORK FOR DAUGHTERS?
DADDY! CAN YOU HEAR ME?!
SCIENCE TIMES
TORRES ROBERTS BLYBERG

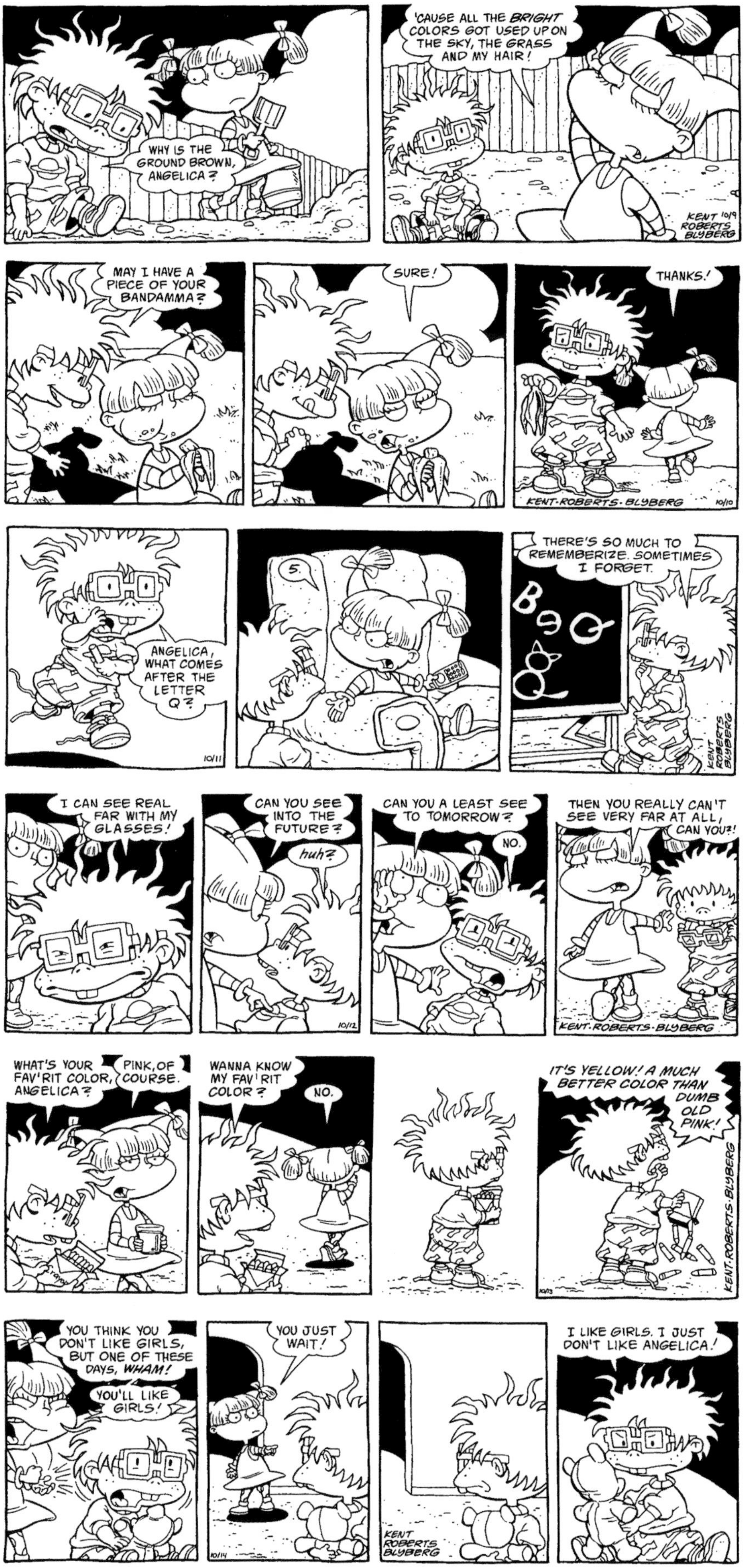
WHY IS THE GROUND BROWN, ANGELICA?
'CAUSE ALL THE *BRIGHT* COLORS GOT USED UP ON THE SKY, THE GRASS AND MY HAIR!
KENT 10/9 ROBERTS BLYBERG
MAY I HAVE A PIECE OF YOUR BANDAMMA?
SURE!
THANKS!
KENT·ROBERTS·BLYBERG 10/10
ANGELICA, WHAT COMES AFTER THE LETTER Q?
10/11
5.
THERE'S SO MUCH TO REMEMBERIZE. SOMETIMES I FORGET.
KENT ROBERTS BLYBERG
I CAN SEE REAL FAR WITH MY GLASSES!
CAN YOU SEE INTO THE FUTURE?
huh?
10/12
CAN YOU A LEAST SEE TO TOMORROW?
NO.
THEN YOU REALLY CAN'T SEE VERY FAR AT ALL, CAN YOU?!
KENT·ROBERTS·BLYBERG
WHAT'S YOUR FAV'RIT COLOR, ANGELICA?
PINK, OF COURSE.
WANNA KNOW MY FAV'RIT COLOR?
NO.
IT'S YELLOW! A MUCH BETTER COLOR THAN DUMB OLD PINK!
10/13
KENT·ROBERTS·BLYBERG
YOU THINK YOU DON'T LIKE GIRLS, BUT ONE OF THESE DAYS, *WHAM!*
YOU'LL LIKE GIRLS!
YOU JUST WAIT!
10/14
KENT ROBERTS BLYBERG
I LIKE GIRLS. I JUST DON'T LIKE ANGELICA!

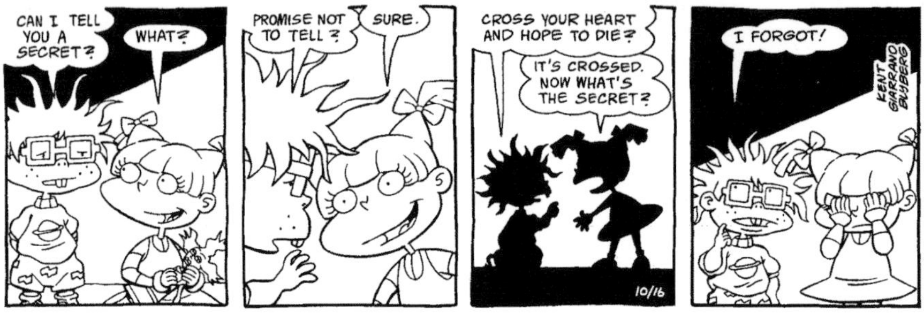
CAN I TELL YOU A SECRET?
WHAT?
PROMISE NOT TO TELL?
SURE.
CROSS YOUR HEART AND HOPE TO DIE?
IT'S CROSSED. NOW WHAT'S THE SECRET?
10/16
I FORGOT!
KENT GIARRANO BLYBERG

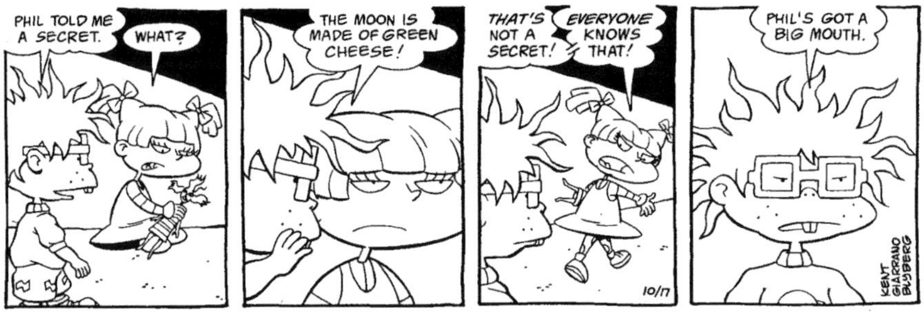
PHIL TOLD ME A SECRET.
WHAT?
THE MOON IS MADE OF GREEN CHEESE!
THAT'S NOT A SECRET!
EVERYONE KNOWS THAT!
10/17
PHIL'S GOT A BIG MOUTH.
KENT GIARRANO BLYBERG

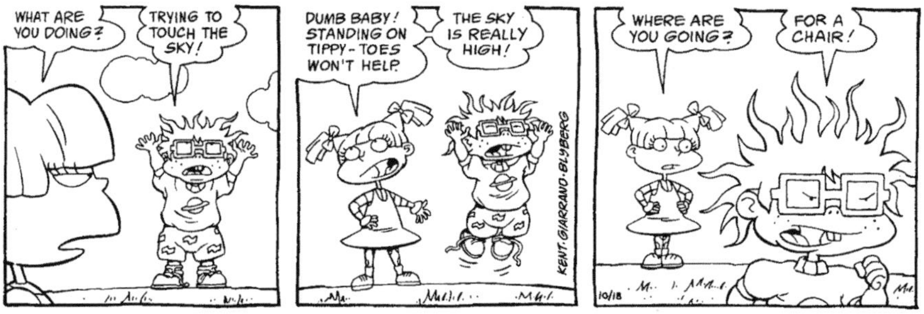
WHAT ARE YOU DOING?
TRYING TO TOUCH THE SKY!
DUMB BABY! STANDING ON TIPPY-TOES WON'T HELP.
THE SKY IS REALLY HIGH!
KENT·GIARRANO·BLYBERG
WHERE ARE YOU GOING?
FOR A CHAIR!
10/18

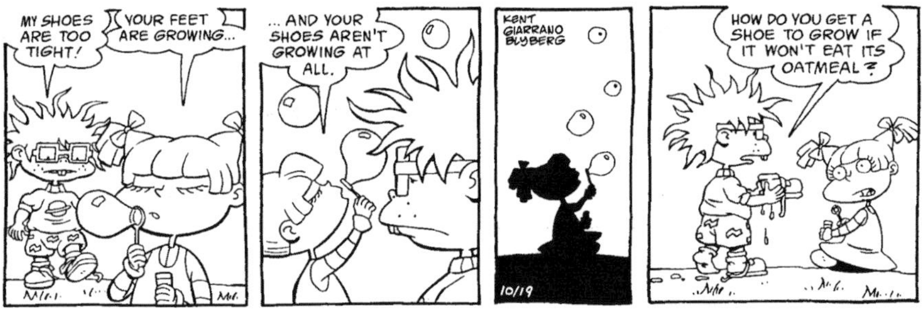
MY SHOES ARE TOO TIGHT!
YOUR FEET ARE GROWING...
... AND YOUR SHOES AREN'T GROWING AT ALL.
KENT GIARRANO BLYBERG
10/19
HOW DO YOU GET A SHOE TO GROW IF IT WON'T EAT ITS OATMEAL?

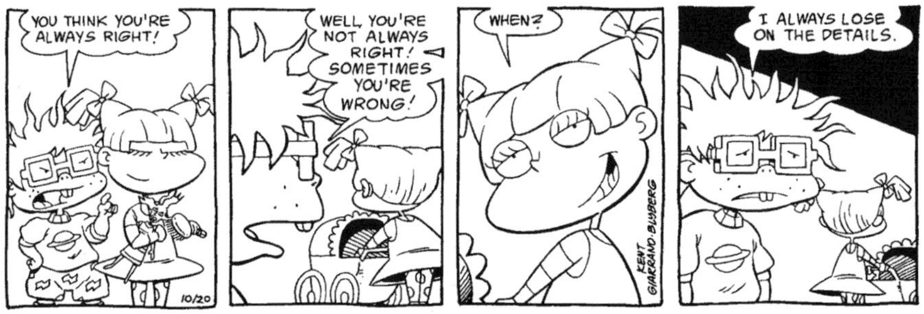
YOU THINK YOU'RE ALWAYS RIGHT!
10/20
WELL, YOU'RE NOT ALWAYS RIGHT! SOMETIMES YOU'RE WRONG!
WHEN?
KENT GIARRANO·BLYBERG
I ALWAYS LOSE ON THE DETAILS.

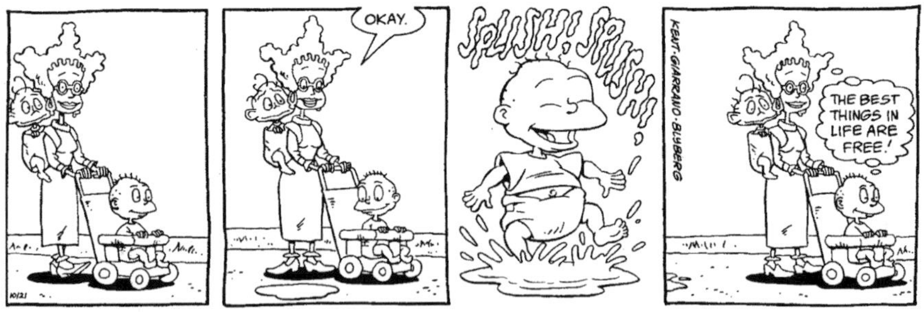
10/21
OKAY.
SPLISH! SPLISH!
KENT·GIARRANO·BLYBERG
THE BEST THINGS IN LIFE ARE FREE!

2000

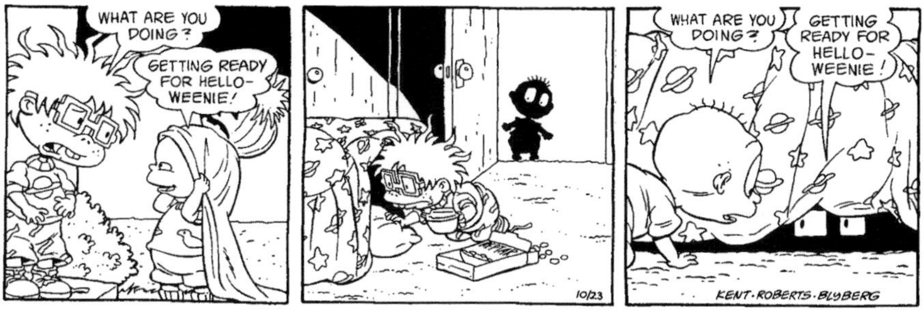
WHAT ARE YOU DOING?
GETTING READY FOR HELLO-WEENIE!
10/23
WHAT ARE YOU DOING?
GETTING READY FOR HELLO-WEENIE!
KENT·ROBERTS·BLYBERG

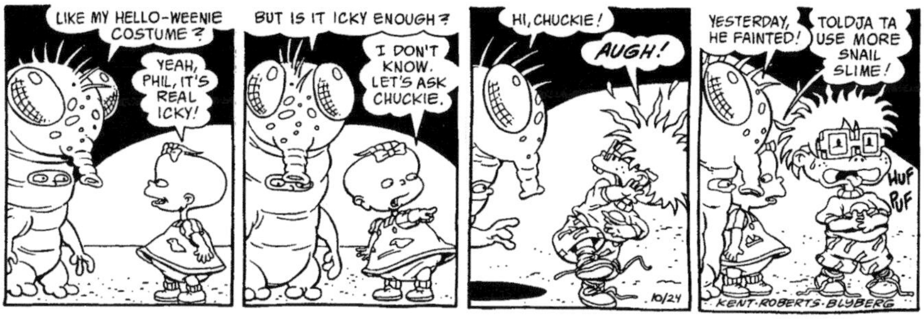
LIKE MY HELLO-WEENIE COSTUME?
YEAH, PHIL, IT'S REAL ICKY!
BUT IS IT ICKY ENOUGH?
I DON'T KNOW. LET'S ASK CHUCKIE.
HI, CHUCKIE!
AUGH!
10/24
YESTERDAY, HE FAINTED!
TOLDJA TA USE MORE SNAIL SLIME!
HUF
PUF
KENT·ROBERTS·BLYBERG

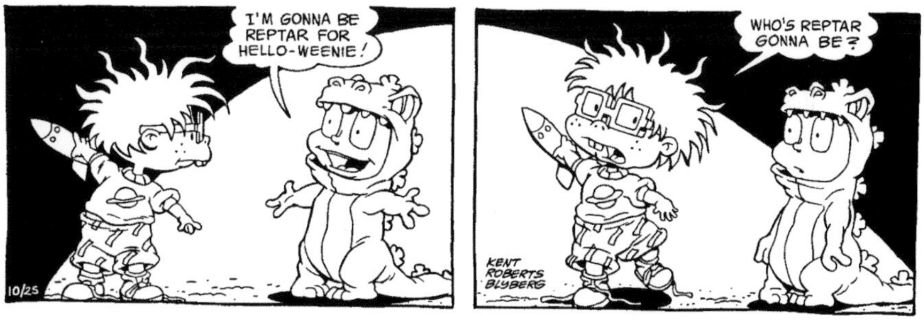
I'M GONNA BE REPTAR FOR HELLO-WEENIE!
10/25
WHO'S REPTAR GONNA BE?
KENT ROBERTS BLYBERG

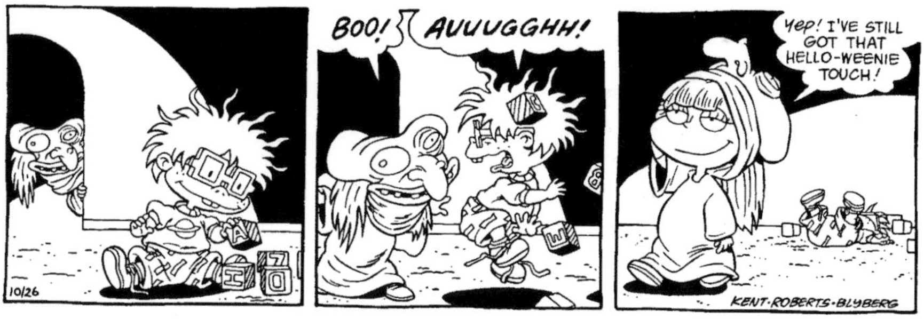
10/26
BOO!
AUUUGGHH!
YEP! I'VE STILL GOT THAT HELLO-WEENIE TOUCH!
KENT·ROBERTS·BLYBERG

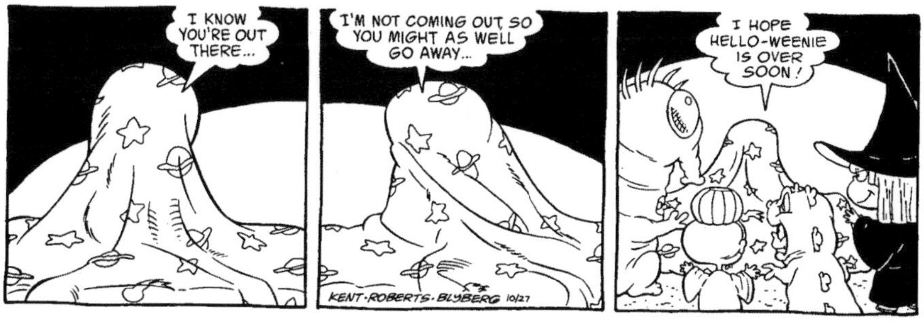
I KNOW YOU'RE OUT THERE...
I'M NOT COMING OUT SO YOU MIGHT AS WELL GO AWAY...
KENT·ROBERTS·BLYBERG 10/27
I HOPE HELLO-WEENIE IS OVER SOON!

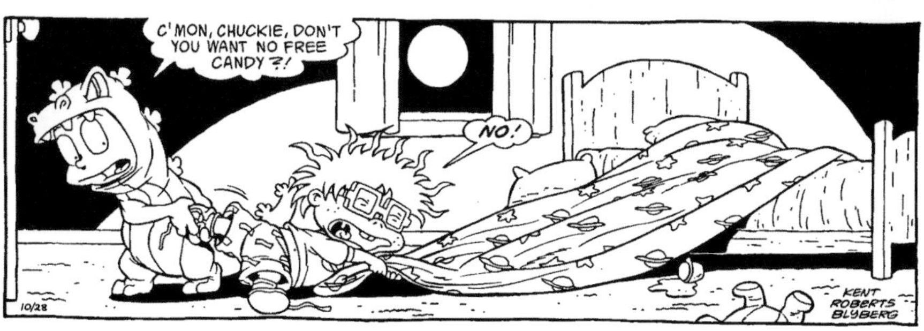
C'MON, CHUCKIE, DON'T YOU WANT NO FREE CANDY?!
NO!
10/28
KENT ROBERTS BLYBERG

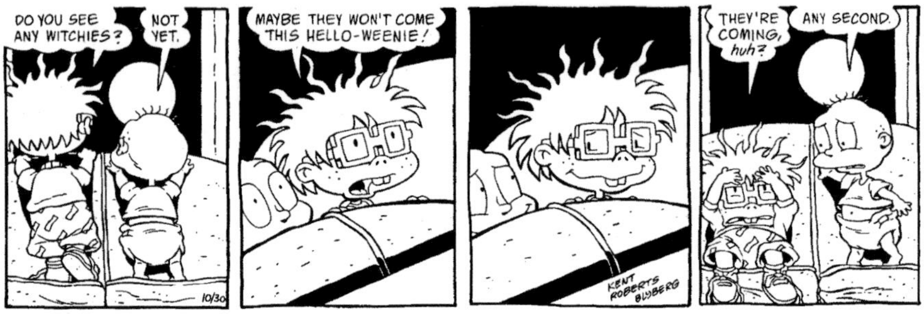
DO YOU SEE ANY WITCHIES?
NOT YET.
10/30
MAYBE THEY WON'T COME THIS HELLO-WEENIE!
KENT ROBERTS BLYBERG
THEY'RE COMING, huh?
ANY SECOND.

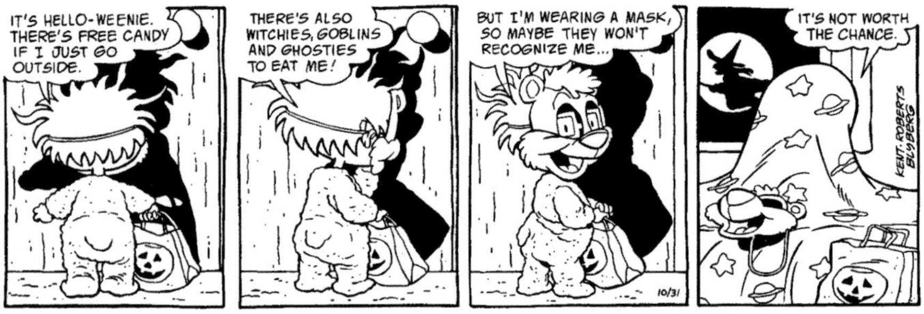
IT'S HELLO-WEENIE. THERE'S FREE CANDY IF I JUST GO OUTSIDE.
THERE'S ALSO WITCHIES, GOBLINS AND GHOSTIES TO EAT ME!
BUT I'M WEARING A MASK, SO MAYBE THEY WON'T RECOGNIZE ME...
10/31
IT'S NOT WORTH THE CHANCE.
KENT·ROBERTS BLYBERG

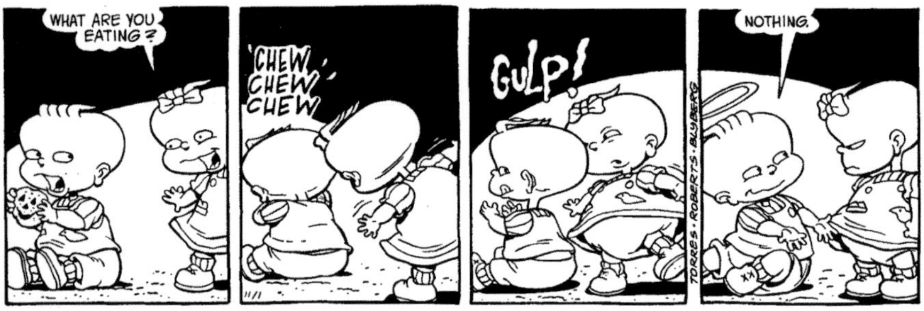
WHAT ARE YOU EATING?
CHEW CHEW CHEW
11/1
GULP!
TORRES·ROBERTS·BLYBERG
NOTHING.

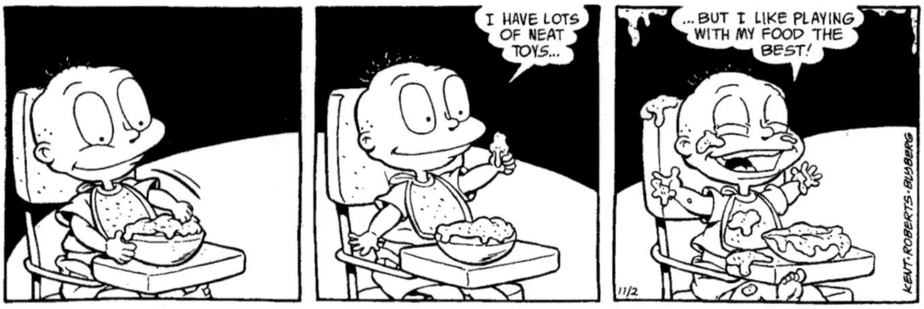
I HAVE LOTS OF NEAT TOYS...
...BUT I LIKE PLAYING WITH MY FOOD THE BEST!
11/2
KENT·ROBERTS·BLYBERG

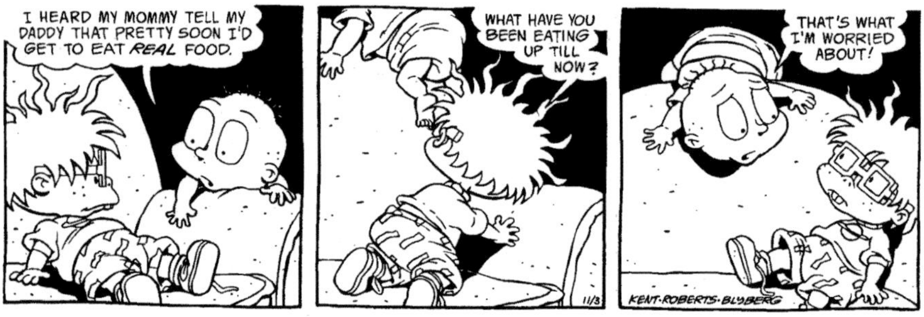
I HEARD MY MOMMY TELL MY DADDY THAT PRETTY SOON I'D GET TO EAT REAL FOOD.
WHAT HAVE YOU BEEN EATING UP TILL NOW?
11/3
THAT'S WHAT I'M WORRIED ABOUT!
KENT·ROBERTS·BLYBERG

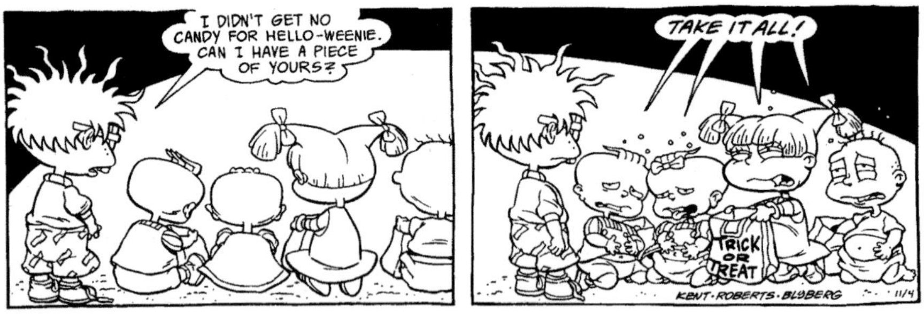
I DIDN'T GET NO CANDY FOR HELLO-WEENIE. CAN I HAVE A PIECE OF YOURS?
TAKE IT ALL!
TRICK OR TREAT
KENT·ROBERTS·BLYBERG
11/4

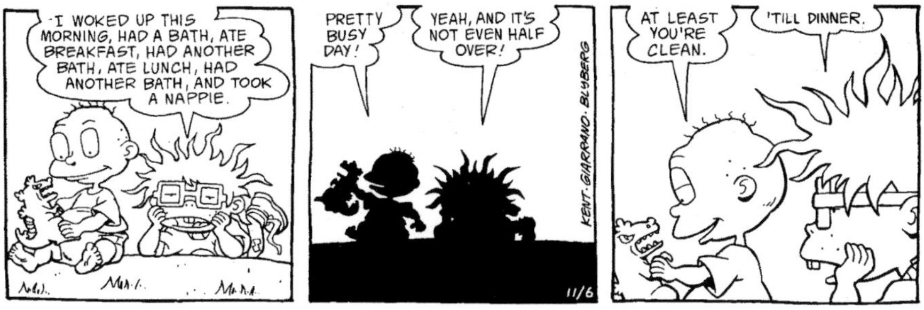
I WOKED UP THIS MORNING, HAD A BATH, ATE BREAKFAST, HAD ANOTHER BATH, ATE LUNCH, HAD ANOTHER BATH, AND TOOK A NAPPIE.
PRETTY BUSY DAY!
YEAH, AND IT'S NOT EVEN HALF OVER!
KENT · GIARRANO · BLYBERG
11/6
AT LEAST YOU'RE CLEAN.
'TILL DINNER.

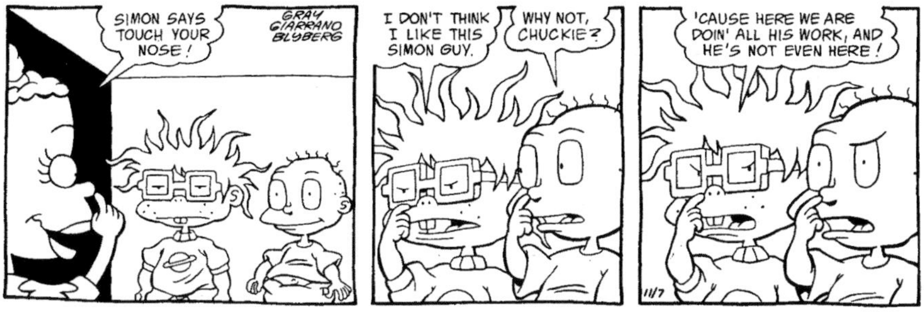
SIMON SAYS TOUCH YOUR NOSE!
GRAY GIARRANO BLYBERG
I DON'T THINK I LIKE THIS SIMON GUY.
WHY NOT, CHUCKIE?
'CAUSE HERE WE ARE DOIN' ALL HIS WORK, AND HE'S NOT EVEN HERE!
11/7

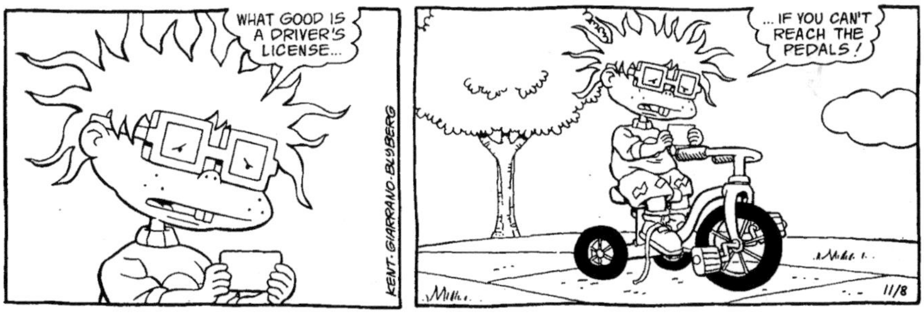
WHAT GOOD IS A DRIVER'S LICENSE...
KENT · GIARRANO · BLYBERG
...IF YOU CAN'T REACH THE PEDALS!
11/8

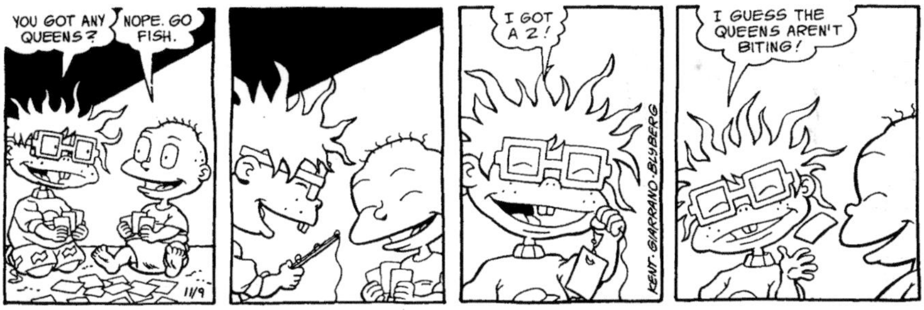
YOU GOT ANY QUEENS?
NOPE. GO FISH.
11/9
I GOT A Z!
KENT · GIARRANO · BLYBERG
I GUESS THE QUEENS AREN'T BITING!

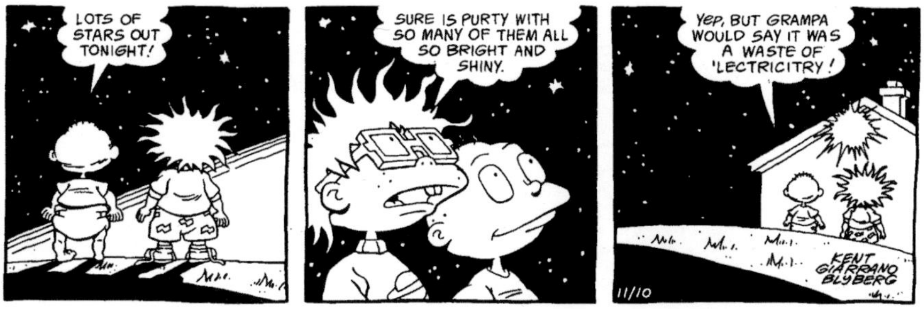
LOTS OF STARS OUT TONIGHT!
SURE IS PURTY WITH SO MANY OF THEM ALL SO BRIGHT AND SHINY.
YEP, BUT GRAMPA WOULD SAY IT WAS A WASTE OF 'LECTRICITRY!
KENT GIARRANO BLYBERG
11/10

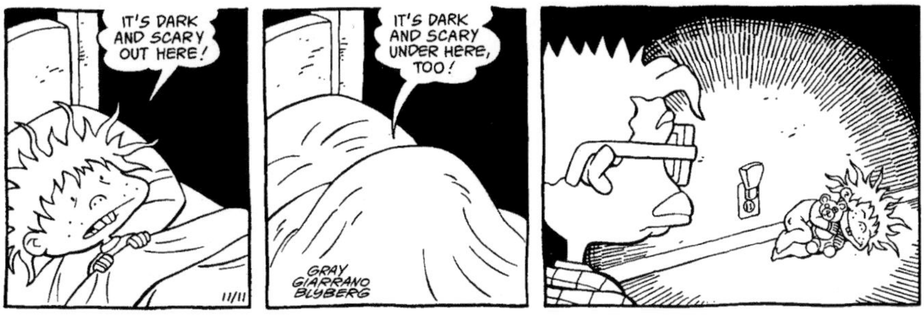
IT'S DARK AND SCARY OUT HERE!
11/11
IT'S DARK AND SCARY UNDER HERE, TOO!
GRAY GIARRANO BLYBERG

2000

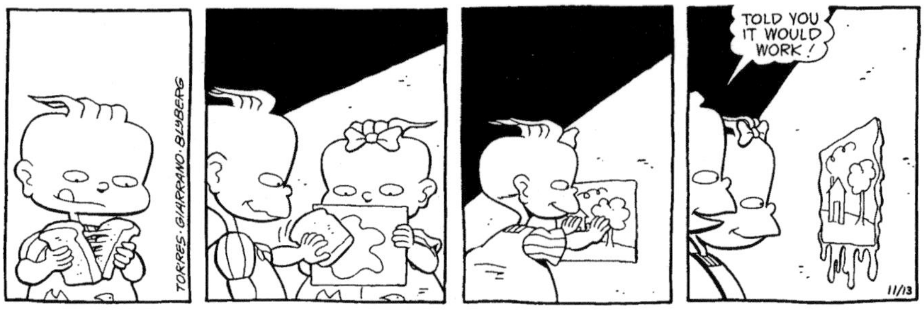
TORRES · GIARRANO · BLYBERG
TOLD YOU IT WOULD WORK!
11/13

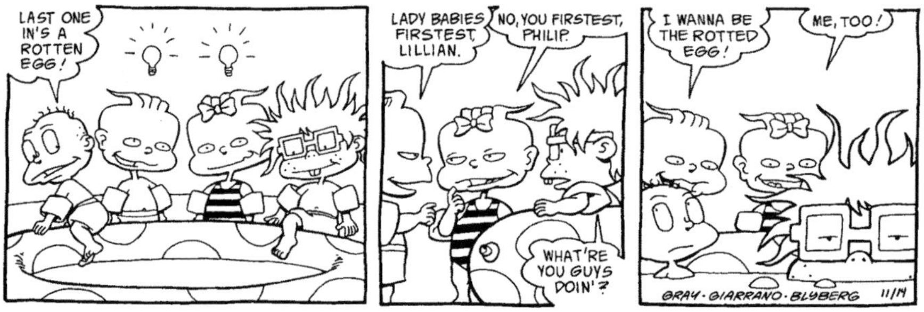
LAST ONE IN'S A ROTTEN EGG!
LADY BABIES FIRSTEST, LILLIAN.
NO, YOU FIRSTEST, PHILIP.
WHAT'RE YOU GUYS DOIN'?
I WANNA BE THE ROTTED EGG!
ME, TOO!
GRAY · GIARRANO · BLYBERG 11/14

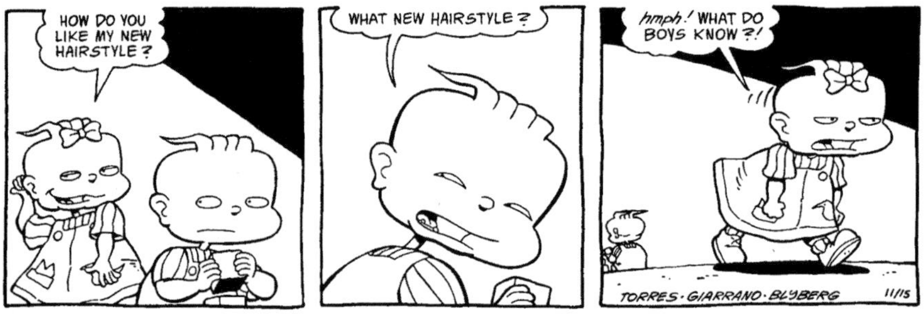
HOW DO YOU LIKE MY NEW HAIRSTYLE?
WHAT NEW HAIRSTYLE?
hmph! WHAT DO BOYS KNOW?!
TORRES · GIARRANO · BLYBERG 11/15

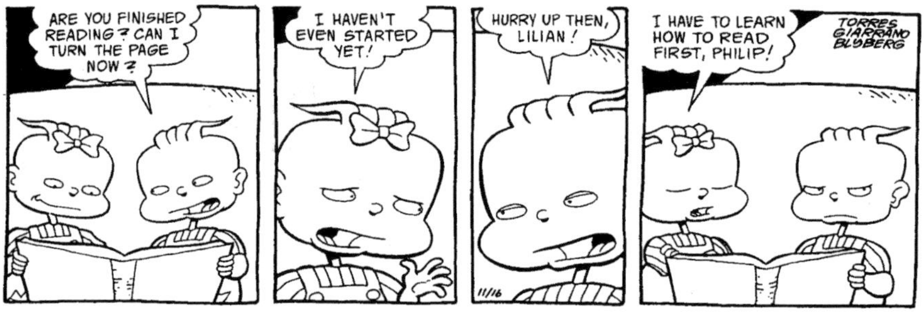
ARE YOU FINISHED READING? CAN I TURN THE PAGE NOW?
I HAVEN'T EVEN STARTED YET!
11/16
HURRY UP THEN, LILIAN!
I HAVE TO LEARN HOW TO READ FIRST, PHILIP!
TORRES GIARRANO BLYBERG

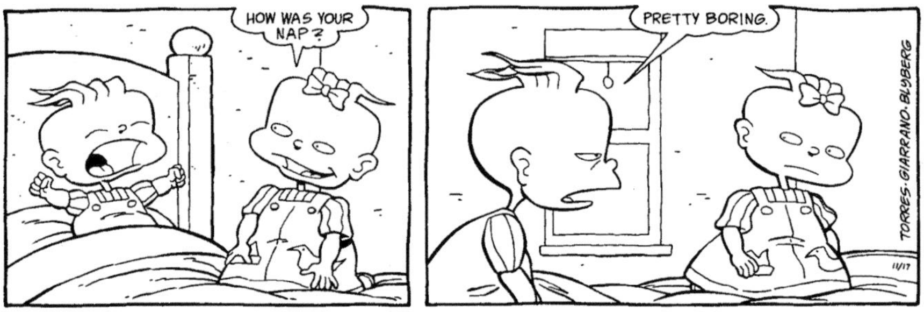
HOW WAS YOUR NAP?
PRETTY BORING.
TORRES · GIARRANO · BLYBERG
11/17

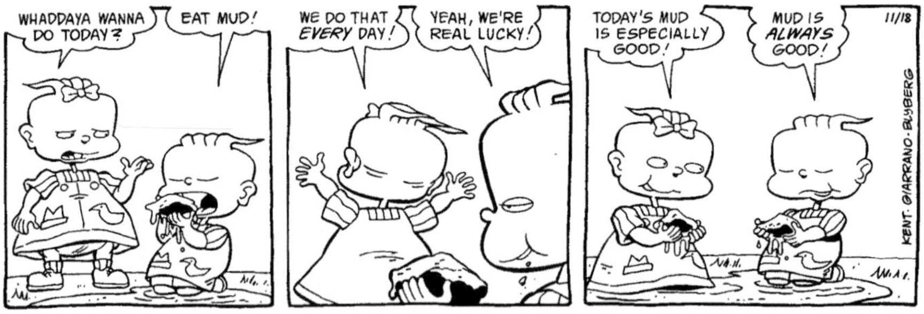
WHADDAYA WANNA DO TODAY?
EAT MUD!
WE DO THAT EVERY DAY!
YEAH, WE'RE REAL LUCKY!
TODAY'S MUD IS ESPECIALLY GOOD!
MUD IS ALWAYS GOOD!
11/18
KENT · GIARRANO · BLYBERG

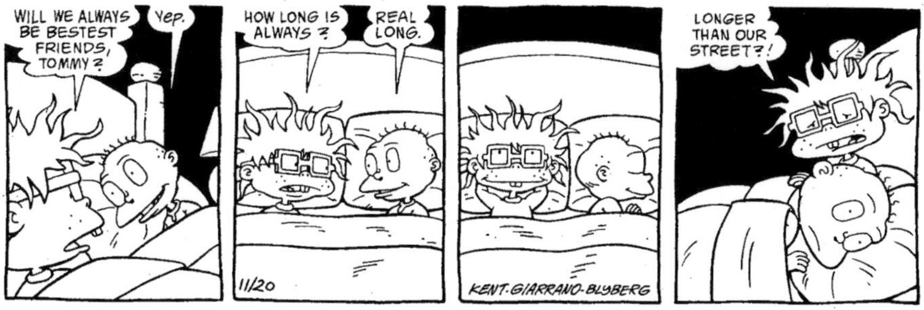
WILL WE ALWAYS BE BESTEST FRIENDS, TOMMY?
Yep.
HOW LONG IS ALWAYS?
REAL LONG.
11/20
KENT·GIARRANO·BLYBERG
LONGER THAN OUR STREET?!

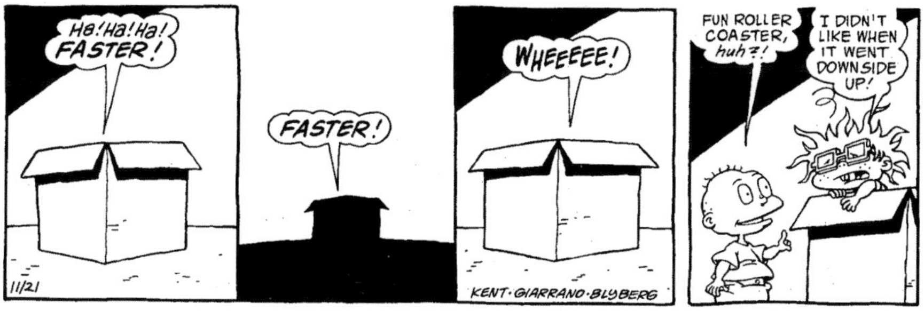
Ha! Ha! Ha! FASTER!
11/21
FASTER!
WHEEEEE!
KENT·GIARRANO·BLYBERG
FUN ROLLER COASTER, huh?!
I DIDN'T LIKE WHEN IT WENT DOWNSIDE UP!

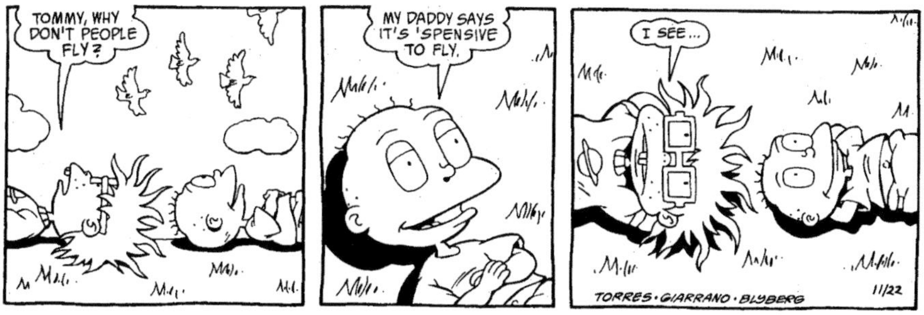
TOMMY, WHY DON'T PEOPLE FLY?
MY DADDY SAYS IT'S 'SPENSIVE TO FLY.
I SEE...
TORRES·GIARRANO·BLYBERG
11/22

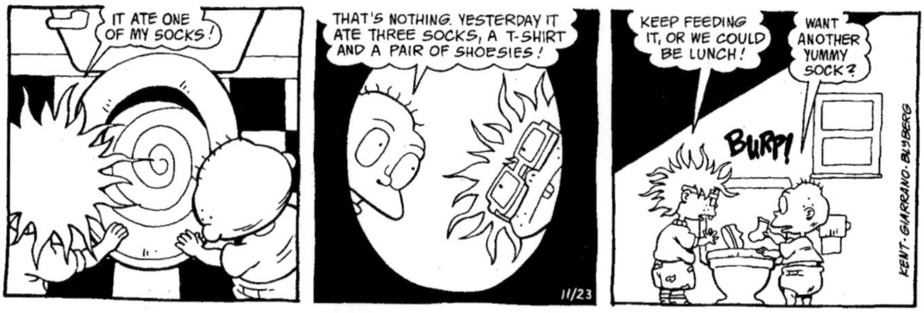
IT ATE ONE OF MY SOCKS!
THAT'S NOTHING. YESTERDAY IT ATE THREE SOCKS, A T-SHIRT AND A PAIR OF SHOESIES!
11/23
KEEP FEEDING IT, OR WE COULD BE LUNCH!
WANT ANOTHER YUMMY SOCK?
BURP!
KENT·GIARRANO·BLYBERG

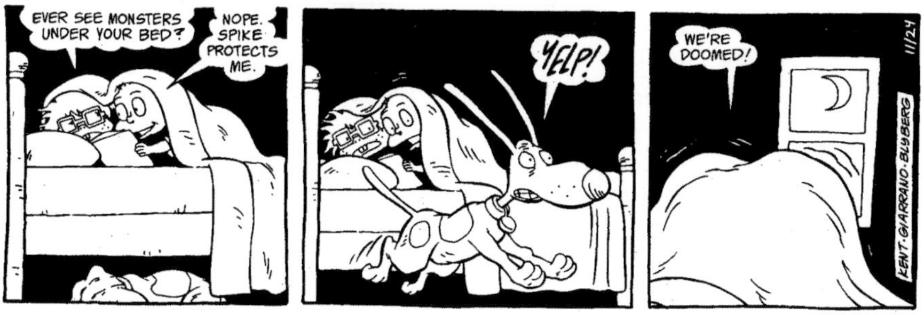
EVER SEE MONSTERS UNDER YOUR BED?
NOPE. SPIKE PROTECTS ME.
YELP!
WE'RE DOOMED!
11/24
KENT·GIARRANO·BLYBERG

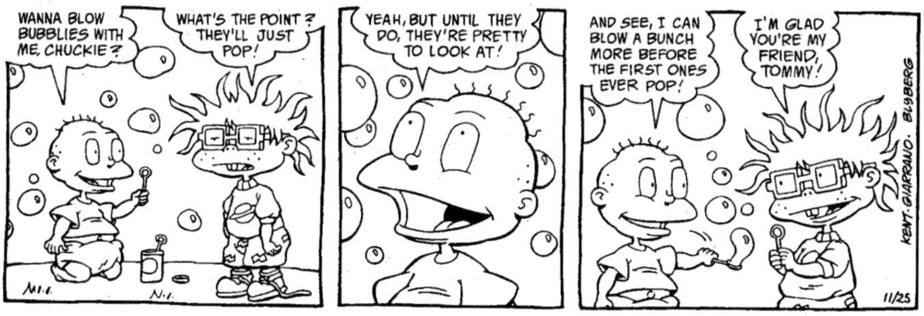
WANNA BLOW BUBBLIES WITH ME, CHUCKIE?
WHAT'S THE POINT? THEY'LL JUST POP!
YEAH, BUT UNTIL THEY DO, THEY'RE PRETTY TO LOOK AT!
AND SEE, I CAN BLOW A BUNCH MORE BEFORE THE FIRST ONES EVER POP!
I'M GLAD YOU'RE MY FRIEND, TOMMY!
KENT·GIARRANO·BLYBERG
11/25

2000

2000

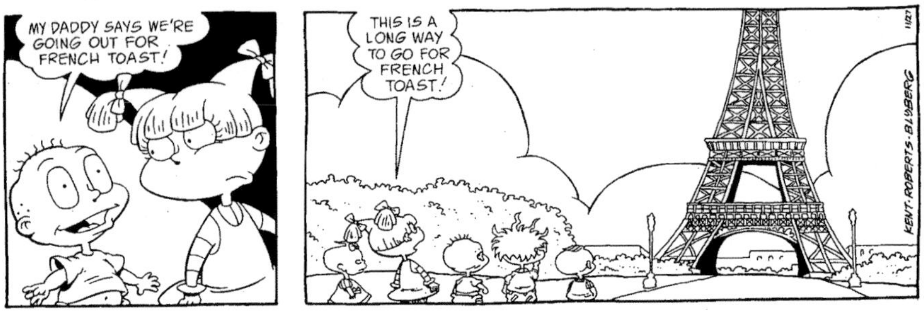
MY DADDY SAYS WE'RE GOING OUT FOR FRENCH TOAST!
THIS IS A LONG WAY TO GO FOR FRENCH TOAST!
KENT·ROBERTS·BLYBERG
11/27

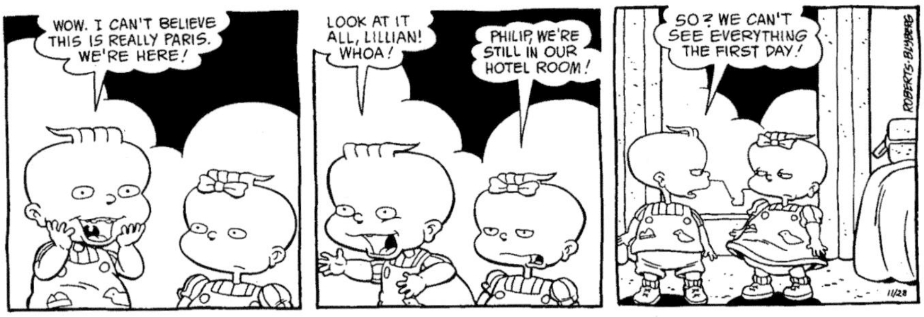
WOW. I CAN'T BELIEVE THIS IS REALLY PARIS. WE'RE HERE!
LOOK AT IT ALL, LILLIAN! WHOA!
PHILIP, WE'RE STILL IN OUR HOTEL ROOM!
SO? WE CAN'T SEE EVERYTHING THE FIRST DAY!
ROBERTS·BLYBERG
11/28

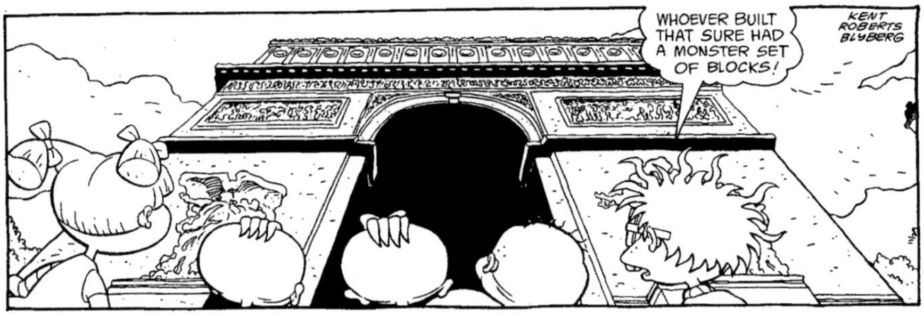
WHOEVER BUILT THAT SURE HAD A MONSTER SET OF BLOCKS!
KENT ROBERTS BLYBERG

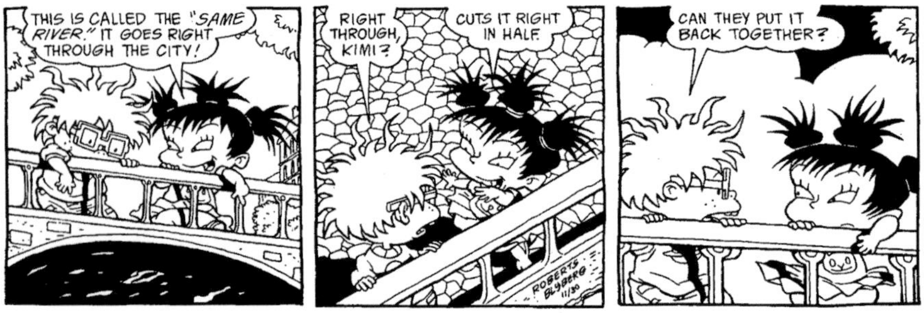
THIS IS CALLED THE "SAME RIVER." IT GOES RIGHT THROUGH THE CITY!
RIGHT THROUGH, KIMI?
CUTS IT RIGHT IN HALF.
CAN THEY PUT IT BACK TOGETHER?
ROBERTS BLYBERG 11/30

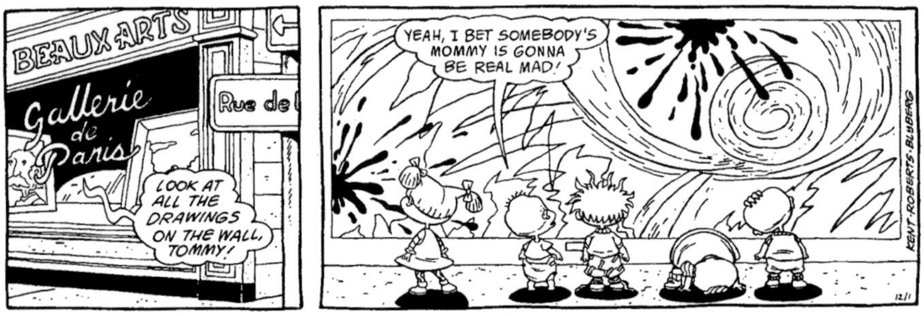
BEAUX ARTS
Gallerie de Paris
Rue de
LOOK AT ALL THE DRAWINGS ON THE WALL, TOMMY!
YEAH, I BET SOMEBODY'S MOMMY IS GONNA BE REAL MAD!
KENT·ROBERTS·BLYBERG
12/1

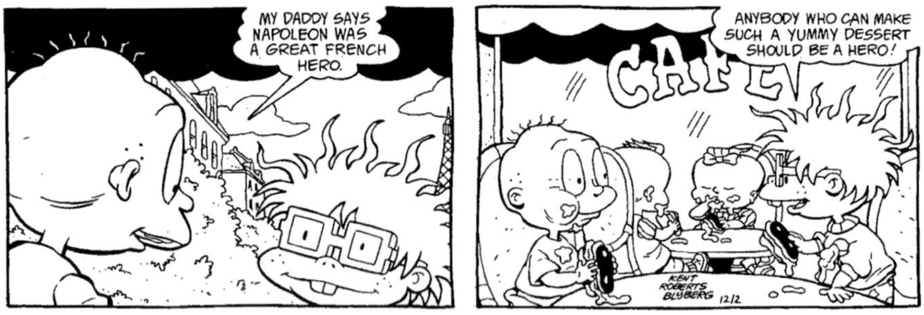
MY DADDY SAYS NAPOLEON WAS A GREAT FRENCH HERO.
ANYBODY WHO CAN MAKE SUCH A YUMMY DESSERT SHOULD BE A HERO!
KENT ROBERTS BLYBERG 12/2

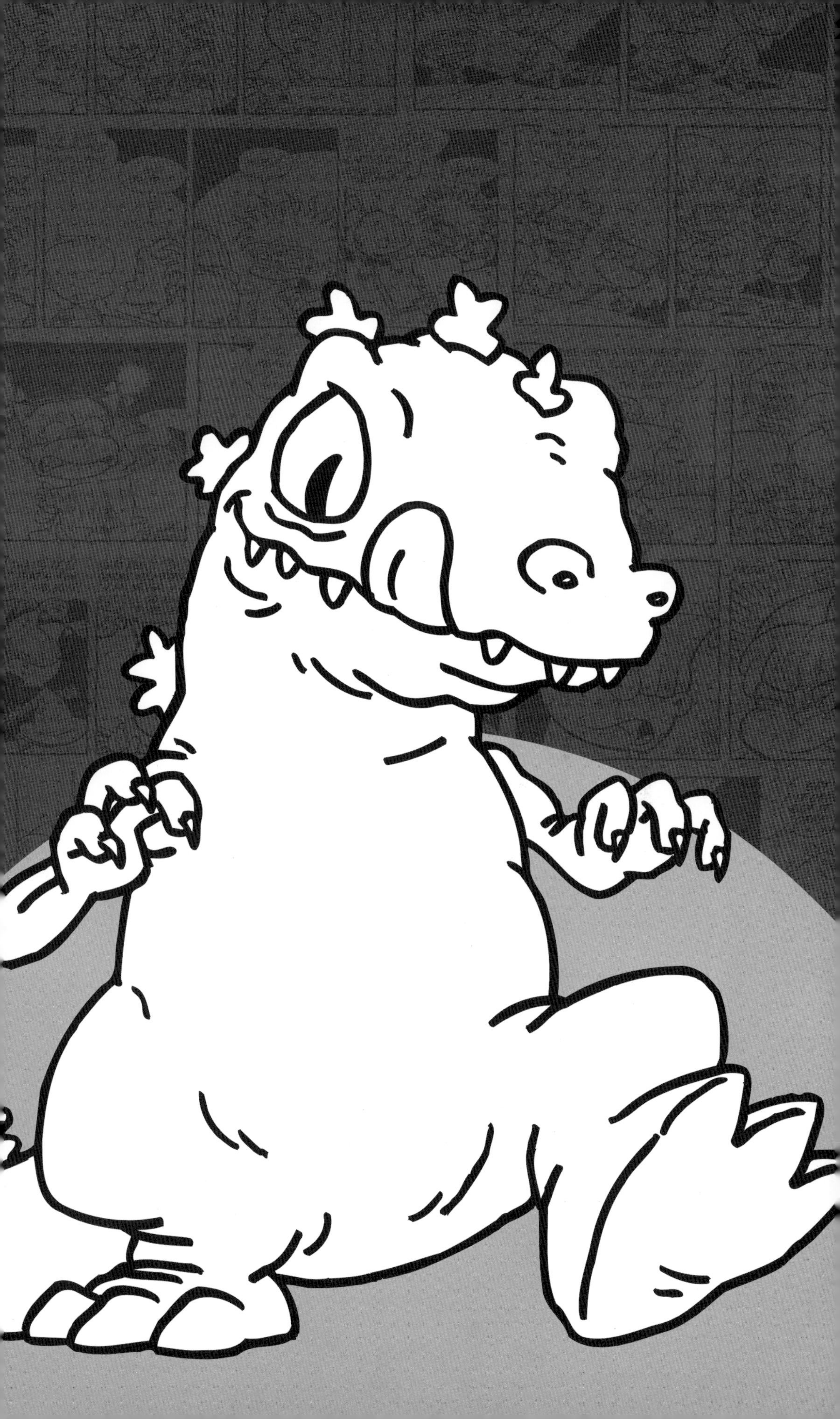

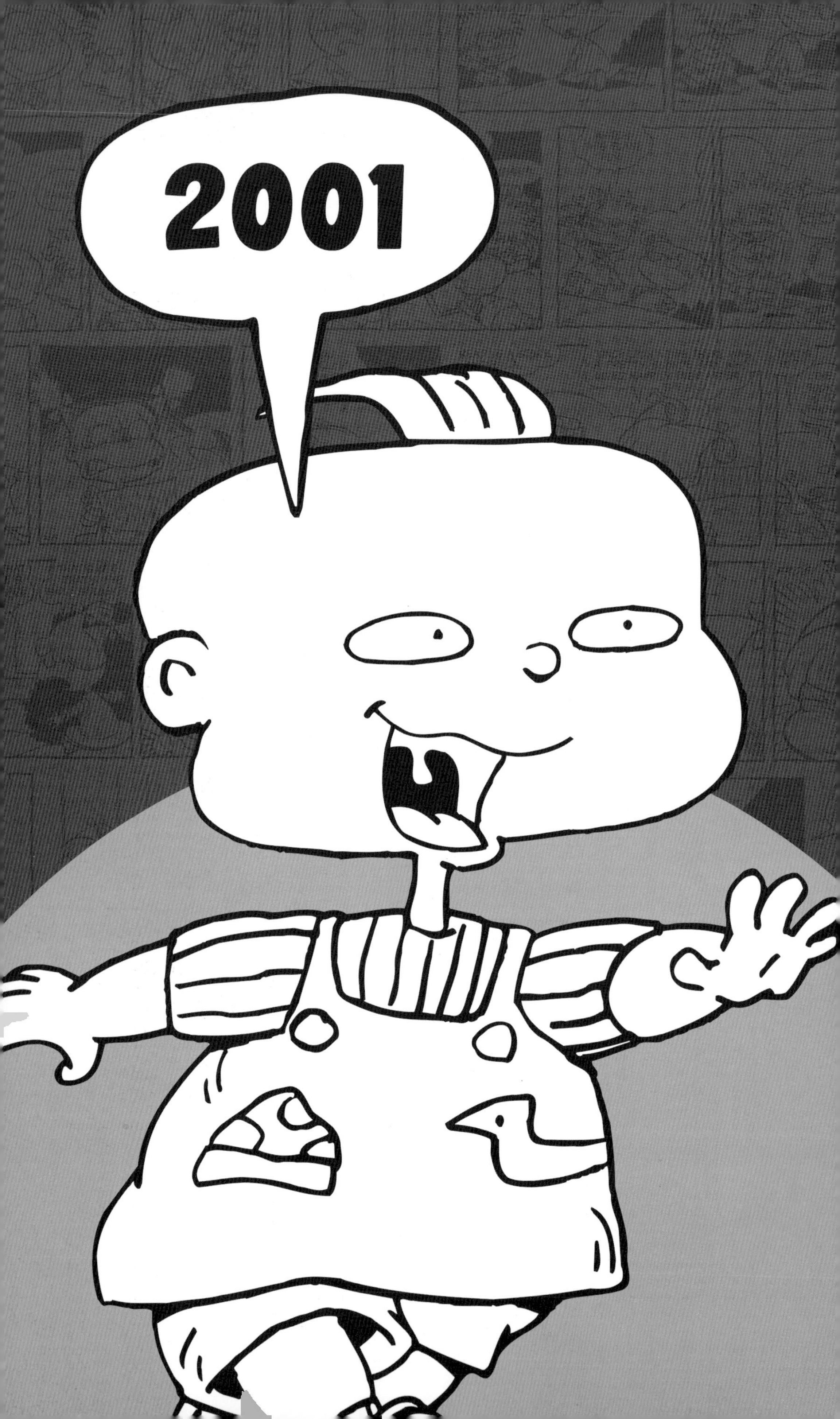
2001

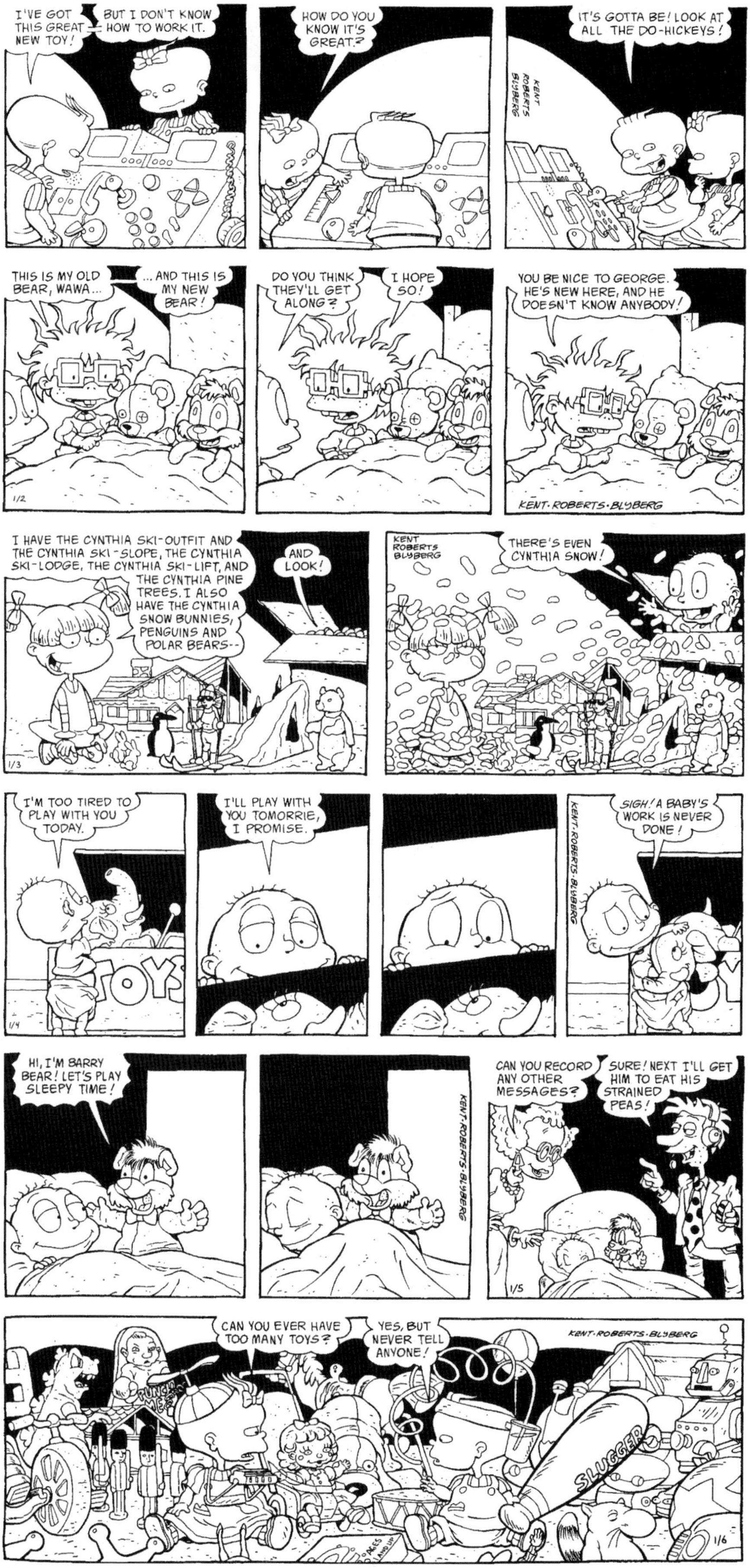

I'VE GOT THIS GREAT NEW TOY!
BUT I DON'T KNOW HOW TO WORK IT.
HOW DO YOU KNOW IT'S GREAT?
KENT ROBERTS BLYBERG
IT'S GOTTA BE! LOOK AT ALL THE DO-HICKEYS!
THIS IS MY OLD BEAR, WAWA...
...AND THIS IS MY NEW BEAR!
1/2
DO YOU THINK THEY'LL GET ALONG?
I HOPE SO!
YOU BE NICE TO GEORGE. HE'S NEW HERE, AND HE DOESN'T KNOW ANYBODY!
KENT·ROBERTS·BLYBERG
I HAVE THE CYNTHIA SKI-OUTFIT AND THE CYNTHIA SKI-SLOPE, THE CYNTHIA SKI-LODGE, THE CYNTHIA SKI-LIFT, AND THE CYNTHIA PINE TREES. I ALSO HAVE THE CYNTHIA SNOW BUNNIES, PENGUINS AND POLAR BEARS--
AND LOOK!
1/3
KENT ROBERTS BLYBERG
THERE'S EVEN CYNTHIA SNOW!
I'M TOO TIRED TO PLAY WITH YOU TODAY.
TOYS
1/4
I'LL PLAY WITH YOU TOMORRIE, I PROMISE.
KENT·ROBERTS·BLYBERG
SIGH! A BABY'S WORK IS NEVER DONE!
HI, I'M BARRY BEAR! LET'S PLAY SLEEPY TIME!
KENT·ROBERTS·BLYBERG
CAN YOU RECORD ANY OTHER MESSAGES?
SURE! NEXT I'LL GET HIM TO EAT HIS STRAINED PEAS!
1/5
CAN YOU EVER HAVE TOO MANY TOYS?
YES, BUT NEVER TELL ANYONE!
KENT·ROBERTS·BLYBERG
SLUGGER
1/6

2001

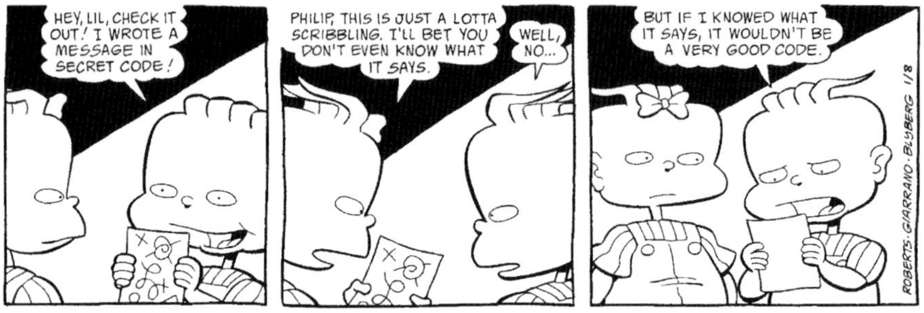
HEY, LIL, CHECK IT OUT! I WROTE A MESSAGE IN SECRET CODE!
PHILIP, THIS IS JUST A LOTTA SCRIBBLING. I'LL BET YOU DON'T EVEN KNOW WHAT IT SAYS.
WELL, NO...
BUT IF I KNOWED WHAT IT SAYS, IT WOULDN'T BE A VERY GOOD CODE.
ROBERTS·GIARRANO·BLYBERG 1/8

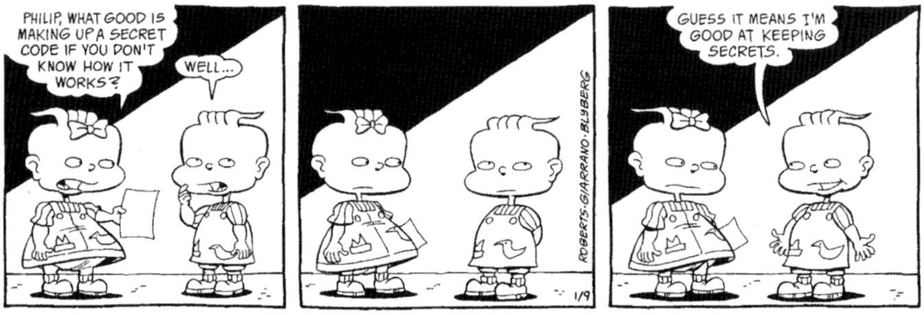
PHILIP, WHAT GOOD IS MAKING UP A SECRET CODE IF YOU DON'T KNOW HOW IT WORKS?
WELL...
ROBERTS·GIARRANO·BLYBERG
1/9
GUESS IT MEANS I'M GOOD AT KEEPING SECRETS.

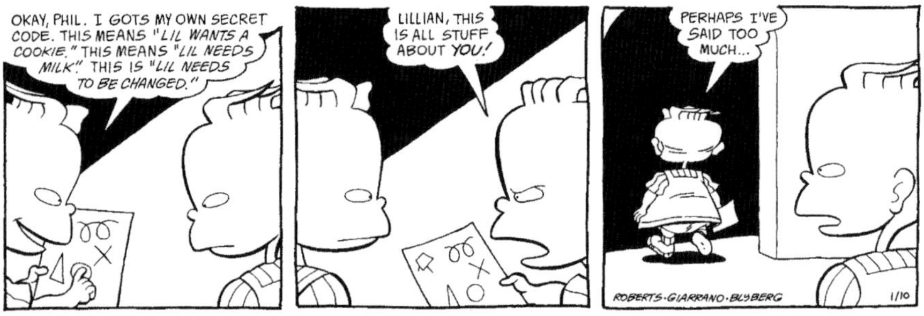
OKAY, PHIL. I GOTS MY OWN SECRET CODE. THIS MEANS "LIL WANTS A COOKIE." THIS MEANS "LIL NEEDS MILK." THIS IS "LIL NEEDS TO BE CHANGED."
LILLIAN, THIS IS ALL STUFF ABOUT YOU!
PERHAPS I'VE SAID TOO MUCH...
ROBERTS·GIARRANO·BLYBERG
1/10

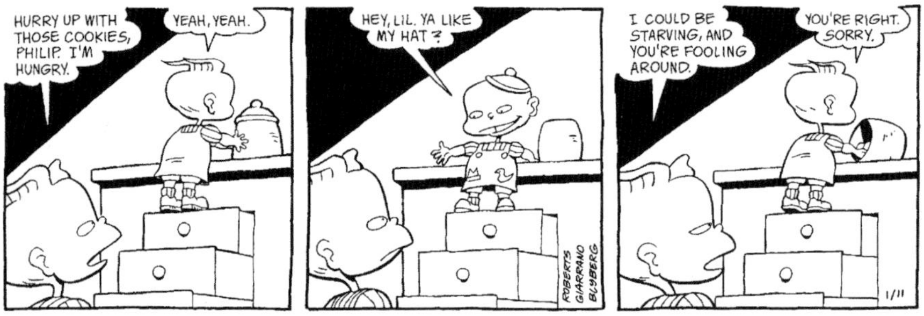
HURRY UP WITH THOSE COOKIES, PHILIP. I'M HUNGRY.
YEAH, YEAH.
HEY, LIL. YA LIKE MY HAT?
ROBERTS GIARRANO BLYBERG
I COULD BE STARVING, AND YOU'RE FOOLING AROUND.
YOU'RE RIGHT. SORRY.
1/11

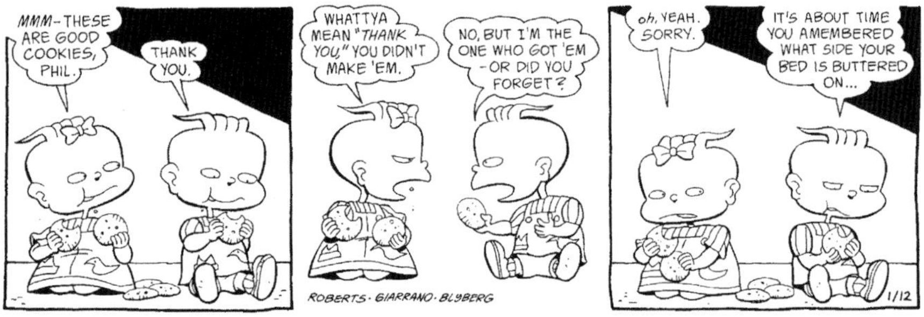
MMM-THESE ARE GOOD COOKIES, PHIL.
THANK YOU.
WHATTYA MEAN "THANK YOU," YOU DIDN'T MAKE 'EM.
NO, BUT I'M THE ONE WHO GOT 'EM -OR DID YOU FORGET?
ROBERTS·GIARRANO·BLYBERG
oh, YEAH. SORRY.
IT'S ABOUT TIME YOU AMEMBERED WHAT SIDE YOUR BED IS BUTTERED ON...
1/12

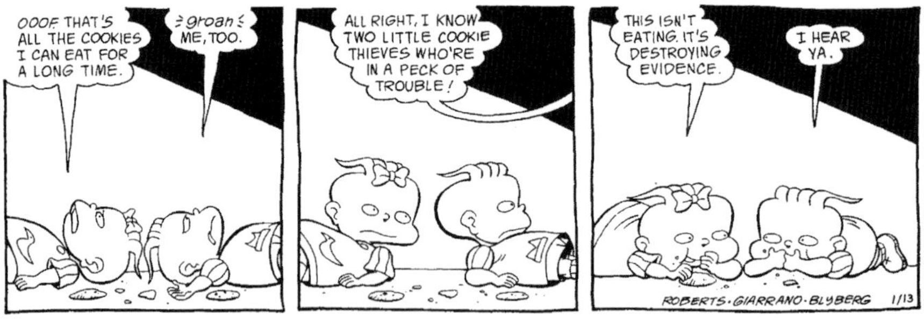
OOOF. THAT'S ALL THE COOKIES I CAN EAT FOR A LONG TIME.
groan ME, TOO.
ALL RIGHT, I KNOW TWO LITTLE COOKIE THIEVES WHO'RE IN A PECK OF TROUBLE!
THIS ISN'T EATING. IT'S DESTROYING EVIDENCE.
I HEAR YA.
ROBERTS·GIARRANO·BLYBERG 1/13

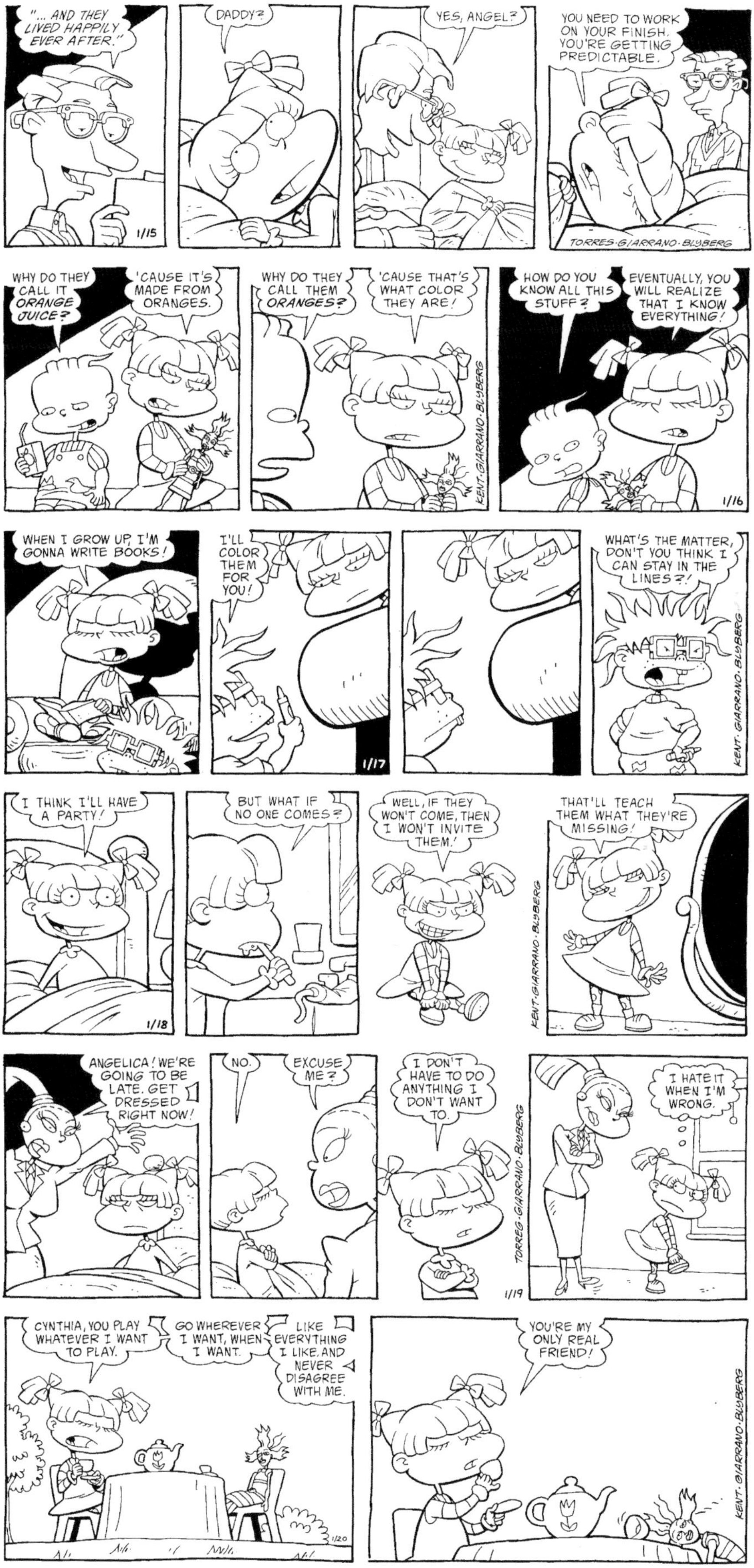

"... AND THEY LIVED HAPPILY EVER AFTER."
1/15
DADDY?
YES, ANGEL?
YOU NEED TO WORK ON YOUR FINISH. YOU'RE GETTING PREDICTABLE.
TORRES·GIARRANO·BLYBERG
WHY DO THEY CALL IT ORANGE JUICE?
'CAUSE IT'S MADE FROM ORANGES.
WHY DO THEY CALL THEM ORANGES?
'CAUSE THAT'S WHAT COLOR THEY ARE!
KENT·GIARRANO·BLYBERG
HOW DO YOU KNOW ALL THIS STUFF?
EVENTUALLY, YOU WILL REALIZE THAT I KNOW EVERYTHING!
1/16
WHEN I GROW UP, I'M GONNA WRITE BOOKS!
I'LL COLOR THEM FOR YOU!
1/17
WHAT'S THE MATTER, DON'T YOU THINK I CAN STAY IN THE LINES?!
KENT·GIARRANO·BLYBERG
I THINK I'LL HAVE A PARTY!
1/18
BUT WHAT IF NO ONE COMES?
WELL, IF THEY WON'T COME, THEN I WON'T INVITE THEM!
KENT·GIARRANO·BLYBERG
THAT'LL TEACH THEM WHAT THEY'RE MISSING!
ANGELICA! WE'RE GOING TO BE LATE. GET DRESSED RIGHT NOW!
NO.
EXCUSE ME?
I DON'T HAVE TO DO ANYTHING I DON'T WANT TO.
TORRES·GIARRANO·BLYBERG
1/19
I HATE IT WHEN I'M WRONG.
CYNTHIA, YOU PLAY WHATEVER I WANT TO PLAY.
GO WHEREVER I WANT, WHEN I WANT.
LIKE EVERYTHING I LIKE, AND NEVER DISAGREE WITH ME.
1/20
YOU'RE MY ONLY REAL FRIEND!
KENT·GIARRANO·BLYBERG

2001

2001

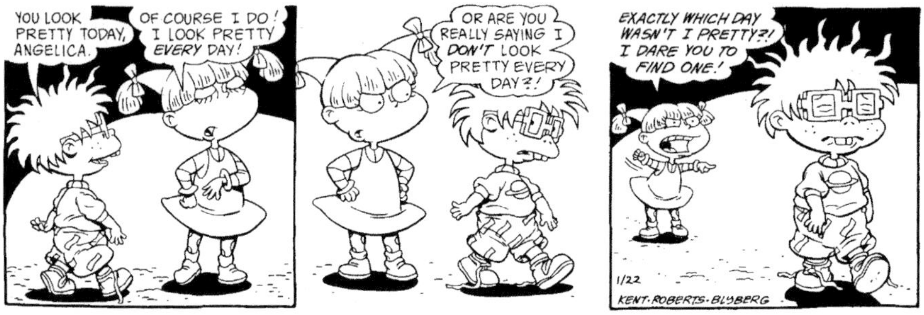

YOU LOOK PRETTY TODAY, ANGELICA.
OF COURSE I DO! I LOOK PRETTY *EVERY* DAY!
OR ARE YOU REALLY SAYING I *DON'T* LOOK PRETTY EVERY DAY?!
EXACTLY WHICH DAY WASN'T I PRETTY?! I DARE YOU TO FIND ONE!
1/22
KENT·ROBERTS·BLYBERG

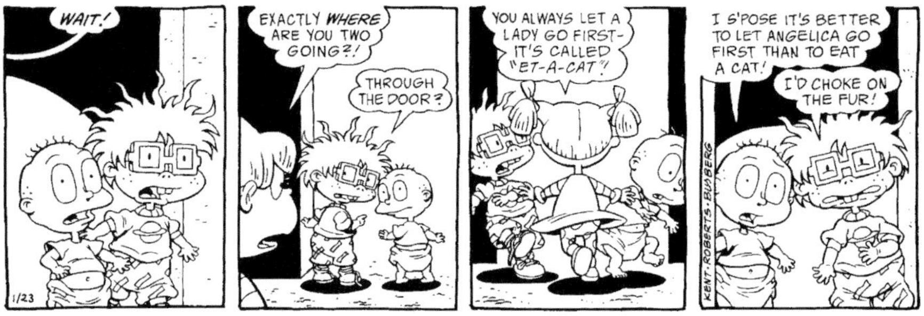

WAIT!
1/23
EXACTLY *WHERE* ARE YOU TWO GOING?!
THROUGH THE DOOR?
YOU ALWAYS LET A LADY GO FIRST– IT'S CALLED "*ET-A-CAT*"!
I S'POSE IT'S BETTER TO LET ANGELICA GO FIRST THAN TO EAT A CAT!
I'D CHOKE ON THE FUR!
KENT·ROBERTS·BLYBERG

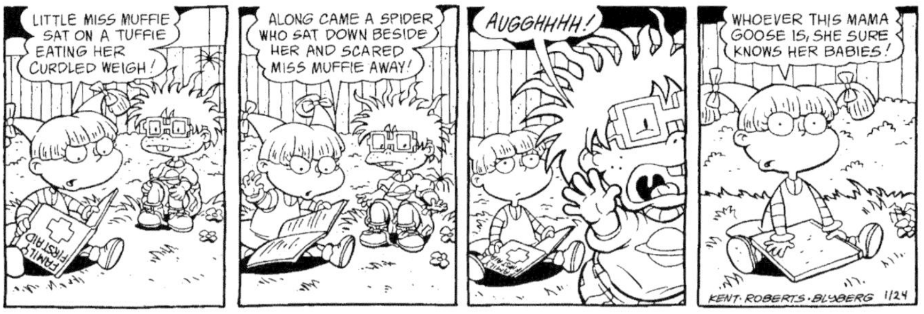

LITTLE MISS MUFFIE SAT ON A TUFFIE EATING HER CURDLED WEIGH!
FAMILY FIRST AID
ALONG CAME A SPIDER WHO SAT DOWN BESIDE HER AND SCARED MISS MUFFIE AWAY!
AUGGHHHH!
WHOEVER THIS MAMA GOOSE IS, SHE SURE KNOWS HER BABIES!
KENT·ROBERTS·BLYBERG 1/24

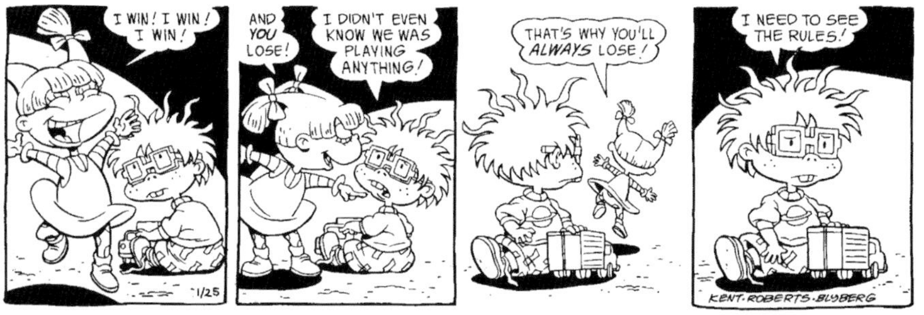

I WIN! I WIN! I WIN!
1/25
AND *YOU* LOSE!
I DIDN'T EVEN KNOW WE WAS PLAYING ANYTHING!
THAT'S WHY YOU'LL *ALWAYS* LOSE!
I NEED TO SEE THE RULES!
KENT·ROBERTS·BLYBERG

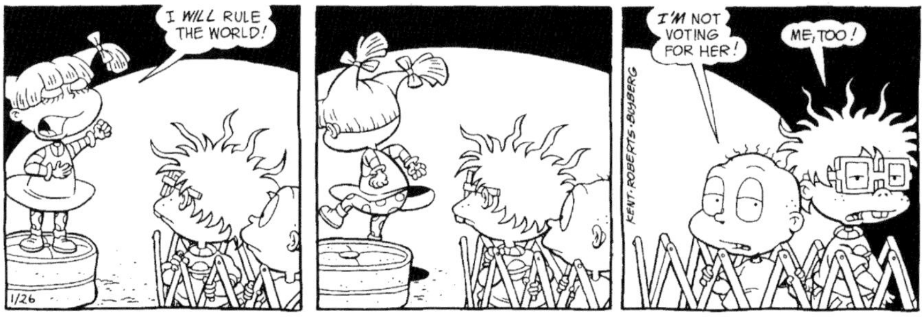

I *WILL* RULE THE WORLD!
1/26
I'M NOT VOTING FOR HER!
ME, TOO!
KENT·ROBERTS·BLYBERG

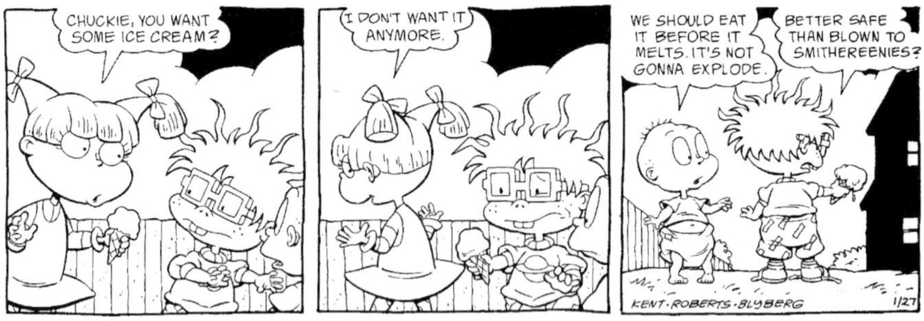

CHUCKIE, YOU WANT SOME ICE CREAM?
I DON'T WANT IT ANYMORE.
WE SHOULD EAT IT BEFORE IT MELTS. IT'S NOT GONNA EXPLODE.
BETTER SAFE THAN BLOWN TO SMITHEREENIES?
KENT·ROBERTS·BLYBERG 1/27

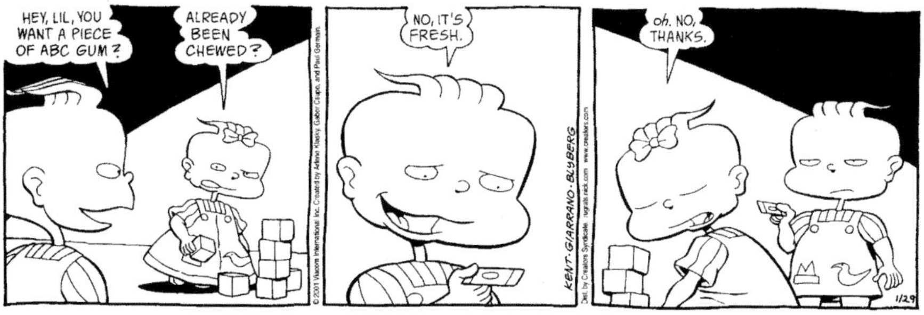
HEY, LIL, YOU WANT A PIECE OF ABC GUM?
ALREADY BEEN CHEWED?
NO, IT'S FRESH.
oh. NO, THANKS.
KENT·GIARRANO·BLYBERG
1/29

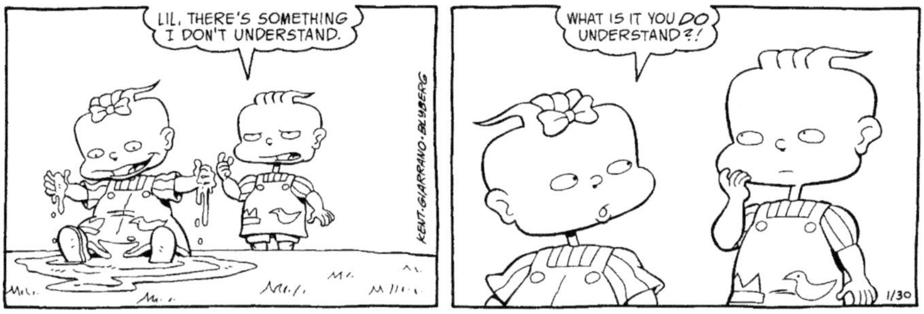
LIL, THERE'S SOMETHING I DON'T UNDERSTAND.
WHAT IS IT YOU *DO* UNDERSTAND?!
KENT·GIARRANO·BLYBERG
1/30

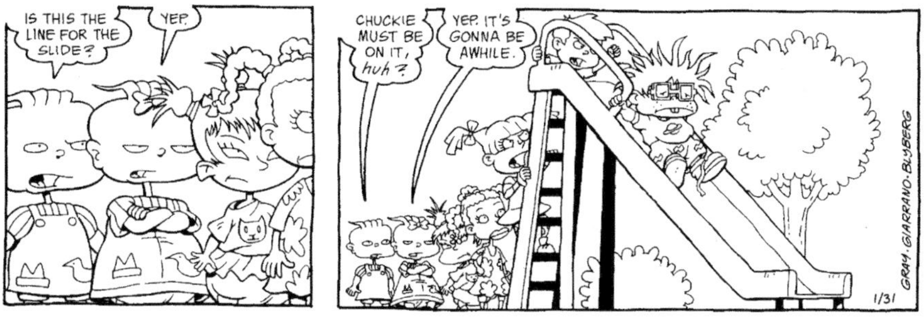
IS THIS THE LINE FOR THE SLIDE?
YEP.
CHUCKIE MUST BE ON IT, *huh*?
YEP. IT'S GONNA BE AWHILE.
GRAY·GIARRANO·BLYBERG
1/31

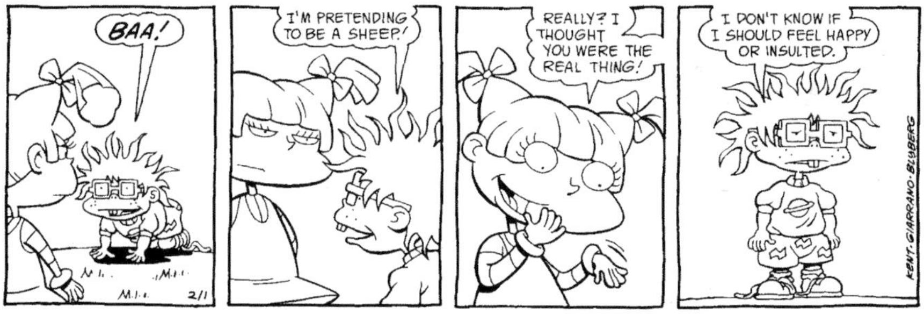
BAA!
2/1
I'M PRETENDING TO BE A SHEEP!
REALLY? I THOUGHT YOU WERE THE REAL THING!
I DON'T KNOW IF I SHOULD FEEL HAPPY OR INSULTED.
KENT·GIARRANO·BLYBERG

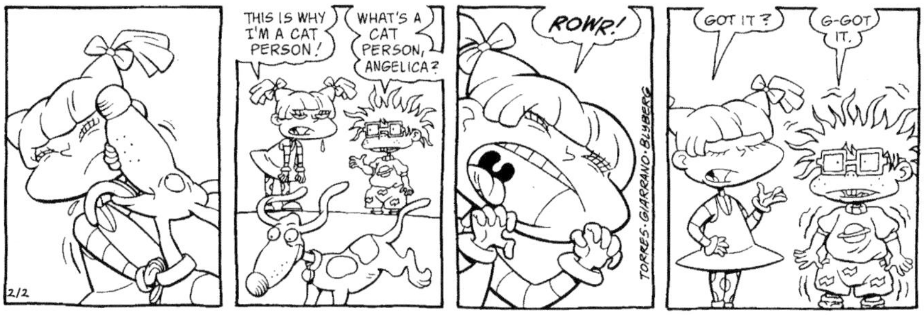
2/2
THIS IS WHY I'M A CAT PERSON!
WHAT'S A CAT PERSON, ANGELICA?
ROWR!
TORRES·GIARRANO·BLYBERG
GOT IT?
G-GOT IT.

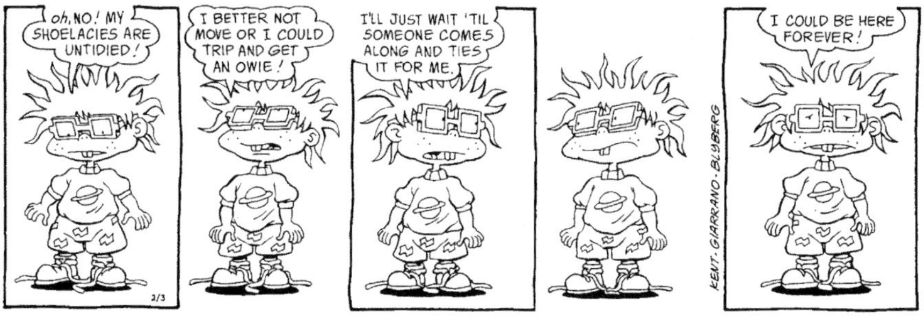
oh, NO! MY SHOELACIES ARE UNTIDIED!
2/3
I BETTER NOT MOVE OR I COULD TRIP AND GET AN OWIE!
I'LL JUST WAIT 'TIL SOMEONE COMES ALONG AND TIES IT FOR ME.
KENT·GIARRANO·BLYBERG
I COULD BE HERE FOREVER!

2001

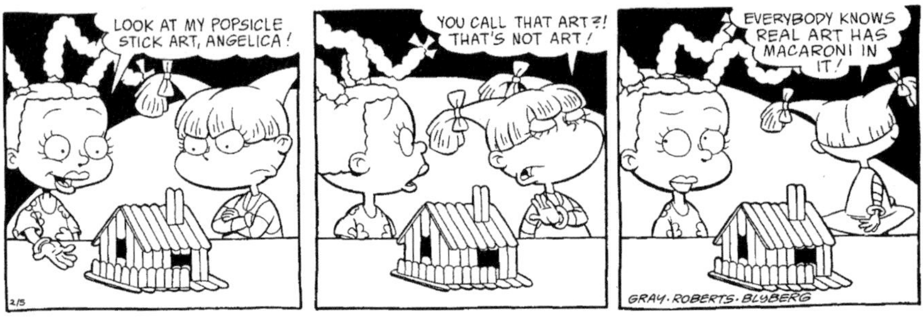
LOOK AT MY POPSICLE STICK ART, ANGELICA!
YOU CALL THAT ART?! THAT'S NOT ART!
EVERYBODY KNOWS REAL ART HAS MACARONI IN IT!
2/5
GRAY·ROBERTS·BLYBERG

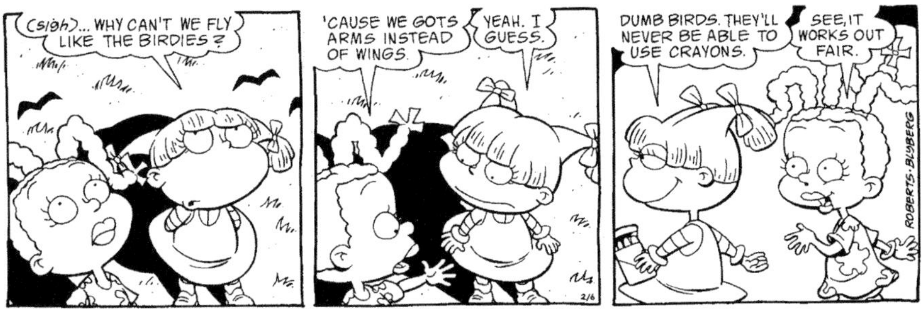
(sigh)... WHY CAN'T WE FLY LIKE THE BIRDIES?
'CAUSE WE GOTS ARMS INSTEAD OF WINGS.
YEAH. I GUESS.
DUMB BIRDS. THEY'LL NEVER BE ABLE TO USE CRAYONS.
SEE, IT WORKS OUT FAIR.
2/6
ROBERTS·BLYBERG

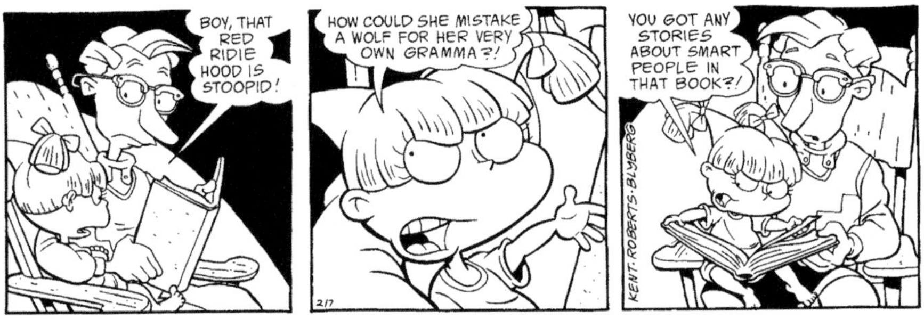
BOY, THAT RED RIDIE HOOD IS STOOPID!
HOW COULD SHE MISTAKE A WOLF FOR HER VERY OWN GRAMMA?!
YOU GOT ANY STORIES ABOUT SMART PEOPLE IN THAT BOOK?!
2/7
KENT·ROBERTS·BLYBERG

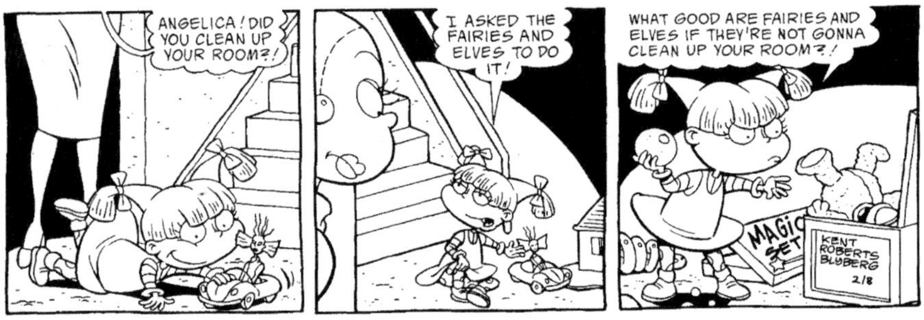
ANGELICA! DID YOU CLEAN UP YOUR ROOM?!
I ASKED THE FAIRIES AND ELVES TO DO IT!
WHAT GOOD ARE FAIRIES AND ELVES IF THEY'RE NOT GONNA CLEAN UP YOUR ROOM?!
MAGIC SET
KENT ROBERTS BLYBERG 2/8

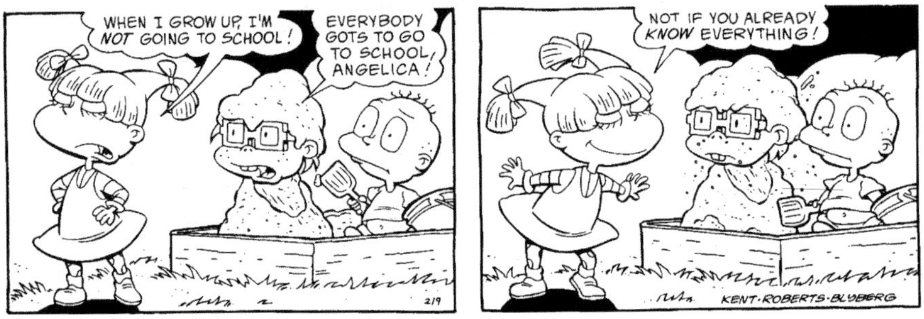
WHEN I GROW UP, I'M *NOT* GOING TO SCHOOL!
EVERYBODY GOTS TO GO TO SCHOOL, ANGELICA!
2/9
NOT IF YOU ALREADY *KNOW* EVERYTHING!
KENT·ROBERTS·BLYBERG

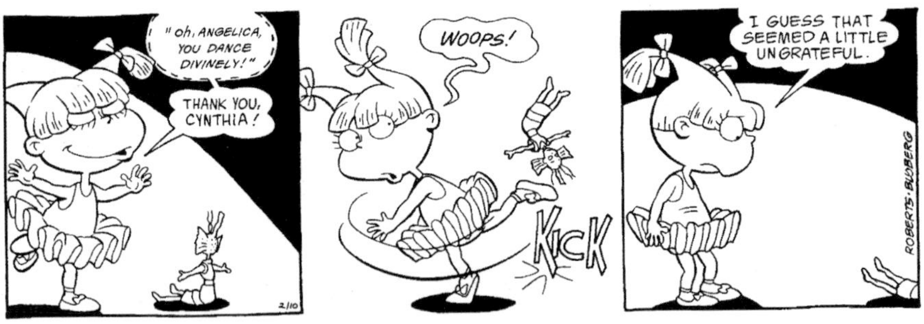
"oh, ANGELICA, YOU DANCE DIVINELY!"
THANK YOU, CYNTHIA!
2/10
WOOPS!
KICK
I GUESS THAT SEEMED A LITTLE UNGRATEFUL.
ROBERTS·BLYBERG

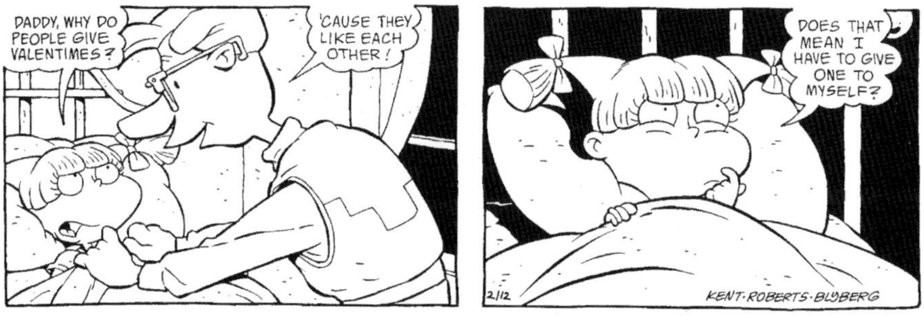
DADDY, WHY DO PEOPLE GIVE VALENTIMES?
'CAUSE THEY LIKE EACH OTHER!
DOES THAT MEAN I HAVE TO GIVE ONE TO MYSELF?
2/12
KENT·ROBERTS·BLYBERG

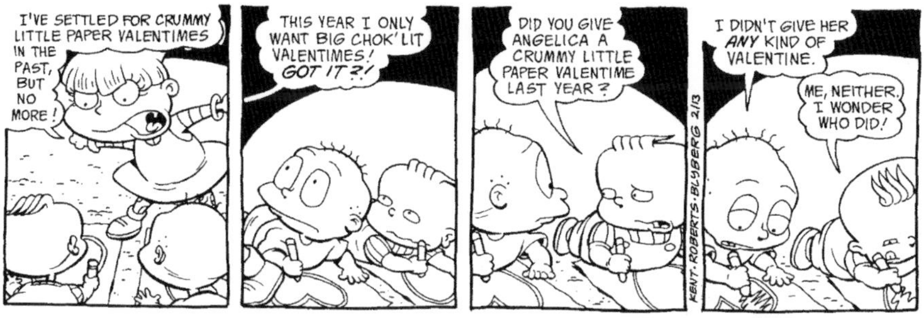
I'VE SETTLED FOR CRUMMY LITTLE PAPER VALENTIMES IN THE PAST, BUT NO MORE!
THIS YEAR I ONLY WANT BIG CHOK'LIT VALENTIMES! GOT IT?!
DID YOU GIVE ANGELICA A CRUMMY LITTLE PAPER VALENTIME LAST YEAR?
KENT·ROBERTS·BLYBERG 2/13
I DIDN'T GIVE HER ANY KIND OF VALENTINE.
ME, NEITHER. I WONDER WHO DID!

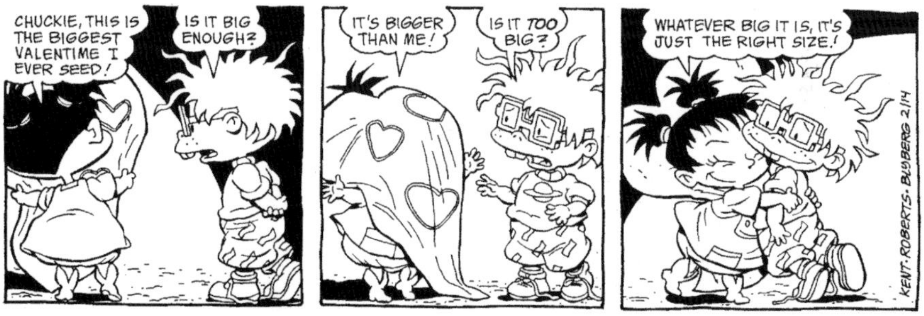
CHUCKIE, THIS IS THE BIGGEST VALENTIME I EVER SEED!
IS IT BIG ENOUGH?
IT'S BIGGER THAN ME!
IS IT TOO BIG?
WHATEVER BIG IT IS, IT'S JUST THE RIGHT SIZE!
KENT·ROBERTS·BLYBERG 2/14

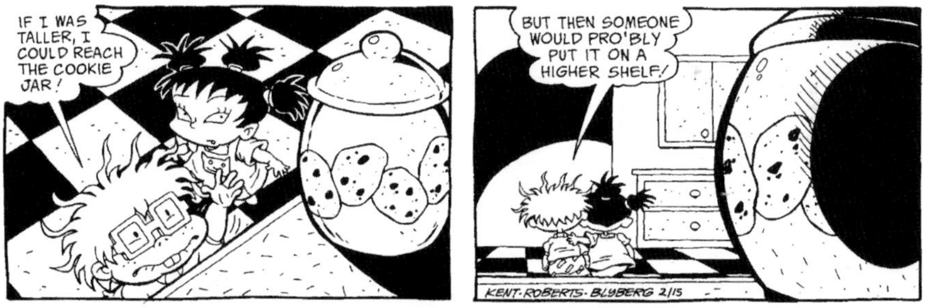
IF I WAS TALLER, I COULD REACH THE COOKIE JAR!
BUT THEN SOMEONE WOULD PRO'BLY PUT IT ON A HIGHER SHELF!
KENT·ROBERTS·BLYBERG 2/15

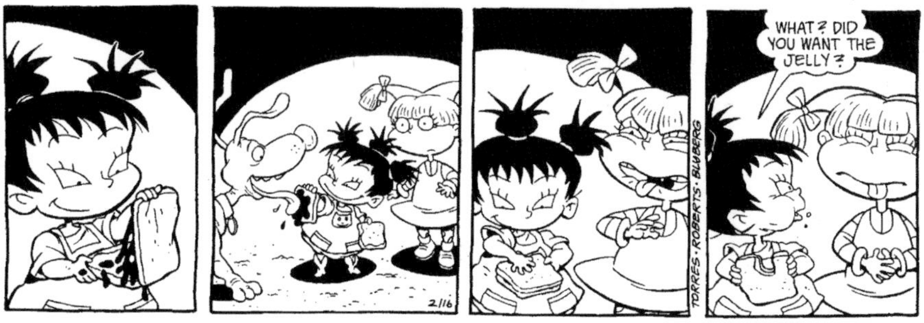
2/16
TORRES·ROBERTS·BLYBERG
WHAT? DID YOU WANT THE JELLY?

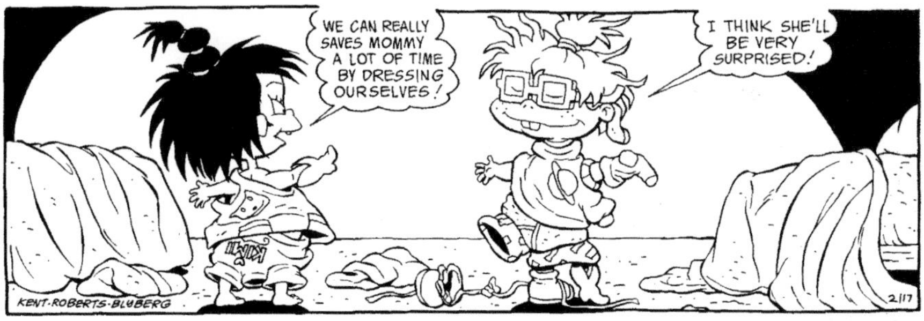
WE CAN REALLY SAVES MOMMY A LOT OF TIME BY DRESSING OURSELVES!
I THINK SHE'LL BE VERY SURPRISED!
KENT·ROBERTS·BLYBERG
2/17

2001

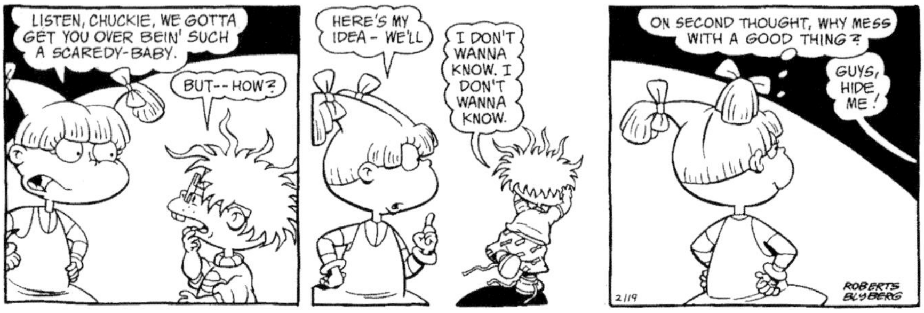
LISTEN, CHUCKIE, WE GOTTA GET YOU OVER BEIN' SUCH A SCAREDY-BABY.
BUT--HOW?
HERE'S MY IDEA - WE'LL
I DON'T WANNA KNOW. I DON'T WANNA KNOW.
ON SECOND THOUGHT, WHY MESS WITH A GOOD THING?
GUYS, HIDE ME!
2/19
ROBERTS BLYBERG

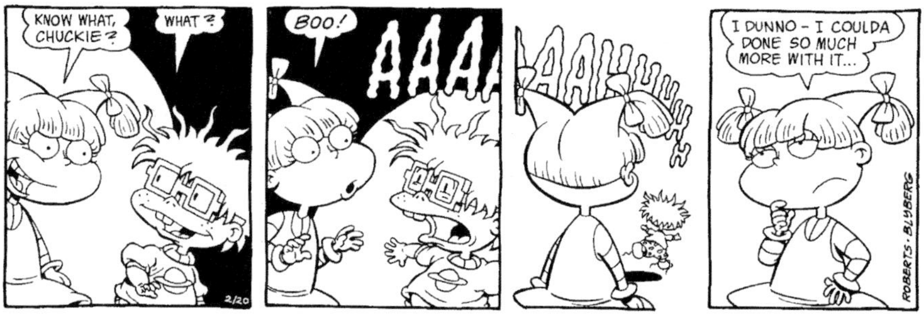
KNOW WHAT, CHUCKIE?
WHAT?
2/20
BOO!
AAAA
I DUNNO - I COULDA DONE SO MUCH MORE WITH IT...
ROBERTS · BLYBERG

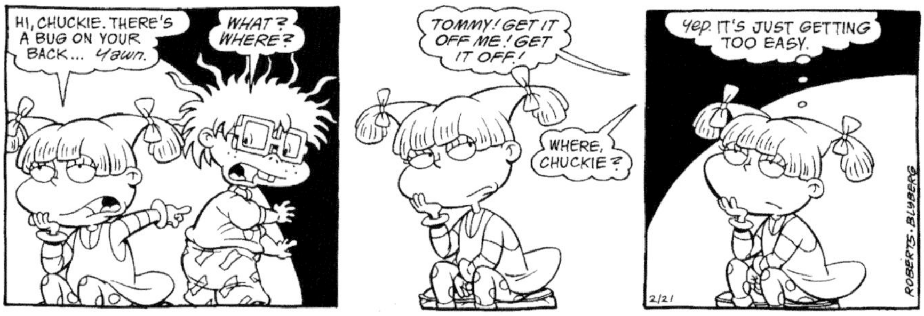
HI, CHUCKIE. THERE'S A BUG ON YOUR BACK... yawn.
WHAT? WHERE?
TOMMY! GET IT OFF ME! GET IT OFF!
WHERE, CHUCKIE?
yep. IT'S JUST GETTING TOO EASY.
2/21
ROBERTS · BLYBERG

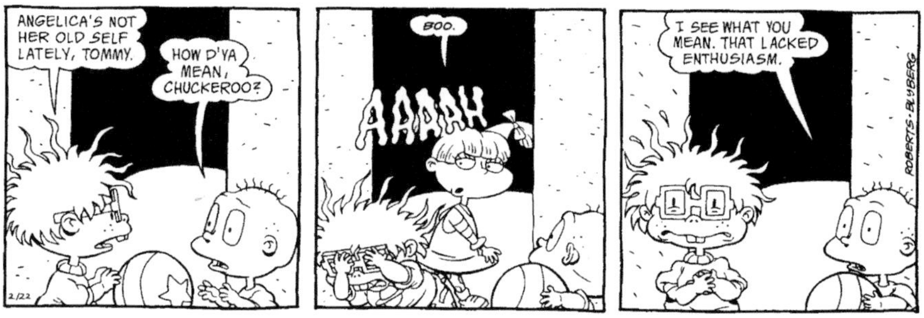
ANGELICA'S NOT HER OLD SELF LATELY, TOMMY.
HOW D'YA MEAN, CHUCKEROO?
2/22
BOO.
AAARH
I SEE WHAT YOU MEAN. THAT LACKED ENTHUSIASM.
ROBERTS · BLYBERG

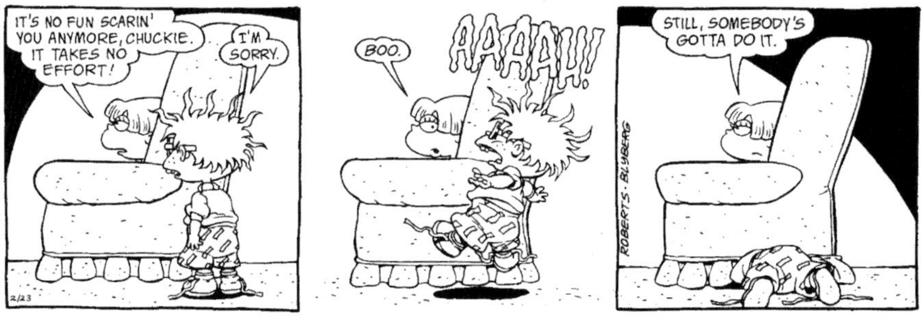
IT'S NO FUN SCARIN' YOU ANYMORE, CHUCKIE. IT TAKES NO EFFORT!
I'M SORRY.
2/23
BOO.
STILL, SOMEBODY'S GOTTA DO IT.
ROBERTS · BLYBERG

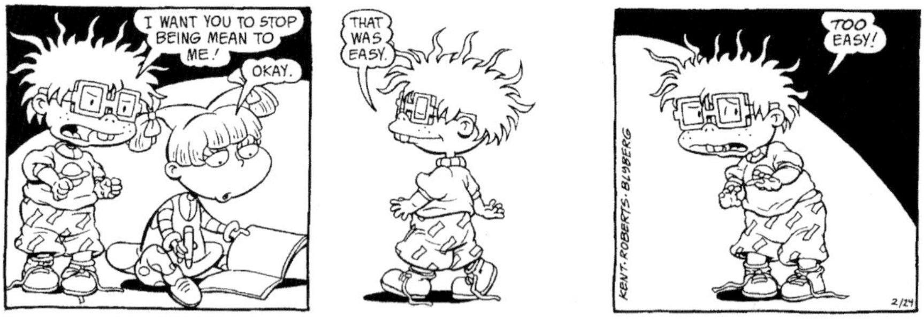
I WANT YOU TO STOP BEING MEAN TO ME!
OKAY.
THAT WAS EASY.
TOO EASY!
KENT · ROBERTS · BLYBERG
2/24

2001

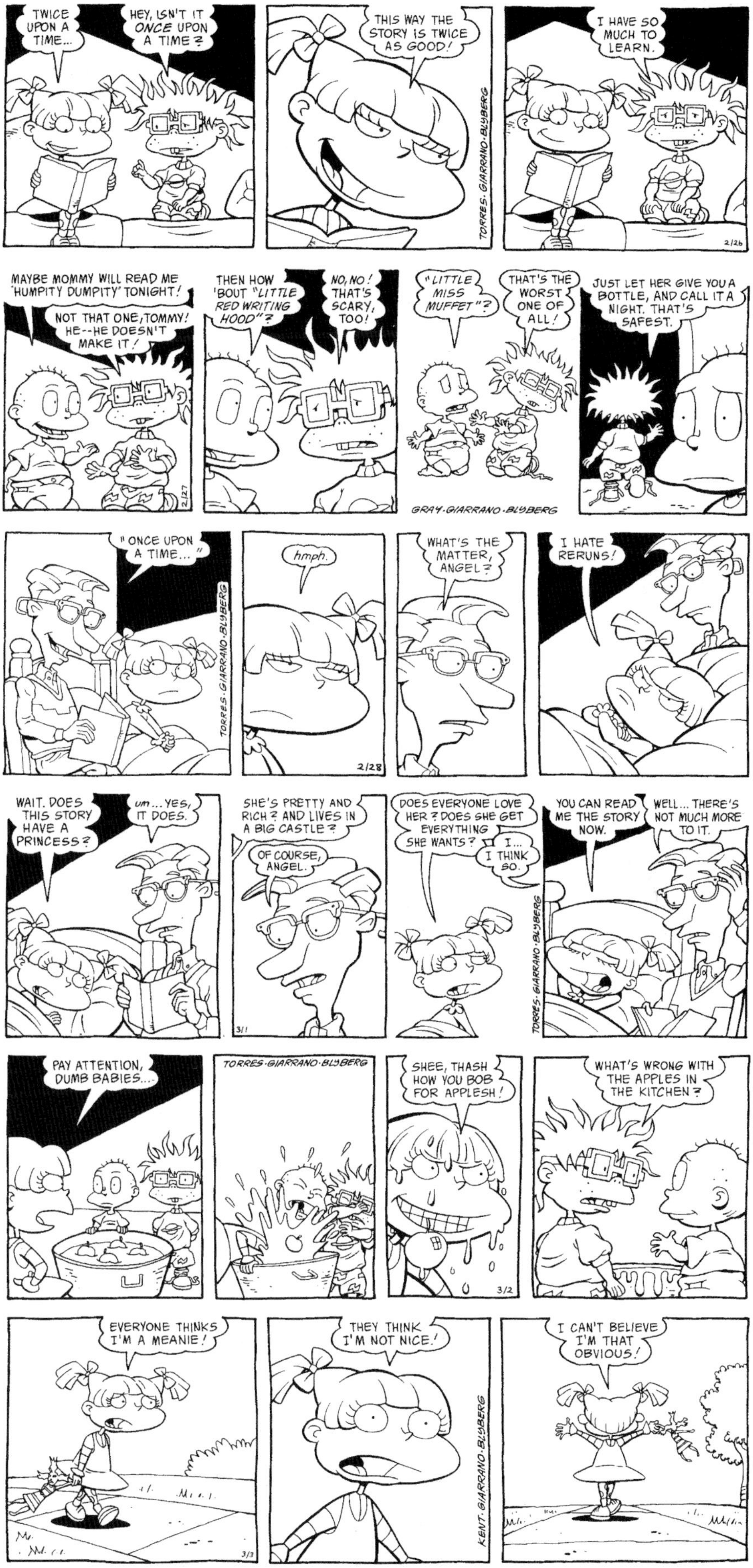
TWICE UPON A TIME...
HEY, ISN'T IT ONCE UPON A TIME?
THIS WAY THE STORY IS TWICE AS GOOD!
TORRES·GIARRANO·BLYBERG
I HAVE SO MUCH TO LEARN.
2/26
MAYBE MOMMY WILL READ ME 'HUMPITY DUMPITY' TONIGHT!
NOT THAT ONE, TOMMY! HE--HE DOESN'T MAKE IT!
2/27
THEN HOW 'BOUT "LITTLE RED WRITING HOOD"?
NO, NO! THAT'S SCARY, TOO!
"LITTLE MISS MUFFET"?
THAT'S THE WORST ONE OF ALL!
JUST LET HER GIVE YOU A BOTTLE, AND CALL IT A NIGHT. THAT'S SAFEST.
GRAY·GIARRANO·BLYBERG
"ONCE UPON A TIME..."
TORRES·GIARRANO·BLYBERG
hmph.
2/28
WHAT'S THE MATTER, ANGEL?
I HATE RERUNS!
WAIT. DOES THIS STORY HAVE A PRINCESS?
um... YES, IT DOES.
SHE'S PRETTY AND RICH? AND LIVES IN A BIG CASTLE?
OF COURSE, ANGEL.
3/1
DOES EVERYONE LOVE HER? DOES SHE GET EVERYTHING SHE WANTS?
I... I THINK SO.
TORRES·GIARRANO·BLYBERG
YOU CAN READ ME THE STORY NOW.
WELL... THERE'S NOT MUCH MORE TO IT.
PAY ATTENTION, DUMB BABIES...
TORRES·GIARRANO·BLYBERG
SHEE, THASH HOW YOU BOB FOR APPLESH!
3/2
WHAT'S WRONG WITH THE APPLES IN THE KITCHEN?
EVERYONE THINKS I'M A MEANIE!
3/3
THEY THINK I'M NOT NICE!
KENT·GIARRANO·BLYBERG
I CAN'T BELIEVE I'M THAT OBVIOUS!

2001

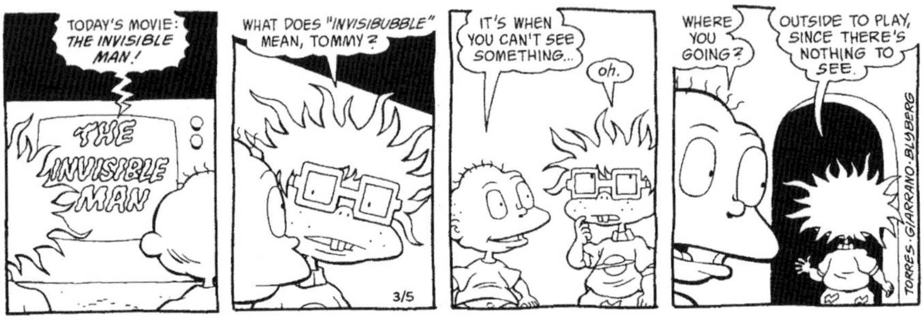
TODAY'S MOVIE: THE INVISIBLE MAN!
THE INVISIBLE MAN
WHAT DOES "INVISIBUBBLE" MEAN, TOMMY?
3/5
IT'S WHEN YOU CAN'T SEE SOMETHING...
oh.
WHERE YOU GOING?
OUTSIDE TO PLAY, SINCE THERE'S NOTHING TO SEE.
TORRES · GIARRANO · BLYBERG

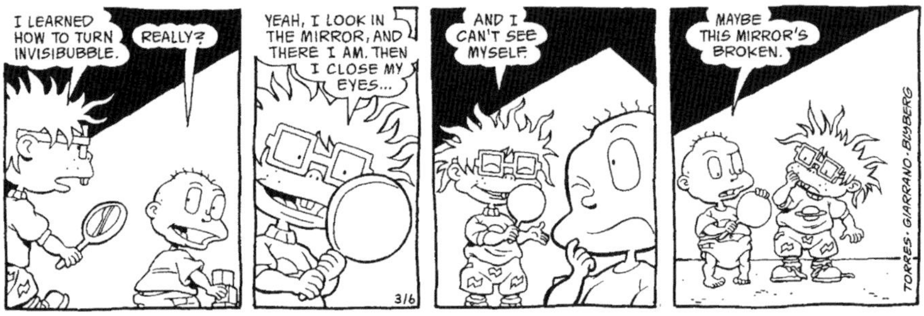
I LEARNED HOW TO TURN INVISIBUBBLE.
REALLY?
YEAH, I LOOK IN THE MIRROR, AND THERE I AM. THEN I CLOSE MY EYES...
3/6
AND I CAN'T SEE MYSELF.
MAYBE THIS MIRROR'S BROKEN.
TORRES · GIARRANO · BLYBERG

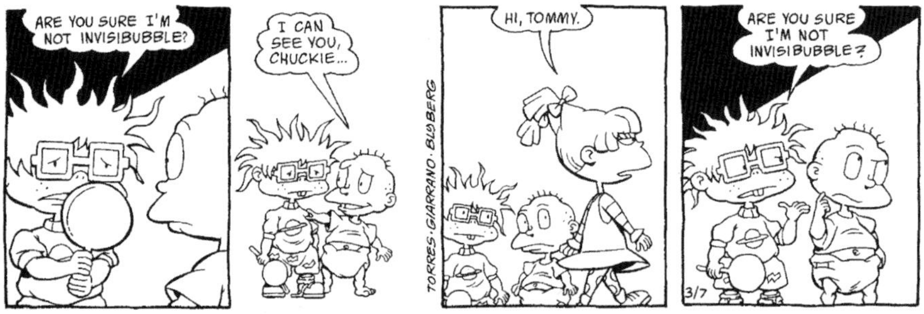
ARE YOU SURE I'M NOT INVISIBUBBLE?
I CAN SEE YOU, CHUCKIE...
TORRES · GIARRANO · BLYBERG
HI, TOMMY.
ARE YOU SURE I'M NOT INVISIBUBBLE?
3/7

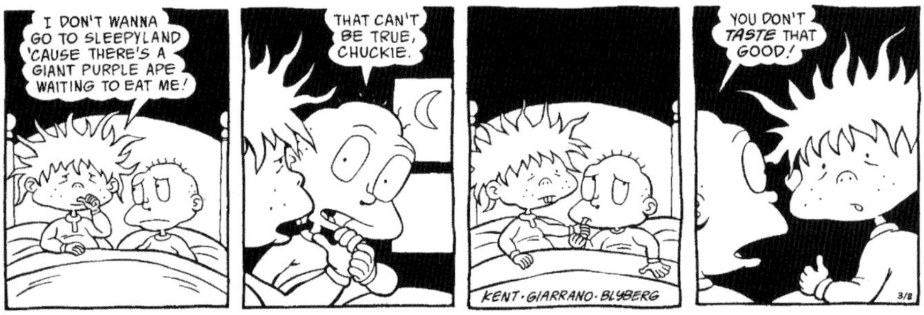
I DON'T WANNA GO TO SLEEPYLAND 'CAUSE THERE'S A GIANT PURPLE APE WAITING TO EAT ME!
THAT CAN'T BE TRUE, CHUCKIE.
KENT · GIARRANO · BLYBERG
YOU DON'T TASTE THAT GOOD!
3/8

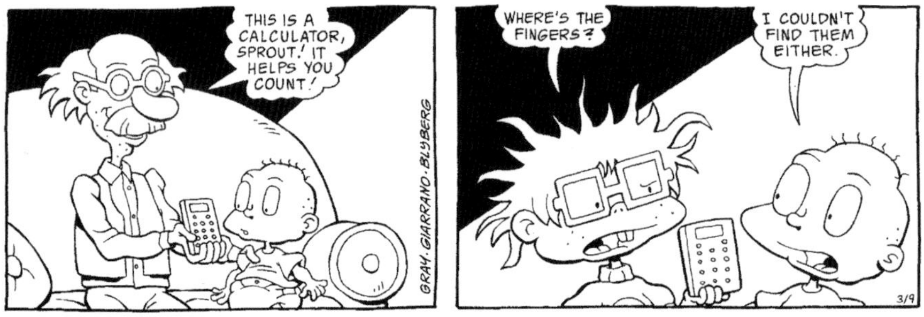
THIS IS A CALCULATOR, SPROUT! IT HELPS YOU COUNT!
GRAY · GIARRANO · BLYBERG
WHERE'S THE FINGERS?
I COULDN'T FIND THEM EITHER.
3/9

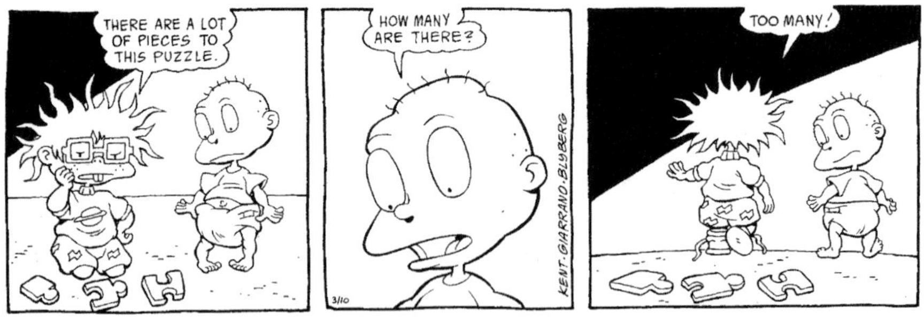
THERE ARE A LOT OF PIECES TO THIS PUZZLE.
HOW MANY ARE THERE?
3/10
KENT · GIARRANO · BLYBERG
TOO MANY!

2001

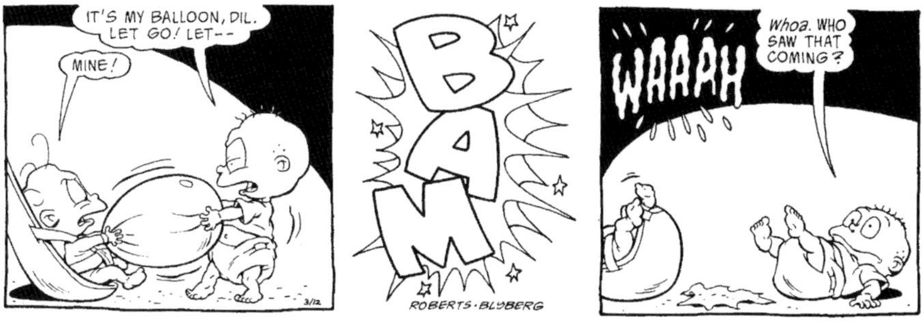
IT'S MY BALLOON, DIL. LET GO! LET--
MINE!
3/12
BAM
ROBERTS·BLYBERG
WAAAH
Whoa. WHO SAW THAT COMING?

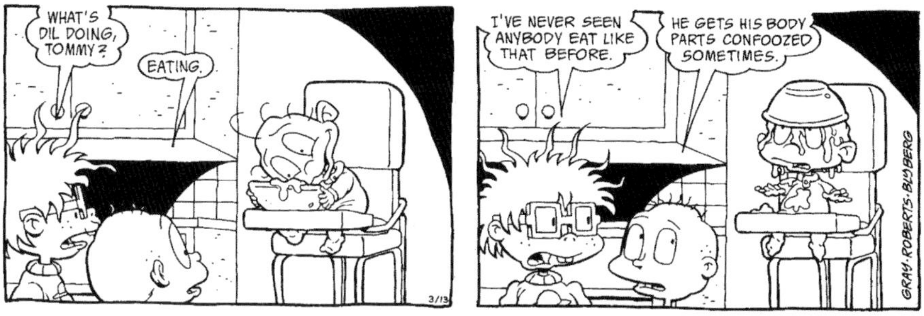
WHAT'S DIL DOING, TOMMY?
EATING.
3/13
I'VE NEVER SEEN ANYBODY EAT LIKE THAT BEFORE.
HE GETS HIS BODY PARTS CONFOOZED SOMETIMES.
GRAY·ROBERTS·BLYBERG

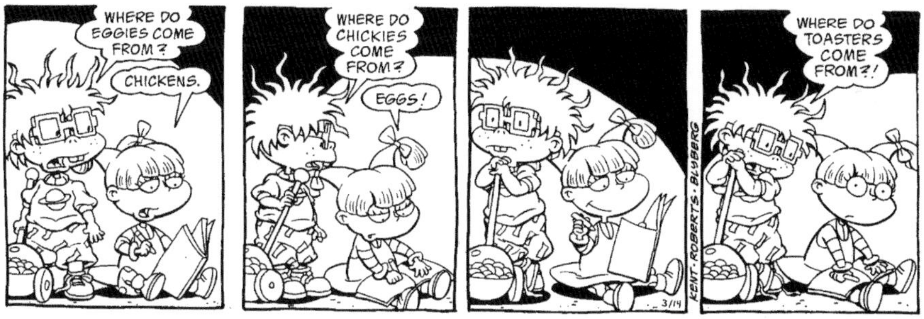
WHERE DO EGGIES COME FROM?
CHICKENS.
WHERE DO CHICKIES COME FROM?
EGGS!
KENT·ROBERTS·BLYBERG
3/14
WHERE DO TOASTERS COME FROM?!

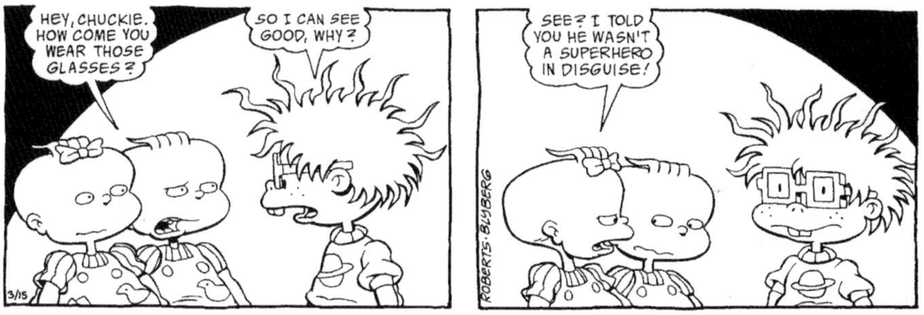
HEY, CHUCKIE. HOW COME YOU WEAR THOSE GLASSES?
SO I CAN SEE GOOD, WHY?
3/15
ROBERTS·BLYBERG
SEE? I TOLD YOU HE WASN'T A SUPERHERO IN DISGUISE!

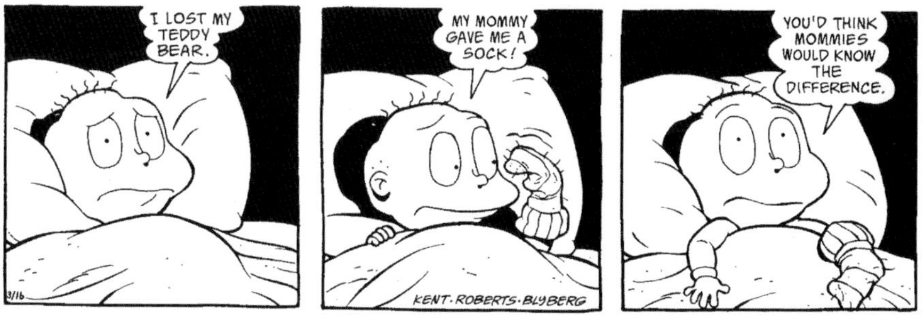
I LOST MY TEDDY BEAR.
3/16
MY MOMMY GAVE ME A SOCK!
KENT·ROBERTS·BLYBERG
YOU'D THINK MOMMIES WOULD KNOW THE DIFFERENCE.

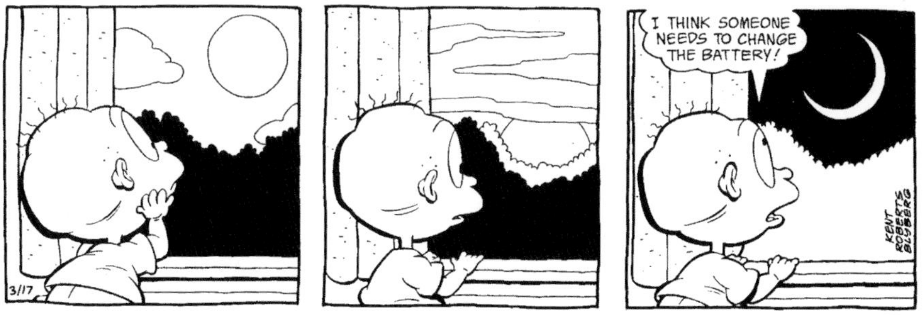
3/17
I THINK SOMEONE NEEDS TO CHANGE THE BATTERY!
KENT ROBERTS BLYBERG

2001

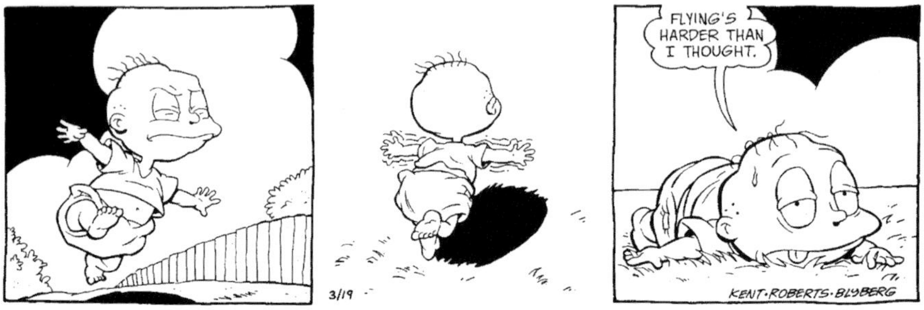
3/19
FLYING'S HARDER THAN I THOUGHT.
KENT·ROBERTS·BLYBERG

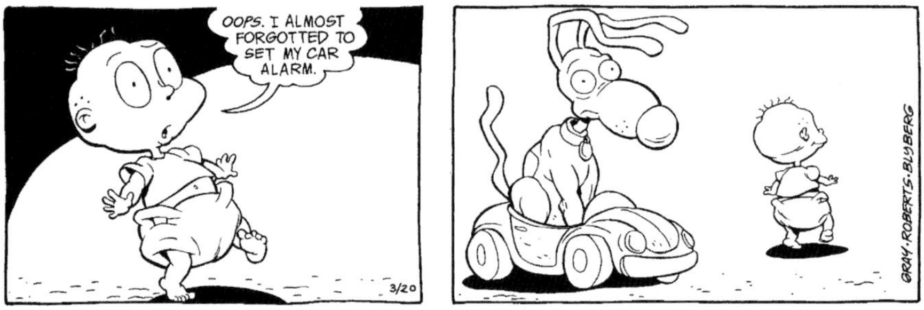
OOPS. I ALMOST FORGOTTED TO SET MY CAR ALARM.
3/20
GRAY·ROBERTS·BLYBERG

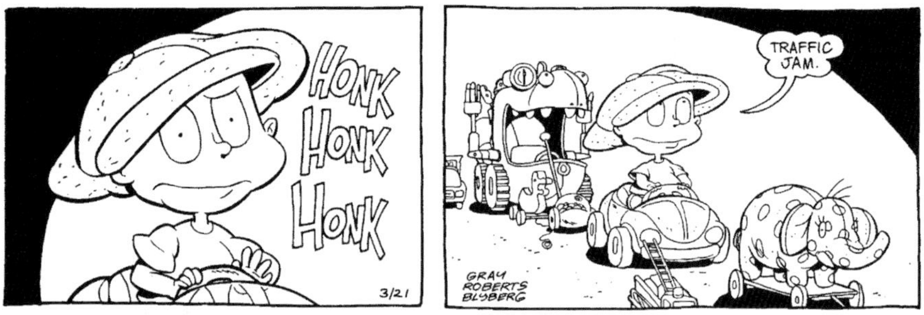
HONK
HONK
HONK
3/21
TRAFFIC JAM.
GRAY ROBERTS BLYBERG

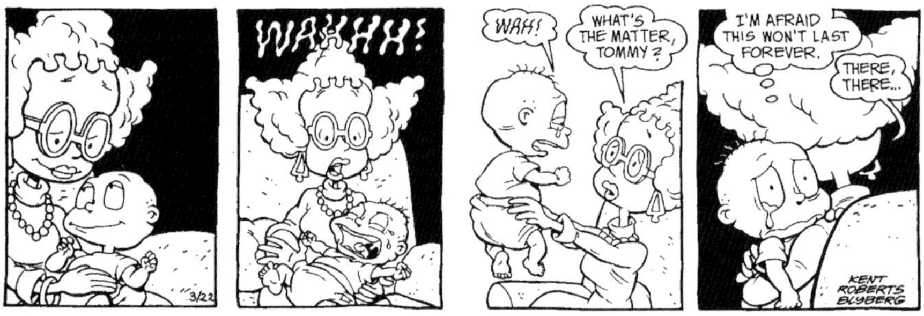
3/22
WAHHH!
WAH!
WHAT'S THE MATTER, TOMMY?
I'M AFRAID THIS WON'T LAST FOREVER.
THERE, THERE...
KENT ROBERTS BLYBERG

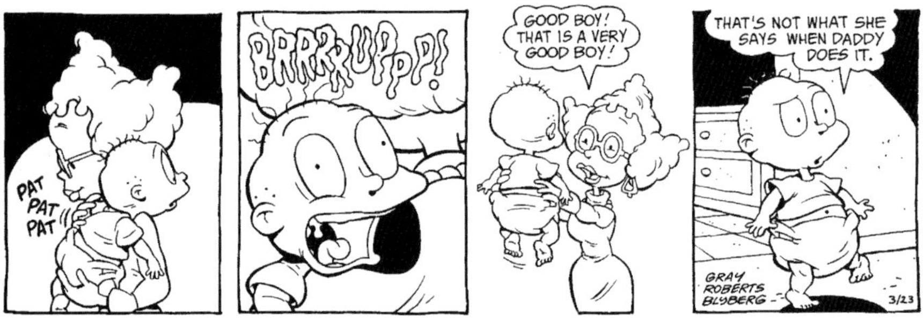
PAT
PAT
PAT
BRRRRUPPP!
GOOD BOY! THAT IS A VERY GOOD BOY!
THAT'S NOT WHAT SHE SAYS WHEN DADDY DOES IT.
GRAY ROBERTS BLYBERG
3/23

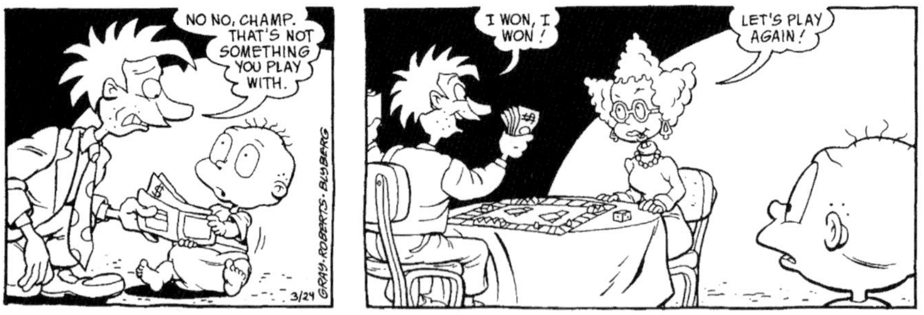
NO NO, CHAMP. THAT'S NOT SOMETHING YOU PLAY WITH.
GRAY·ROBERTS·BLYBERG
3/24
I WON, I WON!
LET'S PLAY AGAIN!

2001

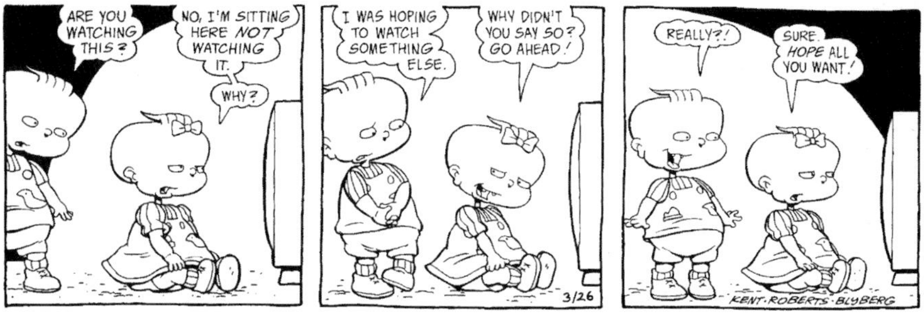
ARE YOU WATCHING THIS?
NO, I'M SITTING HERE *NOT* WATCHING IT.
WHY?
I WAS HOPING TO WATCH SOMETHING ELSE.
WHY DIDN'T YOU SAY SO? GO AHEAD!
REALLY?!
SURE. *HOPE* ALL YOU WANT!
3/26
KENT·ROBERTS·BLYBERG

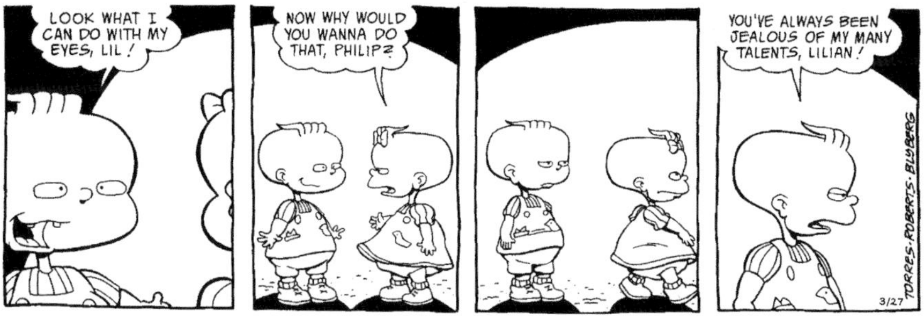
LOOK WHAT I CAN DO WITH MY EYES, LIL!
NOW WHY WOULD YOU WANNA DO THAT, PHILIP?
YOU'VE ALWAYS BEEN JEALOUS OF MY MANY TALENTS, LILIAN!
TORRES·ROBERTS·BLYBERG
3/27

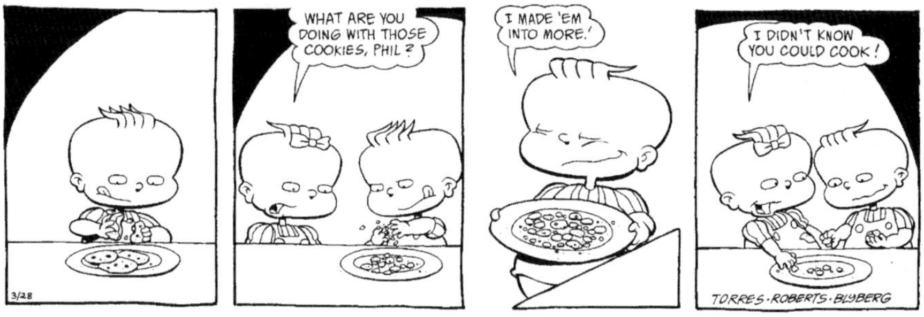
3/28
WHAT ARE YOU DOING WITH THOSE COOKIES, PHIL?
I MADE 'EM INTO MORE!
I DIDN'T KNOW YOU COULD COOK!
TORRES·ROBERTS·BLYBERG

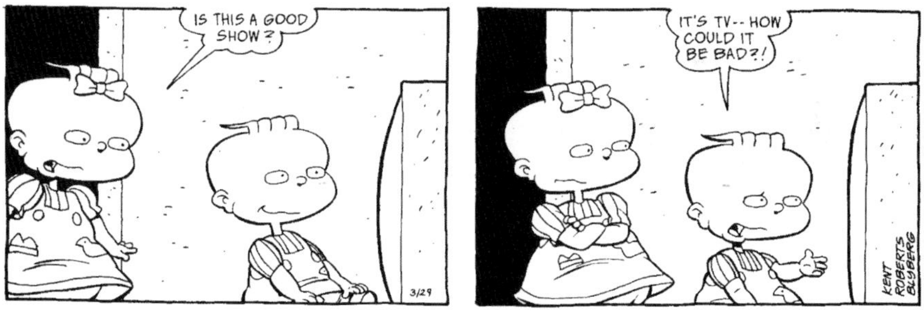
IS THIS A GOOD SHOW?
3/29
IT'S TV-- HOW COULD IT BE BAD?!
KENT ROBERTS BLYBERG

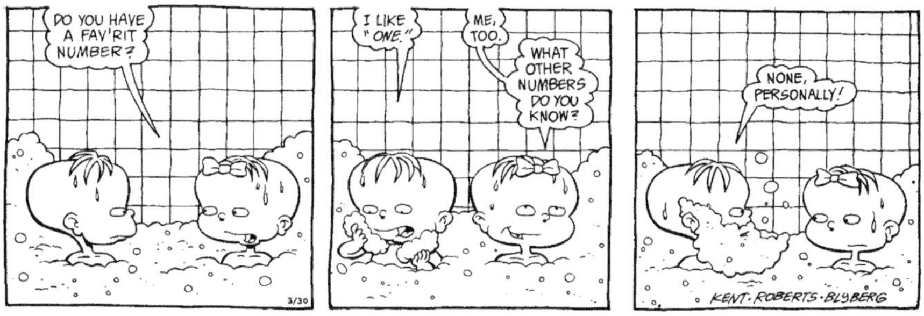
DO YOU HAVE A FAV'RIT NUMBER?
3/30
I LIKE "*ONE*."
ME, TOO.
WHAT OTHER NUMBERS DO YOU KNOW?
NONE, PERSONALLY!
KENT·ROBERTS·BLYBERG

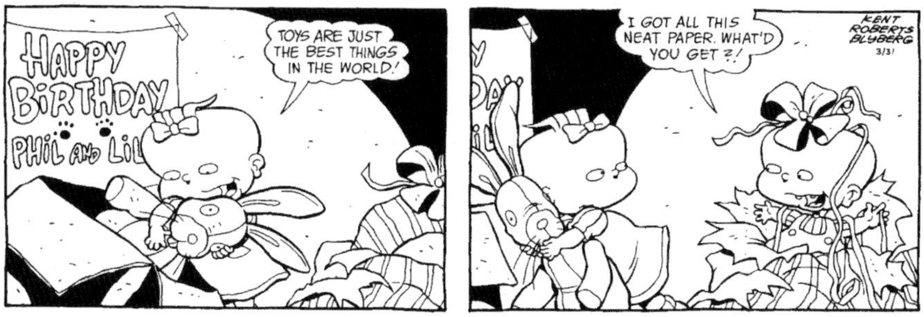
HAPPY BIRTHDAY PHIL AND LIL
TOYS ARE JUST THE BEST THINGS IN THE WORLD!
I GOT ALL THIS NEAT PAPER. WHAT'D YOU GET?!
KENT ROBERTS BLYBERG
3/31

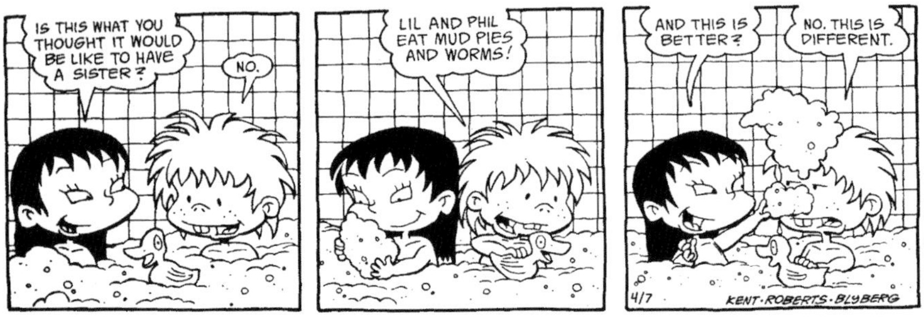
IS THIS WHAT YOU THOUGHT IT WOULD BE LIKE TO HAVE A SISTER?
NO.
LIL AND PHIL EAT MUD PIES AND WORMS!
AND THIS IS BETTER?
NO. THIS IS DIFFERENT.
4/7
KENT·ROBERTS·BLYBERG

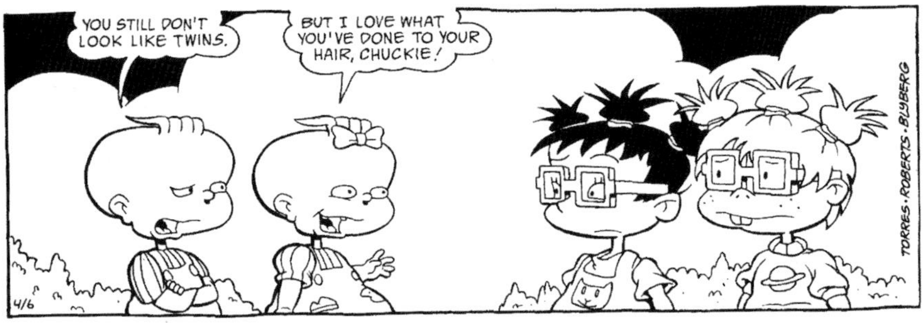
YOU STILL DON'T LOOK LIKE TWINS.
BUT I LOVE WHAT YOU'VE DONE TO YOUR HAIR, CHUCKIE!
TORRES·ROBERTS·BLYBERG
4/6

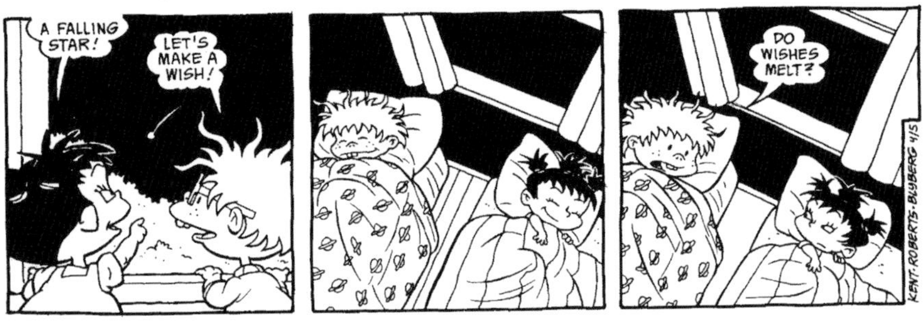
A FALLING STAR!
LET'S MAKE A WISH!
DO WISHES MELT?
KENT·ROBERTS·BLYBERG 4/5

2001

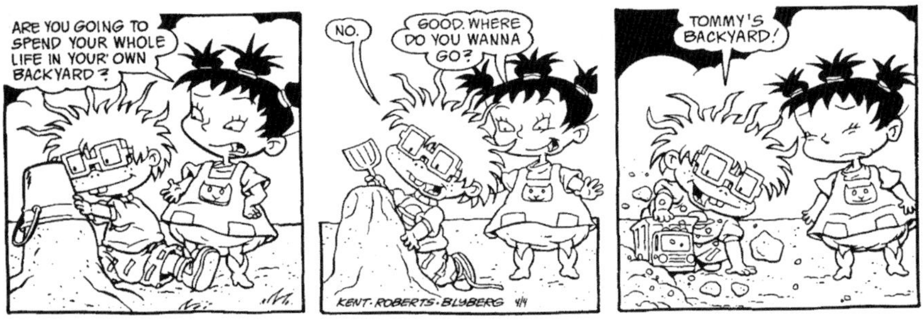
ARE YOU GOING TO SPEND YOUR WHOLE LIFE IN YOUR OWN BACKYARD?
NO.
GOOD. WHERE DO YOU WANNA GO?
KENT·ROBERTS·BLYBERG 4/4
TOMMY'S BACKYARD!

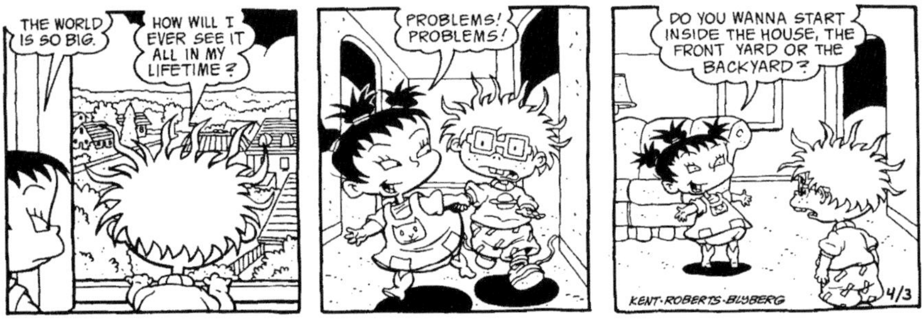
THE WORLD IS SO BIG.
HOW WILL I EVER SEE IT ALL IN MY LIFETIME?
PROBLEMS! PROBLEMS!
DO YOU WANNA START INSIDE THE HOUSE, THE FRONT YARD OR THE BACKYARD?
KENT·ROBERTS·BLYBERG
4/3

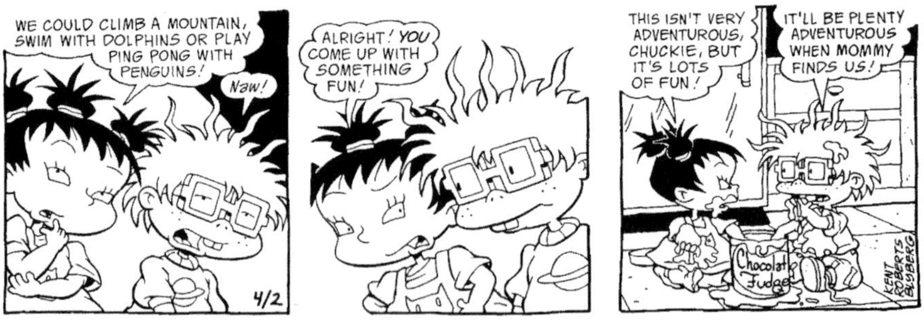
WE COULD CLIMB A MOUNTAIN, SWIM WITH DOLPHINS OR PLAY PING PONG WITH PENGUINS!
NAW!
4/2
ALRIGHT! YOU COME UP WITH SOMETHING FUN!
THIS ISN'T VERY ADVENTUROUS, CHUCKIE, BUT IT'S LOTS OF FUN!
IT'LL BE PLENTY ADVENTUROUS WHEN MOMMY FINDS US!
Chocolate Fudge
KENT ROBERTS BLYBERG

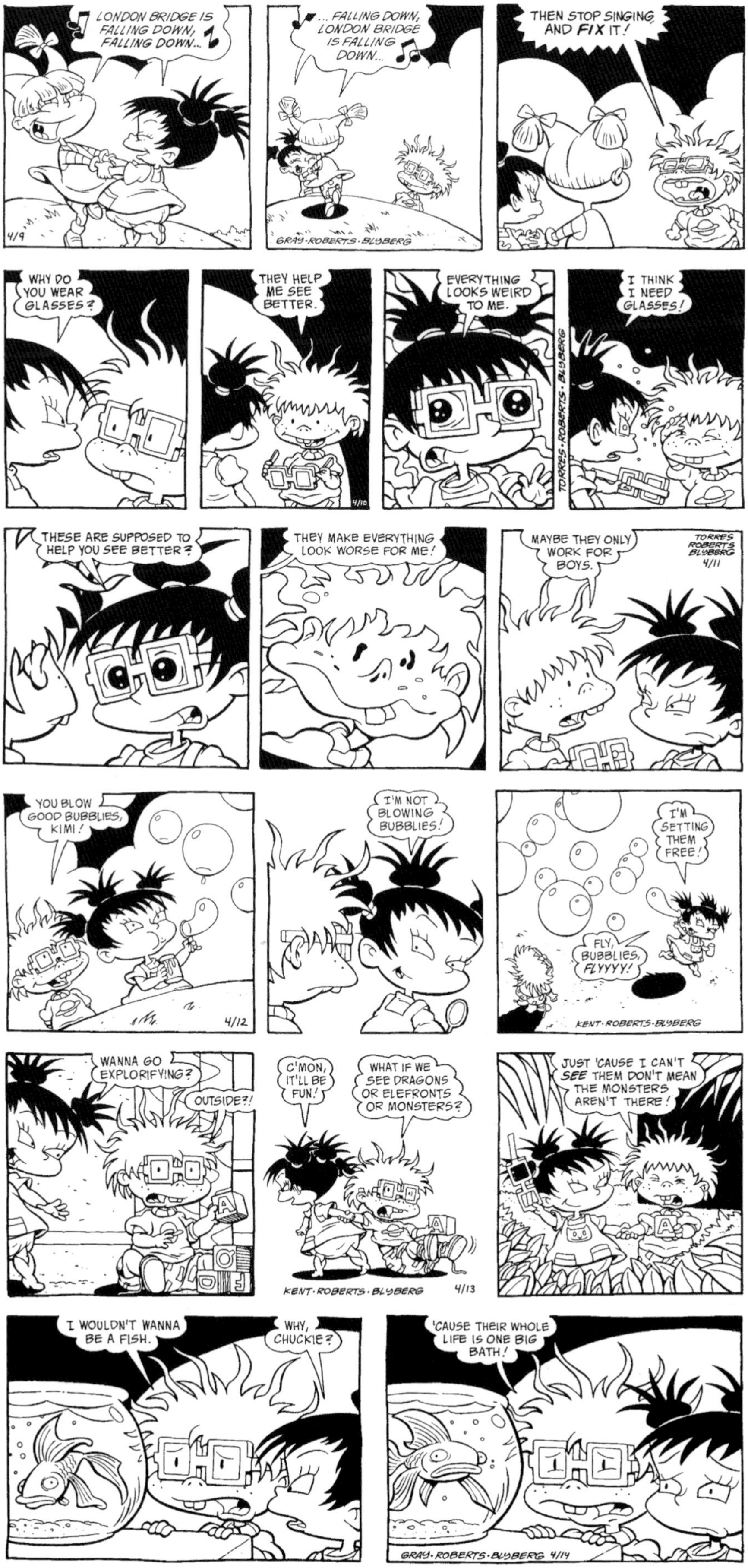
LONDON BRIDGE IS FALLING DOWN, FALLING DOWN...
4/9
...FALLING DOWN, LONDON BRIDGE IS FALLING DOWN...
GRAY·ROBERTS·BLYBERG
THEN STOP SINGING AND FIX IT!
WHY DO YOU WEAR GLASSES?
THEY HELP ME SEE BETTER.
4/10
EVERYTHING LOOKS WEIRD TO ME.
TORRES·ROBERTS·BLYBERG
I THINK I NEED GLASSES!
THESE ARE SUPPOSED TO HELP YOU SEE BETTER?
THEY MAKE EVERYTHING LOOK WORSE FOR ME!
MAYBE THEY ONLY WORK FOR BOYS.
TORRES ROBERTS BLYBERG 4/11
YOU BLOW GOOD BUBBLIES, KIMI!
4/12
I'M NOT BLOWING BUBBLIES!
I'M SETTING THEM FREE!
FLY, BUBBLIES, FLYYYY!
KENT·ROBERTS·BLYBERG
WANNA GO EXPLORIFYING?
OUTSIDE?!
C'MON, IT'LL BE FUN!
WHAT IF WE SEE DRAGONS OR ELEFRONTS OR MONSTERS?
KENT·ROBERTS·BLYBERG 4/13
JUST 'CAUSE I CAN'T SEE THEM DON'T MEAN THE MONSTERS AREN'T THERE!
I WOULDN'T WANNA BE A FISH.
WHY, CHUCKIE?
'CAUSE THEIR WHOLE LIFE IS ONE BIG BATH!
GRAY·ROBERTS·BLYBERG 4/14

2001

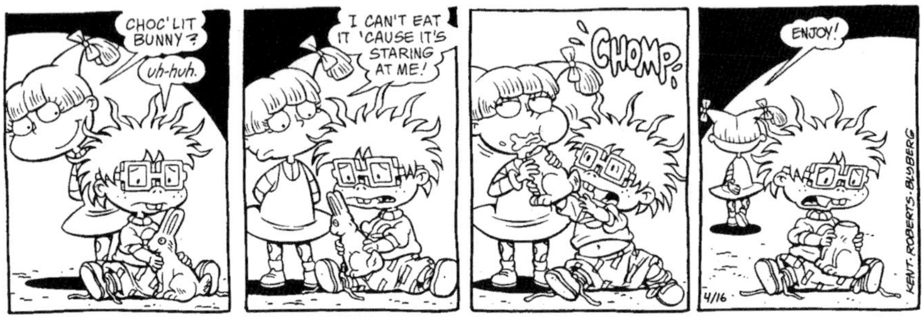
CHOC'LIT BUNNY?
uh-huh.
I CAN'T EAT IT 'CAUSE IT'S STARING AT ME!
CHOMP
ENJOY!
4/16
KENT·ROBERTS·BLYBERG

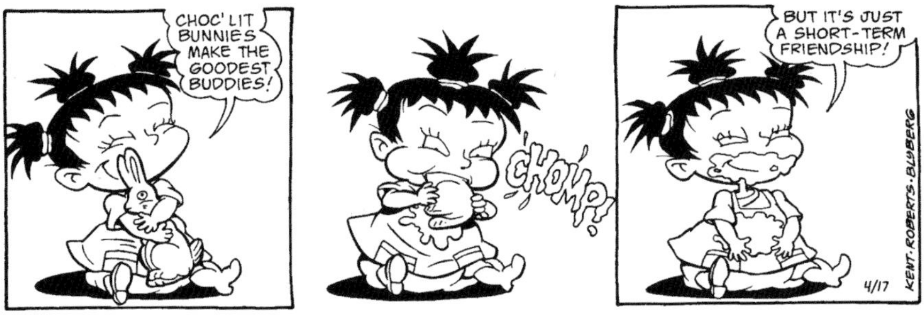
CHOC'LIT BUNNIES MAKE THE GOODEST BUDDIES!
CHOMP!
BUT IT'S JUST A SHORT-TERM FRIENDSHIP!
4/17
KENT·ROBERTS·BLYBERG

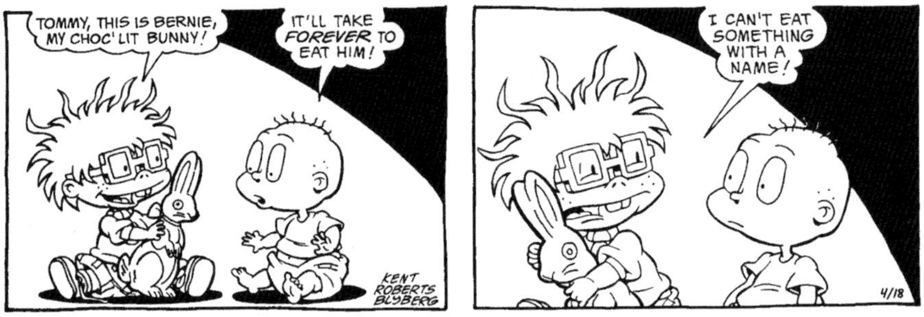
TOMMY, THIS IS BERNIE, MY CHOC'LIT BUNNY!
IT'LL TAKE FOREVER TO EAT HIM!
KENT ROBERTS BLYBERG
I CAN'T EAT SOMETHING WITH A NAME!
4/18

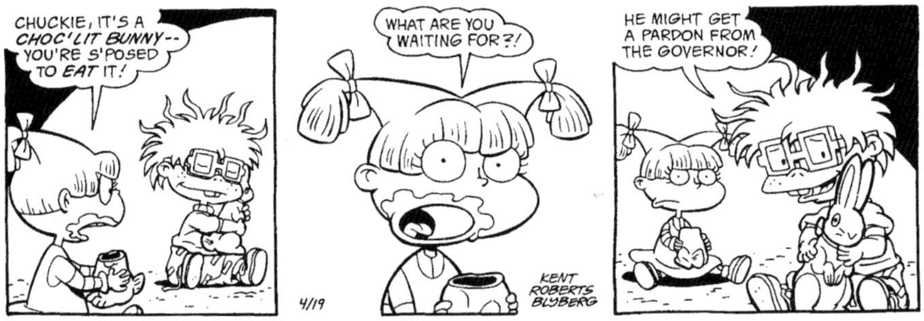
CHUCKIE, IT'S A CHOC'LIT BUNNY-- YOU'RE S'POSED TO EAT IT!
4/19
WHAT ARE YOU WAITING FOR?!
KENT ROBERTS BLYBERG
HE MIGHT GET A PARDON FROM THE GOVERNOR!

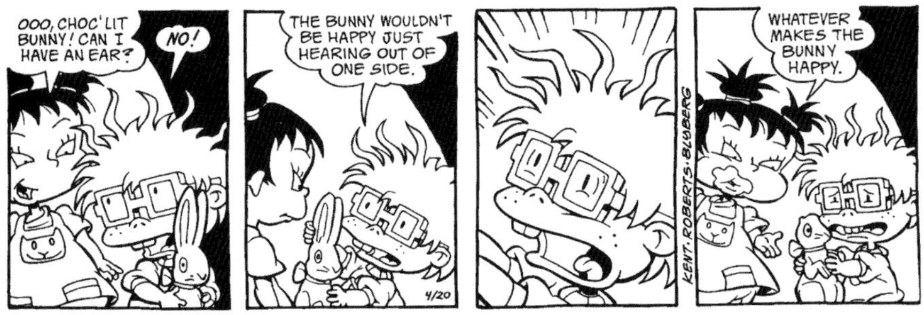
OOO, CHOC'LIT BUNNY! CAN I HAVE AN EAR?
NO!
THE BUNNY WOULDN'T BE HAPPY JUST HEARING OUT OF ONE SIDE.
4/20
KENT·ROBERTS·BLYBERG
WHATEVER MAKES THE BUNNY HAPPY.

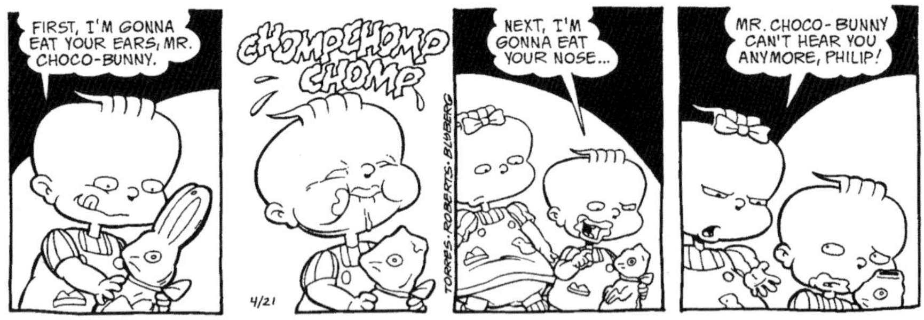
FIRST, I'M GONNA EAT YOUR EARS, MR. CHOCO-BUNNY.
CHOMPCHOMP CHOMP
4/21
TORRES·ROBERTS·BLYBERG
NEXT, I'M GONNA EAT YOUR NOSE...
MR. CHOCO-BUNNY CAN'T HEAR YOU ANYMORE, PHILIP!

2001

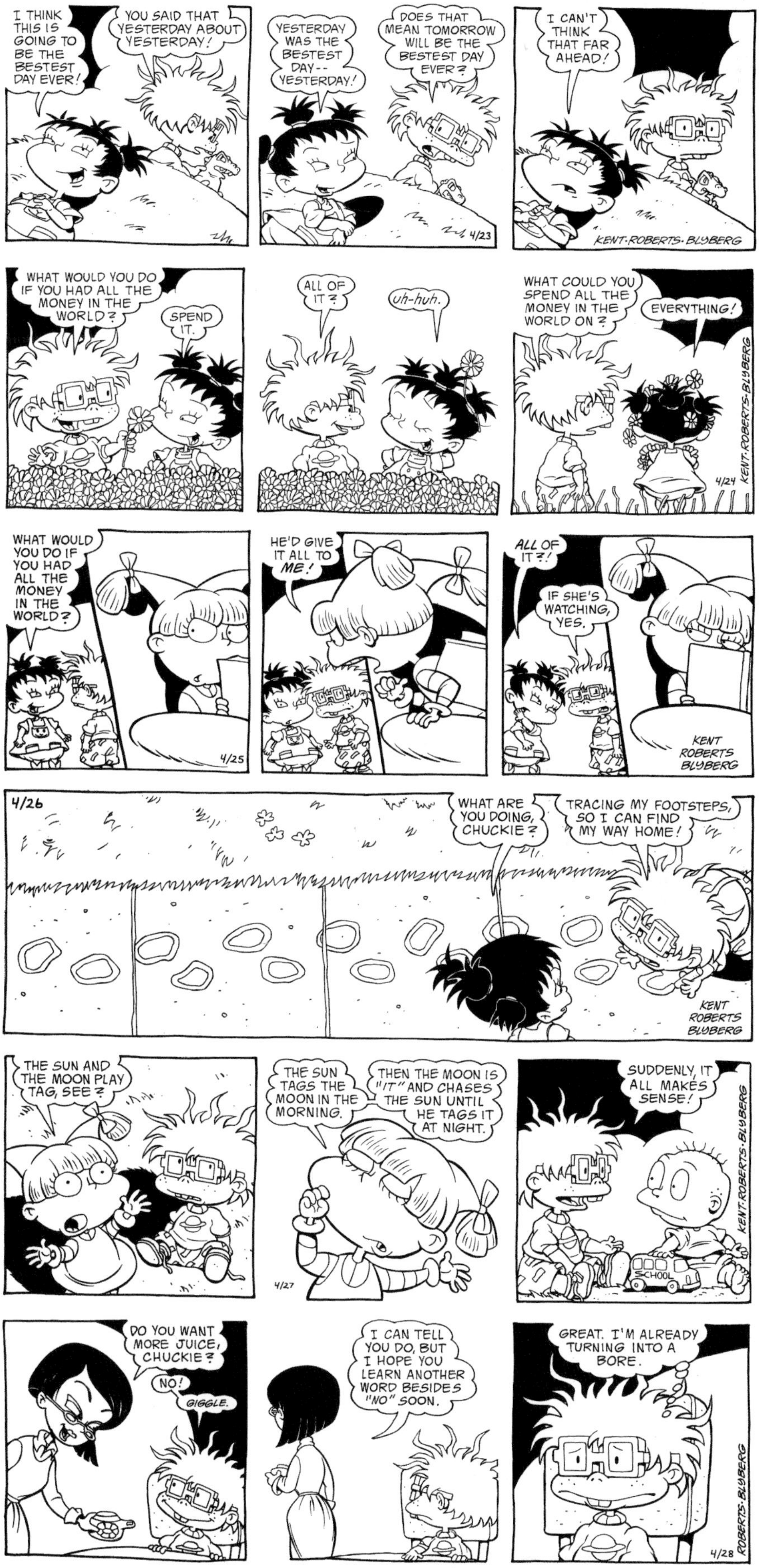
I THINK THIS IS GOING TO BE THE BESTEST DAY EVER!
YOU SAID THAT YESTERDAY ABOUT YESTERDAY!
YESTERDAY WAS THE BESTEST DAY-- YESTERDAY!
DOES THAT MEAN TOMORROW WILL BE THE BESTEST DAY EVER?
4/23
I CAN'T THINK THAT FAR AHEAD!
KENT·ROBERTS·BLYBERG
WHAT WOULD YOU DO IF YOU HAD ALL THE MONEY IN THE WORLD?
SPEND IT.
ALL OF IT?
uh-huh.
WHAT COULD YOU SPEND ALL THE MONEY IN THE WORLD ON?
EVERYTHING!
4/24
KENT·ROBERTS·BLYBERG
WHAT WOULD YOU DO IF YOU HAD ALL THE MONEY IN THE WORLD?
4/25
HE'D GIVE IT ALL TO ME!
ALL OF IT?!
IF SHE'S WATCHING, YES.
KENT ROBERTS BLYBERG
4/26
WHAT ARE YOU DOING, CHUCKIE?
TRACING MY FOOTSTEPS, SO I CAN FIND MY WAY HOME!
KENT ROBERTS BLYBERG
THE SUN AND THE MOON PLAY TAG, SEE?
THE SUN TAGS THE MOON IN THE MORNING.
THEN THE MOON IS "IT" AND CHASES THE SUN UNTIL HE TAGS IT AT NIGHT.
4/27
SUDDENLY, IT ALL MAKES SENSE!
SCHOOL
KENT·ROBERTS·BLYBERG
DO YOU WANT MORE JUICE, CHUCKIE?
NO!
GIGGLE.
I CAN TELL YOU DO, BUT I HOPE YOU LEARN ANOTHER WORD BESIDES "NO" SOON.
GREAT. I'M ALREADY TURNING INTO A BORE.
ROBERTS·BLYBERG
4/28

2001

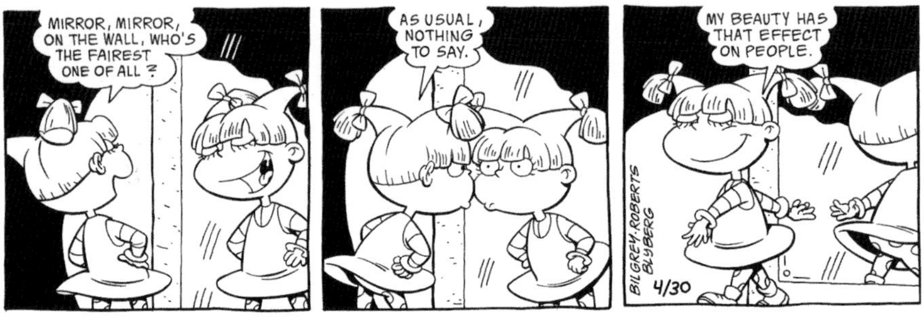
MIRROR, MIRROR, ON THE WALL, WHO'S THE FAIREST ONE OF ALL?
AS USUAL, NOTHING TO SAY.
MY BEAUTY HAS THAT EFFECT ON PEOPLE.
BILGREY·ROBERTS BLYBERG
4/30

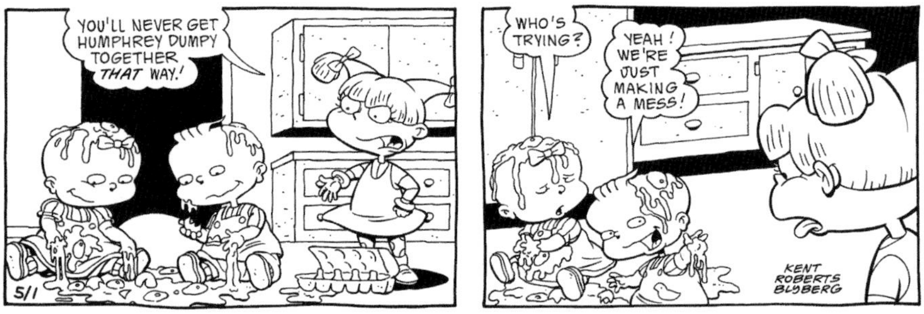
YOU'LL NEVER GET HUMPHREY DUMPY TOGETHER *THAT* WAY!
5/1
WHO'S TRYING?
YEAH! WE'RE JUST MAKING A MESS!
KENT ROBERTS BLYBERG

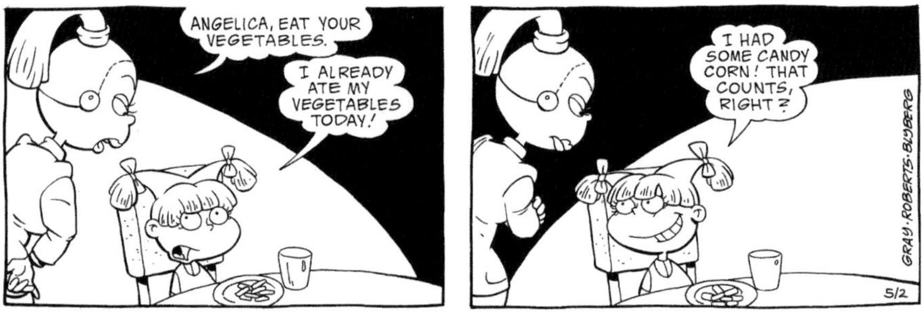
ANGELICA, EAT YOUR VEGETABLES.
I ALREADY ATE MY VEGETABLES TODAY!
I HAD SOME CANDY CORN! THAT COUNTS, RIGHT?
GRAY·ROBERTS·BLYBERG
5/2

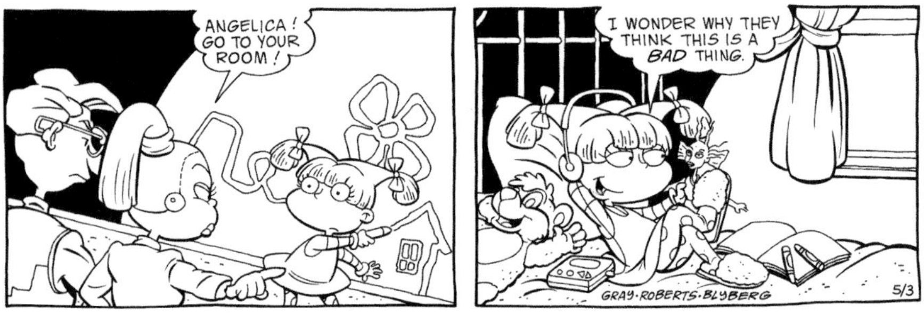
ANGELICA! GO TO YOUR ROOM!
I WONDER WHY THEY THINK THIS IS A *BAD* THING.
GRAY·ROBERTS·BLYBERG
5/3

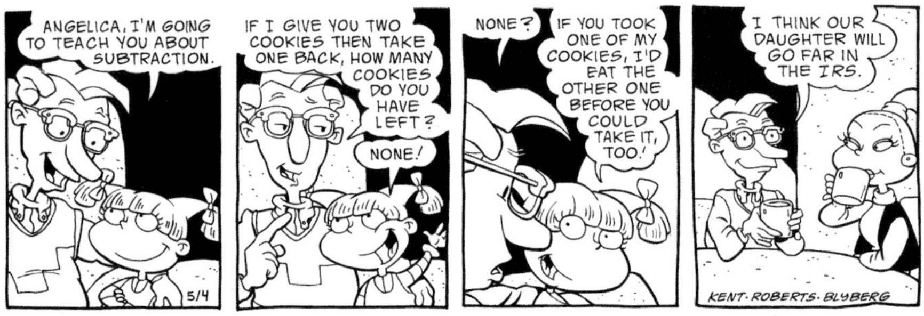
ANGELICA, I'M GOING TO TEACH YOU ABOUT SUBTRACTION.
5/4
IF I GIVE YOU TWO COOKIES THEN TAKE ONE BACK, HOW MANY COOKIES DO YOU HAVE LEFT?
NONE!
NONE?
IF YOU TOOK ONE OF MY COOKIES, I'D EAT THE OTHER ONE BEFORE YOU COULD TAKE IT, TOO!
I THINK OUR DAUGHTER WILL GO FAR IN THE *IRS*.
KENT·ROBERTS·BLYBERG

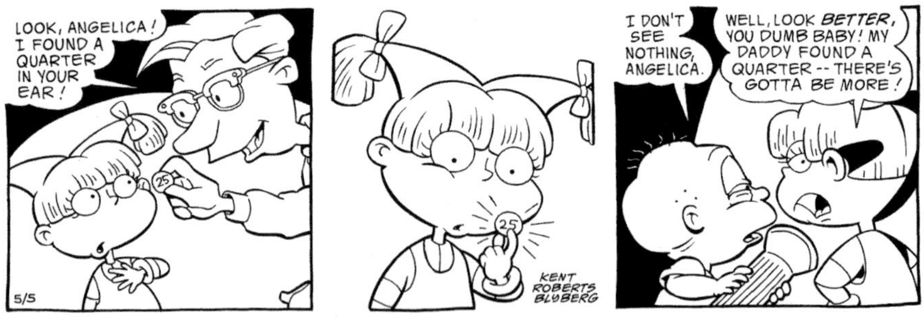
LOOK, ANGELICA! I FOUND A QUARTER IN YOUR EAR!
25
5/5
KENT ROBERTS BLYBERG
I DON'T SEE NOTHING, ANGELICA.
WELL, LOOK *BETTER*, YOU DUMB BABY! MY DADDY FOUND A QUARTER -- THERE'S GOTTA BE MORE!

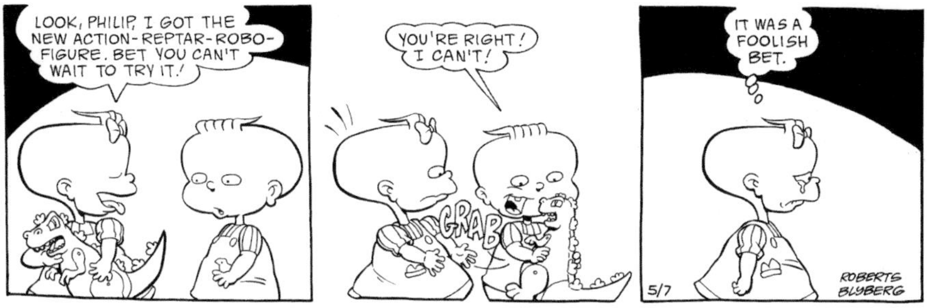
LOOK, PHILIP, I GOT THE NEW ACTION-REPTAR-ROBO-FIGURE. BET YOU CAN'T WAIT TO TRY IT!
YOU'RE RIGHT! I CAN'T!
GRAB
IT WAS A FOOLISH BET.
5/7
ROBERTS BLYBERG

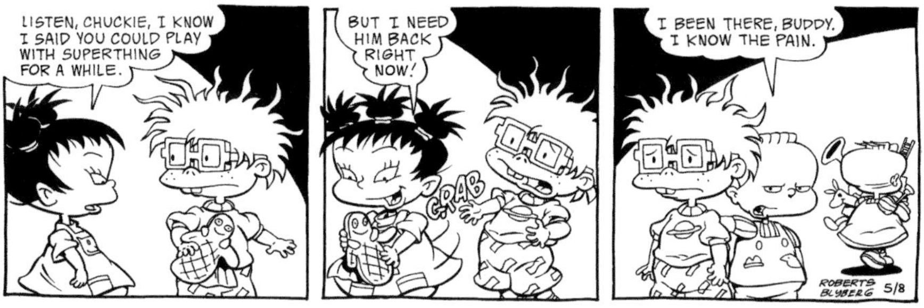
LISTEN, CHUCKIE, I KNOW I SAID YOU COULD PLAY WITH SUPERTHING FOR A WHILE.
BUT I NEED HIM BACK RIGHT NOW!
GRAB
I BEEN THERE, BUDDY. I KNOW THE PAIN.
ROBERTS BLYBERG 5/8

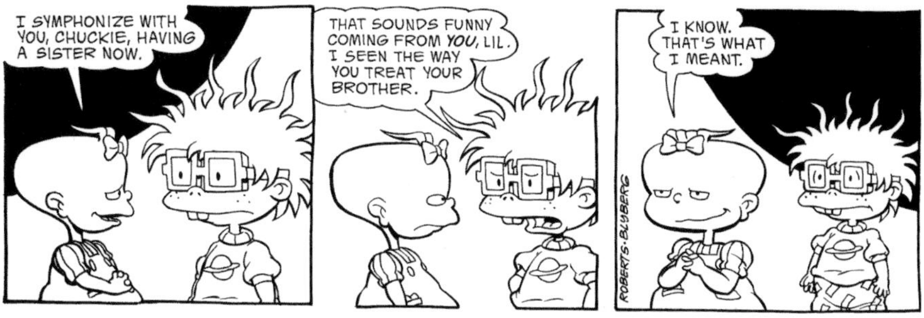
I SYMPHONIZE WITH YOU, CHUCKIE, HAVING A SISTER NOW.
THAT SOUNDS FUNNY COMING FROM YOU, LIL. I SEEN THE WAY YOU TREAT YOUR BROTHER.
ROBERTS·BLYBERG
I KNOW. THAT'S WHAT I MEANT.

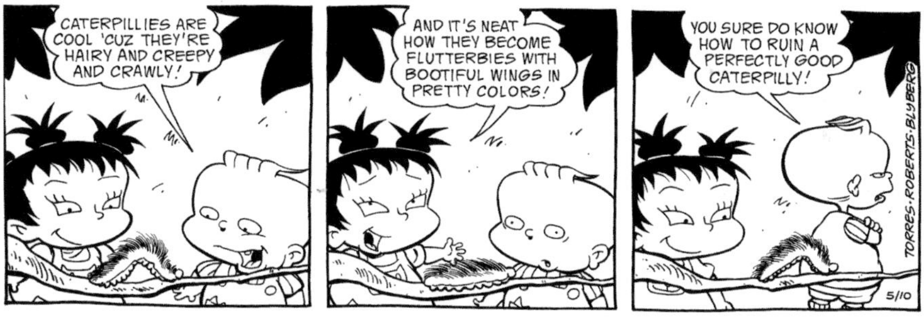
CATERPILLIES ARE COOL 'CUZ THEY'RE HAIRY AND CREEPY AND CRAWLY!
AND IT'S NEAT HOW THEY BECOME FLUTTERBIES WITH BOOTIFUL WINGS IN PRETTY COLORS!
YOU SURE DO KNOW HOW TO RUIN A PERFECTLY GOOD CATERPILLY!
TORRES·ROBERTS·BLYBERG
5/10

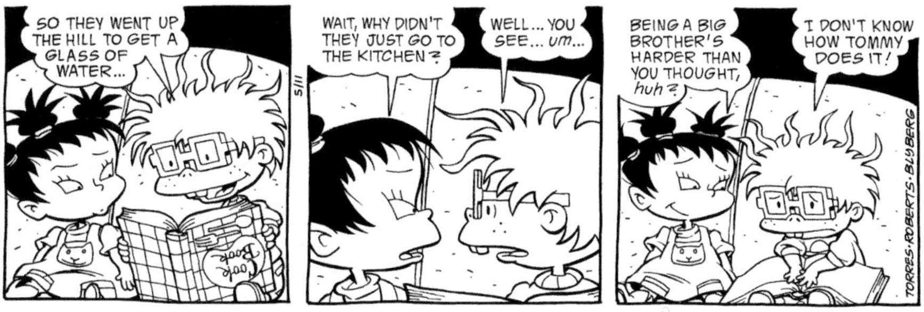
SO THEY WENT UP THE HILL TO GET A GLASS OF WATER...
5/11
WAIT, WHY DIDN'T THEY JUST GO TO THE KITCHEN?
WELL... YOU SEE... um...
BEING A BIG BROTHER'S HARDER THAN YOU THOUGHT, huh?
I DON'T KNOW HOW TOMMY DOES IT!
TORRES·ROBERTS·BLYBERG

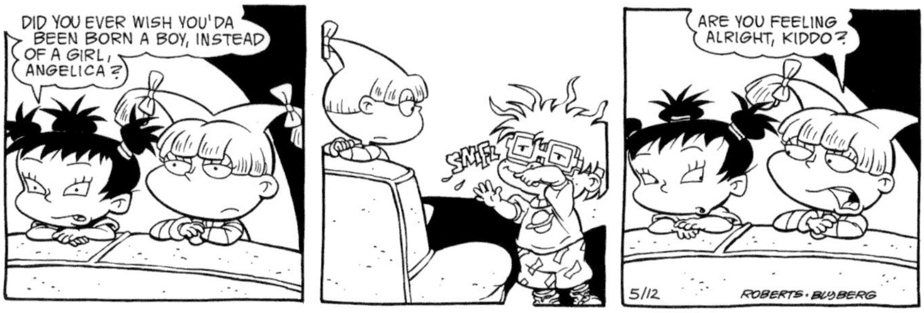
DID YOU EVER WISH YOU'DA BEEN BORN A BOY, INSTEAD OF A GIRL, ANGELICA?
SNIFL
ARE YOU FEELING ALRIGHT, KIDDO?
5/12
ROBERTS·BLYBERG

2001

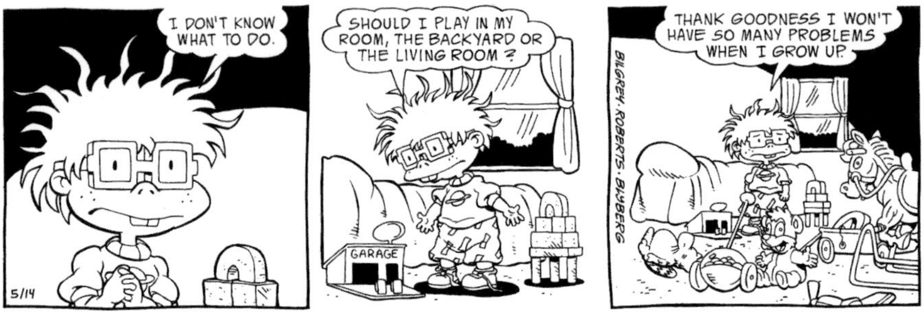
I DON'T KNOW WHAT TO DO.
5/14
SHOULD I PLAY IN MY ROOM, THE BACKYARD OR THE LIVING ROOM?
GARAGE
BILGREY·ROBERTS·BLYBERG
THANK GOODNESS I WON'T HAVE SO MANY PROBLEMS WHEN I GROW UP.

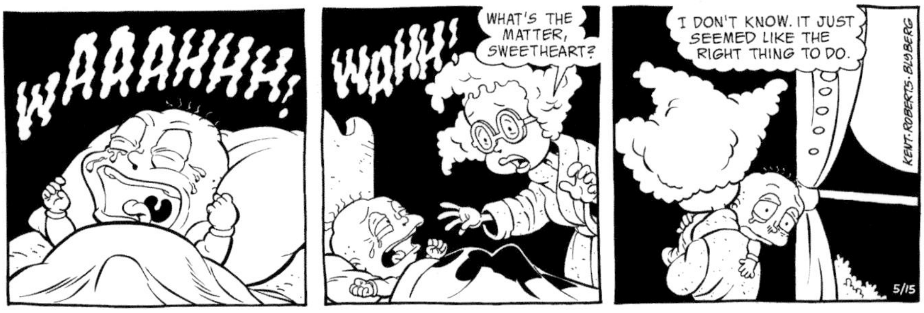
WAAAHHH!
WAHH!
WHAT'S THE MATTER, SWEETHEART?
I DON'T KNOW. IT JUST SEEMED LIKE THE RIGHT THING TO DO.
KENT·ROBERTS·BLYBERG
5/15

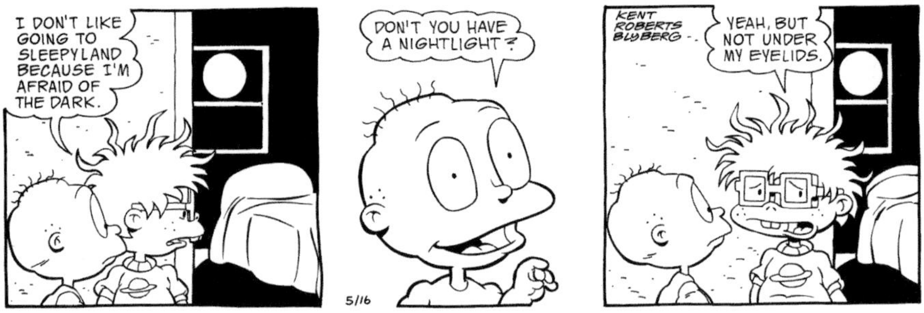
I DON'T LIKE GOING TO SLEEPYLAND BECAUSE I'M AFRAID OF THE DARK.
DON'T YOU HAVE A NIGHTLIGHT?
5/16
KENT ROBERTS BLYBERG
YEAH, BUT NOT UNDER MY EYELIDS.

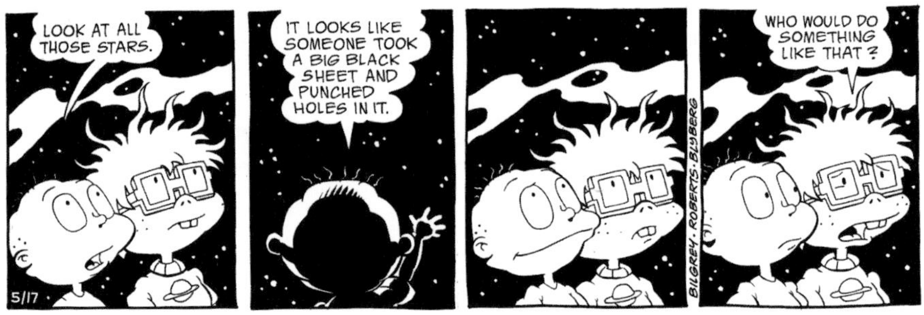
LOOK AT ALL THOSE STARS.
5/17
IT LOOKS LIKE SOMEONE TOOK A BIG BLACK SHEET AND PUNCHED HOLES IN IT.
BILGREY·ROBERTS·BLYBERG
WHO WOULD DO SOMETHING LIKE THAT?

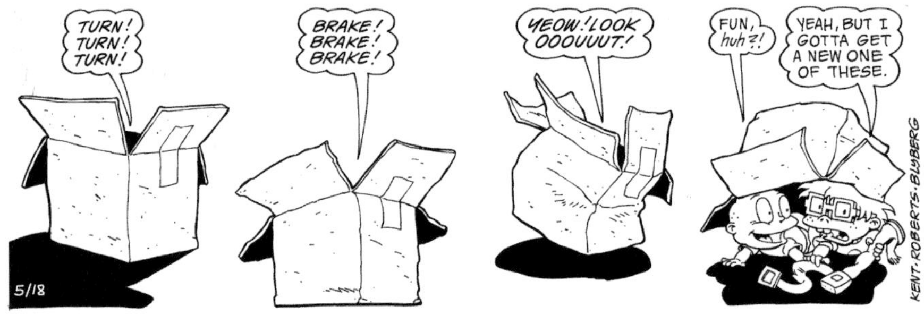
TURN! TURN! TURN!
5/18
BRAKE! BRAKE! BRAKE!
YEOW! LOOK OOOUUUT!
FUN, huh?!
YEAH, BUT I GOTTA GET A NEW ONE OF THESE.
KENT·ROBERTS·BLYBERG

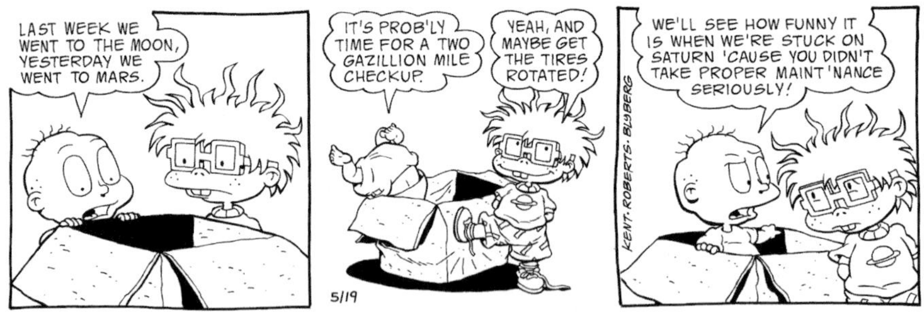
LAST WEEK WE WENT TO THE MOON, YESTERDAY WE WENT TO MARS.
IT'S PROB'LY TIME FOR A TWO GAZILLION MILE CHECKUP.
YEAH, AND MAYBE GET THE TIRES ROTATED!
5/19
KENT·ROBERTS·BLYBERG
WE'LL SEE HOW FUNNY IT IS WHEN WE'RE STUCK ON SATURN 'CAUSE YOU DIDN'T TAKE PROPER MAINT'NANCE SERIOUSLY!

2001

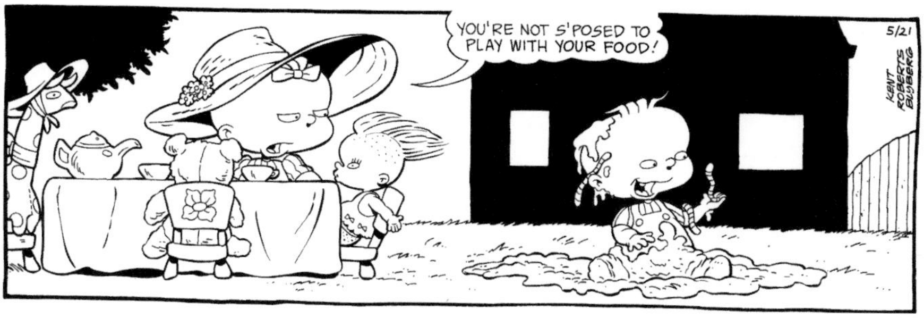
5/21
YOU'RE NOT S'POSED TO PLAY WITH YOUR FOOD!
KENT ROBERTS BLYBERG

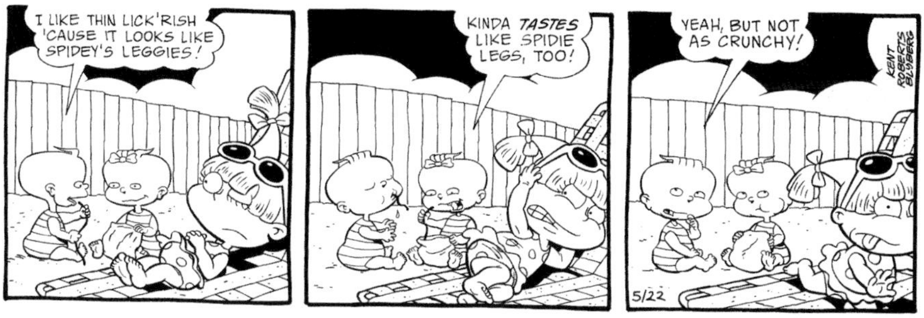
I LIKE THIN LICK'RISH 'CAUSE IT LOOKS LIKE SPIDEY'S LEGGIES!
KINDA *TASTES* LIKE SPIDIE LEGS, TOO!
5/22
YEAH, BUT NOT AS CRUNCHY!
KENT ROBERTS BLYBERG

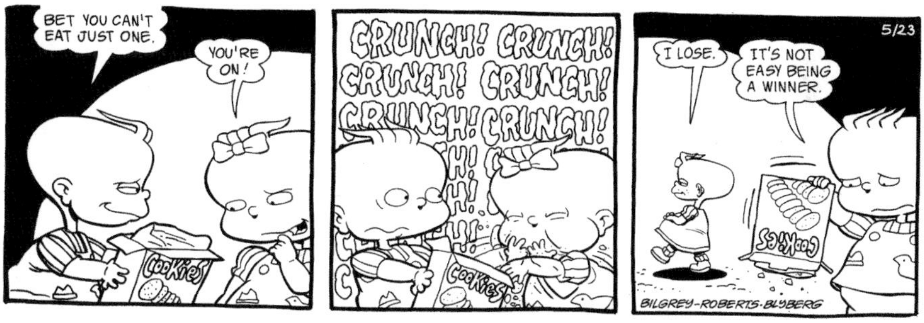
BET YOU CAN'T EAT JUST ONE.
YOU'RE ON!
COOKIES
CRUNCH! CRUNCH! CRUNCH! CRUNCH! CRUNCH! CRUNCH!
COOKIES
5/23
I LOSE.
IT'S NOT EASY BEING A WINNER.
COOKIES
BILGREY-ROBERTS-BLYBERG

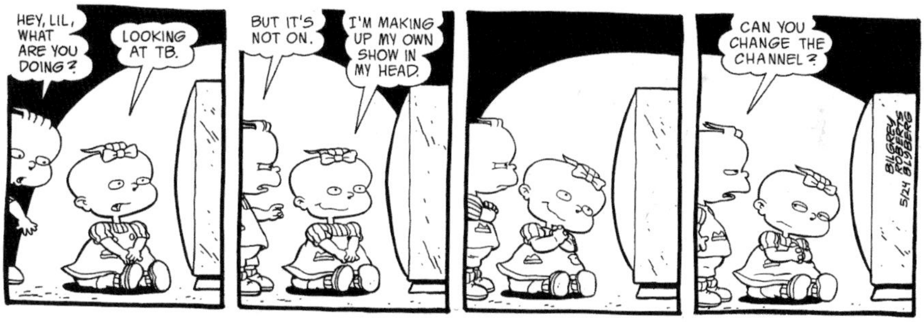
HEY, LIL, WHAT ARE YOU DOING?
LOOKING AT TB.
BUT IT'S NOT ON.
I'M MAKING UP MY OWN SHOW IN MY HEAD.
CAN YOU CHANGE THE CHANNEL?
BILGREY ROBERTS BLYBERG 5/24

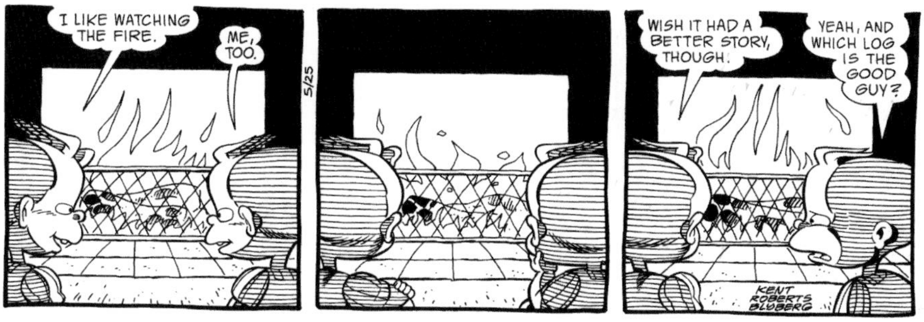
I LIKE WATCHING THE FIRE.
ME, TOO.
5/25
WISH IT HAD A BETTER STORY, THOUGH.
YEAH, AND WHICH LOG IS THE GOOD GUY?
KENT ROBERTS BLYBERG

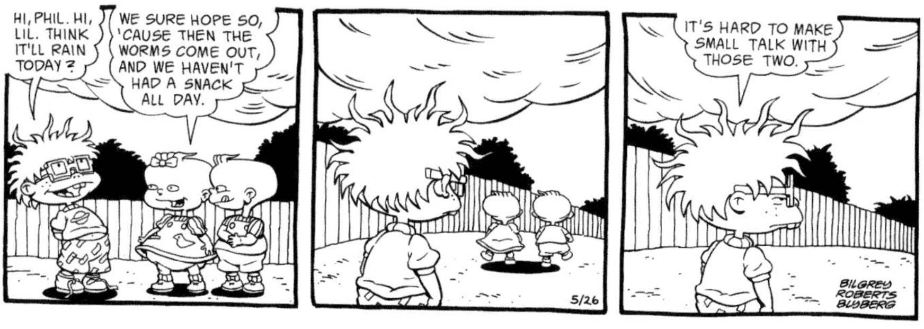
HI, PHIL. HI, LIL. THINK IT'LL RAIN TODAY?
WE SURE HOPE SO, 'CAUSE THEN THE WORMS COME OUT, AND WE HAVEN'T HAD A SNACK ALL DAY.
5/26
IT'S HARD TO MAKE SMALL TALK WITH THOSE TWO.
BILGREY ROBERTS BLYBERG

2001

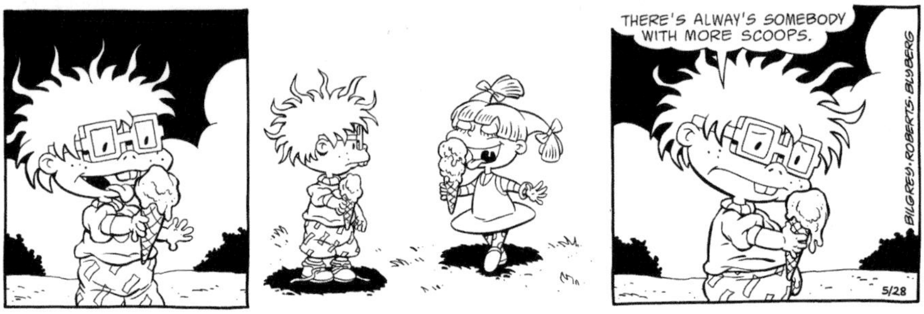
THERE'S ALWAY'S SOMEBODY WITH MORE SCOOPS.
BILGREY · ROBERTS · BLYBERG
5/28

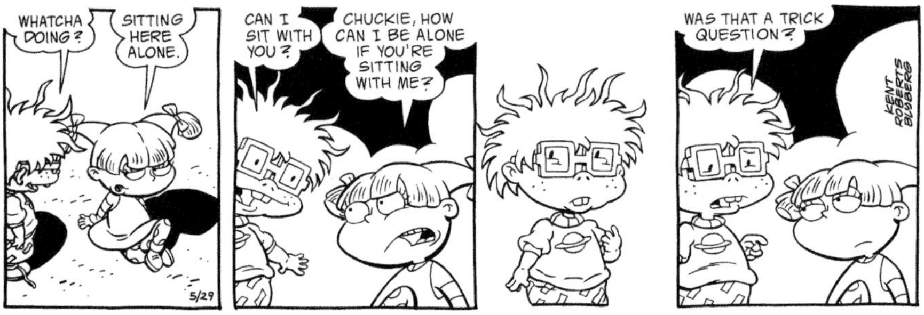
WHATCHA DOING?
SITTING HERE ALONE.
5/29
CAN I SIT WITH YOU?
CHUCKIE, HOW CAN I BE ALONE IF YOU'RE SITTING WITH ME?
WAS THAT A TRICK QUESTION?
KENT ROBERTS BLYBERG

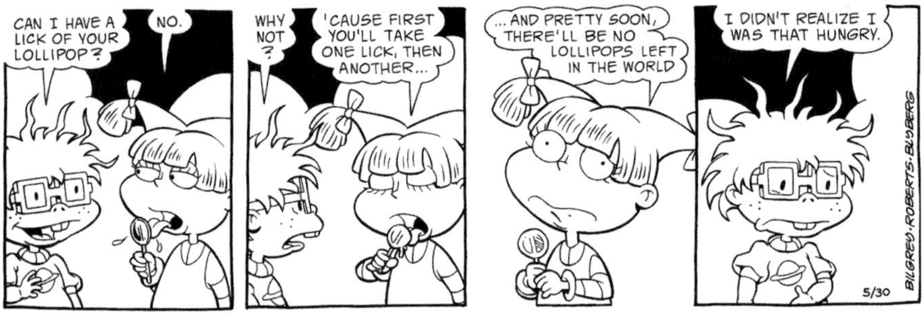
CAN I HAVE A LICK OF YOUR LOLLIPOP?
NO.
WHY NOT?
'CAUSE FIRST YOU'LL TAKE ONE LICK, THEN ANOTHER...
...AND PRETTY SOON, THERE'LL BE NO LOLLIPOPS LEFT IN THE WORLD
I DIDN'T REALIZE I WAS THAT HUNGRY.
BILGREY · ROBERTS · BLYBERG
5/30

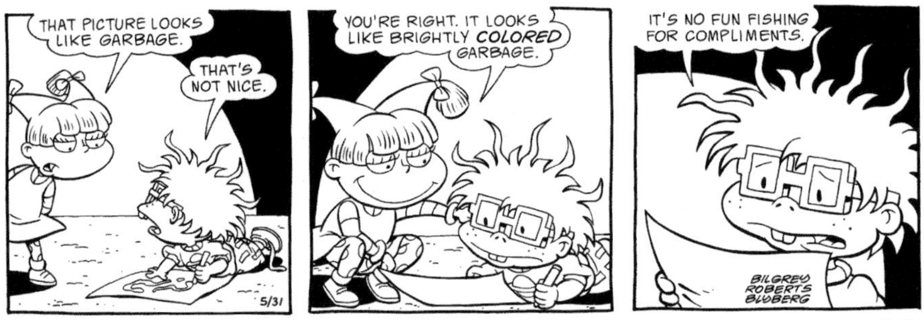
THAT PICTURE LOOKS LIKE GARBAGE.
THAT'S NOT NICE.
5/31
YOU'RE RIGHT. IT LOOKS LIKE BRIGHTLY COLORED GARBAGE.
IT'S NO FUN FISHING FOR COMPLIMENTS.
BILGREY ROBERTS BLYBERG

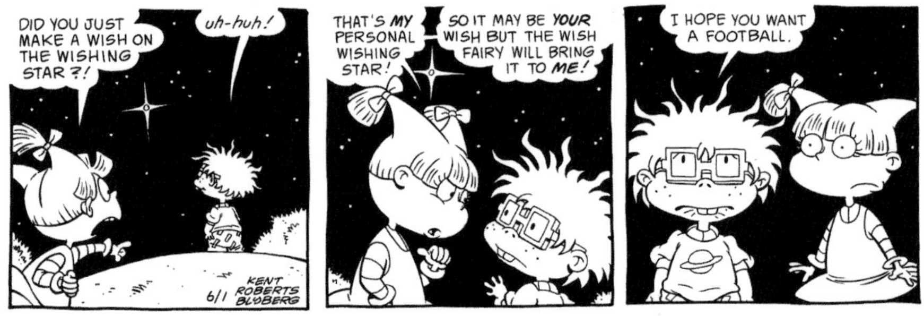
DID YOU JUST MAKE A WISH ON THE WISHING STAR?!
uh-huh!
6/1
KENT ROBERTS BLYBERG
THAT'S MY PERSONAL WISHING STAR!
SO IT MAY BE YOUR WISH BUT THE WISH FAIRY WILL BRING IT TO ME!
I HOPE YOU WANT A FOOTBALL.

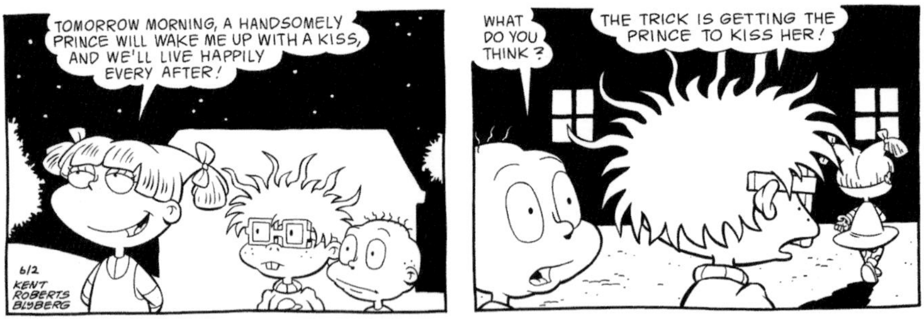
TOMORROW MORNING, A HANDSOMELY PRINCE WILL WAKE ME UP WITH A KISS, AND WE'LL LIVE HAPPILY EVERY AFTER!
6/2
KENT ROBERTS BLYBERG
WHAT DO YOU THINK?
THE TRICK IS GETTING THE PRINCE TO KISS HER!

2001

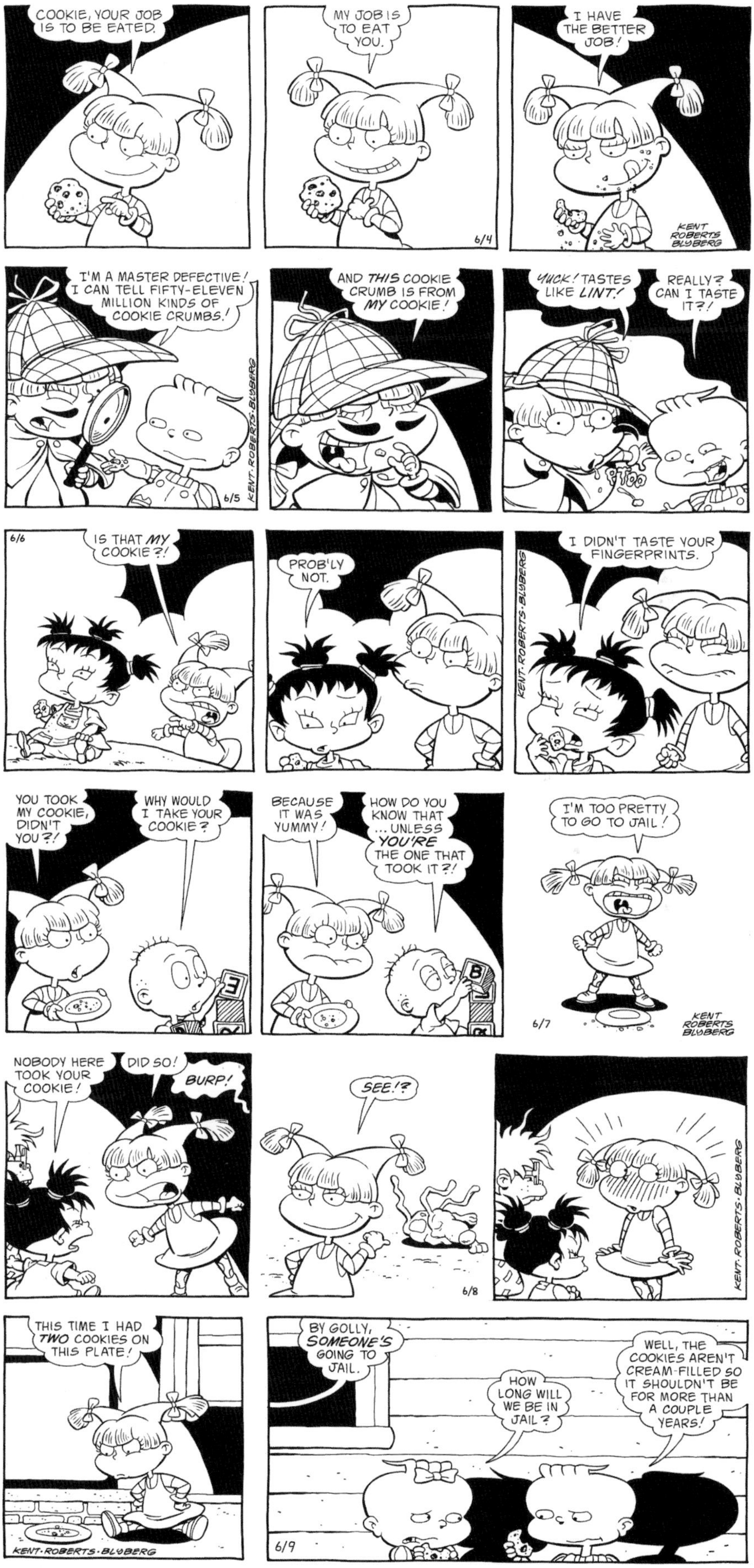
COOKIE, YOUR JOB IS TO BE EATED.
MY JOB IS TO EAT YOU.
6/4
I HAVE THE BETTER JOB!
KENT ROBERTS BLYBERG
I'M A MASTER DEFECTIVE! I CAN TELL FIFTY-ELEVEN MILLION KINDS OF COOKIE CRUMBS!
KENT·ROBERTS·BLYBERG
6/5
AND THIS COOKIE CRUMB IS FROM MY COOKIE!
YUCK! TASTES LIKE LINT!
REALLY? CAN I TASTE IT?!
PTOO
6/6
IS THAT MY COOKIE?!
PROB'LY NOT.
KENT·ROBERTS·BLYBERG
I DIDN'T TASTE YOUR FINGERPRINTS.
YOU TOOK MY COOKIE, DIDN'T YOU?!
WHY WOULD I TAKE YOUR COOKIE?
BECAUSE IT WAS YUMMY!
HOW DO YOU KNOW THAT ... UNLESS YOU'RE THE ONE THAT TOOK IT?!
I'M TOO PRETTY TO GO TO JAIL!
6/7
KENT ROBERTS BLYBERG
NOBODY HERE TOOK YOUR COOKIE!
DID SO!
BURP!
SEE!?
6/8
KENT·ROBERTS·BLYBERG
THIS TIME I HAD TWO COOKIES ON THIS PLATE!
KENT·ROBERTS·BLYBERG
BY GOLLY, SOMEONE'S GOING TO JAIL.
HOW LONG WILL WE BE IN JAIL?
WELL, THE COOKIES AREN'T CREAM-FILLED SO IT SHOULDN'T BE FOR MORE THAN A COUPLE YEARS!
6/9

2001

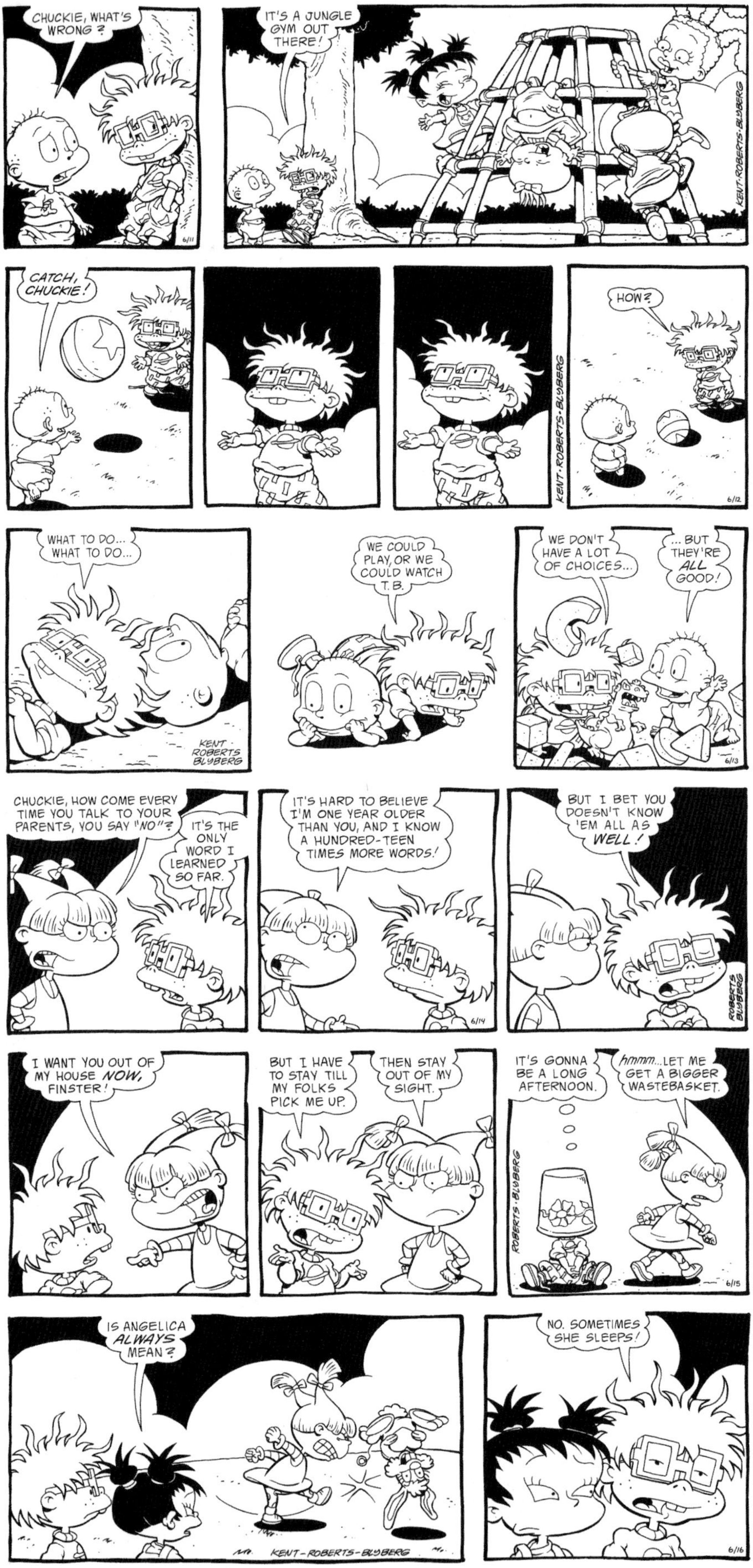
CHUCKIE, WHAT'S WRONG?
IT'S A JUNGLE GYM OUT THERE!
KENT·ROBERTS·BLYBERG
6/11
CATCH, CHUCKIE!
KENT·ROBERTS·BLYBERG
HOW?
6/12
WHAT TO DO... WHAT TO DO...
KENT ROBERTS BLYBERG
WE COULD PLAY, OR WE COULD WATCH T.B.
WE DON'T HAVE A LOT OF CHOICES...
... BUT THEY'RE ALL GOOD!
6/13
CHUCKIE, HOW COME EVERY TIME YOU TALK TO YOUR PARENTS, YOU SAY "NO"?
IT'S THE ONLY WORD I LEARNED SO FAR.
IT'S HARD TO BELIEVE I'M ONE YEAR OLDER THAN YOU, AND I KNOW A HUNDRED-TEEN TIMES MORE WORDS!
6/14
BUT I BET YOU DOESN'T KNOW 'EM ALL AS WELL!
ROBERTS BLYBERG
I WANT YOU OUT OF MY HOUSE NOW, FINSTER!
BUT I HAVE TO STAY TILL MY FOLKS PICK ME UP.
THEN STAY OUT OF MY SIGHT.
IT'S GONNA BE A LONG AFTERNOON.
hmmm...LET ME GET A BIGGER WASTEBASKET.
ROBERTS·BLYBERG
6/15
IS ANGELICA ALWAYS MEAN?
KENT-ROBERTS-BLYBERG
NO. SOMETIMES SHE SLEEPS!
6/16

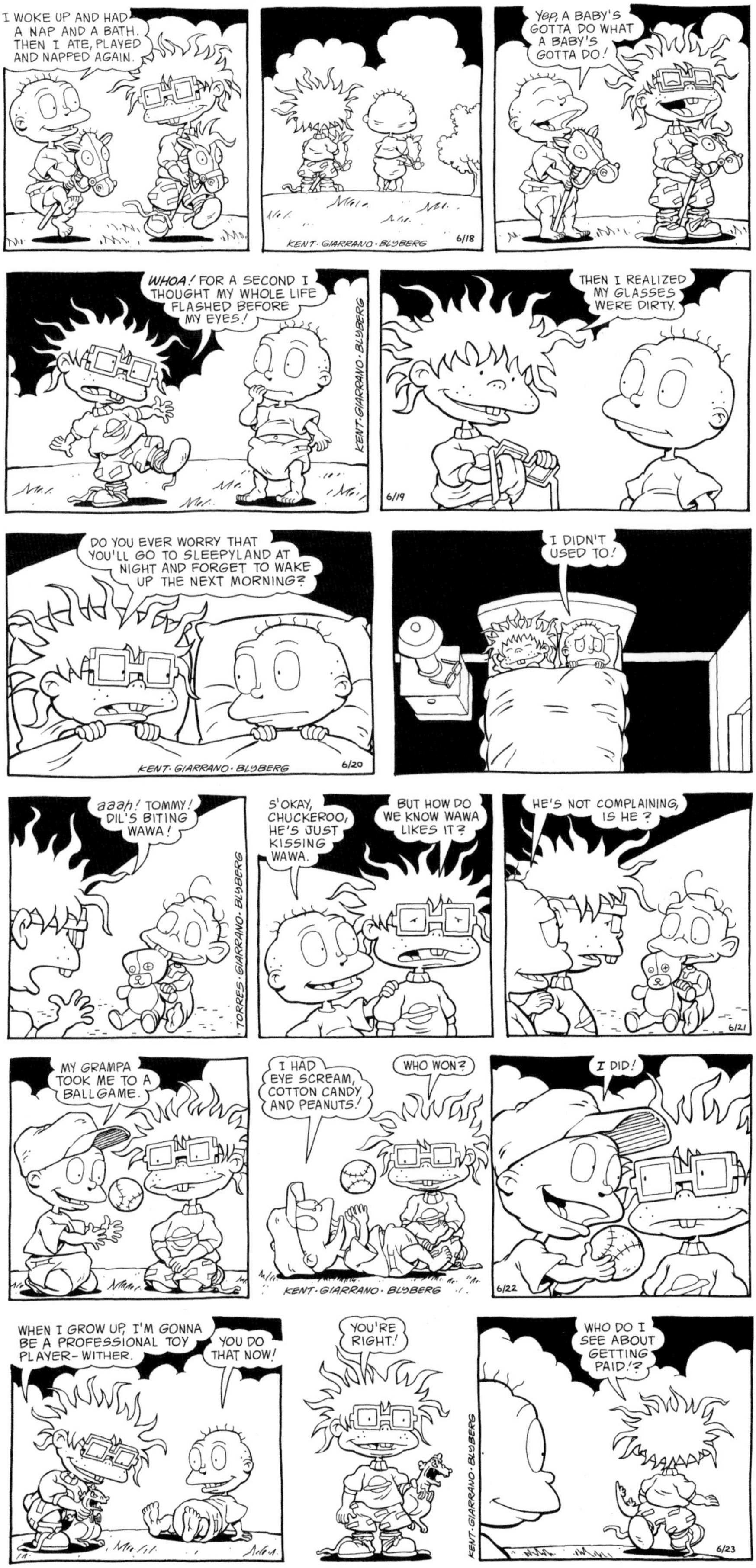
I WOKE UP AND HAD A NAP AND A BATH. THEN I ATE, PLAYED AND NAPPED AGAIN.
KENT · GIARRANO · BLYBERG 6/18
YEP, A BABY'S GOTTA DO WHAT A BABY'S GOTTA DO!
WHOA! FOR A SECOND I THOUGHT MY WHOLE LIFE FLASHED BEFORE MY EYES!
KENT · GIARRANO · BLYBERG
THEN I REALIZED MY GLASSES WERE DIRTY.
6/19
DO YOU EVER WORRY THAT YOU'LL GO TO SLEEPYLAND AT NIGHT AND FORGET TO WAKE UP THE NEXT MORNING?
KENT · GIARRANO · BLYBERG 6/20
I DIDN'T USED TO!
aaah! TOMMY! DIL'S BITING WAWA!
TORRES · GIARRANO · BLYBERG
S'OKAY, CHUCKEROO, HE'S JUST KISSING WAWA.
BUT HOW DO WE KNOW WAWA LIKES IT?
HE'S NOT COMPLAINING, IS HE?
6/21
MY GRAMPA TOOK ME TO A BALLGAME.
I HAD EYE SCREAM, COTTON CANDY AND PEANUTS!
WHO WON?
KENT · GIARRANO · BLYBERG
I DID!
6/22
WHEN I GROW UP, I'M GONNA BE A PROFESSIONAL TOY PLAYER-WITHER.
YOU DO THAT NOW!
YOU'RE RIGHT!
KENT · GIARRANO · BLYBERG
WHO DO I SEE ABOUT GETTING PAID!?
6/23

2001

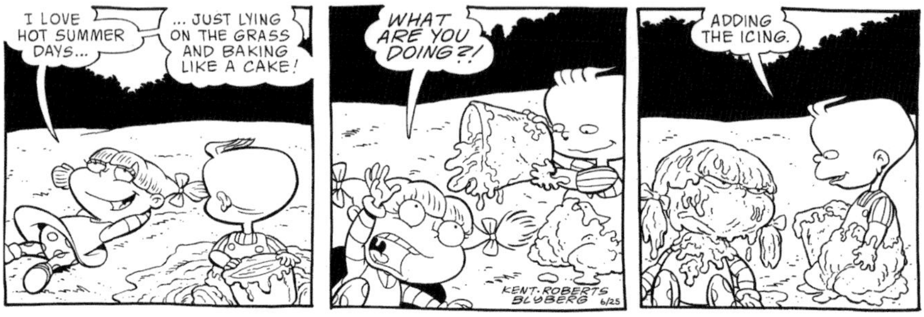
I LOVE HOT SUMMER DAYS...
... JUST LYING ON THE GRASS AND BAKING LIKE A CAKE!
WHAT ARE YOU DOING?!
KENT·ROBERTS BLYBERG 6/25
ADDING THE ICING.

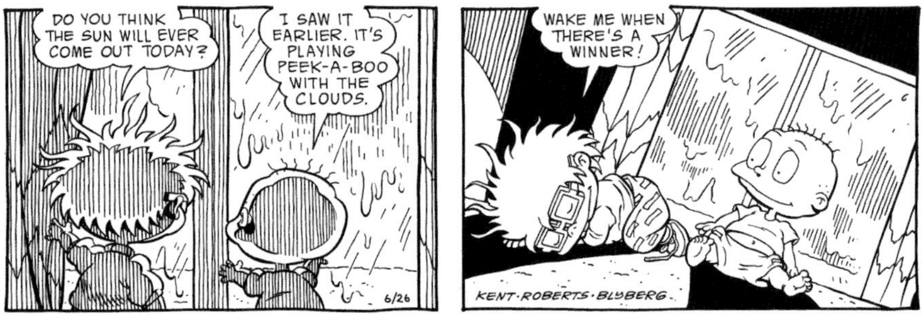
DO YOU THINK THE SUN WILL EVER COME OUT TODAY?
I SAW IT EARLIER. IT'S PLAYING PEEK-A-BOO WITH THE CLOUDS.
6/26
WAKE ME WHEN THERE'S A WINNER!
KENT·ROBERTS·BLYBERG

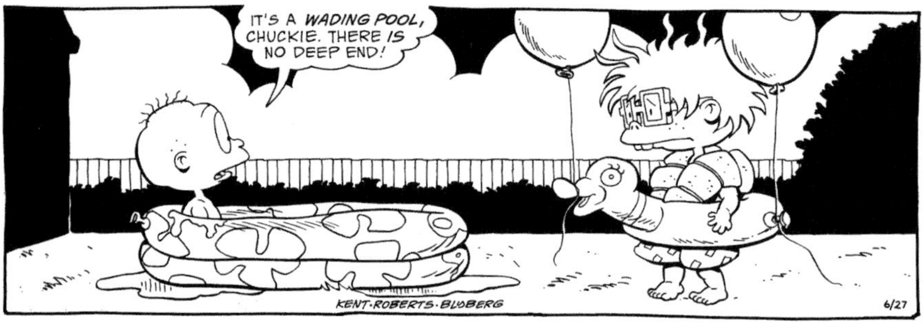
IT'S A WADING POOL, CHUCKIE. THERE IS NO DEEP END!
KENT·ROBERTS·BLYBERG
6/27

2001

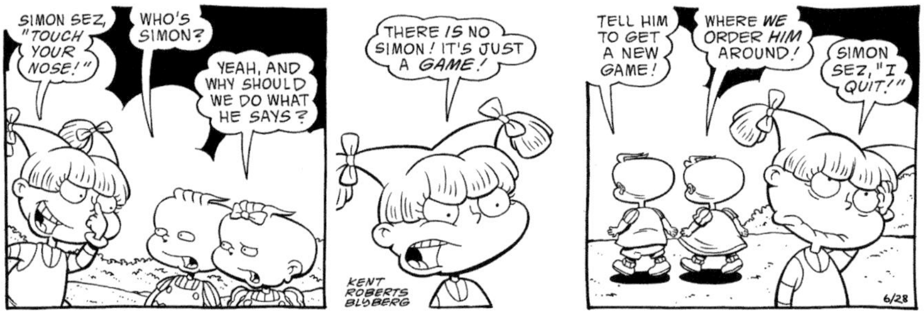
SIMON SEZ, "TOUCH YOUR NOSE!"
WHO'S SIMON?
YEAH, AND WHY SHOULD WE DO WHAT HE SAYS?
THERE IS NO SIMON! IT'S JUST A GAME!
KENT ROBERTS BLYBERG
TELL HIM TO GET A NEW GAME!
WHERE WE ORDER HIM AROUND!
SIMON SEZ, "I QUIT!"
6/28

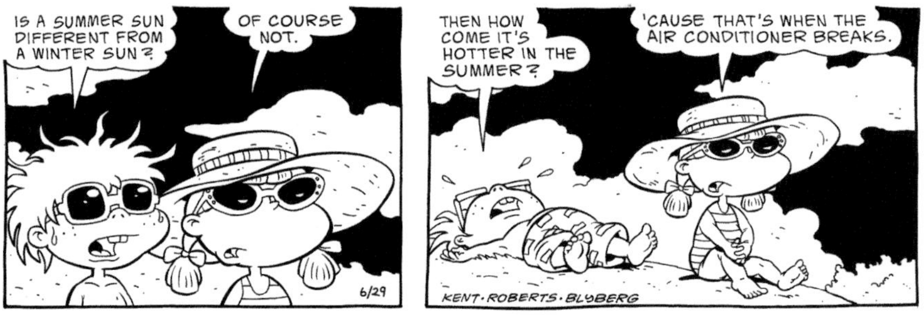
IS A SUMMER SUN DIFFERENT FROM A WINTER SUN?
OF COURSE NOT.
6/29
THEN HOW COME IT'S HOTTER IN THE SUMMER?
'CAUSE THAT'S WHEN THE AIR CONDITIONER BREAKS.
KENT·ROBERTS·BLYBERG

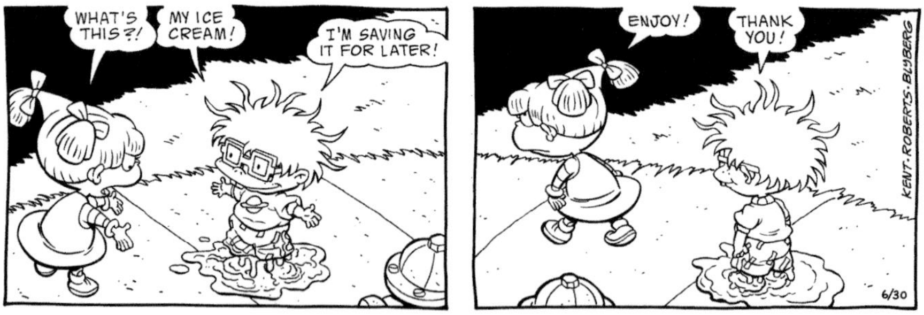
WHAT'S THIS?!
MY ICE CREAM!
I'M SAVING IT FOR LATER!
ENJOY!
THANK YOU!
KENT·ROBERTS·BLYBERG
6/30

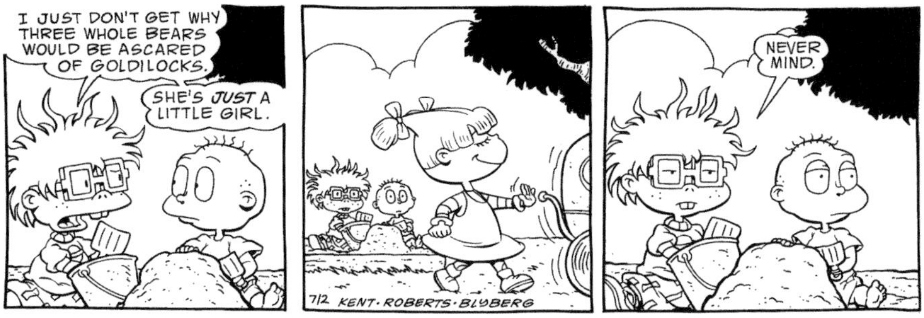
I JUST DON'T GET WHY THREE WHOLE BEARS WOULD BE ASCARED OF GOLDILOCKS.
SHE'S *JUST* A LITTLE GIRL.
7/2 KENT·ROBERTS·BLYBERG
NEVER MIND.

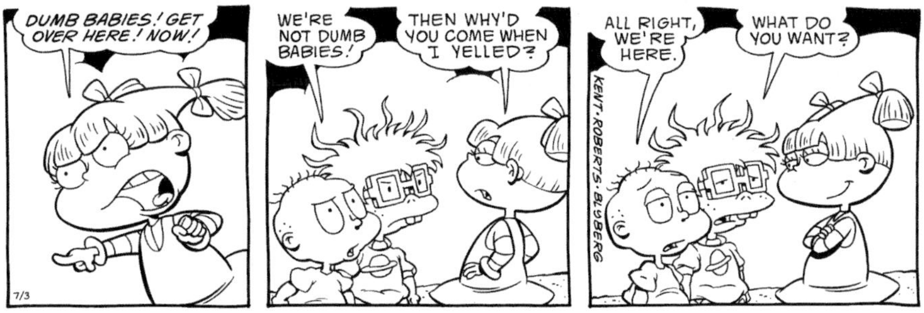
DUMB BABIES! GET OVER HERE! NOW!
7/3
WE'RE NOT DUMB BABIES!
THEN WHY'D YOU COME WHEN I YELLED?
KENT·ROBERTS·BLYBERG
ALL RIGHT, WE'RE HERE.
WHAT DO YOU WANT?

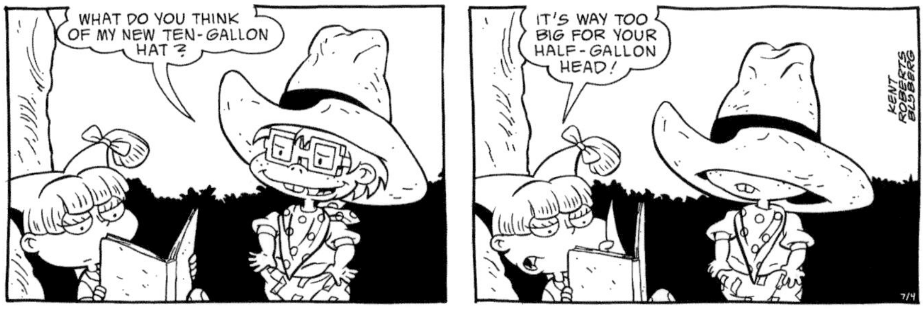
WHAT DO YOU THINK OF MY NEW TEN-GALLON HAT?
IT'S WAY TOO BIG FOR YOUR HALF-GALLON HEAD!
KENT ROBERTS BLYBERG
7/4

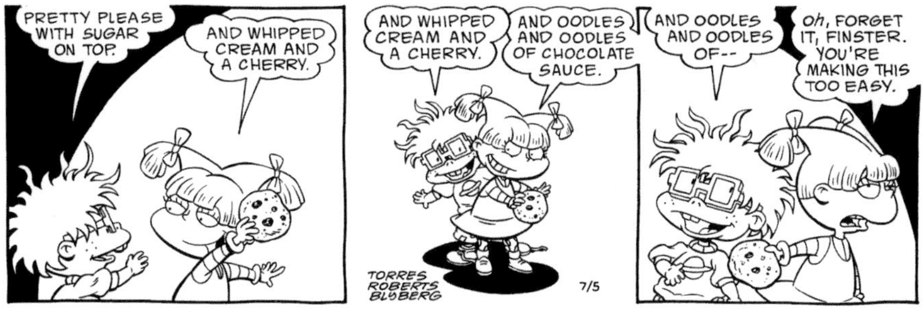
PRETTY PLEASE WITH SUGAR ON TOP.
AND WHIPPED CREAM AND A CHERRY.
AND WHIPPED CREAM AND A CHERRY.
AND OODLES AND OODLES OF CHOCOLATE SAUCE.
TORRES ROBERTS BLYBERG
7/5
AND OODLES AND OODLES OF--
Oh, FORGET IT, FINSTER. YOU'RE MAKING THIS TOO EASY.

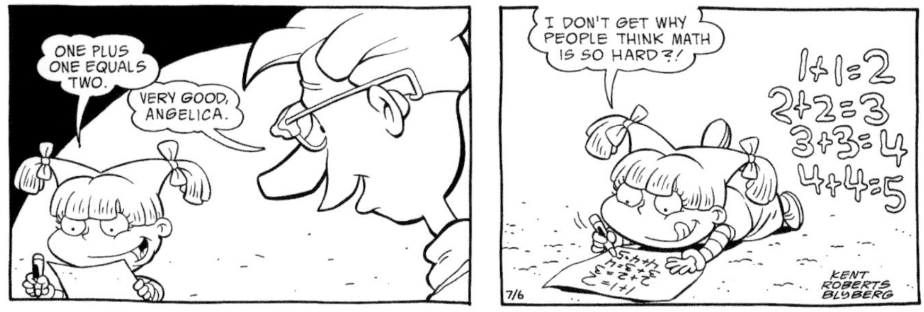
ONE PLUS ONE EQUALS TWO.
VERY GOOD, ANGELICA.
7/6
I DON'T GET WHY PEOPLE THINK MATH IS SO HARD?!
1+1=2
2+2=3
3+3=4
4+4=5
KENT ROBERTS BLYBERG

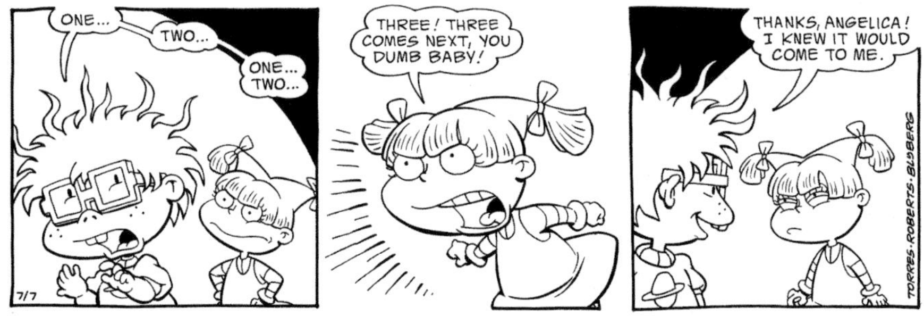
ONE...
TWO...
ONE... TWO...
7/7
THREE! THREE COMES NEXT, YOU DUMB BABY!
THANKS, ANGELICA! I KNEW IT WOULD COME TO ME.
TORRES·ROBERTS·BLYBERG

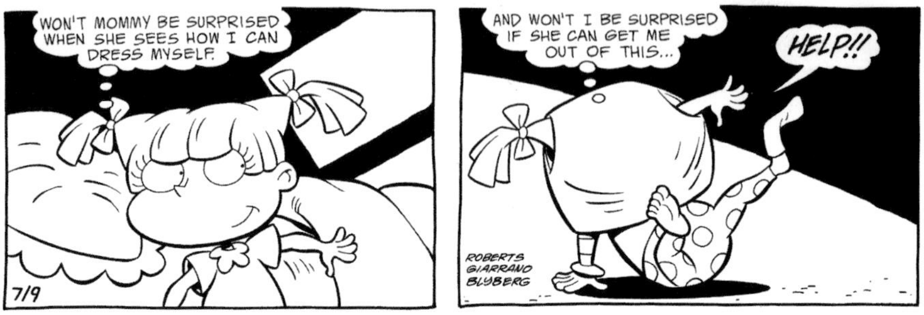
WON'T MOMMY BE SURPRISED WHEN SHE SEES HOW I CAN DRESS MYSELF.
7/9
AND WON'T I BE SURPRISED IF SHE CAN GET ME OUT OF THIS...
HELP!!
ROBERTS GIARRANO BLYBERG

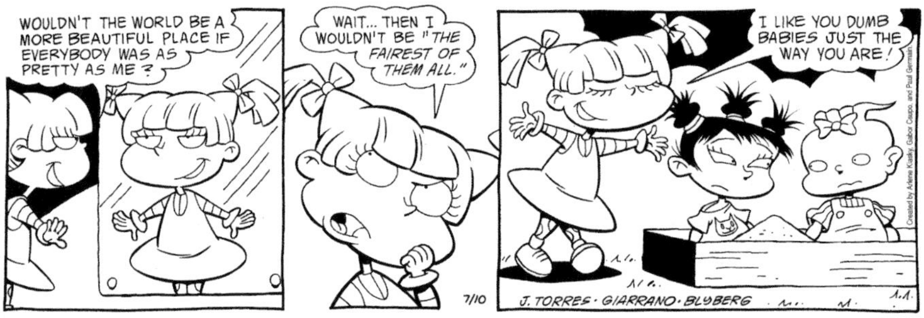
WOULDN'T THE WORLD BE A MORE BEAUTIFUL PLACE IF EVERYBODY WAS AS PRETTY AS ME ?
WAIT... THEN I WOULDN'T BE "THE FAIREST OF THEM ALL."
7/10
I LIKE YOU DUMB BABIES JUST THE WAY YOU ARE!
Created by Arlene Klasky, Gabor Csupo, and Paul Germain
J. TORRES · GIARRANO · BLYBERG

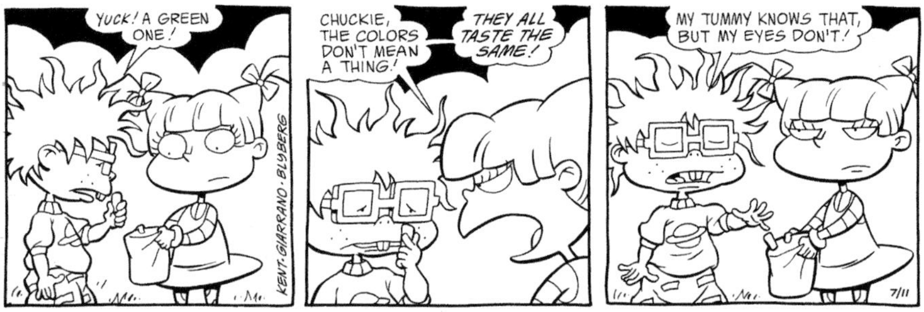
YUCK! A GREEN ONE!
KENT · GIARRANO · BLYBERG
CHUCKIE, THE COLORS DON'T MEAN A THING!
THEY ALL TASTE THE SAME!
MY TUMMY KNOWS THAT, BUT MY EYES DON'T!
7/11

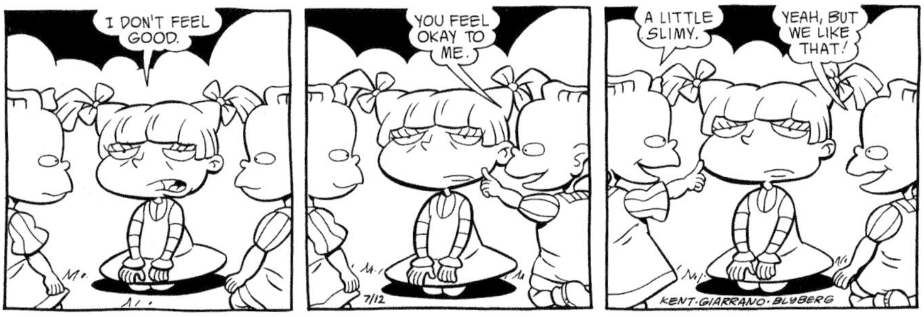
I DON'T FEEL GOOD.
YOU FEEL OKAY TO ME.
7/12
A LITTLE SLIMY.
YEAH, BUT WE LIKE THAT!
KENT · GIARRANO · BLYBERG

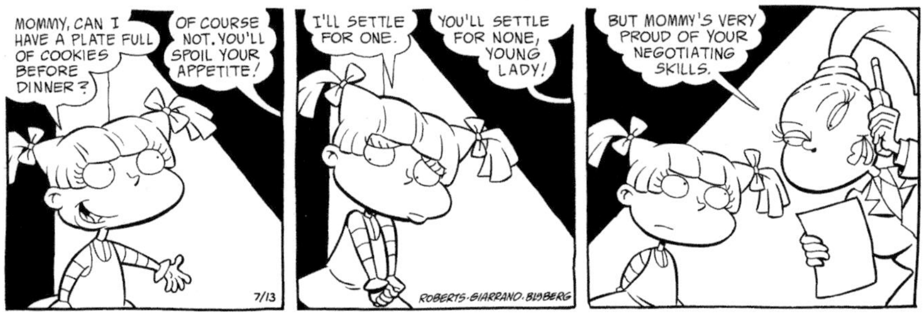
MOMMY, CAN I HAVE A PLATE FULL OF COOKIES BEFORE DINNER ?
OF COURSE NOT. YOU'LL SPOIL YOUR APPETITE!
7/13
I'LL SETTLE FOR ONE.
YOU'LL SETTLE FOR NONE, YOUNG LADY!
ROBERTS · GIARRANO · BLYBERG
BUT MOMMY'S VERY PROUD OF YOUR NEGOTIATING SKILLS.

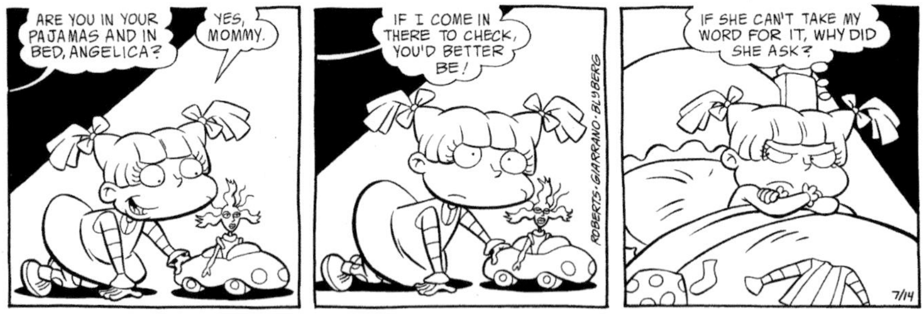
ARE YOU IN YOUR PAJAMAS AND IN BED, ANGELICA ?
YES, MOMMY.
IF I COME IN THERE TO CHECK, YOU'D BETTER BE!
ROBERTS · GIARRANO · BLYBERG
IF SHE CAN'T TAKE MY WORD FOR IT, WHY DID SHE ASK ?
7/14

2001

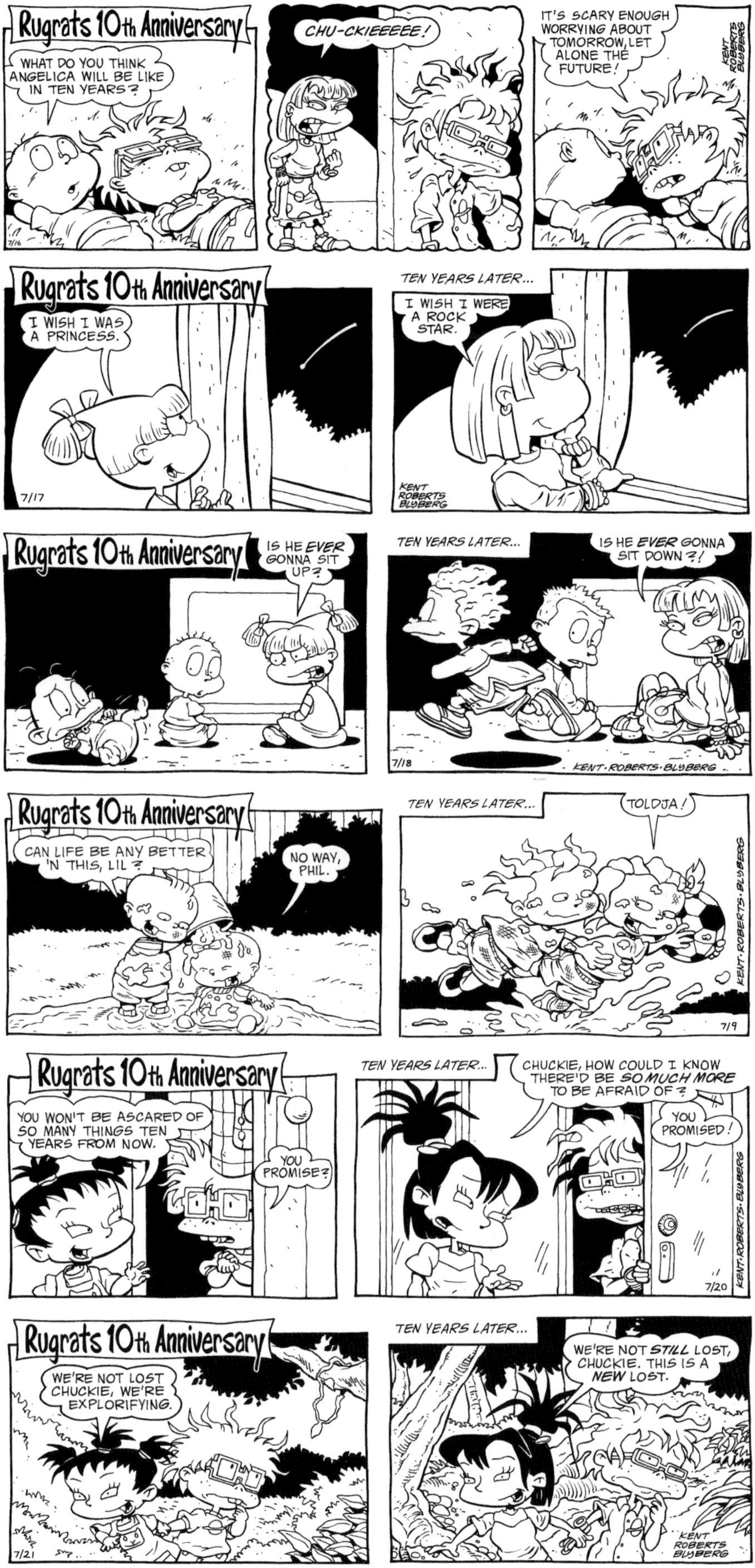

Rugrats 10th Anniversary
WHAT DO YOU THINK ANGELICA WILL BE LIKE IN TEN YEARS?
7/16
CHU-CKIEEEEE!
IT'S SCARY ENOUGH WORRYING ABOUT TOMORROW, LET ALONE THE FUTURE!
KENT ROBERTS BLYBERG
Rugrats 10th Anniversary
I WISH I WAS A PRINCESS.
7/17
TEN YEARS LATER...
I WISH I WERE A ROCK STAR.
KENT ROBERTS BLYBERG
Rugrats 10th Anniversary
IS HE EVER GONNA SIT UP?
TEN YEARS LATER...
IS HE EVER GONNA SIT DOWN?!
7/18
KENT·ROBERTS·BLYBERG
Rugrats 10th Anniversary
CAN LIFE BE ANY BETTER 'N THIS, LIL?
NO WAY, PHIL.
TEN YEARS LATER...
TOLDJA!
KENT·ROBERTS·BLYBERG
7/19
Rugrats 10th Anniversary
YOU WON'T BE ASCARED OF SO MANY THINGS TEN YEARS FROM NOW.
YOU PROMISE?
TEN YEARS LATER...
CHUCKIE, HOW COULD I KNOW THERE'D BE SO MUCH MORE TO BE AFRAID OF?
YOU PROMISED!
7/20
KENT·ROBERTS·BLYBERG
Rugrats 10th Anniversary
WE'RE NOT LOST CHUCKIE, WE'RE EXPLORIFYING.
7/21
TEN YEARS LATER...
WE'RE NOT STILL LOST, CHUCKIE. THIS IS A NEW LOST.
KENT ROBERTS BLYBERG

2001

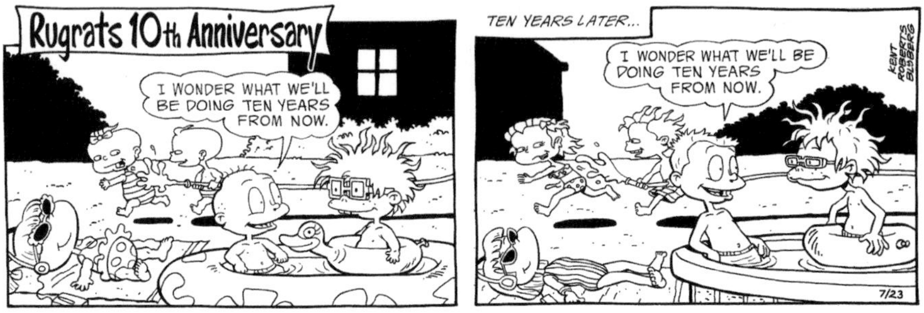
Rugrats 10th Anniversary
I WONDER WHAT WE'LL BE DOING TEN YEARS FROM NOW.
TEN YEARS LATER...
I WONDER WHAT WE'LL BE DOING TEN YEARS FROM NOW.
KENT ROBERTS BLYBERG
7/23

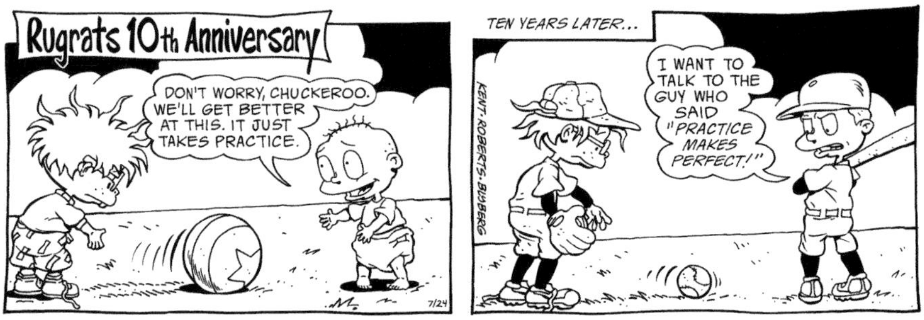
Rugrats 10th Anniversary
DON'T WORRY, CHUCKEROO. WE'LL GET BETTER AT THIS. IT JUST TAKES PRACTICE.
7/24
TEN YEARS LATER...
KENT·ROBERTS·BLYBERG
I WANT TO TALK TO THE GUY WHO SAID "PRACTICE MAKES PERFECT!"

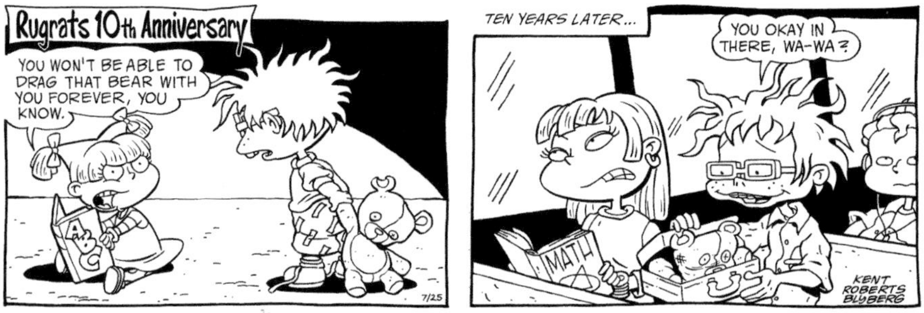
Rugrats 10th Anniversary
YOU WON'T BE ABLE TO DRAG THAT BEAR WITH YOU FOREVER, YOU KNOW.
7/25
TEN YEARS LATER...
YOU OKAY IN THERE, WA-WA?
MATH
KENT ROBERTS BLYBERG

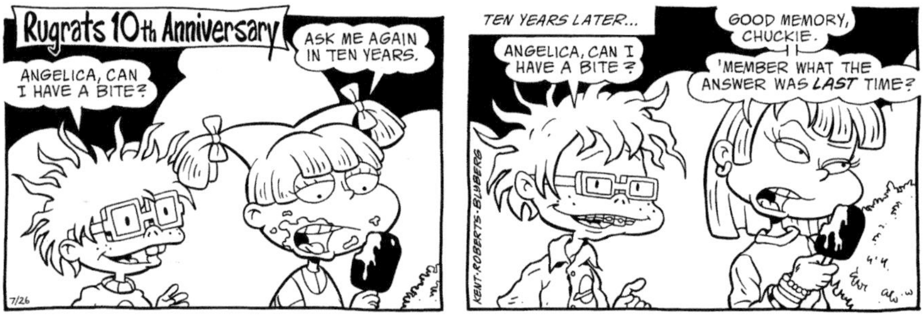
Rugrats 10th Anniversary
ANGELICA, CAN I HAVE A BITE?
ASK ME AGAIN IN TEN YEARS.
7/26
TEN YEARS LATER...
KENT·ROBERTS·BLYBERG
ANGELICA, CAN I HAVE A BITE?
GOOD MEMORY, CHUCKIE.
'MEMBER WHAT THE ANSWER WAS LAST TIME?

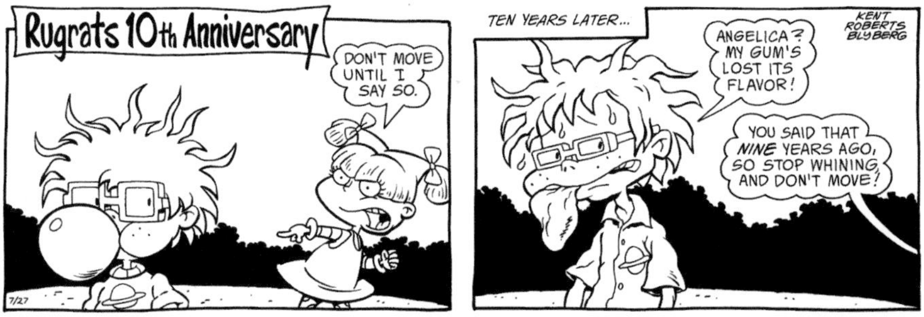
Rugrats 10th Anniversary
DON'T MOVE UNTIL I SAY SO.
7/27
TEN YEARS LATER...
KENT ROBERTS BLYBERG
ANGELICA? MY GUM'S LOST ITS FLAVOR!
YOU SAID THAT NINE YEARS AGO, SO STOP WHINING, AND DON'T MOVE!

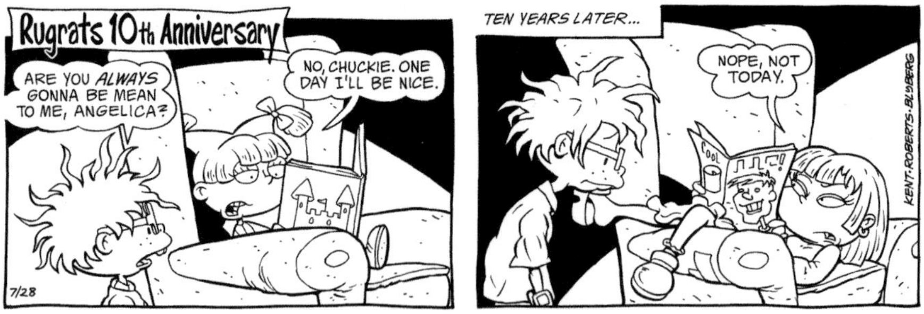
Rugrats 10th Anniversary
ARE YOU ALWAYS GONNA BE MEAN TO ME, ANGELICA?
NO, CHUCKIE. ONE DAY I'LL BE NICE.
7/28
TEN YEARS LATER...
NOPE, NOT TODAY.
KENT·ROBERTS·BLYBERG

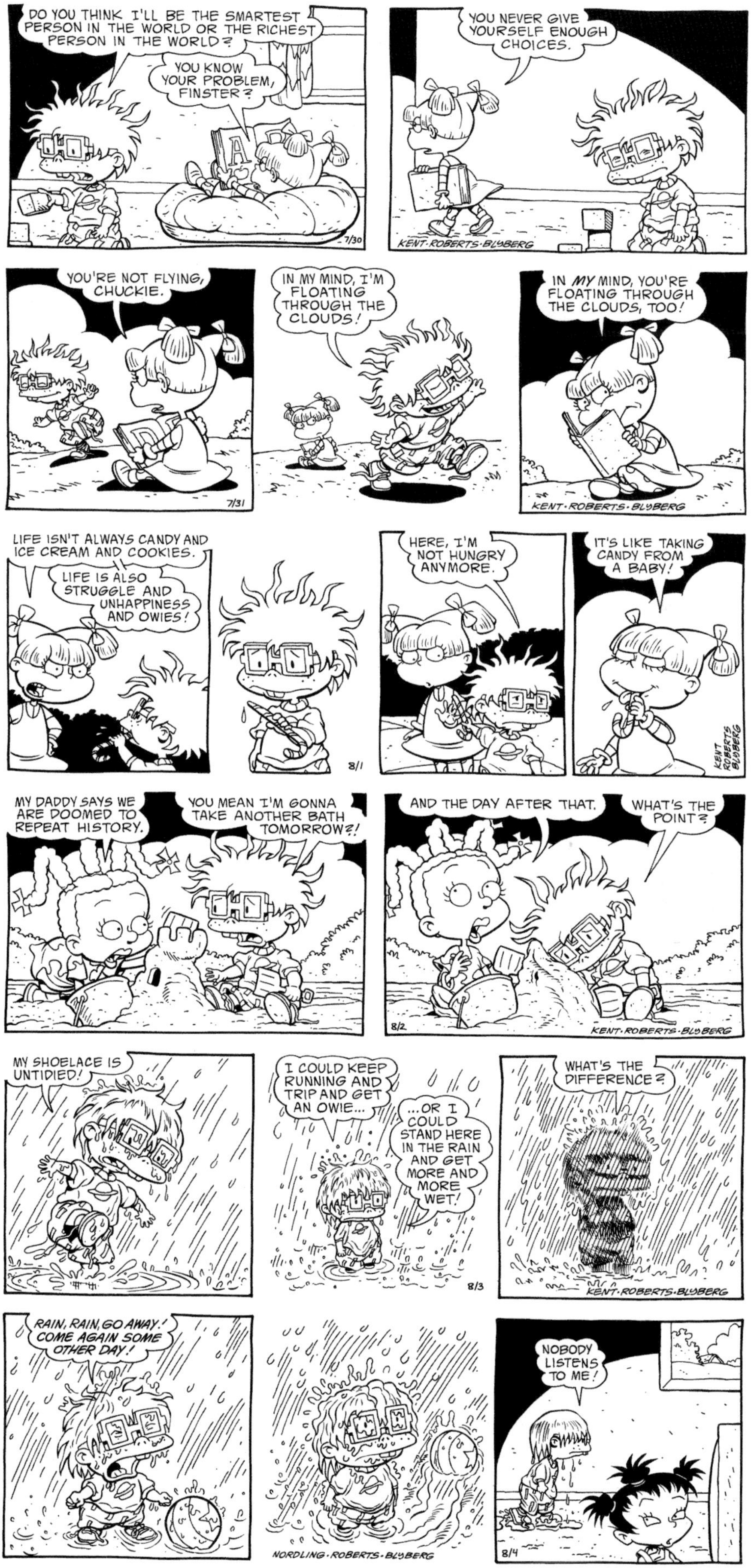
DO YOU THINK I'LL BE THE SMARTEST PERSON IN THE WORLD OR THE RICHEST PERSON IN THE WORLD?
YOU KNOW YOUR PROBLEM, FINSTER?
7/30
YOU NEVER GIVE YOURSELF ENOUGH CHOICES.
KENT·ROBERTS·BLYBERG
YOU'RE NOT FLYING, CHUCKIE.
7/31
IN MY MIND, I'M FLOATING THROUGH THE CLOUDS!
IN MY MIND, YOU'RE FLOATING THROUGH THE CLOUDS, TOO!
KENT·ROBERTS·BLYBERG
LIFE ISN'T ALWAYS CANDY AND ICE CREAM AND COOKIES.
LIFE IS ALSO STRUGGLE AND UNHAPPINESS AND OWIES!
8/1
HERE, I'M NOT HUNGRY ANYMORE.
IT'S LIKE TAKING CANDY FROM A BABY!
KENT ROBERTS BLYBERG
MY DADDY SAYS WE ARE DOOMED TO REPEAT HISTORY.
YOU MEAN I'M GONNA TAKE ANOTHER BATH TOMORROW?!
AND THE DAY AFTER THAT.
WHAT'S THE POINT?
8/2
KENT·ROBERTS·BLYBERG
MY SHOELACE IS UNTIDIED!
I COULD KEEP RUNNING AND TRIP AND GET AN OWIE...
...OR I COULD STAND HERE IN THE RAIN AND GET MORE AND MORE WET!
8/3
WHAT'S THE DIFFERENCE?
KENT·ROBERTS·BLYBERG
RAIN, RAIN, GO AWAY! COME AGAIN SOME OTHER DAY!
NORDLING·ROBERTS·BLYBERG
NOBODY LISTENS TO ME!
8/4

2001

2001

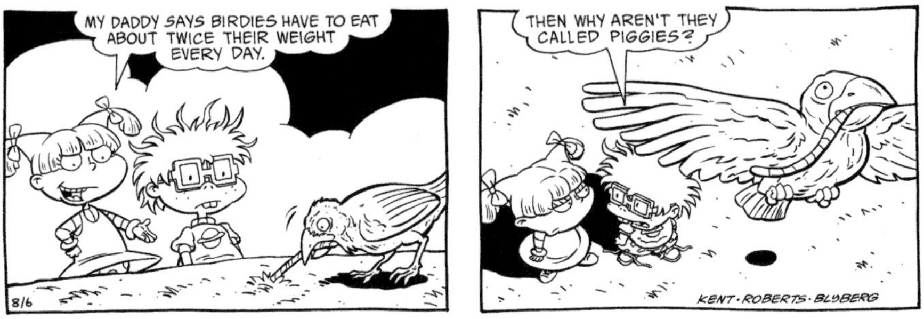
MY DADDY SAYS BIRDIES HAVE TO EAT ABOUT TWICE THEIR WEIGHT EVERY DAY.
8/6
THEN WHY AREN'T THEY CALLED PIGGIES?
KENT·ROBERTS·BLYBERG

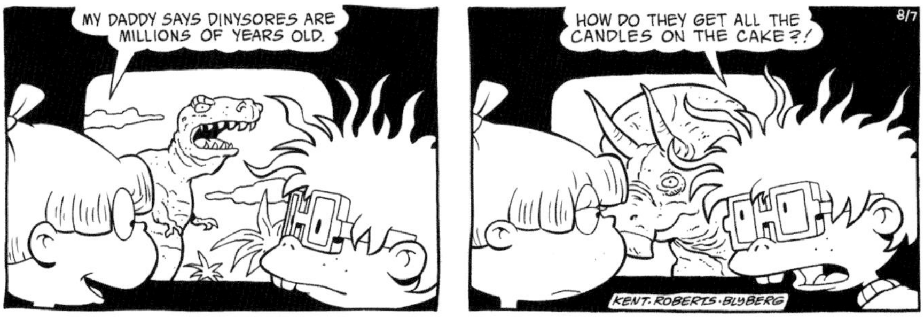
MY DADDY SAYS DINYSORES ARE MILLIONS OF YEARS OLD.
HOW DO THEY GET ALL THE CANDLES ON THE CAKE?!
8/7
KENT·ROBERTS·BLYBERG

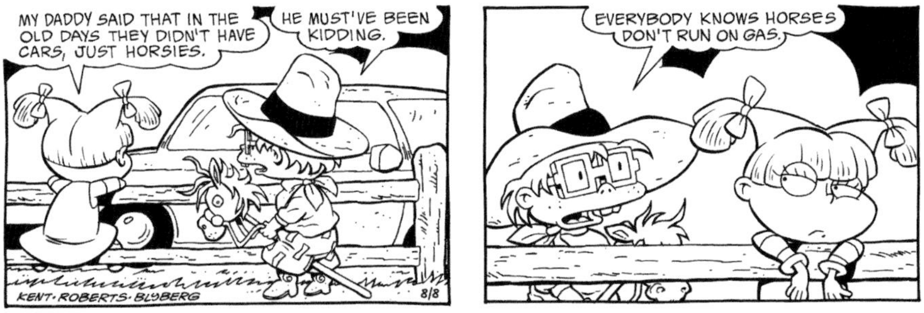
MY DADDY SAID THAT IN THE OLD DAYS THEY DIDN'T HAVE CARS, JUST HORSIES.
HE MUST'VE BEEN KIDDING.
KENT·ROBERTS·BLYBERG
8/8
EVERYBODY KNOWS HORSES DON'T RUN ON GAS.

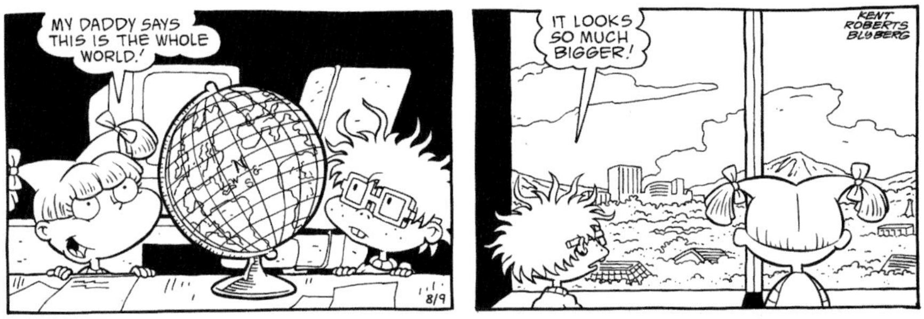
MY DADDY SAYS THIS IS THE WHOLE WORLD!
8/9
IT LOOKS SO MUCH BIGGER!
KENT ROBERTS BLYBERG

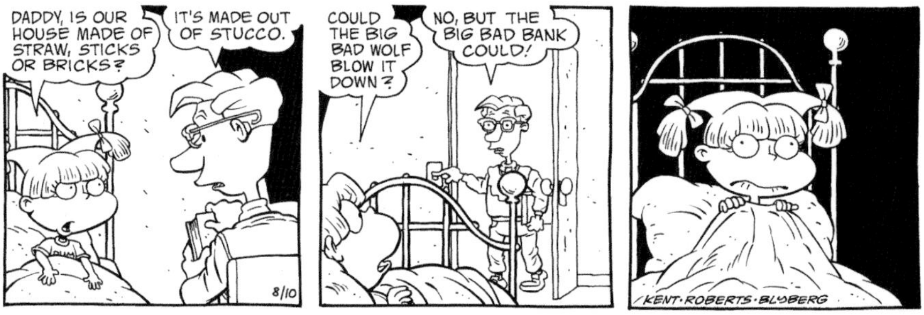
DADDY, IS OUR HOUSE MADE OF STRAW, STICKS OR BRICKS?
IT'S MADE OUT OF STUCCO.
8/10
COULD THE BIG BAD WOLF BLOW IT DOWN?
NO, BUT THE BIG BAD BANK COULD!
KENT·ROBERTS·BLYBERG

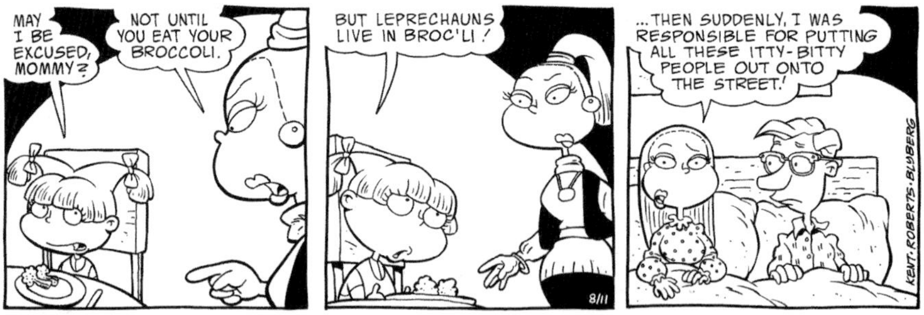
MAY I BE EXCUSED, MOMMY?
NOT UNTIL YOU EAT YOUR BROCCOLI.
BUT LEPRECHAUNS LIVE IN BROC'LI!
8/11
...THEN SUDDENLY, I WAS RESPONSIBLE FOR PUTTING ALL THESE ITTY-BITTY PEOPLE OUT ONTO THE STREET!
KENT·ROBERTS·BLYBERG

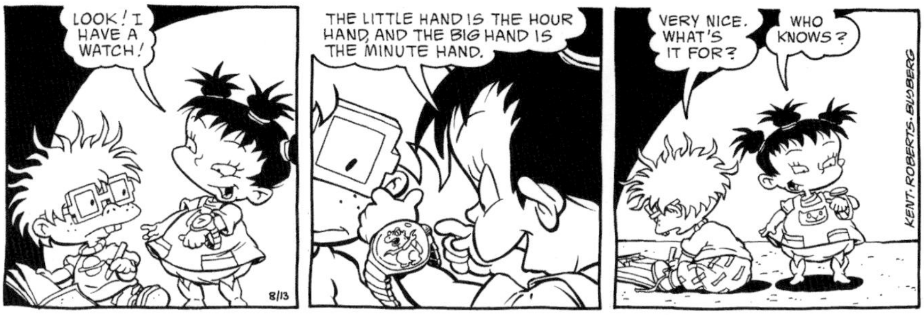
LOOK! I HAVE A WATCH!
THE LITTLE HAND IS THE HOUR HAND, AND THE BIG HAND IS THE MINUTE HAND.
VERY NICE. WHAT'S IT FOR?
WHO KNOWS?
8/13
KENT·ROBERTS·BLYBERG

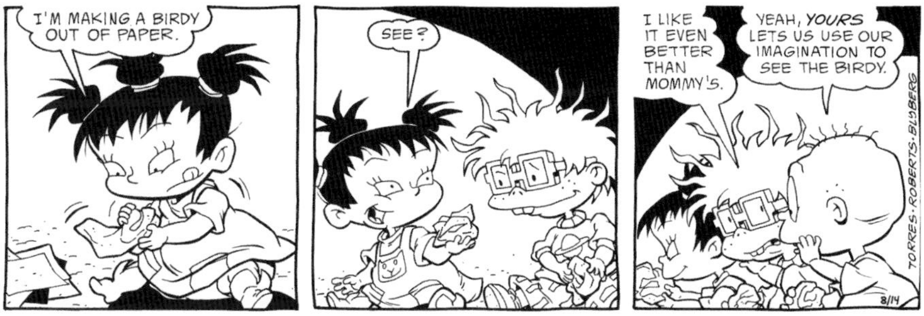
I'M MAKING A BIRDY OUT OF PAPER.
SEE?
I LIKE IT EVEN BETTER THAN MOMMY'S.
YEAH, *YOURS* LETS US USE OUR IMAGINATION TO SEE THE BIRDY.
TORRES·ROBERTS·BLYBERG
8/14

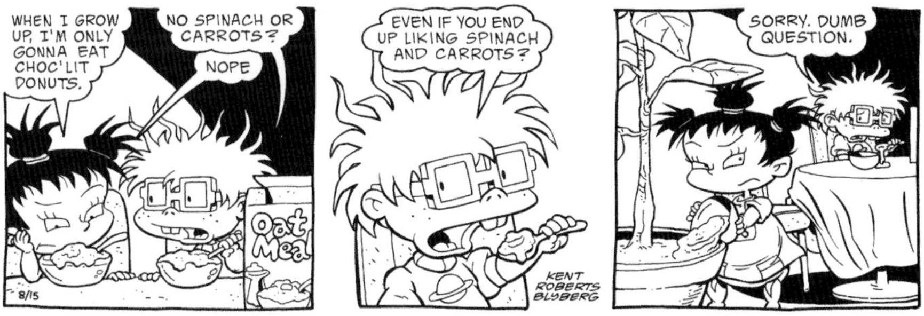
WHEN I GROW UP, I'M ONLY GONNA EAT CHOC'LIT DONUTS.
NO SPINACH OR CARROTS?
NOPE
Oat Meal
8/15
EVEN IF YOU END UP LIKING SPINACH AND CARROTS?
KENT ROBERTS BLYBERG
SORRY. DUMB QUESTION.

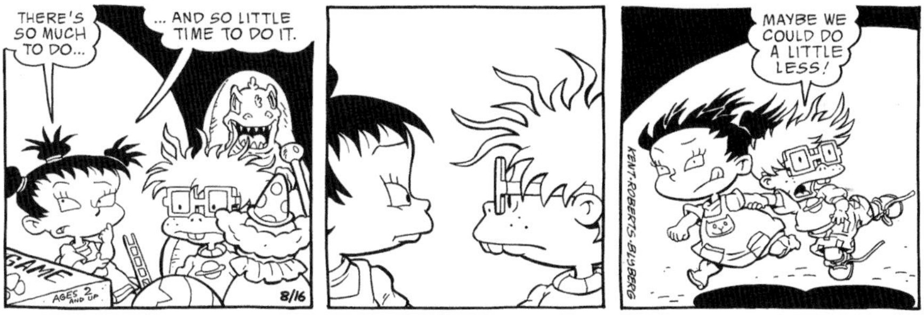
THERE'S SO MUCH TO DO...
... AND SO LITTLE TIME TO DO IT.
GAME
AGES 2 AND UP
8/16
MAYBE WE COULD DO A LITTLE LESS!
KENT·ROBERTS·BLYBERG

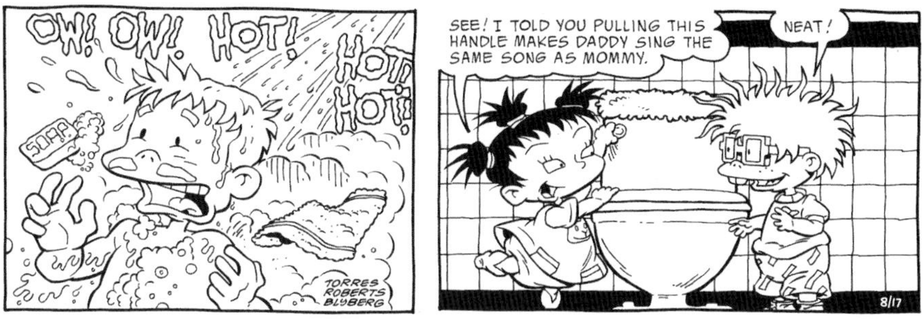
OW! OW! HOT!
HOT! HOT!
SOAP
TORRES ROBERTS BLYBERG
SEE! I TOLD YOU PULLING THIS HANDLE MAKES DADDY SING THE SAME SONG AS MOMMY.
NEAT!
8/17

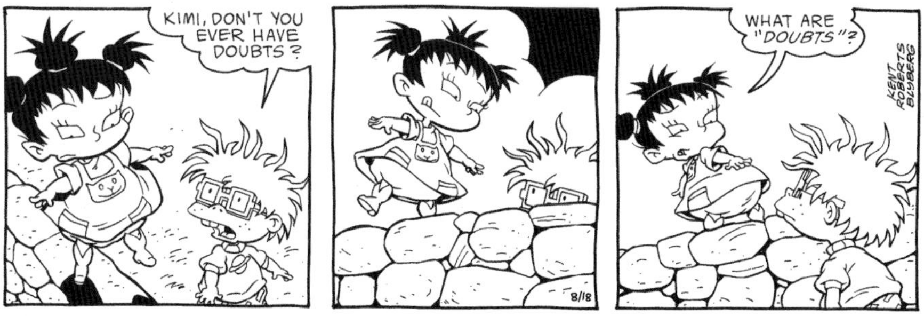
KIMI, DON'T YOU EVER HAVE DOUBTS?
8/18
WHAT ARE "*DOUBTS*"?
KENT ROBERTS BLYBERG

2001

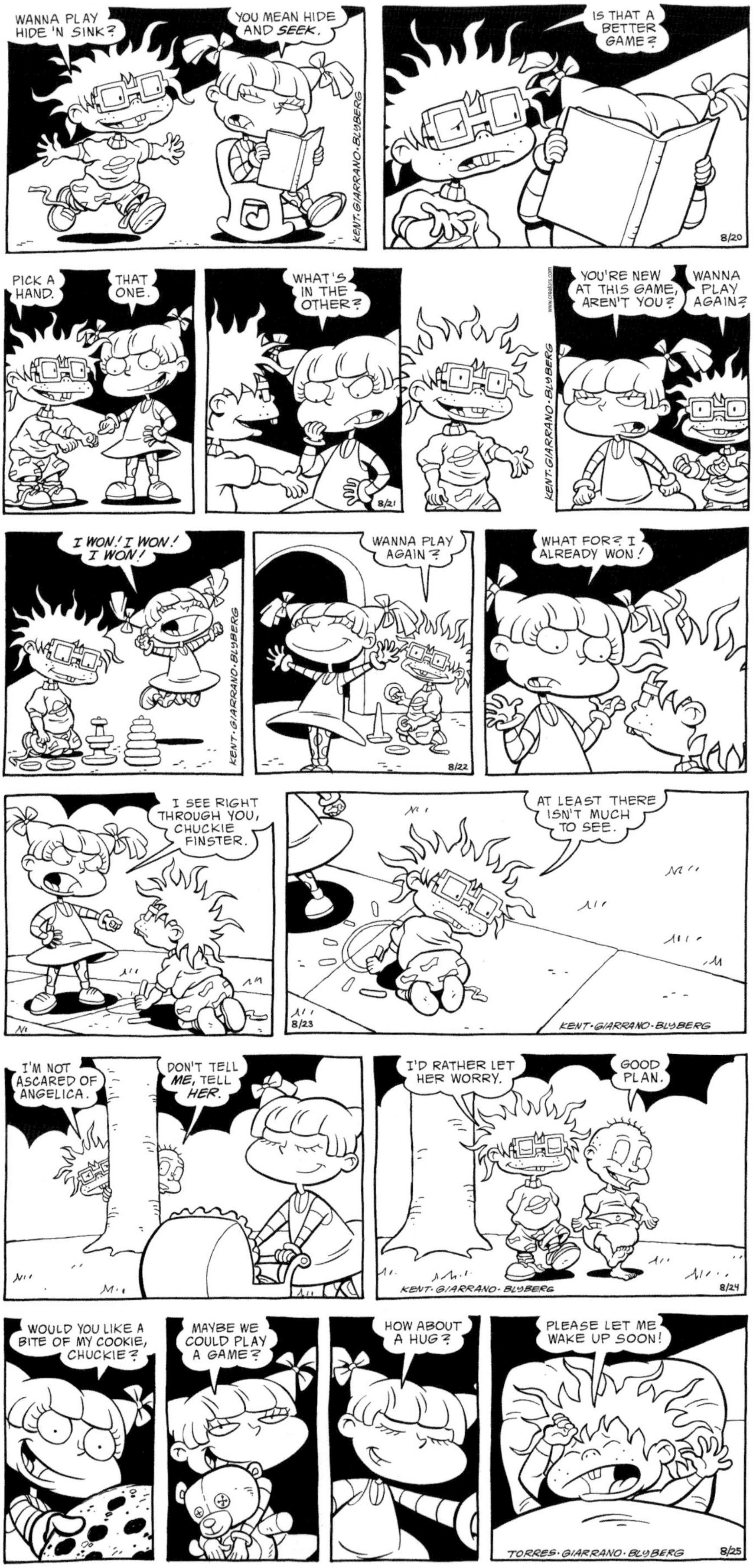
WANNA PLAY HIDE 'N SINK?
YOU MEAN HIDE AND SEEK.
KENT·GIARRANO·BLYBERG
IS THAT A BETTER GAME?
8/20
PICK A HAND.
THAT ONE.
WHAT'S IN THE OTHER?
8/21
YOU'RE NEW AT THIS GAME, AREN'T YOU?
WANNA PLAY AGAIN?
KENT·GIARRANO·BLYBERG
I WON! I WON! I WON!
KENT·GIARRANO·BLYBERG
WANNA PLAY AGAIN?
8/22
WHAT FOR? I ALREADY WON!
I SEE RIGHT THROUGH YOU, CHUCKIE FINSTER.
AT LEAST THERE ISN'T MUCH TO SEE.
8/23
KENT·GIARRANO·BLYBERG
I'M NOT ASCARED OF ANGELICA.
DON'T TELL ME, TELL HER.
I'D RATHER LET HER WORRY.
GOOD PLAN.
KENT·GIARRANO·BLYBERG
8/24
WOULD YOU LIKE A BITE OF MY COOKIE, CHUCKIE?
MAYBE WE COULD PLAY A GAME?
HOW ABOUT A HUG?
PLEASE LET ME WAKE UP SOON!
TORRES·GIARRANO·BLYBERG
8/25

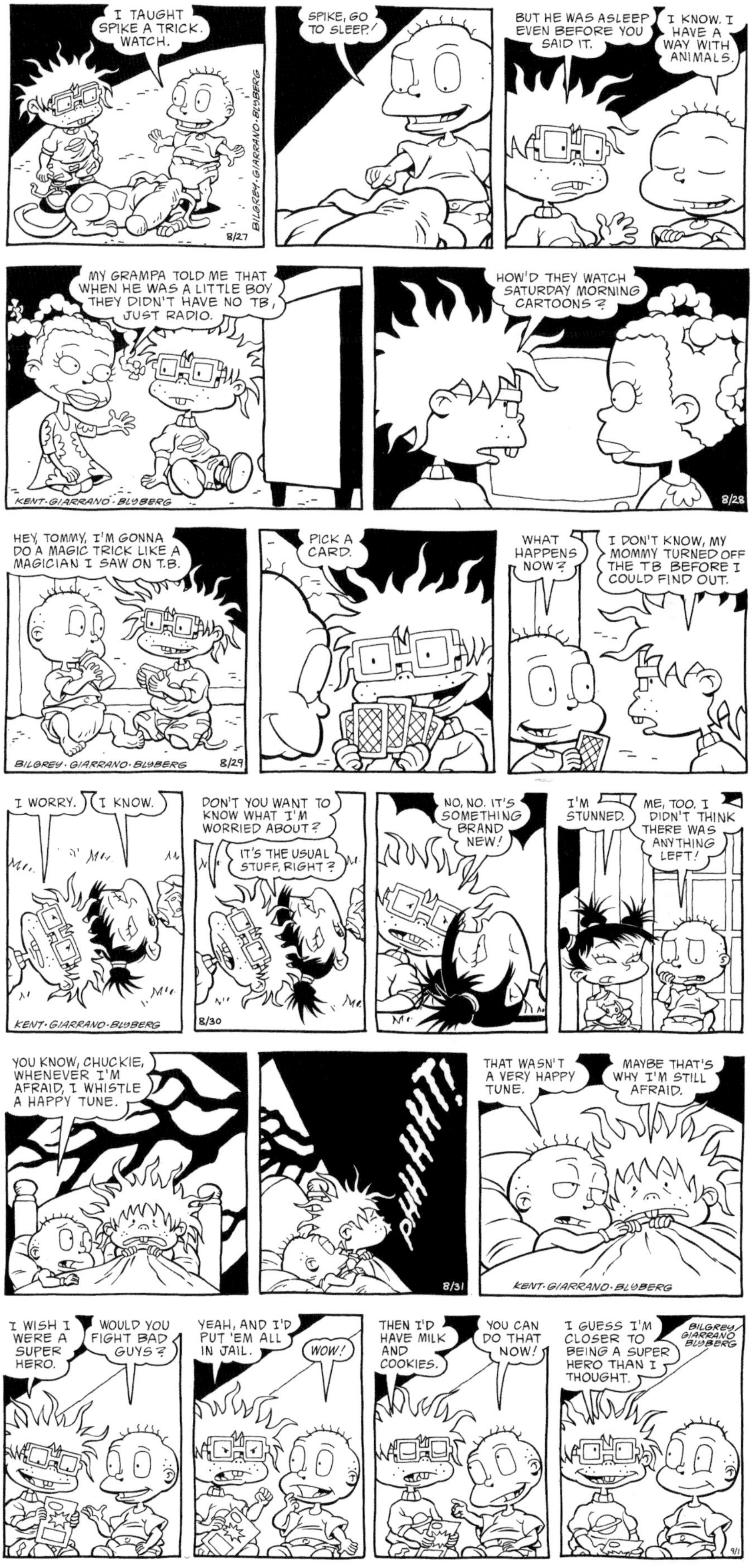
I TAUGHT SPIKE A TRICK. WATCH.
BILGREY·GIARRANO·BLYBERG
8/27
SPIKE, GO TO SLEEP!
BUT HE WAS ASLEEP EVEN BEFORE YOU SAID IT.
I KNOW. I HAVE A WAY WITH ANIMALS.
MY GRAMPA TOLD ME THAT WHEN HE WAS A LITTLE BOY THEY DIDN'T HAVE NO TB, JUST RADIO.
KENT·GIARRANO·BLYBERG
HOW'D THEY WATCH SATURDAY MORNING CARTOONS?
8/28
HEY, TOMMY, I'M GONNA DO A MAGIC TRICK LIKE A MAGICIAN I SAW ON T.B.
BILGREY·GIARRANO·BLYBERG
8/29
PICK A CARD.
WHAT HAPPENS NOW?
I DON'T KNOW, MY MOMMY TURNED OFF THE TB BEFORE I COULD FIND OUT.
I WORRY.
I KNOW.
KENT·GIARRANO·BLYBERG
DON'T YOU WANT TO KNOW WHAT I'M WORRIED ABOUT?
IT'S THE USUAL STUFF, RIGHT?
8/30
NO, NO. IT'S SOMETHING BRAND NEW!
I'M STUNNED.
ME, TOO. I DIDN'T THINK THERE WAS ANYTHING LEFT!
YOU KNOW, CHUCKIE, WHENEVER I'M AFRAID, I WHISTLE A HAPPY TUNE.
PHHHHT!
8/31
THAT WASN'T A VERY HAPPY TUNE.
MAYBE THAT'S WHY I'M STILL AFRAID.
KENT·GIARRANO·BLYBERG
I WISH I WERE A SUPER HERO.
WOULD YOU FIGHT BAD GUYS?
YEAH, AND I'D PUT 'EM ALL IN JAIL.
WOW!
THEN I'D HAVE MILK AND COOKIES.
YOU CAN DO THAT NOW!
I GUESS I'M CLOSER TO BEING A SUPER HERO THAN I THOUGHT.
BILGREY/GIARRANO/BLYBERG
9/1

2001

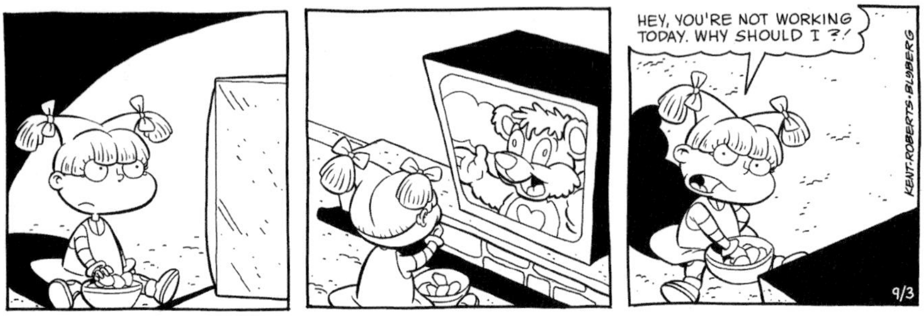
HEY, YOU'RE NOT WORKING TODAY. WHY SHOULD I ?!
KENT·ROBERTS·BLYBERG
9/3

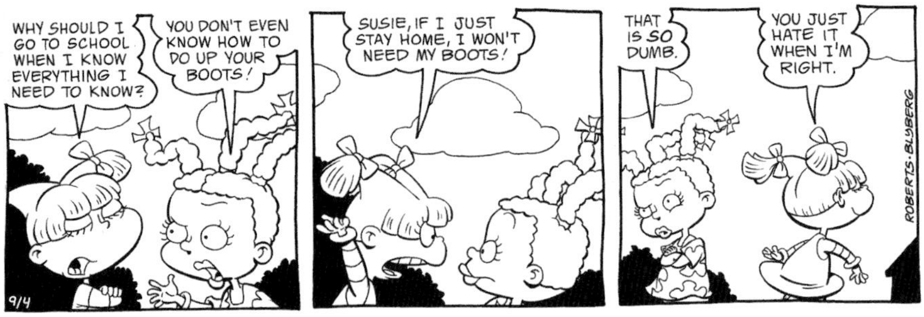
WHY SHOULD I GO TO SCHOOL WHEN I KNOW EVERYTHING I NEED TO KNOW?
YOU DON'T EVEN KNOW HOW TO DO UP YOUR BOOTS!
SUSIE, IF I JUST STAY HOME, I WON'T NEED MY BOOTS!
THAT IS SO DUMB.
YOU JUST HATE IT WHEN I'M RIGHT.
ROBERTS·BLYBERG
9/4

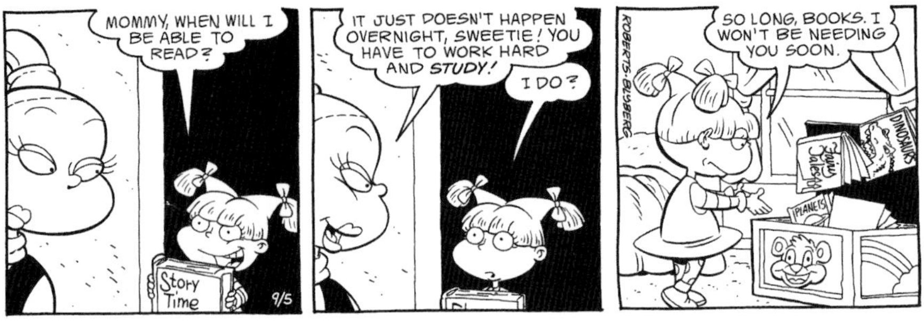
MOMMY, WHEN WILL I BE ABLE TO READ?
Story Time
9/5
IT JUST DOESN'T HAPPEN OVERNIGHT, SWEETIE! YOU HAVE TO WORK HARD AND STUDY!
I DO?
ROBERTS·BLYBERG
SO LONG, BOOKS. I WON'T BE NEEDING YOU SOON.
DINOSAURS
PLANETS

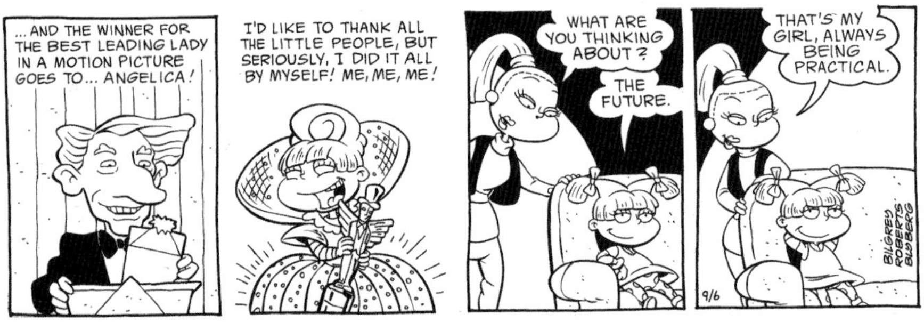
...AND THE WINNER FOR THE BEST LEADING LADY IN A MOTION PICTURE GOES TO... ANGELICA!
I'D LIKE TO THANK ALL THE LITTLE PEOPLE, BUT SERIOUSLY, I DID IT ALL BY MYSELF! ME, ME, ME!
WHAT ARE YOU THINKING ABOUT?
THE FUTURE.
THAT'S MY GIRL, ALWAYS BEING PRACTICAL.
BILGREY ROBERTS BLYBERG
9/6

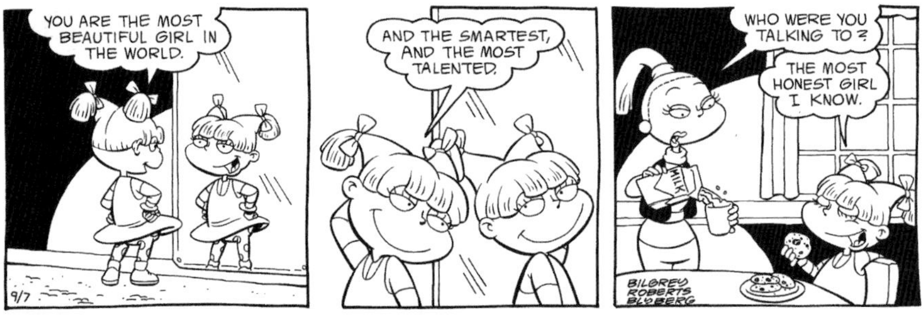
YOU ARE THE MOST BEAUTIFUL GIRL IN THE WORLD.
9/7
AND THE SMARTEST, AND THE MOST TALENTED.
WHO WERE YOU TALKING TO?
THE MOST HONEST GIRL I KNOW.
MILK
BILGREY ROBERTS BLYBERG

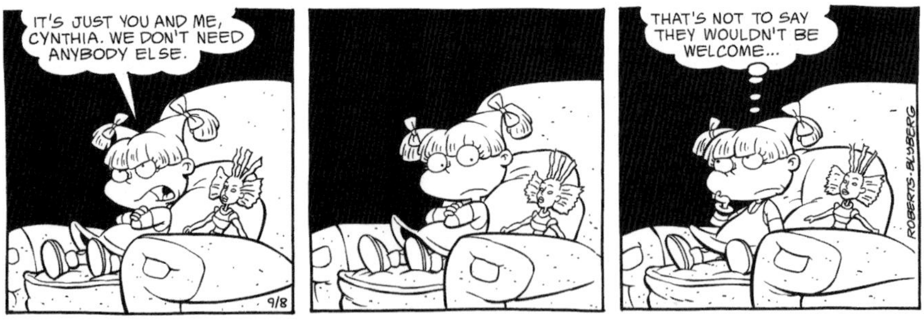
IT'S JUST YOU AND ME, CYNTHIA. WE DON'T NEED ANYBODY ELSE.
9/8
THAT'S NOT TO SAY THEY WOULDN'T BE WELCOME...
ROBERTS·BLYBERG

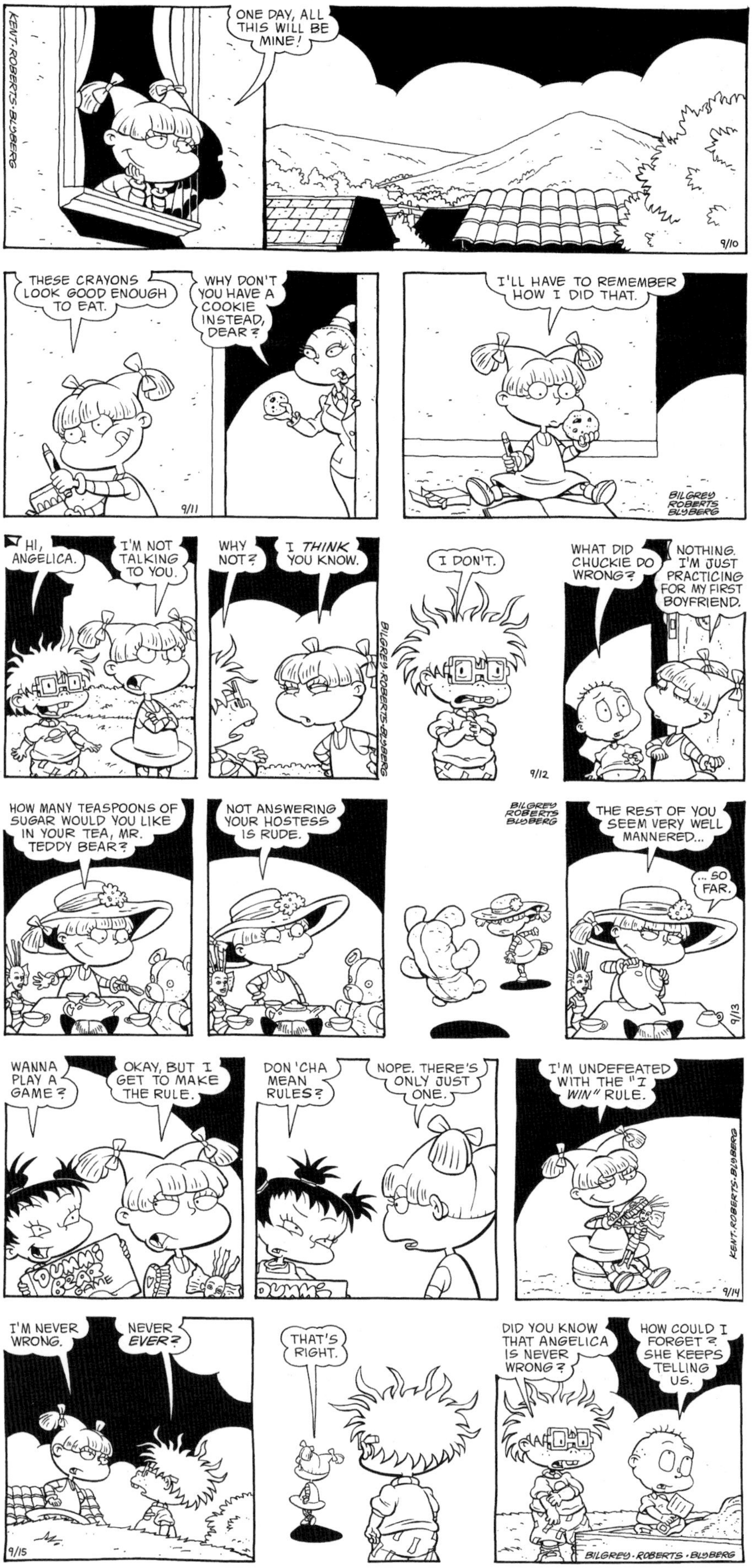
KENT·ROBERTS·BLYBERG
ONE DAY, ALL THIS WILL BE MINE!
9/10
THESE CRAYONS LOOK GOOD ENOUGH TO EAT.
WHY DON'T YOU HAVE A COOKIE INSTEAD, DEAR?
I'LL HAVE TO REMEMBER HOW I DID THAT.
9/11
BILGREY ROBERTS BLYBERG
HI, ANGELICA.
I'M NOT TALKING TO YOU.
WHY NOT?
I *THINK* YOU KNOW.
BILGREY·ROBERTS·BLYBERG
I DON'T.
WHAT DID CHUCKIE DO WRONG?
NOTHING. I'M JUST PRACTICING FOR MY FIRST BOYFRIEND.
9/12
HOW MANY TEASPOONS OF SUGAR WOULD YOU LIKE IN YOUR TEA, MR. TEDDY BEAR?
NOT ANSWERING YOUR HOSTESS IS RUDE.
BILGREY ROBERTS BLYBERG
THE REST OF YOU SEEM VERY WELL MANNERED...
...SO FAR.
9/13
WANNA PLAY A GAME?
OKAY, BUT I GET TO MAKE THE RULE.
DON'CHA MEAN RULES?
NOPE. THERE'S ONLY JUST ONE.
I'M UNDEFEATED WITH THE "I *WIN*" RULE.
KENT·ROBERTS·BLYBERG
9/14
I'M NEVER WRONG.
NEVER *EVER*?
THAT'S RIGHT.
DID YOU KNOW THAT ANGELICA IS NEVER WRONG?
HOW COULD I FORGET? SHE KEEPS TELLING US.
9/15
BILGREY·ROBERTS·BLYBERG

2001

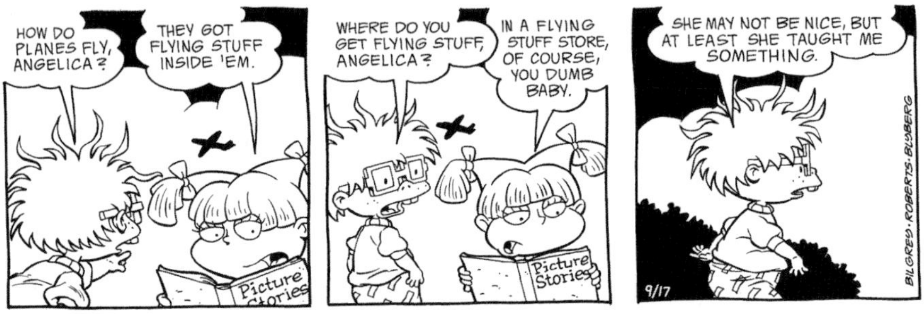
HOW DO PLANES FLY, ANGELICA?
THEY GOT FLYING STUFF INSIDE 'EM.
Picture Stories
WHERE DO YOU GET FLYING STUFF, ANGELICA?
IN A FLYING STUFF STORE, OF COURSE, YOU DUMB BABY.
Picture Stories
SHE MAY NOT BE NICE, BUT AT LEAST SHE TAUGHT ME SOMETHING.
9/17
BILGREY·ROBERTS·BLYBERG

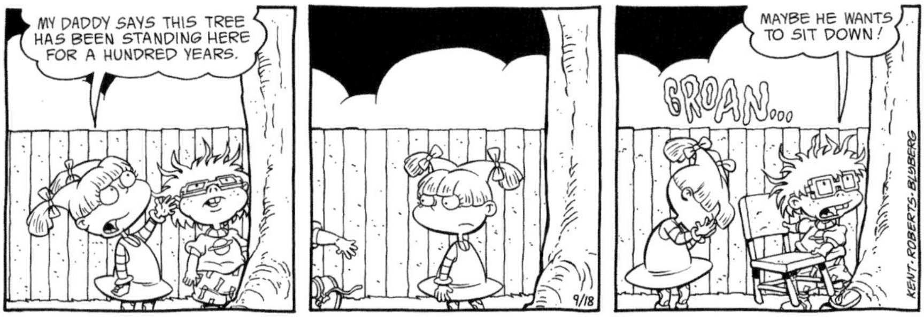
MY DADDY SAYS THIS TREE HAS BEEN STANDING HERE FOR A HUNDRED YEARS.
9/18
GROAN...
MAYBE HE WANTS TO SIT DOWN!
KENT·ROBERTS·BLYBERG

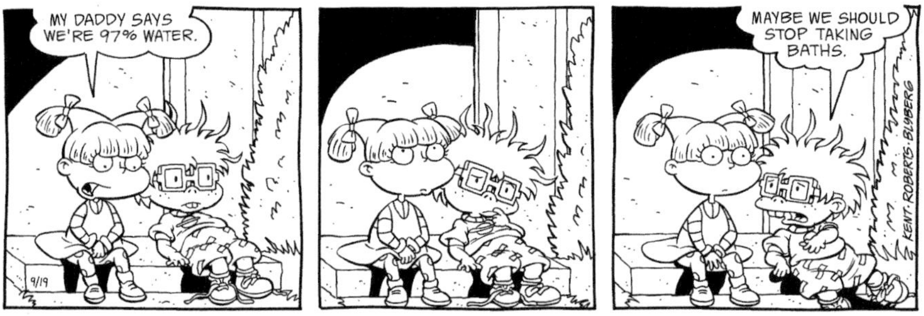
MY DADDY SAYS WE'RE 97% WATER.
9/19
MAYBE WE SHOULD STOP TAKING BATHS.
KENT·ROBERTS·BLYBERG

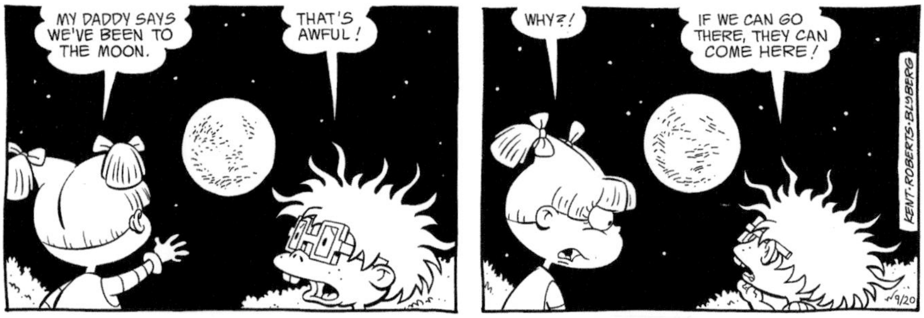
MY DADDY SAYS WE'VE BEEN TO THE MOON.
THAT'S AWFUL!
WHY?!
IF WE CAN GO THERE, THEY CAN COME HERE!
KENT·ROBERTS·BLYBERG
9/20

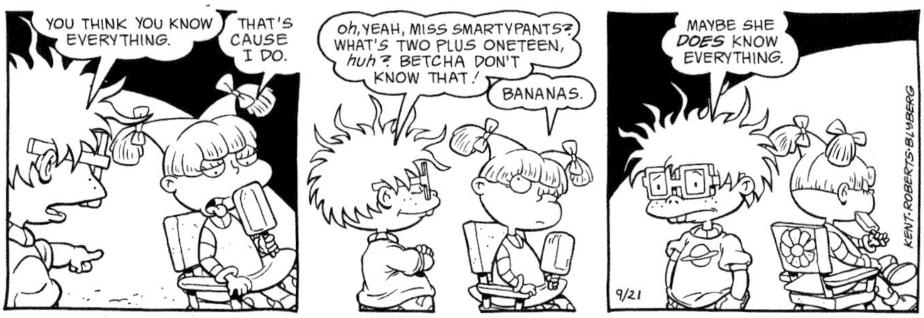
YOU THINK YOU KNOW EVERYTHING.
THAT'S CAUSE I DO.
oh, YEAH, MISS SMARTYPANTS? WHAT'S TWO PLUS ONETEEN, huh? BETCHA DON'T KNOW THAT!
BANANAS.
MAYBE SHE DOES KNOW EVERYTHING.
9/21
KENT·ROBERTS·BLYBERG

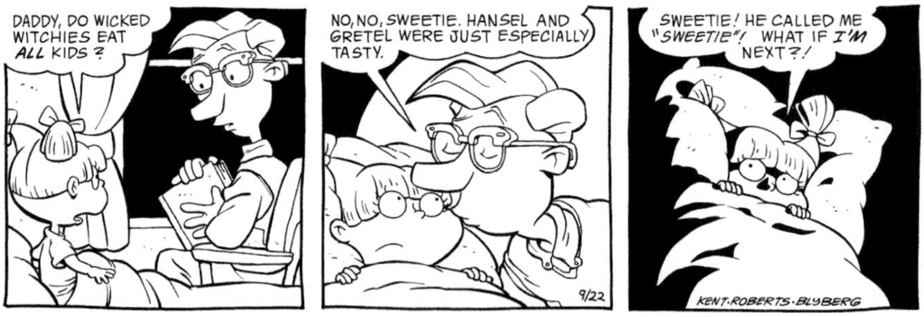
DADDY, DO WICKED WITCHIES EAT ALL KIDS?
NO, NO, SWEETIE. HANSEL AND GRETEL WERE JUST ESPECIALLY TASTY.
9/22
SWEETIE! HE CALLED ME "SWEETIE"! WHAT IF I'M NEXT?!
KENT·ROBERTS·BLYBERG

2001

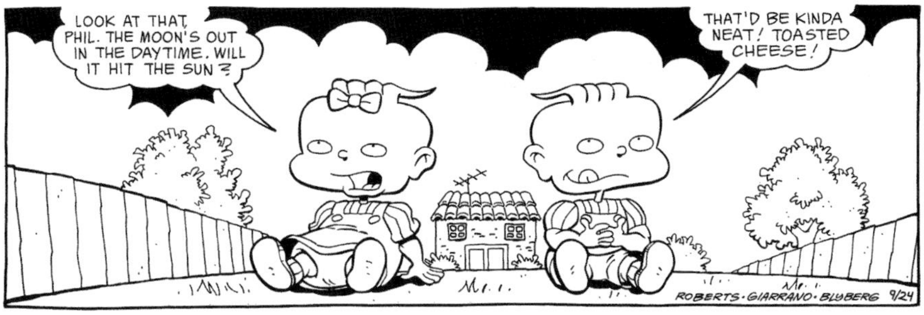
LOOK AT THAT, PHIL. THE MOON'S OUT IN THE DAYTIME. WILL IT HIT THE SUN?
THAT'D BE KINDA NEAT! TOASTED CHEESE!
ROBERTS·GIARRANO·BLYBERG 9/24

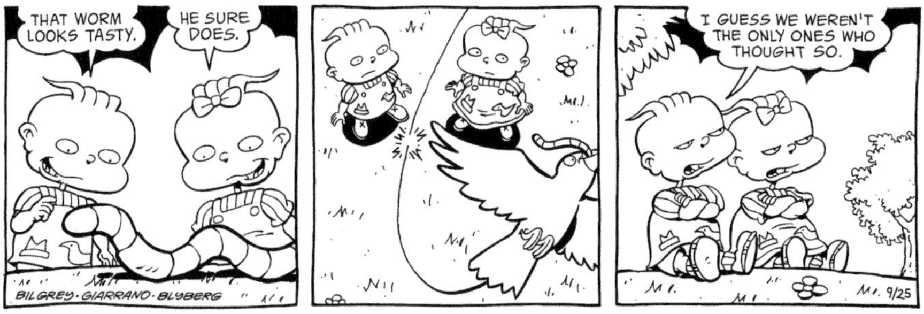
THAT WORM LOOKS TASTY.
HE SURE DOES.
BILGREY·GIARRANO·BLYBERG
I GUESS WE WEREN'T THE ONLY ONES WHO THOUGHT SO.
9/25

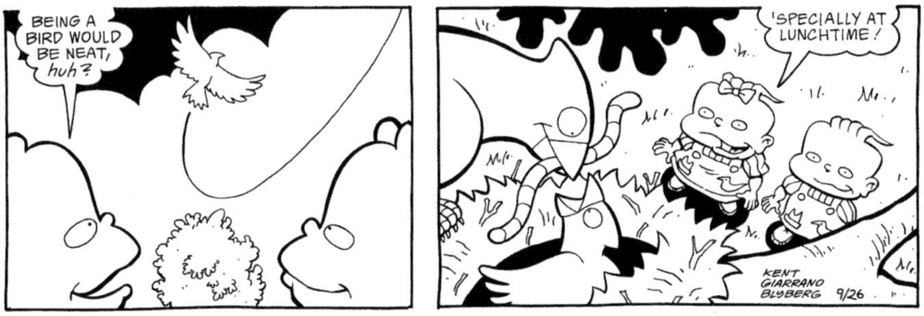
BEING A BIRD WOULD BE NEAT, *huh*?
'SPECIALLY AT LUNCHTIME!
KENT GIARRANO BLYBERG 9/26

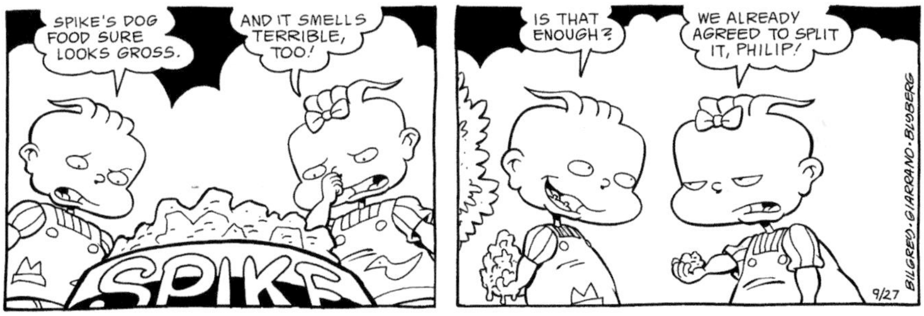
SPIKE'S DOG FOOD SURE LOOKS GROSS.
AND IT SMELLS TERRIBLE, TOO!
SPIKE
IS THAT ENOUGH?
WE ALREADY AGREED TO SPLIT IT, PHILIP!
BILGREY·GIARRANO·BLYBERG
9/27

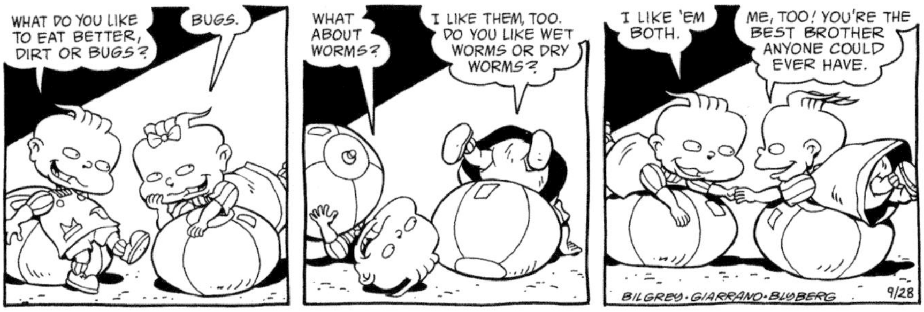
WHAT DO YOU LIKE TO EAT BETTER, DIRT OR BUGS?
BUGS.
WHAT ABOUT WORMS?
I LIKE THEM, TOO. DO YOU LIKE WET WORMS OR DRY WORMS?
I LIKE 'EM BOTH.
ME, TOO! YOU'RE THE BEST BROTHER ANYONE COULD EVER HAVE.
BILGREY·GIARRANO·BLYBERG 9/28

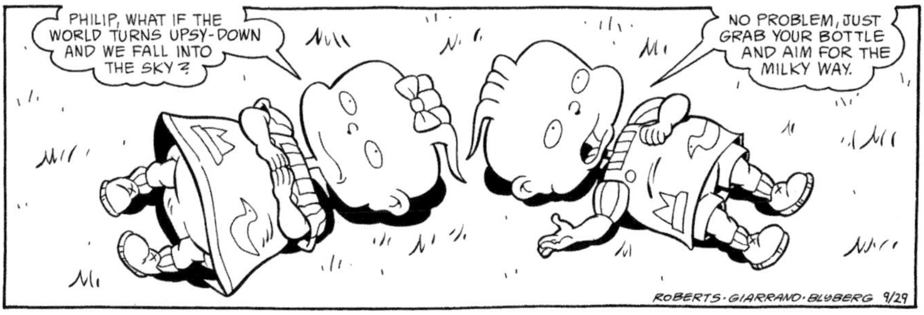
PHILIP, WHAT IF THE WORLD TURNS UPSY-DOWN AND WE FALL INTO THE SKY?
NO PROBLEM, JUST GRAB YOUR BOTTLE AND AIM FOR THE MILKY WAY.
ROBERTS·GIARRANO·BLYBERG 9/29

2001

2001

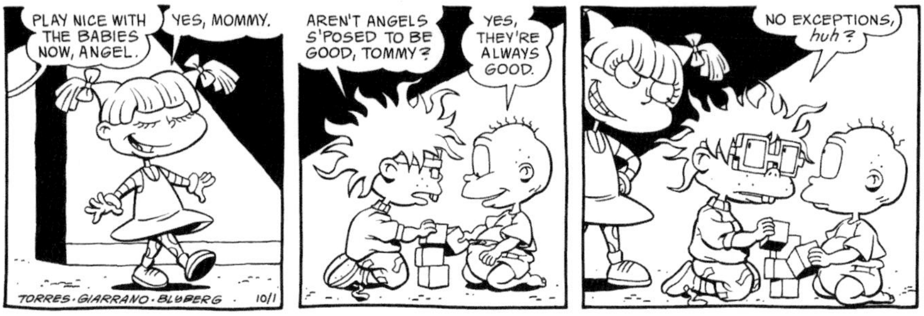
PLAY NICE WITH THE BABIES NOW, ANGEL.
YES, MOMMY.
TORRES · GIARRANO · BLYBERG 10/1
AREN'T ANGELS S'POSED TO BE GOOD, TOMMY?
YES, THEY'RE ALWAYS GOOD.
NO EXCEPTIONS, *huh*?

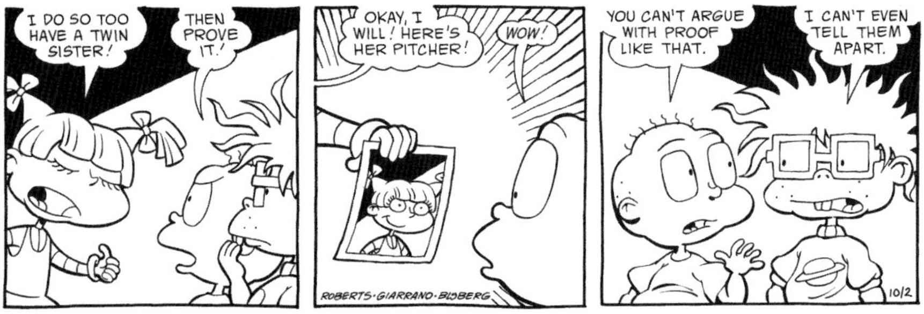
I DO SO TOO HAVE A TWIN SISTER!
THEN PROVE IT!
OKAY, I WILL! HERE'S HER PITCHER!
WOW!
ROBERTS · GIARRANO · BLYBERG
YOU CAN'T ARGUE WITH PROOF LIKE THAT.
I CAN'T EVEN TELL THEM APART.
10/2

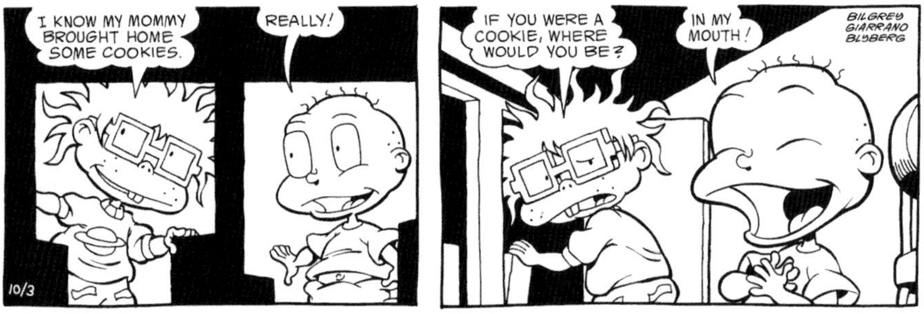
I KNOW MY MOMMY BROUGHT HOME SOME COOKIES.
REALLY!
10/3
IF YOU WERE A COOKIE, WHERE WOULD YOU BE?
IN MY MOUTH!
BILGREY GIARRANO BLYBERG

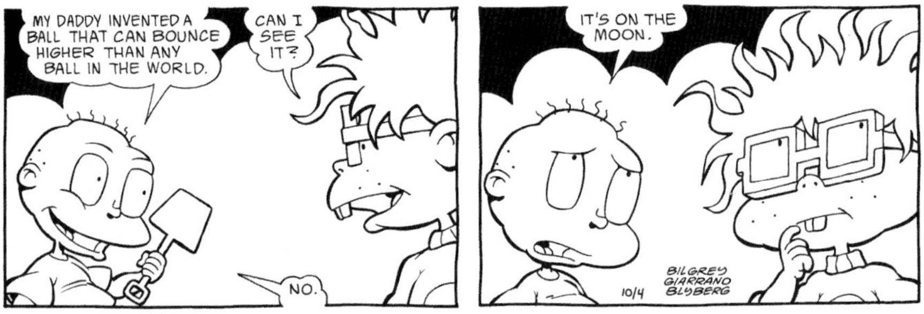
MY DADDY INVENTED A BALL THAT CAN BOUNCE HIGHER THAN ANY BALL IN THE WORLD.
CAN I SEE IT?
NO.
IT'S ON THE MOON.
BILGREY GIARRANO BLYBERG
10/4

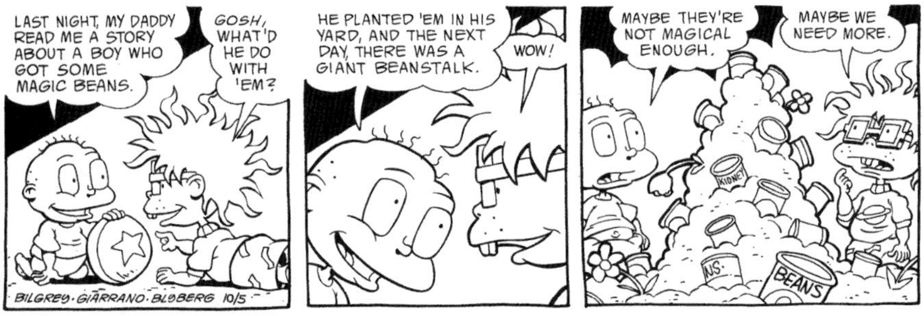
LAST NIGHT, MY DADDY READ ME A STORY ABOUT A BOY WHO GOT SOME MAGIC BEANS.
GOSH, WHAT'D HE DO WITH 'EM?
BILGREY · GIARRANO · BLYBERG 10/5
HE PLANTED 'EM IN HIS YARD, AND THE NEXT DAY, THERE WAS A GIANT BEANSTALK.
WOW!
MAYBE THEY'RE NOT MAGICAL ENOUGH.
MAYBE WE NEED MORE.
KIDNEY
BEANS

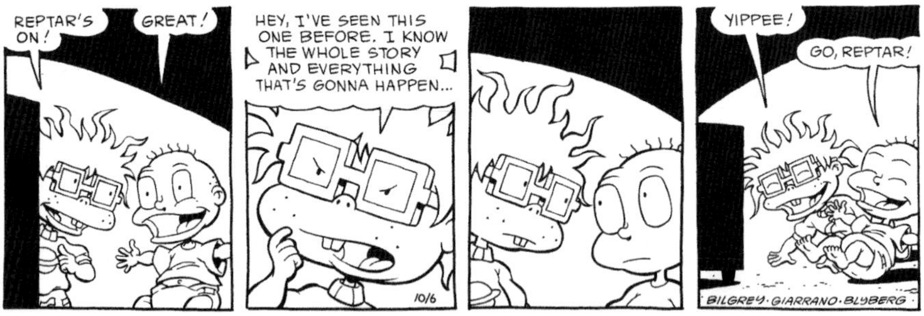
REPTAR'S ON!
GREAT!
HEY, I'VE SEEN THIS ONE BEFORE. I KNOW THE WHOLE STORY AND EVERYTHING THAT'S GONNA HAPPEN...
10/6
YIPPEE!
GO, REPTAR!
BILGREY · GIARRANO · BLYBERG

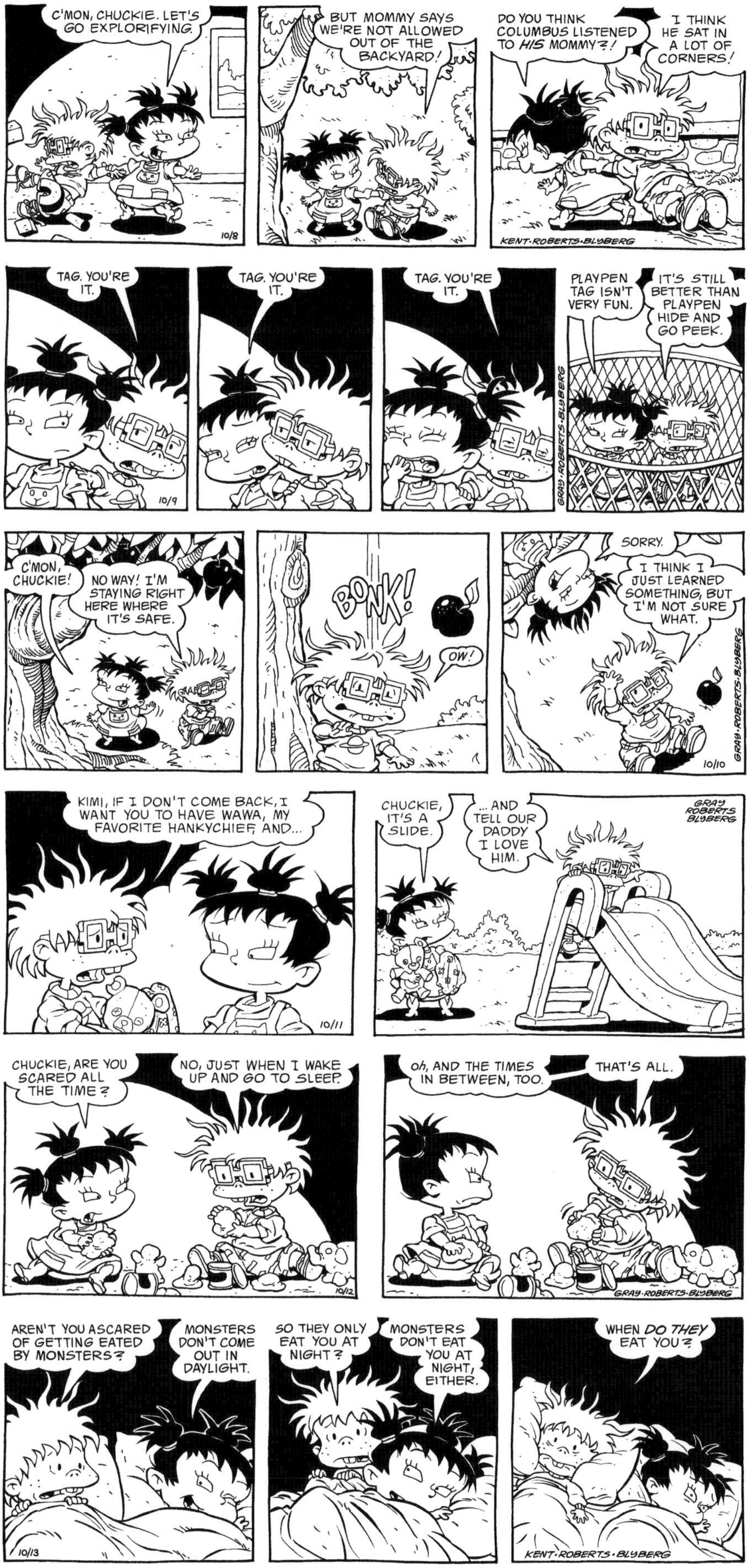
C'MON, CHUCKIE. LET'S GO EXPLORIFYING.
BUT MOMMY SAYS WE'RE NOT ALLOWED OUT OF THE BACKYARD!
DO YOU THINK COLUMBUS LISTENED TO HIS MOMMY?!
I THINK HE SAT IN A LOT OF CORNERS!
10/8
KENT·ROBERTS·BLYBERG
TAG. YOU'RE IT.
TAG. YOU'RE IT.
TAG. YOU'RE IT.
PLAYPEN TAG ISN'T VERY FUN.
IT'S STILL BETTER THAN PLAYPEN HIDE AND GO PEEK.
10/9
GRAY·ROBERTS·BLYBERG
C'MON, CHUCKIE!
NO WAY! I'M STAYING RIGHT HERE WHERE IT'S SAFE.
BONK!
OW!
SORRY.
I THINK I JUST LEARNED SOMETHING, BUT I'M NOT SURE WHAT.
10/10
GRAY·ROBERTS·BLYBERG
KIMI, IF I DON'T COME BACK, I WANT YOU TO HAVE WAWA, MY FAVORITE HANKYCHIEF, AND...
10/11
CHUCKIE, IT'S A SLIDE.
...AND TELL OUR DADDY I LOVE HIM.
GRAY ROBERTS BLYBERG
CHUCKIE, ARE YOU SCARED ALL THE TIME?
NO, JUST WHEN I WAKE UP AND GO TO SLEEP.
10/12
oh, AND THE TIMES IN BETWEEN, TOO.
THAT'S ALL.
GRAY·ROBERTS·BLYBERG
AREN'T YOU ASCARED OF GETTING EATED BY MONSTERS?
MONSTERS DON'T COME OUT IN DAYLIGHT.
10/13
SO THEY ONLY EAT YOU AT NIGHT?
MONSTERS DON'T EAT YOU AT NIGHT, EITHER.
WHEN DO THEY EAT YOU?
KENT·ROBERTS·BLYBERG

2001

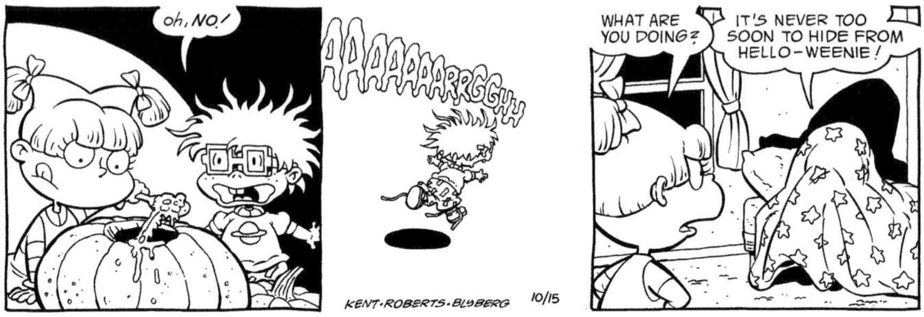
oh, NO!
AAAAAAAARRGGHH
WHAT ARE YOU DOING?
IT'S NEVER TOO SOON TO HIDE FROM HELLO-WEENIE!
KENT·ROBERTS·BLYBERG
10/15

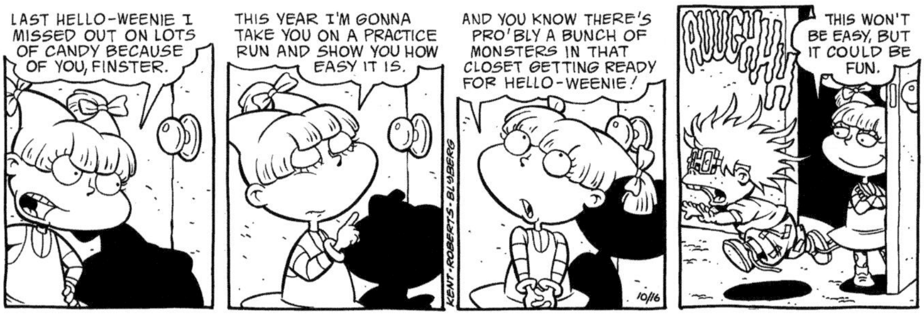
LAST HELLO-WEENIE I MISSED OUT ON LOTS OF CANDY BECAUSE OF YOU, FINSTER.
THIS YEAR I'M GONNA TAKE YOU ON A PRACTICE RUN AND SHOW YOU HOW EASY IT IS.
AND YOU KNOW THERE'S PRO'BLY A BUNCH OF MONSTERS IN THAT CLOSET GETTING READY FOR HELLO-WEENIE!
AUUGHHH
THIS WON'T BE EASY, BUT IT COULD BE FUN.
KENT·ROBERTS·BLYBERG
10/16

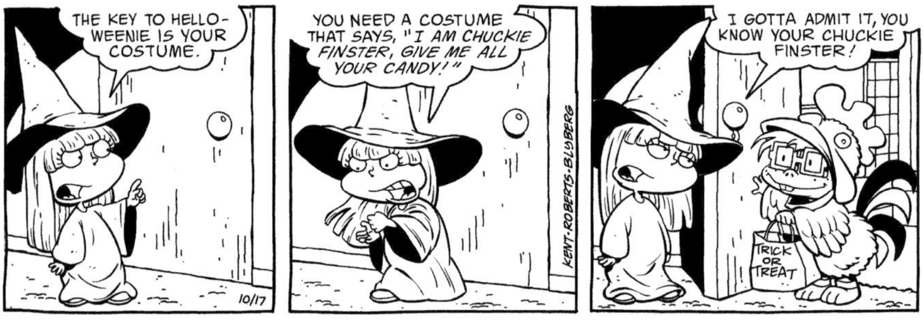
THE KEY TO HELLO-WEENIE IS YOUR COSTUME.
YOU NEED A COSTUME THAT SAYS, "I AM CHUCKIE FINSTER, GIVE ME ALL YOUR CANDY!"
I GOTTA ADMIT IT, YOU KNOW YOUR CHUCKIE FINSTER!
TRICK OR TREAT
KENT·ROBERTS·BLYBERG
10/17

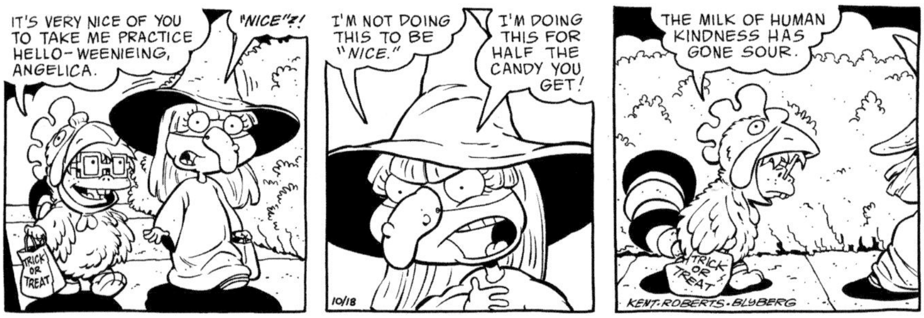
IT'S VERY NICE OF YOU TO TAKE ME PRACTICE HELLO-WEENIEING, ANGELICA.
"NICE"?!
I'M NOT DOING THIS TO BE "NICE."
I'M DOING THIS FOR HALF THE CANDY YOU GET!
THE MILK OF HUMAN KINDNESS HAS GONE SOUR.
TRICK OR TREAT
KENT·ROBERTS·BLYBERG
10/18

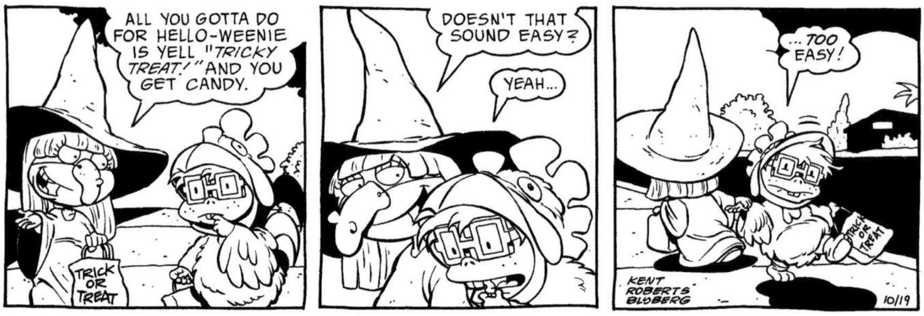
ALL YOU GOTTA DO FOR HELLO-WEENIE IS YELL "TRICKY TREAT!" AND YOU GET CANDY.
DOESN'T THAT SOUND EASY?
YEAH...
...TOO EASY!
TRICK OR TREAT
KENT ROBERTS BLYBERG
10/19

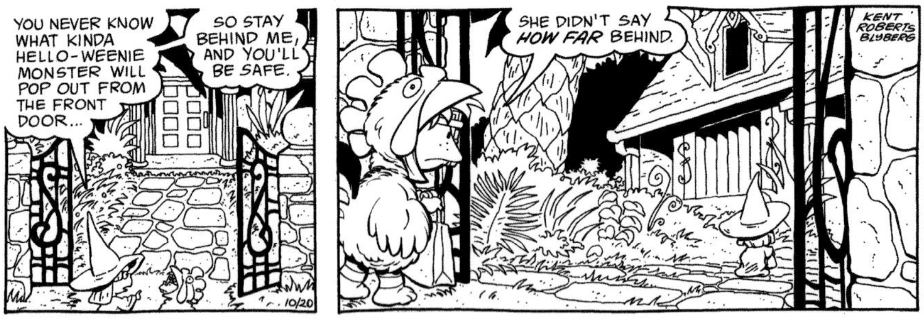
YOU NEVER KNOW WHAT KINDA HELLO-WEENIE MONSTER WILL POP OUT FROM THE FRONT DOOR...
SO STAY BEHIND ME, AND YOU'LL BE SAFE.
SHE DIDN'T SAY HOW FAR BEHIND.
KENT ROBERTS BLYBERG
10/20

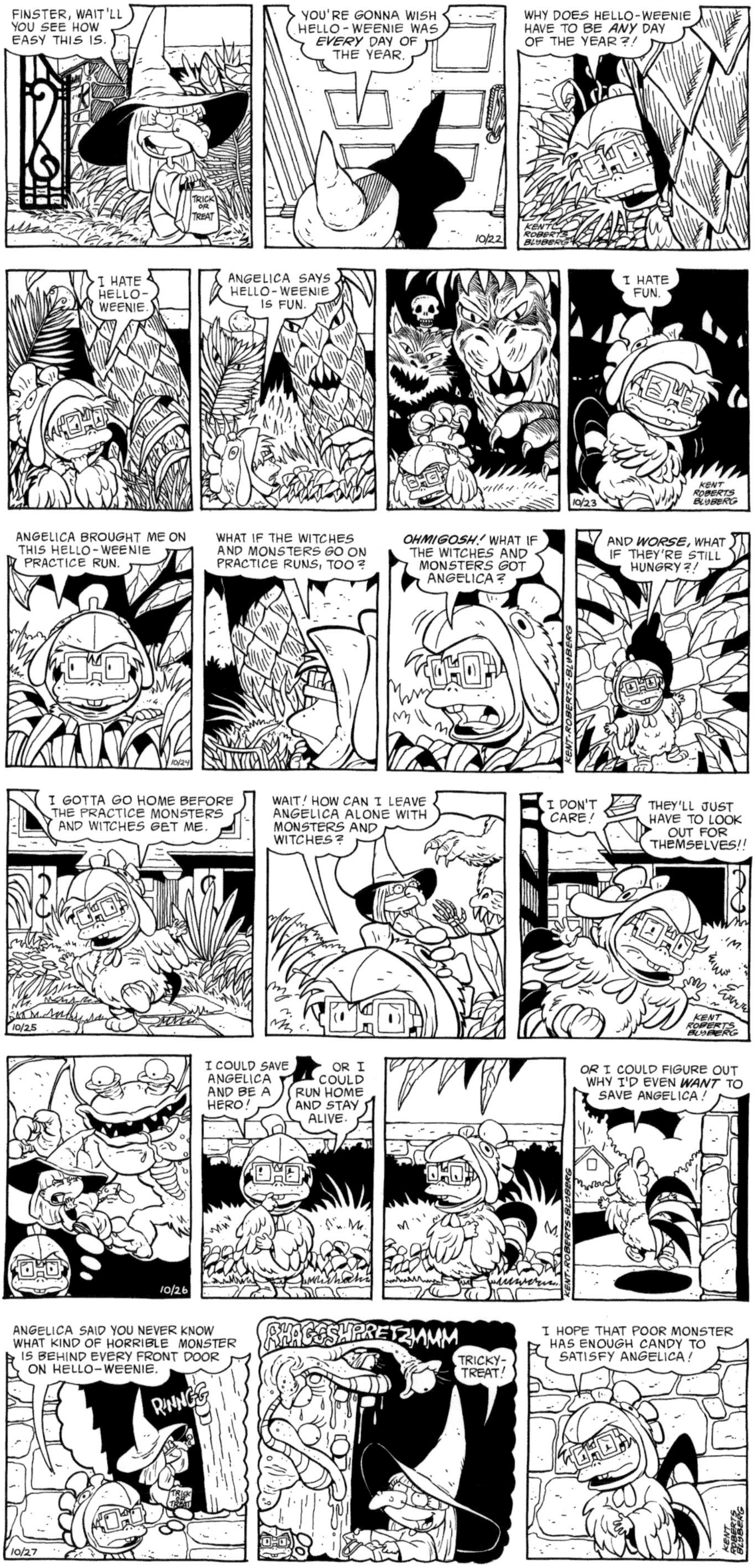

FINSTER, WAIT'LL YOU SEE HOW EASY THIS IS.
TRICK OR TREAT
YOU'RE GONNA WISH HELLO-WEENIE WAS EVERY DAY OF THE YEAR.
10/22
WHY DOES HELLO-WEENIE HAVE TO BE ANY DAY OF THE YEAR?!
KENT ROBERTS BLYBERG
I HATE HELLO-WEENIE.
ANGELICA SAYS HELLO-WEENIE IS FUN.
I HATE FUN.
10/23
KENT ROBERTS BLYBERG
ANGELICA BROUGHT ME ON THIS HELLO-WEENIE PRACTICE RUN.
10/24
WHAT IF THE WITCHES AND MONSTERS GO ON PRACTICE RUNS, TOO?
OHMIGOSH! WHAT IF THE WITCHES AND MONSTERS GOT ANGELICA?
KENT-ROBERTS-BLYBERG
AND WORSE, WHAT IF THEY'RE STILL HUNGRY?!
I GOTTA GO HOME BEFORE THE PRACTICE MONSTERS AND WITCHES GET ME.
10/25
WAIT! HOW CAN I LEAVE ANGELICA ALONE WITH MONSTERS AND WITCHES?
I DON'T CARE!
THEY'LL JUST HAVE TO LOOK OUT FOR THEMSELVES!!
KENT ROBERTS BLYBERG
10/26
I COULD SAVE ANGELICA AND BE A HERO!
OR I COULD RUN HOME AND STAY ALIVE.
KENT-ROBERTS-BLYBERG
OR I COULD FIGURE OUT WHY I'D EVEN WANT TO SAVE ANGELICA!
ANGELICA SAID YOU NEVER KNOW WHAT KIND OF HORRIBLE MONSTER IS BEHIND EVERY FRONT DOOR ON HELLO-WEENIE.
RINNGG
TRICK OR TREAT
10/27
BHAGGSHPRETZAMM
TRICKY-TREAT!
I HOPE THAT POOR MONSTER HAS ENOUGH CANDY TO SATISFY ANGELICA!
KENT ROBERTS BLYBERG

2001

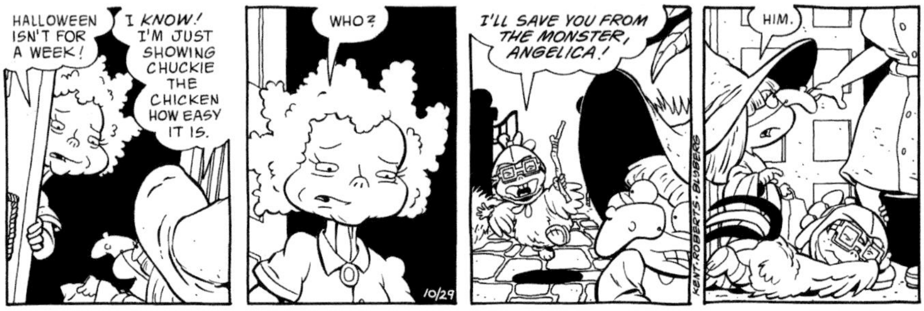
HALLOWEEN ISN'T FOR A WEEK!
I *KNOW*! I'M JUST SHOWING CHUCKIE THE CHICKEN HOW EASY IT IS.
WHO?
I'LL SAVE YOU FROM THE MONSTER, ANGELICA!
HIM.
KENT·ROBERTS·BLYBERG
10/29

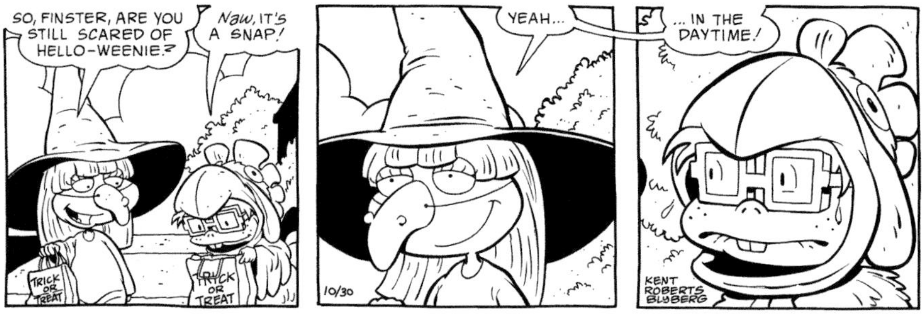
SO, FINSTER, ARE YOU STILL SCARED OF HELLO-WEENIE?
NAW, IT'S A SNAP!
TRICK OR TREAT
TRICK OR TREAT
YEAH...
... IN THE DAYTIME!
10/30
KENT ROBERTS BLYBERG

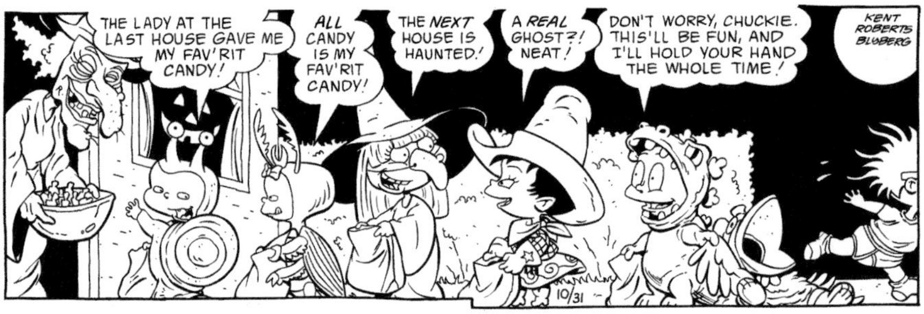
THE LADY AT THE LAST HOUSE GAVE ME MY FAV'RIT CANDY!
ALL CANDY IS MY FAV'RIT CANDY!
THE *NEXT* HOUSE IS HAUNTED!
A *REAL* GHOST?! NEAT!
DON'T WORRY, CHUCKIE. THIS'LL BE FUN, AND I'LL HOLD YOUR HAND THE WHOLE TIME!
KENT ROBERTS BLYBERG
10/31

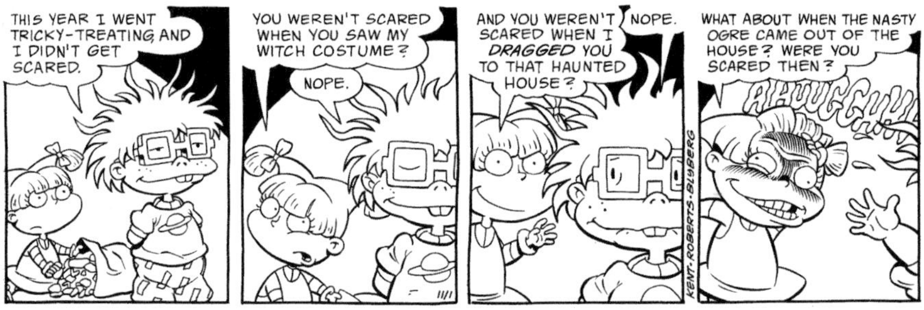
THIS YEAR I WENT TRICKY-TREATING AND I DIDN'T GET SCARED.
YOU WEREN'T SCARED WHEN YOU SAW MY WITCH COSTUME?
NOPE.
AND YOU WEREN'T SCARED WHEN I *DRAGGED* YOU TO THAT HAUNTED HOUSE?
NOPE.
WHAT ABOUT WHEN THE NASTY OGRE CAME OUT OF THE HOUSE? WERE YOU SCARED THEN?
AHUUGGHH
11/1
KENT·ROBERTS·BLYBERG

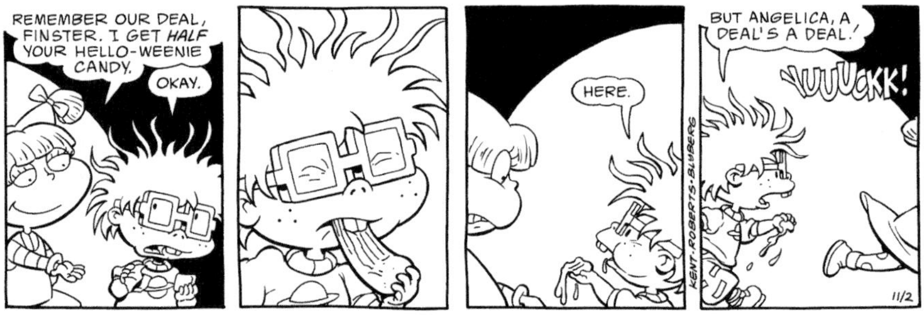
REMEMBER OUR DEAL, FINSTER. I GET *HALF* YOUR HELLO-WEENIE CANDY.
OKAY.
HERE.
KENT·ROBERTS·BLYBERG
BUT ANGELICA, A DEAL'S A DEAL!
YUUUCKK!
11/2

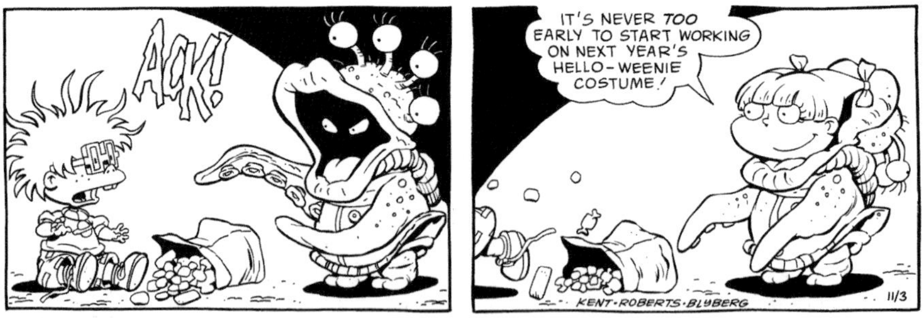
ACK!
IT'S NEVER *TOO* EARLY TO START WORKING ON NEXT YEAR'S HELLO-WEENIE COSTUME!
KENT·ROBERTS·BLYBERG
11/3

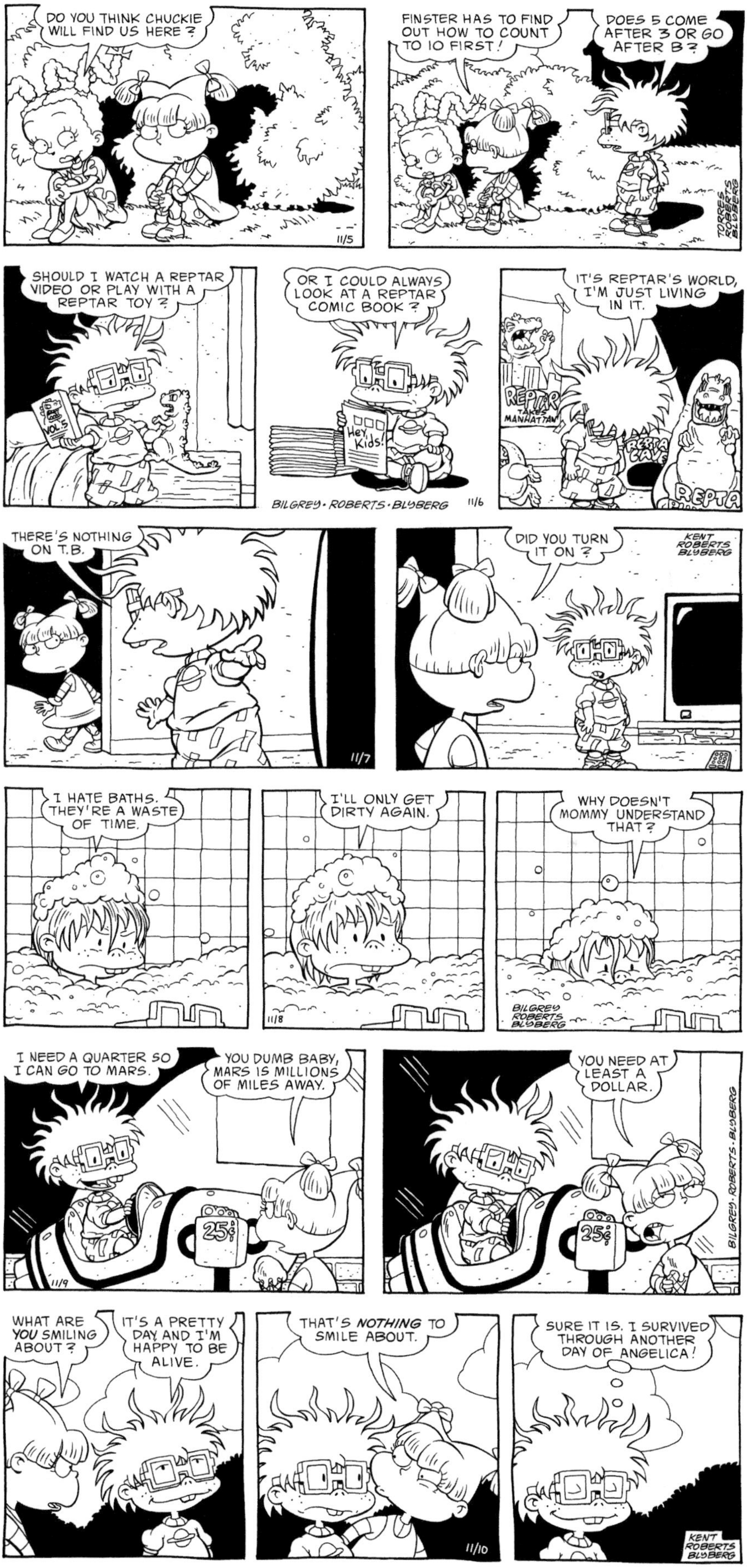
DO YOU THINK CHUCKIE WILL FIND US HERE?
11/5
FINSTER HAS TO FIND OUT HOW TO COUNT TO 10 FIRST!
DOES 5 COME AFTER 3 OR GO AFTER B?
TORRES ROBERTS BLYBERG
SHOULD I WATCH A REPTAR VIDEO OR PLAY WITH A REPTAR TOY?
VOL. 5
OR I COULD ALWAYS LOOK AT A REPTAR COMIC BOOK?
Hey Kids!
IT'S REPTAR'S WORLD, I'M JUST LIVING IN IT.
REPTAR TAKES MANHATTAN
BILGREY · ROBERTS · BLYBERG
11/6
THERE'S NOTHING ON T.B.
11/7
DID YOU TURN IT ON?
KENT ROBERTS BLYBERG
I HATE BATHS. THEY'RE A WASTE OF TIME.
I'LL ONLY GET DIRTY AGAIN.
11/8
WHY DOESN'T MOMMY UNDERSTAND THAT?
BILGREY ROBERTS BLYBERG
I NEED A QUARTER SO I CAN GO TO MARS.
YOU DUMB BABY, MARS IS MILLIONS OF MILES AWAY.
25¢
11/9
YOU NEED AT LEAST A DOLLAR.
25¢
BILGREY · ROBERTS · BLYBERG
WHAT ARE YOU SMILING ABOUT?
IT'S A PRETTY DAY AND I'M HAPPY TO BE ALIVE.
THAT'S NOTHING TO SMILE ABOUT.
11/10
SURE IT IS. I SURVIVED THROUGH ANOTHER DAY OF ANGELICA!
KENT ROBERTS BLYBERG

2001

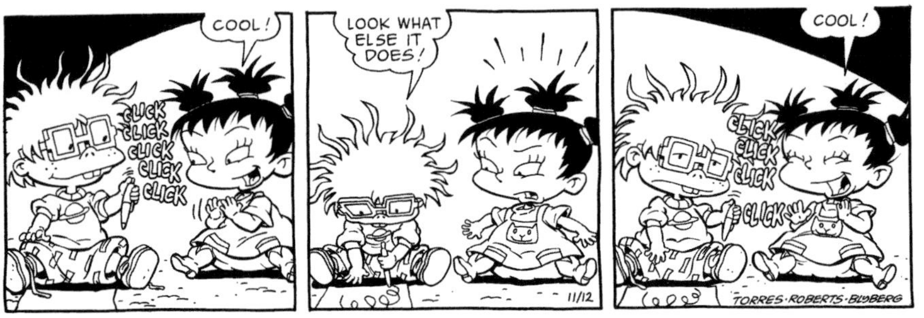
COOL!
CLICK
CLICK
CLICK
CLICK
CLICK
LOOK WHAT ELSE IT DOES!
11/12
COOL!
CLICK
CLICK
CLICK
CLICK
TORRES·ROBERTS·BLYBERG

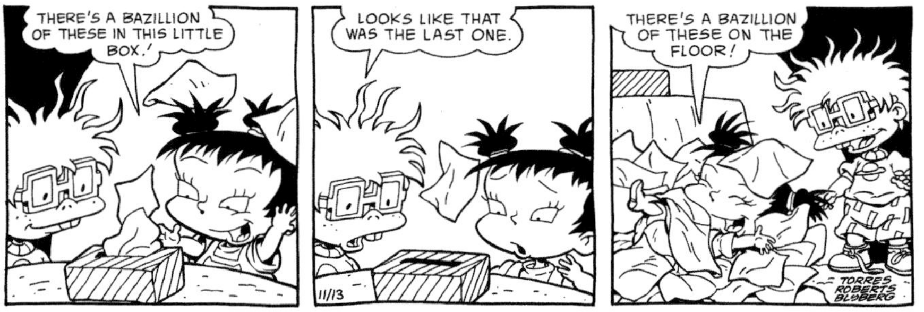
THERE'S A BAZILLION OF THESE IN THIS LITTLE BOX!
LOOKS LIKE THAT WAS THE LAST ONE.
11/13
THERE'S A BAZILLION OF THESE ON THE FLOOR!
TORRES ROBERTS BLYBERG

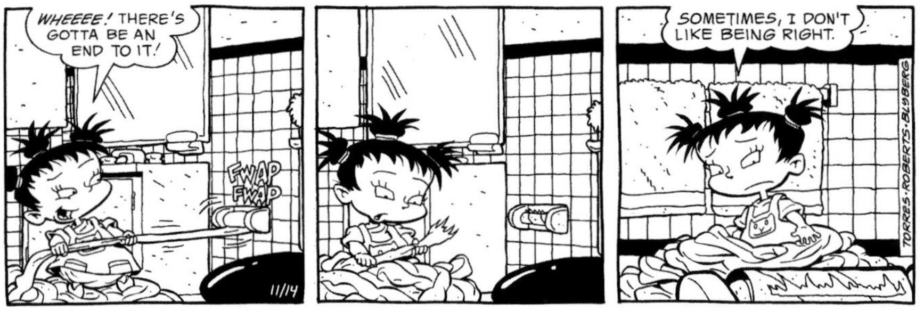
WHEEEE! THERE'S GOTTA BE AN END TO IT!
FWAP
FWAP
11/14
SOMETIMES, I DON'T LIKE BEING RIGHT.
TORRES·ROBERTS·BLYBERG

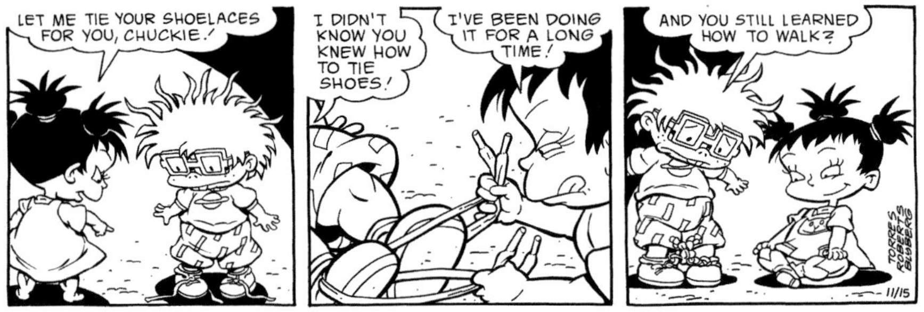
LET ME TIE YOUR SHOELACES FOR YOU, CHUCKIE!
I DIDN'T KNOW YOU KNEW HOW TO TIE SHOES!
I'VE BEEN DOING IT FOR A LONG TIME!
AND YOU STILL LEARNED HOW TO WALK?
TORRES ROBERTS BLYBERG
11/15

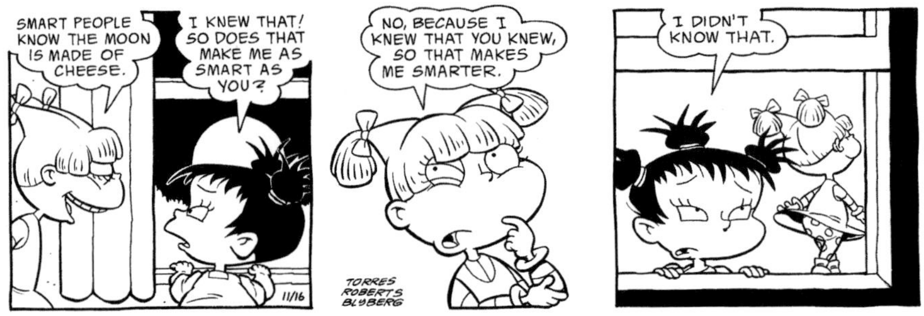
SMART PEOPLE KNOW THE MOON IS MADE OF CHEESE.
I KNEW THAT! SO DOES THAT MAKE ME AS SMART AS YOU?
11/16
NO, BECAUSE I KNEW THAT YOU KNEW, SO THAT MAKES ME SMARTER.
TORRES ROBERTS BLYBERG
I DIDN'T KNOW THAT.

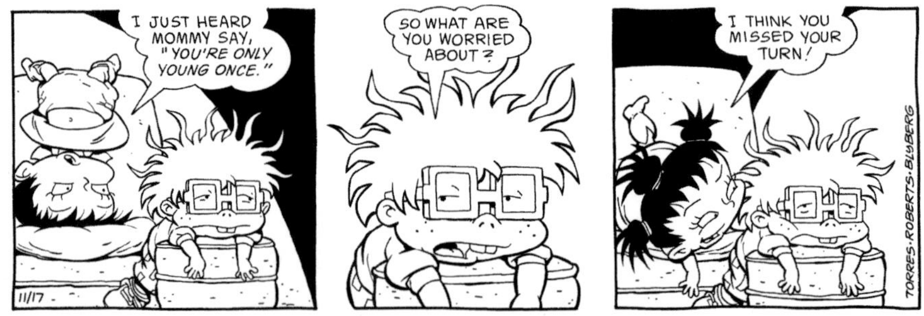
I JUST HEARD MOMMY SAY, "YOU'RE ONLY YOUNG ONCE."
11/17
SO WHAT ARE YOU WORRIED ABOUT?
I THINK YOU MISSED YOUR TURN!
TORRES·ROBERTS·BLYBERG

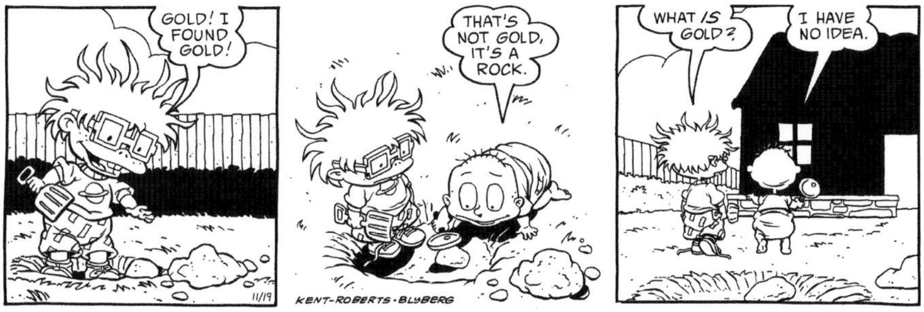
GOLD! I FOUND GOLD!
11/19
THAT'S NOT GOLD, IT'S A ROCK.
KENT-ROBERTS-BLYBERG
WHAT IS GOLD?
I HAVE NO IDEA.

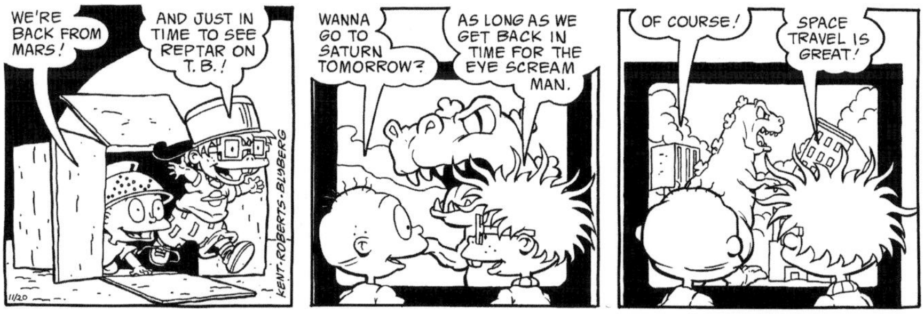
WE'RE BACK FROM MARS!
AND JUST IN TIME TO SEE REPTAR ON T.B.!
KENT-ROBERTS-BLYBERG
11/20
WANNA GO TO SATURN TOMORROW?
AS LONG AS WE GET BACK IN TIME FOR THE EYE SCREAM MAN.
OF COURSE!
SPACE TRAVEL IS GREAT!

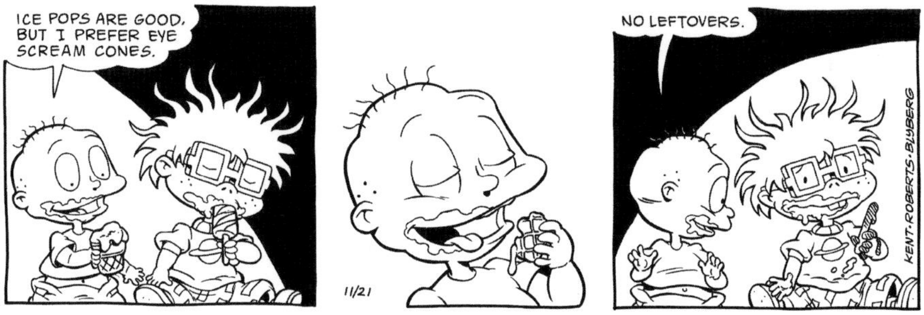
ICE POPS ARE GOOD, BUT I PREFER EYE SCREAM CONES.
11/21
NO LEFTOVERS.
KENT-ROBERTS-BLYBERG

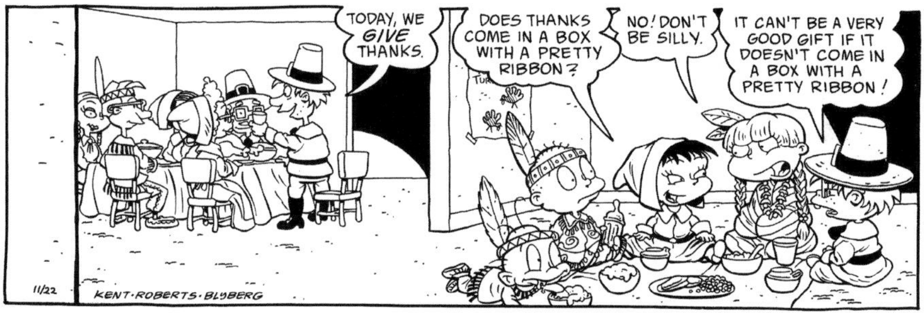
11/22
KENT-ROBERTS-BLYBERG
TODAY, WE GIVE THANKS.
DOES THANKS COME IN A BOX WITH A PRETTY RIBBON?
NO! DON'T BE SILLY.
IT CAN'T BE A VERY GOOD GIFT IF IT DOESN'T COME IN A BOX WITH A PRETTY RIBBON!

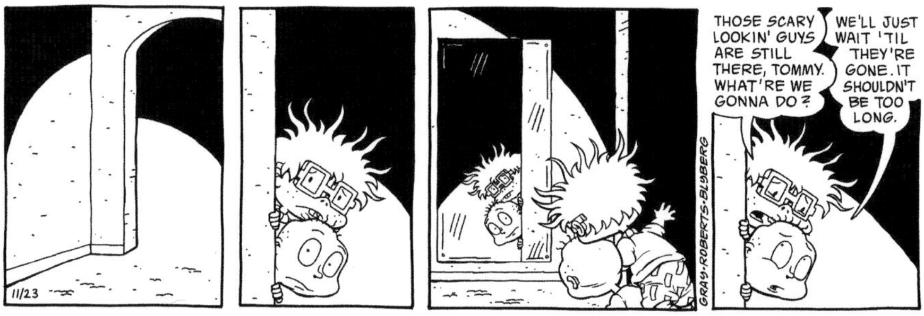
11/23
GRAY-ROBERTS-BLYBERG
THOSE SCARY LOOKIN' GUYS ARE STILL THERE, TOMMY. WHAT'RE WE GONNA DO?
WE'LL JUST WAIT 'TIL THEY'RE GONE. IT SHOULDN'T BE TOO LONG.

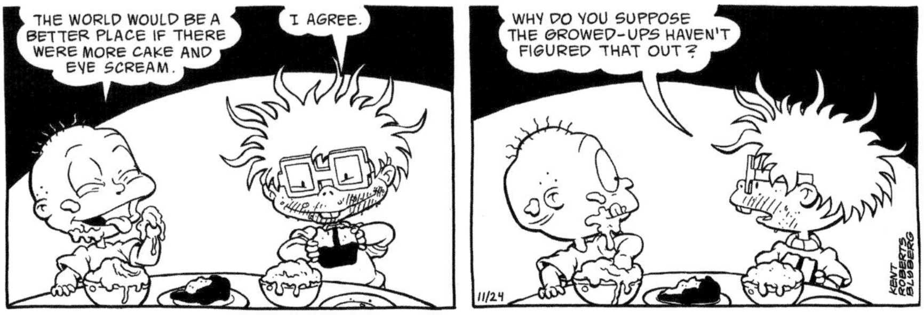
THE WORLD WOULD BE A BETTER PLACE IF THERE WERE MORE CAKE AND EYE SCREAM.
I AGREE.
WHY DO YOU SUPPOSE THE GROWED-UPS HAVEN'T FIGURED THAT OUT?
11/24
KENT ROBERTS BLYBERG

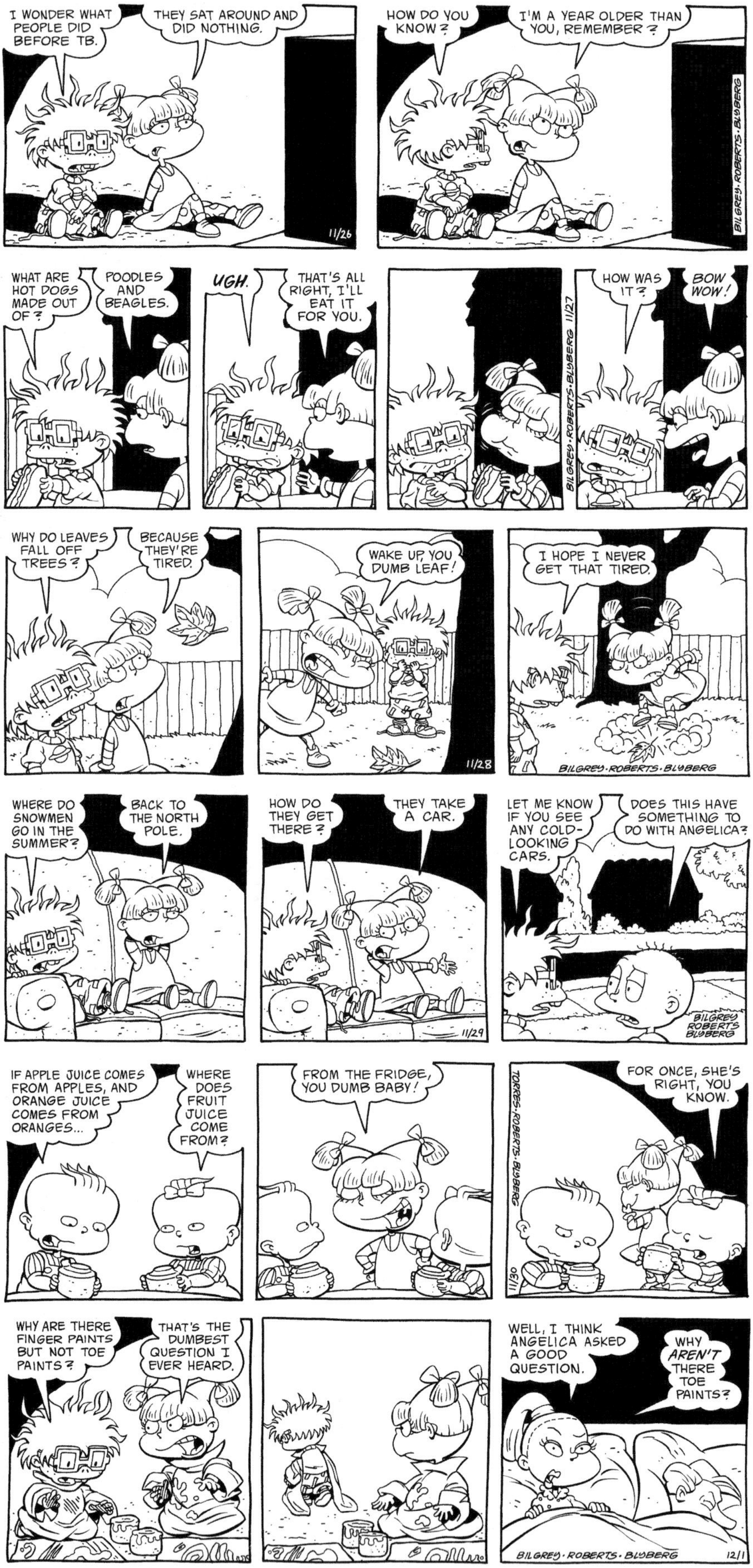
I WONDER WHAT PEOPLE DID BEFORE TB.
THEY SAT AROUND AND DID NOTHING.
11/26
HOW DO YOU KNOW?
I'M A YEAR OLDER THAN YOU, REMEMBER?
BILGREY·ROBERTS·BLYBERG
WHAT ARE HOT DOGS MADE OUT OF?
POODLES AND BEAGLES.
UGH.
THAT'S ALL RIGHT, I'LL EAT IT FOR YOU.
BILGREY·ROBERTS·BLYBERG 11/27
HOW WAS IT?
BOW WOW!
WHY DO LEAVES FALL OFF TREES?
BECAUSE THEY'RE TIRED.
WAKE UP, YOU DUMB LEAF!
11/28
I HOPE I NEVER GET THAT TIRED.
BILGREY·ROBERTS·BLYBERG
WHERE DO SNOWMEN GO IN THE SUMMER?
BACK TO THE NORTH POLE.
HOW DO THEY GET THERE?
THEY TAKE A CAR.
11/29
LET ME KNOW IF YOU SEE ANY COLD-LOOKING CARS.
DOES THIS HAVE SOMETHING TO DO WITH ANGELICA?
BILGREY ROBERTS BLYBERG
IF APPLE JUICE COMES FROM APPLES, AND ORANGE JUICE COMES FROM ORANGES...
WHERE DOES FRUIT JUICE COME FROM?
FROM THE FRIDGE, YOU DUMB BABY!
TORRES·ROBERTS·BLYBERG
11/30
FOR ONCE, SHE'S RIGHT, YOU KNOW.
WHY ARE THERE FINGER PAINTS BUT NOT TOE PAINTS?
THAT'S THE DUMBEST QUESTION I EVER HEARD.
WELL, I THINK ANGELICA ASKED A GOOD QUESTION.
WHY AREN'T THERE TOE PAINTS?
BILGREY·ROBERTS·BLYBERG
12/1

2001

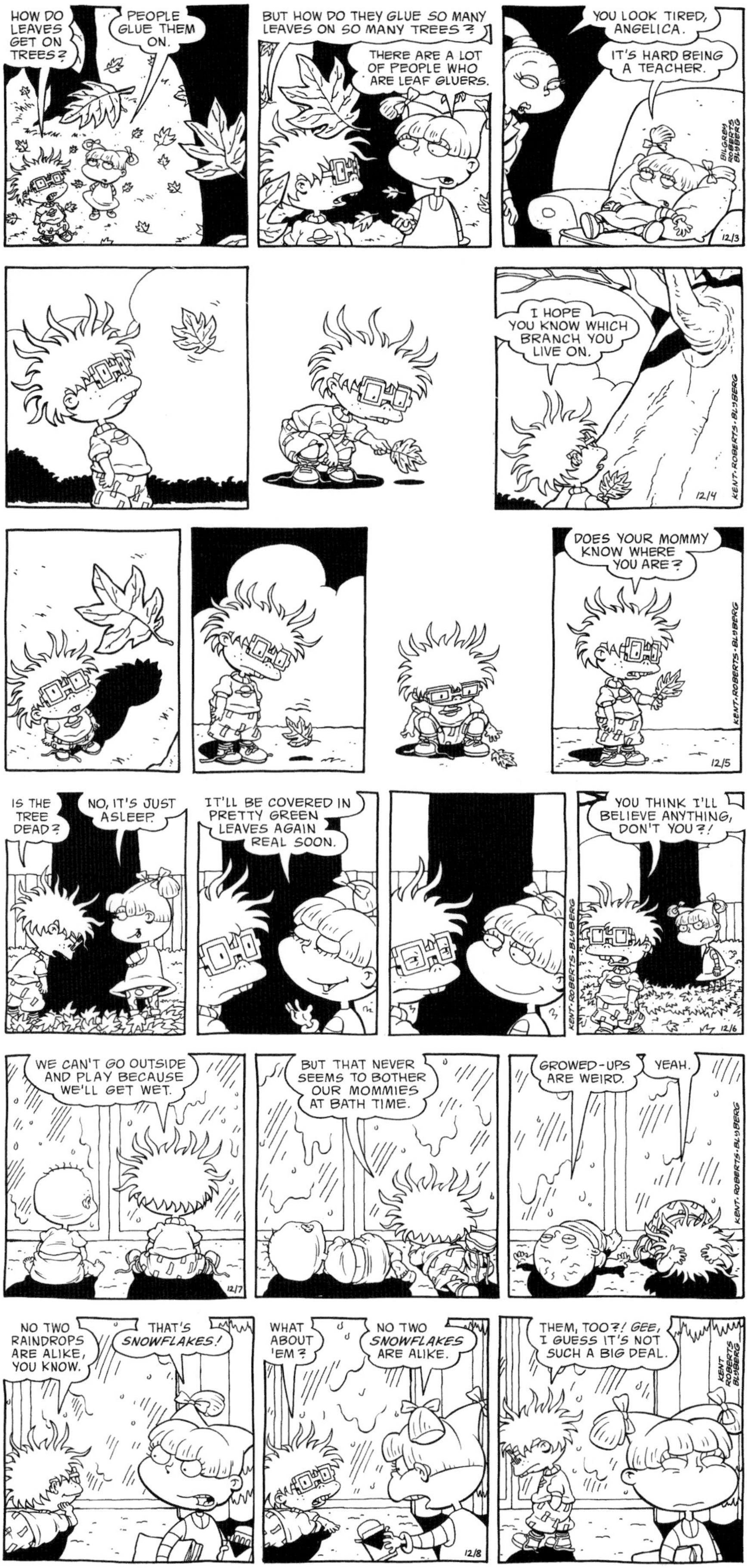
HOW DO LEAVES GET ON TREES?
PEOPLE GLUE THEM ON.
BUT HOW DO THEY GLUE *SO* MANY LEAVES ON SO MANY TREES?
THERE ARE A LOT OF PEOPLE WHO ARE LEAF GLUERS.
YOU LOOK TIRED, ANGELICA.
IT'S HARD BEING A TEACHER.
BILGREY ROBERTS BLYBERG
12/3
I HOPE YOU KNOW WHICH BRANCH YOU LIVE ON.
12/4
KENT·ROBERTS·BLYBERG
DOES YOUR MOMMY KNOW WHERE YOU ARE?
KENT·ROBERTS·BLYBERG
12/5
IS THE TREE DEAD?
NO, IT'S JUST ASLEEP.
IT'LL BE COVERED IN PRETTY GREEN LEAVES AGAIN REAL SOON.
KENT·ROBERTS·BLYBERG
YOU THINK I'LL BELIEVE ANYTHING, DON'T YOU?!
12/6
WE CAN'T GO OUTSIDE AND PLAY BECAUSE WE'LL GET WET.
12/7
BUT THAT NEVER SEEMS TO BOTHER OUR MOMMIES AT BATH TIME.
GROWED-UPS ARE WEIRD.
YEAH.
KENT·ROBERTS·BLYBERG
NO TWO RAINDROPS ARE ALIKE, YOU KNOW.
THAT'S *SNOWFLAKES!*
WHAT ABOUT 'EM?
NO TWO *SNOWFLAKES* ARE ALIKE.
12/8
THEM, TOO?! *GEE,* I GUESS IT'S NOT SUCH A BIG DEAL.
KENT ROBERTS BLYBERG

2001

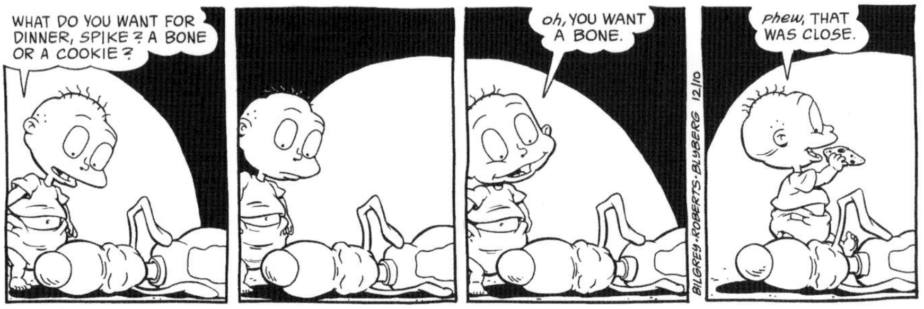
WHAT DO YOU WANT FOR DINNER, SPIKE? A BONE OR A COOKIE?
oh, YOU WANT A BONE.
phew, THAT WAS CLOSE.
BILGREY·ROBERTS·BLYBERG 12/10

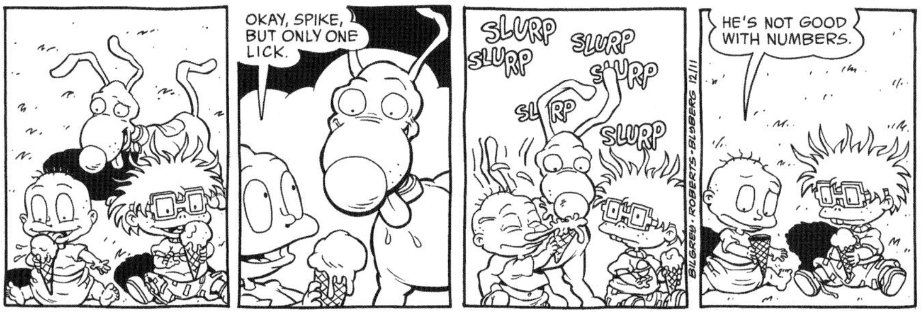
OKAY, SPIKE, BUT ONLY ONE LICK.
SLURP
SLURP
SLURP
SLURP
SLURP
SLURP
BILGREY·ROBERTS·BLYBERG 12/11
HE'S NOT GOOD WITH NUMBERS.

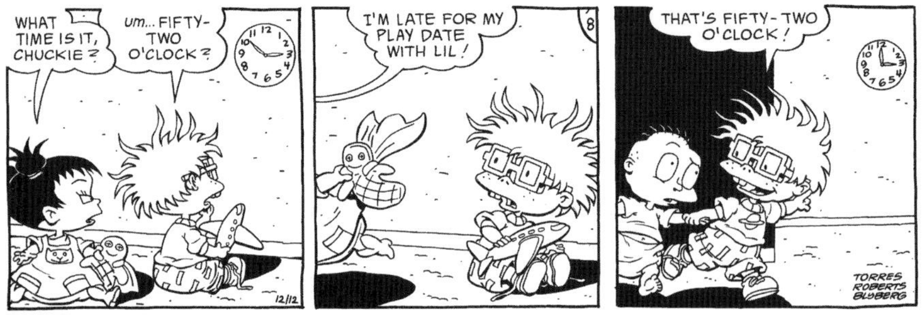
WHAT TIME IS IT, CHUCKIE?
um... FIFTY-TWO O'CLOCK?
12/12
I'M LATE FOR MY PLAY DATE WITH LIL!
THAT'S FIFTY-TWO O'CLOCK!
TORRES ROBERTS BLYBERG

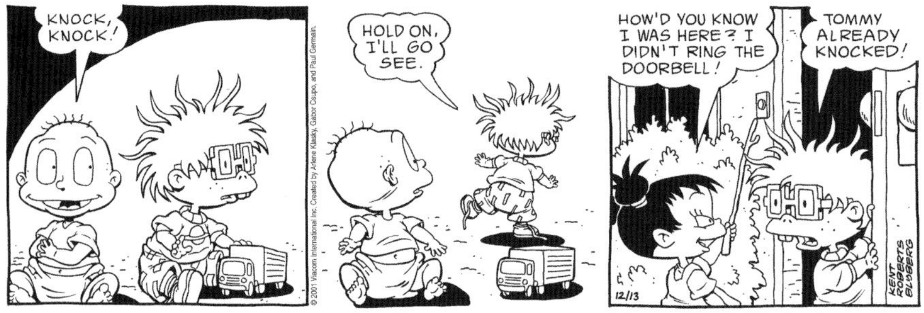
KNOCK, KNOCK!
HOLD ON, I'LL GO SEE.
HOW'D YOU KNOW I WAS HERE? I DIDN'T RING THE DOORBELL!
TOMMY ALREADY KNOCKED!
12/13
KENT ROBERTS BLYBERG

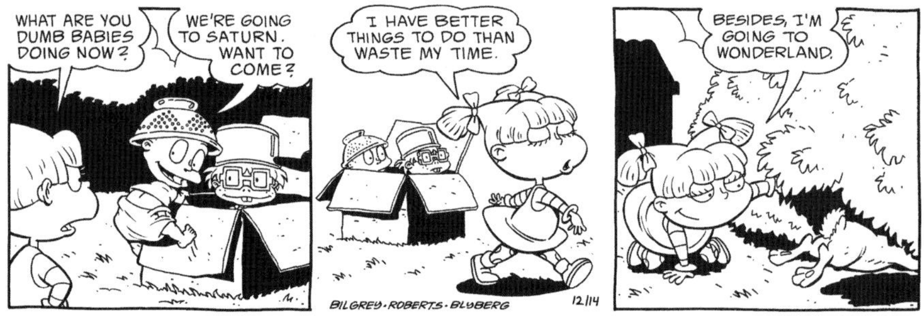
WHAT ARE YOU DUMB BABIES DOING NOW?
WE'RE GOING TO SATURN. WANT TO COME?
I HAVE BETTER THINGS TO DO THAN WASTE MY TIME.
BESIDES, I'M GOING TO WONDERLAND.
BILGREY·ROBERTS·BLYBERG
12/14

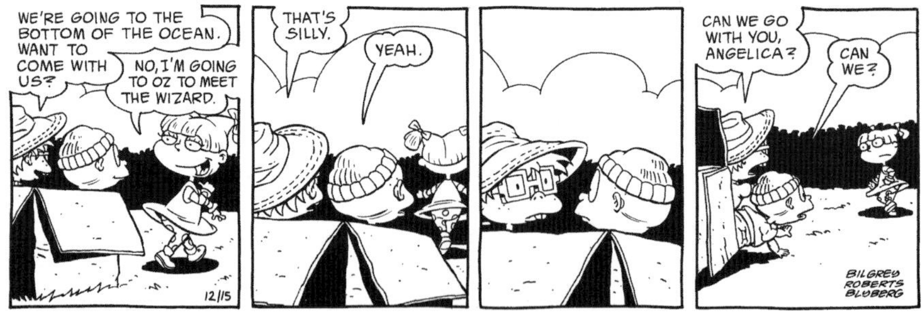
WE'RE GOING TO THE BOTTOM OF THE OCEAN. WANT TO COME WITH US?
NO, I'M GOING TO OZ TO MEET THE WIZARD.
12/15
THAT'S SILLY.
YEAH.
CAN WE GO WITH YOU, ANGELICA?
CAN WE?
BILGREY ROBERTS BLYBERG

2001

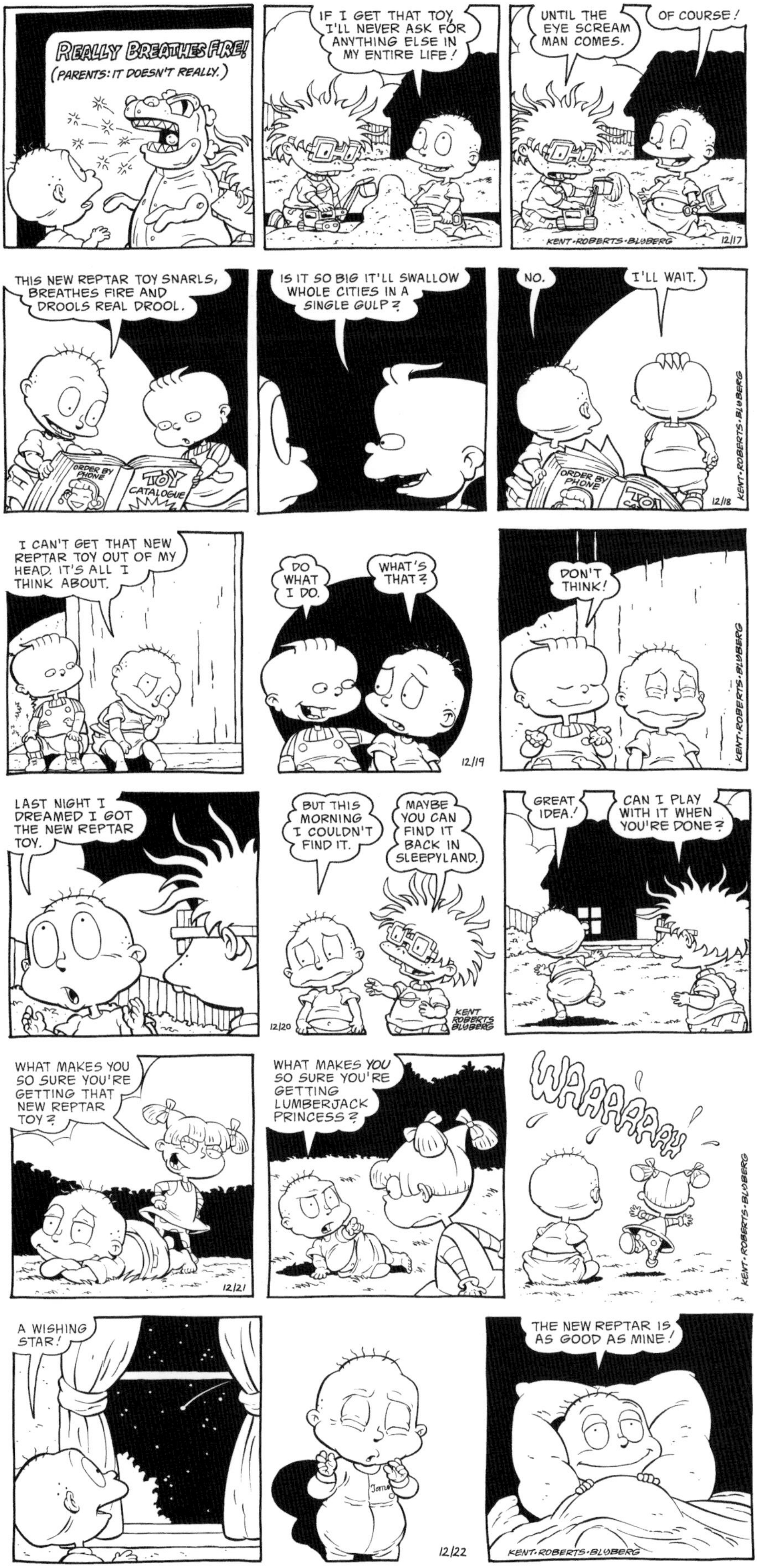
REALLY BREATHES FIRE!
(PARENTS: IT DOESN'T REALLY.)
IF I GET THAT TOY, I'LL NEVER ASK FOR ANYTHING ELSE IN MY ENTIRE LIFE!
UNTIL THE EYE SCREAM MAN COMES.
OF COURSE!
KENT·ROBERTS·BLUBERG 12/17
THIS NEW REPTAR TOY SNARLS, BREATHES FIRE AND DROOLS REAL DROOL.
ORDER BY PHONE
TOY CATALOGUE
IS IT SO BIG IT'LL SWALLOW WHOLE CITIES IN A SINGLE GULP?
NO.
I'LL WAIT.
KENT·ROBERTS·BLUBERG 12/18
I CAN'T GET THAT NEW REPTAR TOY OUT OF MY HEAD. IT'S ALL I THINK ABOUT.
DO WHAT I DO.
WHAT'S THAT?
12/19
DON'T THINK!
KENT·ROBERTS·BLUBERG
LAST NIGHT I DREAMED I GOT THE NEW REPTAR TOY.
BUT THIS MORNING I COULDN'T FIND IT.
MAYBE YOU CAN FIND IT BACK IN SLEEPYLAND.
12/20 KENT ROBERTS BLUBERG
GREAT IDEA!
CAN I PLAY WITH IT WHEN YOU'RE DONE?
WHAT MAKES YOU SO SURE YOU'RE GETTING THAT NEW REPTAR TOY?
12/21
WHAT MAKES YOU SO SURE YOU'RE GETTING LUMBERJACK PRINCESS?
WAAAAAAH!
KENT·ROBERTS·BLUBERG
A WISHING STAR!
12/22
THE NEW REPTAR IS AS GOOD AS MINE!
KENT·ROBERTS·BLUBERG

2001

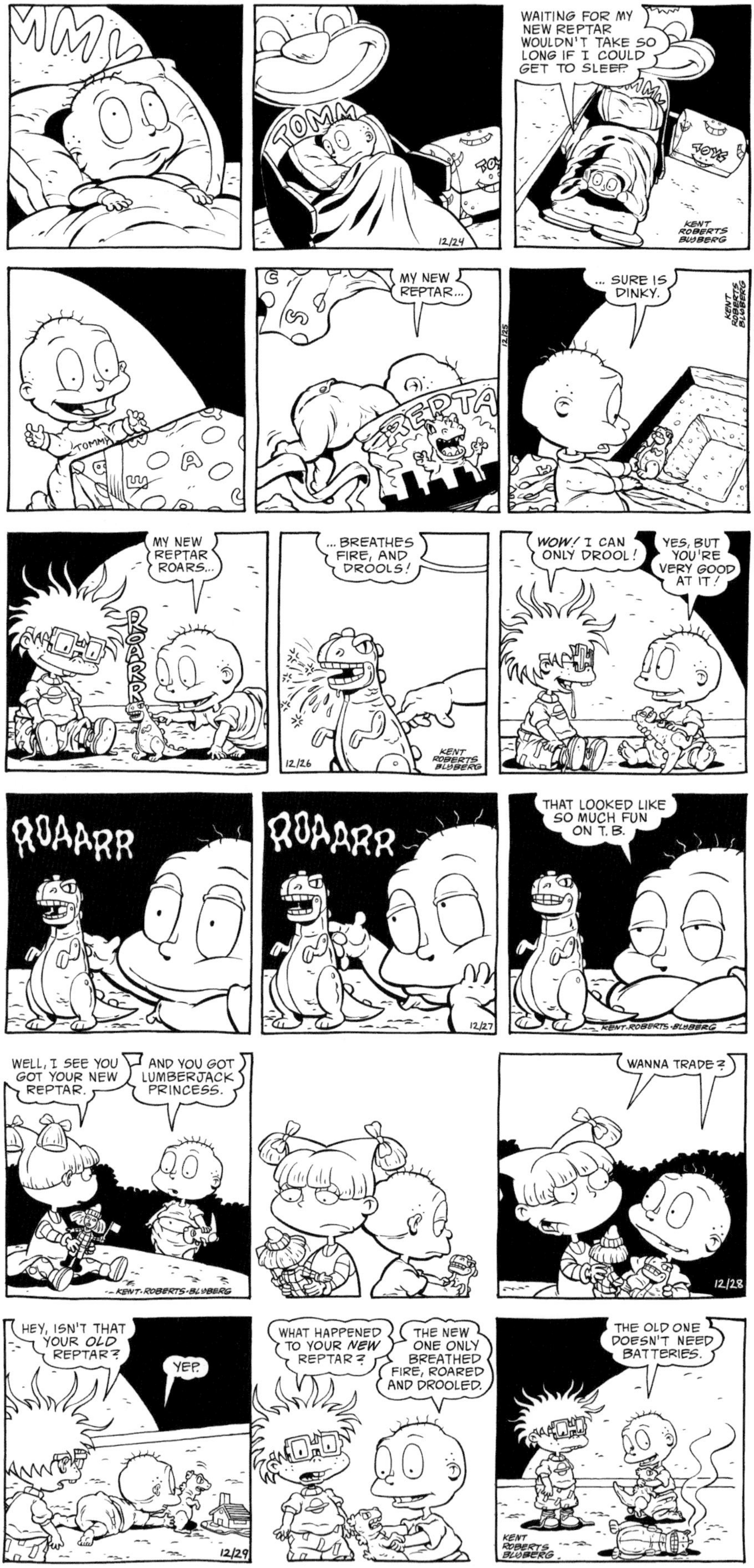
TOMMY
WAITING FOR MY NEW REPTAR WOULDN'T TAKE SO LONG IF I COULD GET TO SLEEP.
12/24
KENT ROBERTS BLYBERG
MY NEW REPTAR...
... SURE IS DINKY.
12/25
KENT ROBERTS BLYBERG
MY NEW REPTAR ROARS...
ROARR
...BREATHES FIRE, AND DROOLS!
12/26
KENT ROBERTS BLYBERG
WOW! I CAN ONLY DROOL!
YES, BUT YOU'RE VERY GOOD AT IT!
ROAARR
ROAARR
THAT LOOKED LIKE SO MUCH FUN ON T. B.
12/27
KENT-ROBERTS-BLYBERG
WELL, I SEE YOU GOT YOUR NEW REPTAR.
AND YOU GOT LUMBERJACK PRINCESS.
KENT-ROBERTS-BLYBERG
WANNA TRADE?
12/28
HEY, ISN'T THAT YOUR OLD REPTAR?
YEP.
12/29
WHAT HAPPENED TO YOUR NEW REPTAR?
THE NEW ONE ONLY BREATHED FIRE, ROARED AND DROOLED.
THE OLD ONE DOESN'T NEED BATTERIES.
KENT ROBERTS BLYBERG

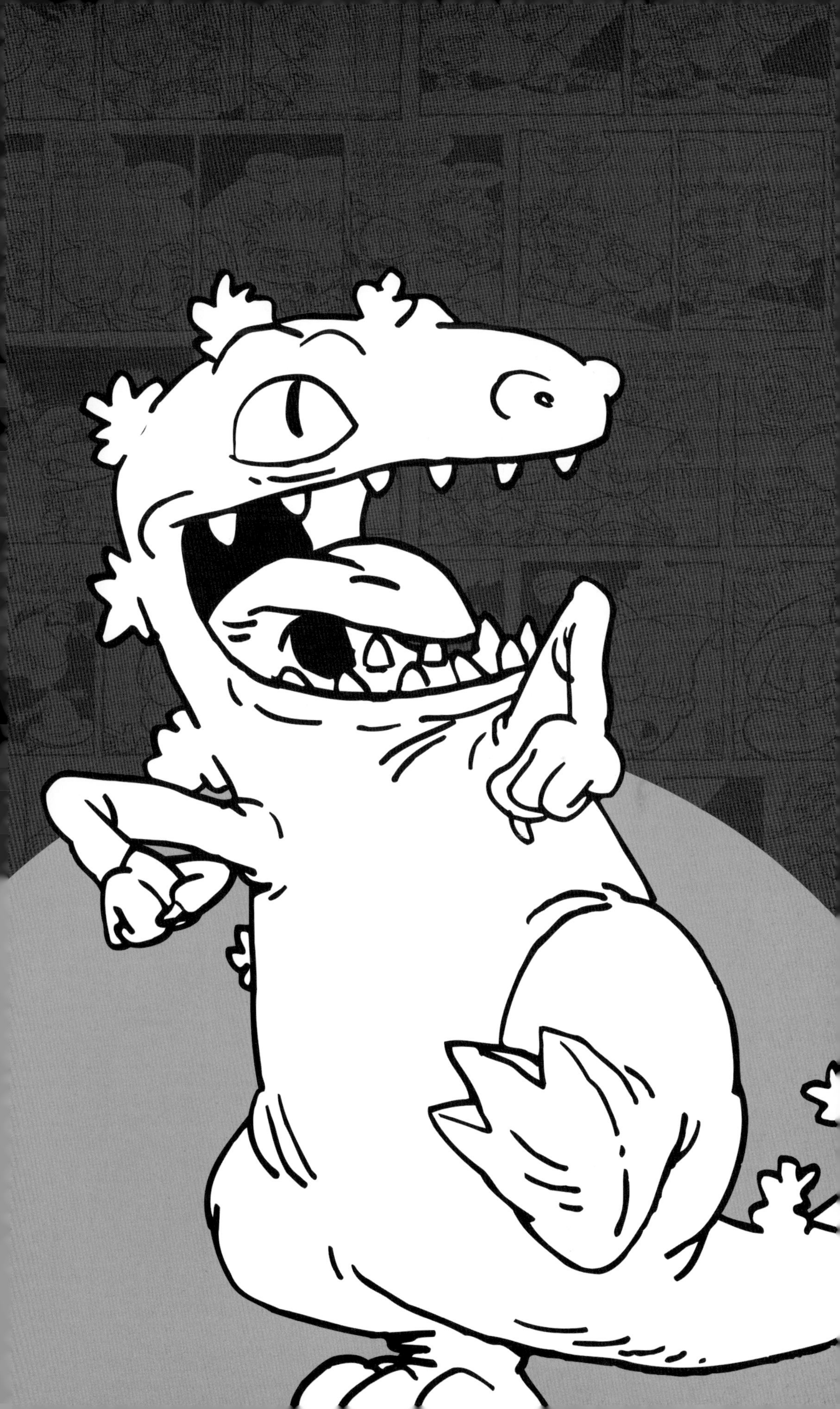

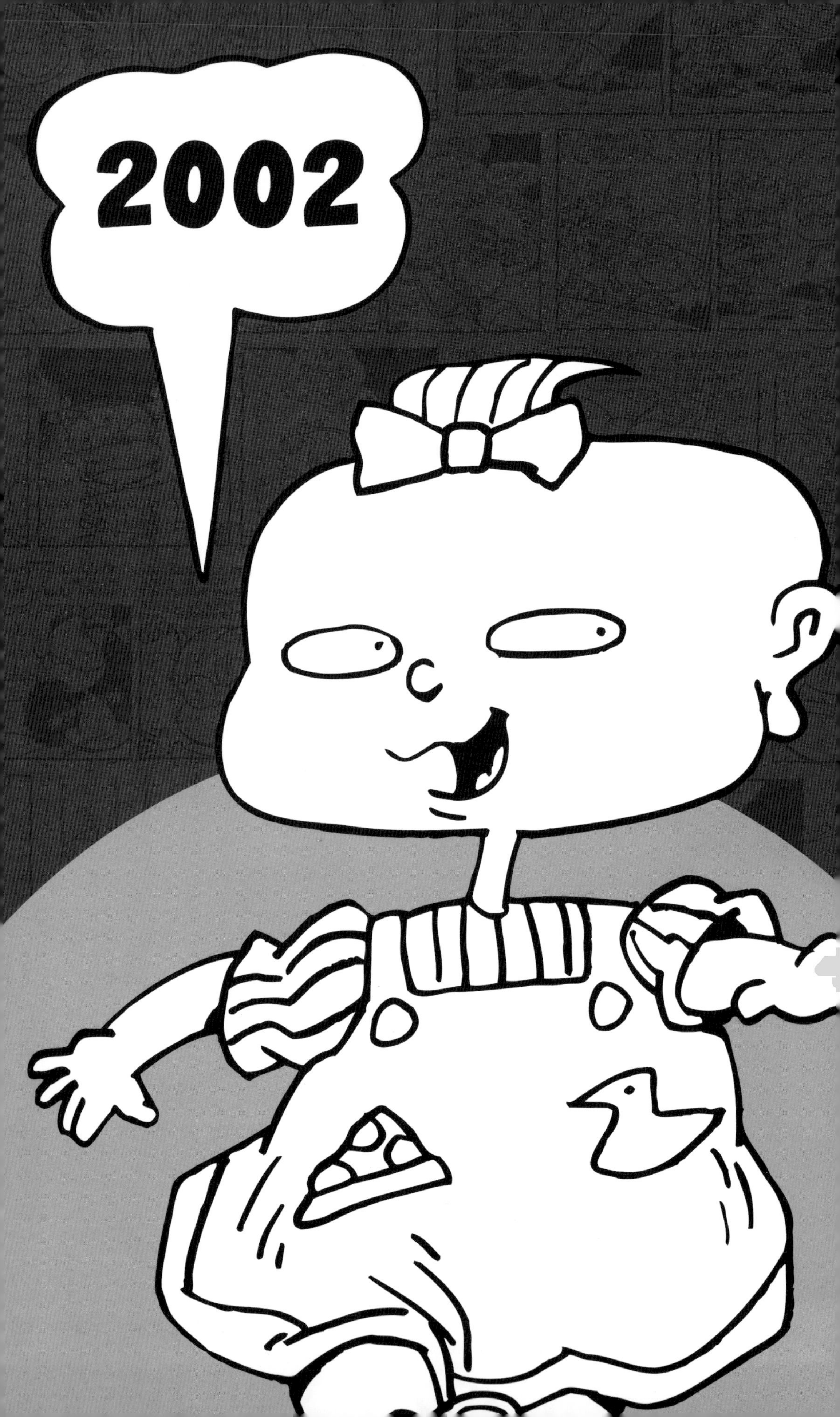
2002

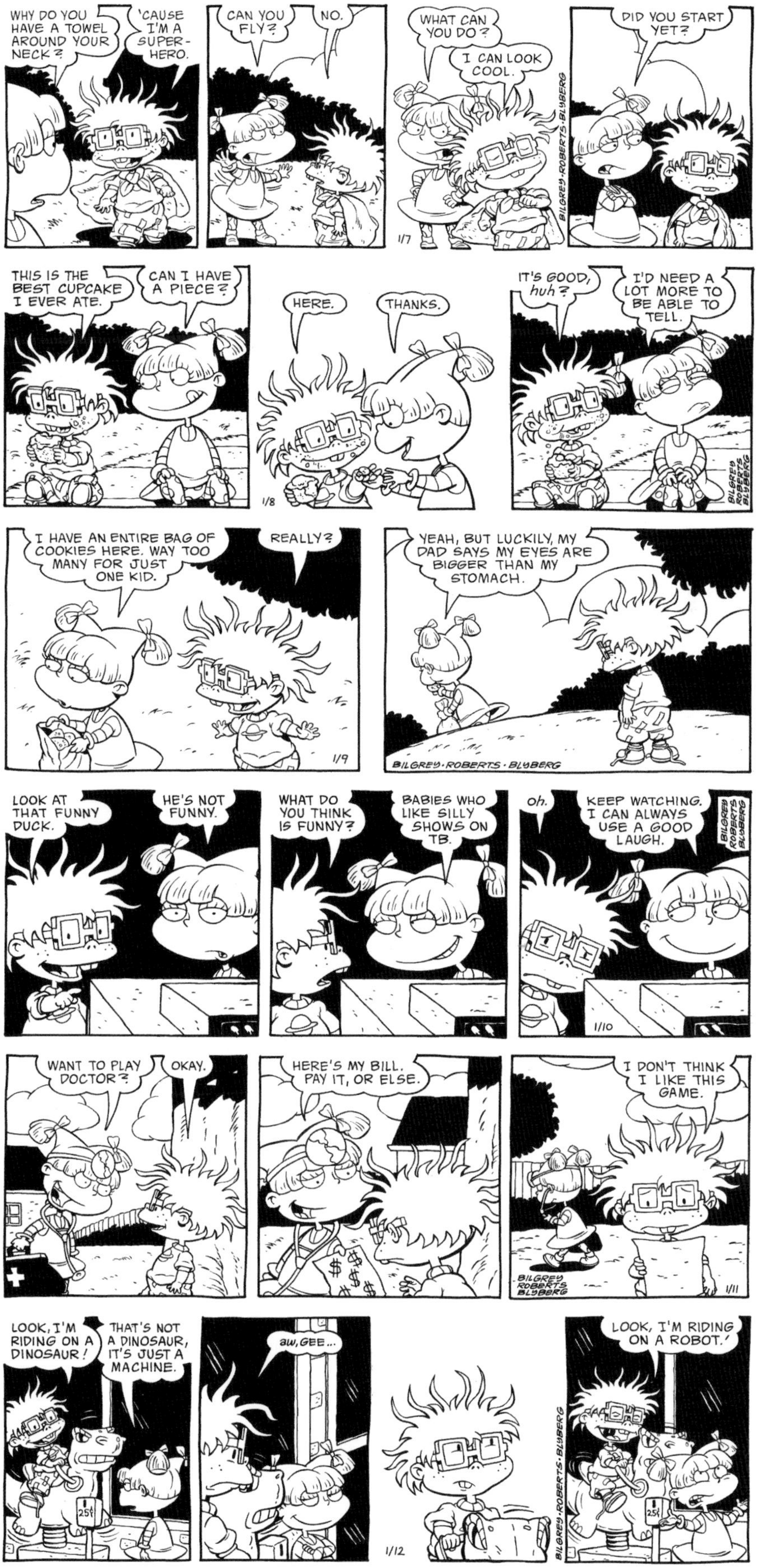
WHY DO YOU HAVE A TOWEL AROUND YOUR NECK?
'CAUSE I'M A SUPER-HERO.
CAN YOU FLY?
NO.
WHAT CAN YOU DO?
I CAN LOOK COOL.
DID YOU START YET?
BILGREY·ROBERTS·BLYBERG
1/7
THIS IS THE BEST CUPCAKE I EVER ATE.
CAN I HAVE A PIECE?
HERE.
THANKS.
IT'S GOOD, huh?
I'D NEED A LOT MORE TO BE ABLE TO TELL.
1/8
BILGREY ROBERTS BLYBERG
I HAVE AN ENTIRE BAG OF COOKIES HERE. WAY TOO MANY FOR JUST ONE KID.
REALLY?
1/9
YEAH, BUT LUCKILY, MY DAD SAYS MY EYES ARE BIGGER THAN MY STOMACH.
BILGREY·ROBERTS·BLYBERG
LOOK AT THAT FUNNY DUCK.
HE'S NOT FUNNY.
WHAT DO YOU THINK IS FUNNY?
BABIES WHO LIKE SILLY SHOWS ON TB.
oh.
KEEP WATCHING. I CAN ALWAYS USE A GOOD LAUGH.
BILGREY ROBERTS BLYBERG
1/10
WANT TO PLAY DOCTOR?
OKAY.
HERE'S MY BILL. PAY IT, OR ELSE.
I DON'T THINK I LIKE THIS GAME.
BILGREY ROBERTS BLYBERG
1/11
LOOK, I'M RIDING ON A DINOSAUR!
THAT'S NOT A DINOSAUR, IT'S JUST A MACHINE.
25¢
aw, GEE...
1/12
BILGREY·ROBERTS·BLYBERG
LOOK, I'M RIDING ON A ROBOT.'
25¢

2002

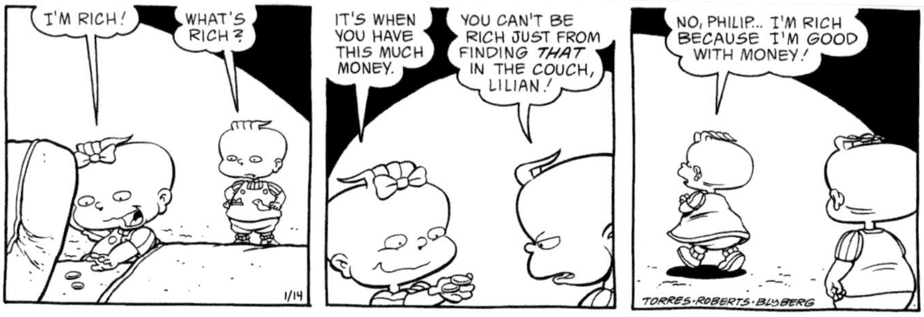
I'M RICH!
WHAT'S RICH?
1/14
IT'S WHEN YOU HAVE THIS MUCH MONEY.
YOU CAN'T BE RICH JUST FROM FINDING *THAT* IN THE COUCH, LILIAN!
NO, PHILIP... I'M RICH BECAUSE I'M GOOD WITH MONEY!
TORRES·ROBERTS·BLYBERG

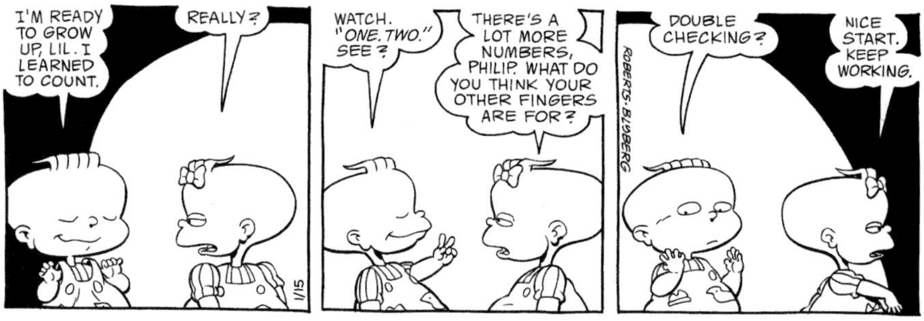
I'M READY TO GROW UP, LIL. I LEARNED TO COUNT.
REALLY?
1/15
WATCH. "*ONE. TWO.*" SEE?
THERE'S A LOT MORE NUMBERS, PHILIP. WHAT DO YOU THINK YOUR OTHER FINGERS ARE FOR?
ROBERTS·BLYBERG
DOUBLE CHECKING?
NICE START. KEEP WORKING.

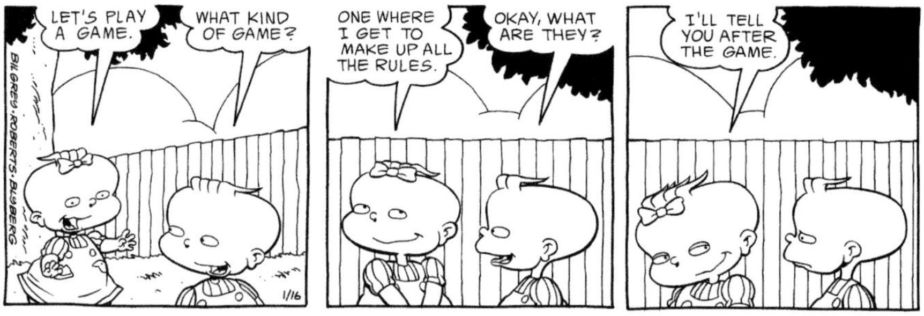
BILGREY·ROBERTS·BLYBERG
LET'S PLAY A GAME.
WHAT KIND OF GAME?
1/16
ONE WHERE I GET TO MAKE UP ALL THE RULES.
OKAY, WHAT ARE THEY?
I'LL TELL YOU AFTER THE GAME.

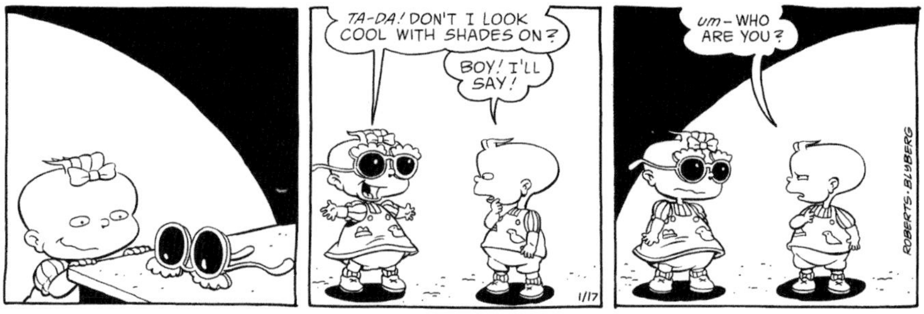
TA-DA! DON'T I LOOK COOL WITH SHADES ON?
BOY! I'LL SAY!
1/17
um-WHO ARE YOU?
ROBERTS·BLYBERG

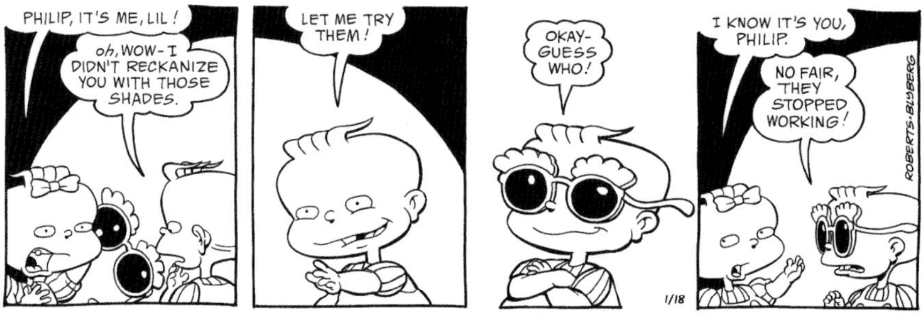
PHILIP, IT'S ME, LIL!
oh, WOW-I DIDN'T RECKANIZE YOU WITH THOSE SHADES.
LET ME TRY THEM!
OKAY- GUESS WHO!
1/18
I KNOW IT'S YOU, PHILIP.
NO FAIR, THEY STOPPED WORKING!
ROBERTS·BLYBERG

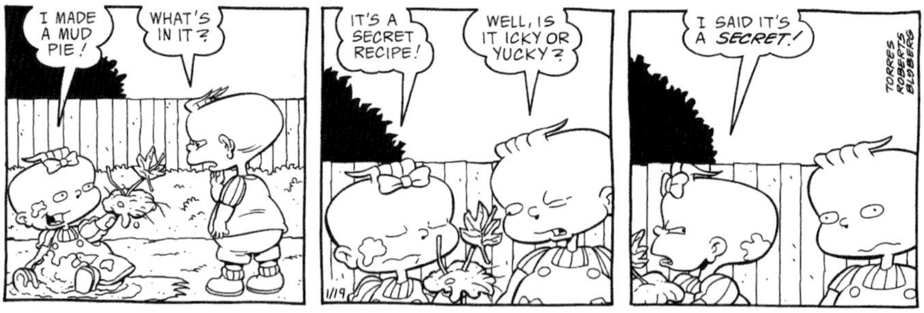
I MADE A MUD PIE!
WHAT'S IN IT?
IT'S A SECRET RECIPE!
WELL, IS IT ICKY OR YUCKY?
1/19
I SAID IT'S A *SECRET!*
TORRES ROBERTS BLYBERG

2002

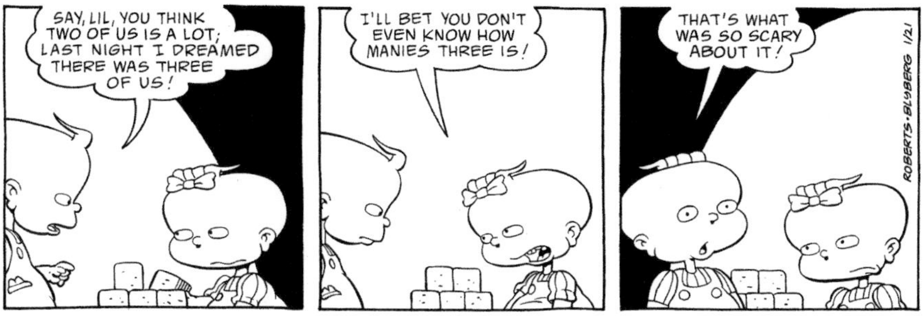
SAY, LIL, YOU THINK TWO OF US IS A LOT; LAST NIGHT I DREAMED THERE WAS THREE OF US!
I'LL BET YOU DON'T EVEN KNOW HOW MANIES THREE IS!
THAT'S WHAT WAS SO SCARY ABOUT IT!
ROBERTS•BLYBERG 1/21

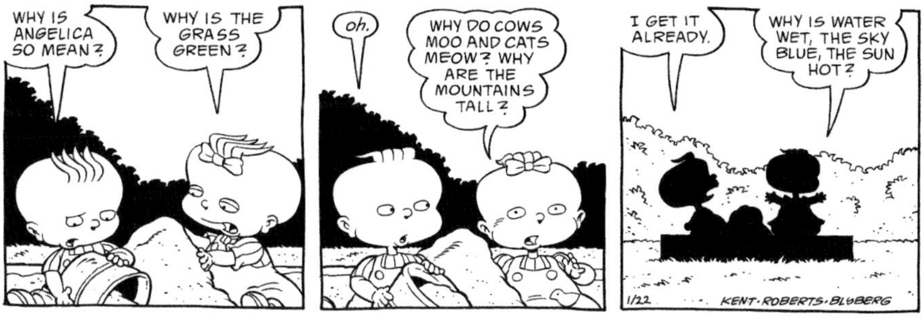
WHY IS ANGELICA SO MEAN?
WHY IS THE GRASS GREEN?
oh.
WHY DO COWS MOO AND CATS MEOW? WHY ARE THE MOUNTAINS TALL?
I GET IT ALREADY.
WHY IS WATER WET, THE SKY BLUE, THE SUN HOT?
1/22 KENT•ROBERTS•BLYBERG

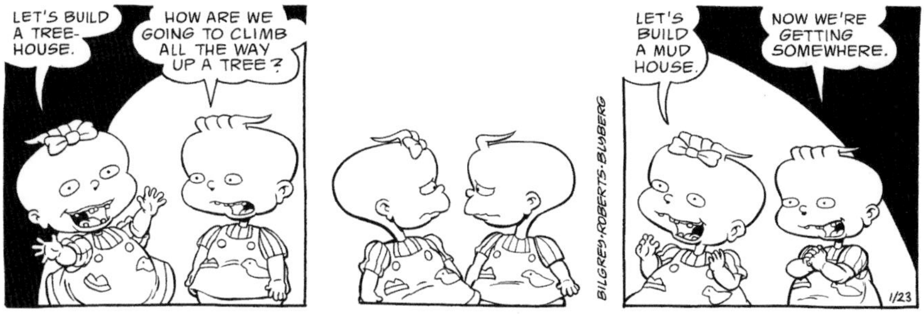
LET'S BUILD A TREE-HOUSE.
HOW ARE WE GOING TO CLIMB ALL THE WAY UP A TREE?
BILGREY•ROBERTS•BLYBERG
LET'S BUILD A MUD HOUSE.
NOW WE'RE GETTING SOMEWHERE.
1/23

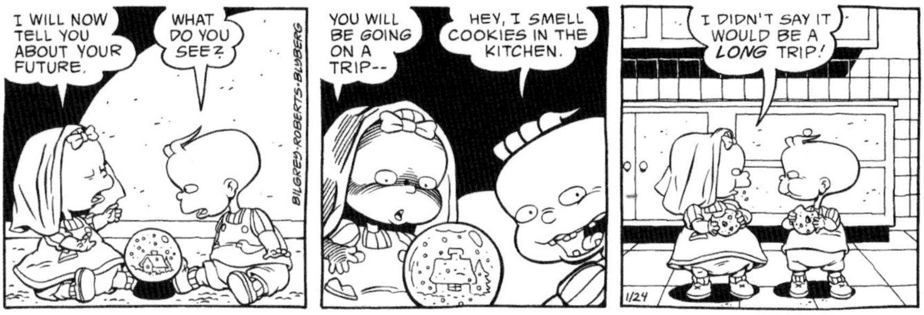
I WILL NOW TELL YOU ABOUT YOUR FUTURE.
WHAT DO YOU SEE?
BILGREY•ROBERTS•BLYBERG
YOU WILL BE GOING ON A TRIP--
HEY, I SMELL COOKIES IN THE KITCHEN.
I DIDN'T SAY IT WOULD BE A LONG TRIP!
1/24

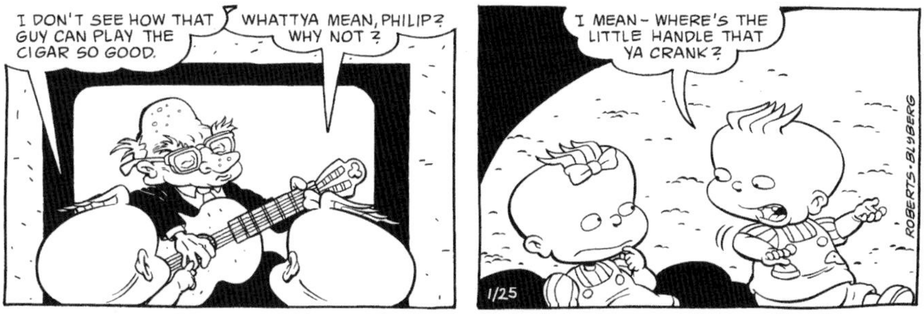
I DON'T SEE HOW THAT GUY CAN PLAY THE CIGAR SO GOOD.
WHATTYA MEAN, PHILIP? WHY NOT?
I MEAN - WHERE'S THE LITTLE HANDLE THAT YA CRANK?
ROBERTS•BLYBERG
1/25

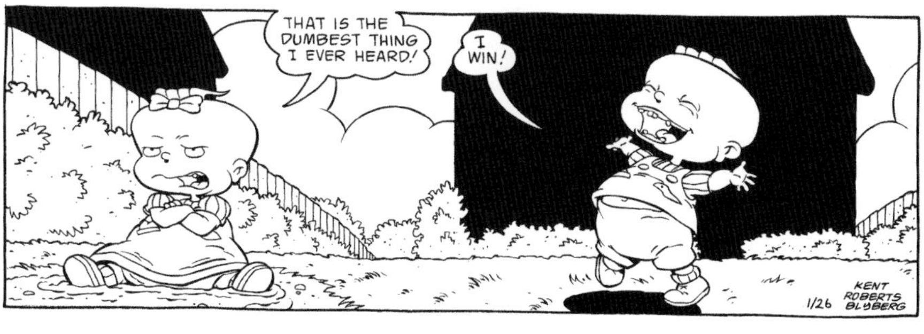
THAT IS THE DUMBEST THING I EVER HEARD!
I WIN!
KENT ROBERTS BLYBERG
1/26

2002

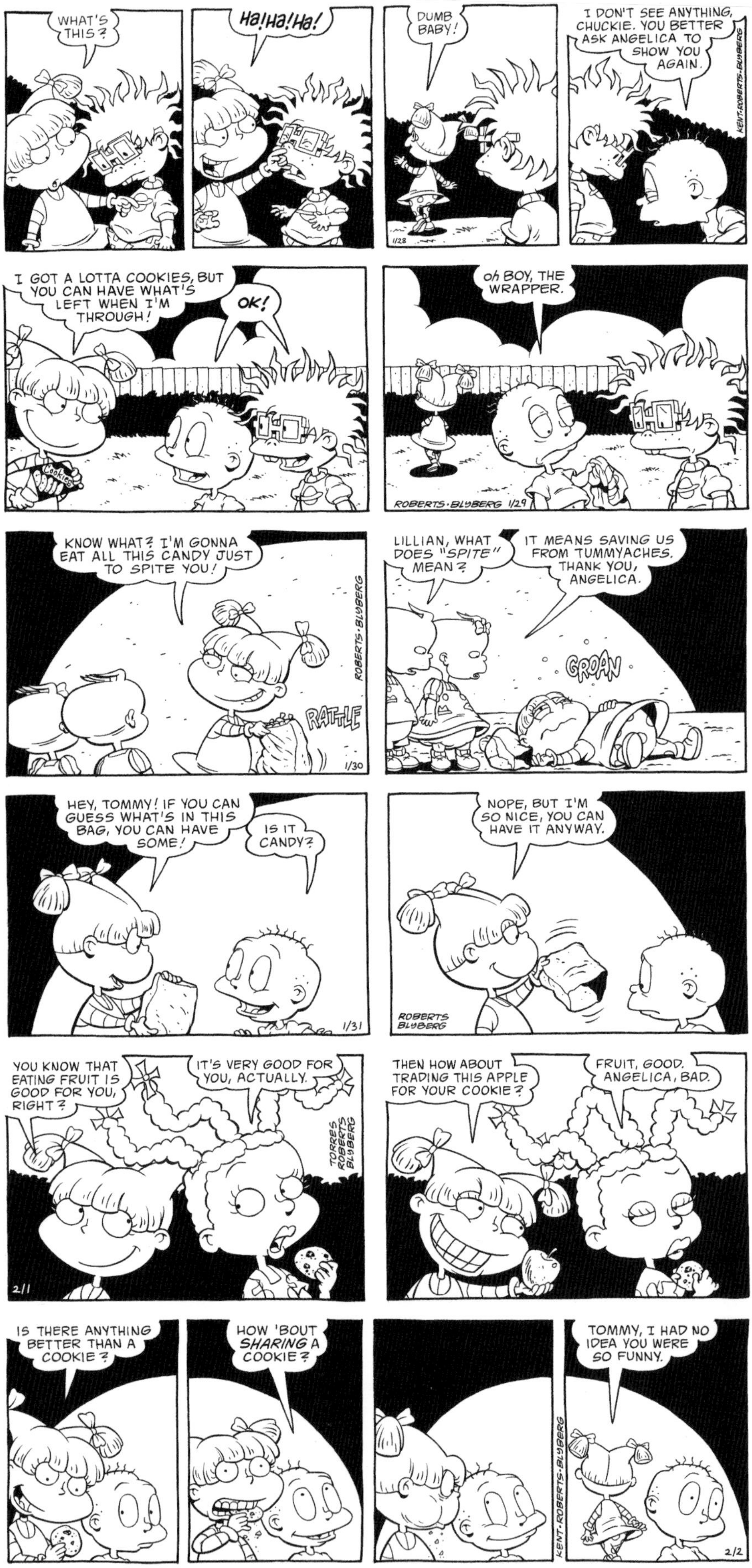

WHAT'S THIS?
HA!HA!HA!
DUMB BABY!
I DON'T SEE ANYTHING, CHUCKIE. YOU BETTER ASK ANGELICA TO SHOW YOU AGAIN.
KENT·ROBERTS·BLYBERG
1/28
I GOT A LOTTA COOKIES, BUT YOU CAN HAVE WHAT'S LEFT WHEN I'M THROUGH!
OK!
COOKIES
OH BOY, THE WRAPPER.
ROBERTS·BLYBERG 1/29
KNOW WHAT? I'M GONNA EAT ALL THIS CANDY JUST TO SPITE YOU!
ROBERTS·BLYBERG
RATTLE
1/30
LILLIAN, WHAT DOES "SPITE" MEAN?
IT MEANS SAVING US FROM TUMMYACHES. THANK YOU, ANGELICA.
GROAN
HEY, TOMMY! IF YOU CAN GUESS WHAT'S IN THIS BAG, YOU CAN HAVE SOME!
IS IT CANDY?
1/31
NOPE, BUT I'M SO NICE, YOU CAN HAVE IT ANYWAY.
ROBERTS BLYBERG
YOU KNOW THAT EATING FRUIT IS GOOD FOR YOU, RIGHT?
IT'S VERY GOOD FOR YOU, ACTUALLY.
TORRES ROBERTS BLYBERG
2/1
THEN HOW ABOUT TRADING THIS APPLE FOR YOUR COOKIE?
FRUIT, GOOD. ANGELICA, BAD.
IS THERE ANYTHING BETTER THAN A COOKIE?
HOW 'BOUT SHARING A COOKIE?
KENT·ROBERTS·BLYBERG
TOMMY, I HAD NO IDEA YOU WERE SO FUNNY.
2/2

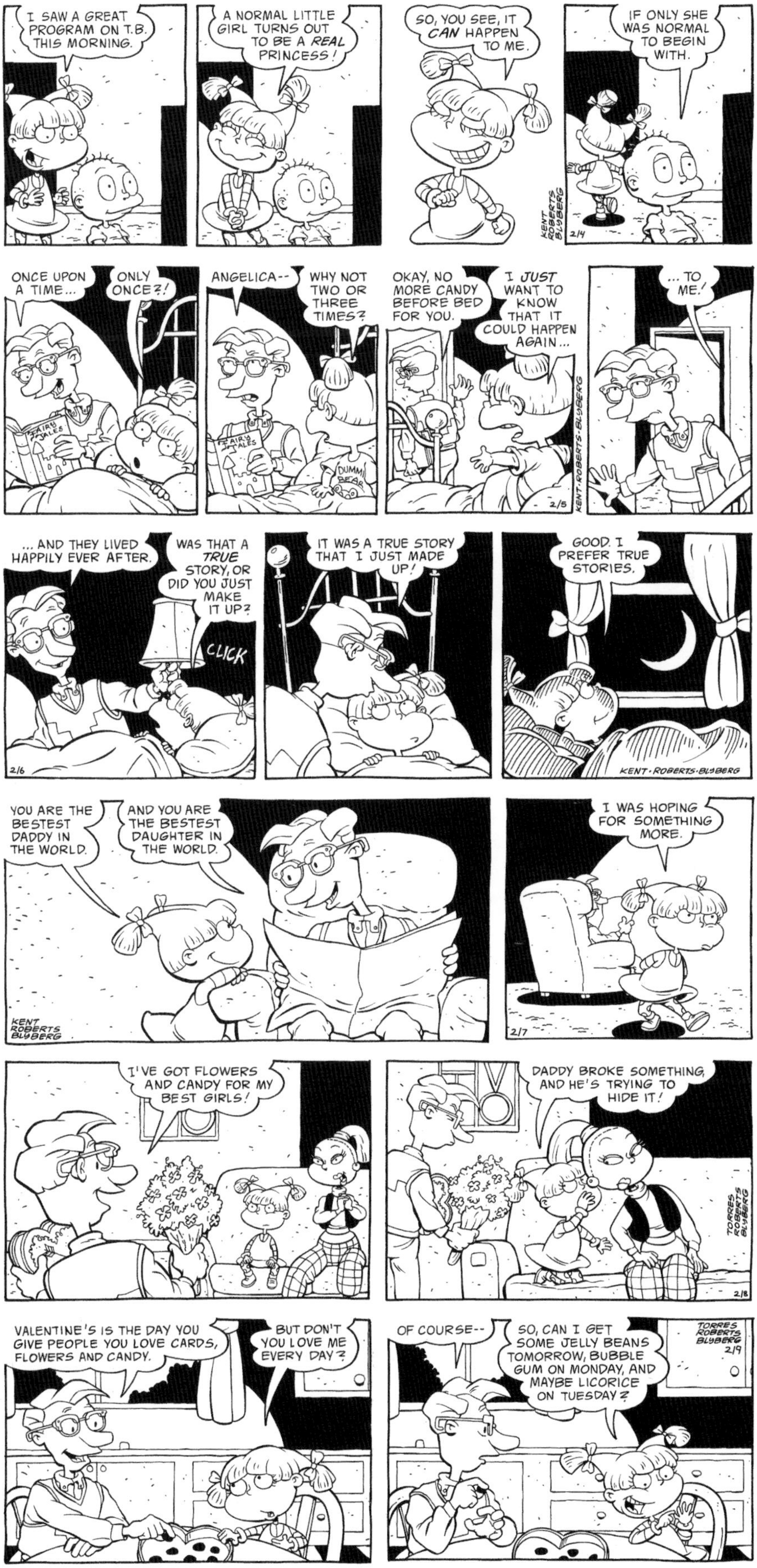
I SAW A GREAT PROGRAM ON T.B. THIS MORNING.
A NORMAL LITTLE GIRL TURNS OUT TO BE A *REAL* PRINCESS!
SO, YOU SEE, IT *CAN* HAPPEN TO ME.
KENT ROBERTS BLYBERG 2/4
IF ONLY SHE WAS NORMAL TO BEGIN WITH.
ONCE UPON A TIME...
ONLY ONCE?!
FAIRY TALES
ANGELICA--
WHY NOT TWO OR THREE TIMES?
DUMMI BEAR
OKAY, NO MORE CANDY BEFORE BED FOR YOU.
I *JUST* WANT TO KNOW THAT IT COULD HAPPEN AGAIN...
KENT·ROBERTS·BLYBERG 2/5
... TO ME!
... AND THEY LIVED HAPPILY EVER AFTER.
WAS THAT A *TRUE* STORY, OR DID YOU JUST MAKE IT UP?
CLICK
2/6
IT WAS A TRUE STORY THAT I JUST MADE UP!
GOOD. I PREFER TRUE STORIES.
KENT·ROBERTS·BLYBERG
YOU ARE THE BESTEST DADDY IN THE WORLD.
AND YOU ARE THE BESTEST DAUGHTER IN THE WORLD.
KENT ROBERTS BLYBERG
2/7
I WAS HOPING FOR SOMETHING MORE.
I'VE GOT FLOWERS AND CANDY FOR MY BEST GIRLS!
DADDY BROKE SOMETHING, AND HE'S TRYING TO HIDE IT!
TORRES ROBERTS BLYBERG
2/8
VALENTINE'S IS THE DAY YOU GIVE PEOPLE YOU LOVE CARDS, FLOWERS AND CANDY.
BUT DON'T YOU LOVE ME EVERY DAY?
OF COURSE--
SO, CAN I GET SOME JELLY BEANS TOMORROW, BUBBLE GUM ON MONDAY, AND MAYBE LICORICE ON TUESDAY?
TORRES ROBERTS BLYBERG 2/9

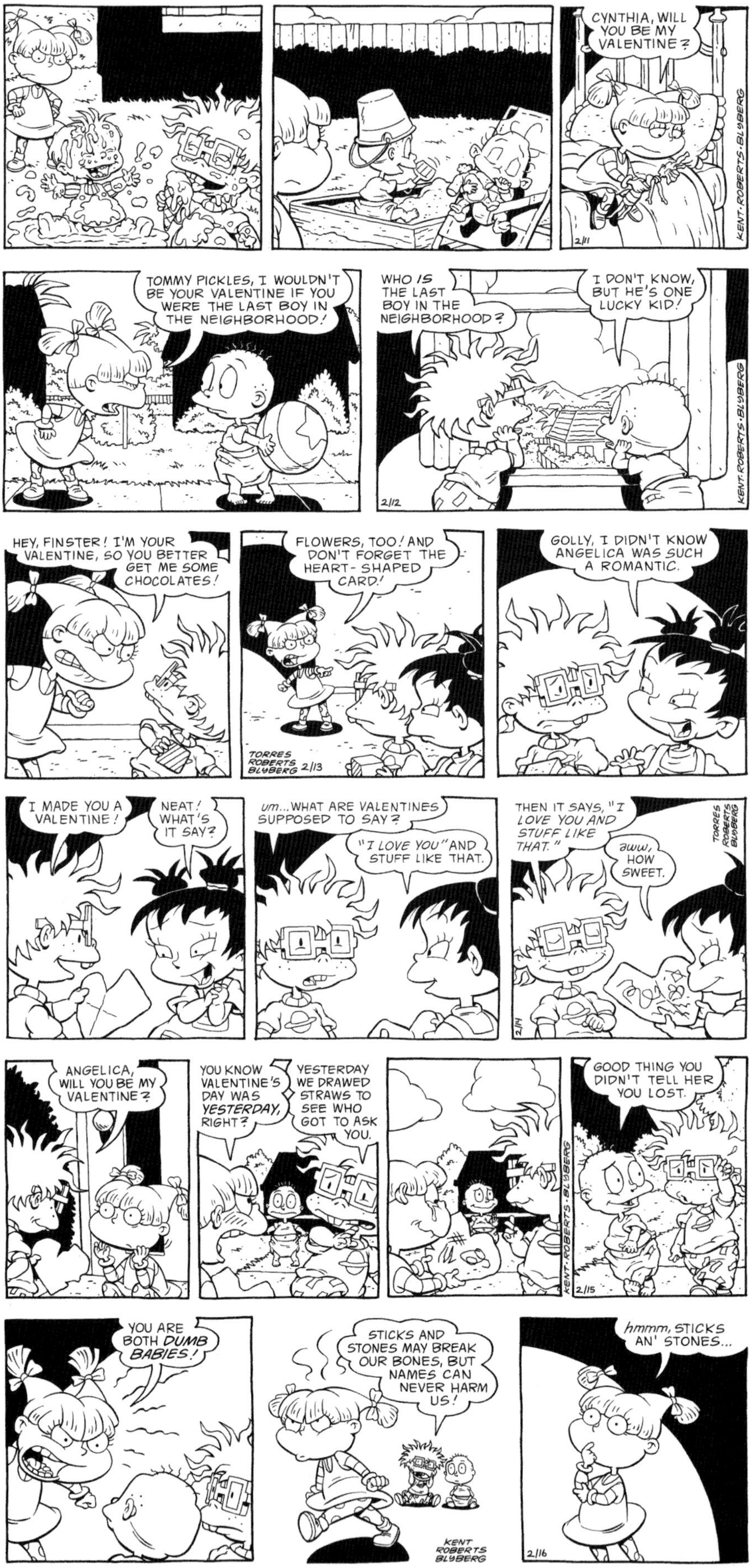
CYNTHIA, WILL YOU BE MY VALENTINE?
2/11
KENT·ROBERTS·BLYBERG
TOMMY PICKLES, I WOULDN'T BE YOUR VALENTINE IF YOU WERE THE LAST BOY IN THE NEIGHBORHOOD!
WHO *IS* THE LAST BOY IN THE NEIGHBORHOOD?
I DON'T KNOW, BUT HE'S ONE LUCKY KID!
2/12
KENT·ROBERTS·BLYBERG
HEY, FINSTER! I'M YOUR VALENTINE, SO YOU BETTER GET ME SOME CHOCOLATES!
FLOWERS, TOO! AND DON'T FORGET THE HEART-SHAPED CARD!
TORRES ROBERTS BLYBERG 2/13
GOLLY, I DIDN'T KNOW ANGELICA WAS SUCH A ROMANTIC.
I MADE YOU A VALENTINE!
NEAT! WHAT'S IT SAY?
um... WHAT ARE VALENTINES SUPPOSED TO SAY?
"I LOVE YOU" AND STUFF LIKE THAT.
THEN IT SAYS, "I LOVE YOU AND STUFF LIKE THAT."
aww, HOW SWEET.
TORRES ROBERTS BLYBERG
2/14
ANGELICA, WILL YOU BE MY VALENTINE?
YOU KNOW VALENTINE'S DAY WAS *YESTERDAY*, RIGHT?
YESTERDAY WE DRAWED STRAWS TO SEE WHO GOT TO ASK YOU.
KENT·ROBERTS·BLYBERG
2/15
GOOD THING YOU DIDN'T TELL HER YOU LOST.
YOU ARE BOTH *DUMB BABIES*!
STICKS AND STONES MAY BREAK OUR BONES, BUT NAMES CAN NEVER HARM US!
KENT ROBERTS BLYBERG
hmmm, STICKS AN' STONES...
2/16

2002

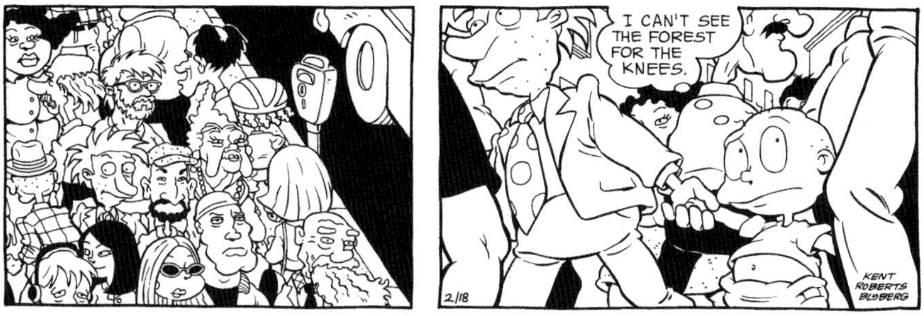
I CAN'T SEE THE FOREST FOR THE KNEES.
2/18
KENT ROBERTS BLYBERG

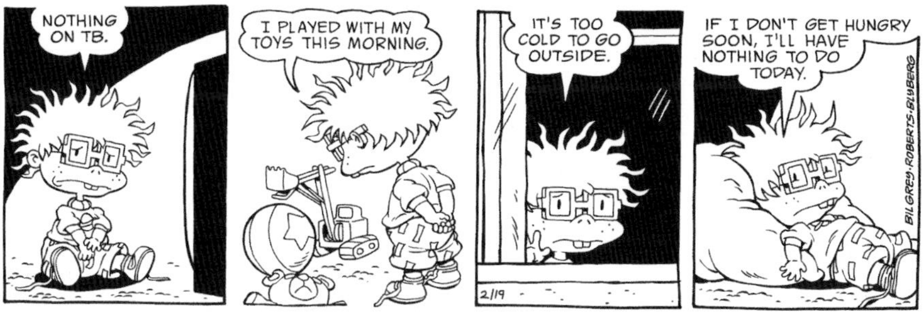
NOTHING ON TB.
I PLAYED WITH MY TOYS THIS MORNING.
IT'S TOO COLD TO GO OUTSIDE.
2/19
IF I DON'T GET HUNGRY SOON, I'LL HAVE NOTHING TO DO TODAY.
BILGREY·ROBERTS·BLYBERG

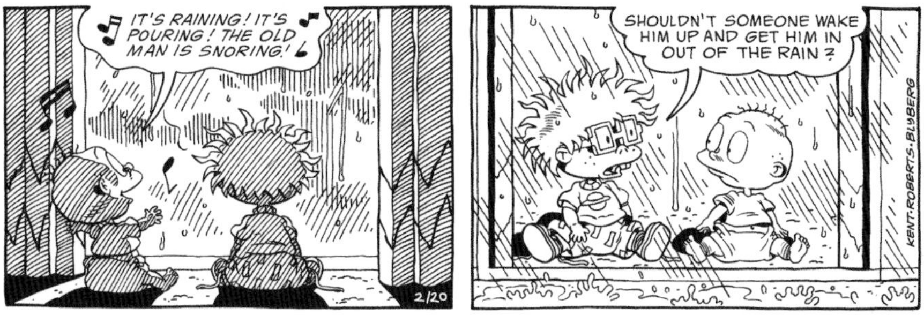
IT'S RAINING! IT'S POURING! THE OLD MAN IS SNORING!
2/20
SHOULDN'T SOMEONE WAKE HIM UP AND GET HIM IN OUT OF THE RAIN?
KENT·ROBERTS·BLYBERG

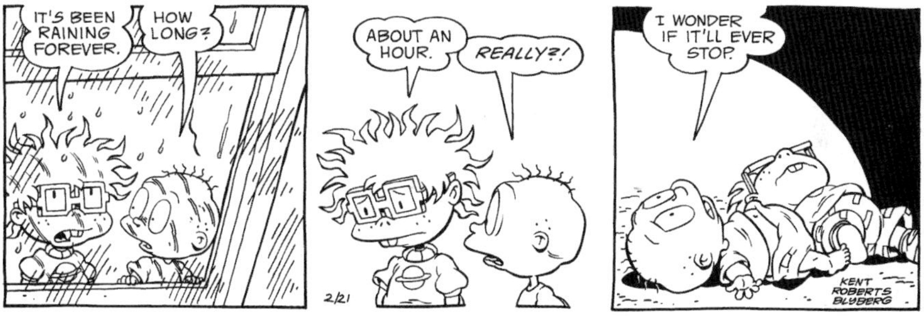
IT'S BEEN RAINING FOREVER.
HOW LONG?
ABOUT AN HOUR.
REALLY?!
2/21
I WONDER IF IT'LL EVER STOP.
KENT ROBERTS BLYBERG

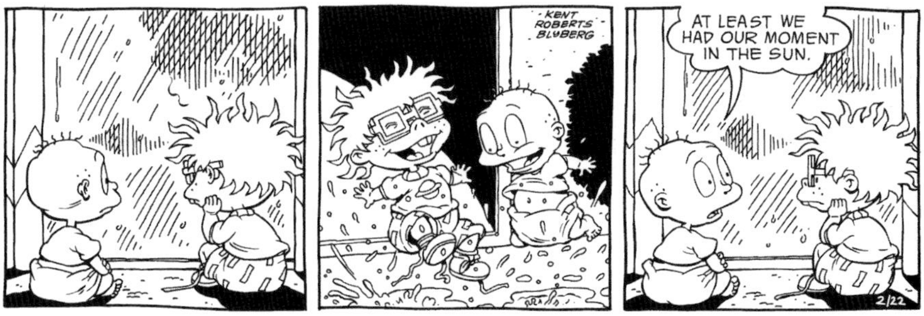
KENT ROBERTS BLYBERG
AT LEAST WE HAD OUR MOMENT IN THE SUN.
2/22

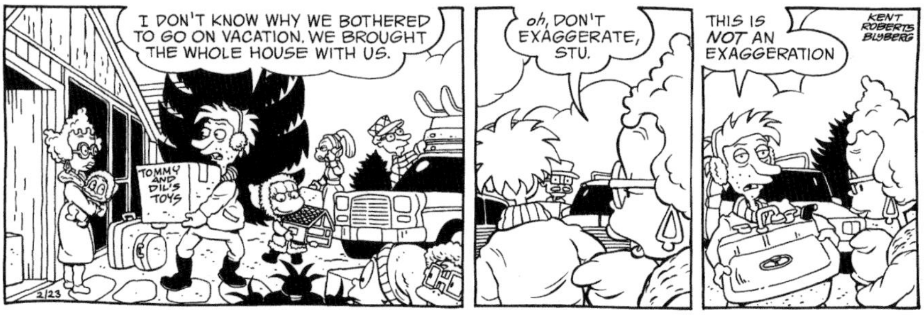
I DON'T KNOW WHY WE BOTHERED TO GO ON VACATION. WE BROUGHT THE WHOLE HOUSE WITH US.
TOMMY AND DIL'S TOYS
2/23
oh, DON'T EXAGGERATE, STU.
THIS IS NOT AN EXAGGERATION
KENT ROBERTS BLYBERG

2002

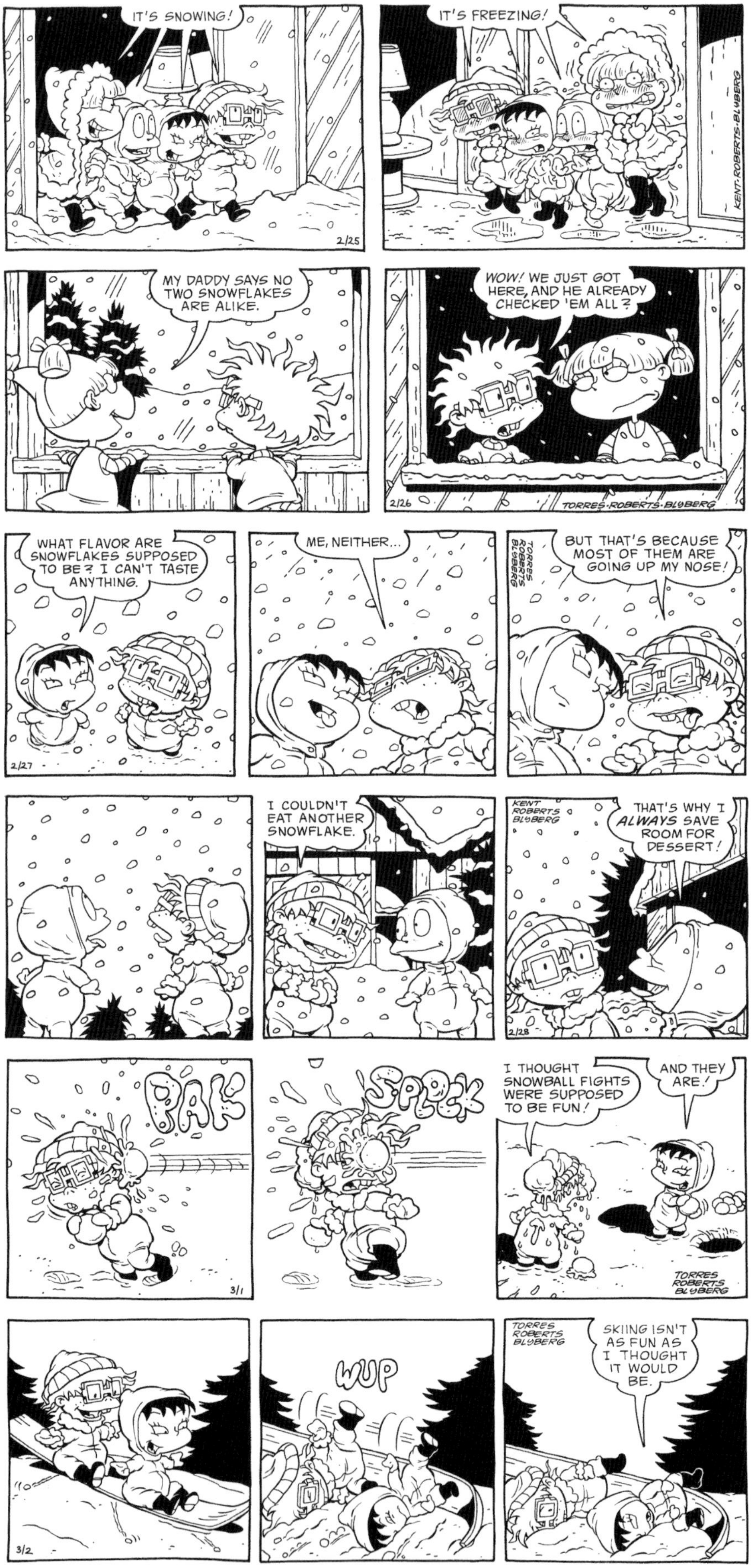

IT'S SNOWING!
IT'S FREEZING!
KENT·ROBERTS·BLYBERG
2/25
MY DADDY SAYS NO TWO SNOWFLAKES ARE ALIKE.
WOW! WE JUST GOT HERE, AND HE ALREADY CHECKED 'EM ALL?
2/26
TORRES·ROBERTS·BLYBERG
WHAT FLAVOR ARE SNOWFLAKES SUPPOSED TO BE? I CAN'T TASTE ANYTHING.
2/27
ME, NEITHER...
TORRES ROBERTS BLYBERG
BUT THAT'S BECAUSE MOST OF THEM ARE GOING UP MY NOSE!
I COULDN'T EAT ANOTHER SNOWFLAKE.
KENT ROBERTS BLYBERG
THAT'S WHY I *ALWAYS* SAVE ROOM FOR DESSERT!
2/28
PAK
3/1
SPLOCK
I THOUGHT SNOWBALL FIGHTS WERE SUPPOSED TO BE FUN!
AND THEY ARE!
TORRES ROBERTS BLYBERG
3/2
WUP
TORRES ROBERTS BLYBERG
SKIING ISN'T AS FUN AS I THOUGHT IT WOULD BE.

2002

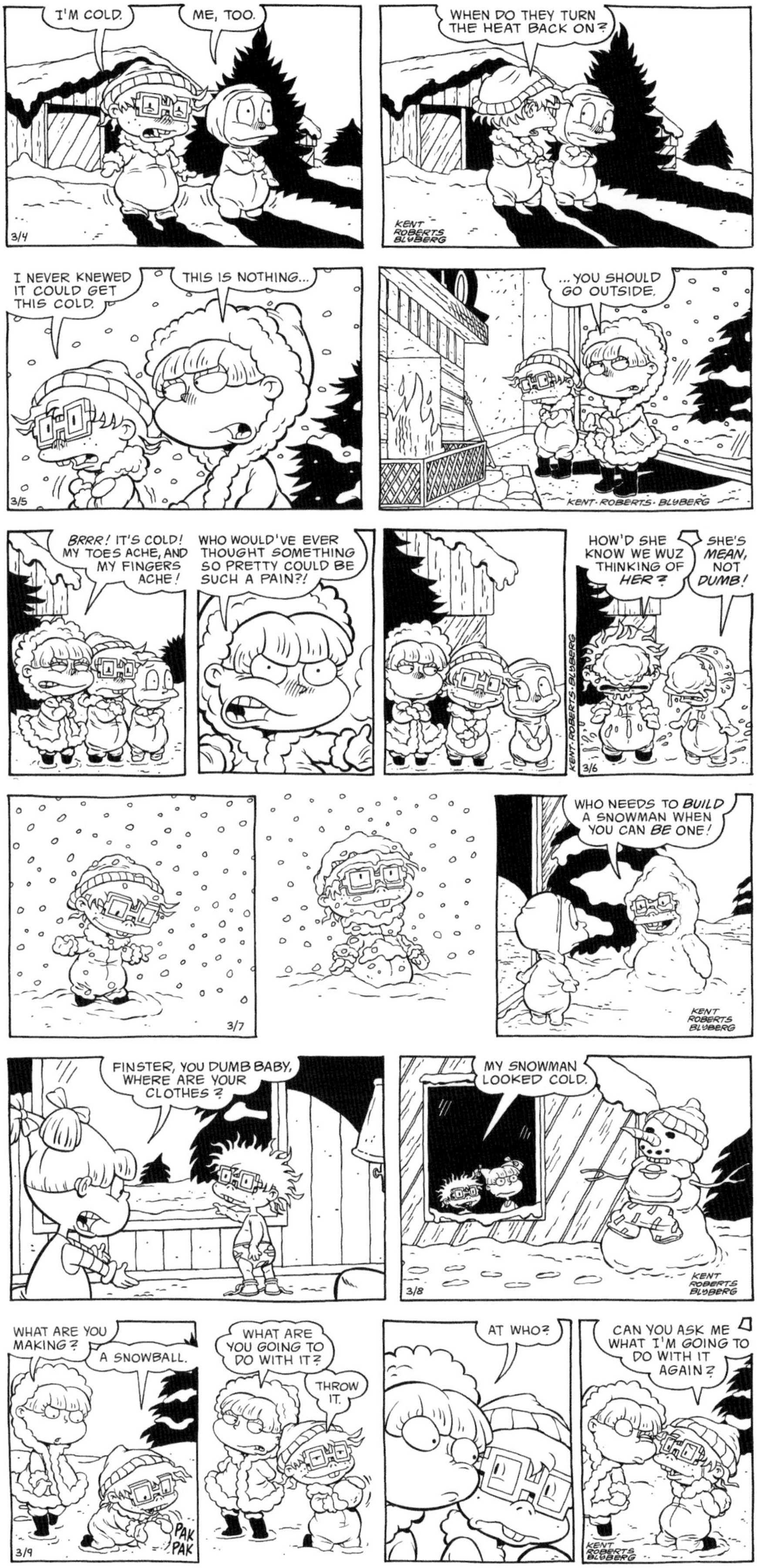
I'M COLD.
ME, TOO.
WHEN DO THEY TURN THE HEAT BACK ON?
3/4
KENT ROBERTS BLYBERG
I NEVER KNEWED IT COULD GET THIS COLD.
THIS IS NOTHING...
...YOU SHOULD GO OUTSIDE.
3/5
KENT·ROBERTS·BLYBERG
BRRR! IT'S COLD! MY TOES ACHE, AND MY FINGERS ACHE!
WHO WOULD'VE EVER THOUGHT SOMETHING SO PRETTY COULD BE SUCH A PAIN?!
KENT·ROBERTS·BLYBERG
HOW'D SHE KNOW WE WUZ THINKING OF HER?
SHE'S MEAN, NOT DUMB!
3/6
3/7
WHO NEEDS TO BUILD A SNOWMAN WHEN YOU CAN BE ONE!
KENT ROBERTS BLYBERG
FINSTER, YOU DUMB BABY, WHERE ARE YOUR CLOTHES?
MY SNOWMAN LOOKED COLD.
3/8
KENT ROBERTS BLYBERG
WHAT ARE YOU MAKING?
A SNOWBALL.
PAK PAK
3/9
WHAT ARE YOU GOING TO DO WITH IT?
THROW IT.
AT WHO?
CAN YOU ASK ME WHAT I'M GOING TO DO WITH IT AGAIN?
KENT ROBERTS BLYBERG

2002

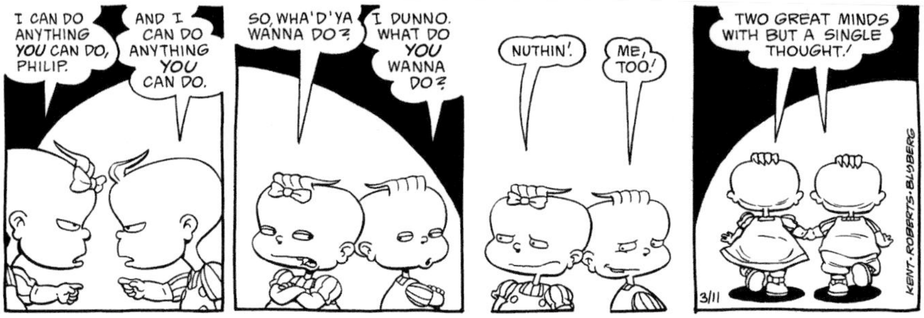
I CAN DO ANYTHING *YOU* CAN DO, PHILIP.
AND I CAN DO ANYTHING *YOU* CAN DO.
SO, WHA'D'YA WANNA DO?
I DUNNO. WHAT DO *YOU* WANNA DO?
NUTHIN'!
ME, TOO!
TWO GREAT MINDS WITH BUT A SINGLE THOUGHT!
3/11
KENT·ROBERTS·BLYBERG

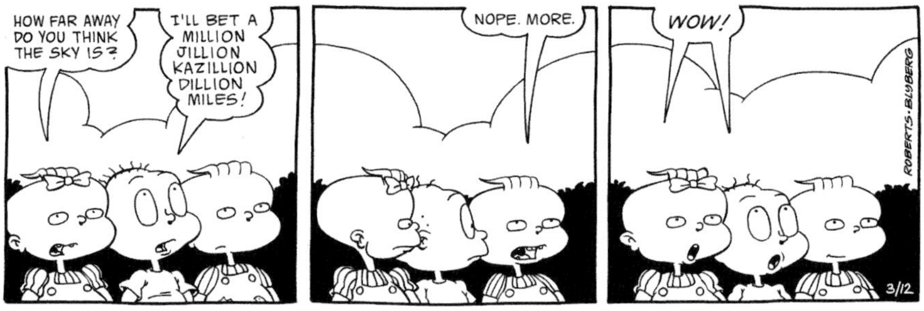
HOW FAR AWAY DO YOU THINK THE SKY IS?
I'LL BET A MILLION JILLION KAZILLION DILLION MILES!
NOPE. MORE.
WOW!
ROBERTS·BLYBERG
3/12

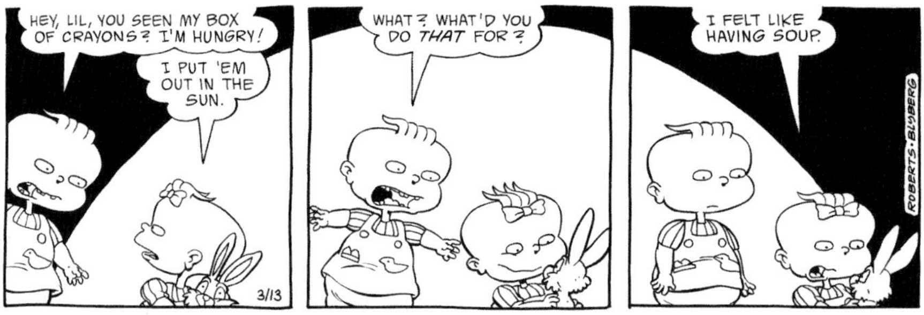
HEY, LIL, YOU SEEN MY BOX OF CRAYONS? I'M HUNGRY!
I PUT 'EM OUT IN THE SUN.
3/13
WHAT? WHAT'D YOU DO *THAT* FOR?
I FELT LIKE HAVING SOUP.
ROBERTS·BLYBERG

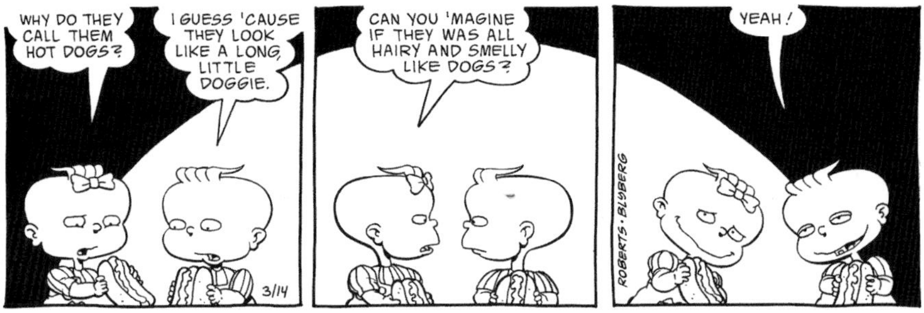
WHY DO THEY CALL THEM HOT DOGS?
I GUESS 'CAUSE THEY LOOK LIKE A LONG, LITTLE DOGGIE.
3/14
CAN YOU 'MAGINE IF THEY WAS ALL HAIRY AND SMELLY LIKE DOGS?
ROBERTS·BLYBERG
YEAH!

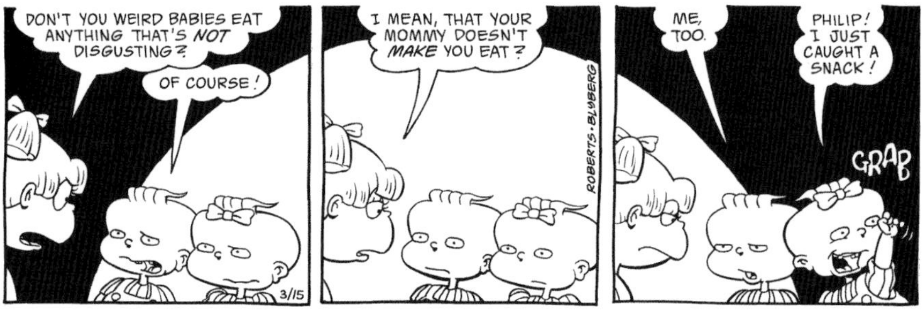
DON'T YOU WEIRD BABIES EAT ANYTHING THAT'S *NOT* DISGUSTING?
OF COURSE!
3/15
I MEAN, THAT YOUR MOMMY DOESN'T *MAKE* YOU EAT?
ROBERTS·BLYBERG
ME, TOO.
PHILIP! I JUST CAUGHT A SNACK!
GRAB

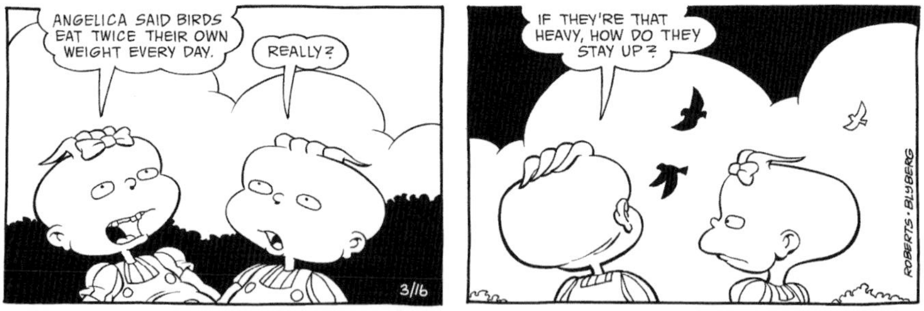
ANGELICA SAID BIRDS EAT TWICE THEIR OWN WEIGHT EVERY DAY.
REALLY?
3/16
IF THEY'RE THAT HEAVY, HOW DO THEY STAY UP?
ROBERTS·BLYBERG

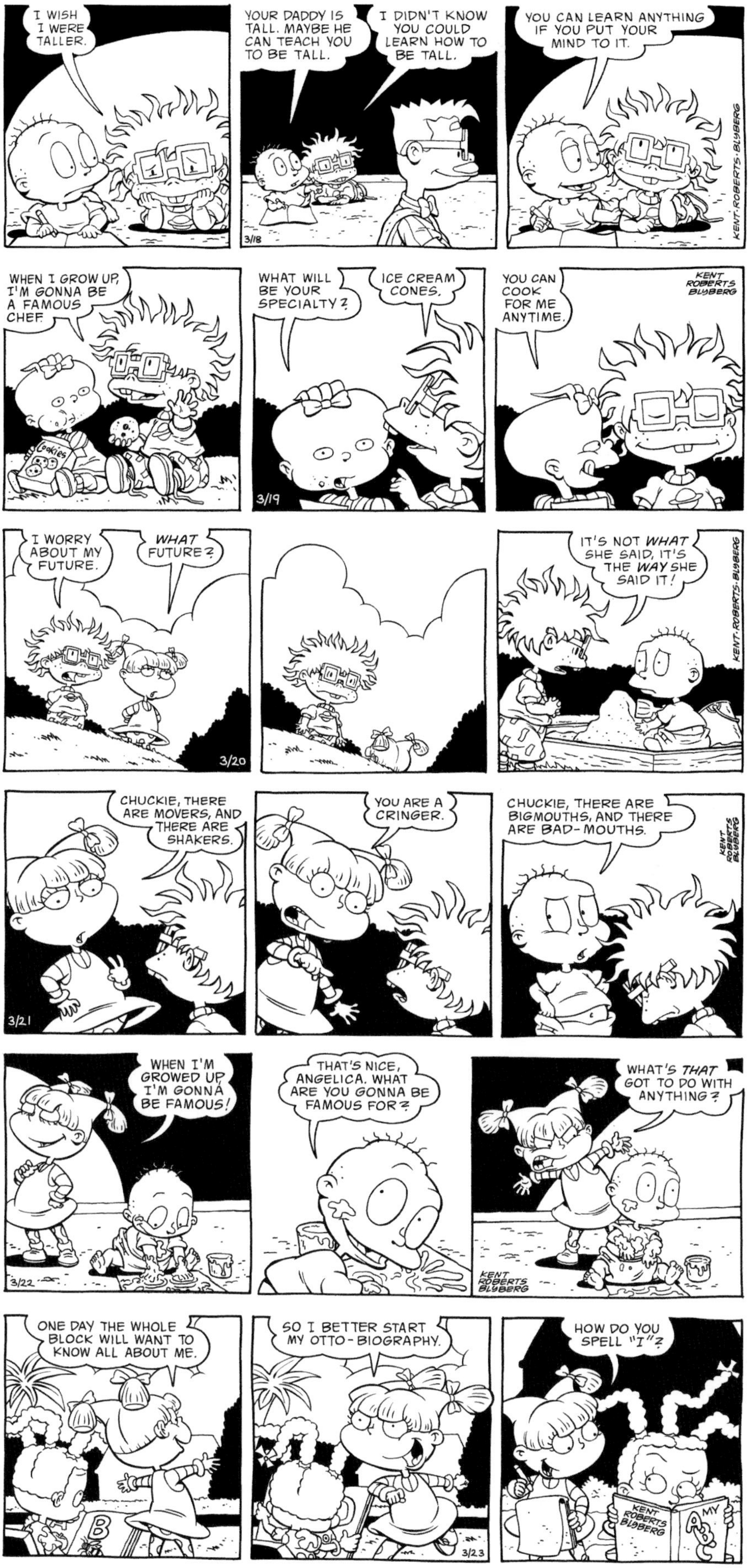
I WISH I WERE TALLER.
YOUR DADDY IS TALL. MAYBE HE CAN TEACH YOU TO BE TALL.
I DIDN'T KNOW YOU COULD LEARN HOW TO BE TALL.
3/18
YOU CAN LEARN ANYTHING IF YOU PUT YOUR MIND TO IT.
KENT·ROBERTS·BLYBERG
WHEN I GROW UP, I'M GONNA BE A FAMOUS CHEF.
COOKIES
WHAT WILL BE YOUR SPECIALTY?
ICE CREAM CONES.
3/19
YOU CAN COOK FOR ME ANYTIME.
KENT ROBERTS BLYBERG
I WORRY ABOUT MY FUTURE.
WHAT FUTURE?
3/20
IT'S NOT WHAT SHE SAID, IT'S THE WAY SHE SAID IT!
KENT·ROBERTS·BLYBERG
CHUCKIE, THERE ARE MOVERS, AND THERE ARE SHAKERS.
3/21
YOU ARE A CRINGER.
CHUCKIE, THERE ARE BIGMOUTHS, AND THERE ARE BAD-MOUTHS.
KENT ROBERTS BLYBERG
WHEN I'M GROWED UP I'M GONNA BE FAMOUS!
3/22
THAT'S NICE, ANGELICA. WHAT ARE YOU GONNA BE FAMOUS FOR?
KENT ROBERTS BLYBERG
WHAT'S THAT GOT TO DO WITH ANYTHING?
ONE DAY THE WHOLE BLOCK WILL WANT TO KNOW ALL ABOUT ME.
B
SO I BETTER START MY OTTO-BIOGRAPHY.
3/23
HOW DO YOU SPELL "I"?
KENT ROBERTS BLYBERG
MY
A B

2002

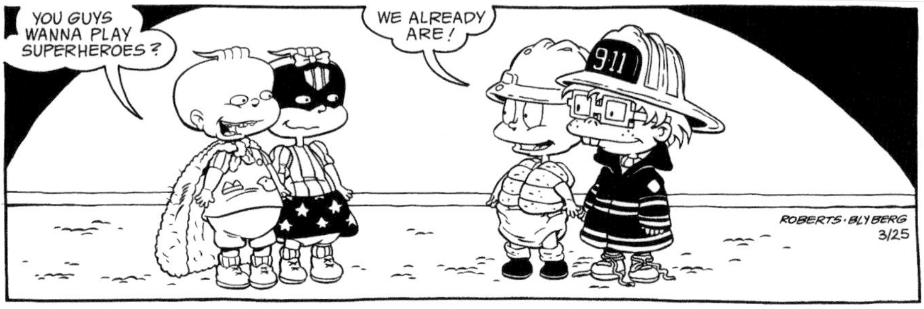
YOU GUYS WANNA PLAY SUPERHEROES?
WE ALREADY ARE!
9·11
ROBERTS·BLYBERG 3/25

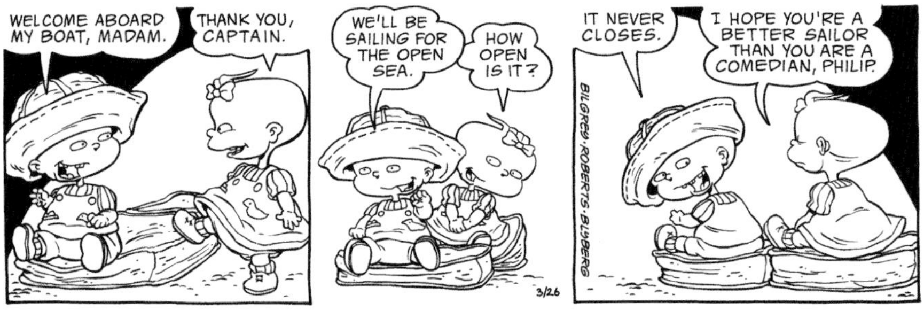
WELCOME ABOARD MY BOAT, MADAM.
THANK YOU, CAPTAIN.
WE'LL BE SAILING FOR THE OPEN SEA.
HOW OPEN IS IT?
IT NEVER CLOSES.
I HOPE YOU'RE A BETTER SAILOR THAN YOU ARE A COMEDIAN, PHILIP.
BILGREY·ROBERTS·BLYBERG
3/26

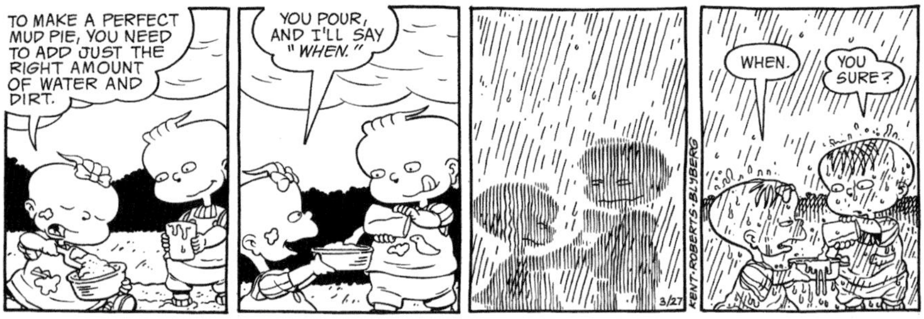
TO MAKE A PERFECT MUD PIE, YOU NEED TO ADD JUST THE RIGHT AMOUNT OF WATER AND DIRT.
YOU POUR, AND I'LL SAY "WHEN."
3/27
KENT·ROBERTS·BLYBERG
WHEN.
YOU SURE?

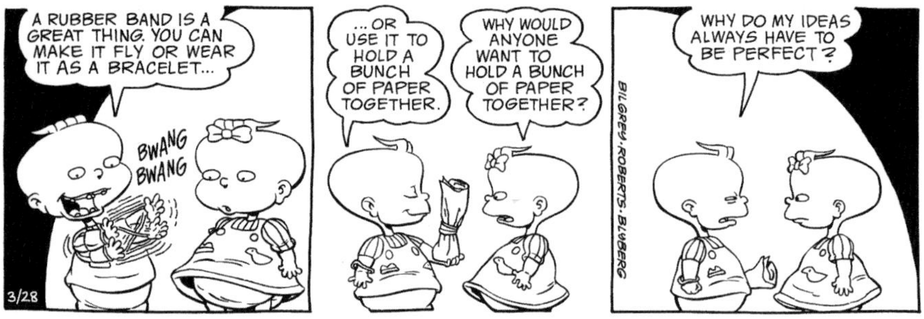
A RUBBER BAND IS A GREAT THING. YOU CAN MAKE IT FLY OR WEAR IT AS A BRACELET...
BWANG BWANG
3/28
...OR USE IT TO HOLD A BUNCH OF PAPER TOGETHER.
WHY WOULD ANYONE WANT TO HOLD A BUNCH OF PAPER TOGETHER?
BILGREY·ROBERTS·BLYBERG
WHY DO MY IDEAS ALWAYS HAVE TO BE PERFECT?

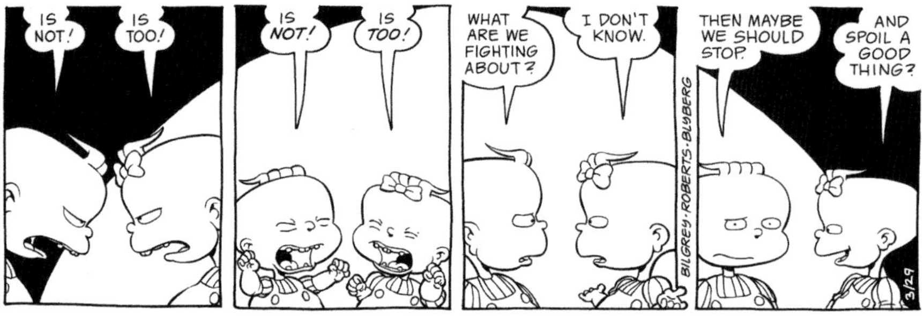
IS NOT!
IS TOO!
IS NOT!
IS TOO!
WHAT ARE WE FIGHTING ABOUT?
I DON'T KNOW.
BILGREY·ROBERTS·BLYBERG
THEN MAYBE WE SHOULD STOP.
AND SPOIL A GOOD THING?
3/29

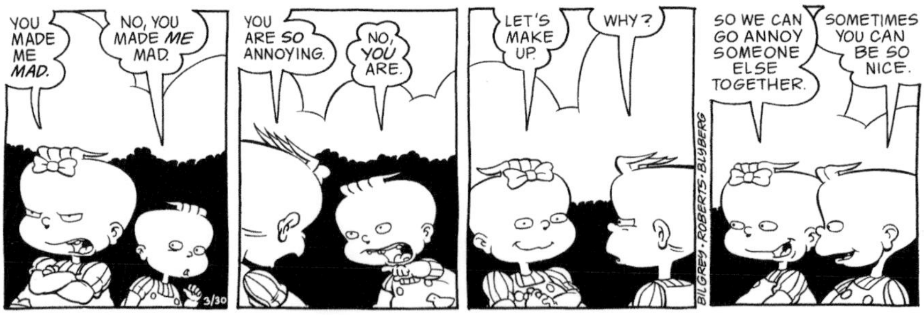
YOU MADE ME MAD.
NO, YOU MADE ME MAD.
3/30
YOU ARE SO ANNOYING.
NO, YOU ARE.
LET'S MAKE UP.
WHY?
BILGREY·ROBERTS·BLYBERG
SO WE CAN GO ANNOY SOMEONE ELSE TOGETHER.
SOMETIMES YOU CAN BE SO NICE.

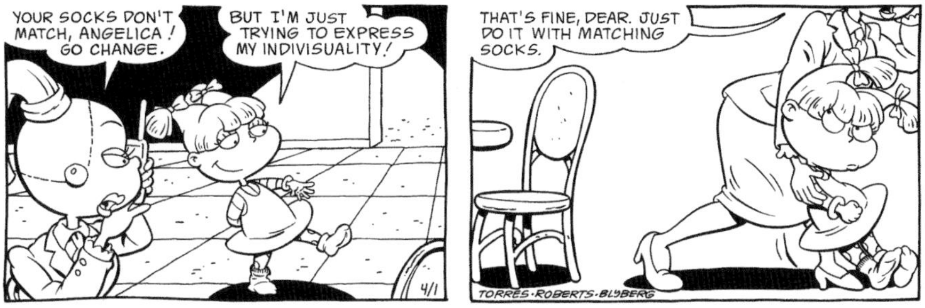
YOUR SOCKS DON'T MATCH, ANGELICA! GO CHANGE.
BUT I'M JUST TRYING TO EXPRESS MY INDIVISUALITY!
4/1
THAT'S FINE, DEAR. JUST DO IT WITH MATCHING SOCKS.
TORRES·ROBERTS·BLYBERG

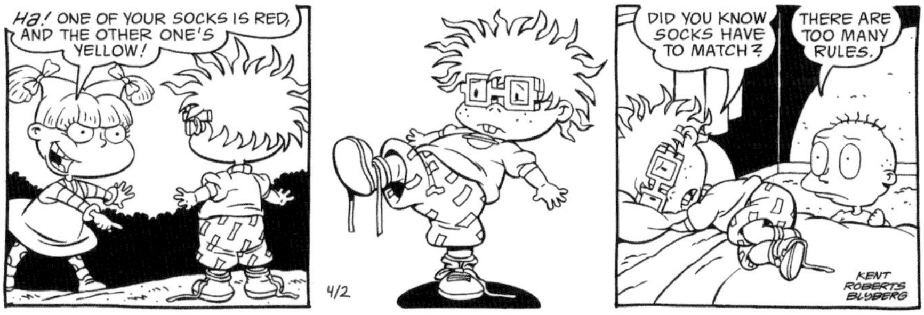
HA! ONE OF YOUR SOCKS IS RED, AND THE OTHER ONE'S YELLOW!
4/2
DID YOU KNOW SOCKS HAVE TO MATCH?
THERE ARE TOO MANY RULES.
KENT ROBERTS BLYBERG

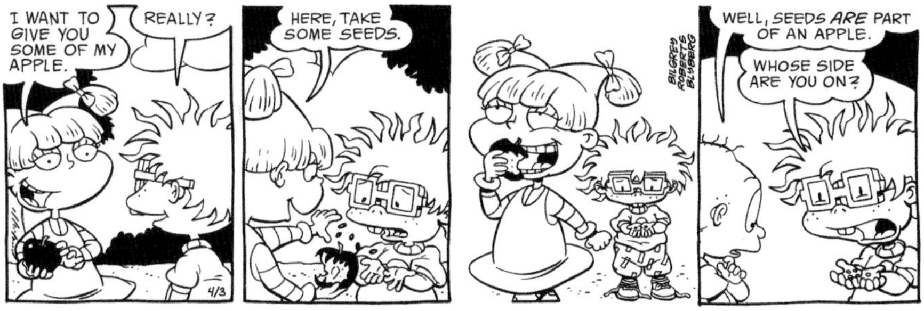
I WANT TO GIVE YOU SOME OF MY APPLE.
REALLY?
4/3
HERE, TAKE SOME SEEDS.
BILGREY ROBERTS BLYBERG
WELL, SEEDS ARE PART OF AN APPLE.
WHOSE SIDE ARE YOU ON?

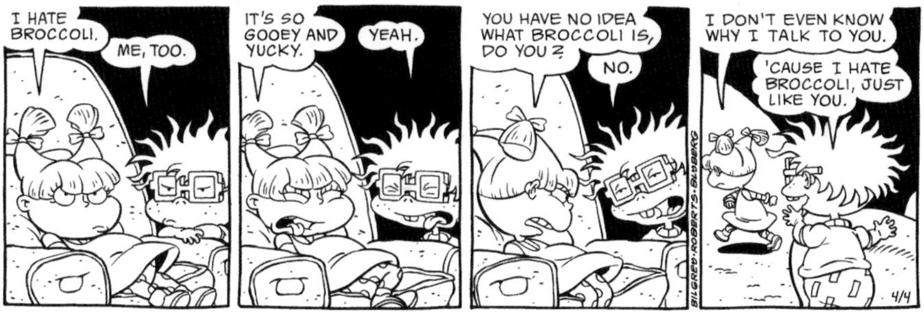
I HATE BROCCOLI.
ME, TOO.
IT'S SO GOOEY AND YUCKY.
YEAH.
YOU HAVE NO IDEA WHAT BROCCOLI IS, DO YOU?
NO.
BILGREY·ROBERTS·BLYBERG
I DON'T EVEN KNOW WHY I TALK TO YOU.
'CAUSE I HATE BROCCOLI, JUST LIKE YOU.
4/4

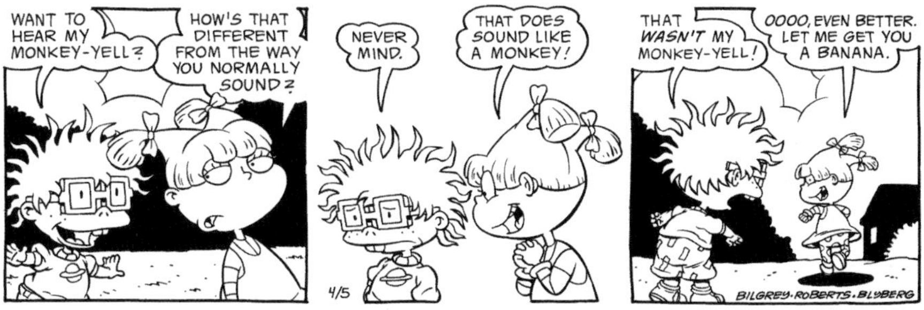
WANT TO HEAR MY MONKEY-YELL?
HOW'S THAT DIFFERENT FROM THE WAY YOU NORMALLY SOUND?
NEVER MIND.
THAT DOES SOUND LIKE A MONKEY!
4/5
THAT WASN'T MY MONKEY-YELL!
OOOO, EVEN BETTER. LET ME GET YOU A BANANA.
BILGREY·ROBERTS·BLYBERG

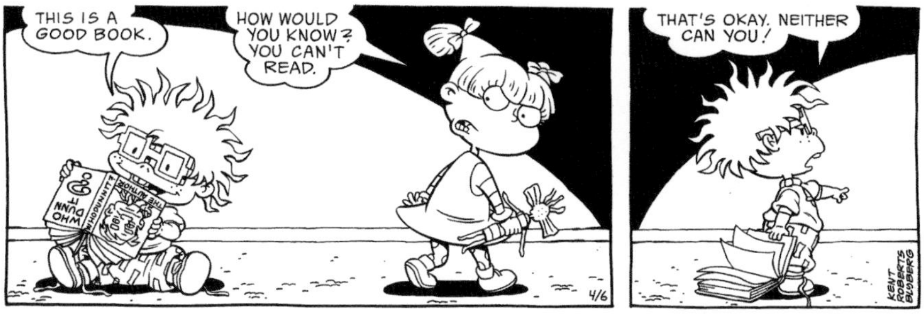
THIS IS A GOOD BOOK.
HOW WOULD YOU KNOW? YOU CAN'T READ.
WHO DUNN IT
4/6
THAT'S OKAY. NEITHER CAN YOU!
KENT ROBERTS BLYBERG

2002

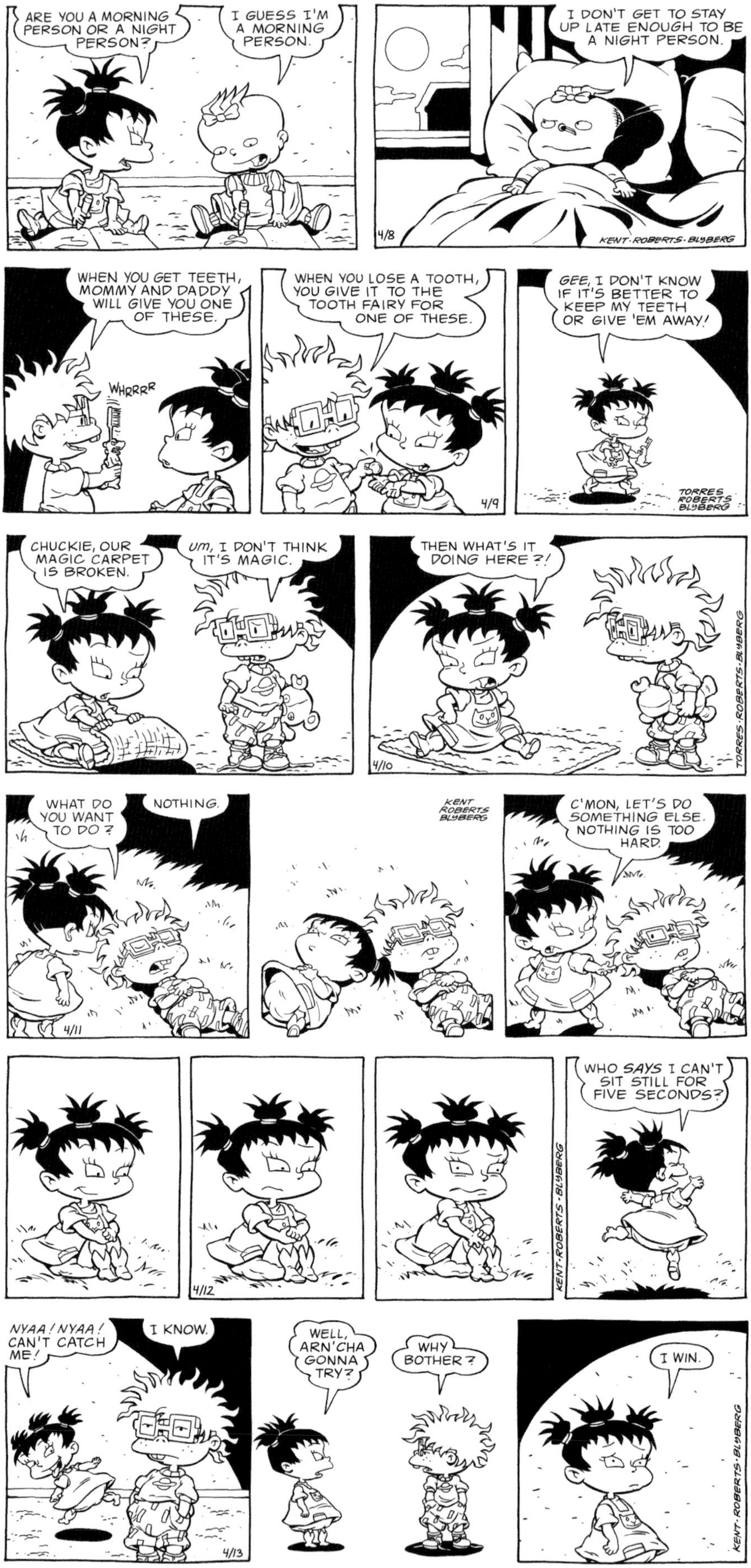
ARE YOU A MORNING PERSON OR A NIGHT PERSON?
I GUESS I'M A MORNING PERSON.
I DON'T GET TO STAY UP LATE ENOUGH TO BE A NIGHT PERSON.
4/8
KENT·ROBERTS·BLYBERG
WHEN YOU GET TEETH, MOMMY AND DADDY WILL GIVE YOU ONE OF THESE.
WHRRRR
WHEN YOU LOSE A TOOTH, YOU GIVE IT TO THE TOOTH FAIRY FOR ONE OF THESE.
4/9
GEE, I DON'T KNOW IF IT'S BETTER TO KEEP MY TEETH OR GIVE 'EM AWAY!
TORRES ROBERTS BLYBERG
CHUCKIE, OUR MAGIC CARPET IS BROKEN.
UM, I DON'T THINK IT'S MAGIC.
THEN WHAT'S IT DOING HERE?!
4/10
TORRES·ROBERTS·BLYBERG
WHAT DO YOU WANT TO DO?
NOTHING.
4/11
KENT ROBERTS BLYBERG
C'MON, LET'S DO SOMETHING ELSE. NOTHING IS TOO HARD.
4/12
KENT·ROBERTS·BLYBERG
WHO SAYS I CAN'T SIT STILL FOR FIVE SECONDS?
NYAA! NYAA! CAN'T CATCH ME!
I KNOW.
4/13
WELL, ARN'CHA GONNA TRY?
WHY BOTHER?
I WIN.
KENT·ROBERTS·BLYBERG

2002

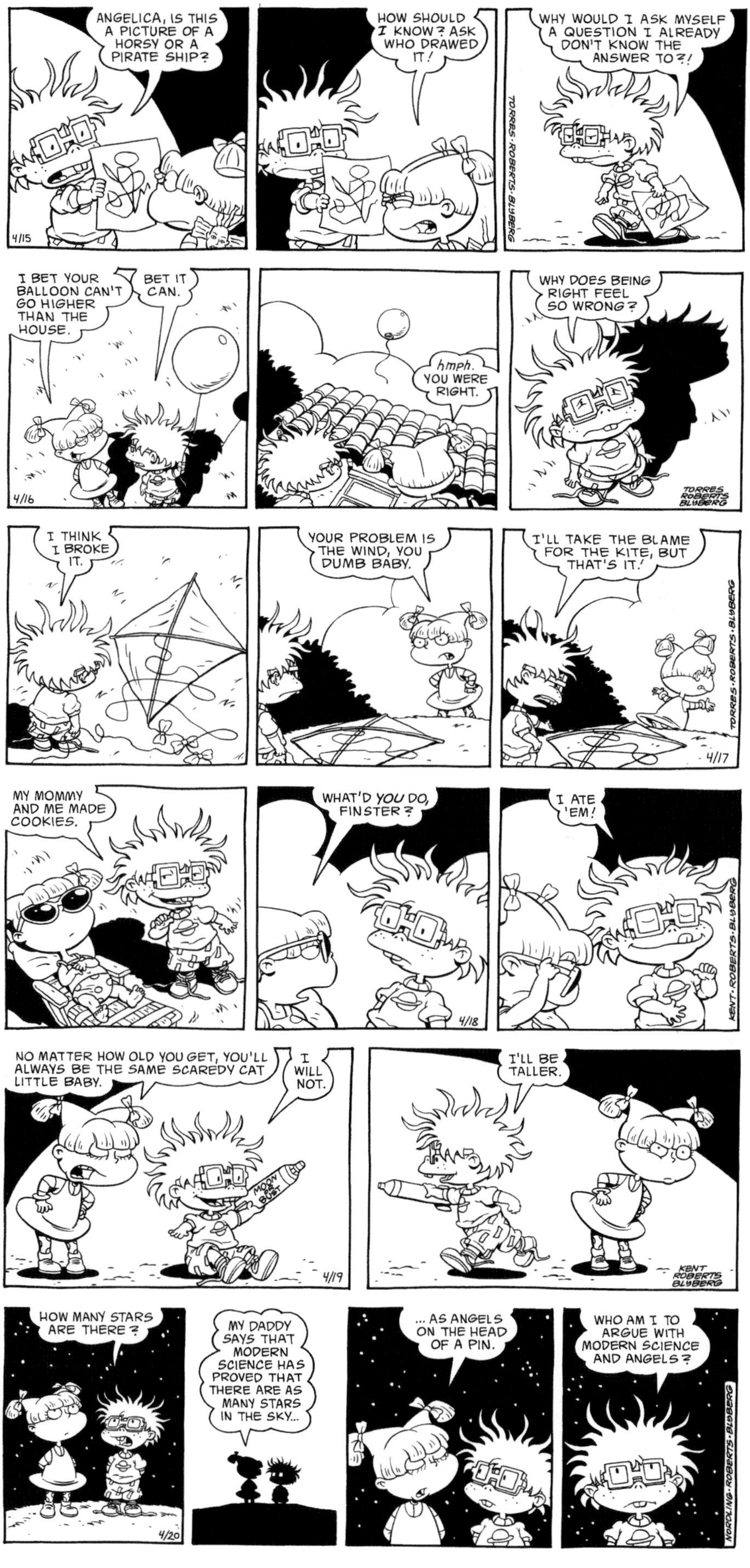

ANGELICA, IS THIS A PICTURE OF A HORSY OR A PIRATE SHIP?
HOW SHOULD I KNOW? ASK WHO DRAWED IT!
WHY WOULD I ASK MYSELF A QUESTION I ALREADY DON'T KNOW THE ANSWER TO?!
TORRES·ROBERTS·BLYBERG
4/15
I BET YOUR BALLOON CAN'T GO HIGHER THAN THE HOUSE.
BET IT CAN.
hmph. YOU WERE RIGHT.
WHY DOES BEING RIGHT FEEL SO WRONG?
TORRES ROBERTS BLYBERG
4/16
I THINK I BROKE IT.
YOUR PROBLEM IS THE WIND, YOU DUMB BABY.
I'LL TAKE THE BLAME FOR THE KITE, BUT THAT'S IT!
TORRES·ROBERTS·BLYBERG
4/17
MY MOMMY AND ME MADE COOKIES.
WHAT'D YOU DO, FINSTER?
I ATE 'EM!
KENT·ROBERTS·BLYBERG
4/18
NO MATTER HOW OLD YOU GET, YOU'LL ALWAYS BE THE SAME SCAREDY CAT LITTLE BABY.
I WILL NOT.
MOON OR BUST
I'LL BE TALLER.
KENT ROBERTS BLYBERG
4/19
HOW MANY STARS ARE THERE?
MY DADDY SAYS THAT MODERN SCIENCE HAS PROVED THAT THERE ARE AS MANY STARS IN THE SKY...
... AS ANGELS ON THE HEAD OF A PIN.
WHO AM I TO ARGUE WITH MODERN SCIENCE AND ANGELS?
NORDLING·ROBERTS·BLYBERG
4/20

2002

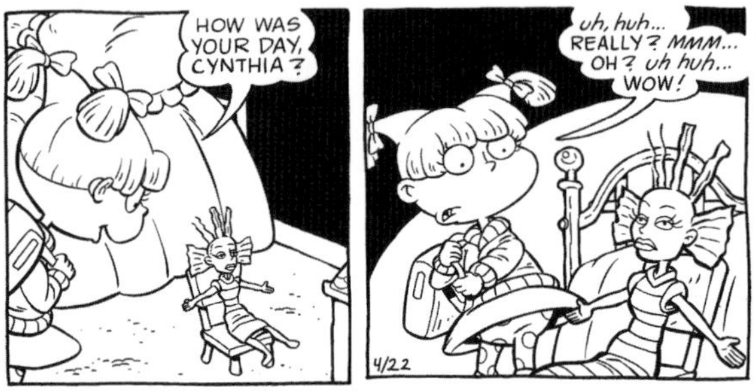
HOW WAS YOUR DAY, CYNTHIA?
uh, huh... REALLY? MMM... OH? uh huh... WOW!
4/22
I CAN'T BELIEVE MY DOLL HAD A MORE INTERESTING DAY THAN I DID.
BILGREY ROBERTS BLYBERG

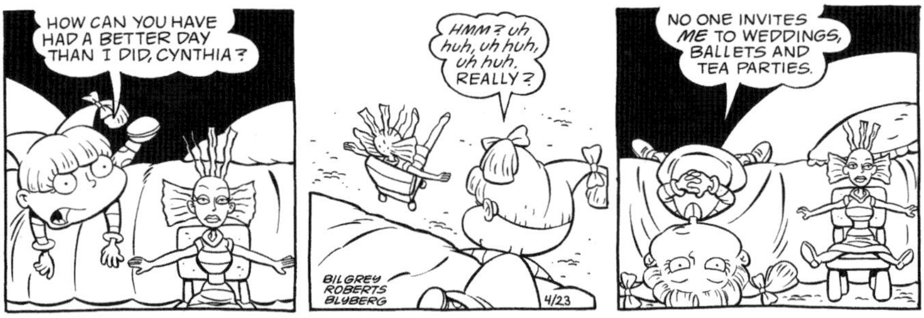
HOW CAN YOU HAVE HAD A BETTER DAY THAN I DID, CYNTHIA?
HMM? uh huh, uh huh, uh huh. REALLY?
BILGREY ROBERTS BLYBERG
4/23
NO ONE INVITES ME TO WEDDINGS, BALLETS AND TEA PARTIES.

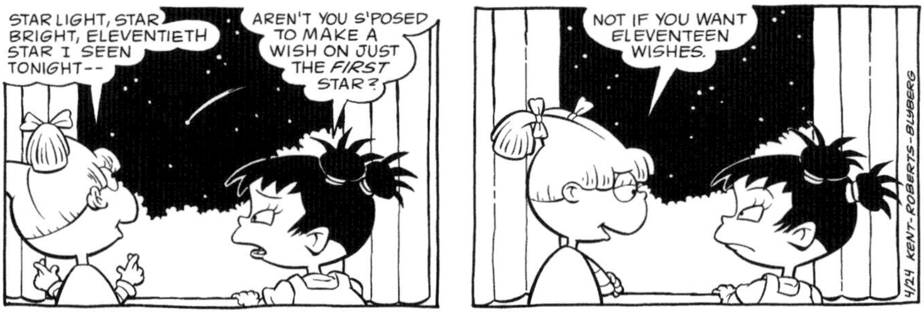
STAR LIGHT, STAR BRIGHT, ELEVENTIETH STAR I SEEN TONIGHT--
AREN'T YOU S'POSED TO MAKE A WISH ON JUST THE FIRST STAR?
NOT IF YOU WANT ELEVENTEEN WISHES.
4/24 KENT-ROBERTS-BLYBERG

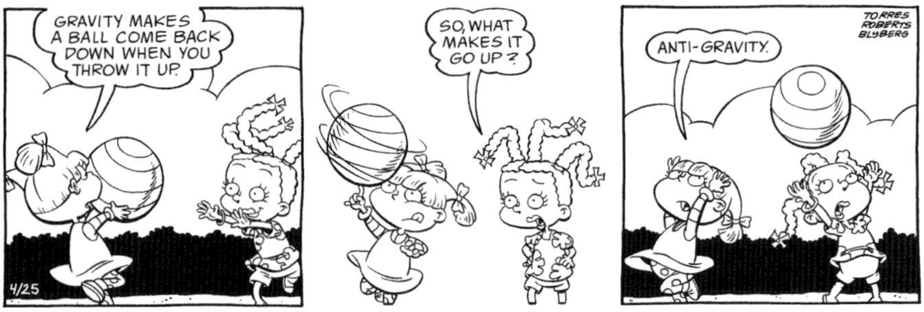
GRAVITY MAKES A BALL COME BACK DOWN WHEN YOU THROW IT UP.
4/25
SO, WHAT MAKES IT GO UP?
TORRES ROBERTS BLYBERG
ANTI-GRAVITY.

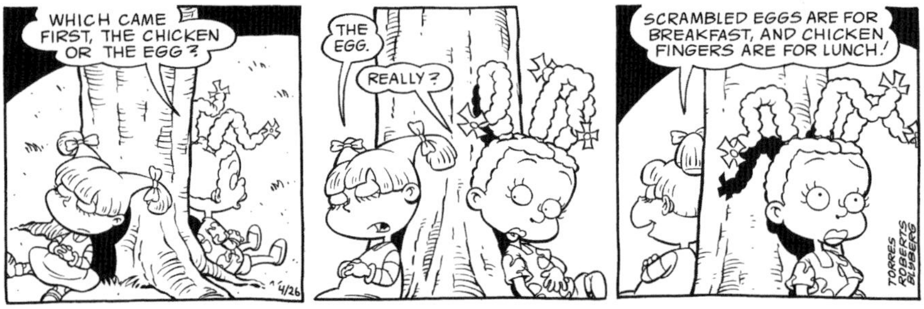
WHICH CAME FIRST, THE CHICKEN OR THE EGG?
4/26
THE EGG.
REALLY?
SCRAMBLED EGGS ARE FOR BREAKFAST, AND CHICKEN FINGERS ARE FOR LUNCH!
TORRES ROBERTS BLYBERG

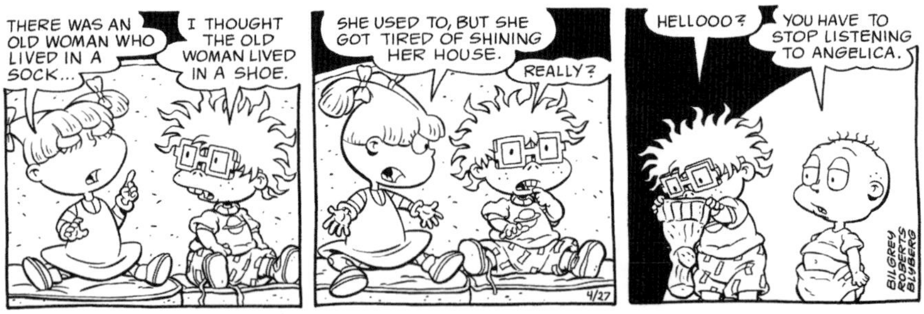
THERE WAS AN OLD WOMAN WHO LIVED IN A SOCK...
I THOUGHT THE OLD WOMAN LIVED IN A SHOE.
SHE USED TO, BUT SHE GOT TIRED OF SHINING HER HOUSE.
REALLY?
4/27
HELLOOO?
YOU HAVE TO STOP LISTENING TO ANGELICA.
BILGREY ROBERTS BLYBERG

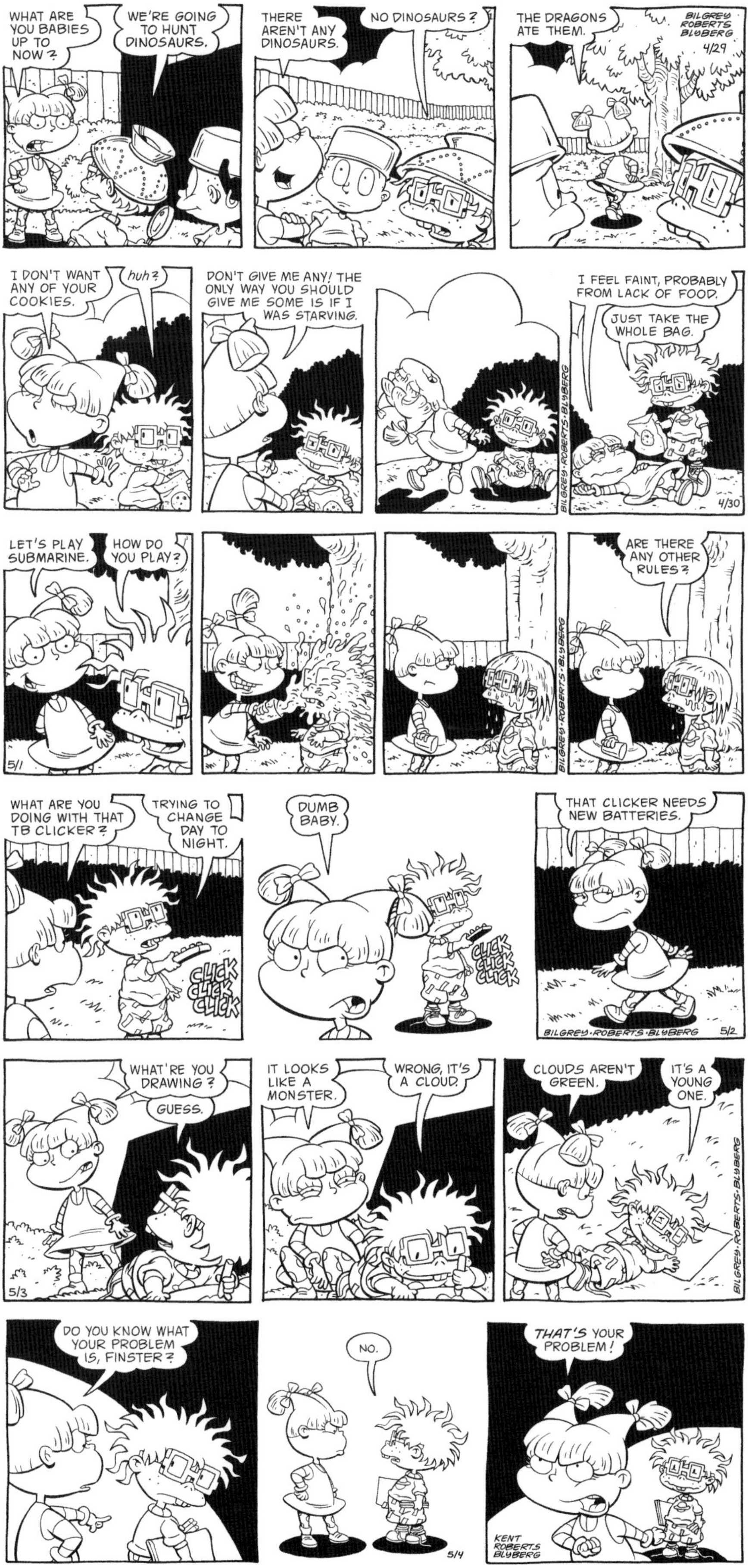
WHAT ARE YOU BABIES UP TO NOW?
WE'RE GOING TO HUNT DINOSAURS.
THERE AREN'T ANY DINOSAURS.
NO DINOSAURS?
THE DRAGONS ATE THEM.
BILGREY ROBERTS BLYBERG 4/29
I DON'T WANT ANY OF YOUR COOKIES.
huh?
DON'T GIVE ME ANY! THE ONLY WAY YOU SHOULD GIVE ME SOME IS IF I WAS STARVING.
BILGREY·ROBERTS·BLYBERG
I FEEL FAINT, PROBABLY FROM LACK OF FOOD.
JUST TAKE THE WHOLE BAG.
4/30
LET'S PLAY SUBMARINE.
HOW DO YOU PLAY?
5/1
BILGREY·ROBERTS·BLYBERG
ARE THERE ANY OTHER RULES?
WHAT ARE YOU DOING WITH THAT TB CLICKER?
TRYING TO CHANGE DAY TO NIGHT.
CLICK CLICK CLICK
DUMB BABY.
CLICK CLICK CLICK
THAT CLICKER NEEDS NEW BATTERIES.
BILGREY·ROBERTS·BLYBERG 5/2
WHAT'RE YOU DRAWING?
GUESS.
5/3
IT LOOKS LIKE A MONSTER.
WRONG, IT'S A CLOUD.
CLOUDS AREN'T GREEN.
IT'S A YOUNG ONE.
BILGREY·ROBERTS·BLYBERG
DO YOU KNOW WHAT YOUR PROBLEM IS, FINSTER?
NO.
5/4
THAT'S YOUR PROBLEM!
KENT ROBERTS BLYBERG

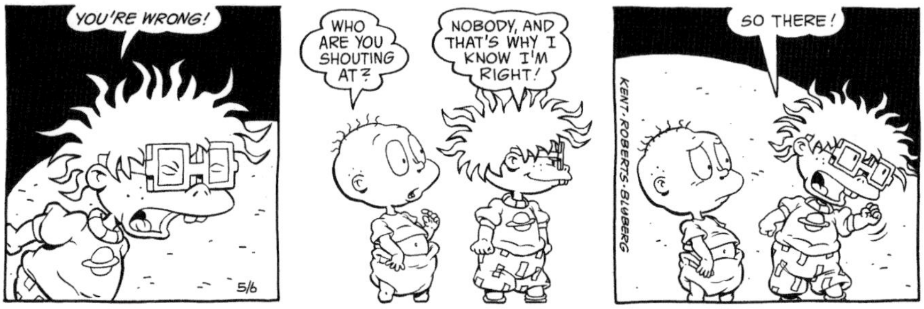
YOU'RE WRONG!
5/6
WHO ARE YOU SHOUTING AT?
NOBODY, AND THAT'S WHY I KNOW I'M RIGHT!
KENT·ROBERTS·BLYBERG
SO THERE!

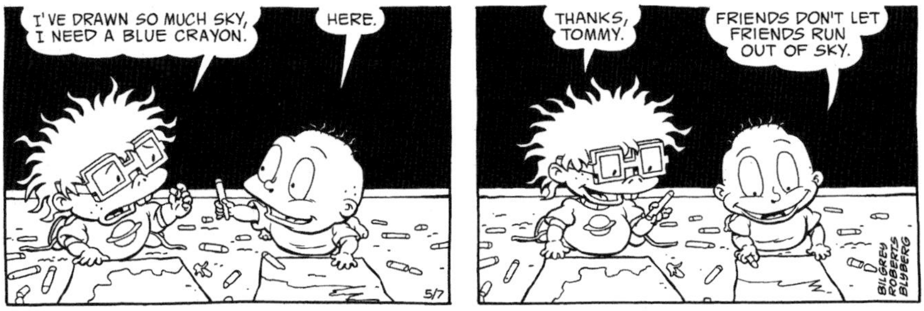
I'VE DRAWN SO MUCH SKY, I NEED A BLUE CRAYON.
HERE.
5/7
THANKS, TOMMY.
FRIENDS DON'T LET FRIENDS RUN OUT OF SKY.
BILGREY ROBERTS BLYBERG

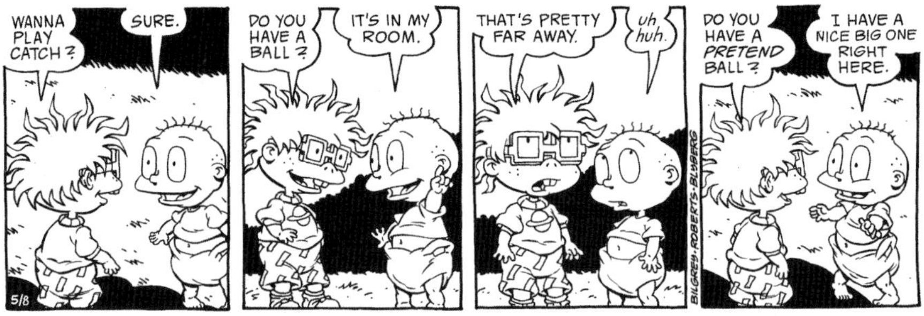
WANNA PLAY CATCH?
SURE.
5/8
DO YOU HAVE A BALL?
IT'S IN MY ROOM.
THAT'S PRETTY FAR AWAY.
uh huh.
BILGREY·ROBERTS·BLYBERG
DO YOU HAVE A PRETEND BALL?
I HAVE A NICE BIG ONE RIGHT HERE.

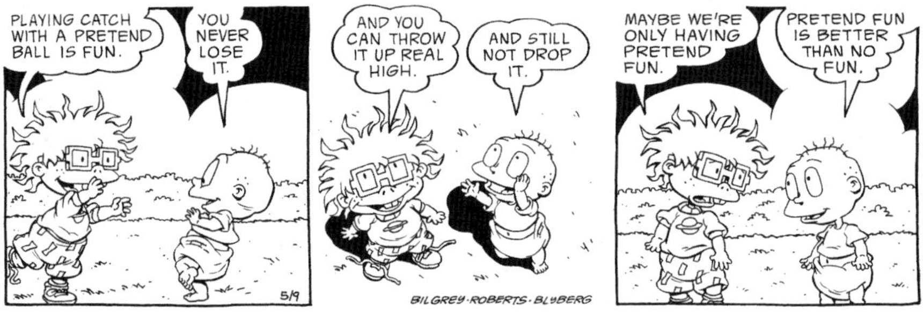
PLAYING CATCH WITH A PRETEND BALL IS FUN.
YOU NEVER LOSE IT.
5/9
AND YOU CAN THROW IT UP REAL HIGH.
AND STILL NOT DROP IT.
BILGREY·ROBERTS·BLYBERG
MAYBE WE'RE ONLY HAVING PRETEND FUN.
PRETEND FUN IS BETTER THAN NO FUN.

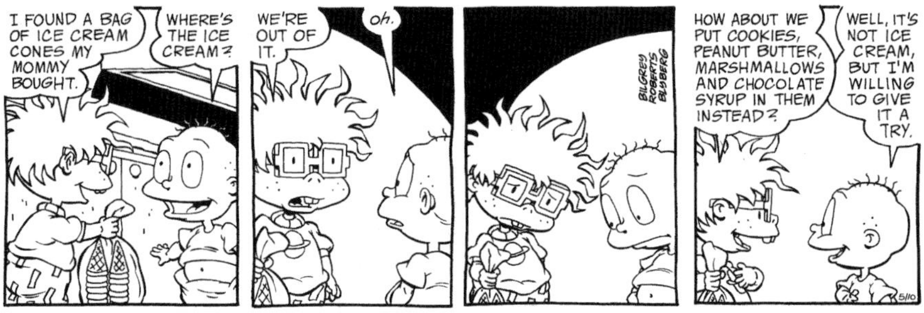
I FOUND A BAG OF ICE CREAM CONES MY MOMMY BOUGHT.
WHERE'S THE ICE CREAM?
WE'RE OUT OF IT.
oh.
BILGREY ROBERTS BLYBERG
HOW ABOUT WE PUT COOKIES, PEANUT BUTTER, MARSHMALLOWS AND CHOCOLATE SYRUP IN THEM INSTEAD?
WELL, IT'S NOT ICE CREAM, BUT I'M WILLING TO GIVE IT A TRY.
5/10

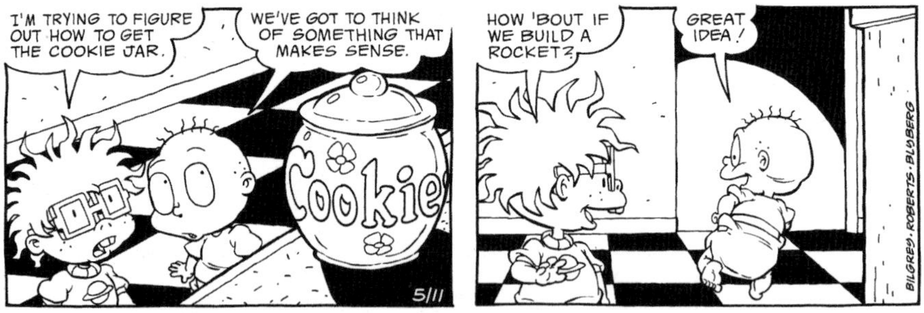
I'M TRYING TO FIGURE OUT HOW TO GET THE COOKIE JAR.
WE'VE GOT TO THINK OF SOMETHING THAT MAKES SENSE.
Cookie
5/11
HOW 'BOUT IF WE BUILD A ROCKET?
GREAT IDEA!
BILGREY·ROBERTS·BLYBERG

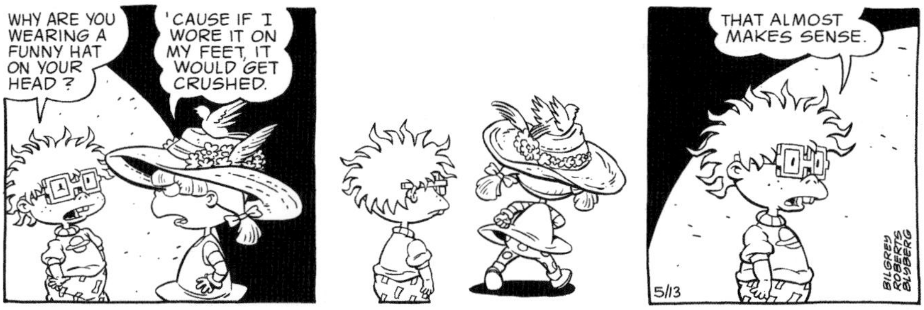
WHY ARE YOU WEARING A FUNNY HAT ON YOUR HEAD?
'CAUSE IF I WORE IT ON MY FEET, IT WOULD GET CRUSHED.
THAT ALMOST MAKES SENSE.
5/13
BILGREY ROBERTS BLYBERG

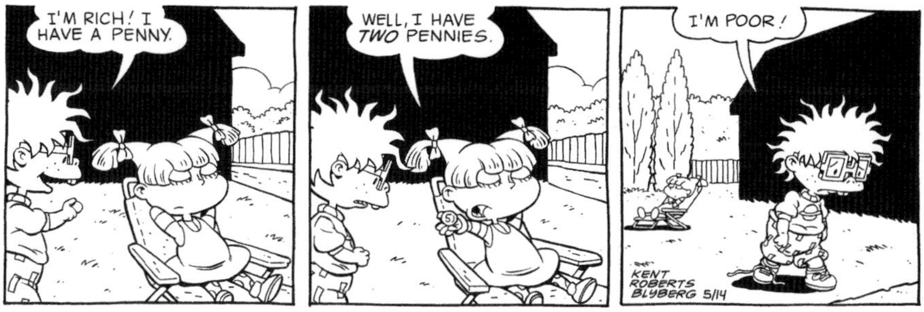
I'M RICH! I HAVE A PENNY.
WELL, I HAVE *TWO* PENNIES.
I'M POOR!
KENT ROBERTS BLYBERG 5/14

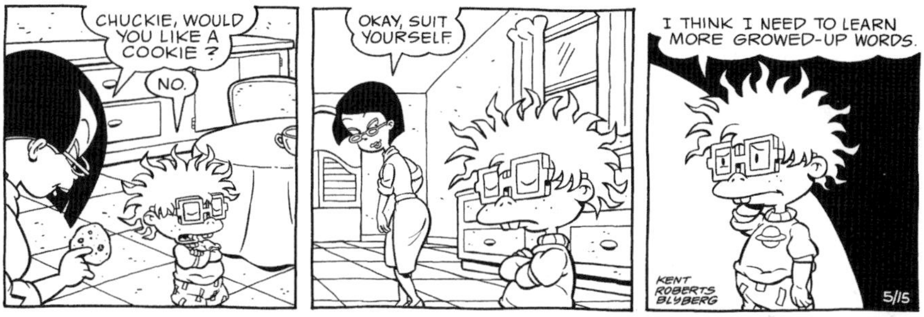
CHUCKIE, WOULD YOU LIKE A COOKIE?
NO.
OKAY, SUIT YOURSELF.
I THINK I NEED TO LEARN MORE GROWED-UP WORDS.
KENT ROBERTS BLYBERG
5/15

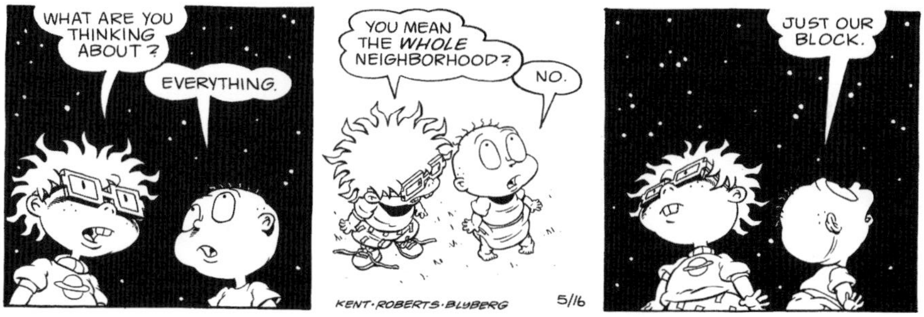
WHAT ARE YOU THINKING ABOUT?
EVERYTHING.
YOU MEAN THE *WHOLE* NEIGHBORHOOD?
NO.
KENT · ROBERTS · BLYBERG
5/16
JUST OUR BLOCK.

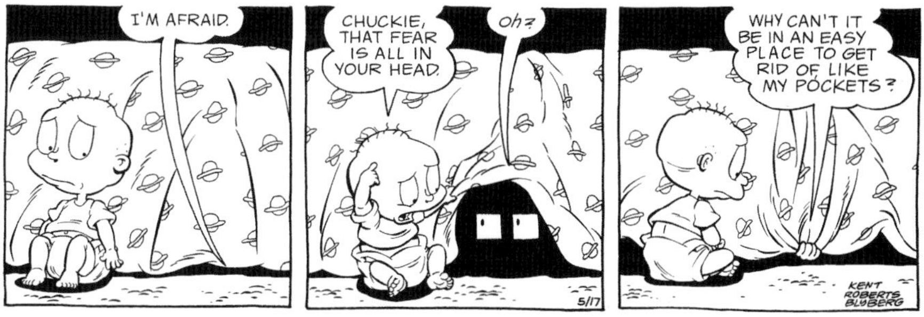
I'M AFRAID.
CHUCKIE, THAT FEAR IS ALL IN YOUR HEAD.
oh?
5/17
WHY CAN'T IT BE IN AN EASY PLACE TO GET RID OF LIKE MY POCKETS?
KENT ROBERTS BLYBERG

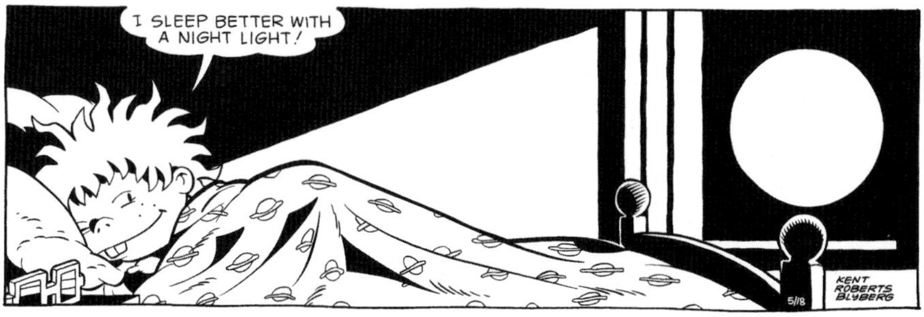
I SLEEP BETTER WITH A NIGHT LIGHT!
5/18
KENT ROBERTS BLYBERG

2002

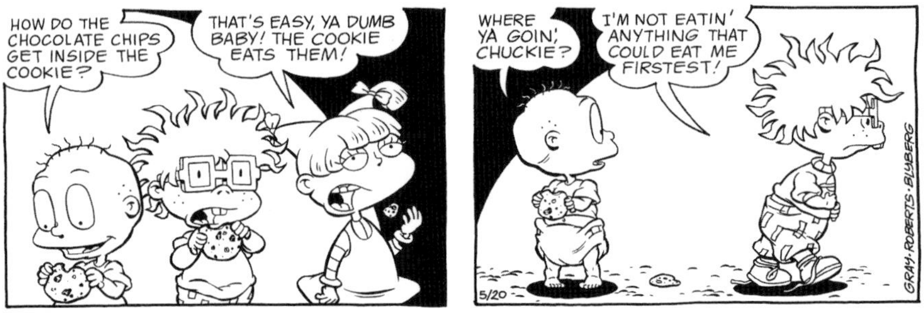
HOW DO THE CHOCOLATE CHIPS GET INSIDE THE COOKIE?
THAT'S EASY, YA DUMB BABY! THE COOKIE EATS THEM!
WHERE YA GOIN', CHUCKIE?
I'M NOT EATIN' ANYTHING THAT COULD EAT ME FIRSTEST!
5/20
GRAY·ROBERTS·BLYBERG

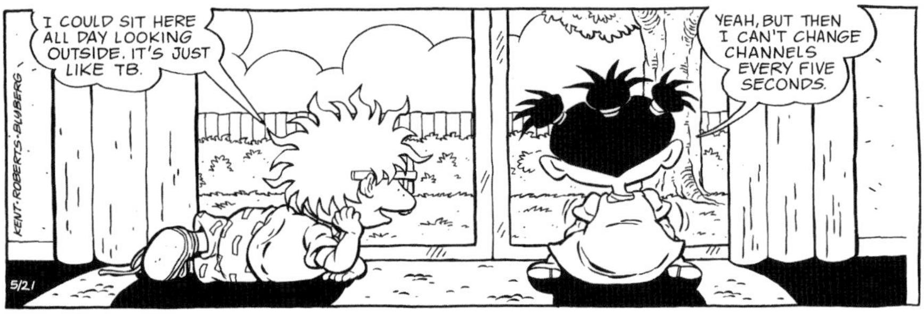
KENT·ROBERTS·BLYBERG
I COULD SIT HERE ALL DAY LOOKING OUTSIDE. IT'S JUST LIKE TB.
YEAH, BUT THEN I CAN'T CHANGE CHANNELS EVERY FIVE SECONDS.
5/21

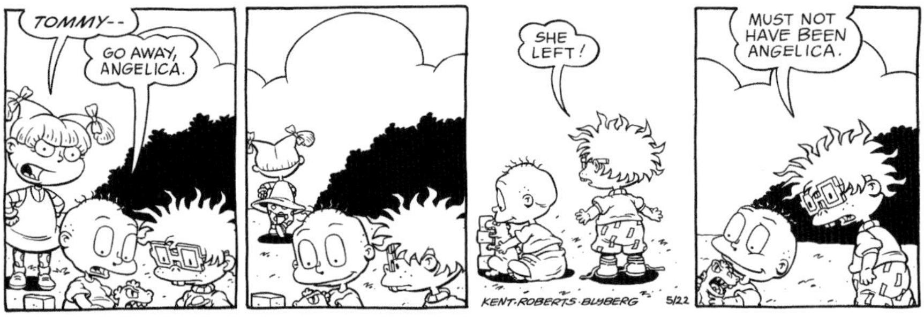
TOMMY--
GO AWAY, ANGELICA.
SHE LEFT!
KENT·ROBERTS·BLYBERG
5/22
MUST NOT HAVE BEEN ANGELICA.

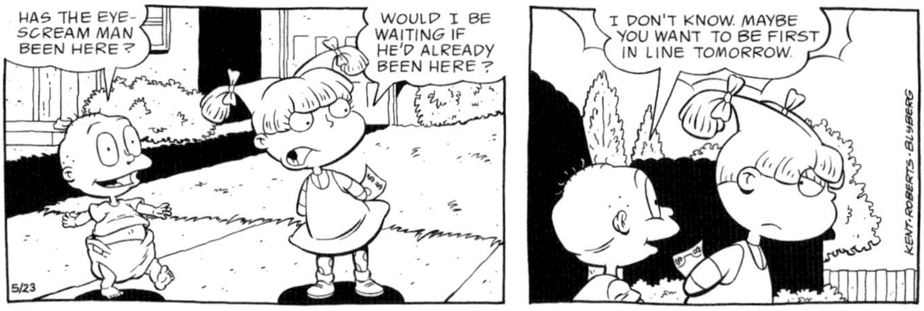
HAS THE EYE-SCREAM MAN BEEN HERE?
WOULD I BE WAITING IF HE'D ALREADY BEEN HERE?
5/23
I DON'T KNOW. MAYBE YOU WANT TO BE FIRST IN LINE TOMORROW.
KENT·ROBERTS·BLYBERG

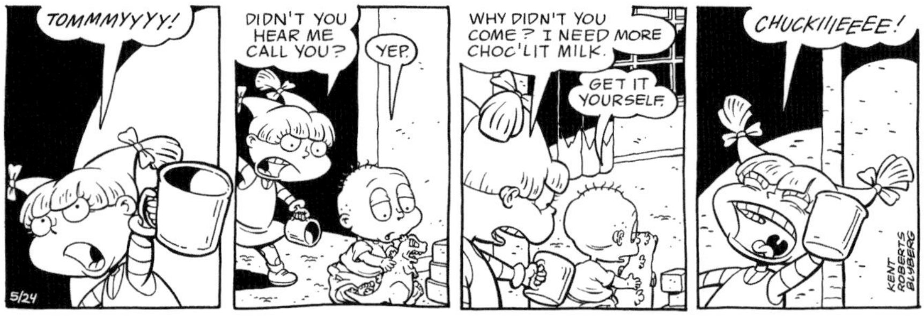
TOMMMYYYY!
5/24
DIDN'T YOU HEAR ME CALL YOU?
YEP.
WHY DIDN'T YOU COME? I NEED MORE CHOC'LIT MILK.
GET IT YOURSELF.
CHUCKIIIEEEE!
KENT ROBERTS BLYBERG

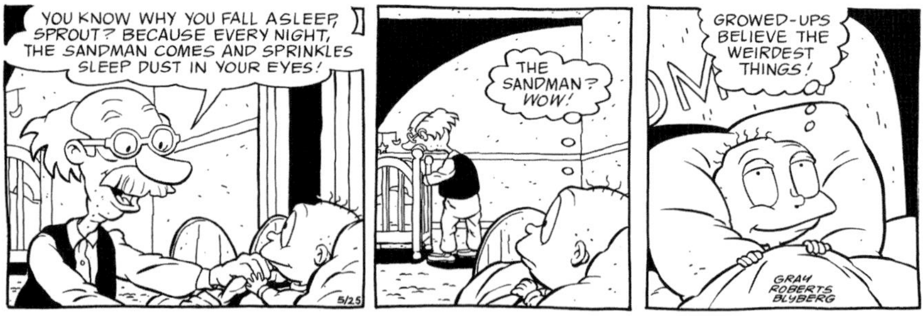
YOU KNOW WHY YOU FALL ASLEEP, SPROUT? BECAUSE EVERY NIGHT, THE SANDMAN COMES AND SPRINKLES SLEEP DUST IN YOUR EYES!
THE SANDMAN? WOW!
5/25
GROWED-UPS BELIEVE THE WEIRDEST THINGS!
GRAY ROBERTS BLYBERG

2002

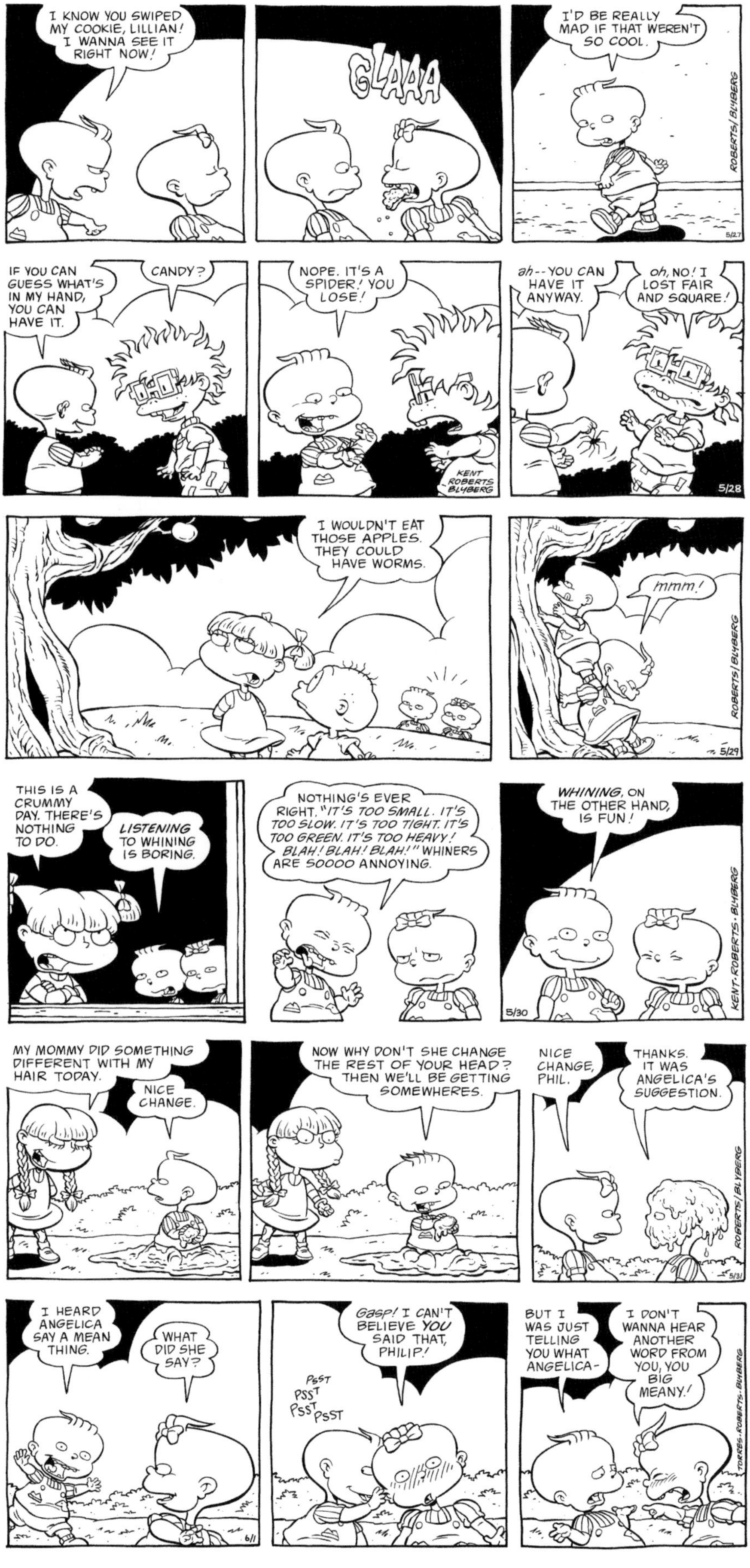
I KNOW YOU SWIPED MY COOKIE, LILLIAN! I WANNA SEE IT RIGHT NOW!
GLAAAA
I'D BE REALLY MAD IF THAT WEREN'T SO COOL.
ROBERTS/BLYBERG
5/27
IF YOU CAN GUESS WHAT'S IN MY HAND, YOU CAN HAVE IT.
CANDY?
NOPE. IT'S A SPIDER! YOU LOSE!
KENT ROBERTS BLYBERG
ah-- YOU CAN HAVE IT ANYWAY.
oh, NO! I LOST FAIR AND SQUARE!
5/28
I WOULDN'T EAT THOSE APPLES. THEY COULD HAVE WORMS.
mmm!
ROBERTS/BLYBERG
5/29
THIS IS A CRUMMY DAY. THERE'S NOTHING TO DO.
LISTENING TO WHINING IS BORING.
NOTHING'S EVER RIGHT. "IT'S TOO SMALL. IT'S TOO SLOW. IT'S TOO TIGHT. IT'S TOO GREEN. IT'S TOO HEAVY! BLAH! BLAH! BLAH!" WHINERS ARE SOOOO ANNOYING.
WHINING, ON THE OTHER HAND, IS FUN!
5/30
KENT·ROBERTS·BLYBERG
MY MOMMY DID SOMETHING DIFFERENT WITH MY HAIR TODAY.
NICE CHANGE.
NOW WHY DON'T SHE CHANGE THE REST OF YOUR HEAD? THEN WE'LL BE GETTING SOMEWHERES.
NICE CHANGE, PHIL.
THANKS. IT WAS ANGELICA'S SUGGESTION.
ROBERTS/BLYBERG
5/31
I HEARD ANGELICA SAY A MEAN THING.
WHAT DID SHE SAY?
6/1
PSST PSST PSST PSST
Gasp! I CAN'T BELIEVE YOU SAID THAT, PHILIP!
BUT I WAS JUST TELLING YOU WHAT ANGELICA-
I DON'T WANNA HEAR ANOTHER WORD FROM YOU, YOU BIG MEANY!
TORRES·ROBERTS·BLYBERG

2002

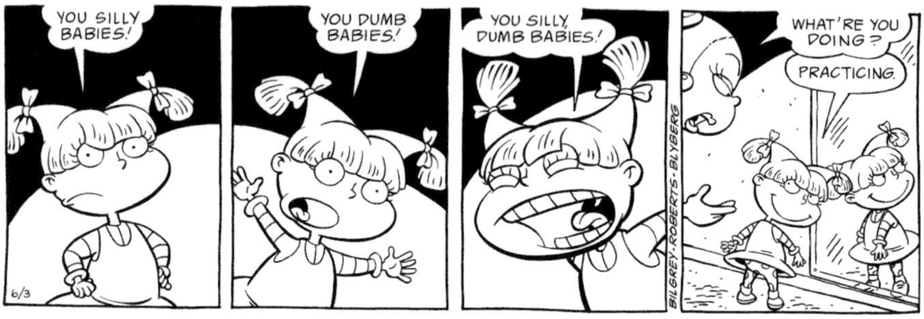
YOU SILLY BABIES!
YOU DUMB BABIES!
YOU SILLY, DUMB BABIES!
BILGREY·ROBERTS·BLYBERG
WHAT'RE YOU DOING?
PRACTICING.
6/3

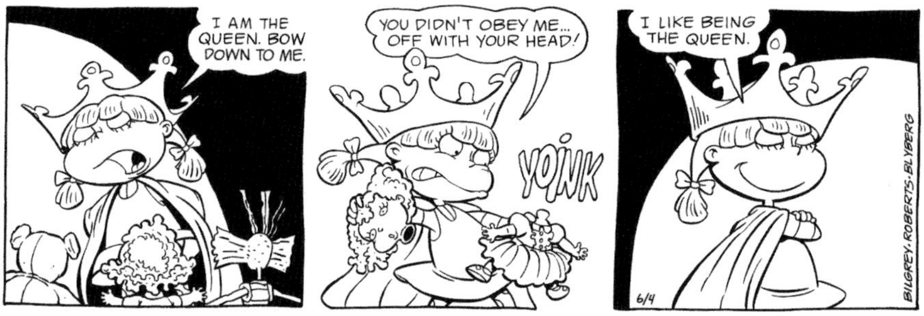
I AM THE QUEEN. BOW DOWN TO ME.
YOU DIDN'T OBEY ME... OFF WITH YOUR HEAD!
YOINK
I LIKE BEING THE QUEEN.
BILGREY·ROBERTS·BLYBERG
6/4

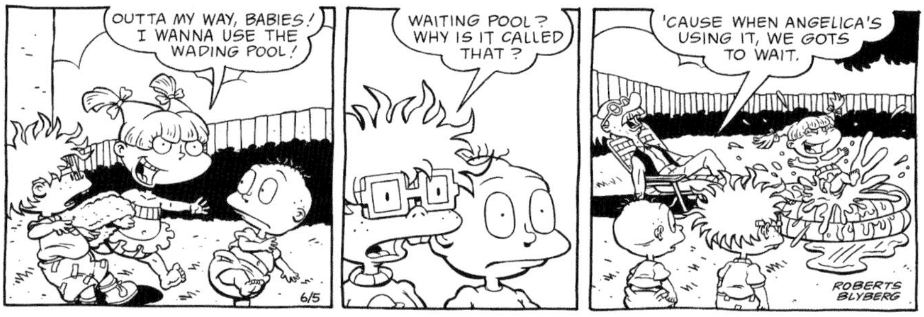
OUTTA MY WAY, BABIES! I WANNA USE THE WADING POOL!
6/5
WAITING POOL? WHY IS IT CALLED THAT?
'CAUSE WHEN ANGELICA'S USING IT, WE GOTS TO WAIT.
ROBERTS BLYBERG

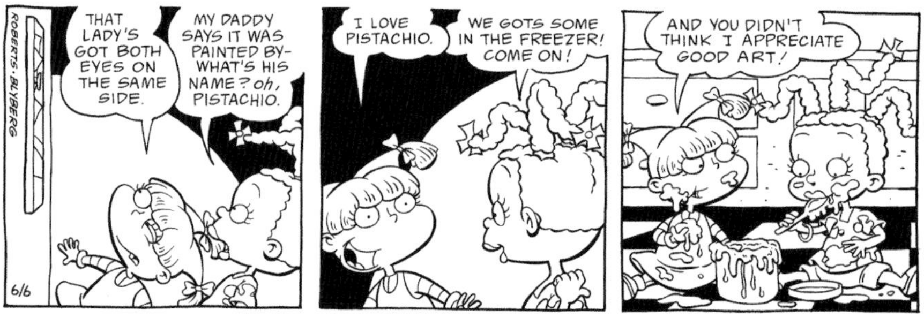
ROBERTS·BLYBERG
THAT LADY'S GOT BOTH EYES ON THE SAME SIDE.
MY DADDY SAYS IT WAS PAINTED BY- WHAT'S HIS NAME? oh, PISTACHIO.
6/6
I LOVE PISTACHIO.
WE GOTS SOME IN THE FREEZER! COME ON!
AND YOU DIDN'T THINK I APPRECIATE GOOD ART!

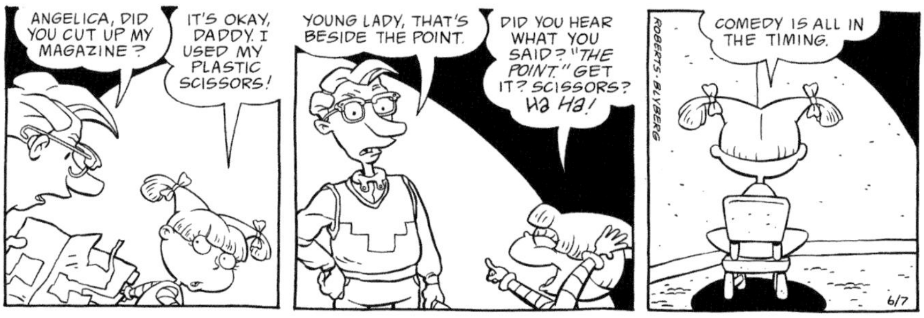
ANGELICA, DID YOU CUT UP MY MAGAZINE?
IT'S OKAY, DADDY. I USED MY PLASTIC SCISSORS!
YOUNG LADY, THAT'S BESIDE THE POINT.
DID YOU HEAR WHAT YOU SAID? "THE POINT." GET IT? SCISSORS? HA HA!
ROBERTS·BLYBERG
COMEDY IS ALL IN THE TIMING.
6/7

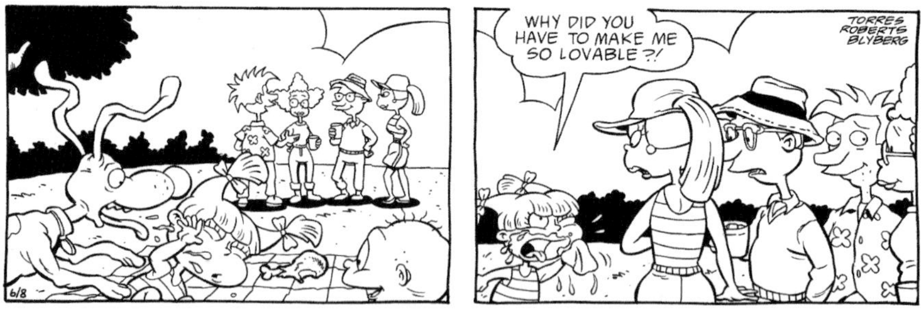
6/8
WHY DID YOU HAVE TO MAKE ME SO LOVABLE?!
TORRES ROBERTS BLYBERG

2002

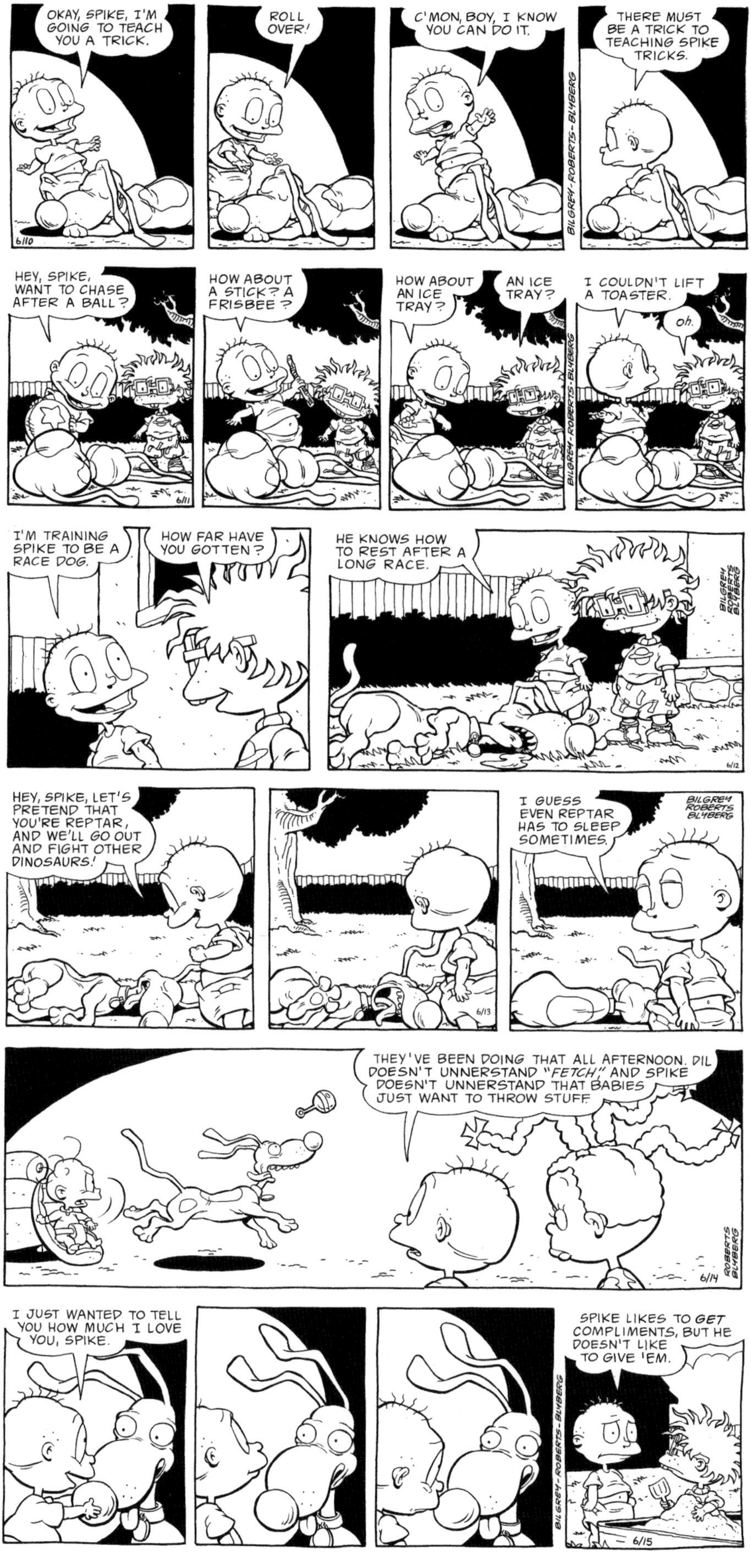
OKAY, SPIKE, I'M GOING TO TEACH YOU A TRICK.
ROLL OVER!
C'MON, BOY, I KNOW YOU CAN DO IT.
BILGREY-ROBERTS-BLYBERG
THERE MUST BE A TRICK TO TEACHING SPIKE TRICKS.
6/10
HEY, SPIKE, WANT TO CHASE AFTER A BALL?
6/11
HOW ABOUT A STICK? A FRISBEE?
HOW ABOUT AN ICE TRAY?
AN ICE TRAY?
BILGREY-ROBERTS-BLYBERG
I COULDN'T LIFT A TOASTER.
oh.
I'M TRAINING SPIKE TO BE A RACE DOG.
HOW FAR HAVE YOU GOTTEN?
HE KNOWS HOW TO REST AFTER A LONG RACE.
BILGREY ROBERTS BLYBERG
6/12
HEY, SPIKE, LET'S PRETEND THAT YOU'RE REPTAR, AND WE'LL GO OUT AND FIGHT OTHER DINOSAURS!
6/13
I GUESS EVEN REPTAR HAS TO SLEEP SOMETIMES.
BILGREY ROBERTS BLYBERG
THEY'VE BEEN DOING THAT ALL AFTERNOON. DIL DOESN'T UNNERSTAND "FETCH," AND SPIKE DOESN'T UNNERSTAND THAT BABIES JUST WANT TO THROW STUFF.
6/14
ROBERTS BLYBERG
I JUST WANTED TO TELL YOU HOW MUCH I LOVE YOU, SPIKE.
BILGREY-ROBERTS-BLYBERG
SPIKE LIKES TO GET COMPLIMENTS, BUT HE DOESN'T LIKE TO GIVE 'EM.
6/15

2002

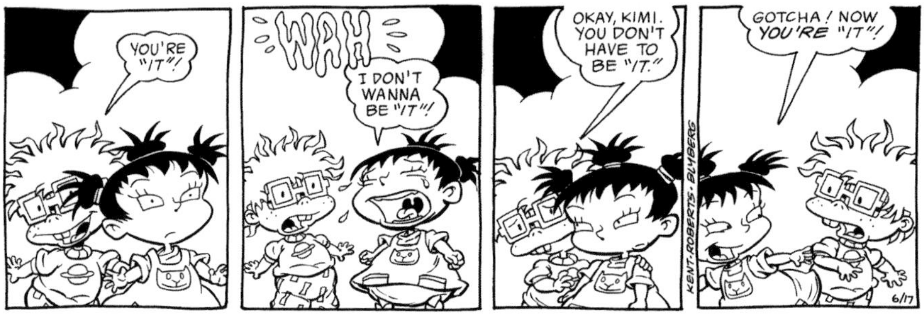
YOU'RE "IT"!
WAH
I DON'T WANNA BE "IT"!
OKAY, KIMI. YOU DON'T HAVE TO BE "IT."
KENT·ROBERTS·BLYBERG
GOTCHA! NOW YOU'RE "IT"!
6/17

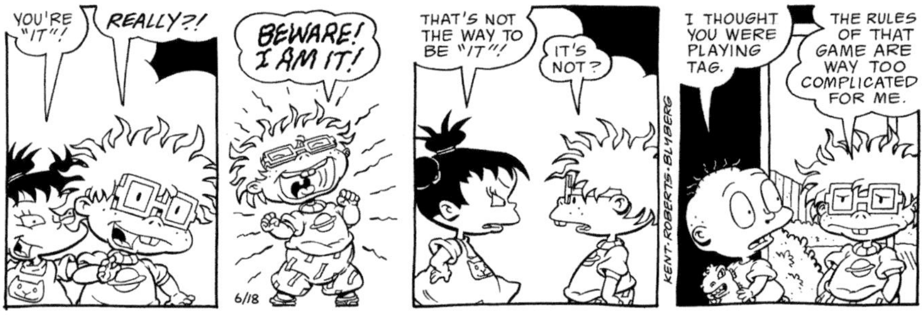
YOU'RE "IT"!
REALLY?!
BEWARE! I AM IT!
6/18
THAT'S NOT THE WAY TO BE "IT"!
IT'S NOT?
KENT·ROBERTS·BLYBERG
I THOUGHT YOU WERE PLAYING TAG.
THE RULES OF THAT GAME ARE WAY TOO COMPLICATED FOR ME.

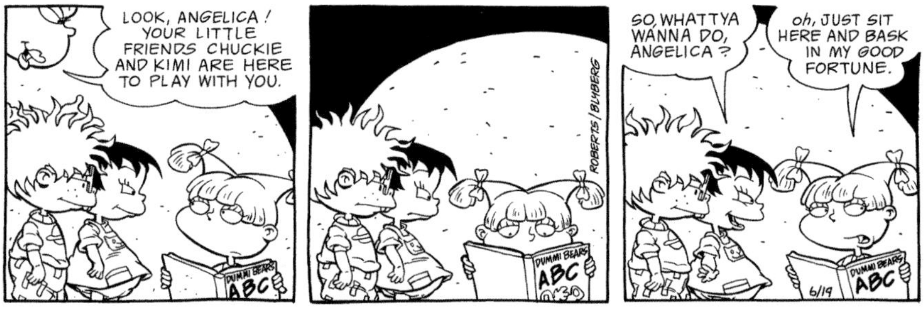
LOOK, ANGELICA! YOUR LITTLE FRIENDS CHUCKIE AND KIMI ARE HERE TO PLAY WITH YOU.
DUMMI BEARS ABC
ROBERTS | BLYBERG
SO, WHATTYA WANNA DO, ANGELICA?
oh, JUST SIT HERE AND BASK IN MY GOOD FORTUNE.
6/19

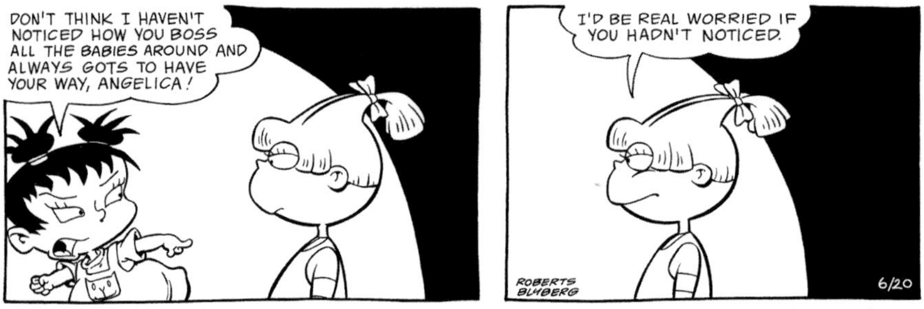
DON'T THINK I HAVEN'T NOTICED HOW YOU BOSS ALL THE BABIES AROUND AND ALWAYS GOTS TO HAVE YOUR WAY, ANGELICA!
I'D BE REAL WORRIED IF YOU HADN'T NOTICED.
ROBERTS BLYBERG
6/20

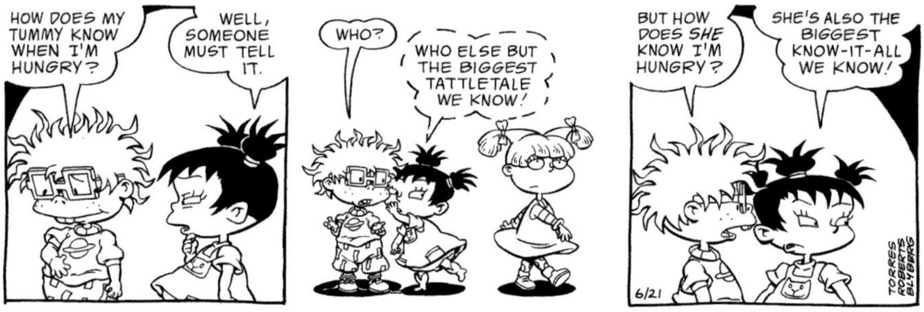
HOW DOES MY TUMMY KNOW WHEN I'M HUNGRY?
WELL, SOMEONE MUST TELL IT.
WHO?
WHO ELSE BUT THE BIGGEST TATTLETALE WE KNOW!
BUT HOW DOES SHE KNOW I'M HUNGRY?
SHE'S ALSO THE BIGGEST KNOW-IT-ALL WE KNOW!
6/21
TORRES ROBERTS BLYBERG

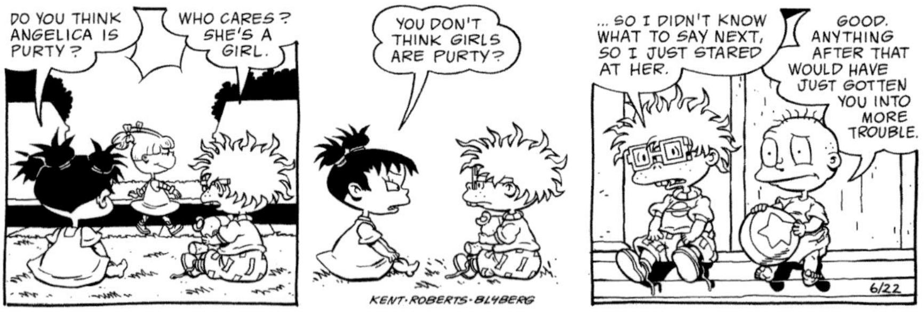
DO YOU THINK ANGELICA IS PURTY?
WHO CARES? SHE'S A GIRL.
YOU DON'T THINK GIRLS ARE PURTY?
KENT·ROBERTS·BLYBERG
... SO I DIDN'T KNOW WHAT TO SAY NEXT, SO I JUST STARED AT HER.
GOOD. ANYTHING AFTER THAT WOULD HAVE JUST GOTTEN YOU INTO MORE TROUBLE.
6/22

2002

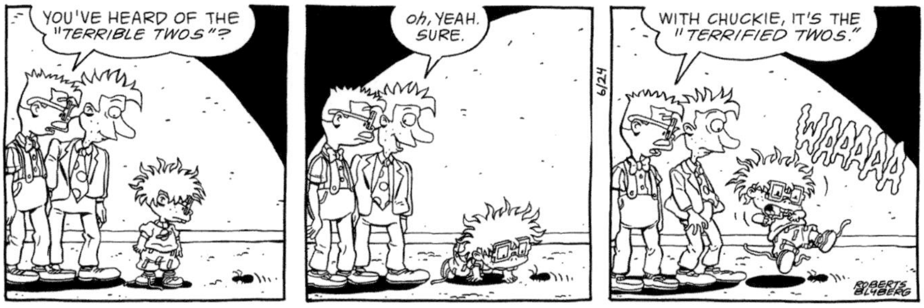
YOU'VE HEARD OF THE "TERRIBLE TWOS"?
Oh, YEAH. SURE.
6/24
WITH CHUCKIE, IT'S THE "TERRIFIED TWOS."
WAAAAA
ROBERTS BLYBERG

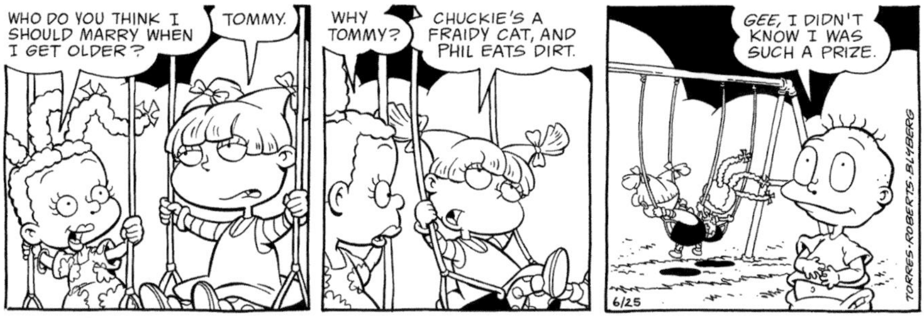
WHO DO YOU THINK I SHOULD MARRY WHEN I GET OLDER?
TOMMY.
WHY TOMMY?
CHUCKIE'S A FRAIDY CAT, AND PHIL EATS DIRT.
GEE, I DIDN'T KNOW I WAS SUCH A PRIZE.
6/25
TORRES·ROBERTS·BLYBERG

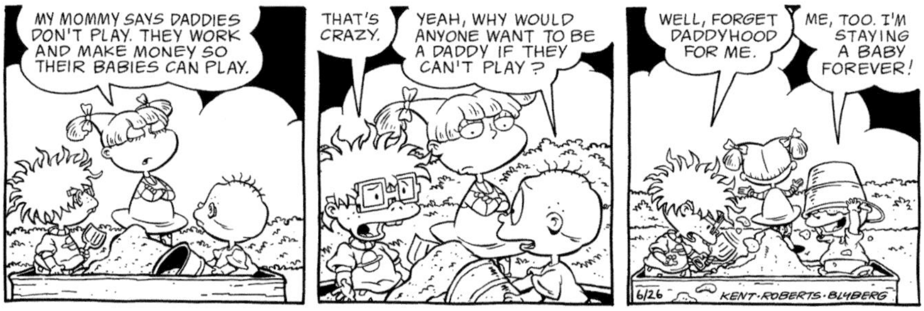
MY MOMMY SAYS DADDIES DON'T PLAY. THEY WORK AND MAKE MONEY SO THEIR BABIES CAN PLAY.
THAT'S CRAZY.
YEAH, WHY WOULD ANYONE WANT TO BE A DADDY IF THEY CAN'T PLAY?
WELL, FORGET DADDYHOOD FOR ME.
ME, TOO. I'M STAYING A BABY FOREVER!
6/26
KENT·ROBERTS·BLYBERG

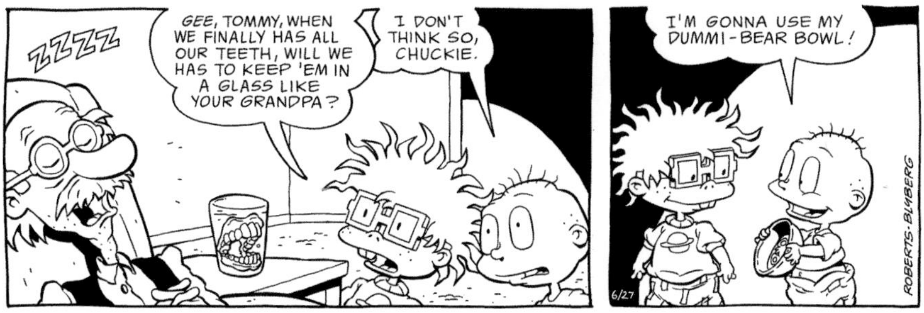
ZZZZ
GEE, TOMMY, WHEN WE FINALLY HAS ALL OUR TEETH, WILL WE HAS TO KEEP 'EM IN A GLASS LIKE YOUR GRANDPA?
I DON'T THINK SO, CHUCKIE.
I'M GONNA USE MY DUMMI-BEAR BOWL!
6/27
ROBERTS·BLYBERG

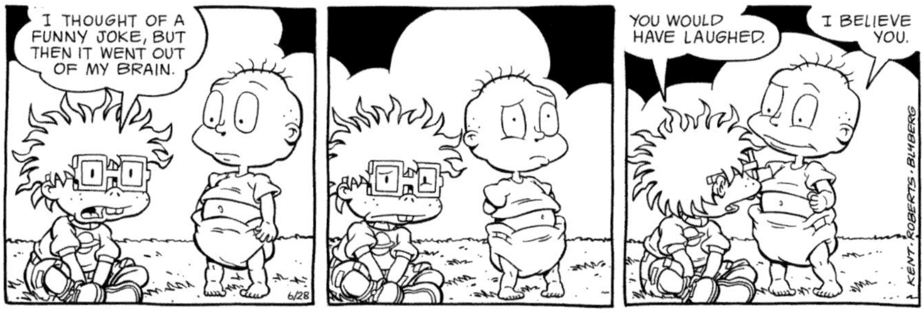
I THOUGHT OF A FUNNY JOKE, BUT THEN IT WENT OUT OF MY BRAIN.
6/28
YOU WOULD HAVE LAUGHED.
I BELIEVE YOU.
KENT·ROBERTS·BLYBERG

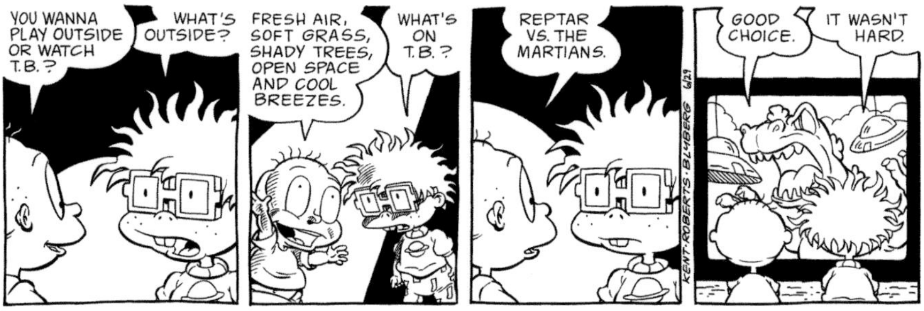
YOU WANNA PLAY OUTSIDE OR WATCH T.B.?
WHAT'S OUTSIDE?
FRESH AIR, SOFT GRASS, SHADY TREES, OPEN SPACE AND COOL BREEZES.
WHAT'S ON T.B.?
REPTAR VS. THE MARTIANS.
6/29
KENT·ROBERTS·BLYBERG
GOOD CHOICE.
IT WASN'T HARD.

2002

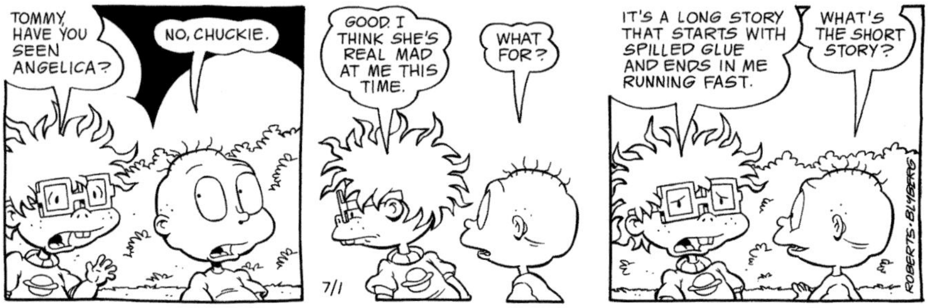
TOMMY, HAVE YOU SEEN ANGELICA?
NO, CHUCKIE.
GOOD. I THINK *SHE'S* REAL MAD AT ME THIS TIME.
WHAT FOR?
7/1
IT'S A LONG STORY THAT STARTS WITH SPILLED GLUE AND ENDS IN ME RUNNING FAST.
WHAT'S THE SHORT STORY?
ROBERTS·BLYBERG

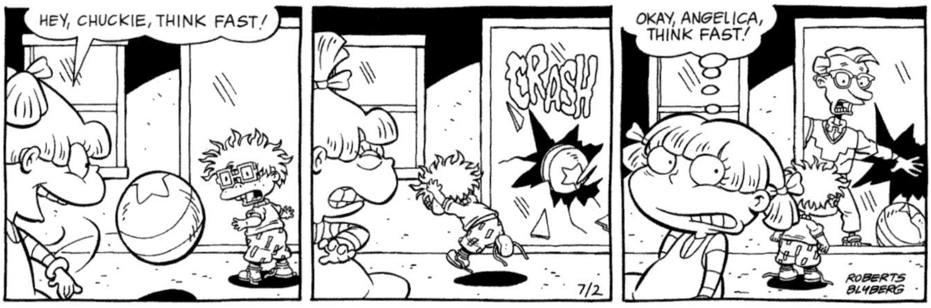
HEY, CHUCKIE, THINK FAST!
CRASH
7/2
OKAY, ANGELICA, THINK FAST!
ROBERTS BLYBERG

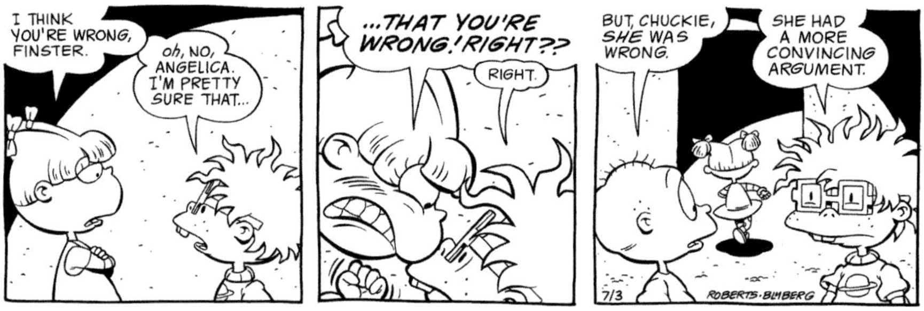
I THINK YOU'RE WRONG, FINSTER.
oh, NO, ANGELICA. I'M PRETTY SURE THAT...
...THAT YOU'RE WRONG! RIGHT??
RIGHT.
BUT, CHUCKIE, *SHE* WAS WRONG.
SHE HAD A MORE CONVINCING ARGUMENT.
7/3
ROBERTS·BLYBERG

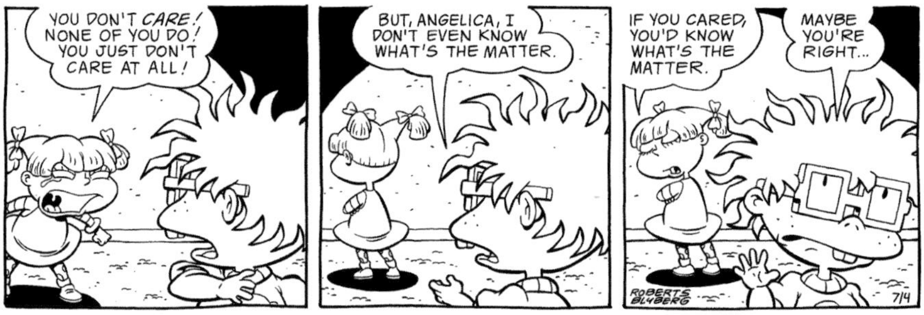
YOU DON'T *CARE*! NONE OF YOU DO! YOU JUST DON'T CARE AT ALL!
BUT, ANGELICA, I DON'T EVEN KNOW WHAT'S THE MATTER.
IF YOU CARED, YOU'D KNOW WHAT'S THE MATTER.
MAYBE YOU'RE RIGHT...
ROBERTS BLYBERG
7/4

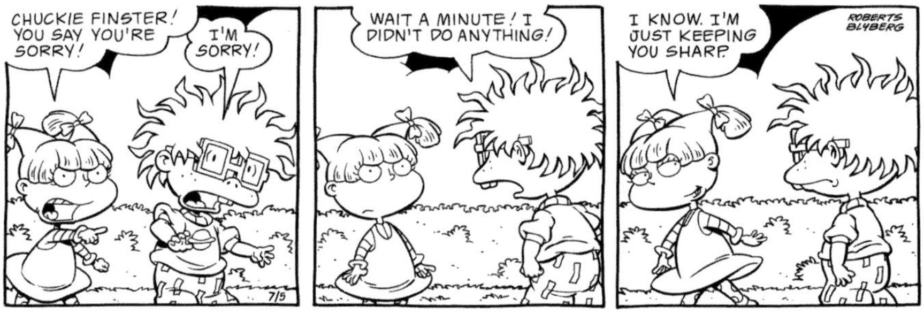
CHUCKIE FINSTER! YOU SAY YOU'RE SORRY!
I'M SORRY!
7/5
WAIT A MINUTE! I DIDN'T DO ANYTHING!
I KNOW. I'M JUST KEEPING YOU SHARP.
ROBERTS BLYBERG

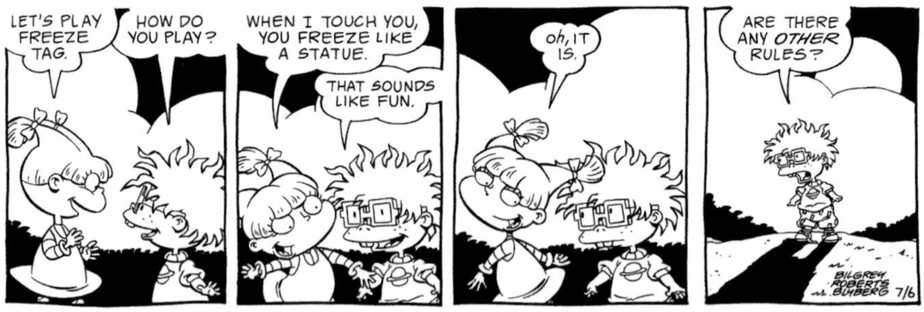
LET'S PLAY FREEZE TAG.
HOW DO YOU PLAY?
WHEN I TOUCH YOU, YOU FREEZE LIKE A STATUE.
THAT SOUNDS LIKE FUN.
oh, IT IS.
ARE THERE ANY *OTHER* RULES?
BILGREY ROBERTS BLYBERG 7/6

2002

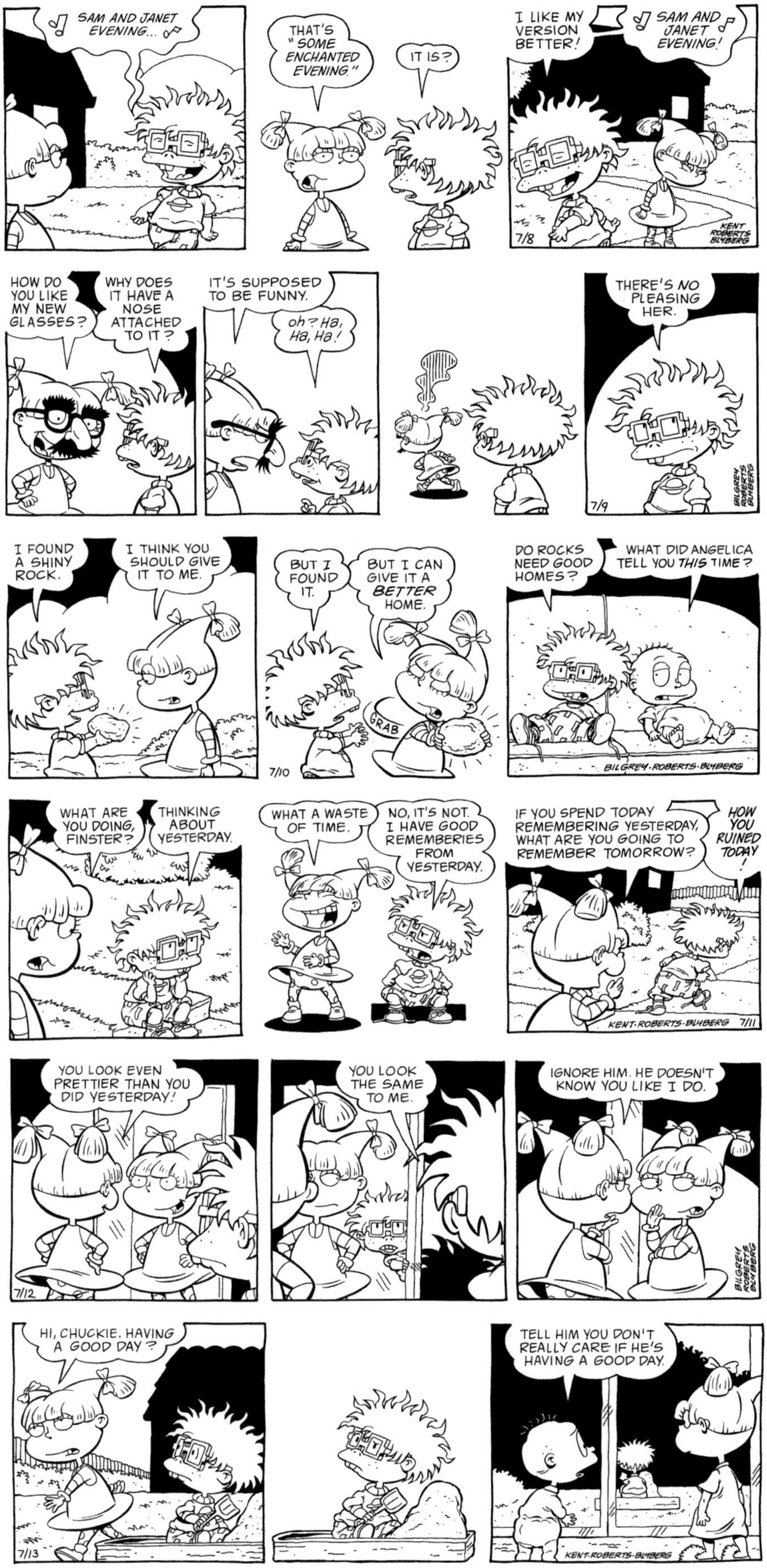
SAM AND JANET EVENING...
THAT'S "SOME ENCHANTED EVENING."
IT IS?
I LIKE MY VERSION BETTER!
SAM AND JANET EVENING!
7/8
KENT ROBERTS BLYBERG
HOW DO YOU LIKE MY NEW GLASSES?
WHY DOES IT HAVE A NOSE ATTACHED TO IT?
IT'S SUPPOSED TO BE FUNNY.
oh? Ha, Ha, Ha!
THERE'S NO PLEASING HER.
7/9
BILGREY ROBERTS BLYBERG
I FOUND A SHINY ROCK.
I THINK YOU SHOULD GIVE IT TO ME.
BUT I FOUND IT.
BUT I CAN GIVE IT A BETTER HOME.
GRAB
7/10
DO ROCKS NEED GOOD HOMES?
WHAT DID ANGELICA TELL YOU THIS TIME?
BILGREY·ROBERTS·BLYBERG
WHAT ARE YOU DOING, FINSTER?
THINKING ABOUT YESTERDAY.
WHAT A WASTE OF TIME.
NO, IT'S NOT. I HAVE GOOD REMEMBERIES FROM YESTERDAY.
IF YOU SPEND TODAY REMEMBERING YESTERDAY, WHAT ARE YOU GOING TO REMEMBER TOMORROW?
HOW YOU RUINED TODAY!
KENT·ROBERTS·BLYBERG 7/11
YOU LOOK EVEN PRETTIER THAN YOU DID YESTERDAY!
7/12
YOU LOOK THE SAME TO ME.
IGNORE HIM. HE DOESN'T KNOW YOU LIKE I DO.
BILGREY ROBERTS BLYBERG
HI, CHUCKIE. HAVING A GOOD DAY?
7/13
TELL HIM YOU DON'T REALLY CARE IF HE'S HAVING A GOOD DAY.
KENT·ROBERTS·BLYBERG

2002

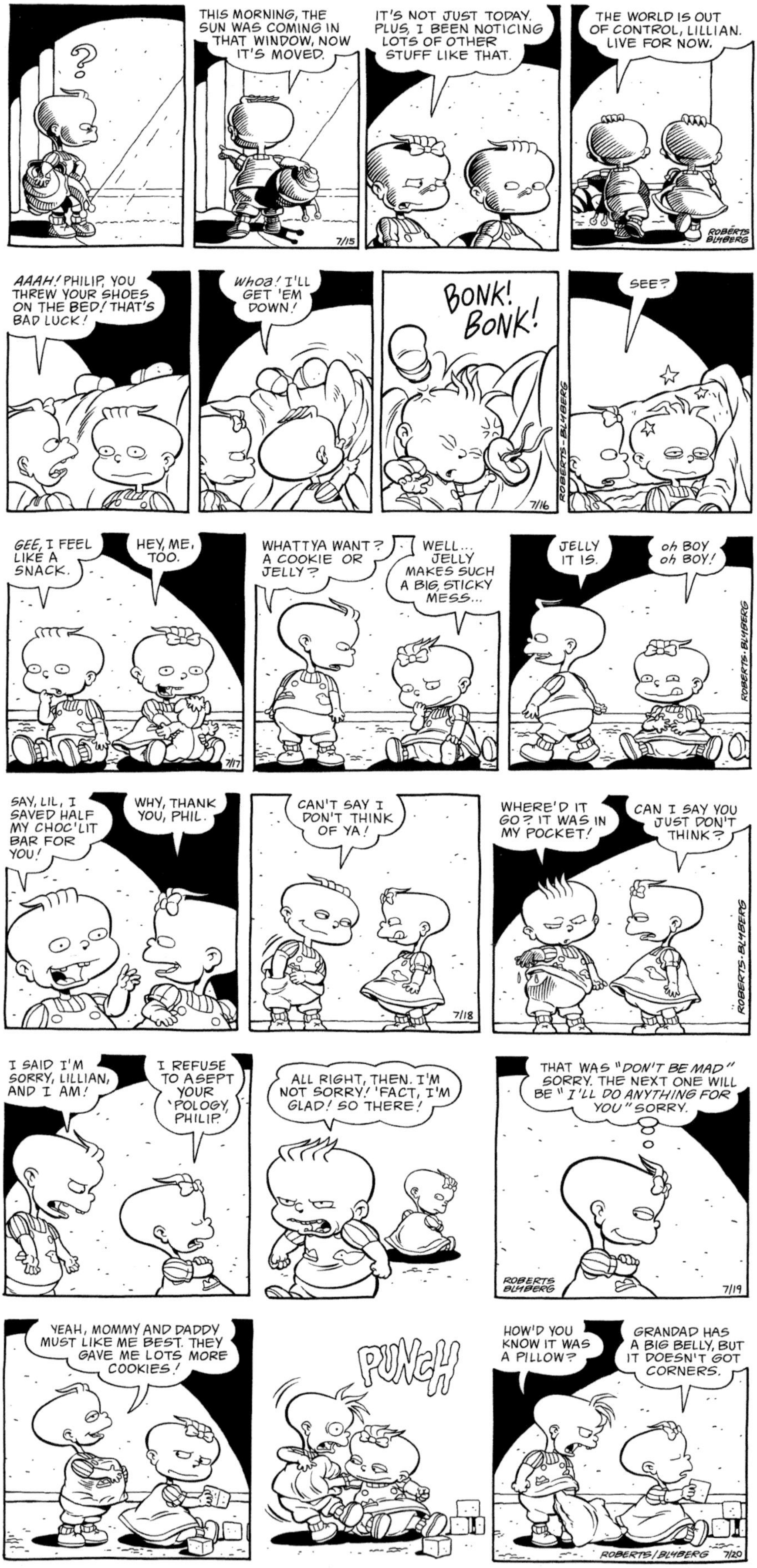
?
THIS MORNING, THE SUN WAS COMING IN THAT WINDOW, NOW IT'S MOVED.
7/15
IT'S NOT JUST TODAY. PLUS, I BEEN NOTICING LOTS OF OTHER STUFF LIKE THAT.
THE WORLD IS OUT OF CONTROL, LILLIAN. LIVE FOR NOW.
ROBERTS BLYBERG
AAAH! PHILIP, YOU THREW YOUR SHOES ON THE BED! THAT'S BAD LUCK!
Whoa! I'LL GET 'EM DOWN!
BONK! BONK!
ROBERTS · BLYBERG
7/16
SEE?
GEE, I FEEL LIKE A SNACK.
HEY, ME, TOO.
7/17
WHATTYA WANT? A COOKIE OR JELLY?
WELL... JELLY MAKES SUCH A BIG, STICKY MESS...
JELLY IT IS.
oh BOY oh BOY!
ROBERTS · BLYBERG
SAY, LIL, I SAVED HALF MY CHOC'LIT BAR FOR YOU!
WHY, THANK YOU, PHIL.
CAN'T SAY I DON'T THINK OF YA!
7/18
WHERE'D IT GO? IT WAS IN MY POCKET!
CAN I SAY YOU JUST DON'T THINK?
ROBERTS · BLYBERG
I SAID I'M SORRY, LILLIAN, AND I AM!
I REFUSE TO ASEPT YOUR 'POLOGY, PHILIP.
ALL RIGHT, THEN. I'M NOT SORRY! 'FACT, I'M GLAD! SO THERE!
THAT WAS "DON'T BE MAD" SORRY. THE NEXT ONE WILL BE "I'LL DO ANYTHING FOR YOU" SORRY.
ROBERTS BLYBERG
7/19
YEAH, MOMMY AND DADDY MUST LIKE ME BEST. THEY GAVE ME LOTS MORE COOKIES!
PUNCH
HOW'D YOU KNOW IT WAS A PILLOW?
GRANDAD HAS A BIG BELLY, BUT IT DOESN'T GOT CORNERS.
ROBERTS/BLYBERG
7/20

2002

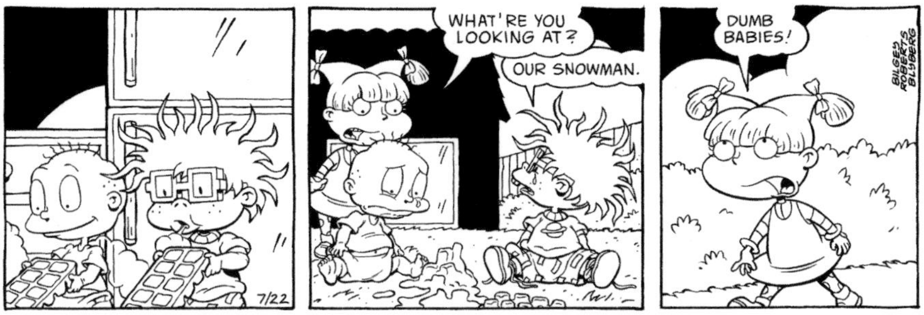
WHAT'RE YOU LOOKING AT?
OUR SNOWMAN.
DUMB BABIES!
BILGREY ROBERTS BLYBERG
7/22

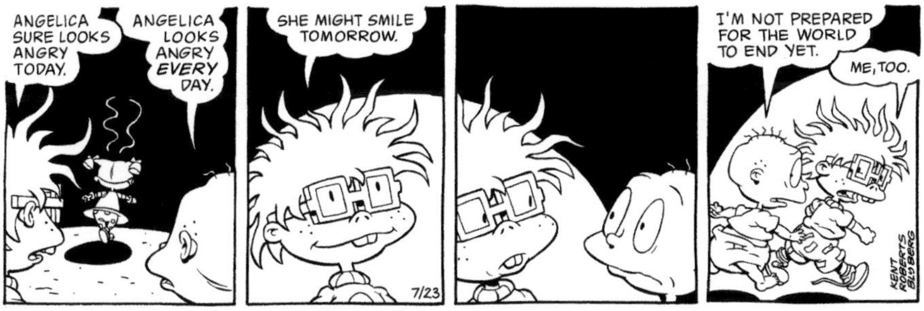
ANGELICA SURE LOOKS ANGRY TODAY.
ANGELICA LOOKS ANGRY EVERY DAY.
SHE MIGHT SMILE TOMORROW.
I'M NOT PREPARED FOR THE WORLD TO END YET.
ME, TOO.
KENT ROBERTS BLYBERG
7/23

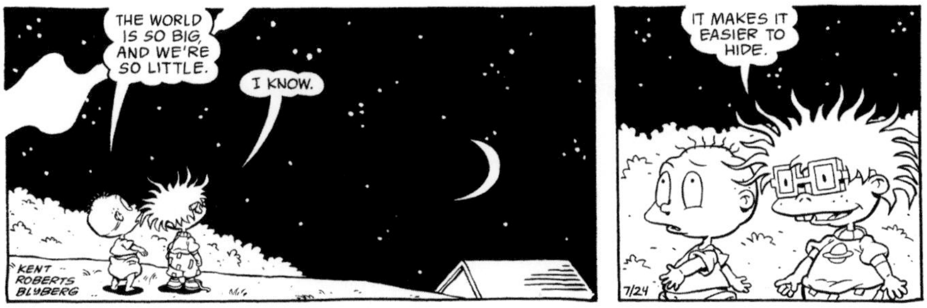
THE WORLD IS SO BIG, AND WE'RE SO LITTLE.
I KNOW.
IT MAKES IT EASIER TO HIDE.
KENT ROBERTS BLYBERG
7/24

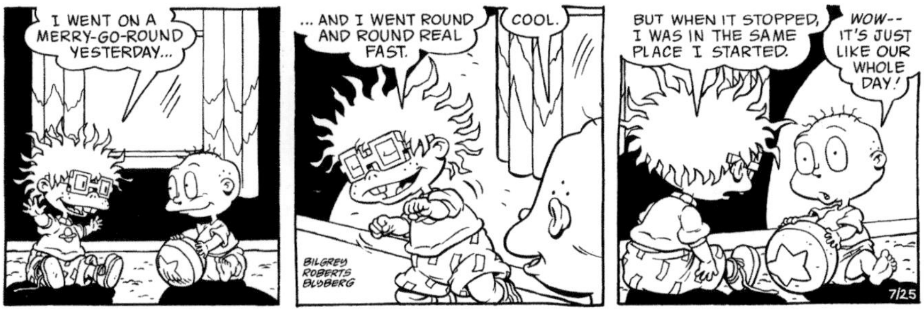
I WENT ON A MERRY-GO-ROUND YESTERDAY...
... AND I WENT ROUND AND ROUND REAL FAST.
COOL.
BUT WHEN IT STOPPED, I WAS IN THE SAME PLACE I STARTED.
WOW-- IT'S JUST LIKE OUR WHOLE DAY!
BILGREY ROBERTS BLYBERG
7/25

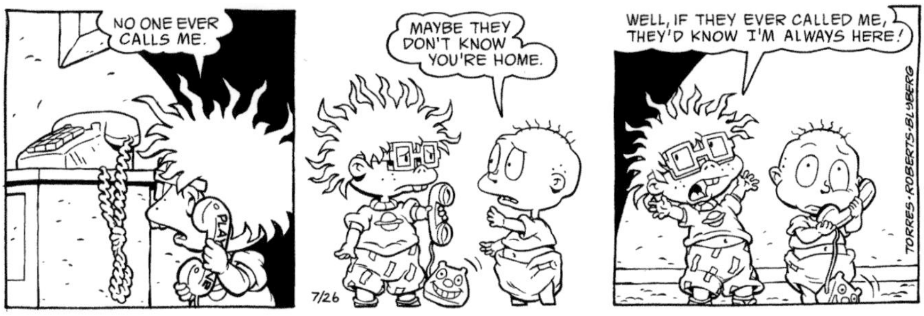
NO ONE EVER CALLS ME.
MAYBE THEY DON'T KNOW YOU'RE HOME.
WELL, IF THEY EVER CALLED ME, THEY'D KNOW I'M ALWAYS HERE!
TORRES·ROBERTS·BLYBERG
7/26

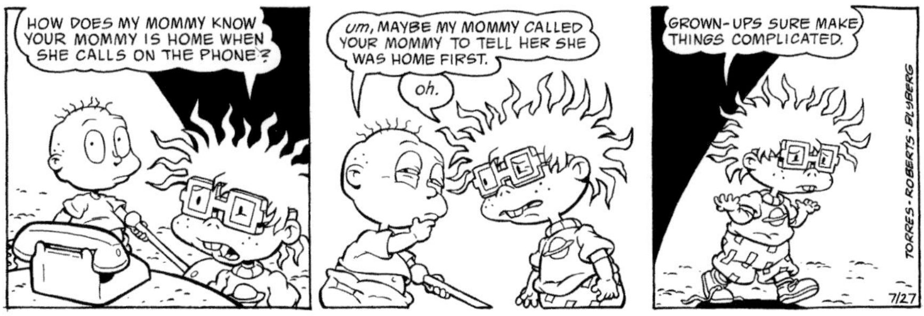
HOW DOES MY MOMMY KNOW YOUR MOMMY IS HOME WHEN SHE CALLS ON THE PHONE?
um, MAYBE MY MOMMY CALLED YOUR MOMMY TO TELL HER SHE WAS HOME FIRST.
oh.
GROWN-UPS SURE MAKE THINGS COMPLICATED.
TORRES·ROBERTS·BLYBERG
7/27

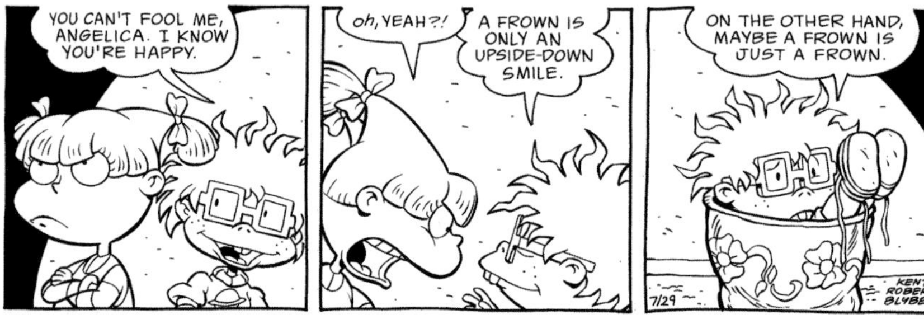
YOU CAN'T FOOL ME, ANGELICA. I KNOW YOU'RE HAPPY.
oh, YEAH?!
A FROWN IS ONLY AN UPSIDE-DOWN SMILE.
ON THE OTHER HAND, MAYBE A FROWN IS JUST A FROWN.
7/29
KENT ROBERTS BLYBERG

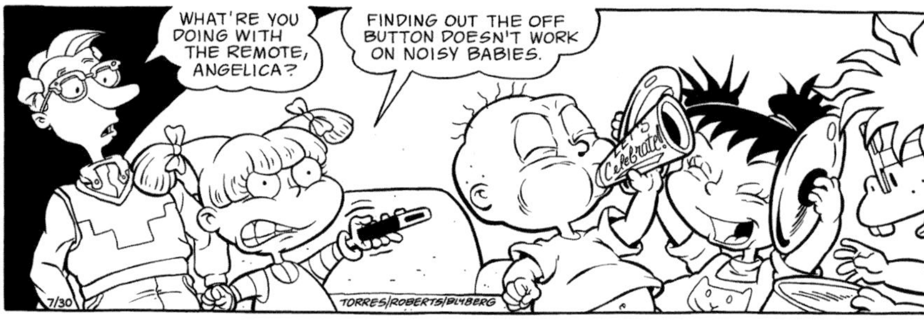
WHAT'RE YOU DOING WITH THE REMOTE, ANGELICA?
FINDING OUT THE OFF BUTTON DOESN'T WORK ON NOISY BABIES.
Let's Celebrate!
7/30
TORRES|ROBERTS|BLYBERG

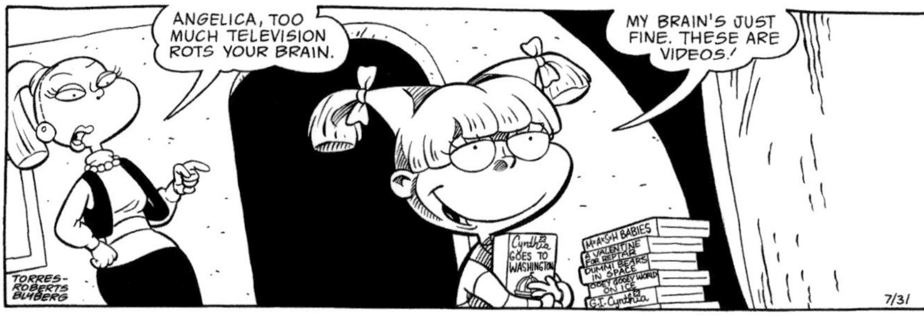
ANGELICA, TOO MUCH TELEVISION ROTS YOUR BRAIN.
MY BRAIN'S JUST FINE. THESE ARE VIDEOS!
Cynthia GOES TO WASHINGTON
TORRES-ROBERTS BLYBERG
7/31

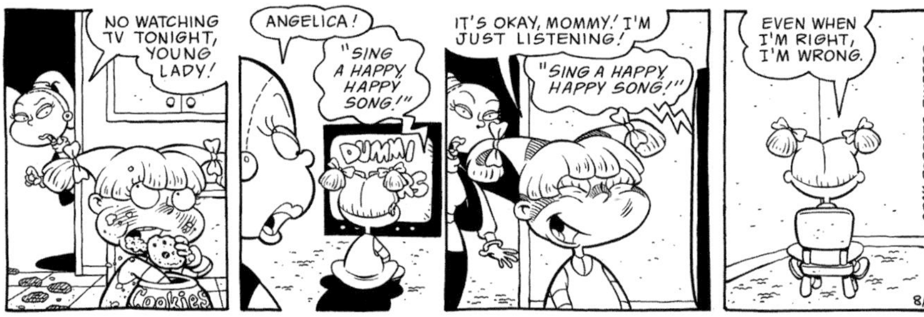
NO WATCHING TV TONIGHT, YOUNG LADY!
Cookies
ANGELICA!
"SING A HAPPY, HAPPY SONG!"
DUMMI
IT'S OKAY, MOMMY! I'M JUST LISTENING!
"SING A HAPPY, HAPPY SONG!"
EVEN WHEN I'M RIGHT, I'M WRONG.
GRAY·ROBERTS·BLYBERG
8/1

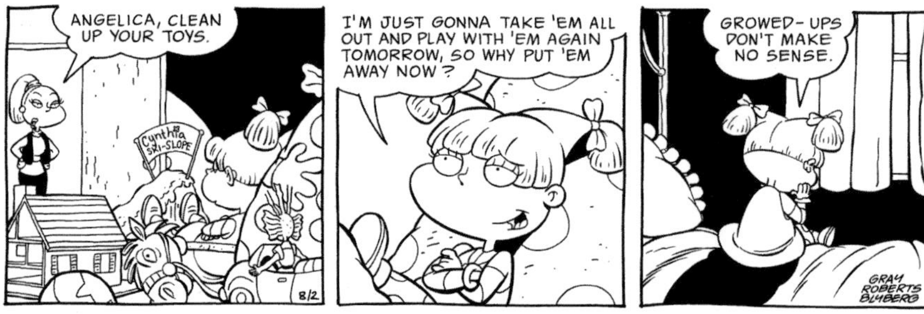
ANGELICA, CLEAN UP YOUR TOYS.
Cynthia SKI-SLOPE
8/2
I'M JUST GONNA TAKE 'EM ALL OUT AND PLAY WITH 'EM AGAIN TOMORROW, SO WHY PUT 'EM AWAY NOW?
GROWED-UPS DON'T MAKE NO SENSE.
GRAY ROBERTS BLYBERG

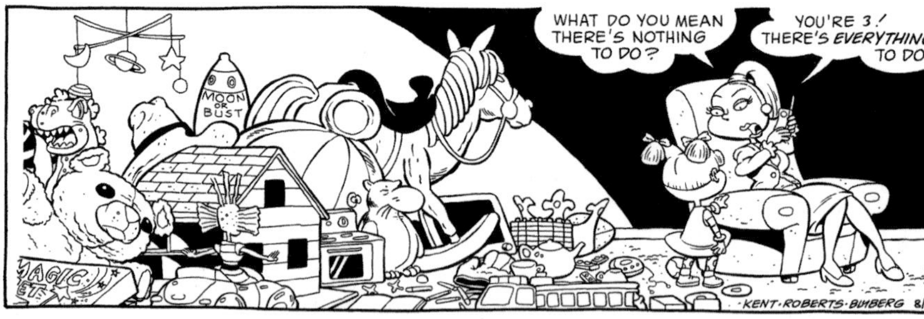
MOON OR BUST
WHAT DO YOU MEAN THERE'S NOTHING TO DO?
YOU'RE 3! THERE'S EVERYTHING TO DO!
KENT·ROBERTS·BLYBERG 8/3

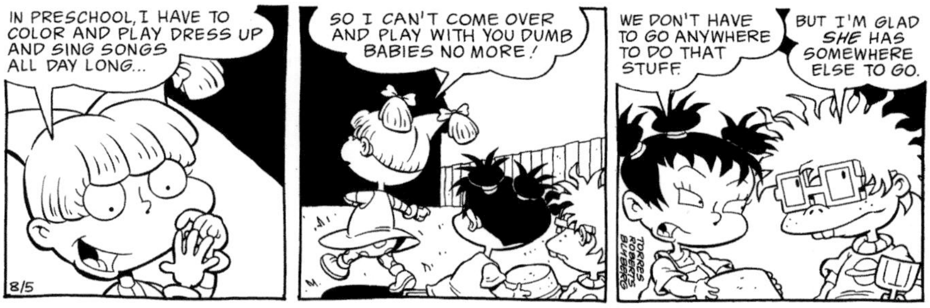
IN PRESCHOOL, I HAVE TO COLOR AND PLAY DRESS UP AND SING SONGS ALL DAY LONG...
SO I CAN'T COME OVER AND PLAY WITH YOU DUMB BABIES NO MORE!
WE DON'T HAVE TO GO ANYWHERE TO DO THAT STUFF.
BUT I'M GLAD SHE HAS SOMEWHERE ELSE TO GO.
TORRES ROBERTS BLYBERG
8/5

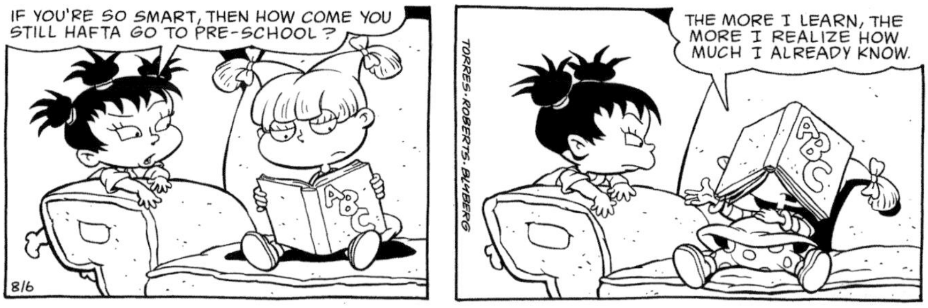
IF YOU'RE SO SMART, THEN HOW COME YOU STILL HAFTA GO TO PRE-SCHOOL?
ABC
TORRES·ROBERTS·BLYBERG
THE MORE I LEARN, THE MORE I REALIZE HOW MUCH I ALREADY KNOW.
8/6

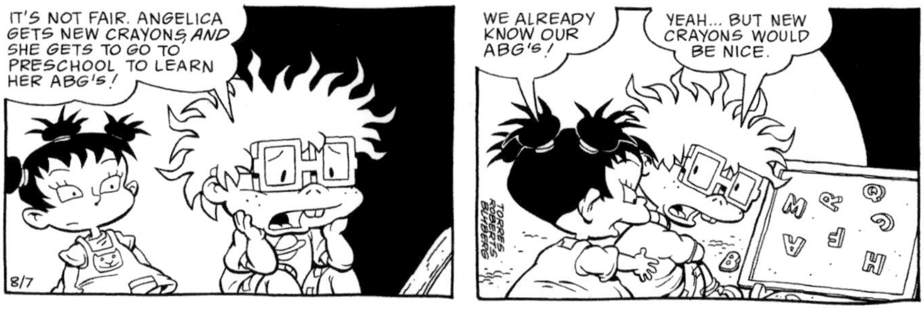
IT'S NOT FAIR. ANGELICA GETS NEW CRAYONS, AND SHE GETS TO GO TO PRESCHOOL TO LEARN HER ABC'S!
WE ALREADY KNOW OUR ABC'S!
YEAH... BUT NEW CRAYONS WOULD BE NICE.
TORRES ROBERTS BLYBERG
8/7

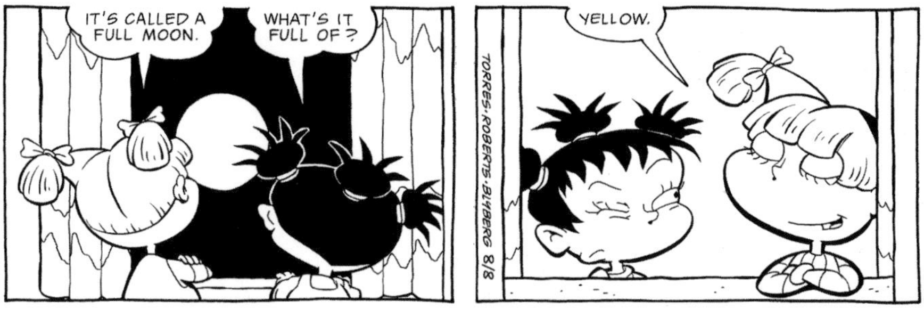
IT'S CALLED A FULL MOON.
WHAT'S IT FULL OF?
TORRES·ROBERTS·BLYBERG 8/8
YELLOW.

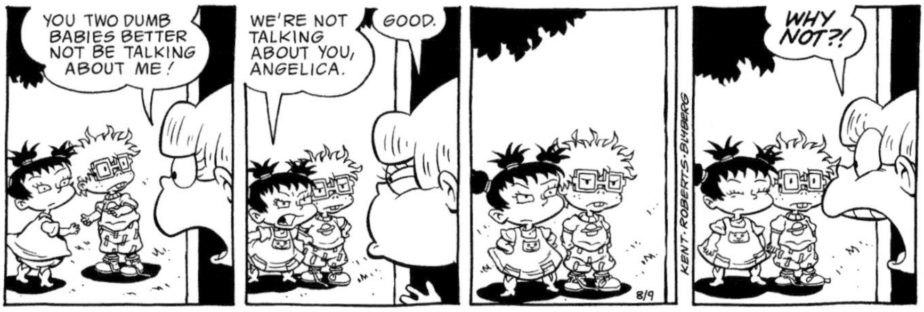
YOU TWO DUMB BABIES BETTER NOT BE TALKING ABOUT ME!
WE'RE NOT TALKING ABOUT YOU, ANGELICA.
GOOD.
8/9
KENT·ROBERTS·BLYBERG
WHY NOT?!

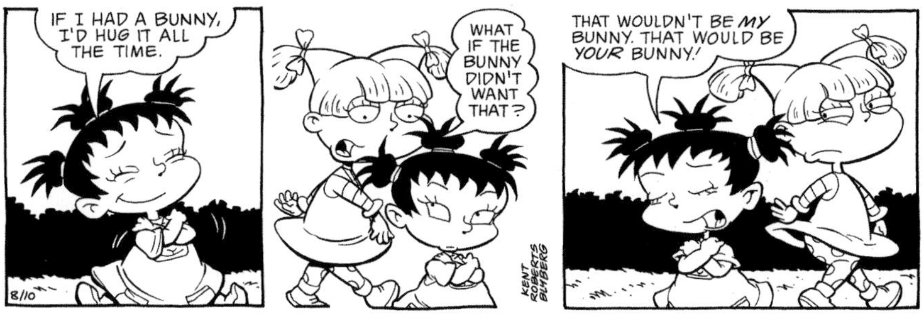
IF I HAD A BUNNY, I'D HUG IT ALL THE TIME.
8/10
WHAT IF THE BUNNY DIDN'T WANT THAT?
KENT ROBERTS BLYBERG
THAT WOULDN'T BE MY BUNNY. THAT WOULD BE YOUR BUNNY!

2002

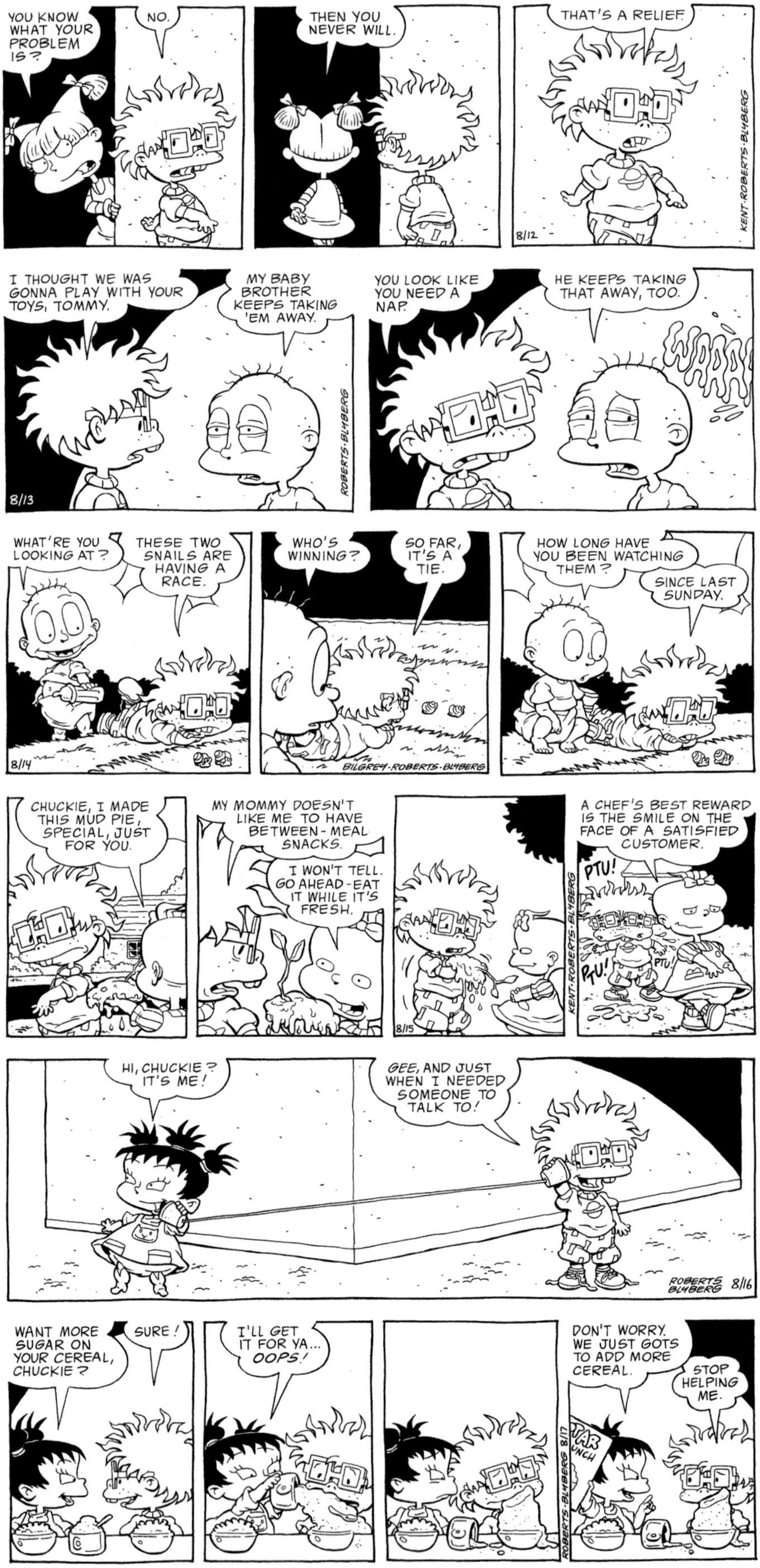
YOU KNOW WHAT YOUR PROBLEM IS?
NO.
THEN YOU NEVER WILL.
THAT'S A RELIEF.
8/12
KENT·ROBERTS·BLYBERG
I THOUGHT WE WAS GONNA PLAY WITH YOUR TOYS, TOMMY.
MY BABY BROTHER KEEPS TAKING 'EM AWAY.
8/13
ROBERTS·BLYBERG
YOU LOOK LIKE YOU NEED A NAP.
HE KEEPS TAKING THAT AWAY, TOO.
WAAAA!
WHAT'RE YOU LOOKING AT?
THESE TWO SNAILS ARE HAVING A RACE.
8/14
WHO'S WINNING?
SO FAR, IT'S A TIE.
BILGREY·ROBERTS·BLYBERG
HOW LONG HAVE YOU BEEN WATCHING THEM?
SINCE LAST SUNDAY.
CHUCKIE, I MADE THIS MUD PIE, SPECIAL, JUST FOR YOU.
MY MOMMY DOESN'T LIKE ME TO HAVE BETWEEN-MEAL SNACKS.
I WON'T TELL. GO AHEAD-EAT IT WHILE IT'S FRESH.
8/15
KENT·ROBERTS·BLYBERG
A CHEF'S BEST REWARD IS THE SMILE ON THE FACE OF A SATISFIED CUSTOMER.
PTU!
PTU!
PTU!
HI, CHUCKIE? IT'S ME!
GEE, AND JUST WHEN I NEEDED SOMEONE TO TALK TO!
ROBERTS BLYBERG 8/16
WANT MORE SUGAR ON YOUR CEREAL, CHUCKIE?
SURE!
I'LL GET IT FOR YA... OOPS!
ROBERTS·BLYBERG 8/17
DON'T WORRY. WE JUST GOTS TO ADD MORE CEREAL.
STOP HELPING ME.

2002

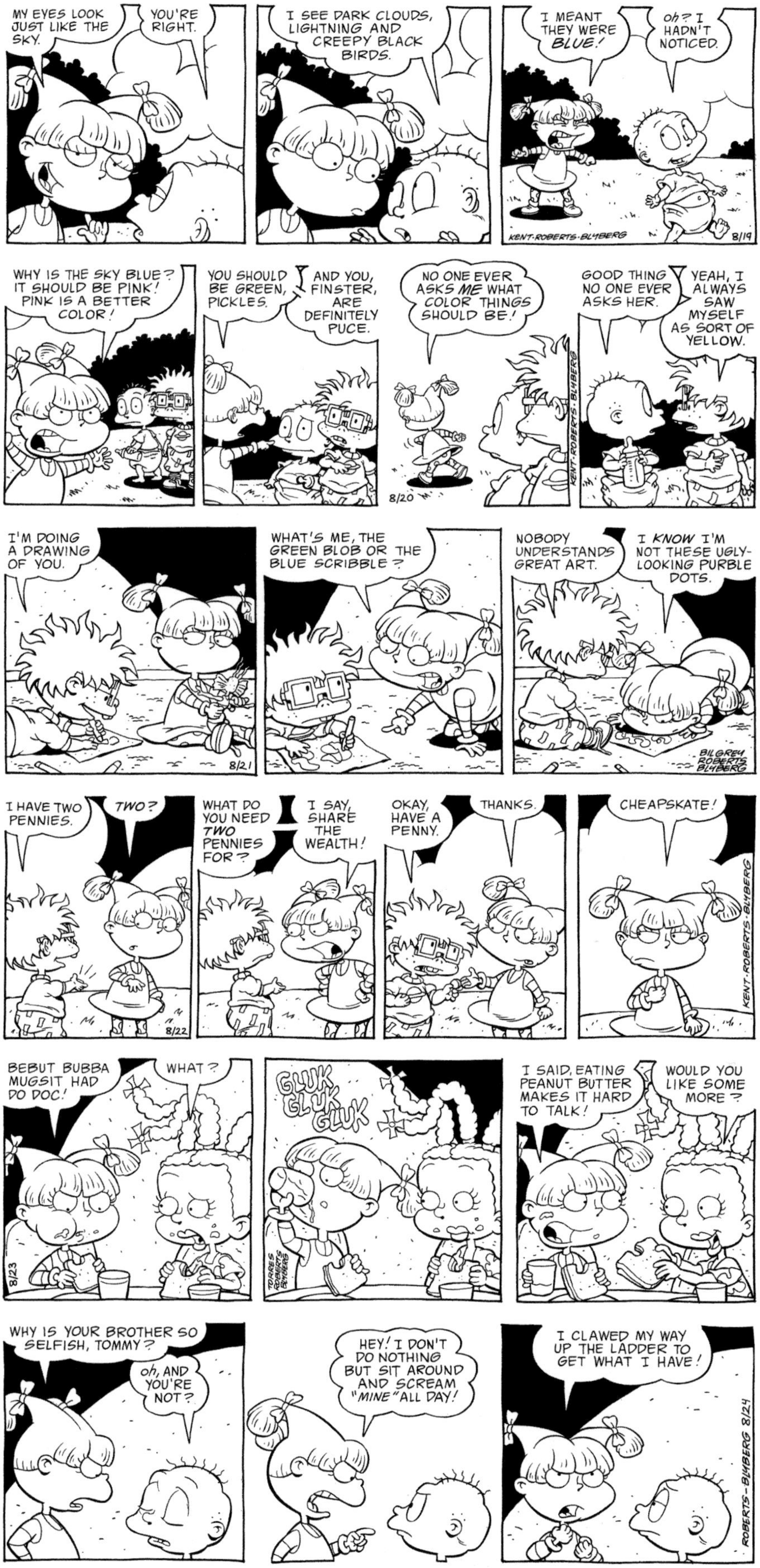
MY EYES LOOK JUST LIKE THE SKY.
YOU'RE RIGHT.
I SEE DARK CLOUDS, LIGHTNING AND CREEPY BLACK BIRDS.
I MEANT THEY WERE BLUE!
oh? I HADN'T NOTICED.
WHY IS THE SKY BLUE? IT SHOULD BE PINK! PINK IS A BETTER COLOR!
YOU SHOULD BE GREEN, PICKLES.
AND YOU, FINSTER, ARE DEFINITELY PUCE.
NO ONE EVER ASKS ME WHAT COLOR THINGS SHOULD BE!
GOOD THING NO ONE EVER ASKS HER.
YEAH, I ALWAYS SAW MYSELF AS SORT OF YELLOW.
I'M DOING A DRAWING OF YOU.
WHAT'S ME, THE GREEN BLOB OR THE BLUE SCRIBBLE?
NOBODY UNDERSTANDS GREAT ART.
I KNOW I'M NOT THESE UGLY-LOOKING PURBLE DOTS.
I HAVE TWO PENNIES.
TWO?
WHAT DO YOU NEED TWO PENNIES FOR?
I SAY, SHARE THE WEALTH!
OKAY, HAVE A PENNY.
THANKS.
CHEAPSKATE!
BEBUT BUBBA MUGSIT HAD DO DOC!
WHAT?
GLUK GLUK GLUK
I SAID, EATING PEANUT BUTTER MAKES IT HARD TO TALK!
WOULD YOU LIKE SOME MORE?
WHY IS YOUR BROTHER SO SELFISH, TOMMY?
oh, AND YOU'RE NOT?
HEY! I DON'T DO NOTHING BUT SIT AROUND AND SCREAM "MINE" ALL DAY!
I CLAWED MY WAY UP THE LADDER TO GET WHAT I HAVE!

2002

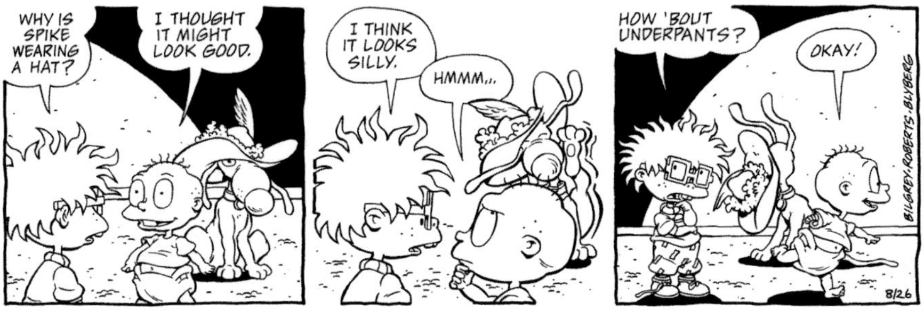
WHY IS SPIKE WEARING A HAT?
I THOUGHT IT MIGHT LOOK GOOD.
I THINK IT LOOKS SILLY.
HMMM...
HOW 'BOUT UNDERPANTS?
OKAY!
BILGREY·ROBERTS·BLYBERG
8/26

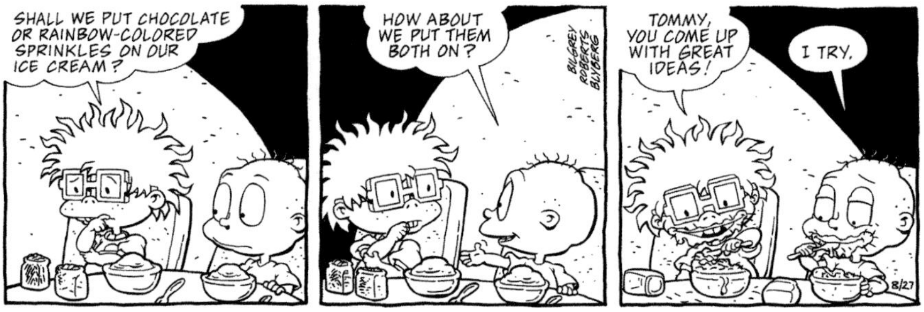
SHALL WE PUT CHOCOLATE OR RAINBOW-COLORED SPRINKLES ON OUR ICE CREAM?
HOW ABOUT WE PUT THEM BOTH ON?
BILGREY ROBERTS BLYBERG
TOMMY, YOU COME UP WITH GREAT IDEAS!
I TRY.
8/27

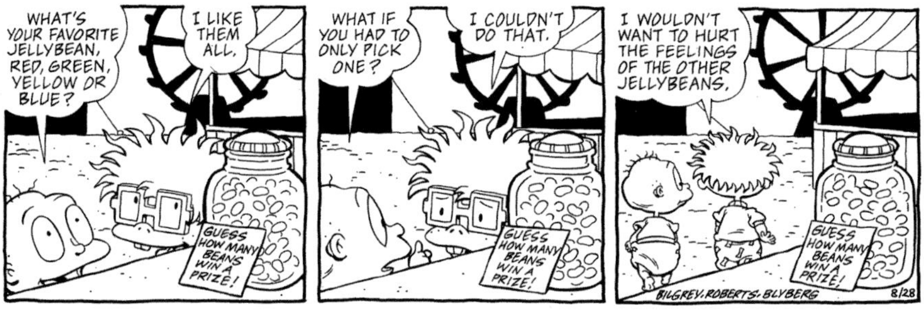
WHAT'S YOUR FAVORITE JELLYBEAN, RED, GREEN, YELLOW OR BLUE?
I LIKE THEM ALL.
GUESS HOW MANY BEANS WIN A PRIZE!
WHAT IF YOU HAD TO ONLY PICK ONE?
I COULDN'T DO THAT.
GUESS HOW MANY BEANS WIN A PRIZE!
I WOULDN'T WANT TO HURT THE FEELINGS OF THE OTHER JELLYBEANS.
GUESS HOW MANY BEANS WIN A PRIZE!
BILGREY·ROBERTS·BLYBERG
8/28

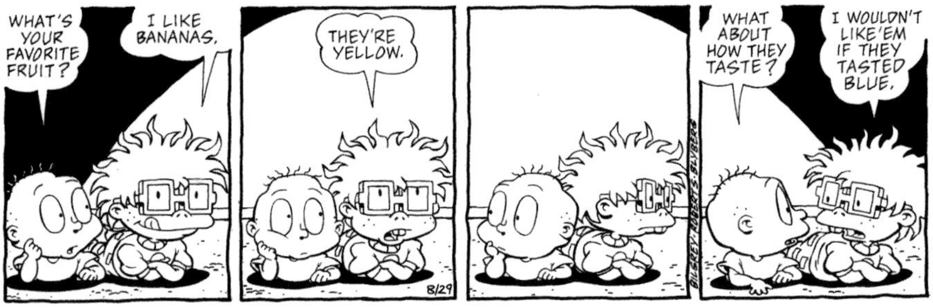
WHAT'S YOUR FAVORITE FRUIT?
I LIKE BANANAS.
THEY'RE YELLOW.
8/29
BILGREY·ROBERTS·BLYBERG
WHAT ABOUT HOW THEY TASTE?
I WOULDN'T LIKE'EM IF THEY TASTED BLUE.

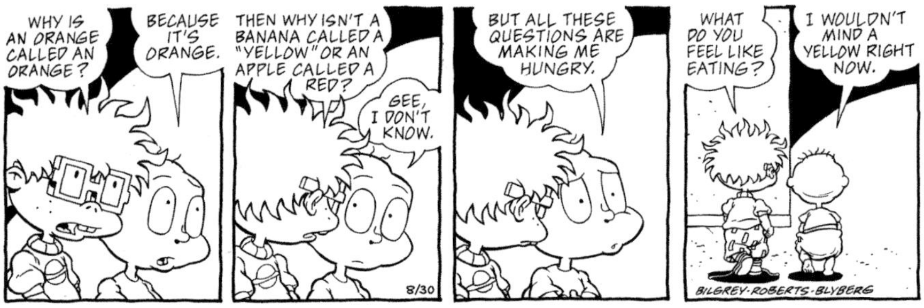
WHY IS AN ORANGE CALLED AN ORANGE?
BECAUSE IT'S ORANGE.
THEN WHY ISN'T A BANANA CALLED A "YELLOW" OR AN APPLE CALLED A RED?
GEE, I DON'T KNOW.
8/30
BUT ALL THESE QUESTIONS ARE MAKING ME HUNGRY.
WHAT DO YOU FEEL LIKE EATING?
I WOULDN'T MIND A YELLOW RIGHT NOW.
BILGREY·ROBERTS·BLYBERG

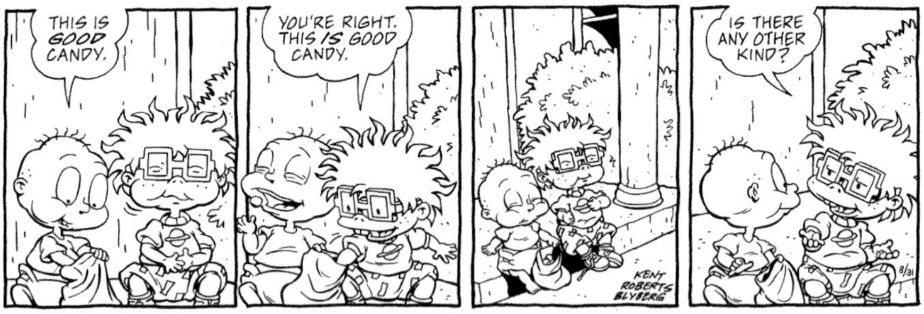
THIS IS GOOD CANDY.
YOU'RE RIGHT. THIS IS GOOD CANDY.
KENT ROBERTS BLYBERG
IS THERE ANY OTHER KIND?
8/31

2002

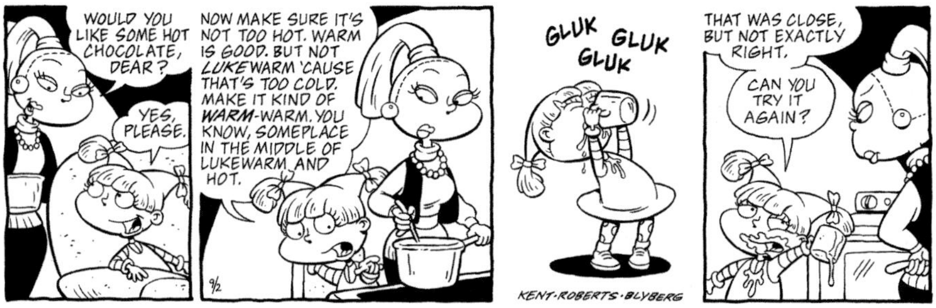
WOULD YOU LIKE SOME HOT CHOCOLATE, DEAR?
YES, PLEASE.
NOW MAKE SURE IT'S NOT TOO HOT. WARM IS GOOD. BUT NOT *LUKE*WARM 'CAUSE THAT'S TOO COLD. MAKE IT KIND OF *WARM*-WARM. YOU KNOW, SOMEPLACE IN THE MIDDLE OF LUKEWARM AND HOT.
9/2
GLUK GLUK GLUK
KENT·ROBERTS·BLYBERG
THAT WAS CLOSE, BUT NOT EXACTLY RIGHT.
CAN YOU TRY IT AGAIN?

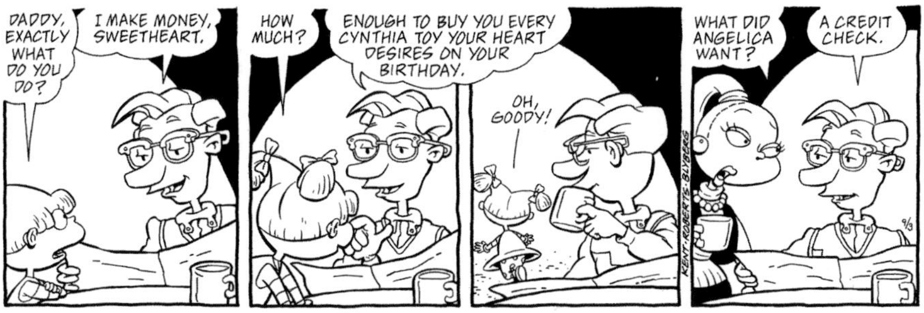
DADDY, EXACTLY WHAT DO YOU DO?
I MAKE MONEY, SWEETHEART.
HOW MUCH?
ENOUGH TO BUY YOU EVERY CYNTHIA TOY YOUR HEART DESIRES ON YOUR BIRTHDAY.
OH, GOODY!
KENT·ROBERTS·BLYBERG
WHAT DID ANGELICA WANT?
A CREDIT CHECK.
9/3

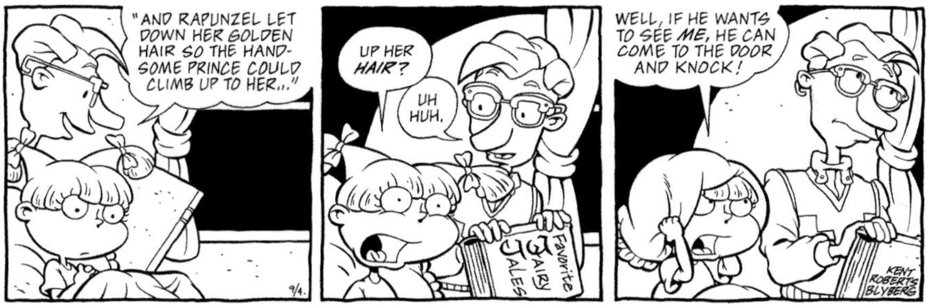
"AND RAPUNZEL LET DOWN HER GOLDEN HAIR SO THE HAND-SOME PRINCE COULD CLIMB UP TO HER..."
9/4
UP HER *HAIR*?
UH HUH.
Favorite FAIRY TALES
WELL, IF HE WANTS TO SEE *ME*, HE CAN COME TO THE DOOR AND KNOCK!
KENT ROBERTS BLYBERG

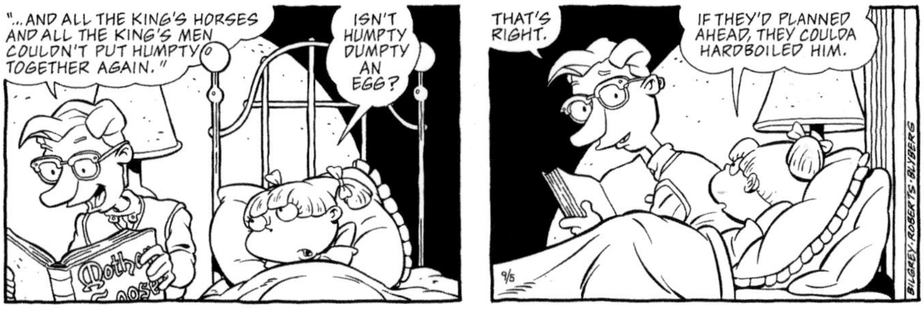
"...AND ALL THE KING'S HORSES AND ALL THE KING'S MEN COULDN'T PUT HUMPTY TOGETHER AGAIN."
ISN'T HUMPTY DUMPTY AN EGG?
Mother Goose
THAT'S RIGHT.
IF THEY'D PLANNED AHEAD, THEY COULDA HARDBOILED HIM.
9/5
BILGREY·ROBERTS·BLYBERG

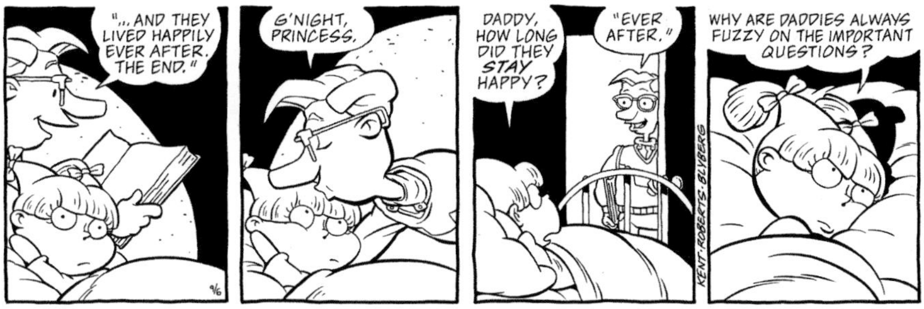
"...AND THEY LIVED HAPPILY EVER AFTER. THE END."
9/6
G'NIGHT, PRINCESS.
DADDY, HOW LONG DID THEY *STAY* HAPPY?
"EVER AFTER."
KENT·ROBERTS·BLYBERG
WHY ARE DADDIES ALWAYS FUZZY ON THE IMPORTANT QUESTIONS?

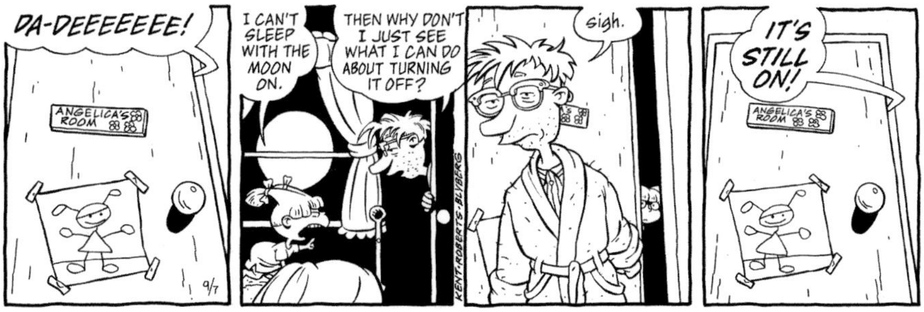
DA-DEEEEEEE!
ANGELICA'S ROOM
9/7
I CAN'T SLEEP WITH THE MOON ON.
THEN WHY DON'T I JUST SEE WHAT I CAN DO ABOUT TURNING IT OFF?
KENT·ROBERTS·BLYBERG
sigh.
IT'S STILL ON!
ANGELICA'S ROOM

2002

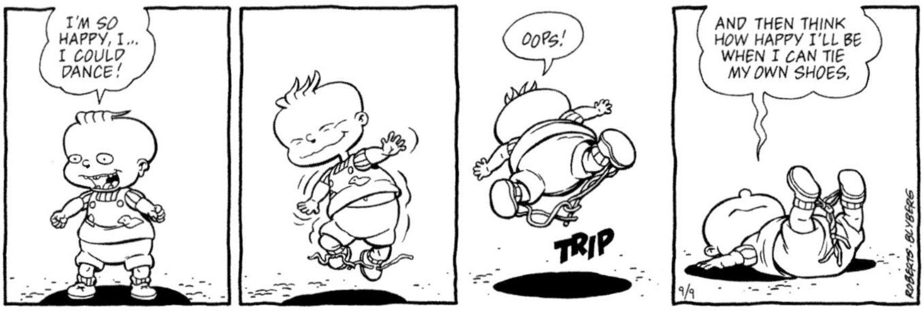
I'M SO HAPPY, I... I COULD DANCE!
OOPS!
TRIP
AND THEN THINK HOW HAPPY I'LL BE WHEN I CAN TIE MY OWN SHOES.
9/9
ROBERTS·BLYBERG

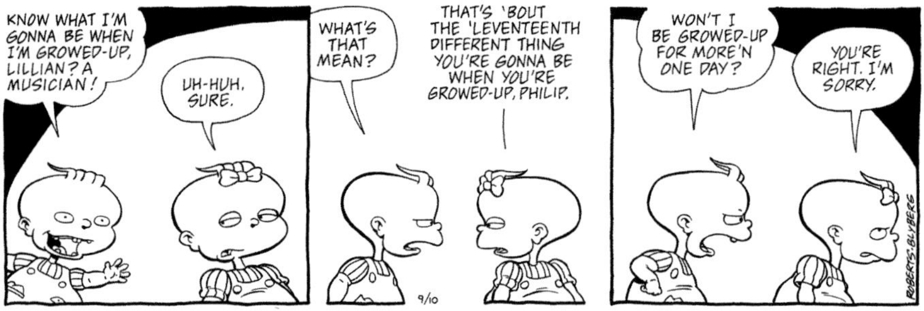
KNOW WHAT I'M GONNA BE WHEN I'M GROWED-UP, LILLIAN? A MUSICIAN!
UH-HUH. SURE.
WHAT'S THAT MEAN?
THAT'S 'BOUT THE 'LEVENTEENTH DIFFERENT THING YOU'RE GONNA BE WHEN YOU'RE GROWED-UP, PHILIP.
9/10
WON'T I BE GROWED-UP FOR MORE'N ONE DAY?
YOU'RE RIGHT. I'M SORRY.
ROBERTS·BLYBERG

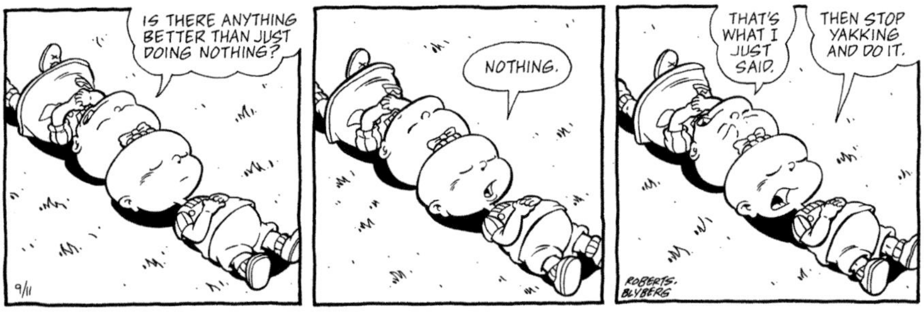
IS THERE ANYTHING BETTER THAN JUST DOING NOTHING?
9/11
NOTHING.
THAT'S WHAT I JUST SAID.
THEN STOP YAKKING AND DO IT.
ROBERTS·BLYBERG

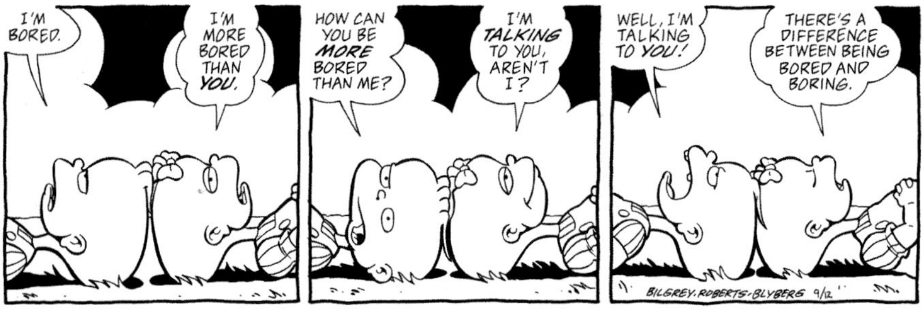
I'M BORED.
I'M MORE BORED THAN YOU.
HOW CAN YOU BE MORE BORED THAN ME?
I'M TALKING TO YOU, AREN'T I?
WELL, I'M TALKING TO YOU!
THERE'S A DIFFERENCE BETWEEN BEING BORED AND BORING.
BILGREY·ROBERTS·BLYBERG 9/12

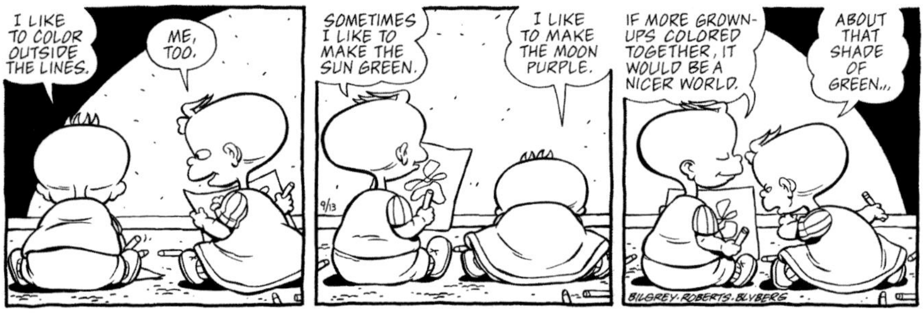
I LIKE TO COLOR OUTSIDE THE LINES.
ME, TOO.
SOMETIMES I LIKE TO MAKE THE SUN GREEN.
I LIKE TO MAKE THE MOON PURPLE.
9/13
IF MORE GROWN-UPS COLORED TOGETHER, IT WOULD BE A NICER WORLD.
ABOUT THAT SHADE OF GREEN...
BILGREY·ROBERTS·BLYBERG

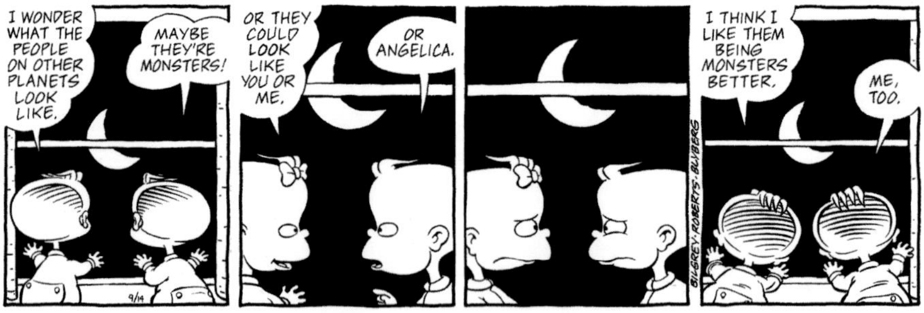
I WONDER WHAT THE PEOPLE ON OTHER PLANETS LOOK LIKE.
MAYBE THEY'RE MONSTERS!
9/14
OR THEY COULD LOOK LIKE YOU OR ME.
OR ANGELICA.
BILGREY·ROBERTS·BLYBERG
I THINK I LIKE THEM BEING MONSTERS BETTER.
ME, TOO.

2002

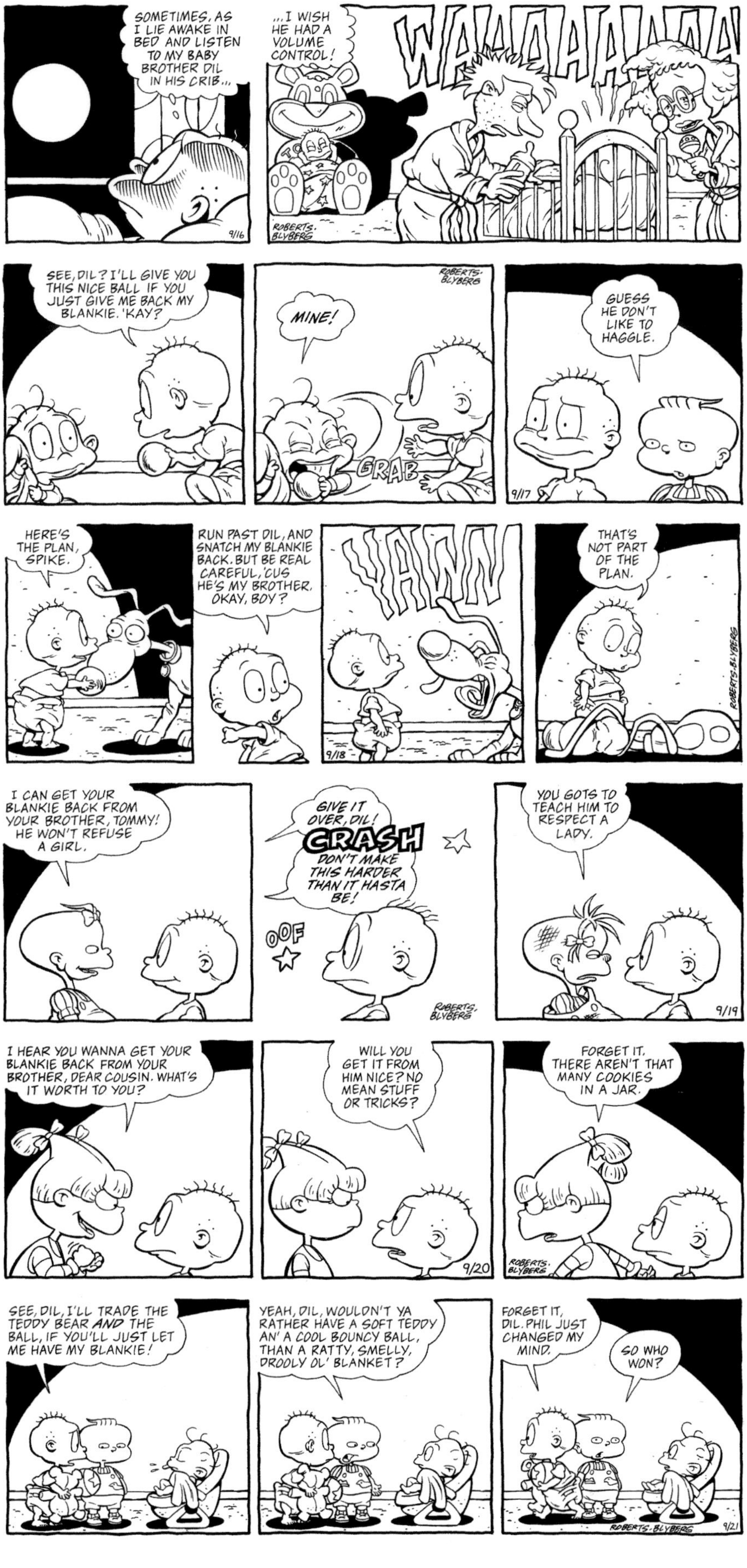
SOMETIMES, AS I LIE AWAKE IN BED AND LISTEN TO MY BABY BROTHER DIL IN HIS CRIB...
9/16
...I WISH HE HAD A VOLUME CONTROL!
WAAAAAAAA
ROBERTS-BLYBERG
SEE, DIL? I'LL GIVE YOU THIS NICE BALL IF YOU JUST GIVE ME BACK MY BLANKIE. 'KAY?
ROBERTS-BLYBERG
MINE!
GRAB
GUESS HE DON'T LIKE TO HAGGLE.
9/17
HERE'S THE PLAN, SPIKE.
RUN PAST DIL, AND SNATCH MY BLANKIE BACK. BUT BE REAL CAREFUL, 'CUS HE'S MY BROTHER. OKAY, BOY?
YAWN
9/18
THAT'S NOT PART OF THE PLAN.
ROBERTS-BLYBERG
I CAN GET YOUR BLANKIE BACK FROM YOUR BROTHER, TOMMY! HE WON'T REFUSE A GIRL.
GIVE IT OVER, DIL!
CRASH
DON'T MAKE THIS HARDER THAN IT HASTA BE!
OOF
ROBERTS-BLYBERG
YOU GOTS TO TEACH HIM TO RESPECT A LADY.
9/19
I HEAR YOU WANNA GET YOUR BLANKIE BACK FROM YOUR BROTHER, DEAR COUSIN. WHAT'S IT WORTH TO YOU?
WILL YOU GET IT FROM HIM NICE? NO MEAN STUFF OR TRICKS?
9/20
FORGET IT. THERE AREN'T THAT MANY COOKIES IN A JAR.
ROBERTS-BLYBERG
SEE, DIL, I'LL TRADE THE TEDDY BEAR AND THE BALL, IF YOU'LL JUST LET ME HAVE MY BLANKIE!
YEAH, DIL, WOULDN'T YA RATHER HAVE A SOFT TEDDY AN' A COOL BOUNCY BALL, THAN A RATTY, SMELLY, DROOLY OL' BLANKET?
FORGET IT, DIL. PHIL JUST CHANGED MY MIND.
SO WHO WON?
ROBERTS-BLYBERG
9/21

2002

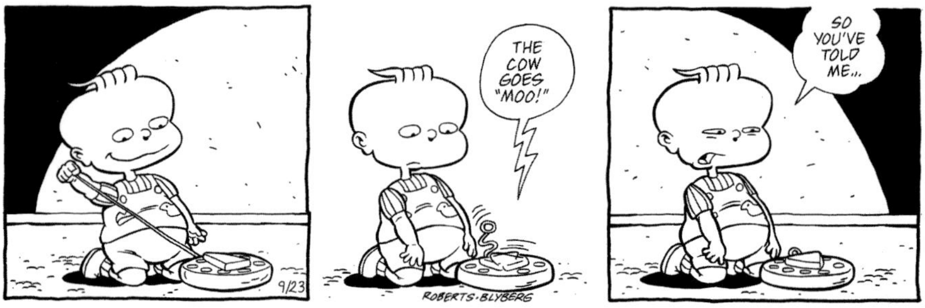

9/23
THE COW GOES "MOO!"
ROBERTS·BLYBERG
SO YOU'VE TOLD ME...

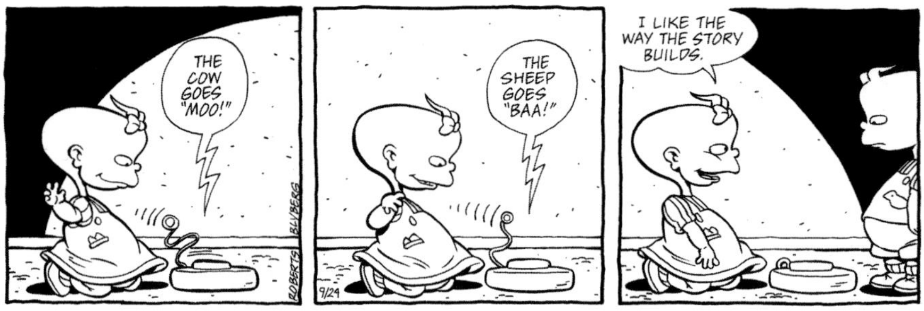

THE COW GOES "MOO!"
ROBERTS·BLYBERG
9/24
THE SHEEP GOES "BAA!"
I LIKE THE WAY THE STORY BUILDS.

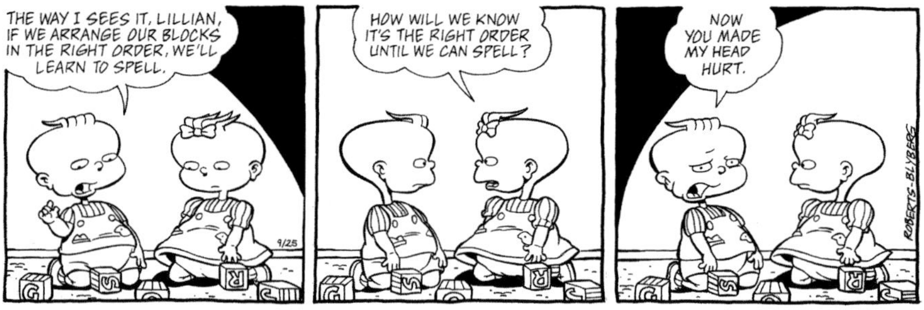

THE WAY I SEES IT, LILLIAN, IF WE ARRANGE OUR BLOCKS IN THE RIGHT ORDER, WE'LL LEARN TO SPELL.
9/25
HOW WILL WE KNOW IT'S THE RIGHT ORDER UNTIL WE CAN SPELL?
NOW YOU MADE MY HEAD HURT.
ROBERTS·BLYBERG

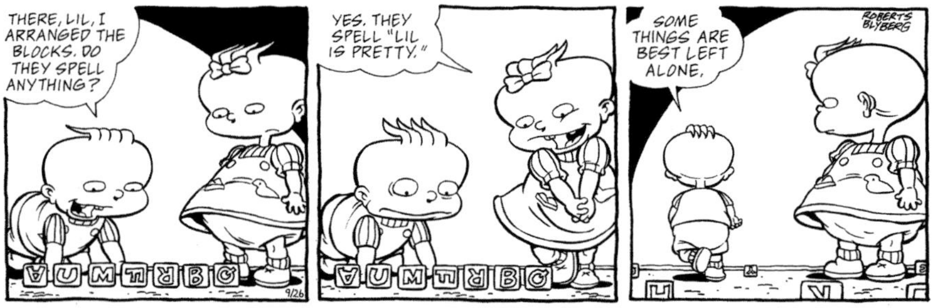

THERE, LIL, I ARRANGED THE BLOCKS. DO THEY SPELL ANYTHING?
9/26
YES. THEY SPELL "LIL IS PRETTY."
SOME THINGS ARE BEST LEFT ALONE.
ROBERTS BLYBERG

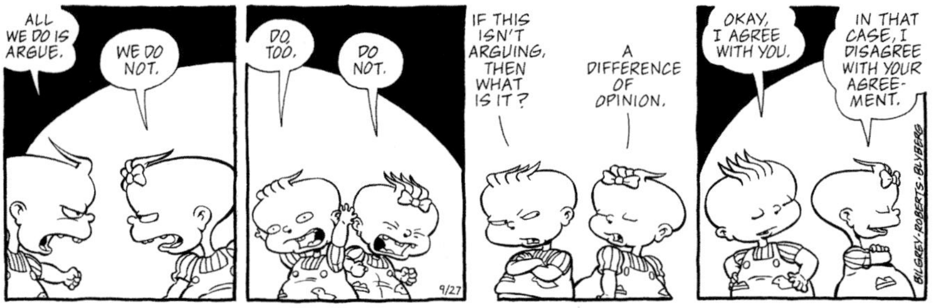

ALL WE DO IS ARGUE.
WE DO NOT.
DO, TOO.
DO NOT.
9/27
IF THIS ISN'T ARGUING, THEN WHAT IS IT?
A DIFFERENCE OF OPINION.
OKAY, I AGREE WITH YOU.
IN THAT CASE, I DISAGREE WITH YOUR AGREEMENT.
BILGREY·ROBERTS·BLYBERG

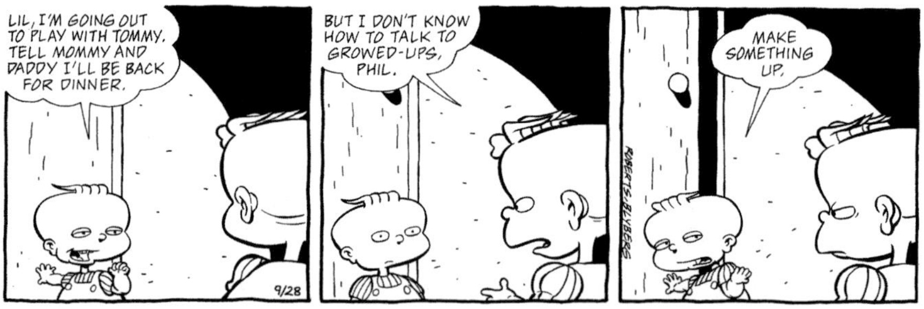

LIL, I'M GOING OUT TO PLAY WITH TOMMY. TELL MOMMY AND DADDY I'LL BE BACK FOR DINNER.
9/28
BUT I DON'T KNOW HOW TO TALK TO GROWED-UPS, PHIL.
ROBERTS·BLYBERG
MAKE SOMETHING UP.

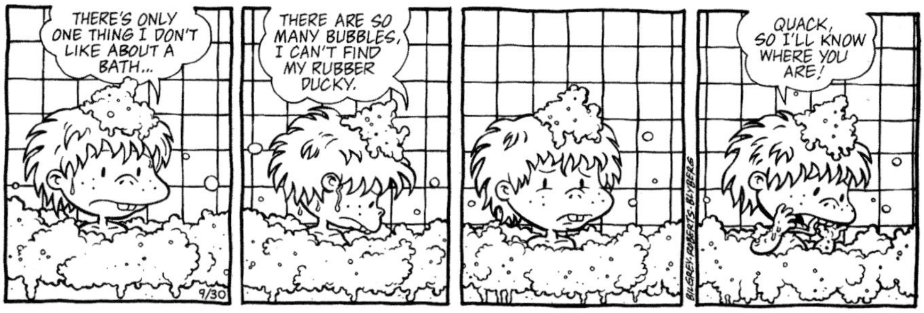
THERE'S ONLY ONE THING I DON'T LIKE ABOUT A BATH...
9/30
THERE ARE SO MANY BUBBLES, I CAN'T FIND MY RUBBER DUCKY.
BILGREY·ROBERTS·BLYBERG
QUACK, SO I'LL KNOW WHERE YOU ARE!

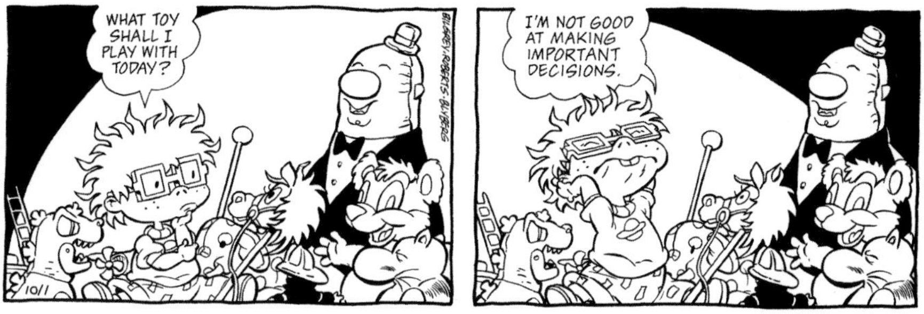
WHAT TOY SHALL I PLAY WITH TODAY?
BILGREY·ROBERTS·BLYBERG
10/1
I'M NOT GOOD AT MAKING IMPORTANT DECISIONS.

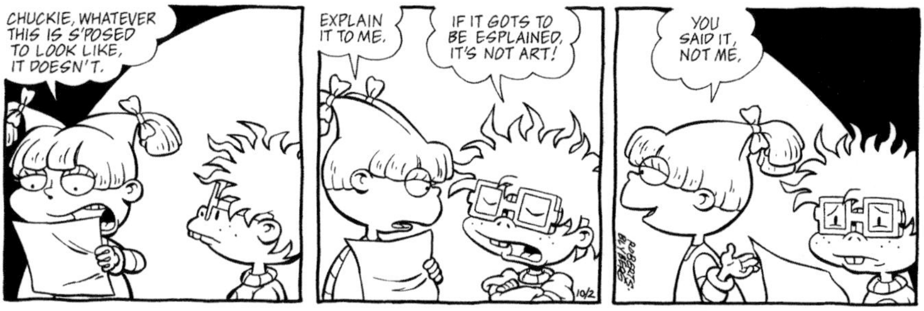
CHUCKIE, WHATEVER THIS IS S'POSED TO LOOK LIKE, IT DOESN'T.
EXPLAIN IT TO ME.
IF IT GOTS TO BE ESPLAINED, IT'S NOT ART!
10/2
ROBERTS·BLYBERG
YOU SAID IT, NOT ME.

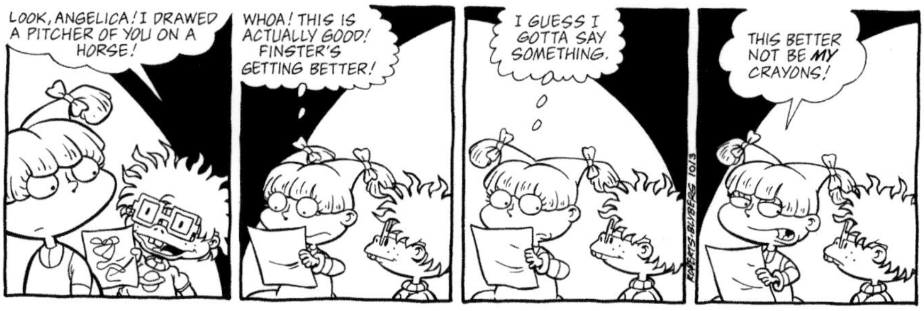
LOOK, ANGELICA! I DRAWED A PITCHER OF YOU ON A HORSE!
WHOA! THIS IS ACTUALLY GOOD! FINSTER'S GETTING BETTER!
I GUESS I GOTTA SAY SOMETHING.
ROBERTS·BLYBERG 10/3
THIS BETTER NOT BE MY CRAYONS!

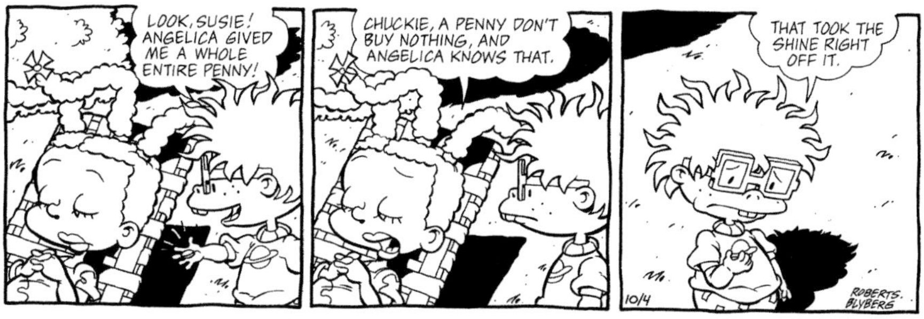
LOOK, SUSIE! ANGELICA GIVED ME A WHOLE ENTIRE PENNY!
CHUCKIE, A PENNY DON'T BUY NOTHING, AND ANGELICA KNOWS THAT.
THAT TOOK THE SHINE RIGHT OFF IT.
10/4
ROBERTS·BLYBERG

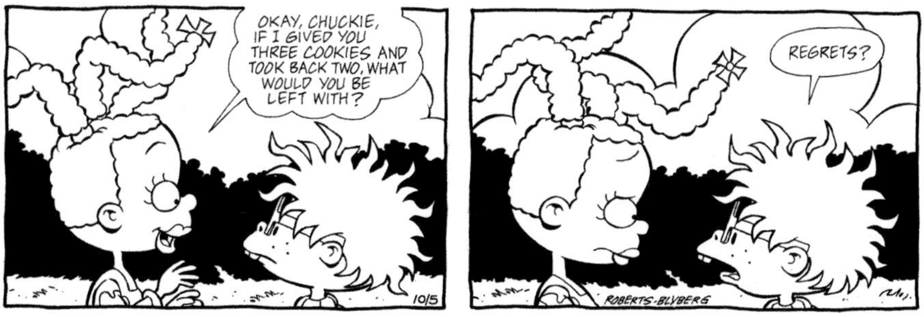
OKAY, CHUCKIE, IF I GIVED YOU THREE COOKIES AND TOOK BACK TWO, WHAT WOULD YOU BE LEFT WITH?
10/5
REGRETS?
ROBERTS·BLYBERG

2002

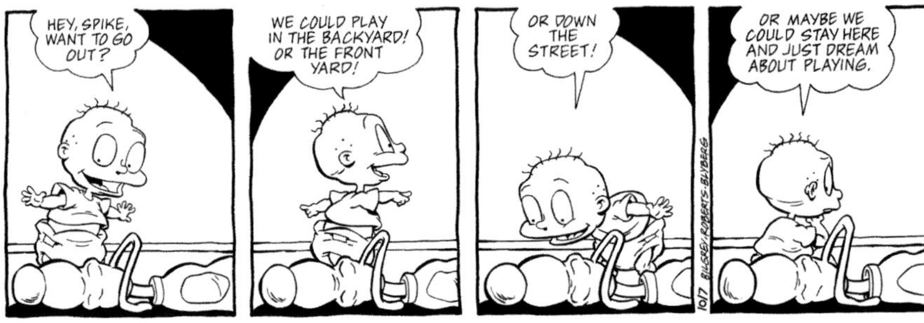
HEY, SPIKE, WANT TO GO OUT?
WE COULD PLAY IN THE BACKYARD! OR THE FRONT YARD!
OR DOWN THE STREET!
OR MAYBE WE COULD STAY HERE AND JUST DREAM ABOUT PLAYING.
10/7

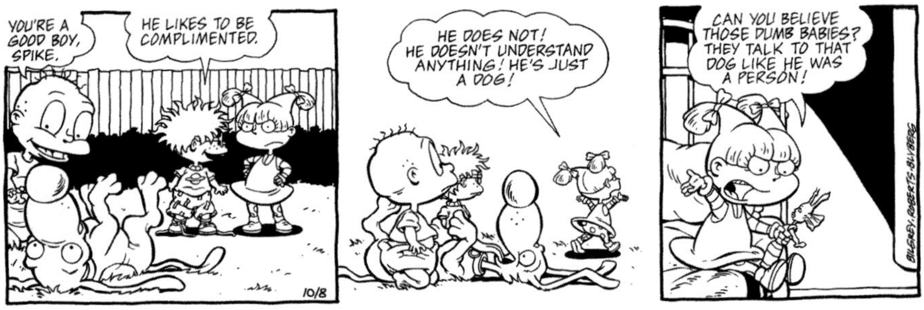
YOU'RE A GOOD BOY, SPIKE.
HE LIKES TO BE COMPLIMENTED.
10/8
HE DOES NOT! HE DOESN'T UNDERSTAND ANYTHING! HE'S JUST A DOG!
CAN YOU BELIEVE THOSE DUMB BABIES? THEY TALK TO THAT DOG LIKE HE WAS A PERSON!

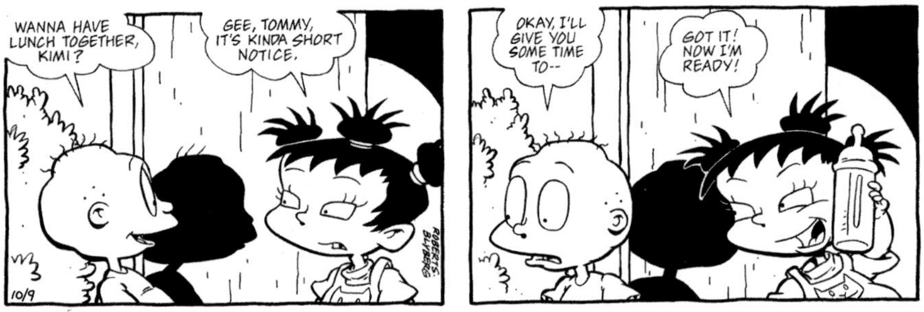
WANNA HAVE LUNCH TOGETHER, KIMI?
GEE, TOMMY, IT'S KINDA SHORT NOTICE.
10/9
OKAY, I'LL GIVE YOU SOME TIME TO--
GOT IT! NOW I'M READY!

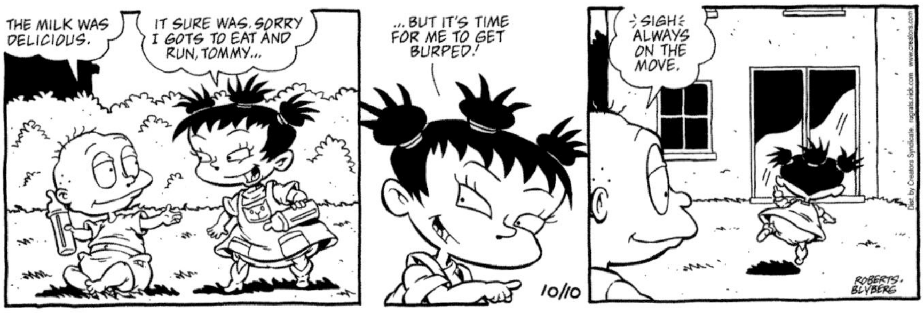
THE MILK WAS DELICIOUS.
IT SURE WAS. SORRY I GOTS TO EAT AND RUN, TOMMY...
...BUT IT'S TIME FOR ME TO GET BURPED!
10/10
SIGH ALWAYS ON THE MOVE.

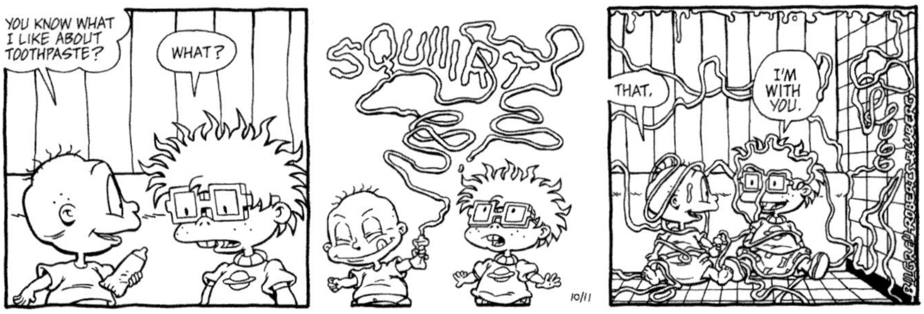
YOU KNOW WHAT I LIKE ABOUT TOOTHPASTE?
WHAT?
SQUIIIRT
10/11
THAT.
I'M WITH YOU.

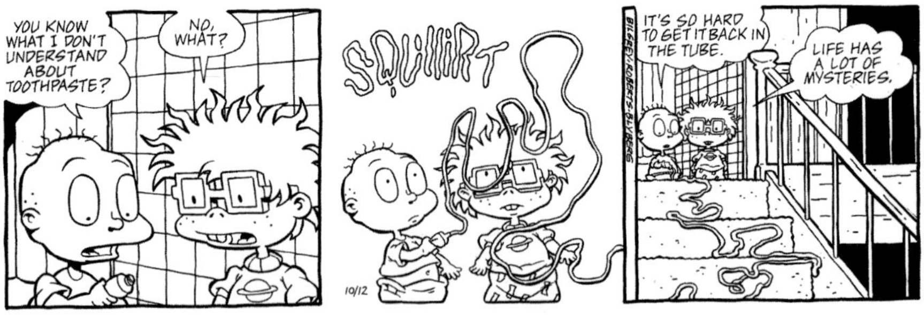
YOU KNOW WHAT I DON'T UNDERSTAND ABOUT TOOTHPASTE?
NO, WHAT?
SQUIIIRT
10/12
IT'S SO HARD TO GET IT BACK IN THE TUBE.
LIFE HAS A LOT OF MYSTERIES.

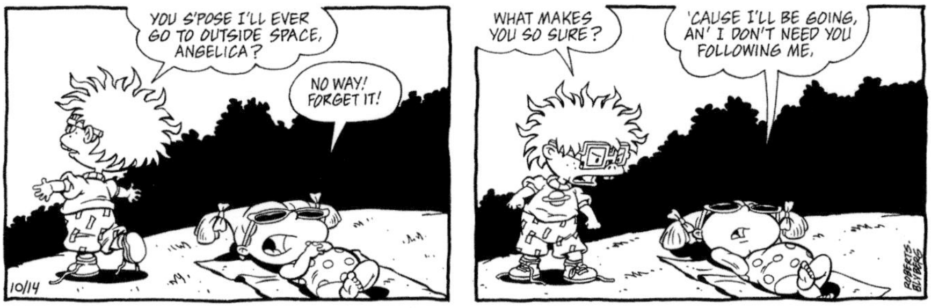

YOU S'POSE I'LL EVER GO TO OUTSIDE SPACE, ANGELICA?
NO WAY! FORGET IT!
10/14
WHAT MAKES YOU SO SURE?
'CAUSE I'LL BE GOING, AN' I DON'T NEED YOU FOLLOWING ME.
ROBERTS-BLYBERG

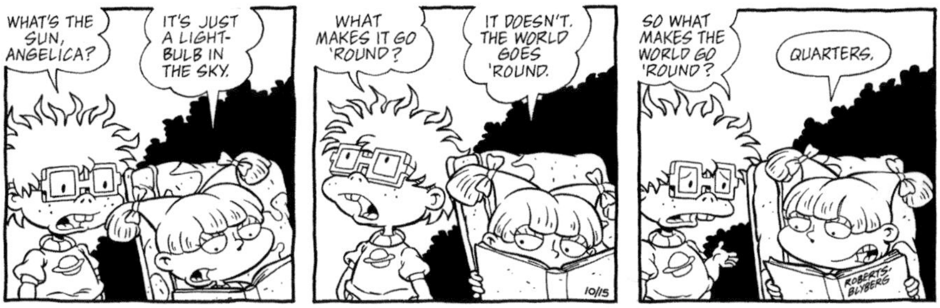

WHAT'S THE SUN, ANGELICA?
IT'S JUST A LIGHT-BULB IN THE SKY.
WHAT MAKES IT GO 'ROUND?
IT DOESN'T. THE WORLD GOES 'ROUND.
10/15
SO WHAT MAKES THE WORLD GO 'ROUND?
QUARTERS.
ROBERTS-BLYBERG

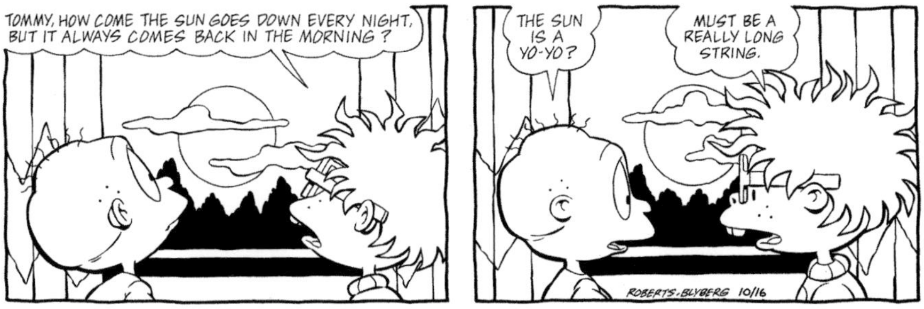

TOMMY, HOW COME THE SUN GOES DOWN EVERY NIGHT, BUT IT ALWAYS COMES BACK IN THE MORNING?
THE SUN IS A YO-YO?
MUST BE A REALLY LONG STRING.
ROBERTS-BLYBERG 10/16

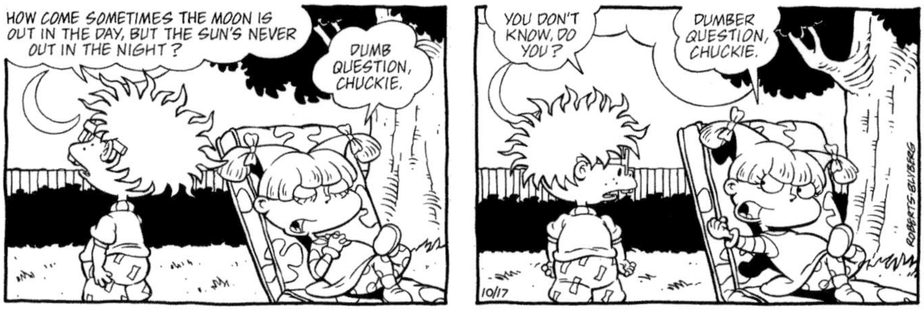

HOW COME SOMETIMES THE MOON IS OUT IN THE DAY, BUT THE SUN'S NEVER OUT IN THE NIGHT?
DUMB QUESTION, CHUCKIE.
YOU DON'T KNOW, DO YOU?
DUMBER QUESTION, CHUCKIE.
10/17
ROBERTS-BLYBERG

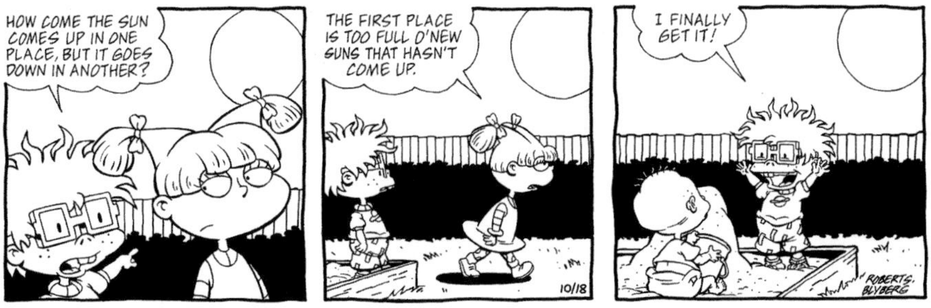

HOW COME THE SUN COMES UP IN ONE PLACE, BUT IT GOES DOWN IN ANOTHER?
THE FIRST PLACE IS TOO FULL O'NEW SUNS THAT HASN'T COME UP.
10/18
I FINALLY GET IT!
ROBERTS-BLYBERG

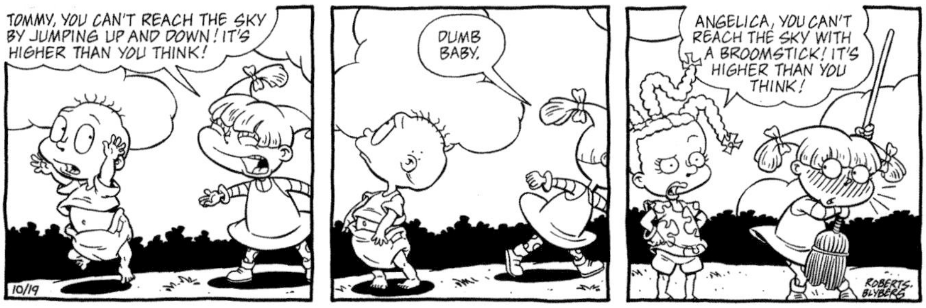

TOMMY, YOU CAN'T REACH THE SKY BY JUMPING UP AND DOWN! IT'S HIGHER THAN YOU THINK!
10/19
DUMB BABY.
ANGELICA, YOU CAN'T REACH THE SKY WITH A BROOMSTICK! IT'S HIGHER THAN YOU THINK!
ROBERTS-BLYBERG

2002

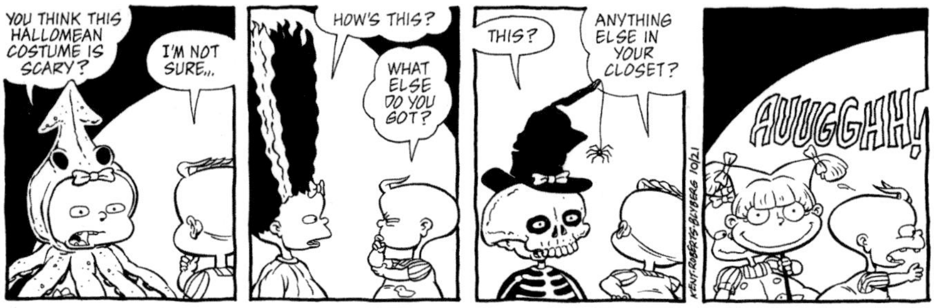
YOU THINK THIS HALLOMEAN COSTUME IS SCARY?
I'M NOT SURE...
HOW'S THIS?
WHAT ELSE DO YOU GOT?
THIS?
ANYTHING ELSE IN YOUR CLOSET?
KENT·ROBERTS·BLYBERG 10/21
AUUGGHH!

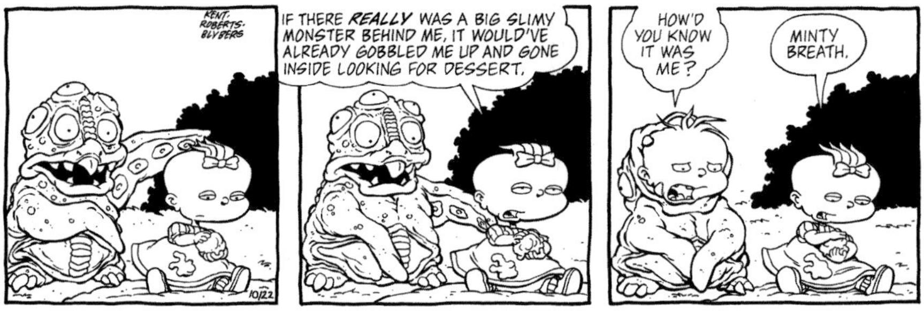
KENT· ROBERTS· BLYBERG
10/22
IF THERE REALLY WAS A BIG SLIMY MONSTER BEHIND ME, IT WOULD'VE ALREADY GOBBLED ME UP AND GONE INSIDE LOOKING FOR DESSERT.
HOW'D YOU KNOW IT WAS ME?
MINTY BREATH.

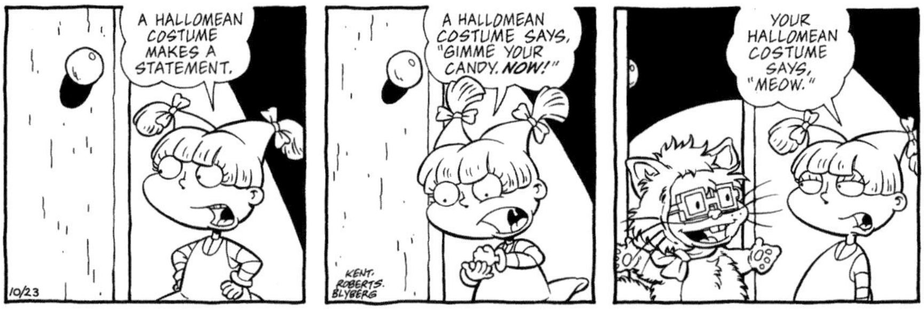
A HALLOMEAN COSTUME MAKES A STATEMENT.
10/23
A HALLOMEAN COSTUME SAYS, "GIMME YOUR CANDY. NOW!"
KENT· ROBERTS· BLYBERG
YOUR HALLOMEAN COSTUME SAYS, "MEOW."

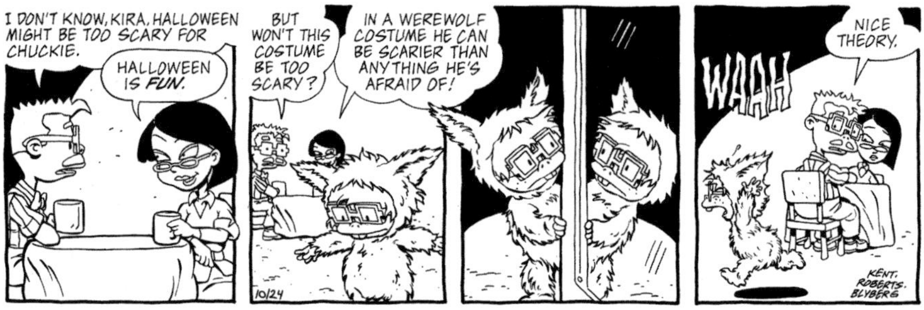
I DON'T KNOW, KIRA, HALLOWEEN MIGHT BE TOO SCARY FOR CHUCKIE.
HALLOWEEN IS FUN.
BUT WON'T THIS COSTUME BE TOO SCARY?
IN A WEREWOLF COSTUME HE CAN BE SCARIER THAN ANYTHING HE'S AFRAID OF!
10/24
WAAH
NICE THEORY.
KENT· ROBERTS· BLYBERG

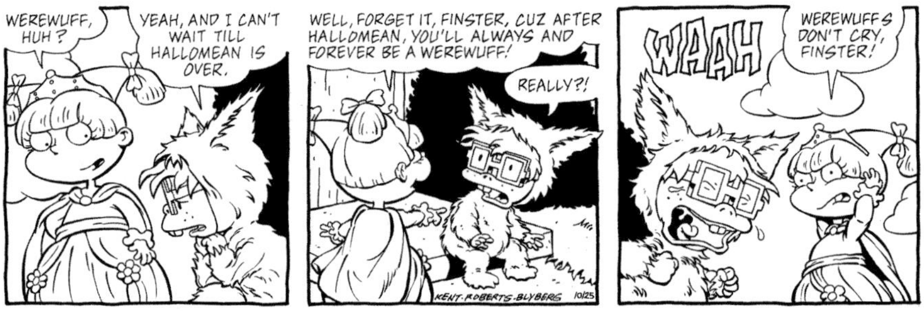
WEREWUFF, HUH?
YEAH, AND I CAN'T WAIT TILL HALLOMEAN IS OVER.
WELL, FORGET IT, FINSTER, CUZ AFTER HALLOMEAN, YOU'LL ALWAYS AND FOREVER BE A WEREWUFF!
REALLY?!
KENT·ROBERTS·BLYBERG 10/25
WAAH
WEREWUFFS DON'T CRY, FINSTER!

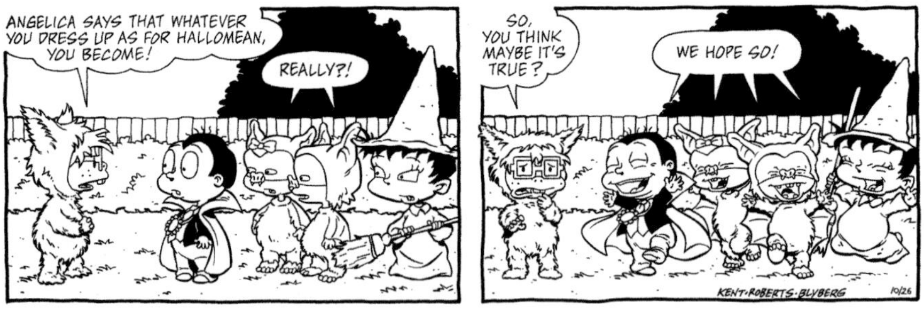
ANGELICA SAYS THAT WHATEVER YOU DRESS UP AS FOR HALLOMEAN, YOU BECOME!
REALLY?!
SO, YOU THINK MAYBE IT'S TRUE?
WE HOPE SO!
KENT·ROBERTS·BLYBERG 10/26

2002

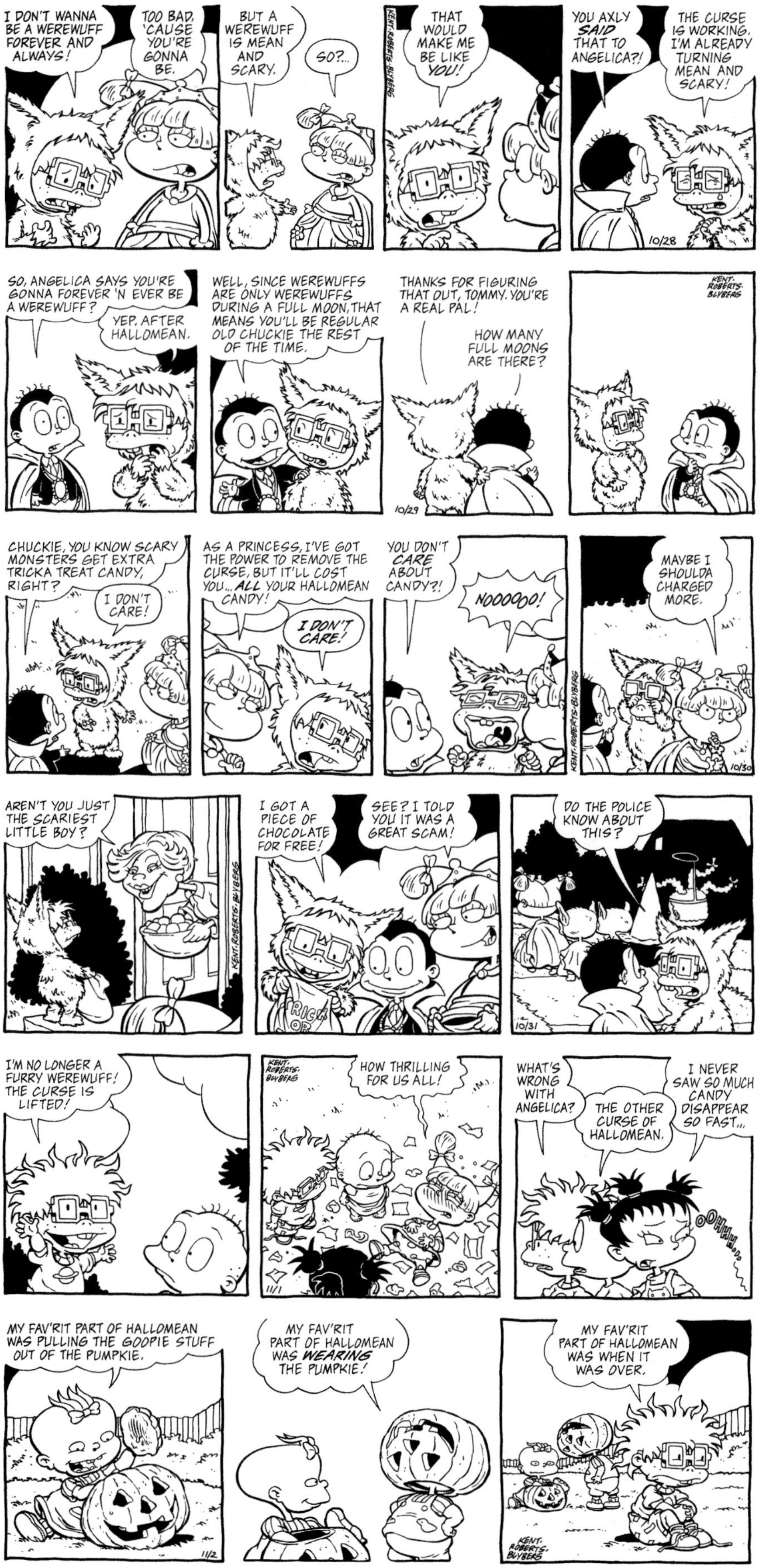
I DON'T WANNA BE A WEREWUFF FOREVER AND ALWAYS!
TOO BAD, 'CAUSE YOU'RE GONNA BE.
BUT A WEREWUFF IS MEAN AND SCARY.
SO?...
KENT. ROBERTS. BLYBERG
THAT WOULD MAKE ME BE LIKE *YOU!*
YOU AXLY *SAID* THAT TO ANGELICA?!
THE CURSE IS WORKING. I'M ALREADY TURNING MEAN AND SCARY!
10/28
SO, ANGELICA SAYS YOU'RE GONNA FOREVER 'N EVER BE A WEREWUFF?
YEP. AFTER HALLOMEAN.
WELL, SINCE WEREWUFFS ARE ONLY WEREWUFFS DURING A FULL MOON, THAT MEANS YOU'LL BE REGULAR OLD CHUCKIE THE REST OF THE TIME.
THANKS FOR FIGURING THAT OUT, TOMMY. YOU'RE A REAL PAL!
HOW MANY FULL MOONS ARE THERE?
10/29
KENT. ROBERTS. BLYBERG
CHUCKIE, YOU KNOW SCARY MONSTERS GET EXTRA TRICKA TREAT CANDY, RIGHT?
I DON'T CARE!
AS A PRINCESS, I'VE GOT THE POWER TO REMOVE THE CURSE, BUT IT'LL COST YOU... *ALL* YOUR HALLOMEAN CANDY!
I DON'T CARE!
YOU DON'T *CARE* ABOUT CANDY?!
NOOOOOO!
KENT. ROBERTS. BLYBERG
MAYBE I SHOULDA CHARGED MORE.
10/30
AREN'T YOU JUST THE SCARIEST LITTLE BOY?
KENT. ROBERTS. BLYBERG
I GOT A PIECE OF CHOCOLATE FOR FREE!
SEE? I TOLD YOU IT WAS A GREAT SCAM!
TRICK OR
DO THE POLICE KNOW ABOUT THIS?
10/31
I'M NO LONGER A FURRY WEREWUFF! THE CURSE IS LIFTED!
KENT. ROBERTS. BLYBERG
HOW THRILLING FOR US ALL!
11/1
WHAT'S WRONG WITH ANGELICA?
THE OTHER CURSE OF HALLOMEAN.
I NEVER SAW SO MUCH CANDY DISAPPEAR SO FAST...
OOHHH...
MY FAV'RIT PART OF HALLOMEAN WAS PULLING THE GOOPIE STUFF OUT OF THE PUMPKIE.
11/2
MY FAV'RIT PART OF HALLOMEAN WAS *WEARING* THE PUMPKIE!
MY FAV'RIT PART OF HALLOMEAN WAS WHEN IT WAS OVER.
KENT. ROBERTS. BLYBERG

2002

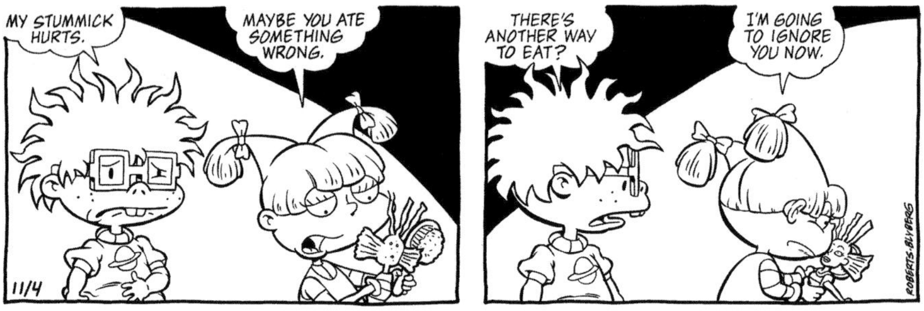
MY STUMMICK HURTS.
MAYBE YOU ATE SOMETHING WRONG.
THERE'S ANOTHER WAY TO EAT?
I'M GOING TO IGNORE YOU NOW.
11/4
ROBERTS·BLYBERG

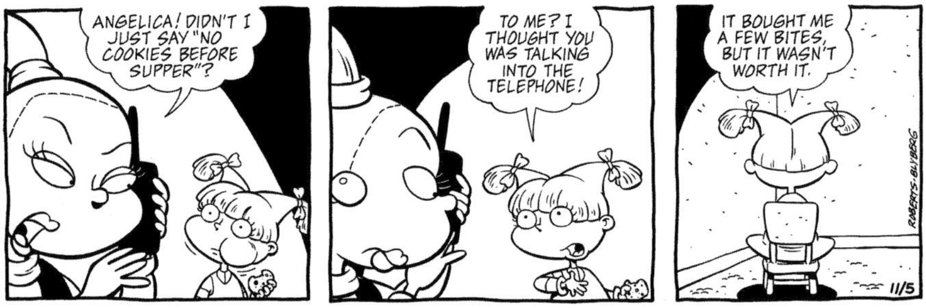
ANGELICA! DIDN'T I JUST SAY "NO COOKIES BEFORE SUPPER"?
TO ME? I THOUGHT YOU WAS TALKING INTO THE TELEPHONE!
IT BOUGHT ME A FEW BITES, BUT IT WASN'T WORTH IT.
ROBERTS·BLYBERG
11/5

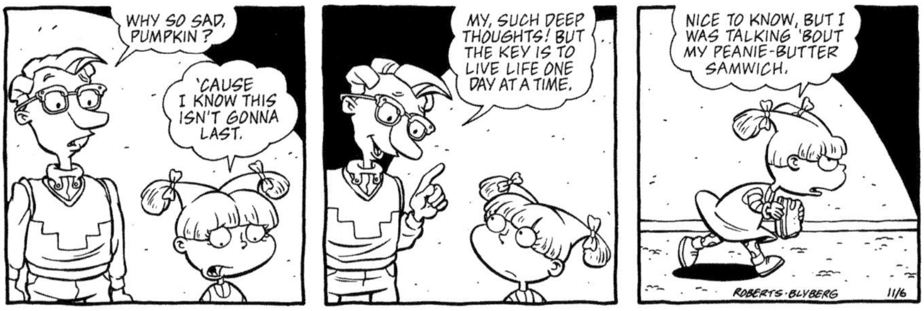
WHY SO SAD, PUMPKIN?
'CAUSE I KNOW THIS ISN'T GONNA LAST.
MY, SUCH DEEP THOUGHTS! BUT THE KEY IS TO LIVE LIFE ONE DAY AT A TIME.
NICE TO KNOW, BUT I WAS TALKING 'BOUT MY PEANIE-BUTTER SAMWICH.
ROBERTS·BLYBERG
11/6

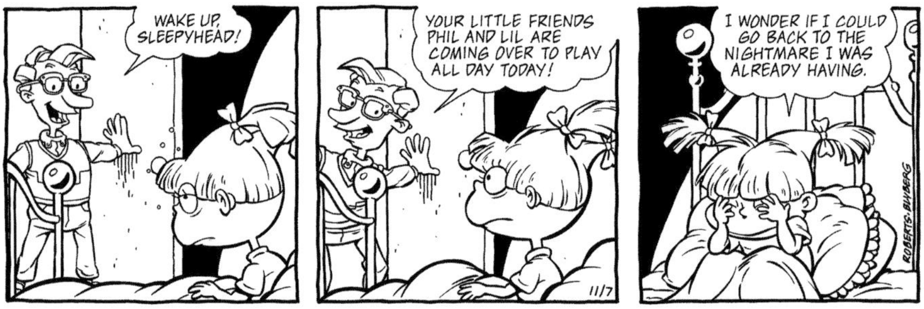
WAKE UP, SLEEPYHEAD!
YOUR LITTLE FRIENDS PHIL AND LIL ARE COMING OVER TO PLAY ALL DAY TODAY!
11/7
I WONDER IF I COULD GO BACK TO THE NIGHTMARE I WAS ALREADY HAVING.
ROBERTS·BLYBERG

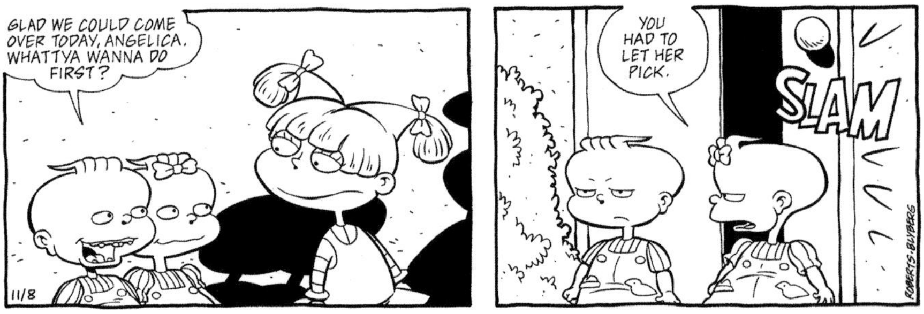
GLAD WE COULD COME OVER TODAY, ANGELICA. WHATTYA WANNA DO FIRST?
11/8
YOU HAD TO LET HER PICK.
SLAM
ROBERTS·BLYBERG

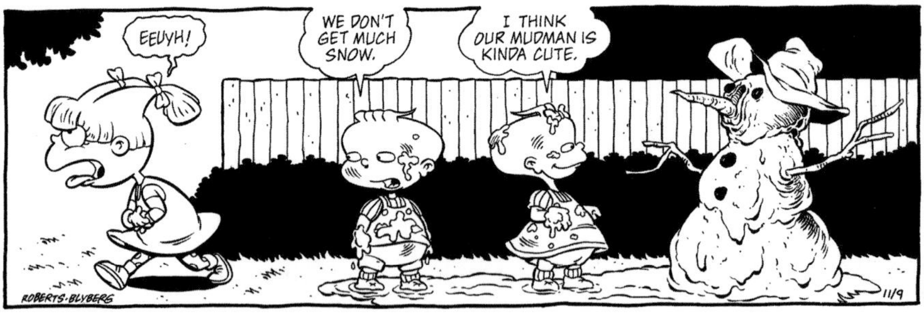
EEUYH!
WE DON'T GET MUCH SNOW.
I THINK OUR MUDMAN IS KINDA CUTE.
ROBERTS·BLYBERG
11/9

2002

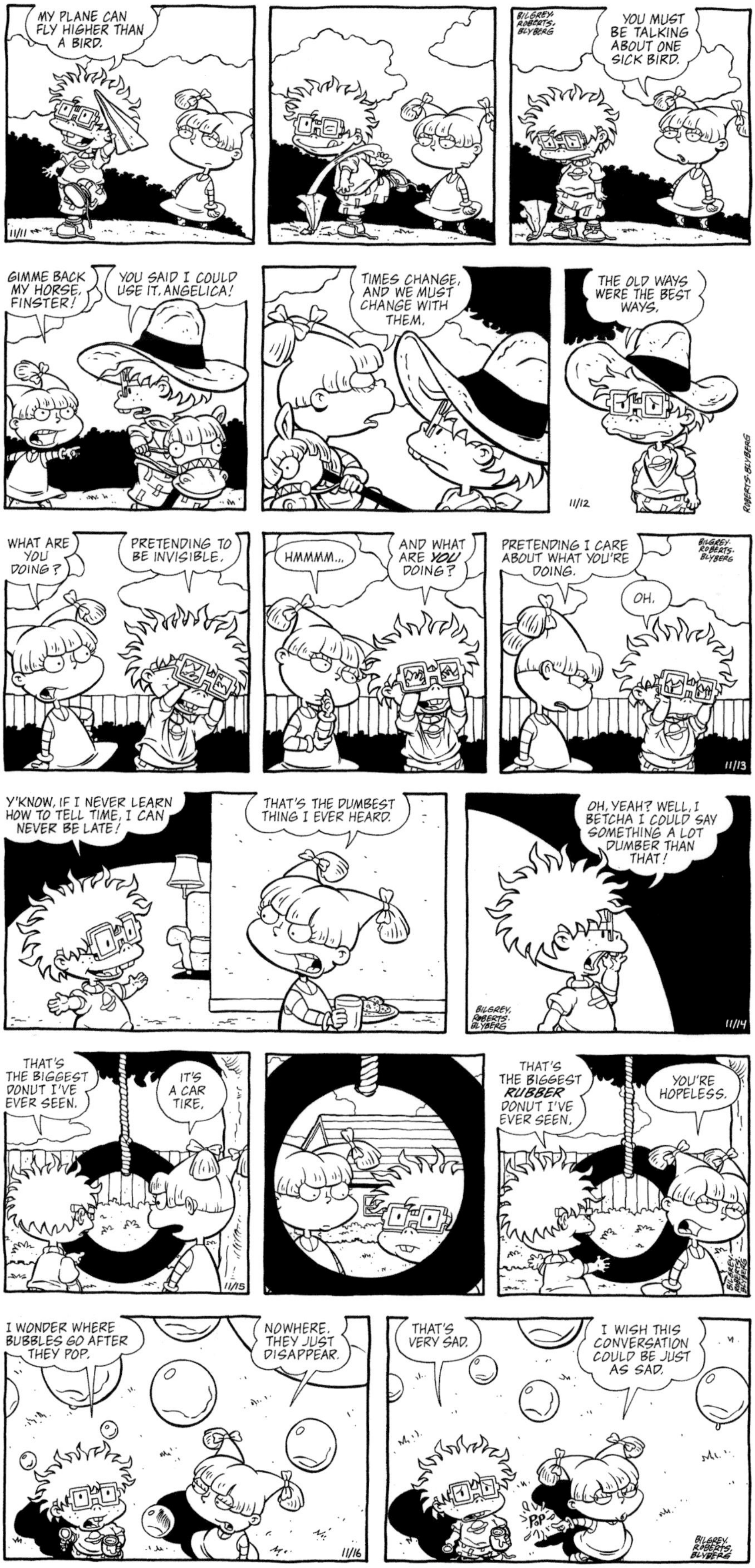

MY PLANE CAN FLY HIGHER THAN A BIRD.
11/11
BILGREY-ROBERTS-BLYBERG
YOU MUST BE TALKING ABOUT ONE SICK BIRD.
GIMME BACK MY HORSE, FINSTER!
YOU SAID I COULD USE IT, ANGELICA!
TIMES CHANGE, AND WE MUST CHANGE WITH THEM.
THE OLD WAYS WERE THE BEST WAYS.
11/12
ROBERTS-BLYBERG
WHAT ARE YOU DOING?
PRETENDING TO BE INVISIBLE.
HMMMM...
AND WHAT ARE *YOU* DOING?
PRETENDING I CARE ABOUT WHAT YOU'RE DOING.
BILGREY-ROBERTS-BLYBERG
OH.
11/13
Y'KNOW, IF I NEVER LEARN HOW TO TELL TIME, I CAN NEVER BE LATE!
THAT'S THE DUMBEST THING I EVER HEARD.
OH, YEAH? WELL, I BETCHA I COULD SAY SOMETHING A LOT DUMBER THAN THAT!
BILGREY-ROBERTS-BLYBERG
11/14
THAT'S THE BIGGEST DONUT I'VE EVER SEEN.
IT'S A CAR TIRE.
11/15
THAT'S THE BIGGEST ***RUBBER*** DONUT I'VE EVER SEEN.
YOU'RE HOPELESS.
BILGREY-ROBERTS-BLYBERG
I WONDER WHERE BUBBLES GO AFTER THEY POP.
NOWHERE. THEY JUST DISAPPEAR.
11/16
THAT'S VERY SAD.
I WISH THIS CONVERSATION COULD BE JUST AS SAD.
POP
BILGREY-ROBERTS-BLYBERG

2002

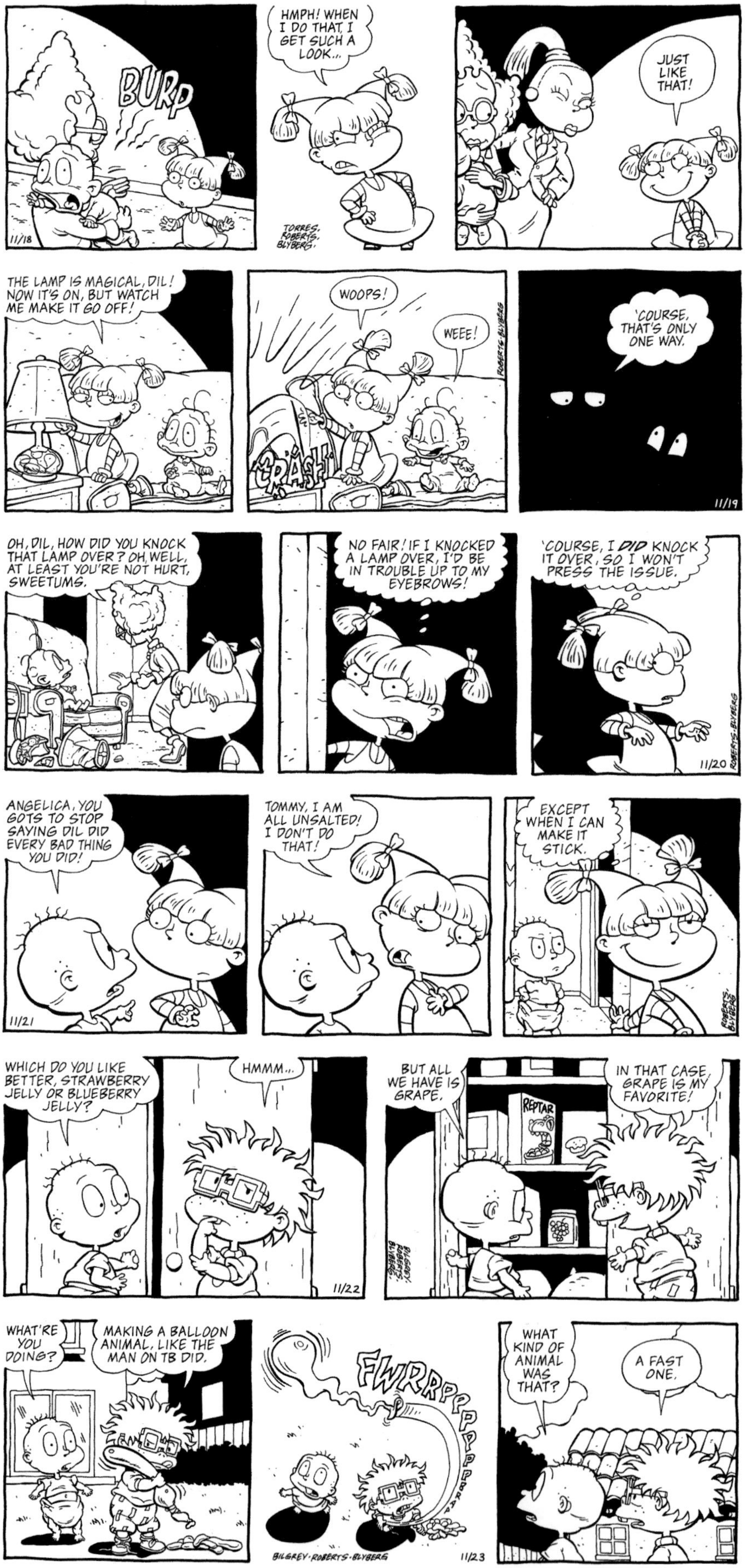
BURP
11/18
HMPH! WHEN I DO THAT, I GET SUCH A LOOK...
TORRES, ROBERTS, BLYBERG.
JUST LIKE THAT!
THE LAMP IS MAGICAL, DIL! NOW IT'S ON, BUT WATCH ME MAKE IT GO OFF!
WOOPS!
WEEE!
CRASH!
ROBERTS·BLYBERG
'COURSE, THAT'S ONLY ONE WAY.
11/19
OH, DIL, HOW DID YOU KNOCK THAT LAMP OVER? OH, WELL, AT LEAST YOU'RE NOT HURT, SWEETUMS.
NO FAIR! IF I KNOCKED A LAMP OVER, I'D BE IN TROUBLE UP TO MY EYEBROWS!
'COURSE, I DID KNOCK IT OVER, SO I WON'T PRESS THE ISSUE.
ROBERTS·BLYBERG
11/20
ANGELICA, YOU GOTS TO STOP SAYING DIL DID EVERY BAD THING YOU DID!
11/21
TOMMY, I AM ALL UNSALTED! I DON'T DO THAT!
EXCEPT WHEN I CAN MAKE IT STICK.
ROBERTS·BLYBERG
WHICH DO YOU LIKE BETTER, STRAWBERRY JELLY OR BLUEBERRY JELLY?
HMMM...
11/22
BILGREY, ROBERTS, BLYBERG
BUT ALL WE HAVE IS GRAPE.
REPTAR
IN THAT CASE, GRAPE IS MY FAVORITE!
WHAT'RE YOU DOING?
MAKING A BALLOON ANIMAL, LIKE THE MAN ON TB DID.
FWRRPPPPPPPPRRRR
BILGREY·ROBERTS·BLYBERG
11/23
WHAT KIND OF ANIMAL WAS THAT?
A FAST ONE.

2002

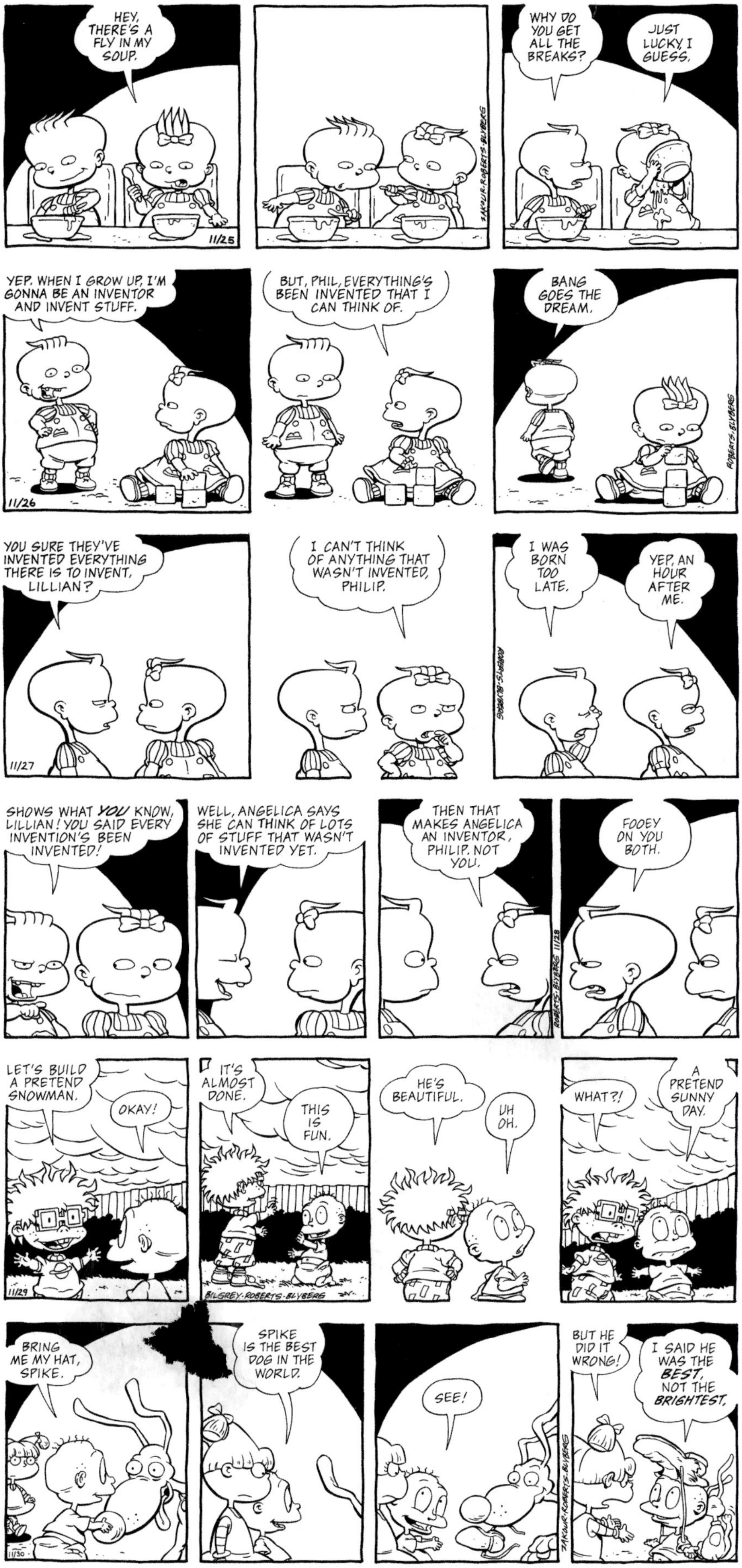
HEY, THERE'S A FLY IN MY SOUP.
WHY DO YOU GET ALL THE BREAKS?
JUST LUCKY, I GUESS.
YEP. WHEN I GROW UP, I'M GONNA BE AN INVENTOR AND INVENT STUFF.
BUT, PHIL, EVERYTHING'S BEEN INVENTED THAT I CAN THINK OF.
BANG GOES THE DREAM.
YOU SURE THEY'VE INVENTED EVERYTHING THERE IS TO INVENT, LILLIAN?
I CAN'T THINK OF ANYTHING THAT WASN'T INVENTED, PHILIP.
I WAS BORN TOO LATE.
YEP, AN HOUR AFTER ME.
SHOWS WHAT YOU KNOW, LILLIAN! YOU SAID EVERY INVENTION'S BEEN INVENTED!
WELL, ANGELICA SAYS SHE CAN THINK OF LOTS OF STUFF THAT WASN'T INVENTED YET.
THEN THAT MAKES ANGELICA AN INVENTOR, PHILIP. NOT YOU.
FOOEY ON YOU BOTH.
LET'S BUILD A PRETEND SNOWMAN.
OKAY!
IT'S ALMOST DONE.
THIS IS FUN.
HE'S BEAUTIFUL.
UH OH.
WHAT?!
A PRETEND SUNNY DAY.
BRING ME MY HAT, SPIKE.
SPIKE IS THE BEST DOG IN THE WORLD.
SEE!
BUT HE DID IT WRONG!
I SAID HE WAS THE BEST, NOT THE BRIGHTEST.

2002

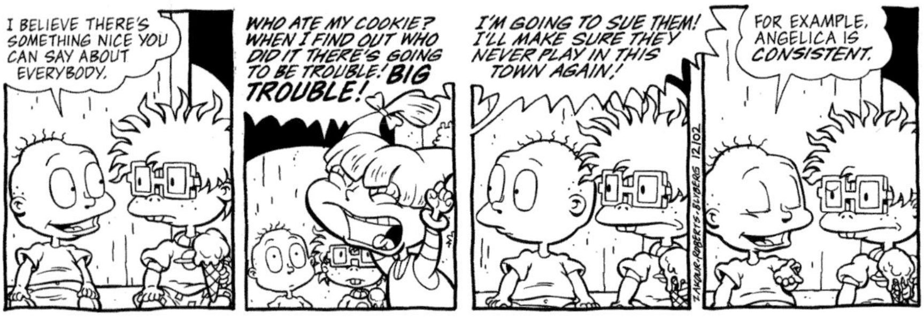
I BELIEVE THERE'S SOMETHING NICE YOU CAN SAY ABOUT EVERYBODY.
WHO ATE MY COOKIE? WHEN I FIND OUT WHO DID IT THERE'S GOING TO BE TROUBLE! BIG TROUBLE!
I'M GOING TO SUE THEM! I'LL MAKE SURE THEY NEVER PLAY IN THIS TOWN AGAIN!
FOR EXAMPLE, ANGELICA IS CONSISTENT.
12/02

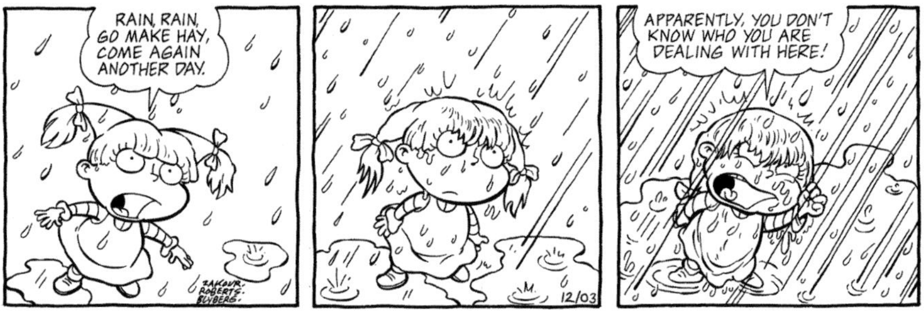
RAIN, RAIN, GO MAKE HAY, COME AGAIN ANOTHER DAY.
APPARENTLY, YOU DON'T KNOW WHO YOU ARE DEALING WITH HERE!
12/03

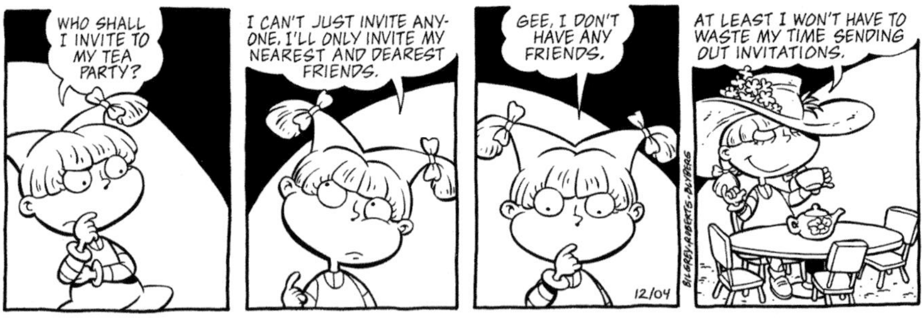
WHO SHALL I INVITE TO MY TEA PARTY?
I CAN'T JUST INVITE ANYONE. I'LL ONLY INVITE MY NEAREST AND DEAREST FRIENDS.
GEE, I DON'T HAVE ANY FRIENDS.
AT LEAST I WON'T HAVE TO WASTE MY TIME SENDING OUT INVITATIONS.
12/04

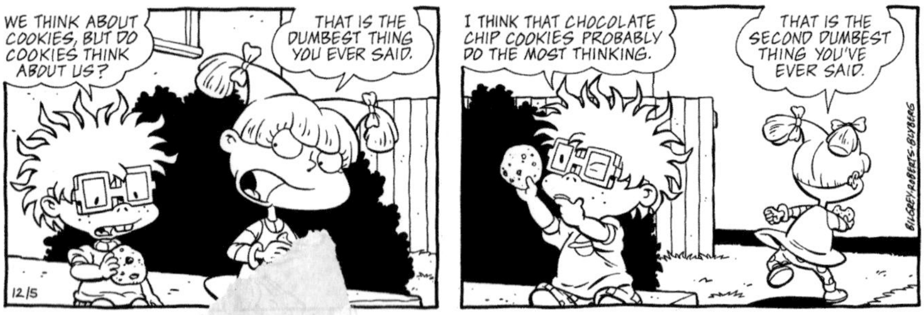
WE THINK ABOUT COOKIES, BUT DO COOKIES THINK ABOUT US?
THAT IS THE DUMBEST THING YOU EVER SAID.
I THINK THAT CHOCOLATE CHIP COOKIES PROBABLY DO THE MOST THINKING.
THAT IS THE SECOND DUMBEST THING YOU'VE EVER SAID.
12/5

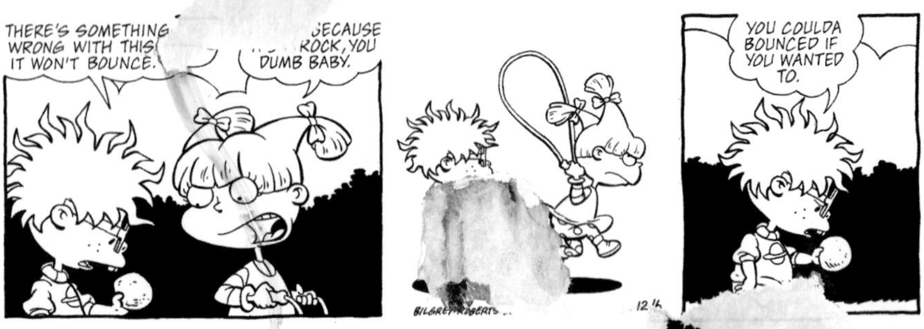
THERE'S SOMETHING WRONG WITH THIS IT WON'T BOUNCE.
ROCK, YOU DUMB BABY.
YOU COULDA BOUNCED IF YOU WANTED TO.

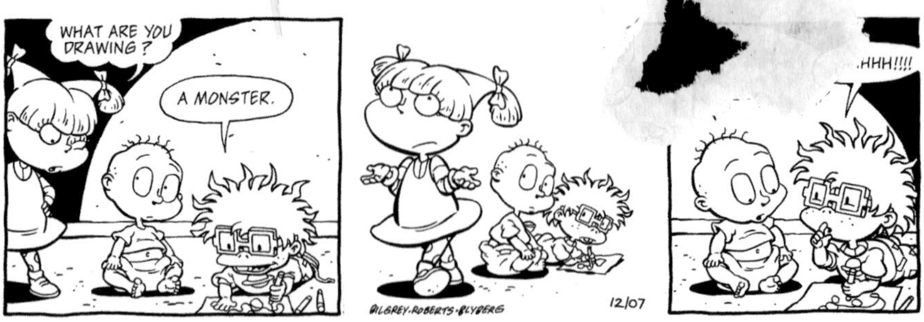
WHAT ARE YOU DRAWING?
A MONSTER.
HHH!!!!
12/07

2002

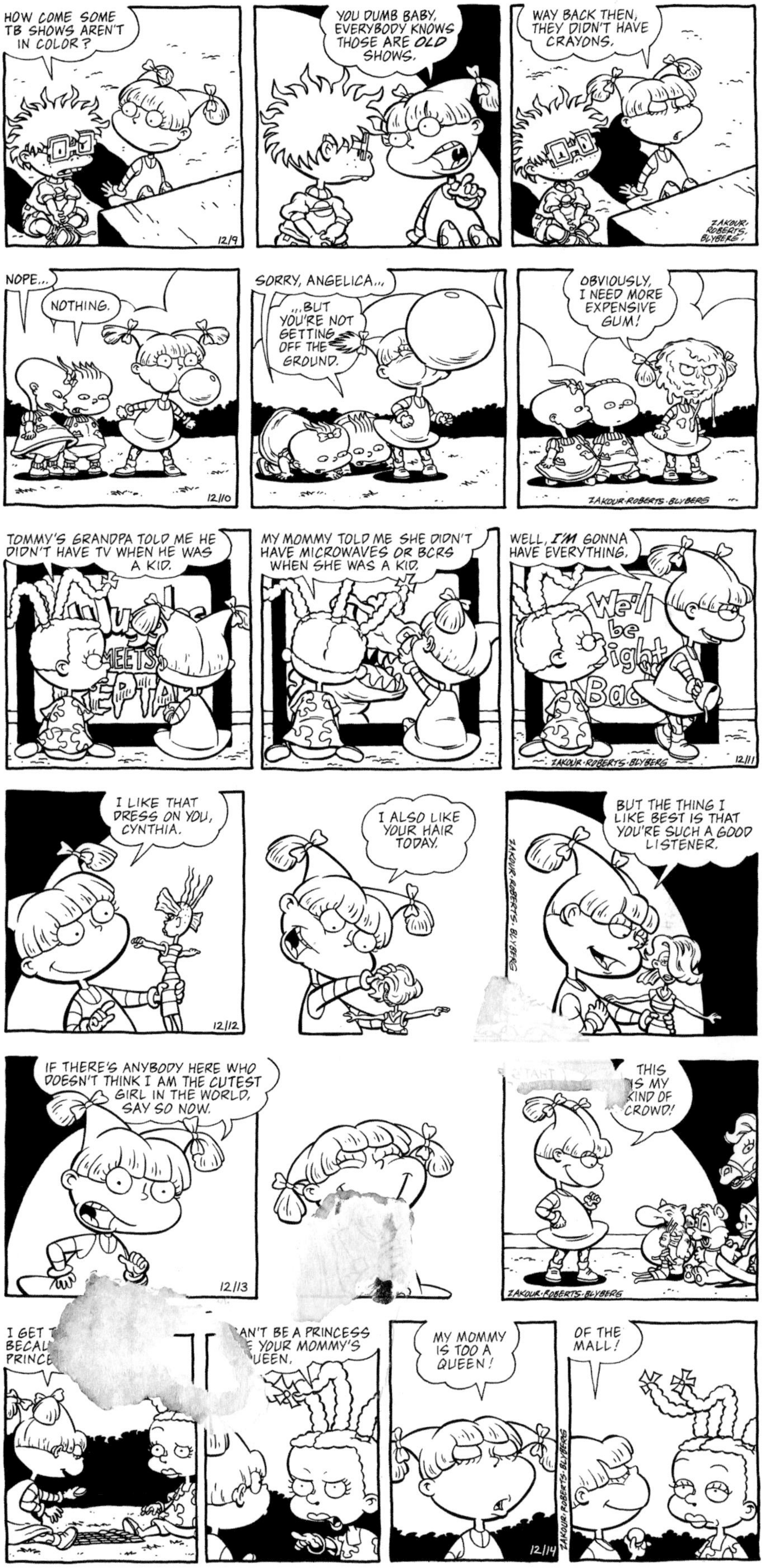
HOW COME SOME TB SHOWS AREN'T IN COLOR?
YOU DUMB BABY, EVERYBODY KNOWS THOSE ARE *OLD* SHOWS.
WAY BACK THEN, THEY DIDN'T HAVE CRAYONS.
12/9
ZAKOUR, ROBERTS, BLYBERG.
NOPE...
NOTHING.
SORRY, ANGELICA...
...BUT YOU'RE NOT GETTING OFF THE GROUND.
OBVIOUSLY, I NEED MORE EXPENSIVE GUM!
12/10
ZAKOUR·ROBERTS·BLYBERG
TOMMY'S GRANDPA TOLD ME HE DIDN'T HAVE TV WHEN HE WAS A KID.
MEETS
MY MOMMY TOLD ME SHE DIDN'T HAVE MICROWAVES OR BCRS WHEN SHE WAS A KID.
WELL, *I'M* GONNA HAVE EVERYTHING.
We'll be
12/11
ZAKOUR·ROBERTS·BLYBERG
I LIKE THAT DRESS ON YOU, CYNTHIA.
12/12
I ALSO LIKE YOUR HAIR TODAY.
ZAKOUR·ROBERTS·BLYBERG
BUT THE THING I LIKE BEST IS THAT YOU'RE SUCH A GOOD LISTENER.
IF THERE'S ANYBODY HERE WHO DOESN'T THINK I AM THE CUTEST GIRL IN THE WORLD, SAY SO NOW.
12/13
THIS S MY KIND OF CROWD!
ZAKOUR·ROBERTS·BLYBERG
I GET T
BECAU
PRINCE
AN'T BE A PRINCESS
E YOUR MOMMY'S
QUEEN.
MY MOMMY IS TOO A QUEEN!
12/14
ZAKOUR·ROBERTS·BLYBERG
OF THE MALL!

2002

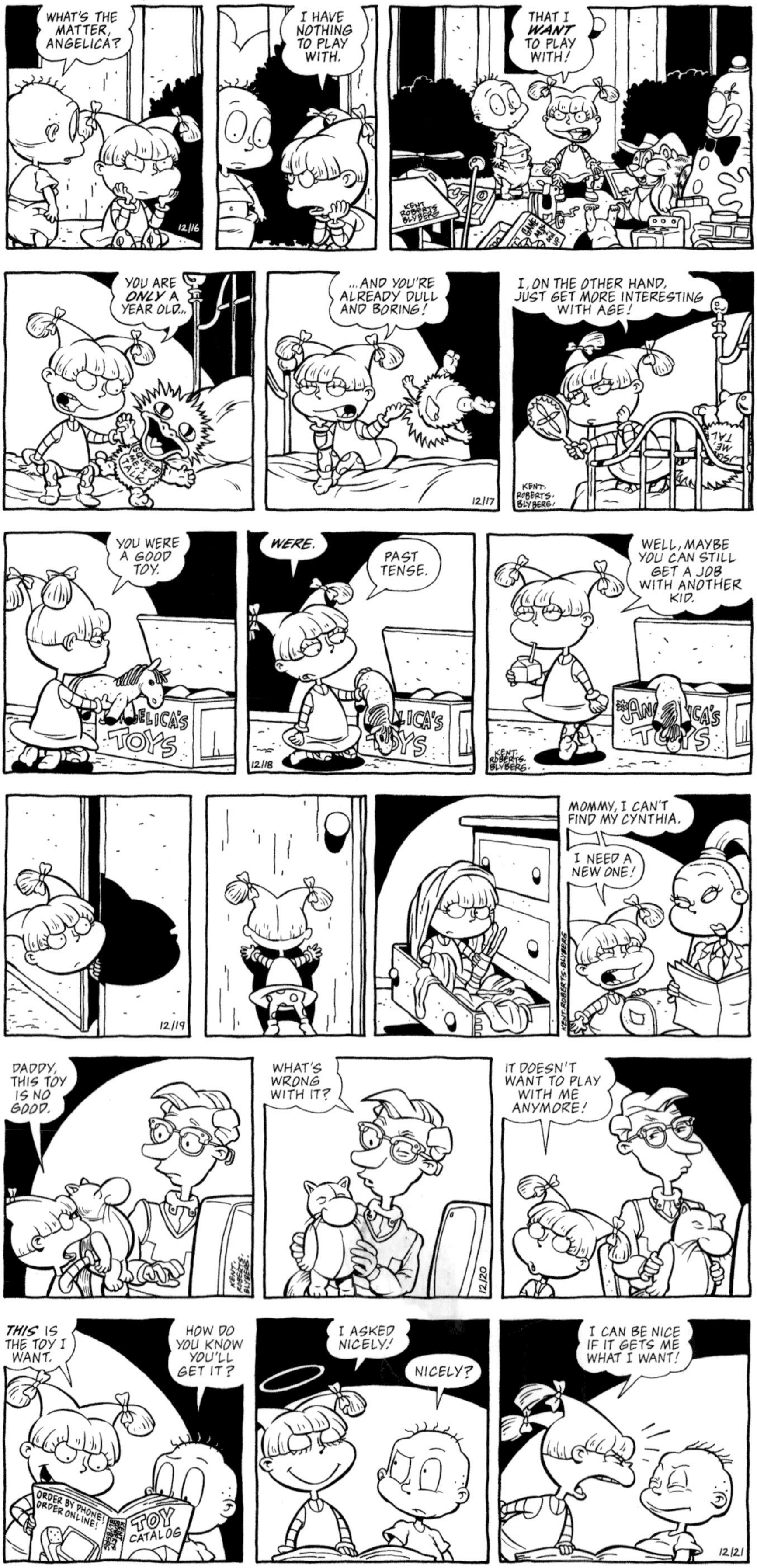
WHAT'S THE MATTER, ANGELICA?
12/16
I HAVE NOTHING TO PLAY WITH.
THAT I WANT TO PLAY WITH!
KENT ROBERTS BLYBERG
YOU ARE ONLY A YEAR OLD...
SQUEEZE ME TALK
...AND YOU'RE ALREADY DULL AND BORING!
12/17
I, ON THE OTHER HAND, JUST GET MORE INTERESTING WITH AGE!
KENT. ROBERTS. BLYBERG.
YOU WERE A GOOD TOY.
WERE.
PAST TENSE.
12/18
WELL, MAYBE YOU CAN STILL GET A JOB WITH ANOTHER KID.
KENT. ROBERTS. BLYBERG.
12/19
MOMMY, I CAN'T FIND MY CYNTHIA.
I NEED A NEW ONE!
KENT.ROBERTS.BLYBERG
DADDY, THIS TOY IS NO GOOD.
KENT. ROBERTS. BLYBERG.
WHAT'S WRONG WITH IT?
12/20
IT DOESN'T WANT TO PLAY WITH ME ANYMORE!
THIS IS THE TOY I WANT.
HOW DO YOU KNOW YOU'LL GET IT?
ORDER BY PHONE! ORDER ONLINE!
TOY CATALOG
I ASKED NICELY!
NICELY?
I CAN BE NICE IF IT GETS ME WHAT I WANT!
12/21

2002

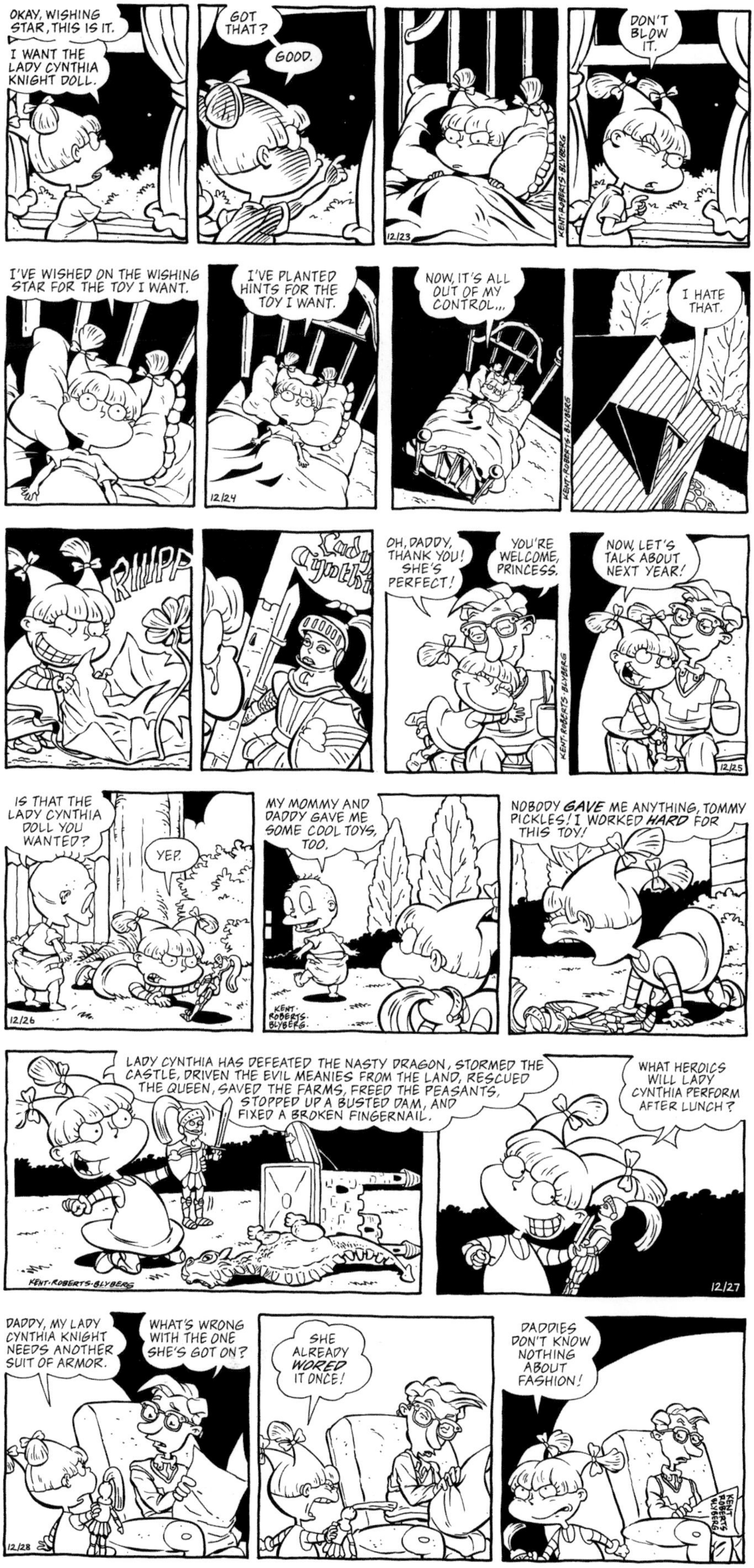
OKAY, WISHING STAR, THIS IS IT.
I WANT THE LADY CYNTHIA KNIGHT DOLL.
GOT THAT?
GOOD.
12/23
KENT·ROBERTS·BLYBERG
DON'T BLOW IT.
I'VE WISHED ON THE WISHING STAR FOR THE TOY I WANT.
I'VE PLANTED HINTS FOR THE TOY I WANT.
12/24
NOW, IT'S ALL OUT OF MY CONTROL...
KENT·ROBERTS·BLYBERG
I HATE THAT.
RIIIPP
Lady Cynthia
OH, DADDY, THANK YOU! SHE'S PERFECT!
YOU'RE WELCOME, PRINCESS.
KENT·ROBERTS·BLYBERG
NOW, LET'S TALK ABOUT NEXT YEAR!
12/25
IS THAT THE LADY CYNTHIA DOLL YOU WANTED?
YEP.
12/26
MY MOMMY AND DADDY GAVE ME SOME COOL TOYS, TOO.
KENT·ROBERTS·BLYBERG
NOBODY GAVE ME ANYTHING, TOMMY PICKLES! I WORKED HARD FOR THIS TOY!
LADY CYNTHIA HAS DEFEATED THE NASTY DRAGON, STORMED THE CASTLE, DRIVEN THE EVIL MEANIES FROM THE LAND, RESCUED THE QUEEN, SAVED THE FARMS, FREED THE PEASANTS, STOPPED UP A BUSTED DAM, AND FIXED A BROKEN FINGERNAIL.
KENT·ROBERTS·BLYBERG
WHAT HEROICS WILL LADY CYNTHIA PERFORM AFTER LUNCH?
12/27
DADDY, MY LADY CYNTHIA KNIGHT NEEDS ANOTHER SUIT OF ARMOR.
WHAT'S WRONG WITH THE ONE SHE'S GOT ON?
12/28
SHE ALREADY WORED IT ONCE!
DADDIES DON'T KNOW NOTHING ABOUT FASHION!
KENT ROBERTS BLYBERG

2002

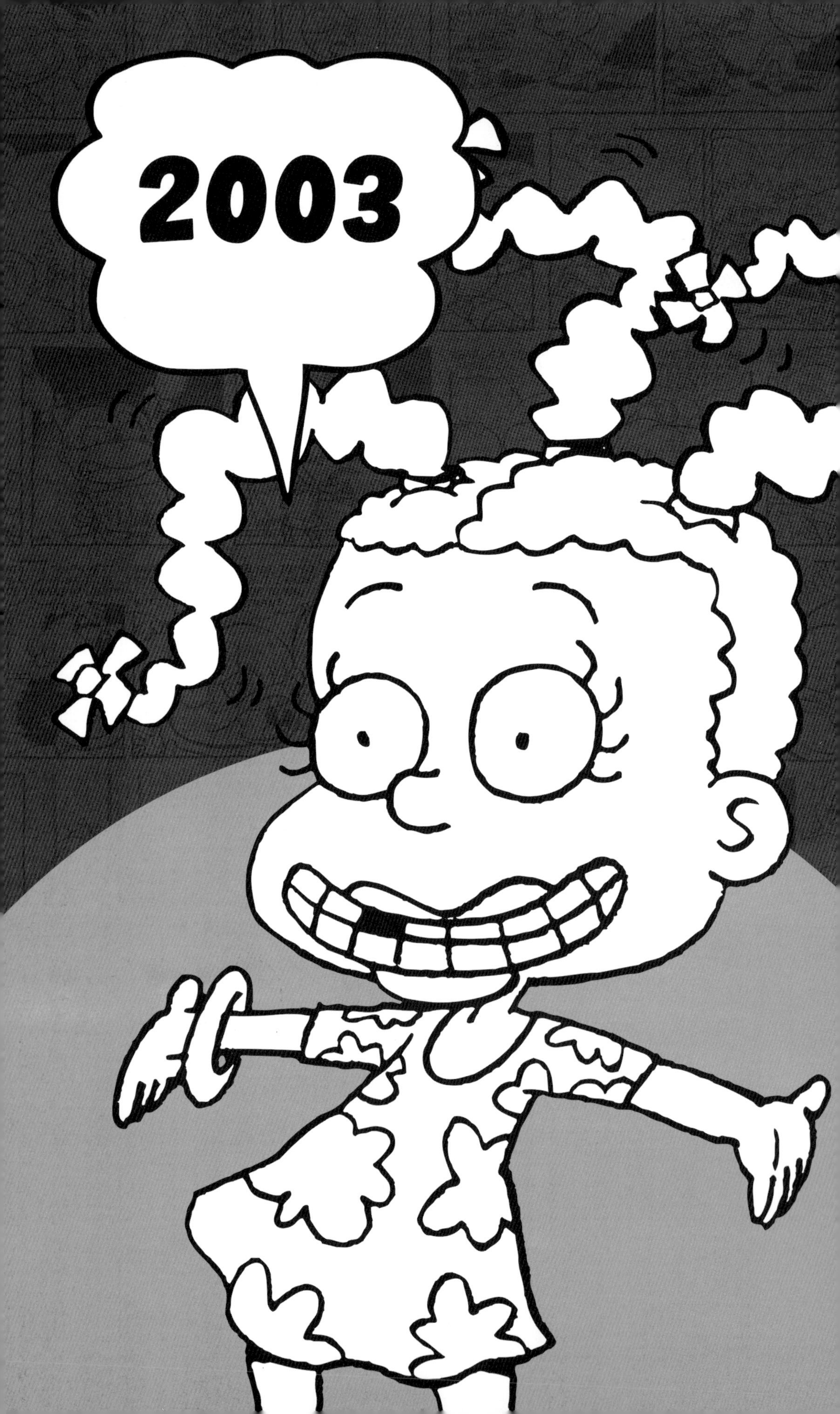
2003

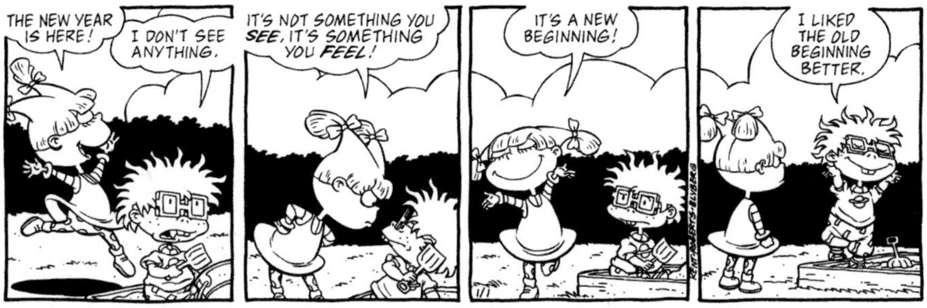
THE NEW YEAR IS HERE!
I DON'T SEE ANYTHING.
IT'S NOT SOMETHING YOU SEE, IT'S SOMETHING YOU FEEL!
IT'S A NEW BEGINNING!
I LIKED THE OLD BEGINNING BETTER.
KENT·ROBERTS·BLYBERG
1/1

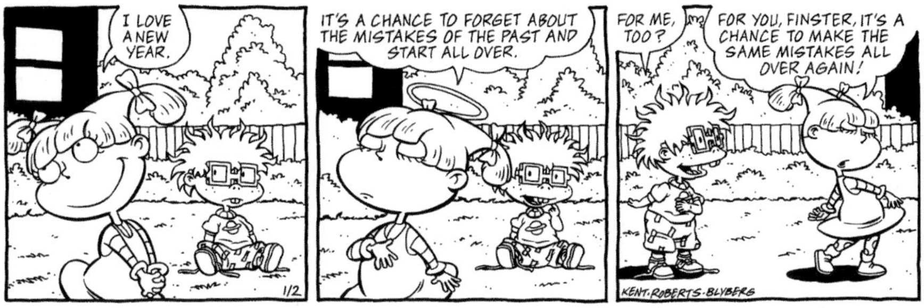
I LOVE A NEW YEAR.
1/2
IT'S A CHANCE TO FORGET ABOUT THE MISTAKES OF THE PAST AND START ALL OVER.
FOR ME, TOO?
FOR YOU, FINSTER, IT'S A CHANCE TO MAKE THE SAME MISTAKES ALL OVER AGAIN!
KENT·ROBERTS·BLYBERG

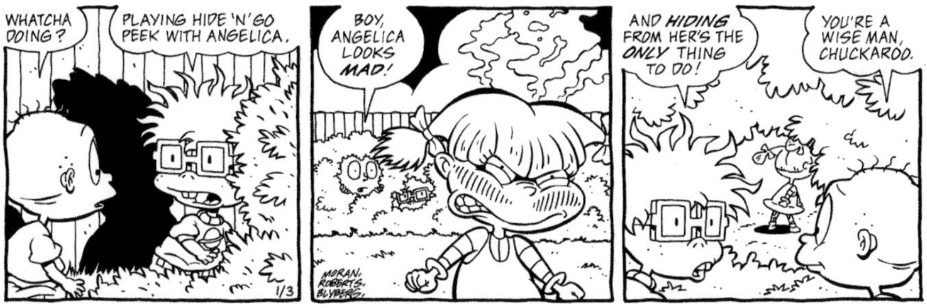
WHATCHA DOING?
PLAYING HIDE 'N' GO PEEK WITH ANGELICA.
1/3
BOY, ANGELICA LOOKS MAD!
MORAN·ROBERTS·BLYBERG
AND HIDING FROM HER'S THE ONLY THING TO DO!
YOU'RE A WISE MAN, CHUCKAROO.

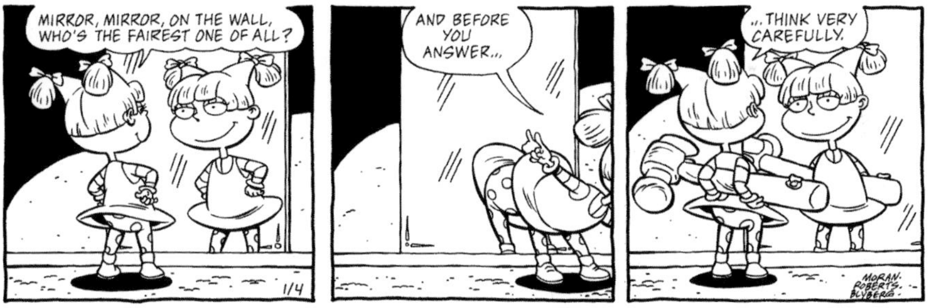
MIRROR, MIRROR, ON THE WALL, WHO'S THE FAIREST ONE OF ALL?
1/4
AND BEFORE YOU ANSWER...
...THINK VERY CAREFULLY.
MORAN·ROBERTS·BLYBERG

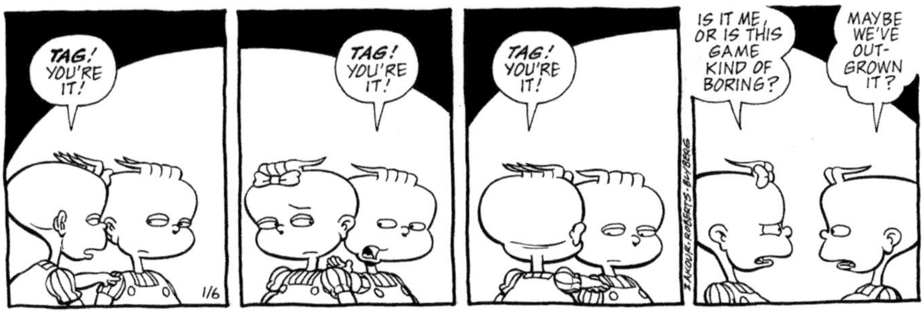
TAG! YOU'RE IT!
1/6
TAG! YOU'RE IT!
TAG! YOU'RE IT!
ZAKOUR·ROBERTS·BLYBERG
IS IT ME, OR IS THIS GAME KIND OF BORING?
MAYBE WE'VE OUT-GROWN IT?

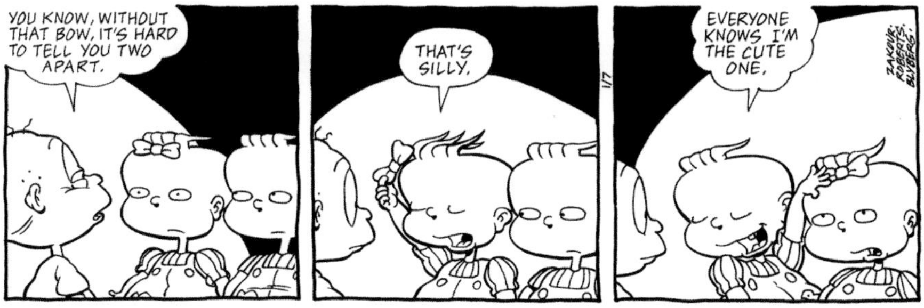
YOU KNOW, WITHOUT THAT BOW, IT'S HARD TO TELL YOU TWO APART.
THAT'S SILLY.
1/7
EVERYONE KNOWS I'M THE CUTE ONE.
ZAKOUR·ROBERTS·BLYBERG

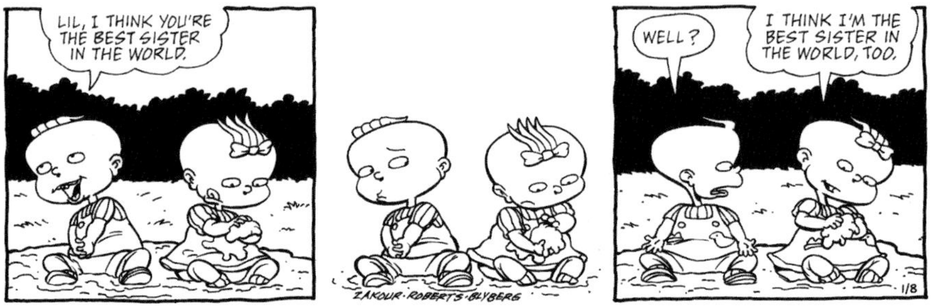
LIL, I THINK YOU'RE THE BEST SISTER IN THE WORLD.
ZAKOUR·ROBERTS·BLYBERG
WELL?
I THINK I'M THE BEST SISTER IN THE WORLD, TOO.
1/8

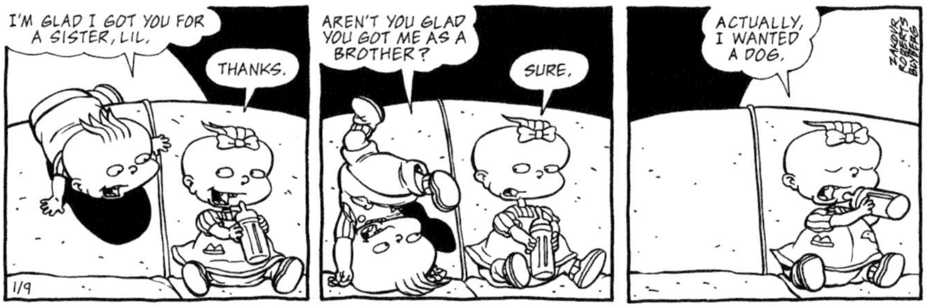
I'M GLAD I GOT YOU FOR A SISTER, LIL.
THANKS.
1/9
AREN'T YOU GLAD YOU GOT ME AS A BROTHER?
SURE.
ACTUALLY, I WANTED A DOG.
ZAKOUR ROBERTS BLYBERG

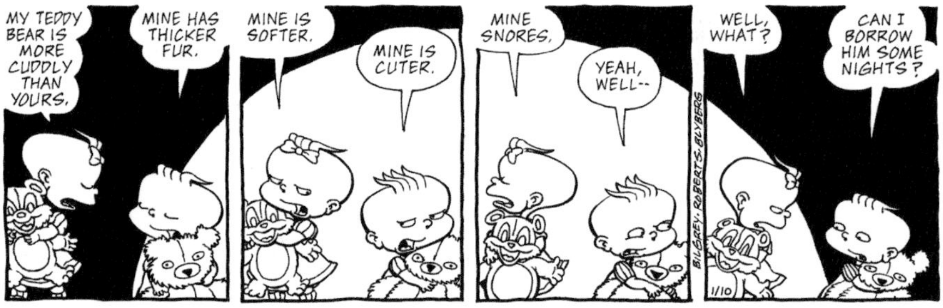
MY TEDDY BEAR IS MORE CUDDLY THAN YOURS.
MINE HAS THICKER FUR.
MINE IS SOFTER.
MINE IS CUTER.
MINE SNORES.
YEAH, WELL--
BILGREY·ROBERTS·BLYBERG
WELL, WHAT?
CAN I BORROW HIM SOME NIGHTS?
1/10

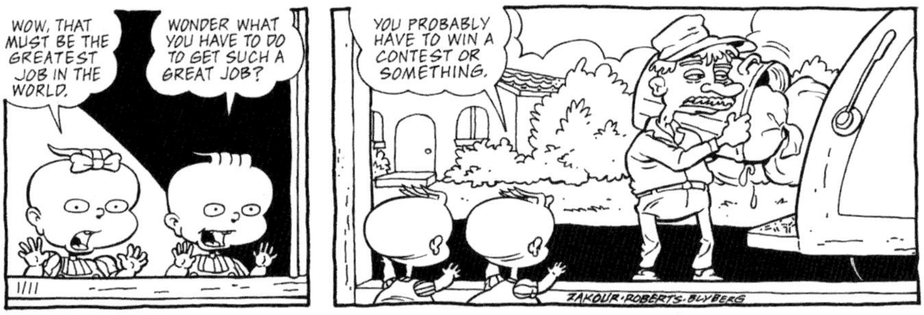
WOW, THAT MUST BE THE GREATEST JOB IN THE WORLD.
WONDER WHAT YOU HAVE TO DO TO GET SUCH A GREAT JOB?
1/11
YOU PROBABLY HAVE TO WIN A CONTEST OR SOMETHING.
ZAKOUR·ROBERTS·BLYBERG

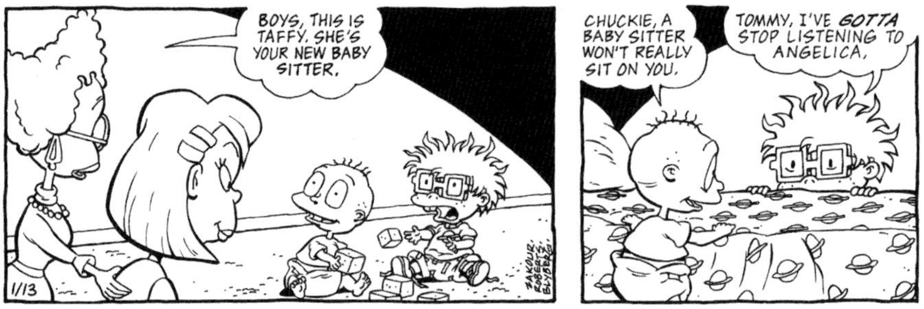
BOYS, THIS IS TAFFY. SHE'S YOUR NEW BABY SITTER.
1/13
ZAKOUR· ROBERTS· BLYBERG
CHUCKIE, A BABY SITTER WON'T REALLY SIT ON YOU.
TOMMY, I'VE GOTTA STOP LISTENING TO ANGELICA.

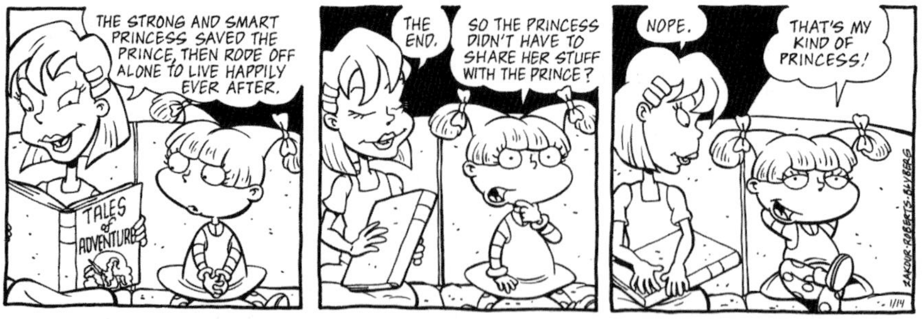
THE STRONG AND SMART PRINCESS SAVED THE PRINCE, THEN RODE OFF ALONE TO LIVE HAPPILY EVER AFTER.
TALES of ADVENTURE
THE END.
SO THE PRINCESS DIDN'T HAVE TO SHARE HER STUFF WITH THE PRINCE?
NOPE.
THAT'S MY KIND OF PRINCESS!
ZAKOUR·ROBERTS·BLYBERG
1/14

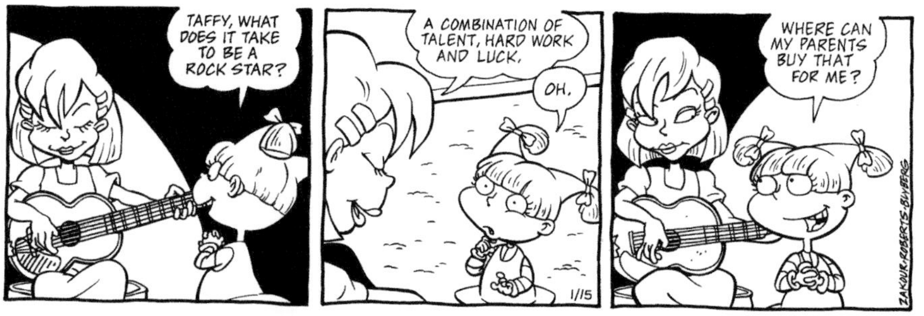
TAFFY, WHAT DOES IT TAKE TO BE A ROCK STAR?
A COMBINATION OF TALENT, HARD WORK AND LUCK.
OH.
1/15
WHERE CAN MY PARENTS BUY THAT FOR ME?
ZAKOUR·ROBERTS·BLYBERG

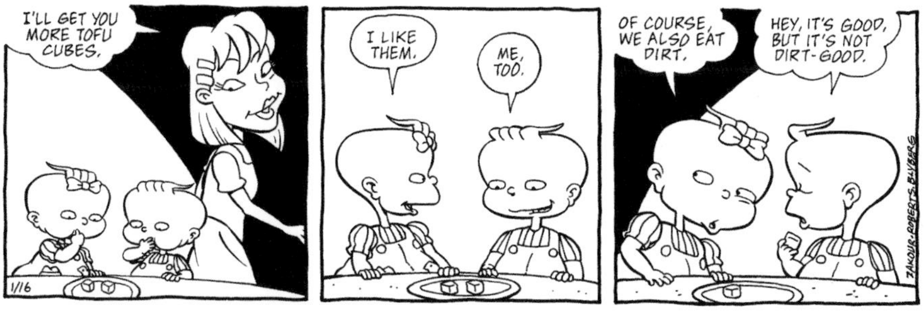
I'LL GET YOU MORE TOFU CUBES.
1/16
I LIKE THEM.
ME, TOO.
OF COURSE, WE ALSO EAT DIRT.
HEY, IT'S GOOD, BUT IT'S NOT DIRT-GOOD.
ZAKOUR·ROBERTS·BLYBERG

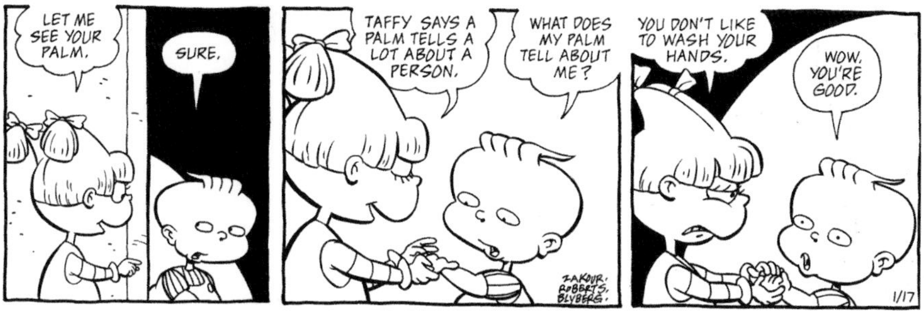
LET ME SEE YOUR PALM.
SURE.
TAFFY SAYS A PALM TELLS A LOT ABOUT A PERSON.
WHAT DOES MY PALM TELL ABOUT ME?
ZAKOUR· ROBERTS· BLYBERG.
YOU DON'T LIKE TO WASH YOUR HANDS.
WOW. YOU'RE GOOD.
1/17

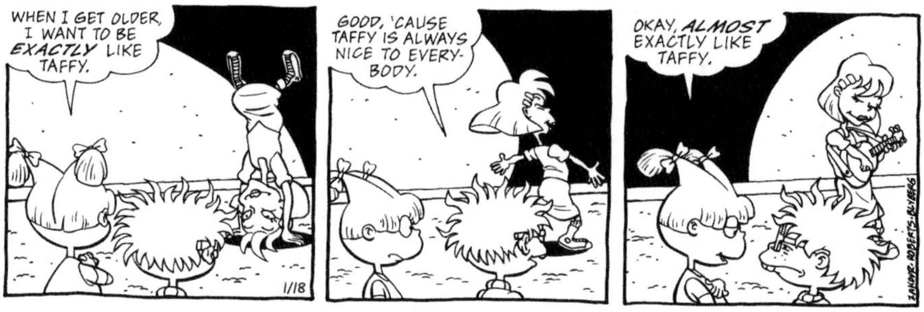
WHEN I GET OLDER, I WANT TO BE EXACTLY LIKE TAFFY.
1/18
GOOD, 'CAUSE TAFFY IS ALWAYS NICE TO EVERY-BODY.
OKAY, ALMOST EXACTLY LIKE TAFFY.
ZAKOUR·ROBERTS·BLYBERG

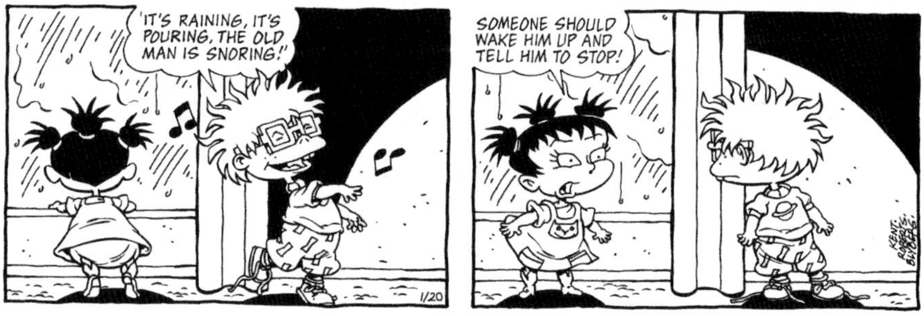
'IT'S RAINING, IT'S POURING, THE OLD MAN IS SNORING!'
1/20
SOMEONE SHOULD WAKE HIM UP AND TELL HIM TO STOP!
KENT· ROBERTS· BLYBERG.

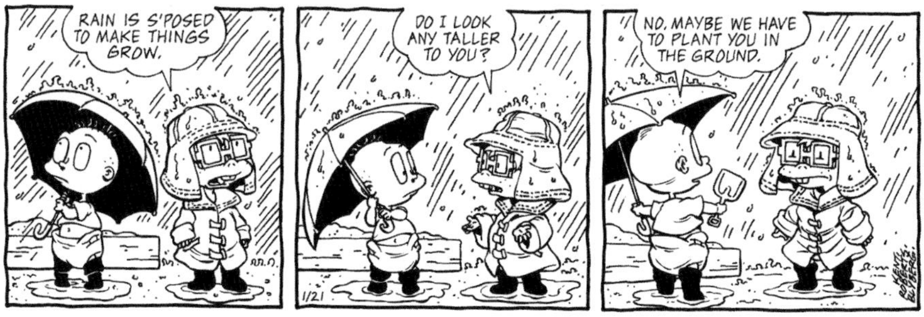
RAIN IS S'POSED TO MAKE THINGS GROW.
DO I LOOK ANY TALLER TO YOU?
1/21
NO, MAYBE WE HAVE TO PLANT YOU IN THE GROUND.
KENT· ROBERTS· BLYBERG.

2003

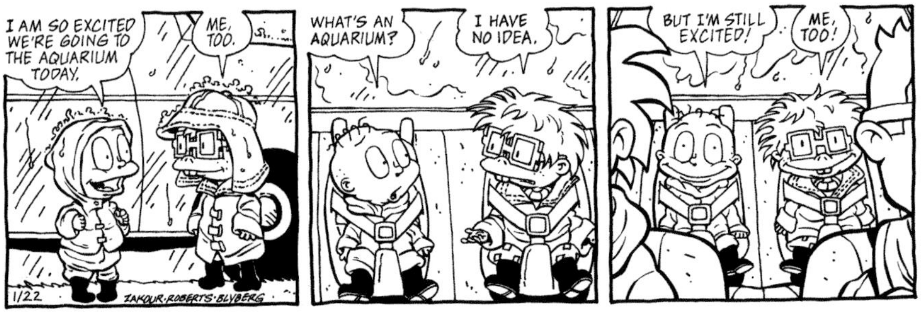
I AM SO EXCITED WE'RE GOING TO THE AQUARIUM TODAY.
ME, TOO.
WHAT'S AN AQUARIUM?
I HAVE NO IDEA.
BUT I'M STILL EXCITED!
ME, TOO!
1/22
ZAKOUR·ROBERTS·BLYBERG

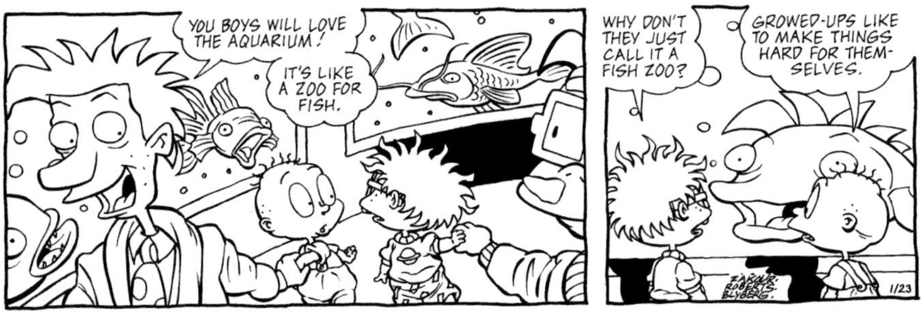
YOU BOYS WILL LOVE THE AQUARIUM!
IT'S LIKE A ZOO FOR FISH.
WHY DON'T THEY JUST CALL IT A FISH ZOO?
GROWED-UPS LIKE TO MAKE THINGS HARD FOR THEMSELVES.
ZAKOUR·ROBERTS·BLYBERG
1/23

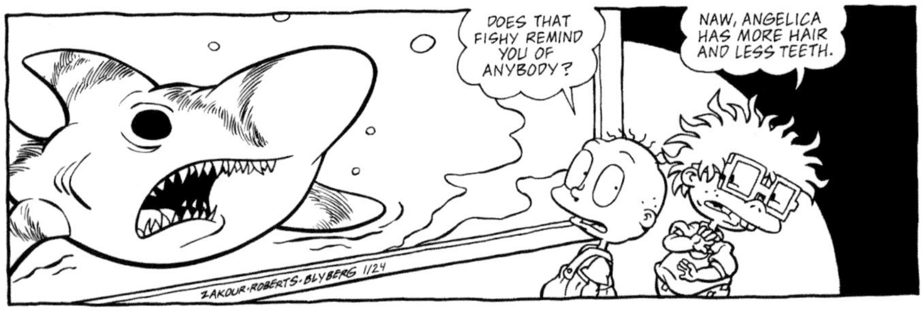
DOES THAT FISHY REMIND YOU OF ANYBODY?
NAW, ANGELICA HAS MORE HAIR AND LESS TEETH.
ZAKOUR·ROBERTS·BLYBERG 1/24

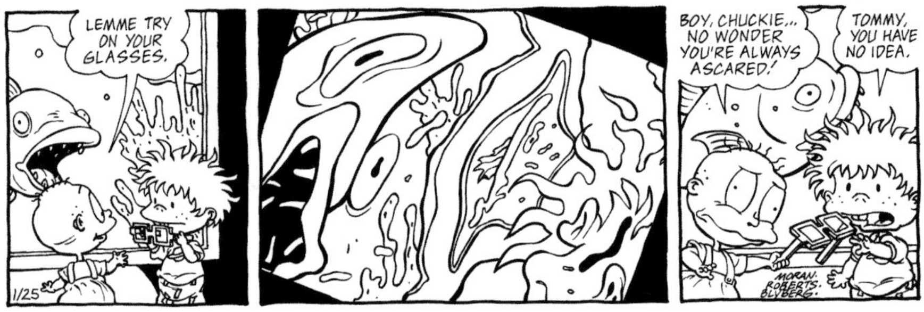
LEMME TRY ON YOUR GLASSES.
1/25
BOY, CHUCKIE... NO WONDER YOU'RE ALWAYS ASCARED!
TOMMY, YOU HAVE NO IDEA.
MORAN·ROBERTS·BLYBERG

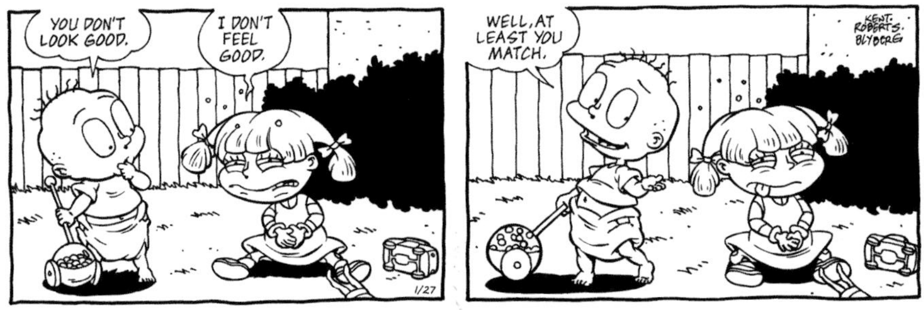
YOU DON'T LOOK GOOD.
I DON'T FEEL GOOD.
1/27
WELL, AT LEAST YOU MATCH.
KENT·ROBERTS·BLYBERG

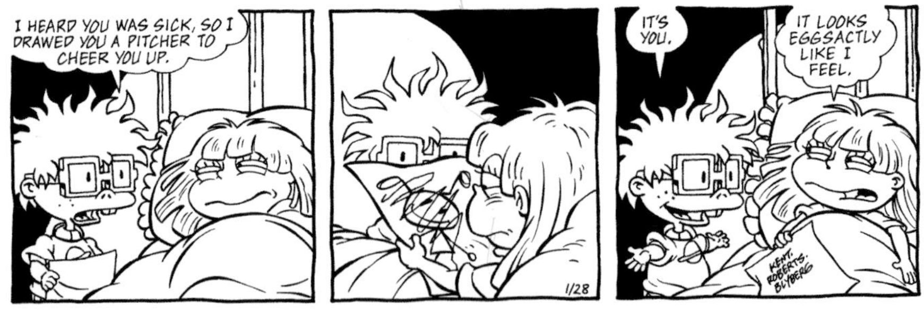
I HEARD YOU WAS SICK, SO I DRAWED YOU A PITCHER TO CHEER YOU UP.
1/28
IT'S YOU.
IT LOOKS EGGSACTLY LIKE I FEEL.
KENT·ROBERTS·BLYBERG

2003

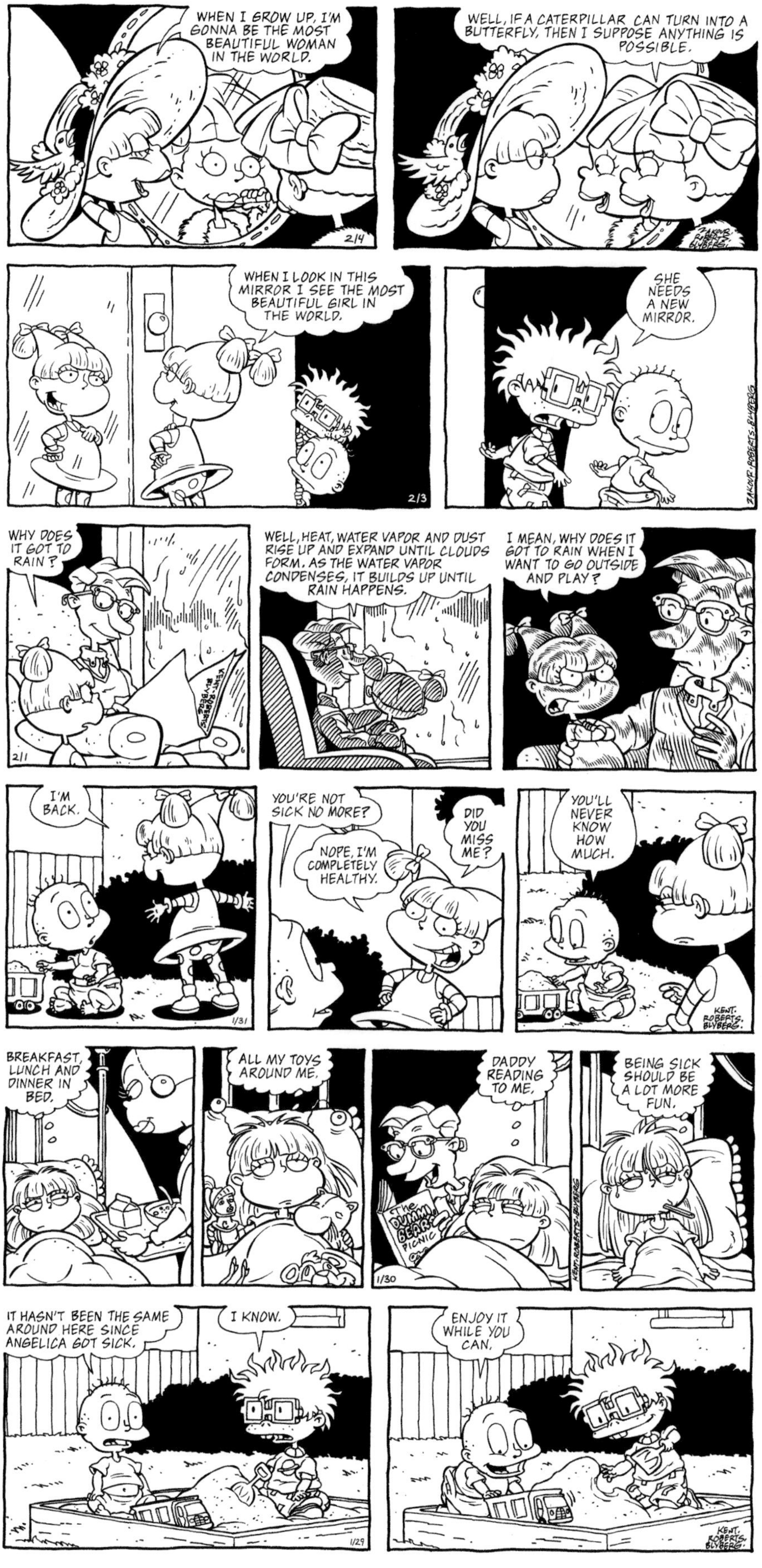
WHEN I GROW UP, I'M GONNA BE THE MOST BEAUTIFUL WOMAN IN THE WORLD.
2/4
WELL, IF A CATERPILLAR CAN TURN INTO A BUTTERFLY, THEN I SUPPOSE ANYTHING IS POSSIBLE.
WHEN I LOOK IN THIS MIRROR I SEE THE MOST BEAUTIFUL GIRL IN THE WORLD.
2/3
SHE NEEDS A NEW MIRROR.
ZAKOUR·ROBERTS·BLYBERG
WHY DOES IT GOT TO RAIN?
2/1
WELL, HEAT, WATER VAPOR AND DUST RISE UP AND EXPAND UNTIL CLOUDS FORM. AS THE WATER VAPOR CONDENSES, IT BUILDS UP UNTIL RAIN HAPPENS.
I MEAN, WHY DOES IT GOT TO RAIN WHEN I WANT TO GO OUTSIDE AND PLAY?
I'M BACK.
1/31
YOU'RE NOT SICK NO MORE?
NOPE, I'M COMPLETELY HEALTHY.
DID YOU MISS ME?
YOU'LL NEVER KNOW HOW MUCH.
KENT. ROBERTS. BLYBERG.
BREAKFAST, LUNCH AND DINNER IN BED.
ALL MY TOYS AROUND ME.
DADDY READING TO ME.
The DUMMI BEARS PICNIC
1/30
KENT·ROBERTS·BLYBERG
BEING SICK SHOULD BE A LOT MORE FUN.
IT HASN'T BEEN THE SAME AROUND HERE SINCE ANGELICA GOT SICK.
I KNOW.
1/29
ENJOY IT WHILE YOU CAN.
KENT. ROBERTS. BLYBERG.

2003

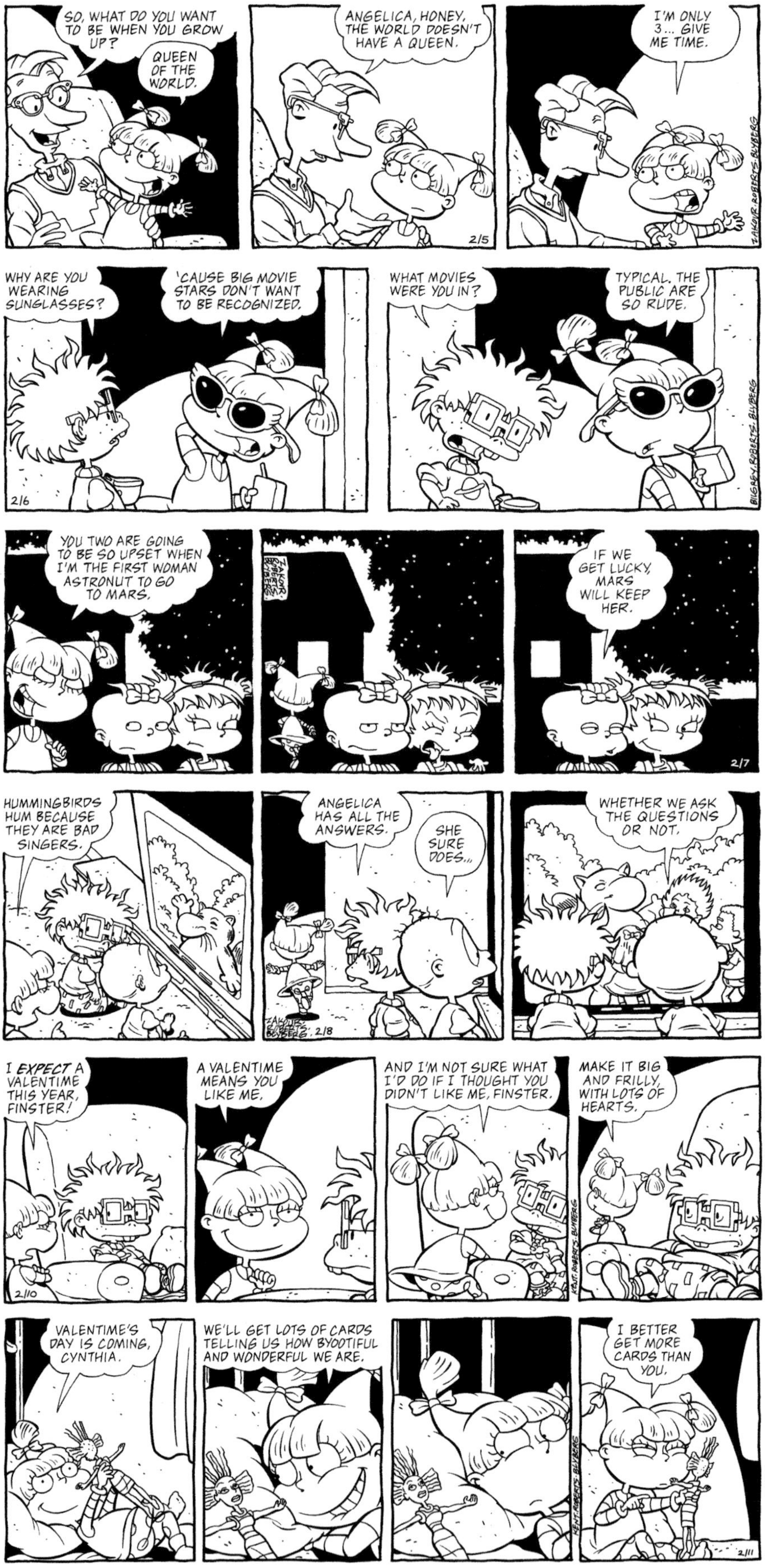
SO, WHAT DO YOU WANT TO BE WHEN YOU GROW UP?
QUEEN OF THE WORLD.
ANGELICA, HONEY, THE WORLD DOESN'T HAVE A QUEEN.
I'M ONLY 3... GIVE ME TIME.
WHY ARE YOU WEARING SUNGLASSES?
'CAUSE BIG MOVIE STARS DON'T WANT TO BE RECOGNIZED.
WHAT MOVIES WERE YOU IN?
TYPICAL. THE PUBLIC ARE SO RUDE.
YOU TWO ARE GOING TO BE SO UPSET WHEN I'M THE FIRST WOMAN ASTRONUT TO GO TO MARS.
IF WE GET LUCKY, MARS WILL KEEP HER.
HUMMINGBIRDS HUM BECAUSE THEY ARE BAD SINGERS.
ANGELICA HAS ALL THE ANSWERS.
SHE SURE DOES...
WHETHER WE ASK THE QUESTIONS OR NOT.
I EXPECT A VALENTIME THIS YEAR, FINSTER!
A VALENTIME MEANS YOU LIKE ME.
AND I'M NOT SURE WHAT I'D DO IF I THOUGHT YOU DIDN'T LIKE ME, FINSTER.
MAKE IT BIG AND FRILLY, WITH LOTS OF HEARTS.
VALENTIME'S DAY IS COMING, CYNTHIA.
WE'LL GET LOTS OF CARDS TELLING US HOW BYOOTIFUL AND WONDERFUL WE ARE.
I BETTER GET MORE CARDS THAN YOU.

2003

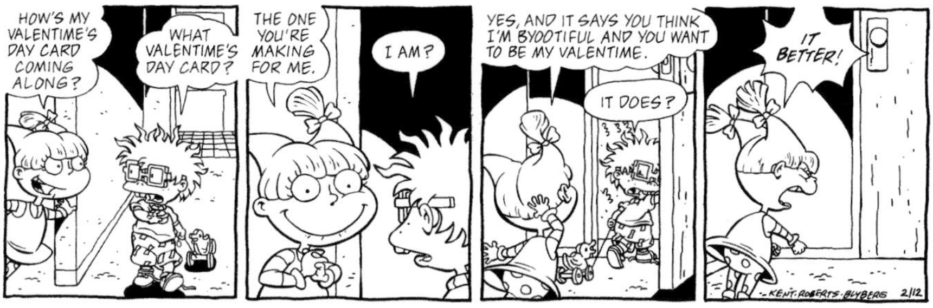
HOW'S MY VALENTINE'S DAY CARD COMING ALONG?
WHAT VALENTINE'S DAY CARD?
THE ONE YOU'RE MAKING FOR ME.
I AM?
YES, AND IT SAYS YOU THINK I'M BYOOTIFUL AND YOU WANT TO BE MY VALENTINE.
IT DOES?
IT BETTER!
KENT·ROBERTS·BLYBERG 2/12

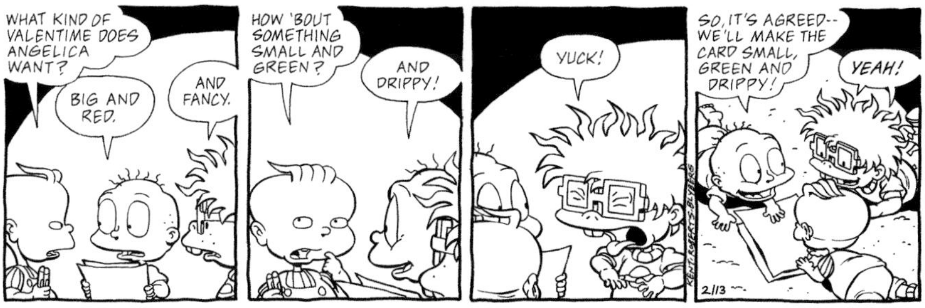
WHAT KIND OF VALENTIME DOES ANGELICA WANT?
BIG AND RED.
AND FANCY.
HOW 'BOUT SOMETHING SMALL AND GREEN?
AND DRIPPY!
YUCK!
SO, IT'S AGREED-- WE'LL MAKE THE CARD SMALL, GREEN AND DRIPPY!
YEAH!
KENT·ROBERTS·BLYBERG
2/13

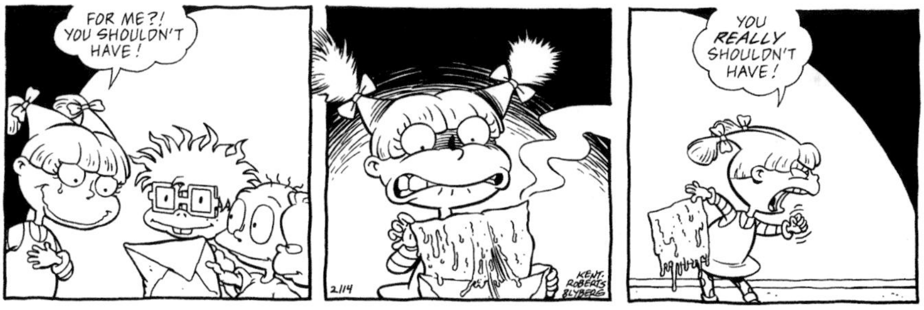
FOR ME?! YOU SHOULDN'T HAVE!
2/14
KENT· ROBERTS· BLYBERG
YOU REALLY SHOULDN'T HAVE!

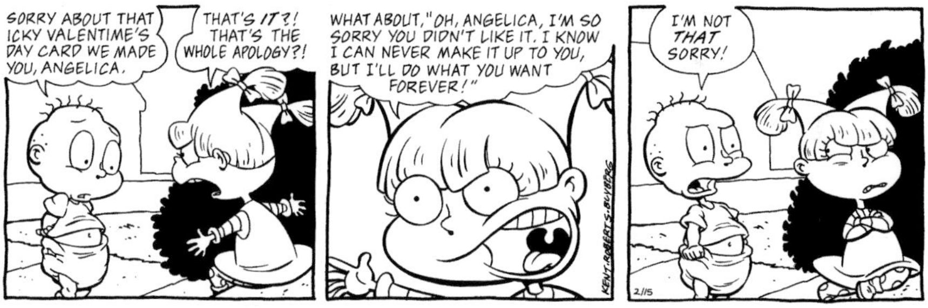
SORRY ABOUT THAT ICKY VALENTIME'S DAY CARD WE MADE YOU, ANGELICA.
THAT'S IT?! THAT'S THE WHOLE APOLOGY?!
WHAT ABOUT, "OH, ANGELICA, I'M SO SORRY YOU DIDN'T LIKE IT. I KNOW I CAN NEVER MAKE IT UP TO YOU, BUT I'LL DO WHAT YOU WANT FOREVER!"
KENT·ROBERTS·BLYBERG
I'M NOT THAT SORRY!
2/15

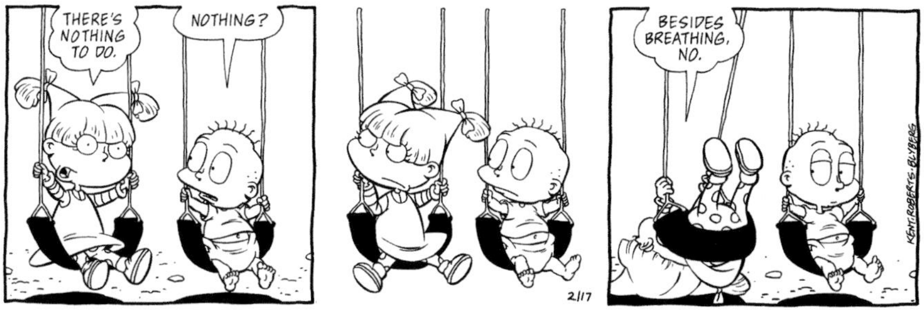
THERE'S NOTHING TO DO.
NOTHING?
2/17
BESIDES BREATHING, NO.
KENT·ROBERTS·BLYBERG

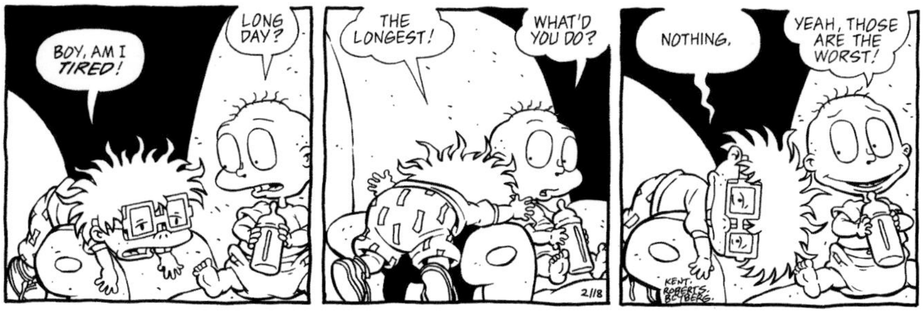
BOY, AM I TIRED!
LONG DAY?
THE LONGEST!
WHAT'D YOU DO?
2/18
NOTHING.
YEAH, THOSE ARE THE WORST!
KENT· ROBERTS· BLYBERG·

2003

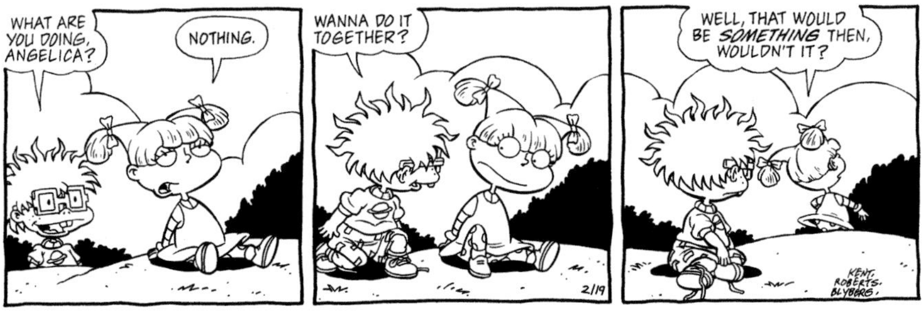
WHAT ARE YOU DOING, ANGELICA?
NOTHING.
WANNA DO IT TOGETHER?
2/19
WELL, THAT WOULD BE *SOMETHING* THEN, WOULDN'T IT?
KENT. ROBERTS. BLYBERG.

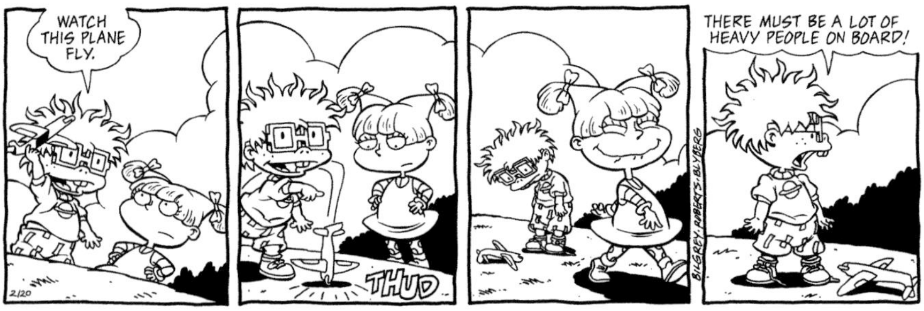
WATCH THIS PLANE FLY.
2/20
THUD
BILGREY. ROBERTS. BLYBERG
THERE MUST BE A LOT OF HEAVY PEOPLE ON BOARD!

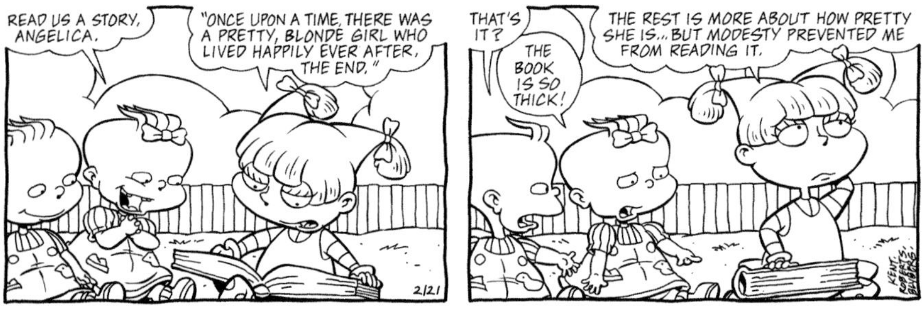
READ US A STORY, ANGELICA.
"ONCE UPON A TIME, THERE WAS A PRETTY, BLONDE GIRL WHO LIVED HAPPILY EVER AFTER. THE END."
2/21
THAT'S IT?
THE BOOK IS SO THICK!
THE REST IS MORE ABOUT HOW PRETTY SHE IS... BUT MODESTY PREVENTED ME FROM READING IT.

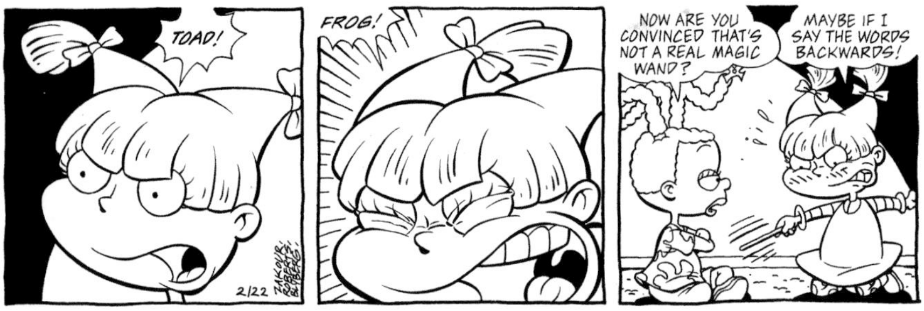
TOAD!
2/22
FROG!
NOW ARE YOU CONVINCED THAT'S NOT A REAL MAGIC WAND?
MAYBE IF I SAY THE WORDS BACKWARDS!

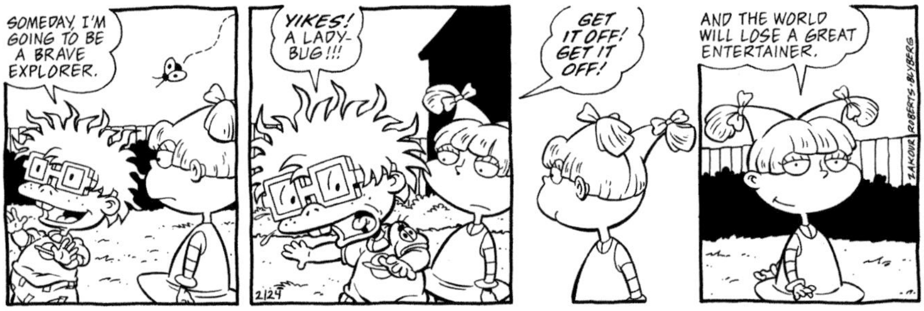
SOMEDAY, I'M GOING TO BE A BRAVE EXPLORER.
YIKES! A LADY-BUG!!!
2/24
GET IT OFF! GET IT OFF!
AND THE WORLD WILL LOSE A GREAT ENTERTAINER.
ZAKOUR. ROBERTS. BLYBERG

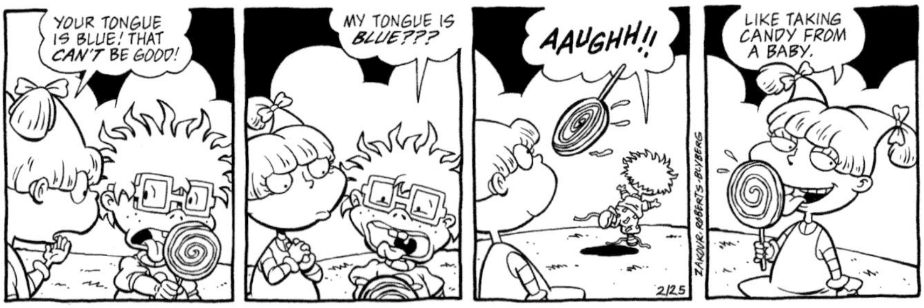
YOUR TONGUE IS BLUE! THAT *CAN'T* BE GOOD!
MY TONGUE IS *BLUE???*
AAUGHH!!
ZAKOUR. ROBERTS. BLYBERG
2/25
LIKE TAKING CANDY FROM A BABY.

2003

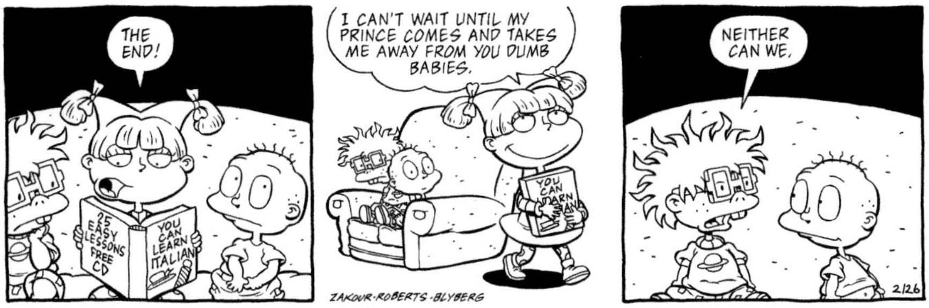
THE END!
25 EASY LESSONS FREE CD
YOU CAN LEARN ITALIAN
I CAN'T WAIT UNTIL MY PRINCE COMES AND TAKES ME AWAY FROM YOU DUMB BABIES.
ZAKOUR·ROBERTS·BLYBERG
NEITHER CAN WE.
2/26

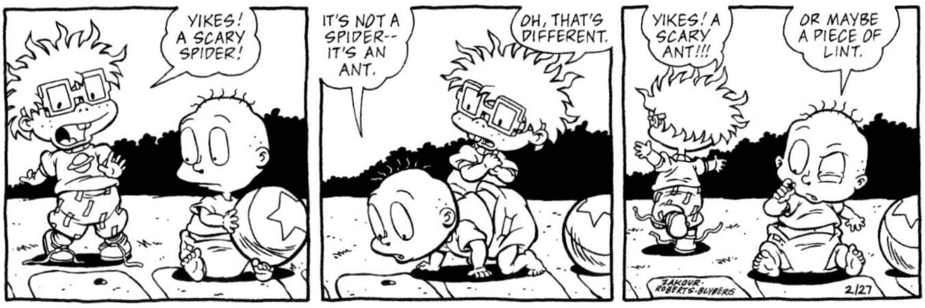
YIKES! A SCARY SPIDER!
IT'S NOT A SPIDER-- IT'S AN ANT.
OH, THAT'S DIFFERENT.
YIKES! A SCARY ANT!!!
OR MAYBE A PIECE OF LINT.
ZAKOUR-ROBERTS-BLYBERG
2/27

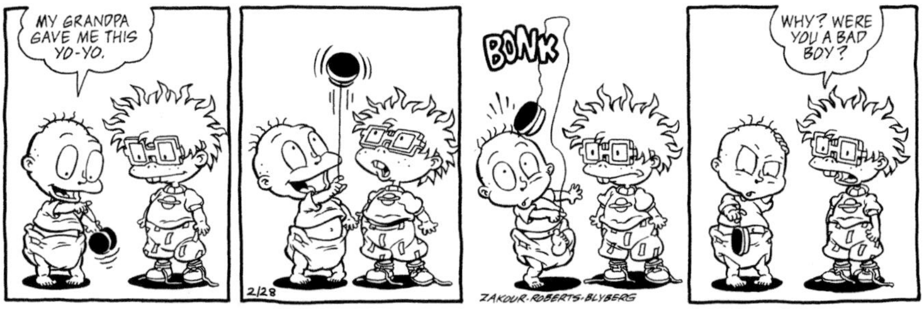
MY GRANDPA GAVE ME THIS YO-YO.
2/28
BONK
ZAKOUR·ROBERTS·BLYBERG
WHY? WERE YOU A BAD BOY?

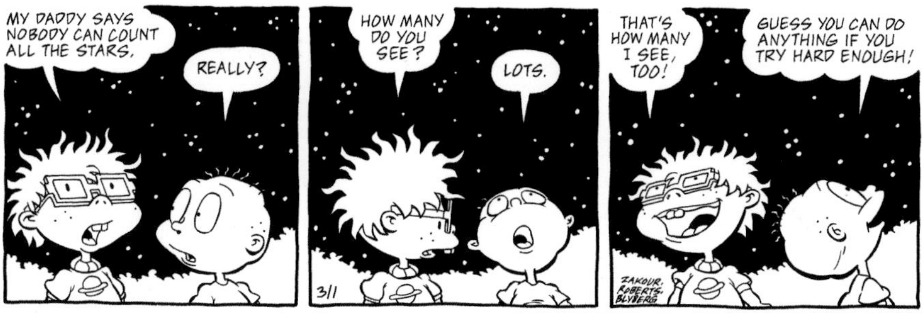
MY DADDY SAYS NOBODY CAN COUNT ALL THE STARS.
REALLY?
HOW MANY DO YOU SEE?
LOTS.
3/1
THAT'S HOW MANY I SEE, TOO!
GUESS YOU CAN DO ANYTHING IF YOU TRY HARD ENOUGH!
ZAKOUR-ROBERTS-BLYBERG

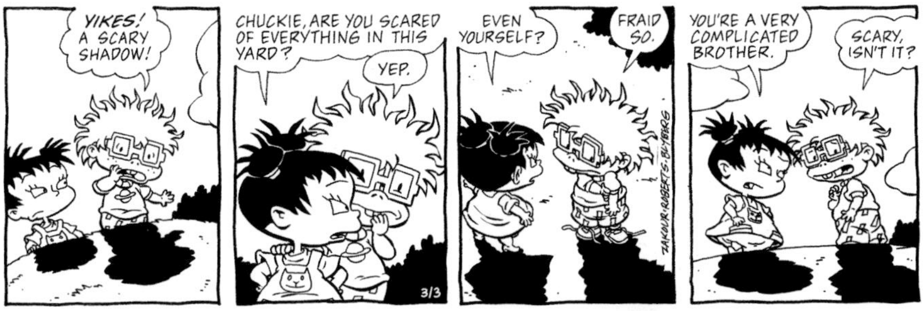
YIKES! A SCARY SHADOW!
CHUCKIE, ARE YOU SCARED OF EVERYTHING IN THIS YARD?
YEP.
3/3
EVEN YOURSELF?
FRAID SO.
ZAKOUR-ROBERTS-BLYBERG
YOU'RE A VERY COMPLICATED BROTHER.
SCARY, ISN'T IT?

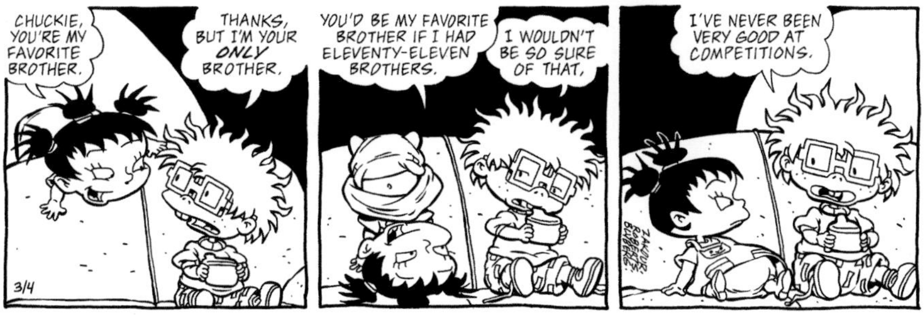
CHUCKIE, YOU'RE MY FAVORITE BROTHER.
THANKS, BUT I'M YOUR *ONLY* BROTHER.
3/4
YOU'D BE MY FAVORITE BROTHER IF I HAD ELEVENTY-ELEVEN BROTHERS.
I WOULDN'T BE SO SURE OF THAT.
ZAKOUR-ROBERTS-BLYBERG
I'VE NEVER BEEN VERY GOOD AT COMPETITIONS.

2003

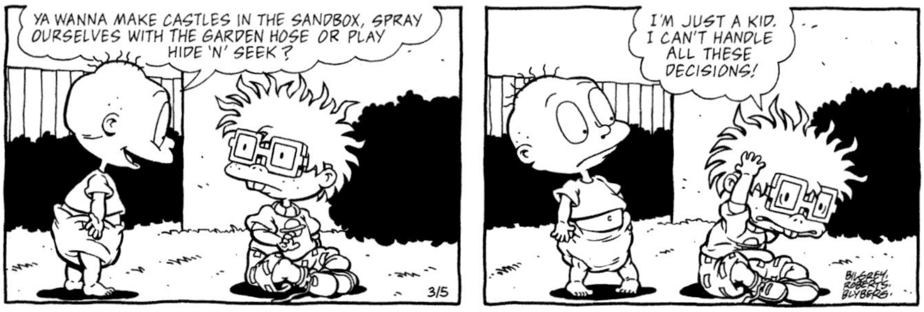
YA WANNA MAKE CASTLES IN THE SANDBOX, SPRAY OURSELVES WITH THE GARDEN HOSE OR PLAY HIDE 'N' SEEK?
3/5
I'M JUST A KID. I CAN'T HANDLE ALL THESE DECISIONS!
BILGREY, ROBERTS, BLYBERG.

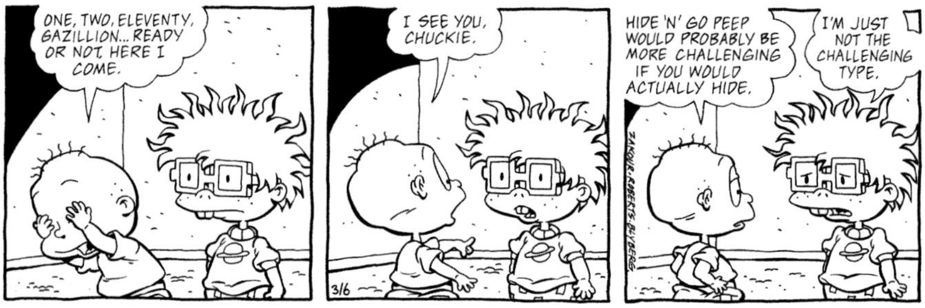
ONE, TWO, ELEVENTY, GAZILLION... READY OR NOT, HERE I COME.
I SEE YOU, CHUCKIE.
3/6
HIDE 'N' GO PEEP WOULD PROBABLY BE MORE CHALLENGING IF YOU WOULD ACTUALLY HIDE.
I'M JUST NOT THE CHALLENGING TYPE.
ZAKOUR, ROBERTS, BLYBERG

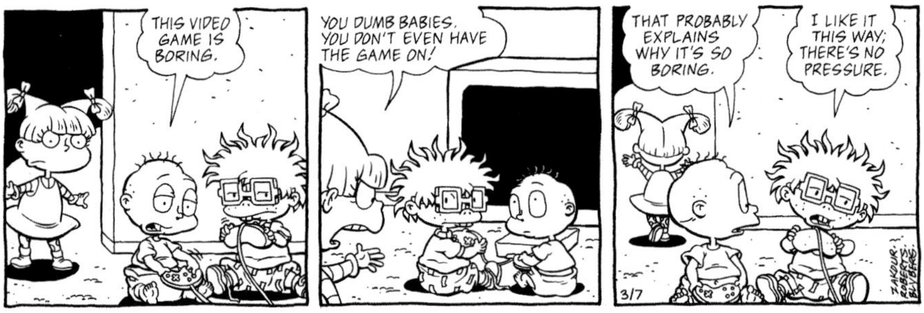
THIS VIDEO GAME IS BORING.
YOU DUMB BABIES. YOU DON'T EVEN HAVE THE GAME ON!
THAT PROBABLY EXPLAINS WHY IT'S SO BORING.
I LIKE IT THIS WAY; THERE'S NO PRESSURE.
3/7
ZAKOUR. ROBERTS. BLYBERG.

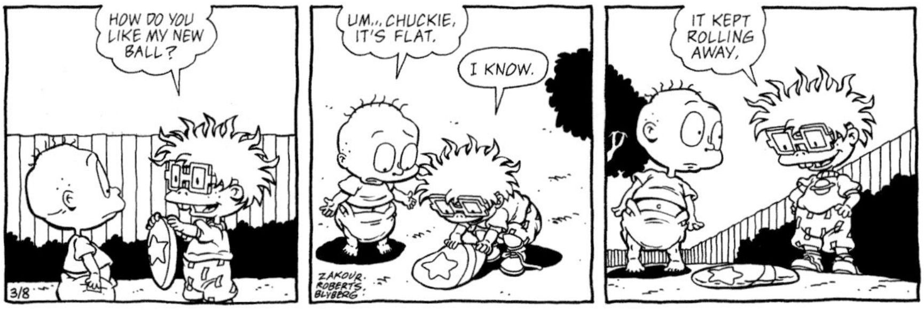
HOW DO YOU LIKE MY NEW BALL?
3/8
UM... CHUCKIE, IT'S FLAT.
I KNOW.
ZAKOUR. ROBERTS. BLYBERG
IT KEPT ROLLING AWAY.

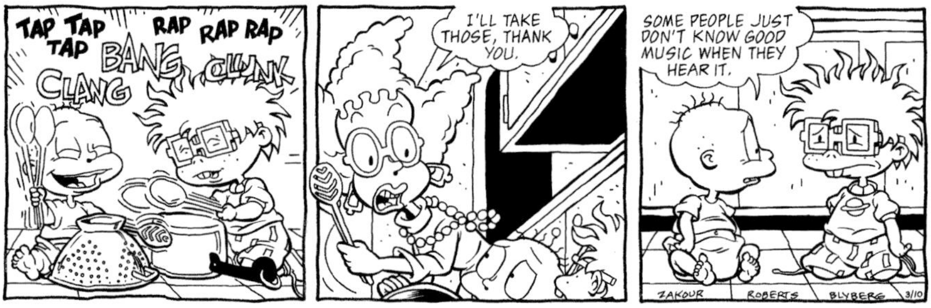
TAP TAP TAP
RAP RAP RAP
BANG
CLUNK
CLANG
I'LL TAKE THOSE, THANK YOU.
SOME PEOPLE JUST DON'T KNOW GOOD MUSIC WHEN THEY HEAR IT.
ZAKOUR ROBERTS BLYBERG 3/10

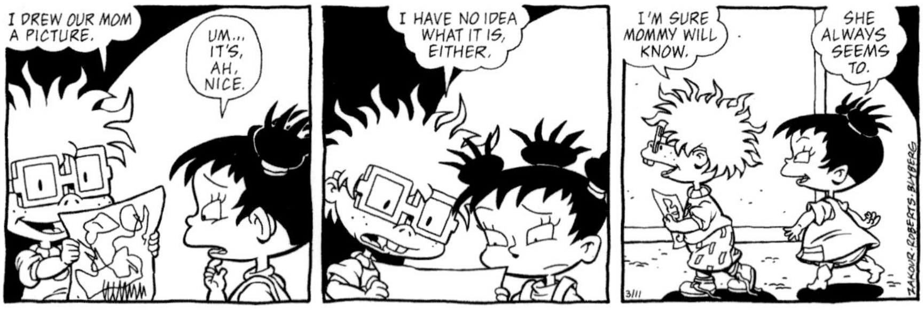
I DREW OUR MOM A PICTURE.
UM... IT'S, AH, NICE.
I HAVE NO IDEA WHAT IT IS, EITHER.
I'M SURE MOMMY WILL KNOW.
SHE ALWAYS SEEMS TO.
3/11
ZAKOUR. ROBERTS. BLYBERG

2003

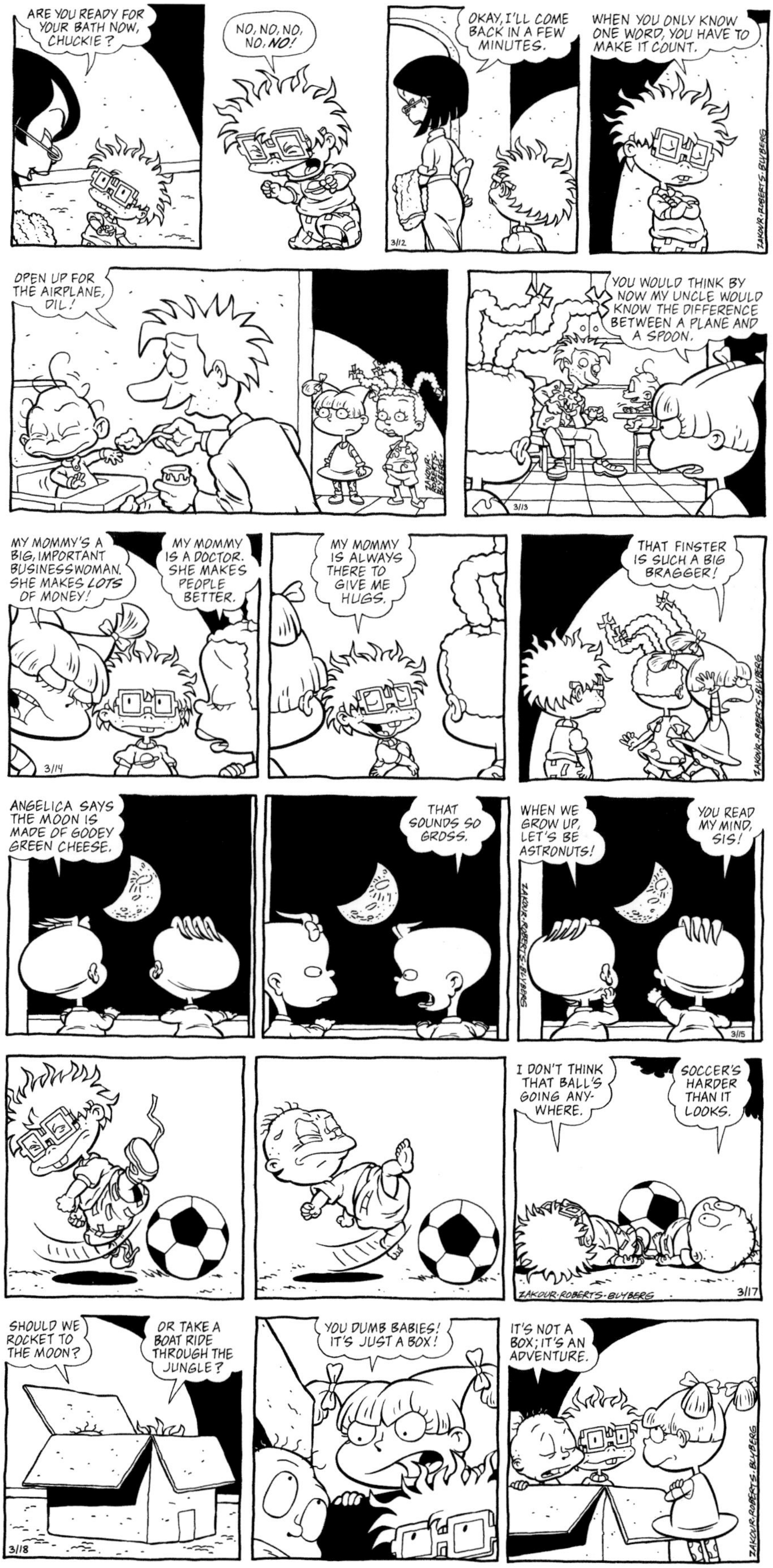
ARE YOU READY FOR YOUR BATH NOW, CHUCKIE?
NO, NO, NO, NO, NO!
OKAY, I'LL COME BACK IN A FEW MINUTES.
3/12
WHEN YOU ONLY KNOW ONE WORD, YOU HAVE TO MAKE IT COUNT.
ZAKOUR-ROBERTS-BLYBERG
OPEN UP FOR THE AIRPLANE, DIL!
ZAKOUR-ROBERTS-BLYBERG
YOU WOULD THINK BY NOW MY UNCLE WOULD KNOW THE DIFFERENCE BETWEEN A PLANE AND A SPOON.
3/13
MY MOMMY'S A BIG, IMPORTANT BUSINESSWOMAN. SHE MAKES LOTS OF MONEY!
MY MOMMY IS A DOCTOR. SHE MAKES PEOPLE BETTER.
3/14
MY MOMMY IS ALWAYS THERE TO GIVE ME HUGS.
THAT FINSTER IS SUCH A BIG BRAGGER!
ZAKOUR-ROBERTS-BLYBERG
ANGELICA SAYS THE MOON IS MADE OF GOOEY GREEN CHEESE.
THAT SOUNDS SO GROSS.
ZAKOUR-ROBERTS-BLYBERG
WHEN WE GROW UP, LET'S BE ASTRONUTS!
YOU READ MY MIND, SIS!
3/15
I DON'T THINK THAT BALL'S GOING ANY-WHERE.
SOCCER'S HARDER THAN IT LOOKS.
ZAKOUR-ROBERTS-BLYBERG
3/17
SHOULD WE ROCKET TO THE MOON?
OR TAKE A BOAT RIDE THROUGH THE JUNGLE?
3/18
YOU DUMB BABIES! IT'S JUST A BOX!
IT'S NOT A BOX; IT'S AN ADVENTURE.
ZAKOUR-ROBERTS-BLYBERG

2003

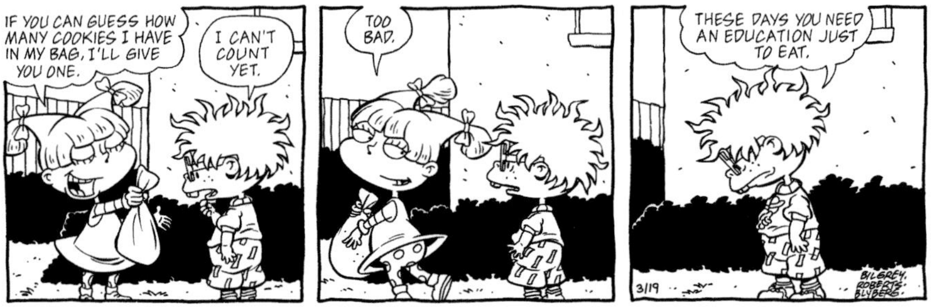
IF YOU CAN GUESS HOW MANY COOKIES I HAVE IN MY BAG, I'LL GIVE YOU ONE.
I CAN'T COUNT YET.
TOO BAD.
THESE DAYS YOU NEED AN EDUCATION JUST TO EAT.
3/19
BILGREY· ROBERTS· BLYBERG

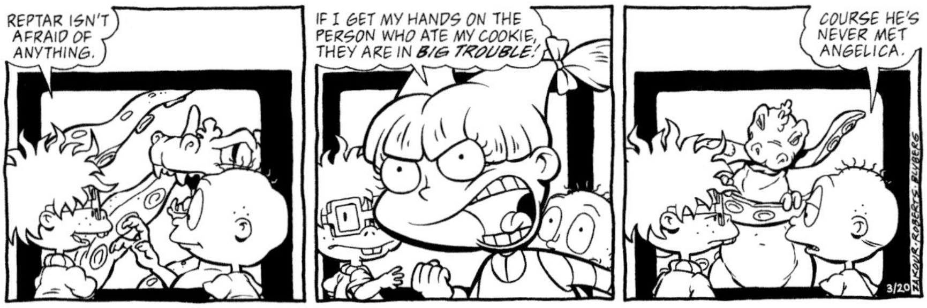
REPTAR ISN'T AFRAID OF ANYTHING.
IF I GET MY HANDS ON THE PERSON WHO ATE MY COOKIE, THEY ARE IN BIG TROUBLE!
COURSE HE'S NEVER MET ANGELICA.
ZAKOUR· ROBERTS· BLYBERG
3/20

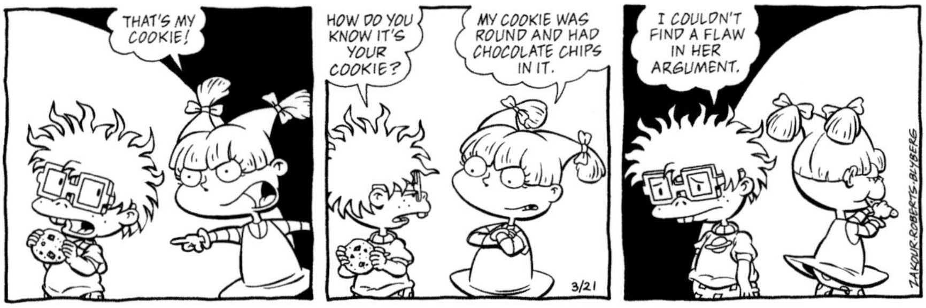
THAT'S MY COOKIE!
HOW DO YOU KNOW IT'S YOUR COOKIE?
MY COOKIE WAS ROUND AND HAD CHOCOLATE CHIPS IN IT.
3/21
I COULDN'T FIND A FLAW IN HER ARGUMENT.
ZAKOUR· ROBERTS· BLYBERG

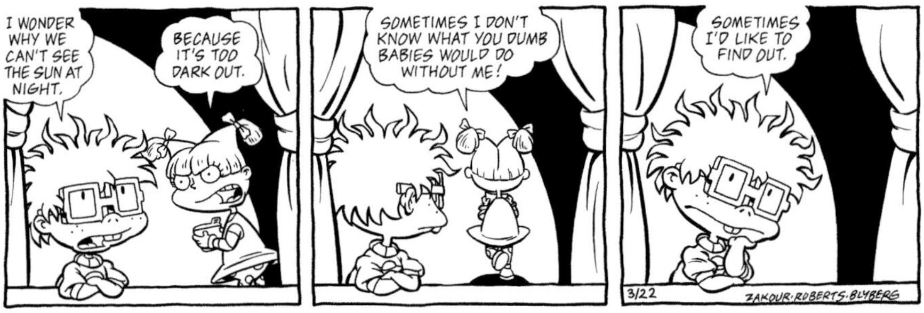
I WONDER WHY WE CAN'T SEE THE SUN AT NIGHT.
BECAUSE IT'S TOO DARK OUT.
SOMETIMES I DON'T KNOW WHAT YOU DUMB BABIES WOULD DO WITHOUT ME!
SOMETIMES I'D LIKE TO FIND OUT.
3/22
ZAKOUR· ROBERTS· BLYBERG

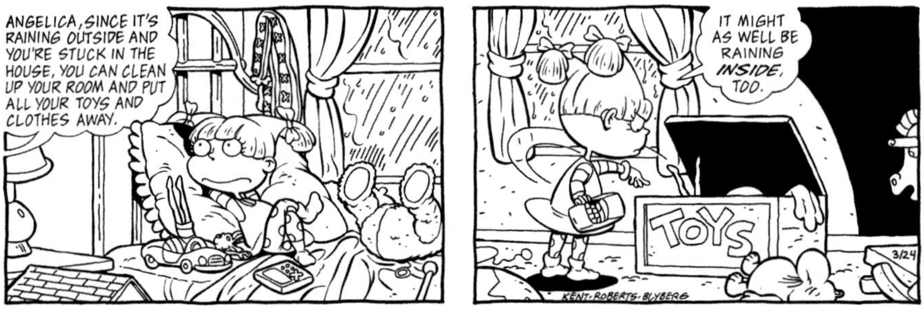
ANGELICA, SINCE IT'S RAINING OUTSIDE AND YOU'RE STUCK IN THE HOUSE, YOU CAN CLEAN UP YOUR ROOM AND PUT ALL YOUR TOYS AND CLOTHES AWAY.
IT MIGHT AS WELL BE RAINING INSIDE, TOO.
TOYS
3/24
KENT· ROBERTS· BLYBERG

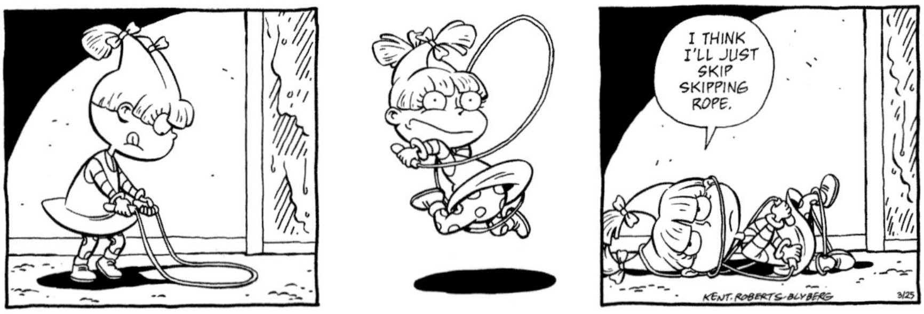
I THINK I'LL JUST SKIP SKIPPING ROPE.
KENT· ROBERTS· BLYBERG
3/25

2003

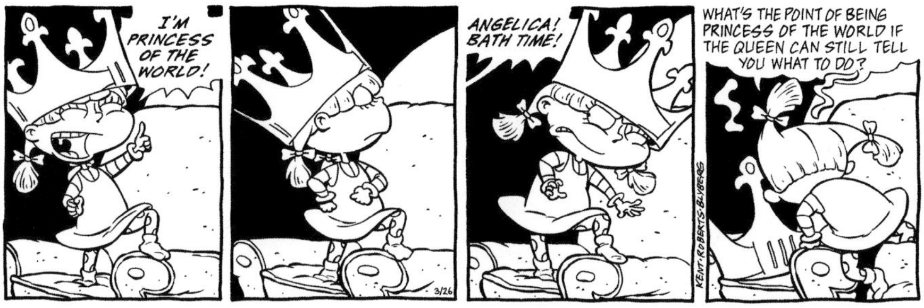
I'M PRINCESS OF THE WORLD!
ANGELICA! BATH TIME!
WHAT'S THE POINT OF BEING PRINCESS OF THE WORLD IF THE QUEEN CAN STILL TELL YOU WHAT TO DO?
3/26
KENT·ROBERTS·BLYBERG

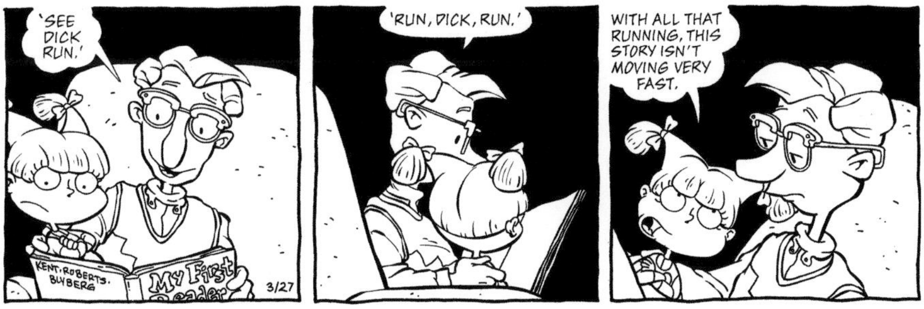
'SEE DICK RUN.'
'RUN, DICK, RUN.'
WITH ALL THAT RUNNING, THIS STORY ISN'T MOVING VERY FAST.
My First
KENT·ROBERTS· BLYBERG
3/27

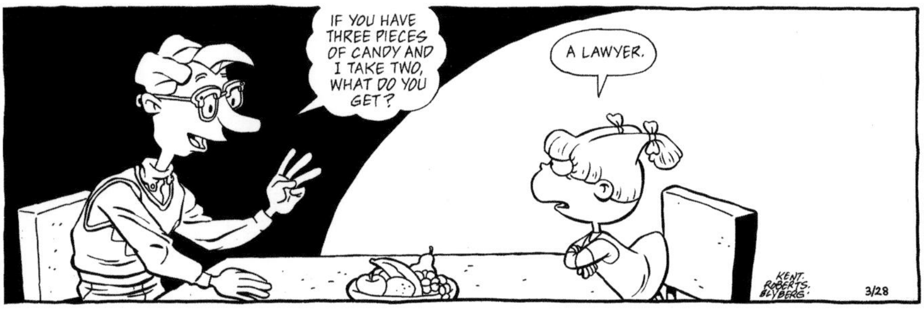
IF YOU HAVE THREE PIECES OF CANDY AND I TAKE TWO, WHAT DO YOU GET?
A LAWYER.
KENT· ROBERTS· BLYBERG·
3/28

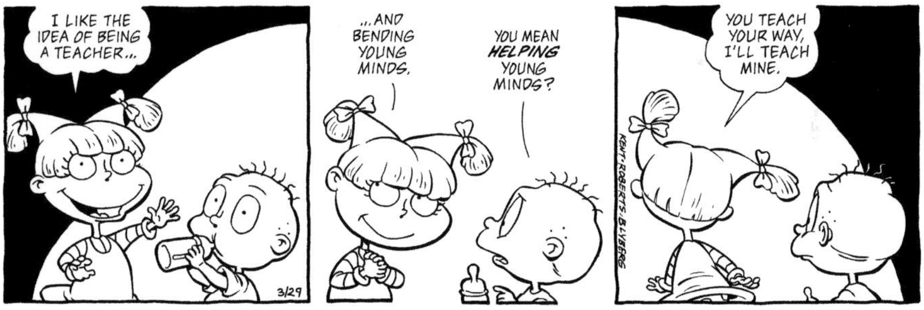
I LIKE THE IDEA OF BEING A TEACHER...
...AND BENDING YOUNG MINDS.
YOU MEAN HELPING YOUNG MINDS?
YOU TEACH YOUR WAY, I'LL TEACH MINE.
3/29
KENT·ROBERTS·BLYBERG

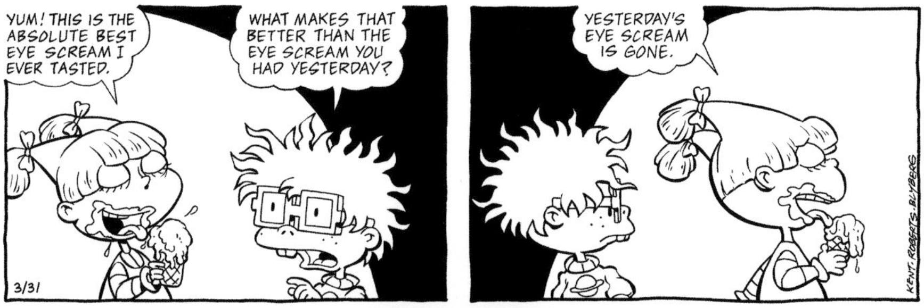
YUM! THIS IS THE ABSOLUTE BEST EYE SCREAM I EVER TASTED.
WHAT MAKES THAT BETTER THAN THE EYE SCREAM YOU HAD YESTERDAY?
YESTERDAY'S EYE SCREAM IS GONE.
3/31
KENT·ROBERTS·BLYBERG

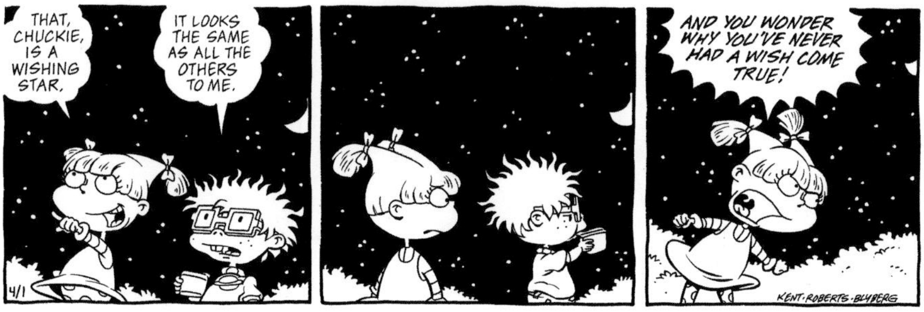
THAT, CHUCKIE, IS A WISHING STAR.
IT LOOKS THE SAME AS ALL THE OTHERS TO ME.
AND YOU WONDER WHY YOU'VE NEVER HAD A WISH COME TRUE!
4/1
KENT·ROBERTS·BLYBERG

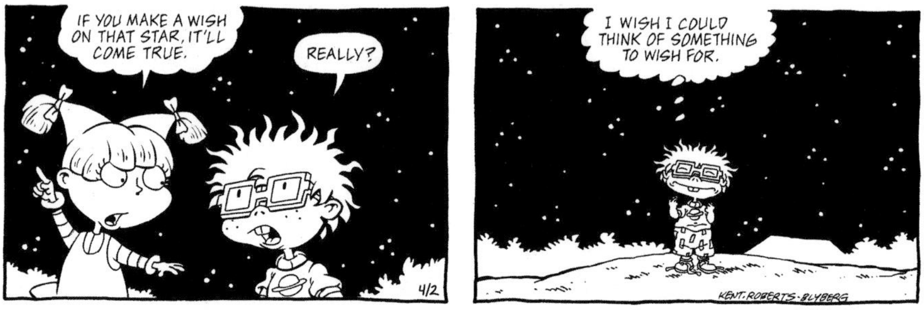
IF YOU MAKE A WISH ON THAT STAR, IT'LL COME TRUE.
REALLY?
4/2
I WISH I COULD THINK OF SOMETHING TO WISH FOR.
KENT.ROBERTS.BLYBERG

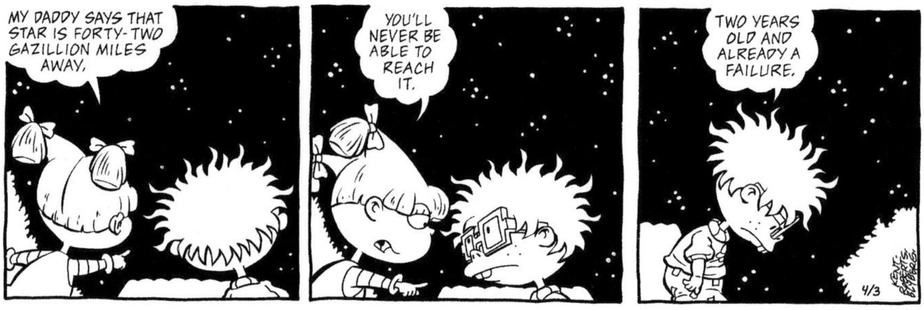
MY DADDY SAYS THAT STAR IS FORTY-TWO GAZILLION MILES AWAY.
YOU'LL NEVER BE ABLE TO REACH IT.
TWO YEARS OLD AND ALREADY A FAILURE.
4/3

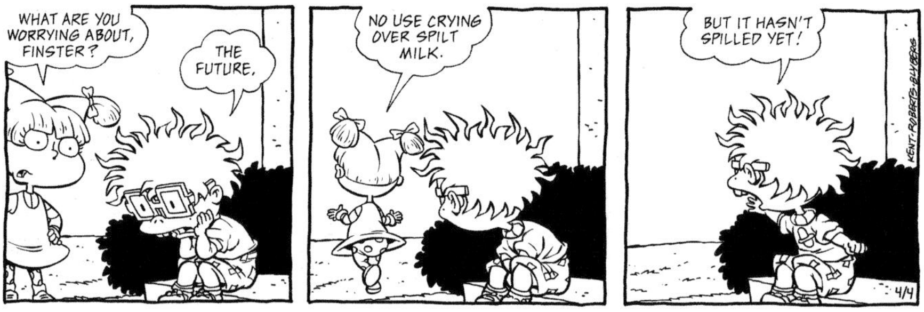
WHAT ARE YOU WORRYING ABOUT, FINSTER?
THE FUTURE.
NO USE CRYING OVER SPILT MILK.
BUT IT HASN'T SPILLED YET!
KENT.ROBERTS.BLYBERG
4/4

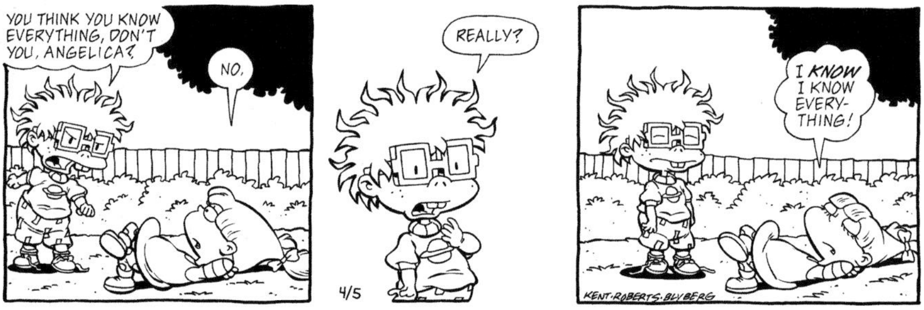
YOU THINK YOU KNOW EVERYTHING, DON'T YOU, ANGELICA?
NO.
REALLY?
4/5
I KNOW I KNOW EVERYTHING!
KENT.ROBERTS.BLYBERG

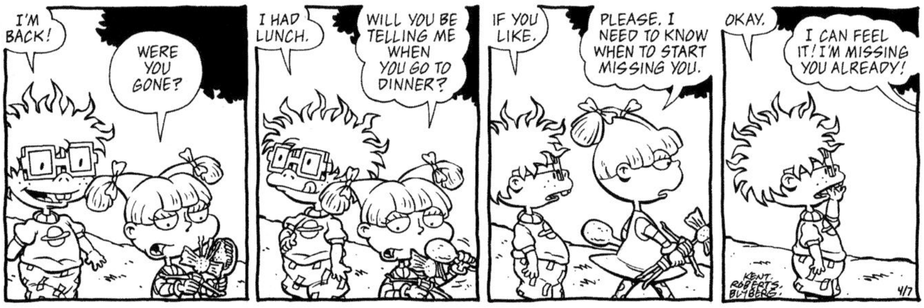
I'M BACK!
WERE YOU GONE?
I HAD LUNCH.
WILL YOU BE TELLING ME WHEN YOU GO TO DINNER?
IF YOU LIKE.
PLEASE. I NEED TO KNOW WHEN TO START MISSING YOU.
OKAY.
I CAN FEEL IT! I'M MISSING YOU ALREADY!
KENT.ROBERTS.BLYBERG
4/7

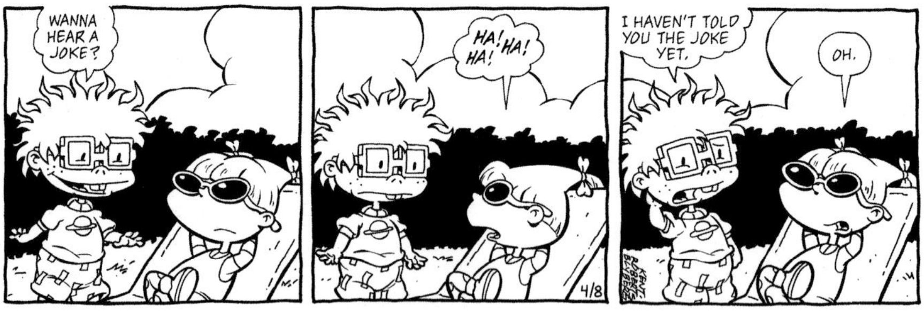
WANNA HEAR A JOKE?
HA! HA! HA!
4/8
I HAVEN'T TOLD YOU THE JOKE YET.
OH.

2003

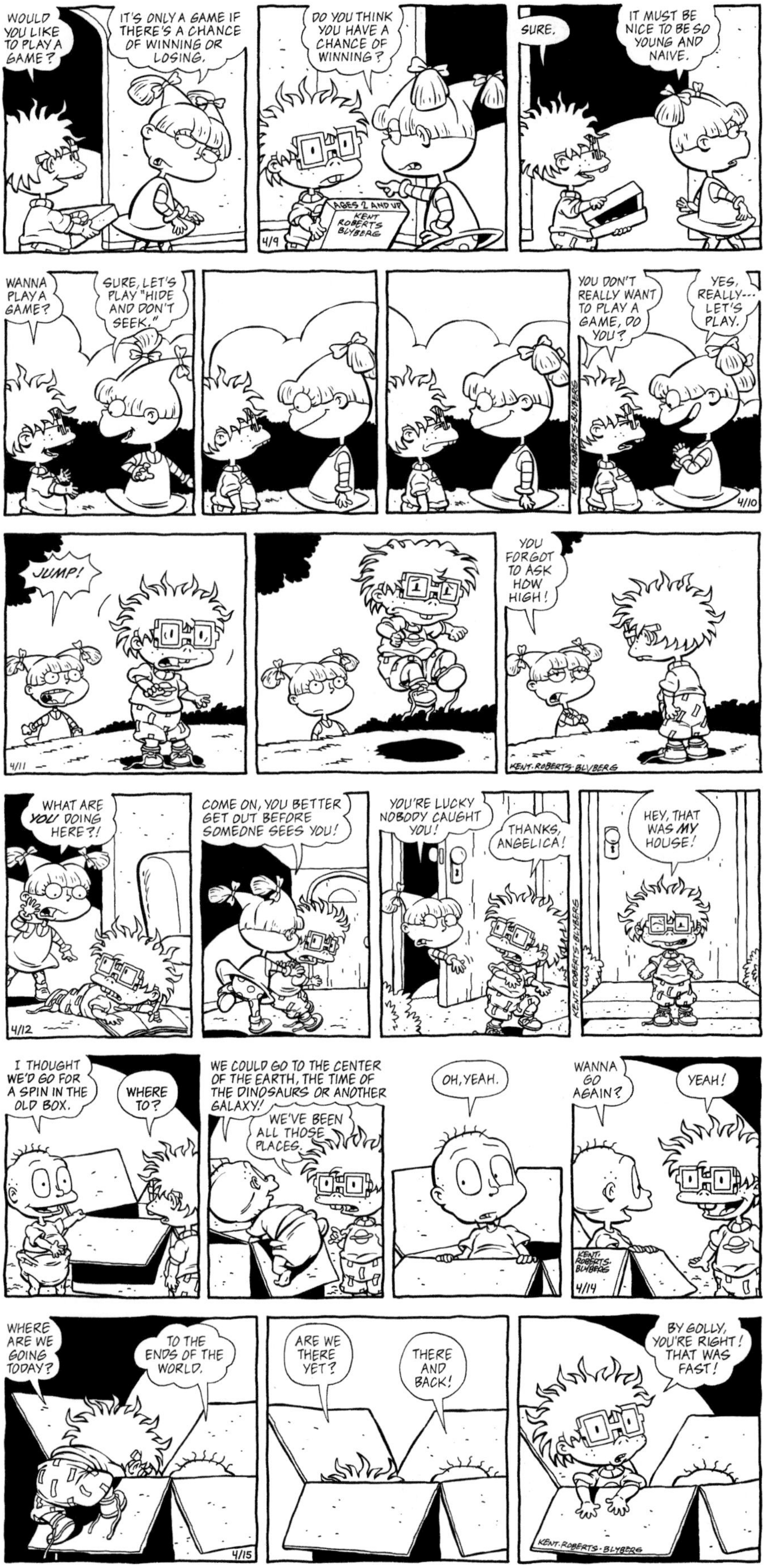
WOULD YOU LIKE TO PLAY A GAME?
IT'S ONLY A GAME IF THERE'S A CHANCE OF WINNING OR LOSING.
DO YOU THINK YOU HAVE A CHANCE OF WINNING?
AGES 2 AND UP
KENT ROBERTS BLYBERG
4/9
SURE.
IT MUST BE NICE TO BE SO YOUNG AND NAIVE.
WANNA PLAY A GAME?
SURE, LET'S PLAY "HIDE AND DON'T SEEK."
KENT-ROBERTS-BLYBERG
YOU DON'T REALLY WANT TO PLAY A GAME, DO YOU?
YES, REALLY--- LET'S PLAY.
4/10
JUMP!
4/11
YOU FORGOT TO ASK HOW HIGH!
KENT-ROBERTS-BLYBERG
WHAT ARE *YOU* DOING HERE?!
4/12
COME ON, YOU BETTER GET OUT BEFORE SOMEONE SEES YOU!
YOU'RE LUCKY NOBODY CAUGHT YOU!
THANKS, ANGELICA!
KENT-ROBERTS-BLYBERG
HEY, THAT WAS *MY* HOUSE!
I THOUGHT WE'D GO FOR A SPIN IN THE OLD BOX.
WHERE TO?
WE COULD GO TO THE CENTER OF THE EARTH, THE TIME OF THE DINOSAURS OR ANOTHER GALAXY!
WE'VE BEEN ALL THOSE PLACES.
OH, YEAH.
WANNA GO AGAIN?
YEAH!
KENT-ROBERTS-BLYBERG
4/14
WHERE ARE WE GOING TODAY?
TO THE ENDS OF THE WORLD.
ARE WE THERE YET?
THERE AND BACK!
4/15
BY GOLLY, YOU'RE RIGHT! THAT WAS FAST!
KENT-ROBERTS-BLYBERG

2003

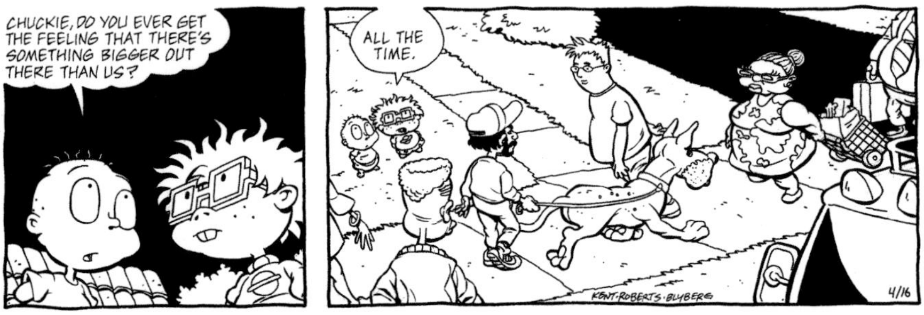
CHUCKIE, DO YOU EVER GET THE FEELING THAT THERE'S SOMETHING BIGGER OUT THERE THAN US?
ALL THE TIME.
KENT·ROBERTS·BLYBERG
4/16

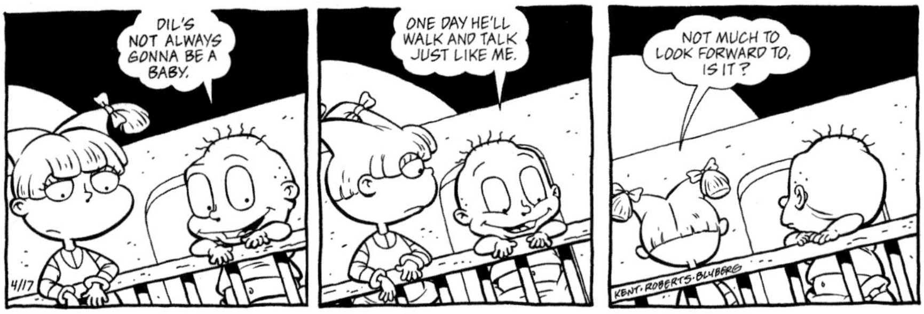
DIL'S NOT ALWAYS GONNA BE A BABY.
ONE DAY HE'LL WALK AND TALK JUST LIKE ME.
NOT MUCH TO LOOK FORWARD TO, IS IT?
4/17
KENT·ROBERTS·BLYBERG

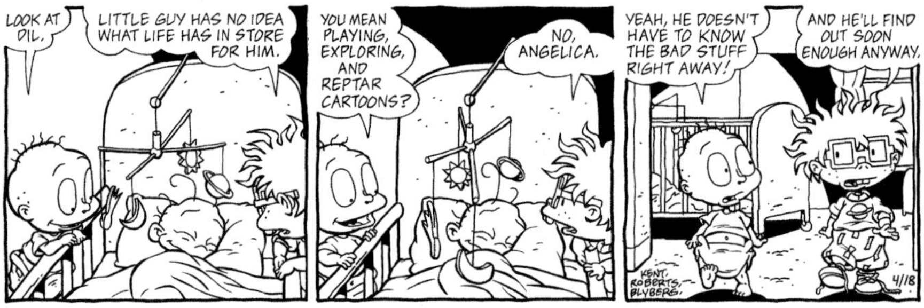
LOOK AT DIL.
LITTLE GUY HAS NO IDEA WHAT LIFE HAS IN STORE FOR HIM.
YOU MEAN PLAYING, EXPLORING, AND REPTAR CARTOONS?
NO, ANGELICA.
YEAH, HE DOESN'T HAVE TO KNOW THE BAD STUFF RIGHT AWAY!
AND HE'LL FIND OUT SOON ENOUGH ANYWAY.
KENT, ROBERTS, BLYBERG.
4/18

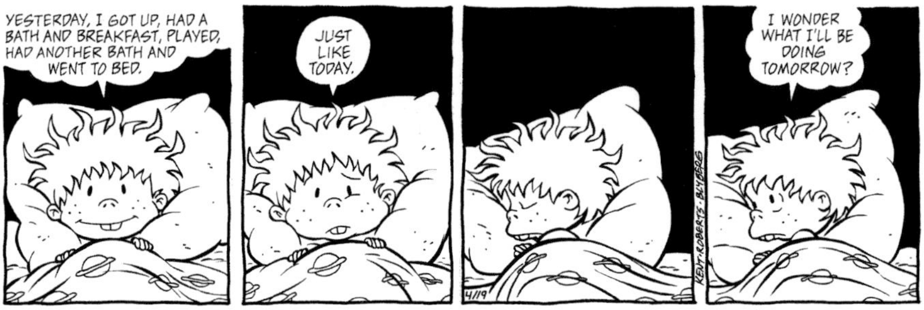
YESTERDAY, I GOT UP, HAD A BATH AND BREAKFAST, PLAYED, HAD ANOTHER BATH AND WENT TO BED.
JUST LIKE TODAY.
4/19
KENT·ROBERTS·BLYBERG
I WONDER WHAT I'LL BE DOING TOMORROW?

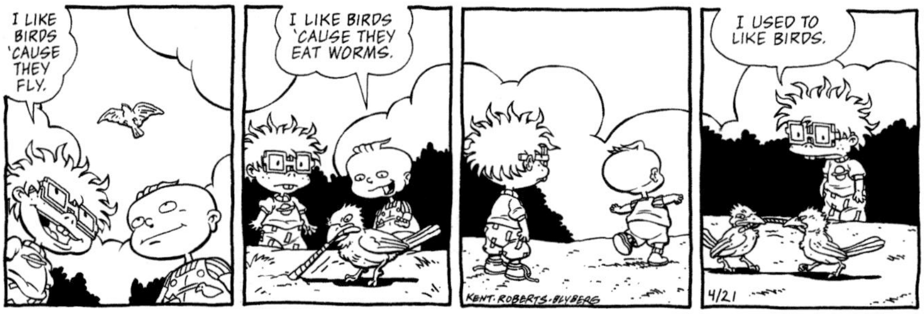
I LIKE BIRDS 'CAUSE THEY FLY.
I LIKE BIRDS 'CAUSE THEY EAT WORMS.
KENT·ROBERTS·BLYBERG
I USED TO LIKE BIRDS.
4/21

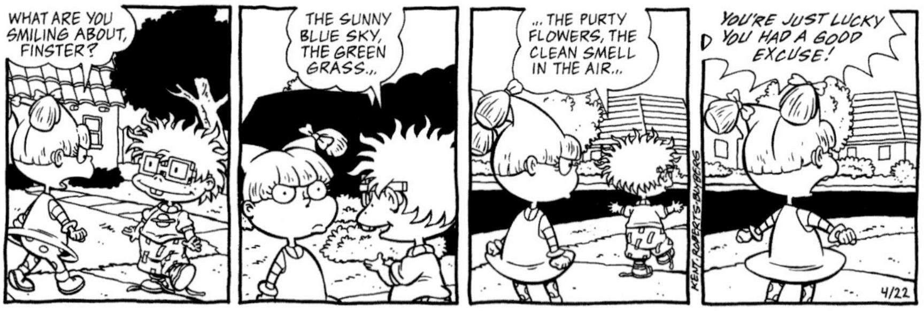
WHAT ARE YOU SMILING ABOUT, FINSTER?
THE SUNNY BLUE SKY, THE GREEN GRASS...
...THE PURTY FLOWERS, THE CLEAN SMELL IN THE AIR...
KENT·ROBERTS·BLYBERG
YOU'RE JUST LUCKY YOU HAD A GOOD EXCUSE!
4/22

2003

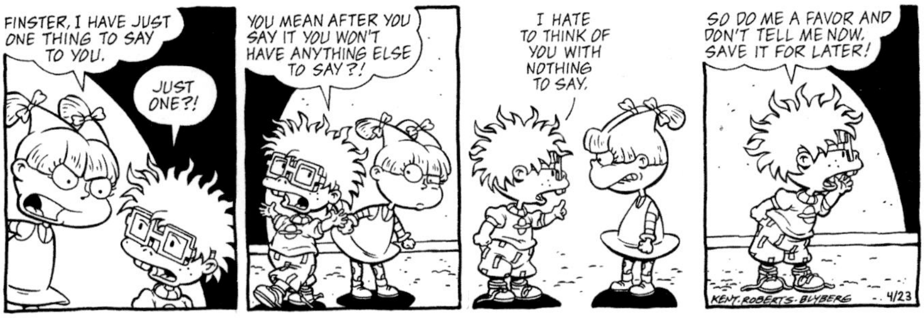
FINSTER, I HAVE JUST ONE THING TO SAY TO YOU.
JUST ONE?!
YOU MEAN AFTER YOU SAY IT YOU WON'T HAVE ANYTHING ELSE TO SAY?!
I HATE TO THINK OF YOU WITH NOTHING TO SAY.
SO DO ME A FAVOR AND DON'T TELL ME NOW. SAVE IT FOR LATER!
KENT·ROBERTS·BLYBERG 4/23

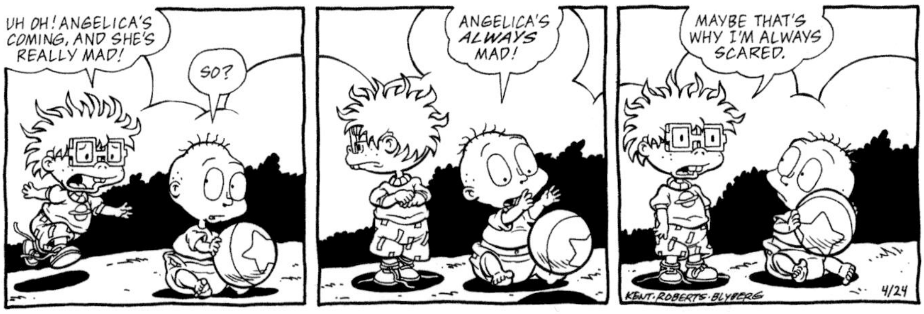
UH OH! ANGELICA'S COMING, AND SHE'S REALLY MAD!
SO?
ANGELICA'S ALWAYS MAD!
MAYBE THAT'S WHY I'M ALWAYS SCARED.
KENT·ROBERTS·BLYBERG 4/24

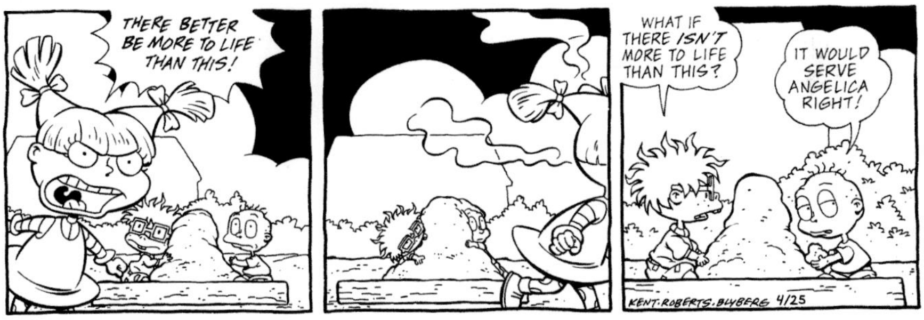
THERE BETTER BE MORE TO LIFE THAN THIS!
WHAT IF THERE ISN'T MORE TO LIFE THAN THIS?
IT WOULD SERVE ANGELICA RIGHT!
KENT·ROBERTS·BLYBERG 4/25

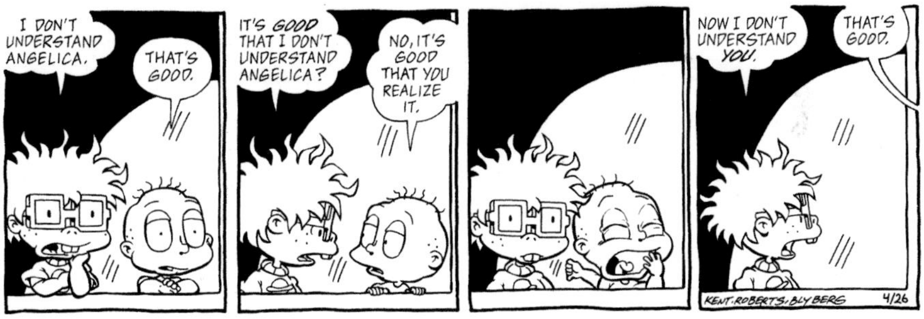
I DON'T UNDERSTAND ANGELICA.
THAT'S GOOD.
IT'S GOOD THAT I DON'T UNDERSTAND ANGELICA?
NO, IT'S GOOD THAT YOU REALIZE IT.
NOW I DON'T UNDERSTAND YOU.
THAT'S GOOD.
KENT·ROBERTS·BLYBERG 4/26

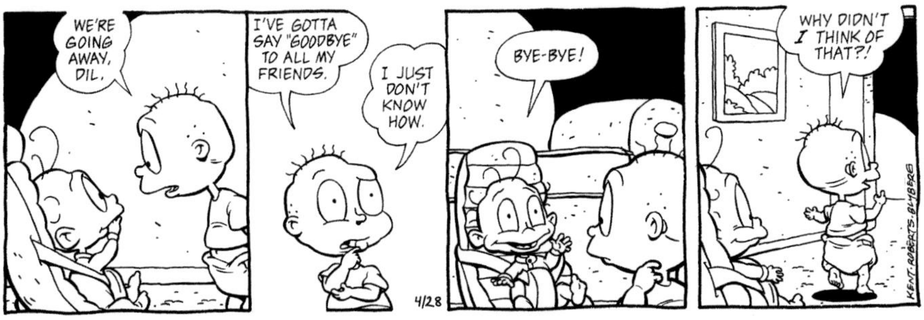
WE'RE GOING AWAY, DIL.
I'VE GOTTA SAY "GOODBYE" TO ALL MY FRIENDS.
I JUST DON'T KNOW HOW.
4/28
BYE-BYE!
WHY DIDN'T I THINK OF THAT?!
KENT·ROBERTS·BLYBERG

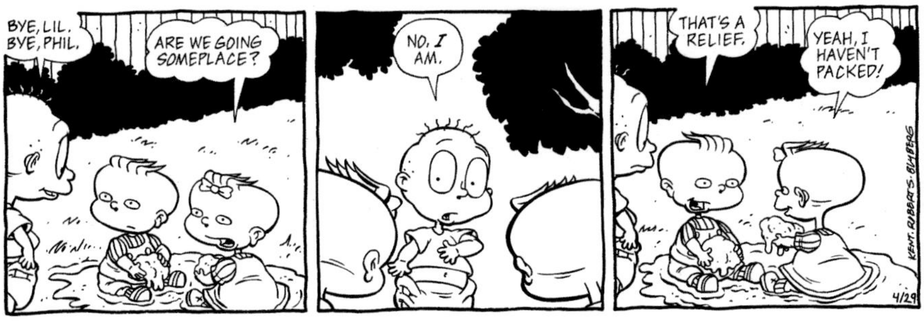
BYE, LIL. BYE, PHIL.
ARE WE GOING SOMEPLACE?
NO, I AM.
THAT'S A RELIEF.
YEAH, I HAVEN'T PACKED!
KENT·ROBERTS·BLYBERG
4/29

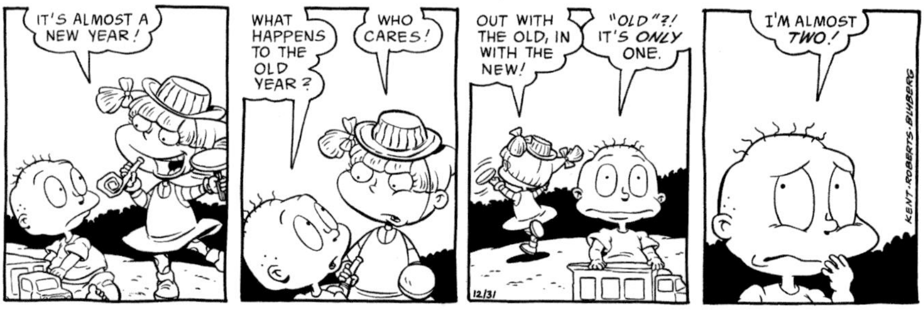
IT'S ALMOST A NEW YEAR!
WHAT HAPPENS TO THE OLD YEAR?
WHO CARES!
OUT WITH THE OLD, IN WITH THE NEW!
"OLD"?! IT'S ONLY ONE.
12/31
I'M ALMOST TWO!
KENT·ROBERTS·BLYBERG

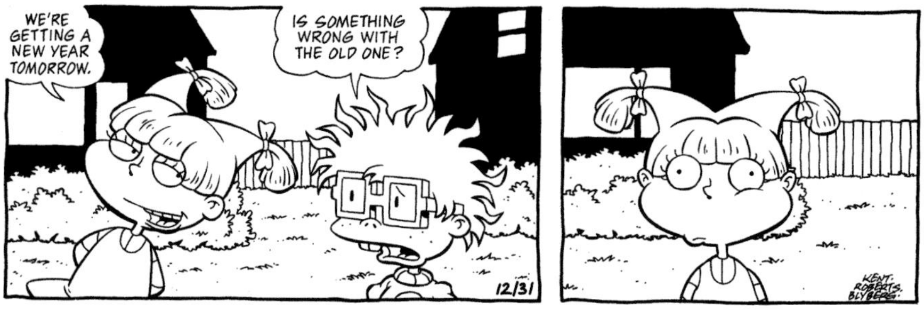
WE'RE GETTING A NEW YEAR TOMORROW.
IS SOMETHING WRONG WITH THE OLD ONE?
12/31
KENT·ROBERTS·BLYBERG

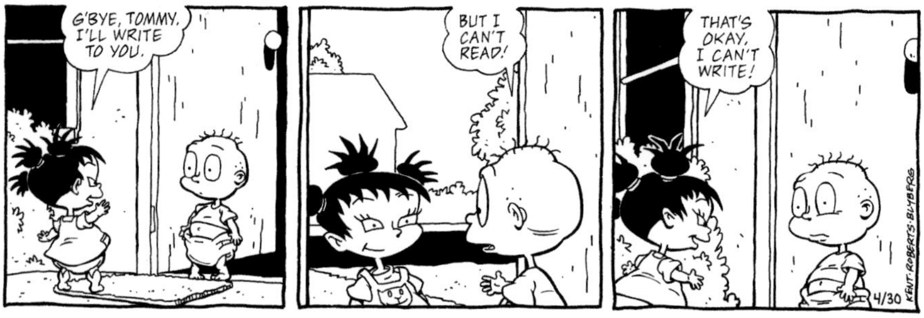
G'BYE, TOMMY. I'LL WRITE TO YOU.
BUT I CAN'T READ!
THAT'S OKAY, I CAN'T WRITE!
KENT·ROBERTS·BLYBERG
4/30

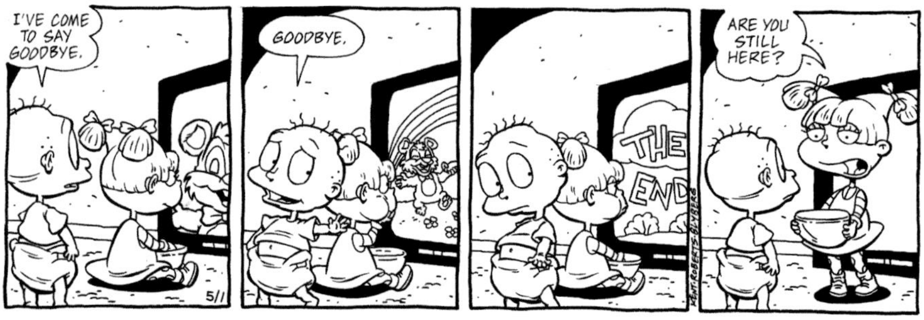
I'VE COME TO SAY GOODBYE.
5/1
GOODBYE.
THE END
KENT·ROBERTS·BLYBERG
ARE YOU STILL HERE?

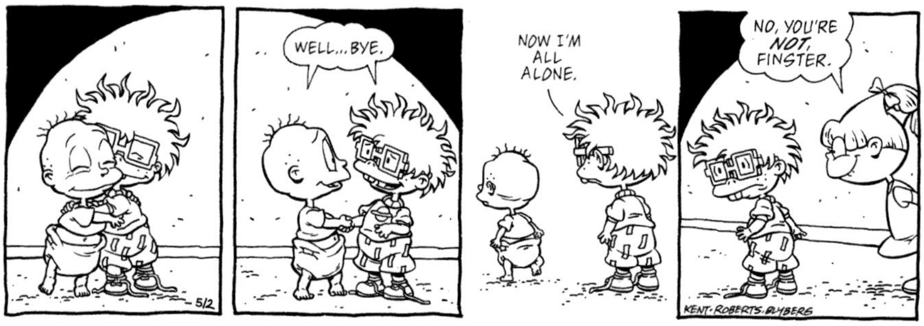
5/2
WELL...BYE.
NOW I'M ALL ALONE.
NO, YOU'RE NOT, FINSTER.
KENT·ROBERTS·BLYBERG

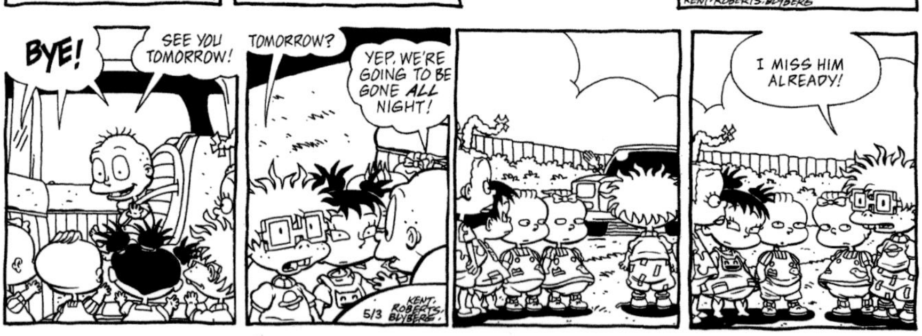
BYE!
SEE YOU TOMORROW!
TOMORROW?
YEP, WE'RE GOING TO BE GONE ALL NIGHT!
5/3
KENT·ROBERTS·BLYBERG
I MISS HIM ALREADY!

2003

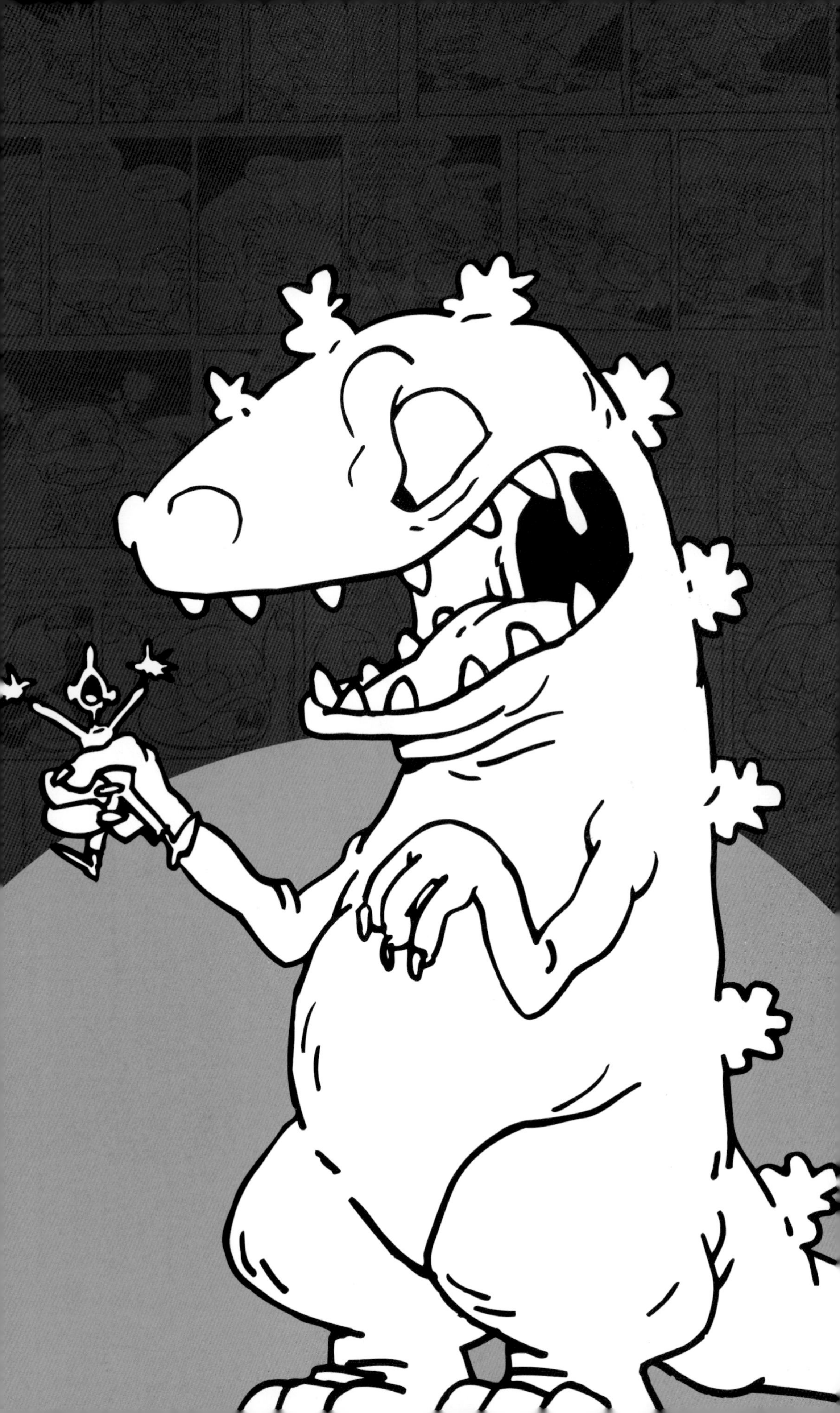

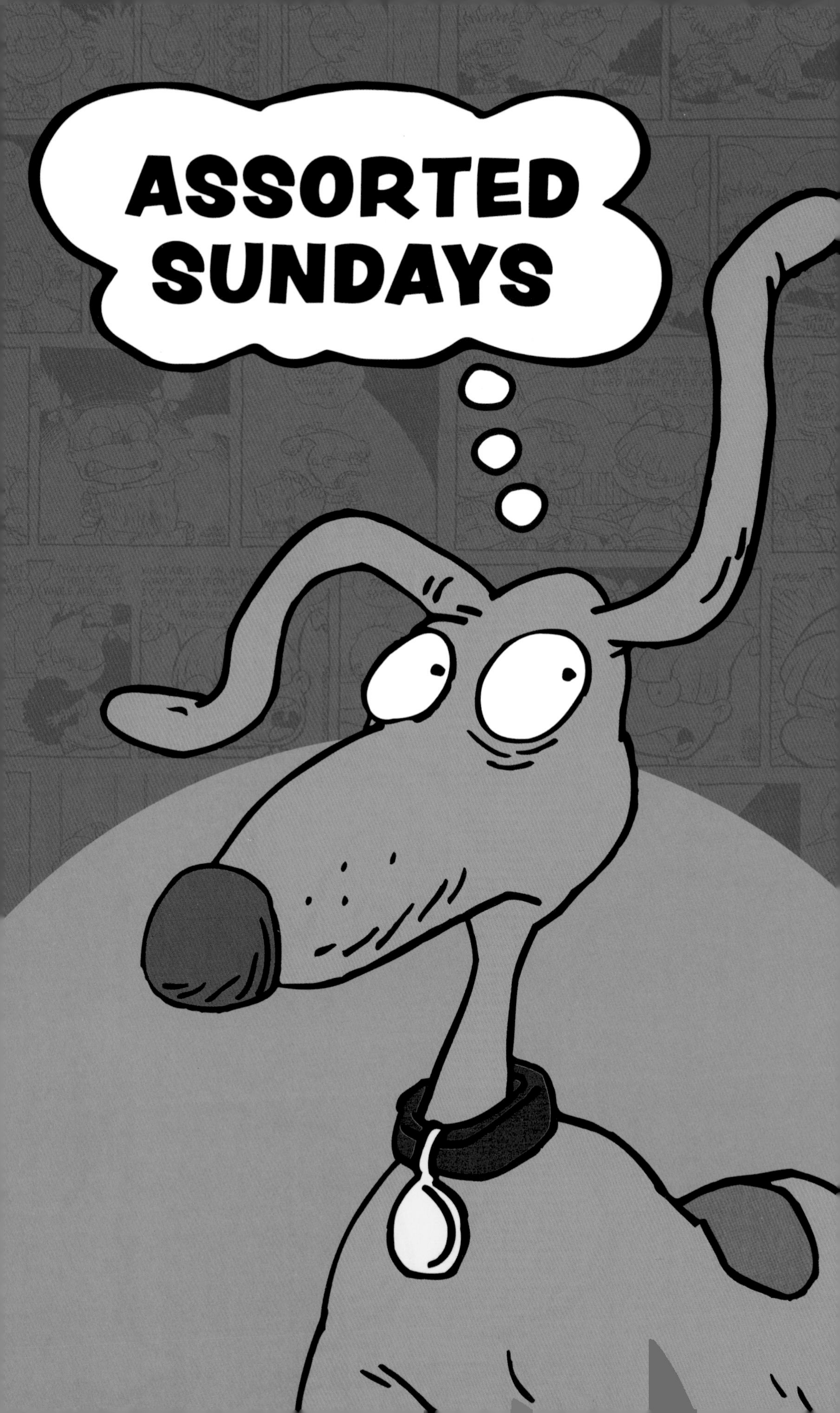
ASSORTED SUNDAYS

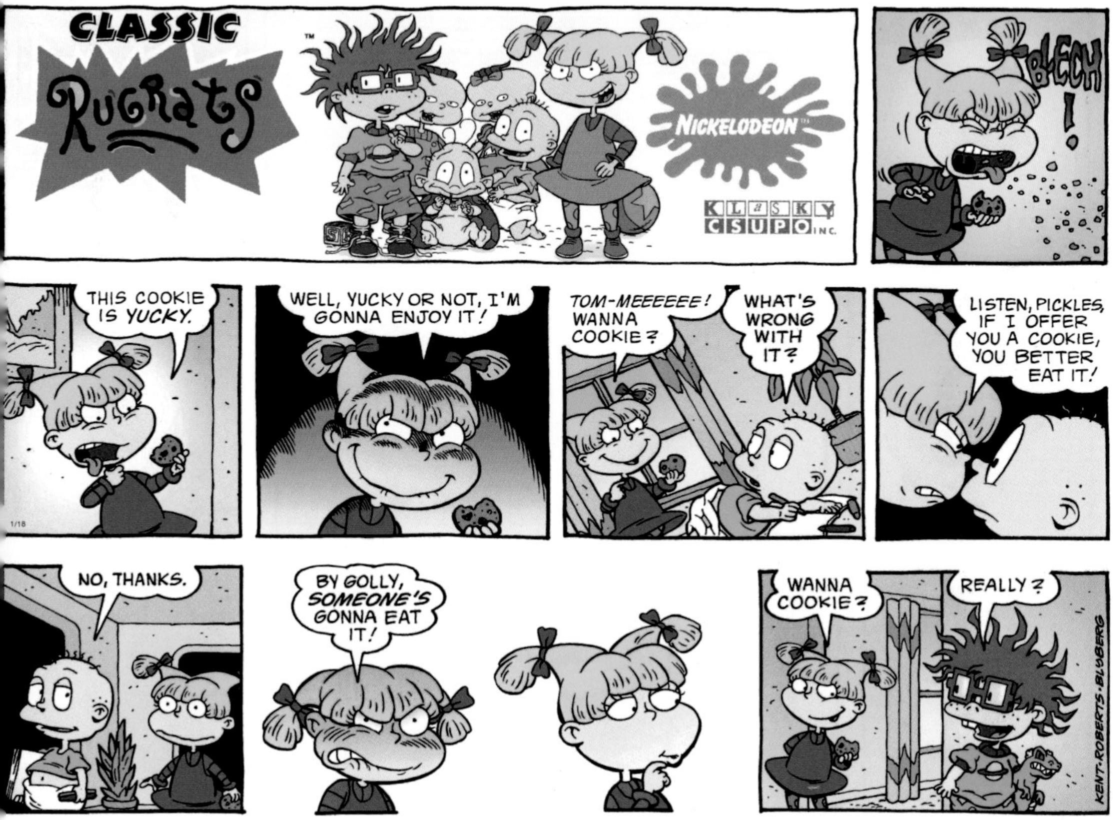
CLASSIC
Rugrats
NICKELODEON
KLaSKY CSUPO INC.
BLECH!
1/18
THIS COOKIE IS *YUCKY.*
WELL, YUCKY OR NOT, I'M GONNA ENJOY IT!
TOM-MEEEEEE! WANNA COOKIE?
WHAT'S WRONG WITH IT?
LISTEN, PICKLES, IF I OFFER YOU A COOKIE, YOU BETTER EAT IT!
NO, THANKS.
BY GOLLY, ***SOMEONE'S*** GONNA EAT IT!
WANNA COOKIE?
REALLY?
KENT·ROBERTS·BLOBERG

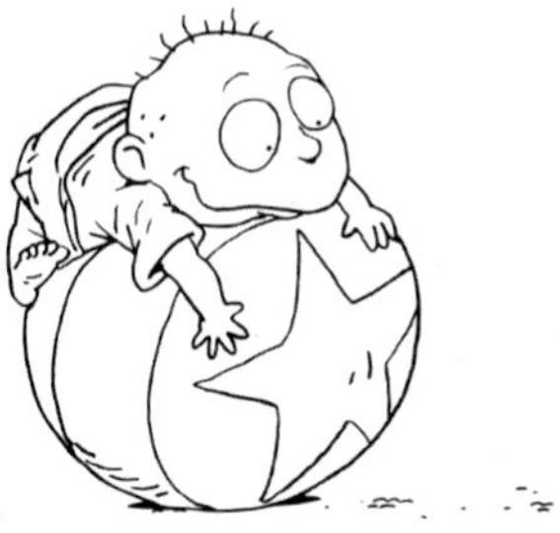

SUNDAYS

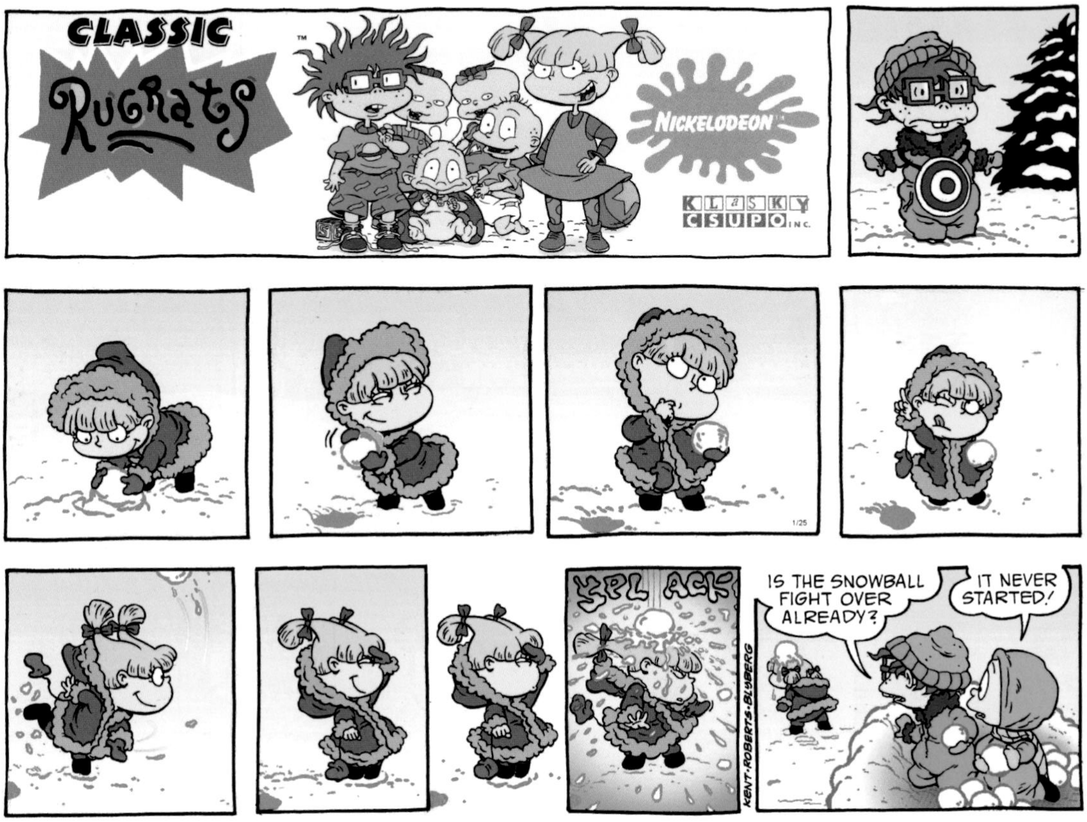

CLASSIC
Rugrats
NICKELODEON
KLASKY CSUPO INC.
1/25
SPLACK
KENT-ROBERTS-BLYBERG
IS THE SNOWBALL FIGHT OVER ALREADY?
IT NEVER STARTED!

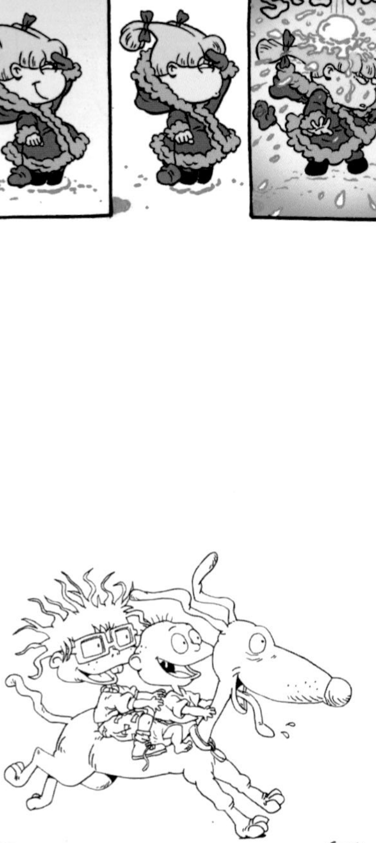

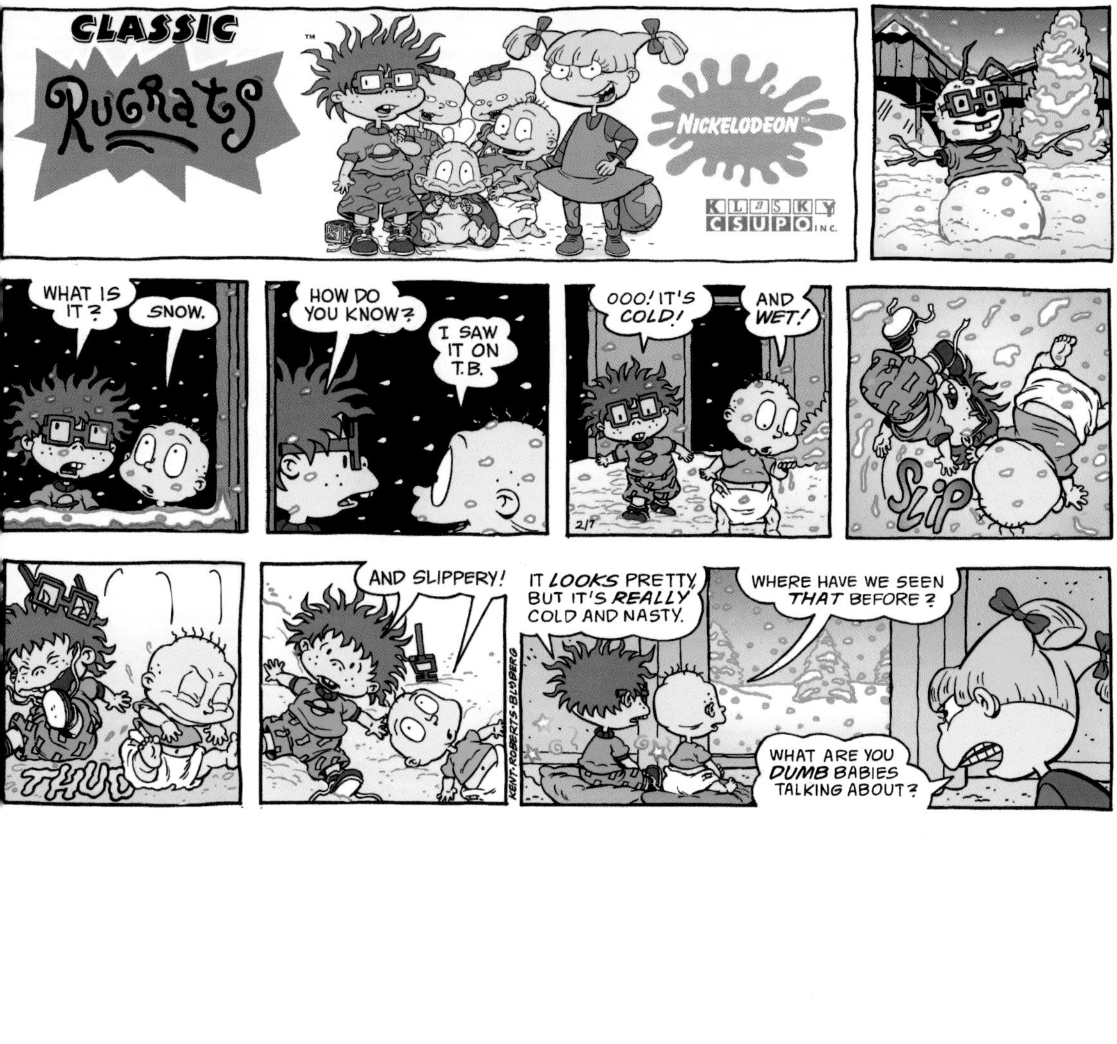
CLASSIC
Rugrats
NICKELODEON
KLASKY CSUPO INC.
WHAT IS IT?
SNOW.
HOW DO YOU KNOW?
I SAW IT ON T.B.
OOO! IT'S *COLD!*
AND *WET!*
2/7
SLIP
THUD
AND SLIPPERY!
KENT·ROBERTS·BLOBERG
IT *LOOKS* PRETTY, BUT IT'S *REALLY* COLD AND NASTY.
WHERE HAVE WE SEEN *THAT* BEFORE?
WHAT ARE YOU *DUMB* BABIES TALKING ABOUT?

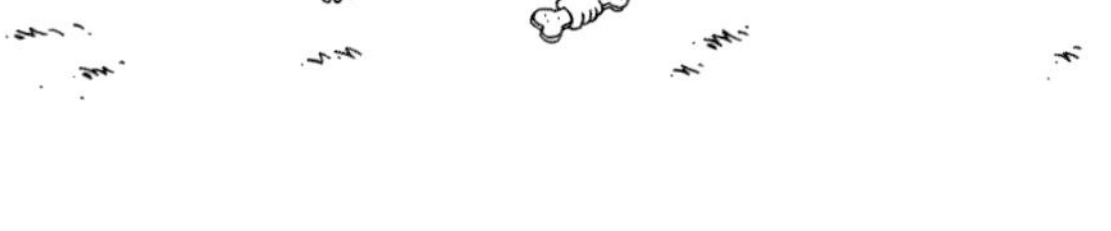

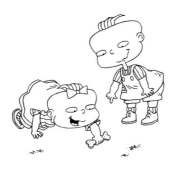

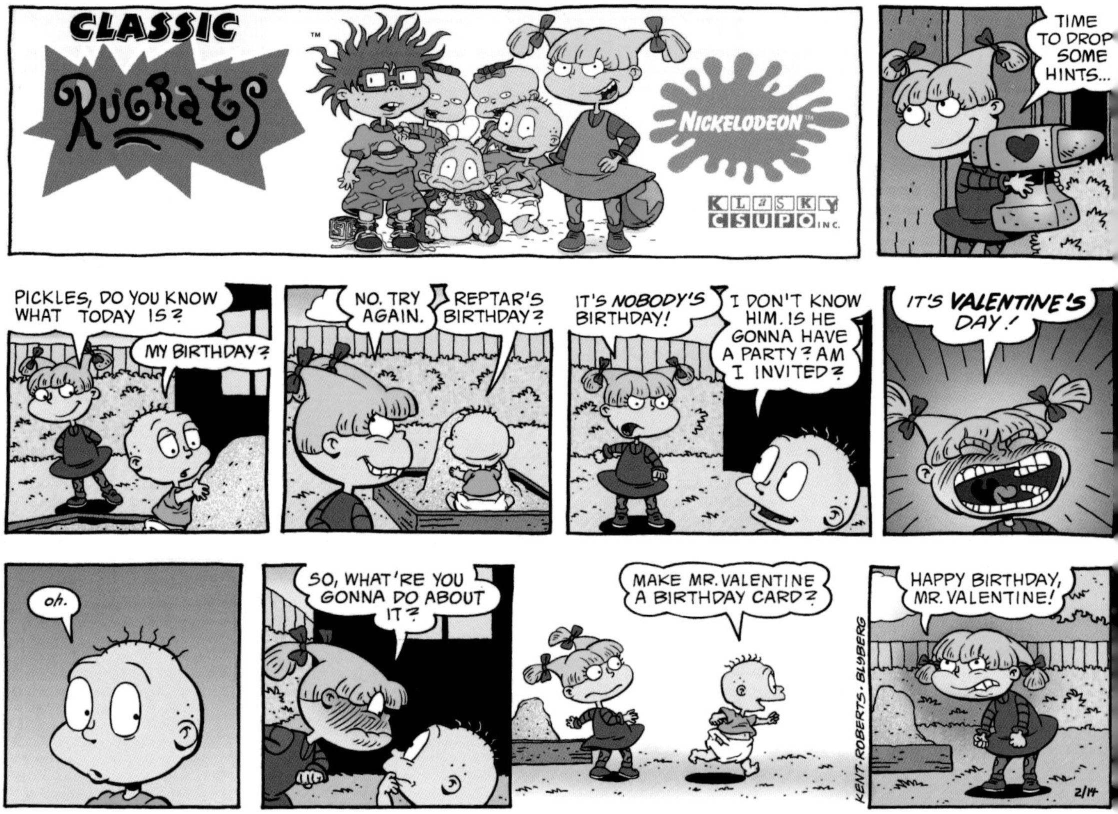
CLASSIC
Rugrats
NICKELODEON
KLASKY CSUPO INC.
TIME TO DROP SOME HINTS...
PICKLES, DO YOU KNOW WHAT TODAY IS?
MY BIRTHDAY?
NO. TRY AGAIN.
REPTAR'S BIRTHDAY?
IT'S *NOBODY'S* BIRTHDAY!
I DON'T KNOW HIM. IS HE GONNA HAVE A PARTY? AM I INVITED?
IT'S **VALENTINE'S** DAY!
oh.
SO, WHAT'RE YOU GONNA DO ABOUT IT?
MAKE MR. VALENTINE A BIRTHDAY CARD?
KENT · ROBERTS · BLYBERG
HAPPY BIRTHDAY, MR. VALENTINE!
2/14

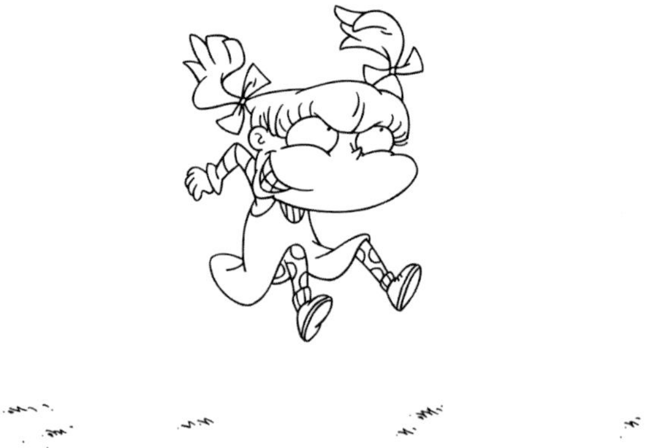

SUNDAYS

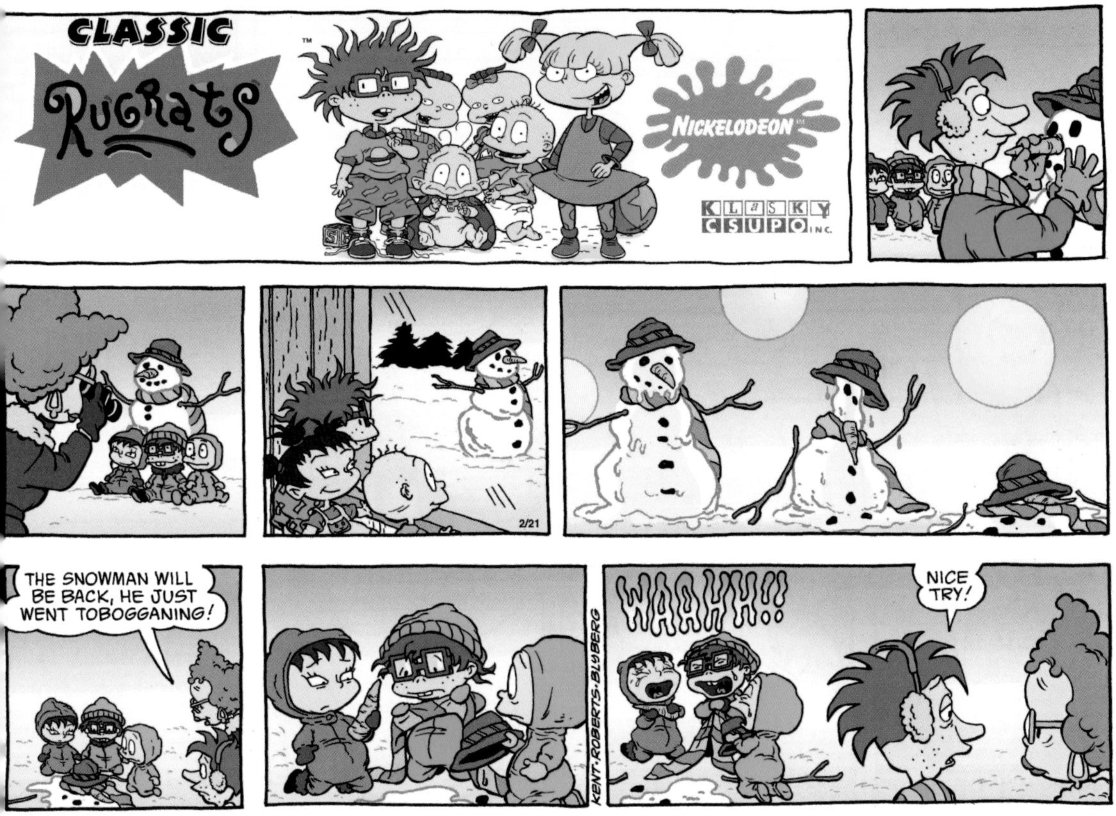
CLASSIC
Rugrats
NICKELODEON
KLASKY CSUPO INC.
2/21
THE SNOWMAN WILL BE BACK, HE JUST WENT TOBOGGANING!
KENT·ROBERTS·BLYBERG
WAAHH!!
NICE TRY!

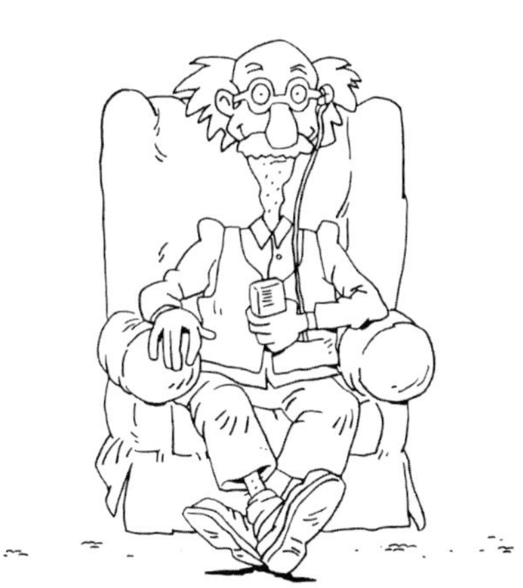

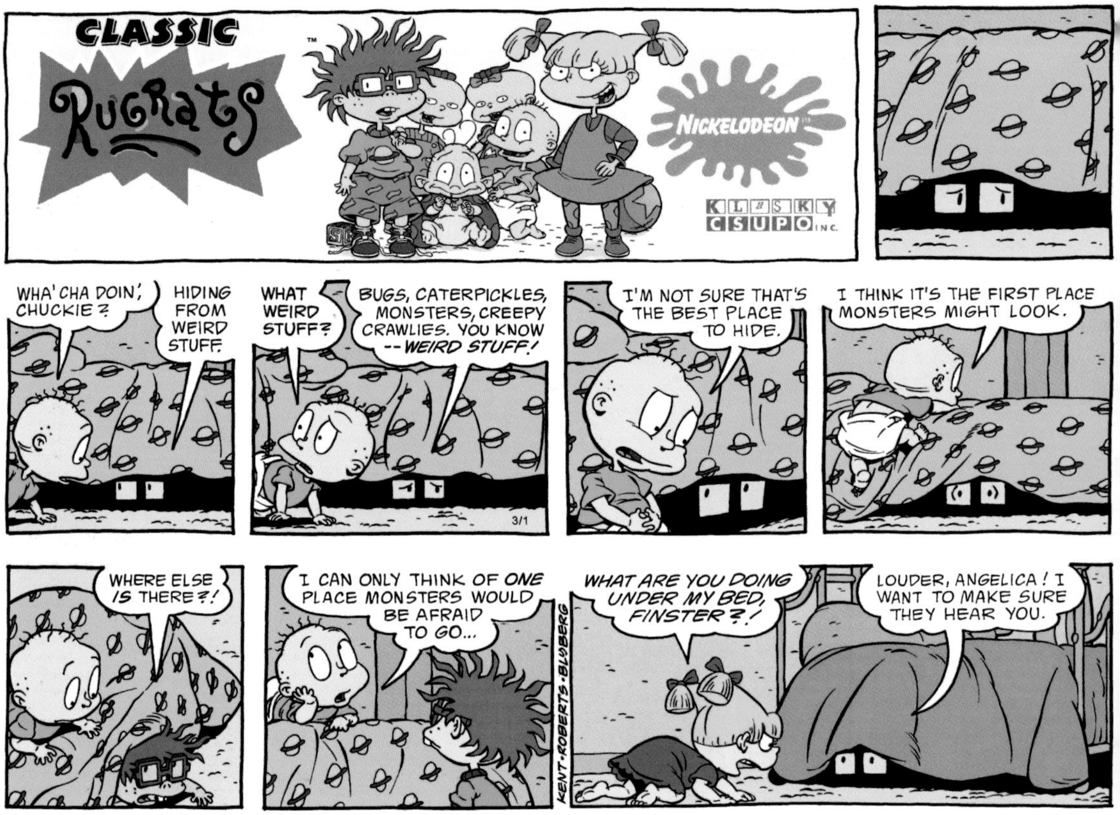
CLASSIC
Rugrats
NICKELODEON
KLASKY CSUPO INC.
WHA'CHA DOIN', CHUCKIE?
HIDING FROM WEIRD STUFF.
WHAT WEIRD STUFF?
BUGS, CATERPICKLES, MONSTERS, CREEPY CRAWLIES. YOU KNOW --WEIRD STUFF!
3/1
I'M NOT SURE THAT'S THE BEST PLACE TO HIDE.
I THINK IT'S THE FIRST PLACE MONSTERS MIGHT LOOK.
WHERE ELSE IS THERE?!
I CAN ONLY THINK OF ONE PLACE MONSTERS WOULD BE AFRAID TO GO...
KENT•ROBERTS•BLYBERG
WHAT ARE YOU DOING UNDER MY BED, FINSTER?!
LOUDER, ANGELICA! I WANT TO MAKE SURE THEY HEAR YOU.

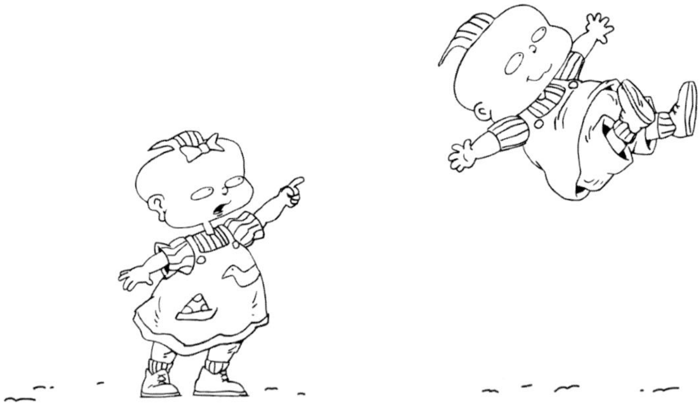

SUNDAYS

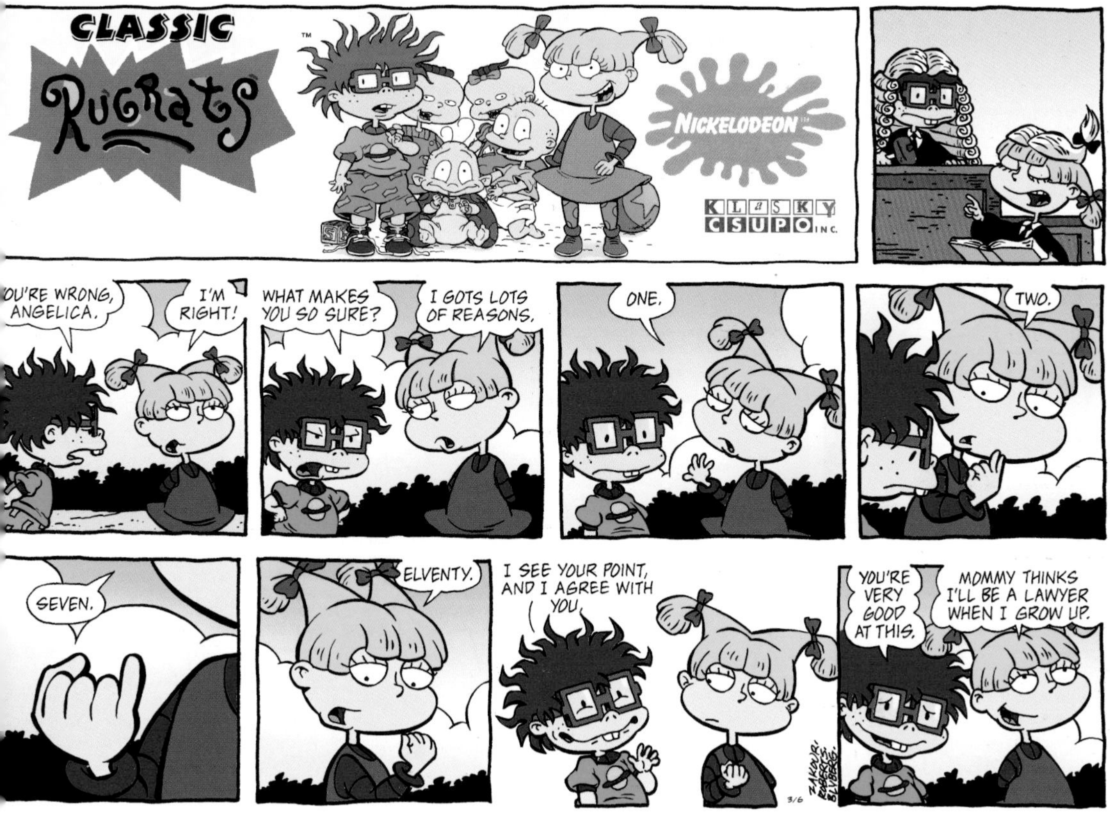
CLASSIC
Rugrats
NICKELODEON
KLaSKY CSUPO INC.
OU'RE WRONG, ANGELICA.
I'M RIGHT!
WHAT MAKES YOU SO SURE?
I GOTS LOTS OF REASONS.
ONE.
TWO.
SEVEN.
ELVENTY.
I SEE YOUR POINT, AND I AGREE WITH YOU.
YOU'RE VERY GOOD AT THIS.
MOMMY THINKS I'LL BE A LAWYER WHEN I GROW UP.
3/6
ZAKOUR/ ROBERTS/ BLYBERG

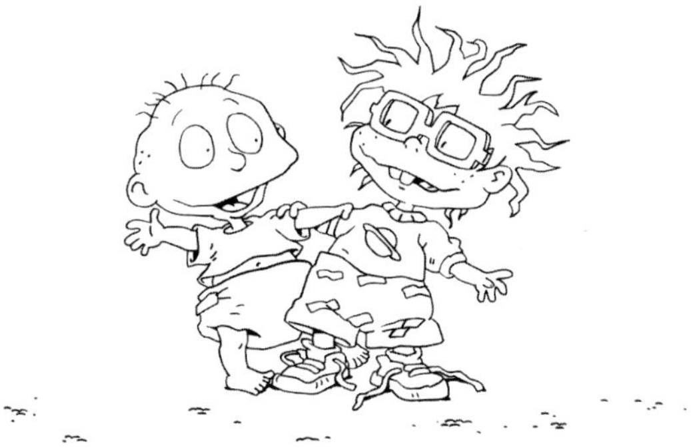

CLASSIC Rugrats™ NICKELODEON™ KLASKY CSUPO INC.

READ US A STORY, ANGELICA.

YEAH, ONE WITH LOTS OF GROSS STUFF!

"THE PRINCE GAVE THE PRINCESS PINK POSIES, WHICH MADE HER EVER SO HAPPY BECAUSE PINK WAS HER FAV'RIT COLOR.

"SO THE PRINCE GAVE HER A PINK HORSIE.

"AND PAINTED HIS CASTLE PINK.

"AND HE DECREED THAT 'FROM NOW ON, ONLY THE COLOR PINK SHALL BE ALLOWED IN MY KINGDOM!'

3/8

"AND THEY LIVED HAPPILY EVER AFTER IN THEIR PINK CASTLE ON PINK, COTTON-CANDY CLOUDS."

I THINK I'M GONNA BE SICK!

THAT WAS THE GROSSEST STORY I EVER HEARD!

YOU'VE GOTTA KNOW YOUR AUDIENCE.

KENT ROBERTS BLYBERG

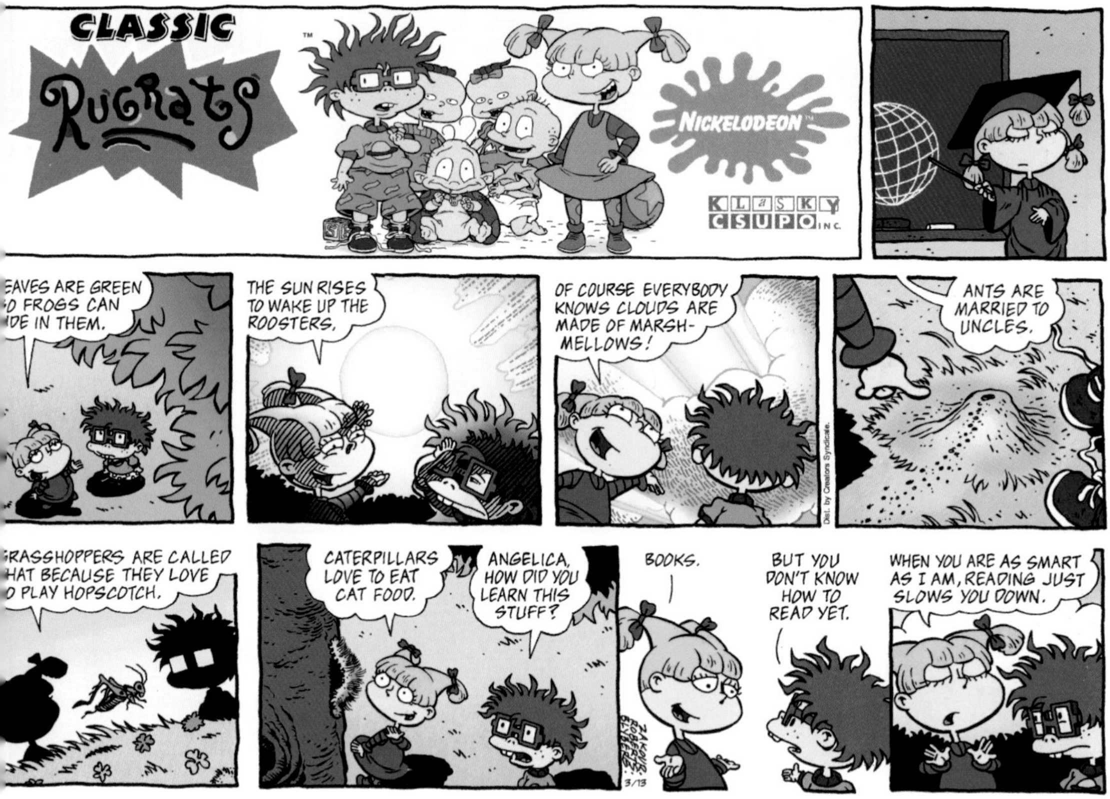
CLASSIC
RUGRATS
NICKELODEON
KLASKY CSUPO INC.
EAVES ARE GREEN O FROGS CAN DE IN THEM.
THE SUN RISES TO WAKE UP THE ROOSTERS.
OF COURSE EVERYBODY KNOWS CLOUDS ARE MADE OF MARSH-MELLOWS!
Dist. by Creators Syndicate.
ANTS ARE MARRIED TO UNCLES.
RASSHOPPERS ARE CALLED HAT BECAUSE THEY LOVE O PLAY HOPSCOTCH.
CATERPILLARS LOVE TO EAT CAT FOOD.
ANGELICA, HOW DID YOU LEARN THIS STUFF?
BOOKS.
BUT YOU DON'T KNOW HOW TO READ YET.
WHEN YOU ARE AS SMART AS I AM, READING JUST SLOWS YOU DOWN.
3/13

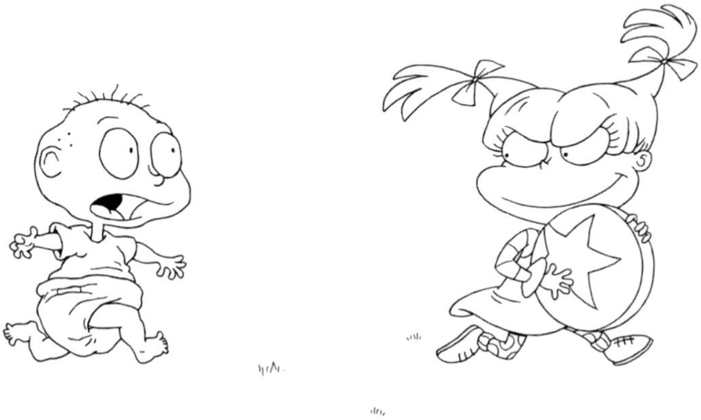

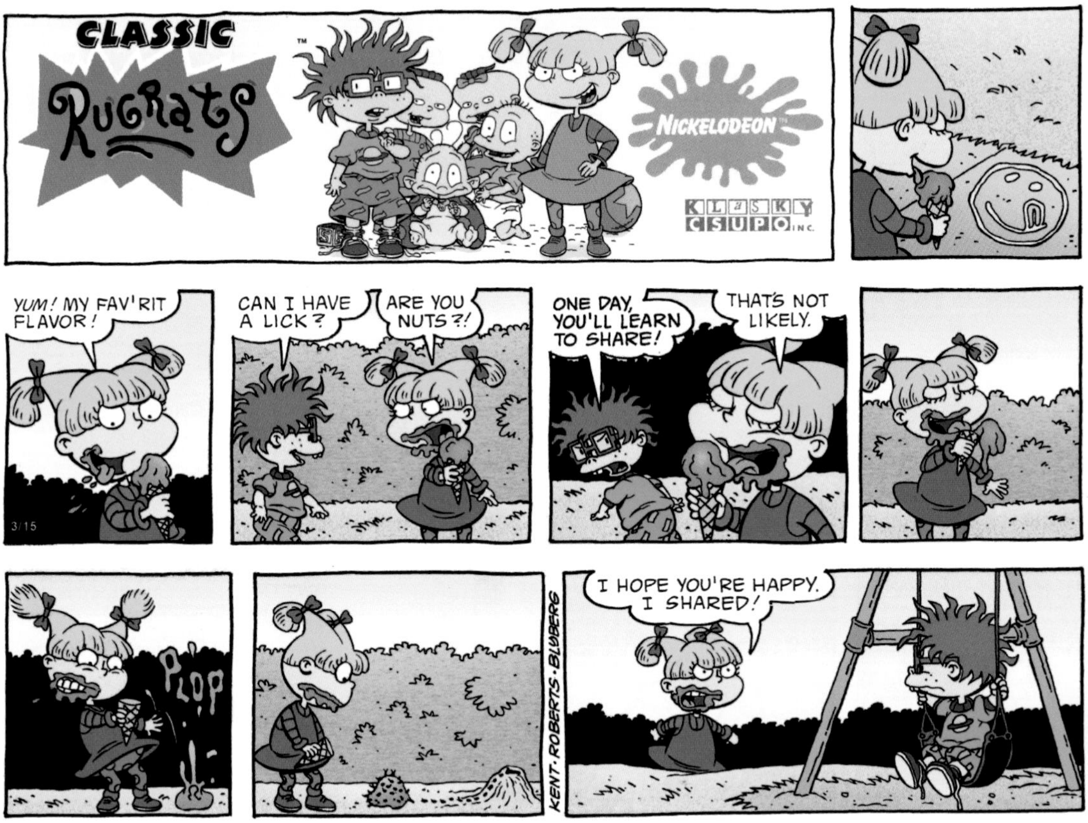
CLASSIC
Rugrats
NICKELODEON
KLASKY CSUPO INC.
YUM! MY FAV'RIT FLAVOR!
3/15
CAN I HAVE A LICK?
ARE YOU NUTS?!
ONE DAY, YOU'LL LEARN TO SHARE!
THAT'S NOT LIKELY.
PLOP
KENT·ROBERTS·BLYBERG
I HOPE YOU'RE HAPPY. I SHARED!

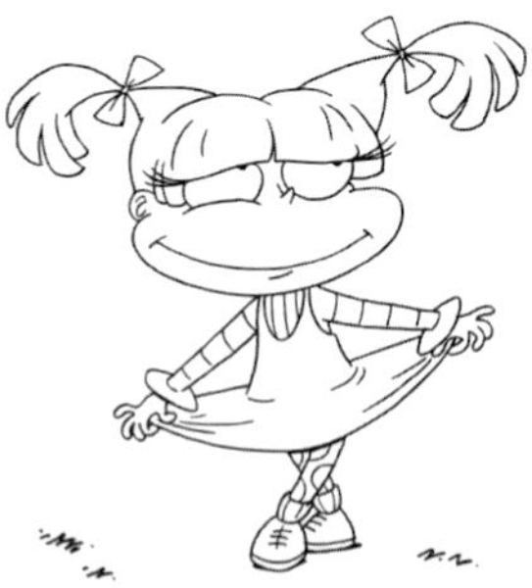

SUNDAYS

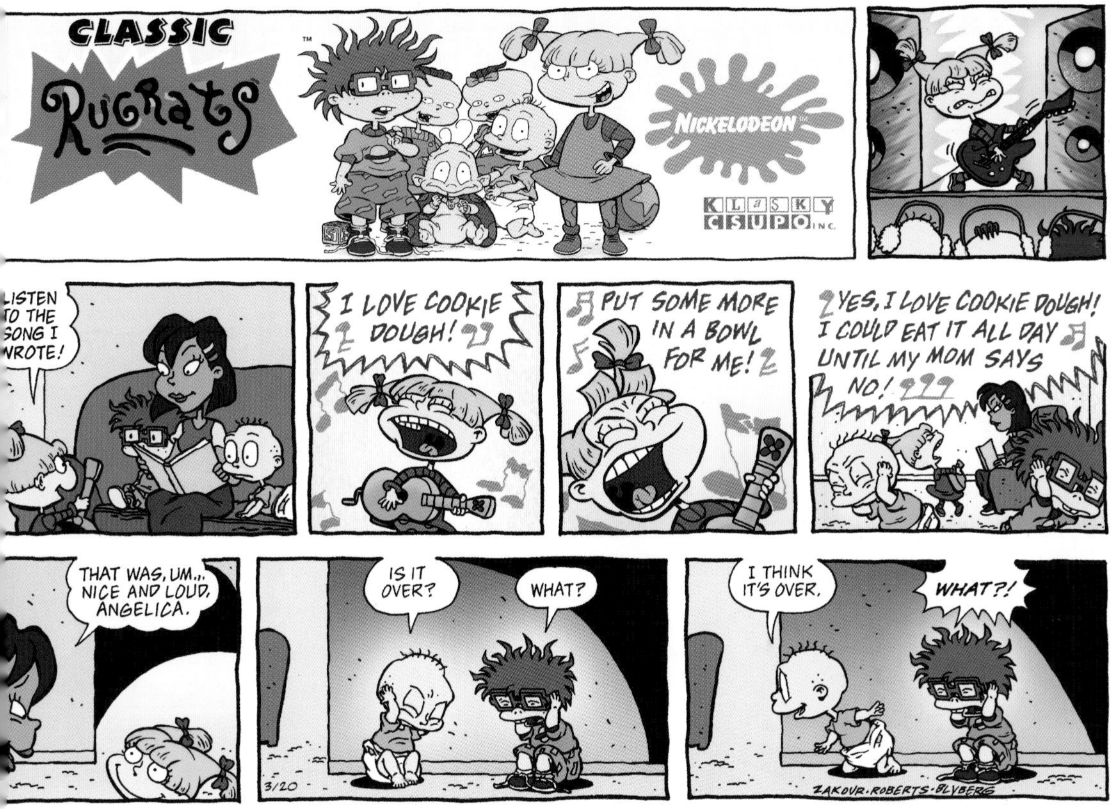
CLASSIC
Rugrats
NICKELODEON
KLASKY CSUPO INC.
LISTEN TO THE SONG I WROTE!
I LOVE COOKIE DOUGH!
PUT SOME MORE IN A BOWL FOR ME!
YES, I LOVE COOKIE DOUGH! I COULD EAT IT ALL DAY UNTIL MY MOM SAYS NO!
THAT WAS, UM... NICE AND LOUD, ANGELICA.
IS IT OVER?
WHAT?
3/20
I THINK IT'S OVER.
WHAT?!
ZAKOUR·ROBERTS·BLYBERG

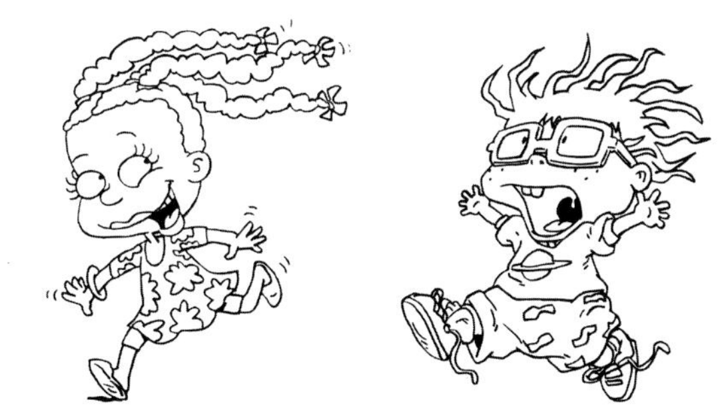

SUNDAYS

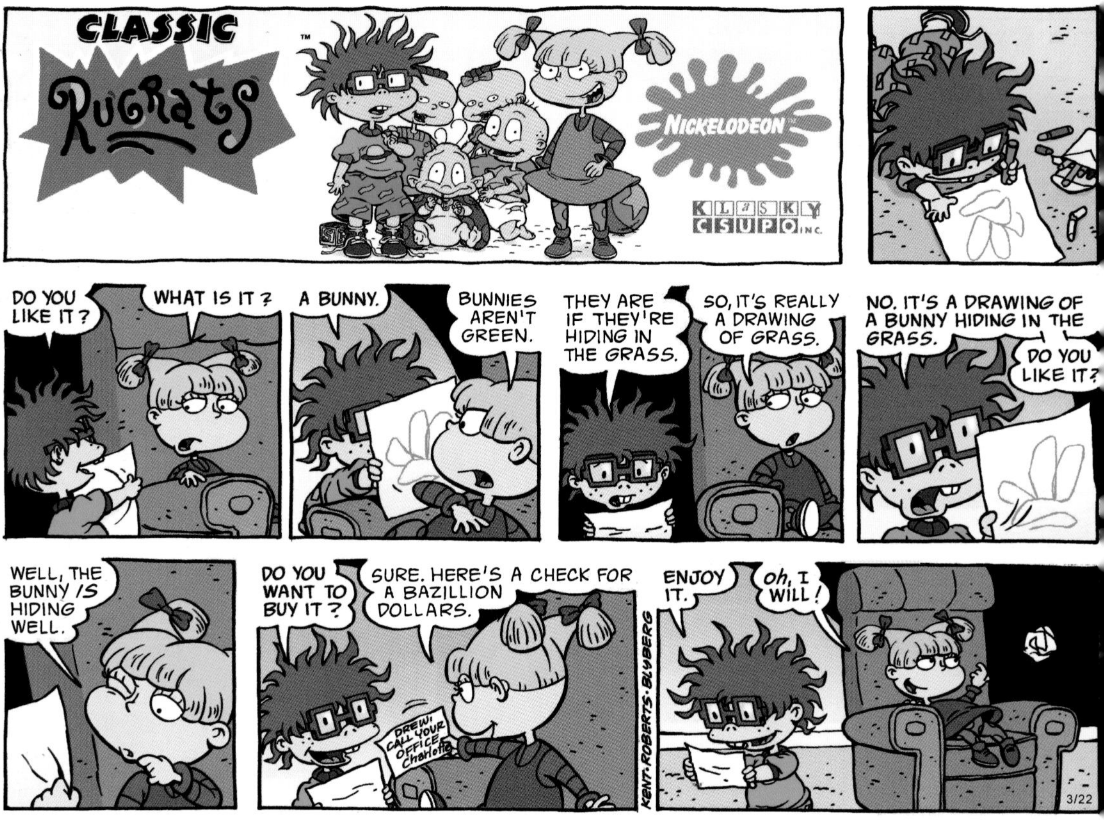
CLASSIC
Rugrats
NICKELODEON
KLASKY CSUPO INC.
DO YOU LIKE IT?
WHAT IS IT?
A BUNNY.
BUNNIES AREN'T GREEN.
THEY ARE IF THEY'RE HIDING IN THE GRASS.
SO, IT'S REALLY A DRAWING OF GRASS.
NO. IT'S A DRAWING OF A BUNNY HIDING IN THE GRASS.
DO YOU LIKE IT?
WELL, THE BUNNY *IS* HIDING WELL.
DO YOU WANT TO BUY IT?
SURE. HERE'S A CHECK FOR A BAZILLION DOLLARS.
DREW: CALL YOUR OFFICE Charlotte
KENT·ROBERTS·BLYBERG
ENJOY IT.
oh, I WILL!
3/22

SUNDAYS

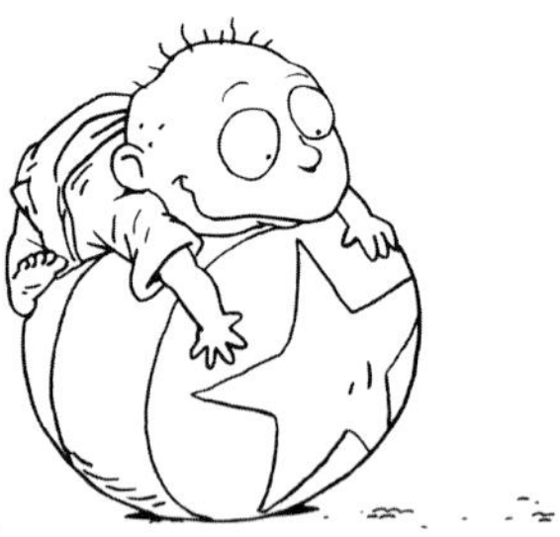

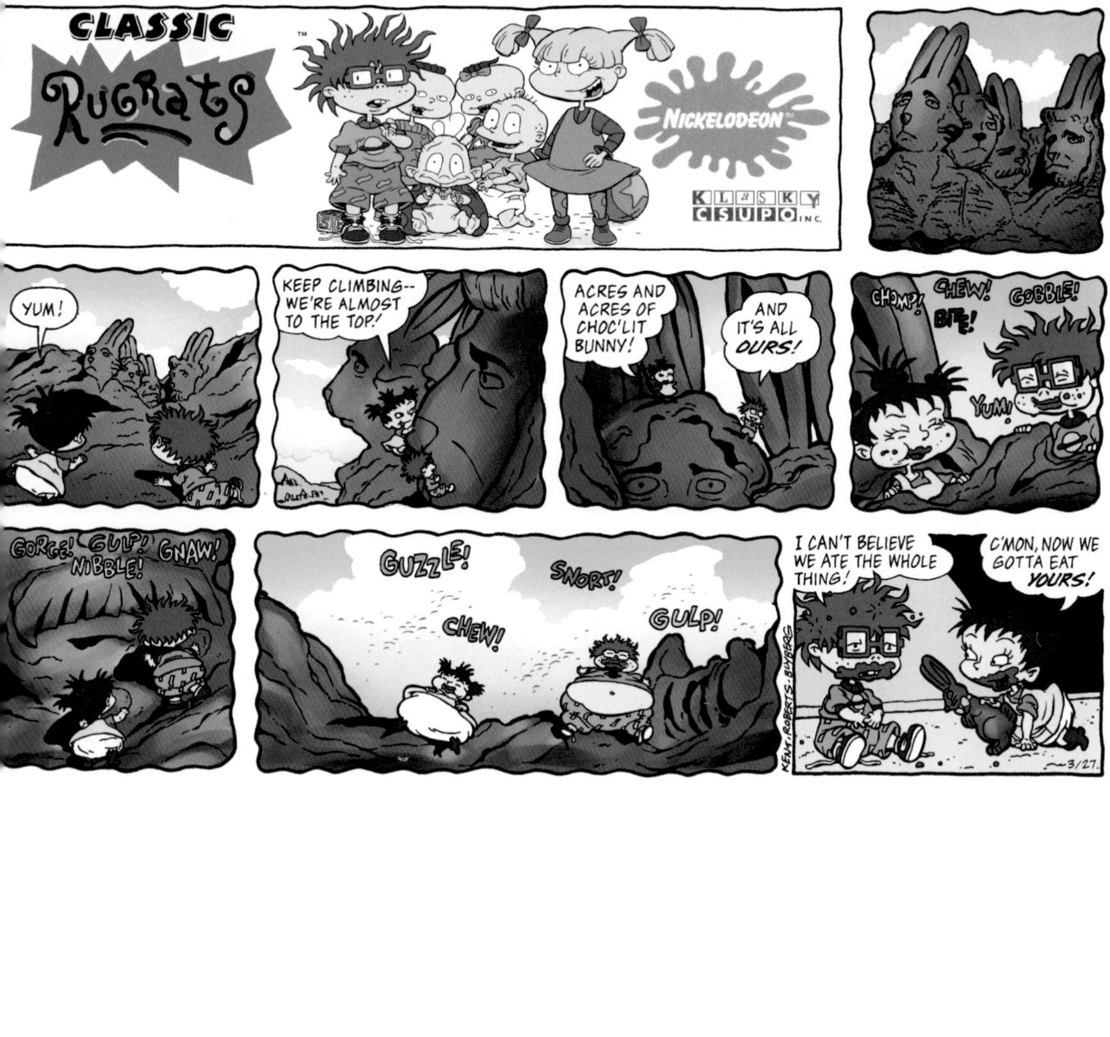
CLASSIC
Rugrats
NICKELODEON
KLASKY CSUPO INC.
YUM!
KEEP CLIMBING-- WE'RE ALMOST TO THE TOP!
ACRES AND ACRES OF CHOC'LIT BUNNY!
AND IT'S ALL OURS!
CHOMP!
CHEW!
GOBBLE!
BITE!
YUM!
GORGE!
GULP!
NIBBLE!
GNAW!
GUZZLE!
SNORT!
CHEW!
GULP!
I CAN'T BELIEVE WE ATE THE WHOLE THING!
C'MON, NOW WE GOTTA EAT YOURS!
3/27

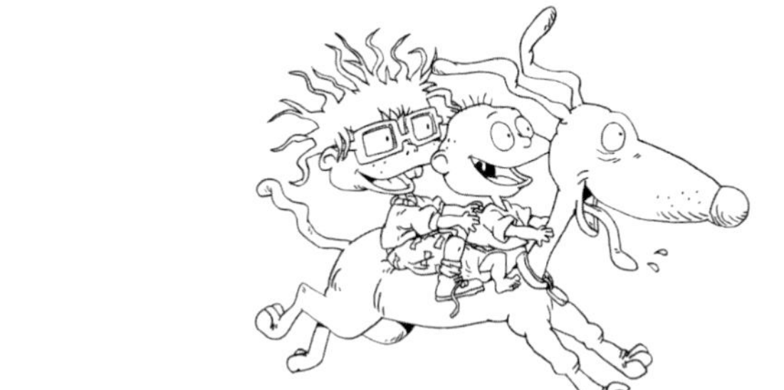

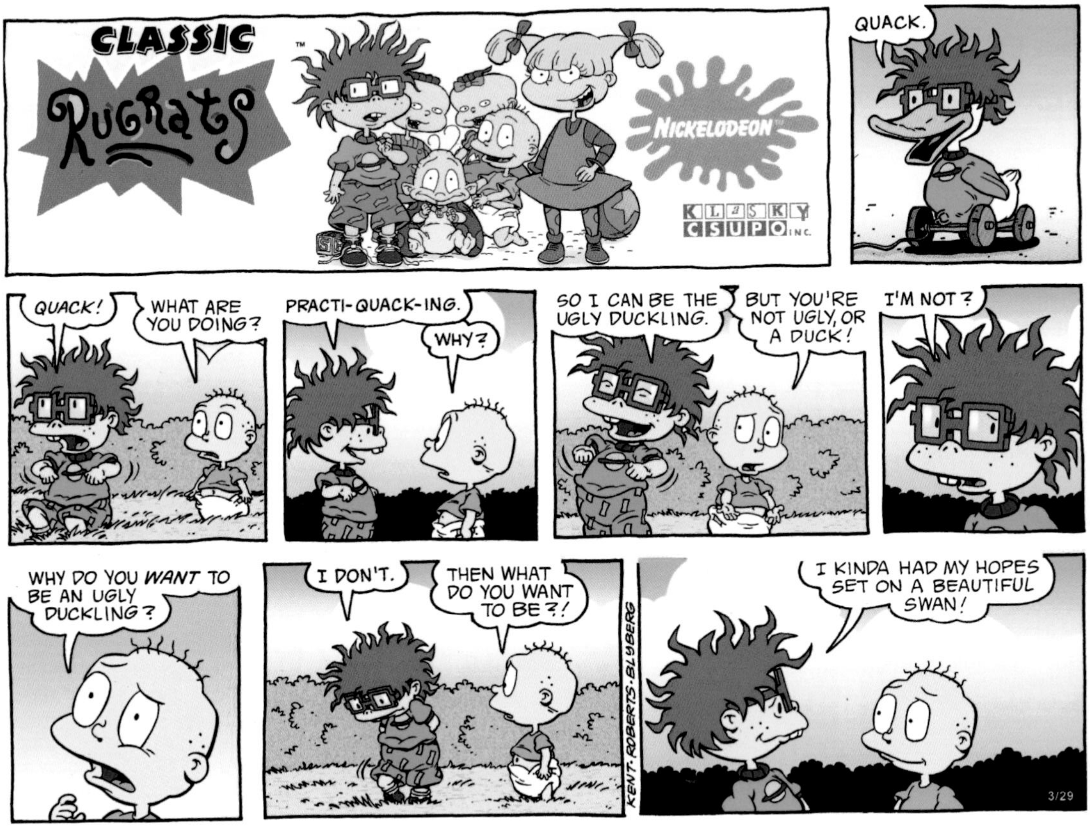
CLASSIC
Rugrats
NICKELODEON
KLASKY CSUPO INC.
QUACK.
QUACK!
WHAT ARE YOU DOING?
PRACTI-QUACK-ING.
WHY?
SO I CAN BE THE UGLY DUCKLING.
BUT YOU'RE NOT UGLY, OR A DUCK!
I'M NOT?
WHY DO YOU *WANT* TO BE AN UGLY DUCKLING?
I DON'T.
THEN WHAT DO YOU WANT TO BE?!
KENT·ROBERTS·BLYBERG
I KINDA HAD MY HOPES SET ON A BEAUTIFUL SWAN!
3/29

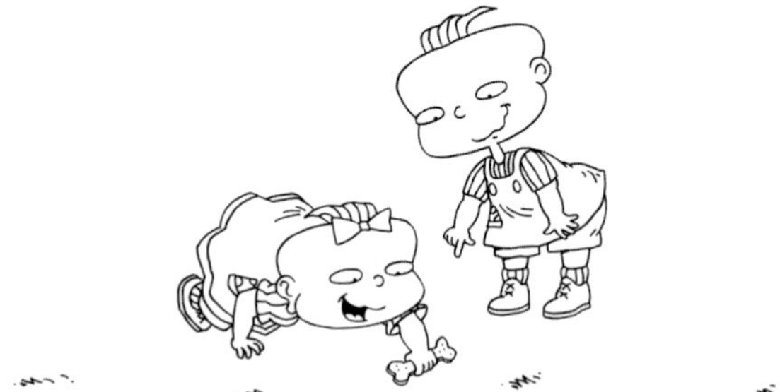

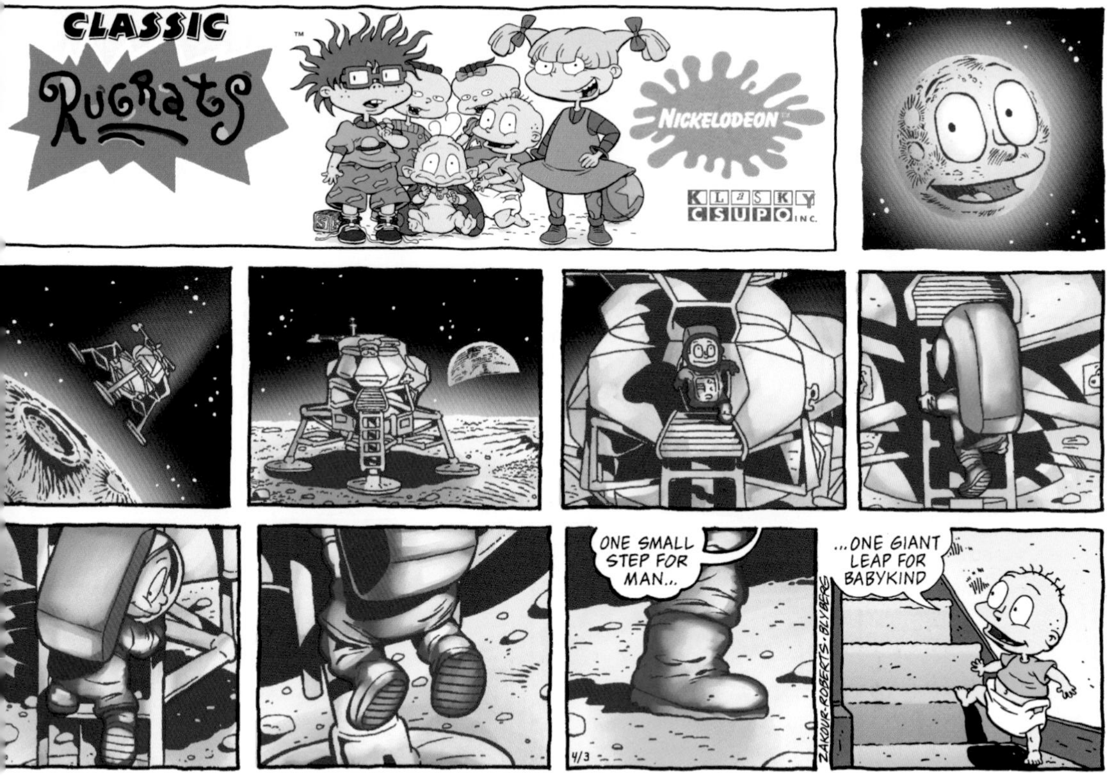
CLASSIC
Rugrats
NICKELODEON
KLASKY CSUPO INC.
ONE SMALL STEP FOR MAN..
...ONE GIANT LEAP FOR BABYKIND
4/3
ZAKOUR-ROBERTS-BLYBERG

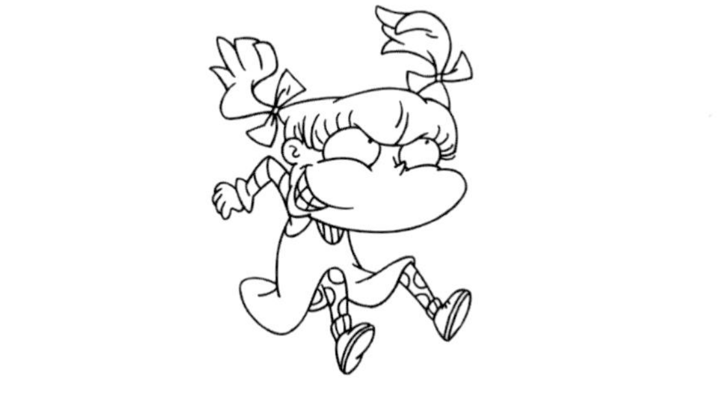

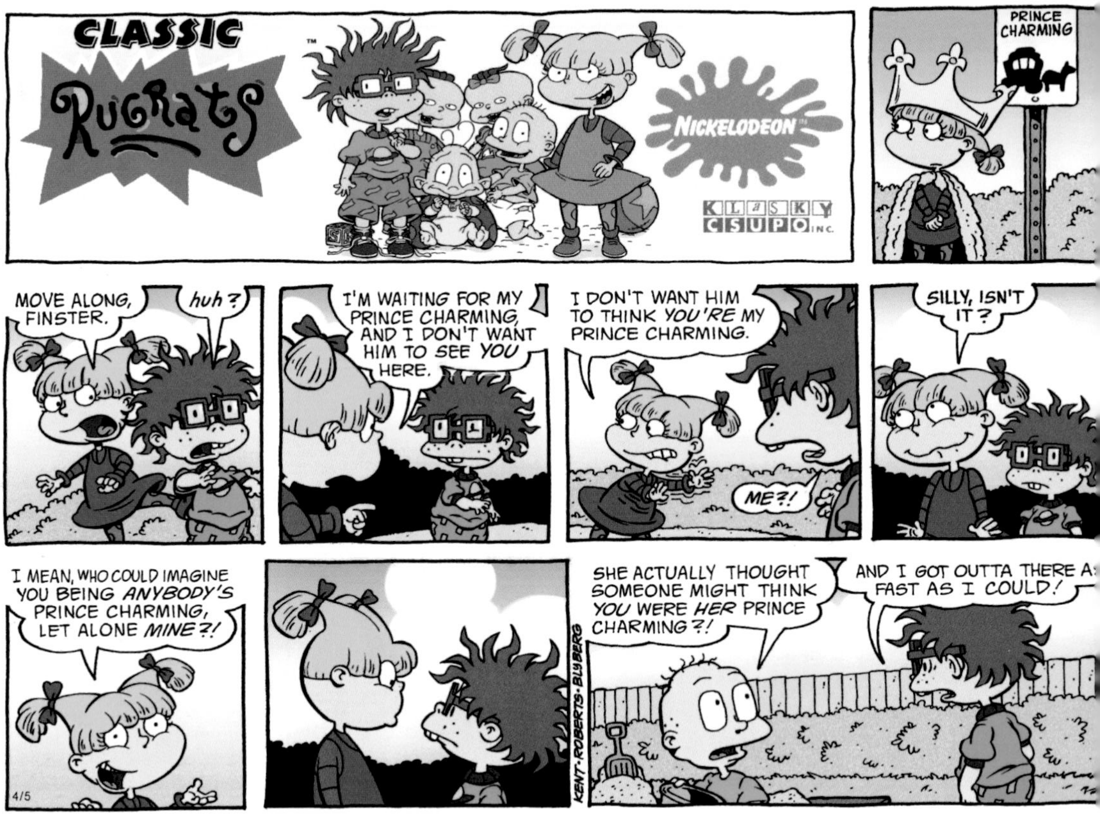
CLASSIC
Rugrats
NICKELODEON
KLASKY CSUPO INC.
PRINCE CHARMING
MOVE ALONG, FINSTER.
huh?
I'M WAITING FOR MY PRINCE CHARMING, AND I DON'T WANT HIM TO SEE YOU HERE.
I DON'T WANT HIM TO THINK YOU'RE MY PRINCE CHARMING.
ME?!
SILLY, ISN'T IT?
I MEAN, WHO COULD IMAGINE YOU BEING ANYBODY'S PRINCE CHARMING, LET ALONE MINE?!
4/5
KENT-ROBERTS-BLYBERG
SHE ACTUALLY THOUGHT SOMEONE MIGHT THINK YOU WERE HER PRINCE CHARMING?!
AND I GOT OUTTA THERE AS FAST AS I COULD!

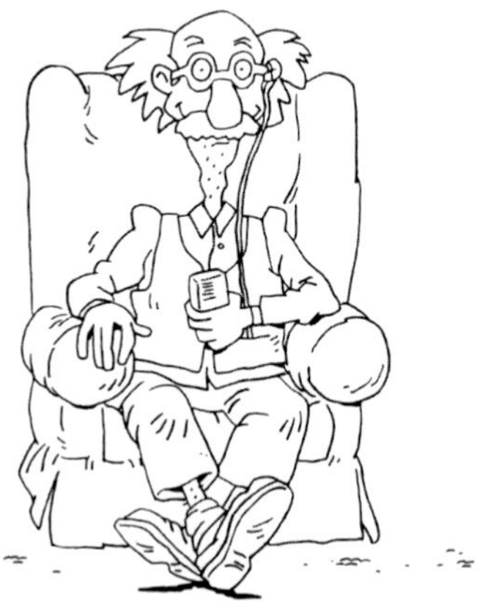

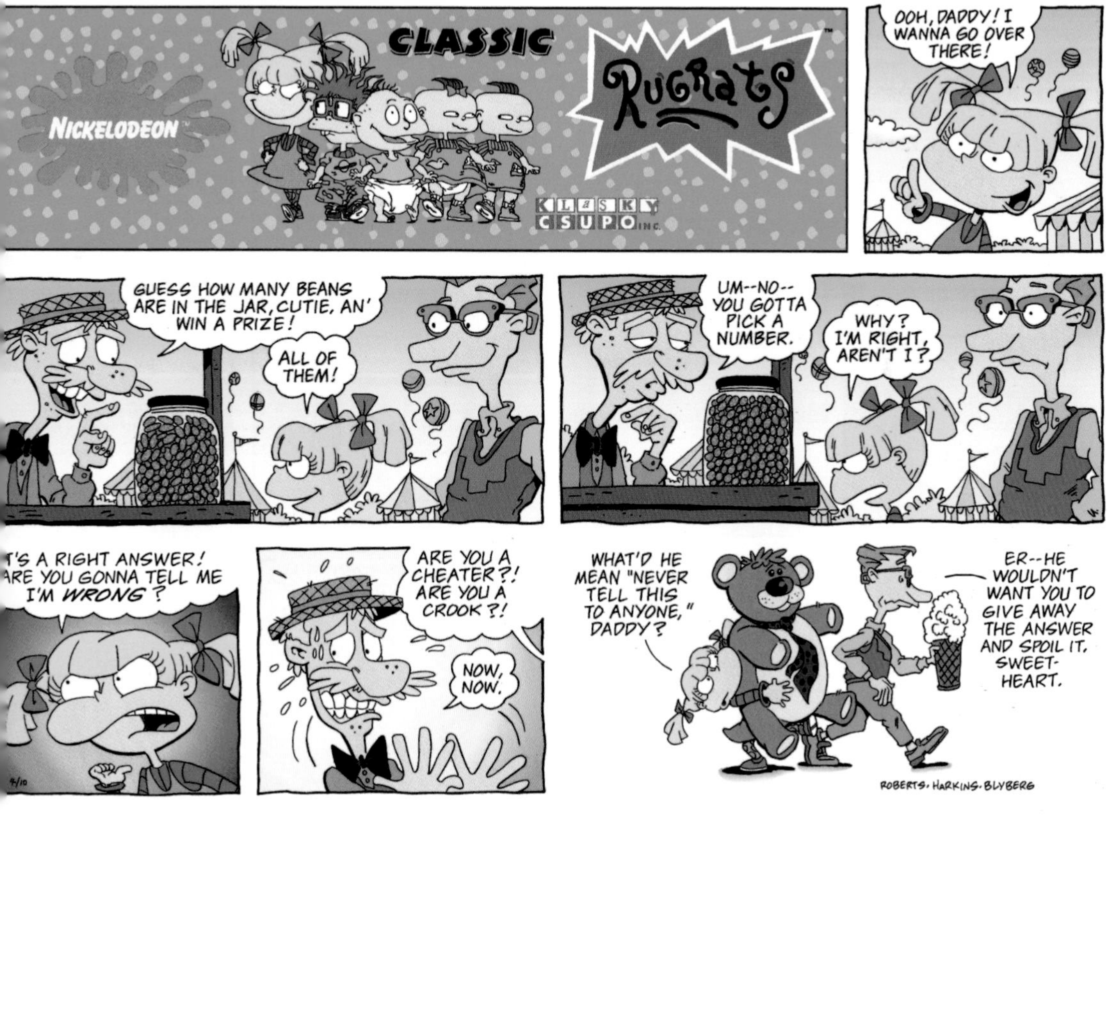
NICKELODEON
CLASSIC
Rugrats
KLASKY CSUPO INC.
OOH, DADDY! I WANNA GO OVER THERE!
GUESS HOW MANY BEANS ARE IN THE JAR, CUTIE, AN' WIN A PRIZE!
ALL OF THEM!
UM--NO-- YOU GOTTA PICK A NUMBER.
WHY? I'M RIGHT, AREN'T I?
T'S A RIGHT ANSWER! ARE YOU GONNA TELL ME I'M *WRONG*?
ARE YOU A CHEATER?! ARE YOU A CROOK?!
NOW, NOW.
WHAT'D HE MEAN "NEVER TELL THIS TO ANYONE," DADDY?
ER--HE WOULDN'T WANT YOU TO GIVE AWAY THE ANSWER AND SPOIL IT, SWEET-HEART.
4/10
ROBERTS · HARKINS · BLYBERG

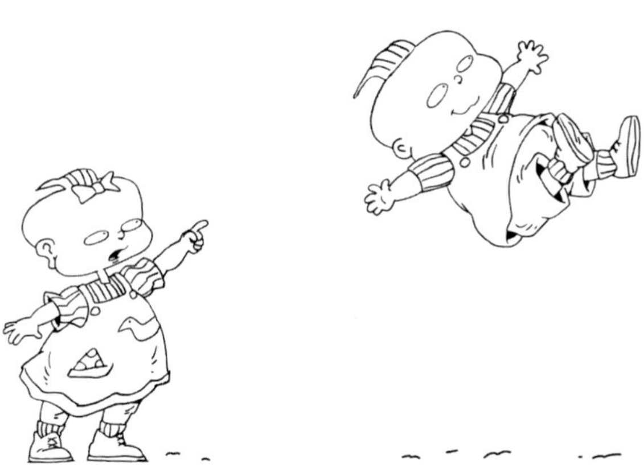

SUNDAYS

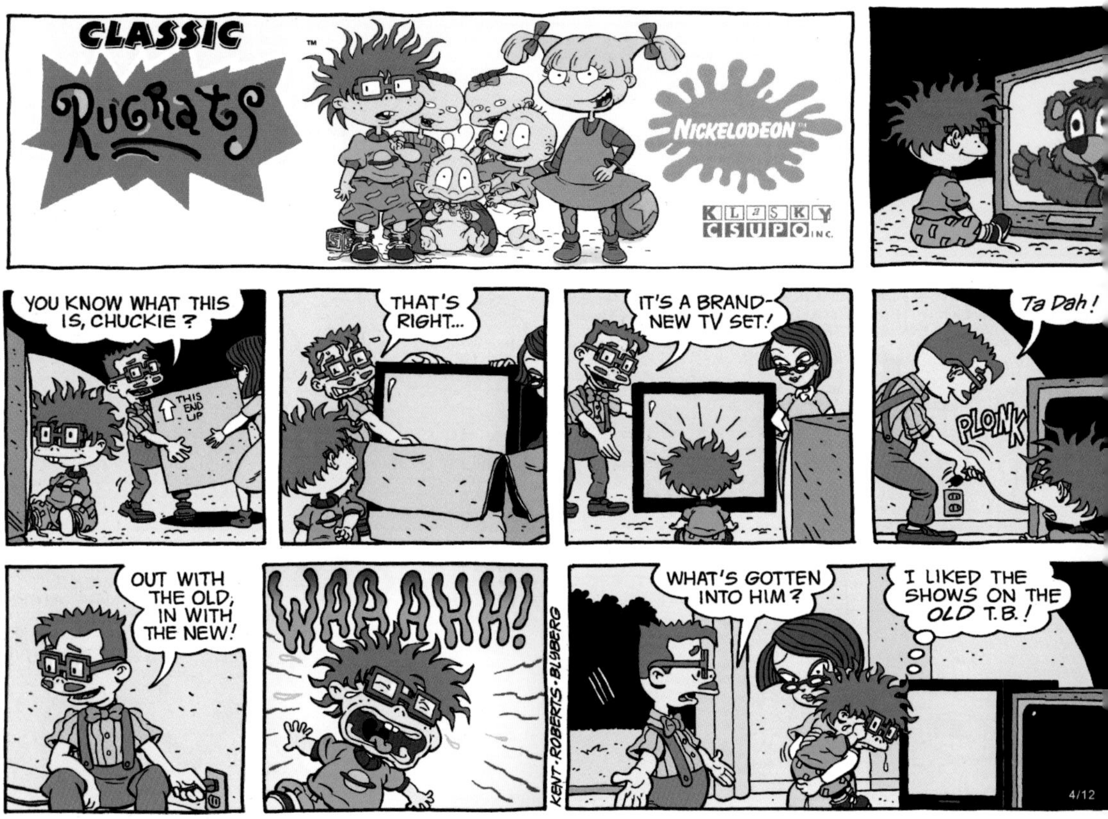
CLASSIC
Rugrats
NICKELODEON
KLASKY CSUPO INC.
YOU KNOW WHAT THIS IS, CHUCKIE?
THIS END UP
THAT'S RIGHT...
IT'S A BRAND-NEW TV SET!
Ta Dah!
PLONK
OUT WITH THE OLD, IN WITH THE NEW!
WAAAHH!
KENT·ROBERTS·BLYBERG
WHAT'S GOTTEN INTO HIM?
I LIKED THE SHOWS ON THE OLD T.B.!
4/12

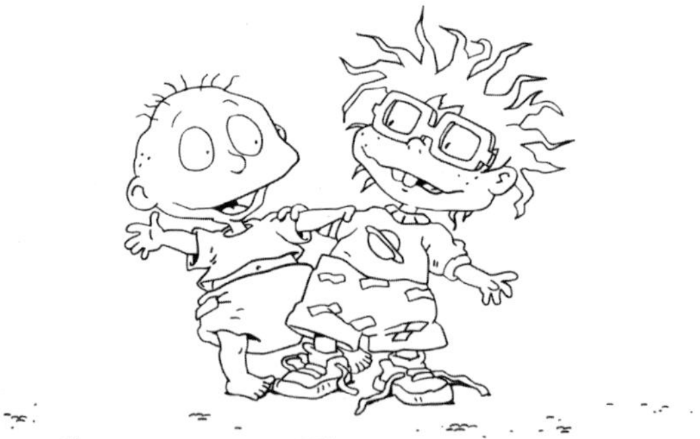

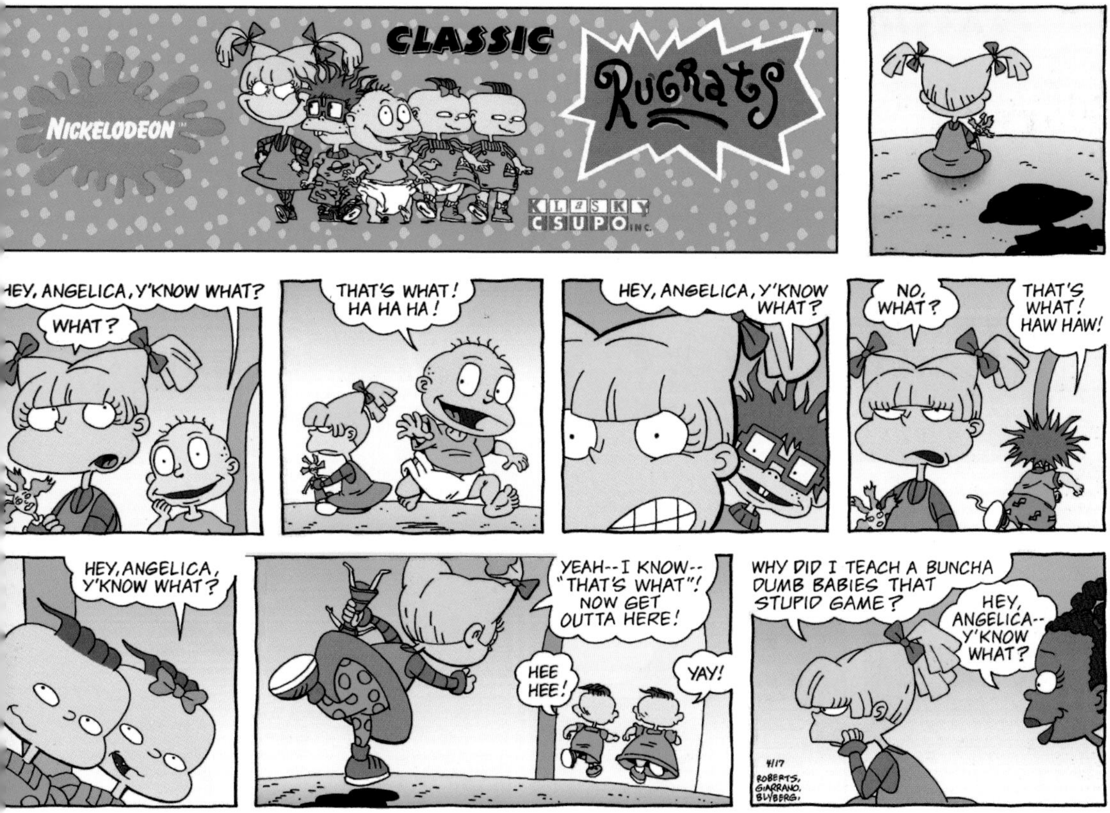
NICKELODEON
CLASSIC
Rugrats
KLASKY CSUPO INC.
HEY, ANGELICA, Y'KNOW WHAT?
WHAT?
THAT'S WHAT! HA HA HA!
HEY, ANGELICA, Y'KNOW WHAT?
NO, WHAT?
THAT'S WHAT! HAW HAW!
HEY, ANGELICA, Y'KNOW WHAT?
YEAH--I KNOW-- "THAT'S WHAT"! NOW GET OUTTA HERE!
HEE HEE!
YAY!
WHY DID I TEACH A BUNCHA DUMB BABIES THAT STUPID GAME?
HEY, ANGELICA-- Y'KNOW WHAT?
4/17
ROBERTS, GIARRANO, BLYBERG.

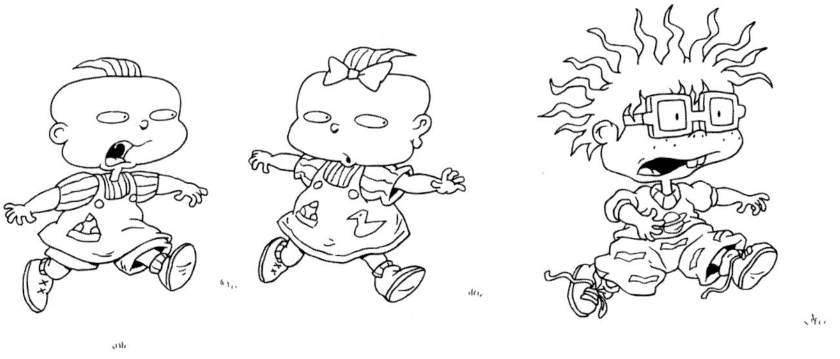

SUNDAYS

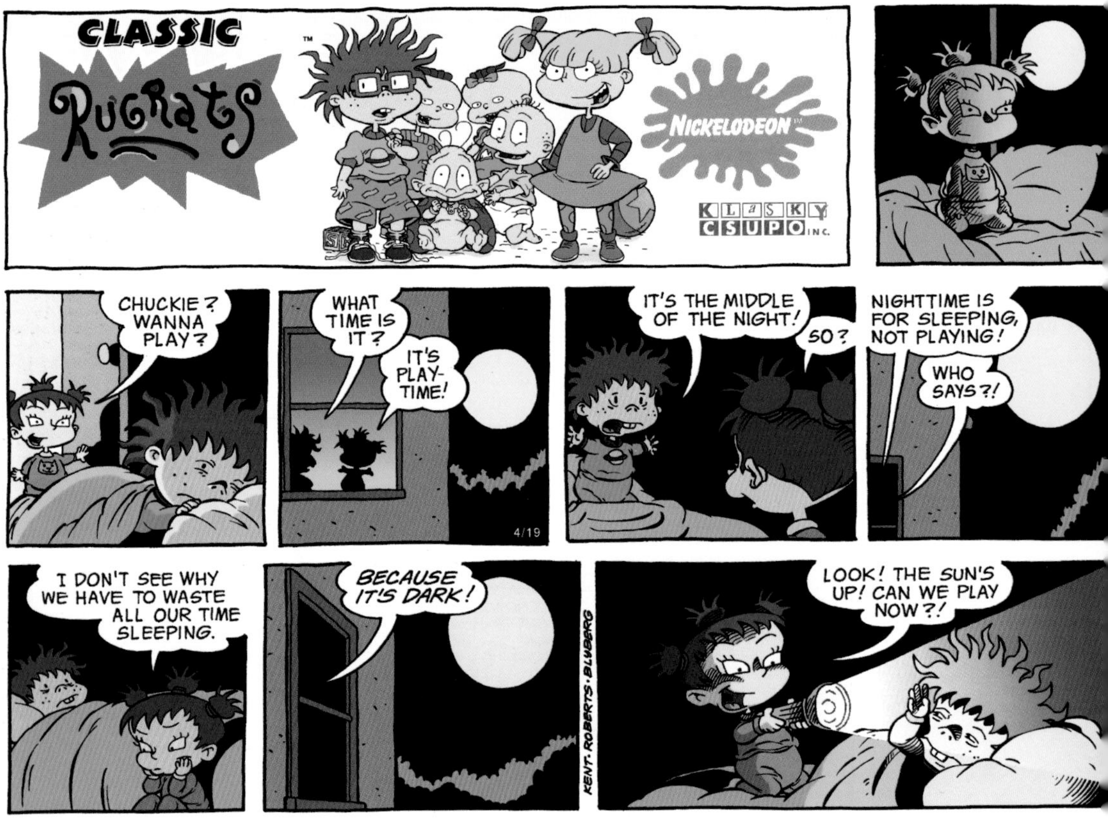
CLASSIC Rugrats
NICKELODEON
KLaSKY CSUPO INC.
CHUCKIE? WANNA PLAY?
WHAT TIME IS IT?
IT'S PLAY-TIME!
4/19
IT'S THE MIDDLE OF THE NIGHT!
SO?
NIGHTTIME IS FOR SLEEPING, NOT PLAYING!
WHO SAYS?!
I DON'T SEE WHY WE HAVE TO WASTE ALL OUR TIME SLEEPING.
BECAUSE IT'S DARK!
KENT·ROBERTS·BLUBERG
LOOK! THE SUN'S UP! CAN WE PLAY NOW?!

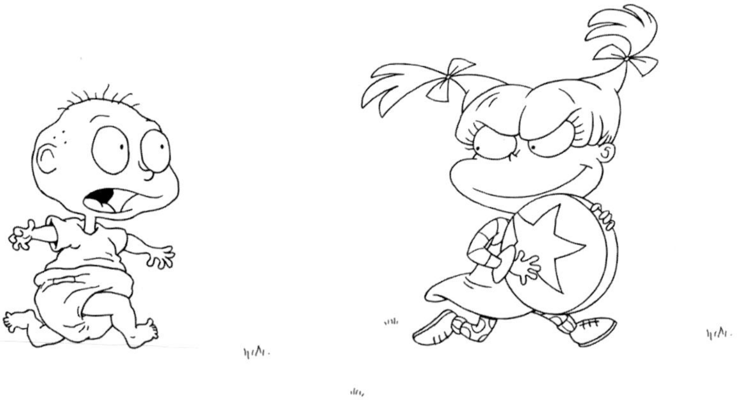

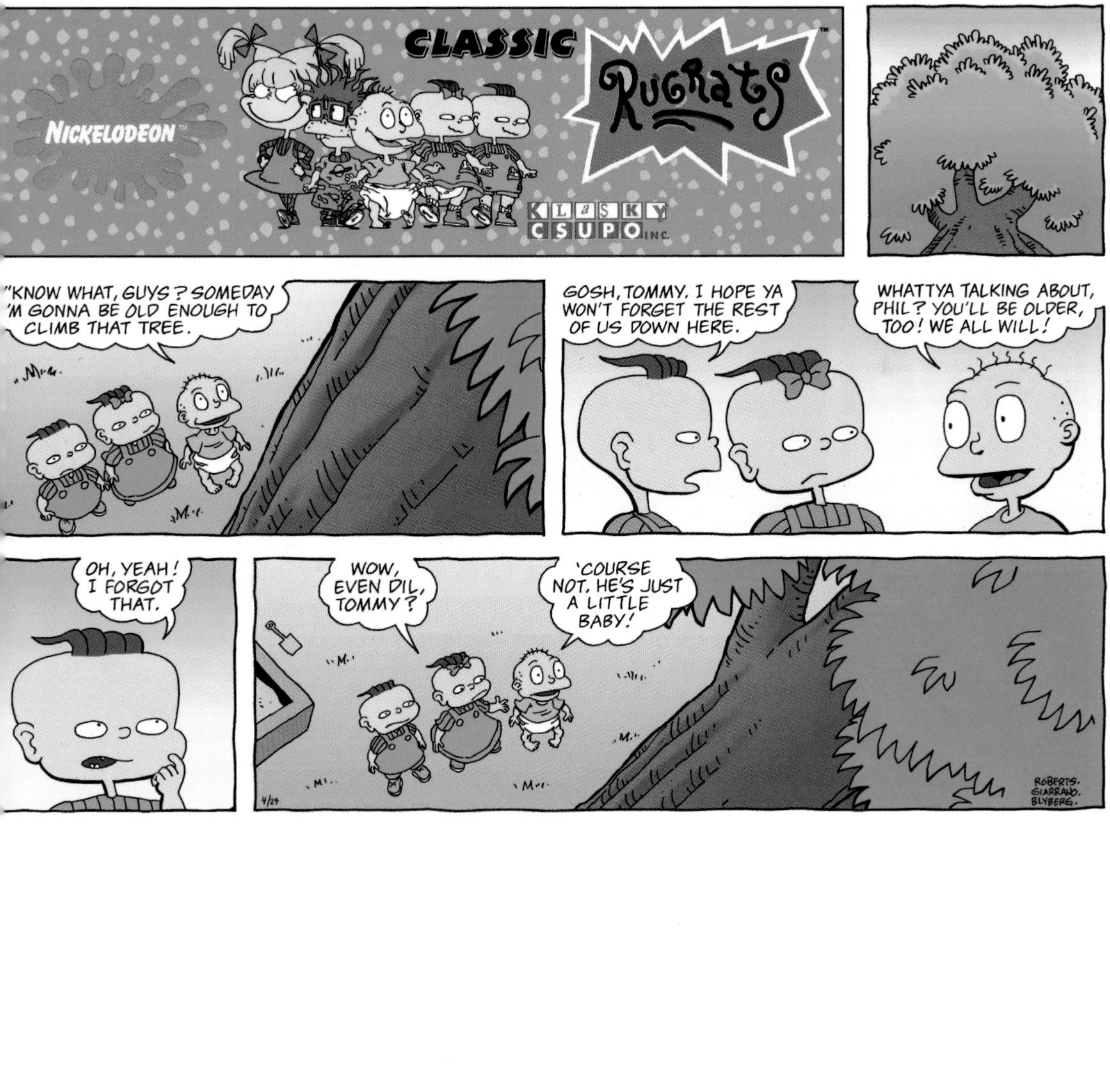
NICKELODEON
CLASSIC
Rugrats
KLASKY CSUPO INC.
KNOW WHAT, GUYS? SOMEDAY
M GONNA BE OLD ENOUGH TO
CLIMB THAT TREE.
GOSH, TOMMY. I HOPE YA WON'T FORGET THE REST OF US DOWN HERE.
WHATTYA TALKING ABOUT, PHIL? YOU'LL BE OLDER, TOO! WE ALL WILL!
OH, YEAH! I FORGOT THAT.
WOW, EVEN DIL, TOMMY?
'COURSE NOT. HE'S JUST A LITTLE BABY!
ROBERTS. GIARRANO. BLYBERG.

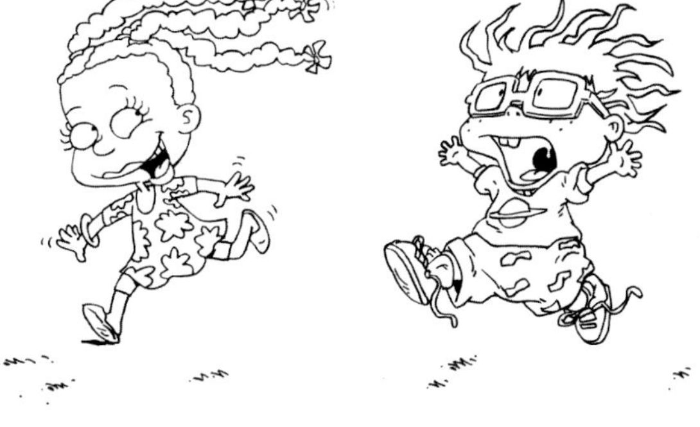

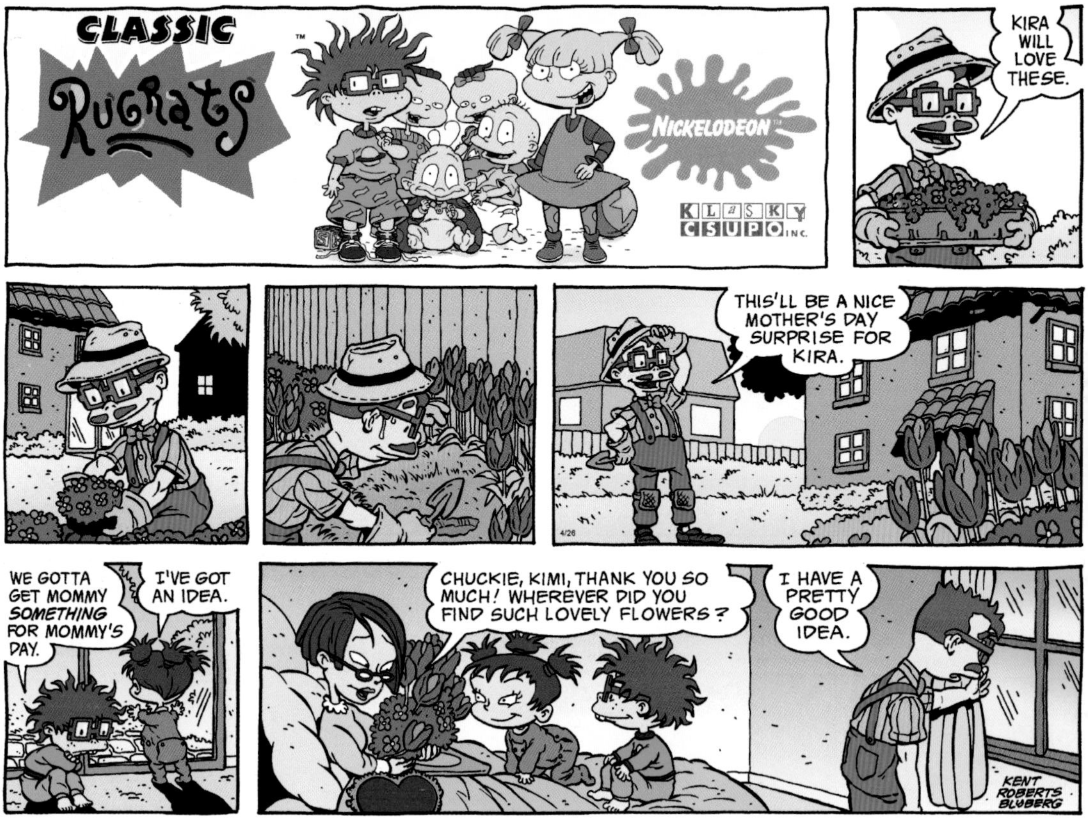
CLASSIC
Rugrats
NICKELODEON
KLASKY CSUPO INC.
KIRA WILL LOVE THESE.
THIS'LL BE A NICE MOTHER'S DAY SURPRISE FOR KIRA.
4/26
WE GOTTA GET MOMMY *SOMETHING* FOR MOMMY'S DAY.
I'VE GOT AN IDEA.
CHUCKIE, KIMI, THANK YOU SO MUCH! WHEREVER DID YOU FIND SUCH LOVELY FLOWERS?
I HAVE A PRETTY GOOD IDEA.
KENT ROBERTS BLUBERG

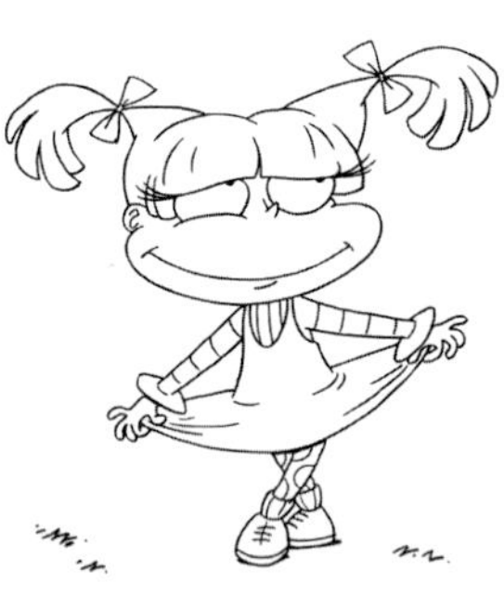

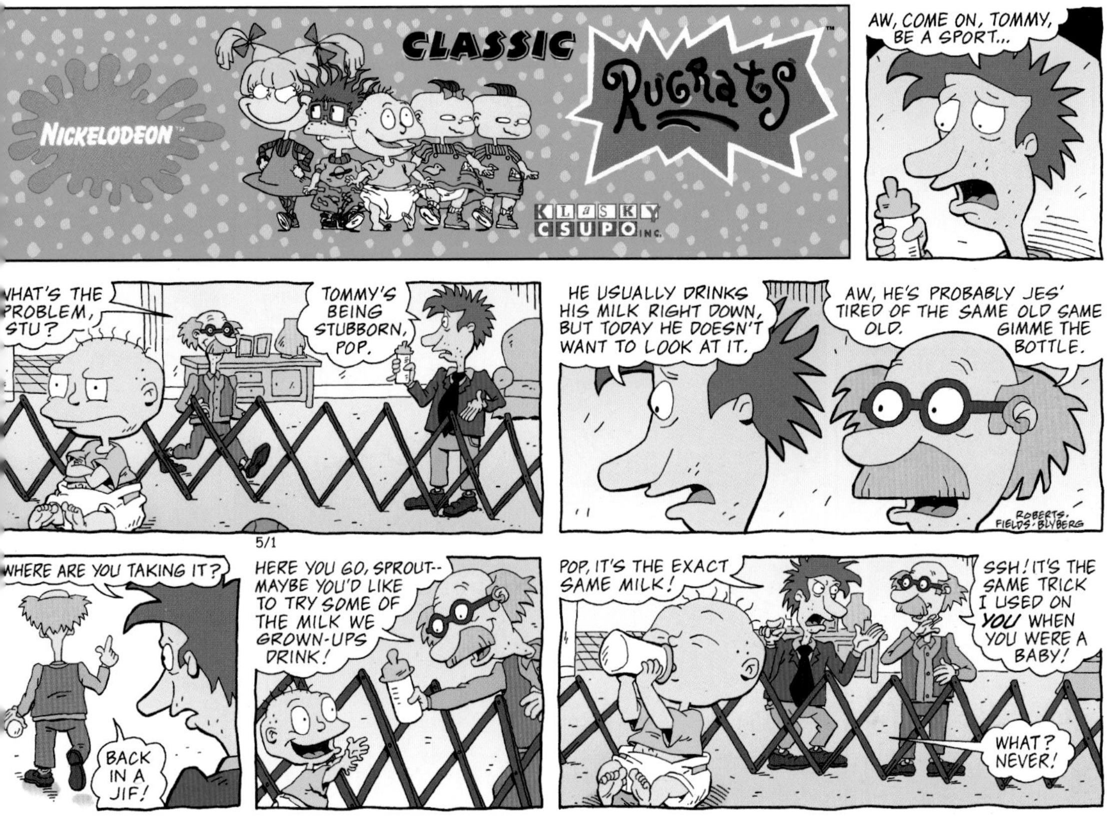
NICKELODEON
CLASSIC
Rugrats
KLaSKY CSUPO INC.
AW, COME ON, TOMMY, BE A SPORT...
WHAT'S THE PROBLEM, STU?
TOMMY'S BEING STUBBORN, POP.
HE USUALLY DRINKS HIS MILK RIGHT DOWN, BUT TODAY HE DOESN'T WANT TO LOOK AT IT.
AW, HE'S PROBABLY JES' TIRED OF THE SAME OLD SAME OLD. GIMME THE BOTTLE.
ROBERTS. FIELDS·BLYBERG
5/1
WHERE ARE YOU TAKING IT?
BACK IN A JIF!
HERE YOU GO, SPROUT-- MAYBE YOU'D LIKE TO TRY SOME OF THE MILK WE GROWN-UPS DRINK!
POP, IT'S THE EXACT SAME MILK!
SSH! IT'S THE SAME TRICK I USED ON YOU WHEN YOU WERE A BABY!
WHAT? NEVER!

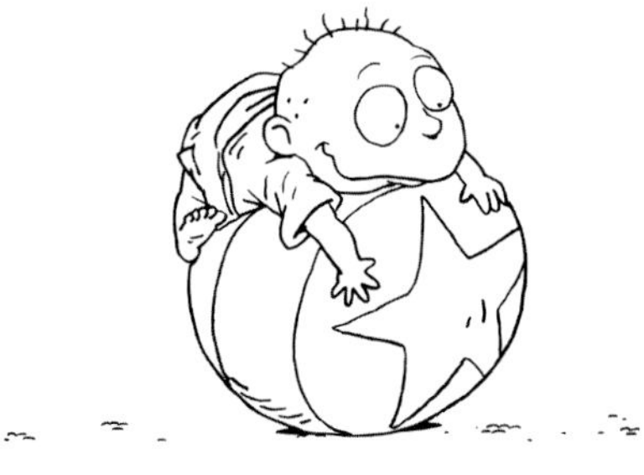

SUNDAYS

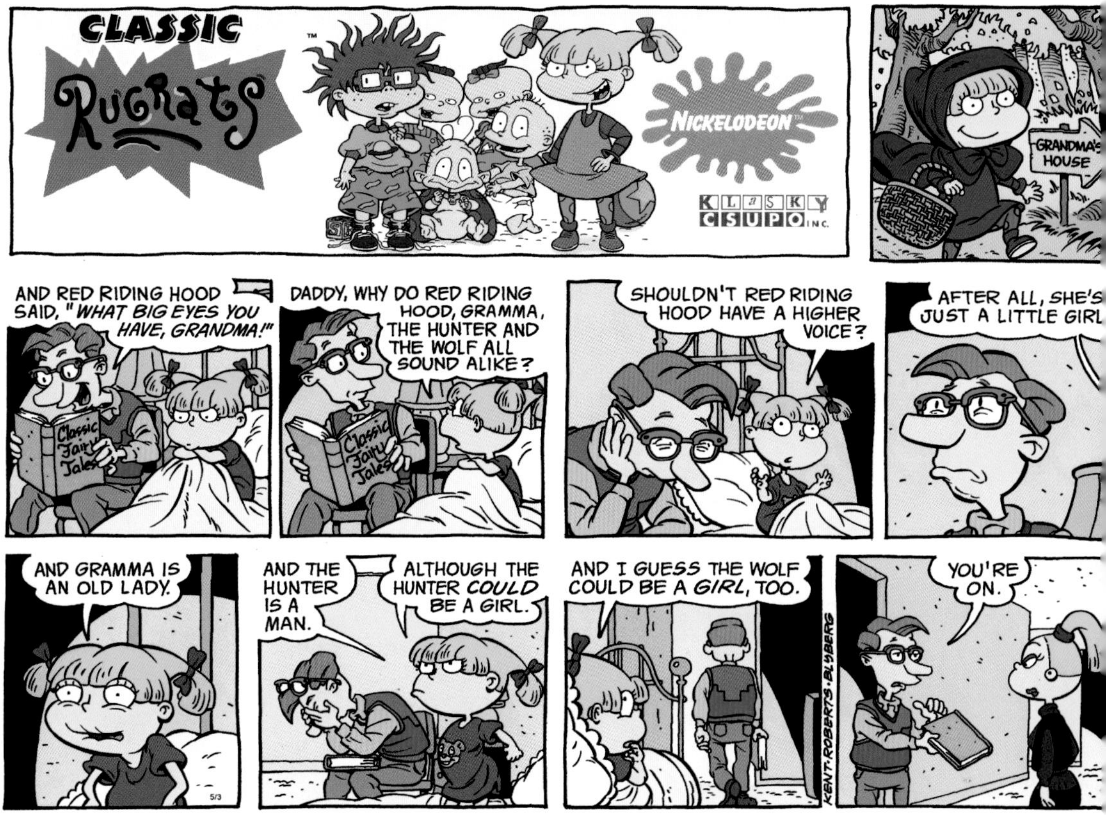
CLASSIC
Rugrats
NICKELODEON
KLASKY CSUPO INC.
GRANDMA'S HOUSE
AND RED RIDING HOOD SAID, "*WHAT BIG EYES YOU HAVE, GRANDMA!*"
Classic Fairy Tales
DADDY, WHY DO RED RIDING HOOD, GRAMMA, THE HUNTER AND THE WOLF ALL SOUND ALIKE?
SHOULDN'T RED RIDING HOOD HAVE A HIGHER VOICE?
AFTER ALL, *SHE'S* JUST A LITTLE GIRL
AND GRAMMA IS AN OLD LADY.
5/3
AND THE HUNTER IS A MAN.
ALTHOUGH THE HUNTER *COULD* BE A GIRL.
AND I GUESS THE WOLF COULD BE A *GIRL*, TOO.
KENT·ROBERTS·BLYBERG
YOU'RE ON.

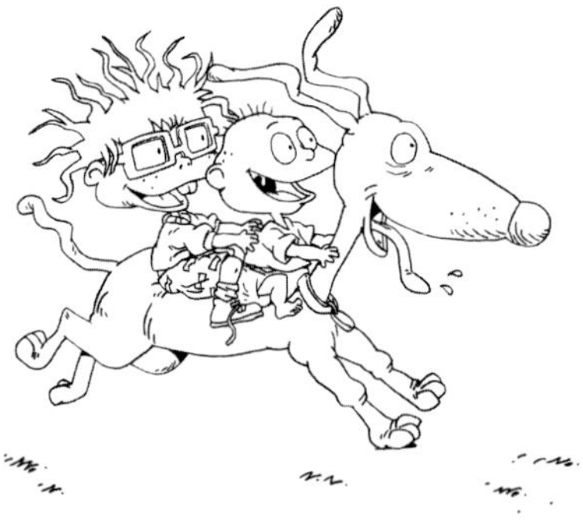

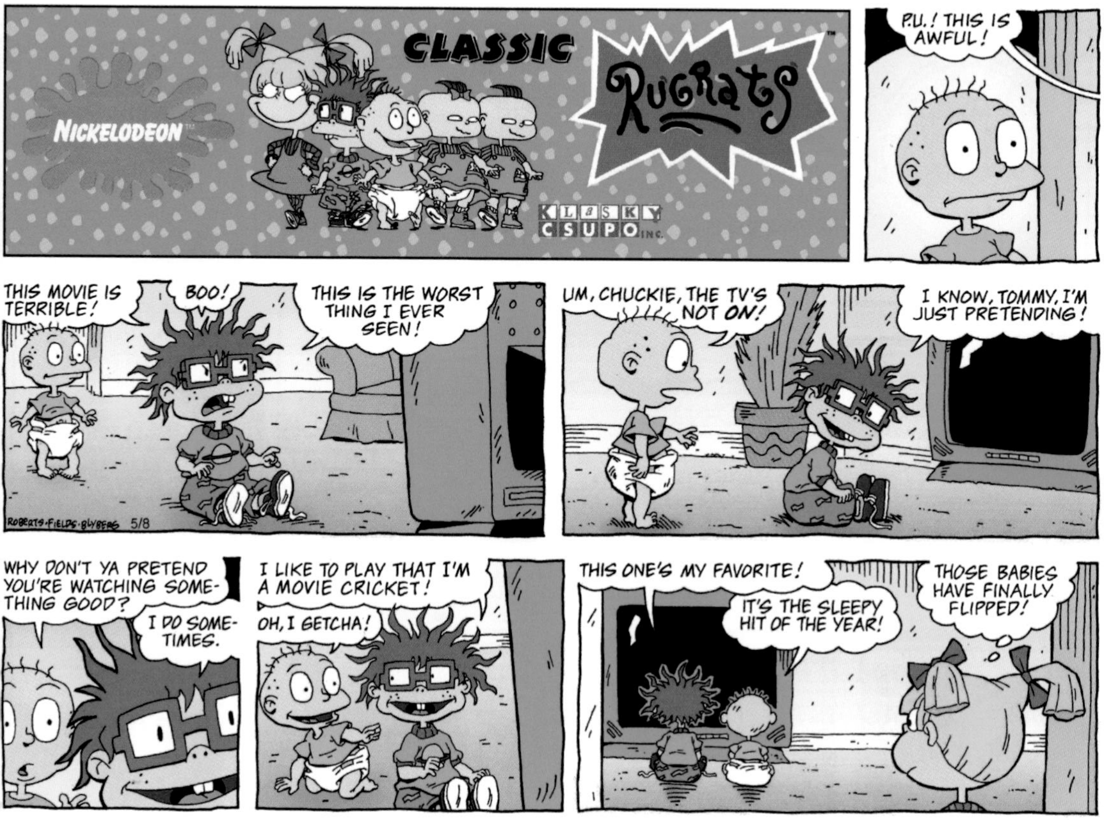
NICKELODEON
CLASSIC
Rugrats
KLASKY CSUPO INC.
P.U.! THIS IS AWFUL!
THIS MOVIE IS TERRIBLE!
BOO!
THIS IS THE WORST THING I EVER SEEN!
ROBERTS·FIELDS·BLYBERG 5/8
UM, CHUCKIE, THE TV'S NOT ON!
I KNOW, TOMMY, I'M JUST PRETENDING!
WHY DON'T YA PRETEND YOU'RE WATCHING SOME-THING GOOD?
I DO SOME-TIMES.
I LIKE TO PLAY THAT I'M A MOVIE CRICKET!
OH, I GETCHA!
THIS ONE'S MY FAVORITE!
IT'S THE SLEEPY HIT OF THE YEAR!
THOSE BABIES HAVE FINALLY FLIPPED!

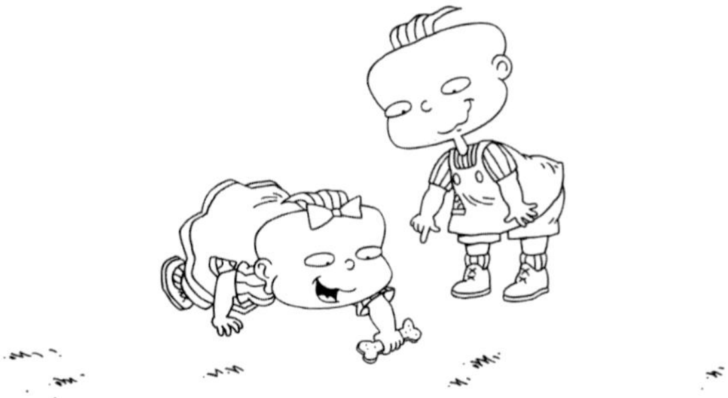

SUNDAYS

CLASSIC
Rugrats
NICKELODEON
KLASKY CSUPO INC.
I'M SLEEPY.
YAWN-- I GUESS IT'S BEDDY-BYE TIME.
5/10
ARE YOU NUTS?! YOU CAN'T GO TO BED YET, FINSTER!
IT'S STILL LIGHT OUT. YOUR BEDTIME ISN'T FOR HOURS!
IF YOU GO TO BED NOW, YOUR MOMMY AND DADDY WILL EXPECT YOU TO GO TO BED THIS EARLY EVERY DAY!
AND THEN YOUR BEDTIME WILL START GETTING EARLIER AND EARLIER!
REALLY?
THAT'S RIGHT, AND IF YOU KEEP THIS UP THEY MIGHT NEVER LET YOU OUT OF BED!
KENT-ROBERTS-BLYBERG
WELL, NOW I'M WIDE AWAKE.

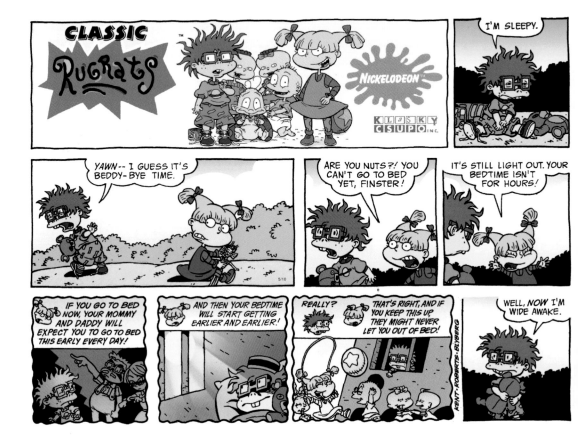

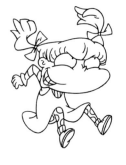

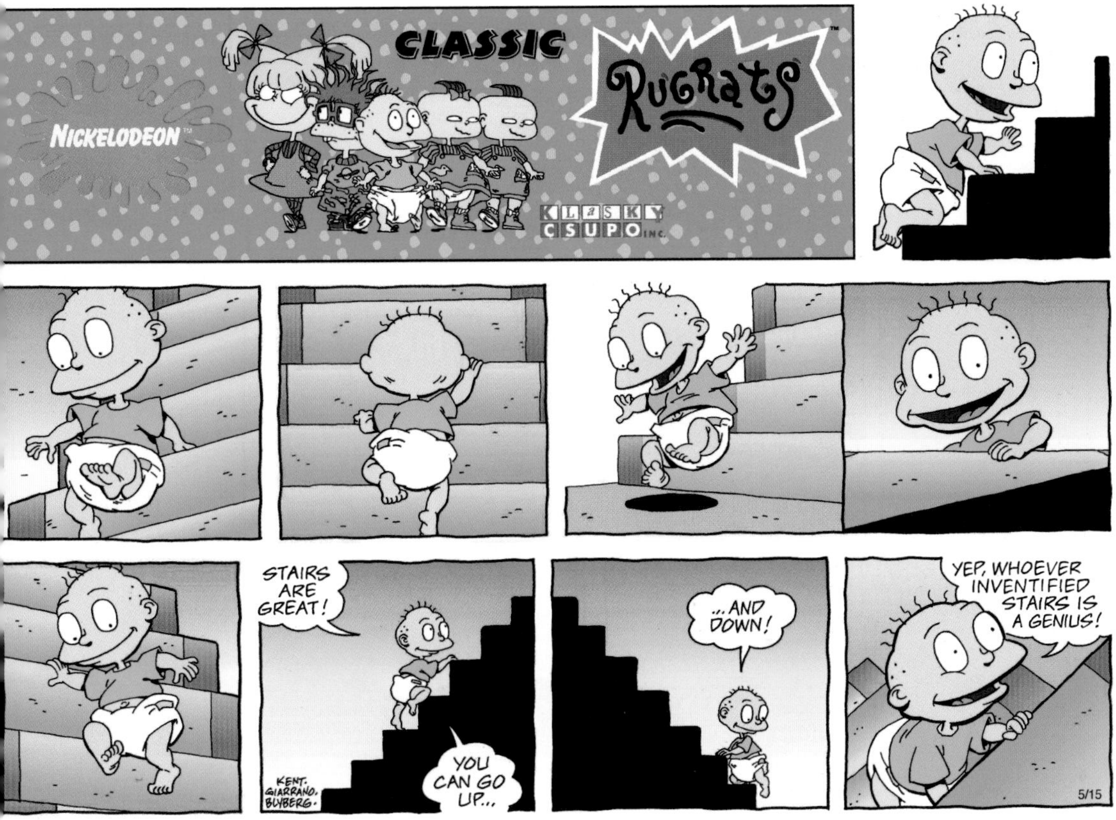
NICKELODEON
CLASSIC
RUGRATS
KLASKY CSUPO INC.
STAIRS ARE GREAT!
YOU CAN GO UP...
KENT. GIARRANO. BLYBERG.
...AND DOWN!
YEP, WHOEVER INVENTIFIED STAIRS IS A GENIUS!
5/15

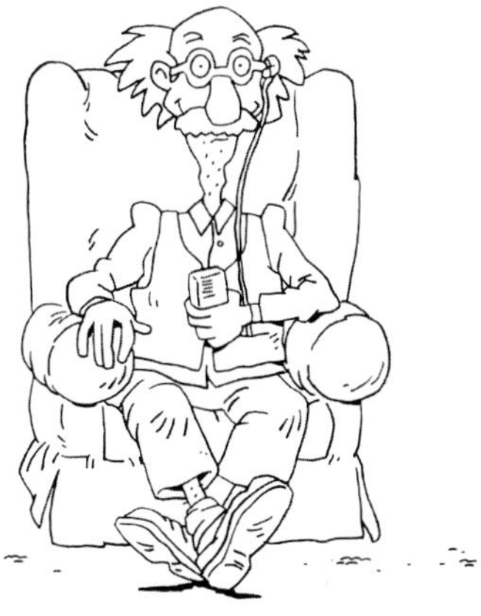

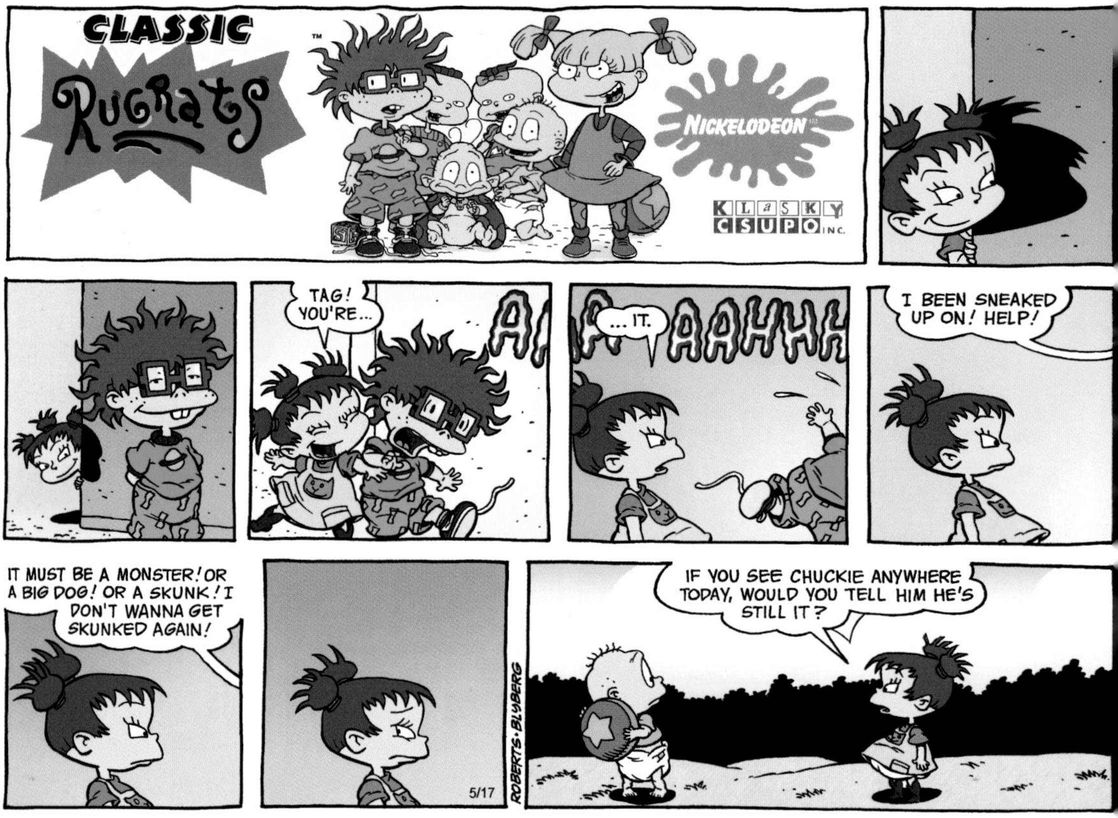

CLASSIC
Rugrats
NICKELODEON
KLASKY CSUPO INC.
TAG! YOU'RE...
... IT.
AAHHH
I BEEN SNEAKED UP ON! HELP!
IT MUST BE A MONSTER! OR A BIG DOG! OR A SKUNK! I DON'T WANNA GET SKUNKED AGAIN!
5/17
ROBERTS·BLYBERG
IF YOU SEE CHUCKIE ANYWHERE TODAY, WOULD YOU TELL HIM HE'S STILL IT?

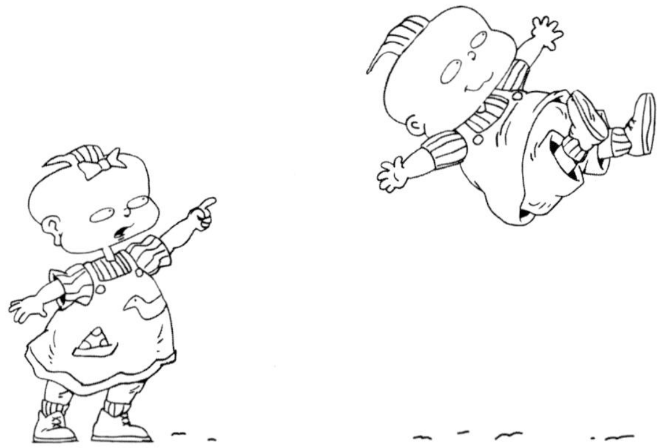

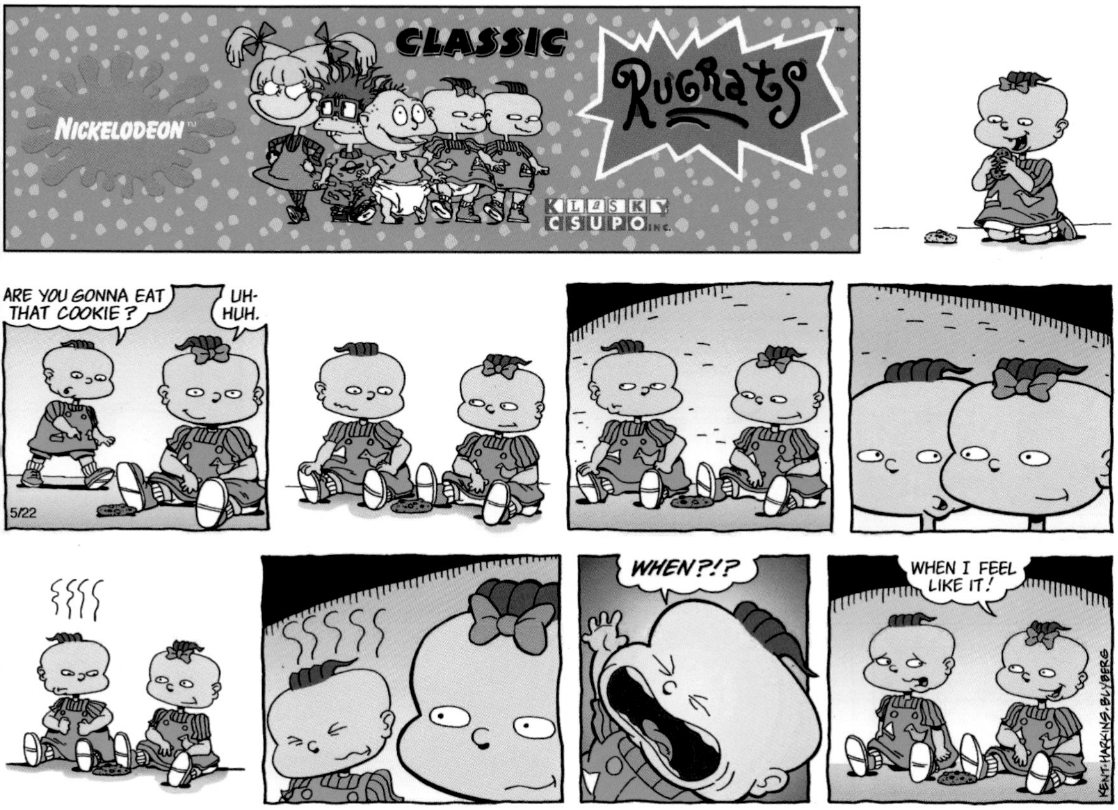
CLASSIC
NICKELODEON
Rugrats
KLASKY CSUPO INC.
ARE YOU GONNA EAT THAT COOKIE?
UH-HUH.
5/22
WHEN?!?
WHEN I FEEL LIKE IT!
KENT·HARKINS.BLYBERG

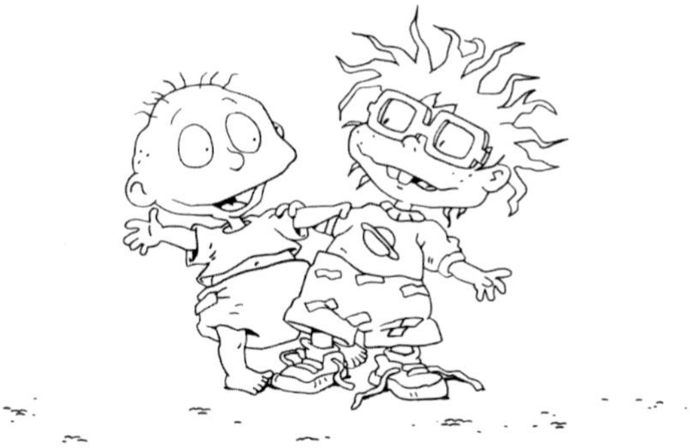

SUNDAYS

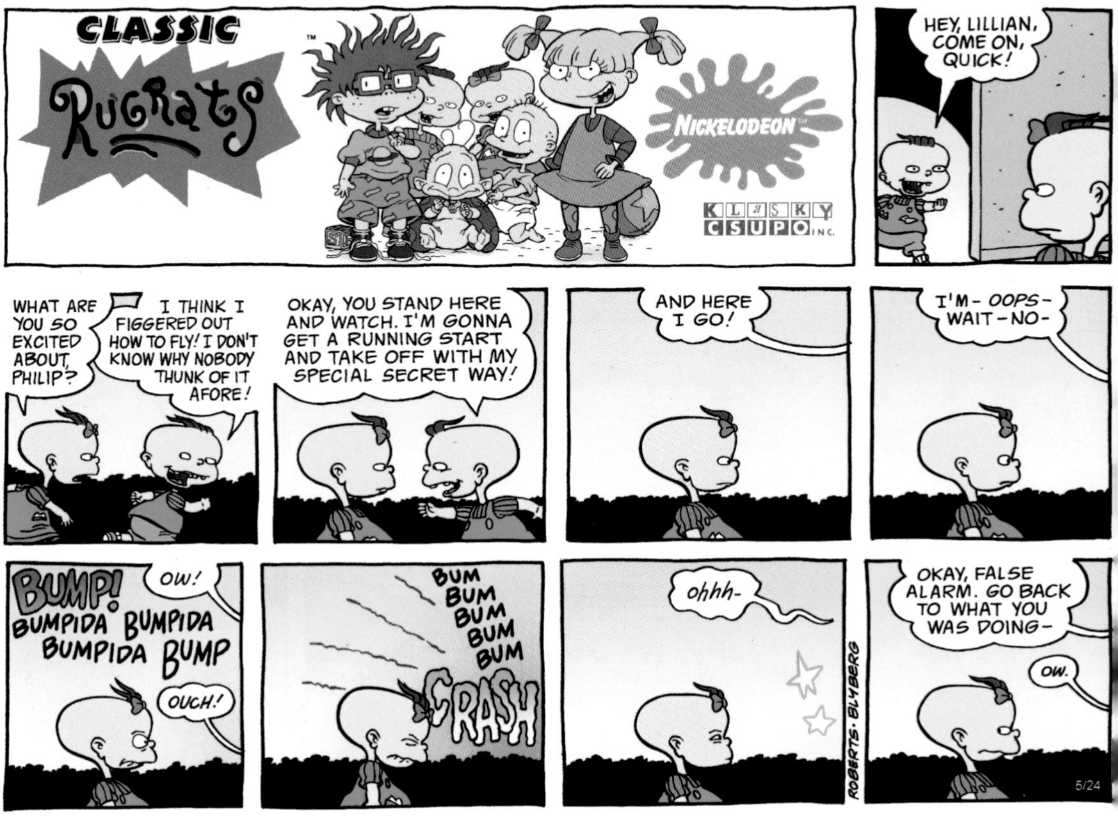
CLASSIC
Rugrats
NICKELODEON
KLASKY CSUPO INC.
HEY, LILLIAN, COME ON, QUICK!
WHAT ARE YOU SO EXCITED ABOUT, PHILIP?
I THINK I FIGGERED OUT HOW TO FLY! I DON'T KNOW WHY NOBODY THUNK OF IT AFORE!
OKAY, YOU STAND HERE AND WATCH. I'M GONNA GET A RUNNING START AND TAKE OFF WITH MY SPECIAL SECRET WAY!
AND HERE I GO!
I'M- OOPS- WAIT-NO-
BUMP! BUMPIDA BUMPIDA BUMPIDA BUMP
OW!
OUCH!
BUM BUM BUM BUM BUM
CRASH
ohhh-
ROBERTS·BLYBERG
OKAY, FALSE ALARM. GO BACK TO WHAT YOU WAS DOING-
OW.
5/24

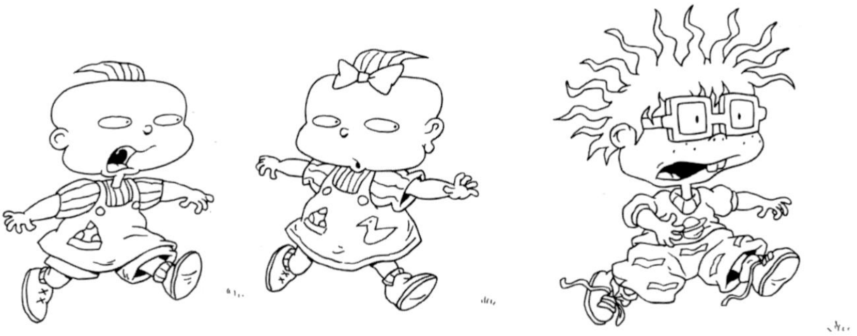

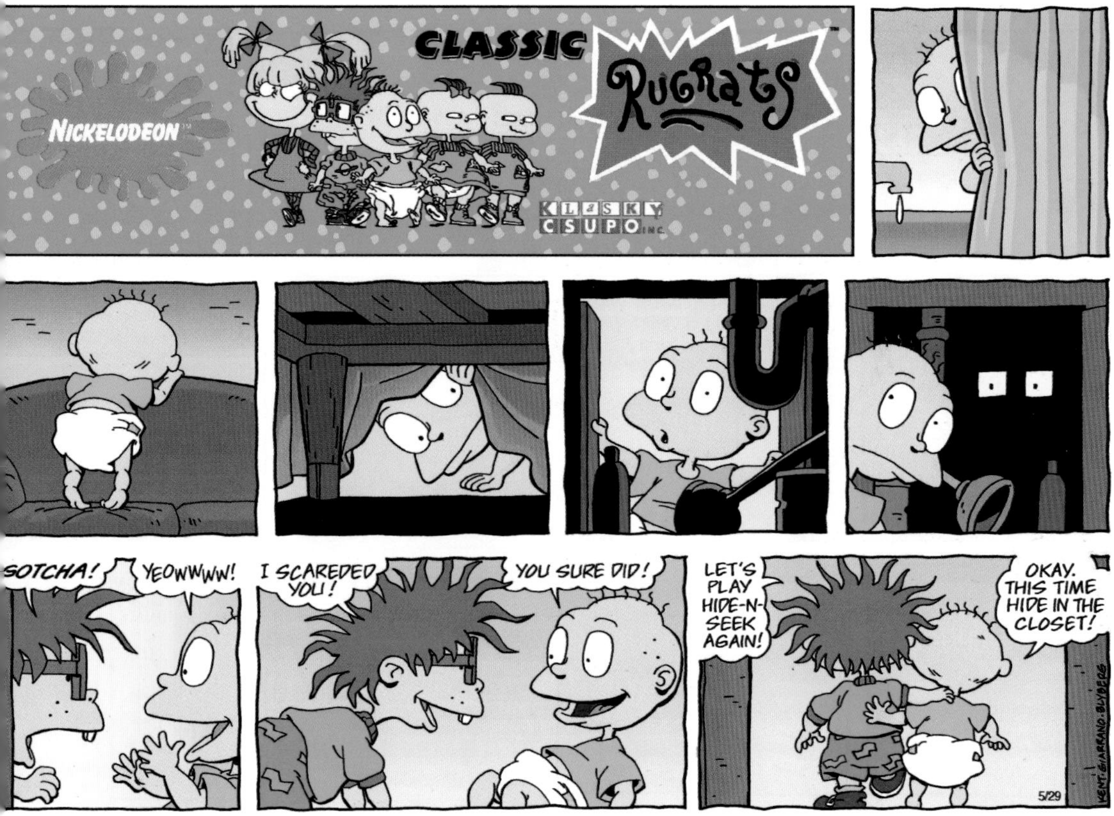

NICKELODEON
CLASSIC
Rugrats
KLASKY CSUPO INC.
GOTCHA!
YEOWWWW!
I SCAREDED YOU!
YOU SURE DID!
LET'S PLAY HIDE-N-SEEK AGAIN!
OKAY. THIS TIME HIDE IN THE CLOSET!
5/29

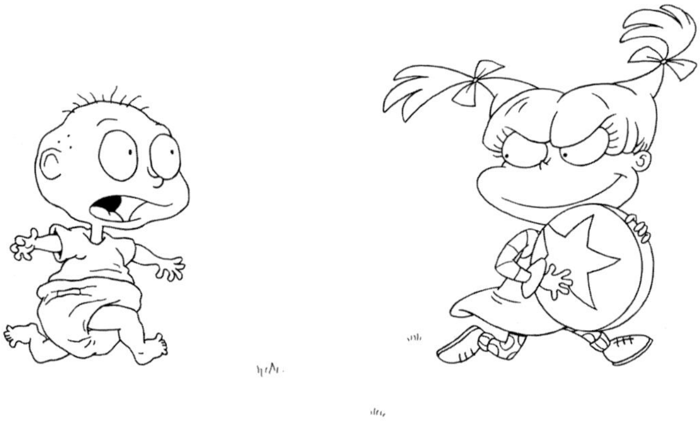

SUNDAYS

CLASSIC
RUGRATS
NICKELODEON
KLASKY CSUPO INC.
OWIE!
PINCH
HEY!
PINCH
JUST AS I THOUGHT.
WHAT WAS *THAT* FOR?
I WAS TESTING OUT A THEORY.
YOUR OWIE IS FUNNY, BUT *MY* OWIE HURTS.
5/31
HEY!
WHACK!
NO, *YOUR* OWIE IS FUNNY, AND *MINE* HURTS!
YOUR OWIE IS FUNNY!
NO, *YOUR* OWIE IS FUNNY!
OW!
OUCH!
HEY!
KENT·ROBERTS·BLYBERG
ACTUALLY, I DON'T THINK *ANYBODY'S* OWIE IS FUNNY.
I KNOW *MINE* ISN'T.

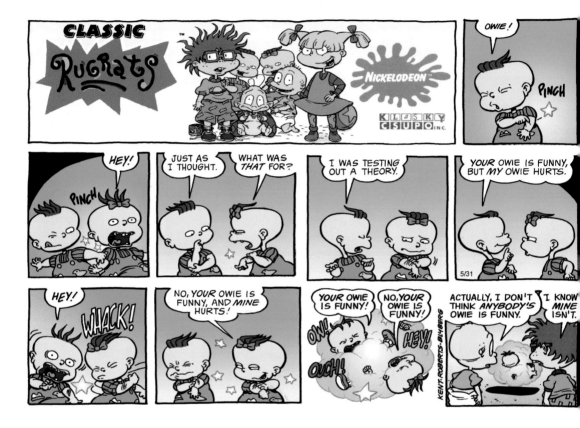

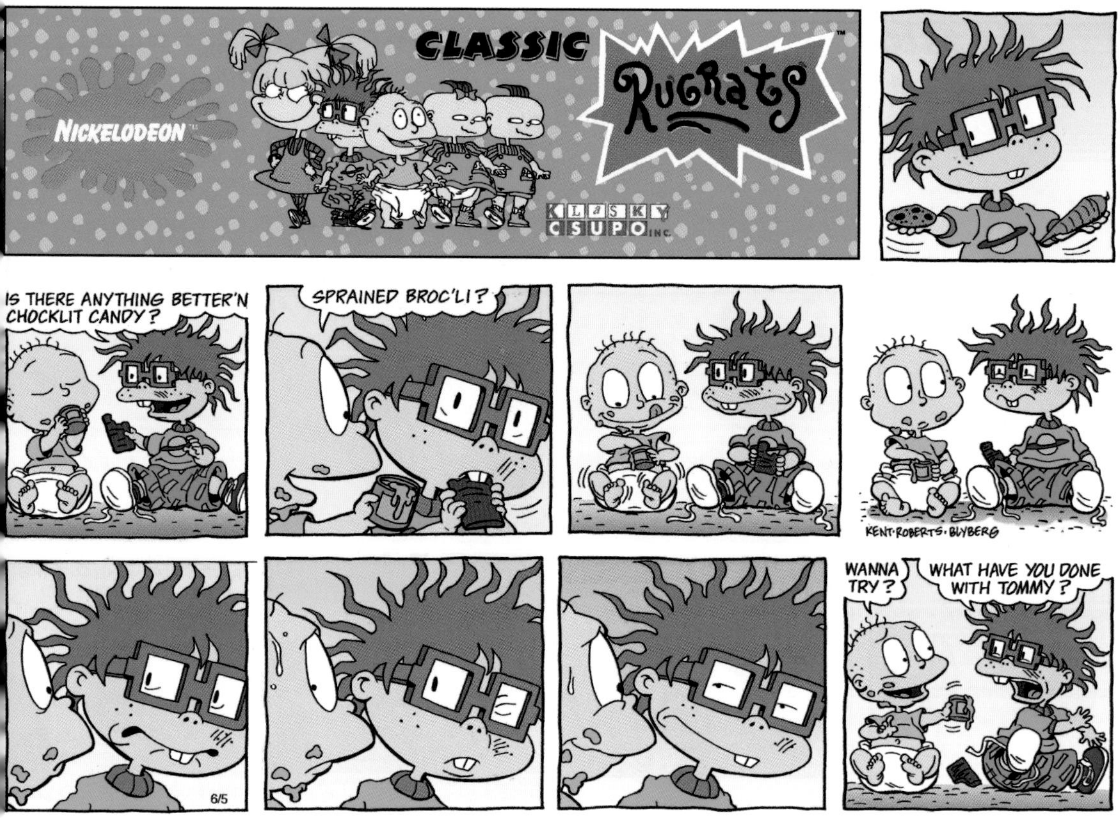
NICKELODEON
CLASSIC
Rugrats
KLASKY CSUPO INC.
IS THERE ANYTHING BETTER'N CHOCKLIT CANDY?
SPRAINED BROC'LI?
KENT·ROBERTS·BLYBERG
6/5
WANNA TRY?
WHAT HAVE YOU DONE WITH TOMMY?

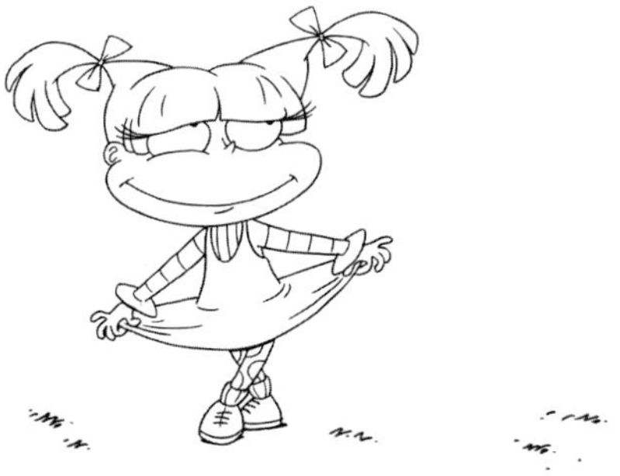

SUNDAYS

CLASSIC
Rugrats
NICKELODEON
KLASKY CSUPO INC.
CAN'T THAT CHILD TAKE A BATH WITHOUT SO MUCH SPLASHING? WHAT DOES SHE DO UP THERE?
ROBERTS BLYBERG
6/7

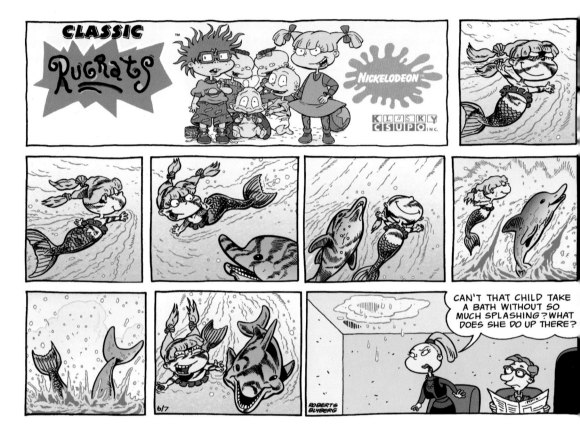

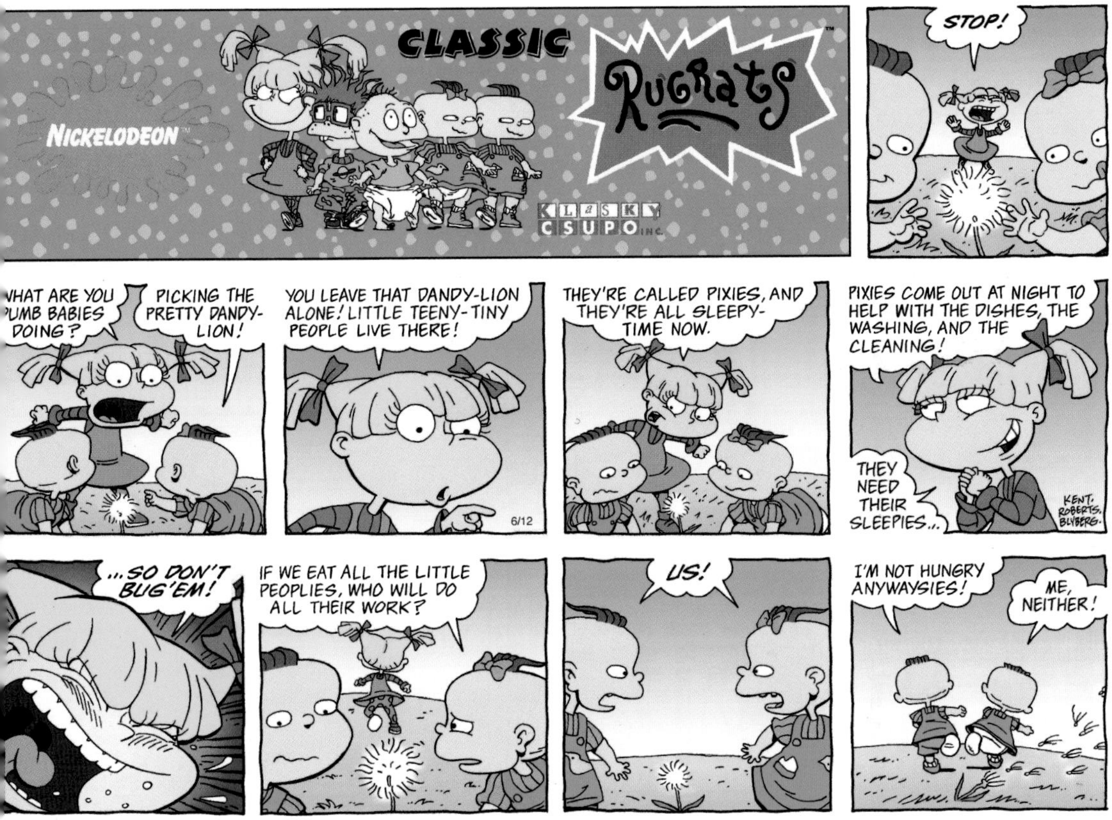
CLASSIC
Rugrats
NICKELODEON
KLASKY CSUPO INC.
STOP!
WHAT ARE YOU DUMB BABIES DOING?
PICKING THE PRETTY DANDY-LION!
YOU LEAVE THAT DANDY-LION ALONE! LITTLE TEENY-TINY PEOPLE LIVE THERE!
6/12
THEY'RE CALLED PIXIES, AND THEY'RE ALL SLEEPY-TIME NOW.
PIXIES COME OUT AT NIGHT TO HELP WITH THE DISHES, THE WASHING, AND THE CLEANING!
THEY NEED THEIR SLEEPIES...
KENT. ROBERTS. BLYBERG.
...SO DON'T BUG'EM!
IF WE EAT ALL THE LITTLE PEOPLIES, WHO WILL DO ALL THEIR WORK?
US!
I'M NOT HUNGRY ANYWAYSIES!
ME, NEITHER!

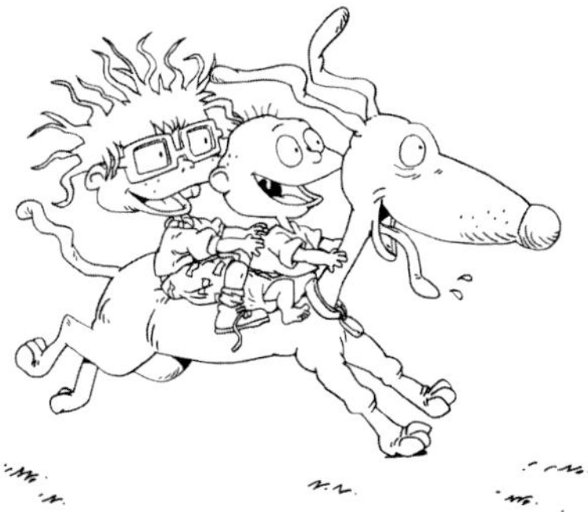

CLASSIC
RUGRATS
™
NICKELODEON™
KLASKY CSUPO INC.
DADDY WILL LOVE THIS.
I LOVE MY DADDY.
I LOVE MY DADDY MORE.
REALLY? HOW MUCH MORE?
I LOVE MY DADDY MORE THAN THE LAVENDER RIBBONS IN MY HAIR.
IS THAT ALL?
NO. I LOVE MY DADDY MORE THAN ALL THE PINK CRAYONS IN THE WORLD.
6/14
hmmm...
WAIT!-- I LOVE MY DADDY MORE THAN THE STASH OF HALLOWEEN CANDY HIDDEN UNDER MY BED!
I LOVE MY DADDY MORE THAN THE ENTIRE CYNTHIA BEACH PARTY PLAY SET–INCLUDING HER PINK DUNE BUGGY!
KENT • ROBERTS • BLYBERG
WHAT'S ANGELICA MAD ABOUT?
HOW MUCH SHE LOVES HER DADDY.
MAYBE SHE SHOULD JUST GIVE HIM A CARD AND A HUG.

SUNDAYS

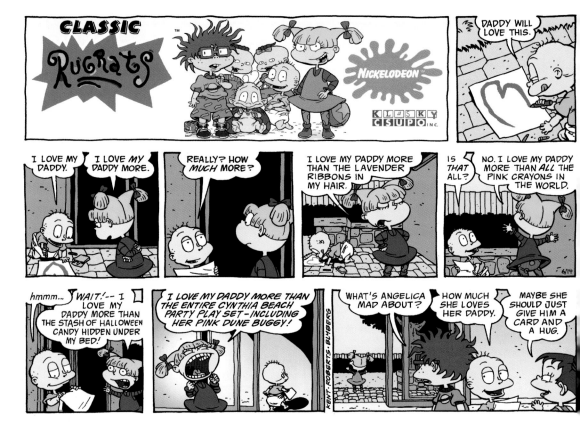

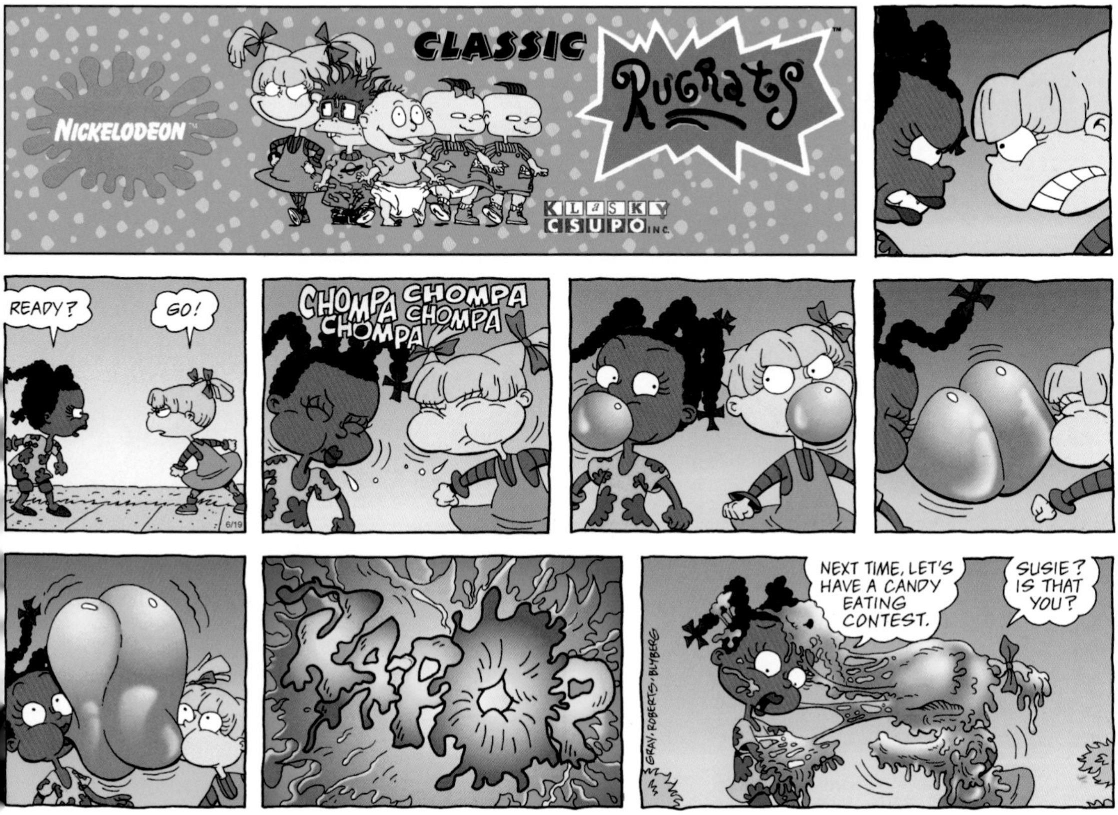
CLASSIC
Rugrats
NICKELODEON
KLASKY CSUPO INC.
READY?
GO!
6/19
CHOMPA CHOMPA CHOMPA CHOMPA
NEXT TIME, LET'S HAVE A CANDY EATING CONTEST.
SUSIE? IS THAT YOU?
GRAY · ROBERTS · BLYBERG

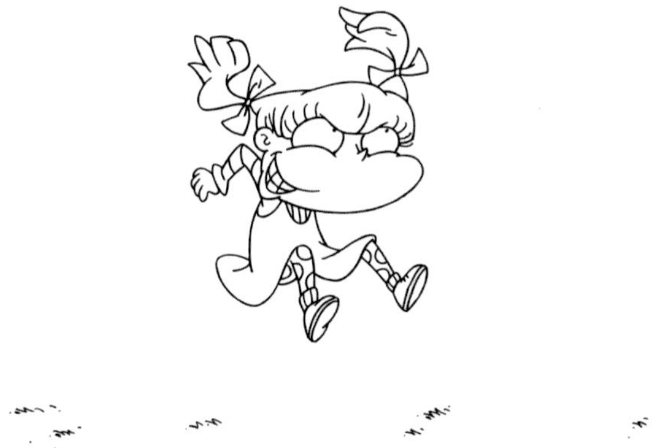

SUNDAYS

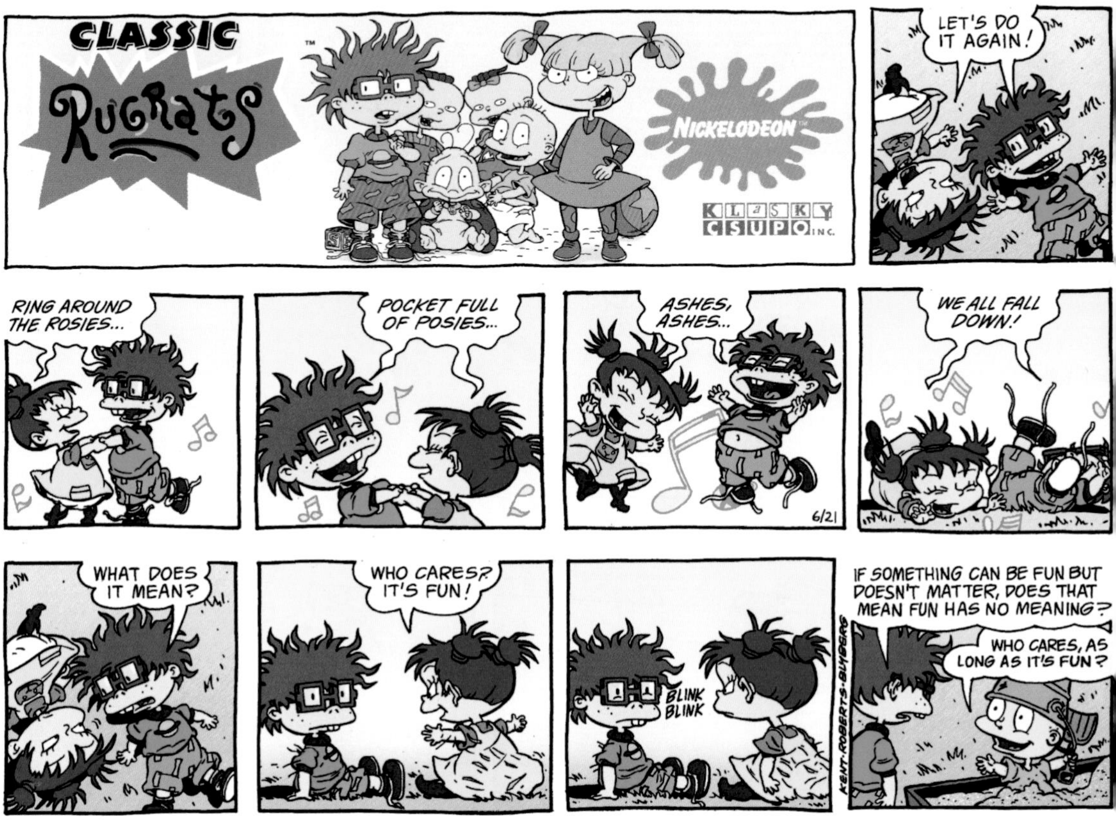
CLASSIC
Rugrats
NICKELODEON
KLASKY CSUPO INC.
LET'S DO IT AGAIN!
RING AROUND THE ROSIES...
POCKET FULL OF POSIES...
ASHES, ASHES...
WE ALL FALL DOWN!
6/21
WHAT DOES IT MEAN?
WHO CARES? IT'S FUN!
BLINK BLINK
KENT·ROBERTS·BUYBERG
IF SOMETHING CAN BE FUN BUT DOESN'T MATTER, DOES THAT MEAN FUN HAS NO MEANING?
WHO CARES, AS LONG AS IT'S FUN?

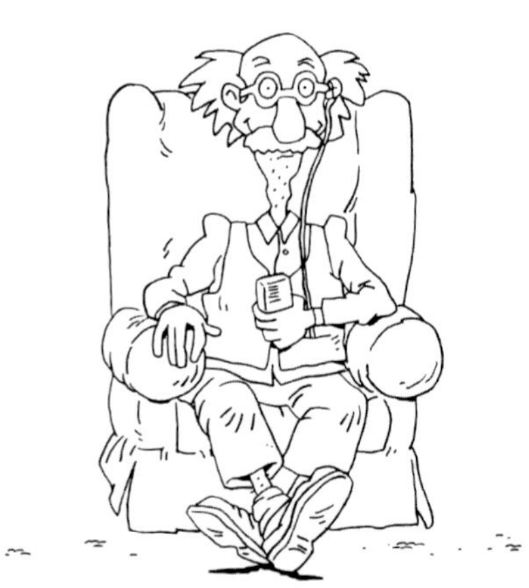

SUNDAYS

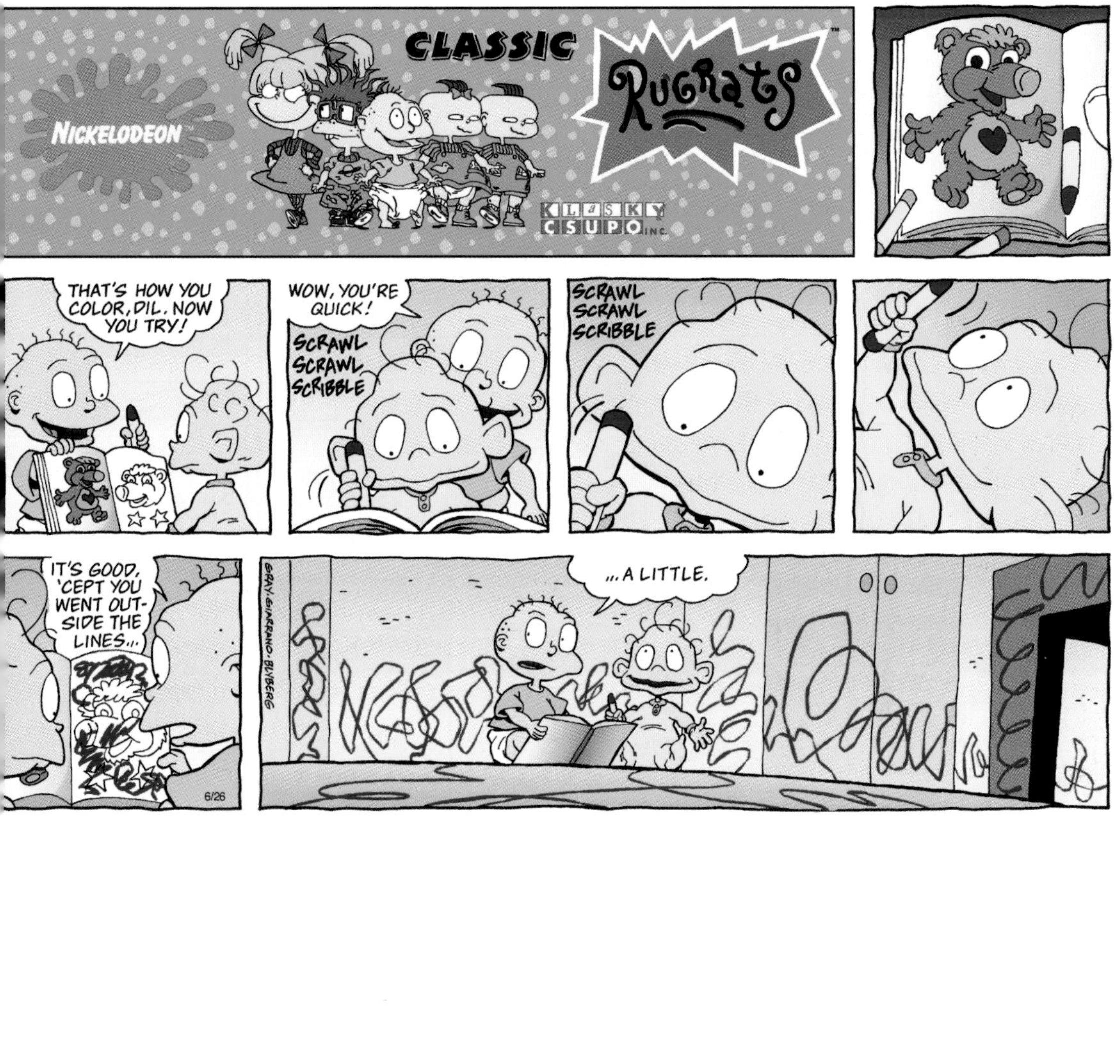
NICKELODEON
CLASSIC
Rugrats
KLASKY CSUPO INC.
THAT'S HOW YOU COLOR, DIL. NOW YOU TRY!
WOW, YOU'RE QUICK!
SCRAWL SCRAWL SCRIBBLE
SCRAWL SCRAWL SCRIBBLE
IT'S GOOD, 'CEPT YOU WENT OUT-SIDE THE LINES...
6/26
GRAY·GIARRANO·BLYBERG
...A LITTLE.

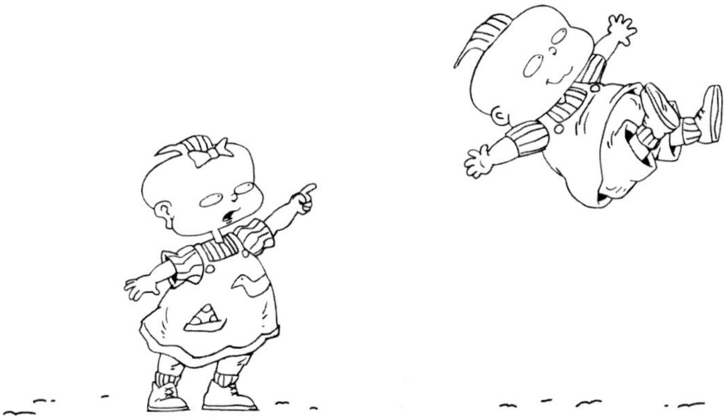

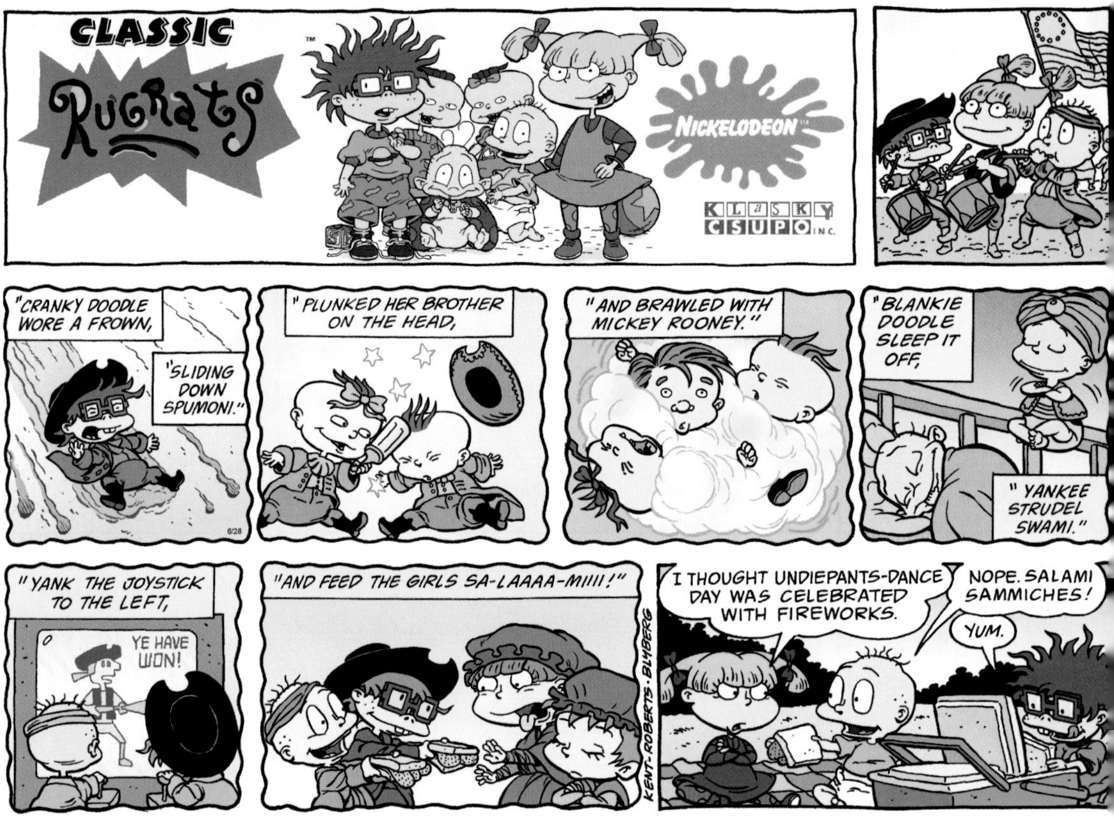
CLASSIC
Rugrats
NICKELODEON
KLaSKY CSUPO INC.
"CRANKY DOODLE WORE A FROWN,
"SLIDING DOWN SPUMONI."
"PLUNKED HER BROTHER ON THE HEAD,
"AND BRAWLED WITH MICKEY ROONEY."
"BLANKIE DOODLE SLEEP IT OFF,
"YANKEE STRUDEL SWAMI."
"YANK THE JOYSTICK TO THE LEFT,
YE HAVE WON!
"AND FEED THE GIRLS SA-LAAAA-MIIII!"
KENT · ROBERTS · BLYBERG
I THOUGHT UNDIEPANTS-DANCE DAY WAS CELEBRATED WITH FIREWORKS.
NOPE. SALAMI SAMMICHES!
YUM.

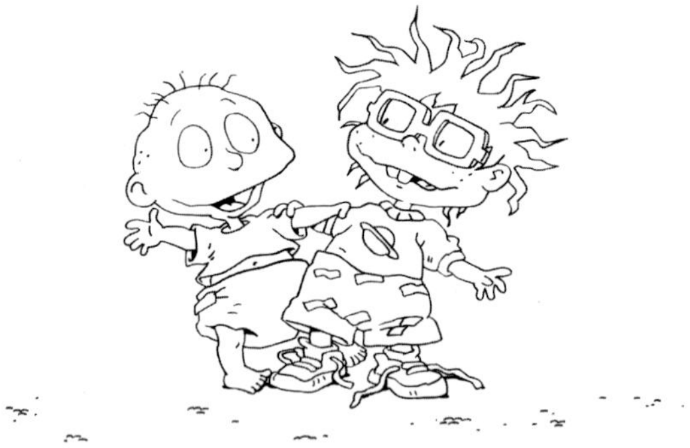

SUNDAYS

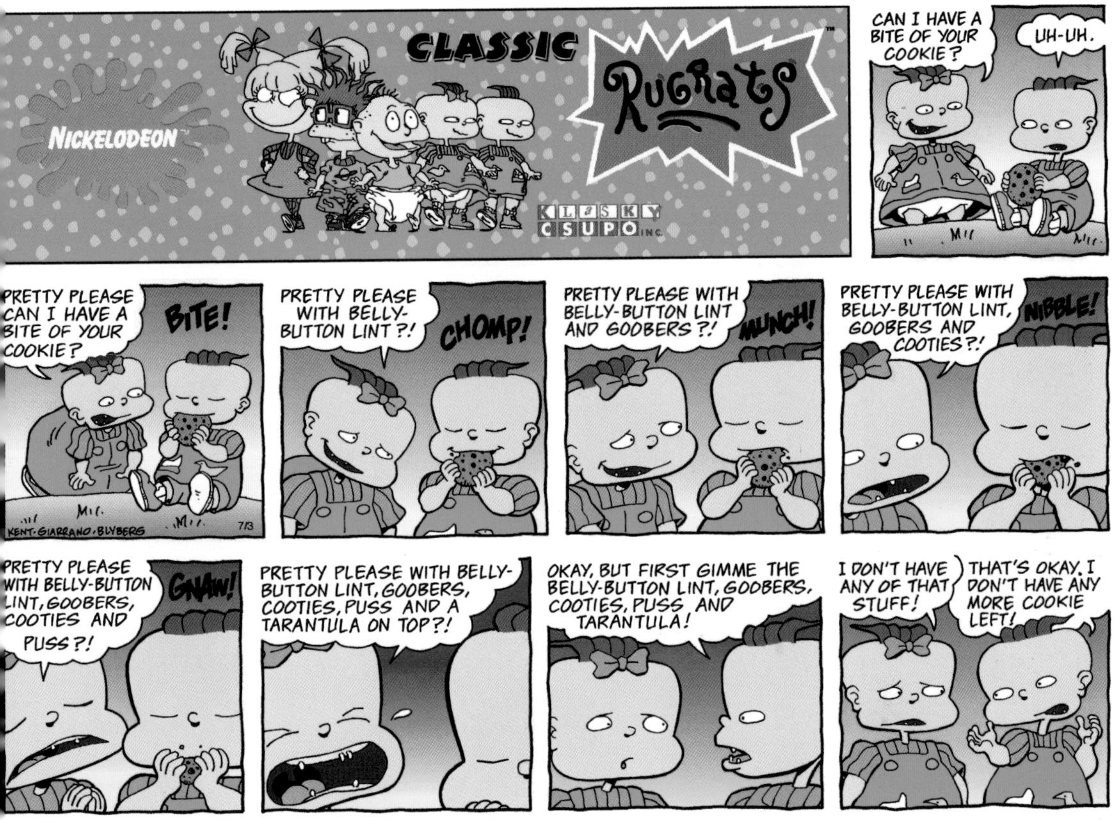
NICKELODEON
CLASSIC
Rugrats
KLASKY CSUPO INC.
CAN I HAVE A BITE OF YOUR COOKIE?
UH-UH.
PRETTY PLEASE CAN I HAVE A BITE OF YOUR COOKIE?
BITE!
KENT·GIARRANO·BLYBERG
7/13
PRETTY PLEASE WITH BELLY-BUTTON LINT?!
CHOMP!
PRETTY PLEASE WITH BELLY-BUTTON LINT AND GOOBERS?!
MUNCH!
PRETTY PLEASE WITH BELLY-BUTTON LINT, GOOBERS AND COOTIES?!
NIBBLE!
PRETTY PLEASE WITH BELLY-BUTTON LINT, GOOBERS, COOTIES AND PUSS?!
GNAW!
PRETTY PLEASE WITH BELLY-BUTTON LINT, GOOBERS, COOTIES, PUSS AND A TARANTULA ON TOP?!
OKAY, BUT FIRST GIMME THE BELLY-BUTTON LINT, GOOBERS, COOTIES, PUSS AND TARANTULA!
I DON'T HAVE ANY OF THAT STUFF!
THAT'S OKAY. I DON'T HAVE ANY MORE COOKIE LEFT!

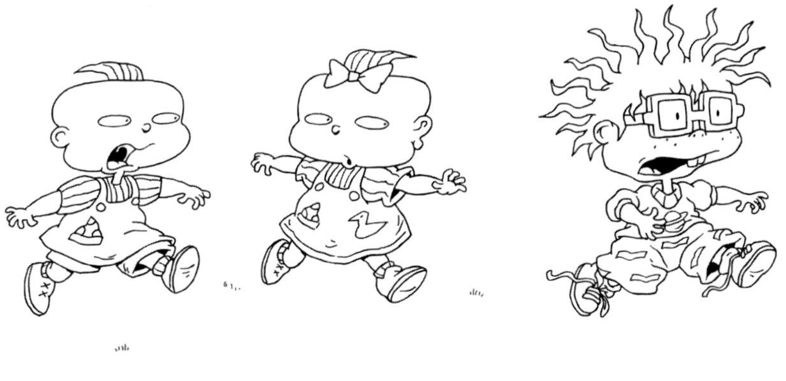

SUNDAYS

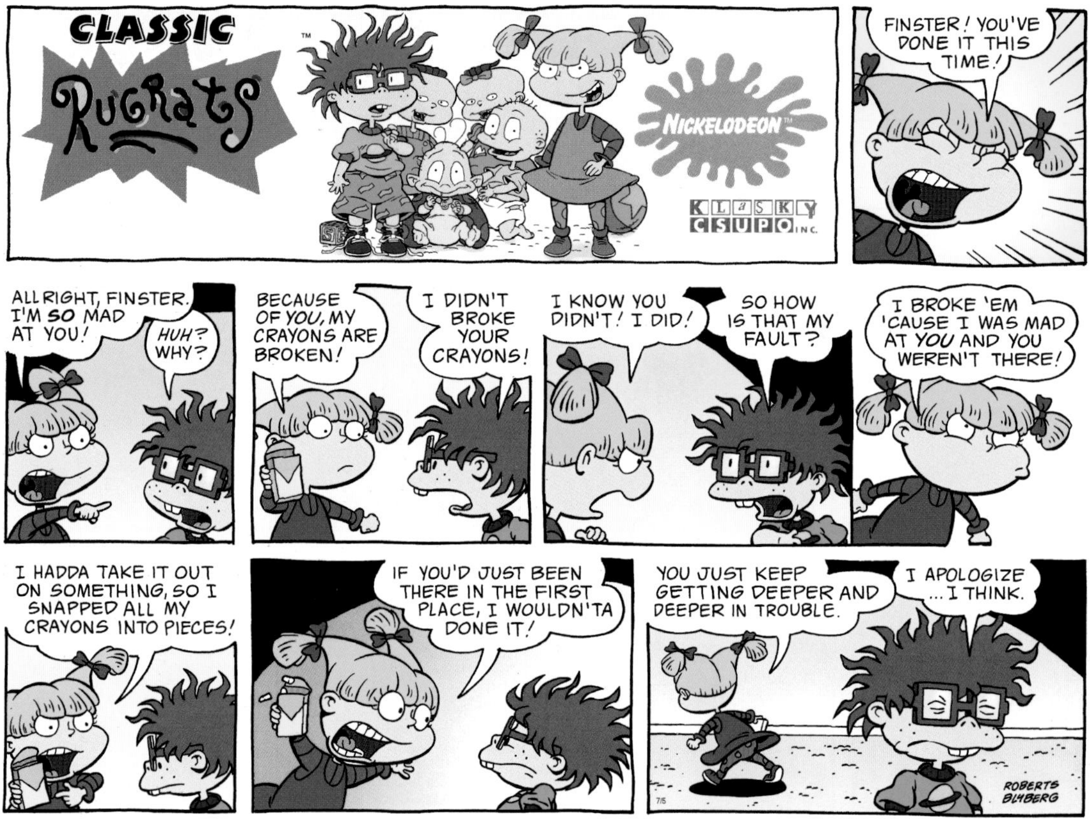
CLASSIC
Rugrats
NICKELODEON
KLASKY CSUPO INC.
FINSTER! YOU'VE DONE IT THIS TIME!
ALL RIGHT, FINSTER. I'M SO MAD AT YOU!
HUH? WHY?
BECAUSE OF YOU, MY CRAYONS ARE BROKEN!
I DIDN'T BROKE YOUR CRAYONS!
I KNOW YOU DIDN'T! I DID!
SO HOW IS THAT MY FAULT?
I BROKE 'EM 'CAUSE I WAS MAD AT YOU AND YOU WEREN'T THERE!
I HADDA TAKE IT OUT ON SOMETHING, SO I SNAPPED ALL MY CRAYONS INTO PIECES!
IF YOU'D JUST BEEN THERE IN THE FIRST PLACE, I WOULDN'TA DONE IT!
YOU JUST KEEP GETTING DEEPER AND DEEPER IN TROUBLE.
I APOLOGIZE ... I THINK.
7/5
ROBERTS BLYBERG

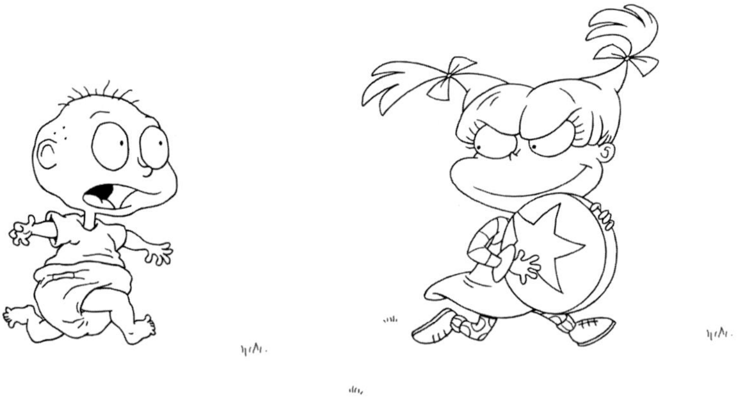

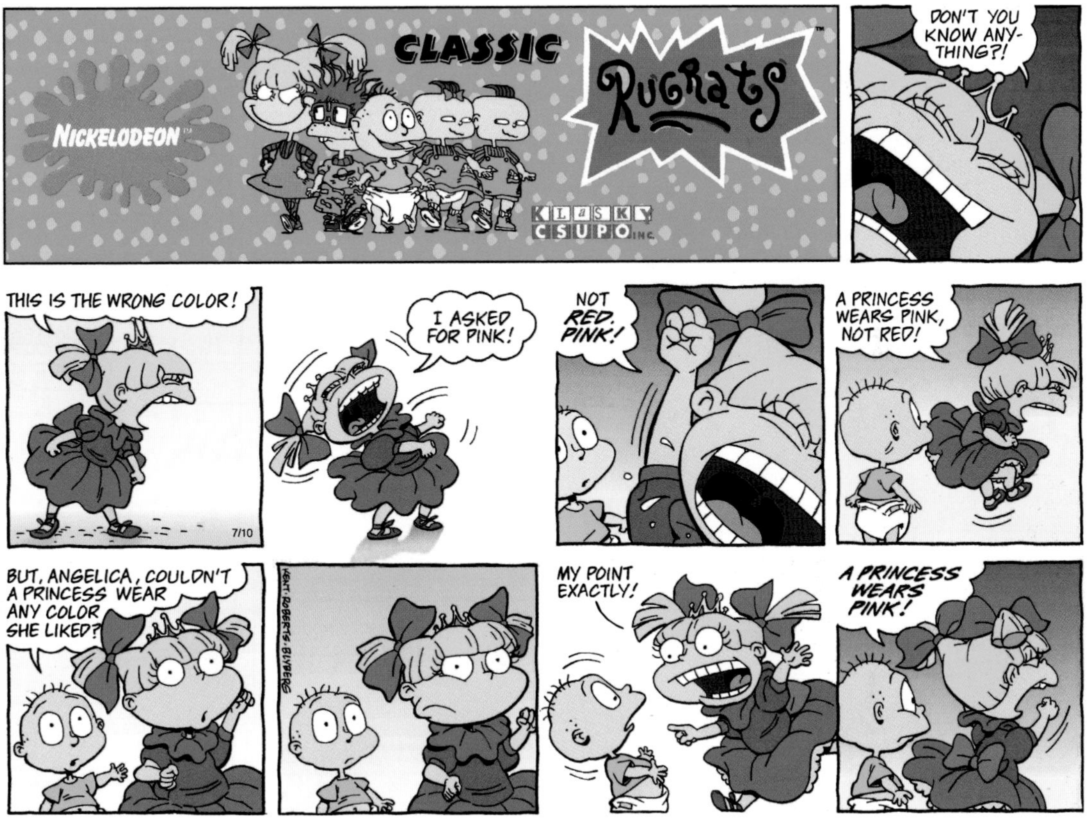
NICKELODEON
CLASSIC
Rugrats
KLASKY CSUPO INC.
DON'T YOU KNOW ANY-THING?!
THIS IS THE WRONG COLOR!
7/10
I ASKED FOR PINK!
NOT RED. PINK!
A PRINCESS WEARS PINK, NOT RED!
BUT, ANGELICA, COULDN'T A PRINCESS WEAR ANY COLOR SHE LIKED?
MY POINT EXACTLY!
A PRINCESS WEARS PINK!

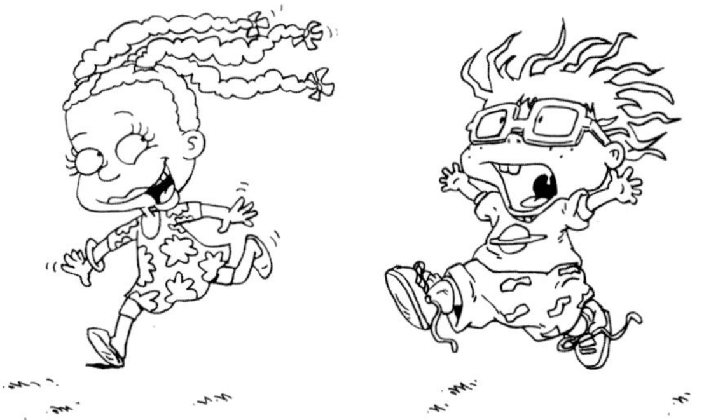

CLASSIC
Rugrats
NICKELODEON
KLaSKY CSUPO INC.
SAY, ANGELICA!
HEY, ANGELICA, WANNA COME TO MY TEA PARTY?
NO, CHUCKIE, I DON'T WANNA...
FINSTER, YOU DUMB BABY, YOU CAN'T HAVE A TEA PARTY!
I CAN'T?
OF COURSE NOT! WHAT'S THE MATTER WITH YOU?
BOYS PLAY BASEBALL, AND ARMY, AND CLIMB STUPID ROCKS, AND SEE WHO CAN BURP LOUDEST!
7/12
oh.
YEAH, "oh."
ROBERTS·BLYBERG
SO, DO YOU WANNA CLIMB ROCKS AND BURP?

SUNDAYS

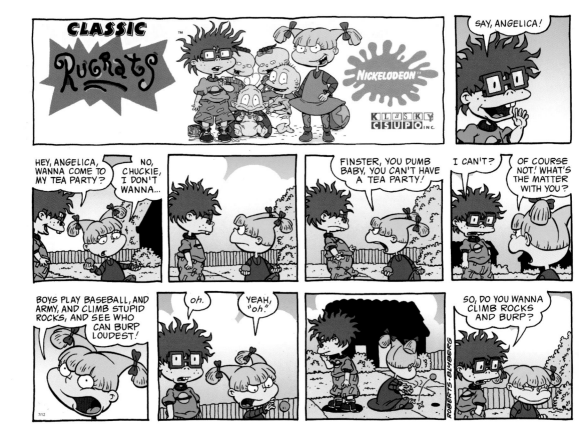

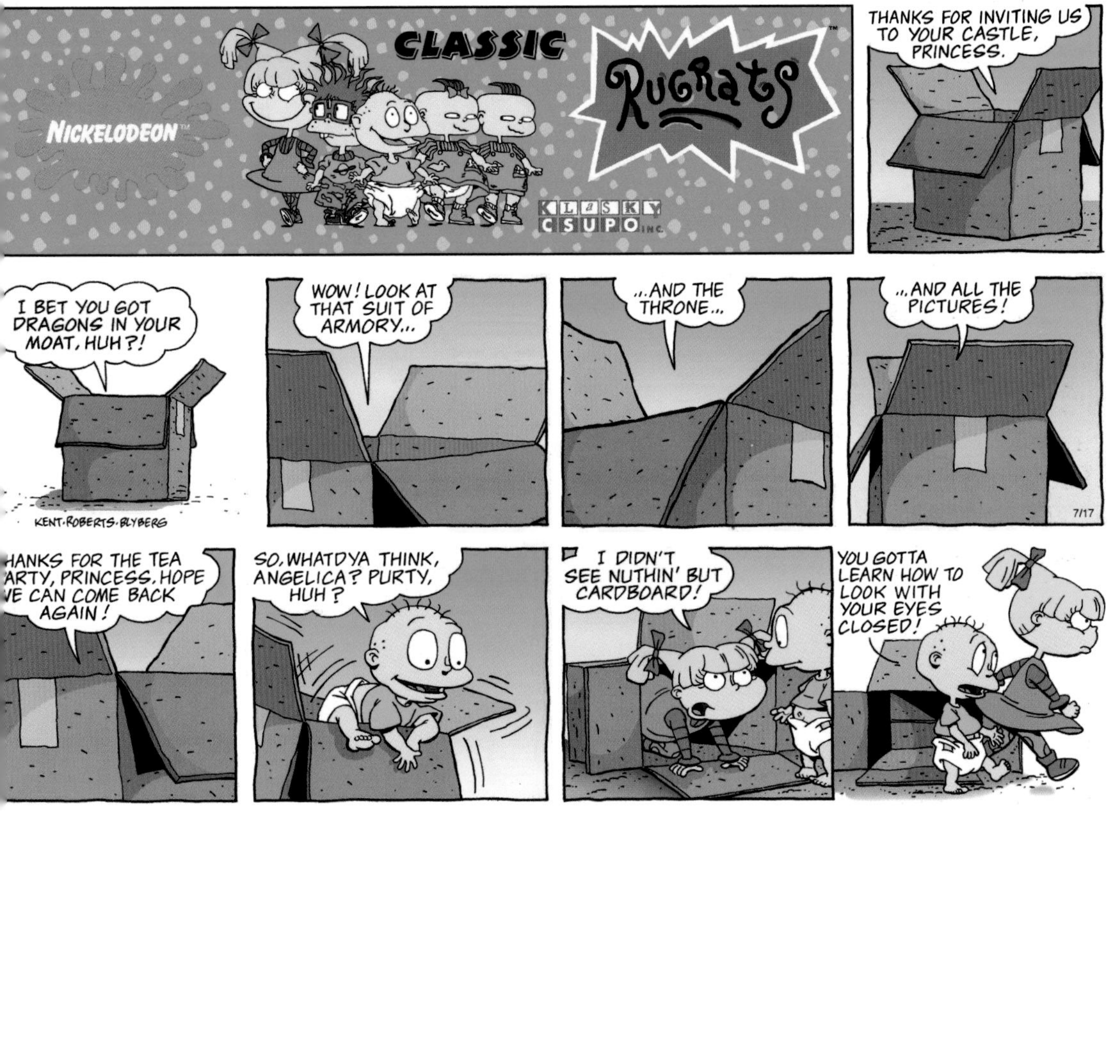
NICKELODEON
CLASSIC
Rugrats
KLASKY CSUPO INC.
THANKS FOR INVITING US TO YOUR CASTLE, PRINCESS.
I BET YOU GOT DRAGONS IN YOUR MOAT, HUH?!
KENT·ROBERTS·BLYBERG
WOW! LOOK AT THAT SUIT OF ARMORY...
...AND THE THRONE...
...AND ALL THE PICTURES!
7/17
HANKS FOR THE TEA ARTY, PRINCESS. HOPE VE CAN COME BACK AGAIN!
SO, WHATDYA THINK, ANGELICA? PURTY, HUH?
I DIDN'T SEE NUTHIN' BUT CARDBOARD!
YOU GOTTA LEARN HOW TO LOOK WITH YOUR EYES CLOSED!

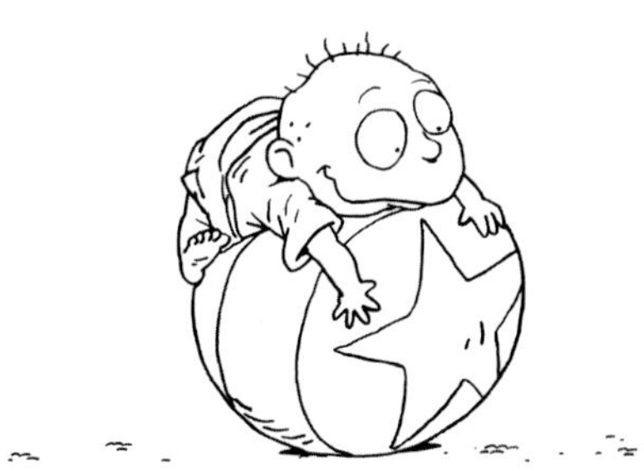

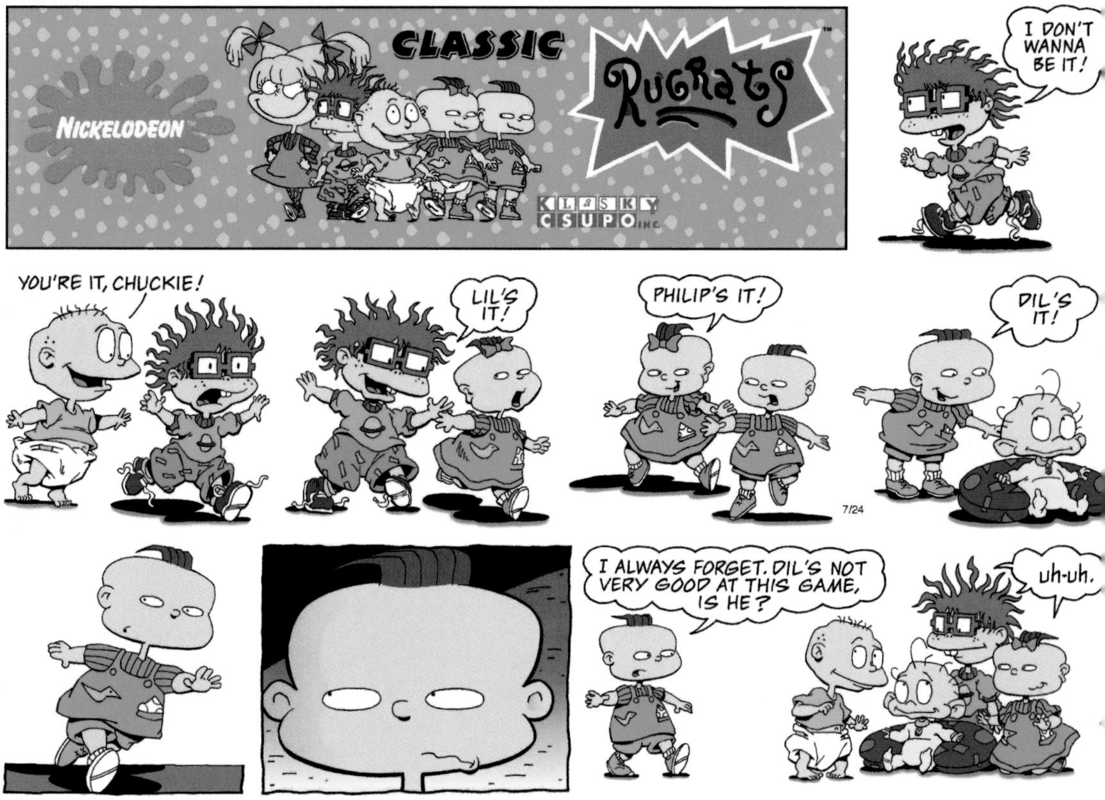
NICKELODEON
CLASSIC
Rugrats
KLASKY CSUPO INC.
I DON'T WANNA BE IT!
YOU'RE IT, CHUCKIE!
LIL'S IT!
PHILIP'S IT!
DIL'S IT!
7/24
I ALWAYS FORGET. DIL'S NOT VERY GOOD AT THIS GAME, IS HE?
uh-uh.

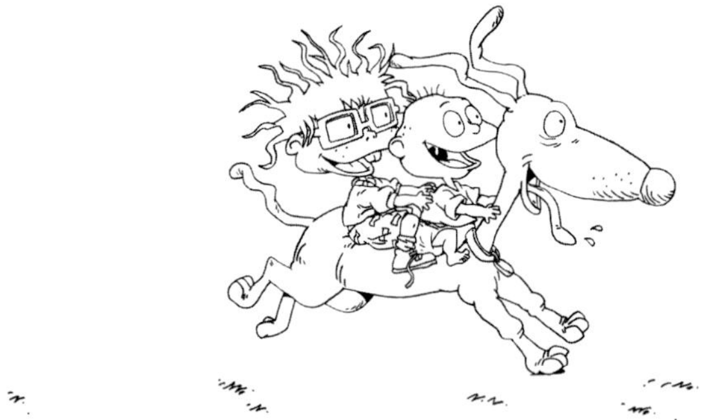

SUNDAYS

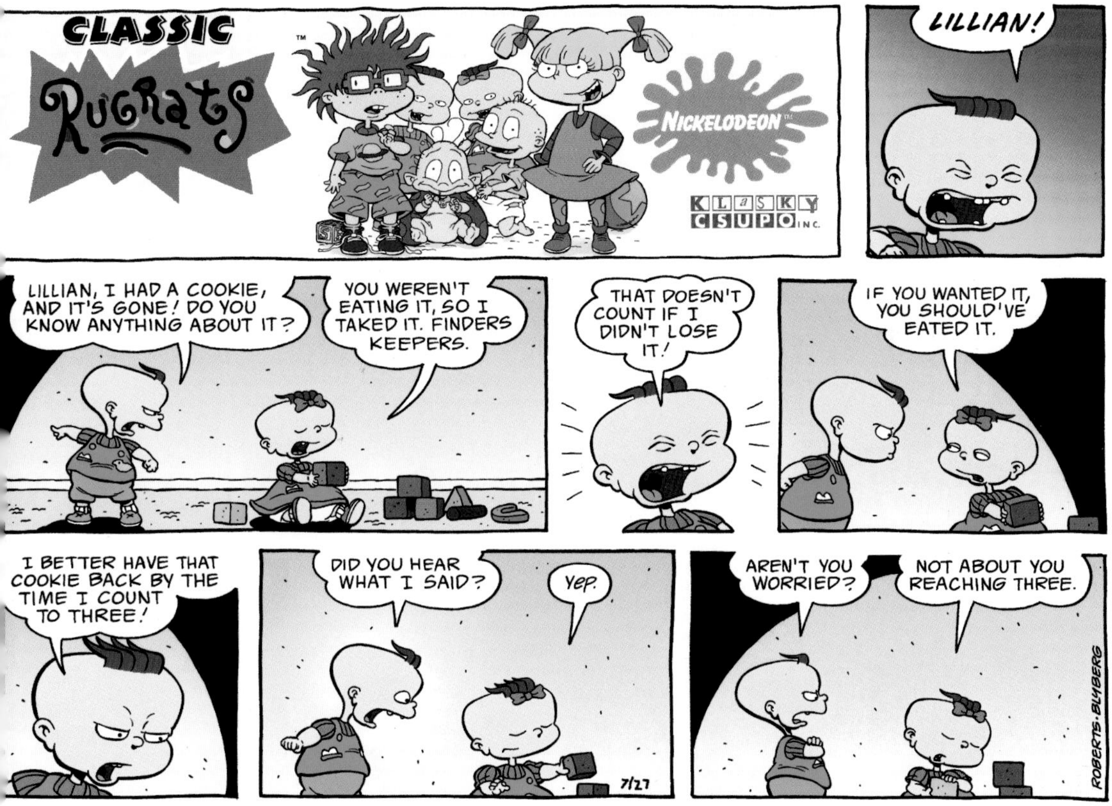
CLASSIC
Rugrats
NICKELODEON
KLaSKY CSUPO INC.
LILLIAN!
LILLIAN, I HAD A COOKIE, AND IT'S GONE! DO YOU KNOW ANYTHING ABOUT IT?
YOU WEREN'T EATING IT, SO I TAKED IT. FINDERS KEEPERS.
THAT DOESN'T COUNT IF I DIDN'T LOSE IT!
IF YOU WANTED IT, YOU SHOULD'VE EATED IT.
I BETTER HAVE THAT COOKIE BACK BY THE TIME I COUNT TO THREE!
DID YOU HEAR WHAT I SAID?
YEP.
7/27
AREN'T YOU WORRIED?
NOT ABOUT YOU REACHING THREE.
ROBERTS·BLYBERG

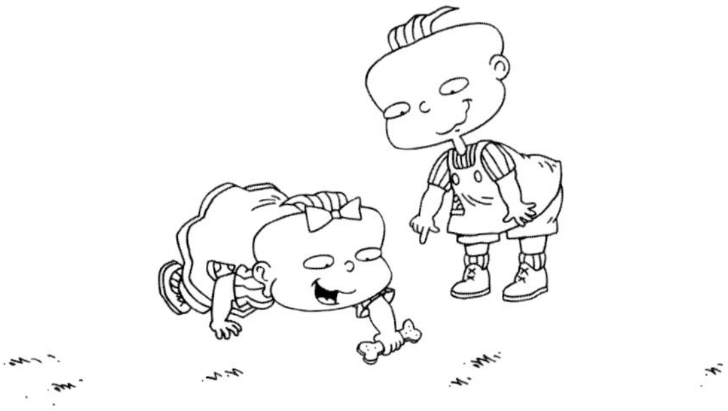

SUNDAYS

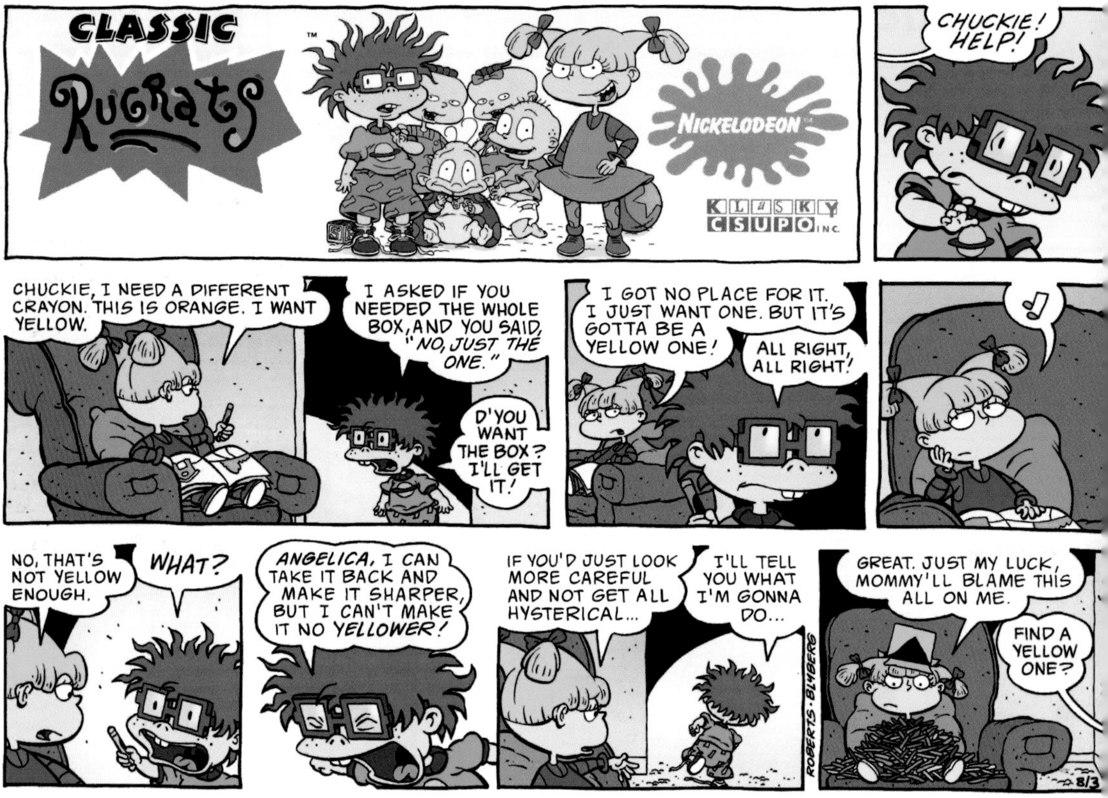
CLASSIC
RUGRATS
NICKELODEON
KLASKY CSUPO INC.
CHUCKIE! HELP!
CHUCKIE, I NEED A DIFFERENT CRAYON. THIS IS ORANGE. I WANT YELLOW.
I ASKED IF YOU NEEDED THE WHOLE BOX, AND YOU SAID, "NO, JUST THE ONE."
D'YOU WANT THE BOX? I'LL GET IT!
I GOT NO PLACE FOR IT. I JUST WANT ONE. BUT IT'S GOTTA BE A YELLOW ONE!
ALL RIGHT, ALL RIGHT!
NO, THAT'S NOT YELLOW ENOUGH.
WHAT?
ANGELICA, I CAN TAKE IT BACK AND MAKE IT SHARPER, BUT I CAN'T MAKE IT NO YELLOWER!
IF YOU'D JUST LOOK MORE CAREFUL AND NOT GET ALL HYSTERICAL...
I'LL TELL YOU WHAT I'M GONNA DO...
ROBERTS · BLYBERG
GREAT. JUST MY LUCK, MOMMY'LL BLAME THIS ALL ON ME.
FIND A YELLOW ONE?
8/3

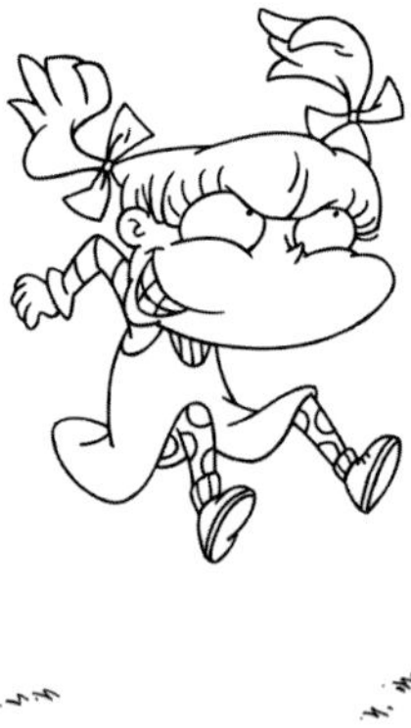

SUNDAYS

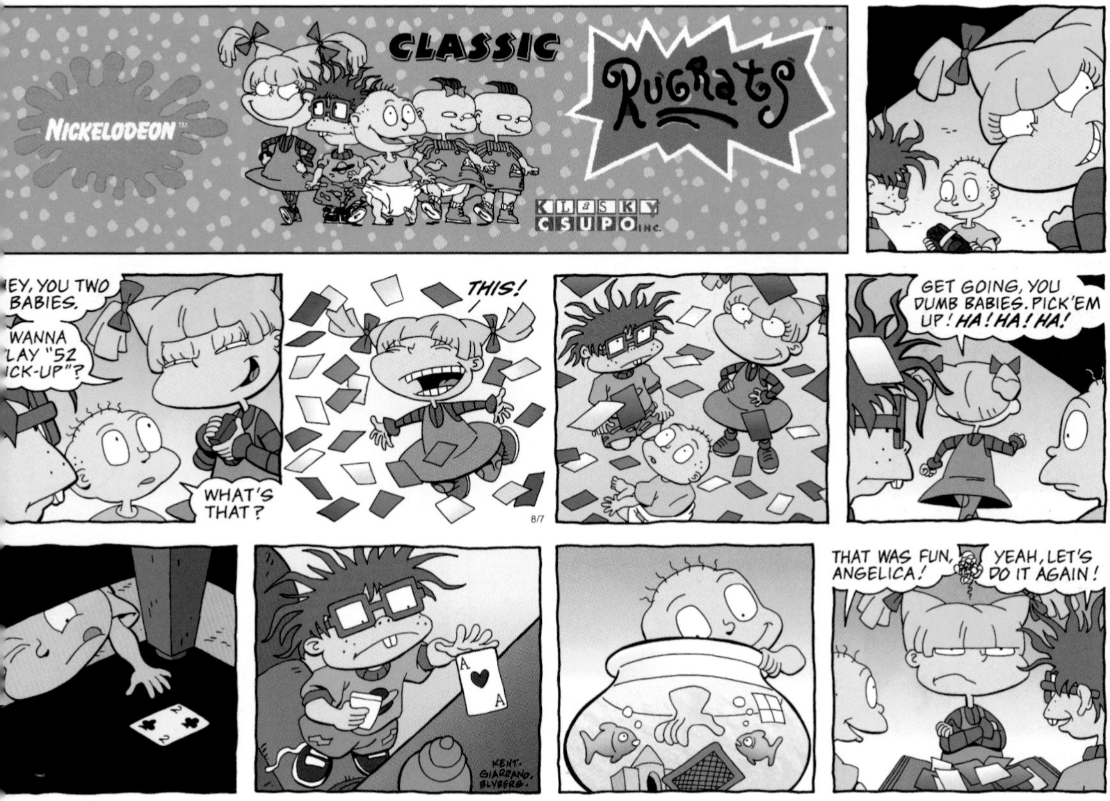
NICKELODEON
CLASSIC
Rugrats
KLASKY CSUPO INC.
EY, YOU TWO BABIES.
WANNA
LAY "52
ICK-UP"?
WHAT'S THAT?
THIS!
8/7
GET GOING, YOU DUMB BABIES. PICK'EM UP! HA! HA! HA!
KENT. GIARRANO. BLYBERG.
THAT WAS FUN, ANGELICA!
YEAH, LET'S DO IT AGAIN!

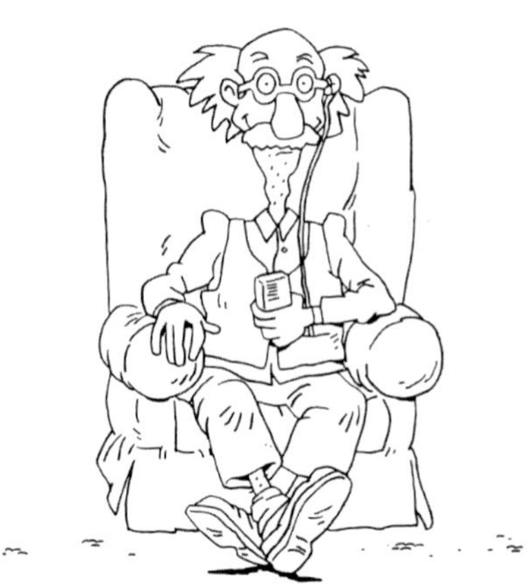

SUNDAYS

CLASSIC
Rugrats
NICKELODEON
KLASKY CSUPO INC.
PHIL, WHAT TIME IS IT ?
DON'T HAVE THE SLIGHTEST IDEA.
YOU DON'T EVEN KNOWS HOW TO TELL TIME, DO YOU ?
UM- NO.
MM-hm.
THEN WHAT'S IT MATTER WHAT TIME IT IS ?
ROBERTS·BLYBERG
8/10
Y'KNOW, PHIL, IN A WAY, WE'RE LUCKY...
WAY AHEAD OF YA, SIS.

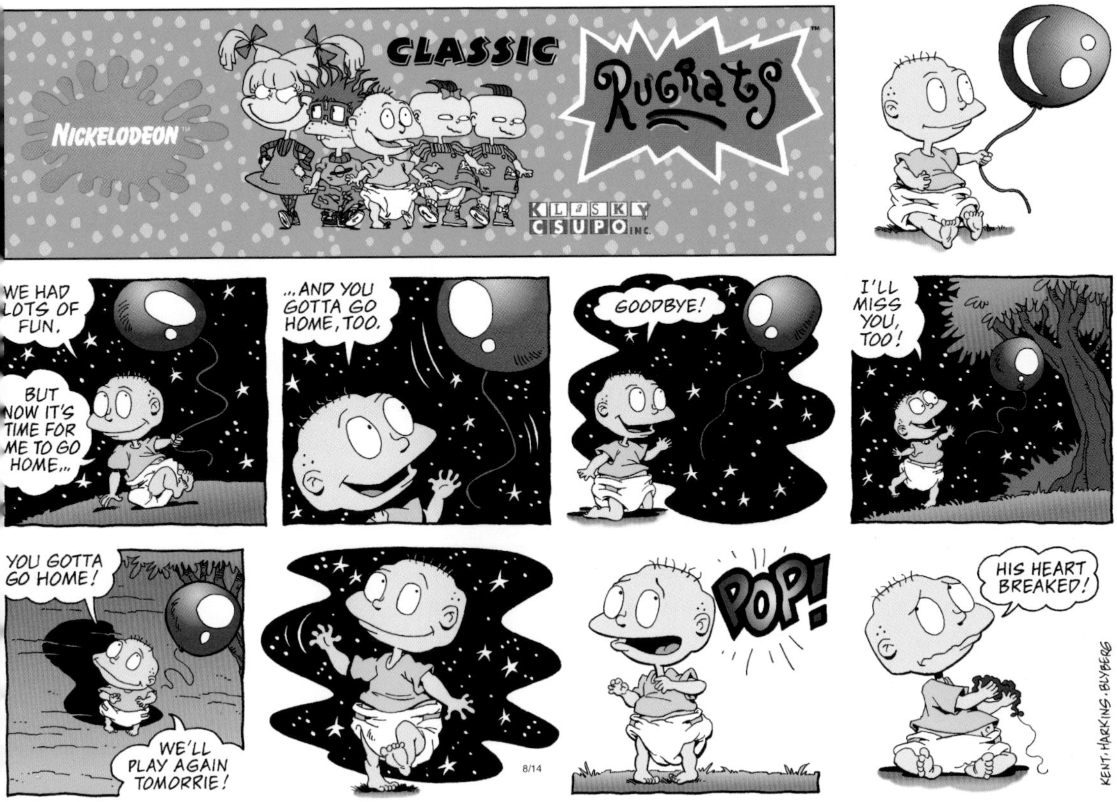
NICKELODEON
CLASSIC
Rugrats
KLASKY CSUPO INC.
WE HAD LOTS OF FUN.
BUT NOW IT'S TIME FOR ME TO GO HOME...
...AND YOU GOTTA GO HOME, TOO.
GOODBYE!
I'LL MISS YOU, TOO!
YOU GOTTA GO HOME!
WE'LL PLAY AGAIN TOMORRIE!
8/14
POP!
HIS HEART BREAKED!
KENT · HARKINS · BLYBERG

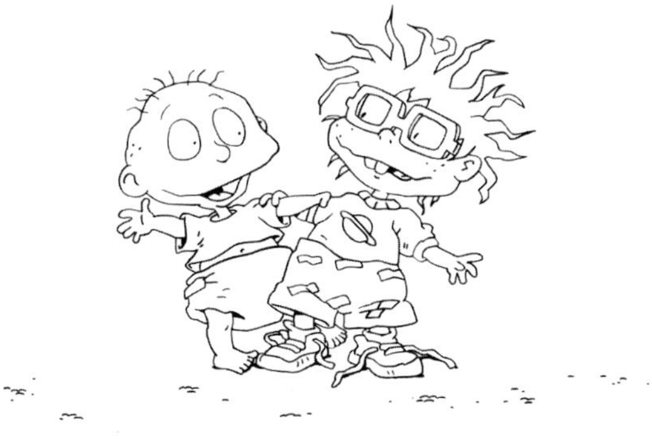

SUNDAYS

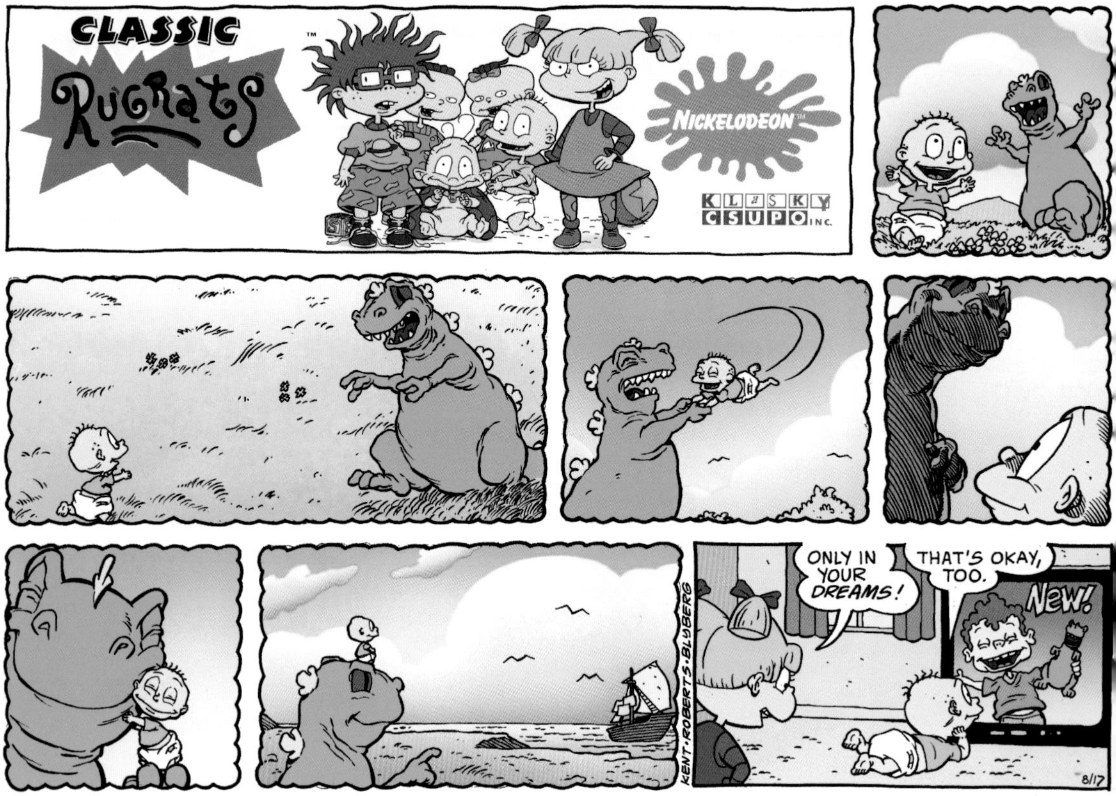
CLASSIC
Rugrats
NICKELODEON
KLASKY CSUPO INC.
KENT·ROBERTS·BLYBERG
ONLY IN YOUR DREAMS!
THAT'S OKAY, TOO.
NEW!
8/17

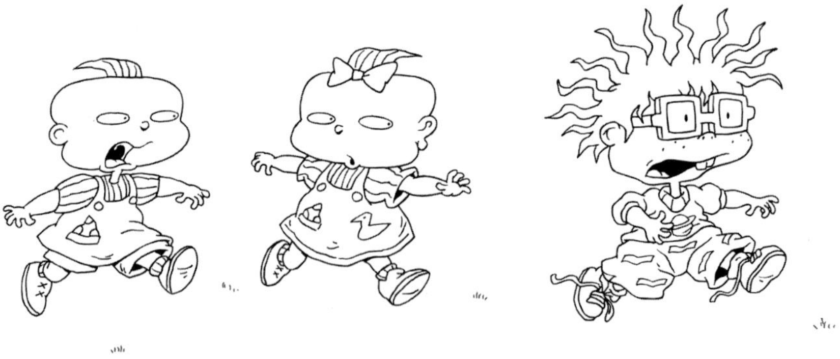

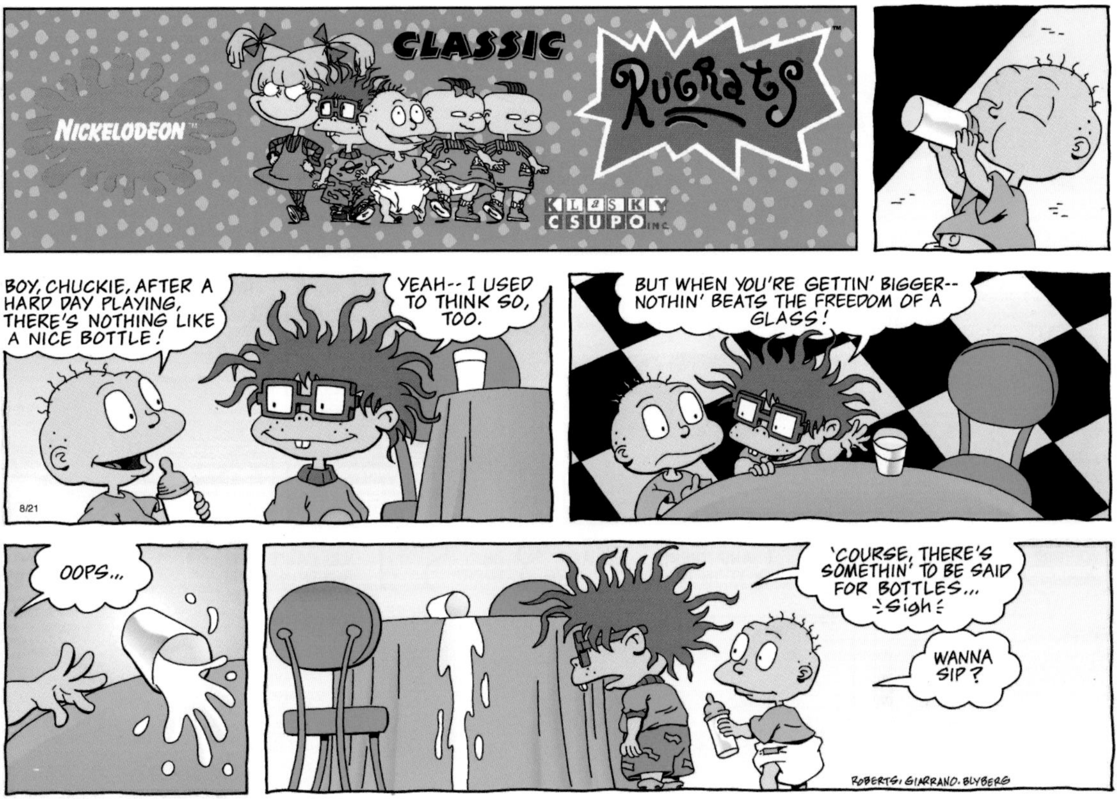
NICKELODEON
CLASSIC
Rugrats
KLASKY CSUPO INC.
BOY, CHUCKIE, AFTER A HARD DAY PLAYING, THERE'S NOTHING LIKE A NICE BOTTLE!
YEAH-- I USED TO THINK SO, TOO.
8/21
BUT WHEN YOU'RE GETTIN' BIGGER-- NOTHIN' BEATS THE FREEDOM OF A GLASS!
OOPS...
'COURSE, THERE'S SOMETHIN' TO BE SAID FOR BOTTLES...
Sigh
WANNA SIP?
ROBERTS. GIARRANO. BLYBERG

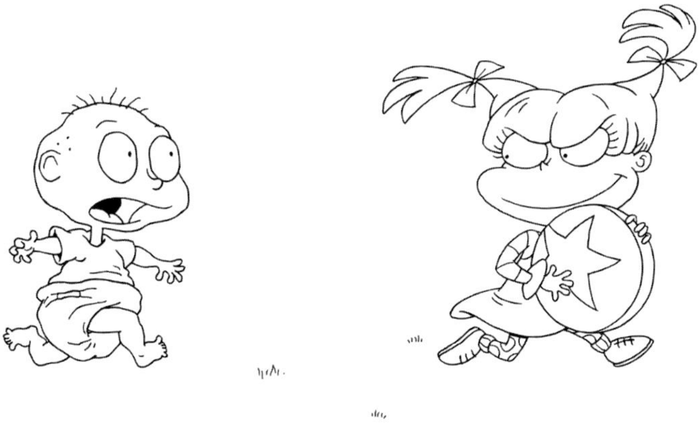

CLASSIC
Rugrats
NICKELODEON
KLaSKY CSUPO INC.
OOOOOOO... NEAT!
?
SEE THAT!
WHAT?
PAY ATTENTION.
THERE!
I DIDN'T SEE ANYTHING.
DID YOU SEE IT *THAT* TIME?
NOPE.
HOW 'BOUT THEN?
I SAW IT.!
YOU DID NOT!
SURE I DID.
AND THERE IT IS AGAIN!
AND THERE...
AND THERE...
AND THERE, TOO!
KENT·ROBERTS·BLYBERG
8/24
YOU CAN'T SEE ANYTHING, 'CAUSE I MADE IT ALL UP!
I SEE'D WHAT I SAID I SAW, 'CAUSE I MADE IT UP, TOO. SO *THERE!*

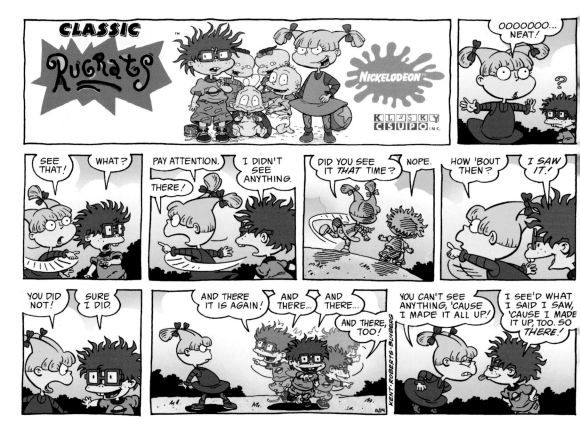

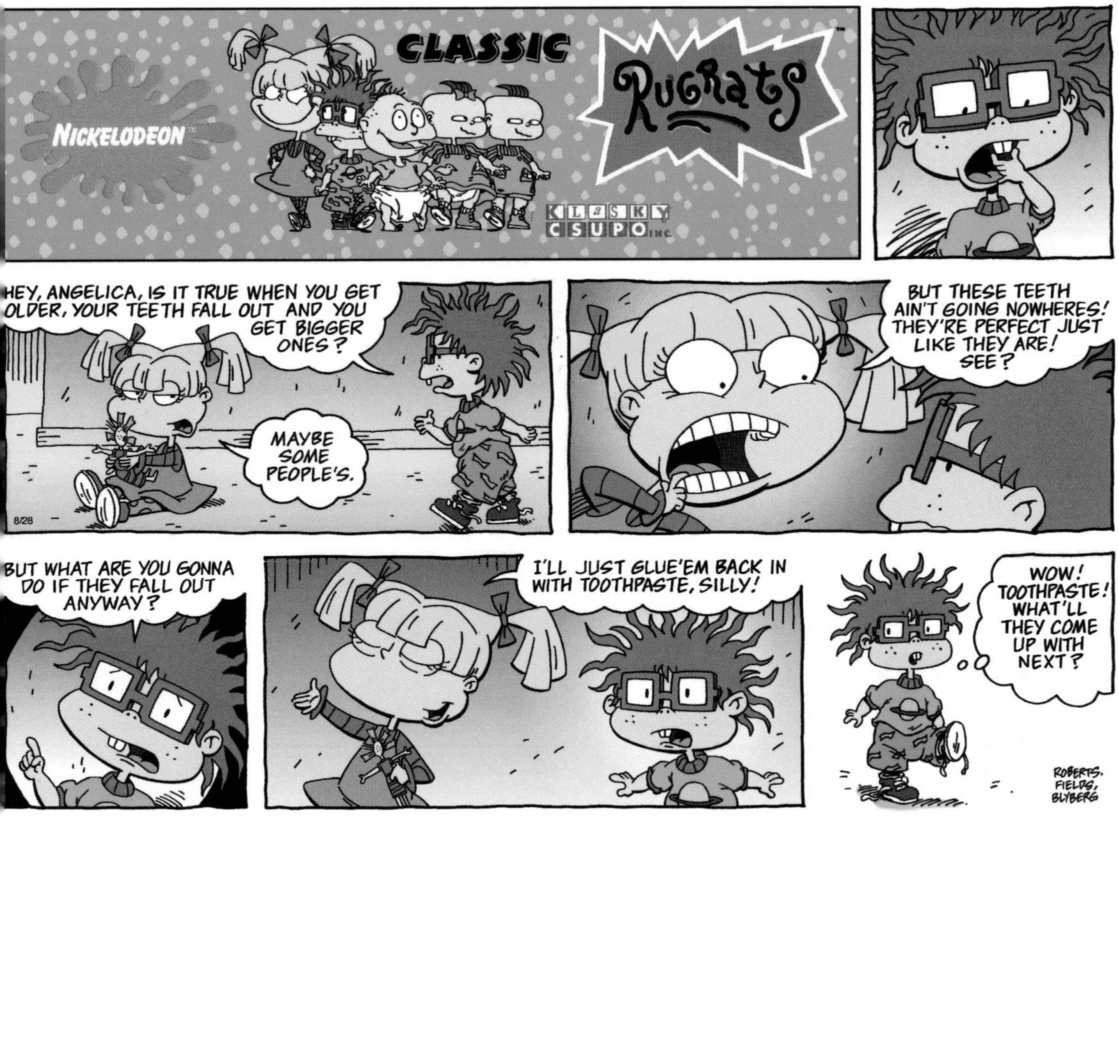
NICKELODEON
CLASSIC
Rugrats
KLASKY CSUPO INC.
HEY, ANGELICA, IS IT TRUE WHEN YOU GET OLDER, YOUR TEETH FALL OUT AND YOU GET BIGGER ONES?
MAYBE SOME PEOPLE'S.
8/28
BUT THESE TEETH AIN'T GOING NOWHERES! THEY'RE PERFECT JUST LIKE THEY ARE! SEE?
BUT WHAT ARE YOU GONNA DO IF THEY FALL OUT ANYWAY?
I'LL JUST GLUE'EM BACK IN WITH TOOTHPASTE, SILLY!
WOW! TOOTHPASTE! WHAT'LL THEY COME UP WITH NEXT?
ROBERTS. FIELDS, BLYBERG

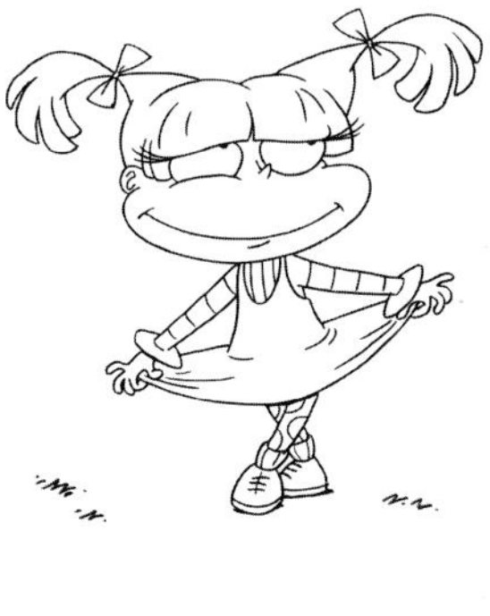

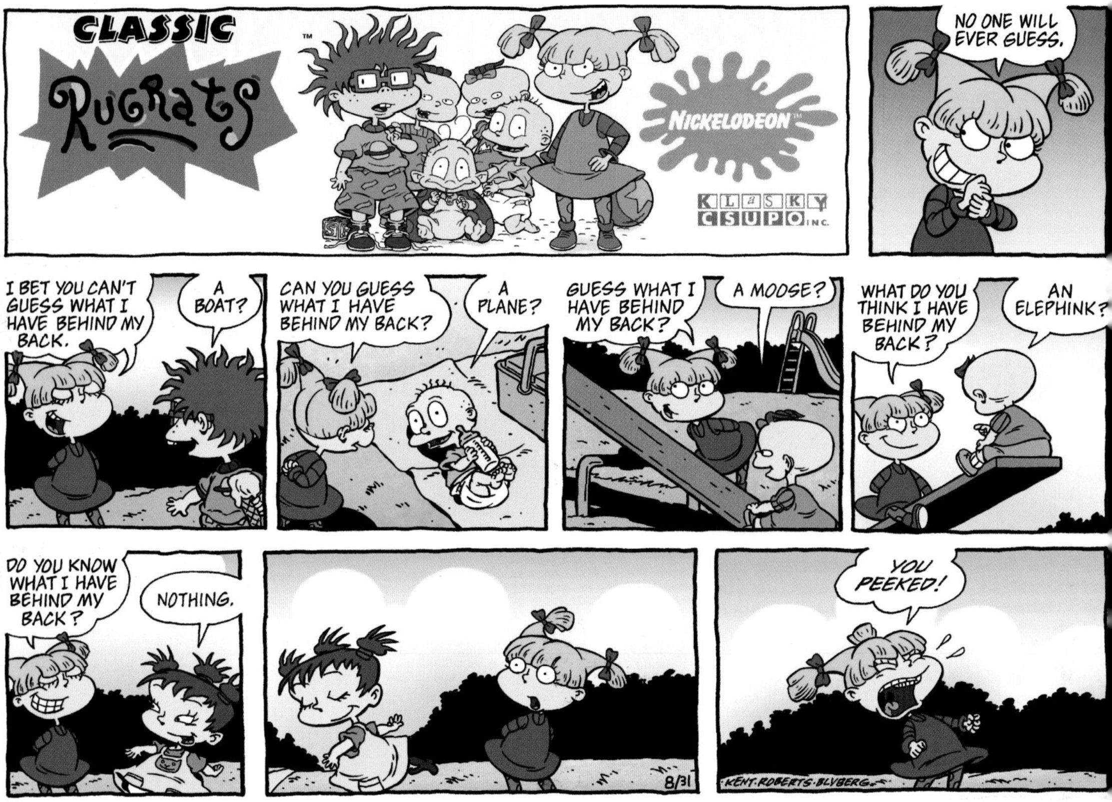
CLASSIC
Rugrats
NICKELODEON
KLASKY CSUPO INC.
NO ONE WILL EVER GUESS.
I BET YOU CAN'T GUESS WHAT I HAVE BEHIND MY BACK.
A BOAT?
CAN YOU GUESS WHAT I HAVE BEHIND MY BACK?
A PLANE?
GUESS WHAT I HAVE BEHIND MY BACK?
A MOOSE?
WHAT DO YOU THINK I HAVE BEHIND MY BACK?
AN ELEPHINK?
DO YOU KNOW WHAT I HAVE BEHIND MY BACK?
NOTHING.
8/31
YOU PEEKED!
KENT.ROBERTS.BLYBERG

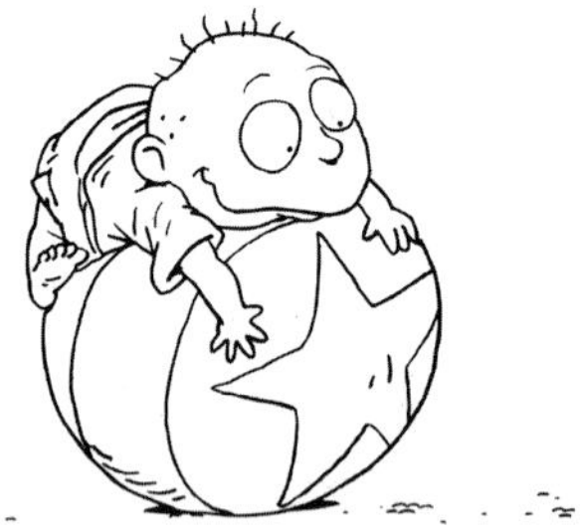

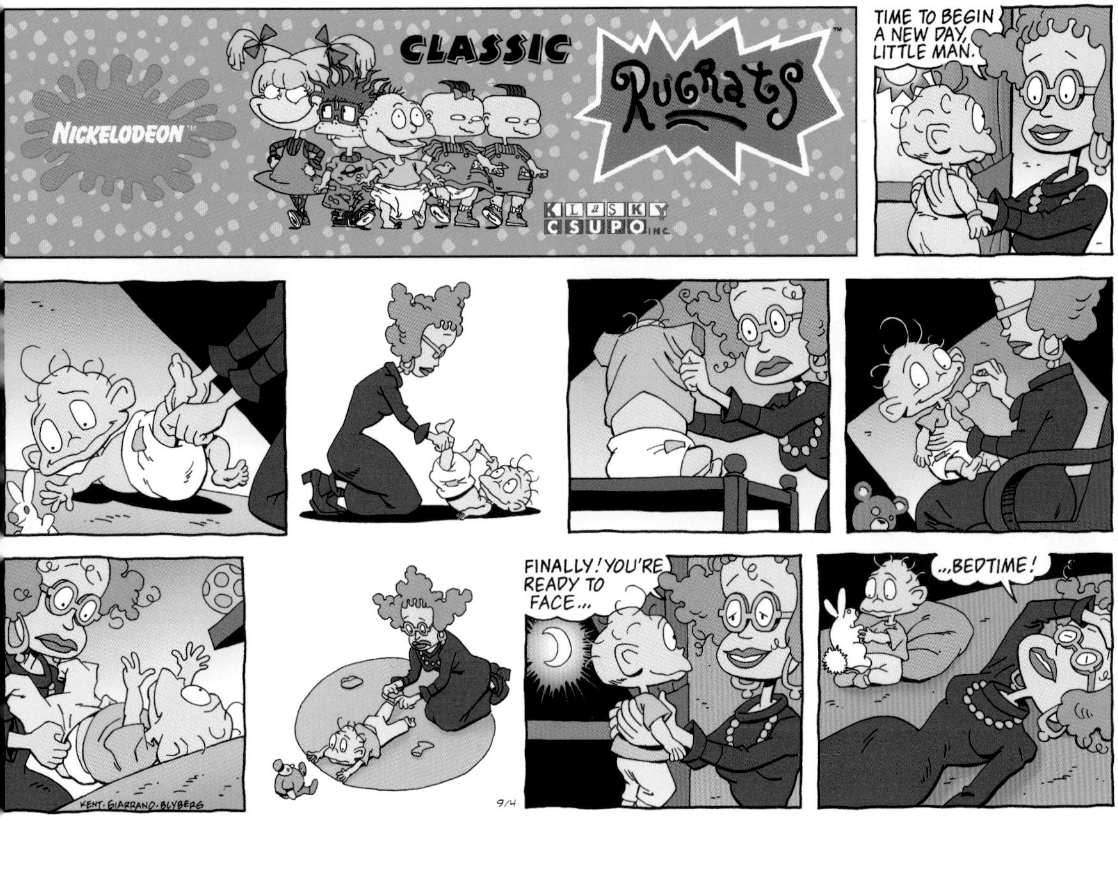
NICKELODEON
CLASSIC
Rugrats
KLASKY CSUPO INC.
TIME TO BEGIN A NEW DAY, LITTLE MAN.
FINALLY! YOU'RE READY TO FACE...
...BEDTIME!
KENT · GIARRANO · BLYBERG

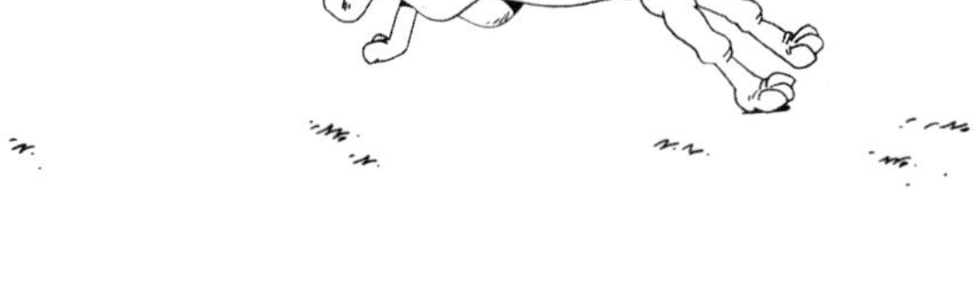

SUNDAYS

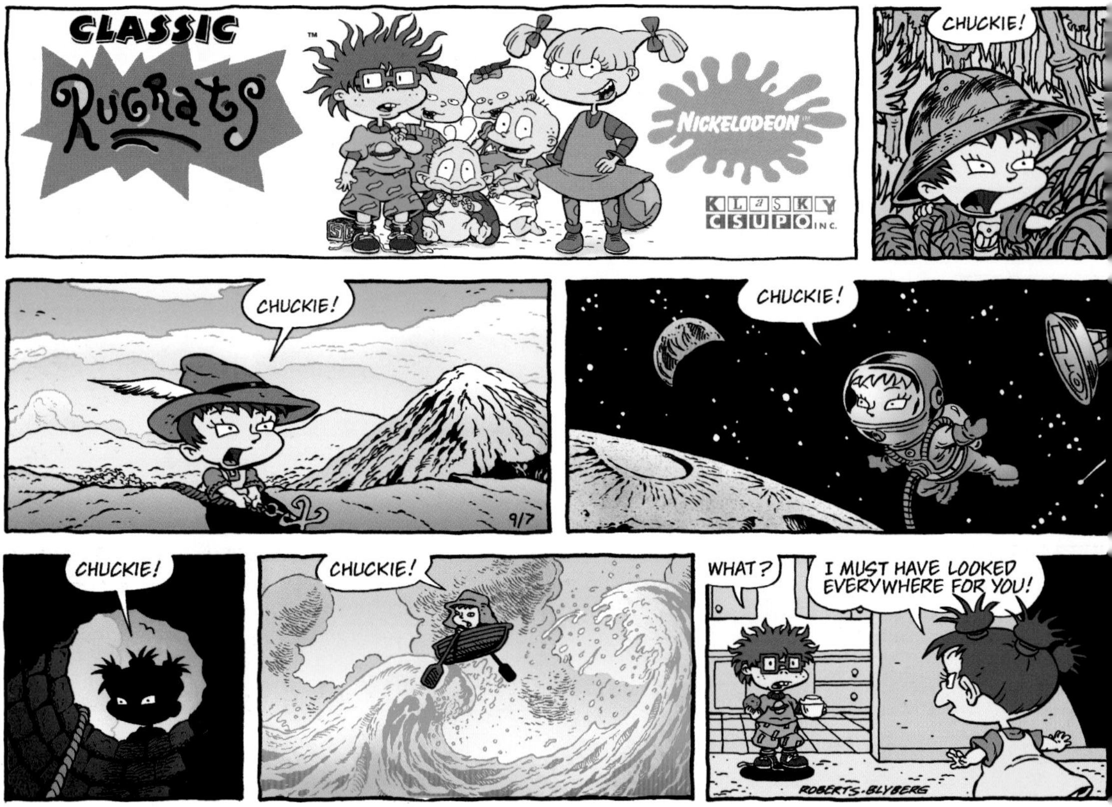
CLASSIC
Rugrats
NICKELODEON
KLASKY CSUPO INC.
CHUCKIE!
CHUCKIE!
9/7
CHUCKIE!
CHUCKIE!
CHUCKIE!
WHAT?
I MUST HAVE LOOKED EVERYWHERE FOR YOU!
ROBERTS-BLYBERG

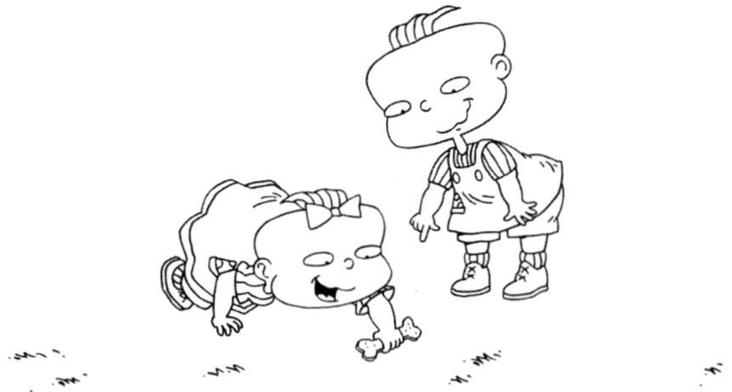

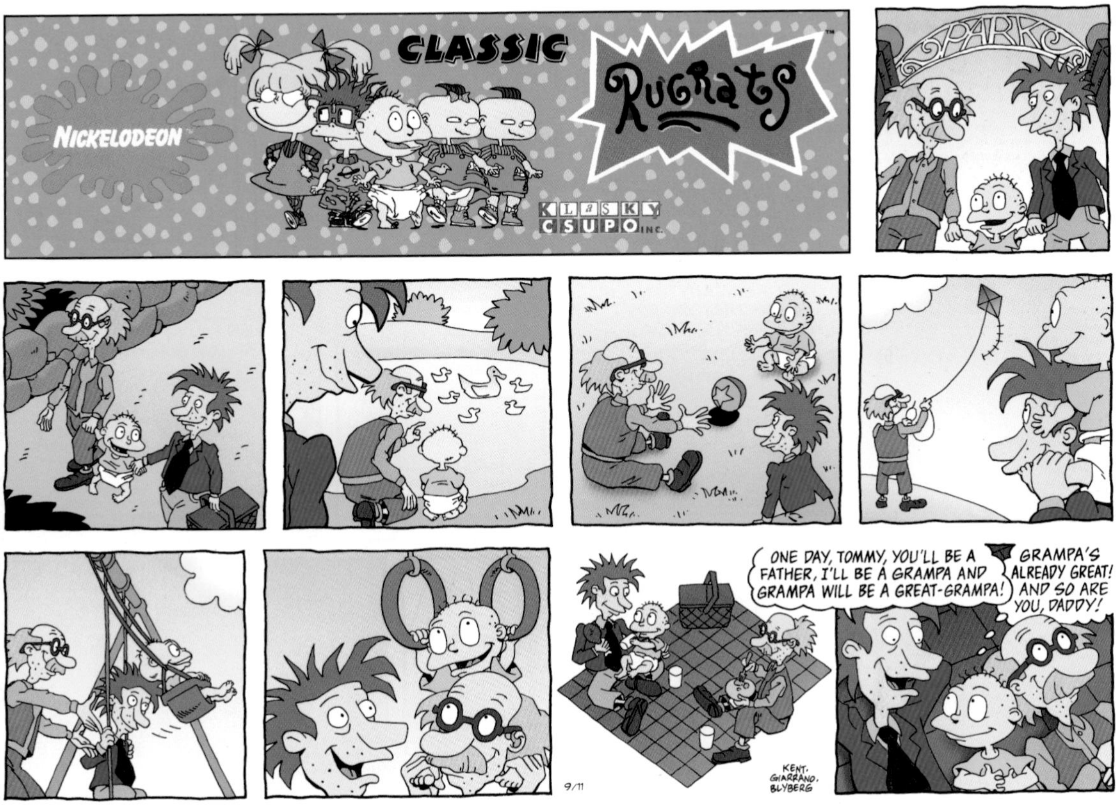
NICKELODEON
CLASSIC
Rugrats
KLASKY CSUPO INC.
PARK
ONE DAY, TOMMY, YOU'LL BE A FATHER, I'LL BE A GRAMPA AND GRAMPA WILL BE A GREAT-GRAMPA!
GRAMPA'S ALREADY GREAT! AND SO ARE YOU, DADDY!
9/11
KENT. GIARRANO. BLYBERG

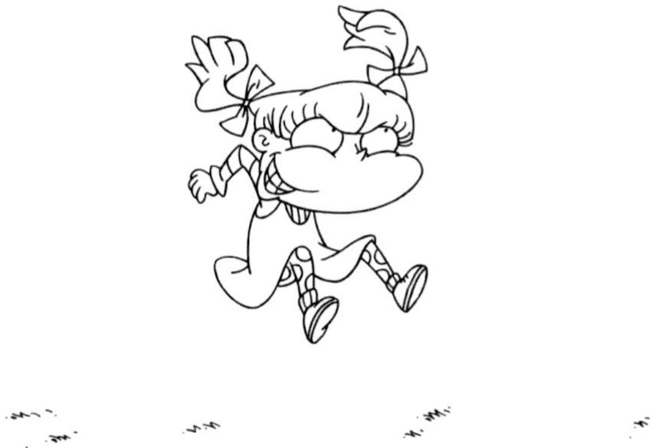

CLASSIC
RUGRATS
NICKELODEON
KLASKY CSUPO INC.
I KNOW YOU THINK I DON'T KNOW ANYTHING, BUT DON'T THINK I DON'T KNOW THAT YOU DON'T KNOW EVERYTHING YOU THINK YOU KNOW!
YOU JUST THINK YOU'RE SMART BECAUSE YOU'RE OLDER, BUT WAIT!
SOMEDAY, I'LL BE OLDER, MAYBE OLDER THAN YOU! THEN YOU'LL SEE! I'LL BE OLD AND WISE!
THEN I'LL TELL YOU STUFF YOU DON'T KNOW, THEN I'LL LAUGH! JUST WAIT! THAT'S ALL! JUST WAIT!
9/14
SLAM
"WHEN ALL IS SAID AND DUMB."
ROBERTS-BLYBERG

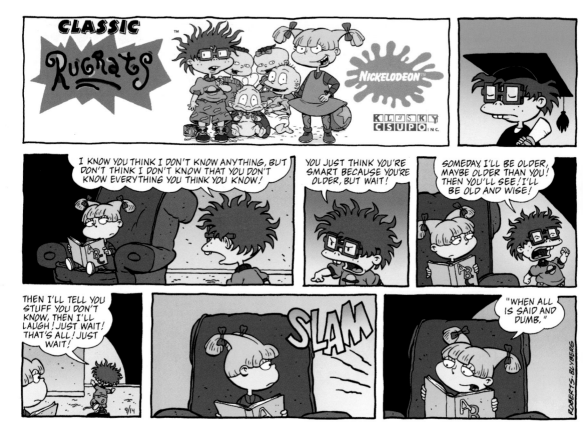

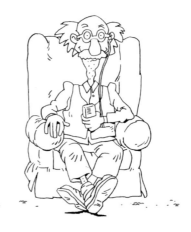

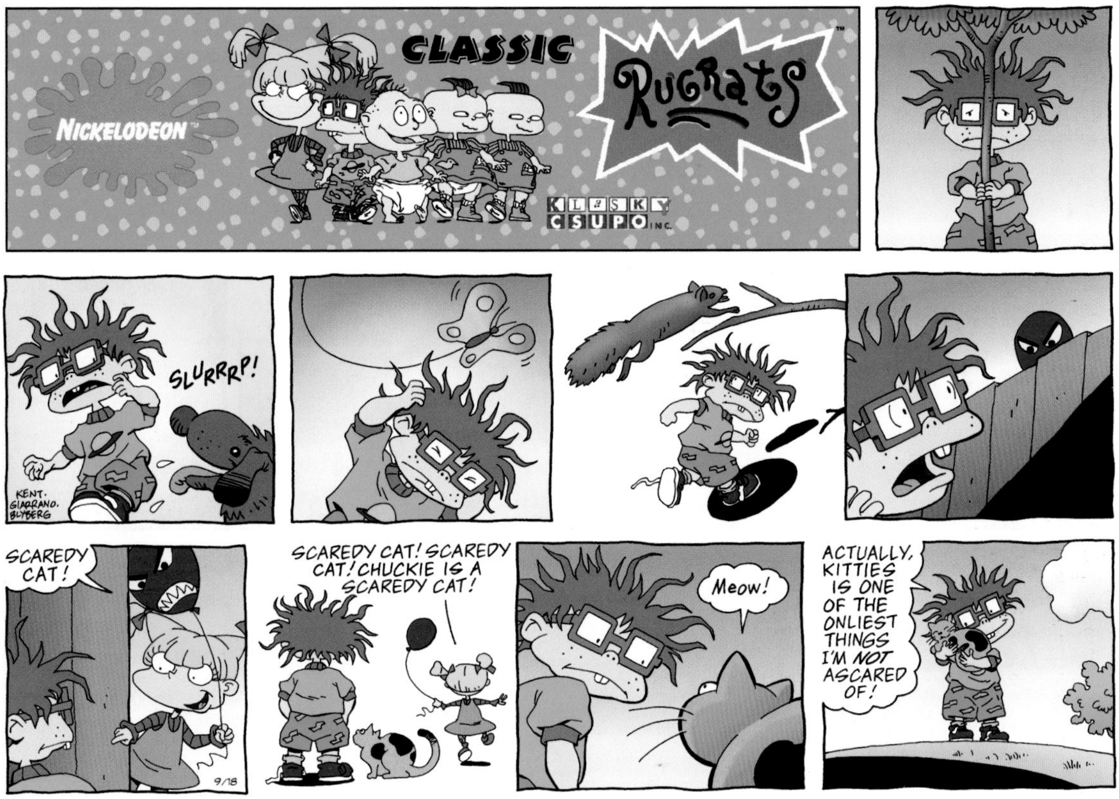
NICKELODEON
CLASSIC
RUGRATS
KLASKY CSUPO INC.
KENT. GIARRANO. BLYBERG
SLURRRP!
SCAREDY CAT!
9/18
SCAREDY CAT! SCAREDY CAT! CHUCKIE IS A SCAREDY CAT!
Meow!
ACTUALLY, KITTIES IS ONE OF THE ONLIEST THINGS I'M NOT ASCARED OF!

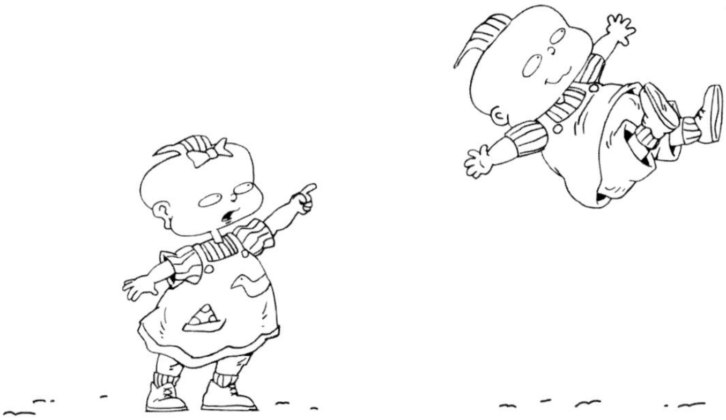

SUNDAYS

CLASSIC
Rugrats
NICKELODEON
KLASKY CSUPO INC.
WHATTYA WANNA DO, CHUCKIE?
HUH?
WANNA PLAY COOKIE CHECKERS, CHUCKIE?
I'D LIKE TO, TOMMY, BUT MY DADDY'LL BE HERE SOON.
THAT'S WHAT HE SAID.
CHUCKIE! "DUMMI BEARS" ARE ON!
I'D LOVE TO WATCH, TOMMY, BUT MY DADDY'LL BE HERE SOON.
SO MUCH FUN STUFF TO DO, AND I GOTTA LEAVE. Sigh.
CHUCKIE! LET'S HAVE A PARTY! I FOUND NOISY-MAKERS!
WHHR CLAK
CLAK
I WANNA DO ALL THAT STUFF, TOMMY, BUT MY DADDY SAID HE'D BE BACK SOON TO PICK ME UP! I GOTS TO BE READY!
9/21
BUT, CHUCKIE, DO YOU KNOW HOW MANY SOONS HAVE GONE BY WHILE YOU BEEN STANDING THERE?
I KNOW. BUT IT COULD BE THE VERY NEXT SOON.
ROBERTS. BLYBERG

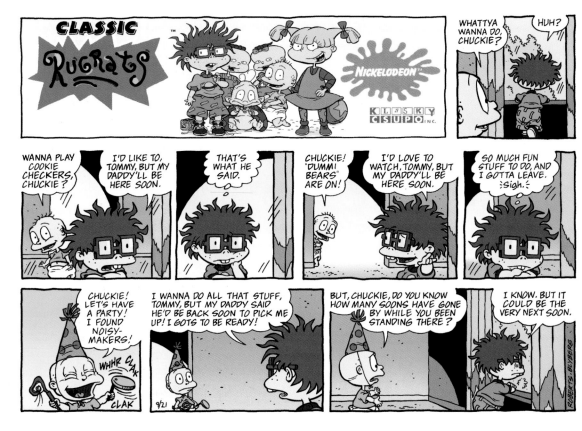

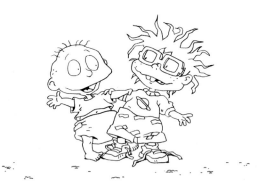

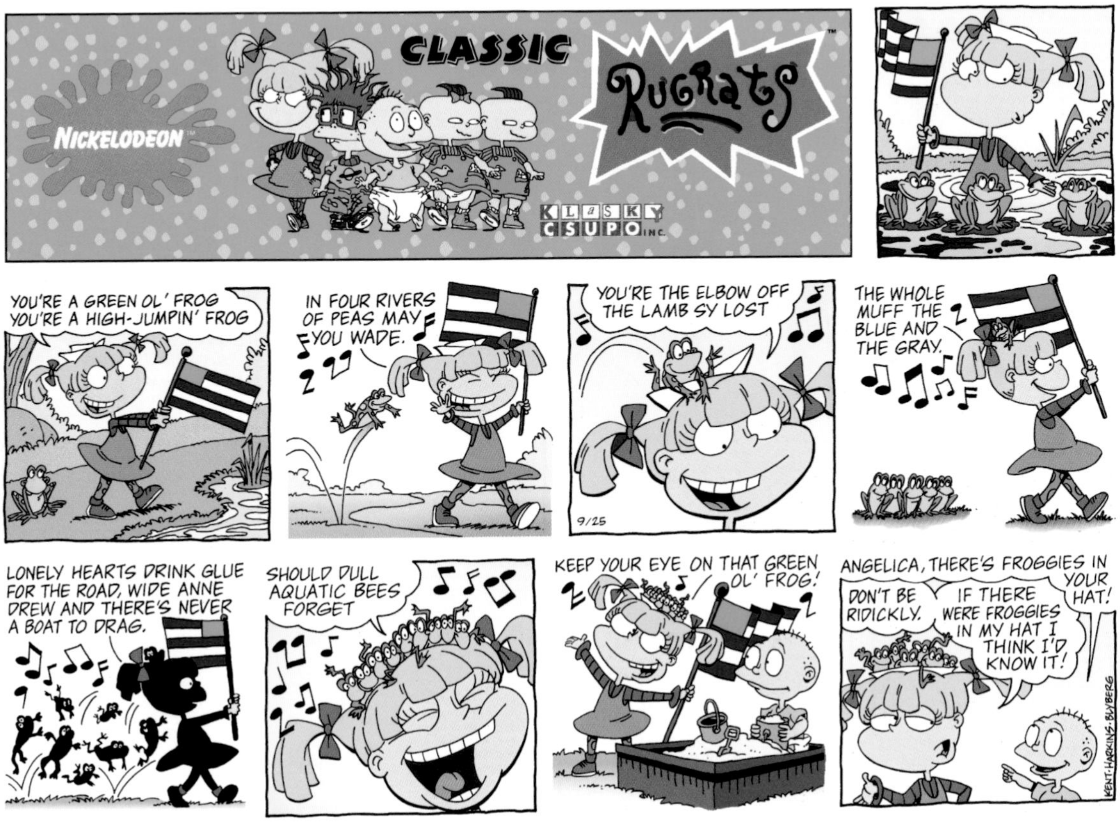

NICKELODEON
CLASSIC
RUGRATS
KLASKY CSUPO INC.
YOU'RE A GREEN OL' FROG YOU'RE A HIGH-JUMPIN' FROG
IN FOUR RIVERS OF PEAS MAY YOU WADE.
YOU'RE THE ELBOW OFF THE LAMB SY LOST
9/25
THE WHOLE MUFF THE BLUE AND THE GRAY.
LONELY HEARTS DRINK GLUE FOR THE ROAD, WIDE ANNE DREW AND THERE'S NEVER A BOAT TO DRAG.
SHOULD DULL AQUATIC BEES FORGET
KEEP YOUR EYE ON THAT GREEN OL' FROG!
ANGELICA, THERE'S FROGGIES IN YOUR HAT!
DON'T BE RIDICKLY.
IF THERE WERE FROGGIES IN MY HAT I THINK I'D KNOW IT!
KENT·HARKINS·BLYBERG

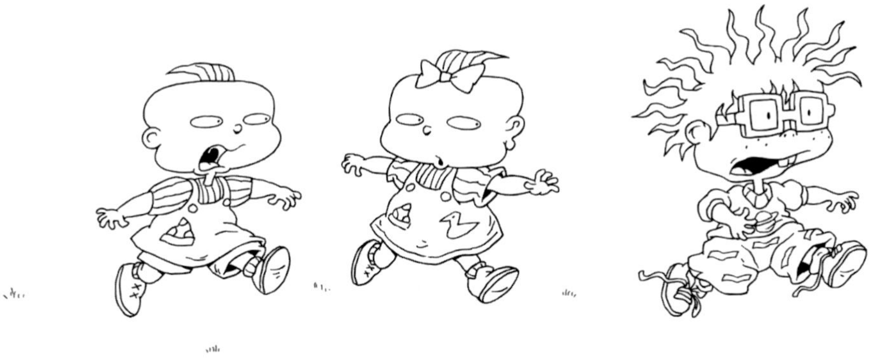

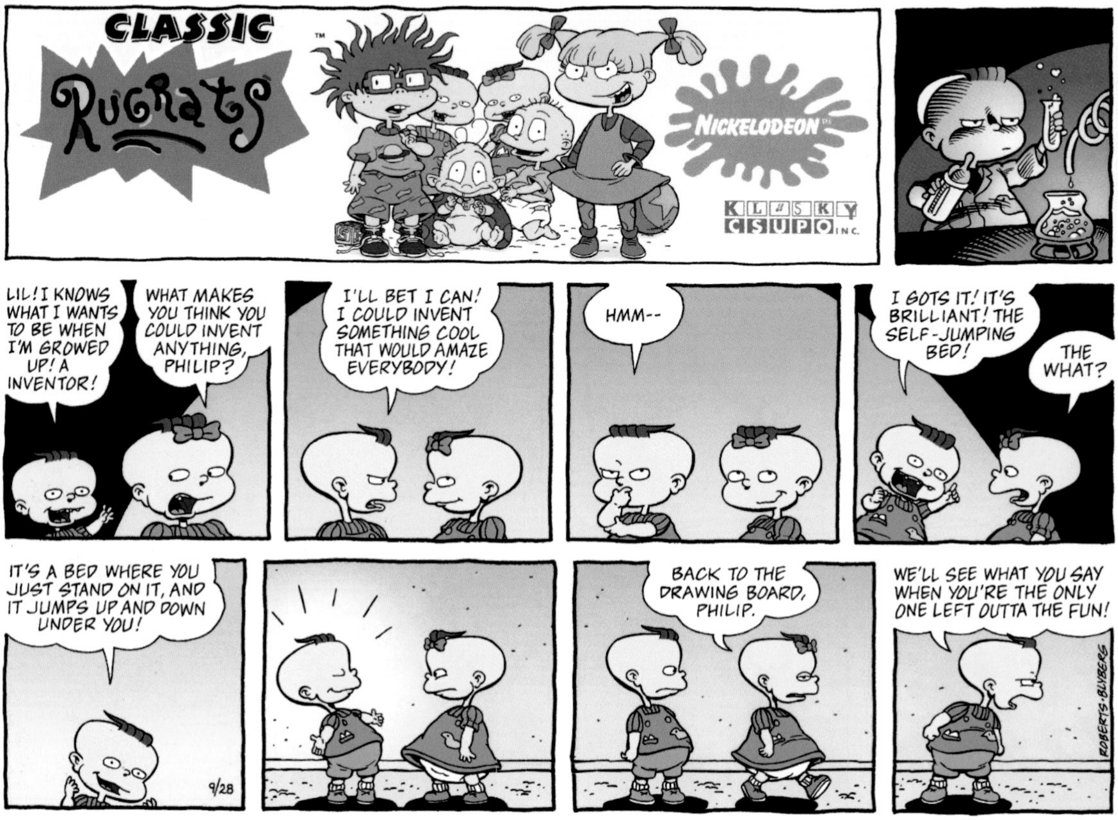
CLASSIC
RUGRATS
NICKELODEON
KLASKY CSUPO INC.
LIL! I KNOWS WHAT I WANTS TO BE WHEN I'M GROWED UP! A INVENTOR!
WHAT MAKES YOU THINK YOU COULD INVENT ANYTHING, PHILIP?
I'LL BET I CAN! I COULD INVENT SOMETHING COOL THAT WOULD AMAZE EVERYBODY!
HMM--
I GOTS IT! IT'S BRILLIANT! THE SELF-JUMPING BED!
THE WHAT?
IT'S A BED WHERE YOU JUST STAND ON IT, AND IT JUMPS UP AND DOWN UNDER YOU!
9/28
BACK TO THE DRAWING BOARD, PHILIP.
WE'LL SEE WHAT YOU SAY WHEN YOU'RE THE ONLY ONE LEFT OUTTA THE FUN!
ROBERTS·BLYBERG

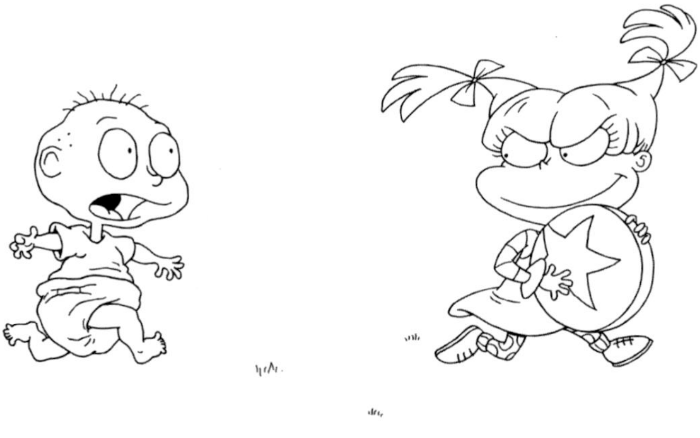

NICKELODEON
CLASSIC
Rugrats
KLASKY CSUPO INC.
THANKS FOR LETTING ME SLEEP OVER, TOMMY.
IF THERE'S TWO OF US, THE MONSTERS MIGHT NOT COME!
KENT·ROBERTS·BLYBERG
DID YOU HEAR THAT?!
IT'S THE MONSTERS!
WHAT'LL WE DO?! WHAT'LL WE DO?!
HIDE UNDER THE BED!
NO! THAT'S THE FIRSTEST PLACE MONSTERS LOOK!
HIDE IN THE CLOSET!
NO! THAT'S WHERE MONSTERS LIVE!
WHAT DO WE DO?!
SHUT YOUR EYES TIGHT!
THINK THEY'RE STILL OUT THERE?
DOESN'T MATTER.
AS LONG AS WE'VE GOT OUR EYES CLOSED, THE MONSTERS CAN'T SEE US!

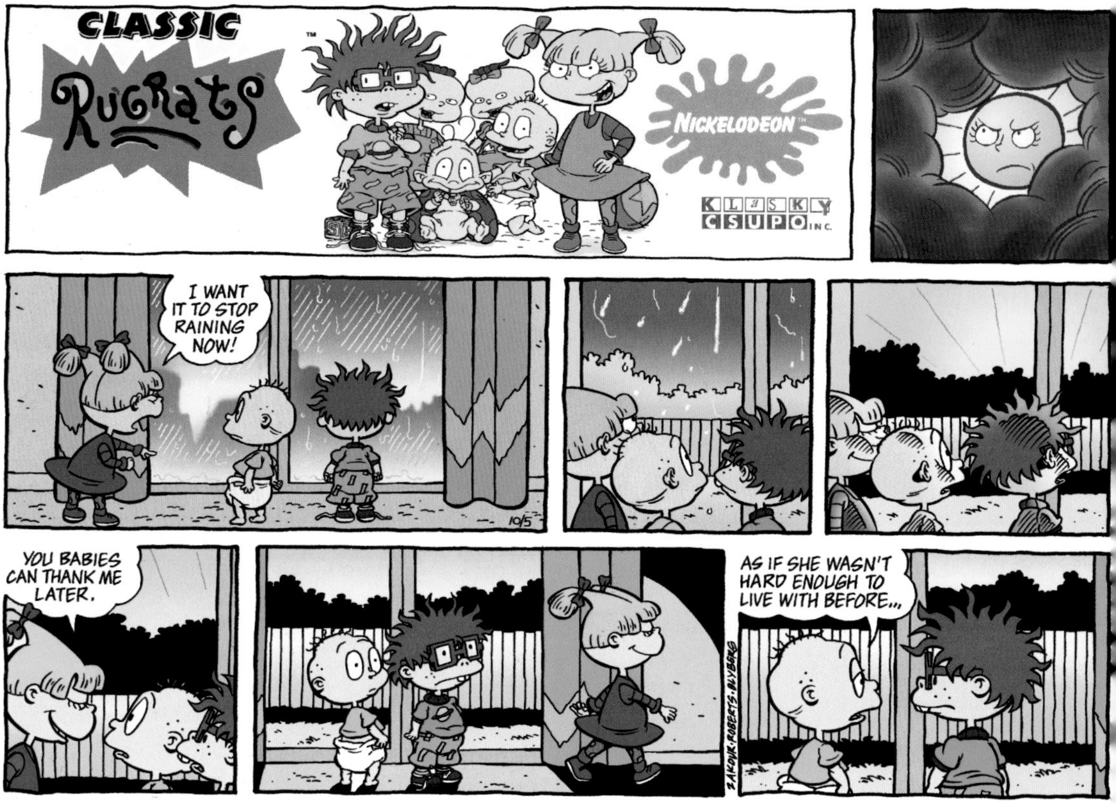
CLASSIC
Rugrats
NICKELODEON
KLASKY CSUPO INC.
I WANT IT TO STOP RAINING NOW!
10/5
YOU BABIES CAN THANK ME LATER.
AS IF SHE WASN'T HARD ENOUGH TO LIVE WITH BEFORE...

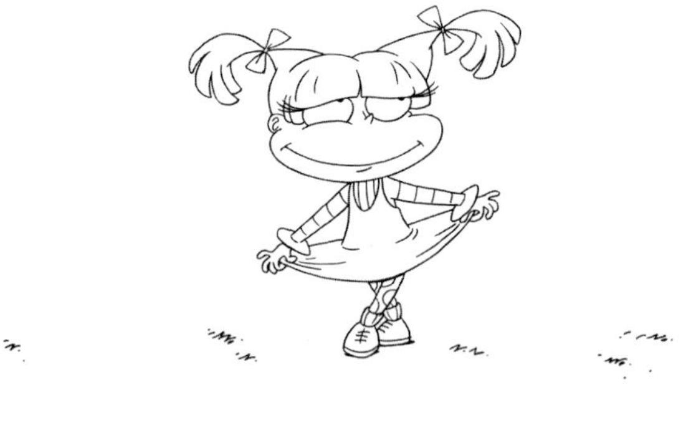

CLASSIC
Rugrats
NICKELODEON
KLASKY CSUPO INC.
C'MON, ANGELICA, TWO MORE BITES.
FOR DADDY. JUST TWO MORE BITES.
ALL RIGHT, HAVE IT YOUR WAY. JUST THREE BITES.
THAT'S ALL, JUST THREE.
OKAY, PRINCESS, YOU WIN.
YOU JUST HAVE TO EAT FOUR BITES AND YOU'RE DONE.
TELL YOU WHAT, HONEY. YOU EAT TEN BITES AND WE'LL CALL IT EVEN.
DADDY, HOW MANY BITES IS TEN?
JUST TWENTY MORE.
GOOD!
10/9
KENT. GIARRANO. BLYBERG

SUNDAYS

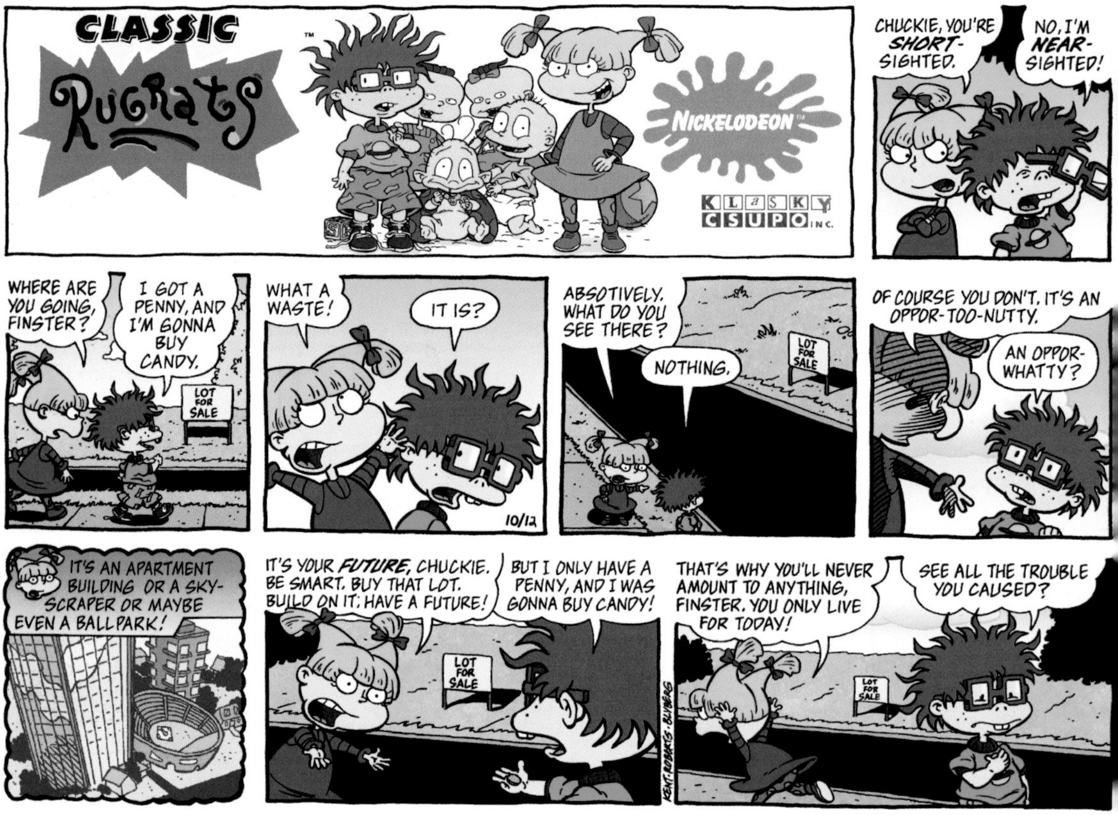
CLASSIC
Rugrats
NICKELODEON
KLASKY CSUPO INC.
CHUCKIE, YOU'RE *SHORT*-SIGHTED.
NO, I'M *NEAR*-SIGHTED!
WHERE ARE YOU GOING, FINSTER?
I GOT A PENNY, AND I'M GONNA BUY CANDY.
LOT FOR SALE
WHAT A WASTE!
IT IS?
10/12
ABSOTIVELY. WHAT DO YOU SEE THERE?
NOTHING.
LOT FOR SALE
OF COURSE YOU DON'T. IT'S AN OPPOR-TOO-NUTTY.
AN OPPOR-WHATTY?
IT'S AN APARTMENT BUILDING OR A SKY-SCRAPER OR MAYBE EVEN A BALLPARK!
IT'S YOUR *FUTURE*, CHUCKIE. BE SMART. BUY THAT LOT. BUILD ON IT; HAVE A FUTURE!
BUT I ONLY HAVE A PENNY, AND I WAS GONNA BUY CANDY!
LOT FOR SALE
KENT ROBERTS · BLYBERG
THAT'S WHY YOU'LL NEVER AMOUNT TO ANYTHING, FINSTER. YOU ONLY LIVE FOR TODAY!
SEE ALL THE TROUBLE YOU CAUSED?
LOT FOR SALE

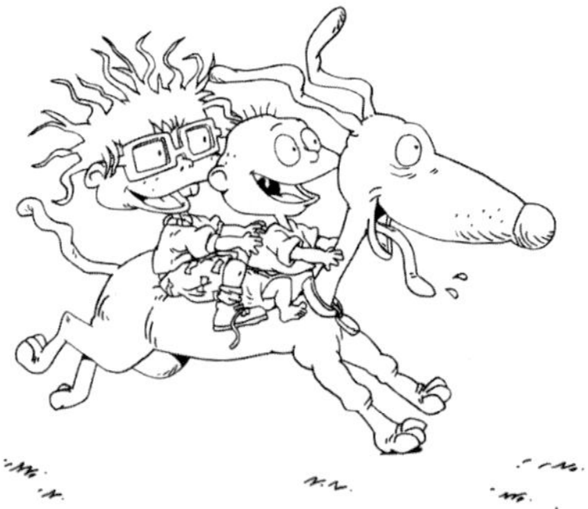

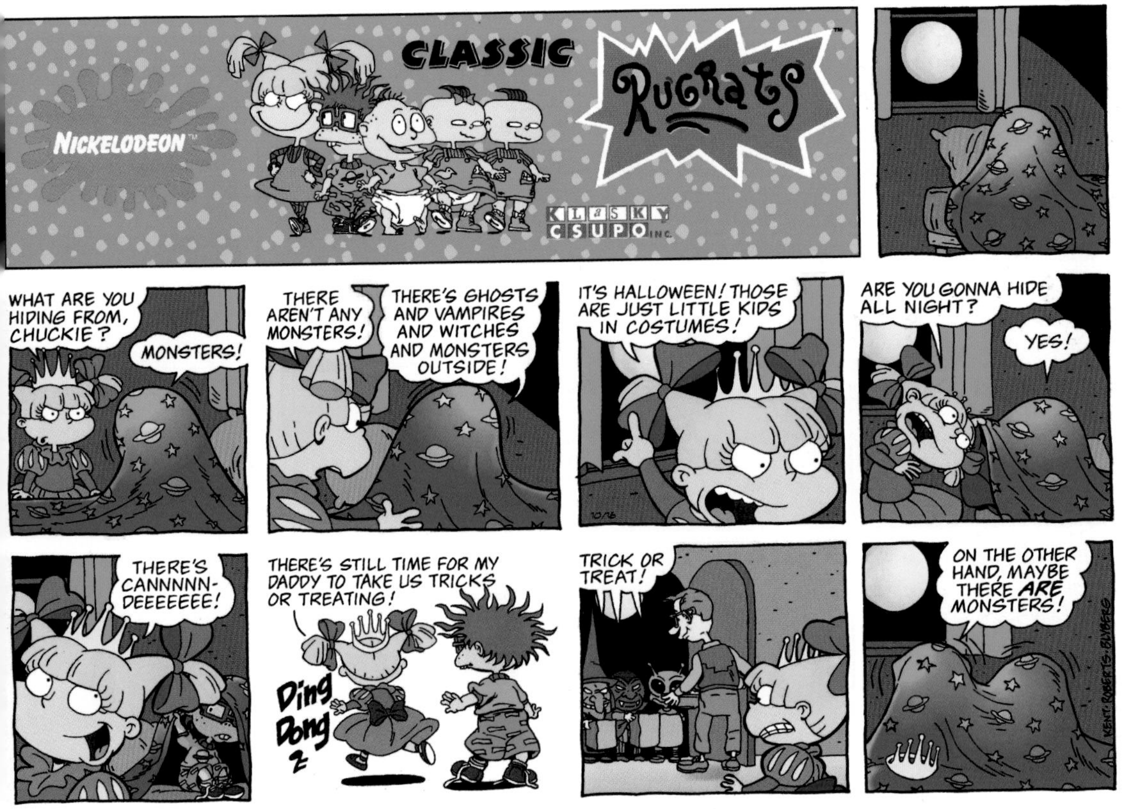
NICKELODEON
CLASSIC
Rugrats
KLASKY CSUPO INC.
WHAT ARE YOU HIDING FROM, CHUCKIE?
MONSTERS!
THERE AREN'T ANY MONSTERS!
THERE'S GHOSTS AND VAMPIRES AND WITCHES AND MONSTERS OUTSIDE!
IT'S HALLOWEEN! THOSE ARE JUST LITTLE KIDS IN COSTUMES!
ARE YOU GONNA HIDE ALL NIGHT?
YES!
THERE'S CANNNNN-DEEEEEEE!
THERE'S STILL TIME FOR MY DADDY TO TAKE US TRICKS OR TREATING!
Ding Dong
TRICK OR TREAT!
ON THE OTHER HAND, MAYBE THERE *ARE* MONSTERS!

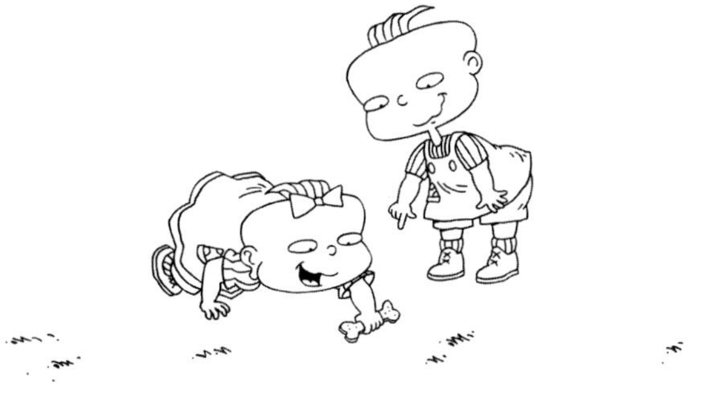

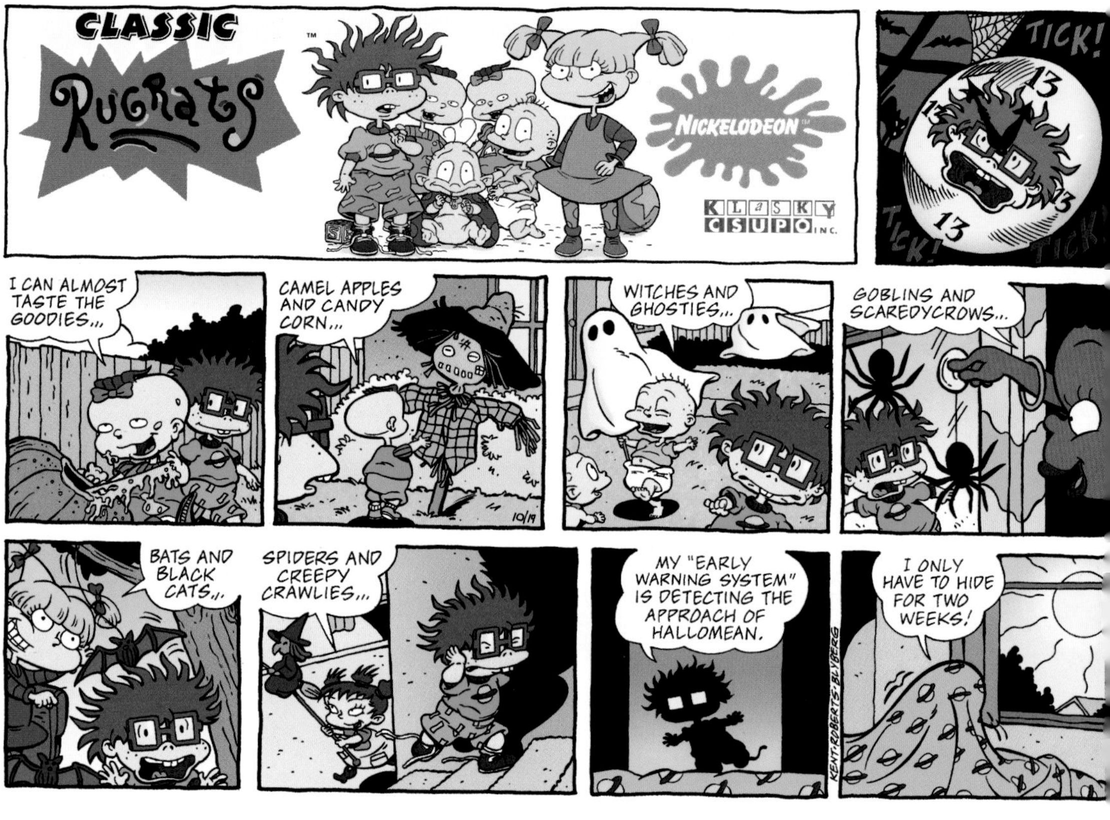

CLASSIC
RUGRATS
NICKELODEON
KLASKY CSUPO INC.
TICK!
TICK!
TICK!
13
13
13
13
I CAN ALMOST TASTE THE GOODIES...
CAMEL APPLES AND CANDY CORN...
10/19
WITCHES AND GHOSTIES...
GOBLINS AND SCAREDYCROWS...
BATS AND BLACK CATS...
SPIDERS AND CREEPY CRAWLIES...
MY "EARLY WARNING SYSTEM" IS DETECTING THE APPROACH OF HALLOMEAN.
KENT ROBERTS · BLYBERG
I ONLY HAVE TO HIDE FOR TWO WEEKS!

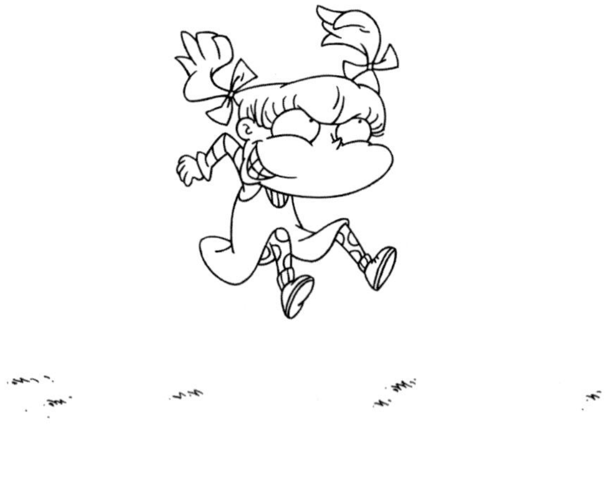

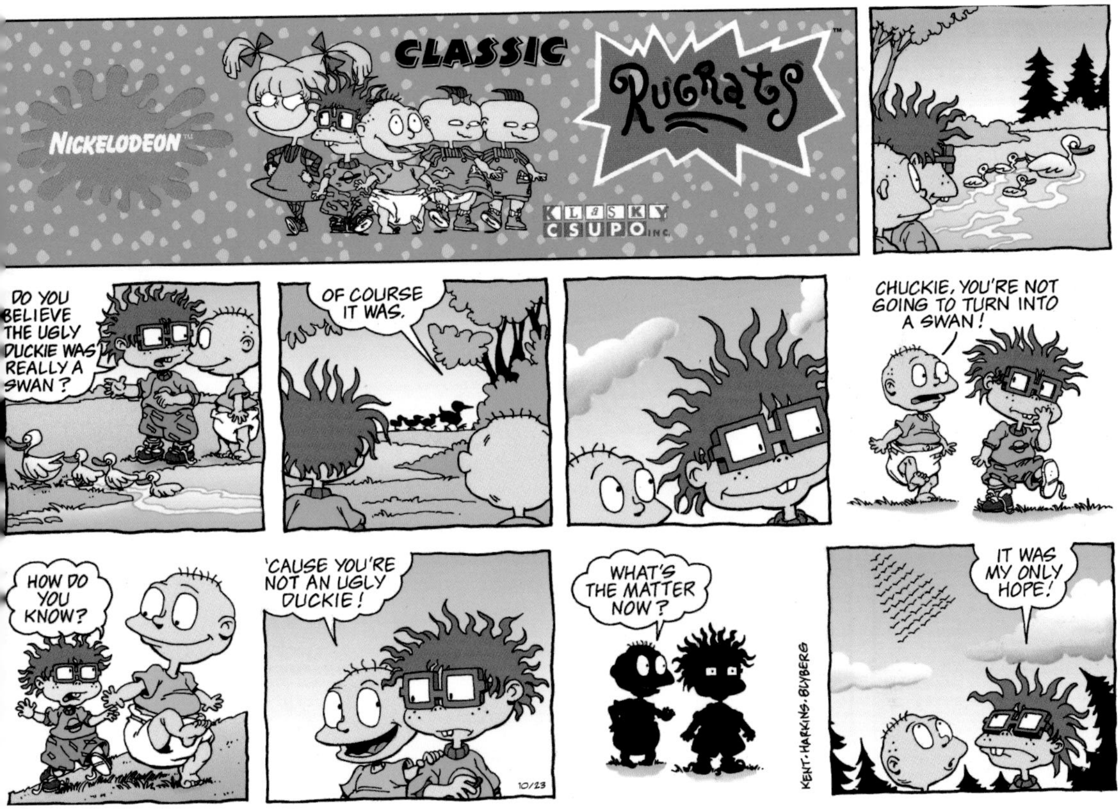

NICKELODEON
CLASSIC
Rugrats
KLASKY CSUPO INC.
DO YOU BELIEVE THE UGLY DUCKIE WAS REALLY A SWAN?
OF COURSE IT WAS.
CHUCKIE, YOU'RE NOT GOING TO TURN INTO A SWAN!
HOW DO YOU KNOW?
'CAUSE YOU'RE NOT AN UGLY DUCKIE!
10/23
WHAT'S THE MATTER NOW?
KENT·HARKINS·BLYBERG
IT WAS MY ONLY HOPE!

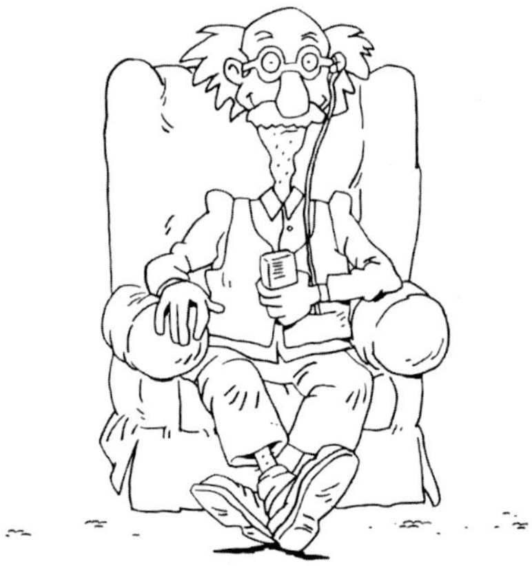

SUNDAYS

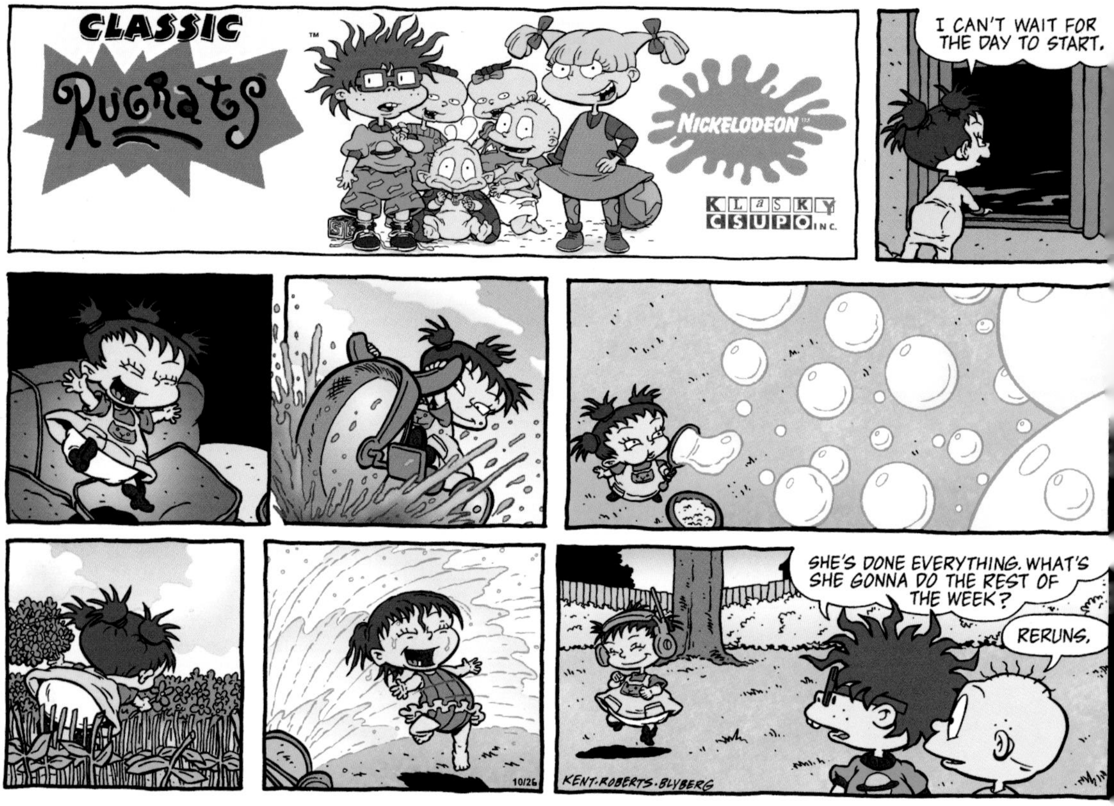
CLASSIC
Rugrats
NICKELODEON
KLASKY CSUPO INC.
I CAN'T WAIT FOR THE DAY TO START.
SHE'S DONE EVERYTHING. WHAT'S SHE GONNA DO THE REST OF THE WEEK?
RERUNS.
10/26
KENT·ROBERTS·BLYBERG

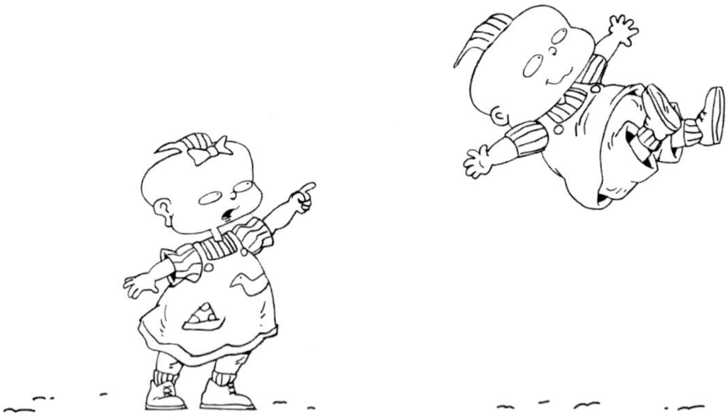

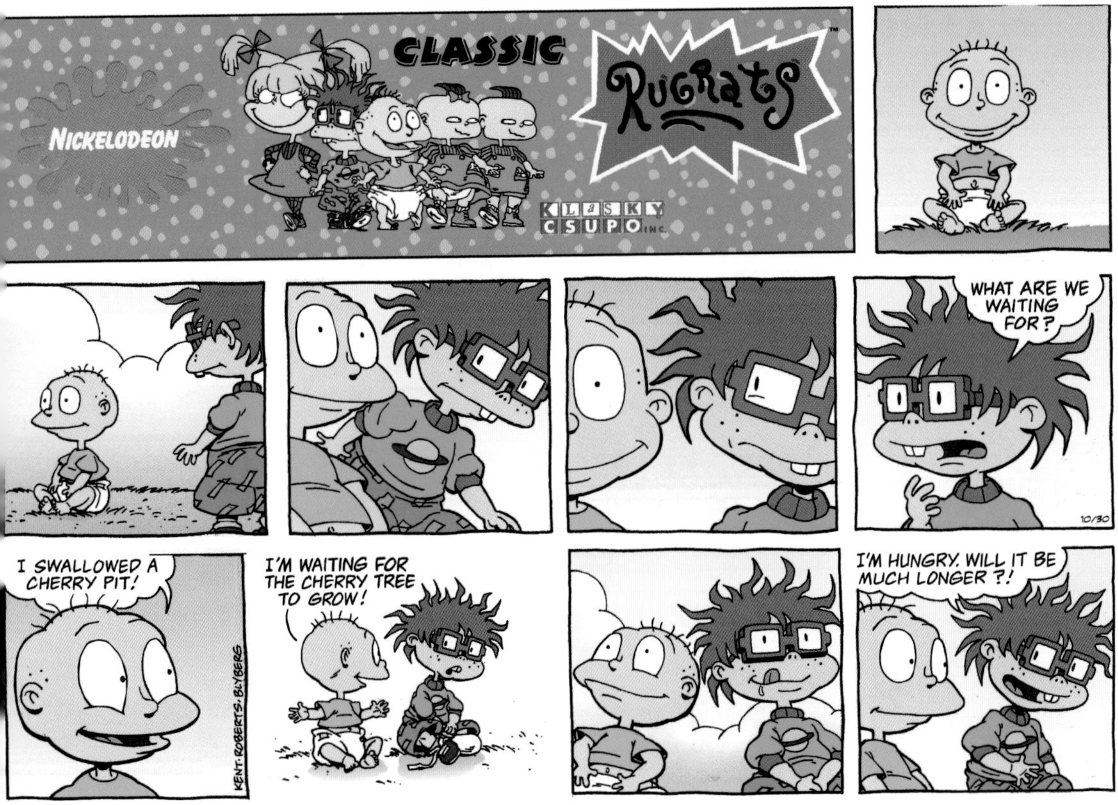
NICKELODEON
CLASSIC
Rugrats
KLASKY CSUPO INC.
WHAT ARE WE WAITING FOR?
10/30
I SWALLOWED A CHERRY PIT!
I'M WAITING FOR THE CHERRY TREE TO GROW!
I'M HUNGRY. WILL IT BE MUCH LONGER?!

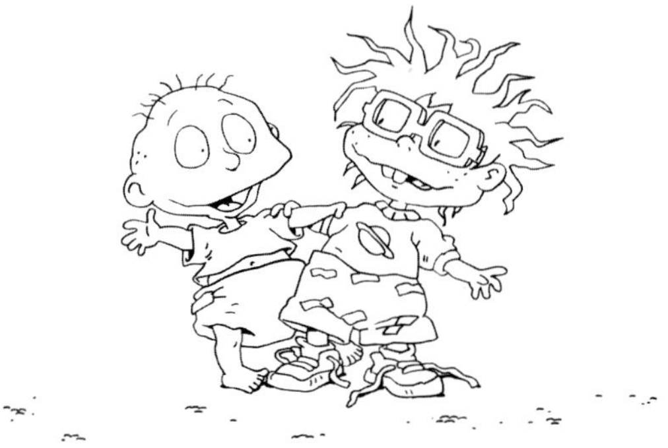

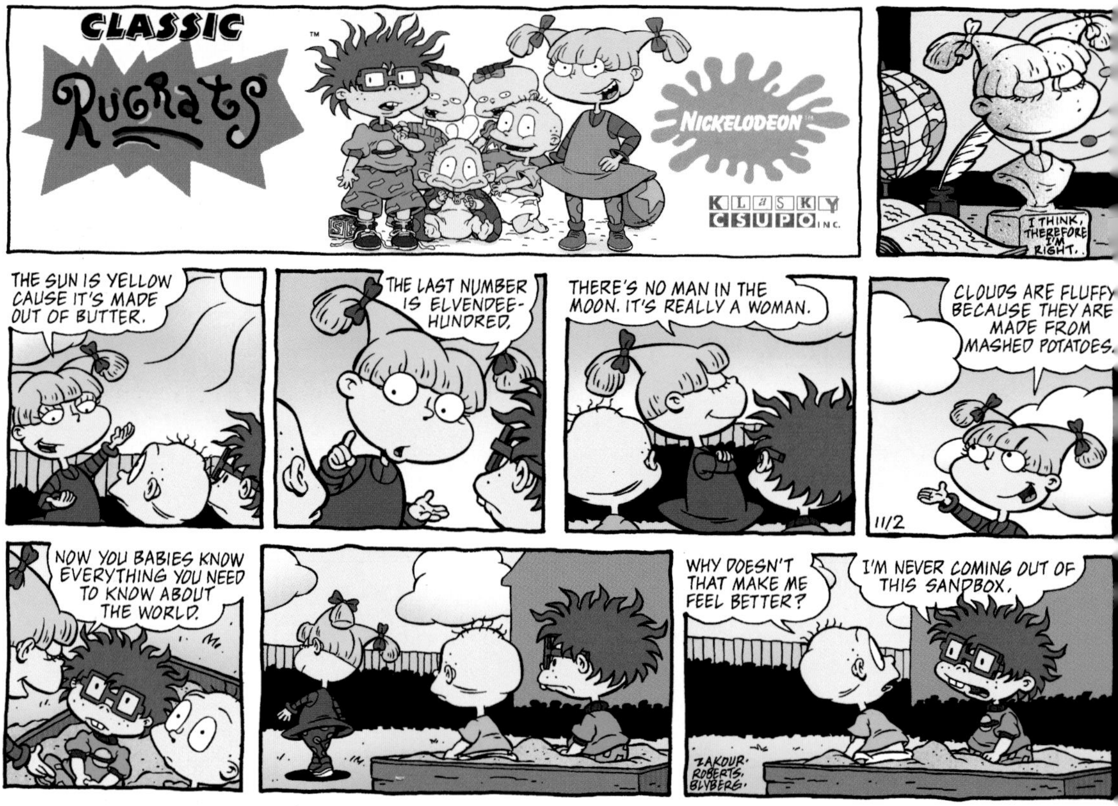
CLASSIC
Rugrats
NICKELODEON
KLASKY CSUPO INC.
I THINK, THEREFORE I'M RIGHT.
THE SUN IS YELLOW CAUSE IT'S MADE OUT OF BUTTER.
THE LAST NUMBER IS ELVENDEE-HUNDRED.
THERE'S NO MAN IN THE MOON. IT'S REALLY A WOMAN.
CLOUDS ARE FLUFFY BECAUSE THEY ARE MADE FROM MASHED POTATOES.
11/2
NOW YOU BABIES KNOW EVERYTHING YOU NEED TO KNOW ABOUT THE WORLD.
WHY DOESN'T THAT MAKE ME FEEL BETTER?
I'M NEVER COMING OUT OF THIS SANDBOX.
ZAKOUR· ROBERTS· BLYBERG·

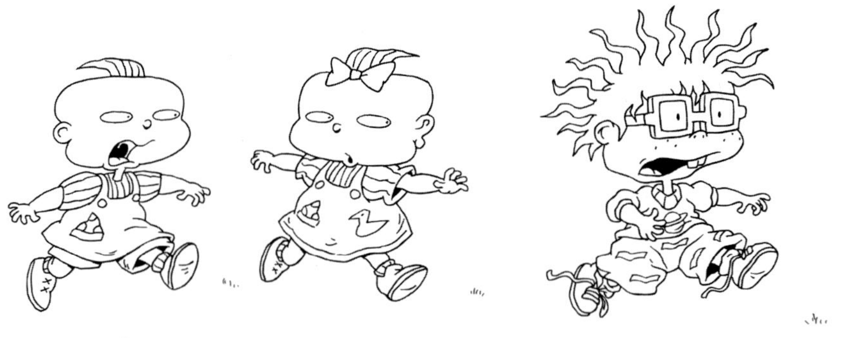

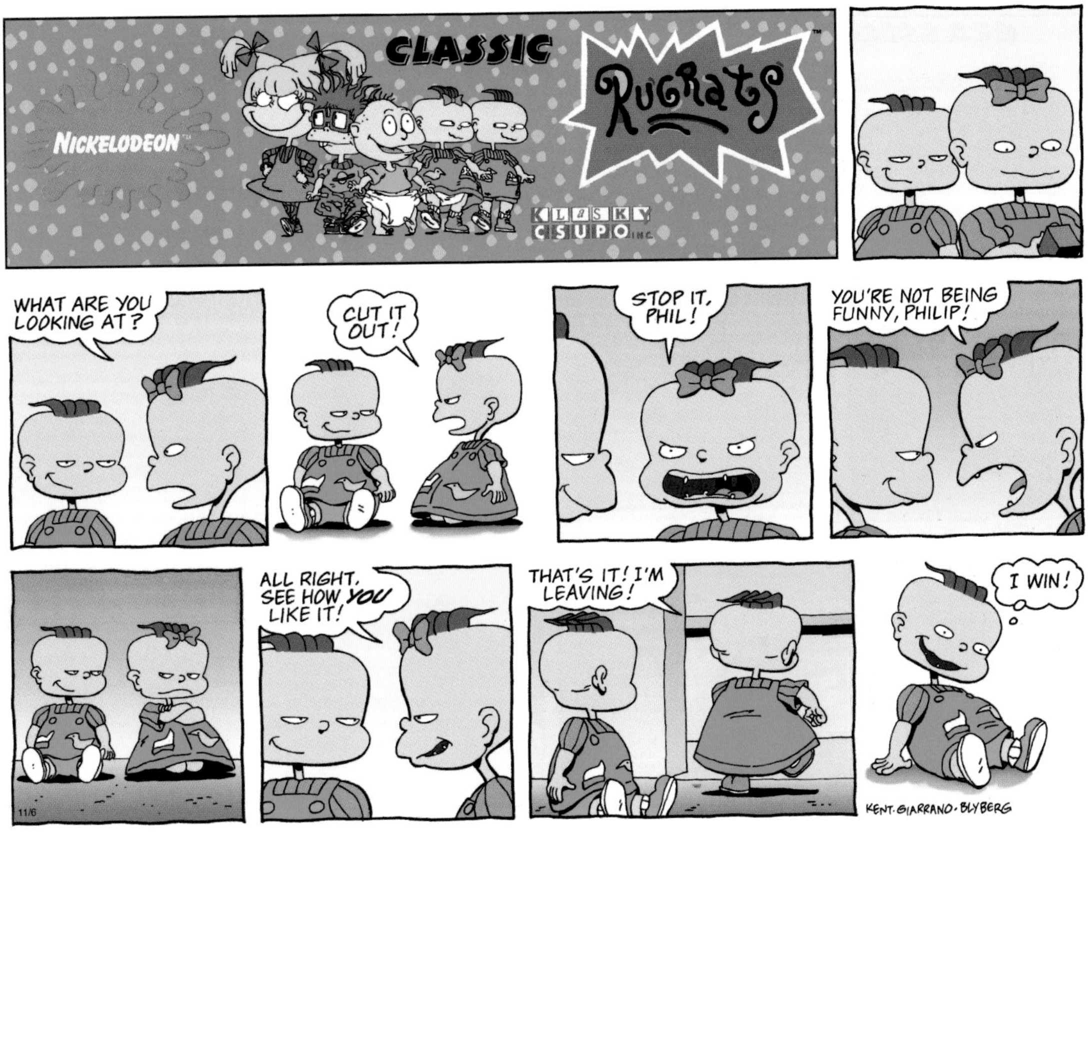
NICKELODEON
CLASSIC
Rugrats
KLASKY CSUPO INC.
WHAT ARE YOU LOOKING AT?
CUT IT OUT!
STOP IT, PHIL!
YOU'RE NOT BEING FUNNY, PHILIP!
11/6
ALL RIGHT, SEE HOW YOU LIKE IT!
THAT'S IT! I'M LEAVING!
I WIN!
KENT·GIARRANO·BLYBERG

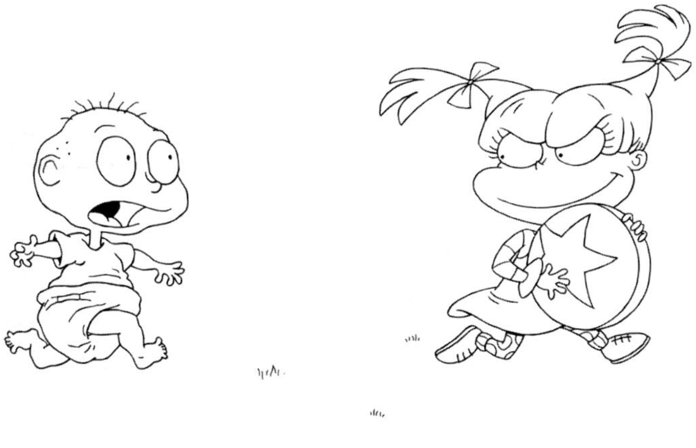

SUNDAYS

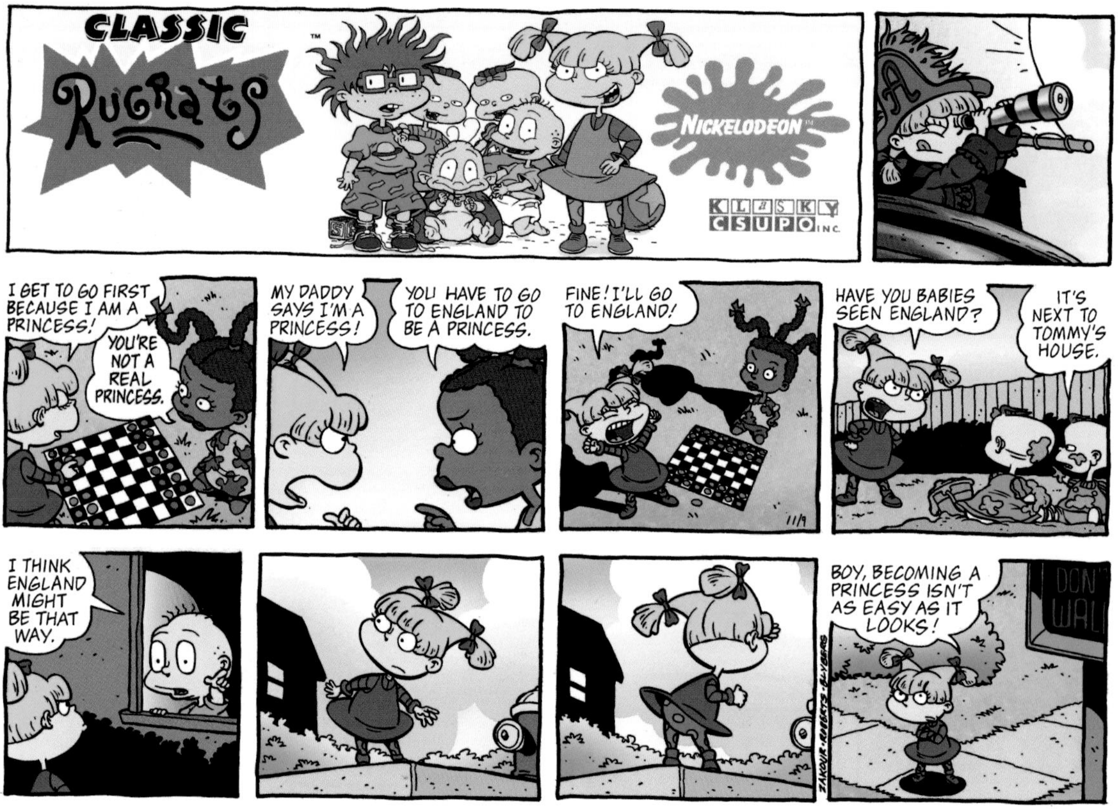
CLASSIC
Rugrats
NICKELODEON
KLASKY CSUPO INC.
I GET TO GO FIRST BECAUSE I AM A PRINCESS!
YOU'RE NOT A REAL PRINCESS.
MY DADDY SAYS I'M A PRINCESS!
YOU HAVE TO GO TO ENGLAND TO BE A PRINCESS.
FINE! I'LL GO TO ENGLAND!
11/9
HAVE YOU BABIES SEEN ENGLAND?
IT'S NEXT TO TOMMY'S HOUSE.
I THINK ENGLAND MIGHT BE THAT WAY.
BOY, BECOMING A PRINCESS ISN'T AS EASY AS IT LOOKS!

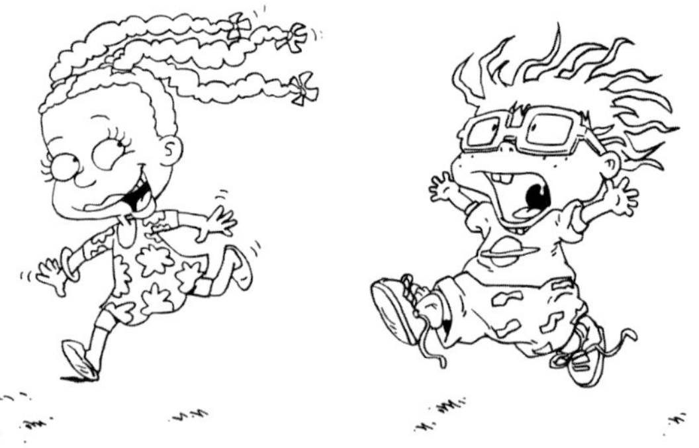

CLASSIC
Rugrats
NICKELODEON
KLASKY CSUPO INC.
LOOK, TOMMY AND CHUCKIE! THAT CLOUD LOOKS LIKE A DUCKY!
THAT CLOUD LOOKS LIKE A RHINOSAMOOSE!
AND THAT ONE LOOKS LIKE A BANDAMA SPLIT WITH A CHERRY ON TOP!
THAT'S GREAT, SUSIE. WHAT DO YOU SEE, CHUCKIE?
WELL?
KENT
11/12
I KNOW! I KNOW!
FIELDS
THAT ONE LOOKS LIKE A BIG BOWL OF OATMEAL THAT'S JUST ABOUT TO...
BLYBERG
...SPILL.

SUNDAYS

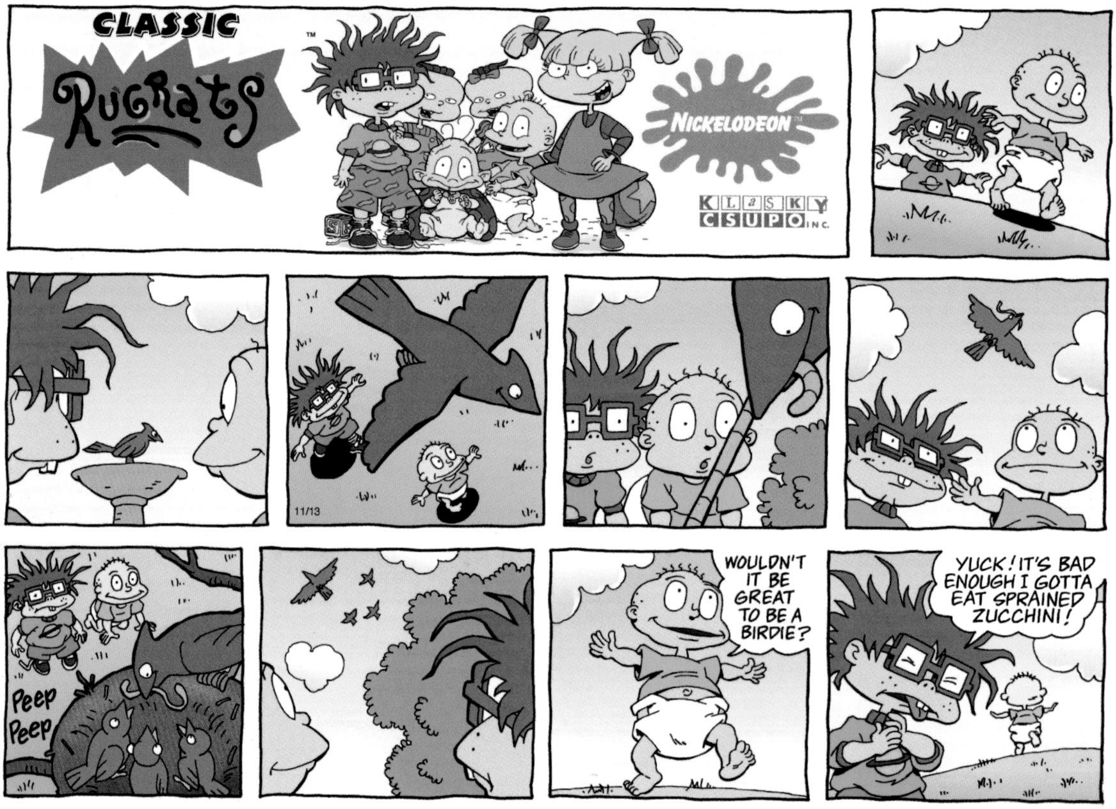
CLASSIC
Rugrats
NICKELODEON
KLaSKY CSUPO INC.
11/13
Peep Peep
WOULDN'T IT BE GREAT TO BE A BIRDIE?
YUCK! IT'S BAD ENOUGH I GOTTA EAT SPRAINED ZUCCHINI!

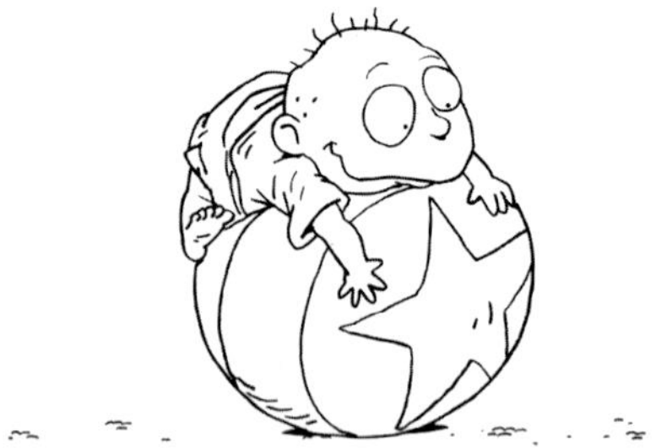

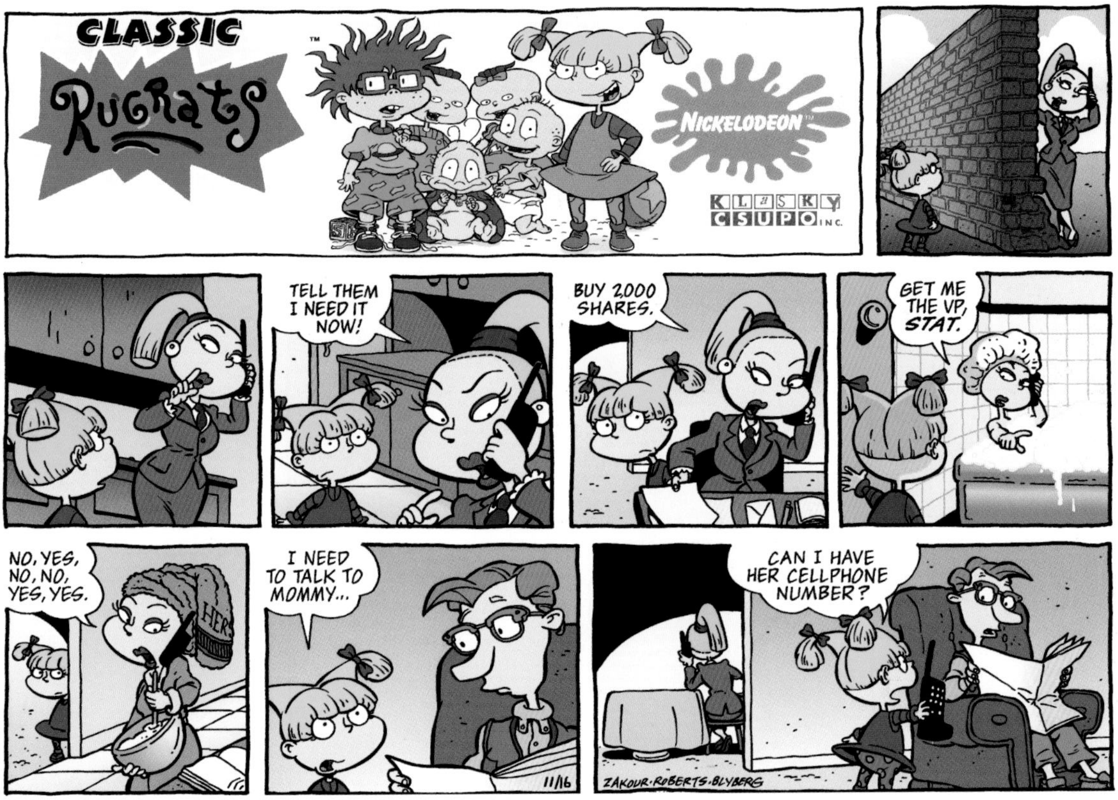
CLASSIC
Rugrats
NICKELODEON
KLASKY CSUPO INC.
TELL THEM I NEED IT NOW!
BUY 2000 SHARES.
GET ME THE VP, STAT.
NO, YES, NO, NO, YES, YES.
HER$
I NEED TO TALK TO MOMMY...
11/16
CAN I HAVE HER CELLPHONE NUMBER?
ZAKOUR·ROBERTS·BLYBERG

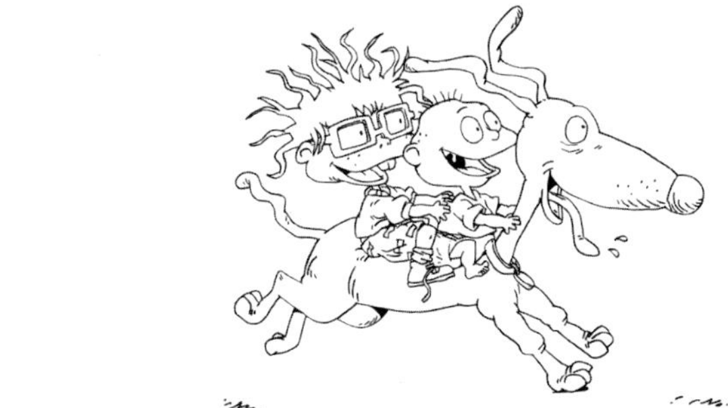

SUNDAYS

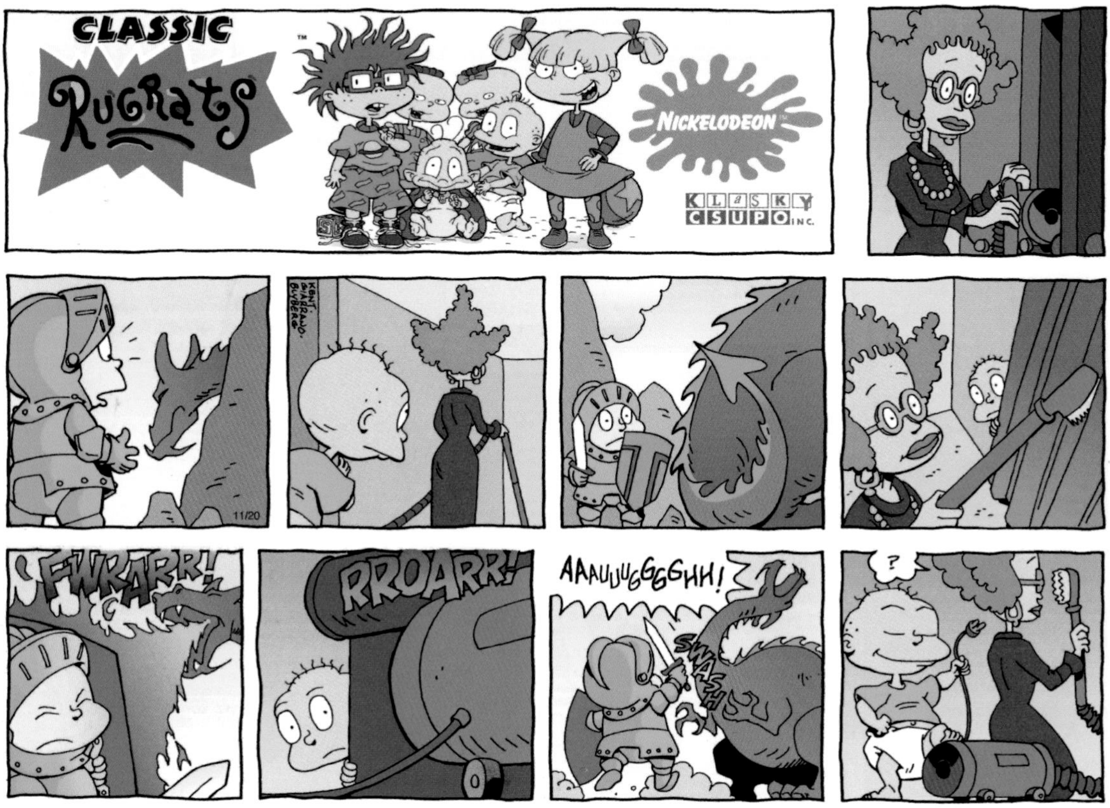
CLASSIC
Rugrats
NICKELODEON
KLASKY CSUPO INC.
11/20
FWRARR!
RROARR!
AAAUUUGGGGHH!
SWASH
?

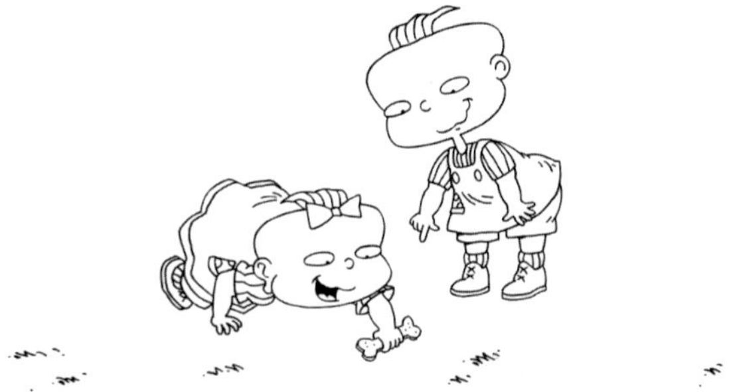

SUNDAYS

CLASSIC
Rugrats
NICKELODEON
KLASKY CSUPO INC.
C'MON, SPIKE. LET'S PLAY CATCH.
SIT UP, SPIKE.
SPEAK, SPIKE.
BEG, SPIKE.
ROLL OVER, SPIKE.
STAY, SPIKE.
GOOD BOY, SPIKE.
KENT·ROBERTS·BLYBERG
YOU COULD GO ON T.B. WITH THAT ACT, TOMMY!
NOT YET, BUT PRETTY SOON!
11/23

SUNDAYS

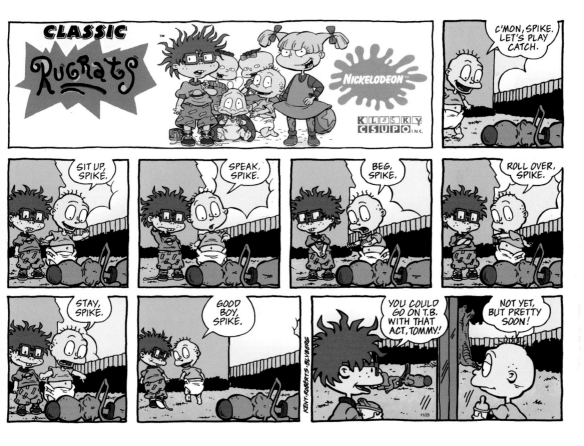

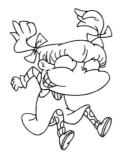

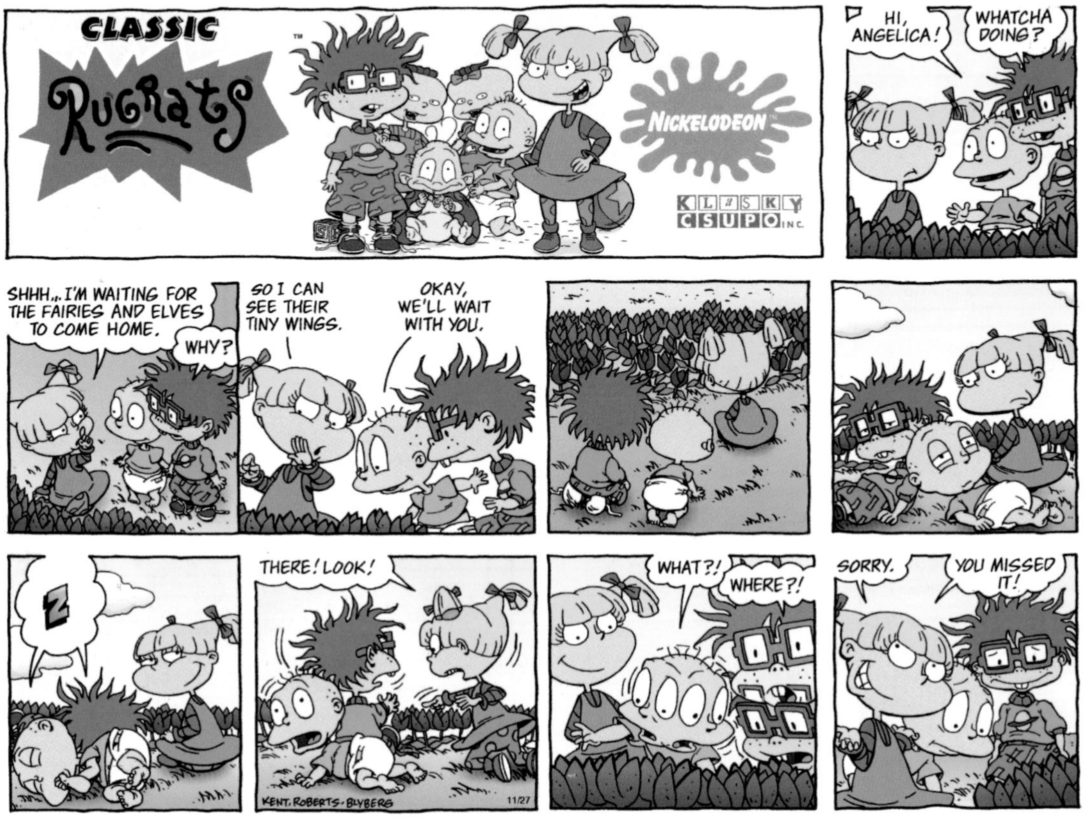
CLASSIC
Rugrats
NICKELODEON
KLASKY CSUPO INC.
HI, ANGELICA!
WHATCHA DOING?
SHHH... I'M WAITING FOR THE FAIRIES AND ELVES TO COME HOME.
WHY?
SO I CAN SEE THEIR TINY WINGS.
OKAY, WE'LL WAIT WITH YOU.
Z
THERE! LOOK!
KENT. ROBERTS. BLYBERG
11/27
WHAT?!
WHERE?!
SORRY.
YOU MISSED IT!

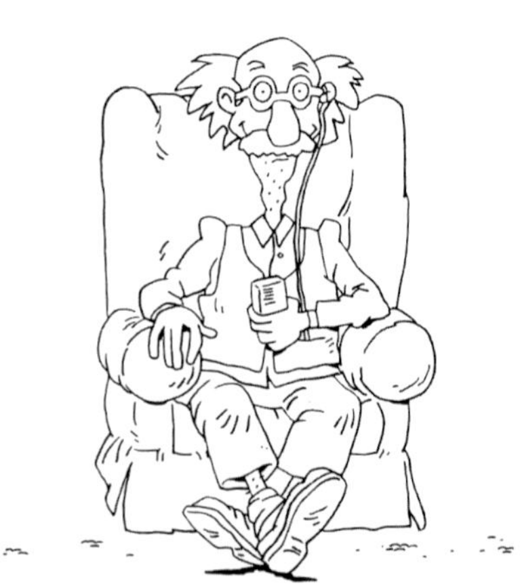

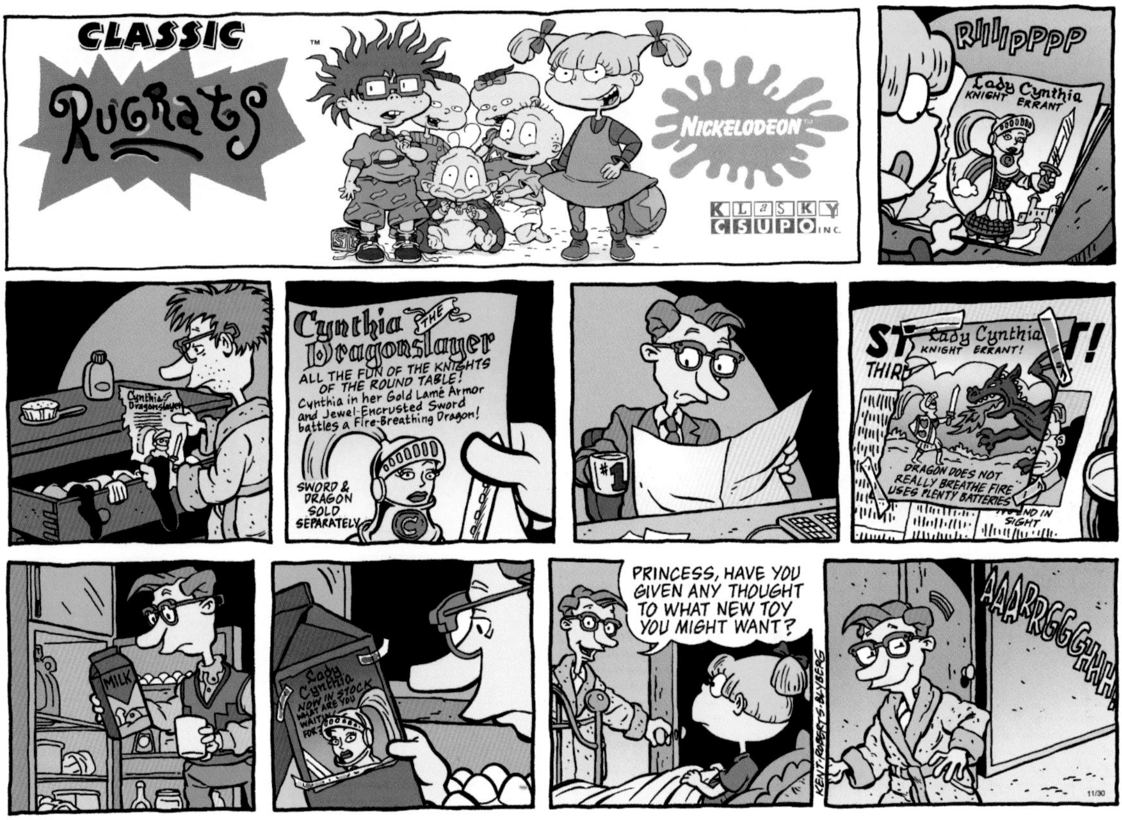

CLASSIC
RUGRATS
NICKELODEON
KLASKY CSUPO INC.
RIIIPPPP
Lady Cynthia
KNIGHT ERRANT
Cynthia The Dragonslayer
Cynthia the Dragonslayer
ALL THE FUN OF THE KNIGHTS OF THE ROUND TABLE!
Cynthia in her Gold Lamé Armor and Jewel-Encrusted Sword battles a Fire-Breathing Dragon!
SWORD & DRAGON SOLD SEPARATELY
#1
Lady Cynthia
KNIGHT ERRANT!
DRAGON DOES NOT REALLY BREATHE FIRE USES PLENTY BATTERIES
SIGHT
MILK
Lady Cynthia
NOW IN STOCK
WHAT ARE YOU
PRINCESS, HAVE YOU GIVEN ANY THOUGHT TO WHAT NEW TOY YOU MIGHT WANT?
KENT·ROBERTS·S·BLYBERG
AAARRGGGHHH
11/30

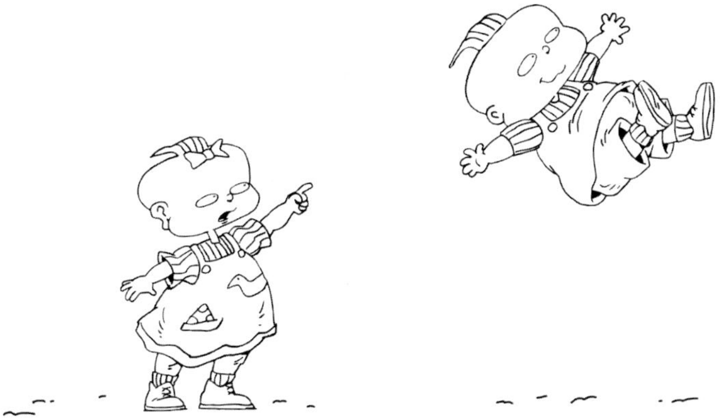

SUNDAYS

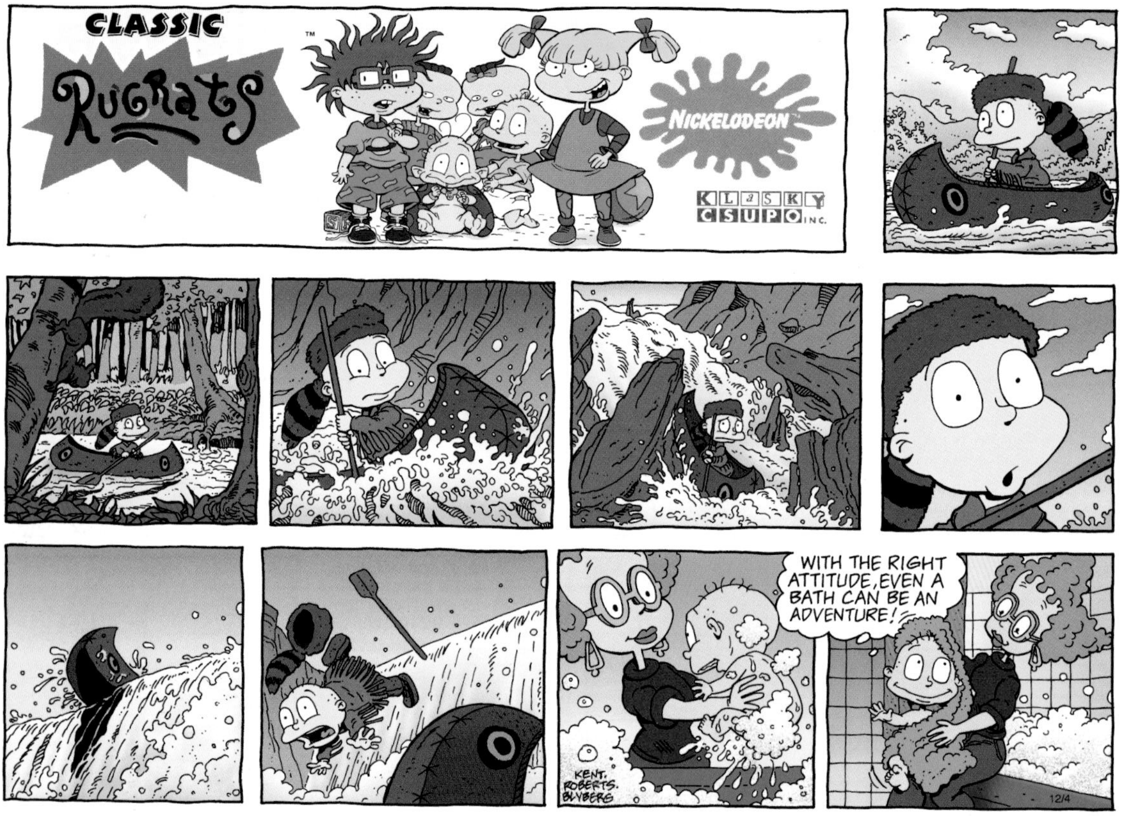
CLASSIC
Rugrats
NICKELODEON
KLaSKY CSUPO INC.
WITH THE RIGHT ATTITUDE, EVEN A BATH CAN BE AN ADVENTURE!
KENT. ROBERTS. BLYBERG
12/4

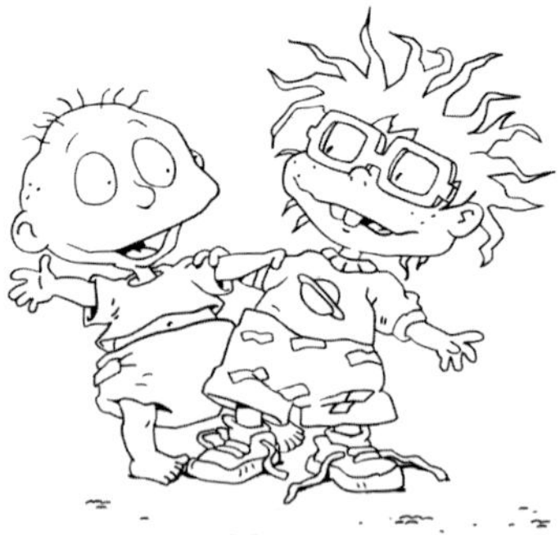

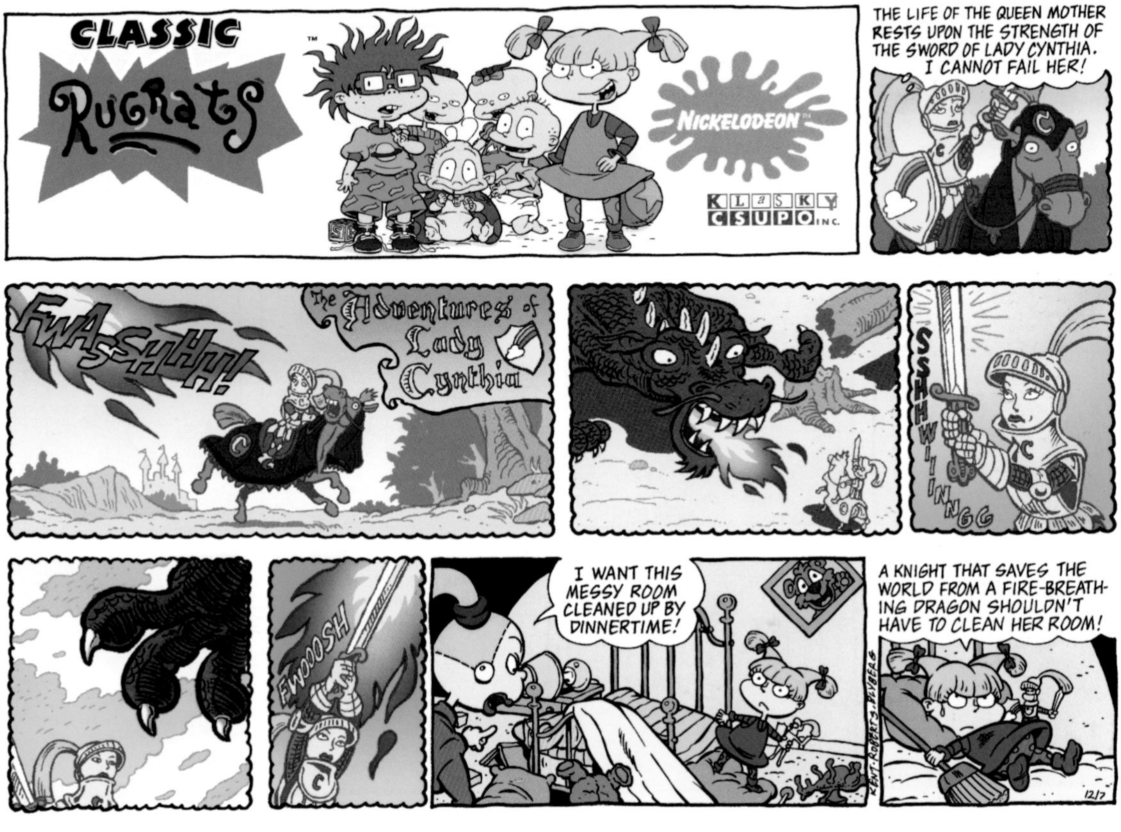
CLASSIC
Rugrats
NICKELODEON
KLASKY CSUPO INC.
THE LIFE OF THE QUEEN MOTHER RESTS UPON THE STRENGTH OF THE SWORD OF LADY CYNTHIA. I CANNOT FAIL HER!
FWASHHH!
The Adventures of Lady Cynthia
SSHHWIIINNGG
FWOOOSH
I WANT THIS MESSY ROOM CLEANED UP BY DINNERTIME!
A KNIGHT THAT SAVES THE WORLD FROM A FIRE-BREATHING DRAGON SHOULDN'T HAVE TO CLEAN HER ROOM!
12/7

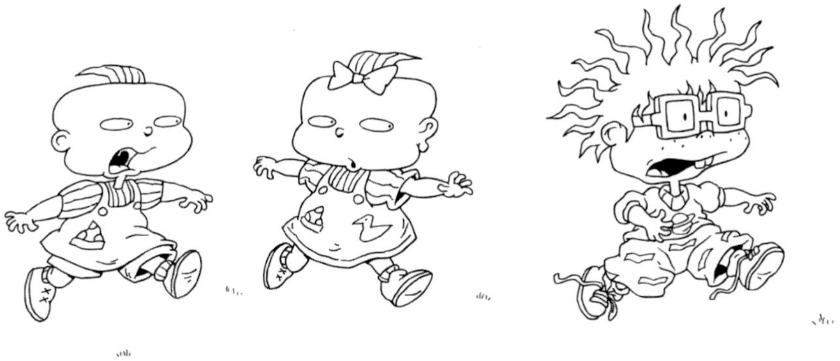

SUNDAYS

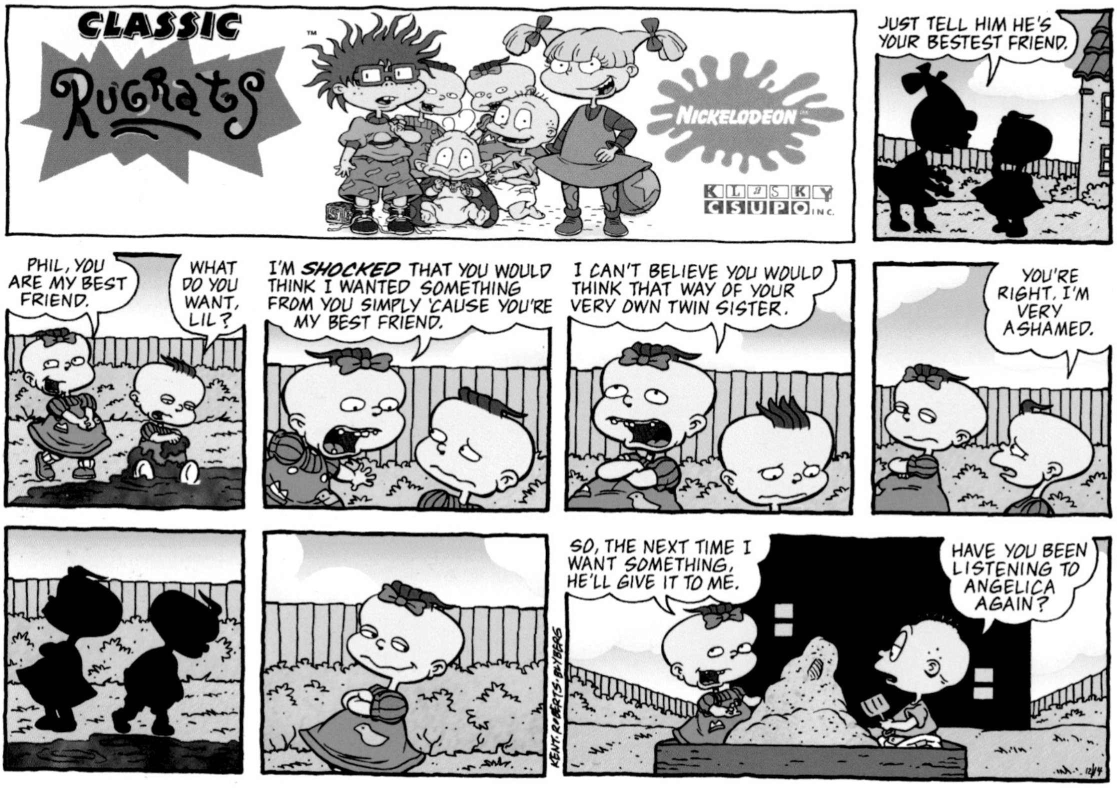
CLASSIC
Rugrats
NICKELODEON
KLASKY CSUPO INC.
JUST TELL HIM HE'S YOUR BESTEST FRIEND.
PHIL, YOU ARE MY BEST FRIEND.
WHAT DO YOU WANT, LIL?
I'M *SHOCKED* THAT YOU WOULD THINK I WANTED SOMETHING FROM YOU SIMPLY 'CAUSE YOU'RE MY BEST FRIEND.
I CAN'T BELIEVE YOU WOULD THINK THAT WAY OF YOUR VERY OWN TWIN SISTER.
YOU'RE RIGHT. I'M VERY ASHAMED.
KENT. ROBERTS. BUYBERG
SO, THE NEXT TIME I WANT SOMETHING, HE'LL GIVE IT TO ME.
HAVE YOU BEEN LISTENING TO ANGELICA AGAIN?
12/14

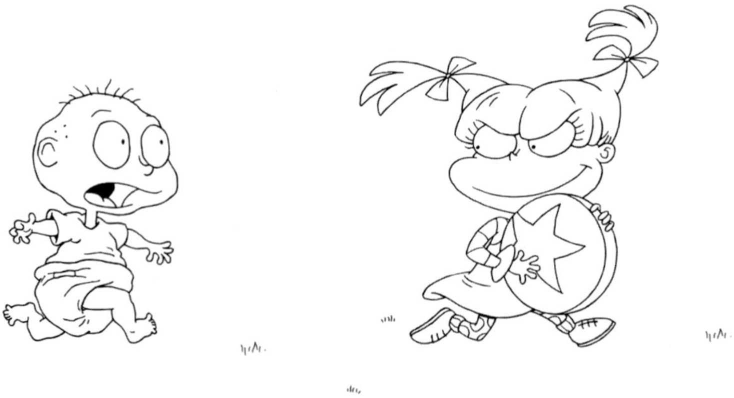

SUNDAYS

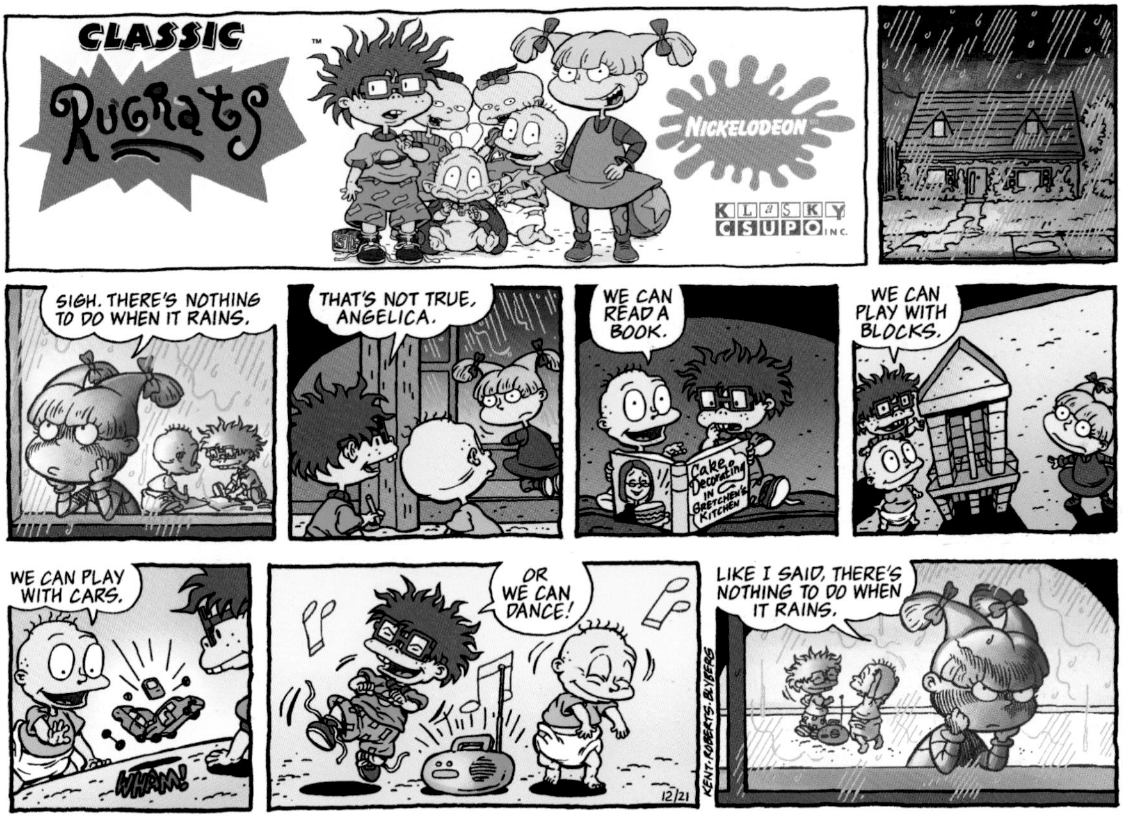
CLASSIC
Rugrats
NICKELODEON
KLASKY CSUPO INC.
SIGH. THERE'S NOTHING TO DO WHEN IT RAINS.
THAT'S NOT TRUE, ANGELICA.
WE CAN READ A BOOK.
Cake Decorating IN GRETCHEN'S KITCHEN
WE CAN PLAY WITH BLOCKS.
WE CAN PLAY WITH CARS.
WHAM!
OR WE CAN DANCE!
KENT·ROBERTS·BLYBERG
12/21
LIKE I SAID, THERE'S NOTHING TO DO WHEN IT RAINS.

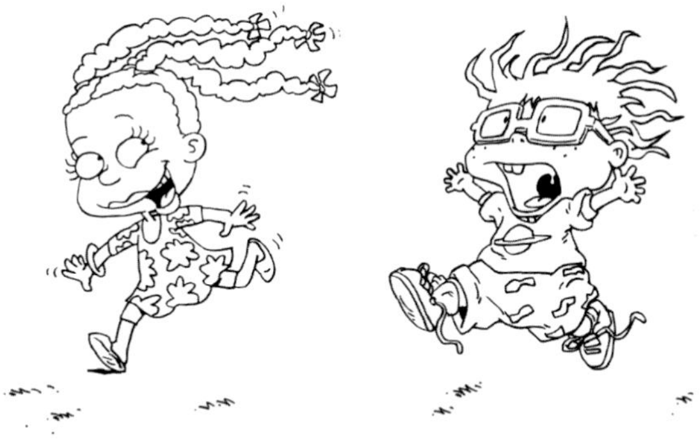

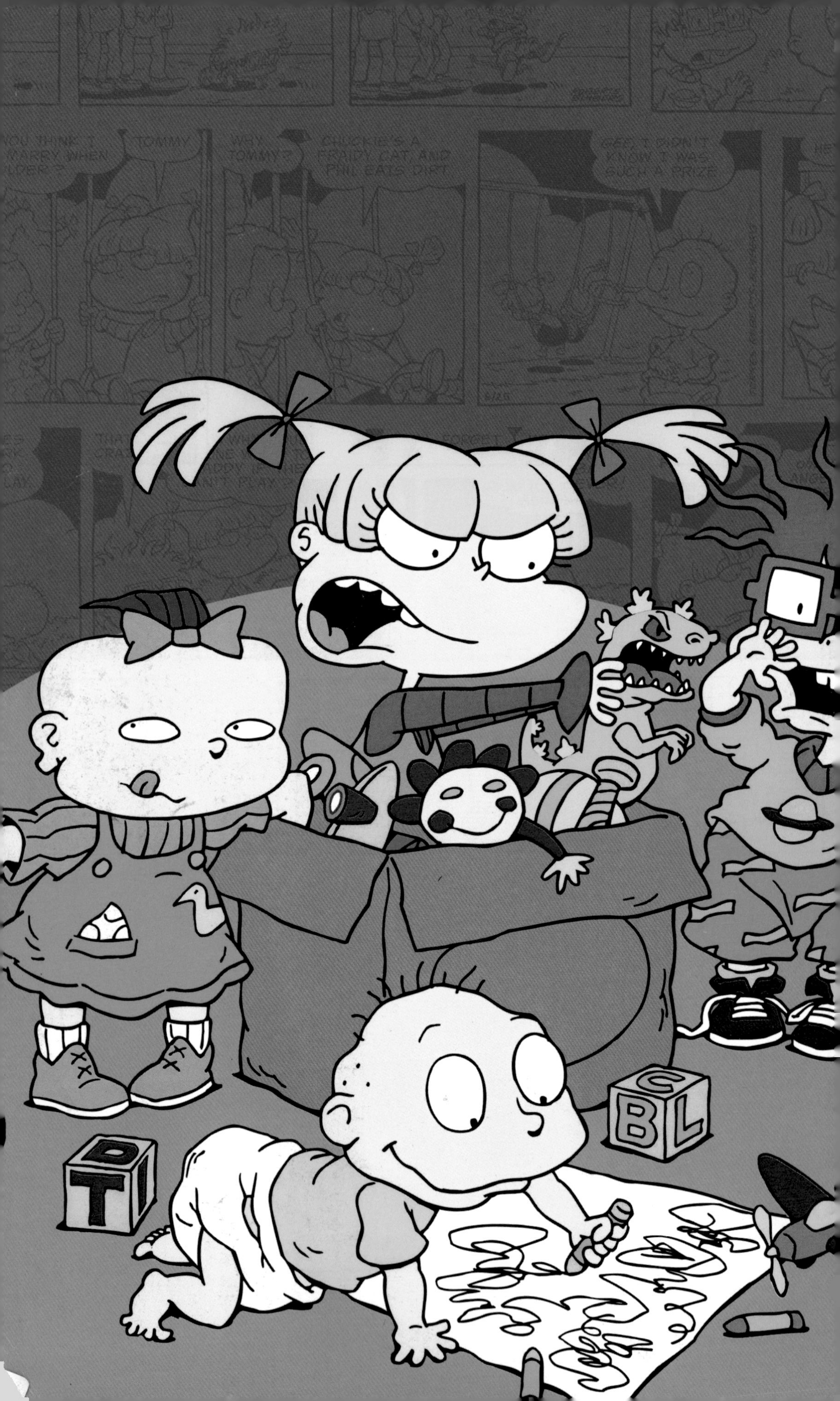
WHY TOMMY?
CHUCKIE'S A FRAIDY CAT AND PHIL EATS DIRT
GEE, I DIDN'T KNOW I WAS SUCH A PRIZE
D
T
C
B
L

HOLD ON TO YOUR DIAPERS, THERE'S MORE

RUGRATS Volume One
ISBN: 978-1-68415-176-9
$14.99 US

RUGRATS Volume Two
ISBN: 978-1-68415-256-8
$14.99 US

RUGRATS: BUILDING BLOCKS
ISBN: 978-1-68415-460-9
$14.99 US

RUGRATS: THE LAST TOKEN
ISBN: 978-1-68415-462-3
$14.99 US

DISCOVER
EXPLOSIVE NEW WORLDS

Adventure Time
Pendleton Ward and Others
Volume 1
ISBN: 978-1-60886-280-1 | $14.99 US
Volume 2
ISBN: 978-1-60886-323-5 | $14.99 US
Adventure Time: Islands
ISBN: 978-1-60886-972-5 | $9.99 US

The Amazing World of Gumball
Ben Bocquelet and Others
Volume 1
ISBN: 978-1-60886-488-1 | $14.99 US
Volume 2
ISBN: 978-1-60886-793-6 | $14.99 US

Brave Chef Brianna
Sam Sykes, Selina Espiritu
ISBN: 978-1-68415-050-2 | $14.99 US

Mega Princess
Kelly Thompson, Brianne Drouhard
ISBN: 978-1-68415-007-6 | $14.99 US

The Not-So Secret Society
Matthew Daley, Arlene Daley,
Wook Jin Clark
ISBN: 978-1-60886-997-8 | $9.99 US

Over the Garden Wall
Patrick McHale, Jim Campbell
and Others
Volume 1
ISBN: 978-1-60886-940-4 | $14.99 US
Volume 2
ISBN: 978-1-68415-006-9 | $14.99 US

Steven Universe
Rebecca Sugar and Others
Volume 1
ISBN: 978-1-60886-706-6 | $14.99 US
Volume 2
ISBN: 978-1-60886-796-7 | $14.99 US

Steven Universe & The Crystal Gems
ISBN: 978-1-60886-921-3 | $14.99 US

Steven Universe: Too Cool for School
ISBN: 978-1-60886-771-4 | $14.99 US

AVAILABLE AT YOUR LOCAL COMICS SHOP AND BOOKSTORE
To find a comics shop in your area, visit www.comicshoplocator.com
WWW.**BOOM-STUDIOS**.COM

kaboom!™

ADVENTURE TIME, OVER THE GARDEN WALL, STEVEN UNIVERSE, CARTOON NETWORK, the logos, and all related characters and elements are trademarks of and © Cartoon Network. A WarnerMedia Company. All rights reserved. (S19) THE AMAZING WORLD OF GUMBALL and all related characters and elements are trademarks of and © 2019 Turner Broadcasting System Europe Limited & Cartoon Network, WarnerMedia. All Rights Reserved. All works © their respective creators and licensors. KaBOOM! © and the KaBOOM! logo are trademarks of Boom Entertainment, Inc. All rights reserved.